W9-BLO-419

McDOUGAL, LITTELL

LITERATURE
AND LANGUAGE

· **ORANGE LEVEL** ·

BLUE LEVEL

YELLOW LEVEL
American Literature

PURPLE LEVEL
English and World Literature

McDOUGAL, LITTELL

LITERATURE AND LANGUAGE

Orange Level

Senior Consultants

Arthur N. Applebee
State University of New York at Albany

Andrea B. Bermudez
University of Houston—Clear Lake

Judith A. Langer
State University of New York at Albany

James Marshall
University of Iowa, Iowa City

Author

Jane N. Beatty

McDOUGAL, LITTELL & COMPANY

Evanston, Illinois
New York · Dallas · Sacramento · Columbia, SC

Acknowledgments

Margaret Walker Alexander: "Lineage," from *For My People* by Margaret Walker, Yale University Press, 1942.

Rudolfo A. Anaya: Abridged from "A Celebration of Grandfathers" by Rudolfo A. Anaya. Copyright © 1983, *New Mexico Magazine*, Santa Fe. Reprinted by permission of the author.

Virginia Barber Literary Agency for Alice Munro and McGraw-Hill Ryerson Ltd.: "Red Dress---1946," from *Dance of the Happy Shades*. Copyright © 1968 by Alice Munro. Originally published by McGraw-Hill Ryerson Limited. Reprinted by permission of Virginia Barber Literary Agency and McGraw-Hill Ryerson Ltd. All rights reserved.

Bantam Books, Inc.: Excerpt(s) from *War Party* by Louis L'Amour, copyright © 1975 by Bantam Books, Inc. "The Gift of Cochise," from *Collier's*, July 5, 1952, copyright © 1952 by The Crowell-Collier Publishing Company. Used by permission of Bantam Books, a division of Bantam, Doubleday, Dell Publishing Group, Inc.

Susan Bergholz Literary Services for Sandra Cisneros: "Three Wise Guys: Un Cuentos de Navidad/A Christmas Story," from *Woman Hollering Creek* by Sandra Cisneros, Random House. Copyright © 1990 by Sandra Cisneros. Reprinted by permission of Susan Bergholz Literary Services.

Curtis Brown Ltd.: "The Way Up" by William Hoffman, from *Scholastic Teacher*, May 6, 1966 issue. Copyright © 1966 by William Hoffman. Reprinted by permission of Curtis Brown, Ltd.

Caxton Printers, Ltd.: "Say It with Flowers," from *Yokohama, California* by Toshio Mori. Reprinted by permission of The Caxton Printers, Ltd., Caldwell, Idaho 83605.

Diana Chang: "Saying Yes" by Diana Chang. By permission of the author.

Don Congdon Associates, Inc.: "Button, Button" by Richard Matheson, appeared in *Playboy*. Copyright © 1970 by Richard Matheson. Reprinted by permission of Don Congdon Associates, Inc.

Continued on page 988

Cover Art: *Echo Park Lake* (detail—panel 4 of 4)   1982   Carlos Almaraz
Courtesy of Mark Bautzer, Beverly Hills and Jan Turner Gallery, Los Angeles.
Photograph by Douglas M. Parker.

Frontispiece: *High School Students #3* (detail)   1974   Isabel Bishop
Private collection   Courtesy of Midtown Galleries, New York.

ISBN: 0-8123-7102-X

LMN-DWO-00

Senior Consultants

The senior consultants guided conceptual development for the *Literature and Language* series. They participated actively in shaping prototype materials for major components, and they reviewed completed units to ensure consistency with current research and the philosophy of the series.

Arthur N. Applebee
Professor of Education, State University of New York at Albany; Director, Center for the Learning and Teaching of Literature

Andrea B. Bermudez
Professor of Multicultural Education; Director, Research Center for Language and Culture; University of Houston—Clear Lake

Judith A. Langer
Professor of Education, State University of New York at Albany; Co-Director, Center for the Learning and Teaching of Literature

James Marshall
Associate Professor of English and Education, University of Iowa, Iowa City

Author

The author of this text participated in the conceptual development of the series and wrote lessons for the literary selections.

Jane N. Beatty
Reading Specialist; formerly, Haverford High School, Haverford, Pennsylvania

Consultants

The consultants worked with the senior consultants to establish the theoretical framework for the series. They reviewed completed units and made specific recommendations according to their areas of specialization.

Jerry Conrath
Educational consultant specializing in drop-out prevention and discouraged learners; Adjunct Instructor, Portland State University, Seattle Pacific University, University of Idaho; Director, Our Other Youth conferences

William Sweigart
Assistant Professor of English, Indiana University Southeast, New Albany; formerly Research Associate, Center for the Study of Writing, University of California at Berkeley

Special Contributors

Writer's Workshops
Stephen Kern
English and Humanities Teacher, New Trier Township High School, Winnetka, Illinois

Sherry Medwin
English Teacher, New Trier Township High School, Winnetka, Illinois; Adjunct Instructor, School of Education, Northwestern University, Evanston, Illinois

Design
Design 5
New York, New York

Contents

Unit Two

OBSTACLES: FACING THE CHALLENGE 148

Unit Three

RELATIONSHIPS: PORTRAITS FROM LIFE 292

Unit Four

HIGH EXPECTATIONS: UNEXPECTED RESULTS

Unit Five

TURNING POINTS: MOMENTS TO REMEMBER 544

LANGUAGE FROM
LITERATURE

Unit Six

THE CLASSIC TRADITION 714

Handbook Section

Organization of Selections by Genre

■ Detail, untitled illustration, John Martin, 1981

LITERATURE AND LANGUAGE AND YOU

The book you are holding is unlike any textbook you have ever used. It is based on a unique philosophy—that what you bring to this book is just as important as what the book brings to you. This means that your own experiences become the basis for your involvement with the literature and activities. The special features in *Literature and Language* promote this relationship between you and the text.

ꟲPECIAL FEATURES

Great Literature   The selections in this book represent some of the finest examples of unadapted traditional and contemporary literature. There are classics that have been read and enjoyed again and again, as well as exciting pieces that have never before appeared in a literature textbook. What you read will challenge your ways of thinking, illustrate the cultural and ethnic variety of your world, and relate to experiences in your own life. If you look at the acknowledgments in the front of the book, you will see that students just like you were involved in choosing these selections.

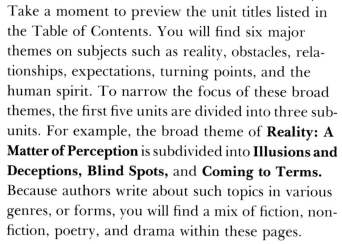

Important Themes   *Literature and Language* is organized by unit themes chosen for their connections to your life and the world around you. Take a moment to preview the unit titles listed in the Table of Contents. You will find six major themes on subjects such as reality, obstacles, relationships, expectations, turning points, and the human spirit. To narrow the focus of these broad themes, the first five units are divided into three sub-units. For example, the broad theme of **Reality: A Matter of Perception** is subdivided into **Illusions and Deceptions, Blind Spots,** and **Coming to Terms.** Because authors write about such topics in various genres, or forms, you will find a mix of fiction, non-fiction, poetry, and drama within these pages.

Respect for Your Experiences

Your understanding of what you read is based on your previous experience with the subject. For this reason, an **Explore** page comes before each literary selection. The first section of this page will help you discover what you already know and help you recall previous experiences that may relate to the selection.

Information and Strategies for Learning

The second section of the **Explore** page contains important background information about the literary selection. At the bottom of the page you will find a third section, which provides a specific reading or writing activity to help you better understand the literature you are about to read.

Practical Vocabulary Study   Most selections contain underlined vocabulary words. These are useful words to know. Making them part of your permanent vocabulary can improve your writing, reading, and communication skills. In most literature books, definitions are located in a glossary at the back. In *Literature and Language,* however, the vocabulary words are defined in a special box on the page where they appear. Words that are rarely used, as well as other terms and references whose meanings will enhance your understanding of the selection, are footnoted and defined separately.

A Personal Response   Unlike other literature texts that ask you unimportant questions about minor details in a piece of literature, *Literature and Language* focuses on your unique personal response to what you have read. An **Explain** page provides the framework for this response. The first question on the page always asks for your immediate impression after you finish reading. The remaining questions allow you to build on your initial reactions and to explore the larger issues and themes covered in the selection. Some questions are supported by "think abouts," which will help you focus your answers. It is important to understand that there are never "right" or "wrong" answers to these questions. Any thoughtful response is acceptable as long as it can be supported by examples.

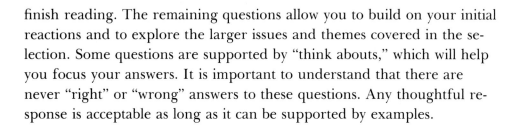

Respect for the Way You Learn

Each person has a "best" way of learning and of demonstrating what he or she has learned. Perhaps your strength is in reading and writing. Maybe you learn best by listening and discussing. Do you express yourself best by drawing, acting, building something, or giving an oral presentation? An **Extend** page, occurring at the end of many of the literature selections, will tap your unique learning and communicating styles. This page contains Options for Learning activities that offer a variety of exciting ways to show what you have learned.

Integration of Literature and Language

The authors, editors, and educators who developed this textbook believe that the various parts of an English program should be related to each other, or **integrated.** Therefore, literature, writing, and grammar are combined in this one book. What you read is used as a basis for related writing and language activities. Each subunit is followed by a **Writer's Workshop,** a **Language Workshop,** and a third workshop that varies in content.

The **Writer's Workshop** presents a guided writing assignment that is linked to the ideas and themes of the literature in a particular subunit. This assignment stresses that you work with your classmates as a community of writers in developing writing ideas and revising your work. In addition, each assignment comes with a PASSkey that provides a framework for your writing.

The **Language Workshop** is a mini-lesson that helps you revise and improve your work. Along with regular practice exercises, two special activities are often included. The exercise called Style directs you to look back at the literature to see how other writers have used the concepts taught in the workshop mini-lesson. The Analyzing and Revising Your Writing activity asks you to review your own writing based on what you have learned. The third workshop provides a mini-lesson on any of a variety of useful topics.

A Reading/Thinking Model   An important feature of this textbook is the **Strategies for Reading** lesson that follows this introduction. Built around W. C. Heinz's baseball story "One Throw," this reading lesson lets you see what a good reader thinks about as he or she reads. You can use the same strategies to become a more effective reader and to enjoy more of what you read.

The people who worked on this book truly believe that it offers some exciting new ways to learn about and enjoy literature and language. Since responding and communicating are important parts of our program, we invite you to share your impressions and experiences with us.

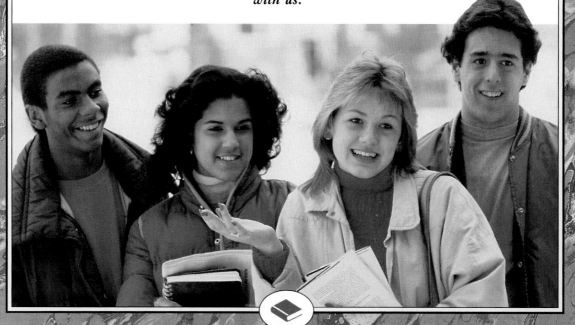

Strategies for
READING

What kind of reader are you? Passive readers let words slide by. Their eyes are moving, but their thoughts are often elsewhere. Active readers, on the other hand, keep their attention focused on what they are reading. They not only understand words and sentences, they also make constant mental connections, comments, and predictions about the selection.

While it is not easy to classify thoughts, the general categories in the list below show the types of connections active readers make in order to enjoy and understand what they read. To improve your own reading skills, try using these strategies. Although this kind of thinking and reacting may seem strange to you at first, it will soon become a natural part of your reading.

- **Questioning:** When a word, statement, or action is unclear, question it. It may become clear later.

- **Connecting:** Make connections with people, places, and things you know.

- **Predicting:** Try to figure out what will happen.

- **Clarifying:** Watch for answers to questions you had earlier.

- **Evaluating:** Respond to what you have read. Draw your own conclusions about characters, actions, and the whole story.

To understand how thinking and reading work together, look at the story that begins on the next page. You will see what one student was thinking as she read. Although the connections she makes with the story will be different from yours or anyone else's, they will give you an example of what it means to be an active reader.

One Throw

W. C. HEINZ

I checked into a hotel called the Olympia,
which is right on the main street and the only
hotel in the town. After lunch I was hanging
around the lobby, and I got to talking to the
guy at the desk. I asked him if this wasn't the town
where that kid named Maneri played ball.

"That's right," the guy said. "He's a pretty good
ballplayer."

"He should be," I said. "I read that he was the new
Phil Rizzuto."[1]

"That's what they said," the guy said.

"What's the matter with him?" I said. "I mean if he's
such a good ballplayer what's he doing in this league?"

"I don't know," the guy said. "I guess the Yankees
know what they're doing."

"What kind of a kid is he?"

"He's a nice kid," the guy said. "He plays good ball,
but I feel sorry for him. He thought he'd be playing
for the Yankees soon, and here he is in this town. You
can see it's got him down."

"He lives here in this hotel?"

"That's right," the guy said. "Most of the older
ballplayers stay in rooming houses, but Pete and a
couple other kids live here."

He was leaning on the desk, talking to me and
looking across the hotel lobby. He nodded his head.
"This is a funny thing," he said. "Here he comes now."

The kid had come through the door from the street.
He had on a light gray sport shirt and a pair of gray
flannel slacks.

I could see why, when he showed up with the
Yankees in spring training, he made them all think of
Rizzuto. He isn't any bigger than Rizzuto, and he looks
just like him.

> One hotel in town—must be a really small town. *(Connecting)*

> I've heard of him—reminds me of a TV car salesman I've seen. *(Connecting)*

> Why does he want to know all this stuff about the kid? *(Questioning)*

> I'd be down too if I had to live in a hotel. *(Connecting)*

---

1. **Phil Rizzuto:** one of the best bunters and shortstops of all time.
Rizzuto was a New York Yankee from 1941 to 1956 and winner of the
1950 Most Valuable Player Award for the American League. After
retirement he became an announcer for the Yankees.

"Hello, Nick," he said to the guy at the desk.

"Hello, Pete," the guy at the desk said. "How goes it today?"

"All right," the kid said but you could see he was exaggerating.

"I'm sorry, Pete," the guy at the desk said, "but no mail today."

"That's all right, Nick," the kid said. "I'm used to it."

"Excuse me," I said, "but you're Pete Maneri?"

"That's right," the kid said, turning and looking at me.

"Excuse me," the guy at the desk said, introducing us. "Pete, this is Mr. Franklin."

"Harry Franklin," I said.

"I'm glad to know you," the kid said, shaking my hand.

"I recognize you from your pictures," I said.

"Pete's a good ballplayer," the guy at the desk said.

"Not very," the kid said.

"Don't take his word for it, Mr. Franklin," the guy said.

"I'm a great ball fan," I said to the kid. "Do you people play tonight?"

"We play two games," the kid said.

"The first game's at six o'clock," the guy at the desk said. "They play pretty good ball."

"I'll be there," I said. "I used to play a little ball myself."

"You did?" the kid said.

"With Columbus," I said. "That's twenty years ago."

"Is that right?" the kid said. . . .

That's the way I got to talking with the kid. They had one of those pine-paneled taprooms in the basement of the hotel, and we went down there. I had a couple and the kid had a Coke, and I told him a few stories and he turned out to be a real good listener.

"But what do you do now, Mr. Franklin?" he said after a while.

"I sell hardware," I said. "I can think of some things I'd like better, but I was going to ask you how you like playing in this league."

"Well," the kid said. "I suppose it's all right. I guess I've got no kick coming."

"Oh, I don't know," I said. "I understand you're too

STRETCHING AT FIRST 1976 John Dobbs
Collection of Gilbert Kinney, Washington, D.C.

➤ What does he mean? [I had a couple]
(Questioning)
Oh, I get it, a couple of drinks.
(Clarifying)

good for this league. What are they trying to do to you?"

"I don't know," the kid said. "I can't understand it."

"What's the trouble?"

"Well," the kid said, "I don't get along very well here. I mean there's nothing wrong with my playing. I'm hitting .365 right now. I lead the league in stolen bases. There's nobody can field with me, but who cares?"

"Who manages this ball club?"

"Al Dall," the kid said. "You remember, he played in the outfield for the Yankees for about four years."

"I remember."

"Maybe he is all right," the kid said, "but I don't get along with him. He's on my neck all the time."

"Well," I said, "that's the way they are in the minors sometimes. You have to remember the guy is looking out for himself and his ball club first. He's not worried about you."

"I know that," the kid said. "If I get a big hit or make the play he never says anything. The other night I tried to take second on a loose ball and I got caught in the rundown. He bawls me out in front of everybody. There's nothing I can do."

"Oh, I don't know," I said. "This is probably a guy who knows he's got a good thing in you, and he's looking to keep you around. You people lead the league, and that makes him look good. He doesn't want to lose you to Kansas City or the Yankees."

➤ Why doesn't Dall want him to go on? Is it discrimination?
(Questioning)
➤ Aha, he doesn't get along with the manager.
(Clarifying)

"That's what I mean," the kid said. "When the Yankees sent me down here they said, 'Don't worry. We'll keep an eye on you.' So Dall never sends a good report on me. Nobody ever comes down to look me over. What chance is there for a guy like Eddie Brown or somebody like that coming down to see me in this town?"

➤ Who's Eddie Brown?
(Questioning)

"You have to remember that Eddie Brown's the big shot," I said, "the great Yankee scout."

"Sure," the kid said. "I never even saw him, and I'll never see him in this place. I have an idea that if they ever ask Dall about me he keeps knocking me down."

➤ Oh, that's who he is.
(Clarifying)

"Why don't you go after Dall?" I said. "I had trouble like that once myself, but I figured out a way to get attention."

"You did?" the kid said.

"I threw a couple of balls over the first baseman's head," I said. "I threw a couple of games away, and that really got the manager sore. I was lousing up his ball club and his record. So what does he do? He blows the whistle on me, and what happens? That gets the brass curious, and they send down to see what's wrong?"

"Is that so?" the kid said. "What happened?"

"Two weeks later," I said, "I was up with Columbus."

"Is that right?" the kid said.

"Sure," I said, egging him on. "What have you got to lose?"

"Nothing," the kid said. "I haven't got anything to lose."

"I'd try it," I said.

"I might try it," the kid said. "I might try it tonight if the spot comes up."

I could see from the way he said it that he was madder than he'd said. Maybe you think this is mean to steam a kid up like this, but I do some strange things.

"Take over," I said. "Don't let this guy ruin your career."

"I'll try it," the kid said. "Are you coming out to the park tonight?"

"I wouldn't miss it," I said. "This will be better than making out route sheets and sales orders."

It's not much ball park in this town—old wooden bleachers and an old wooden fence and about four hundred people in the stands. The first game wasn't much either, with the home club winning something like 8 to 1.

The kid didn't have any hard chances, but I could see he was a ballplayer, with a double and a couple of walks and a lot of speed.

The second game was different, though. The other club got a couple of runs and then the home club picked up three runs in one, and they were in the top of the ninth with a 3–2 lead and two outs when the pitching began to fall apart and they loaded the bases.

I was trying to wish the ball down to the kid, just to see what he'd do with it, when the batter drives one on one big bounce to the kid's right.

The kid was off for it when the ball started. He made a backhand stab and grabbed it. He was deep now, and

> What's up with this guy? What's his motivation—to make Pete lose the game?
(Questioning)
> Maybe it's a gambling scheme.
(Predicting)

> Is this guy Eddie Brown?
(Predicting)

> What does he mean? [wish the ball down] Strange way to say it.
(Questioning)

he turned in the air and fired. If it goes over the first baseman's head, it's two runs in and a panic—but it's the prettiest throw you'd want to see. It's right on a line, and the runner is out by a step, and it's the ball game.

I walked back to the hotel, thinking about the kid. I sat around the lobby until I saw him come in, and then I walked toward the elevator like I was going to my room, but so I'd meet him. And I could see he didn't want to talk.

"How about a Coke?" I said.

"No," he said. "Thanks, but I'm going to bed."

"Look," I said. "Forget it. You did the right thing. Have a Coke."

We were sitting in the taproom again. The kid wasn't saying anything.

"Why didn't you throw that ball away?" I said.

"I don't know," the kid said. "I had it in my mind before he hit it, but I couldn't."

"Why?"

"I don't know why."

"I know why," I said.

The kid didn't say anything. He just sat looking down.

"Do you know why you couldn't throw that ball away?" I said.

"No," the kid said.

"You couldn't throw that ball away," I said, "because you're going to be a major-league ballplayer someday."

The kid just looked at me. He had that same sore expression.

"Do you know why you're going to be a major-league ballplayer?" I said.

The kid was just looking down again, shaking his head. I never got more of a kick out of anything in my life.

"You're going to be a major-league ballplayer," I said, "because you couldn't throw that ball away, and because I'm not a hardware salesman and my name's not Harry Franklin."

"What do you mean?" the kid said.

"I mean," I explained to him, "that I tried to needle you into throwing that ball away because I'm Eddie Brown."

➤ Good for the kid—not to try to lose on purpose.
(Evaluating)

➤ I understand why he didn't throw it, especially if the team is depending on him—puts guilt on you.
(Connecting)

➤ Aha! I was right! I thought there was something funny about Harry Franklin—most fans would want autographs instead of telling him stuff.
(Clarifying)

➤ I like the twist at the end. It's a good ending.
(Evaluating)

REALITY: A MATTER OF PERCEPTION

"*Human kind cannot bear very much reality.*"

T.S. Eliot

WOODLAND ENCOUNTER (detail)
1980 Bev Doolittle
© 1980 The Greenwich Workshop, Inc.,
Trumbull, Connecticut.

ℐLLUSIONS AND DECEPTIONS

How can two eyewitnesses have different accounts of an accident? Both see the same event. However, their perceptions, or the ways they understand what happened, can be quite different. The title of Unit 1, "Reality: A Matter of Perception," suggests that reality, or the "true" facts and events of the real world, is interpreted in different ways.

"Illusions and Deceptions" refers to faulty perceptions. Illusions are mistaken or false ideas, or misunderstandings on the part of the observer. Deceptions, on the other hand, are deliberate attempts by someone to mislead or to create a wrong perception in another person.

As you read the following selections, try to figure out who is under an illusion or who is creating a deception. Notice how the personalities and life experiences of the characters influence how they perceive what happens to or around them.

Elements of
FICTION

When people read for relaxation or fun, they generally choose **fiction**—writing that comes from an author's imagination. Fiction is not factual, but it may be based on facts, on real experiences, or on people the writer has known. Most of the pieces of fiction you will read in this book are short stories. A **short story** is a work of fiction that centers on a single idea and can be read in one sitting. A **novel**, on the other hand, focuses on several ideas, and it is much longer and more complex than a short story.

Both forms of fiction—short stories and novels—have certain elements in common.

*U*nderstanding Fiction

Characters are the people or animals about whom the story is told. **Main characters** are those who are most important in the story; **minor characters** play a less important role.

The **setting** of a story is the time and place in which the action occurs. A story may be set in the past, the present, or the future; during the day or at night; during a particular time of year or in a certain historical period. The place may be real or imaginary. Sometimes the setting is clear and well-defined; at other times it is left to the reader's imagination.

The **plot** is the series of events in a story, that is, what happens in the story. Almost all plots center on at least one conflict, or problem, that the characters struggle to resolve. Plots usually follow a specific pattern, made up of five steps. You will see the steps of this pattern develop as you read "A Mother in Mannville."

Exposition   The exposition, at the beginning of a story, gives background information that the reader needs to know. The exposition introduces the setting, the characters, and the conflict. Sometimes it tells what happened in the past.

Rising Action   During this part of a story, the conflict is obvious. Complications arise and suspense begins to build as the main characters struggle to resolve their problem.

Climax   The climax is the turning point of a story, that point at which the conflict is resolved. The climax may occur because of a decision the characters reach or because of a discovery or an event that turns the situation. The climax usually results in a change in the characters or a solution to the problem.

Falling Action   In this part, the effects of the climax are shown. The suspense is over, but the results of the decision or action that caused the climax are worked out.

Resolution   The resolution tells how the struggle ends. It ties up any loose ends of the plot.

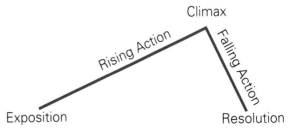

The **theme** of a story is the message the writer presents through the characters and the plot. Often the theme is a generalization about life, or a lesson the characters learn. The theme is not usually stated; the reader has to figure it out.

Strategies for Reading Fiction

1. Remember that your main purpose in reading fiction is to **enjoy a good story.** Sometimes you gain insight or new understanding, but mainly you want to lose yourself in the story and find out what happens.
2. Before you read, **preview** the story. How long is it? Do the title and pictures suggest what it might be about?
3. As you read the first few paragraphs, **visualize,** or picture in your mind, the setting and characters. Compare them to places and people you know. In this way the story will seem more real to you.
4. While you are reading, **make observations** and **ask questions** about the story. In other words, think about what you are reading. If you think a character behaves strangely, ask yourself why. Make a mental note when a character says something that you think is significant or when you notice a detail that might be important later. Some people write down their thoughts in a reading log as they read. The notes in the margin of the thinking model on page 9 show what kinds of thoughts you might have while you are reading a story.
5. As you become more involved in the story, **predict** what will happen next. Let yourself guess beforehand who will win a battle or what choice a character will make. This makes reading much more exciting.
6. As you read along, **refine your understanding** of what's going on. At first, you may not easily understand a character or an event. As you read further, however, things become more clear. Your impressions of characters change, and actions take on new meaning. Don't be frustrated when you don't understand something immediately; read on and see how misunderstandings are cleared up. Sometimes you may even need to go back and reread a part that confuses you.
7. After you finish reading a story, **think about it** for a few minutes. What is your initial impression? How did the story make you feel? What did you think of the main character? What is the underlying meaning of the story, the message about life that the writer is sharing?
8. To make sure that you have understood the story, answer the following **Story Grammar Questions.**

Story Grammar Questions

1. What is the story about?
2. What does the main character want or need to do?
3. How does he or she try to do it?
4. What happens in the end?

Fiction

A *Mother in Mannville*

MARJORIE KINNAN RAWLINGS

Examine What You Know

The narrator of "A Mother in Mannville" describes another character in the story as someone who has integrity. She goes on to say that *integrity* means "more than brave . . . more than honesty." Explore what *integrity* means by using a diagram like the one below. Begin with a dictionary definition of the word, then add synonyms. Think of people you know or characters you have read about who have acted with integrity. Then decide if you feel any characters in the story act with integrity.

INTEGRITY

(Dictionary Definition)

(Synonyms)

(Examples of People Who Have Shown Integrity)

Expand Your Knowledge

Jerry, the boy in this story, lives in an orphanage. An orphanage is an institution for children whose parents have died, or have deserted them, or can no longer care for them. Traditionally, orphanages kept children for a number of years and trained them to care for themselves in the outside world. Few, if any, orphanages for large groups of children still exist in the United States, although such orphanages can still be found in many other countries. In America, orphaned children are now usually placed in small group homes or with foster families.

Write Before You Read

■ *A biography of the author can be found on page 29.*

What is the difference between being lonely and being alone? Describe the difference in your journal or notebook. Try to use examples from your own life to make your explanation more exact.

A Mother in Mannville

MARJORIE KINNAN RAWLINGS

The orphanage is high in the Carolina mountains. Sometimes in winter the snowdrifts are so deep that the institution is cut off from the village below, from all the world. Fog hides the mountain peaks, the snow swirls down the valleys, and a wind blows so bitterly that the orphanage boys who take the milk twice daily to the baby cottage reach the door with fingers stiff in an agony of numbness.

"Or when we carry trays from the cookhouse for the ones that are sick," Jerry said, "we get our faces frostbit, because we can't put our hands over them. I have gloves," he added. "Some of the boys don't have any."

He liked the late spring, he said. The rhododendron was in bloom, a carpet of color, across the mountainsides, soft as the May winds that stirred the hemlocks. He called it laurel.

"It's pretty when the laurel blooms," he said. "Some of it's pink and some of it's white."

I was there in the autumn. I wanted quiet, isolation, to do some troublesome writing. I wanted mountain air to blow out the malaria from too long a time in the subtropics. I was homesick, too, for the flaming of maples in October, and for corn shocks and pumpkins and black-walnut trees and the lift of hills. I found them all, living in a cabin that belonged to the orphanage, half a mile beyond the orphanage farm. When I took the cabin, I asked for a boy or man to come and chop wood for the fireplace. The first few days were warm, I found what wood I needed about the cabin, no one came, and I forgot the order.

I looked up from my typewriter one late afternoon, a little startled. A boy stood at the door, and my pointer dog, my companion, was at his side and had not barked to warn me. The boy was probably twelve years old but undersized. He wore overalls and a torn shirt, and was barefooted.

He said, "I can chop some wood today."

I said, "But I have a boy coming from the orphanage."

"I'm the boy."

"You? But you're small."

"Size don't matter, chopping wood," he said. "Some of the big boys don't chop good. I've been chopping wood at the orphanage a long time."

I visualized mangled and inadequate

Words to Know and Use | **visualize** (vizh′ o͞o əl īz′) *v.* to form a mental image of something
inadequate (in ad′ i kwət) *adj.* not good enough for what is needed or not equal to what is required

branches for my fires. I was well into my work and not inclined to conversation. I was a little <u>blunt</u>.

"Very well. There's the ax. Go ahead and see what you can do."

I went back to work, closing the door. At first the sound of the boy dragging brush annoyed me. Then he began to chop. The blows were rhythmic and steady, and shortly I had forgotten him, the sound no more of an interruption than a consistent rain. I suppose an hour and a half passed, for when I stopped and stretched, and heard the boy's steps on the cabin stoop, the sun was dropping behind the farthest mountain, and the valleys were purple with something deeper than the asters.

The boy said, "I have to go to supper now. I can come again tomorrow evening."

I said, "I'll pay you now for what you've done," thinking I should probably have to insist on an older boy. "Ten cents an hour?"

"Anything is all right."

We went together back of the cabin. An astonishing amount of solid wood had been cut. There were cherry logs and heavy roots of rhododendron, and blocks from the waste pine and oak left from the building of the cabin.

"But you've done as much as a man," I said. "This is a splendid pile."

I looked at him, actually, for the first time. His hair was the color of the corn shocks, and his eyes, very direct, were like the mountain sky when rain is pending—gray, with a shadowing of that miraculous blue. As I spoke, a light came over him, as though the setting sun had touched him with the same suffused glory with which it touched the mountains. I gave him a quarter.

"You may come tomorrow," I said, "and thank you very much."

He looked at me and the coin, and seemed to want to speak, but could not and turned away.

"I'll split <u>kindling</u> tomorrow," he said over his thin, ragged shoulder. "You'll need kindling and medium wood and logs and backlogs."

At daylight I was half wakened by the sound of chopping. Again it was so even in texture that I went back to sleep. When I left my bed in the cool morning, the boy had come and gone, and a stack of kindling was neat against the cabin wall. He came again after school in the afternoon and worked until time to return to the orphanage. His name was Jerry; he was twelve years old, and he had been at the orphanage since he was four. I could picture him at four, with the same grave gray-blue eyes and the same—independence? No, the word that comes to me is "integrity."

The word means something very special to me, and the quality for which I use it is a rare one. My father had it—there is another of whom I am almost sure—but almost no man of my acquaintance possesses it with the <u>clarity</u>, the purity, the simplicity of a mountain stream. But the boy Jerry had it. It is bedded on courage, but it is more than brave. It is honest, but it is more than honesty. The ax handle broke one day. Jerry said the woodshop at the orphanage would repair it. I brought money to pay for the job, and he refused it.

"I'll pay for it," he said. "I broke it. I brought the ax down careless."

"But no one hits accurately every time," I

told him. "The fault was in the wood of the handle. I'll see the man from whom I bought it."

It was only then that he would take the money. He was standing back of his own carelessness. He was a free-will agent, and he chose to do careful work; and if he failed, he took the responsibility without subterfuge.

And he did for me the unnecessary thing, the gracious thing, that we find done only by the great of heart. Things no training can teach, for they are done on the instant, with no predicated experience. He found a cubbyhole beside the fireplace that I had not noticed. There, of his own accord, he put kindling and "medium" wood, so that I might always have dry fire material ready in case of sudden wet weather. A stone was loose in the rough walk to the cabin. He dug a deeper hole and steadied it, although he came, himself, by a shortcut over the bank. I found that when I tried to return his thoughtfulness with such things as candy and apples, he was wordless. "Thank you" was, perhaps, an expression for which he had no use, for his courtesy was <u>instinctive</u>. He only looked at the gift and at me, and a curtain lifted, so that I saw deep into the clear well of his eyes, and gratitude was there, and affection, soft over the firm granite of his character.

He made simple excuses to come and sit with me. I could no more have turned him away than if he had been physically hungry. I suggested once that the best time for us to visit was just before supper, when I left off my writing. After that, he waited always until my typewriter had been some time quiet. One day I worked until nearly dark. I went outside the cabin, having forgotten him. I saw him going up over the hill in the twilight toward the orphanage. When I sat down on my stoop, a place was warm from his body where he had been sitting.

He became intimate, of course, with my pointer, Pat. There is a strange <u>communion</u> between a boy and a dog. Perhaps they possess the same singleness of spirit, the same kind of wisdom. It is difficult to explain, but it exists. When I went across the state for a weekend, I left the dog in Jerry's charge. I gave him the dog whistle and the key to the cabin, and left sufficient food. He was to come two or three times a day and let out the dog, and feed and exercise him. I should return Sunday night, and Jerry would take out the dog for the last time Sunday afternoon and then leave the key under an agreed hiding place.

My return was belated, and fog filled the mountain passes so treacherously that I dared not drive at night. The fog held the next morning, and it was Monday noon before I reached the cabin. The dog had been fed and cared for that morning. Jerry came early in the afternoon, anxious.

"The superintendent said nobody would drive in the fog," he said. "I came just before bedtime last night and you hadn't come. So I brought Pat some of my breakfast this morning. I wouldn't have let anything happen to him."

"I was sure of that. I didn't worry."

"When I heard about the fog, I thought you'd know."

He was needed for work at the orphanage, and he had to return at once. I gave him a dollar in payment, and he looked at it

Words to Know and Use

instinctive (in stiŋk′ tiv) *adj.* having a natural tendency; spontaneous
communion (kə myo͞on′ yən) *n.* a close relationship with deep understanding; intimacy

ALBERT'S SON   1959   Andrew Wyeth   National Gallery of Oslo.   Photograph by Jacques Lathion.

and went away. But that night he came in the darkness and knocked at the door.

"Come in, Jerry," I said, "if you're allowed to be away this late."

"I told maybe a story," he said. "I told them I thought you would want to see me."

"That's true," I assured him, and I saw his relief. "I want to hear about how you managed with the dog."

He sat by the fire with me, with no other light, and told me of their two days together. The dog lay close to him, and found a comfort there that I did not have for him. And it seemed to me that being with my dog, and caring for him, had brought the boy and me, too, together, so that he felt that he belonged to me as well as to the animal.

"He stayed right with me," he told me, "except when he ran in the laurel. He likes the laurel. I took him up over the hill and we both ran fast. There was a place where the grass was high and I lay down in it and hid. I could hear Pat hunting for me. He found my trail and he barked. When he found me, he acted crazy, and he ran around and around me, in circles."

We watched the flames.

"That's an apple log," he said. "It burns the prettiest of any wood."

We were very close.

He was suddenly impelled to speak of things he had not spoken of before, nor had I cared to ask him.

"You look a little bit like my mother," he said. "Especially in the dark, by the fire."

"But you were only four, Jerry, when you came here. You have remembered how she looked, all these years?"

"My mother lives in Mannville," he said.

For a moment, finding that he had a mother shocked me as greatly as anything in my life has ever done, and I did not know why it disturbed me. Then I understood my distress. I was filled with a passionate resentment that any woman should go away and leave her son. A fresh anger added itself. A son like this one— The orphanage was a wholesome place, the executives were kind, good people, the food was more than adequate, the boys were healthy, a ragged shirt was no hardship, nor the doing of clean labor. Granted, perhaps, that the boy felt no lack, what blood fed the bowels of a woman who did not yearn over this child's lean body that had come in parturition out of her own? At four he would have looked the same as now. Nothing, I thought, nothing in life could change those eyes. His quality must be apparent to an idiot, a fool. I burned with questions I could not ask. In any case, I was afraid, there would be pain.

"Have you seen her, Jerry—lately?"

"I see her every summer. She sends for me."

I wanted to cry out. "Why are you not with her? How can she let you go away again?"

He said, "She comes up here from Mannville whenever she can. She doesn't have a job now."

His face shone in the firelight.

"She wanted to give me a puppy, but they can't let any one boy keep a puppy. You remember the suit I had on last Sunday?" He was plainly proud. "She sent me that for Christmas. The Christmas before that"—he drew a long breath, savoring the memory— "she sent me a pair of skates."

"Roller skates?"

My mind was busy, making pictures of

Words to Know and Use | impel (im pel′) v. to force, drive, or urge

her, trying to understand her. She had not, then, entirely deserted or forgotten him. But why, then—I thought, "I must not condemn her without knowing."

"Roller skates. I let the other boys use them. They're always borrowing them. But they're careful of them."

What circumstance other than poverty—

"I'm going to take the dollar you gave me for taking care of Pat," he said, "and buy her a pair of gloves."

I could only say, "That will be nice. Do you know her size?"

"I think it's 8½," he said.

He looked at my hands.

"Do you wear 8½?" he asked.

"No. I wear a smaller size, a 6."

"Oh! Then I guess her hands are bigger than yours."

I hated her. Poverty or no, there was other food than bread, and the soul could starve as quickly as the body. He was taking his dollar to buy gloves for her big stupid hands, and she lived away from him, in Mannville, and contented herself with sending him skates.

"She likes white gloves," he said. "Do you think I can get them for a dollar?"

"I think so," I said.

I decided that I should not leave the mountains without seeing her and knowing for myself why she had done this thing.

The human mind scatters its interests as though made of thistledown,[1] and every wind stirs and moves it. I finished my work. It did not please me, and I gave my thoughts to another field. I should need some Mexican material.

I made arrangements to close my Florida place. Mexico immediately, and doing the writing there, if conditions were favorable.

Then, Alaska with my brother. After that, heaven knew what or where.

I did not take time to go to Mannville to see Jerry's mother, or even to talk with the orphanage officials about her. I was a trifle abstracted about the boy, because of my work and plans. And after my first fury at her—we did not speak of her again—his having a mother, any sort at all, not far away, in Mannville, relieved me of the ache I had had about him. He did not question the anomalous relation. He was not lonely. It was none of my concern.

He came every day and cut my wood and did small helpful favors and stayed to talk. The days had become cold, and often I let him come inside the cabin. He would lie on the floor in front of the fire, with one arm across the pointer, and they would both doze and wait quietly for me. Other days they ran with a common ecstasy through the laurel, and since the asters were now gone, he brought me back vermillion maple leaves, and chestnut boughs dripping with imperial yellow. I was ready to go.

I said to him, "You have been my good friend, Jerry. I shall often think of you and miss you. Pat will miss you too. I am leaving tomorrow."

He did not answer. When he went away, I remember that a new moon hung over the mountains, and I watched him go in silence up the hill. I expected him the next day, but he did not come. The details of packing my personal belongings, loading my car, arranging the bed over the seat, where the

---

1. **thistledown:** the soft, fluffy down attached to the flower head of a thistle plant.

dog would ride, occupied me until late in the day. I closed the cabin and started the car, noticing that the sun was in the west and I should do well to be out of the mountains by nightfall. I stopped by the orphanage and left the cabin key and money for my light bill with Miss Clark.

"And will you call Jerry for me to say goodbye to him?"

"I don't know where he is," she said. "I'm afraid he's not well. He didn't eat his dinner this noon. One of the other boys saw him going over the hill into the laurel. He was supposed to fire the boiler this afternoon. It's not like him; he's usually <u>reliable</u>."

I was almost relieved, for I knew I should never see him again, and it would be easier not to say goodbye to him.

I said, "I wanted to talk with you about his mother—why he's here—but I'm in more of a hurry than I expected to be. It's out of the question for me to see her now too. But here's some money I'd like to leave with you to buy things for him at Christmas and on his birthday. It will be better than for me to try to send him things. I could so easily duplicate—skates, for instance."

She blinked her eyes.

"There's not much use for skates here," she said.

Her stupidity annoyed me.

"What I mean," I said, "is that I don't want to duplicate things his mother sends him. I might have chosen skates if I didn't know she had already given them to him."

She stared at me.

"I don't understand," she said. "He has no mother. He has no skates." 🍂

THE HOME PLACE   Tony Eubanks   Private collection   From *Art for the Parks,* 1990.

Words to Know and Use | **reliable** (ri līʹə bəl) *adj.* trustworthy; dependable

Responding to Reading

First Impressions

1. How did you feel when you learned the truth about Jerry's "mother in Mannville"?

Second Thoughts

2. Why do you think Jerry makes up the story about his mother?

   Think about
   - Jerry's life as an orphan
   - his behavior toward the narrator
   - the narrator's actions and reactions to Jerry

3. Why do you think the narrator believes Jerry's story?

4. Describe Jerry's feelings when he hears that the narrator is leaving. In your opinion, were his feelings justified?

5. Based on your definition of *integrity,* do you think either character acts with integrity? Explain your answer.

6. The characters in this story seem to have conflicting needs. What does Jerry want from the narrator? What is she looking for?

   Think about
   - Jerry's life in an orphanage
   - Jerry's reactions to the narrator and her dog
   - the reasons that the narrator came to the cabin and why she left
   - the narrator's comments about Jerry

7. Do you blame either character for his or her actions? Explain.

Broader Connections

8. Large orphanages like the one that Jerry lived in have been replaced by small group homes and foster homes. What reasons can you think of for their disappearance? Do you think the smaller residences and foster families of today are a better solution? Why or why not?

Literary Concept: Setting

The **setting,** or time and place in which a story occurs, is more important in some stories than in others. The narrator in this story often refers to the setting. What role does the setting play in bringing the narrator to the cabin? How does the setting influence her first meeting with Jerry? How does it influence her whole way of thinking about Jerry?

Writing Options

1. What do you think Jerry will be like at age twenty-one? What might he be doing? Write a brief profile, or description, of Jerry as a young adult.

2. The narrator states, "Poverty or no, there was other food than bread, and the soul could starve as quickly as the body." Explain the quotation and its meaning in the story.

3. How might the story be different if the narrator had contacted Jerry's mother when she first thought of it? Rewrite the story from the point at which the narrator first thinks of contacting the woman.

4. Write a letter that Jerry might send to the narrator or a letter that the narrator might send to Jerry after the story ends.

Vocabulary Practice

Exercise On a sheet of paper, write the letter of the word or phrase that best completes each sentence below.

1. Jerry used **kindling** to (a) light the electric oven (b) feed the dog when the narrator did not return (c) start a fire.
2. The narrator's comments were **blunt,** or (a) to the point but not very polite (b) polite but indirect (c) unclear.
3. Since her time was **inadequate,** the narrator (a) employed someone who had more time (b) wasted time (c) got more work.
4. The narrator might worry about the **clarity** of her directions if (a) Jerry complimented her (b) she forgot her glasses (c) Jerry looked puzzled.
5. Jerry might shout with **ecstasy** if (a) he lost the dog (b) the narrator adopted him (c) he cut his finger.
6. Jerry's actions were **instinctive** when he acted (a) quickly, without thinking (b) after much thought (c) after a short delay.
7. Jerry was **reliable** because he (a) was never there when needed (b) could be counted on to help out (c) could not be trusted.
8. The **communion** between Jerry and Pat suggested (a) a deep hatred (b) a special closeness (c) an end of the friendship.
9. To help you **visualize** the setting, the writer included (a) dialogue (b) a surprise ending (c) many sensory details.
10. To **impel** the narrator to stay, Jerry might have (a) spoken his true feelings (b) gone home (c) chopped more wood.

> **Words to Know and Use**
> ────────
> blunt
> clarity
> communion
> ecstasy
> impel
> inadequate
> instinctive
> kindling
> reliable
> visualize

extend

Options for Learning

1 • Create a Montage A montage is a picture created from a number of different pictures that have been lapped over one another. Unlike a collage, in which pictures are pasted together without a pattern, a montage combines pictures in such a way as to form a new picture. Skim through "A Mother in Mannville" for information about the setting of the story. Then use photographs and magazine pictures to create a montage that suggests this setting.

2 • "Mother Wanted" Skim through the story "A Mother in Mannville," looking for clues that show what qualities Jerry might want in a mother. List these qualities. Then compose a personal ad that Jerry might write to advertise for a new mother. Before you begin, study personal ads in your local newspaper. You might call the newspaper to find out the maximum length for an ad and the cost of each line. Share your ad in class.

3 • Pick a Poem Find a poem that Jerry might send the narrator as a symbol or as a remembrance of their friendship. Copy and illustrate the poem.

4 • Eye of the Beholder This story is told from the narrator's point of view, or presented as she perceived it to have happened. Choose a scene from the story to act out with a friend. Act it out first from the narrator's point of view; then act out the same scene from Jerry's point of view.

FACT FINDER

What are the meanings of the word laurel? What does it mean "to rest on one's laurels"?

Marjorie Kinnan Rawlings
1896-1953

The character of Jerry was modeled on a real boy whom Marjorie Kinnan Rawlings met in North Carolina while she was writing a novel. "A Mother in Mannville" and many other stories by Rawlings were eventually collected in a book entitled *When the Whippoorwill*.

Rawlings is best known for her stories about conflicts between people and nature. Rawlings preferred to write in a quiet, natural setting. In 1928, at the age of thirty-two, she moved to a farm in Cross Creek, Florida, where she lived until her death. Her life in Cross Creek was difficult; she had few luxuries and lived almost completely off the land. However, her experiences there gave her the ideas for several of her books. Her most famous novel is *The Yearling*, a story about a young boy and his pet fawn. The book won a Pulitzer Prize in 1939, and was later made into a movie.

Fiction

^A *Retrieved Reformation*

O. HENRY

Examine What You Know

The title of this story is an unusual combination of words. What ideas come to your mind when you see the word *retrieved?* Think also about the word *reformation.* Who or what is usually reformed? Draw two word webs on a sheet of paper as shown below. On the spokes around each word, write other words you associate with the center word. Use your dictionary for exact definitions. Then predict what the combination "A Retrieved Reformation" might mean in this story.

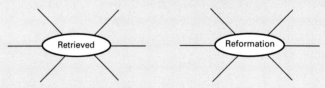

Expand Your Knowledge

Slang is the very informal, everyday speech used by a particular group of people. Slang can be new words or established words and phrases that have taken on new meanings. Slang terms usually go out of date quickly. The word *rap,* for example, currently means "talking to music." This meaning may be out of date in five years.

In his story, O. Henry included slang terms used by criminals of his day. Examples include *stir,* meaning prison; *get sent up,* meaning to be sent to prison; *cracksman,* someone who opens safes illegally; and *rogue-catcher,* a person who captures criminals.

■ *A biography of the author can be found on page 39.*

Enrich Your Reading

Noting Chronological Order   In most stories, events are reported in **chronological order,** the order in which they happen in time. As you read this story, make a time line like the one below, jotting down at least five main events as they occur. Look for phrases—such as "one day" and "at the end of a year"—that signal the passage of time. Watch for events that happen at the same time.

Jimmy is pardoned
and leaves prison.

A Retrieved Reformation

O. HENRY

A guard came to the prison shoe shop, where Jimmy Valentine was assiduously stitching uppers, and escorted him to the front office. There the warden handed Jimmy his pardon, which had been signed that morning by the governor. Jimmy took it in a tired kind of way. He had served nearly ten months of a four-year sentence. He had expected to stay only about three months, at the longest. When a man with as many friends on the outside as Jimmy Valentine had is received in the "stir" it is hardly worthwhile to cut his hair.

"Now, Valentine," said the warden, "you'll go out in the morning. Brace up, and make a man of yourself. You're not a bad fellow at heart. Stop cracking safes, and live straight."

"Me?" said Jimmy, in surprise. "Why, I never cracked a safe in my life."

"Oh, no," laughed the warden. "Of course not. Let's see, now. How was it you happened to get sent up on that Springfield job? Was it because you wouldn't prove an alibi for fear of compromising somebody in extremely high-toned society? Or was it simply a case of a mean old jury that had it in for you? It's always one or the other with you innocent victims."

"Me?" said Jimmy, still blankly virtuous. "Why, warden, I never was in Springfield in my life!"

"Take him back, Cronin," smiled the warden, "and fix him up with outgoing clothes. Unlock him at seven in the morning, and let him come to the bull-pen. Better think over my advice, Valentine."

At a quarter past seven on the next morning Jimmy stood in the warden's outer office. He had on a suit of the villainously fitting, ready-made clothes and a pair of the stiff, squeaky shoes that the state furnishes to its discharged compulsory guests.

The clerk handed him a railroad ticket and the five-dollar bill with which the law expected him to rehabilitate himself into good citizenship and prosperity. The warden gave him a cigar, and shook hands. Valentine, 9762, was chronicled on the books "Pardoned by Governor," and Mr. James Valentine walked out into the sunshine.

Disregarding the song of the birds, the waving green trees, and the smell of the flowers, Jimmy headed straight for a restaurant. There he tasted the first sweet joys of

Words
to Know
and Use

virtuous (vʉr′ cho͞o əs) *adj.* having moral excellence, right action and thinking, goodness
compulsory (kəm pul′ sə rē) *adj.* that must be done, required, or undergone; mandatory, obligatory
rehabilitate (rē′ hə bil′ ə tāt′) *v.* to restore or return to order the privileges or reputation that one has lost

31

liberty in the shape of a broiled chicken and a bottle of white wine—followed by a cigar a grade better than the one the warden had given him. From there he proceeded leisurely to the depot. He tossed a quarter into the hat of a blind man sitting by the door, and boarded his train. Three hours set him down in a little town near the state line. He went to the café of one Mike Dolan and shook hands with Mike, who was alone behind the bar.

"Sorry we couldn't make it sooner, Jimmy, me boy," said Mike. "But we had that protest from Springfield to buck against, and the governor nearly <u>balked</u>. Feeling all right?"

"That's Dandy Jim Valentine's autograph. He's resumed business."

"Fine," said Jimmy. "Got my key?"

He got his key and went upstairs, unlocking the door of a room at the rear. Everything was just as he had left it. There on the floor was still Ben Price's collar-button that had been torn from that <u>eminent</u> detective's shirt-band when they had overpowered Jimmy to arrest him.

Pulling out from the wall a folding-bed, Jimmy slid back a panel in the wall and dragged out a dust-covered suitcase. He opened this and gazed fondly at the finest set of burglar's tools in the East. It was a complete set, made of specially tempered steel, the latest designs in drills, punches, braces and bits, jimmies, clamps, and au-

gers, with two or three novelties invented by Jimmy himself, in which he took pride. Over nine hundred dollars they had cost him to have made at ———, a place where they make such things for the profession.

In half an hour Jimmy went downstairs and through the café. He was now dressed in tasteful and well-fitting clothes, and carried his dusted and cleaned suitcase in his hand.

"Got anything on?" asked Mike Dolan, genially.

"Me?" said Jimmy, in a puzzled tone. "I don't understand. I'm representing the New York Amalgamated Short Snap Biscuit Cracker and Frazzled Wheat Company."

This statement delighted Mike to such an extent that Jimmy had to take a seltzer-and-milk on the spot. He never touched "hard" drinks.

A week after the release of Valentine, 9762, there was a neat job of safe-burglary done in Richmond, Indiana, with no clue to the author. A scant eight hundred dollars was all that was <u>secured</u>. Two weeks after that a patented, improved, burglar-proof safe in Logansport was opened like a cheese to the tune of fifteen hundred dollars, currency; securities and silver untouched. That began to interest the rogue catchers. Then an old-fashioned bank safe in Jefferson City became active and threw out of its crater an eruption of banknotes amounting to five thousand dollars. The losses were now high enough to bring the matter up into Ben Price's class of work. By comparing notes, a remarkable similarity in the methods of the burglaries was noticed. Ben Price investigated the scenes of the robberies, and was heard to remark:

"That's Dandy Jim Valentine's autograph.

RAINY NIGHT   1930   Charles E. Burchfield   San Diego Museum of Art   Donors: Misses Anne R. and Amy Putnam

He's resumed business. Look at that combination knob—jerked out as easy as pulling up a radish in wet weather. He's got the only clamps that can do it. And look how clean those tumblers were punched out! Jimmy never has to drill but one hole. Yes, I guess I want Mr. Valentine. He'll do his bit next time without any short-time or clemency foolishness."

Ben Price knew Jimmy's habits. He had learned them while working up the Springfield case. Long jumps, quick get-aways, no confederates,[1] and a taste for good society—these ways had helped Mr. Valentine to become noted as a successful dodger of retribution. It was given out that Ben Price had taken up the trail of the elusive cracks-

man, and other people with burglar-proof safes felt more at ease.

One afternoon Jimmy Valentine and his suitcase climbed out of the mailhack in Elmore, a little town five miles off the railroad down in the blackjack country of Arkansas. Jimmy, looking like an athletic young senior just home from college, went down the board sidewalk toward the hotel.

A young lady crossed the street, passed him at the corner, and entered a door over which was the sign "The Elmore Bank." Jimmy Valentine looked into her eyes, forgot what he was, and became another man. She lowered her eyes and colored slightly.

---

1. **confederates** (kən fed′ ər its): accomplices or associates in crime.

33

Young men of Jimmy's style and looks were scarce in Elmore.

Jimmy collared a boy that was loafing on the steps of the bank as if he were one of the stockholders, and began to ask him questions about the town, feeding him dimes at intervals. By and by the young lady came out, looking royally unconscious of the young man with the suitcase, and went her way.

"Isn't that young lady Miss Polly Simpson?" asked Jimmy, with specious guile.[2]

"Naw," said the boy. "She's Annabel Adams. Her pa owns this bank. What'd you come to Elmore for? Is that a gold watch-chain? I'm going to get a bulldog. Got any more dimes?"

Jimmy went to the Planters' Hotel, registered as Ralph D. Spencer, and engaged a room. He leaned on the desk and declared his platform to the clerk. He said he had come to Elmore to look for a location to go into business. How was the shoe business, now, in the town? He had thought of the shoe business. Was there an opening?

The clerk was impressed by the clothes and manner of Jimmy. He, himself, was something of a pattern of fashion to the thinly gilded youth of Elmore, but he now perceived his shortcomings. While trying to figure out Jimmy's manner of tying his four-in-hand[3] he cordially gave information.

Yes, there ought to be a good opening in the shoe line. There wasn't an exclusive shoe store in the place. The dry-goods and general stores handled them. Business in all lines was fairly good. Hoped Mr. Spencer would decide to locate in Elmore. He would find it a pleasant town to live in, and the people very sociable.

Mr. Spencer thought he would stop over in the town a few days and look over the situation. No, the clerk needn't call the boy. He would carry up his suitcase, himself; it was rather heavy.

Mr. Ralph Spencer, the phoenix[4] that arose from Jimmy Valentine's ashes—ashes left by the flame of a sudden and alterative attack of love—remained in Elmore, and prospered. He opened a shoe store and secured a good run of trade.

Socially he was also a success and made many friends. And he accomplished the wish of his heart. He met Miss Annabel Adams, and became more and more captivated by her charms.

At the end of a year the situation of Mr. Ralph Spencer was this: he had won the respect of the community, his shoe store was flourishing, and he and Annabel were engaged to be married in two weeks. Mr. Adams, the typical, plodding, country banker, approved of Spencer. Annabel's pride in him almost equalled her affection. He was as much at home in the family of Mr. Adams and that of Annabel's married sister as if he were already a member.

One day Jimmy sat down in his room and wrote this letter, which he mailed to the safe address of one of his old friends in St. Louis:

DEAR OLD PAL:

I want you to be at Sullivan's place, in Little Rock, next Wednesday night, at nine o'clock. I want you to wind up some little matters for me. And, also, I want to make you a present of my kit of tools. I know you'll be glad to get them—you couldn't duplicate the lot for a thousand dollars.

---

2. **specious guile** (spē′ shəs gīl): innocent charm masking real slyness.

3. **four-in-hand:** a necktie tied in the usual way, that is, in a slipknot with the ends left hanging.

4. **phoenix** (fē′ niks): in Egyptian mythology, a beautiful bird that lived for over 500 years and then burned itself to death, only to rise out of its own ashes to live another long life. The phoenix is a symbol of immortality.

Say, Billy, I've quit the old business—a year ago. I've got a nice store. I'm making an honest living, and I'm going to marry the finest girl on earth two weeks from now. It's the only life, Billy—the straight one. I wouldn't touch a dollar of another man's money now for a million. After I get married I'm going to sell out and go West, where there won't be so much danger of having old scores brought up against me. I tell you, Billy, she's an angel. She believes in me; and I wouldn't do another crooked thing for the whole world. Be sure to be at Sully's, for I must see you. I'll bring along the tools with me.

Your old friend,
JIMMY.

On the Monday night after Jimmy wrote this letter, Ben Price jogged unobtrusively into Elmore in a livery buggy. He lounged about town in his quiet way until he found out what he wanted to know. From the drugstore across the street from Spencer's shoe store he got a good look at Ralph D. Spencer.

"Going to marry the banker's daughter are you, Jimmy?" said Ben to himself, softly. "Well, I don't know!"

The next morning Jimmy took breakfast at the Adamses. He was going to Little Rock that day to order his wedding suit and buy something nice for Annabel. That would be the first time he had left town since he came to Elmore. It had been more than a year now since those last professional "jobs," and he thought he could safely venture out.

After breakfast quite a family party went down together—Mr. Adams, Annabel, Jimmy, and Annabel's married sister with her two little girls, aged five and nine. They came by the hotel where Jimmy still boarded, and he ran up to his room and brought along his suitcase. Then they went on to the bank. There stood Jimmy's horse and buggy and Dolph Gibson, who was going to drive him over to the railroad station.

All went inside the high, carved oak railings into the banking room—Jimmy included, for Mr. Adams's future son-in-law was welcome anywhere. The clerks were pleased to be greeted by the good-looking, agreeable young man who was going to marry Miss Annabel. Jimmy set his suitcase down. Annabel, whose heart was bubbling with happiness and lively youth, put on Jimmy's hat and picked up the suitcase. "Wouldn't I make a nice drummer?" said Annabel. "My! Ralph, how heavy it is. Feels like it was full of gold bricks."

"Lot of nickel-plated shoehorns in there," said Jimmy, coolly, "that I'm going to return. Thought I'd save express charges by taking them up. I'm getting awfully economical."

The Elmore Bank had just put in a new safe and vault. Mr. Adams was very proud of it, and insisted on an inspection by everyone. The vault was a small one, but it had a new patented door. It fastened with three solid steel bolts thrown simultaneously with a single handle, and had a time lock. Mr. Adams beamingly explained its workings to Mr. Spencer, who showed a courteous but not too intelligent interest. The two children, May and Agatha, were delighted by the shining metal and funny clock and knobs.

While they were thus engaged Ben Price sauntered in and leaned on his elbow, looking casually inside between the railings. He told the teller that he didn't want anything; he was just waiting for a man he knew.

Suddenly there was a scream or two from the women, and a commotion. <u>Unperceived</u>

**Words
to Know
and Use** | **unperceived** (un′ pər sēvd′) *adj.* not seen

35

by the elders, May, the nine-year-old girl, in a spirit of play, had shut Agatha in the vault. She had then shot the bolts and turned the knob of the combination as she had seen Mr. Adams do.

The old banker sprang to the handle and tugged at it for a moment. "The door can't be opened," he groaned. "The clock hasn't been wound nor the combination set."

Agatha's mother screamed again, hysterically.

"Hush!" said Mr. Adams, raising his trembling hand. "All be quiet for a moment. Agatha!" he called as loudly as he could. "Listen to me." During the following silence they could just hear the faint sound of the child wildly shrieking in the dark vault in a panic of terror.

"My precious darling!" wailed the mother. "She will die of fright! Open the door! Oh, break it open! Can't you men do something?"

"There isn't a man nearer than Little Rock who can open that door," said Mr. Adams, in a shaky voice. "My God! Spencer, what shall we do? That child—she can't stand it long in there. There isn't enough air, and, besides, she'll go into convulsions from fright."

Agatha's mother, frantic now, beat the door of the vault with her hands. Somebody wildly suggested dynamite. Annabel turned to Jimmy, her large eyes full of anguish, but not yet despairing. To a woman nothing seems quite impossible to the powers of the man she worships.

"Can't you do something, Ralph—*try*, won't you?"

He looked at her with a queer, soft smile on his lips and in his keen eyes.

"Annabel," he said, "give me that rose you are wearing, will you?"

Hardly believing that she had heard him aright, she unpinned the bud from the bosom of her dress, and placed it in his hand. Jimmy stuffed it into his vest pocket, threw off his coat and pulled up his shirt sleeves. With that act Ralph D. Spencer passed away and Jimmy Valentine took his place.

"Get away from the door, all of you," he commanded, shortly.

He set his suitcase on the table, and opened it out flat. From that time on he seemed to be unconscious of the presence of anyone else. He laid out the shining, queer implements swiftly and orderly, whistling softly to himself as he always did when at work. In a deep silence and immovable, the others watched him as if under a spell.

In a minute Jimmy's pet drill was biting smoothly into the steel door. In ten minutes—breaking his own burglarious record—he threw back the bolts and opened the door.

Agatha, almost collapsed, but safe, was gathered into her mother's arms.

Jimmy Valentine put on his coat, and walked outside the railings toward the front door. As he went he thought he heard a far-away voice that he once knew call "Ralph!" But he never hesitated.

At the door a big man stood somewhat in his way.

"Hello, Ben!" said Jimmy, still with his strange smile. "Got around at last, have you? Well, let's go. I don't know that it makes much difference, now."

And then Ben Price acted rather strangely.

"Guess you're mistaken, Mr. Spencer," he said. "Don't believe I recognize you. Your buggy's waiting for you, ain't it?"

And Ben Price turned and strolled down the street. 🙢

Responding to Reading

First Impressions

1. As the story closes, what feelings do you have about Jimmy's future?

Second Thoughts

2. Based on what you know about Jimmy, what do you think he will do next?

3. What is your opinion of Ben Price's decision to let Jimmy go? Is his decision wise or unwise?

> **Think about**
> • whether the decision was fair to others
> • whether Jimmy will be a risk in the future
> • how long Jimmy had gone without committing a crime

4. A title can summarize the main idea of a work. Explain the title "A Retrieved Reformation" and tell how it relates to the story.

5. How would you describe the character of Jimmy Valentine?

> **Think about**
> • Jimmy's successful career as a criminal and the code by which he lives
> • whether or not Jimmy changes during the story
> • Annabel's effects on Jimmy
> • how he is alike or different from a "typical" criminal

6. In your opinion, is the reformation of Jimmy Valentine believable? In forming your opinion, use your time line to review the order of events.

Broader Connections

7. Like Jimmy, many prisoners are released from prison before their sentences are up. How do you feel about prisoners' serving shortened sentences? Discuss the advantages and disadvantages of this situation.

Literary Concept: Plot and Climax

As you know, the plot of a story centers on how the characters will deal with a problem, or conflict. Suspense builds to a **climax,** or turning point. The climax may be a decision or an event that solves the conflict and ends the suspense. The climax usually leads to a solution to the problem or to a change in the characters. Look back at the time line you made. What is the climax in "A Retrieved Reformation"? Be prepared to explain your answer.

*W*riting Options

1. Write a headline for the *Elmore Daily News* article that describes the rescue of Agatha. The headline may be up to two lines long, with a maximum of 32 letters in each line.

2. An **interior monologue** is a discussion a person has in his or her mind as a way of sorting out a problem. Write the interior monologue Jimmy might have had as he decided whether he should crack the safe to save Agatha.

3. Imagine that you are Detective Ben Price. Write a report to your superiors explaining why you are closing the case on Jimmy Valentine.

4. Why do you think the criminal's name is Jimmy Valentine? Think of all that is associated with valentines. List reasons why the name is or is not appropriate.

*V*ocabulary Practice

Exercise Read each sentence below. On your paper, write *true* if the statement is true. Write *false* if the statement is false. Explain why each false statement is incorrect.

1. A common **retribution** for criminals like Jimmy is a prison sentence.
2. A **compulsory** prison term would have kept Jimmy out of prison.
3. Most thieves would not **balk** at stealing jewels.
4. A **virtuous** person like Miss Annabel often breaks the law.
5. Jimmy's **unperceived** actions were not noticed.
6. Bank officers sometimes help people **secure** business loans.
7. To **rehabilitate** a criminal like Jimmy means to restore the person to honest, law-abiding ways of living.
8. An **elusive** criminal would be easy to catch.
9. One kind of **retribution** that bank robbers often receive from the courts is money.
10. Since Ben Price was an **eminent** detective, he was not well known.

> *Words to Know and Use*
>
> balk
> compulsory
> elusive
> eminent
> rehabilitate
> retribution
> secure
> unperceived
> virtuous

extend

Options for Learning

1 • Making Movies Create a script based on the last scene in the bank. Cast at least six students to act out the scene. If possible, use realistic costumes, props, and scenery. Then videotape the scene. Present your movie to your class and ask your classmates to critique it.

2 • Draw a Dandy A dandy dresses in the latest styles and looks sharp. Research the clothes of the late 1800's, the setting of this story, by examining costume books in the library. Then find details in the story that describe Jimmy. Finally, draw or paint a portrait of Jimmy Valentine.

3 • A Musical Valentine Write a poem that summarizes the story of Jimmy Valentine. If you can, make the lines rhyme; add a refrain, or lines that are repeated. Set the poem to music and sing it to the class.

4 • Vanity Plates Many states allow car owners to display vanity plates, or license plates with a personal message, on their cars. Find out how many letters or numbers and spaces are allowed on a license plate in your state. Then write a slogan Jimmy might order for his vanity plates.

FACT FINDER

Find out what percentage of criminals in your state are repeat offenders.

O. Henry
1862-1910

O. Henry is the pen name of William Sydney Porter, author of nearly three hundred short stories and novels. Like his character Jimmy Valentine, Porter himself spent time in jail. In Texas, Porter was accused of embezzling funds from a bank at which he had been a teller. Although his "crime" may have been a technical mistake rather than intentional stealing, he fled to Central America to avoid trial. However, when he returned to Austin to visit his dying wife, he was captured and spent three years in prison.

Porter moved to Texas from Greensboro, North Carolina, at the age of twenty. He worked as a ranch hand, bank clerk, newspaper publisher, and newspaper columnist. In prison, Porter began writing short stories, many of which tell about victims of coincidence or fate and are famous for their surprise endings, irony, and humor. After his release, he spent the rest of his life in New York, working as a newspaper columnist and writer of fiction.

Elements of
NONFICTION

Many people prefer to read factual material rather than fiction. They like the idea that what they are reading really happened.

Nonfiction is writing about real people, places, things, and ideas. Although nonfiction usually provides information, it may have several purposes and may come in different forms. The four main purposes of nonfiction are **to inform, to give an opinion, to persuade,** and **to entertain.** A single work often combines two or more of these purposes; for example, it entertains while informing, or it gives the writer's opinion while persuading. The main purpose of the work determines how the information it presents is organized.

Although it is sometimes difficult to divide nonfiction writing into neat categories, there are several types, each of which does have certain characteristic elements. The list below describes a few types of nonfiction that you will read in this book.

Types of Nonfiction

Biography   A biography is the true story of a real person's life. The writer studies all the information that is available about the person, called the subject, including letters, books by and about the subject, diaries, even interviews. A biographer chooses which facts and which parts of the subject's life he or she will include.

Autobiography   An autobiography is the true account of a person's life told by that person. Since the writer is telling his or her own story, he or she can report remembered thoughts and feelings, as you will notice when you read "Fool's Paradise." Biographies and autobiographies are usually organized in chronological order. When a writer presents only one incident from his or her life, the account is called a **personal narrative.**

Informative Article   Informative articles give facts about a specific subject. This type of writing is found in textbooks, newspapers, magazines, pamphlets, books, directions, encyclopedias, and so on. The information is generally organized around main ideas supported by details.

True-Life Adventure   Often found in magazines and books, these true tales of heroic deeds or exciting adventures are similar to stories. The tales are usually told chronologically.

Essay   An essay is a short nonfiction work about one subject. The author might give an opinion, persuade, or simply narrate an interesting event. Essays can be formal or informal. **Formal essays** examine a topic in a thorough, serious, and highly organized manner. **Informal essays,** such as "A Celebration of Grandfathers," reflect the writer's feelings and personality.

Strategies for Reading Nonfiction

You know from experience that reading nonfiction requires you to read and think differently than you do when you read fiction. The following tips will help you tailor your reading.

1. **Set a purpose for reading.** Once you decide *why* you are reading, you can decide *how* to read. If your purpose is to get information, you will need to read slowly, taking notes when necessary, and reread difficult passages. If your purpose is to be entertained, you can usually read at a faster pace.

2. **Preview the reading material.** By looking at the title, subtitles, pictures, and organization of an article, you can get a good idea of what it is about. For example, if you are looking for information about a specific topic for a report, you can tell by previewing a selection whether it will help you. If it will not help, don't waste your time on it; find a more appropriate book or article.

3. **Understand the organization of the work.** Some nonfiction writing has **subtitles,** or small titles in dark print, which show how the information is organized. At other times, you can read the first sentence of each of several paragraphs to get a grasp of the organization.

4. **Look for main ideas or topic sentences.** Often the first or last sentence in a paragraph is the topic sentence, that is, the statement that tells the main idea of the paragraph. The other sentences in the paragraph provide details about that main idea.

5. **Separate facts from opinions.** You remember that **facts** are statements that can be proved, such as "Minnesota contains many lakes." **Opinions** are statements that express a writer's belief and cannot be proved, such as "Minnesota is the most beautiful of the fifty states." As you read nonfiction, be sure to separate in your own mind which of the writer's statements are facts and which are opinions. Writers usually use facts to support their opinions, but sometimes they present an opinion as if it were a fact. You as a reader will want to form your own opinion based on facts. For more about fact and opinion, see the Thinking Skills Workshop, page 630.

6. **Be aware of the writer's tone.** The writer's attitude toward his or her subject matter is called **tone.** The tone might be humorous, admiring, sad, angry, bitter—reflecting almost any emotion that a writer could feel about a subject. Tone is not measurable, but you can get a feeling for it by noticing the writer's choice of words and the kinds of statements that he or she makes.

7. **Summarize the information.** To make sure you understand what you read, summarize the main points. Briefly state in your own words what you learned. Do not hesitate to go back and reread parts of a selection. No reader is able to understand everything he or she reads the first time.

Remember that nonfiction can be just as enjoyable as fiction. You can find nonfiction that amazes you, angers you, teaches you, or makes you laugh or cry. You may even get hooked on nonfiction permanently!

Autobiography

Fool's Paradise

FLOYD DELL

*E*xamine What You Know

In "Fool's Paradise," the writer recalls an incident in which his image of himself was badly shaken and he no longer felt like a respectable person. In a small group, discuss what it means to be respectable. Then copy and complete the chart below by listing examples of people, actions, or qualities that describe your concept of respectability. Compare your idea of respectability with that presented by the author in this selection.

RESPECTABILITY

What It Is	What It Is Not

*E*xpand Your Knowledge

This selection is set soon after the Panic of 1893, when the woolen mills in Floyd Dell's hometown of Barry, Illinois, shut down. A panic occurs when people lose faith in banks and other financial institutions and attempt to withdraw their money quickly. Such a panic can start a chain reaction that eventually causes widespread unemployment and poverty. During the Panic of 1893, fifteen thousand businesses failed and 4 million people lost their jobs. As you read Dell's account, look for more information about this historic time.

*W*rite Before You Read

Like many families today, the Dell family experienced serious financial trouble when the father lost his job. How do you think a parent's inability to find work might affect a family? Make a list of ways such a situation could affect not only the adult who is out of work but other family members as well. Include emotional as well as economic effects.

■ *A biography of the author can be found on page 50.*

Fool's Paradise

FLOYD DELL

It was not considered necessary to tell me anything about the financial status of the family. I was not able to make comparative observations in school because I was sent there immaculately dressed. And I knew that my mother regarded some of the children in the neighborhood as not nice enough for me to play with. I thought we were just a little bit more "respectable" than other people. I did not realize that in the currency of "respectability" a father who used to have a butcher shop was not quite on a par with a father who was cashier of the bank. My father spoke familiarly of the mayor and other city dignitaries. And, as I understood it, his membership in the G.A.R.[1] made him one of what I felt to be the aristocracy of the nation—certainly on Decoration Day[2] he was treated as such. So I had no idea that we were not the very flower of Barry "respectability." There undoubtedly were plenty of things that might have enlightened me about our financial condition. But there was a deceptive parental softening and evasion of harsh facts for my benefit. A child, in their opinion, should be protected from unpleasant things. And the parental gloss marvelously protected me from the facts that were before my eyes. . . .

So, next year, I didn't know there was a Panic. The shutting down of the Barry woolen mills was in my young mind, as in my father's talk, a political and not an economic tragedy. Grover Cleveland[3] was to blame for it all. He was a Democratic President, and that was why he did it. Governor Altgeld was a Democrat, too—that was why he pardoned the Haymarket Anarchists.[4] I wondered why Democrats were allowed to exist. . . .

That fall, before it was discovered that the soles of both my shoes were worn clear through, I still went to Sunday school. And one time the Sunday-school superintendent made a speech to all the classes. He said that these were hard times and that many poor children weren't getting enough to eat. It was the first that I had heard about it. He asked everybody to bring some food for the poor children next Sunday. I felt very sorry for the poor children.

---

1. **G.A.R.:** The Grand Army of the Republic, founded in Illinois in 1866, was a society of Civil War veterans who had fought for the North.

2. **Decoration Day:** Memorial Day, a day to honor the soldiers who have died in America's wars.

3. **Grover Cleveland:** the twenty-second and twenty-fourth President of the United States, who held office from 1885 to 1889 and from 1893 to 1897.

4. **Governor Altgeld . . . Haymarket Anarchists:** This passage refers to a labor meeting held in Haymarket Square in Chicago in 1886 in which seven police officers and ten workers were killed and more than a hundred officers and workers were wounded. The eight people charged with the crime became known as the Haymarket Anarchists; they were later pardoned by John P. Altgeld, governor of Illinois.

Words to Know and Use

respectability (ri spek′ tə bil′ ə tē) *n.* the quality or state of being respectable or honorable
deceptive (dē sep′ tiv) *adj.* not truthful; dishonest
evasion (ə vā′ zhən) *n.* an avoiding, using deceit or cleverness

43

TOM CAFFERTY 1924 Robert Henri Memorial Art Gallery of the University of Rochester Gift of Mrs. Granger A. Hollister.

Also, little envelopes were distributed to all the classes. Each little boy and girl was to bring money for the poor, next Sunday. The pretty Sunday-school teacher explained that we were to write our names, or have our parents write them, up in the left-hand corner of the little envelopes. . . . I told my mother all about it when I came home. And my mother gave me, the next Sunday, a small bag of potatoes to carry to Sunday school. I supposed the poor children's mothers would make potato soup out of them. . . . Potato soup was good. My father, who was quite a joker, would always say, as if he were surprised, "Ah! I see we have some nourishing potato soup today!" It was so good that we had it every day. My father was at home all day long and every day, now; and I liked that, even if he was grumpy as he sat reading Grant's "Memoirs." I had my parents all to myself, too; the others were away. My oldest brother was in Quincy, and memory does not reveal where the others were: perhaps with relatives in the country.

Taking my small bag of potatoes to Sunday school, I looked around for the poor children; I was disappointed not to see them. I had heard about poor children in stories. But I was told just to put my contribution with the others on the big table in the side room.

I had brought with me the little yellow envelope, with some money in it for the poor children. My mother had put the money in it and sealed it up. She wouldn't tell me how much money she had put in it, but it felt like several dimes. Only she wouldn't let me write my name on the envelope. I had learned to write my name, and I was proud of being able to do it. But my mother said firmly, *no,* I must *not* write my name on the envelope; she didn't tell me why. On the way to Sunday school I had pressed the envelope against the coins until I could tell what they were; they weren't dimes but pennies.

When I handed in my envelope, my Sunday-school teacher noticed that my name wasn't on it, and she gave me a pencil; I could write my own name, she said. So I did. But I was confused because my mother had said not to; and when I came home, I confessed what I had done. She looked distressed. "I told you not to!" she said. But she didn't explain why. . . .

I didn't go back to school that fall. My mother said it was because I was sick. I did have a cold the week that school opened; I had been playing in the gutters and had got my feet wet because there were holes in my shoes. My father cut insoles out of card-

The Museum of the City of New York, New York.

board, and I wore those in my shoes. As long as I had to stay in the house anyway, they were all right.

I stayed cooped up in the house, without any companionship. We didn't take a Sunday paper any more, but the *Barry Adage* came every week in the mails; and though I did not read small print, I could see the Santa Clauses and holly wreaths in the advertisements.

There was a calendar in the kitchen. The red days were Sundays and holidays; and that red 25 was Christmas. (It was on a Monday, and the two red figures would come right together in 1893; but this represents research in the World Almanac, not memory.) I knew when Sunday was because I could look out of the window and see the neighbor's children, all dressed up, going to Sunday school. I knew just when Christmas was going to be.

But there was something queer! My father and mother didn't say a word about Christmas. And once, when I spoke of it, there was a strange, embarrassed silence; so I didn't say anything more about it. But I wondered and was troubled. Why didn't they say anything about it? Was what I had said I wanted (memory refuses to supply that detail) too expensive?

I wasn't arrogant and talkative now. I was silent and frightened. What was the matter? Why didn't my father and mother say anything about Christmas? As the day approached, my chest grew tighter with anxiety.

Now it was the day before Christmas. I couldn't be mistaken. But not a word about it from my father and mother. I waited in painful <u>bewilderment</u> all day. I had supper with them and was allowed to sit up for an hour. I was waiting for them to say something. "It's time for you to go to bed," my mother said gently. I *had* to say something.

"This is Christmas Eve, isn't it?" I asked, as if I didn't know.

My father and mother looked at one another. Then my mother looked away. Her face was pale and stony. My father cleared his throat, and his face took on a joking look. He pretended he hadn't known it was Christmas Eve because he hadn't been reading the papers. He said he would go downtown and find out.

My mother got up and walked out of the room. I didn't want my father to have to keep on being funny about it, so I got up and went to bed. I went by myself without having a light. I undressed in the dark and crawled into bed.

I was numb. As if I had been hit by something. It was hard to breathe. I ached all through. I was stunned—with finding out the truth.

My body knew before my mind quite did. In a minute, when I could think, my mind would know. And as the pain in my body ebbed, the pain in my mind began. I *knew*. I couldn't put it into words yet. But I knew why I had taken only a little bag of potatoes to Sunday school that fall. I knew why there had been only pennies in my little yellow envelope. I knew why I hadn't gone to school that fall—why I hadn't any new shoes—why we had been living on potato soup all winter. All these things, and others, many others, fitted themselves together in my mind and meant something.

Then the words came into my mind and I whispered them into the darkness:

"We're poor!"

Words to Know and Use | **bewilderment** (bē wil′ dər mənt) *n.* hopeless confusion

46

That was it. I was one of those poor children I had been sorry for when I heard about them in Sunday school. My mother hadn't told me. My father was out of work, and we hadn't any money. That was why there wasn't going to be any Christmas at our house.

Then I remembered something that made me squirm with shame—a boast. (Memory will not yield this up. Had I said to some Nice little boy, "I'm going to be President of the United States"? or to a Nice little girl, "I'll marry you when I grow up"? It was some boast as horribly shameful to remember.)

"We're poor." There in bed in the dark, I whispered it over and over to myself. I was making myself get used to it. (Or—just torturing myself, as one presses the tongue against a sore tooth? No, memory says not like that—but to keep myself from ever being such a fool again: suffering now, to keep this awful thing from ever happening again. Memory is clear on that; it was more like pulling the tooth to get it over with—never mind the pain, this will be the end!)

It wasn't so bad, now that I knew. I just *hadn't known!* I had thought all sorts of foolish things: that I was going to Ann Arbor—going to be a lawyer—going to make speeches in the square, going to be President. Now I knew better.

I had wanted (something) for Christmas. I didn't want it now. I didn't want anything.

I lay there in the dark, feeling the cold emotion of <u>renunciation</u>. (The tendrils of desire unfold their clasp on the outer world of objects, withdraw, shrivel up. Wishes shrivel up, turn black, die. It is like that.)

It hurt. But nothing would ever hurt again. I would never let myself want anything again.

I lay there stretched out straight and stiff in the dark, my fists clenched hard upon Nothing. . . .

In the morning it had been like a nightmare that is not clearly remembered—that one wishes to forget. Though I hadn't hung up any stocking, there was one hanging at the foot of my bed. A bag of popcorn and a lead pencil, for me. They had done the best they could, now they realized that I knew about Christmas. But they needn't have thought they had to. I didn't want anything. ❧

| *Words to Know and Use* | **renunciation** (ri nun' sē a' shən) *n.* the act of giving up or denying an idea or claim to something |

Responding to Reading

First Impressions

1. What was your reaction to Dell's discovery on Christmas Eve? Explain.

Second Thoughts

2. Why is Dell surprised by this discovery?

   Think about
   - how Dell's parents want others to see them
   - how they handle their economic situation
   - how they think they should raise their son
   - what Dell's life is like before his discovery

3. Is Dell's reaction to learning that he is poor justified? Why or why not?

4. What part does pride play in this selection?

   Think about
   - how Dell's mother shows pride
   - how Dell shows pride before his discovery
   - why Dell is so hurt when his illusion is shattered

5. Dell suggests that it would have been better if he had known his family was poor. Would his knowing sooner have made a difference? Explain.

6. Why do you think Dell's parents choose to deceive their son about their financial situation?

Broader Connections

7. Do you think children should know what their parents earn, how much they have saved, and what they have borrowed? Explain your opinion.

Literary Concept: Autobiography

An **autobiography** is the account of a person's life written by that person. It is told from a first-person point of view, using the first-person pronouns *I* and *me.* Since the writer is writing about himself or herself, an autobiography can provide inside information that only the writer knows. Because the writer chooses what incidents to include, the account reveals the author's self-image. In this excerpt from his autobiography, Dell invites readers to relive a painful incident from his childhood. Why do you think he chose to include this incident? What do you think he wanted the reader to learn about him from this account?

Writing Options

1. Review the chart you made on the meaning of respectability. Compare your thoughts with those of Dell. Present your findings in paragraph form or on a Venn diagram (two overlapping circles), writing your ideas on respectability in the left-hand circle, Dell's ideas in the right-hand circle, and the ideas you and Dell have in common in the space where the circles overlap.

2. In a paragraph, explain what you think the title "Fool's Paradise" means. How does the title relate to this selection?

3. Dell's parents kept him home from school when they could no longer afford to buy him new clothes and shoes. Write a paragraph stating whether you agree or disagree with their decision. State your opinion in a topic sentence; then give reasons for your opinion.

4. List at least five ways Dell's discovery may affect him in the future. Consider the effect on his self-image, his relationships with other children, and his plans for the future.

Vocabulary Practice

Exercise On your paper, write the word from the list that best completes each sentence below.

1. Dell felt _____ when his mother was upset with him for writing his name on the envelope.
2. Dell's concept of _____ was based on the standards of those around him, outward appearance, and material wealth.
3. When Dell found out the truth, he felt that his parents had been _____ about their financial situation.
4. Dell blamed his disappointment and hurt on his parents' _____ of economic discussions.
5. The _____ of his old lifestyle and standards made Dell swear that he would never allow pride to hurt him again.

Words to Know and Use

bewilderment
deceptive
evasion
renunciation
respectability

*O*ptions for Learning

1 • **On Stage** A pantomime is a play or skit acted out by using only gestures and actions to tell the story. Plan a pantomime that shows the moments before, during, and after the point at which Dell discovers the truth about his family's financial situation. Present your pantomime for the class.

2 • **Singing the Blues** Collect four to six songs, old or new, that express the feelings of Dell or his father about their financial situation. Think of lyrics to songs you know, listen to songs from the 1890's era, or ask your parents or music teachers for suggestions. Copy the lyrics and share them or play the songs for your class.

3 • **The Perfect Gift** Think of the perfect gift for Dell and each of his parents for the Christmas described in the selection. Be sure to consider the personality and needs of each character when making your choices.

4 • **Setting the Scene** Using history books, encyclopedias, and other resources, create a time line of the events that led to the Panic of 1893. For an example of a time line, see page 30. List the events beside the vertical lines in the order in which they happened.

 **FACT FINDER**

What percentage of the population of the United States was unemployed last year?

*F*loyd Dell
1887-1969

Floyd Dell's memory of his sixth Christmas affected his entire life. His attempts to come to terms with his working-class background led him to adopt a socialist point of view. Dell believed strongly that government, rather than individuals, should control the means of production and that everyone should share equally in both work and profits. To this end, he tried to use his writings to influence others.

Dell wrote poetry and fiction while living as a sort of early hippie in New York City's Greenwich Village, but he is best known for his nonfiction work. During his career as a journalist, Dell worked for several radical literary magazines. In 1918 he even stood trial along with three other editors of a radical magazine called *The Masses* for articles criticizing American policies during World War I. The charges were finally dropped, and Dell continued to write about and fight for social justice and high ideals.

WORKSHOP

FIRST-PERSON NARRATIVE

Like the characters in the selections you have just read, most of us have experienced illusions or deceptions. Perhaps we believed something that wasn't true. In some instances we ourselves may have been the ones doing the deceiving or creating the illusion.

For the following assignment you will write a first-person autobiographical narrative about such an incident. "Fool's Paradise" by Floyd Dell is an example of this type of writing. In this selection, the writer **narrates**, or tells, his story from what is called **first-person point of view.** Look at the following paragraph.

> I didn't go back to school that fall. My mother said it was because I was sick. I did have a cold the week that school opened; I had been playing in the gutters and had got my feet wet because there were holes in my shoes.

The use of first-person pronouns such as *I* and *my* signals that the writing is in the first person. "Fool's Paradise" is also **autobiographical**, which means that the events in the story actually happened to the writer.

> Here is your PASSkey to this assignment.

**GUIDED ASSIGNMENT:
THE AUTOBIOGRAPHICAL
INCIDENT**

Narrate an incident in your life when you experienced an illusion or deception that taught you an important lesson.

PURPOSE: To narrate a true story

AUDIENCE: Your teacher and classmates

SUBJECT: An illusion or deception

STRUCTURE: A multi-paragraph composition

Prewriting

STEP **1** **Explore ideas** With a partner or small group, brainstorm illusions or deceptions each of you has experienced. Don't be shy about relating your experiences, but remember to listen, too. Your peers' thoughts may bring more of your own experiences to mind. Summarize your ideas in a list like the one this student created:

—the time I thought a store detective was actually a shoplifter
—when one of my best friends spread a rumor about me behind
my back
—the time I pretended to be sick on the day of my piano recital

STEP 2 Select the best idea   Discuss your list with your peers. Use the following questions to help judge the merits of each idea. Then, choose the topic that seems best to you.

1. Will the idea be interesting to my audience?
2. Can the idea be developed into a good narrative?
3. Does the idea truly contain an illusion or deception?
4. Does the idea lead to a lesson that I or someone else learned from the experience?

STEP 3 Organize your narrative   After you've selected your topic, break the incident down into various parts and decide what should come first, second, and so on. A common way to organize a narrative is to tell the story in the order in which the events actually happened. This organizing plan is known as **chronological order**.

List the parts of your incident in order on a separate piece of paper. Along with each part, include details that explain and illustrate exactly what happened.

Finally, write down what you or someone else learned from this encounter with deception or illusion.

Drafting

STEP 1 Use a strong introduction   An interesting beginning that grabs the reader's attention and makes him or her want to read on is crucial in all kinds of writing, but it is especially important for narratives. All sorts of openings are possible. You might start with a vivid description, a dramatic point in the action, or a preview of the lesson that was learned. If you need ideas, skim through this book to see how other writers started their narratives.

NOTE: Some writers like to write their introductions later in the writing process. Decide which method seems most comfortable for you.

STEP 2 Use vivid details   Make sure that as you write you include all the details necessary to make your reader see and feel what you experienced when the incident actually happened.

STEP **3** **Tie up loose ends**   The conclusion of the composition should tie up any loose ends in your story. If you have not previously explained the lesson that was learned, make it part of your conclusion.

Revising and Editing

Use the following checklist to help you evaluate and revise your work, or ask a classmate to review your work according to the checklist.

Revision Checklist

. . . .

1. Is the opening lively and interesting? Does it make the reader want to read on?

2. Is the narrative told in a clear, logical order? Do there seem to be any parts missing? Are there any unnecessary details?

3. Can the descriptions be improved?

4. Is the illusion or deception obvious?

5. Will the reader understand what lesson was learned? Is the connection between the event and the lesson clear?

Editing   When you have finished revising, exchange drafts with a peer editor. Proofread each other's papers for spelling, clarity, and mechanics. Then make a clean, final copy.

Here is the final version of one student's autobiographical incident.

Playtime

◀ STUDENT MODEL

I woke up with a stomachache, but it wasn't because I was really sick. I had the shakes, but I wasn't cold. I was sweating like a marathon runner, but I was still in bed. When my mother came in to wake me up, I knew what I had to do.

Tonight was the night of my first recital. I was scared.

My mother felt my forehead, but there was no fever.

"I don't care," I said. "I'm sick. I can't play at the recital."

"Your teacher will be so disappointed," she said. "Are you sure you're not just nervous?"

She was right about that, but I couldn't tell her. "I'm sure. I'm sure that if I play at that recital, I'll be sick all over the keys."

She said OK and left me alone. That morning passed slowly. I tried many things to keep my mind off the recital. I tried going back to sleep, but it didn't work. I stared at the ceiling. I counted everything in my room. A little while before the recital was to start, my mom came back in. I knew she was giving me one more chance to go, but I told her I was still feeling terrible. She sighed and walked out.

By now I really <u>was</u> feeling terrible. I looked at the clock. It was too late. I had missed the beginning of the recital. There was no way I could go late. I imagined myself playing the piano, hitting all the notes, and I realized that I really could have done it. I learned that it is much better to face what you fear. Avoiding it just makes it worse. I let down my mother, my teacher, but most of all, myself.

Presenting

Read your completed essay to the class. If you feel that the illusion or deception you describe is too personal, you might ask your teacher to read it to the class anonymously.

Reflecting on Your Writing

Answer the following questions about this assignment. Hand in your answers with your paper.

1. What part of your paper do you like best? Why?
2. Which part do you think could be improved?
3. Did working with a peer group help or hinder your writing? What could make your peer group more effective?

LANGUAGE
WORKSHOP

USING PRONOUNS CORRECTLY

> A **pronoun** is a word that replaces a noun or another pronoun. When choosing pronouns, consider your point of view and whether the pronoun is the subject or the object of the sentence.

Writers use pronouns to replace nouns and to let readers know their narrative method, or point of view. If a writer uses the pronouns *I, me,* or *we,* the narrator is a character in the story and the writer is using the first-person point of view.

> *I* looked up from *my* typewriter late one afternoon, a little startled.

In the third-person point of view, the story is told from the point of view of someone who is not one of the characters. This narrator refers to all the characters as *he, she,* or *they* and functions as an outside observer keeping a sharp eye on the action of the story.

> Jimmy Valentine looked into her *eyes,* forgot what *he* was, and became another name.

The first two Writer's Workshops in this book ask you to write in the first person and the third person. You must always keep your point of view consistent in a piece of writing by using the correct pronouns throughout. The chart below lists the forms of these pronouns.

	Nominative	Objective	Possessive
First Person	I, we	me, us	my, mine, our, ours
Third Person	he, she, it, they	her, him, it, them	her, hers, his, its, their, theirs

NOTE

The second-person pronouns are *you, your,* and *yours.* The second-person point of view is rarely used in writing because the pronoun *you* sounds too informal. However, this point of view is common in advertising and in other forms of persuasive writing.

Using the Nominative Form of Pronouns

As you can see from the chart, first- and third-person pronouns can also be divided into three forms. Pronouns in the **nominative** form are used as subjects of verbs.

I visualized mangled and inadequate branches for my fires.
(The subject of the verb *visualized* is the pronoun *I*.)
He lounged about town in his quiet way. (The subject of the
verb *lounged* is the pronoun *he*.)

Use the nominative form of a pronoun even if two or more pronouns
or a noun and a pronoun are used as the subject.

He and *I* looked at the growing woodpile.
Dandy Jim and *he* studied the lock together.

Use the nominative form of a pronoun when a pronoun is used
together with a noun as the subject of a sentence.

We students brought food for the poor children in town.

Using the Objective Form of Pronouns

Use the **objective** form of a pronoun for direct objects, indirect
objects, and objects of prepositions. Remember that a direct object is the
person or thing that receives the action of the verb. An indirect object
tells *to whom* or *for whom* the action of the verb is done. An indirect
object always comes before the direct object in a sentence. (For a review
of these sentence elements, see the Language Handbook.)

Jerry asked *me* to visit the orphanage. (*Me* is the direct object
of the verb *visit*.)
Jimmy Valentine lent *him* a set of burglary tools. (*Him* is the
indirect object of the verb *lent*.)

A pronoun can also be the object of a preposition.

Can you deliver the potatoes to *her*? (*Her* is the object of the
preposition *to*.)

Use the objective form of a pronoun even if two or more pronouns or
a noun and a pronoun are used together in the object of a sentence.

My father could not afford new shoes for Mom and *me*.

Exercise 1   Write the correct pronoun from those given in parentheses.

1. (We, Us) orphanage boys were always busy.
2. For example, my friend John and (I, me) carried milk.
3. Working together helped (he, him) and (I, me) to become friends.
4. One fall, a woman writer called the orphanage executives and asked
   (they, them) to send a boy to chop wood for (she, her).

5. The other boys couldn't go, so the orphanage sent (I, me).
6. (She, Her) and her dog, Pat, lived in a cabin in the hills.
7. (They, Them) seemed friendly.
8. However, (she, her) doubted that (I, me) could do the work.
9. Eventually, (us, we) three got along fine.
10. When (she, her) was busy writing, Pat and (I, me) went for walks.
11. For some reason I told (she, her) a story that was not true.
12. I didn't want (she, her) to pity me.
13. I said, "I have a mother in Mannville, and (she, her) and (me, I) get together each summer."
14. "My mother buys things for (I, me)," I continued.
15. "(We, Us) boys at the orphanage share the things (she, her) sends."
16. Suddenly, (she, her) and Pat were leaving.
17. I was too sad to say goodbye to (she, her).
18. (She, Her) and the people at the orphanage talked about (I, me).
19. (They, Them) and (she, her) discovered that I had lied.
20. I hope (she, her) and the others aren't disappointed in (I, me).

Exercise 2   Work in groups to decide whether the italicized pronouns in the following passage are used correctly or incorrectly. Have one group member copy the passage on a piece of paper, inserting the correct pronouns as determined by the group. Then compare your work with that of the other groups in your class.

I loved O. Henry's story about Jimmy Valentine's safecracking career. It reminded *me* of the time Jane and *me* created quite a scene at a party. Most of the other girls were from another school and *them* seemed snobby. All the boys kept asking a redheaded girl named Sara to dance with *they*. *Us* two girls couldn't stand to watch *them* and *she* dance for one more minute, so *we* escaped to a quiet room. As *her* and *me* closed the door, it made a definite clicking sound. Then when *us* two tried to open it, *we* discovered that the door was locked! Jane and *me* banged and banged until a crowd gathered outside the door. Our problem certainly gave *they* a good laugh.

Exercise 3 Analyzing and Revising Your Writing

1. Review the first-person writing you did for the autobiographical workshop assignment on pages 51-54.
2. Reread the piece and correct any pronoun errors.
3. Remember to check for correct pronoun usage the next time you proofread your writing.

LANGUAGE HANDBOOK

For review and practice:
nominative pronouns,
    pages 906–09
objective pronouns,
    pages 909–11
objects, page 894

STUDY SKILLS
WORKSHOP

WORKING WITH PEERS

In many of the assignments in this book, you will be asked to work in groups or pairs. The following guidelines will help you work more effectively with your peers.

1. **Be an active listener.** Avoid daydreaming. Concentrate on what other group members are saying. As a group member, you are expected to make meaningful suggestions and contribute to the success of each person in the group. When it is your turn to speak or read your work, you will want others to listen attentively to you.

2. **Be an active contributor.** Nothing creates more tension in a group than one or two members who don't participate.

3. **Don't underestimate yourself or others.** Each group member has something important to contribute. A person does not need to know every grammar rule in order to offer useful ideas and suggestions.

4. **Be sensitive and courteous.** Have concern for others' feelings and treat them the way you wish to be treated. Avoid destructive or sarcastic comments. Such statements, even when made as a joke, can hurt others deeply.

5. **Offer constructive criticism.** There are many ways to be constructive while discussing a peer's work. Tell a peer what part of his or her work you like best before you point out the part you like least. Ask questions such as "Can you explain what you mean here?" instead of "Where did you get this ridiculous idea?"

Exercise Working in a group, try to compose a first-person story. Brainstorm a list of details describing an imaginary character who is an orphan in America sometime in the past. Also list details describing the setting. Decide as a group which of the details about character and setting are appropriate. Choose one person to record the story. Have a member of the group begin the story by composing aloud the first two or three sentences. Then proceed in a circle, having each group member add a sentence or two until a story has been told. Each member should have at least two turns to add sentences.

▶ **GROUP EVALUATION**
Name two things your group did well and one thing your group needs to improve on.

When your group is completely satisfied with its story, share it with the other groups by reading it aloud or by making copies for them to read. As a class, critique each of the stories, keeping in mind the interpersonal skills you have been practicing.

58   UNIT ONE   ILLUSIONS AND DECEPTIONS

BLIND SPOTS

There is a small area in your eye called a blind spot, from which you are unable to see. Technically, the blind spot is the point at which the optic nerve joins the retina of the eye. However, people have other kinds of blind spots as well. These blind spots are weaknesses or faults that people are unable to recognize in themselves or others. For example, someone might be blind to his or her own prejudice, ignorance, or weakness or may fail to recognize such flaws in someone else.

As you read the next set of selections, look for blind spots in the characters. Which characters are not "seeing" accurately? What are they failing to see?

Elements of
POETRY

Poetry is a special type of literature in which words are arranged and chosen to create a certain effect. Poets carefully select words for their sounds and meanings and combine them in different and unusual ways in order to communicate ideas, feelings, new ways of looking at things, experiences, and sometimes stories. Poets use the elements of poetry to convey the sounds, emotions, pictures, and ideas they want to express.

*U*nderstanding Poetry

Form   The way a poem looks and is arranged on a page is its form. The words in a poem are written in **lines,** which may or may not be sentences. In some poems, such as ''Annabel Lee,'' lines are grouped into **stanzas.** Each stanza may have a uniform number of lines, or the number of lines may vary.

Sound   Since most poems are meant to be read aloud, poets make many decisions about how the poem should sound. In some poems, words are arranged to form patterns of sound. Some of these patterns are described below.

Rhyme   Rhyme is the repetition of the same sound at the ends of words—*peek* and *creak,* for example. Many traditional poems contain rhyme at the ends of lines. The pattern of such rhyme is called the **rhyme scheme.**

Rhythm   The rhythm of a poem is the pattern of stressed and unstressed syllables. Rhythm brings out the musical quality of language; it can also create mood and emphasize

ideas. Notice the rhythm in this line from ''Annabel Lee.'' The stressed syllables are marked by a /.

   /   /   /   /
It was many and many a year ago.

Poems in which the rhythm is like everyday conversation, without a definite pattern, are called **free verse.** ''Incident in a Rose Garden'' is written in free verse.

Alliteration   Alliteration is the repetition of consonant sounds at the beginnings of words, as in this line from ''Incident in a Rose Garden'':

<u>B</u>lack gloves, a <u>b</u>road <u>b</u>lack hat.

Assonance   The repetition of vowel sounds within words is called assonance, as in this line from ''Annabel Lee'':

And so, all the n<u>i</u>ght-t<u>i</u>de, I l<u>ie</u>
down by the s<u>i</u>de.

Imagery   Language that appeals to the readers' senses of sight, hearing, touch, smell, and taste is called imagery. Most imagery creates visual images for the reader, as in these lines from ''Incident in a Rose Garden'':

Death grinned, and his eyes lit up
With the pale glow of those lanterns
That workmen carry sometimes . . .

Imagery can appeal to other senses as well. These lines from ''Lost'' appeal to the senses of touch and smell:

I brushed by people with every step,
Covered my nose once in a while,
Gasping against the smell of
  perspiration on humid days.

Figurative Language   Language that describes ordinary things in a new way is called figurative language. Poets commonly use figurative language to compare one thing to another. These and other special ways words are combined, called "figures of speech," are explained below.

Simile   A comparison of unlike things using the word *like* or *as* is called a simile. This example from "The Courage That My Mother Had" compares courage to a rock:

> That courage like a rock, which she
> Has no more need of, and I have.

Metaphor   A metaphor compares two unlike things without the word *like* or *as*. In these lines from "Lost," the speaker's head is compared to a signal.

> Lights flashed everywhere
> until my head became a signal,
> flashing on and off.

Personification   In personification, an object, animal, or idea exhibits human qualities. In these lines from "Incident in a Rose Garden," death seems like a person.

> Sir, I encountered Death
> Just now among the roses.
> Thin as a scythe he stood there.

Speaker   The speaker is the voice that talks to the reader. The speaker may or may not be the voice of the poet, even in a poem that uses the pronouns *I* and *me*. The poet might make the speaker a young child or an old woman, or anyone. The speaker often expresses feelings the poet wants to convey.

Theme   The theme of a poem is the message about life or human nature that the poet shares with the reader. For example, the theme might be an idea, such as "Death is inevitable."

Strategies for Reading Poetry

1. **Read the poem aloud.** You hear the sounds of a poem by reading it aloud. As you read, remember that the end of a line is not necessarily the end of a thought. Read to the end punctuation to understand the complete thought. Listen to the rhyme, rhythm, and sounds of the words as you read.

2. **Visualize the images.** Picture the images that the poem suggests. Think about any comparisons the poet makes.

3. **Figure out who the speaker is.** Use clues in the poem to decide if the speaker is male or female, young or old, and so on. The speaker's identity will influence how you feel about his or her message.

4. **Look carefully at individual words and phrases.** Poets try to choose words that convey an exact meaning, feeling, and sound. As you read, try to figure out what each word adds to the poem. Think about why the poet chose those words.

5. **Think about the poem's message or theme.** Ask yourself what idea all the elements of the poem combine to suggest. Paraphrase, or put into your own words, the idea or feeling or picture the poem gives you.

Remember that poetry is very personal. A poem may mean something special to you because you have experienced the feelings it expresses. You may have seen a picture the poem describes, or agree with an idea the poem suggests. Let yourself become involved with poetry and enjoy the new and special way that poetry makes you think and feel.

Poetry

Annabel Lee
EDGAR ALLAN POE

Incident in a Rose Garden
DONALD JUSTICE

Examine What You Know

Down through the ages, people have personified, or given human qualities to, death in many ways. One common image of death in Western cultures is that of a hooded figure dressed in black, often with the body of a skeleton. If death were a person, how do you imagine it would appear? Draw the picture you imagine. Share your sketch with your classmates, and later compare it to the images presented in the poems.

Expand Your Knowledge

Each of the following poems tells a story about someone who is forced to deal with death. Poetry that tells a story is called **narrative poetry.** Narrative poetry has elements of both fiction and poetry. Like all stories, narrative poetry contains the elements of character, setting, plot, and theme. However, unlike a prose story, narrative poetry is written in lines and incorporates the elements of poetry described on pages 60-61. As you read, think about why each writer chose to present his story as poetry rather than prose.

Enrich Your Reading

Identifying the Speaker   The voice that "talks" to the reader in poetry is called the **speaker.** The speaker may be the poet, or it may be someone or something else the poet chooses. For instance, the speaker might be a baby, a dog, or the wind. In a narrative poem, the main speaker is the narrator. Because a narrative poem has characters, it may contain dialogue to show the different characters conversing. For example, in "Incident in a Rose Garden," the main speaker and narrator is the master, but there are two other speakers with whom the master converses, or talks. The dialogue between these characters appears in italics and is indented.

Look for clues to the personality of each speaker in the poems. Use each speaker's actions and words to determine his attitude toward death.

■ *Biographies of the authors can be found on page 68.*

Annabel Lee

EDGAR ALLAN POE

It was many and many a year ago,
   In a kingdom by the sea,
That a maiden there lived whom you may know
   By the name of Annabel Lee;
5 And this maiden she lived with no other thought
   Than to love and be loved by me.

She was a child and *I* was a child,
   In this kingdom by the sea,
But we loved with a love that was more than love—
10   I and my Annabel Lee—
With love that the wingéd seraphs[1] of Heaven
   Coveted[2] her and me.

And this was the reason that, long ago,
   In this kingdom by the sea,
15 A wind blew out of a cloud by night
   Chilling my Annabel Lee;
So that her highborn kinsmen came
   And bore her away from me,
To shut her up in a sepulchre[3]
20   In this kingdom by the sea.

The angels, not half so happy in Heaven,
   Went envying her and me:—
Yes!—that was the reason (as all men know,
   In this kingdom by the sea)
25 That the wind came out of the cloud, chilling
   And killing my Annabel Lee.

ANNABEL LEE c. 1870 James A.
McNeill Whistler Freer Gallery of Art,
Smithsonian Institution, Washington, D.C.
05.129

---

1. **seraphs** (ser′ əfs): any of the highest order of angels.
2. **coveted:** envied.
3. **sepulchre** (sep′ əl kər): a place for burial; tomb.

But our love it was stronger by far than the love
   Of those who were older than we—
   Of many far wiser than we—
30 And neither the angels in Heaven above
   Nor the demons down under the sea,
Can ever dissever[4] my soul from the soul
   Of the beautiful Annabel Lee:—

For the moon never beams, without bringing me dreams
35   Of the beautiful Annabel Lee:—
And the stars never rise but I see the bright eyes
   Of the beautiful Annabel Lee:
And so, all the night-tide, I lie down by the side
Of my darling, my darling, my life and my bride,
40   In her sepulchre there by the sea—
   In her tomb by the side of the sea.

---

4. **dissever:** disunite; separate.

*R*esponding to Reading

First Impressions of "Annabel Lee"

1. How do you feel about the speaker and his story?

Second Thoughts on "Annabel Lee"

2. Who or what does the speaker blame for the death of Annabel Lee? Consider his comments in lines 11-12 and lines 21-22.

3. What do you think caused Annabel Lee's death? Consider the physical evidence presented in lines 13-16 and lines 25-26.

4. In your opinion, how well is the speaker dealing with his bride's death?
   Think about
   • the speaker's description of his relationship with Annabel Lee
   • the information in the fifth stanza
   • the visions described in lines 34-37
   • the speaker's nightly habit, described in lines 38-41

Incident in a Rose Garden

DONALD JUSTICE

THE GARDENER   Reg Cartwright
Collection of the artist.

The gardener came running,
An old man, out of breath.
Fear had given him legs.

    Sir, I encountered Death
5   *Just now among the roses.*
    Thin as a scythe[1] he stood there.
    I knew him by his pictures.
    He had his black coat on,
    Black gloves, a broad black hat.
10   *I think he would have spoken,*
    Seeing his mouth stood open.
    Big it was, with white teeth.
    As soon as he beckoned, I ran.
    I ran until I found you.
15   *Sir, I am quitting my job.*
    I want to see my sons
    Once more before I die.
    I want to see California.
We shook hands; he was off.

20 And there stood Death in the garden,
Dressed like a Spanish waiter.
He had the air of someone
Who because he likes arriving
At all appointments early
25 Learns to think himself patient.
I watched him pinch one bloom off
And hold it to his nose—
A connoisseur[2] of roses—
One bloom and then another.

30 They strewed the earth around him.
    Sir, you must be that stranger
    Who threatened my gardener.
    This is my property, sir.
    I welcome only friends here.
35 Death grinned, and his eyes lit up
With the pale glow of those lanterns
That workmen carry sometimes
To light their way through the dusk.
Now with great care he slid
40 The glove from his right hand
And held that out in greeting,
A little cage of bone.
    Sir, I knew your father,
    And we were friends at the end.
45   *As for your gardener,*
    I did not threaten him.
    Old men mistake my gestures.
    I only meant to ask him
    To show me to his master.
50   *I take it you are he?*

for Mark Strand

---

1. **scythe** (sīth): a tool with a long, curved handle and long, thin blade, used for cutting down tall grass.
2. **connoisseur** (kän′ ə sʉr′): an expert or authority in some field, especially in the fine arts or in matters of taste.

*R*esponding to Reading

First Impressions of "Incident in a Rose Garden"

1. Does this poem leave you with the same feeling you had after reading "Annabel Lee" or a different one? Explain.

Second Thoughts on "Incident in a Rose Garden"

2. What misunderstandings occur in the poem? Why do you suppose they happen?

   Think about
   • for whom the gardener thinks Death has come
   • how the master reacts to the gardener's words
   • what the master says to Death in the garden

3. Contrast the reactions of the gardener and the master toward Death.

   Think about
   • the gardener's action and decision in lines 13-18
   • the master's description of Death in lines 21-25
   • the master's words to Death in lines 31-34

4. Consider the compact style, the use of conversation, and the abrupt ending in this poem. What are the effects of these techniques on you?

Comparing the Poems

5. Compare the images of death presented in each of these poems. Use words or phrases from each poem in your comparison.

6. Which poem do you like better? Why?

Broader Connections

7. What are some ways people react to the death of a loved one? What causes their reactions to vary? Consider such factors as the age of the person who has died and the cause of death.

*L*iterary Concepts: *Rhyme and Rhythm/Personification*

Some poems have a strong, predictable sound pattern caused by a regular rhythm and a repeated pattern of end rhyme. Read aloud the first stanza of "Annabel Lee" and listen to the sound of the words. Which lines **rhyme,** or end with the same sound? Do you hear a regular, almost musical **rhythm,** or pattern of stressed syllables? Now read the rest of the poem and decide if the pattern is the same in all six stanzas.

Personification is a figure of speech in which human qualities are assigned to an object, an animal, or an idea. For example, in lines 35-38 of "Incident in a Rose Garden," the poet personifies death as a smiling man with glowing eyes. Find three other examples of personification in the poem.

Writing Options

1. A **euphemism** is a word or phrase that is used instead of a more direct, but distasteful or offensive, word or phrase. For example, a euphemism like "the grim reaper" might be substituted for the word *death,* while "crossing over" might be used instead of *dying.* List as many euphemisms as you can for the words *death* and *dying.*

2. Both "Annabel Lee" and "Incident in a Rose Garden" are grouped under the subunit title "Blind Spots." Explain why each poem belongs in this grouping.

3. Tell the next part of the story of "Incident in a Rose Garden" by writing (a) another stanza for the poem, (b) a dialogue between Death and the master, or (c) a description of how the master will respond to Death's question.

4. Each of these poems personifies death. Describe Death's personality as presented in either "Annabel Lee" or "Incident in a Rose Garden."

Edgar Allan Poe
1809-1849

Edgar Allan Poe is best known for his dark poems and morbid stories that sometimes feature characters on the edge of madness. His horror stories are among the best ever written. Poe pioneered the short story form and the detective story.

The tragedies that appear in Poe's writings reflect the tragedies that haunted his own life. Poe was the son of traveling actors, but by the time he was two, his father had deserted the family and his mother had died in poverty in Virginia. Mr. and Mrs. John Allan adopted the orphan. However, the relationship between Poe and Mr. Allan was always strained.

After brief studies at the University of Virginia and a dismissal from West Point, Poe became a journalist and an editor. At the age of twenty-six, Poe married his thirteen-year-old cousin, Virginia Clemm. Their life together was a struggle against poverty. When Virginia died after a long illness, Poe was in despair. Deeply depressed, he often sought escape in alcohol.

In spite of these tragedies, or because of them, Poe created a body of work that remains unique and popular. Poe died a poor and unhappy man, three years after his wife. "Annabel Lee" was published two days after his death.

Donald Justice
1925-

Donald Justice's talents as a poet were recognized when he was awarded a Pulitzer Prize in 1980. He has received numerous awards and grants, including fellowships from the Rockefeller and Ford Foundations and a grant from the National Council on the Arts. Justice likes to experiment with different types of poetry. For example, the poem "Incident in a Rose Garden" was originally written using only dialogue. Later, Justice revised the poem to include descriptive passages. The second version of the poem appears in this book.

Fiction

The *Necklace*

GUY DE MAUPASSANT (gē də mō pä sän′)

Examine What You Know

In reading "The Necklace" you will discover what possessions one woman feels she needs in order to be socially accepted. List five things you own that you value highly. Order them from most to least important. Which of these items are important to you because of what others think of them? Where do those items fall on your list?

Expand Your Knowledge

This story takes place in France during the nineteenth century. In those times, a woman's choices—both professional and social—were severely restricted by her wealth and social class. A woman born to poverty rarely escaped to a better life. A woman born into the middle class could only move up by marrying an aristocrat or another member of the upper class. This was difficult, since a bride's family was expected to give her new husband a dowry, a large sum of money or parcel of property, upon marriage.

Enrich Your Reading

Problems and Solutions   The plot of most stories centers around a conflict, or problem, that the characters need to resolve. Sometimes the plot is made up of several separate, but related, problems. In this story, the main characters, Monsieur and Madame Loisel, encounter three main problems. To better understand the story, identify each problem and its solution as you read. You might use a chart like the one below, in which the first problem and solution have been identified.

Problem	Solution
Madame Loisel feels deprived and longs to be part of the upper class.	Monsieur Loisel gets his wife invited to a party for the wealthy.

■ *A biography of the author can be found on page 79.*

The Necklace

GUY DE MAUPASSANT

She was one of those pretty and charming girls, born, as if by an accident of fate, into a family of clerks. With no dowry, no <u>prospects</u>, no way of any kind of being met, understood, loved, and married by a man both prosperous and famous, she was finally married to a minor clerk in the Ministry of Education.

She dressed plainly because she could not afford fine clothes, but was as unhappy as a woman who has come down in the world; for women have no family rank or social class. With them, beauty, grace, and charm take the place of birth and breeding. Their natural poise, their instinctive good taste, and their mental cleverness are the sole guiding principles that make daughters of the common people the equals of ladies in high society.

She grieved incessantly, feeling that she had been born for all the little niceties and luxuries of living. She grieved over the shabbiness of her apartment, the dinginess of the walls, the worn-out appearance of the chairs, the ugliness of the draperies. All these things, which another woman of her class would not even have noticed, gnawed at her and made her furious. The sight of the little Breton[1] girl who did her humble housework roused in her <u>disconsolate</u> regrets and wild daydreams. She would dream of silent chambers, draped with Oriental tapestries and lighted by tall bronze floor lamps, and of two handsome butlers in knee breeches, who, drowsy from the heavy warmth cast by the central stove, dozed in large overstuffed armchairs.

She would dream of great reception halls hung with old silks, of fine furniture filled with priceless curios,[2] and of small, stylish, scented sitting rooms just right for the four o'clock chat with intimate friends, with distinguished and sought-after men whose attention every woman envies and longs to attract.

When dining at the round table, covered for the third day with the same cloth, opposite her husband, who would raise the cover of the soup tureen, declaring delightedly, "Ah! A good stew! There's nothing I like better . . . ," she would dream of fashionable dinner parties, of gleaming silverware, of tapestries making the walls alive with characters out of history and strange birds in a fairyland forest; she would dream of delicious dishes served on wonderful china, of gallant compliments whispered and listened

---

1. **Breton** (bret′ 'n): from the French province of Brittany.
2. **curios:** rare or unusual articles.

Words to Know and Use	**prospects** (prä′ spekts) *n.* chances for success **disconsolate** (dis kän′ sə lit) *adj.* very unhappy, beyond cheering up

to with a sphinxlike[3] smile as one eats the rosy flesh of a trout or nibbles at the wings of a grouse.

She had no evening clothes, no jewels, nothing. But those were the things she wanted: she felt that was the kind of life for her. She so much longed to please, be envied, be fascinating and sought after.

She had a well-to-do friend, a classmate of convent-school days whom she would no longer go to see, simply because she would feel so distressed on returning home. And she would weep for days on end from vexation, regret, despair, and anguish.

clarify   Why is Mme. Loisel so unhappy?

Then one evening, her husband came home proudly holding out a large envelope.

"Look," he said, "I've got something for you."

She excitedly tore open the envelope and pulled out a printed card bearing these words:

"The Minister of Education and Mme. Georges Ramponneau[4] beg M. and Mme. Loisel[5] to do them the honor of attending an evening reception at the Ministerial Mansion on Friday, January 18."

Instead of being delighted, as her husband had hoped, she scornfully tossed the invitation on the table, murmuring, "What good is that to me?"

"But, my dear, I thought you'd be thrilled to death. You never get a chance to go out, and this is a real affair, a wonderful one! I had an awful time getting a card. Everybody wants one; it's much sought after, and not many clerks have a chance at one. You'll see all the most important people there."

She gave him an irritated glance and burst out impatiently, "What do you think I have to go in?"

He hadn't given that a thought. He stammered, "Why, the dress you wear when we go to the theater. That looks quite nice, I think."

He stopped talking, dazed and distracted to see his wife burst out weeping. Two large tears slowly rolled from the corners of her eyes to the corners of her mouth. He gasped, "Why, what's the matter? What's the trouble?"

By sheer willpower she overcame her outburst and answered in a calm voice while wiping the tears from her wet cheeks, "Oh, nothing. Only I don't have an evening dress and therefore I can't go to that affair. Give the card to some friend at the office whose wife can dress better than I can."

Even though she has been invited to a party, why is Mme. Loisel still unhappy?   *clarify*

He was stunned. He resumed. "Let's see, Mathilde.[6] How much would a suitable outfit cost—one you could wear for other affairs too—something very simple?"

She thought it over for several seconds, going over her allowance and thinking also of the amount she could ask for without

_____

3. **sphinxlike:** resembling a famous Egyptian statue with the body of a lion and head of a man.

4. **Mme. Georges Ramponneau** (må däm′ zhorzh räm′ pə nō)

5. **M. and Mme. Loisel** (mə syʉr′ and må däm′ lwä zel′)

6. **Mathilde** (må tēld′)

71

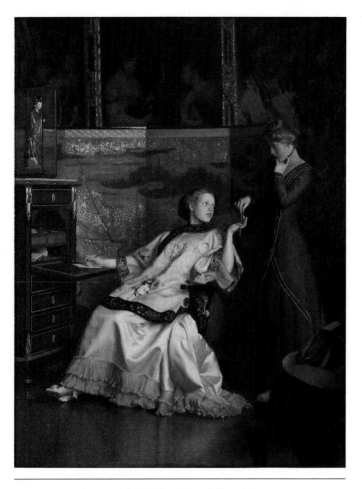

THE NEW NECKLACE 1910 William McGregor
Paxton Museum of Fine Arts, Boston. Zoe Oliver Sherman
Collection

shoot larks on the plain near Nanterre.[8]

However, he said, "All right. I'll give you four hundred francs. But try to get a nice dress."

As the day of the party approached, Mme. Loisel seemed sad, moody, and ill at ease. Her outfit was ready, however. Her husband said to her one evening, "What's the matter? You've been all out of sorts for three days."

And she answered, "It's embarrassing not to have a jewel or a gem—nothing to wear on my dress. I'll look like a pauper; I'd almost rather not go to that party."

He answered, "Why not wear some flowers? They're very fashionable this season. For ten francs you can get two or three gorgeous roses."

She wasn't at all convinced. "No. . . . There's nothing more humiliating than to look poor among a lot of rich women."

But her husband exclaimed, "My, but you're silly! Go see your friend Mme. Forestier[9] and ask her to lend you some jewelry. You and she know each other well enough for you to do that."

She gave a cry of joy, "Why, that's so! I hadn't thought of it."

The next day she paid her friend a visit and told her of her predicament.

Mme. Forestier went toward a large closet with mirrored doors, took out a large jewel box, brought it over, opened it, and said to Mme. Loisel, "Pick something out, my dear."

At first her eyes noted some bracelets, then a pearl necklace, then a Venetian cross,

bringing an immediate refusal and an exclamation of dismay from the thrifty clerk.

Finally, she answered hesitatingly, "I'm not sure exactly, but I think with four hundred francs[7] I could manage it."

He turned a bit pale, for he had set aside just that amount to buy a rifle so that, the following summer, he could join some friends who were getting up a group to

---

7. **francs:** the monetary units of France.
8. **Nanterre** (nän ter′): a town near Paris.
9. **Mme. Forestier** (fo rə stē ā′)

*Words
to Know
and Use*

pauper (pô′ pər) *n.* a poor person
predicament (prē dik′ə mənt) *n.* a difficult or embarrassing situation

gold and gems, of marvelous workmanship. She tried on these adornments in front of the mirror, but hesitated, unable to decide which to part with and put back. She kept on asking, "Haven't you something else?"

"Oh, yes, keep on looking. I don't know just what you'd like."

All at once she found, in a black satin box, a superb diamond necklace; and her pulse beat faster with longing. Her hands trembled as she took it up. Clasping it around her throat, outside her high-necked dress, she stood in ecstasy looking at her reflection.

Then she asked, hesitatingly, pleading, "Could I borrow that, just that and nothing else?"

"Why, of course."

She threw her arms around her friend, kissed her warmly, and fled with her treasure.

The day of the party arrived. Mme. Loisel was a sensation. She was the prettiest one there, fashionable, gracious, smiling, and wild with joy. All the men turned to look at her, asked who she was, begged to be introduced. All the Cabinet officials wanted to waltz with her. The minister took notice of her.

She danced madly, wildly, drunk with pleasure, giving no thought to anything in the triumph of her beauty, the pride of her success, in a kind of happy cloud composed of all the adulation, of all the admiring glances, of all the awakened longings, of a sense of complete victory that is so sweet to a woman's heart.

She left around four o'clock in the morning. Her husband, since midnight, had been dozing in a small empty sitting room with three other gentlemen whose wives were having too good a time to leave.

He threw over her shoulders the wraps he had brought for going home, modest garments of everyday life whose shabbiness clashed with the stylishness of her evening clothes. She felt this and longed to escape, unseen by the other women who were draped in expensive furs.

Loisel held her back.

"Hold on! You'll catch cold outside. I'll call a cab."

But she wouldn't listen to him and went rapidly down the stairs. When they were on the street, they didn't find a carriage; and they set out to hunt for one, hailing drivers whom they saw going by at a distance.

They walked toward the Seine,[10] disconsolate and shivering. Finally on the docks they found one of those carriages that one sees in Paris only after nightfall, as if they were ashamed to show their drabness during daylight hours.

It dropped them at their door in the Rue des Martyrs,[11] and they climbed wearily up to their apartment. For her, it was all over. For him, there was the thought that he would have to be at the Ministry at ten o'clock.

Before the mirror, she let the wraps fall from her shoulders to see herself once again in all her glory. Suddenly she gave a cry. The necklace was gone.

Her husband, already half undressed, said, "What's the trouble?"

She turned toward him despairingly, "I . . . I . . . I don't have Mme. Forestier's necklace."

"What! You can't mean it! It's impossible!"

They hunted everywhere, through the folds of the dress, through the folds of the coat, in the pockets. They found nothing.

---

10. **Seine** (sān): the river that runs through Paris.

11. **Rue des Martyrs** (rōō dā mär tēr′): Street of the Martyrs.

He asked, "Are you sure you had it when leaving the dance?"

"Yes, I felt it when I was in the hall of the Ministry."

"But if you had lost it on the street, we'd have heard it drop. It must be in the cab."

"Yes, quite likely. Did you get its number?"

"No. Didn't you notice it either?"

"No."

They looked at each other aghast. Finally Loisel got dressed again.

"I'll retrace our steps on foot," he said, "to see if I can find it."

And he went out. She remained in her evening clothes, without the strength to go to bed, slumped in a chair in the unheated room, her mind a blank.

Her husband came in about seven o'clock. He had had no luck.

He went to the police station, to the newspapers to post a reward, to the cab companies, everywhere the slightest hope drove him.

That evening Loisel returned, pale, his face lined; still he had learned nothing.

"We'll have to write your friend," he said, "to tell her you have broken the catch and are having it repaired. That will give us a little time to turn around."

She wrote to his dictation.

At the end of a week, they had given up all hope.

And Loisel, looking five years older, declared, "We must take steps to replace that piece of jewelry."

The next day they took the case to the jeweler whose name they found inside. He consulted his records. "I didn't sell that necklace, madame," he said. "I only supplied the case."

Then they went from one jeweler to another hunting for a similar necklace, going over their recollections, both sick with despair and anxiety.

They found, in a shop in Palais Royal,[12] a string of diamonds that seemed exactly like the one they were seeking. It was priced at forty thousand francs. They could get it for thirty-six.

They asked the jeweler to hold it for them for three days. And they reached an agreement that he would take it back for thirty-four thousand if the one lost was found before the end of February.

Loisel had eighteen thousand francs he had inherited from his father. He would borrow the rest.

He went about raising the money, asking a thousand francs from one, four hundred from another, a hundred here, sixty there. He signed notes, made ruinous deals, did business with loan sharks, ran the whole gamut of moneylenders. He compromised the rest of his life, risked his signature without knowing if he'd be able to honor it, and then, terrified by the outlook for the future, by the blackness of despair about to close around him, by the prospect of all the privations of the body and tortures of the spirit, he went to claim the new necklace with the thirty-six thousand francs that he placed on the counter of the shopkeeper.

When Mme. Loisel took the necklace back, Mme. Forestier said to her frostily, "You should have brought it back sooner; I might have needed it."

---

12. **Palais Royal** (pȧ lā′ roi yal′): an expensive shopping area of Paris.

Words to Know and Use	**aghast** (ə gast′) *adj.* horrified, in disbelief **ruinous** (rōō′ə nəs) *adj.* disastrous, bringing ruin **gamut** (gam′ ət) *n.* the entire range or series of something

TOO EARLY 1873 Jacques-Joseph Tissot Guildhall Gallery, London/The Bridgeman Art Library, London.

She didn't open the case, an action her friend was afraid of. If she had noticed the substitution, what would she have thought? What would she have said? Would she have thought her a thief?

Mme. Loisel experienced the horrible life the needy live. She played her part, however, with sudden heroism. That frightful debt had to be paid. She would pay it. She dismissed her maid; they rented a garret[13] under the eaves.

She learned to do the heavy housework, to perform the hateful duties of cooking. She washed dishes, wearing down her shell-pink nails scouring the grease from pots and pans; she scrubbed dirty linen, shirts, and cleaning rags, which she hung on a line to dry; she took the garbage down to the street each morning and brought up water, stopping on each landing to get her breath. And, <u>clad</u> like a peasant woman, basket on arm, guarding sou[14] by sou her scanty allowance, she bargained with the fruit dealers, the grocer, the butcher, and was insulted by them.

How and why has Mme. Loisel's daily life changed?

---

13. **garret:** rooms just below the sloping roof of a building; attic.
14. **sou** (so͞o): a French coin worth about a penny.

Each month notes had to be paid and others renewed to give more time.

Her husband labored evenings to balance a tradesman's accounts, and at night, often, he copied documents at five sous a page.

And this went on for ten years.

Finally, all was paid back, everything including the exorbitant rates of the loan sharks and accumulated compound interest.

Mme. Loisel appeared an old woman now. She became heavy, rough, harsh, like one of the poor. Her hair untended, her skirts <u>askew</u>, her hands red, her voice shrill, she even slopped water on her floors and scrubbed them herself. But, sometimes, while her husband was at work, she would sit near the window and think of that long-ago evening when, at the dance, she had been so beautiful and admired.

What would have happened if she had not lost that necklace? Who knows? Who can say? How strange and unpredictable life is! How little there is between happiness and misery!

Then one Sunday when she had gone for a walk on the Champs Élysées[15] to relax a bit from the week's labors, she suddenly noticed a woman strolling with a child. It was Mme. Forestier, still young-looking, still beautiful, still charming.

Mme. Loisel felt a rush of emotion. Should she speak to her? Of course. And now that everything was paid off, she would tell her the whole story. Why not?

She went toward her. "Hello, Jeanne."

The other, not recognizing her, showed astonishment at being spoken to so familiarly by this common person. She stammered. "But . . . madame . . . I don't recognize . . . You must be mistaken."

"No, I'm Mathilde Loisel."

Her friend gave a cry, "Oh, my poor Mathilde, how you've changed!"

"Yes, I've had a hard time since last seeing you. And plenty of misfortune—and all on account of you!"

"Of me . . . How do you mean?"

"Do you remember that diamond necklace you loaned me to wear to the dance at the Ministry?"

"Yes, but what about it?"

"Well, I lost it."

"You lost it! But you returned it."

"I brought you another just like it. And we've been paying for it for ten years now. You can imagine that wasn't easy for us who had nothing. Well, it's over now, and I am glad of it."

Mme. Forestier stopped short, "You mean to say you bought a diamond necklace to replace mine?"

"Yes. You never noticed, then? They were quite alike."

And she smiled with proud and simple joy.

Mme. Forestier, quite overcome, clasped her by the hands. "Oh, my poor Mathilde. But mine was only paste.[16] Why, at most it was worth only five hundred francs!"

---

15. **Champs Élysées** (shän za lē zā′): a famous boulevard in Paris.

16. **paste:** an artificial gem.

Words to Know and Use | **askew** (ə skyo͞o′) *adj.* crooked; on one side

Responding to Reading

First Impressions

1. What was your reaction to the news that the borrowed necklace was a fake?

Second Thoughts

2. What kind of person is Madame Loisel before she loses the necklace?

   Think about
   • what she values most
   • how she treats her husband
   • how she loses the necklace

3. How is Madame Loisel changed by the loss of the necklace?

   Think about
   • the sacrifices she makes to pay for the new necklace
   • the changes in her appearance
   • whether her values change

4. In your opinion, does Monsieur Loisel change during the story? Explain.

5. Remember the three main problems and solutions that you identified. Decide how wisely the Loisels solved each problem. What other solutions might they have found?

6. Suppose that Madame Loisel had not lost the necklace. Based on her actions and those of her husband up to that point in the story, what do you predict the couple's future would have been like?

Broader Connections

7. The author states that women in nineteenth-century France had "no family rank or social class." Therefore, he says, they were forced to rely on "beauty, grace, and charm" for help in gaining access to the wealthy class. Do you think things are different for women today? Use examples to support your answer.

Literary Concept: Irony

Irony is a contrast between what is expected and what actually exists or happens. For example, it is ironic when a student who has not studied gets an A on a difficult test, since you would expect that student to do poorly. "The Necklace" contains irony. What is ironic about the ten years the Loisels spend working?

Writing Options

1. What do you think will happen now that Madame Loisel knows the real value of the necklace? Write a possible continuation of the story.

2. In a paragraph, compare your values with those of Madame Loisel. You might compare your ideas with hers on such subjects as the importance of possessions, the ways to solve problems, the nature of happiness, and treatment of others.

3. Describe a modern-day teenage version of Madame Loisel. In a few paragraphs, explain how a high school student today might get into a similar predicament.

4. Many gentlemen wished to be introduced to Madame Loisel at the ball. What do you think she told them about herself? Write a possible dialogue between Madame Loisel and one of her admirers.

Vocabulary Practice

Exercise Read each sentence below. On your paper, write *True* if a sentence is true. Write *False* if it is false, and explain why it is false.

1. Madame Loisel was probably **aghast** when she found out that the original necklace was fake.
2. You might expect a **pauper** to own a diamond necklace.
3. The Loisels worked for ten years to get out of their **predicament.**
4. Poor women's **prospects** of marrying above their class were slim.
5. Madame Loisel's glorious time at the party made her feel **disconsolate.**
6. Monsieur Loisel felt very **clad** about going into debt to buy the new necklace.
7. As she dressed for the party, Madame Loisel made sure her hair and skirts were **askew.**
8. Madame Loisel felt great **vexation** about her status in life.
9. The loss of the necklace had a **ruinous** effect on the Loisels.
10. Madame Loisel had to give up her **gamut** in order to save money.

Words to Know and Use

aghast
askew
clad
disconsolate
gamut
pauper
predicament
prospects
ruinous
vexation

extend

Options for Learning

1 • **Create a Pantomime** In groups of three, create a pantomime that tells the entire story of "The Necklace" in no more than three minutes. Remember that pantomimes use only actions and gestures, no words. Rehearse your pantomime and then perform it for the class.

2 • **Jewels Galore** Find out what types of necklaces were popular in the nineteenth century. Look in books on antique jewelry or in costume books, or study paintings of that time. Use what you learn to design the borrowed necklace. Either draw it or make a model from beads.

3 • **Discover a Fake** Do research to discover what materials are used to make artificial copies of jewels and how jewelers can tell real jewels from fakes. You might look in books about costume jewelry or talk to a jeweler. Share your findings with your class.

4 • **Dreams vs. Reality** Although she lives in a run-down apartment, Madame Loisel dreams of a beautiful home filled with luxurious furnishings. Reread page 70 to find details of both her dream home and her actual living quarters. Find a book that shows aristocratic French furnishings and homes of the 1800's. Then draw or use photographs to illustrate her dream home and her real home.

 **FACT FINDER**

The new necklace cost 36,000 francs. How much is that in today's dollars?

Guy de Maupassant
1850-1893

Before Guy de Maupassant died in an insane asylum at age forty-two, he had written six novels and over three hundred short stories.

Maupassant was born in Normandy, a northern region of France. When he was eleven his parents separated, and he was raised by his mother. Although Maupassant felt great loyalty to his mother, the separation affected him deeply and he never married. His writing eventually brought him some degree of wealth, but he led a troubled life in spite of his success. Although he looked healthy, he was deteriorating both physically and mentally. His brother became violently psychotic in 1888 and died a year later. This death greatly upset Maupassant, who felt it foreshadowed his own death. He himself became mentally unbalanced, and died in a Paris asylum.

Fiction

The *Stolen Party*

LILIANA HEKER

Examine What You Know

Other people sometimes view us differently from the way we see ourselves. Their views might be based on our appearance, what we are doing when they see us, whom we are with, what we say, or whom they think we represent. Think about a time when someone made an incorrect assumption about you, or supposed something untrue. What did the person assume? Why did the person draw that conclusion? How did you feel about it? Discuss your experience with your class. Then compare it to the event described in this story.

Expand Your Knowledge

"The Stolen Party" takes place in Argentina, where, as in other South American countries, there have traditionally been only two classes—the rich and the poor. Although many poor people work as servants or laborers for the wealthy, there is rarely any social contact between the two groups. The difference between the incomes and lifestyles of the two classes, often reflected in their attitudes toward each other, prevents social equality.

Enrich Your Reading

Examining Characters   As you read "The Stolen Party," study the main character Rosaura. Notice especially how she reacts to other characters' words and actions. For example, when the magician calls her "little countess," Rosaura feels proud and special. Use a chart like the one below to organize your findings.

Other Characters' Words and Actions	Rosaura's Reactions
magician calls her "little countess"	feels proud and special

■ *A biography of the author can be found on page 89.*

The Stolen Party

LILIANA HEKER

Translated by ALBERTO MANGUEL

As soon as she arrived she went straight to the kitchen to see if the monkey was there. It was: what a relief! She wouldn't have liked to admit that her mother had been right. *Monkeys at a birthday?* her mother had sneered. *Get away with you, believing any nonsense you're told!* She was cross, but not because of the monkey, the girl thought; it's just because of the party.

"I don't like you going," she told her. "It's a rich people's party."

"Rich people go to Heaven too," said the girl, who studied religion at school.

"Get away with Heaven," said the mother.

"You know nothing about being friends!"

The girl didn't approve of the way her mother spoke. She was barely nine, and one of the best in her class.

"I'm going because I've been invited," she said. "And I've been invited because Luciana[1] is my friend. So there."

"Ah yes, your friend," her mother grumbled. She paused. "Listen, Rosaura,"[2] she said at last. "That one's not your friend. You know what you are to them? The maid's daughter, that's what."

Rosaura blinked hard: she wasn't going to cry. Then she yelled: "Shut up! You know nothing about being friends!"

Every afternoon she used to go to Luciana's house and they would both finish their homework while Rosaura's mother did the cleaning. They had their tea in the kitchen and they told each other secrets. Rosaura loved everything in the big house, and she also loved the people who lived there.

"I'm going because it will be the most lovely party in the whole world, Luciana told me it would. There will be a magician, and he will bring a monkey and everything."

The mother swung around to take a good look at her child, and pompously put her hands on her hips.

"Monkeys at a birthday?" she said. "Get away with you, believing any nonsense you're told!"

Rosaura was deeply offended. She thought it unfair of her mother to accuse other people of being liars simply because they were rich. Rosaura too wanted to be

---

1. **Luciana** (lo͞o′ sē ä′ nä)
2. **Rosaura** (rō sou′ rä)

INTRUDER (detail) 1977 Julio Larraz Collection of Saskia Larraz Courtesy of Nohra Haime Gallery, New York.

rich, of course. If one day she managed to live in a beautiful palace, would her mother stop loving her? She felt very sad. She wanted to go to that party more than anything else in the world.

"I'll die if I don't go," she whispered, almost without moving her lips.

And she wasn't sure whether she had been heard, but on the morning of the party she discovered that her mother had starched her Christmas dress. And in the afternoon, after washing her hair, her mother rinsed it in apple vinegar so that it would be all nice and shiny. Before going out, Rosaura admired herself in the mirror, with her white dress and glossy hair, and thought she looked terribly pretty.

Señora Ines[3] also seemed to notice. As soon as she saw her, she said:

"How lovely you look today, Rosaura."

Rosaura gave her starched skirt a slight toss with her hands and walked into the party with a firm step. She said hello to Luciana and asked about the monkey. Luciana put on a secretive look and whispered into Rosaura's ear: "He's in the kitchen. But don't tell anyone, because it's a surprise."

Rosaura wanted to make sure. Carefully she entered the kitchen and there she saw it: deep in thought, inside its cage. It looked so funny that the girl stood there for a while, watching it, and later, every so often, she

---

3. **Señora Ines** (se nyōr′ rä ē nis′)

would slip out of the party unseen and go and admire it. Rosaura was the only one allowed into the kitchen. Señora Ines had said: "You yes, but not the others, they're much too boisterous, they might break something." Rosaura had never broken anything. She even managed the jug of orange juice, carrying it from the kitchen into the dining-room. She held it carefully and didn't spill a single drop. And Señora Ines had said: "Are you sure you can manage a jug as big as that?" Of course she could manage. She wasn't a butterfingers, like the others. Like that blonde girl with the bow in her hair. As soon as she saw Rosaura, the girl with the bow had said:

"And you? Who are you?"

"I'm a friend of Luciana," said Rosaura.

"No," said the girl with the bow, "you are not a friend of Luciana because I'm her cousin and I know all her friends. And I don't know you."

"So what," said Rosaura. "I come here every afternoon with my mother and we do our homework together."

"You and your mother do your homework together?" asked the girl, laughing.

"I and Luciana do our homework together," said Rosaura, very seriously.

The girl with the bow shrugged her shoulders.

"That's not being friends," she said. "Do you go to school together?"

"No."

"So where do you know her from?" said the girl, getting impatient.

Rosaura remembered her mother's words perfectly. She took a deep breath.

"I'm the daughter of the employee," she said.

Her mother had said very clearly: "If someone asks, you say you're the daughter of the employee; that's all." She also told her to add: "And proud of it." But Rosaura thought that never in her life would she dare say something of the sort.

"What employee?" said the girl with the bow. "Employee in a shop?"

"No," said Rosaura angrily. "My mother doesn't sell anything in any shop, so there."

"So how come she's an employee?" said the girl with the bow.

Just then Señora Ines arrived saying *shh shh*, and asked Rosaura if she wouldn't mind helping serve out the hot dogs, as she knew the house so much better than the others.

"See?" said Rosaura to the girl with the bow, and when no one was looking she kicked her in the shin.

Apart from the girl with the bow, all the others were delightful. The one she liked best was Luciana, with her golden birthday crown; and then the boys. Rosaura won the sack race, and nobody managed to catch her when they played tag. When they split into two teams to play charades, all the boys wanted her for their side. Rosaura felt she had never been so happy in all her life.

But the best was still to come. The best came after Luciana blew out the candles. First the cake. Señora Ines had asked her to help pass the cake around, and Rosaura had enjoyed the task immensely, because everyone called out to her, shouting "Me, me!" Rosaura remembered a story in which there was a queen who had the power of life or death over her subjects. She had always loved that, having the power of life or death. To Luciana and the boys she gave the largest pieces, and to the girl with the bow she gave a slice so thin one could see through it.

After the cake came the magician, tall and bony, with a fine red cape. A true magician:

he could untie handkerchiefs by blowing on them and make a chain with links that had no openings. He could guess what cards were pulled out from a pack, and the monkey was his assistant. He called the monkey "partner." "Let's see here, partner," he would say, "Turn over a card." And, "Don't run away, partner: time to work now."

The final trick was wonderful. One of the children had to hold the monkey in his arms and the magician said he would make him disappear.

"What, the boy?" they all shouted.

"No, the monkey!" shouted back the magician.

Rosaura thought that this was truly the most amusing party in the whole world.

The magician asked a small fat boy to come and help, but the small fat boy got frightened almost at once and dropped the monkey on the floor. The magician picked him up carefully, whispered something in his ear, and the monkey nodded almost as if he understood.

"You musn't be so unmanly, my friend," the magician said to the fat boy.

"What's unmanly?" said the fat boy.

The magician turned around as if to look for spies.

"A sissy," said the magician. "Go sit down."

Then he stared at all the faces, one by one. Rosaura felt her heart tremble.

"You, with the Spanish eyes," said the magician. And everyone saw that he was pointing at her.

She wasn't afraid. Neither holding the monkey, nor when the magician made him vanish; not even when, at the end, the magician flung his red cape over Rosaura's head and uttered a few magic words . . . and the monkey reappeared, chattering happily, in her arms. The children clapped furiously. And before Rosaura returned to her seat, the magician said:

"Thank you very much, my little countess."

She was so pleased with the compliment that a while later, when her mother came to fetch her, that was the first thing she told her.

"I helped the magician and he said to me, 'Thank you very much, my little countess.' "

It was strange because up to then Rosaura had thought that she was angry with her mother. All along Rosaura had imagined that she would say to her: "See that the monkey wasn't a lie?" But instead she was so thrilled that she told her mother all about the wonderful magician.

Her mother tapped her on the head and said: "So now we're a countess!"

But one could see that she was beaming.

And now they both stood in the entrance, because a moment ago Señora Ines, smiling, had said: "Please wait here a second."

Her mother suddenly seemed worried.

"What is it?" she asked Rosaura.

"What is what?" said Rosaura. "It's nothing; she just wants to get the presents for those who are leaving, see?"

She pointed at the fat boy and at a girl with pigtails who were also waiting there, next to their mothers. And she explained about the presents. She knew, because she had been watching those who left before her. When one of the girls was about to leave, Señora Ines would give her a bracelet. When a boy left, Señora Ines gave him a yo-yo. Rosaura preferred the yo-yo because it sparkled, but she didn't mention that to her mother. Her mother might have said: "So why don't you ask for one, you blockhead?" That's what her mother was like. Rosaura didn't feel like explaining that she'd be horribly ashamed to be the odd one out. Instead she said:

"I was the best-behaved at the party."

And she said no more because Señora Ines came out into the hall with two bags, one pink and one blue.

First she went up to the fat boy, gave him a yo-yo out of the blue bag, and the fat boy left with his mother. Then she went up to the girl and gave her a bracelet out of the pink bag, and the girl with the pigtails left as well.

Finally she came up to Rosaura and her mother. She had a big smile on her face and Rosaura liked that. Señora Ines looked down at her, then looked up at her mother, and then said something that made Rosaura proud:

"What a marvelous daughter you have, Herminia."[4]

HEAD OF A GIRL (detail) 1905 Paula Modersohn-Becker
Stadlisches Kunstitut, Frankfurt/The Bridgeman Art Library, London.

For an instant, Rosaura thought that she'd give her two presents: the bracelet and the yo-yo. Señora Ines bent down as if about to look for something. Rosaura also leaned forward, stretching out her arm. But she never completed the movement.

Señora Ines didn't look in the pink bag. Nor did she look in the blue bag. Instead she rummaged in her purse. In her hand appeared two bills.

"You really and truly earned this," she said handing them over. "Thank you for all your help, my pet."

Rosaura felt her arms stiffen, stick close to her body, and then she noticed her mother's hand on her shoulder. Instinctively she pressed herself against her mother's body. That was all. Except her eyes. Rosaura's eyes had a cold, clear look that fixed itself on Señora Ines's face.

Señora Ines, motionless, stood there with her hand outstretched. As if she didn't dare draw it back. As if the slightest change might shatter an infinitely delicate balance.

---

4. **Herminia** (er mē′ nē′ ə)

I N S I G H T

The Pocketbook Game

ALICE CHILDRESS

Marge . . . : Day's work is an education! Well, I mean workin' in different homes you learn much more than if you was steady in one place. . . . I tell you, it really keeps your mind sharp tryin' to watch for what folks will put over on you.

What? . . . No, Marge, I do not want to help shell no beans, but I'd be more than glad to stay and have supper with you, and I'll wash the dishes after. Is that all right? . . .

Who put anything over on who? . . . Oh yes! It's like this. . . . I been working for Mrs. E . . . one day a week for several months and I notice that she has some peculiar ways. Well, there was only one thing really bothered me and that was her pocketbook habit. . . . No, not those little novels. . . . I mean her purse—her handbag.

Marge, she's got a big old pocketbook with two long straps on it . . . and whenever I'd go there, she'd be propped up in a chair with her handbag double wrapped tight around her wrist, and from room to room, she'd roam with that purse hugged to her bosom . . . yes, girl! This happens every time! No, there's nobody there but me and her. . . . Marge, I couldn't say nothin' to her! It's her purse, ain't it? She can hold it if she wants to!

I held my peace for months, tryin' to figure out how I'd make my point. . . . Well, bless Bess! Today was the day! . . . Please, Marge, keep shellin' the beans so we can eat! I know you're listenin', but you listen with your ears, not your hands. . . . Well, anyway, I was almost ready to go home when she steps in the room hangin' onto her bag as usual and says, "Mildred, will you ask the super to come up and fix the kitchen faucet?" "Yes, Mrs. E . . ." I says, "as soon as I leave." "Oh, no," she says, "he may be gone by then. Please go now." "All right," I says, and out the door I went, still wearin' my Hoover apron.

I just went down the hall and stood there a few minutes . . . and then I rushed back to the door and knocked on it as hard and frantic as I could. She flung open the door sayin', "What's the matter? Did you see the super?" . . . "No," I says, gaspin' hard for breath, "I was almost downstairs when I remembered . . . I left my pocketbook!"

With that I dashed in, grabbed my purse and then went down to get the super. Later, when I was leavin' she says real timid like, "Mildred, I hope that you don't think I distrust you because . . ." I cut her off real quick. . . . "That's all right, Mrs. E . . . , I understand. 'Cause if I paid anybody as little as you pay me, I'd hold my pocketbook too!"

Marge, you fool . . . look out! . . . You gonna drop the beans on the floor!

Responding to Reading

First Impressions

1. How do you feel about Señora Ines's treatment of Rosaura?

Second Thoughts

2. What thoughts might be going through Rosaura's mind as the story ends?

3. How does your interpretation of the events of the party change once you learn that Señora Ines thought of Rosaura as a servant?

4. Do you think Rosaura had a realistic view of her relationship with Luciana? Explain your opinion.

5. Does Rosaura's attitude toward her mother change during the story? Use the character map you made to help you.

6. What is Rosaura's blind spot? Is she still "blind" at the end of the story? Explain.

7. Why is the story called "The Stolen Party"? How and from whom was the party stolen?

8. At the end of the story, Señora Ines seems afraid to "shatter an infinitely delicate balance." What is this delicate balance?

> **Think about**
> • the relationships among the characters in the story
> • the relationships between the classes of society in Argentina

Broader Connections

9. "The Stolen Party" and "The Pocketbook Game" both involve employers who treat servants as inferior people. Do these stories reflect real modern attitudes toward people—such as housekeepers or waiters—who serve others? Explain your opinion, giving examples to support it.

Literary Concept: Third-Person Limited Point of View

Point of view refers to the perspective from which a story is told. "The Stolen Party" is told from a **third-person limited point of view.** That is, the narrator is someone outside the action, not a character within the story. The characters are referred to by name or by the pronouns *he, she,* or *they.* It is a limited viewpoint because the narrator tells only what one character—Rosaura—sees, thinks, and feels.

Choose a scene from the story, such as the initial conversation between Rosaura and her mother, or the party scene.

1. How does the point of view affect your understanding of the events?
2. How might your understanding have been different if this story had been told from Rosaura's mother's point of view?
3. How might Señora Ines's perspective differ from that of Rosaura and her mother?

Writing Options

1. Some readers see a similarity between the way the monkey is treated and the way Rosaura is treated. Reread passages about the monkey. List any comparisons you make between the two characters.

2. What long-term effects do you think this incident might have on Rosaura? Write your prediction. You might predict how the incident will affect her relationships with her mother, with Luciana, and with Señora Ines or how it will affect her future view of herself and others.

3. List three things Rosaura's mother might have said to her on the way home from the party. Write as if the mother were really speaking. For example, use phrases such as "I told you . . ." or whatever mothers tend to say in your own experience.

4. Think of and write two or three other titles for this story.

Options for Learning

1 • **Graph Personality Traits** Choose at least five words that could describe a character's personality, such as *brave, realistic, self-confident,* and so on. Create a graph that shows how, on a scale of I to 5, you rate Rosaura's personality in each category. You might list the traits along one leg of an L shape and list numbers along the other leg. Then use one color to rate Rosaura as she is in the early part of the story and another color to rate her at the story's end. You might decide that some of her personality traits change while others stay the same. Compare your graph to your classmates' graphs.

2 • **Picture Your Opinion** Prove the old saying "A picture is worth a thousand words." Create a work of art—for example, an ink or pencil drawing, a painting, or a photograph—that portrays the theme of "The Stolen Party." Try to achieve a strong effect. Display your work and take note of others' reactions to it.

3 • **Dear Rosaura** Suppose you host a radio talk-show and that Rosaura, her mother, or Luciana calls you up for advice after the party. Have a classmate play the role of the caller, and present your talk-show conversation to the class.

4 • **A Monologue** A **monologue** is a talk, a reading, or a drama presented by one person. Practice reading "The Pocketbook Game" aloud. Have your voice reflect the emotions of the narrator. Then read the selection aloud or present it from memory to your class.

FACT FINDER

Locate Argentina on a map. How does it compare in size to the other countries in South America?

Liliana Heker

Liliana Heker began her writing career as a young girl. She published her first book of short stories, *Los que vieron la zarza* (Those Who Beheld the Burning Bush), when she was a teenager. It is considered by some to be one of the best collections of short stories published in Argentina since the 1960's.

While many Argentinian writers fled to other countries to preserve their freedom and to escape the dangerous political climate during this period, Heker remained in Argentina to work as editor-in-chief of *El Ornitorrinco* (The Platypus), a literary magazine. Of her decision to stay and work for change, she has said, "To be heard, we must shout from within."

Elements of
DRAMA

The last time you watched a drama, you may have gulped back tears or you may have laughed hysterically. Drama is one of our most enjoyable and common forms of entertainment. We watch drama on television, in movies, in videos, and on stage. We even listen to it on the radio occasionally.

Drama is literature that is meant to be performed for an audience in the form of a play. The elements of drama are very similar to the elements of fiction, but in drama, actors and actresses play the parts of the characters, who tell the story through their words and actions.

Understanding Drama

Cast of Characters   A script, or written form of a drama, usually begins with a list—sometimes including short descriptions—of all the characters in the play. The characters are generally listed in the order in which they will appear. Just as in fiction, some characters are main characters and others are minor characters.

Dialogue   A play is written almost entirely in dialogue, or conversation between two or more characters. The plot of the play and the personalities of the characters are revealed mostly through the dialogue. The words each character says are written in lines next to the character's name, as in the following example from *A Sunny Morning*.

Don Gonzalo. Are you speaking to me, señora?
Doña Laura. Yes, to you.

Stage Directions   A play includes sets of instructions, called **stage directions,** which are often in a different kind of type, such as italic, and are separated from the dialogue by parentheses or brackets. These stage directions give a great deal of information to the reader and to the performers. Stage directions are most often used to explain where and how actors should move and speak. Some also describe the **scenery,** or decorations on stage that help show the setting of the play. Others describe the **props,** objects that the actors need. Still other stage directions describe lighting, costumes, music, or sound effects. The playwright can use the stage directions to give any instructions he or she wants the performers to have.

Read the following stage directions from *A Sunny Morning*. Notice how they are set off visually from the rest of the play.

Doña Laura. Yes, you are only twenty. *(She sits down on the bench.)* Oh, I feel more tired today than usual. *(noticing* Petra, *who seems impatient)* Go, if you wish to chat with your guard.

Scene and Act   In drama, the action is divided into scenes. Each scene has a different setting, either in time or place. In long plays, scenes are grouped into acts, which are almost like chapters in a book. The play *A Sunny Morning* has just one scene, while *The Miracle Worker* has three acts involving many scenes.

The elements of drama are put together in a form that makes a play easy to read. As you read the plays in this book, the following strategies will help you get the most meaning and enjoyment from them.

Strategies for Reading Drama

1. **Read the play silently.** As you know, plays are intended to be performed or read aloud. However, before you take part in reading a play aloud, make sure you read the entire play so that you understand the plot and characters.

2. **Figure out what is happening.** When you read drama, you are plunged into the story with very little explanation. Unlike fiction, drama has no exposition, or quick explanation of setting and characters and introduction to the plot. When you read a play, use what you learn in the dialogue and stage directions to figure out what is going on. Be patient; as you read on, you will gradually learn what the story is about. Just as it takes a while for you to get involved in a movie, it takes a while before you understand the plot and characters when you read a play.

3. **Read the stage directions carefully.** When you see a play performed, you see the action and the scenery. When you read a play, you must read the instructions for the actions and the descriptions of the scenery in order to know what is going on. Visualize how the stage looks and picture the actions in your mind. Imagine that you are seeing the play or the movie.

4. **Get to know the characters.** The characters reveal themselves through their words and actions. Pay careful attention to what they say and do, what others say about them, and how others act toward them.

5. **Analyze the plot.** Remember what you learned about plot in fiction. The plot centers around a conflict that the characters have to resolve. Keep track of the plot events and watch the action rise until a climax is reached. Then notice how the conflict is resolved and the loose ends are tied up.

6. **Read the play aloud.** When you read a play aloud with others, watch for your character's name and be ready ahead of time to read your lines. Do not read the stage directions aloud, but notice the instructions they give about your tone of voice, actions, and so on. Interpret your character. That is, with your voice show the emotions that the character feels. Be sure to show your character's reaction to what other characters say and do. If you act in front of others, let your facial expressions and body language also reflect your character's feelings.

Drama

^A *Sunny Morning*

SERAFÍN AND JOAQUÍN ÁLVAREZ QUINTERO (äl′ vä reth kēn tä′ rō)

Examine What You Know

In this play, one character quotes these words from a poem: "All love is sad, but sad as it is, it is the best thing that we know." Think about the love stories you know from movies, books, or your own experience. What is the best love story you know? Was it sad or happy? Summarize and share the plot of the story with your class.

Expand Your Knowledge

A Sunny Morning is set in Madrid, the capital city of Spain, in the late 1920's. Then, as today, Madrid was a beautiful, sophisticated city with many plazas and parks. Marriages were arranged by a girl's parents. In order to preserve their honor, unmarried Spanish women led strict and sheltered lives; they were chaperoned whenever they went out in public or whenever a young man came to call. Men, too, had a personal code of honor to uphold, and the preservation of their honor sometimes led to duels. In a duel, two men fought, often to the death, with swords or pistols. Since duels were illegal, they usually took place at sunrise in a secluded spot.

You may know that the title *Señor* (se nyôr′) is Spanish for *Mr.*, while *Señora* (se nyô′ rä) is Spanish for *Mrs.* The terms *Don* (dän) and *Doña* (dô′ nyä) are used only before the first names of men and women.

Enrich Your Reading

Understanding the Aside   In this play, the word *aside* appears as a stage direction. In drama, an **aside** is a remark made by a character that is heard by the audience but not by the other characters on stage. Through the use of asides, the audience learns directly what a character is thinking or feeling; as a result, the audience knows more about the characters than the characters know about each other. As you read, notice how the asides reveal the differences between the feelings of the main characters and their behavior, and see how they add excitement, interest, and humor to the plot.

■ *Biographies of the authors can be found on page 104.*

A *Sunny Morning*

SERAFÍN AND JOAQUÍN ÁLVAREZ QUINTERO
Translated by LUCRETIA XAVIER FLOYD

CHARACTERS

Doña Laura (dô′nyä lou′ rä)

Petra (pā′trä), her maid

Don Gonzalo (dän gän zä′ lō)

Juanito (hwän ē′ tō), his servant

Scene: A park in Madrid

Time: The present

A sunny morning in a retired corner of a park in Madrid. Autumn. A bench at right. Doña Laura, *a handsome, white-haired old lady of about seventy,* refined *in appearance, her bright eyes and entire manner giving evidence that despite her age her mental* faculties *are unimpaired, enters leaning upon the arm of her maid,* Petra. *In her free hand she carries a parasol,*[1] *which serves also as a cane.*

Doña Laura. I am so glad to be here. I feared my seat would be occupied. What a beautiful morning!

Petra. The sun is hot.

Doña Laura. Yes, you are only twenty. *(She sits down on the bench.)* Oh, I feel more tired today than usual. *(Noticing* Petra, *who seems impatient)* Go, if you wish to chat with your guard.

Petra. He is not mine, señora; he belongs to the park.

Doña Laura. He belongs more to you than he does to the park. Go find him, but remain within calling distance.

Petra. I see him over there waiting for me.

Doña Laura. Do not remain more than ten minutes.

Petra. Very well, señora. *(walks toward right)*

Doña Laura. Wait a moment.

Petra. What does the señora wish?

Doña Laura. Give me the bread crumbs.

Petra. I don't know what is the matter with me.

Doña Laura *(smiling).* I do. Your head is where your heart is—with the guard.

Petra. Here, señora. *(She hands* Doña Laura *a small bag. Exit* Petra *by right.)*

Doña Laura. Adiós. *(glances toward trees at right)* Here they come! They know just when to expect me. *(She rises, walks toward right, and throws three handfuls of bread crumbs.)* These are for the spryest, these for the gluttons, and these for the little

---

1. **parasol** (par′ ə sôl′): an umbrella used to provide shade.

Words to Know and Use

refined (ri fīnd′) *adj.* elegant and cultivated **refine** *v.*
faculty (fak′ əl tē) *n.* a mental ability or power, such as will or reason
glutton (glut′ ′n) *n.* a person or animal who eats too much because of greed

93

ones which are the most persistent. *(Laughs. She returns to her seat and watches with a pleased expression, the pigeons feeding.)* There, that big one is always first! I know him by his big head. Now one, now another, now two, now three—that little fellow is the least timid. I believe he would eat from my hand. That one takes his piece and flies up to that branch alone. He is a philosopher. But where do they all come from? It seems as if the news has spread. Ha, ha! Don't quarrel. There is enough for all. I'll bring more tomorrow.

(Enter Don Gonzalo *and* Juanito *from left center.* Don Gonzalo *is an old gentleman of seventy, gouty*[2] *and impatient. He leans upon* Juanito's *arm and drags his feet somewhat as he walks.)*

Don Gonzalo. Idling their time away! They should be saying mass.

Juanito. You can sit here, señor. There is only a lady. *(Doña Laura turns her head and listens.)*

Don Gonzalo. I won't, Juanito. I want a bench to myself.

Juanito. But there is none.

Don Gonzalo. That one over there is mine.

Juanito. There are three priests sitting there.

Don Gonzalo. Rout them out. Have they gone?

Juanito. No, indeed. They are talking.

Don Gonzalo. Just as if they were glued to the seat. No hope of their leaving. Come this way, Juanito. *(They walk toward the birds, right.)*

Doña Laura *(indignantly).* Look out!

Don Gonzalo. Are you speaking to me, señora?

Doña Laura. Yes, to you.

Don Gonzalo. What do you wish?

Doña Laura. You have scared away the birds who were feeding on my crumbs.

Don Gonzalo. What do I care about the birds?

Doña Laura. But I do.

Don Gonzalo. This is a public park.

Doña Laura. Then why do you complain that the priests have taken your bench?

Don Gonzalo. Señora, we have not met. I cannot imagine why you take the liberty of addressing me. Come, Juanito. *(Both go out right.)*

Doña Laura. What an ill-natured old man! Why must people get so fussy and cross when they reach a certain age? *(looking toward right)* I am glad. He lost that bench, too. Serves him right for scaring the birds. He is furious. Yes, yes; find a seat if you can. Poor man! He is wiping the perspiration from his face. Here he comes. A carriage would not raise more dust than his feet. *(Enter* Don Gonzalo *and* Juanito *by right and walk toward left.)*

Don Gonzalo. Have the priests gone yet, Juanito?

Juanito. No, indeed, señor. They are still there.

Don Gonzalo. The authorities should place more benches here for these sunny mornings. Well, I suppose I must resign myself and sit on the bench with the old lady. *(Muttering to himself, he sits at the extreme*

---

2. **gouty** (gout' ē): having gout—an illness that causes swelling of the hands and feet.

Words to Know and Use

persistent (pər sist' ənt) *adj.* refusing to give up; stubborn or persevering
indignantly (in dig' nənt lē) *adv.* angrily; resentfully

94

end of Doña Laura's *bench and looks at her indignantly. Touches his hat as he greets her.)* Good morning.

Doña Laura. What, you here again?

Don Gonzalo. I repeat that we have not met.

Doña Laura. I was responding to your salute.

Don Gonzalo. "Good morning" should be answered by "Good morning," and that is all you should have said.

Doña Laura. You should have asked permission to sit on this bench, which is mine.

Don Gonzalo. The benches here are public property.

Doña Laura. Why, you said the one the priests have is yours.

Don Gonzalo. Very well, very well. I have nothing more to say. *(between his teeth)* <u>Senile</u> old lady! She ought to be at home knitting and counting her beads.

LOVERS LANE   1988   Susan Slyman
Jay Johnson America's Folk Heritage Gallery, New York.

Words to Know and Use | **senile** (sē′ nīl) *adj.* showing signs of breakdown caused by old age; especially confusion or loss of memory

95

Doña Laura. Don't grumble any more. I'm not going to leave just to please you.

Don Gonzalo (*brushing the dust from his shoes with his handkerchief*). If the ground were sprinkled a little, it would be an improvement.

Doña Laura. Do you use your handkerchief as a shoe brush?

Don Gonzalo. Why not?

Doña Laura. Do you use a shoe brush as a handkerchief?

Don Gonzalo. What right have you to criticize my actions?

Doña Laura. A neighbor's right.

Don Gonzalo. Juanito, my book. I do not care to listen to nonsense.

Doña Laura. You are very polite.

Don Gonzalo. Pardon me, señora, but never interfere with what does not concern you.

Doña Laura. I generally say what I think.

Don Gonzalo. And more to the same effect. Give me the book, Juanito.

Juanito. Here, señor. (*Juanito takes a book from his pocket, hands it to* Don Gonzalo, *then exits by right.* Don Gonzalo *casting indignant glances at* Doña Laura, *puts on an enormous pair of glasses, takes from his pocket a reading glass, adjusts both to suit him, and opens his book.*)

Doña Laura. I thought you were taking out a telescope.

Don Gonzalo. Was that you?

Doña Laura. Your sight must be keen.

Don Gonzalo. Keener than yours is.

Doña Laura. Yes, evidently.

Don Gonzalo. Ask the hares and partridges.

Doña Laura. Ah! Do you hunt?

Don Gonzalo. I did, and even now—

Doña Laura. Oh, yes, of course!

Don Gonzalo. Yes, señora. Every Sunday I take my gun and dog, you understand, and go to one of my estates near Aravaca[3] and kill time.

Doña Laura. Yes, kill time. That is all you kill.

Don Gonzalo. Do you think so? I could show you a wild boar's head in my study—

Doña Laura. Yes, and I could show you a tiger's skin in my boudoir.[4] What does that prove?

Don Gonzalo. Very well, señora, please allow me to read. Enough conversation.

Doña Laura. Well, you subside, then.

Don Gonzalo. But first I shall take a pinch of snuff.[5] (*takes out snuff box*) Will you have some? (*offers box to* Doña Laura)

Doña Laura. If it is good.

Don Gonzalo. It is of the finest. You will like it.

Doña Laura (*taking pinch of snuff*). It clears my head.

Don Gonzalo. And mine.

Doña Laura. Do you sneeze?

Don Gonzalo. Yes, señora, three times.

Doña Laura. And so do I. What a coincidence!

(*After taking the snuff, they await the sneezes, both anxiously, and sneeze alternately three times each.*)

Don Gonzalo. There, I feel better.

Doña Laura. So do I. (*aside*) The snuff has made peace between us.

Don Gonzalo. You will excuse me if I read aloud?

Doña Laura. Read as loud as you please; you will not disturb me.

---

3. **Aravaca** (ä rə vä′ kə): a village near Madrid.

4. **boudoir** (boo dwär′): a woman's bedroom.

5. **snuff:** powdered tobacco, meant to be taken up into the nose by sniffing.

Don Gonzalo (reading). "All love is sad, but sad as it is, it is the best thing that we know." That is from Campoamor.[6]

Doña Laura. Ah!

Don Gonzalo (reading). "The daughters of the mothers I once loved kiss me now as they would a graven image." Those lines, I take it, are in a humorous vein.

Doña Laura (laughing). I take them so, too.

Don Gonzalo. There are some beautiful poems in this book. Here. "Twenty years pass. He returns."

Doña Laura. You cannot imagine how it affects me to see you reading with all those glasses.

Don Gonzalo. Can you read without any?

Doña Laura. Certainly.

Don Gonzalo. At your age? You're jesting.

Doña Laura. Pass me the book, then. (takes book, reads aloud)

"Twenty years pass. He returns.
And each, beholding the other, exclaims—
Can it be that this is he?
Heavens, is it she?"

(Doña Laura returns the book to Don Gonzalo.)

Don Gonzalo. Indeed, I envy you your wonderful eyesight.

Doña Laura (aside). I know every word by heart.

Don Gonzalo. I am very fond of good verses, very fond. I even composed some in my youth.

Doña Laura. Good ones?

Don Gonzalo. Of all kinds. I was a great friend of Espronceda, Zorrilla, Bécquer,[7] and others. I first met Zorrilla in America.

Doña Laura. Why, have you been in America?

Don Gonzalo. Several times. The first time I went I was only six years old.

Doña Laura. You must have gone with Columbus in one of his caravels![8]

Don Gonzalo (laughing). Not quite as bad as that. I am old, I admit, but I did not know Ferdinand and Isabella.[9] (They both laugh.) I was also a great friend of Campoamor. I met him in Valencia.[10] I am a native of that city.

Doña Laura. You are?

Don Gonzalo. I was brought up there and there I spent my early youth. Have you ever visited that city?

Doña Laura. Yes, señor. Not far from Valencia there was a villa[11] that, if still there, should retain memories of me. I spent several seasons there. It was many, many years ago. It was near the sea, hidden away among lemon and orange trees. They called it—let me see, what did they call it—Maricela.[12]

Don Gonzalo (startled). Maricela?

Doña Laura. Maricela. Is the name familiar to you?

Don Gonzalo. Yes, very familiar. If my memory serves me right, for we forget as we grow old, there lived in that villa the most beautiful woman I have ever seen, and I assure you I have seen many. Let me see—what was her name? Laura—Laura—Laura Llorente.

Doña Laura (startled). Laura Llorente?

---

6. **Campoamor** (kam′ pwä mōr′): Ramón de Campoamor, a nineteenth-century Spanish poet.

7. **Espronceda** (ās′ prôn sä dä), **Zorrilla** (zô rē′ yä), **Bécquer** (bā′ ker): Jośe de Espronceda, Jośe Zorrilla, and Gustavo Adolfo Bécquer, respected nineteenth-century Spanish poets and literary figures.

8. **caravel** (kar′ ə vel′): a 15th century Spanish ship.

9. **Ferdinand and Isabella:** King Ferdinand V and Queen Isabella, the first rulers of a united Spain.

10. **Valencia** (vä len′ sē ə): a city in eastern Spain.

11. **villa** (vē′ yä): a country house.

12. **Maricela** (mar ē sā′ lä).

Don Gonzalo. Yes. *(They look at each other intently.)*

Doña Laura *(recovering herself)*. Nothing. You reminded me of my best friend.

Don Gonzalo. How strange!

Doña Laura. It is strange. She was called "The Silver Maiden."

Don Gonzalo. Precisely, "The Silver Maiden." By that name she was known in that locality. I seem to see her as if she were before me now, at that window with the red roses. Do you remember that window?

Doña Laura. Yes, I remember. It was the window of her room.

Don Gonzalo. She spent many hours there. I mean in my day.

Doña Laura *(sighing)*. And in mine, too.

Don Gonzalo. She was ideal. Fair as a lily, jet-black hair and black eyes, with an uncommonly sweet expression. She seemed to cast a radiance wherever she was. Her figure was beautiful, perfect. "What forms of sovereign beauty God models in human clay!" She was a dream.

Doña Laura *(aside)*. If you but knew that dream was now by your side, you would realize what dreams come to. *(aloud)* She was very unfortunate and had a sad love affair.

Don Gonzalo. Very sad. *(They look at each other)*.

Doña Laura. Did you hear of it?

Don Gonzalo. Yes.

Doña Laura. The ways of Providence[13] are strange. *(aside)* Gonzalo!

Don Gonzalo. The gallant lover, in the same affair—

Doña Laura. Ah, the duel!

Don Gonzalo. Precisely, the duel. The gallant lover was—my cousin, of whom I was very fond.

Doña Laura. Oh, yes, a cousin? My friend told me in one of her letters the story of that affair, which was truly romantic. He, your cousin, passed by on horseback every morning down the rose path under her window, and tossed up to her balcony a bouquet of flowers which she caught.

Don Gonzalo. And later in the afternoon the gallant horseman would return by the same path, and catch the bouquet of flowers she would toss him. Am I right?

Doña Laura. Yes. They wanted to marry her to a merchant whom she would not have.

Don Gonzalo. And one night, when my cousin waited under her window to hear her sing, this other person presented himself unexpectedly.

Doña Laura. And insulted your cousin.

Don Gonzalo. There was a quarrel.

Doña Laura. And later a duel.

Don Gonzalo. Yes, at sunrise, on the beach, and the merchant was badly wounded. My cousin had to conceal himself for a few days and later to fly.

Doña Laura. You seem to know the story well.

Don Gonzalo. And so do you.

Doña Laura. I have explained that a friend repeated it to me.

Don Gonzalo. As my cousin did to me. *(aside)* This is Laura!

Doña Laura *(aside)*. Why tell him? He does not suspect.

Don Gonzalo *(aside)*. She is entirely innocent.

Doña Laura. And was it you, by any chance, who advised your cousin to forget Laura?

---

13. **Providence** (präv′ ə dəns): God, acting as the guiding force behind the universe.

LUXEMBOURG GARDEN 1909 Henri Rousseau Hermitage State Museum, Leningrad, Russia

Don Gonzalo. Why, my cousin never forgot her!

Doña Laura. How do you account, then, for his conduct?

Don Gonzalo. I will tell you. The young man took <u>refuge</u> in my house, fearful of the consequences of a duel with a person highly regarded in that locality. From my home he went to Seville,[14] then came to Madrid. He wrote Laura many letters, some of them in verse. But undoubtedly they were intercepted by her parents, for she never answered at all. Gonzalo then, in despair, believing his love lost to him forever, joined the army, went to Africa, and there, in a trench, met a glorious death, grasping the flag of Spain and whispering the name of his beloved Laura—

Doña Laura *(aside).* What an atrocious lie!

Don Gonzalo *(aside).* I could not have killed myself more gloriously.

Doña Laura. You must have been prostrated by the calamity.

Don Gonzalo. Yes, indeed, señora. As if he were my brother. I presume, though, on the contrary, that Laura in a short time was chasing butterflies in her garden, indifferent to regret.

Doña Laura. No señor, no!

---

14. **Seville** (sə vil′): a city in southern Spain.

Words to Know and Use | **refuge** (ref′ yo͞oj) *n.* a place of safety and protection

99

Don Gonzalo. It is woman's way.

Doña Laura. Even if it were woman's way, "The Silver Maiden" was not of that <u>disposition</u>. My friend awaited news for days, months, a year, and no letter came. One afternoon, just at sunset, as the first stars were appearing, she was seen to leave the house, and with quickening steps wend her way toward the beach, the beach where her beloved had risked his life. She wrote his name on the sand, then sat down upon a rock, her gaze fixed upon the horizon. The waves murmured their eternal threnody[15] and slowly crept up to the rock where the maiden sat. The tide rose with a boom and swept her out to sea.

Don Gonzalo. Good heavens!

Doña Laura. The fishermen of that shore who often tell the story affirm that it was a long time before the waves washed away that name written on the sand. *(aside)* You will not get ahead of me in decorating my own funeral.

Don Gonzalo *(aside)*. She lies worse than I do.

Doña Laura. Poor Laura!

Don Gonzalo. Poor Gonzalo!

Doña Laura *(aside)*. I will not tell him that I married two years later.

Don Gonzalo *(aside)*. In three months I ran off to Paris with a ballet dancer.

Doña Laura. Fate is curious. Here are you and I, complete strangers, met by chance, discussing the romance of old friends of long ago! We have been conversing as if we were old friends.

Don Gonzalo. Yes, it is curious, considering the ill-natured <u>prelude</u> to our conversation.

Doña Laura. You scared away the birds.

Don Gonzalo. I was unreasonable, perhaps.

Doña Laura. Yes, that was evident. *(sweetly)* Are you coming again tomorrow?

Don Gonzalo. Most certainly, if it is a sunny morning. And not only will I not scare away the birds, but I will bring a few crumbs.

Doña Laura. Thank you very much. Birds are grateful and repay attention. I wonder where my maid is? Petra! *(signals for her maid)*

Don Gonzalo *(aside, looking at* Laura, *whose back is turned)*. No, no. I will not reveal myself. I am <u>grotesque</u> now. Better that she recall the gallant horseman who passed daily beneath her window tossing flowers.

Doña Laura. Here she comes.

Don Gonzalo. That Juanito! He plays havoc with the nursemaids. *(looks right and signals with his hand)*

Doña Laura *(aside, looking at* Gonzalo, *whose back is turned)*. No, I am too sadly changed. It is better he should remember me as the black-eyed girl tossing flowers as he passed among the roses in the garden. *(*Juanito *enters by right,* Petra *by left. She has a bunch of violets in her hand.)*

Doña Laura. Well, Petra! At last!

Don Gonzalo. Juanito, you are late.

Petra *(to* Doña Laura*)*. The guard gave me these violets for you, señora.

Doña Laura. How very nice! Thank him for me. They are fragrant. *(As she takes the*

---

15. **threnody** (thren′ ə dē): a tearful song or a song of mourning.

Words to Know and Use

disposition (dis′ pə zish′ ən) *n.* a person's usual nature or frame of mind
prelude (prel′ yōōd′) *n.* an introduction to an event, action, or performance
grotesque (grō tesk′) *adj.* distorted; highly unattractive; ugly

violets from her maid, a few loose ones fall to the ground.)

Don Gonzalo. My dear lady, this has been a great honor and a great pleasure.

Doña Laura. It has also been a pleasure to me.

Don Gonzalo. Goodbye until tomorrow.

Doña Laura. Until tomorrow.

Don Gonzalo. If it is sunny.

Doña Laura. A sunny morning. Will you go to your bench?

Don Gonzalo. No, I will come to this—if you do not object?

Doña Laura. This bench is at your disposal.

Don Gonzalo. And I will surely bring the crumbs.

Doña Laura. Tomorrow, then?

Don Gonzalo. Tomorrow!

(Laura walks away toward right, supported by her maid. Gonzalo, before leaving with Juanito, trembling and with a great effort, stoops to pick up the violets Laura dropped. Just then Laura turns her head and surprises him picking up the flowers.)

Juanito. What are you doing, señor?

Don Gonzalo. Juanito, wait—

Doña Laura *(aside)*. Yes, it is he!

Don Gonzalo *(aside)*. It is she, and no mistake. *(Doña Laura and Don Gonzalo wave farewell.)*

Doña Laura. "Can it be that this is he?"

Don Gonzalo. "Heavens, is it she?" *(They smile once more, as if she were again at the window and he below in the rose garden, and then disappear upon the arms of their servants.)* ❧

Responding to Reading

First Impressions

1. What do you wonder about as you finish reading this play?

Second Thoughts

2. At first, Doña Laura and Don Gonzalo are barely civil to each other. How does their relationship change during the play?

3. Why do you think both main characters decide to keep their true identities a secret?

   Think about
   • why both make up dramatic deaths for the young lovers
   • asides spoken by both characters on page 100 about their appearance

4. By the end of the play, the main characters are no longer blind to who the other really is. Why don't they expose each other?

5. Why are the exchanging of flowers on page 98 and the last lines of the poem Doña Laura recites repeated at the end of the play? What purpose does this repetition serve?

6. Doña Laura and Don Gonzalo talk about meeting the next day. What do you think will happen to their relationship in the future?

Broader Connections

7. Doña Laura and Don Gonzalo are embarrassed by how old age has altered their appearance. To what extent do you think a person is judged by his or her appearance? To whom do you think a person's appearance is more important—the person or those around him or her?

8. Think about all the ways people try to avoid looking old—using face lifts, workouts, hair coloring, makeup, and so on. Should there be so much emphasis on looking young? What are the advantages and disadvantages of people appearing younger than they really are?

Literary Concept: Humor

One purpose of humor is to entertain, but humor can also help to make a serious point. For example, the teasing remarks, or banter, that Doña Laura and Don Gonzalo exchange early in the play might be considered humorous or amusing, but both characters reveal their personalities through these remarks and their reactions to them. What, if anything, struck you as humorous in this play? What was the purpose of the humor?

Writing Options

1. Write a character sketch of either Doña Laura or Don Gonzalo. Be sure to include a description of the person's outward appearance, attitudes, and inner self.

2. Imagine that you are Don Gonzalo and that you want to send a greeting card to Doña Laura. Write the message that you would like to appear on the card. It can be a few sentences or a poem.

3. How does the passage of poetry Doña Laura recites on page 97 relate to the plot of this play? Write a few sentences to explain your ideas.

4. You have met two seventy-year-olds in this play. How are they similar to and different from elderly people you know? List words and phrases that compare and contrast the two characters with your real acquaintances.

Vocabulary Practice

Exercise Some words are associated with certain subjects. For instance, *dribble* is a word you would find in a book about soccer or basketball. Read each book title below. Find a word in the list that you would expect to find in that book. Write the number and the word on your paper.

1. *Before the Game: Preparing to Play Chess*
2. *Saving the Vanishing Buffalo*
3. *The Long Road to the Top*
4. *When Your Parent Becomes a Child*
5. *Fifty Frightful Pumpkin Faces*
6. *How to Take Control of Your Eating*
7. *Nice Guys Can Finish First*
8. *Lucy Lyon's Guide to Modern Manners*
9. *Holding Your Temper*
10. *Keeping Your Mind Sharp and Fit*

Words to Know and Use

disposition
faculty
glutton
grotesque
indignantly
persistent
prelude
refined
refuge
senile

e x t e n d

Options for Learning

1 • **Design a Poster** Imagine that your school is presenting *A Sunny Morning*. Design a poster to advertise the production. Include (1) a picture that expresses the theme, (2) the title of the play, (3) where and when the play will be performed, (4) the price of admission, and (5) something to grab the viewer's attention and create an interest in attending the play.

2 • **Private Lives** People keep mementos such as dried flowers, notes, locks of hair, ticket stubs, and photographs to remember special people and experiences. Gather or make sample mementos Doña Laura or Don Gonzalo might have collected during their lives. Display the mementos for your classmates.

3 • **Anti-Age Ad** Create a magazine advertisement for an anti-aging product. Your product might be anything from wrinkle cream to calcium pills to haircolor to clothing. Aim the ad at older people.

4 • **Ham It Up** With a small group of classmates, improvise a play based on the story of Doña Laura and Don Gonzalo's earlier romance. First, reread the account of the sad love affair as told by the main characters. Roughly plot the main events in the story. Then act out the story. Play the characters broadly, that is, exaggerate their emotions and actions so that they seem almost overly dramatic. Be prepared for laughs, as this technique is often used by comedians to create humor.

 **FACT FINDER**

Find out how to say "a sunny morning" in Spanish, the language in which this play was written.

Serafín and Joaquín Álvarez Quintero
1871-1938; 1873-1944

"Our collaboration is as old as we are . . . we are one person," said Serafín and Joaquín Álvarez Quintero. The brothers were born in Andalusia, an area of southern Spain. They were still teenagers when their first play was produced in Seville, the capital of Andalusia. Their early success caused them to move to the cultural city of Madrid, work in the theater, and continue writing. Together they wrote almost two hundred plays.

The Álvarez brothers are known for the touches of humor in their plays, which strongly reflect their love for the people, the customs, and the speech of Andalusia. Their plays are also noted for their happy endings, sometimes touched with a little regret. Both brothers declared that their goal was to send their audiences home smiling.

WRITER'S WORKSHOP

THIRD-PERSON NARRATIVE

Sometimes for dramatic purposes a writer ends a tale in a way that leaves the reader wondering "What next?" All the selections in this subunit have such endings. You will answer the "what next" question for one of these selections by writing a third-person narrative that picks up where the original story ends.

As you learned earlier, a first-person narrative uses first-person pronouns such as *I* and *me*. The narrator (the *I*) is a character in his or her own story. In contrast, a narrative written from the third-person point of view refers to each of the characters as *he* or *she*, as in this paragraph from "The Necklace."

> Mme. Loisel appeared an old woman now. She became heavy, rough, harsh, like one of the poor. Her hair untended, her skirts askew, her hands red, her voice shrill, she even slopped water on her floors and scrubbed them herself.

A successful third-person narrative presents characters worth caring about who interact in ways that capture the reader's interest. Though many variations are possible, nearly all narratives have a definite structure that includes a beginning, a middle, and an end.

> Here is your PASSkey to this assignment.

GUIDED ASSIGNMENT: THE NEXT CHAPTER

Choose a selection in "Blind Spots" and write a third-person narrative that continues the story.

PURPOSE: To narrate part of a story
AUDIENCE: Readers of the original story
SUBJECT: A fictional character
STRUCTURE: Story chapter

Prewriting

STEP **1** **Choose a story** Review the selections in "Blind Spots." Recall what each main character was like and where the story ended. Select the character whose story you would like to continue.

STEP 2 **Explore plot possibilities** With classmates who have selected the same story you have, brainstorm possible plot developments. Remember that a good plot usually centers around a conflict or problem. Think of as many ideas as you can. You may wish to stay with the setting and characters already in the story, or you may want to add new elements. Here are some suggestions to help you explore.

1. What's your purpose? Do you want to resolve the unanswered questions in the original story, or do you want to create new questions?
2. Try out new settings for the character. Imagine settings from other stories, from TV or movies, from places you've heard about, or from places you know.
3. Introduce a new character or object. Who or what would your character love, hate, or fear?

STEP 3 **Decide on your plot** After your group has come up with a number of possibilities, decide for yourself where you want to take the story. You must consider carefully what you know about the main character. Review the story once again, paying special attention to this character's personality. Your goal is to write a "next chapter" that is believable, and you will not accomplish this if you make your character do something that does not fit his or her personality.

STEP 4 **Develop a story outline** A narrative has a structure that includes a beginning, a middle, and an end. The beginning draws the reader into the story by presenting the characters and the situation. The middle shows the conflict through action, dialogue, and description. The end resolves the conflict. Write an informal outline of your "next chapter" that reveals the beginning, middle, and end of your narrative. Here is the outline one student wrote for the "next chapter" of "A Mother in Mannville."

STUDENT MODEL ▶ BEGINNING--The narrator is shocked to learn that Jerry has no mother. Why did he lie? She can't leave until she talks to him.

MIDDLE--Narrator begins to search for Jerry. She and dog (Pat) search for hours through hills. Pat finds Jerry. Jerry finally confesses he lied because he didn't want narrator to feel sorry for him and didn't want her to know that he wanted to be adopted by her. Narrator can't adopt; she travels too much—but arranges for Jerry to visit her.

END--When Jerry visits, he meets narrator's married sister. The sister and her family love Jerry immediately and adopt him. Just what the narrator wanted!

Remember that your scenes must include details that allow the reader to imagine clearly what is happening. After you have decided generally what each scene is about, outline the details.

Special Tip
....

The events in the plot of a narrative show characters trying to reach a goal or solve a problem.

Drafting

Using your outline, write a draft of your "next chapter."

STEP 1   **Decide on a starting point**   Since you are completing a story that another writer has already begun, you may start right where he or she left off, or you may begin an entirely new scene. Don't forget the importance of a lively, interesting beginning.

STEP 2   **Try adding dialogue**   Most narratives contain dialogue between characters. Try including it in your story chapter to add interest and a true-to-life quality. Here is part of a conversation from one student's "next chapter" of "A Mother in Mannville":

> Jerry sat with his back against a tree, his head turned ◀ **STUDENT MODEL** away from her. "I'm sorry," he whispered. "I'm sorry I lied to you."
>
> "But Jerry," she replied helplessly. "Why? I don't understand. Whatever made you do it?"
>
> He was quiet for a long time. Finally with a deep sigh he raised his eyes and began to explain.

Notice how the conversation is punctuated, where capital letters are placed, and what synonyms are used for the word *said*. When you use dialogue in your story, try to make it sound realistic. Referring to the original story will help you capture the right tone. The Language Workshop that begins on page 109 will show you how to punctuate dialogue correctly.

Revising and Editing

Form small groups and have each group member read his or her story aloud. As one person reads, the others should jot down questions, comments, and suggestions to help the person evaluate and revise his or her work. The following checklist can serve as a guide.

Revision Checklist

1. Is the narrative told from the third-person point of view?
2. Does the narrative have a beginning, a middle, and an end?
3. Are the characters trying to reach a goal or solve a problem?
4. Does the "next chapter" relate clearly to the original story?
5. If dialogue is used, does it sound realistic?

After your story has been discussed, complete your revision.

Editing   Proofread for spelling, clarity, and mechanics. Make sure dialogue is correctly punctuated. Then ask a peer editor to take a final look.

Presenting

In a group with other students who selected the same character as you did, take turns reading your chapters aloud. Discuss these questions: Which narrative seems most like the original story? Which outcome is the most creative or unusual? You might also collect copies of your narratives and put them in a folder for the next class that reads the original stories to enjoy.

Reflecting on Your Writing

Answer the following questions. Turn in your answers with your paper.

1. Was story writing harder or easier for you than other writing?
2. Which part of your story do you like best? least?
3. What did you learn about writing stories that you might think about the next time you read a story?

LANGUAGE
WORKSHOP

PUNCTUATING DIALOGUE

> **Dialogue** is a conversation between two or more people. When you use dialogue in a story, make sure it is punctuated correctly. Careless punctuation can ruin a story by leaving your reader wondering who said what, when.

1. Use quotation marks to enclose direct quotations.

A **direct quotation** is a speaker's exact words. Use quotation marks to show where this speech begins and ends.

> Mme. Loisel said, ''I have nothing to wear to the party.''

When a direct quotation is interrupted by explanatory words, enclose each part of the quotation in quotation marks.

> ''If you need jewelry,'' said her husband, ''why don't you borrow something from your friend?''

Begin the second part of a divided quotation with a small letter unless it is a new sentence, a proper noun, or the pronoun *I*.

> ''Because you're so careful,'' said Señora Ines, ''you can serve the orange juice.''
> ''Go away,'' replied Doña Laura. ''This is my bench.''
> ''Sir,'' said Death, ''I knew your father.''

2. Place commas and periods inside quotation marks.

> The girl said, ''You can't be a friend of Luciana's.''
> ''You can't be a friend of Luciana's,'' said the girl.
> ''It's impossible,'' she continued, ''because I know all of her friends, and I don't know you.''

3. Place exclamation points and question marks inside quotation marks if those marks are part of the quotation itself. Place quotation marks in front of exclamation points and question marks if those marks are not part of the quotation.

> ''Have you seen the monkey?'' asked Luciana.
> Mme. Loisel exclaimed, ''The necklace is gone!''

REMINDER

Quotation marks are not used with **indirect quotations.** The word *that* often signals an indirect quotation. *Mme. Loisel said that she had nothing to wear to the party.*

Did Señora Ines say, "You're not really a guest"?

What a shock it was to hear, "But Mathilde, the necklace was only paste"!

4. Begin a new paragraph every time the speaker changes.

He asked, "Are you sure you had the necklace when you left the dance?"

"Yes, I felt it when I was in the hall."

"But if you had lost it in the street, we'd have heard it drop. It must be in the cab."

Exercise 1 Rewrite the following sentences. Punctuate them correctly with quotation marks, end marks, and commas.

1. Plays about love should always be set in romantic places said Ellen at the beginning of a class discussion Don't you agree
2. Absolutely answered Mr. Brown *A Sunny Morning* takes place in a park in Madrid The combination of Spain, sun, and love seems perfect
3. I don't really think said David that this play is an ordinary love story
4. I agree, David said Mr. Brown The love in this story is bittersweet
5. *Bittersweet* continued Mr. Brown means exactly what it says—bitter and sweet at the same time

Exercise 2 Work in groups to punctuate the following dialogue. Have one person copy the passage, beginning new paragraphs and inserting quotation marks, end marks, and commas as determined by the group.

Americans have always been fascinated by European cities Ms. Diaz said one day in English class Writers like F. Scott Fitzgerald and Ernest Hemingway were drawn to cities like Paris and Madrid for their culture and sophistication Those cities have been the settings for many classic stories, novels, and plays Have you ever visited those cities asked Henry Yes, I have answered Ms. Diaz Which European city is your favorite asked Delores. Well said Ms. Diaz I guess I'd have to say London. What do you do when you're there asked Joe Ms. Diaz laughed and replied I sightsee, visit museums, and window-shop. However, my favorite activity is sitting in parks and people watching

LANGUAGE HANDBOOK
....
For review and practice:
end marks,
   pages 962–65
commas,
   pages 966–67
quotation marks,
   pages 973–74

Exercise 3 Analyzing and Revising Your Writing

1. Find a paper in which you have written dialogue and check your punctuation. Correct any errors that you find.
2. Remember to check for correctly punctuated dialogue the next time you proofread your work.

VOCABULARY
WORKSHOP

DEFINITION AND EXAMPLE CLUES

If you are like most readers, you sometimes come across a word that you do not recognize. One way to find the meaning of such a word is to use the dictionary. Often, however, you can figure out the word's meaning by studying its context. **Context** refers to the words and sentences around an unfamiliar word. Within the context you may find specific clues. Two types of context clues are definition and example.

When **definition** is used, the meaning of the unfamiliar word is stated directly. Sometimes key words such as *or, is called, that is, which is,* or *in other words* signal the definition. A comma or a pair of commas may also be used as a signal.

> Mme. Loisel was *disconsolate,* or extremely unhappy, with her situation in life.

Examples can also help a reader understand an unfamiliar word. The key words *like, such as, for example, for instance,* and *other* alert you to the use of examples.

> Rosaura did not recognize the signs of her *servitude,* such as carrying the jug of juice or helping serve the hot dogs and the cake.

In this case the key words *such as* and the examples from the story suggest the meaning of the word *servitude*—"involuntary service to another person."

Exercise   Use context clues to determine the meaning of each italicized word. Write out your definitions on a piece of paper.

1. Rosaura was *ostracized,* or left out, by the other children.
2. Rosaura's *impudence* was reflected in the way she behaved. For example, she angrily yelled, "Shut up!" at her mother.
3. The magician at the party had an *enigmatic,* or mysterious, smile.
4. The *illusionist,* like other magicians, thrilled his audience with his seemingly impossible tricks.
5. Some monkeys are *arboreal.* In other words, they live in trees.
6. Many monkeys have *opposable* thumbs—that is, the thumb can be placed opposite the other fingers.

COMING TO TERMS

Have you ever faced a problem that seemed to have no solution? Not all problems have answers. Sometimes a person can only accept the situation and come to terms with it. "Coming to terms" means arriving at an understanding or an acceptance of the way things are.

The characters in the following selections face problems both within and outside themselves. As you read, examine each problem and judge how well each character comes to terms with his or her situation. Finally, decide how you would have dealt with each problem.

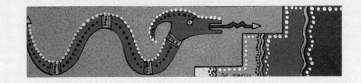

Fiction

Snake Boy

JAMAKE HIGHWATER

(jə mô′ kə hī′ wôt′ ər)

Examine What You Know

In this story, a Cheyenne boy must come to terms with his own destiny. Do you believe in destiny, the idea that your future is predetermined by some outside force, such as God, Fate, or Nature? Or do you believe that you control your own future? Discuss your beliefs with your classmates.

Expand Your Knowledge

A **myth** is a traditional story, usually involving magic or supernatural beings, that explains how something connected with humans or nature came to be. "Snake Boy" is a myth from the Cheyenne tribe. Myths were created to entertain listeners and at the same time teach them the values, traditions, and beliefs of the tribe. Such myths still serve as a cultural link between generations.

Native American myths often explore the balance between nature and humans. In these stories, animals and natural features, such as rocks or water, possess magical powers and are therefore sacred. Nature responds favorably to humans if treated with respect; if harmed, it may punish humans, perhaps through illness or floods. Animals are especially honored because they are a food source and therefore a source of life. Both animals and humans can be transformed, or changed into another form, and can easily communicate with each other. As you read "Snake Boy," notice the role nature plays in one boy's life.

Enrich Your Reading

Visualizing One way to enjoy reading is to **visualize**, or picture in your mind, the settings, characters, and action in a story. To do this, imagine what is happening, as if it were a movie. As you read "Snake Boy," pause at each point listed below to visualize the scene and the action.

- Page 114, column 1, paragraph 3
- Page 116, column 1, paragraph 1
- Page 116, column 2, paragraph 5
- Page 118, column 1, paragraph 6
- Page 119, column 1, paragraph 2
- Page 121, column 1, paragraph 3

■ *A biography of the author can be found on page 124.*

Snake Boy

JAMAKE HIGHWATER

When it was spring, and in the night the men of the clans could be heard singing to the spirits of powerful animals, Anpao and his two friends decided they would explore the lands beyond the village. The brothers had never ventured out of the valley of their people, for the elders often cautioned them about the dangers of the world beyond the meadow. But Anpao loved to explore, and his <u>infatuation</u> with adventure was highly <u>contagious</u>. Before long his two friends wanted to accompany him.

So early one morning the three young men started in the direction of the farthest slope of the little valley. By the time the Sun was high, they were tired and hungry. The brothers complained of the heat and cursed the rocks which bruised their feet through the thin soles of their moccasins. They were not the kind of people who are made for adventure.

Anpao attempted to encourage them, but his high spirits had little effect. The elder brother was especially <u>sullen</u> as they hiked through the rocky, scorched landscape in which nothing grew and there was neither fruit to eat nor water to drink. The three young men searched everywhere for food, but they found absolutely nothing, not even tender roots or green berries. Finally, the sullen elder brother sat down on a rock and refused to go any farther. "I want to turn back," he said angrily.

"No," protested the younger brother. "We have come this far, and what will be the good of it if we turn back before we have seen what lies beyond the valley?"

"It takes nothing to go back," Anpao told them. "That is why people never get anywhere. Do not be so easily disappointed, my friend. We will find food soon. And we will also find a good place to make our camp for the night."

The elder brother grumbled but finally agreed to continue their journey. And so, after resting in the shade of a boulder, they started out again.

"Ah!" shouted the elder brother suddenly. "Just as you said, Anpao, I have found food! Come and see what I have found for us!"

The three young men crowded around a nest built of pebbles among the great rocks. In the nest were four extremely large greenish eggs. "I am very glad," the elder brother said, and laughed. "I have found a blessing. Here is food for us to eat in this place where there is no food!"

"No," Anpao whispered. "Please, my friends, do not eat these eggs. I think there is great power in them. We must come away and continue walking."

114

"You are a fool, Anpao," the elder brother shouted. "You always tell us what to do. If we are tired, you tell us we must continue to walk. If we are hungry, you tell us we must be patient. And when we finally find food, then you tell us we must not eat it. You are a fool and I don't know why I call you my friend!"

"Listen to me . . ." Anpao urged, but the brothers ignored him and gathered dried grass to make a fire. Soon the eggs were roasting. The brothers sang heartily, their voices echoing among the great gray rocks, as they sniffed the cooking food.

"*I* know that something bad will happen if we eat these eggs."

"You must listen to what I am telling you," Anpao pleaded. "I have come to know about such things, and you are doing evil. Already the eggs have died in the fire. Now we must run away quickly. You cannot steal these eggs without a prayer or an offering. A living thing is a vast mystery, and something which is coming into life, like these great eggs, is even more mysterious. I know that something bad will happen if we eat these eggs."

The younger brother looked worriedly at Anpao, and at last he agreed to abandon the eggs. But the elder brother laughed at both of them, as he carefully removed one of the eggs from the fire and broke it open. "Hmm," he sighed, "how good this egg is! Come, see how good they taste. Eat one before you die of hunger!" he mumbled as he ate greedily. But the other two refused to touch the eggs, so the hungry brother ate the two eggs he had cooked for his brother and Anpao as well as his own. After he had finished, he lay down and rested, while his brother and Anpao watched him with great apprehension. He mocked their concern and laughed at them, patting his belly proudly. "You are both starving fools! I am full and you are hungry. Come now, let us continue our journey while there is still light."

After they had walked for a considerable distance and nothing had happened, the younger brother began to regret that he had listened to Anpao's warning. He was so hungry he could think of nothing but how large and delicious-looking the eggs had been. He was about to chide Anpao for his advice when his brother suddenly complained of sharp pains in his stomach. He gradually turned horribly pale and was unwilling to walk.

But there was no place to stop, and nowhere for the sick brother to lie down and rest. Everywhere were sharp stones and the blaze of the Sun. So the young men continued across the white haze of the plain until at last the fierce sunlight withdrew and the world became cool and dark. They finally found a tiny ravine and searched for water. All they found was a muddy little stream flowing sluggishly through the clay and stones. There, among the thorny bushes and dry grass, the three young men made camp.

Just before daybreak, the elder brother awakened Anpao.

"Please help me," he whispered. "I am going to die. I cannot walk. My legs feel

---

Words to Know and Use | **apprehension** (ap're hen'shən) *n.* a feeling of anxiety, worry, or dread
chide (chīd) *v.* to scold

strange. I think something horrible is happening to me! Please," he begged in a strange voice, "you must help me, Anpao!"

"You must relax, my friend," Anpao told him softly. "Come, lie still and let me see what is wrong. Maybe there is something wrong with your legs from our long walk. Perhaps I can help you." So he drew back his friend's robe and took off his moccasins. It was true: something very peculiar was happening. The boy's legs were no longer smooth and brown. His skin had changed . . . not completely, but enough to make it a very curious sight. It had become scaly and seemed to have very faint green stripes.

"What is it, Anpao?" the boy asked in dread. But Anpao could not tell him. "What do you see, Anpao? Are my legs all right?"

"Yes, yes, I think they are fine," Anpao said softly.

"Ah," he sighed. "Then awaken my brother and let's go now. I am so thirsty I can't stand it. The water in the stream has dried up during the night and we have nothing to drink."

Anpao peered at the boy, for the stream was not dry but exactly as it had been when they found it.

"Quickly, quickly, let's go find water," the sick boy said in a daze. "I know I will feel fine if only we can find some water to drink!" Before Anpao could stop him, he had struggled to his feet and started out without waiting for the others. "We must go," he mumbled again and again, "we must go."

Anpao and the younger brother followed as quickly as they could. The elder brother moved quickly across the sharp, stony <u>terrain</u>, and his brother and Anpao could

barely keep up with him. Finally, the boy stopped and looked as if he might collapse.

"Ah, help me!" he cried out. He was feeling worse and could walk no farther. His legs, he told them, were so heavy that they did not seem to be part of his body. They dragged behind him and would not do what he told them to do. Yet he insisted upon continuing, for he said that only water could cure him. So after resting a moment, he hurried on alone. Afraid to argue with him, his brother and Anpao ran after him and tried to support his body with their arms. Slowly the three friends staggered through the rocks and boulders.

"Please," the boy whimpered, "don't leave me—no matter what happens. I know I have been cruel to people. But I will surely die if you leave me here alone."

"We won't leave you," Anpao promised. "Try to walk and don't worry so much. We will stay with you until we find water and you are safe. We both promise this to you."

All that hot day they traveled painfully over the cruel landscape, exhausted from the heat and recoiling from the sharp stones which cut through their moccasins and bruised their feet.

Finally at nightfall they came to the edge of the terrible valley of rocks and found themselves in a beautiful wooded area where a small lake was fed by clear water cascading from the summit of the vast cliff that bordered the valley of rocks.

"Please," pleaded the sick boy, "let's make camp here. I want to be near the water. Perhaps if I sit with my legs in the cool water they will be cured. I am certain that if my

Words to Know and Use | **terrain** (ter rān') *n.* ground, especially with regard to topographical features

PRAYER TO THE SPIRIT OF THE BUFFALO   1920   Joseph Henry Sharp   The Rockwell Museum, Corning, New York.

legs are in the water they will get better." So his brother and Anpao carefully lowered him to the bank of the lake, where he sat and dangled his legs in the cold clear water.

"I will make a fire," Anpao said. "Will you be all right without us? Your brother can look for food while I make the fire, if you can get along for a while." The sick boy assured them that he would be fine now that he was near the water. So they left him and went off to make camp and to find food.

As soon as they were gone, the boy quickly untied his hair ornaments and took off his breechclout and put them with his moccasins on the shore. Then he slipped quietly into the deep water and began to swim in the pale light of the rising Moon. He glided effortlessly through the water, diving gracefully and emerging again, twisting his body as he slithered through the water, and his skin gleamed in the moonlight.

"I feel marvelous!" he shouted to his brother and Anpao. "Now I feel better than I ever have felt in my life! Come and see how well I have learned to swim!"

"No," his young brother called desperately, rushing to the shore and searching the night for him. "Come out of the water! Please come out!"

Anpao had just lighted the campfire when he heard the sick boy calling from somewhere out in the middle of the lake. He too ran to the shore and called out, "Please, come back now and join us at the fire. It is warm and you can dry off."

"Yes, yes, yes," the boy said, laughing, as he dragged himself from the water, flopping down exhausted on the shore and panting for breath. "Ah!" he cried, looking down at his legs for the first time.

His legs had grown together, and the entire lower part of his body was now covered with green scales. "What is happening to me!" he bellowed in panic.

His brother tried to comfort him, and together he and Anpao managed to carry him to the fireside, where they begged him to rest. They did not let the sick boy realize how frightened they were, but when he finally closed his eyes they looked at each other in astonishment and the younger brother sobbed quietly. In the light of the fire they could see stripes gradually covering the body of the sleeping boy.

That night the younger brother and Anpao could not rest. The sick brother whimpered continually, and once he awakened in hysterics and begged them to cast him into the lake and forget him. It was a terrible night and by morning they were resolved that, no matter how hard the journey might be, they would go back through the valley of rocks before the boy's sickness got worse.

But the elder brother could not walk. His legs had turned into a thick green tail covered with scales. The only way the boys could travel was by taking turns carrying him across their shoulders. "Take me home," he cried as they climbed among the ragged rocks. "Please take me home!" And so they went along slowly and painfully until they came to another little lake formed, like the first one, by a waterfall that cascaded over the cliff.

"You must help me into the water," the boy urged them, even before they had put him down. "Please do as I ask and I won't bother you again, I promise. Just put me in the water."

Unwillingly, the two helped him into the water. Immediately he laughed and pulled free of them. Then with a leer he slithered off into the darkness of the water. All that night his brother and Anpao sat shivering beside the lake, unable to find enough wood to keep their fire burning and listening to the elder brother splashing and leaping about in the black lake. They did not speak or look at each other. They waited silently for daylight.

When at last it was dawn, the sick boy giggled at them as he glided glistening from the water and slid effortlessly onto the shore.

"Ah," Anpao groaned, for his friend had been utterly transformed. Only his arms and his head were his own. The rest of his body was that of a giant green snake.

"Do not look so sad," said the snake boy. He laughed, but his voice was almost gone, and when he spoke the sounds he made were gasps and hisses. "Let us continue on our way," he hissed. "Don't be afraid. I

Words to Know and Use

leer (lir) *n.* a sly look revealing triumph or evilness
transform (trans fôrm') *v.* to change the appearance, form, or character of someone or something

know exactly what I am doing," he said confidently.

So the others, horrified and dazed, followed Snake Boy, who slithered among the rocks with ease. His body was very sleek and long, and he hissed and giggled as he hurried along.

When the day was almost over, they reached a vast river at the end of the valley of rocks.

"Here is my home," Snake Boy hissed, as he slid into the water. "But stay here with me a little longer, my friends, because there are things I must tell you before you go. Do not mourn for me or cry for me. Brother, when you return to our village you must tell our people that we must accept whatever it is we are becoming. I have learned this and now I will be all right. Sometimes we grow up to be like everyone else, but sometimes

THE FOUR WORLDS 1954
Joe Herrera
Private Collection.

INDIAN HUNTERS   date unknown   Joseph Henry Sharp   Courtesy of Nedra Metteucci's Fenn Galleries, Santa Fe, New Mexico

we do not. People are always afraid of turning into something unusual, but they must not be afraid. We must be happy with whatever we are becoming. That is the way it is and that is the way it was intended to be."

With that, Snake Boy giggled happily and slipped out of sight. His brother called out to him and begged him not to leave them.

He promised that he would find help—someone with such great power that he could change the snake boy back into a boy. But there was no reply. Anpao stared out into the black lake. "Perhaps," he said, "he does not want to be a boy." And then they were silent.

The two friends paced the banks of the

river all night, crying and offering prayers and peering into the darkness for a sign of Snake Boy, but he did not return to them. When the dawn was near, the two boys could remain awake no longer. Their day's journey and their hunger had weakened them, and finally they fell asleep by the river.

"Sheeeee . . ." came a voice. "Shsss-wake shsss-up! Shsss-wake shsss-up shsss-and shsss-look shsss-at shsss-me!"

"People are always afraid of turning into something unusual . . ."

Anpao jumped to his feet and stared across the river. Rising from the misty water was a gigantic serpent whose body was covered with luminous blue and green scales and whose head was crowned with twin horns. It was the most amazing sight Anpao had ever seen. The younger brother had also awakened and was crouching in fear of the vision in the black river.

"Do not be afraid, my brother. I am still your friend," the serpent hissed across the water.

"Yes, yes." The younger brother wept, as he slowly stood up. "I am not afraid and I still love you, my brother."

"Then do not weep. Be happy because I have finally found the place where I truly belong."

"It cannot be! How could this happen to you, my brother?"

"It is true, and you must accept it, and you must promise not to talk about it. You must tell our people that I am not dead. I am taking care of this great river. When you cross it, you must think about me, and you must bring meat for me and drop it into the river. If you will do this whenever you cross this water, I will bless and protect you."

"I promise," said his brother, weeping. "I will tell them everything you have said."

"Now come to me," the great serpent hissed as he slithered over the water toward the shore. "I will not see you again, my little brother, and I want to kiss you good-by. Do not be afraid; I won't hurt you."

Reluctantly the younger brother crept toward the river's edge, and as Anpao watched in amazement, he put his arms around the giant snake's neck. Then the snake licked his face with its bright red, forked tongue.

For a moment Snake Boy looked intently, perhaps sadly, at Anpao and his brother. Then he vanished into the water. ❧

Responding to Reading

First Impressions

1. What words or phrases describe your mood after reading this selection?

Second Thoughts

2. The elder brother is transformed in more than one way. In what ways does he change?

   Think about
   - his physical appearance at the beginning of the story and at the end
   - the way he treats others early in the story and later on
   - his comments about people and their destiny

3. Why do you think the elder brother disregards Anpao's warning and eats the eggs?

4. The elder brother says that people should not be afraid of growing up to be different, but should be happy with whatever they are becoming. How does this message apply to people in our world today? Do you agree or disagree with it?

5. What purpose do you think this myth serves in Cheyenne culture?

   Think about
   - why the elder brother becomes a snake, rather than some other animal
   - Snake Boy's comments about change
   - the role of animals in the Cheyenne culture

Broader Connections

6. Think about people in your school or community who are seen as "different." How are they treated by others? What adjustments do you think they might make in order to be happy? Is it hardest for people to be different as children, as teenagers, or as adults? Why?

Literary Concept: Theme

The **theme** is the message or insight about life or human nature that an author presents in a work of literature. To understand the theme of a story, notice how the characters change as the story progresses. Decide what they learn about themselves and about life. There are several themes in "Snake Boy." Describe one theme about a person's relationship with nature and one about the nature of people.

Writing Options

1. Anpao tells his friends, "It takes nothing to go back. That is why people never get anywhere." What does his comment mean in the story? What meaning might these words have for people in general? Write your opinion.

2. Imagine that you are a scientist recording the elder brother's transformation from boy to snake. Review the story, making detailed, step-by-step notes about the changes in the elder brother as you go.

3. Write the conversation that might have taken place between the boys and their families or the elders of the tribe on the boys' return home. Be sure the boys explain what happened, why the elder brother will not be returning, and his feelings about his transformation.

4. List at least three details or events from the story that help identify it as a myth.

Vocabulary Practice

Exercise Read each phrase below and write the word from the list suggested by the phrase. Some words will be used twice.

1. what angry elders might do if the boys disobey them
2. how the boys might act if they were not allowed to explore
3. the strong feelings that the boys might have toward girls
4. what a frightened boy might feel if his body started changing
5. the nature of the excitement spreading among the boys
6. the land formations the boys travel through
7. what eating the eggs could do to Snake Boy's body
8. a triumphant, evil look that Snake Boy gives the boys
9. what a major experience might do to a boy's outlook on life
10. the worry that Snake Boy's parents might feel when they find out that their son is missing

Words to Know and Use

apprehension
chide
contagious
infatuation
leer
sullen
terrain
transform

extend

Options for Learning

1 • Mapmaker, Mapmaker Draw the map the boys might create to show where they traveled. Skim the story for details about specific locations. Include important markers such as the nest of eggs, the stream where the elder brother's transformation was first noticed, and the two waterfalls. Study a United States Forest Service map to see how trails, lakes, and mountains are marked. On your map, include a legend that explains your symbols.

2 • Serpentine Symbolism Snakes appear in the myths and legends of several Native American tribes. Research what snakes symbolize by examining Indian paintings and sculpture and the myths and legends of other tribes. If possible, interview Native Americans. Share your findings orally and show examples of snake symbols to your class.

3 • A Buffalo Robe The Cheyenne, who created this myth, made winter robes from buffalo skins and sometimes decorated these robes with illustrations. Create such a robe on paper or from material and decorate it with drawings or symbols depicting the story of Snake Boy.

4 • Picture This Draw or paint a full-figure portrait of Snake Boy, as he appeared to the other boys at the end of the story. Make your interpretation as detailed and accurate as possible.

 **FACT FINDER**

Where do most Cheyenne live today?

Jamake Highwater
1942?-

"I am adopted." So begins Jamake Highwater's story of his life. "I do not know when or where I was born, because I was adopted at a time when adoption was still a covert [secret] matter." As a young child, Highwater traveled the carnival and rodeo circuits with his parents before he was left in an orphanage. He was adopted when he was about nine years old and grew up in southern California.

After Highwater's unhappy childhood, a teacher motivated him and he began to achieve, even putting himself through college. As an adult, Highwater has written, hosted, and helped produce several television documentaries and has written twenty books, including numerous nonfiction books and articles about Native American culture. He is a noted critic and commentator on the arts. About the novel *Anpao: An American Indian Odyssey*, from which "Snake Boy" comes, Highwater says "I wrote the one and only draft of a novel I had wanted to write for so long that when I finally sat down at my typewriter it wrote itself in less than six weeks."

Fiction

The
Scholarship
Jacket

MARTA SALINAS

*E*xamine What You Know

In your school, what kinds of awards are given for achievements in sports, academics, and music and for service? Do some awards seem more important than others? Explain your opinion of your school's awards system and then compare it to the one in this story.

*E*xpand Your Knowledge

The main character in this story is the valedictorian, or the graduating student with the highest grades. Often the valedictorian gives a speech at the graduation ceremony. The word *valedictorian* comes from two Latin words, *vale,* meaning "farewell," and *dicere,* meaning "to say." The valedictorian says farewell to the school.

The salutatorian has the second-highest grades, and sometimes he or she also gives a graduation speech. The word *salutatorian* comes from the Latin word *salutare,* meaning "salute." The origin of *salute* is the Latin *salus,* meaning "health and safety." The salutatorian's speech salutes, or wishes health and safety to, the graduating class.

*E*nrich Your Reading

Cause and Effect Events in a story are often related to each other by cause and effect. That is, the first event in time—the cause— is the reason why a later event—the effect—happens. For example, in the sentence "Al chuckled because the raccoon ate the cake," the raccoon's action is the cause of Al's chuckling. Al's chuckling is the effect. The word *because* is a clue that indicates cause and effect. Other clue words that show cause and effect are *so/that, if/then, since,* and *therefore.* Even if there are no clue words, you can still recognize that one event causes another. As you read, list events linked by cause and effect in a chart like the one below.

Cause	Effect	Clue Words (if any)
Martha's father did not have enough money to support her	Martha lived with her grandparents	so

The *Scholarship Jacket*

MARTA SALINAS

The small Texas school that I went to had a tradition carried out every year during the eighth-grade graduation: a beautiful gold and green jacket (the school colors) was awarded to the class valedictorian, the student who had maintained the highest grades for eight years. The scholarship jacket had a big gold *S* on the left front side and your name written in gold letters on the pocket.

My oldest sister Rosie had won the jacket a few years back, and I fully expected to also. I was fourteen and in the eighth grade. I had been a straight A student since the first grade and this last year had looked forward very much to owning that jacket. My father was a farm laborer who couldn't earn enough money to feed eight children, so when I was six I was given to my grandparents to raise. We couldn't participate in sports at school because there were registration fees, uniform costs, and trips out of town; so, even though our family was quite agile and athletic, there would never be a school sports jacket for us. This one, the scholarship jacket, was our only chance.

In May, close to graduation, spring fever had struck as usual with a vengeance.[1] No one paid any attention in class; instead we stared out the windows and at each other wanting to speed up the last few weeks of school. I despaired every time I looked in the mirror. Pencil thin, not a curve anywhere. I was called "beanpole" and "string bean," and I knew that's what I looked like. A flat chest, no hips, and a brain; that's what I had. That really wasn't much for a four-teen-year-old to work with, I thought, as I absentmindedly wandered from my history class to the gym. Another hour of sweating in basketball and displaying my toothpick legs was coming up. Then I remembered my P.E. shorts were still in a bag under my desk where I'd forgotten them. I had to walk all the way back and get them. Coach Thompson was a real bear if someone wasn't dressed for P.E. She had said I was a good forward and even tried to talk Grandma into letting me join the team once. Of course Grandma said no.

I was almost back at my classroom door when I heard voices raised in anger as if in some sort of argument. I stopped. I didn't mean to <u>eavesdrop</u>, I just hesitated, not knowing what to do. I needed those shorts

---

1. **with a vengeance:** with great force.

Words to Know and Use | **eavesdrop** (ēvz'drŏp') *v.* to listen secretly to a private conversation

and I was going to be late, but I didn't want to interrupt an argument between my teachers. I recognized the voices: Mr. Schmidt, my history teacher, and Mr. Boone, my math teacher. They seemed to be arguing about me. I couldn't believe it. I still remember the feeling of shock that rooted me flat against the wall as if I were trying to blend in with the graffiti written there.

"I refuse to do it! I don't care who her father is, her grades don't even begin to compare to Martha's. I won't lie or falsify records. Martha has a straight A-plus average and you know it." That was Mr. Schmidt and he sounded very angry. Mr. Boone's voice sounded calm and quiet.

"Look. Joann's father is not only on the Board, he owns the only store in town: we could say it was a close tie and—"

The pounding in my ears drowned out the rest of the words, only a word here and there filtered through. ". . . Martha is Mexican . . . resign . . . won't do it. . . ." Mr. Schmidt came rushing out and luckily for me went down the opposite way toward the auditorium, so he didn't see me. Shaking, I waited a few minutes and then went in and grabbed my bag and fled from the room. Mr. Boone looked up when I came in but didn't say anything. To this day I don't remember if I got in trouble in P.E. for being late or how I made it through the rest of the afternoon. I went home very sad and cried into my pillow that night so Grandmother wouldn't hear me. It seemed a cruel coincidence that I had overheard that conversation.

The next day when the principal called me into his office I knew what it would be about. He looked uncomfortable and un-

happy. I decided I wasn't going to make it any easier for him so I looked him straight in the eyes. He looked away and fidgeted with the papers on his desk.

"Martha," he said, "there's been a change in policy this year regarding the scholarship jacket. As you know, it has always been free." He cleared his throat and continued. "This year the Board has decided to charge fifteen dollars, which still won't cover the complete cost of the jacket."

I stared at him in shock and a small sound of dismay escaped my throat. I hadn't expected this. He still avoided looking in my eyes.

"So if you are unable to pay the fifteen dollars for the jacket it will be given to the next one in line." I didn't need to ask who that was.

Standing with all the dignity I could muster, I said, "I'll speak to my grandfather about it, sir, and let you know tomorrow." I cried on the walk home from the bus stop. The dirt road was a quarter mile from the highway, so by the time I got home, my eyes were red and puffy.

"Where's Grandpa?" I asked Grandma, looking down at the floor so she wouldn't ask me why I'd been crying. She was sewing on a quilt as usual and didn't look up.

"I think he's out back working in the bean field."

I went outside and looked out at the fields. There he was. I could see him walking between the rows, his body bent over the little plants, hoe in hand. I walked slowly out to him, trying to think how I could best ask him for the money. There was a cool breeze blowing and a sweet smell of mesquite fruit in the air

Words to Know and Use

falsify (fôl′sə fī′) *v.* to make untrue
coincidence (kō in′sə dəns) *n.* an accidental occurrence of related events at about the same time
dignity (dig′nə tē) *n.* self-respect

BERNADITA 1922 Robert Henri
San Diego Museum of Art Donated by The Wednesday Club.

ing. "Grandpa, I have a big favor to ask you," I said in Spanish, the only language he knew. He still waited silently. I tried again. "Grandpa, this year the principal said the scholarship jacket is not going to be free. It's going to cost fifteen dollars, and I have to take the money in tomorrow, otherwise it'll be given to someone else." The last words came out in an eager rush. Grandpa straightened up tiredly and leaned his chin on the hoe handle. He looked out over the field that was filled with the tiny green bean plants. I waited, desperately hoping he'd say I could have the money.

He turned to me and asked quietly, "What does a scholarship jacket mean?"

I answered quickly; maybe there was a chance. "It means you've earned it by having the highest grades for eight years and that's why they're giving it to you." Too late I realized the <u>significance</u> of my words. Grandpa knew that I understood it was not a matter of money. It wasn't that. He went back to hoeing the weeds that sprang up between the delicate little bean plants. It was a time-consuming job; sometimes the small shoots were right next to each other. Finally he spoke again as I turned to leave, crying.

"Then if you pay for it, Marta, it's not a scholarship jacket, is it? Tell your principal I will not pay the fifteen dollars."

I walked back to the house and locked myself in the bathroom for a long time. I was angry with Grandfather even though I knew he was right, and I was angry with the Board, whoever they were. Why did they have to change the rules when it was my turn to win the jacket? Those were the days of belief and innocence.

It was a very sad and <u>withdrawn</u> girl who

but I didn't appreciate it. I kicked at a dirt clod. I wanted that jacket so much. It was more than just being a valedictorian and giving a little thank you speech for the jacket on graduation night. It represented eight years of hard work and expectation. I knew I had to be honest with Grandpa; it was my only chance. He saw my shadow and looked up.

He waited for me to speak. I cleared my throat nervously and clasped my hands behind my back so he wouldn't see them shak-

Words to Know and Use | **significance** (sig nif′ ə kəns) *n.* importance
withdrawn (with drôn′) *adj.* shy, reserved

dragged into the principal's office the next day. This time he did look me in the eyes.

"What did your grandfather say?"

I sat very straight in my chair.

"He said to tell you he won't pay the fifteen dollars."

The principal muttered something I couldn't understand under his breath and walked over to the window. He stood looking out at something outside. He looked bigger than usual when he stood up; he was a tall, gaunt man with gray hair, and I watched the back of his head while I waited for him to speak.

"Why?" he finally asked. "Your grandfather has the money. He owns a two-hundred acre ranch."

I looked at him, forcing my eyes to stay dry. "I know, sir, but he said if I had to pay for it, then it wouldn't be a scholarship jacket." I stood up to leave. "I guess you'll just have to give it to Joann." I hadn't meant to say that, it had just slipped out. I was almost to the door when he stopped me.

"Martha—wait."

I turned and looked at him, waiting. What did he want now? I could feel my heart pounding loudly in my chest. . . . Something bitter and vile tasting was coming up in my mouth; I was afraid I was going to be sick. I didn't need any sympathy speeches. He sighed loudly and went back to his big desk. He watched me, biting his lip.

"Okay. We'll make an exception in your case. I'll tell the Board, you'll get your jacket."

I could hardly believe my ears. I spoke in a trembling rush. "Oh, thank you, sir!" Suddenly I felt great. I didn't know about adrenalin in those days, but I knew something was pumping through me, making me feel as tall as the sky. I wanted to yell, jump, run the mile, do something. I ran out so I could cry in the hall where there was no one to see me.

At the end of the day, Mr. Schmidt winked at me and said, "I hear you're getting the scholarship jacket this year."

His face looked as happy and innocent as a baby's, but I knew better. Without answering I gave him a quick hug and ran to the bus. I cried on the walk home again but this time because I was so happy. I couldn't wait to tell Grandpa and ran straight to the field. I joined him in the row where he was working, and without saying anything I crouched down and started pulling up the weeds with my hands. Grandpa worked alongside me for a few minutes and he didn't ask what had happened. After I had a little pile of weeds between the rows, I stood up and faced him.

"The principal said he's making an exception for me, Grandpa, and I'm getting the jacket after all. That's after I told him what you said."

Grandpa didn't say anything, he just gave me a pat on the shoulder and a smile. He pulled out the crumpled red handkerchief that he always carried in his back pocket and wiped the sweat off his forehead.

"Better go see if your grandmother needs any help with supper."

I gave him a big grin. He didn't fool me. I skipped and ran back to the house whistling some silly tune. ❧

129

Responding to Reading

First Impressions

1. What is your impression of the character of Martha's grandfather?

Second Thoughts

2. Martha's grandfather refuses to pay fifteen dollars for the scholarship jacket. Do you agree or disagree with his decision?

   Think about
   - the effect he says paying for the jacket would have
   - what he feels might be best for Martha

3. What does the jacket mean to Martha? Why does she want it?

4. Why is Martha asked to pay for the jacket?

   Think about
   - the overheard remark "Martha is Mexican"
   - the assumption made about Martha's financial situation
   - who would receive the jacket if Martha could not pay for it

5. Why do you think the principal finally awards Martha the jacket?

6. Martha goes along with her grandfather's wishes. Would you have reacted differently, or did she react the only possible way?

Broader Connections

7. Does it cost money to participate in sports at your school? Think of the cost of uniforms, special shoes, and bus trips and other "hidden" costs. Does the school provide for those unable to pay? Is it fair that some athletes are unable to participate for financial reasons?

Literary Concept: Realistic Fiction

Although all fiction comes from a writer's imagination, it is divided into several categories. **Fantasy** is highly imaginative and could not really happen; it might contain magic, be set in an imaginary world, or involve characters who employ extrahuman powers. An example is *The Wizard of Oz.* **Historical fiction** is set in real times and places from the past, but the story itself did not happen. The characters use ordinary human abilities to confront a problem from that historical period. *Little House on the Prairie* is an example of historical fiction. **Realistic fiction** is set in the real, modern world. The characters act like real people who face problems typical of the modern world using ordinary human abilities. Why is "The Scholarship Jacket" classified as realistic fiction?

Writing Options

1. As valedictorian of the class, Martha will have to give a short speech at graduation. Write a speech for her. What might she most like to say to her class? Would she mention the jacket incident and what she learned from it?

2. If Martha had not received the jacket, how might she have protested? Make a list of possible actions.

3. Martha heard only bits of the conversation between Mr. Schmidt and Mr. Boone. Write out in dialogue form their complete conversation as you imagine it.

4. Imagine that you are Mr. Schmidt or Mr. Boone. Write a memo to the school board president saying who you think should win the jacket and why.

Vocabulary Practice

Exercise Read each sentence. Decide whether the boldfaced word is used correctly. On your paper, write *Correct* or *Incorrect.*

1. Grandpa helped Martha maintain her **dignity** in the face of prejudice.
2. Though she did not intend to **eavesdrop,** Martha heard much of the conversation between her math and history teachers.
3. Martha acted very **withdrawn** as she joyfully came home with the jacket.
4. Grandpa's refusal to pay was a **coincidence.**
5. Like many who work hard physically, Grandpa was **gaunt;** his body was lean and well muscled.
6. Martha's surge of **adrenalin** caused her to feel sleepy.
7. If the teachers wanted to **falsify** the records, they would have to change Joann's grades.
8. The principal understood the **significance** of Martha's refusal to pay for the jacket.
9. In the early part of the story, the principal acted with **dignity.**
10. It was a **coincidence** that Martha went to the classroom at the time that her teachers were discussing her.

> *Words to Know and Use*
>
> **adrenalin
> coincidence
> dignity
> eavesdrop
> falsify
> gaunt
> significance
> withdrawn**

*O*ptions for Learning

1 • Stage an Argument The principal seems to have made the final decision about the jacket on his own. Suppose Joann's father called him up after hearing the decision to give Martha the jacket. With another student, act out this conversation for the class. Plan the conversation ahead of time, making sure that each speaker gives reasons to back his argument. Remember that Joann's father is both a member of the school board and owner of the only store in town.

2 • Design the Scholarship Jacket Design a scholarship jacket that Martha would be proud to wear. Decide what materials would be durable and appropriate for Martha's climate. Decide how to decorate the jacket using the school colors mentioned early in the story. Sketch both the front and the back of the jacket and write a brief description of the materials that would be used to make it.

3 • A Realistic Setting Skim the story for details about the farm. Look through books of photographs or paintings of the Southwest. Then paint or use another medium to illustrate the grandfather working in the field of bean plants, or Martha's home with the fields in the background, or some other scene that represents the natural setting of the story. Aim for realism in your painting.

4 • Make a Mandala Originally, a mandala was a circular design that symbolized the universe in the Hindu and Buddhist religions. Today the word has been broadened in art to mean a circular design containing images that are intended to be a symbol for a person, idea, or place. Make a mandala showing the personality of either Martha or her grandfather. You may make the mandala flat, using paints and other colors, or three-dimensional, by gluing on objects that represent either personality.

 **FACT FINDER**

Find out who pays for athletic uniforms and trips at your school.

e x p l o r e

Poetry

Saying Yes
DIANA CHANG

*E*xamine *What You Know*

Americans tend to identify one another with one-word labels, such as *jock, Democrat, brain, Irish,* and *nerd.* Why do you think we categorize people in this way rather than describe them in a way that shows their many qualities, interests, and diversities?

*E*xpand *Your Knowledge*

While this selection may not fit your idea of a "normal" poem, it is a good example of how the **form** of poetry can vary greatly. Notice the shape of the poem on the page. You will see that the lines vary in length and that the number of lines in a stanza varies. The poem does not rhyme, nor does it have an even pattern of rhythm. The capitalization and punctuation vary from usual poetic form. The strangest thing about the poem is that the first half is written in dialogue, or conversation, while the second half tells the main speaker's thoughts. As you read the poem, think about what the dialogue contributes to the poem's meaning.

*W*rite *Before You Read*

How would you describe your cultural or national heritage? For example, are you an Irish American, a Mexican American, a Vietnamese American? In your journal or on a piece of paper, explain what aspects of your life today, if any, are traditions your family has retained from the "old country." Maybe you celebrate Chinese New Year or Cinco de Mayo, eat pancakes on Shrove Tuesday like your Irish father, or remember lullabies sung by your Haitian grandparents.

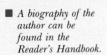

■ *A biography of the author can be found in the Reader's Handbook.*

Saying Yes

DIANA CHANG

SEATED GIRL WITH DOG 1944 Milton Avery
Collection of Roy R. Neuberger, New York.

"Are you Chinese?"
"Yes."

"American?"
"Yes."

5   "*Really* Chinese?"
"No . . . not quite."

"*Really* American?"
"Well, actually, you see . . ."

But I would rather say
10   yes

Not neither-nor,
not maybe,
but both, and not only

The homes I've had,
15   the ways I am

I'd rather say it
twice,
yes

Responding to Reading

First Impressions

1. What is your first impression of the main speaker?

Second Thoughts

2. What idea is the main speaker trying to explain?

   Think about
   - the questions she is asked
   - how her answers change as the questions become more specific
   - the meaning of lines 9-13
   - the main speaker's conclusion

3. Who might be asking the questions in this poem and why?

4. Why do you think the first half of the poem is written in dialogue?

5. Based on the title and the last three lines of the poem, how do you think the main speaker feels about being both Chinese and American?

6. What is the theme, or message about life, of this poem?

Broader Connections

7. Do you think it is possible to hold onto the culture of your immigrant ancestors and still be an American? Explain.

Writing Options

1. Think about public service slogans you have heard, such as "Give a hoot, don't pollute" or "Just Say No!" Write a public service slogan that promotes pride in one's cultural heritage or that celebrates the United States as a melting pot of various cultures.

2. Write a brief essay about an episode in which belonging to a particular ethnic group helped or hurt you or someone you know.

3. How do you think the speaker should answer the questions posed in this poem? Write a letter to the speaker suggesting how you might handle the situation if you were in her shoes.

4. Write a poem about a label such as the ones you discussed earlier. Use "Saying Yes" as a model or create your own format.

Essay

On Being Seventeen, Bright, and Unable to Read

DAVID RAYMOND

Examine What You Know

Each of us, even the most talented, has trouble doing something—push-ups, vocal solos before a group, math problems: What is one thing you find difficult to do? How do you feel when you must do this thing?

Expand Your Knowledge

hondno
(London)

grib
(girl)

Kat
(Kate)

ʲℓℓ
(is)

c q r b ℓ
(cards)

Examples of
dyslexic writing.

David Raymond, the author of this essay, has dyslexia, a type of learning disability that makes it difficult to read and write. Most people with dyslexia have average or above-average intelligence; they simply cannot learn to read the way most people learn. Dyslexia often causes people to make mistakes in one or more of the following areas:

1. Recognizing and remembering printed words and numbers.
2. Reading and writing letters and numerals. Some dyslexics reverse letters and numerals, for example mistaking the letter *b* for *d* or *p*.
3. Reading a word as it is written. Some dyslexics reverse the order of the letters when they read or write, such as seeing the word *saw* as *was*.
4. Reading a sentence as it is written, without leaving out or adding words.
5. Interpreting sounds correctly. Sometimes dyslexics confuse vowel sounds or substitute one consonant for another.

Research on dyslexia has resulted in techniques and programs that help most dyslexics manage their disability.

Write Before You Read

■ *A biography of the author can be found in the Reader's Handbook.*

How would your life be different if you couldn't read? Think of all the things you read daily, such as the television guide, food labels, street signs, as well as school texts. Jot down the difficulties you would encounter and how those difficulties would affect you.

On *Being Seventeen, Bright, and Unable to Read*

DAVID RAYMOND

One day a substitute teacher picked me to read aloud from the textbook. When I told her, "No, thank you," she came unhinged. She thought I was acting smart and told me so. I kept calm, and that got her madder and madder. We must have spent 10 minutes trying to solve the problem, and finally she got so red in the face I thought she'd blow up. She told me she'd see me after class.

Maybe someone like me was a new thing for that teacher. But she wasn't new to me. I've been through scenes like that all my life. You see, even though I'm 17 and a junior in high school, I can't read because I have dyslexia. I'm told I read "at a fourth-grade level," but from where I sit, that's not reading. You can't know what that means unless you've been there. It's not easy to tell how it feels when you can't read your homework assignments or the newspaper or a menu in a restaurant or even notes from your own friends.

My family began to suspect I was having problems almost from the first day I started school. My father says my early years in school were the worst years of his life. They weren't so good for me, either. As I look back on it now, I can't find the words to express how bad it really was. I wanted to die. I'd come home from school screaming,

"I'm dumb. I'm dumb—I wish I were dead!"

I guess I couldn't read anything at all then—not even my own name—and they tell me I didn't talk as good as other kids. But what I remember about those days is that I couldn't throw a ball where it was supposed to go, I couldn't learn to swim, and I wouldn't learn to ride a bike, because no matter what anyone told me, I knew I'd fail.

Sometimes my teachers would try to be encouraging. When I couldn't read the words on the board, they'd say, "Come on, David, you know that word." Only I didn't. And it was embarrassing. I just felt dumb. And dumb was how the kids treated me. They'd make fun of me every chance they got, asking me to spell *cat* or something like that. Even if I knew how to spell it, I wouldn't; they'd only give me another word. Anyway, it was awful, because more than anything I wanted friends. On my birthday when I blew out the candles I didn't wish I could learn to read; what I wished for was that the kids would like me.

With the bad reports coming from school, and with me moaning about wanting to die and how everybody hated me, my parents began looking for help. That's when the testing started. The school tested me, the child-guidance center tested me, private

BELLAMY 9 1988 Glenn Priestley Gerold-Wunderlich Gallery, New York

psychiatrists tested me. Everybody knew something was wrong—especially me.

It didn't help much when they stuck a fancy name onto it. I couldn't pronounce it then—I was only in second grade—and I was ashamed to talk about it. Now it rolls off my tongue, because I've been living with it for a lot of years—dyslexia.

Elementary School

All through elementary school it wasn't easy. I was always having to do things that were "different," things the other kids didn't have to do. I had to go to a child psychiatrist, for instance.

One summer my family forced me to go to a camp for children with reading problems. I hated the idea, but the camp turned out pretty good, and I had a good time. I met a lot of kids who couldn't read and somehow that helped. The director of the camp said I had a higher IQ than 90 percent of the population. I didn't believe him.

About the worst thing I had to do in fifth and sixth grade was go to a special education class in another school in our town. A bus picked me up, and I didn't like that at all. The bus also picked up emotionally disturbed kids and retarded kids. It was like going to a school for the retarded. I always worried that someone I knew would see me on that bus. It was a relief to go to the regular junior high school.

Junior High School

Life began to change a little for me, then, because I began to feel better about myself. I found the teachers cared; they had meetings about me and I worked harder for them for a while. I began to work on the potter's wheel, making vases and pots that the teachers said were pretty good. Also, I got a letter for being on the track team. I could always run pretty fast.

High School

At high school the teachers are good and everyone is trying to help me. I've gotten honors some marking periods, and I've won a letter on the cross-country team. Next quarter I think the school might hold a show of my pottery. I've got some friends. But there are still some embarrassing times. For instance, every time there is writing in the class, I get up and go to the special education room. Kids ask me where I go all the time. Sometimes I say, "to Mars."

Homework is a real problem. During free periods in school I go into the special ed room, and staff members read assignments to me. When I get home, my mother reads to me. Sometimes she reads an assignment into a tape recorder, and then I go into my room and listen to it. If we have a novel or something like that to read, she reads it out loud to me. Then I sit down with her and we do the assignment. She'll write, while I talk my answers to her. Lately I've taken to dictating into a tape recorder, and then someone—my father, a private tutor, or my mother—types up what I've dictated. Whatever homework I do takes someone else's time, too. That makes me feel bad.

We had a big meeting in school the other day—eight of us, four from the guidance department, my private tutor, my parents and me. The subject was me. I said I wanted to go to college, and they told me about colleges that have facilities and staff to handle people like me. That's nice to hear.

As for what happens after college, I don't know and I'm worried about that. How can I make a living if I can't read? Who will hire me? How will I fill out the application form? The only thing that gives me any courage is the fact that I've learned about well-known people who couldn't read or had other problems and still made it. Like Albert Einstein, who didn't talk until he was 4 and flunked math. Like Leonardo da Vinci, who everyone seems to think had dyslexia.

I've told this story because maybe some teacher will read it and go easy on a kid in the classroom who has what I've got. Or, maybe some parent will stop nagging his kid and stop calling him lazy. Maybe he's not lazy or dumb. Maybe he just can't read and doesn't know what's wrong. Maybe he's scared, like I was. 🙠

Editor's Note

This essay first appeared in *The New York Times* in 1976. Raymond later attended college and graduated *cum laude*, with honors.

Responding to Reading

First Impressions

1. What words would you use to describe David Raymond?

Second Thoughts

2. The author, David Raymond, has had dyslexia all his life. What has bothered him most about his disability?

   Think about
   - the way other students treated him
   - his birthday wish
   - his experiences in fifth and sixth grade
   - his comment about going "to Mars"

3. Although the author was very unhappy as a young boy, his life finally began to improve. What do you think was the turning point in Raymond's life? Explain your answer.

4. Even though the author seems to feel better about himself, what continuing problems does dyslexia present for him?

5. In your opinion, how well has David Raymond come to terms with his dyslexia by the end of this essay? Use examples from the essay to support your opinion.

6. Do you consider David Raymond to be handicapped? Why or why not?

Broader Connections

7. With help, most dyslexics learn to cope with their disability; however, it cannot be cured. Think of ways in which dyslexia might affect a young person's future. For example, what kinds of jobs might a dyslexic person have difficulty performing? In what kinds of jobs might he or she be likely to find success?

Writing Options

1. List facts that you learned about dyslexia that you did not know before. Then write at least three questions you have about dyslexia, about the essay, or both.

2. Suppose that David is running for student council president and you are his campaign manager. Write a brief speech aimed at convincing others to vote for him.

WRITER'S WORKSHOP

DESCRIPTION

Description, like narration, is a central feature in many types of writing. You will find descriptions in letters, reports, short stories, poems, travelogues, personal narratives, textbooks, menus, advertisements, repair manuals, catalogs and so on. Being able to create verbal pictures of people, places, and objects accurately and vividly is an important skill every writer must master.

In some high schools, yearbook writers are called upon to use their descriptive writing skills to create brief descriptions or **sketches** of graduating seniors. For this workshop, you will write a yearbook sketch.

> Here is your PASSkey to this assignment.

GUIDED ASSIGNMENT: YEARBOOK SKETCH

Compose a yearbook sketch for one of the characters in this book. Include a physical description, the highlights of your character's high school years, and a quotation that illustrates your character's main personality trait.

PURPOSE: To describe a person

AUDIENCE: High school students

SUBJECT: A character from one of the selections

STRUCTURE: A yearbook sketch

Prewriting

STEP 1 **Choose a character**   Review the characters you've read about in this book. Try to imagine what each one might have been like or would be like as a high school student. Consider characters of all ages. Then, choose the one that offers the best writing possibilities.

STEP 2 **List descriptive details**   Scan the selection for clues about your character's appearance and personality. The story may contain specific descriptions of your subject, or you may have to use your imagination to visualize how he or she might appear. Make a list of words, phrases, and images that describe your character.

STEP 3 **Create a history**   Make a list of school activities for your character. Consider sports, clubs, hobbies, awards, jobs, and so on. Would your character have been an athlete? a student council officer? a club president? What other qualities would have made this character memorable in high school? Was he or she a prankster, an artist, a troublemaker, always after the boys (girls)?

STEP 4 **Get suggestions from peers**   With a partner or in a small group, exchange lists of details, activities, and qualities. Ask your peers to suggest ways your ideas can be made even more specific and vivid. Also ask if your ideas fit your character.

STEP 5 **Search for a quote**   Finally, find a quotation that illustrates some important aspect of your character. Possible sources include books of quotations from the library, old yearbooks, and calendars and date books that contain quotes.

NOTE: While finding a quote at this point may help you focus on your character, you may also postpone this step until later in the writing process.

Drafting

Write a draft of your yearbook sketch combining the lists you've made.

STEP 1 **Start with a name**   Begin with your character's name and the quotation, if available at this point. If the author did not give your character a name, make one up.

STEP 2 **Organize the details**   Using the student model at the end of the workshop as a guide, include the physical and personality description first, then list the activities.

Special Tip

A comparison between two unlike things (such as eyes and strobe lights) that uses the word *like* or *as* is called a **simile**. If the comparison does not use *like* or *as*, it is a **metaphor**. These figures of speech help make descriptions more interesting and vivid.

STEP 3 **Use transitions** Try to find ways to link the different parts of your description. Look over the student model on page 144. How did that writer make a smooth transition from the physical description to the activities?

STEP 4 **Consider your audience** Remember that you are writing material for other students to read. Choose words, phrases, and ideas that will appeal to them. Your tone should be light, informal, and possibly humorous.

Revising and Editing

Review the draft you composed. Ask a classmate to read your draft using the following questions as a guide:

Revision Checklist

1. Are the different parts of the yearbook sketch included in the proper order? Is the character's name first, followed by the quotation, the physical and personality description, and activities?
2. Does the description fit the original character?
3. Does the quotation capture an important aspect of the character?
4. Is the description vivid? Are the descriptive words strong, clear, and specific? If similes or metaphors are used, are they appropriate?
5. Will the sketch interest other high school students?

Editing When you have finished revising your draft, exchange papers with a peer editor to proofread for spelling, clarity, and mechanics.

Publishing

Publish a yearbook that includes all of the yearbook sketches. If your teacher agrees, divide the class into small groups to work on different aspects of the project. For instance, one group could include artists who would draw pictures of the characters and a second group might design the layout of the yearbook.

Here is a yearbook sketch one student wrote about a character you will meet later in this book in a story called "Fish Eyes."

David Brenner (Kingy)

"Life's too serious to take too seriously."
Look out world. Here comes "Kingy" Brenner—king of the practical jokes, that is. No one is safe when this skinny senior with hair like an untrimmed bramble bush lurks in the halls. His flashing dark eyes are strobe lights in search of victims for his never-ending string of gags and practical jokes. When that devilishly clever wit starts churning and Kingy's wicked smile begins to crinkle the corners of his mouth, you know there's trouble ahead! What student can ever forget David's two most famous exploits: the incredibly foul "War of the Dirty Socks" and the fiendish "Fish-Eyes Escapade"?
When he's not busy scheming, David writes editorials and commentary for the school paper. He has participated in the all-school variety show for four years, the junior and senior play for two, and even managed to make the track team in his freshman year.

Reflecting on Your Writing

Briefly answer the following questions about your writing. Attach your answers to your paper before handing it in.

1. What was the hardest part of this assignment?
2. What are you doing better now than you did at the beginning of the year?
3. What areas of your writing would you like to improve?

USING VIVID MODIFIERS

> Words that change the meanings of other words are called **modifiers.**
> An **adjective** is a word that modifies a noun or a pronoun.
> An **adverb** is a word that modifies a verb, an adjective, or another adverb.

Bicycle-racing enthusiasts spend hours modifying their bikes. They change parts in the frames to make them lighter. They add gears to make riding uphill less strenuous. In the end, their bicycles are fine-tuned, high-performance, one-of-a-kind vehicles modified to be specifically theirs.

Authors also spend hours fine-tuning. They modify the frames of their sentences by adding adjectives and adverbs. In this way they create unique word pictures. Adjectives and adverbs can make a description come alive.

Using Adjectives

An **adjective** tells *which one, what kind, how much,* or *how many* about a noun or pronoun.

> *these* eggs   *red, forked* tongue   *plentiful* water   *both* brothers ◀

Many adjectives are trite and overused. Use fresh, original adjectives to create vivid images in your reader's mind. What do *big* and *little* tell a reader? What about *huge, colossal,* and *monstrous* and *tiny, petite,* and *microscopic*?

Using Adverbs

An **adverb** tells *how, when, where,* or *to what extent* about a verb, an adjective, or another adverb.

> The boy glided *effortlessly.* (adverb modifying a verb)
> They were *extremely* large eggs. (adverb modifying an adjective)
> The snake boy hissed *very* loudly. (adverb modifying an adverb)

PUNCTUATION

When one adjective follows another, a comma may be needed to separate them. If saying "and" between the adjectives sounds natural, and if you can switch their order without changing meaning, use a comma.

REMINDER

Many adverbs are formed by adding -*ly* to adjectives.

Adj.	Adv.
loud	loudly
nervous	nervously
crisp	crisply

Exercise 1 Each of the italicized adjectives and adverbs in the following sentences is overused or vague. Rewrite the sentences, replacing these modifiers with more interesting, more vivid ones. If you wish, use a thesaurus for help.

1. The three *sad* boys hiked through the *hot, brown* desert.
2. The *hungry* brothers sang as they cooked the *big* egg.
3. Anpao spoke *nicely* to the *sick* elder brother.
4. The *unhappy* brother laughed in a *very strange* way.
5. Snake Boy had *really* turned into a *large, mad* monster.

Exercise 2 In small groups brainstorm a list of vivid modifiers that could fill each blank in the passage below. Use a thesaurus to strengthen your lists. Then, from each list, choose a word that brings the image in the passage to life. Compare your work with that of other groups to see the variety of modifiers writers have at their disposal.

There are _____ legends about sea monsters in many lands and cultures. Off the _____ coast of the _____ Sea, a _____ monster has been seen riding the _____ waves two or three times in this century. One _____ fisherman reported that he saw a _____, _____ head with _____ jaws twelve feet above the bow of his _____ boat. The _____ monster _____ dove under the boat, reappearing in the _____, _____ sea half a mile away. The _____ sailor told his story to the _____ townspeople, who _____ made him a _____ hero.

Exercise 3 Style Open this book to any page with a descriptive passage. Read the passage, paying special attention to the adjectives and adverbs the author has used. Write the five sentences you think show the best use of modifiers. Circle the modifiers that you think are the most striking.

Exercise 4 Analyzing and Revising Your Writing

1. Take a piece of writing from your portfolio.
2. Reread the piece, looking for vague, uninteresting adjectives and adverbs.
3. Choose two paragraphs and rewrite them with new modifiers.
4. Compare your revision with the original piece of writing. Which one do you prefer? Why?

LANGUAGE HANDBOOK

For review and practice:
adjectives, pages 917–20
adverbs, pages 917–20
commas between
    adjectives, page 964

VOCABULARY
WORKSHOP

INFERENCE CLUES

You have already learned about context clues that give definitions or examples of new words. Sometimes, however, you will find that there is no single clue to a word's meaning. When this occurs you may be able to **infer,** or figure out, what a word means by piecing together several ideas in the context. These hints or suggestions about meaning are called **inference clues.** Use the context below to make educated guesses about the meanings of the italicized words.

> I started making an iceball—a perfect iceball, from perfectly white snow, perfectly *spherical,* and squeezed perfectly *translucent* so no snow remained all the way through.

From reading the paragraph you know that the iceball was perfect. You can guess what shape a perfect iceball would be, and you might be familiar with the word *sphere.* Both of these clues could lead to the definition of *spherical,* which means "round." What does the context tell you about the meaning of *translucent*?

Exercise   Use the context in the following sentences to infer the meaning of each italicized word. Write out your definitions.

1. Due to Martha's *pre-eminence* in all her classes, everyone assumed that she would be the class valedictorian.
2. When Martha overheard two of her teachers arguing about her school records, she understood the *gravity* of the situation.
3. The loud *altercation* between the two men involved a disagreement about falsifying the records.
4. One of the teachers proposed *embellishing* Joann's record so that her grades would appear to be the best in the class.
5. Martha's grandfather was not *parsimonious* with his money. He refused to pay for the jacket because it was the wrong thing to do.
6. Her grandfather was kind but *implacable.* Nothing she could say would convince him to pay for the jacket.
7. Would the principal admit that giving the jacket to Joann was *inequitable* after Martha had excelled for eight years?
8. If Martha had been forced to pay for the jacket, its value would have been *depreciated.*

OBSTACLES: FACING THE CHALLENGE

"*We are made strong by what we overcome.*"

John Burroughs

ULYSSES DERIDING POLYPHEMUS
1829 Joseph Mallord William Turner
National Gallery, London/Art Resource, New York.

IN THE HEROIC TRADITION

In traditional literature, heroes battled monsters that threatened society. Such heroes were strong, brave, and clever. They outwitted and outfought enemies who were clearly evil and dangerous. Modern heroes, on the other hand, often fight faceless enemies such as pollution, bureaucracy, or hunger; these heroes are sometimes harder to identify.

You are about to meet one of the most popular heroes of all time—Odysseus, the Greek hero of the epic poem *The Odyssey*. The word *odyssey* is Greek for "journey"; *The Odyssey* is the story of one man's ten-year journey home after the Trojan War. Think about Odysseus' character and evaluate his decisions. How does he compare with your image of a hero?

Poetry

from **The Odyssey**

HOMER
translated by ROBERT FITZGERALD

Examine What You Know

One of the most dramatic, action-packed adventure stories ever told is the ancient Greek epic, *The Odyssey*. The hero of this story is Odysseus (ō dis′ ē əs), who was called Ulysses by the Romans. What have you heard about Odysseus, the Trojan War, or *The Odyssey?* What do you know about Greek gods and goddesses or mythical creatures like the Cyclopes or the Sirens? Share your knowledge with your classmates. As you read these episodes from *The Odyssey,* look for insights into the culture and ideals of the ancient Greeks. Decide for yourself what qualities make Odysseus such a memorable hero.

Expand Your Knowledge

The Epic Poem

The Odyssey is the most famous epic poem in Western literature. An **epic** is a long, narrative poem that tells the adventures of a hero whose actions help decide the fate of a nation or of a group of people. Some characteristics of epic poems are the following:

1. The hero is a well-known character of high social position whose qualities represent those valuable to his or her society. Odysseus, for example, is King of Ithaca and a respected chieftain and warrior. The hero of an epic is usually pitted against monsters and must therefore be strong and courageous, often to the point of seeming superhuman. The hero often displays cleverness and guile, that is, cunning and craftiness, in dealing with others. At the same time, since the hero represents all humans, he or she must struggle to overcome human weaknesses such as pride or temptation.

2. Supernatural forces play an important role in the plot of an epic. Odysseus faces supernatural monsters, and is, at the same time, under the influence of the gods and goddesses.

■ *Biographies of the author and translator can be found on page 197.*

3. The action in an epic involves many great deeds and is set in many locations across a wide area. As you can see from the map on page 153, the setting for *The Odyssey* includes places all across the Mediterranean Sea. The setting can be real or imaginary.

4. The style of an epic is formal and grand. Although the language of the poetry is lofty, it is clear and easy to follow, since epics were originally recited to an audience.

The Story of *The Odyssey*

The Odyssey was composed sometime around 700 B.C. Although it is probably based on stories created by several poets, the Greek minstrel and poet Homer is considered to be the author. He is also credited with composing *The Iliad,* a companion epic that tells the story of the Trojan War, the war that caused Odysseus to lose favor with the gods.

In about 1200 B.C., a war was fought in Troy, also known as Ilion, an ancient city in what is now the country of Turkey. Legend explains that the war began when Paris, a prince of Troy, kidnapped the beautiful Helen, queen of the Greek city of Sparta. Her husband, King Menelaus, called upon kings and soldiers from all over Greece to avenge his honor and bring back Helen. Odysseus, King of Ithaca, is one of the Greek kings who fought for Menelaus. The war went on for ten years before the Trojans were finally defeated. In the end, it was Odysseus' trick involving a giant wooden horse filled with men that allowed the Greeks to enter Troy and win the war.

The Greeks believed that gods and goddesses, who resembled humans in many ways, controlled all things and took an active interest in human affairs. They believed that mortals must respect the gods or suffer the consequences. Because Odysseus' actions angered the gods who wanted the Trojans to win, the gods decreed that Odysseus should not return home to his wife Penelope and his young son Telemachus without enduring many hardships. Odysseus then angered Poseidon, the lord of the sea, who in revenge further delayed his return. *The Odyssey* is the story of Odysseus' attempts to reach home after the war.

Odysseus began his journey home with 720 men and 12 ships. Ten years later, after many adventures and misadventures, Odysseus alone survived. The goddess Athena, who felt sorry for Odysseus, finally persuaded Zeus, king of the gods, to force Poseidon into allowing Odysseus to return home to his family in Ithaca.

Places and Names to Know

The map shows the real and imaginary places Odysseus visited during his ten years of wandering. Use it to follow Odysseus' journey.

Although some of the characters in *The Odyssey* really existed, many came from the myths of the time. The most important characters you will meet in the episodes you are about to read are listed on page 154. This chart will serve as a quick reference while you read and discuss each adventure. Other characters and places may be identified in the annotations that accompany the poem. When you come to names that are not on this list, you can assume that they are not important to the plot.

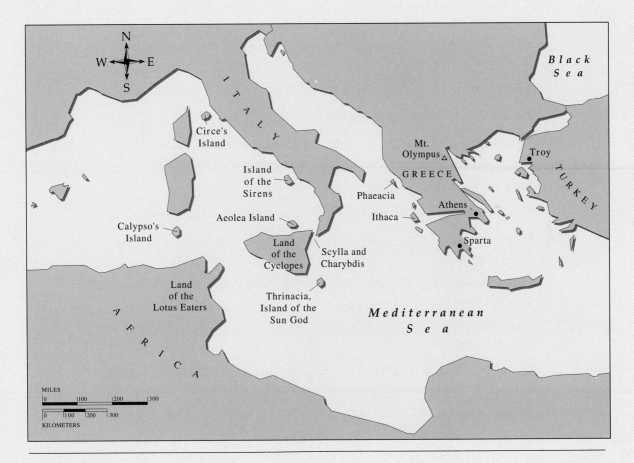

Reading a Map
This map shows the real and imaginary lands that Odysseus visits. The map identifies some current place names as well. The distance shows the length of line that represents three hundred miles on the map. The compass indicates which direction is north.

CHARACTERS

Achaeans (ə kē′ ənz)—Greeks from Achaea, in northern Greece

Apollo (ə päl′ ō)—god of music, poetry, prophecy, and medicine

Athena (ə thē′ nə)—goddess of wisdom, skills, and warfare; Odysseus' protector

Calypso (kə lip′ sō)—a sea goddess who keeps Odysseus on her island for seven years

Charybdis (kə rib′ dis)—a dangerous whirlpool in the Straits of Messina, personified as a female monster

Circe (sur′ sē)—a goddess and an enchantress

Cyclops (sī′ kläps)—a member of a race of one-eyed giants; plural, **Cyclopes** (sī klō′ pēz)

Eurylochus (yoo ril′ ə kəs)—Odysseus' relative and a trusted officer

Helios (hē′ lē äs′)—the sun god

Hermes (hur′ mēz)—the god who serves as messenger to the other gods; the god of science, commerce, eloquence, and cunning

Laertes (lā ur′ tēz)—Odysseus' father

Lotus Eaters (lō′ təs ēt′ ərz)—inhabitants of an island Odysseus visits

Odysseus (ō dis′ ē əs)—king of the Greek island of Ithaca and hero of *The Odyssey*

Polyphemos (päl′ i fē′ məs)—the Cyclops who imprisons Odysseus and his crew; son of Poseidon

Poseidon (pō sī′ d'n)—god of sea, earthquakes, and horses; father of Polyphemos

Scylla (sil′ ə)—a dangerous rock believed to be the Straits of Messina; personified as a six-headed sea monster of gray rock

Sirens (sī′ rənz)—creatures whose songs lure sailors to their death

Telemos (tə lē′ məs)—a prophet of the Cyclopes

Zeus (zoos)—king of all the Greek gods and goddesses; father of Athena and Apollo

READING FROM HOMER   1885   Sir Lawrence Alma-Tadema   Philadelphia Museum of Art.   George W. Elkins Collection.

*E*nrich Your Reading

Reading an Epic   *The Odyssey* may seem difficult at first, but there are several things you can do to make it easy to read and enjoy. First, read the poem as if it were prose. That is, do not stop at the end of each line, but read to the end punctuation to understand each complete thought. For example, notice how the first two lines appear on the page:

What shall I
say first? What shall I keep until the end?

Read these lines like this:

What shall I say first? What shall I keep until the end?

Second, use the annotations as an aid to understanding. These notes provide definitions of difficult words, summaries, and important background knowledge. Some questions appear to help you follow the action.

Third, don't hesitate to reread sections if you don't understand them the first time. Finally, since *The Odyssey* was originally recited aloud to an audience, reading it aloud might help you.

from *The Odyssey*

HOMER

Translated by Robert Fitzgerald

During seven of Odysseus' ten years on the Mediterranean Sea, he is held captive by the sorceress Calypso. Odysseus finally persuades Calypso to let him go, and she helps him build a raft to leave her island. After Odysseus sails away, his raft is destroyed by storms.

Alone and exhausted, Odysseus is washed up on the shores of Phaeacia, where Alcinous (al sin' ō əs) is king. Alcinous gives a banquet in honor of Odysseus and asks him to reveal who he is and where he came from. Odysseus relates to the king his adventures up to that time. His account makes up Books Nine through Twelve of The Odyssey. *The sections of* The Odyssey *you will read are from these books. In this first section, Odysseus introduces himself and relates one short adventure.*

BOOK NINE

New Coasts

"What shall I
say first? What shall I keep until the end?
The gods have tried me in a thousand ways.
But first my name: let that be known to you,
5 and if I pull away from pitiless death,
friendship will bind us, though my land lies far.

I am Laertes' son, Odysseus.
   Men hold me
formidable for guile in peace and war:
10 this fame has gone abroad to the sky's rim.
My home is on the peaked sea-mark of Ithaca
under Mount Neion's wind-blown robe of leaves,
in sight of other islands—Dulichium
Same, wooded Zacynthos—Ithaca
15 being most lofty in that coastal sea,
and northwest, while the rest lie east and south.
A rocky isle, but good for a boy's training;
I shall not see on earth a place more dear,

GUIDE FOR READING

3 *tried:* tested.

9 *formidable:* awe-inspiring.

though I have been detained long by Calypso,
20 loveliest among goddesses, who held me
in her smooth caves, to be her heart's delight,
as Circe of Aeaea, the enchantress,
desired me, and detained me in her hall.
But in my heart I never gave consent.
25 Where shall a man find sweetness to surpass
his own home and his parents? In far lands
he shall not, though he find a house of gold.

What of my sailing, then, from Troy?
   What of those years
30 of rough adventure, weathered under Zeus? . . .

19–21 Calypso fell in love with Odysseus and kept him on her island for seven years.

30 *What part does Odysseus feel Zeus plays in his adventures?*

GREEK COASTLINE © 1984 Larry Dale Gordon/Image Bank, Chicago

Soon after leaving Troy, Odysseus and his crew land at Ismarus, the land of the Cicones. The Cicones are allies of the Trojans, and, therefore, enemies of Odysseus. Odysseus and his crew raid the Cicones, robbing and killing people, until the Ciconian army kills seventy-two of Odysseus' men and drives the rest out to sea. Delayed by a storm for two days, Odysseus and his remaining twelve ships continue their journey.

The Lotus Eaters

I might have made it safely home, that time,
but as I came round Malea the current
took me out to sea, and from the north
a fresh gale drove me on, past Cythera.
35   Nine days I drifted on the teeming sea
before dangerous high winds. Upon the tenth
we came to the coastline of the Lotus Eaters,
who live upon that flower. We landed there
to take on water. All ships' companies
40   mustered alongside for the mid-day meal.
Then I sent out two picked men and a runner
to learn what race of men that land sustained.
They fell in, soon enough, with Lotus Eaters,
who showed no will to do us harm, only
45   offering the sweet Lotus to our friends—
but those who ate this honeyed plant, the Lotus,
never cared to report, nor to return:
they longed to stay forever, browsing on
that native bloom, forgetful of their homeland.
50   I drove them, all three wailing, to the ships,
tied them down under their rowing benches,
and called the rest: 'All hands aboard;
come, clear the beach and no one taste
the Lotus, or you lose your hope of home.'
55   Filing in to their places by the rowlocks
my oarsmen dipped their long oars in the surf,
and we moved out again on our sea faring."

40 mustered: gathered together or assembled.

46–49 The lotus flower acts like a drug that makes the men happy and lazy. *How is this a threat to Odysseus and his men?*

explain

Responding to Reading

First Impressions

1. What are your first impressions of Odysseus? Jot down words and phrases that come to mind and share them with your classmates.

Second Thoughts

2. From Odysseus' introduction, how do you think he sees himself?

3. Why do you think Odysseus talks about his home, his boyhood, and his family? What purpose might this information serve?

4. In your opinion, how dangerous is the land of the Lotus Eaters to Odysseus and his crew? Explain.

5. What qualities of a hero and leader does Odysseus reveal in his adventure with the Lotus Eaters? Use details to support your answer.

Broader Connections

6. Do you think Odysseus' way of dealing with the problem of drug abuse would work in today's world? Why or why not?

Writing Options

1. Imagine that Odysseus encounters one of the Lotus Eaters as he tries to convince his crew members to leave. Write the conversation that might take place.

2. At some time you may be asked to introduce yourself to a group. Study Odysseus' introduction. Consider the types of background information he includes. Then write an introduction of yourself that is modeled after that of Odysseus.

3. Explain why it is or is not right for Odysseus to force his men off the island of the Lotus Eaters.

Reading On

Odysseus's next adventure is probably his most famous one. In this episode, Odysseus enters into a battle of wits with a one-eyed giant. As this confrontation unfolds, look for ways each tries to outwit the other. Watch for descriptions of the Cyclops and his way of life. Note details of the setting that affect the plot. Follow the chain of events carefully.

The Land of the Cyclopes

"In the next land we found were Cyclopes,
giants, louts, without a law to bless them.
In ignorance leaving the fruitage of the earth in mystery
to the immortal gods, they neither plow
5 nor sow by hand, nor till the ground, though grain—
wild wheat and barley—grows untended, and
wine-grapes, in clusters, ripen in heaven's rain.
Cyclopes have no muster and no meeting,
no consultation or old tribal ways,
10 but each one dwells in his own mountain cave
dealing out rough justice to wife and child,
indifferent to what the others do. . . .

2 louts: clumsy, stupid people.

12 *Because the Cyclopes live separately from one another and do not farm their land, what does Odysseus think of them?*

HEAD OF POLYPHEMUS c. 150 B.C.
Hellenistic Marble
Museum of Fine Arts, Boston
Gift in honor of Edward W.
Forbes from his friends.

Across the bay from the land of the Cyclopes is a lush, deserted island. Odysseus and his crew land on the island in a dense fog and spend several days feasting on wine and wild goats and observing the mainland, where the Cyclopes live. On the third day, Odysseus and his company of men set out to learn if the Cyclopes are friends or foes.

As we rowed on, and nearer to the mainland,
at one end of the bay, we saw a cavern
15 yawning above the water, screened with laurel,
and many rams and goats about the place
inside a sheepfold—made from slabs of stone
earthfast between tall trunks of pine and rugged
towering oak trees.
20   A prodigious man
slept in this cave alone, and took his flocks
to graze afield—remote from all companions,
knowing none but savage ways, a brute
so huge, he seemed no man at all of those
25 who eat good wheaten bread; but he seemed rather
a shaggy mountain reared in solitude.
We beached there, and I told the crew
to stand by and keep watch over the ship;
as for myself I took my twelve best fighters
30 and went ahead. I had a goatskin full
of that sweet liquor that Euanthes' son,
Maron, had given me. He kept Apollo's
holy grove at Ismarus; for kindness
we showed him there, and showed his wife and child,
35 he gave me seven shining golden talents
perfectly formed, a solid silver winebowl,
and then this liquor—twelve two-handled jars
of brandy, pure and fiery. Not a slave
in Maron's household knew this drink; only
40 he, his wife and the storeroom mistress knew;
and they would put one cupful—ruby-colored,
honey-smooth—in twenty more of water,
but still the sweet scent hovered like a fume
over the winebowl. No man turned away
45 when cups of this came round.

20 *prodigious* (prō dij′ əs): enormous, huge.

23–26 *What does Odysseus imply with the two comparisons he makes?*

35 *talents:* a talent was a unit of money in ancient Greece.

A wineskin full
I brought along, and victuals in a bag,
for in my bones I knew some towering brute
would be upon us soon—all outward power,
50 a wild man, ignorant of civility.

We climbed, then, briskly to the cave. But Cyclops
had gone afield, to pasture his fat sheep,
so we looked round at everything inside:
a drying rack that sagged with cheeses, pens
55 crowded with lambs and kids, each in its class:
firstlings apart from middlings, and the 'dewdrops,'
or newborn lambkins, penned apart from both.
And vessels full of whey were brimming there—
bowls of earthenware and pails for milking.
60 My men came pressing round me, pleading:

'Why not
take these cheeses, get them stowed, come back,
throw open all the pens, and make a run for it?
We'll drive the kids and lambs aboard. We say
65 put out again on good salt water!'

Ah,
how sound that was! Yet I refused, I wished
to see the caveman, what he had to offer—
no pretty sight, it turned out, for my friends.
70 We lit a fire, burnt an offering,
and took some cheese to eat; then sat in silence
around the embers, waiting. When he came
he had a load of dry boughs on his shoulder
to stoke his fire at suppertime. He dumped it
75 with a great crash into that hollow cave,
and we all scattered fast to the far wall.
Then over the broad cavern floor he ushered
the ewes he meant to milk. He left his rams
and he-goats in the yard outside, and swung
80 high overhead a slab of solid rock
to close the cave. Two dozen four-wheeled wagons,
with heaving wagon teams, could not have stirred
the tonnage of that rock from where he wedged it
over the doorsill. Next he took his seat
85 and milked his bleating ewes. A practiced job
he made of it, giving each ewe her suckling;

47 victuals (vit' 'lz): food or other provisions.

58 whey: the watery part of milk that separates from the curds, or thick parts, during the making of cheese.

70 burnt an offering: burned an animal or food as a gift to a god as a symbol of respect and goodwill.

78 ewes: female sheep.

81–84 *How does Odysseus give a sense of the size of the rock?*

thickened his milk, then, into curds and whey,
sieved out the curds to drip in withy baskets,
and poured the whey to stand in bowls
90   cooling until he drank it for his supper.
When all these chores were done, he poked the fire,
heaping on brushwood. In the glare he saw us.

'Strangers,' he said, 'who are you? And where from?
What brings you here by sea ways—a fair traffic?
95   Or are you wandering <u>rogues</u>, who cast your lives
like dice, and ravage other folk by sea?'

We felt a pressure on our hearts, in dread
of that deep rumble and that mighty man.
But all the same I spoke up in reply:

100   'We are from Troy, Achaeans, blown off course
by shifting gales on the Great South Sea;
homeward bound, but taking routes and ways
uncommon; so the will of Zeus would have it.
We served under Agamemnon, son of Atreus—
105   the whole world knows what city
he laid waste, what armies he destroyed.
It was our luck to come here; here we stand,
beholden for your help, or any gifts
you give—as custom is to honor strangers.
110   We would entreat you, great Sir, have a care
for the gods' courtesy; Zeus will avenge
the unoffending guest.'

   He answered this
from his brute chest, unmoved:

115   'You are a ninny,
or else you come from the other end of nowhere,
telling me, mind the gods! We Cyclopes
care not a whistle for your thundering Zeus
or all the gods in bliss; we have more force by far.
120   I would not let you go for fear of Zeus—
you or your friends—unless I had a whim to.

88 *withy* (with' ē): made of slender twigs.

95 The Cyclops asks whether the men are honest traders or wandering beggars who steal from those they meet.

104 *Agamemnon* (ag ə mem' nän'): Greek king who led the Greeks against the Trojans.

110 It was a Greek custom for a host to honor strangers with gifts. Odysseus reminds the Cyclops of his duties as a host and of the consequences of offending a guest.

Words to Know and Use | **rogue** (rōg) *n.* **1** an archaic term for a wandering beggar or tramp **2** a rascal

Tell me, where was it, now, you left your ship—
around the point, or down the shore, I wonder?'

He thought he'd find out, but I saw through this,
125   and answered with a ready lie:

'My ship?
Poseidon Lord, who sets the earth a-tremble,
broke it up on the rocks at your land's end.
A wind from seaward served him, drove us there.
130   We are survivors, these good men and I.'

Neither reply nor pity came from him,
but in one stride he clutched at my companions
and caught two in his hands like squirming puppies
to beat their brains out, spattering the floor.
135   Then he dismembered them and made his meal,
gaping and crunching like a mountain lion—
everything: innards, flesh, and marrow bones.
We cried aloud, lifting our hands to Zeus,
powerless, looking on at this, appalled;
140   but Cyclops went on filling up his belly
with manflesh and great gulps of whey,
then lay down like a mast among his sheep.
My heart beat high now at the chance of action,
and drawing the sharp sword from my hip I went
145   along his flank to stab him where the midriff
holds the liver. I had touched the spot
when sudden fear stayed me: if I killed him
we perished there as well, for we could never
move his ponderous doorway slab aside.
150   So we were left to groan and wait for morning.

When the young Dawn with finger tips of rose
lit up the world, the Cyclops built a fire
and milked his handsome ewes, all in due order,
putting the sucklings to the mothers. Then,
155   his chores being all dispatched, he caught
another brace of men to make his breakfast,
and whisked away his great door slab

137 *innards:* the body's internal organs.

151 Watch for this personification of dawn to appear again in the poem.

156 *brace:* pair.

*Words
to Know
and Use*

appalled (ə pôld´) *adj.* filled with horror; shocked
ponderous (pän´ dər əs) *adj.* heavy and massive

HEAD OF ODYSSEUS   late second century B.C.   Agesander, Athanadoros, and Polydoros   Sperlonga Museum, Italy.

to let his sheep go through—but he, behind,
reset the stone as one would cap a quiver.

160 There was a din of whistling as the Cyclops
rounded his flock to higher ground, then stillness.
And now I pondered how to hurt him worst,
if but Athena granted what I prayed for.
Here are the means I thought would serve my turn:

165 a club, or staff, lay there along the fold—
an olive tree, felled green and left to season
for Cyclops' hand. And it was like a mast
a lugger of twenty oars, broad in the beam—
a deep-sea-going craft—might carry:
170 so long, so big around, it seemed. Now I
chopped out a six-foot section of this pole
and set it down before my men, who scraped it;
and when they had it smooth, I hewed again
to make a stake with pointed end. I held this
175 in the fire's heart and turned it, toughening it,
then hid it, well back in the cavern, under
one of the dung piles in profusion there.
Now came the time to toss for it: who ventured
along with me? whose hand could bear to thrust
180 and grind that spike in Cyclops' eye, when mild
sleep had mastered him? As luck would have it,
the men I would have chosen won the toss—
four strong men, and I made five as captain.

At evening came the shepherd with his flock,
185 his woolly flock. The rams as well, this time,
entered the cave: by some sheep-herding whim—
or a god's bidding—none were left outside.
He hefted his great boulder into place
and sat him down to milk the bleating ewes
190 in proper order, put the lambs to suck,
and swiftly ran through all his evening chores.
Then he caught two more men and feasted on them.
My moment was at hand, and I went forward
holding an ivy bowl of my dark drink,
195 looking up, saying:

159 cap a quiver: place the cap on a container of arrows.

163 *To whom does Odysseus call for help?*

Words to Know and Use | **profusion** (prō fyoo̅' zhən) *n.* an abundance; a large amount

'Cyclops, try some wine.
Here's liquor to wash down your scraps of men.
Taste it, and see the kind of drink we carried
under our planks. I meant it for an offering
200   if you would help us home. But you are mad,
unbearable, a bloody monster! After this,
will any other traveller come to see you?'

He seized and drained the bowl, and it went down
so fiery and smooth he called for more:

205   'Give me another, thank you kindly. Tell me,
how are you called? I'll make a gift will please you.
Even Cyclopes know the wine-grapes grow
out of grassland and loam in heaven's rain,
but here's a bit of nectar and ambrosia!'

210   Three bowls I brought him, and he poured them down.
I saw the fuddle and flush come over him,
then I sang out in cordial tones:

'Cyclops,
you ask my honorable name? Remember
215   the gift you promised me, and I shall tell you.
My name is Nohbdy: mother, father, and friends,
everyone calls me Nohbdy.'

And he said:

'Nohbdy's my meat, then, after I eat his friends.
220   Others come first. There's a noble gift, now.'

Even as he spoke, he reeled and tumbled backward,
his great head lolling to one side; and sleep
took him like any creature. Drunk, hiccuping,
he dribbled streams of liquor and bits of men.

225   Now, by the gods, I drove my big hand spike
deep in the embers, charring it again,
and cheered my men along with battle talk
to keep their courage up: no quitting now.

202 *Why does Odysseus lure the Cyclops into drinking the potent liquor he brought from the ship?*

209 *nectar and ambrosia:* the drink and food of the gods.

211 *fuddle and flush:* state of confusion and reddening of the face caused by drinking alcohol.

The pike of olive, green though it had been,
230 reddened and glowed as if about to catch.
I drew it from the coals and my four fellows
gave me a hand, lugging it near the Cyclops
as more than natural force nerved them; straight
forward they sprinted, lifted it, and rammed it
235 deep in his crater eye, and I leaned on it
turning it as a shipwright turns a drill
in planking, having men below to swing
the two-handled strap that spins it in the groove.
So with our brand we bored that great eye socket
240 while blood ran out around the red hot bar.
Eyelid and lash were seared; the pierced ball
hissed broiling, and the roots popped.

    In a smithy
one sees a white-hot axehead or an adze
245 plunged and wrung in a cold tub, screeching steam—
the way they make soft iron hale and hard—:
just so that eyeball hissed around the spike.

243 *smithy:* a blacksmith's shop.

ULYSSES BLINDING POLYPHEMUS P. Tibaldi Scala/Art Resource, New York.

The Cyclops bellowed and the rock roared round him,
and we fell back in fear. Clawing his face
250 he tugged the bloody spike out of his eye,
threw it away, and his wild hands went groping;
then he set up a howl for Cyclopes
who lived in caves on windy peaks nearby.
Some heard him; and they came by divers ways
255 to clump around outside and call:

254 *divers* (dī' verz): various.

'What ails you,
Polyphemos? Why do you cry so sore
in the starry night? You will not let us sleep.
Sure no man's driving off your flock? No man
260 has tricked you, ruined you?'

Out of the cave
the mammoth Polyphemos roared in answer:

'Nohbdy, Nohbdy's tricked me, Nohbdy's ruined me!'

To this rough shout they made a sage reply:
265 'Ah well, if nobody has played you foul
there in your lonely bed, we are no use in pain
given by great Zeus. Let it be your father,
Poseidon Lord, to whom you pray.'

264 *sage:* wise.

So saying
270 they trailed away. And I was filled with laughter
to see how like a charm the name deceived them.
Now Cyclops, wheezing as the pain came on him,
fumbled to wrench away the great doorstone
and squatted in the breach with arms thrown wide
275 for any silly beast or man who bolted—
hoping somehow I might be such a fool.
But I kept thinking how to win the game:
death sat there huge; how could we slip away?
I drew on all my wits, and ran through tactics,
280 reasoning as a man will for dear life,
until a trick came—and it pleased me well.
The Cyclops' rams were handsome, fat, with heavy
fleeces, a dark violet.
Three abreast
285 I tied them silently together, twining
cords of willow from the ogre's bed;

274 *breach:* an entranceway or doorway.

then slung a man under each middle one
to ride there safely, shielded left and right.
So three sheep could convey each man. I took
290 the woolliest ram, the choicest of the flock,
and hung myself under his kinky belly,
pulled up tight, with fingers twisted deep
in sheepskin ringlets for an iron grip.
So, breathing hard, we waited until morning.

295 When Dawn spread out her finger tips of rose
the rams began to stir, moving for pasture,
and peals of bleating echoed round the pens
where dams with udders full called for a milking.
Blinded, and sick with pain from his head wound,
300 the master stroked each ram, then let it pass,
but my men riding on the pectoral fleece
the giant's blind hands blundering never found.
Last of them all my ram, the leader, came,
weighted by wool and men with my meditations.
305 The Cyclops patted him, and then he said:

'Sweet cousin ram, why lag behind the rest
in the night cave? You never linger so,
but graze before them all, and go afar
to crop sweet grass, and take your stately way
310 leading along the streams, until at evening
you run to be the first one in the fold.
Why, now, so far behind? Can you be grieving
over your Master's eye? That carrion rogue
and his accurst companions burnt it out
315 when he had conquered all my wits with wine.
Nohbdy will not get out alive, I swear.
Oh, had you brain and voice to tell
where he may be now, dodging all my fury!
Bashed by this hand and bashed on this rock wall
320 his brains would strew the floor, and I should have
rest from the outrage Nohbdy worked upon me.'
He sent us into the open, then. Close by,
I dropped and rolled clear of the ram's belly,
going this way and that to untie the men.
325 With many glances back, we rounded up
his fat, stiff-legged sheep to take aboard,
and drove them down to where the good ship lay.

CYCLOPS AND SHEEP 1973 Eric Fraser
From *The Voyage of Odysseus*.
retold by James Reeves,
Bedrick/Blackie, New York.

301 *pectoral fleece:* wool covering a
sheep's chest.

313 *carrion* (kar' ē ən) ***rogue:*** rotten
scoundrel.

We saw, as we came near, our fellows' faces
shining; then we saw them turn to grief
330 tallying those who had not fled from death.
I hushed them, jerking head and eyebrows up,
and in a low voice told them: 'Load this herd;
move fast, and put the ship's head toward the breakers.'
They all pitched in at loading, then embarked
335 and struck their oars into the sea. Far out,
as far off shore as shouted words would carry,
I sent a few back to the <u>adversary</u>:

'O Cyclops! Would you feast on my companions?
Puny, am I, in a Caveman's hands?
340 How do you like the beating that we gave you,
you damned cannibal? Eater of guests
under your roof! Zeus and the gods have paid you!'

The blind thing in his doubled fury broke
a hilltop in his hands and heaved it after us.
345 Ahead of our black prow it struck and sank
whelmed in a spuming geyser, a giant wave
that washed the ship stern foremost back to shore.
I got the longest boathook out and stood
fending us off, with furious nods to all
350 to put their backs into a racing stroke—
row, row, or perish. So the long oars bent
kicking the foam sternward, making head
until we drew away, and twice as far.
Now when I cupped my hands I heard the crew
355 in low voices protesting:

   'Godsake, Captain!
Why bait the beast again? Let him alone!'
'That tidal wave he made on the first throw all but
beached us.'

360   'All but stove us in!'

'Give him our bearing with your trumpeting,
he'll get the range and lob a boulder.'

346 The hilltop that Polyphemos throws lands directly in front of Odysseus' ship, causing a foaming column of water to gush skyward and a giant wave to push the ship back toward the shore.

361 The men complain that Odysseus' shouting will tell the giant their position.

*Words
to Know
and Use* **adversary** (ad′ vər ser′ ē) *n.* an opponent; enemy

'Aye
He'll smash our timbers and our heads together!'

365 I would not heed them in my glorying spirit,
but let my anger flare and yelled:

'Cyclops
if ever mortal man inquire
how you were put to shame and blinded, tell him
370 Odysseus, raider of cities, took your eye:
Laertes' son, whose home's on Ithaca!'

At this he gave a mighty sob and rumbled:

'Now comes the weird upon me, spoken of old.   **373 weird:** fate or destiny.
A wizard, grand and wondrous, lived here—Telemos,
375 a son of Eurymos; great length of days
he had in wizardry among the Cyclopes,
and these things he foretold for time to come:
my great eye lost, and at Odysseus' hands.
Always I had in mind some giant, armed
380 in giant force, would come against me here.
But this, but you—small, pitiful and twiggy—
you put me down with wine, you blinded me.
Come back, Odysseus, and I'll treat you well,
praying the god of earthquake to befriend you—   **384 god of earthquake:** Poseidon.
385 his son I am, for he by his avowal   **385 avowal:** honest admission.
fathered me, and, if he will, he may
heal me of this black wound—he and no other
of all the happy gods or mortal men.'

Few words I shouted in reply to him:
390 'If I could take your life I would and take
your time away, and hurl you down to hell!
The god of earthquake could not heal you there!'

At this he stretched his hands out in his darkness
toward the sky of stars, and prayed Poseidon:
395 'O hear me, lord, blue girdler of the islands,
if I am thine indeed, and thou art father:
grant that Odysseus, raider of cities, never
see his home: Laertes' son, I mean,
who kept his hall on Ithaca. Should destiny
400 intend that he shall see his roof again

among his family in his fatherland,
far be that day, and dark the years between.
Let him lose all companions, and return
under strange sail to bitter days at home.'

405 In these words he prayed, and the god heard him.
Now he laid hands upon a bigger stone
and wheeled around, titanic for the cast,
to let it fly in the black-prowed vessel's track.
But it fell short, just aft the steering oar,
410 and whelming seas rose giant above the stone
to bear us onward toward the island.
    There
as we ran in we saw the squadron waiting,
the trim ships drawn up side by side, and all
415 our troubled friends who waited, looking seaward.
We beached her, grinding keel in the soft sand,
and waded in, ourselves, on the sandy beach.
Then we unloaded all the Cyclops' flock
to make division, share and share alike,
420 only my fighters voted that my ram,
the prize of all, should go to me. I slew him
by the sea side and burnt his long thighbones
to Zeus beyond the stormcloud, Kronos' son,
who rules the world. But Zeus disdained my offering;
425 destruction for my ships he had in store
and death for those who sailed them, my companions.
Now all day long until the sun went down
we made our feast on mutton and sweet wine,
till after sunset in the gathering dark
430 we went to sleep above the wash of ripples.

When the young Dawn with finger tips of rose
touched the world, I roused the men, gave orders
to man the ships, cast off the mooring lines;
and filing in to sit beside the rowlocks
435 oarsmen in line dipped oars in the gray sea.
So we moved out, sad in the vast offing,
having our precious lives, but not our friends."

404 Polyphemos begs Poseidon to avenge his injury by making Odysseus suffer.

*R*esponding to Reading

First Impressions

1. Review the notes you have made about Odysseus. What new impressions can you add to your list? Have any impressions changed? If so, why?

Second Thoughts

2. Odysseus disregards his crew's warnings and waits for the Cyclops. What motivates Odysseus to risk his life and the lives of his men? What price does he pay for his adventure?

3. Odysseus says that he is known for his guile. Find examples that show how he is both cunning and crafty in dealing with others.

4. What is there about Polyphemos and his lifestyle that makes him a threat to Odysseus and his men?

   Think about
   • the Cyclops' lack of society in lines 1–12
   • Polyphemos' feelings about Zeus and the gods in lines 115–121
   • Polyphemos' strength and appetite
   • Polyphemos' relationship to Poseidon in lines 392–404

5. Do you feel that the Cyclops is a villain? Are Odysseus' actions toward him justified? Explain.

6. How heroic are Odysseus' acts in this episode? Explain your answer.

Broader Connections

7. Odysseus looks down on the Cyclopes for being less civilized than the Greeks. What does it mean to be civilized? Does any race or group have a right to think of themselves as more civilized than any other group? Give examples to support your opinions.

*L*iterary Concept: Epic Simile

   A **simile** is a figure of speech that uses the word *like* or *as* to make a comparison between two dissimilar things. The expressions "eyes as dark as night" and "hair like spun gold" are examples of similes. **Epic similes** are long comparisons that often go on for several lines; they do not always use *like* or *as.* Homer sprinkles epic similes throughout *The Odyssey.* Study the two epic similes in lines 233–247. What is being compared in each? How do the similes add to the description of the action?

Concept Review: Epic Poetry Review the definition of an epic poem on pages 151–152. Find an example of each of the characteristics in the first two episodes.

*W*riting Options

1. The story is told from Odysseus' point of view. Imagine how the Cyclops might interpret the events. Write the story as he might have told it.

2. The Cyclops says that the wizard Telemos predicted Odysseus' coming. Write a poem that tells the prophecy. Choose a poetic form that best suits your ideas. Your poem may or may not rhyme.

3. Odysseus and his crew face several problems in this episode. Create a diagram that identifies each problem and explains how it is solved. The problem-solution diagram used for "The Necklace," on page 69, shows one approach you might use.

4. The ancient Greeks believed that the gods observed life on earth and discussed what was happening just as we might discuss a sporting event or television show. Write the conversation that might occur between Zeus and Athena as they watch the conflict between Odysseus and the Cyclops.

*V*ocabulary Practice

Exercise On your paper, write the letter of the word or phrase that best completes each sentence below.

Words to Know and Use

adversary
appalled
ponderous
profusion
rogue

1. In this story, Odysseus' main **adversary** is his (a) loyal crew (b) ship (c) enemy, the Cyclops.
2. Odysseus was **appalled** when he saw the Cyclops (a) eat the men (b) pat his sheep (c) fall asleep.
3. The stone blocking the cave's opening was so **ponderous** that Odysseus could (a) move it easily (b) not move it (c) not see it.
4. The Cyclops had a **profusion** of sheep, that is, (a) very few (b) none at all (c) many.
5. At first, the Cyclops thought Odysseus was a **rogue,** or (a) Greek god (b) wandering rascal (c) lost king.

*R*eading On

In this next adventure, pay close attention to Odysseus' weaknesses as well as his strengths. Notice whether his weaknesses ever lead the crew into trouble. Try to see Odysseus through the eyes of the crew member Eurylochus. Compare and contrast Eurylochus and Odysseus.

BOOK TEN

Circe, the Enchantress

*With the Cyclops' threats echoing in their ears, Odysseus and his men
flee to their ships and set sail. For a month, they stay with Aeolus, the
wind king. Finally, Aeolus sends Odysseus off, with the west wind
blowing the ships toward Ithaca and a great bag holding all the
unfavorable, stormy winds. In sight of home, while Odysseus sleeps, the
men open the bag, thinking it contains gold and silver. The bad winds
escape and blow the ships back to King Aeolus. The king refuses to help
them again, believing now that their voyage has been cursed by the
gods.*

*The discouraged voyagers next stop in the land of the cannibals known
as the Laistrygones, who bombard their ships with boulders. Only
Odysseus, his ship, and its crew of forty-five survive the shower of
boulders. The lone ship then sails to Aeaea, home of the goddess Circe.
There, Odysseus divides his men into two groups. Eurylochus leads one
platoon and Odysseus the other. Eurylochus' group sets out to explore
the island.*

"In the wild wood they found an open glade,
around a smooth stone house—the hall of Circe—
and wolves and mountain lions lay there, mild
in her soft spell, fed on her drug of evil.
5 None would attack—oh, it was strange, I tell you—
but switching their long tails they faced our men
like hounds, who look up when their master comes
with tidbits for them—as he will—from table.
Humbly those wolves and lions with mighty paws
10 fawned on our men—who met their yellow eyes
and feared them.
      In the entrance way they stayed
to listen there: inside her quiet house
they heard the goddess Circe.

10 fawned: acted in a flattering, servantlike way.

11 *What is unusual about the behavior of the wolves and lions?*

*Words
to Know
and Use* | **glade** (glād) *n.* an open space in a wood or forest

15   Low she sang
in her beguiling voice, while on her loom
she wove ambrosial fabric sheer and bright,
by that craft known to the goddesses of heaven.
No one would speak, until Polites—most
20 faithful and likable of my officers, said:

'Dear friends, no need for <u>stealth</u>: here's a young weaver
singing a pretty song to set the air
a-tingle on these lawns and paven courts.
Goddess she is, or lady. Shall we greet her?'

25 So reassured, they all cried out together,
and she came swiftly to the shining doors
to call them in. All but Eurylochus—
who feared a <u>snare</u>—the innocents went after her.
On thrones she seated them, and lounging chairs,
30 while she prepared a meal of cheese and barley
and amber honey mixed with Pramnian wine,
adding her own <u>vile</u> pinch, to make them lose
desire or thought of our dear fatherland.
Scarce had they drunk when she flew after them
35 with her long stick and shut them in a pigsty—
bodies, voices, heads, and bristles, all
swinish now, though minds were still unchanged.
So, squealing, in they went. And Circe tossed them
acorns, mast, and cornel berries—fodder
40 for hogs who rut and slumber on the earth.

Down to the ship Eurylochus came running
to cry alarm, foul magic doomed his men!
But working with dry lips to speak a word
he could not, being so shaken; blinding tears
45 welled in his eyes; <u>foreboding</u> filled his heart.
When we were frantic questioning him, at last
we heard the tale: our friends were gone. . . .

17 ambrosial (am brō′ zhəl): fit for the gods.

28 *Who are the "innocents"?*

37 swinish: like a swine, which is a pig or hog.

Words to Know and Use	**stealth** (stelth) *n.* secret behavior **snare** (snar) *n.* a trap; anything dangerous that tempts people **vile** (vīl) *adj.* evil; offensive **foreboding** (fôr bōd′ iŋ) *n.* a feeling that something bad is about to happen

ULYSSES AT THE PALACE OF CIRCE (detail) 1667
Wilhelm Schubert van Ehrenberg   The J. Paul Getty Museum, Malibu, California.

*Eurylochus tells Odysseus what has happened and begs the captain to
sail away from Circe's land. Against Eurylochus' advice, Odysseus rushes
to save his men from the enchantress. On the way, he meets the god
Hermes, who gives him a special flower—a molu—to protect him from
Circe's power. Now she will not be able to turn Odysseus into a pig as
she has the others. Still, Hermes warns, Odysseus must make the
enchantress swear that she will play no "witches' tricks." Even more
determined, Odysseus continues toward Circe's palace. Once he arrives,
Circe welcomes him and leads him to a magnificent silver-studded chair.*

    The lady Circe
mixed me a golden cup of honeyed wine,
50 adding in mischief her unholy drug.
I drank, and the drink failed. But she came forward
aiming a stroke with her long stick, and whispered:

'Down in the sty and snore among the rest!'

Without a word, I drew my sharpened sword
55 and in one bound held it against her throat.
She cried out, then slid under to take my knees,
catching her breath to say, in her distress:

'What champion, of what country, can you be?
Where are your kinsmen and your city?
60 Are you not sluggish with my wine? Ah, wonder!
Never a mortal man that drank this cup
but when it passed his lips he had <u>succumbed</u>.
Hale must your heart be and your tempered will.
Odysseus then you are, O great contender,
65 of whom the glittering god with golden wand
spoke to me ever, and foretold
the black swift ship would carry you from Troy.
Put up your weapon in the sheath. We two
shall mingle and make love upon our bed.
70 So mutual trust may come of play and love.'
To this I said:

   'Circe, am I a boy,
that you should make me soft and <u>doting</u> now?
Here in this house you turned my men to swine;
75 now it is I myself you hold, enticing
into your chamber, to your dangerous bed,
to take my manhood when you have me stripped.
I mount no bed of love with you upon it.
Or swear me first a great oath, if I do,
80 you'll work no more enchantment to my harm.'

She swore at once, outright, as I demanded,
and after she had sworn, and bound herself,
I entered Circe's flawless bed of love. . . .

64–67 *How does Circe know who Odysseus is?*

Words to Know and Use | **succumb** (sə kum′) *v.* to give in
doting (dōt′ iŋ) *adj.* foolishly or overly fond

179

Circe's maidens bathe Odysseus and offer him a tempting meal, yet his mind remains on his captive men.

Circe regarded me, as there I sat
85 <u>disconsolate</u>, and never touched a crust.
Then she stood over me and chided me:

'Why sit at table mute, Odysseus?
Are you mistrustful of my bread and drink?
Can it be treachery that you fear again,
90 after the gods' great oath I swore for you?'
I turned to her at once, and said:

   'Circe,
where is the captain who could bear to touch
this banquet, in my place? A decent man
95 would see his company before him first.
Put heart in me to eat and drink—you may,
by freeing my companions. I must see them.'

But Circe had already turned away.
Her long staff in her hand, she left the hall
100 and opened up the sty. I saw her enter,
driving those men turned swine to stand before me.
She stroked them, each in turn, with some new chrism;   **102 *chrism:*** a holy oil.
and then, behold! their bristles fell away,
the coarse pelt grown upon them by her drug
105 melted away, and they were men again,
younger, more handsome, taller than before.
Their eyes upon me, each one took my hands,
and wild regret and longing pierced them through,
so the room rang with sobs, and even Circe
110 pitied that transformation. Exquisite
the goddess looked as she stood near me, saying:

'Son of Laertes and the gods of old,
Odysseus, master mariner and soldier,
go to the sea beach and sea-breasting ship;
115 drag it ashore, full length upon the land;

*Words
to Know
and Use*   **disconsolate** (dis cän' sə lit) *adj.* dejected; extremely unhappy

180

stow gear and stores in rock-holes under cover;
return; be quick; bring all your dear companions.'
Now, being a man, I could not help consenting.
So I went down to the sea beach and the ship,
120   where I found all my other men on board,
weeping, in despair along the benches.
Sometimes in farmyards when the cows return
well fed from pasture to the barn, one sees
the pens give way before the calves in tumult,
125   breaking through to cluster about their mothers,
bumping together, bawling. Just that way
my crew poured round me when they saw me come—
their faces wet with tears as if they saw
their homeland, and the crags of Ithaca,
130   even the very town where they were born.
And weeping still they all cried out in greeting:

'Prince, what joy this is, your safe return!
Now Ithaca seems here, and we in Ithaca!
But tell us now, what death befell our friends?"

135   And, speaking gently, I replied:

'First we must get the ship high on the shingle,
and stow our gear and stores in clefts of rock
for cover. Then come follow me, to see
your shipmates in the magic house of Circe
140   eating and drinking, endlessly regaled.'

They turned back, as commanded, to this work;
only one lagged, and tried to hold the others:
Eurylochus it was, who blurted out:

'Where now, poor remnants? Is it devil's work
145   you long for? Will you go to Circe's hall?
Swine, wolves, and lions she will make us all,
beasts of her courtyard, bound by her enchantment.
Remember those the Cyclops held, remember
shipmates who made that visit with Odysseus!
150   The daring man! They died for his foolishness!'

118 Odysseus says that, "being a man," he had to go along with Circe's request. *What does Odysseus imply in this line?*

122–130 *What is being compared in this epic simile?*

140 *regaled:* entertained; delighted with something pleasing.

When I heard this I had a mind to draw
the blade that swung against my side and chop him,
bowling his head upon the ground—kinsman
or no kinsman, close to me though he was.
155 But others came between, saying, to stop me,

'Prince, we can leave him, if you say the word;
let him stay here on guard. As for ourselves,
show us the way to Circe's magic hall.'

So all turned inland, leaving shore and ship,
160 and Eurylochus—he, too, came on behind,
fearing the rough edge of my tongue. Meanwhile
at Circe's hands the rest were gently bathed,
anointed with sweet oil, and dressed afresh
in tunics and new cloaks with fleecy linings.
165 We found them all at supper when we came.
But greeting their old friends once more, the crew
could not hold back their tears; and now again
the rooms rang with sobs. Then, Circe, loveliest
of all immortals, came to counsel me:

170 'Son of Laertes and the gods of old,
Odysseus, master mariner and soldier,
enough of weeping fits. I know—I, too—
what you endured upon the inhuman sea,
what odds you met on land from hostile men.
175 Remain with me, and share my meat and wine;
restore behind your ribs those gallant hearts
that served you in the old days, when you sailed
from stony Ithaca. Now parched and spent,
your cruel wandering is all you think of,
180 never of joy, after so many blows.'

As we were men we could not help consenting.
So day by day we lingered, feasting long
on roasts and wine, until a year grew fat.
But when the passing months and wheeling seasons
185 brought the long summery days, the pause of summer,
my shipmates one day summoned me and said:

151–154 *Why is Odysseus so violently angry with Eurylochus?*

178 *spent:* worn out.

Words to Know and Use	**parched** (parchd) *adj.* very hot and thirsty

'Captain, shake off this trance, and think of home—
if home indeed awaits us,
   if we shall ever see
190 your own well-timbered hall on Ithaca.'

They made me feel a <u>pang</u>, and I agreed.
That day, and all day long, from dawn to sundown,
we feasted on roast meat and ruddy wine,
and after sunset when the dusk came on
195 my men slept in the shadowy hall, but I
went through the dark to Circe's flawless bed
and took the goddess' knees in supplication,
urging, as she bent to hear:

   'O Circe,
200 now you must keep your promise; it is time.
Help me make sail for home. Day after day
my longing quickens, and my company
give me no peace, but wear my heart away
pleading when you are not at hand to hear.'

205 The loveliest of goddesses replied:

'Son of Laertes and the gods of old,
Odysseus, master mariner and soldier,
you shall not stay here longer against your will;
but home you may not go
210 unless you take a strange way round and come
to the cold homes of Death and pale Persephone.
You shall hear prophecy from the rapt shade
of blind Tiresias of Thebes, forever
charged with reason even among the dead;
215 to him alone, of all the flitting ghosts,
Persephone has given a mind undarkened.'

At this I felt a weight like stone within me,
and, moaning, pressed my length against the bed,
with no desire to see the daylight more. . . ."

197 *supplication:* a humble request or prayer.

211 *the cold homes of Death:* the underworld, or home of the dead, where Hades rules. *Persephone:* the wife of Hades.

212–213 *rapt shade of blind Tiresias of Thebes:* a spirit from the underworld who counsels Odysseus.

217–219 *What is Odysseus' mood when he hears he must visit the "cold homes of Death"?*

Responding to Reading

First Impressions

1. What new impressions of Odysseus have you gotten from this story? Have your thoughts about him changed? Add your new ideas to your list.

Second Thoughts

2. In what ways is Circe a danger to Odysseus and his men? Is she more or less dangerous to them than the Cyclops? Explain.

3. Early in this section, Eurylochus avoids Circe's trap while the other men are snared. What qualities do you think allow Eurylochus to remain free? Explain.

4. Odysseus decides to trust Circe, so he beaches his ship and brings the rest of the men to her hall. Do you think this decision is wise? Give reasons for your answer.

5. How are Odysseus and Eurylochus alike and different?

   Think about
   • how each feels about beaching the ship and staying
   • Eurylochus' opinion of Odysseus' past decisions
   • the decisions each one makes

6. How much control does Odysseus have over his fate?

   Think about
   • how he begs Circe to set him and his men free
   • how he responds to her prophecy at the end
   • whether he could have acted differently

Broader Connections

7. Both Circe and Odysseus consciously manipulate, or use, others to achieve their goals. In what ways are you manipulated by those around you? In what ways do you manipulate others?

Literary Concept: Conflict

The struggle between opposing forces that is the basis of the plot of a story is called **conflict. External conflict** occurs between a character and a force of nature, between two characters, or between a character and society. **Internal conflict** occurs when a character has a struggle within himself or herself, such as trying to make a decision. Identify two conflicts that Odysseus faces in this episode and tell whether each is external or internal.

Writing Options

1. Skim this adventure to find descriptive details of Circe's hall. Use these details and your imagination to write a poem about the luxury of the enchantress's home.

2. Write a part of the story from Eurylochus' point of view, showing how he sees things differently than Odysseus.

3. Write a magic spell Circe might have used to turn Odysseus' men into swine.

4. When Eurylochus and his men arrive at Circe's hall, they find wolves and lions. Write to explain why you think Homer chose to have Circe turn men into swine, wolves, and lions rather than into other animals.

Vocabulary Practice

Exercise Decide whether each of the following pairs of words are synonyms or antonyms. On your paper, write *S* for synonyms or *A* for antonyms.

1. stealth—openness
2. vile—evil
3. disconsolate—cheerful
4. doting—unfriendly
5. pang—twinge
6. foreboding—forewarning
7. glade—clearing
8. parched—dry
9. snare—trap
10. succumb—conquer

> *Words to Know and Use*
>
> **disconsolate
> doting
> foreboding
> glade
> pang
> parched
> snare
> stealth
> succumb
> vile**

Reading On

In the last episodes you will read, much is demanded of Odysseus and his men. Their lives hang in the balance. To appreciate the forces that Odysseus and his crew are up against, take time to visualize the sights, sounds, and characters that Homer describes. Consider what each monster represents in the real world. As you read, think about what you would do in Odysseus' place.

BOOK TWELVE

Sea Perils and Defeat

In Book Eleven, Odysseus and his men visit the underworld, where the spirits of the dead, the shades, reside. During Odysseus' visit there, the spirit of the prophet Tiresias warns him that death and destruction will follow unless he and his crew act with restraint and control. Tiresias also reveals what Odysseus must do on his return to Ithaca.

In the underworld, Odysseus also speaks with the spirit of his mother, who died of grief because Odysseus was away for so long. He promises the spirit of Elpenor, his crewman who died on Circe's island, that he will bury Elpenor's body.

Odysseus and his men then leave the underworld and return to Circe's island to fulfill the promise to Elpenor. While his men sleep, Circe takes Odysseus aside to hear about the underworld and to offer advice.

"Then said the Lady Circe:

'So: all those trials are over.
　Listen with care to this, now, and a god will arm your
mind.
5　Square in your ship's path are Sirens, crying
　beauty to bewitch men coasting by;
　woe to the innocent who hears that sound!
　He will not see his lady nor his children
　in joy, crowding about him, home from sea;
10　the Sirens will sing his mind away
　on their sweet meadow lolling. There are bones
　of dead men rotting in a pile beside them
　and flayed skins shrivel around the spot.
　　Steer wide;
15　keep well to seaward; plug your oarsmen's ears
　with beeswax kneaded soft; none of the rest
　should hear that song.
　　But if you wish to listen,
　let the men tie you in the lugger, hand

3 Circe warns Odysseus to do as she says if he wants the help of the gods.

13 *flayed:* torn off; stripped.

19 *lugger* (lug' ər): a small ship with four-sided sails.

THE SHIP OF ULYSSES BETWEEN
SCYLLA AND CHARYBDIS
Engraving
The Bettmann Archive, New York.

20 and foot, back to the mast, lashed to the mast,
so you may hear those harpies' thrilling voices;
shout as you will, begging to be untied,
your crew must only twist more line around you
and keep their stroke up, till the singers fade. . . .
25 What then? One of two courses you may take,
and you yourself must weigh them. I shall not
plan the whole action for you now, but only
tell you of both.

      Ahead are beetling rocks
30 and dark blue glancing Amphitrite, surging,
roars around them. Prowling Rocks, or Drifters,
the gods in bliss have named them—named them well.
Not even birds can pass them by. . . .

      A second course
35 lies between headlands. One is a sharp mountain
piercing the sky, with stormcloud round the peak
dissolving never, not in the brightest summer,
to show heaven's azure there, nor in the fall.
No mortal man could scale it, nor so much
40 as land there, not with twenty hands and feet,
so sheer the cliffs are—as of polished stone.

21 harpies: winged monsters that are
part woman and part bird.

30 Amphitrite (am′ fi trīt′ ē): goddess
of the sea and wife of Poseidon.

Midway that height, a cavern full of mist
opens toward Erebos and evening. Skirting
this in the lugger, great Odysseus,
45   your master bowman, shooting from the deck,
would come short of the cavemouth with his shaft;
but that is the den of Scylla, where she yaps
<u>abominably</u>, a newborn whelp's cry,
though she is huge and monstrous. God or man,
50   no one could look on her in joy. Her legs—
and there are twelve—are like great tentacles,
unjointed, and upon her serpent necks
are borne six heads like nightmares of ferocity,
with triple serried rows of fangs and deep
55   gullets of black death. Half her length, she sways
her heads in air, outside her horrid cleft,
hunting the sea around that promontory
for dolphins, dogfish, or what bigger game
thundering Amphitrite feeds in thousands.
60   And no ship's company can claim
to have passed her without loss and grief; she takes,
from every ship, one man for every gullet.

The opposite point seems more a tongue of land
you'd touch with a good bowshot, at the narrows.
65   A great wild fig, a shaggy mass of leaves,
grows on it, and Charybdis lurks below
to swallow down the dark sea tide. Three times
from dawn to dusk she spews it up
and sucks it down again three times, a whirling
70   maelstrom; if you come upon her then,
the god who makes earth tremble could not save you.
No, hug the cliff of Scylla, take your ship
through on a racing stroke. Better to mourn six men
than lose them all, and the ship, too.'

75   So her advice ran; but I faced her, saying:

'Only instruct me, goddess, if you will,
how, if possible, can I pass Charybdis,
or fight off Scylla when she raids my crew?'

43 _Erebos_ (er′ ə bəs): darkness; the dark place under the earth leading to the land of the dead.

48 Scylla sounds like a crying puppy or cub.

51 _tentacles:_ long, grasping, flexible feelers like the arms of an octopus.

55 _gullets:_ throats leading to stomachs.

56 _cleft:_ opening or crevice.

57 _promontory:_ a point of high land that extends out into a body of water.

70 _maelstrom_ (māl′ strəm): a large, violent whirlpool.

Words to Know and Use | **abominably** (ə bäm′ə nə b'lē) _adv._ disgustingly

Swiftly that loveliest goddess answered me:

80 'Must you have battle in your heart forever?
The bloody toil of combat? Old <u>contender</u>,
will you not yield to the immortal gods?
That nightmare cannot die, being eternal
evil itself—horror, and pain, and <u>chaos</u>;
85 there is no fighting her, no power can fight her,
all that <u>avails</u> is flight.
    Lose headway there
along that rockface while you break out arms,
and she'll swoop over you, I fear, once more,
90 taking one man again for every gullet.
No, no, put all your backs into it, row on;
invoke Blind Force, that bore this <u>scourge</u> of men,
to keep her from a second strike against you.

Then you will coast Thrinakia, the island
95 where Helios' cattle graze, fine herds, and flocks
of goodly sheep. The herds and flocks are seven,
with fifty beasts in each.
    No lambs are dropped,
or calves, and these fat cattle never die.
100 Immortal, too, their cowherds are—their shepherds—
Phaethousa and Lampetia, sweetly braided
nymphs that divine Neaira bore
to the overlord of high noon, Helios.
These nymphs their gentle mother bred and placed
105 upon Thrinakia, the distant land,
in care of flocks and cattle for their father.
Now give those kine a wide berth, keep your thoughts
intent upon your course for home,
and hard seafaring brings you all to Ithaca.
110 But if you raid the beeves, I see destruction
for ship and crew.
    Rough years then lie between you and your
homecoming, alone and old, the one survivor, all
companions lost.' . . .

107 *kine:* cattle; also called beeves.
Circe warns Odysseus to stay far away
from them.

Words	**contender** (kən tend′ ər) *n.* an opposer; one who fights against someone or
to Know	something else
and Use	**chaos** (kā äs) *n.* disorder; confusion
	avail (ə vāl′) *v.* to be of help or advantage to, as in achieving an end
	scourge (skʉrj) *n.* a means of harsh punishment or great suffering

The Sirens

At dawn, Odysseus and his men continue their journey. Odysseus decides to tell the men only of Circe's warnings about the Sirens, whom they will soon encounter. He is fairly sure that they can survive this peril if he keeps their spirits up. Suddenly, the wind stops.

115   The crew were on their feet
    briskly, to furl the sail, and stow it; then,
    each in place, they poised the smooth oar blades
    and sent the white foam scudding by. I carved
    a massive cake of beeswax into bits
120 and rolled them in my hands until they softened—
    no long task, for a burning heat came down
    from Helios, lord of high noon. Going forward
    I carried wax along the line, and laid it
    thick on their ears. They tied me up, then, plumb
125 amidships, back to the mast, lashed to the mast,
    and took themselves again to rowing. Soon,
    as we came smartly within hailing distance,
    the two Sirens, noting our fast ship
    off their point, made ready, and they sang . . .
130 The lovely voices in ardor appealing over the water
    made me crave to listen, and I tried to say
    'Untie me!' to the crew, jerking my brows;
    but they bent steady to the oars. Then Perimedes
    got to his feet, he and Eurylochus,
135 and passed more line about, to hold me still.
    So all rowed on, until the Sirens
    dropped under the sea rim, and their singing
    dwindled away.
        My faithful company
140 rested on their oars now, peeling off
    the wax that I had laid thick on their ears;
    then set me free.

125 *plumb amidships:* exactly in the center of the ship.

130 *ardor:* passion.

ODYSSEUS AND THE SIRENS
5th cent. B.C.
The Granger Collection, New York.

Scylla and Charybdis

But scarcely had that island
faded in blue air than I saw smoke
145 and white water, with sound of waves in tumult—
a sound the men heard, and it terrified them.
Oars flew from their hands; the blades went knocking
wild alongside till the ship lost way,
with no oarblades to drive her through the water.

150 Well, I walked up and down from bow to stern,
trying to put heart into them, standing over
every oarsman, saying gently,

'Friends,
have we never been in danger before this?
155 More fearsome, is it now, than when the Cyclops
penned us in his cave? What power he had!
Did I not keep my nerve, and use my wits
to find a way out for us?
Now I say
160 by hook or crook this peril too shall be
something that we remember.
Heads up, lads!
We must obey the orders as I give them.
Get the oarshafts in your hands, and lay back
165 hard on your benches; hit these breaking seas.
Zeus help us pull away before we founder.

145 *tumult:* noisy confusion.

You at the tiller, listen, and take in
all that I say—the rudders are your duty;
keep her out of the combers and the smoke;
170 steer for that headland; watch the drift, or we
fetch up in the smother, and you drown us.'

That was all, and it brought them round to action.
But as I sent them on toward Scylla, I
told them nothing, as they could do nothing.
175 They would have dropped their oars again, in panic,
to roll for cover under the decking. Circe's
bidding against arms had slipped my mind,
so I tied on my cuirass and took up
two heavy spears, then made my way along
180 to the foredeck—thinking to see her first from there,
the monster of the gray rock, harboring
torment for my friends. I strained my eyes
upon that cliffside veiled in cloud, but nowhere
could I catch sight of her.
185   And all this time,
in travail, sobbing, gaining on the current,
we rowed into the strait—Scylla to port
and on our starboard beam Charybdis, dire
gorge of the salt sea tide. By heaven! when she
190 vomited, all the sea was like a cauldron
seething over intense fire, when the mixture
suddenly heaves and rises.
        The shot spume
soared to the landside heights, and fell like rain.

195 But when she swallowed the sea water down
we saw the funnel of the maelstrom, heard
the rock bellowing all around, and dark
sand raged on the bottom far below.
My men all blanched against the gloom, our eyes
200 were fixed upon that yawning mouth in fear
of being devoured.
        Then Scylla made her strike,
whisking six of my best men from the ship.
I happened to glance aft at ship and oarsmen
205 and caught sight of their arms and legs, dangling
high overhead. Voices came down to me
in anguish, calling my name for the last time.

176–180 Odysseus forgets Circe's warning not to try to fight, and he grabs his cuirass, or body armor, and spears. *What effects might his actions have?*

188–189 *dire gorge:* dreadful, devouring throat or mouth.

199 *blanched:* became pale.

A man surfcasting on a point of rock
for bass or mackerel, whipping his long rod
210   to drop the sinker and the bait far out,
will hook a fish and rip it from the surface
to dangle wriggling through the air:
    so these
were borne aloft in spasms toward the cliff.

215 She ate them as they shrieked there, in her den,
in the dire grapple, reaching still for me—
and deathly pity ran me through
at that sight—far the worst I ever suffered,
questing the passes of the strange sea.
220   We rowed on.
The Rocks were now behind; Charybdis, too,
and Scylla dropped astern. . . ."

214 *spasms:* violent motions.

216 *grapple:* hand-to-hand fight.

*Odysseus tries to persuade the men to bypass Thrinacia
(thri nā' shē ə), the island of the sun god Helios, but the men
insist on landing. They ignore Odysseus' warning not to feast on the
cattle they find there. This disobedience angers Lord Helios, who
threatens to stop shining if payment is not made for the loss of his
cattle. Zeus tries to appease Helios and sends down a thunderbolt to
sink Odysseus' ship.*

*Odysseus alone survives. He eventually drifts to the Isle of Ogygia,
the home of Calypso, a dangerous sea nymph who keeps him on her
island for seven years.*

The End of The Odyssey

*With the help of King Alcinous and the Phaeacians, Odysseus
eventually returns home, only to find his kingdom in chaos and his
wife pursued by several arrogant suitors, who are after his wealth.
Odysseus tricks the suitors into challenging him and, in a test of skills,
he regains his land.*

Responding to Reading

First Impressions

1. Do Odysseus' actions in these episodes change your previous impressions of him in any way? Explain.

Second Thoughts

2. Circe becomes annoyed with Odysseus in lines 80–86. What is she saying about his character? Do you agree or disagree with her reaction? Why?

3. Odysseus chooses to tell his crew only part of what Circe reveals about the dangers ahead. Does this decision show strength or weakness in his character? What would you have done? Explain.

4. What dangers do the Sirens, Scylla, and Charybdis represent to Odysseus and his crew? What dangers or forces do you think they represent in the real world?

5. In what ways, if any, does Odysseus exhibit the qualities of a leader and a hero in these three adventures at sea? In which adventure do you think he is most heroic? Why?

6. From the parts of *The Odyssey* that you have read, what do you think is Odysseus' greatest strength? What is his most dangerous weakness? Support your opinion with details from the text.

Broader Connections

7. Odysseus holds back from his crew vital information about their upcoming adventures. Consequently, his men meet terrible deaths. In what ways might leaders today be placed in similar situations? Is it sometimes better for a leader not to tell "the whole truth" to those in his or her command? Explain.

Literary Concept: Imagery

Imagery refers to words and phrases that appeal to the reader's senses. Although images may appeal to the senses of hearing, touch, taste, or smell, most images appeal to the sense of sight. The imagery in lines 11–13, for example, creates a visual picture of dead bodies around the Sirens. To what senses does the image in lines 189–192 appeal? Find three other examples of imagery in this section of *The Odyssey* and decide to what sense each appeals.

Concept Review: Theme Homer used *The Odyssey* to pass down lessons about life and human nature that were important to Greeks in his time. Identify at least three themes found in these episodes of *The Odyssey*.

Writing Options

1. Write encyclopedia entries for two of the creatures Odysseus and his crew encounter. Look at several encyclopedia entries for guidance about what kinds of information to include. Then skim the text for facts about each creature. Include graphics with your finished work.

2. A **eulogy** is a formal speech praising someone who has died. Write a eulogy for one of Odysseus' lost crew members. Use facts about the character's death and ideas from your imagination to make the deceased man seem real.

3. Epic similes are used in lines 233–247 in the Cyclops episode and lines 122–130 of the Circe episode. Write an epic simile in which you compare yourself to someone or something else.

4. Write another adventure Odysseus and his crew might have had. Devise an original plot in which Odysseus is portrayed as an epic hero. Consider the ways that Athena, Zeus, Poseidon, and the other gods might get involved. Read your story aloud to your classmates.

5. The Greeks believed strongly in divine intervention, or the idea that gods and goddesses interfere in the lives of humans. Explain how the gods and goddesses influence the action in these episodes of *The Odyssey*.

6. Write a character sketch for Odysseus based on these episodes and any notes you made. Include details about his appearance, attitudes, and heroic acts.

Vocabulary Practice

Exercise Write the letter of the word that is not related in meaning to the other words in the set.

1. (a) benefit (b) continue (c) aid (d) avail
2. (a) chaos (b) confusion (c) emptiness (d) disorder
3. (a) survivor (b) combatant (c) contender (d) contestant
4. (a) horribly (b) abominably (c) terribly (d) amazingly
5. (a) vengeance (b) scourge (c) punishment (d) indifference

Words to Know and Use

abominably
avail
chaos
contender
scourge

*O*ptions for Learning

1 • **A Capsule Summary** Explore ways of visually summarizing the main events in one or all of these adventures. Skim each episode, jotting down the main events and where they take place. Then decide whether to present the events on a time line, in a picture graph, or in some other way.

2 • **Your Turn to Play** Create a board game based on the adventures of Odysseus. To get ideas, review each adventure and study the map on page 153. Study the rules for games you already know for tips on writing the rules for your game. Decide whether players will move by choosing a card, spinning a wheel, or rolling dice. Design a board that allows for both forward and backward movement.

3 • **Who Were the Greeks?** At one time, *The Odyssey* was used as the basis for all Greek education, much as we use textbooks today to pass on basic knowledge. What can you learn about the ancient Greeks from this epic poem? Make a chart or diagram that shows what Homer reveals about his society's morals, values, religious beliefs, rules of hospitality, physical ideals, and views of other societies.

4 • **Shipshape Models** Odysseus reveals many facts about his ships during his narrative. For example, we know that the ships had sails and that at least part of the hull was black. Research the kinds of ships the Greeks used in 800 B.C. and use your findings to make a model of a ship Odysseus might have sailed. Investigate the work of British navigator Tim Severin.

5 • **Meet the Press** Imagine that on Odysseus' return to Ithaca he holds a press conference. Consider whether the members of the press would be friendly or antagonistic and what questions they might ask Odysseus. Think about how he might defend his actions. With classmates, act out the press conference.

6 • **Tell a Tale** Suppose that you are Odysseus relating your adventures to King Alcinous. Choose one episode from *The Odyssey* to present. Practice reading it with an appropriate tone and feeling, pauses, and changes in pitch and volume. Tape your reading and play it for your class. Invite your listeners to critique it.

7 • **Siren's Song** The Siren's song was so beautiful and alluring that mortals could not resist its message. It promised happiness, knowledge, and peace, but instead it led sailors to their death. Compose and perform the song they might have sung.

8 • **Story in Dance** With several classmates, choreograph a dance that tells your favorite adventure from *The Odyssey*. Use your movements to show what is happening in the story.

9 • **3-D Art** Choose a character from *The Odyssey* to portray in a three-dimensional work of art. For example, you might sculpt the Cyclops from clay, or create Scylla from tin cans and tubes.

📕 FACT FINDER

What were the Latin names the Romans had for these Greek deities: Zeus, Poseidon, Hermes, and Athena?

Homer

Credit for writing *The Iliad* and *The Odyssey* is usually given to Homer, a poet who is thought to have lived sometime between 900 and 700 B.C. Little is known about Homer. In fact, some scholars today question whether or not he really existed, suggesting that the creator of these epics was actually a woman or that the works resulted from the efforts of a team of people.

It is believed that Homer lived on the Ionian island of Chios and that he may have been blind. He was most likely a traveling poet and minstrel who made his living by telling exciting tales to large audiences that included kings and other members of the nobility. By 300 B.C., there were many written versions of these oral tales.

Homer's epic poems became models for many later writers, such as the Roman poet Virgil. With the possible exception of Shakespeare, Homer's works have been quoted more often than those of any other poet in the Western world.

Robert Fitzgerald
1910-1985

Robert Fitzgerald is probably best known for his translations of *The Iliad* and *The Odyssey*. Although he received the Bollinger Award in 1961 for best translation of a poem into English, Fitzgerald claimed that *The Odyssey* "can no more be translated into English than rhododendron can be translated into dogwood." When asked why he chose to attempt such a monumental task, Fitzgerald replied, "I suppose that the pleasure of hearing a story in words has [not] quite gone out. Even movies and TV make use of words. *The Odyssey* at all events was made for your pleasure, in Homer's words and in mine."

Fitzgerald was born in Geneva, New York, and grew up in Springfield, Illinois. He began writing when he was in high school and published his first poems while attending Harvard University. After graduating, Fitzgerald worked as a reporter and an editor. He gained recognition as a poet, translator, and professor at Harvard University.

DESCRIPTION AND PERSUASION

A brief description, like the character sketch you wrote for an earlier workshop, provides a picture of a single subject. Sometimes, however, description focuses on a much broader subject. To describe a vacation spot, for example, you will have to choose from a wide variety of possibilities. Which features will you describe? How will you arrange your information?

In this workshop you will use description to write a travel brochure about one of the locations in *The Odyssey*. Your brochure will be used to give prospective tourists a preview of an exciting vacation spot and to persuade them to visit there. Most brochures include descriptions of the geographical location and climate, a picture of the local inhabitants, and suggestions for sightseeing, dining, and other activities.

To get an idea of this type of writing, read this first paragraph from a travel brochure for Cozumel, Mexico. Notice how the writer chooses details of geography and climate to suggest vacationing activities. Pay particular attention to word choice. What words and phrases make you "see" and "feel" the location? What words make you want to visit Cozumel?

COZUMEL

Lying just off the eastern coast of Mexico is Cozumel, a lush tropical island surrounded by the warm Caribbean Sea. Miles of magnificent beaches of bright white sand—many of them isolated—stand out brilliantly against the inviting blue-green of the sea. Palm trees dip and bend in the refreshing trade winds.

Cozumel ranks as one of the top scuba spots in the world. Particularly fabulous are the sights of the Palancar Reef—second only to Australia's Great Barrier Reef—with its red coral formations and exotic fish species. Several diving shops offer equipment and lessons for novices. And if you prefer to stay on top of the water, sailing and windsurfing are popular alternatives.

GUIDED ASSIGNMENT:
***ODYSSEY* TRAVEL BROCHURE**

Choose a location from *The Odyssey*. Write a travel brochure that "sells" your location as a perfect vacation spot.

PURPOSE: To describe and persuade

AUDIENCE: Tourists considering a vacation

SUBJECT: A location in *The Odyssey*

STRUCTURE: A travel brochure

Prewriting

STEP 1 **Choose a location**   In small groups review the locations in *The Odyssey*. Discuss the pros and cons of each location as a possible tourist attraction. Choose the spot you think offers the most interesting possibilities.

STEP 2 **List and organize details**   List all the details in *The Odyssey* that describe your location. You might organize the details by separating them into columns with headings such as "Location's Physical Details," "Details About Inhabitants," and "Things to Do."

STEP 3 **Consult with a classmate**   Team up with a classmate who is describing the same location. Compare lists of physical details and add to your own list if necessary. Brainstorm activities you can recommend to visitors. Finally, work together to create a list of intriguing descriptive words and phrases for your brochure.

STEP 4 **Research for more details**   Using an encyclopedia, atlas, geography book, or other source, find out more about the climate and landscapes of the western Greek islands. Add these details to your list. For the exact location of your vacation spot, see the map on page 153.

STEP 5 **Be creative**   "Sell" your trip to tourists. Keeping in mind the physical details, use your imagination to suggest activities. For example, clear sparkling water is perfect for scuba diving and underwater photography of exotic marine life.

Drafting

Write a draft of your travel brochure using the lists of details and images you created.

STEP 1 **Organize your description** One way to organize your description is to match physical details with related activities. Look back at your list of physical details and pick out the ones that belong together, such as all the water details. From your Things to Do column, pick out the water activities. Write a paragraph that describes the water and suggests the activities that go with it. In this way you describe the place at the same time that you make it sound appealing.

Notice how one student combined physical details and suggested activities.

STUDENT MODEL ▶

Numerous tidepools dot the rocky beaches, offering you the chance to spend endless hours observing the comings and goings of exotic marine life.

STEP 2 **Remember your purpose** You want to persuade people to vacation in this wonderful place. Use vivid and enticing language. Add sensory details when possible. Replace some general, over-used adjectives such as *exciting* and *sunny* with hyphenated words such as *spine-chilling* and *sun-splashed*.

Revising and Editing

When you have completed your draft, ask a classmate to evaluate it according to the following checklist. Then revise your paper using any ideas that you think will improve it.

Editing   When you have finished revising your draft, proofread for spelling, clarity, and mechanics. Make a clean, final copy and, if you wish, add pictures or illustrations to your brochure.

Publishing

Form a travel agency in your class to assemble the various brochures into a travel guide. You might call it "Retracing the Steps of Odysseus." You could also create a bulletin board display that combines the brochures with a map of the locations.

Reflecting on Your Writing

Briefly answer these questions about your writing. Attach your answers to your paper before putting it in your writing portfolio.

1. Is description becoming easier for you to write?
2. Were you able to keep focused on your purpose and audience?
3. Which part of the writing process did you like most? least?

LANGUAGE
WORKSHOP

AVOIDING FRAGMENTS AND RUN-ONS

> A group of words that is only part of a sentence is a **sentence fragment**. A **run-on sentence** is two or more sentences written, incorrectly, as one.

Sentence Fragments

What if you were asked to explain a story when you had only read the title? Of course, you could make a guess, but based on only a fragment of information such as the title, how accurate could your prediction be?

On a smaller scale, the same problem can occur with sentences. When only a fragment of information is provided, the reader can only guess at what the writer really means.

You already know that a sentence needs both a subject and a predicate. When one or both are missing, a fragment results. To correct a sentence fragment, you must add the missing information.

Fragment	Wanted desperately to hear the Sirens. (In this case the subject is missing and the reader is left wondering, *Who wanted?*)
Sentence	Odysseus wanted desperately to hear the Sirens.
Fragment	The Cyclops, his only eye blinded. (Now, because the predicate is missing, the reader wonders, *What happened?* or *What did he do?*)
Sentence	The Cyclops, his only eye blinded, could not see the men who were escaping from his cave.

Exercise 1 Write *S* for each group of words that is a sentence. Write *F* for each fragment. Then add words and end marks to make each fragment a sentence.

1. Odysseus, curious about who lived in the cave
2. Waiting in the shadows for the giant's return

3. The Cyclops, son of Poseidon, feared neither man nor god
4. Ate two of Odysseus's men as if they were nothing more than a snack
5. With strong wine to make the Cyclops sleep
6. Drove a burning stake into his eye
7. In the morning, needed to let the sheep out to eat
8. The stone that blocked the entrance to the cave
9. Odysseus and his men, cleverly hiding under the sheep
10. As the sailors escaped, Odysseus could not resist laughing at the giant

NOTE: Fragments are acceptable for personal writing such as notetaking and journals. Also, some professional writers use fragments deliberately for special purposes. In most writing, however, complete sentences should be used.

Run-on Sentences

Unlike a fragment, which has too little information, a **run-on sentence** has too much. This happens because two or more sentences are written, incorrectly, as one. You probably know someone who has a "motor mouth"—a person who talks on and on until the listener becomes tired and tunes out. A run-on, a sentence that goes on and on without necessary punctuation breaks, can create the same problem for a reader. Eventually the reader tunes out because the words stop making sense.

There are two kinds of run-ons. In the first, two or more sentences are strung together without any punctuation marks to separate them. In the second, the writer makes the mistake of using a comma instead of a period. This second type of run-on is sometimes called a **comma splice.** To correct run-ons, end each complete thought with a period or other end mark and begin the next idea with a capital letter.

Run-on	Circe offered wine to the sailors they immediately turned into animals.
Correct	Circe offered wine to the sailors. They immediately turned into animals.
Comma Splice	His men wanted to leave Circe's island, Odysseus, however, was determined to stay.
Correct	His men wanted to leave Circe's island. Odysseus, however, was determined to stay.

EXCEPTION

Dialogue is one place where fragments are appropriate. Written dialogue imitates real-life conversation; since fragments are a natural part of speaking, they are always acceptable in written dialogue.

SAY IT ALOUD!

Sometimes you can detect run-on sentences by reading your writing aloud. Notice where you pause naturally, at the end of a complete thought. Be sure you have used the correct punctuation at that point.

Exercise 2 Correct the following run-on sentences. For each, be sure your choice of end mark is appropriate.

1. The Sirens sang a haunting song, no man could resist it.
2. When men got close they learned the truth, they called to the gods to save them.
3. The Sirens were not as beautiful as their songs, in fact, they were horrible monsters.
4. Piles of bones surrounded the Sirens, they were the remains of other unfortunate sailors.
5. Odysseus put wax in his men's ears and had himself tied to the mast, he was determined to hear the Sirens' song.

Exercise 3 Work in groups to correct the following passage. Be sure you have punctuated the sentences appropriately. Then compare your work with the other groups in your class to see how different writers work.

> While Odysseus was at sea. His wife Penelope waited patiently at home. After many years, eager suitors gathered at the palace. They urged Penelope to marry again, the suitors told her Odysseus was dead, and Ithaca needed a new king. Penelope, wanting to remain loyal to her husband. Thought up a clever plan. She told the suitors she would marry. When she had finished weaving a tapestry. Penelope worked at the weaving each day, each night she undid her work. The suitors grew impatient, they could not understand why the tapestry was taking so long to complete.

Exercise 4 Style Find five fragments in the selections you have read or in other writing. Rewrite the fragments as complete sentences. In groups or as a class, discuss why a writer might have chosen to use fragments, how their use affects the tone of the writing, and how the writing would be different if fragments were not used.

LANGUAGE HANDBOOK
....
For review and practice:
subjects/predicates,
    page 894
fragments,
    pages 895–96, 898, 900
run-on sentences,
    pages 896–98, 900
end marks,
    pages 962–65

Exercise 5 Analyzing and Revising Your Writing

1. Take a paper from your writing portfolio.
2. Skim your work, looking for fragments and run-ons.
3. Correct any fragments and run-ons, using appropriate punctuation.
4. Remember to check for fragments and run-ons in your future writing.

THINKING SKILLS
WORKSHOP

THE LANGUAGE OF ADVERTISING

Everyday you are bombarded by advertising. To avoid being overwhelmed by all this information, you must become a smart consumer. Listen to, or read, ads carefully and critically. Don't be fooled by misleading claims.

Advertising often relies on **loaded language** and **persuasive techniques** to sway your thinking. Loaded language appeals to your emotions; it is often used in place of facts to shape your opinion about a product. There are two common types of loaded language: **snarl words** and **purr words.** A snarl word creates a negative impression and a purr word creates a positive impression. Look at the examples below.

> This *affordable, compact* AM-FM receiver delivers *superb* sound. This *cheap, little* radio delivers good sound.

Advertisers use a variety of persuasive techniques to convince you to buy their products. **Testimonials,** or statements from famous people, attest to the merits of a product. You should realize, however, that these "experts" are almost always paid handsomely for their endorsements. Using **polling results** is another persuasive technique. "Four out of five doctors surveyed" is a familiar refrain in the advertising world. But beware! Companies often do their own research and report only the data that support their product. The **bandwagon appeal,** or the use of statements such as "Everybody's wearing Gold Medal jeans," urges you to join the crowd. Many ads are designed to elicit an **emotional response.** A variety of emotional appeals is listed in the margin.

Exercise   List the persuasive techniques you find in each of the following ads. Then write down any snarl or purr words. Note that ads may use more than one persuasive technique.

1. Keep fit—have fun in Radical Racer Roller Blades, the first choice of all-star hockey great Jeff "High Stick" Lamont.
2. Still brown-bagging it? Join the lunch bunch that knows what's hot! Insulated Brag bags in six screamin' neon colors.
3. Eight out of ten pediatricians agree! Nice 'n' Dry diapers keep babies drier and prevent diaper rash.
4. Unbelievable offer! Six of the latest and greatest cassettes or CD's for just one penny when you join Hit Parade's exclusive music club.

EMOTIONAL APPEALS

Ads may appeal to one or more of the following needs, desires, or feelings:
physical comfort
concern for loved ones
financial security
friendship
social approval
individuality
◄ health
fun and laughter
safety
power
beauty
patriotism
romance
adventure
creativity
escape

NOTE

◄ Sentence fragments are commonly used in advertising. Why do you think this is so?

$\mathscr{S}$MALL VICTORIES

Not all obstacles are life-threatening. Sometimes just getting through a day can be a challenge—a sometimes humorous, sometimes difficult challenge. Victories in such circumstances might seem small in comparison to life-threatening tests of survival, but they are important just the same.

You are about to read about several small challenges of everyday life. As you read each of these selections, try to imagine yourself in the place of the main character. Decide which characters win victories and how large or small you think each victory is.

Autobiography

from All Things
Bright and Beautiful

JAMES HERRIOT

Examine What You Know

You are about to read a story by a country veterinarian, a doctor who cares for both farm animals and pets. Think about the kinds of things a veterinarian does. List qualities you think a person needs to become a good veterinarian. As you read, add new qualities to your list.

Expand Your Knowledge

This selection is from James Herriot's bestselling book *All Things Bright and Beautiful*. Herriot, whose real name is James Alfred Wight, began writing about his career when he was in his fifties. His books describe his life as a British country veterinarian with warmth, tenderness, and a great deal of humor, and even became the basis of a television series. In this selection, Herriot first encounters a very stubborn bull, and then treats a terrified budgie, a small Australian parrot.

Enrich Your Reading

Using Context Clues When you read about a specific profession, you may come across unfamiliar terms. Use context clues to understand such words. Words may be defined or explained in the same sentence or in the next one, or there may be clues that help you infer the meaning of the words. Locate the word *calipers* in the third paragraph on page 209. Using that sentence and the one before it, you can infer that calipers are a kind of instrument used to measure thickness.

You may not always find the exact definition in the context, but often, getting the general idea is enough. Use a chart like the one below to help you understand unfamiliar words through context clues.

Word	Clues	Probable Meaning
pelt		
flank		

■ *A biography of the author can be found in the Reader's Handbook.*

from *All Things Bright and Beautiful*

JAMES HERRIOT

Photograph by Derry Brabbs   From *James Herriot's Yorkshire*,
published by Michael Joseph, Great Britain and St. Martin's Press, U.S.A.

"Move over, Bill!" Mr. Dacre cried . . . as he tweaked the big bull's tail.

Nearly every farmer kept a bull in those days, and they were all called Billy or Bill. I suppose it was because this was a very mature animal that he received the adult version. Being a <u>docile</u> beast, he responded to the touch on his tail by shuffling his great bulk to one side, leaving me enough space to push in between him and the wooden partition against which he was tied by a chain.

I was reading a tuberculin test, and all I wanted to do was to measure the intradermal[1] reaction. I had to open my calipers very wide to take in the thickness of the skin on the enormous neck.

"Thirty," I called out to the farmer.

He wrote the figure down on the testing book and laughed.

"By heck, he's got some pelt on 'im."

"Yes," I said, beginning to squeeze my way out. "But he's a big fellow, isn't he?"

Just how big he was was brought home to me immediately because the bull suddenly swung round, pinning me against the partition. Cows did this regularly, and I moved them by bracing my back against whatever was behind me and pushing them away. But it was different with Bill.

Gasping, I pushed with all my strength against the rolls of fat which covered the vast roan-colored flank, but I might as well have tried to shift a house.

The farmer dropped his book and seized the tail again, but this time the bull showed no response. There was no <u>malice</u> in his behavior—he was simply having a comfortable lean against the boards, and I don't suppose he even noticed the morsel of <u>puny</u> humanity wriggling frantically against <u>his</u> rib cage.

Still, whether he meant it or not, the end result was the same; I was having the life crushed out of me. Pop-eyed, groaning, scarcely able to breathe, I struggled with everything I had, but I couldn't move an inch. And just when I thought things couldn't get any worse, Bill started to rub himself up and down against the partition. So that was what he had come round for; he had an itch and he just wanted to scratch it.

The effect on me was <u>catastrophic</u>. I was certain my internal organs were being steadily ground to pulp, and as I thrashed about in complete panic the huge animal leaned even more heavily.

I don't like to think what would have happened if the wood behind me had not been old and rotten, but just as I felt my senses leaving me there was a cracking and splintering, and I fell through into the next stall. Lying there like a stranded fish on a bed of shattered timbers, I looked up at Mr. Dacre, waiting till my lungs started to work again.

The farmer, having got over his first alarm, was rubbing his upper lip vigorously in a polite attempt to stop himself laughing. His little girl who had watched the whole thing from her vantage point in one of the hay racks had no such inhibitions. Screaming with delight, she pointed at me.

"Ooo, Dad, Dad, look at that man! Did you see him, Dad, did you see him? Ooo,

---

1. **intradermal** (in′ trə dʉr′ məl): inside the skin.

Words to Know and Use

docile (dös′ əl) *adj.* easy to manage; obedient
malice (mal′ is) *n.* the desire to harm or hurt another
puny (pyo͞o′ nē) *adj.* of very little size or strength; slight; weak
catastrophic (kat′ ə sträf′ ik) *adj.* disastrous; tragic

209

what a funny man!" She went into helpless convulsions.[2] She was only about five, but I had a feeling she would remember my performance all her life.

At length I picked myself up and managed to brush the matter off lightly, but after I had driven a mile or so from the farm I stopped the car and looked myself over. My ribs ached pretty uniformly as though a light road roller had passed over them, and there was a tender area of my left buttock where I had landed on my calipers, but otherwise I seemed to have escaped damage. I removed a few spicules of wood from my trousers, got back into the car, and consulted my list of visits.

And when I read my next call, a gentle smile of relief spread over my face. "Mrs. Tompkin, 14 Jasmine Terrace. Clip budgie's beak."

Thank heaven for the infinite variety of veterinary practice. After that bull I needed something small and weak and harmless, and really you can't ask for much better in that line than a budgie.

Number 14 was one of a row of small, mean houses built of the cheap bricks so beloved of the jerry-builders[3] after the first world war. I armed myself with a pair of clippers and stepped onto the narrow strip of pavement which separated the door from the road. A pleasant-looking red-haired woman answered my knock.

"I'm Mrs. Dodds from next door," she said. "I keep an eye on t'old lady. She's over eighty and lives alone. I've just been out gettin' her pension[4] for her."

She led me into the cramped little room. "Here y'are, love," she said to the old woman who sat in a corner. She put the pension book and money on the mantelpiece.

"And here's Mr. Herriot come to see Peter for you."

Mrs. Tompkin nodded and smiled. "Oh, that's good. Poor little feller can't hardly eat with 'is long beak and I'm worried about him. He's me only companion, you know."

"Yes, I understand, Mrs. Tompkin." I looked at the cage by the window with the green budgie perched inside. "These little birds can be wonderful company when they start chattering."

She laughed. "Aye, but it's a funny thing. Peter never has said owt much. I think he's lazy! But I just like havin' him with me."

"Of course you do," I said. "But he certainly needs attention now."

The beak was greatly overgrown, curving away down till it touched the feathers of the breast. I would be able to revolutionize his life with one quick snip from my clippers. The way I was feeling, this job was right up my street.

I opened the cage door and slowly inserted my hand.

"Come on, Peter," I wheedled as the bird fluttered away from me. And I soon cornered him and enclosed him gently in my fingers. As I lifted him out I felt in my pocket with the other hand for the clippers, but as I poised them I stopped.

The tiny head was no longer poking cheekily[5] from my fingers but had fallen loosely to one side. The eyes were closed. I stared at the bird uncomprehendingly for a moment, then opened my hand. He lay quite motionless on my palm. He was dead.

---

2. **convulsions** (kən vul′ shənz): violent laughing fits.

3. **jerry-builders:** builders who make cheap, poorly constructed houses.

4. **pension** (pen′ shən): a payment to an elderly, retired person.

5. **cheekily** (chēk′ ə lē): without respect.

Dry mouthed, I continued to stare; at the beautiful iridescence[6] of the plumage,[7] the long beak which I didn't have to cut now, but mostly at the head dropping down over my forefinger. I hadn't squeezed him or been rough with him in any way, but he was dead. It must have been sheer fright.

Mrs. Dodds and I looked at each other in horror, and I hardly dared turn my head toward Mrs. Tompkin. When I did, I was surprised to see that she was still nodding and smiling.

I drew her neighbor to one side. "Mrs. Dodds, how much does she see?"

"Oh, she's very shortsighted, but she's right vain despite her age. Never would wear glasses. She's hard of hearin', too."

"Well look," I said. My heart was still pounding. "I just don't know what to do. If I tell her about this, the shock will be terrible. Anything could happen."

Mrs. Dodds nodded, stricken faced. "Aye, you're right. She's that attached to the little thing."

"I can only think of one alternative," I whispered. "Do you know where I can get another budgie?"

Mrs. Dodds thought for a moment. "You could try Jack Almond at t'town end. I think he keeps birds."

I cleared my throat, but even then my voice came out in a dry croak. "Mrs. Tompkin, I'm just going to take Peter along to the surgery to do this job. I won't be long."

I left her still nodding and smiling and, cage in hand, fled into the street. I was at the town end and knocking at Jack Almond's door within three minutes.

"Mr. Almond?" I asked of the stout, shirt-sleeved man who answered.

"That's right, young man." He gave me a slow, placid smile.

Hans Reinhard/Bruce Coleman Ltd., Uxbridge, England.

"Do you keep birds?"

He drew himself up with dignity. "I do, and I'm t'president of the Darrowby and Houlton Cage Bird Society."

"Fine," I said breathlessly. "Have you got a green budgie?"

"Ah've got Canaries, Budgies, Parrots, Parraqueets. Cockatoos . . ."

"I just want a budgie."

"Well ah've got Albinos, Blue-greens, Barreds, Lutinos . . ."

"I just want a green one."

A slightly pained expression flitted across

---

6. **iridescence** (ir′ i des′ əns): shifting, rainbowlike colors.

7. **plumage** (plo͞om′ ij): feathers.

the man's face as though he found my attitude of haste somewhat unseemly.

"Aye . . . well, we'll go and have a look," he said.

I followed him as he paced unhurriedly through the house into the back yard, which was largely given over to a long shed containing a bewildering variety of birds.

Mr. Almond gazed at them with gentle pride, and his mouth opened as though he was about to launch into a dissertation;[8] then he seemed to remember that he had an impatient chap to deal with and dragged himself back to the job in hand.

"There's a nice little green 'un here. But he's a bit older than t'others. Matter of fact I've got 'im talkin'."

"All the better, just the thing. How much do you want for him?"

"But . . . there's some nice 'uns along here. Just let me show you . . ."

I put a hand on his arm. "I want that one. How much?"

He pursed his lips in frustration, then shrugged his shoulders.

"Ten bob.[9]"

"Right. Bung him in this cage."

As I sped back up the road, I looked in the driving mirror and could see the poor man regarding me sadly from his doorway.

Mrs. Dodds was waiting for me back at Jasmine Terrace.

"Do you think I'm doing the right thing?" I asked her in a whisper.

"I'm sure you are," she replied. "Poor awd[10] thing, she hasn't much to think about, and I'm sure she'd fret over Peter."

"That's what I thought." I made my way into the living room.

Mrs. Tompkin smiled at me as I went in. "That wasn't a long job, Mr. Herriot."

"No," I said, hanging the cage with the new bird up in its place by the window. "I think you'll find all is well now."

It was months before I had the courage to put my hand into a budgie's cage again. In fact to this day I prefer it if the owners will lift the birds out for me. People look at me strangely when I ask them to do this; I believe they think I am scared the little things might bite me.

It was a long time, too, before I dared go back to Mrs. Tompkin's, but I was driving down Jasmine Terrace one day, and on an impulse I stopped outside Number 14.

The old lady herself came to the door. "How . . ." I said, "How is . . . er . . .?"

She peered at me closely for a moment, then laughed. "Oh, I see who it is now. You mean Peter, don't you, Mr. Herriot. Oh, 'e's just grand. Come in and see 'im."

In the little room the cage still hung by the window, and Peter the Second took a quick look at me, then put on a little act for my benefit; he hopped around the bars of the cage, ran up and down his ladder, and rang his little bell a couple of times before returning to his perch.

His mistress reached up, tapped the metal, and looked lovingly at him.

"You know, you wouldn't believe it," she said. "He's like a different bird."

I swallowed. "Is that so? In what way?"

"Well, he's so active now. Lively as can be. You know, 'e chatters to me all day long. It's wonderful what cuttin' a beak can do." ▪

ANGLESEY FARMLAND   Charles Tunnicliffe   Courtesy of the Tunnicliffe Trustees, London.

---

8. **dissertation** (dis′ ər tā′ shən): a long speech.

9. **bob:** slang for *shilling*, a British coin.

10. **awd:** *dialect*, old.

explain

Responding to Reading

First Impressions

1. Jot down phrases that describe your impression of Mr. Herriot.

Second Thoughts

2. What obstacles and victories do you see in Herriot's two visits?

3. When Herriot sees that Mrs. Tompkin's budgie is dead, he makes a quick decision. Do you agree or disagree with his decision? Explain.

4. Based on the incidents he reports and how he describes them, what do you think is Herriot's attitude toward himself and others?

   Think about
   • his feelings toward the animals that he cares for
   • his view of himself as a veterinarian
   • his reaction to Mrs. Tompkin's situation

5. From this selection, why do you think Herriot's books are so popular?

Literary Concept: Style

The way a writer uses words and sentences is called **style.** Style does not describe what is said, but rather how it is said. Find examples of each of the following techniques that make up Herriot's style: humor, descriptive details, dialect, tone, and choice of words.

Writing Options

1. Based on this selection, your list of qualities, and your experience, would you want to be a veterinarian? Explain why or why not.

2. Write a new title for this selection and explain why you chose it.

Vocabulary Practice

Exercise Answer each question and explain the reason.
1. Which animal might make a man look **puny,** a bull or a bird?
2. Which animal would be more **docile,** a cow or a bull?
3. Which place would be more **placid,** a bullring or a farm?
4. If a bull felt **malice** toward you, would you be happy, sad, or afraid?
5. Which event is **catastrophic,** a bad accident, an opera, or a party?

Words to Know and Use

catastrophic
docile
malice
placid
puny

Fiction

Everybody Knows Tobie

DANIEL GARZA (gär′ za)

Examine What You Know

Acts of prejudice can be extreme or they can be subtle and hard to identify. With your class, list ways prejudice is exhibited in your school or community. As you read, look for subtle ways prejudice is shown by people in Joey's town.

Expand Your Knowledge

This story is set in a small farming town in northern Texas. In this town migrant workers—traveling farm laborers—are hired for a short time to help harvest the crops. Migrant workers often work in Florida, Texas, or California during the winter and spring and then travel north for the summer to work in the Midwest. Because the work is seasonal, they do not live in any one spot long enough to become a part of the community.

Enrich Your Reading

Recognizing Connotations A dictionary provides the **denotations,** or precise meanings, of a word, but it does not supply the connotations of the word. **Connotations** are the feelings and ideas that come to be associated with a word over a period of time. A word can have a positive, negative, or neutral connotation. For example, to most people, the noun *smell* has a negative connotation, while *aroma* implies an enjoyable odor. Words with positive or negative connotations influence your response to what they describe.

Watch for words in this story that suggest positive or negative feelings about a character or group. List them on a chart like that below.

Positive Connotation	Negative Connotation
	gringos

■ *A biography of the author can be found on page 223.*

Everybody Knows Tobie

DANIEL GARZA

When I was thirteen years old, my older brother, Tobie, had the town newspaper route. Everyone in the town knew him well because he had been delivering papers for a year and a half. Tobie used to tell me that he had the best route of all because his customers would pay promptly each month, and sometimes he used to brag that the nice people of the town would tip him a quarter or maybe fifty cents at the end of the month because he would trudge up many stairs to deliver the paper personally.

The other newspaper boys were not as lucky as Tobie because sometimes their customers would not be at home when they went by to collect payment for that month's newspaper, or maybe at the end of the month the customers would just try to avoid the paper boys to keep from paying.

Yes, Tobie had it good. The biggest advantage, I thought, that Tobie had over all the newspaper boys was that he knew the gringos[1] of the town so well that he could go into a gringo barbershop and get a haircut without having the barber tell him to go to the Mexican barber in our town or maybe just embarrassing him in front of all the gringo customers in the shop, as they often did when Chicano cotton pickers came into their places during the fall months.

The gringo barbers of my town were careful whom they allowed in their shops during the cotton-harvest season in the fall. September and October and cotton brought Chicanos from the south to the north of Texas where I lived, and where the cotton was sometimes plentiful and sometimes scarce. *Chicanos* is what we say in our language, and it is slang among our people. It means the Mexicans of Texas. These Chicano cotton pickers came from the Rio Grande Valley in South Texas, and sometimes even people from Mexico made the trip to the north of Texas. All these Chicanos came to my little town in which many gringos lived, and a few of us who spoke both English and Spanish.

When the Chicanos came to my town on Saturdays after working frightfully in the cotton fields all week, they would go to the town market for food, and the fathers would buy candy and ice cream for their flocks of little black-headed ones. The younger ones, the *jovenes*,[2] would go to the local movie house. And then maybe those who had never been to the north of Texas before would go to the gringos' barbershops for haircuts, not knowing that they would be

1. **gringos** (grĭŋ′ gōs): a slang term, sometimes derogatory, used by Latin Americans to refer to North Americans or Europeans.
2. *jovenes* (hô ve′ nes) *Spanish*.

refused. The gringo barbers would be very careful not to let them come too close to their shops because the regular gringo customers would get mad, and sometimes they would curse the Chicanos.

"It's them darn pepper bellies again. Can't seem to get rid of 'em in the fall," the prejudiced gringos of my town would say. Some of the nicer people would only become uneasy at seeing so many Chicanos with long, black, greasy hair wanting haircuts.

The barbers of the town liked Tobie, and they invited him to their shops for haircuts. Tobie said that the barbers told him that they would cut his hair because he did not belong to that group of people who came from the south of Texas. Tobie understood. And he did not argue with the barbers because he knew how Chicanos from South Texas were and how maybe gringo scissors would get all greasy from cutting their hair.

During that fall, Tobie encouraged me to go to the gringo's place for a haircut. "Joey, when are you going to get rid of that mop of hair?" he asked.

"I guess I'll get rid of it when Mr. Lopez learns how to cut flattops."

"Golly, Joey, Mr. Lopez is a good ole guy and all that, but if he doesn't know how to give flattops, then you should go to some other barber for flattops. Really, Kid Brother, that hair looks awful."

"Yeah, but I'm afraid."

"Afraid of what?" Tobie asked.

"I'm afraid the barber will mistake me for one of those guys from South Texas and run me out of his shop."

"Oh, forget it," Tobie said. "Mr. Brewer . . . you know, the barber who cuts my hair . . . is a nice man, and he'll cut your hair. Just tell him you're my kid brother."

I thought about this new adventure for several days, and then on a Saturday, when there was no school, I decided on the haircut at Mr. Brewer's. I hurriedly rode my bike to town and parked it in the alley close to the barbershop. As I walked into the shop, I noticed that all of a sudden the gringos inside stopped their conversation and looked at me. The shop was silent for a moment. I thought then that maybe this was not too good and that I should leave. I remembered what Tobie had told me about being his brother, and about Mr. Brewer being a nice man. I was convinced that I belonged in the gringo barbershop.

I was convinced that I belonged in the gringo barbershop.

I found an empty chair and sat down to wait my turn for a haircut. One gringo customer sitting next to me rose and explained to the barber that he had to go to the courthouse for something. Another customer left without saying anything. And then one, who was dressed in dirty coveralls and a faded khaki shirt, got up from Mr. Brewer's chair and said to him, "Say, Tom, looks like you got yourself a little tamale to clip."

Mr. Brewer smiled only.

My turn was next, and I was afraid. But I remembered again that this was all right because I was Tobie's brother, and everybody liked Tobie. I went to Mr. Brewer's chair. As I started to sit down, he looked at me and smiled a nice smile.

He said, "I'm sorry, Sonny, but I can't cut your hair. You go to Mr. Lopez's. He'll cut your hair."

Mr. Brewer took me to the door and pointed the way to Lopez's barbershop. He pointed with his finger and said, "See, over there behind that service station. That's his place. You go there. He'll clip your hair."

Tears were welling up in my eyes. I felt a lump in my throat. I was too choked up to tell him I was Tobie's brother and that it was all right to cut my hair. I only looked at him as he finished giving directions. He smiled again and patted me on the back. As I left, Mr. Brewer said, "Say hello to Mr. Lopez for me, will you, Sonny?"

I did not turn back to look at Mr. Brewer. I kept my head bowed as I walked to Mr. Lopez's because tears filled my eyes, and these tears were tears of hurt to the pride and confidence that I had slowly gained in my gringo town.

I thought of many things as I walked slowly. Maybe this was a foolish thing that I had done. There were too many gringos in the town and too few of us who lived there all the year long. This was a bad thing because the gringos had the right to say yes or no, and we could only follow what they said. It was useless to go against them. It was foolish. But I was different from the Chicanos who came from the south, much different. I did live in the town the ten months of the year when the other Chicanos were in the south or in Mexico. Then I remembered what the barber had told my brother about the South Texas people, and why the gringo customers had left while I was in Mr. Brewer's shop. I began to understand. But it was very hard for me to realize that even though I had lived among gringos all of my life I still had to go to my own people for such things as haircuts. Why wouldn't gringos cut my hair? I was clean. My hair was not long and greasy.

I walked into Mr. Lopez's shop. There were many Chicanos sitting in the chairs and even on the floor, waiting their turn for a haircut. Mr. Lopez paused from his work

PORTRAIT OF NITO 1961 Peter Hurd
Phoenix Art Museum, Arizona.

as he saw me enter and said, "Sorry, Joey, full up. Come back in a couple of hours."

I shrugged my shoulders and said OK. As I started to leave, I remembered what Mr. Brewer had told me to say to Mr. Lopez. "Mr. Lopez," I said, and all the Chicanos, the ones who were waiting, turned and looked at me with curious eyes. "Mr. Brewer told me to tell you hello."

Mr. Lopez shook his head approvingly, not digesting the content of my statement. The Chicanos looked at me again and began to whisper among themselves. I did not hear, but I understood.

I told Mr. Lopez that I would return later in the day, but I did not because there would be other Chicanos wanting haircuts on Saturday. I could come during the week when he had more time and when all the Chicanos would be in the fields working.

I went away, feeling rejected both by the gringos and even my people, the entire world I knew.

Back in the alley where my bike was parked, I sat on the curb for a long while thinking how maybe I did not fit into this town. Maybe my place was in the south of Texas where there were many of my kind of people, and where there were more Chicano barbershops and fewer gringo barbers. Yes, I thought, I needed a land where I could belong to one race. I was so concerned with myself that I did not notice a Chicano, a middle-aged man dressed in a new chambray shirt and faded denim pants, studying me.

I needed a land where I could belong to one race.

He asked, *"Que paso, Chamaco?"*[3]

"Nada,"[4] I answered.

"Maybe the cotton has not been good for you this year."

"No, Señor. I live here in the town."

And then the Chicano said, "Chico, I mistook you for one of us."

Suddenly the Chicano became less interested in me and walked away unconcerned.

I could not have told him that I had tried for a haircut at the gringo's because he would have laughed at me, and called me a *pocho,*[5] a Chicano who prefers gringo ways. These experienced Chicanos knew the ways of the gringos in the north of Texas.

After the Chicano had left me, I thought that maybe these things that were happening to me in the town would all pass in a short time. The entire cotton crop would soon be harvested, and the farmers around my town would have it baled and sold. Then the Chicanos would leave the north of Texas and journey back to their homes in the Valley in the south and to Mexico.

My town would be left alone for ten more months of the year, and in this time everything and everybody would be all right again. The gringo barbers would maybe think twice before sending me to Mr. Lopez's.

Early in November, the last of the cotton around my town had been harvested. The people of South Texas climbed aboard their big trucks with tall sideboards and canvas on the top to shield the sun, and they began their long journey to their homes in the border country.

The streets of the little town were now empty on Saturday. A few farmers came to town on Saturday and brought their families to do their shopping. Still, the streets were quiet and empty.

In my home there was new excitement for me. Tobie considered leaving his newspaper route for another job, one that would pay more money. And I thought that maybe he would let me take over his route. This was something very good. By taking his route, I would know all the gringos of the town, and maybe . . . maybe then the barbers would invite me to their shops as they had invited Tobie.

At supper that night I asked Tobie if he would take me on his delivery for a few days and then let me deliver the newspaper on my own.

Tobie said, "No, Joey. You're too young to handle money. Besides, the newspaper bag would be too heavy for you to carry on your shoulder all over town. No, I think I'll turn the route over to Red."

---

3. *Que paso, Chamaco?* (kä pä′ sô chä mä′ kō) *Spanish:* What happened, boy?

4. *nada* (nä dä) *Spanish:* nothing.

5. *pocho* (pôch′ ô) *Spanish.*

IN THE BARBER SHOP 1934 Ilya Bolotowsky National Museum of American Art, Smithsonian Institution, Washington, D.C./Art Resource, New York

My father was quiet during this time, but soon he spoke, "Tobie, you give the route to Joey. He knows about money. And he needs to put a little muscle on his shoulders."

The issue was settled.

The next day Tobie took me to the newspaper office. Tobie's boss, a nice elderly man wearing glasses, studied me carefully, scratched his white head, and then asked Tobie, "Well, what do you think?"

"Oh," Tobie said, "I told him he was too young to handle this job, but he says he can do it."

"Yes, sir," I butted in enthusiastically.

Tobie's boss looked at me and chuckled, "Well, he's got enough spunk."

He thought some more.

Tobie spoke, "I think he'll make you a good delivery boy, sir."

A short silence followed while Tobie's boss put his thoughts down on a scratch pad on his desk.

Finally, the boss said. "We'll give him a try, Tobie." He looked at me. "But, Young'un, you'd better be careful with that money. It's your responsibility."

"Yes, sir," I gulped.

"OK, that's settled," the boss said.

Tobie smiled and said, "Sir, I'm taking him on my delivery for a few days so he can get the hang of it, and then I'll let him take it over."

The boss agreed. I took his hand and shook it, and promised him that I would do my extra best. Then Tobie left, and I followed behind.

In a few days I was delivering the *Daily News* to all the gringos of the town and also to Mr. Brewer.

Each afternoon, during my delivery, I was careful not to go into Mr. Brewer's with the newspaper. I would carefully open the door and drop the paper in. I did this because I thought that maybe Mr. Brewer would remember me, and this might cause an embarrassing incident. But I did this a very few times because one afternoon Mr. Brewer was standing at the door. He saw me. I opened the door and quickly handed him the newspaper, but before I could shut the door he said, "Say, Sonny, aren't you the one I sent to Mr. Lopez's a while back?"

"Yes, sir," I said.

"Why'd you stay around here? Didn't your people go back home last week? You do belong to 'em, don't you?"

"No, sir," I said. "I live here in the town."

"You mean to say you're not one of those . . .?"

"No, sir."

"Well, I'll be durned." He paused and thought. "You know, Sonny, I have a young Meskin[6] boy who lives here in town come to this here shop for haircuts every other Saturday. His name is . . . durn, can't think of his name to save my soul. . . ."

"Tobie?"

"Yeah, yeah, that's his name. Fine boy. You know him?"

"Yes, sir. He's my older brother."

Then Mr. Brewer's eyes got bigger in astonishment. "Well, I'll be doubly durned." He paused and shook his head unbelievingly. "And I told you to go to Mr. Lopez's. Why didn't you speak up and tell me you

was Tobie's brother? I woulda put you in that there chair and clipped you a pretty head of hair."

"Oh, I guess I forgot to tell you," I said.

"Well, from now on, Sonny, you come to this here shop, and I'll cut your hair."

"But what about your customers? Won't they get mad?"

"Naw. I'll tell 'em you're Tobie's brother, and everything will be all right. Everybody in town knows Tobie, and everybody likes him."

Then a customer walked into the barbershop. He looked at Mr. Brewer, and then at me, and then at my newspaper bag. And then the gringo customer smiled a nice smile at me.

"Well, excuse me, Sonny, got a customer waitin'. Remember now, come Saturday, and I'll clip your hair."

"OK, Mr. Brewer. Bye."

Mr. Brewer turned and said goodbye.

As I continued my delivery, I began to chuckle small bits of contentment to myself because Mr. Brewer had invited me to his shop for haircuts, and because the gringo customer had smiled at me, and because now all the gringos of the town would know me and maybe accept me.

Those incidents that had happened to me during the cotton harvest in my town—Mr. Brewer sending me to Mr. Lopez's for the haircut, and the Chicano cotton picker avoiding me after discovering that I was not one of his people, and the gringo customers leaving Mr. Brewer's barbershop because of me—all seemed so insignificant. And now I felt that delivering the *Daily News* to the businessmen had given me a place among them and all because of the fact that everybody in my town knew Tobie. 🦋

---

6. **Meskin:** mispronunciation of *Mexican*.

explain

Responding to Reading

First Impressions

1. Jot down your thoughts about Joey, the narrator of this story.

Second Thoughts

2. What image do you think Joey has of himself? Explain your answer.

> **Think about**
> - his relationships with Mr. Brewer and Mr. Brewer's customers
> - how he views himself in comparison to the migrant workers
> - how he views himself in comparison to his brother Tobie

3. How do Mr. Brewer and the other gringos show their prejudice toward migrant workers? Do you think that they are prejudiced toward the Chicanos who live in town? Tell why you think as you do.

> **Think about**
> - their actions toward the migrant workers
> - the connotations of the words they use to talk about migrant workers
> - their treatment of Tobie and Joey

4. In your opinion, do Tobie and Joey share the gringos' prejudice toward migrant workers? Why or why not?

5. Why does Tobie have a privileged status? Do you think that he is truly accepted in the gringo society? Explain.

6. In your opinion, why does the writer use a barber to present his message about prejudice? Consider the importance of outward appearance and hairstyles in society.

7. At the end of the story, Joey feels he has won a small victory. Do you agree? Explain why you think as you do.

Broader Connections

8. You know that many of today's prejudices have actually been passed down from previous generations. What are the origins of prejudice? Do you think prejudices like those between Catholics and Protestants in Northern Ireland, between blacks and whites in South Africa, and between ethnic groups in this country can be resolved? If so, how?

9. Wages for migrant workers are extremely low—often falling below the poverty level. Would you favor mandatory higher wages even if it meant paying more for food? Why or why not?

Literary Concept: Setting

The importance of the setting varies from story to story. How important is the setting to this story? Consider these questions:

- What does the writer tell you about the setting and how much must you visualize on your own?

- In what ways are the characters affected by the setting?

- How does the setting help the writer convey his theme?

- Could the story happen in a different setting? If so, what about the plot or characters would have to change?

Concept Review: Conflict In this story the main conflict is between the main character and society. Use the call-outs, or highlighted quotes from the story, on pages 216 and 218 to help you explain the problems Joey faces in this story. Do you think that the conflict is resolved by the end of the story? Why or why not?

Writing Options

1. Imagine that you live in Joey's town and witness Joey's first encounter with Mr. Brewer. Write two letters to the editor of a local newspaper, one from the viewpoint of a gringo and one from that of a Chicano, expressing your opinion of the incident.

2. Skim the story for details that describe Tobie's appearance, behavior, opinions, and feelings. Note how others speak of him and react to him. Then summarize your notes to create a character sketch of Tobie.

3. Joey feels good about himself as the story closes. From what you know about Joey and the people in his town and from your own experience, what do you predict Joey's future will hold? Write your prediction in the form of a paragraph or poem.

4. Joey wants to be like Tobie. Whom would you like to emulate? Explain why you wish to be like this person and how achieving this dream might change your life.

Options for Learning

1 • **Rooting Out Prejudice** Investigate a local incident that resulted from prejudice, or research one of the following historic cases: Rosa Parks and the Montgomery bus boycott, the story of Felix Longoria and the American GI Forum of the United States, the work of Cesar Chavez and the United Farm Workers of America, or Jose Angel Gutierrez and La Raza Unida (Unity of Races). Find out what caused the problem, how the trouble started, and how the problem was (or was not) resolved. Present your information orally, as a written report, or as a photo essay.

2 • **Roving Reporters** Imagine that you are a reporter whose assignment is to uncover stories that have human interest. You have just witnessed a young boy leaving Mr. Brewer's barbershop in tears. The boy is Joey. With other students, act out your interview with Joey and your subsequent interviews with Mr. Brewer and any other people you wish to include to present a balanced report. Present your interviews as a special report for radio or television.

3 • **Debating the Issue** Should Mr. Brewer be forced to cut the hair of anyone who can pay for a haircut? Have three students support one side of the issue while you and two other students support the other. List reasons that support your position, including legal aspects of the question and any other facts that contribute to your argument. Then hold a debate for your class.

4 • **A Television Story** Rewrite this story as a play for television and videotape your production. Invite classmates to play the characters.

 **FACT FINDER**

What is the estimated number of migrant workers in the United States?

Daniel Garza
1938–

Daniel Garza was born near Hillsboro, Texas. His family had emigrated from Mexico not many years earlier. Educated at Texas Christian University, he later served as an officer in the United States Army. Garza's works focus primarily on the relationship between Mexican Americans and Anglos, or white Americans, in the rural communities of the Southwest. He received the *Harper's Magazine* Southwest Literature Award in 1962 for his article "Saturday Belongs to the *Palomia.*" Since then, his works have been widely reprinted.

Autobiography

from
An
American Childhood
ANNIE DILLARD

Examine What You Know

Have you ever thrown something at somebody and then run away? Or dared to pull some other risky prank and hoped you wouldn't get caught? Remember your feelings at that time. Were you more scared than excited? What were the consequences for you and others? Was the prank worth the risk? Share your story with your classmates.

Expand Your Knowledge

"See the world in a grain of sand," said English poet and artist William Blake (1757-1827). Annie Dillard, a modern writer who seems to follow Blake's advice, often uses simple images to make sense of life, to understand the universe. In her autobiography, *An American Childhood*, she looks at moments of pure joy from her years of growing up in Pittsburgh, Pennsylvania. As you read, notice how Dillard pulls deep meaning from what might seem like an unimportant incident.

Enrich Your Reading

Visualizing Action Fast-paced action fills this brief sketch of a scene from Annie Dillard's childhood. On each page vivid details bring the action to life. You will enjoy the chase scene more if you visualize the action, imagining what the narrator sees, hears, and feels.

■ *A biography of the author can be found on page 231.*

from An American Childhood

ANNIE DILLARD

Some boys taught me to play football. This was fine sport. You thought up a new strategy for every play and whispered it to the others. You went out for a pass, fooling everyone. Best, you got to throw yourself mightily at someone's running legs. Either you brought him down or you hit the ground flat out on your chin, with your arms empty before you. It was all or nothing. If you hesitated in fear, you would miss and get hurt: you would take a hard fall while the kid got away, or you would get kicked in the face while the kid got away. But if you flung yourself wholeheartedly at the back of his knees—if you gathered and joined body and soul and pointed them, diving fearlessly—then you likely wouldn't get hurt, and you'd stop the ball. Your fate, and your team's score, depended on your concentration and courage. Nothing girls did could compare with it.

Boys welcomed me at baseball, too, for I had, through enthusiastic practice, what was weirdly known as a boy's arm. In winter, in the snow, there was neither baseball nor football, so the boys and I threw snowballs at passing cars. I got in trouble throwing snowballs and have seldom been happier since.

On one weekday morning after Christmas, six inches of new snow had just fallen.

We were standing up to our boot tops in snow on a front yard on trafficked Reynolds Street, waiting for cars. The cars traveled Reynolds Street slowly and evenly; they were targets all but wrapped in red ribbons, cream puffs. We couldn't miss.

I was seven; the boys were eight, nine, and ten. The oldest two Fahey boys were there—Mikey and Peter—polite, blond boys who lived near me on Lloyd Street and who already had four brothers and sisters. My parents approved Mikey and Peter Fahey. Chickie McBride was there, a tough kid, and Billy Paul and Mackie Kean too, from across Reynolds, where the boys grew up dark and furious, grew up skinny, knowing, and skilled. We had all drifted from our houses that morning looking for action and had found it here on Reynolds Street.

It was cloudy but cold. The cars' tires laid behind them on the snowy street a complex trail of beige chunks like crenelated[1] castle walls. I had stepped on some earlier; they squeaked. We could have wished for more traffic. When a car came, we all popped it one. In the intervals between cars, we <u>reverted</u> to the natural <u>solitude</u> of children.

I started making an ice ball—a perfect ice

---

1. **crenelated** (kren′ ə lāt′ id): having a series of squared notches.

ball, from perfectly white snow, perfectly spherical and squeezed perfectly translucent so no snow remained all the way through. (The Fahey boys and I considered it unfair actually to throw an ice ball at somebody, but it had been known to happen.)

I had just embarked on the ice ball project when we heard tire chains come clanking from afar. A black Buick was moving toward us down the street. We all spread out, banged together some regular snowballs, took aim, and, when the Buick drew nigh, fired.

A soft snowball hit the driver's windshield right before the driver's face. It made a smashed star with a hump in the middle.

Often, of course, we hit our target, but this time, the only time in all of life, the car pulled over and stopped. Its wide black door opened; a man got out of it, running. He didn't even close the car door.

He ran after us, and we ran away from him, up the snowy Reynolds sidewalk. At the corner, I looked back; incredibly, he was still after us. He was in city clothes: a suit and tie, street shoes. Any normal adult would have quit, having sprung us into flight and made his point. This man was gaining on us. He was a thin man, all action. All of a sudden, we were running for our lives.

Wordless, we split up. We were on our turf; we could lose ourselves in the neighborhood back yards, everyone for himself. I paused and considered. Everyone had vanished except Mikey Fahey, who was just rounding the corner of a yellow brick house. Poor Mikey, I trailed him. The driver of the Buick sensibly picked the two of us to follow. The man apparently had all day.

He chased Mikey and me around the yellow house and up a back-yard path we knew by heart: under a low tree, up a bank, through a hedge, down some snowy steps, and across the grocery store's delivery driveway. We smashed through a gap in another hedge, entered a scruffy back yard and ran around its back porch and tight between houses to Edgerton Avenue; we

HOME FOR CHRISTMAS
(STOCKBRIDGE MAIN
STREET AT CHRISTMAS) 1967
Norman Rockwell ©1967 Estate
of Norman Rockwell The Norman
Rockwell Museum at Stockbridge.

ran across Edgerton to an alley and up our own sliding woodpile to the Halls' front yard; he kept coming. We ran up Lloyd Street and wound through mazy back yards toward the steep hilltop at Willard and Lang.

He chased us silently, block after block. He chased us silently over picket fences, through thorny hedges, between houses, around garbage cans, and across streets. Every time I glanced back, choking for breath, I expected he would have quit. He must have been as breathless as we were. His jacket strained over his body. It was an immense discovery, pounding into my hot head with every sliding, joyous step, that this ordinary adult evidently knew what I thought only children who trained at football knew: that you have to fling yourself at what you're doing, you have to point yourself, forget yourself, aim, dive.

Mikey and I had nowhere to go, in our own neighborhood or out of it, but away from this man who was chasing us. He impelled us forward; we compelled him to follow our route. The air was cold; every breath tore my throat. We kept running, block after block; we kept improvising, back yard after back yard, running a frantic course and choosing it simultaneously, failing always to find small places or hard places to slow him down, and discovering always, <u>exhilarated</u>, dismayed, that only bare speed could save us—for he would never give up, this man—and we were losing speed.

He chased us through the back yard labyrinths[2] of ten blocks before he caught us by our jackets. He caught us and we all stopped.

We three stood staggering, half blinded, coughing, in an obscure hilltop back yard: a man in his twenties, a boy, a girl. He had released our jackets, our pursuer, our captor, our hero: he knew we weren't going anywhere. We all played by the rules. Mikey and I unzipped our jackets. I pulled off my sopping mittens. Our tracks multiplied in

2. **labyrinths** (lab' ə rinths'): mazes of confusing passageways.

227

the back yard's new snow. We had been breaking new snow all morning. We didn't look at each other. I was cherishing my excitement. The man's lower pants legs were wet; his cuffs were full of snow, and there was a prow of snow beneath them on his shoes and socks. Some trees bordered the little, flat back yard, some messy winter trees. There was no one around: a clearing in a grove and we the only players.

It was a long time before he could speak. I had some difficulty at first recalling why we were there. My lips felt swollen; I couldn't see out of the sides of my eyes; I kept coughing.

"You stupid kids," he began perfunctorily.[3]

We listened perfunctorily indeed, if we listened at all, for the chewing out was <u>redundant</u>, a mere formality, and beside the point. The point was that he had chased us passionately without giving up, and so he had caught us. Now he came down to earth. I wanted the glory to last forever.

But how could the glory have lasted forever? We could have run through every back yard in North America until we got to Panama. But when he trapped us at the lip of the Panama Canal, what precisely could he have done to prolong the drama of the chase and cap[4] its glory? I brooded about this for the next few years. He could only have fried Mike Fahey and me in boiling oil, say, or dismembered us piecemeal, or staked us to anthills. None of which I really wanted, and none of which any adult was likely to do, even in the spirit of fun. He could only chew us out there in the Panamanian jungle, after months or years of exalting pursuit. He could only begin, "You stupid kids" and continue in his ordinary Pittsburgh accent with his normal, righteous anger and the usual common sense.

If in that snowy back yard the driver of the black Buick had cut off our heads, Mikey's and mine, I would have died happy, for nothing has required so much of me since as being chased all over Pittsburgh in the middle of winter—running terrified, exhausted—by this sainted, skinny, furious redheaded man who wished to have a word with us. I don't know how he found his way back to his car. ໒

---

3. **perfunctorily** (pər fuŋk′ tə rə lē′): in a very routine or superficial way.

4. **cap:** outdo; surpass.

Words to Know and Use | **redundant** (ri dun′ dənt) *adj.* more than enough; superfluous

explain

Responding to Reading

First Impressions

1. Jot down words and phrases that describe your reaction to the chase.

Second Thoughts

2. What did you think of Annie's feelings about the chase? Explain your answer.

   Think about
   - what she has learned from playing football
   - how she feels about the man
   - what the chase requires of her

3. What do you learn about Annie's personality and values from this story?

4. Annie suggests that the man might have chased her and Mikey all the way to the Panama Canal and dismembered them or staked them to anthills. Why do you think she uses such extreme examples?

5. Who do you think wins a small victory as a result of the chase? Explain.

Broader Connections

6. The narrator and her friends do not seem to think about the consequences of throwing snowballs at cars. Make a list of the possible consequences of their actions. What pranks can you think of that have backfired, causing unexpected results such as damage to property or injury to people?

Literary Concept: Descriptive Details

One way writers add life to a piece of writing is by vividly describing details. The details of the chase, for example, help you visualize that scene. What details especially help you picture the chase? What other details help you picture the setting?

Concept Review: Theme *An American Childhood* is nonfiction, yet it is still a story that Annie Dillard tells us. What theme, or message about life, does she present in this story? How did you determine her theme?

Writing Options

1. The narrator doesn't tell us what the man said after his words "You stupid kids." Based on his actions to that point, and using your imagination, write the lecture he might have given Annie.

2. Dillard did not title each chapter in *An American Childhood*. Write two or three possible titles for this chapter that capture the event, the theme, or Annie's character.

3. The narrator likes football because it is "all or nothing," something you "flung yourself into wholeheartedly." She admires the man because he flings himself into the chase in just such a way. Write about an experience you have had that required these qualities.

4. Consider what you have learned about the young Annie. Write a character sketch describing the adult you imagine she has become.

Vocabulary Practice

Exercise On your paper, write the word from the list that best completes each sentence. Some words will be used more than once.

1. The man had already made his point, so the lecture seemed _____.
2. Annie seemed to prefer the excitement of team sports to the _____ of quiet activities like reading.
3. A perfect snowball is _____ in shape.
4. The wild excitement of the chase made Annie feel quite _____.
5. Do you predict that the children will _____ to the practice of throwing snowballs at cars?
6. An ice ball is _____ because you can see light through it.
7. The man left the _____ of his car to chase the kids.
8. The thrill of the chase probably made the man feel as _____ as Annie felt.
9. Frosted glass, ice, and most jewels are _____.
10. A baseball is _____.

> *Words to Know and Use*
>
> exhilarated
> redundant
> revert
> solitude
> spherical
> translucent

e x t e n d

O ptions for Learning

1 • Cartoon Story Plan and draw a cartoon strip of this story. Select the scenes you think are important. Use details from the story and your imagination to depict the characters and background. Write the characters' words in balloons.

2 • Map the Chase Draw a map of the chase. Review the author's description, especially of details like fences and hedges. Use these details as well as your imagination, to guide you. Show landmarks and trace the path of the chase. Write brief comments along the route, such as, "This is where the snowball hit the car."

3 • Design a Computer Game Create a computer game based on the chase. Design a screen and figures to represent Annie, Mikey, and the man. Include the obstacles mentioned in the story and add some of your own. Decide on a way of scoring the game.

4 • Mood Music Please Select some background music for this story. Imagine that you are planning a movie or a reading of the story. Find music that will capture the feeling of each scene. Select pieces of music to accompany playing football, throwing snowballs, hitting the car, the chase, and the capture. Play each piece for your class and ask them to guess which scene it matches.

 **FACT FINDER**

The narrator exaggerates, saying that the chase could have stretched from Pittsburgh to the Panama Canal. How far is that?

A nnie Dillard
1945-

Writing *An American Childhood* required "a lot of remembering," Annie Dillard says. The memories included the comfortable, roomy house in which she grew up with her two sisters and her parents—"a house full of comedians," she says. Then there were the recollections of biking, playing sports, collecting rocks and insects, drawing, learning to tell jokes. She also remembered reading. "Reading showed me an enormous number of worlds," she says.

As Dillard grew up, she continued to store up interesting memories. She has been an artist, lived alone in the woods, taught at universities, married, and had a daughter named Rosie. But mostly Dillard writes—often in her secluded Cape Cod, Massachusetts, writing shed. And she still views the world with excitement and wonder.

Dillard expresses her enthusiasm for life in her books. Her second published book, *Pilgrim at Tinker Creek*, won a Pulitzer Prize.

W RITER'S
WORKSHOP

PERSUASION AND EVALUATION

In persuasive writing the writer attempts to convince the reader that a particular idea, goal, or course of action is the best possible alternative among several. Persuasion sometimes involves **evaluation.** The writer makes a judgment about the worth of something (for example, an object, story, or movie), gives reasons for the judgment, and convinces the reader that the judgment is sound. The key lies in developing solid and meaningful standards, or **criteria,** for the judgment. If the criteria are sound and reasonable, there is an excellent chance that the writer will succeed in persuading the reader.

Suppose that next year there will be only enough time to read and study one of the selections from this subunit. In this workshop you will recommend which selection should be chosen, based on sensible criteria by which you can evaluate the selections. In a letter, you will persuade next year's teacher to choose your recommendation.

Here is your PASSkey to
this assignment.

**GUIDED ASSIGNMENT:
LITERARY RECOMMENDATION**

Write a letter to next year's teacher explaining which selection in this subunit should be taught.

PURPOSE: To persuade and evaluate

AUDIENCE: Next year's teacher

SUBJECT: Selections from this subunit

STRUCTURE: Letter of recommendation

Prewriting

STEP **1** **Determine the criteria** When you make judgments about something, you must have sound reasons, or criteria, on which to base your judgment. When someone shops for a car, for example, that buyer determines what criteria are important to him or her. The criteria might include price, options, and the purpose for which the vehicle will be used. The buyer reviews the different cars and compares them on the basis of those criteria. He or she might finally choose one car over another because it is less expensive, has more options, and carries a large family more comfortably.

Your first task, then, is to determine some basic criteria for recommending one selection over the others. What makes one selection more enjoyable than another? Your criteria might be qualities that make selections fun to read.

In a small group list stories or books each group member has enjoyed. Then discuss what qualities, such as suspense or humor, make those stories worth reading. Choose four or five qualities that are important to your own reading enjoyment and list them as your criteria. They will serve as the basis for your evaluation.

STEP 2 **Choose a selection** Review the selections in the subunit and rate them according to the criteria you have chosen. You might find it helpful to use a chart like the one below:

Criteria	*All Things . . .*	*" . . . Tobie"*	*. . . Childhood*
humor			

Rate each selection for each criterion. Give a rating of *3* if you think a selection meets the criterion extremely well. Write a *2* if it partially meets the criterion, and *1* if it fails to meet the criterion. The selection with the highest total score will probably be the one that you recommend.

STEP 3 **Find supporting examples** In order to persuade someone that your evaluation is sound, you need good examples that illustrate how your choice meets your criteria. Read the paragraph below:

> Cassette Player X is the best buy because it has more features and is less expensive than either Player Y or Player Z. Player X not only costs five dollars less than the others, but it can record and it includes an AM/FM radio. Player Y has a radio but cannot record; Player Z can record but does not have a radio.

◀ STUDENT MODEL

Notice that the writer mentions two criteria—features and cost—and explains how Player X meets those criteria better than the others do.

Skim through the selection you chose. List the criteria you decided were most important. Beneath each one, give specific examples from the story that show how the criterion is met.

Drafting

Using your chart and notes, draft your letter of recommendation. For correct letter form, see the **Writer's Handbook,** Correct Business Letter Form.

Begin your first paragraph by stating your reason for writing and your recommended selection. Next state the criteria on which you have based your recommendation.

You might organize your letter by giving each criterion its own paragraph. Explain what the criterion is and why it is relevant to your evaluation; then give examples from the selection that meet the criterion.

Special Tip

A recommendation of one option over others is more persuasive if you compare the choices. Strengthen your case by referring specifically to the others and showing how yours is better.

Revising and Editing

Evaluate and revise your draft using the following checklist. Also ask a classmate to review your work using the checklist. Use those suggestions you think will improve your letter.

Revision Checklist

1. Does the letter begin by stating the reason for writing, the recommended selection, and the criteria used in evaluating?
2. Are the criteria relevant to the task at hand? Are any important criteria missing?
3. Does each paragraph focus on a different criterion?
4. Are there specific examples of how the recommended selection meets each criterion? Should any other examples be included?
5. Are the examples clear? Do any need further explaining?

Editing   When you finish revising your draft, proofread for spelling, clarity, and mechanics. Make sure you have used correct letter form.

Presenting

Read your letter to the whole class or to a small group. Try to persuade the others that your recommendation is the best one. The group should vote on which recommendation to accept and give the reasons.

Reflecting on Your Writing

Jot down answers to the following questions. Attach your responses to your paper before putting it into your writing portfolio.

1. Which part of the assignment was hardest for you?
2. What did you learn that might help you with other writing?
3. What did you learn about evaluating literature selections?

LANGUAGE
WORKSHOP

MAKING CORRECT COMPARISONS

> Adjectives and adverbs have three forms, or degrees: **positive, comparative,** and **superlative.**

"I like comedies *better* than action movies."
"Today's soccer practice was the *longest* of the season."

Every time you go shopping, go to the movies, or talk about anything from sports to music, you use adjectives and adverbs to make comparisons. Most of the time when you make these comparisons, you automatically choose the correct form of the modifier. Occasionally, however, you may run into difficulty.

Remember, in the **positive degree** an adjective or adverb describes people, places, things, ideas, or actions but does not make a comparison. In the **comparative degree** an adjective or adverb compares two of anything; in the **superlative degree** an adjective or adverb compares three or more of anything.

Positive   That bull is *big.*

Comparative   That bull is *bigger* than a cow.

Superlative   That bull is the *biggest* animal on the farm.

Don't get confused between the comparative and superlative. In the following sentence the phrase *all other bulls* is considered one unit or one group. Therefore, the comparison is between two things, and the comparative form *bigger* is correct.

Bill was *bigger* than *all other bulls.*

Most modifiers form their comparative and superlative degrees in regular ways.

1. A one-syllable modifier is made comparative or superlative by adding *-er* or *-est.*

Positive	Comparative	Superlative
small	smaller	smallest
kind	kinder	kindest

2. Most two-syllable modifiers are made comparative or superlative by adding -*er* or -*est*. Sometimes, however, a two-syllable modifier sounds awkward with these endings. In such cases, use *more* and *most* to form the comparative and superlative. Note that *more* and *most* are always used to form comparisons involving two-syllable adverbs that end in -*ly*.

Positive	Comparative	Superlative
gentle	gentler	gentlest
pretty	prettier	prettiest
hopeful	more hopeful	most hopeful
swiftly	more swiftly	most swiftly

SPELLING
....
When words of two syllables end in *y*, the *y* is almost always changed to *i* when -*er* or -*est* is added.

> happy   happier
> fancy   fanciest

3. Modifiers of three or more syllables are made comparative or superlative using *more* or *most*.

Positive	Comparative	Superlative
agreeable	more agreeable	most agreeable
rapidly	more rapidly	most rapidly

For some modifiers the comparative and superlative forms are completely different words from the positive forms. Study the chart on the side of the page to learn these special forms.

IRREGULAR COMPARISONS
....

Pos.	Comp.	Super.
good	better	best
well	better	best
bad	worse	worst
much	more	most
many	more	most
little	less *or* lesser	least

Exercise 1   Correct the errors in comparison in the following sentences. If a sentence has no errors, write *Correct.*

1. In the excerpt from *All Things Bright and Beautiful,* was the author describing his most worst day as a veterinarian?
2. On the other hand, perhaps he was narrating the funnier day he had ever experienced.
3. Bill the Bull was more big than most of Herriot's patients.
4. Of all the animals Herriot had ever treated, that bull was the stronger.
5. Bill pinned Herriot to the wall tightlyer than a sumo wrestler pins his opponent.
6. To the desperate vet, Bill felt more heavier than a ton of bricks.
7. The farmer's daughter laughed loudlier than her father did.
8. Herriot hoped that the budgie would be easier to treat than Bill the bull had been.
9. However, the budgie was more bad than Bill the bull; the poor bird actually died of fright at Herriot's touch.
10. Peter was quickly replaced by a satisfyinger bird.

REMINDER
....
To make a negative comparison, use *less* or *least* before the positive form of the modifier: hopeful, less hopeful, least hopeful; funny, less funny, least funny.

Exercise 2 Write the form of the modifier given in parentheses.

1. Tobie was (old—comparative) than his brother Joey.
2. Joey believed that Tobie's newspaper route was the (great—superlative) job in town.
3. Tobie bragged that he knew the gringos in the town (well—comparative) than any other Chicano paperboy.
4. Of all the paperboys, Joey believed that Tobie was the (good—superlative).
5. Because he was Tobie's brother, Joey believed that Mr. Brewer would be (nice—comparative) to him than the other gringo barbers.
6. Mr. Lopez's shop was (busy—comparative) than Mr. Brewer's shop.
7. Of all the days of the week, Saturday was (busy—superlative) for Mr. Lopez.
8. Once Mr. Brewer realized that Joey was Tobie's brother, he reacted to Joey (graciously—comparative) than he had before.
9. To Tobie, Mr. Brewer's "acceptance" of him was the (important—superlative) thing in the world.
10. To maintain his "acceptance" by the gringo world, Joey may work even (hard—comparative) than his brother did.

COLLABORATIVE LEARNING
....
This exercise may be done in groups. One person should record the revised sentences.

Exercise 3 Proofreading Rewrite the following paragraphs correctly.

Of all my childhood jobs I still remember my paper route vividlyest. Each morning at 5:00 A.M., I got up the most earliest of all the members of my family. Within ten minutes, I was riding through the deserted streets, tossing papers onto porches accuratelyer than a major league pitcher.

Of all the mornings, Sunday was the most bad. The Sunday paper, filled with advertisements, was more heavier than the weekly edition. The pitiful payment I gave my sister to help me on Sundays was least than the cost of a comic book. Still, each Sunday morning she came, skipping through the dawn, much more happilyer than I was.

Exercise 4 Analyzing and Revising Your Writing

1. Review the paper you wrote for the workshop on page 232.
2. Make sure all comparisons are correctly worded.
3. Remember to check for comparison errors the next time you proofread your work.

LANGUAGE HANDBOOK
....
For review and practice: modifiers in comparison, pages 922–27

STUDY SKILLS
WORKSHOP

READING RATES

How you read depends on what you're reading and why you're reading it. Sometimes you'll want to read quickly. At other times, you'll need to read much more carefully and slowly.

For example, to find a specific fact or definition, you can quickly **scan** a reading selection, sweeping your eyes across each page until you spot what you're looking for.

If you want to find the main idea in a piece of reading or get an overview of its contents, you can **skim** fairly quickly, reading only the title, headlines, highlighted words or phrases, and topic sentences. If there's a summary section, slow down and read it more carefully.

When you need to do some **in-depth** learning or studying, you'll need to read more slowly. Skim the entire piece first, noting the main ideas. Then identify the details that support each main idea. Make sure you know all the key words, dates, and facts. Take notes as you read.

HOW TO SCAN

To train yourself to scan, try this method.
1. Choose a familiar textbook.
2. Place a folded paper or a 3×5-inch card over the first line of any page and move the paper or card quickly down the page.
3. Look for key words or phrases that indicate you are near the information you need.
4. When you locate such a clue, stop scanning and begin to read slowly.

Exercise   Follow the directions below, step by step. Do not read through all the directions at once.

Step 1   Skim the following article. Write one sentence that summarizes the main idea of the passage.

Step 2   Scan the article to find two examples of zoonoses. Write these examples on your paper.

Step 3   Read the article in depth. Write at least three facts or reasons that support the main idea of the article.

> **Veterinary medicine** is the branch of medicine that deals with the diseases of animals. Animal doctors are called *veterinarians.* Their work is especially valuable because many animal diseases can be transmitted to human beings. Such diseases are *zoonoses.* Some examples of zoonoses are rabies and tuberculosis. **In cities** most veterinarians are associated with pet hospitals. Many animal hospitals contain equipment much like that used in hospitals for human beings. **On farms** perhaps the most important activity of the veterinarian is the care and treatment of livestock. Veterinarians help keep farm animals in good health to prevent outbreaks of animal diseases.
>
> —*The World Book Encyclopedia*

$\mathscr{T}$ESTS OF ENDURANCE

Tests of endurance are long trials that challenge an individual's will to survive. Unlike Odysseus' battles with mythical monsters and gods, many characters in literature face obstacles caused by man or nature. Their challenge is to survive despite these obstacles; their survival depends on their ability to outlast the danger.

In this subunit you will read several selections about people who battle with nature, disease, and human enemies. Some of these pieces are true stories while others are fiction based on facts. As you read, look for clues that explain why some individuals find the courage to continue fighting in spite of overwhelming odds.

Article

ᴬ*Trip to the Edge of Survival*

RON ARIAS (är′ ē əs)

Examine What You Know

From the title of this selection and its place-
ment in the subunit "Tests of Endurance," what
do you suppose it is about? Examine the pictures included with the selection. Based on this preview and
your own knowledge, what dangers do you think the men
in this account might face? Jot down your predictions.

Expand Your Knowledge

This article is a true account of an ordeal five men endured during a
fishing trip in the Pacific Ocean. The men set sail from Puntarenas (po͞on′
tä rä′ näs), Costa Rica, and sailed west with the steadily blowing trade
winds. Along this part of the Pacific coast, a strong, dry, seasonal wind
known as El Norte comes down from the north, causing brief, violent
windstorms called squalls and large waves called swells, which can reach
the height of a three-story building. For fishermen and others who make
their living at sea, El Norte is a force to be feared and respected.

Enrich Your Reading

Understanding Magazine Articles This selection first appeared in
People magazine. Magazine writers must capture their readers' interest
and present many facts in a limited amount of space.

Notice how information in this article is organized and presented. The
article includes excerpts from a letter written by a crew member,
quotations from survivors, and third-person narration. Events are
sometimes presented out of order. In a list like the one below, describe
the type of information given in each of the first seven paragraphs and
the form in which it is presented. Then see whether these techniques
are used throughout the article.

Paragraph 1—letter from Joel to his wife
**Paragraph 2—background on how ship was disabled/3rd-person
narrative**

■ *A biography of the
author can be
found on page 253.*

A Trip to the Edge of Survival

RON ARIAS

To My Beloved Wife, I want to write you so bad but I don't know what to say. Only that I feel this great desire to live, which is all that gives me strength. But I don't think I can resist because God is making it very difficult for me. But what can I do? I love you and my four daughters so much. I only know that if I die, you won't have bad memories nor will you tell my daughters I was a bad man. My strength is ending, and if I die, I hope someone will be able to send you this.

—Joel González[1]

On January 24, as the dawn's first light brightened the cloudless sky twenty miles off the coast of Costa Rica, Joel González, twenty-seven, stood at the helm of the *Cairo III*, maneuvering the squat, 29½-foot fishing boat through light swells in the Pacific Ocean. Suddenly, Joel felt a squall send the vessel shuddering and lurching to one side. Within minutes, the dreaded north wind, a 50-to-60-mph seasonal scourge of the coastal area, struck with full force, heaving up thirty-foot swells that bashed in doors and windows, swamped the cabin,

and left the wooden craft bobbing wildly and close to foundering.[2]

"That was the beginning of our nightmare," says Joel, who was alone on deck until his four panicked crew mates scrambled from their bunks. "There was so much noise, I thought the boat was breaking up. The guys looked like monkeys, hanging on to anything they could grab. It's a miracle we didn't go down. The boat was half filled with water, and we bailed like madmen. We lost our net, the radio went out, and before long the engine overheated and gave out. All day the water poured in. We'd nail the doors shut, but the waves would just smash them open again. We fought and fought, bailing and working the pump. From that day we never saw the coast again."

Eventually, the five fishermen, who had left the port city of Puntarenas January 19 on a routine, week-long trip near the coast, would remember the 22-day storm as one of the most terrifying chapters in the five months they were lost at sea. They would still have to face many desperate bouts of

---

1. **Joel González** (hô′ el gôn zäl′ es).
2. **foundering** (foun′ dər iŋ): filling with water and sinking.

Words to Know and Use	**maneuvering** (mə noo̅′ vər iŋ) *adj.* directing or guiding in a skillful manner **maneuver** *v.*

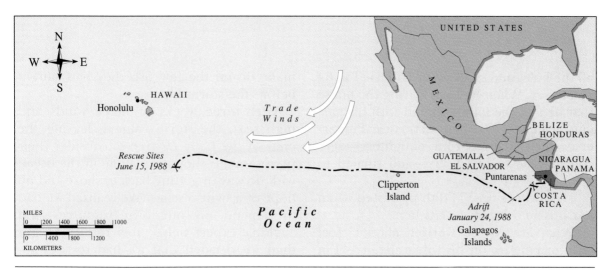

This map shows the westward voyage of the *Cairo III*.

hunger and thirst, a badly leaking hull, the constant danger of shark attacks, and the threat of mental collapse. But amazingly, they would battle on for a total of 144 days, to be rescued near the end of their endurance June 15 by a Japanese fishing ship about seven hundred miles from Honolulu and four thousand miles from Costa Rica. Their odyssey would set a world record for survivors cast adrift, surpassing the 133 days a Chinese seaman spent alone in the Atlantic in 1942–43. Shaky but miraculously healthy after such an ordeal, they would return home as heroes. "I never thought I'd see my wife and kids again," says Joel. "That's why I started to write her a note explaining how we died. I kept it in a little bottle with my gold ring tied to the top. With my last strength, I was going to throw the bottle into the water, hoping someone would find it and send her the note."

The captain of the *Cairo III* on its epic voyage into maritime history was Gerardo Obregón,[3] thirty-three, a quiet, <u>affable</u> man with five years' experience as a skipper. Except for Pastor López,[4] twenty-seven, the small, talkative fisherman who joined the group in December and who would become its spiritual leader in the crisis, the crew had sailed together for a year. The veterans included Joel, the poet of the group; Jorge Hernández,[5] twenty-six, a tall, sober-faced young man; and Juan Bolívar,[6] the crew's elder at forty-seven, with more than thirty years of seagoing experience.

I only know one thing—that if it's possible to love after life, I will love you. This is the last I'll write you, since I see things are so difficult that I no longer have the illusion or the strength to go on. We're out here two months now and nothing has happened to lift our spirits.

The day the *Cairo III* put out to sea, Joel's wife, Edith, twenty-six, awoke with a strange feeling. Though her husband had gone on many fishing tours with Captain Obregón, on this morning she feared unreasonably for Joel's safety. She was worried about the condition of the boat's wooden hull, about

---

3. **Gerardo Obregón** (her är' dô ô' brē gôn').
4. **Pastor López** (päs' tôr lô' pes).
5. **Jorge Hernández** (hôr' hä her nän' des).
6. **Juan Bolívar** (hwän bô lē' vär).

all the holes and cracks they had tried to fix in a hurry. When Joel was leaving the house that he and the family shared with his parents in an <u>impoverished</u> <u>barrio</u> near Puntarenas, he kissed his four daughters—ages two months to five years—and turned to go.

"Hey, what's this?" Edith protested when her husband forgot to kiss her.

"What are you so worried about?" Joel said, picking up on his wife's anxiety. "I'm not going as far as Panama."

"Well, you never know," Edith said. And with that, Joel gave her a kiss and departed.

Eight days later, Edith and Gerardo's wife, Lydia, twenty-seven, knew something had happened to their husbands; all the fishing-fleet boats except the *Cairo III* had fled into port to escape the rough seas and winds that had been pounding the coast for several days. Alarmed, the women asked the local coast guard office to begin an air-and-sea search for the boat. Officials assured them that they would scour the adjacent Gulf of Nicoya and the ocean beyond.

While the coast guard hunted for them in vain, Joel, Gerardo, Jorge, Juan, and Pastor were battling crashing waves and their own exhaustion, bailing continuously, eating or resting when they could, crawling about on all fours to keep their balance on the dizzily pitching deck of their five-ton vessel. "We were desperate, terrified that at any minute we would sink," says Joel. "Until the end of the storm all we did was bail, crawl into our bunks for a few hours' sleep, and bail some more." The provisions—rice, flour, beans, crackers, sugar, and some meat—ran out on the third day of the storm. The men had to make do on the few fish they had caught before the storm hit.

After three weeks of fierce winds and high seas, the storm calmed, leaving the crew of the *Cairo III* free to consider their predicament; they were alone in the ocean with no way of getting back to shore and no hope of a swift rescue. "We realized we had to depend on our own resources and couldn't expect help," Joel recalls. "Right then we decided that we had to stick together. We made rules to ration food and water and agreed to bail in four-hour shifts, day and night." They began dismantling the wooden cabin and its four sleeping berths to provide fuel for their cooking fire. With the bunks gone, the crew found that the most protected <u>niche</u> on board was the hatch-covered icebox set under the rear deck. No longer used to store their catch, the icebox was barely large enough to accommodate four men in a crouch or lying down. All but the captain, who would lie down in a sheltered spot in the bow, would sleep here.

After the cabin was torn down, the icebox, once used to keep fish, became the sleeping area.
Directions, International, Inc., Los Angeles.

A daily struggle for food and survival had begun. All they had was a long, trailing fishing line with a lot of dangling hooks and no bait. As soon as the swells began to <u>abate</u>, they decided to try to catch some of the turtles they had seen inquisitively approaching the boat. Though a half dozen twelve-foot sharks were already circling nearby, catching them would require baited hooks. The turtles, some measuring up to three feet in width, could be gaffed[7] with a big hook tied to a pole.

"My job," Joel explains, "was to hide behind the side rail; and, before they could see me and be scared away, I'd have to spring up and hook them. As soon as we pulled one onto the deck, Gerardo would kill it and open the bottom part with his knife. Then Jorge would clean the meat, Pastor would cook us something like a stew in seawater, and Juan would divide up the pieces. I guess we trusted Juan the most to be fair. This was very important because some days we wouldn't catch anything, and when we finally did, even if it was a fish no bigger than a man's hand, it was Juan who'd cut up and distribute the little pieces that would tease our stomachs for another day." Some days when their luck was running they would eat well; other days they caught nothing and went hungry. Their only source of fresh water being rain, they measured their chances of survival by the weather.

The rainwater that we had is about used up. We have no food. And all around us, the same thing, water and more water. We have suffered so much that I believe, with death, God will finally allow us to rest. I know you may never get this note, Edith, but anything is possible. And if I can't hang on, I hope you will find out exactly how and when it was that I died.

After three weeks of waiting with no news from the coast guard, Edith and Lydia hitched a two-hour ride to the capital city of San José. There they spoke with a government official who told them that the coast guard had been unable to make a search beyond the gulf because their large patrol boat had broken down. "He made all these excuses," says Edith, "and when we suggested that the *Cairo III* might have drifted into Nicaraguan waters, he said it was out of his hands. He also said there were no clues about our husbands' whereabouts and that they couldn't invest a lot of money on a search when the chances of finding something were so small."

By late February, the men were drifting with the westward current and tradewinds. The boat's compass, the only navigational device on board, now showed their course was almost due west. On a day of relative calm, Juan, whom the others nicknamed "the old man," suggested they make a mast and sail. The only one among them who had worked on a sailboat, he volunteered to design and direct the project. "On our own, the way we were, we couldn't get anywhere," he recalls having told them. "Only God could take us there, but it wouldn't hurt if we helped Him a bit. The wind and current were too strong for us to get back home, but a sail would move us to the west faster." With a thick crossbeam wrenched out of the cabin roof, the men fashioned a 21-foot mast, tore away planks to make a boom, and sewed together blankets and pieces of vinyl cushion covers to create a crude, triangular sail. After the sail was fastened to the boom and mast with fishing line and wire, Juan

---

7. **gaffed** (gaft): caught or hooked.

Words to Know and Use | **abate** (ə bāt') *v.* to lessen or decrease; subside

had them make a rudder.[8] While prying out nails for reuse in these tasks, the crew found themselves blessing the thoroughness of *Cairo III*'s original builders. "The boat turned into a floating hardware store," says Pastor. "We had so much wire and nails of all sizes." The makeshift rudder worked well at first, but like the sail it had to be constantly repaired.

Getting the boat back underway was a <u>psychological</u> boost and allowed the five to weather the storms and towering seas they encountered frequently. The men confess they had little idea of world geography or where they might wash ashore. By mid-March they must have crossed a couple of time zones, because they knew from their watches that the sun was setting much later than it did in Costa Rica. The crew's two-date wristwatches also helped them keep track of their voyage. "The watches gave us an idea of how far we had gone and how many days we'd been out," says Gerardo. "By keeping them set to Costa Rican time, they were also a reminder, or a way of tying us to our country." Gathering food—usually turtles, sometimes a shark they would snare with a baited hook and fishing line—had become almost an <u>obsession</u>. And since the thought of eating raw flesh was repulsive to all five, they took extreme care in safeguarding and cleaning what became their most cherished possession—a plastic Bic lighter that Joel, a nonsmoker, absent-mindedly threw in his suitcase before the trip. "I was chosen to cook," says Pastor, "because I was the most careful in lighting the wood. It's funny now, but during the trip that lighter seemed like life itself for us. Late in the trip, when we had torn down the cabin and the wood was running out, we could just barely warm up the meat. But it still made all the difference to our stomachs." The moment when Pastor flicked the lighter into flame became an important, hope-affirming ritual. With the other four watching intently, Pastor would start the fire with fragments of a sponge mattress and nurse it to glowing life with splinters of wood. Once, the Bic slipped from Pastor's grasp and fell to the bottom of the flooded engine well; without hesitating, he dived into the oily slop to retrieve it. "We were angry at him for being so clumsy," says Joel, "but I think he felt worse than we did."

Edith, don't spend the rest of your life suffering and wondering what happened to me. Be courageous and try to overcome life's hardships, since from the time of our birth we know we're going to die sooner or later. And if God takes me first, what can I do? I fought till the end and did everything I could to return to you. But finally I was defeated. Yet even now, on the brink of death, there's still a little flame in me that refuses to go out.

Sometime in April Edith dreamed that she received letters from Joel, postmarked in Korea, instructing her to take care of the children. Desperate for news of Joel, she clung to her faith that he was still alive and hid her anxiety from the children. Emily, their two-year-old daughter, who was especially close to her father, also had dreams that Joel was still alive. In one dream, she was stranded on a rock in the sea and he came to save her. In another, he returned home and, complaining of hunger, asked for a plate of rice, beans, and fried eggs.

---

8. **rudder** (rud′ ər): a broad, flat, movable piece of wood hinged vertically at the stern, or back end, of a boat, used for steering.

Words to Know and Use | **psychological** (sī′ kə laj′ i kəl) *adj.* of the mind; mental
obsession (əb sesh′ ən) *n.* the state of being preoccupied with an idea or desire

A replica of the *Cairo III*
Directions, International, Inc., Los Angeles.

By this time, most of the boat's cabin had been torn apart to be used as firewood in the small, cylindrical stove they had made out of a gas tank. All that remained above deck was a flat, wooden awning held up by four posts. They used the awning for shade from the intense tropical sun and to catch rainwater, which they trapped in a gutter on one side by tilting the boat with their weight; the runoff spilled into a forty-gallon barrel.

Gradually the stress and punishing hardship of life aboard the *Cairo III* began to distort the crew's sense of reality. Food deprivation became a maddening fixation. At first they had argued over choice pieces of turtle liver, but now, increasingly, the bickering was centering on their dreams of favorite meals. At night, ravenous and unable to sleep, they lay under the stars, their thoughts plagued by tantalizing visions of heavenly dishes. In a lunatic game, the men would find themselves haggling endlessly over an ideal plate of food, "buying" the fruits of their imagination with the little money each man carried on board. Upset that the others were only torturing themselves, Juan pleaded with them to stop, but they refused, finding some humor in taunting the older man.

A ship came on the morning of April 15, as a few small birds flitted low over the foam-tipped swells. Jorge was brushing his teeth near the stern when he glimpsed a freighter about two miles away. "Look!" he shouted. "A ship! A ship!" For a long time the men shouted and waved their arms. "I dropped my toothbrush in the water, I was so happy," Jorge recalls. Alas, no one aboard the freighter spotted the tiny speck of the *Cairo III* in the vast ocean, and the ship disappeared over the horizon. The

---

Words to Know and Use

cylindrical (sə lin′ dri kəl) *adj.* having the tubelike shape of a cylinder
deprivation (dep′ rə vā′ shən) *n.* a forcible taking away or loss of something
ravenous (rav′ ə nəs) *adj.* wildly hungry; famished

247

men fell silent and despondent, their disappointment all the more acute because it was the second time a distant ship had passed them by. "We thought it was another of God's tests for us," says Pastor. "After that, we just assumed that we'd be saved or hit land if God meant us to."

The day of that second boat sighting, Juan suffered a crippling attack of stomach pains. Although they all contended with constant diarrhea, the normally stoic Juan finally asked Joel, the crew's designated "doctor," for some antacid pills. "I was the doctor only because I happened to bring along some aspirin and a handful of other pills," he says. "Poor Juan. He was hurting the most, but the pills helped. He also had to have a tooth pulled, which we yanked out with a piece of twine."

In mid-May, Gerardo ordered the dismantling of the engine. It was dumped overboard, along with batteries and a gas tank, to reduce the boat's weight. They had been riding ever lower in the water, bailing around the clock to control the flooding below decks, and now Gerardo began going into the water to plug holes and cracks in the hull from the outside, tethered to *Cairo III* by a rope. Wary of the sharks that circled the boat with nerve-racking constancy, the others would keep a close lookout while the captain stuffed rags and pieces of plastic and mattress sponge into the vessel's leaking skin.

It was after completing this chore, after Gerardo had been pulled up and the men were sitting down to rest under the awning, when Pastor shouted: "My God, look at that!" The others started, then froze at the sight of a monstrous whale.

"It was about twenty feet away, so big it looked like a piece of land," Gerardo recalls. "The tail alone was as big as our boat. All we could do was hold on and watch. If it touched us, we would sink in a minute. There were other whales but never that big or that close. I was ready to poke it with a little harpoon we'd made, just to shoo it away. But as it came closer, it dove under us and stayed there for about twenty minutes. We held our breath and prayed, and then, thank God, it went away."

May 10. My beloved. Incredibly I'm still alive, since by this date I thought I would have been rescued or dead. But so great is God's power that even from here I can wish you a happy birthday and my mother, a happy Mother's Day.

Not long after the day the whale appeared, Jorge was on deck, about to clean the severed head of a ten-foot shark. As he stooped to pick it up, the jaws reflexively snapped shut on one of his fingers. Yelling in pain, he yanked his hand free and saw that a tooth had punctured a finger. "It shocked him so much his legs wouldn't stop trembling," Joel remembers. "You could bash a shark over and over with a club, cut his insides out, and he would still go flopping around and twitching for an hour. We all had cuts from those fights, but Jorge's wound was the worst."

On May 31, they once again rationed out the last dregs of water. "There were many days when we had no rain," says Joel. "By the end, we cherished the water we could drink more than food." Tormented by thirst, the men lay about on the deck in their tattered shorts, looking at the faraway, dark clouds that seemed to taunt them with the promise of rain. They had begun to eat their

---

Words to Know and Use

despondent (di spän' dənt) *adj.* having lost hope; depressed
stoic (stō' ik) *adj.* calm and unemotional, especially while in pain; uncomplaining
severed (sev' ərd) *adj.* cut apart or cut off **sever** *v.*

fish raw, something they had sworn they wouldn't do. "We had to," says Pastor, "because we'd used up all the wood to make a fire. If we ripped up any more of the boat, we'd probably sink, since there wasn't much left of it." But now their tongues and throats were so parched that they could hardly swallow. They had killed about 200 turtles so far, and the creature that had saved them from starving was no longer of use.

For four days they waited for rain. Some thought of suicide, and all five passed into a kind of delirious stupor. But at their lowest ebb, Pastor gave a rousing talk to get the men moving again. "The sail was down and we had been drifting," Pastor remembers. "I told them that God was tempting us to die the way the devil tempted Jesus. 'Fight back, get up, and let's raise the sail,' I said. And somehow we did and we started moving again."

Though Pastor's brave talk rallied his friends, he too was feeling almost overwhelmed by despair. "A lot of the time I thought of suicide, how wonderful it would be to find a way out of this situation," he says. "But I knew it was better to fight like a man than die like a coward."

I don't know how much life remains in me, Edith. I pray with all my will to be reunited with you. You and my daughters are everything. I love you without limits. I can't accept reality, but that's the way the end is. I don't regret what I had in life, because it was the best—a great woman, beautiful children and a wonderful mother. I love you, Edith. I love you.

As death became increasingly likely, the crew of the *Cairo III* began to prepare for it. Joel scribbled the last entry in his letter to his wife—something he had shown only to

Pastor, thinking the others would find it overly sentimental—and Pastor carved a loving message to his family on a plank, weeping as he did so. The five men carefully put on their best clothes, the ones they had been saving for their rescue, which now seemed a futile hope. Then they lay down, closed their eyes, and readied themselves for the end.

After a while, a light rain began to sprinkle their faces. Their hopes reborn, the men became nearly hysterical with joy, licking moisture from the surface of the awning roof. "We were afraid it would stop," says Joel, "but our prayers were answered, and it started to rain hard. At that point we were all crying."

Ten days later, on the afternoon of June 15, a crewman on the bridge of the *Kinei Maru*, a Japanese fishing vessel, spotted the bobbing, sea-stained white hull of the *Cairo III.*

Joel saw the ship first: "I'd just caught a shark when I looked up and saw it," he says. "I remember saying, 'Hey, a boat! A boat!' and screaming to them to wave to it. We were all leaping with joy. I cut loose the shark, and I remember thinking, 'Thank you, God, thank you, thank you.' Tears came to my eyes; I realized I wasn't going to die."

At home in Costa Rica, Edith was the first of the wives to receive the news from the boat's owner, Carlos Rohman, of their rescue. When she heard the words "alive" and "saved," she dropped the telephone receiver and collapsed on the sofa.

The five survivors, who regretted leaving their boat behind—probably to sink in a matter of hours—were taken by the Japanese to Honolulu, where U.S. Army physician Dr. Fred Thaler examined them, proclaiming the Costa Ricans surprisingly fit.

Words to Know and Use | **stupor** (stoo′ pər) *n.* a condition in which the mind and senses are dulled

The rescued crew of the *Cairo III* pose on the beach in Puntarenas, Costa Rica. From left to right. Top row: Gerardo Obregón, Joel Gonzáles; Bottom row: Jorge Hernández, Juan Bolívar, Pastor López. © Peter Serling, New York.

"There were no obvious signs of scurvy,[9] nor did they seem terribly emaciated[10]," says Thaler. "For what they had been through, they were in superb shape."

After a flight back to their country by way of Los Angeles, the men were given a hero's welcome home, especially in the port of Puntarenas. There, after sharing tears and hugs with their families, hundreds of cheering fishermen and other townsfolk paraded them through the streets.

Joel and Edith clung to each other, in the grip of emotions they hardly dared to voice. Edith's eyes followed Joel wherever he went, as if she were afraid he might disappear again. Some days later he showed her the note from the bottle. She sat down and read it, crying softly, and telling him finally, "You touch my heart with your words."

Today, two days after the tumultuous homecoming, Joel sits on the deck of *Cairo III*'s sister boat, the *Cairo V*. He's just finished eating his third ham and cheese sandwich of the morning (like the other survivors, he eats often now, throughout the day). Fingering the bottle and the note to Edith, which is deeply creased from many foldings and unfoldings, he says he hasn't returned to work yet but he will. He likes how it feels to be on a boat again. He has decided to keep the bottle as a memento of the voyage that nearly cost him his life—but also as a symbol of what the experience taught him. "During those days," he says, "I realized how much I love my wife and children. And now I want to show them that without the family, there is no reason to live." ❧

9. **scurvy** (skʉr′ vē): a disease caused by a deficiency of vitamin C in the body and characterized by weakness, anemia, spongy gums, and nosebleeds.

10. **emaciated** (ē mā′ shē āt′ əd): abnormally lean or underweight, as by starvation.

Responding to Reading

First Impressions

1. If you had been with the men on the *Cairo III,* what would have been the worst part of the trip for you? Explain your choice.

Second Thoughts

2. Why do you think the men of the *Cairo III* survived their ordeal?

3. What additions can you make to the list of dangers you predicted the men would face? Which were the most serious? Why?

4. What did each man contribute to the survival of the group? Did anyone emerge as a leader? Why or why not?

5. What part did family members play in the men's survival? Consider the families' psychological influences as well as their actions.

Broader Connections

6. The crew of the *Cairo III* had no idea of the ordeal they would face. However, many Vietnamese and Cubans knowingly chance dangerous voyages to escape their homelands. How willing would you be to escape in a small boat on the ocean? How does this article affect your view of boat people?

Literary Concepts: Author's Purpose and Conflict

You know that writers write for a variety of **purposes,** including entertainment, information, persuasion, or sharing an opinion. What are the purposes of this article? How do those purposes affect the way the facts are presented? Use your notes about the first seven paragraphs to answer these questions:

- What purpose do the excerpts from Joel's letter to his wife serve?
- Why do you think Arias chose to present events out of sequence?
- How did the many forms—letters, narrative writing, interviews, dialogue—affect your understanding of and interest in the article?

Most **conflicts** can be classified in one of three ways: (1) a conflict between a person and nature; (2) a conflict between two people or between a person and society; or (3) a conflict within a person. What conflicts do the men face in this account?

Writing Options

1. Imagine that you are Edith. Write a letter to Joel, telling him of your thoughts, dreams, and efforts to find him.

2. The captain keeps a daily log of the speed and progress of the ship and of any important events that occur. Write Captain Gerardo Obregón's log entries for two or three days of the trip. Use the map on page 243 and facts from the article as the basis for your entries.

3. Write a headline for the *Puntarenas Daily News* announcing the rescue of the crew of the *Cairo III*. Describe or sketch a photograph, chart, or map to put below the headline.

4. If you could invite one of the members of the *Cairo III* crew to accompany you on a fishing expedition, which one would you choose? Give the reasons for your choice.

Vocabulary Practice

Exercise On your paper, write the word from the list that best completes each sentence.

1. Joel and his family lived in a _____ near Puntarenas.
2. Although Joel's family was economically _____, they were rich in other ways.
3. While _____ the *Cairo III* through the storm, Joel must have wondered if he would survive.
4. Finally the weather improved and the waves began to _____.
5. The captain slept in a small but safe _____ under the bow.
6. The captain's _____ and considerate nature cheered the men.
7. Pastor's job was to tend the fire in the _____ stove.
8. The crew felt _____, or depressed, when a second ship passed them by.
9. The starving men were _____ for food of any kind.
10. _____ of food and water became the greatest threat to the survival of the crew.
11. Weak from starvation and thirst, the men fell into a _____, in which they felt dazed and lazy.
12. Wishing for rain became an _____ with the thirsty men.
13. When Juan, who was usually _____ and calm, asked for medical assistance, the men finally realized he was truly in pain.
14. Jorge almost had a _____ finger due to a shark.
15. The crew hit a _____ low and lay down in the boat, ready to die.

Words to Know and Use

abate
affable
barrio
cylindrical
deprivation
despondent
impoverished
maneuvering
niche
obsession
psychological
ravenous
severed
stoic
stupor

e x t e n d

Options for Learning

1 • **Pack a Survival Kit** Assume that you are facing a dangerous ocean voyage. Other than clothing and a two-week supply of food, you are only allowed to pack fifteen items in your survival kit. What will you take? Number your items in order of importance.

2 • **How to Survive** Create a humorous or serious pamphlet on how to survive a shipwreck, using information from this article and other sources. Use a variety of lettering styles and include graphic aids, such as cartoons, photographs, and diagrams.

3 • **Before and After** Construct a model of the *Cairo III* with removable pieces so that you can show what the boat looked like by the end of the voyage. Or draw a detailed illustration of the boat both before and after the voyage. Use descriptions in the article as your source of information.

4 • **Sketch a Storyboard** A storyboard is a series of sketches that shows the sequence of scenes or camera shots that will make up a film. Filmmakers use storyboards to plan what the sets will look like, where the actors will stand, what action will take place, and so on. Create a storyboard of at least five scenes that shows how you would film this story. Have your class decide whether your film would have box office appeal.

 **FACT FINDER**

If it traveled 4,000 miles total, how many miles did the Cairo III *average daily?*

Ron Arias
1941–

Ron Arias first met the crew of the *Cairo III* when he interviewed them in Los Angeles on their return home to Costa Rica. "None of them spoke English, so when I walked in and introduced myself in Spanish, it was as if they were welcoming a brother." Arias believes that his close ties to his Latin heritage helped him understand the fishermen and their point of view. He later expanded the account of their adventure into a book, *Five Against the Sea.*

Arias began writing at the age of nine, when he was hospitalized with tonsillitis. Although he has a master's degree in journalism, he feels that his true education—at least where writing is concerned—came from travel, work, and the books he has read.

Arias, who enjoys the adventure in changing places and jobs, has been a newspaper reporter, a Peace Corps volunteer, a teacher, and a senior writer for *People* magazine. He has written short stories, novels, screenplays, and many types of nonfiction.

Fiction

Giving Blood

ROBERTA SILMAN

*E*xamine What You Know

"Giving Blood" tells of a mother's efforts to find blood donors for her daughter, who has leukemia (loo kē′ mē ə). What do you know about the process of giving blood? For what reasons do people need blood donations? How do hospitals maintain a sufficient blood supply? Pool your knowledge about these questions with your class. As you read, note the new things you learn about giving blood.

*E*xpand Your Knowledge

The young girl in "Giving Blood" has leukemia, a cancer that causes abnormal growth of the white blood cells and reduces the body's ability to produce red blood cells. Leukemia is the most frequent cancer among children. In the past, leukemia was fatal to the great majority of its victims. Today, however, many more patients survive because of early treatment with drugs. Such treatment, known as chemotherapy, has advanced greatly since this story was written. Still, leukemia patients need frequent blood transfusions to replenish red blood cells and platelets, elements in the blood that allow it to clot to prevent the patient from bleeding to death.

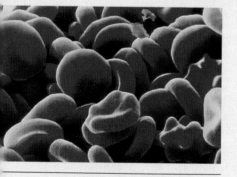

Blood cells
© CNRI/SPL/Photo
Researchers, Inc., New York

Donating blood takes about an hour. After making sure a donor is healthy enough to give blood, a nurse or technician inserts a needle into the donor's arm for seven to twelve minutes to extract a pint of blood. The rest of the hour the donor spends resting and sometimes eating a snack. In order to give, a potential donor must be at least seventeen years old and weigh no less than 110 pounds.

*W*rite Before You Read

Have you ever asked neighbors or friends to contribute money or buy something to support your athletic team, a school project, or a charity? How did your asking make you feel? In your journal or on a piece of paper, record your thoughts about participating in fund-raising and asking others for donations.

■ *A biography of the author can be found on page 265.*

Giving Blood

ROBERTA SILMAN

My little girl has leukemia; she has had it for over a year, and now she needs at least five pints of blood a day. Not the whole blood, just the platelets. Most of our relatives and friends have given at least a few times. But we need more. Now I have to go to strangers.

Alexander wanted to play with a new toy, but I was firm and dressed him and said, "Come on, Alexander, we're going for a walk. It's a beautiful day."

At the first house no one was home.

The next house was smaller, friendlier looking. Hyacinths[1] lined the front path. When she opened the door, she smiled. "I know you," she said. "You moved in about a year ago. I've seen you walking along the road with the children."

I nodded. "My daughter is in the hospital." She was still smiling. "She needs blood. I was wondering if you could give blood. She has leukemia."

"Oh, I'm so sorry." Her face was filled with pity. My hopes rose. "But I can't give blood now," she said and stepped backward, her fingers touching her throat. "My brother-in-law had surgery a few months ago and I gave for him."

"But you could give platelets," I persisted. "She needs just the platelets, and in an hour they can take them and return your blood to you. You rebuild the platelets."

"No. No. I told you, I just gave." Quickly she closed the door.

We passed a clump of Red Emperor tulips. Everyone makes such a fuss over them, I guess because of the color, but all I could see were splotches of blood. Blood in a garden, blood on the road being washed off by those powerful fire hoses, blood in the delivery room, covered with blood when they showed her to me. I was so surprised, I didn't think she'd look that messy. "Don't worry, dear, she's a beautiful baby; she just needs to be washed off and then you can hold her," the nurse said. Katharine we called her, thinking she would be Kate, but somehow it became Kathy.

Alexander started to cry. He had to go to the bathroom. I carried him to the door of the next house. She was still in her robe and her hair was disheveled.

"Can we use the bathroom?"

"Come in." We followed her down the hall.

"He was just trained."

"I remember those days," she said but didn't smile.

When we came out of the bathroom, she said, "Are you new here?"

"No, we moved in a year ago." I took a quick breath determined not to lose my chance. Her hand was on the doorknob.

---

1. **hyacinths** (hī′ə sinths′): plants of the lily family with bell-shaped flowers of white, yellow, red, blue, or purple.

"I didn't ring your bell just for Alexander. I was coming to ask if you could give blood. My little girl, Kathy, has leukemia." Her face didn't change.

"It takes only an hour."

Her eyes were vacant. Silence. Then, "I don't give for anyone but my family. It's a rule I made a long time ago." We were dismissed.

I look as though I'm collecting for charity. That turns them off, I guess. People don't give the way they used to. My mother never refused anyone; she kept a jug of change in the kitchen and always gave a little. Money is easy, though, you just put your hand into the jug. Blood, that's another thing.

Long ago, when we were first married, Matt and I discussed it. Someone we knew was having open-heart surgery. "Giving blood is a tremendously complicated matter for some people," he said then. "I once knew a man who said he could give it but never accept it. He was a Scot and afraid of getting Irish blood, or something like that." We had laughed.

Giving blood is a tremendously complicated matter for some people.

And now—sometimes I don't even feel real.

What do you want? their eyes say.

Blood.

What d'ya want, *blood?*

Yes! I want to yell. There's nothing wrong with asking for it. It's OK. Legitimate. Even good. You all have it. Everyone! Flowing through your bodies. It's almost blue until it hits the air. A red ocean in my dreams, but it's blue, like the sea. Salt in the sea. Salt in your blood. They say that's proof of evolution.

The next house was gray with a yellow door. Colors seem to jump out at me these days.

"Yes?" she said.

"We came because we need . . . ," I began.

"Come in, it's chilly." She smiled at Alexander. "How old is he?"

"Three."

"Our baby's a year. But she's down for a nap now." She pulled some toys from the bookcase. "What's your name?" She looked at Alexander.

"Alexander," he said.

"Here you go, Alexander." She handed him a Tonka truck.

"When did you move here?" she asked.

"A year ago; we're from the state of Washington."

"Oh, it's so lovely out there; why did you move?"

"We had to." I always try to sound casual but it never works. "Our little girl has leukemia and there's this marvelous doctor . . ." She couldn't say anything. She felt guilty—why me and not her, her eyes asked. I don't know.

"We need blood for her. She needs five pints a day and it's thirty dollars a pint, and what we don't get donated we have to pay for."

"Thirty dollars a pint?" She frowned. "What about the blood banks?"

"They don't have that quantity of blood. It's lasted so long."

"Of course I'll give. So will my husband.

Words to Know and Use | **legitimate** (lə jit′ ə mət) *adj.* legal; acceptable
evolution (ev′ ə lōō′ shən) *n.* the process of development, as from a simple to a complex form

And I'll call some of my friends. I'm sure they'll help," she said casually. I wasn't so sure, but let her try. When Matt asked people at the college, he thought everyone would help. Each night his face seemed grayer when he came home. He must have asked a hundred people. Thirty gave. His office mate said, "I'll do anything." When Matt asked him, he turned green and said, "Oh, no, anything but that. I'm scared of needles."

She gave me a hot cup of coffee; it was good. She said her name was Lois.

"Where do you go to give?" she said.

"To the city. The hospital has a donor room."

"I just learned to drive and I've never driven in New York. Could you . . ." She hesitated.

"Of course I'll take you. I have to go tomorrow to give platelets. I'll pick you up at ten. Eat some breakfast at eight."

"I could try to drive."

"No, it's OK. I do it every day. It's easier for me to take my car. They give us stickers, and there's a special parking lot for us."

I took Alexander's hand; she smiled as we left.

One. One out of three. It was only ten-thirty. For a second I thought of going home and pretending to be like everyone else—maybe I could finish the beds and do a wash and take down the bathroom curtain, which looks so gray. But then that tightening at the back of my neck. No. I still had time before the baby sitter came and I left for the hospital. Maybe I could get more.

Alexander's hand was suddenly heavy in mine. He started to shuffle.

"Let's sing, Alexander,"

Row, row, row your boat,
Gently down the stream,
Merrily, merrily, merrily, merrily,
Life is but a dream.

"No," he protested. "Kathy's way."
"Which way?"
"Kathy's way. Putt. Putt."
"Oh." I smiled, then we sang,

Row, row, row your boat,
Gently down the stream,
Putt, putt, putt, putt,
I'm a submarine.

"I want Kathy," he said. It was six weeks since he had seen her. He went into her bedroom every morning to see if she had come home. I picked him up, and he held on to me very tightly all the way home.

The waiting room was empty. The irises had <u>shriveled</u>.

"I'll be right back," I said to Lois. They looked even worse in the wastebasket than in the vase. I went back and put them into the basket flowers down, hearing my grandmother's voice. "I won't have them in the garden; I can't stand to watch them die."

The nurse came into the waiting room.

"Hi, Miss O'Neill. This is Lois Slater; she's come to give blood for Kathy." Miss O'Neill smiled.

"Have you seen her yet?" she asked. I shook my head.

"Oh, she looks beautiful, sitting up, pleased as punch and fresh as a daisy today. Someone sent her a set of homemade dolls."

"We'll see her later." I went ahead of Lois because giving platelets takes longer. She

---

Words to Know and Use | **shrivel** (shriv′ əl) *v.* to wither; waste

257

looked a little frightened. She couldn't get another soul besides her husband to give blood; they all said they couldn't give for someone they didn't know. One woman told her she'd be lucky to get out of here alive.

The Markeseys were in the donor room. They give platelets together; they say it gives them a chance to talk, but it's too much for Matt and me. We tried it once; I couldn't watch him watch Kathy. Then she was well enough to come down and visit with us.

The Markeseys' boy Chris is still up, but from his color, well, who can tell, maybe he'll be lucky.

"How are you?" They were glad to see me. "Did you drive in?" They live near the hospital.

"Yes. It was a little windy along the river, but the forsythia[2] is gorgeous."

"How's Alexander?" Chris is always interested in Alexander.

"Oh, he's fine. All trained and knows how to sing 'Row, row, row your boat.'" Chris grinned. Lois came in.

"Chris, this is Mrs. Slater—she's a friend of mine—and Marjorie and Tom Markesey, Lois Slater." Lois lay down and watched Chris help the other nurse tie up the packets of blood from his parents. The kids are amazing, so casual. Then Chris took the blood up to the lab. In a few minutes he was back.

"Don't know if I should let you in, Chris, after you cut me to the quick the other day." Miss O'Neill winked at Lois and me. "He doesn't like redheads any more; he prefers blondes."

"Blondes have more fun, Maggie."

"Traitor!"

A voice from the door boomed: "Well, well, if it isn't Christopher Columbus Markesey." It was Teddy. Brisk, matter-of-fact Teddy. It was always good to see him. He lay on the remaining table and beckoned

Chris to him. Teddy usually says he doesn't care who gets his blood, but last week I heard him tell one of the nurses he'd like Chris to have it for a while.

"Is he—does he have a child?" Lois hesitated.

"Oh, no, Teddy's a construction worker on the job nearby. He comes every few days to give platelets," Miss O'Neill explained.

"Are there any others like Teddy?" Lois was amazed.

"Oh, about five, a group of friends—all young and in construction. They say they've no money but lots of blood. They're all so happy-go-lucky; wonderful to have them around." Miss O'Neill held the orange juice for Lois. Lois looked at me and shook her head.

"Better stay there awhile, my girl," Miss O'Neill cautioned her, then turned to me. "She has very low blood pressure, but since you're driving, I let her give. We need whatever we can get, God knows," she said softly. I smiled gratefully and closed my eyes.

It's weird that the only rest I get these days is in this room, on a hard table, giving blood for my child. When I'm here I feel fine; it's where I should be. At home, sleep never comes easily. Matt and I lie next to each other, pretending, yet Miss O'Neill told me that he fell asleep the other day with the needle in his arm.

"I'll go into the waiting room now, Anne," Lois said. I opened my eyes.

"I shouldn't be too long; they've already taken the blood up to the lab," I told her. I could have gone with her, but it was more comfortable to be with the Markeseys and Teddy.

"Now don't forget to concentrate on the math," Mr. Markesey said to Chris as they

---

2. **forsythia** (fôr si*th*′ ē ə): a shrub whose yellow star-shaped flowers appear in the early spring.

NANCY 1981 Alice Neel Robert Miller Gallery, New York.

were leaving. Marjorie Markesey straightened Chris's sailor hat before she kissed him. All the kids are so sensitive about the hats and wigs under them. Having their hair fall out because of the drugs is the worst part of it for some of them. Now that she's in bed almost all the time, Kathy doesn't bother with her hat, but she wears her wig when she isn't sleeping.

" 'Bye now, we'll see you," the Markeseys said. I waved. Chris saw them out, then asked Teddy, "Now what color?" He was coloring a large poster that was hanging on the far wall. He held up the magic markers.

"Orange."

"Great, Teddy, an orange alligator!"

I was finished. In exactly an hour. So what I tell people is true, but so few ever come back once they've given whole blood just to give the platelets. No time, they say.

Sometimes all I can see in my dreams is a huge pot, an ocean really, but contained in a pot—the stockpot of humanity—and the nurses and lab assistants dipping into it. No individuals, no asking, no packets. Just everyone's blood for anyone who needs it.

As we walked out of the waiting room, I took Lois's arm. "Come on, I want you to meet Kathy. She's beautiful."

I could see that she didn't believe me, but when we stopped at the foot of Kathy's bed I saw that she understood. Kathy's wig is a poor imitation of her thick brown hair, but even in her wig she's lovely. Good bones, deep green eyes, such an intelligent expression. She was wearing new pajamas, purple, her favorite color. When she looked up, her face was flushed.

"Look, Mommy, Jill sent them; aren't they great?" I bent to kiss her; she had a temperature, hard to tell how much.

"Yes they are, darling, and look at all the clothes." I turned to Lois. "Her best friend from Seattle. She sends something every few weeks; they're a wonderful family."

"Honey, this is Lois Slater; she lives up the road. She came to give blood."

"Oh, thank you. Do you have any children?"

"Yes, two boys and a girl. My younger boy is your age."

"Who does he have?" Kathy was so eager for any information about school. She had gone for a few months in the fall, but only for a couple of hours a day.

"Mrs. Blackfield."

"Oh, I got Miss Owens." Then her eyes brightened. "What's your son's name?"

"Peter."

"Could you ask Peter to tell Miss Owens I said hello?"

"Of course, Kathy, I'll be happy to."

"Grandma send the pajamas?" I poured some water into a glass and held it out for her to drink.

"Um hm." She put the glass down and began to dress one of the dolls. Her schoolwork was piled at the foot of the bed. Each Friday I picked it up from school, and the volunteers in the hospital corrected it. "Excellent," "excellent," "very good," a smile face, the usual.

"It looks like you had a good morning."

"Yes," she said absently. Then she remembered something. She pulled a large piece of construction paper out of her night table. On it she had written, first in capital letters, then in lower-case, the word "quack." Underneath it said, "Quack begins with *Q*. Mother ducks teach their babies how to quack. That is how ducks speak. Mother ducks take good care of their babies." Below that was a drawing of a large white mother duck and, trailing behind her, four small gray ducklings.

LOBBY OF THE
UNIVERSITY
HOSPITAL   May H. Lesser
From *An Artist in the
University Medical Center,*
Tulane University Press,
New Orleans, Louisiana.

"That's great, Kathy." Lois handed me the drawing. Kathy had started this project the day after she went to the hospital. She was now on her second trip through the alphabet. Almost six weeks of drawings cover the walls in Alexander's room. The first *Q* says: "*Q* is for quiet. In the hospital it is too quiet at night." The drawing shows several kids asleep in identical beds. Now Kathy is more used to the hospital, and there are times when I know it is a relief for her to be here. If only she could see Alexander.

"Alexander will love it, darling. I can't wait to show it to him." But she was back to her dolls. We went out to the hall. Lois looked at the children's artwork; I talked to the nurse.

"Yes, a little bit of fever, nothing serious, a good night; today seems to be another good day."

I went back to kiss Kathy goodbye, just to feel her, to see her eyes bright, to know that blood was still moving through her. It was so discouraging at night not to be able to go in and check her, watch her sleep. It's such a unique pleasure—watching your child sleep. Okay, Anne, enough of that, I told myself. Lois looked tired; she had had it.

"Goodbye, puss. See you tomorrow." We waved.

No traffic, and the sun was strong; the warmer weather was coming. Now the river was calm, the wind had subsided, and everything sparkled. Except Lois. She was very pale.

"Are you all right?"

"Fine, just a little tired," she whispered. Then she leaned forward and put her head between her knees. I pulled over and grabbed a pillow from the back seat. After a few minutes she lay back on the pillow. Her hairline was ringed with sweat.

I handed her a Life Saver. "Here, this will help. You didn't tell me about your low blood pressure."

"I didn't realize it would matter, but I'll be all right. You know, Anne, I didn't believe you at first, but what an unusual child Kathy is! How pretty and bright . . ." Her voice trailed.

"I know. I have to admit it even if I am her mother. But all those kids are special. Some creepy doctor is writing a paper on how high the IQ's of children with leukemia are. He's convinced there's something in their blood; the same thing that gives them leukemia gives them a high intelligence. No one agrees with him, but he thinks he has something and keeps questioning the parents." Lois looked at me <u>incredulously</u>. We were silent.

After a while she murmured. "I'm glad I gave." Then she slept.

I'm glad I gave. I gave. I gave. I gave; stop bothering me. I gave. When? Once in your life? Twice? Did you know you could give blood every six months, and they say it's good for you, it's a cleansing mechanism for your body? I could feel my hands tightening on the wheel. But anger is no help. I tried to relax.

After we paid the toll on the Henry Hudson Bridge, Lois sighed. "Oh." Her voice was filled with disappointment.

"What's the matter?"

"I had the most wonderful dream, and it was so real. I guess it was really a fantasy. I was lying in the donor room and Chris took my blood up to the lab, and then there was a call, and we all went upstairs, and everyone took turns looking into a microscope. Then the doctor said, 'I think we've found it,' and the nurses touched my arm and I felt very happy . . ." She shrugged.

Tears filled her eyes. She wanted me to comfort her, but what could I say? Silently I pulled up to her house.

"Won't you come in, Anne? I'll make some coffee." Lois's eyes told me she wanted us to share the pain we both felt. How could I disappoint her? She, a stranger, who had given blood for my child. But it was too much to ask. My nerves were ragged; I was beginning to get angry.

"I'm sorry, Lois, I have to get home." I avoided her eyes, hating myself. As I pulled the car out of the driveway, I waved.

"Thanks."

"What?" She frowned.

"Thanks for giving blood," I called.

The next morning was another magnificent day. We were out at nine. The tight magnolia buds reminded me of hungry infants' fists. At the bottom of our driveway, some daffodils had bloomed in the night. Alexander pushed his new toy lawn mower as we walked down another road looking for blood. ❧

Words to Know and Use | **incredulously** (in krej′ o͞o ləs lē′) *adv.* in an unbelieving way; skeptically

explain

Responding to Reading

First Impressions

1. What is your attitude about giving blood after reading this story? Jot down your thoughts in your journal or on a piece of paper.

Second Thoughts

2. Why were people so reluctant to donate blood for Anne's daughter? Consider their stated as well as unstated reasons for refusing.

3. Anne and her husband must pay for blood that is not donated, and they have difficulty finding donors. What is Anne's reaction to this problem?

   Think about
   • how asking for blood makes her feel
   • her attitude toward people who donate blood and those who refuse
   • the thoughts you noted earlier about asking for help

4. Explain Anne's reactions and feelings toward Lois.

   Think about
   • when Lois is in the hospital
   • when Lois says, "I'm glad I gave"
   • when Lois tells Anne of her dream
   • why Anne refuses Lois's invitation for coffee

5. How and why does Kathy's attitude toward Lois differ from Anne's?

6. What is your opinion of Anne? Are there clues that Kathy's illness and the burden of asking for blood may have changed her? Explain.

Broader Connections

7. Hospitals need a plentiful supply of blood. What new methods do you think hospitals, governments, and individuals might use to ensure a constant supply?

Literary Concept: Tone

The **tone** of any piece of writing expresses the writer's attitude toward the subject. A writer communicates tone through his or her choice of words and details. The tone may be amusing, angry, bitter, hopeful, or objective, for example. Think about Silman's word choice and the incidents and details on which she focuses. How would you describe her tone in this story? How does the tone make you feel?

Concept Review: Author's Purpose You remember that an author may write for more than one purpose. What do you think is the main purpose of "Giving Blood"? Does Silman's tone help carry out her purpose?

Writing Options

1. A slogan is a short, peppy phrase or sentence written to persuade. Write two or three slogans that might inspire people to give blood.

2. What do you predict will happen in the relationship between Lois and the narrator? Do you think Lois will give blood again? Write your prediction about Lois.

3. Skim the story and list new facts you have learned about blood donation. Then list any questions you still have about giving blood.

4. Anne might have written letters explaining her need for blood donations. Write a letter that Anne could have sent to persuade her neighbors to give blood.

Vocabulary Practice

Exercise Write the letter of the situation that best shows the meaning of the boldfaced word.

1. **evolution**
   (a) Anne's daughter Kathy needs blood platelets.
   (b) Anne wonders whether we descended from sea animals, since our blood contains salt.
   (c) In the donor room, the Markeseys give blood together.

2. **incredulously**
   (a) Lois listens with serious doubts to the doctor's theory about leukemia.
   (b) Anne is not surprised when someone refuses to give blood.
   (c) One woman refuses because she has given blood recently.

3. **legitimate**
   (a) Matt knows a Scot who is afraid of getting Irish blood.
   (b) Some neighbors will not even talk about giving blood.
   (c) Anne insists that it is all right to ask for blood.

4. **shrivel**
   (a) Anne watches the flowers die in the waiting room.
   (b) Kathy beams as Anne and Lois enter her room.
   (c) Anne gives Kathy a pair of purple pajamas.

5. **unique**
   (a) Watching Kathy sleep is a joy unlike any other for Anne.
   (b) Alexander starts to cry and has to go to the bathroom.
   (c) Anne feels some people are annoyed by her pleas.

> *Words to Know and Use*
> ———
> **evolution**
> **incredulously**
> **legitimate**
> **shrivel**
> **unique**

Options for Learning

1 • **Become a Photojournalist** A magazine has asked you to photograph the story told in "Giving Blood." Ask other students to take the roles of the characters. Plan the situations you will need to photograph and locate appropriate settings and props. Take the photographs, develop them, and choose the ones that best tell this story. Write a caption for each picture and display the photos in your classroom.

2 • **Improvise an Apology** Put yourself in Anne's shoes. You have dropped Lois at her house and gone home. You wish you had been kinder to Lois after she gave blood for Kathy. Act out your apology to her. Ask another student to improvise Lois's response.

3 • **Paint a Bouquet** Silman mentions a number of different kinds of flowers in this story. Find out what some of these flowers look like and paint them.

4 • **Giving Blood** To educate other students about giving blood, make a poster, comic strip, filmstrip, or diagram that shows each step involved. Interview a Red Cross worker, a hospital worker, or someone who has given blood to get a complete description of the process. Find out about the special procedure used to donate platelets. Collect questions other students had after reading and ask them in your interview.

 FACT FINDER

How many pints of blood does the average person have in his or her body?

Roberta Silman
1934-

"Horrified"—that was Roberta Silman's reaction to the reluctance of people to give blood to a child dying of leukemia. Even though it was not her own child, Silman still "felt rage at people for not giving blood." Her anger and her sympathy led Silman to volunteer as a caller for blood donations, to donate her own blood, and to write "Giving Blood." A number of magazines turned down the story, saying it was "too depressing, too controversial." It was finally published in *Blood Relations*, an anthology of Silman's short stories. Silman often deals with such emotional issues in her writing. Her only children's book, *Somebody Else's Child*, tells the story of an adopted boy. Since one of her own children is adopted, Silman wrote from her own experience. In 1976 the book won an award from the Child Study Association.

Silman has also written stories for *The Atlantic*, *McCall's*, *The New Yorker*, and *Redbook*. Whenever she is asked for advice on writing, she responds, "The only way people learn to write is by reading really good writing."

Fiction

The *Gift* of *Cochise*

LOUIS L'AMOUR (lä moor')

*E*xamine What You Know

The setting for this story is the Old West in the late 1800's. What mental pictures does this time and place in American history give you? What do you know about the people who lived there? Jot down your ideas and where you learned what you know. As you read, see if your vision of the Old West matches that of Louis L'Amour.

*E*xpand Your Knowledge

One of the most famous figures from the Old West is Cochise (kō chēs'), a chief of the Chiricahua Apache (chir i kä' wə ə pach' ē) tribe. The Chiricahua Apaches were at peace with the white settlers in the Southwest through the 1850's. Then in 1861, Cochise was falsely accused of kidnapping a white settler's child and arrested. He escaped and led his tribe in a war against the settlers that lasted eleven years. This story takes place toward the end of this war, in 1871 and 1872. Famous for his bravery and skill in war strategies, Cochise was also known for courtesy and gentleness. Finally, he agreed to move his tribe to a reservation in southeastern Arizona, where he died in 1874. His warriors carried his body to the Dragoon Mountains of Arizona. The location of his burial place remains a secret to this day.

Although there were periods of peace between the Apaches and the settlers, the Apaches had a reputation for being the most warlike of all the North American Indians. Part of the Apaches' territory is shown on the map on page 268, which you can follow as you read.

*E*nrich Your Reading

A biography of the author can be found on page 283.

Reading a Long Short Story Although this story is longer than most, it is not difficult to read. Keep in mind that two separate stories are interwoven to form the plot. Because of this, the action sometimes switches abruptly from place to place. Also, the action moves forward and backward in time in order to give the characters' background. As you read, watch for intersections between the two stories.

The *Gift of Cochise*

LOUIS L'AMOUR

Tense, and white to the lips, Angie Lowe stood in the door of her cabin with a double-barreled shotgun in her hands. Beside the door was a Winchester '73,[1] and on the table inside the house were two Walker Colts.[2]

Facing the cabin were twelve Apaches on ragged calico ponies, and one of the Indians had lifted his hand palm outward. The Apache sitting on the white-splashed bay pony was Cochise.

Beside Angie were her seven-year-old son, Jimmy, and her five-year-old daughter, Jane.

Cochise sat on his pony in silence. His black, unreadable eyes studied the woman, the children, the cabin, and the small garden. He looked at the two ponies in the corral and the three cows. His eyes strayed to the small stack of hay cut from the meadow and to the few steers farther up the canyon.

Three times the warriors of Cochise had attacked this solitary cabin, and three times they had been turned back. In all, they had lost seven men, and three had been wounded. Four ponies had been killed. His braves reported that there was no man in the house, only a woman and two children, so Cochise had come to see for himself this woman who was so certain a shot with a rifle and who killed his fighting men.

These were some of the same fighting men who had outfought, outguessed, and outrun the finest American army on record, an army outnumbering the Apaches by a hundred to one. Yet a lone woman with two small children had fought them off, and the woman was scarcely more than a girl. And she was prepared to fight now. There was a glint of admiration in the old eyes that appraised her. The Apache was a fighting man, and he respected fighting blood.

"Where is your man?"

"He has gone to El Paso." Angie's voice was steady, but she was frightened as she had never been before. She recognized Cochise from descriptions, and she knew that if he decided to kill or capture her it would be done. Until now, the sporadic attacks she had fought off had been those of casual bands of warriors who raided her in passing.

1. **Winchester '73:** trademark for a type of repeating rifle.
2. **Walker Colts:** revolvers or handguns of a certain type.

| Words to Know and Use | **solitary** (säl′ ə ter′ ē) *adj.* **1** unfrequented; remote **2** single; alone
sporadic (spə rad′ ik) *adj.* occurring from time to time; occasional |

267

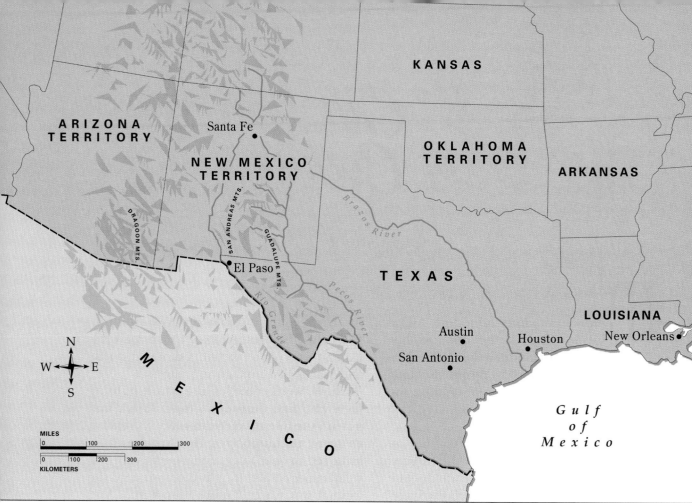

Map of the Southwest during the mid-1800's.

"He has been gone a long time. How long?"

Angie hesitated, but it was not in her to lie. "He has been gone four months."

Cochise considered that. No one but a fool would leave such a woman and such fine children. Only one thing could have prevented his return. "Your man is dead," he said.

Angie waited, her heart pounding with heavy, measured beats. She had guessed long ago that Ed had been killed, but the way Cochise spoke did not imply that Apaches had killed him, only that he must be dead or he would have returned.

"You fight well," Cochise said. "You have killed my young men."

"Your young men attacked me." She hes-

itated, then added, "They stole my horses."

"Your man is gone. Why do you not leave?"

Angie looked at him with surprise. "Leave? Why, this is my home. This land is mine. This spring is mine. I shall not leave."

"This was an Apache spring," Cochise reminded her reasonably.

"The Apache lives in the mountains," Angie replied. "He does not need this spring. I have two children, and I do need it."

"But when the Apache comes this way, where shall he drink? His throat is dry and you keep him from water."

The very fact that Cochise was willing to talk raised her hopes. There had been a time when the Apache made no war on the white man. "Cochise speaks with a forked tongue," she said. "There is water yonder." She gestured toward the hills, where Ed had told her there were springs. "But if the people of Cochise come in peace, they may drink at this spring."

The Apache leader smiled faintly. Such a woman would rear a nation of warriors. He nodded at Jimmy. "The small one—does he also shoot?"

"He does," Angie said proudly, "and well, too!" She pointed at an upthrust leaf of prickly pear. "Show them, Jimmy."

The prickly pear was an easy two hundred yards away, and the Winchester was long and heavy, but he lifted it eagerly and steadied it against the doorjamb[3] as his father had taught him, held his sight an instant, then fired. The bud on top of the prickly pear disintegrated.

There were grunts of appreciation from the dark-faced warriors. Cochise chuckled.

"The little warrior shoots well. It is well you have no man. You might raise an army of little warriors to fight my people."

"I have no wish to fight your people," Angie said quietly. "Your people have your ways, and I have mine. I live in peace when I am left in peace. I did not think," she added with dignity, "that the great Cochise made war on women!"

The Apache looked at her, then turned his pony away. "My people will trouble you no longer," he said. "You are the mother of a strong son."

"What about my two ponies?" she called after him. "Your young men took them from me."

Cochise did not turn or look back, and the little cavalcade of riders followed him away.

Angie stepped back into the cabin and closed the door. Then she sat down abruptly, her face white, the muscles in her legs trembling.

When morning came, she went cautiously to the spring for water. Her ponies were back in the corral. They had been returned during the night.

Slowly, the days drew on. Angie broke a small piece of the meadow and planted it. Alone, she cut hay in the meadow and built another stack. She saw Indians several times, but they did not bother her. One morning, when she opened her door, a quarter of antelope lay on the step, but no Indian was in sight. Several times, during the weeks that followed, she saw moccasin tracks near the spring.

Once, going out at daybreak, she saw an Indian girl dipping water from the spring. Angie called to her, and the girl turned quickly, facing her. Angie walked toward her, offering a bright red silk ribbon. Pleased at the gift, the Apache girl left.

And the following morning there was another quarter of antelope on her step—but she saw no Indian.

Ed Lowe had built the cabin in West Dog Canyon in the spring of 1871, but it was Angie who chose the spot, not Ed. In Santa Fe they would have told you that Ed Lowe was good-looking, shiftless, and agreeable. He was also, unfortunately, handy with a pistol.

Angie's father had come from County Mayo[4] to New York and from New York to the Mississippi, where he became a tough,

---

3. **doorjamb:** a vertical piece of wood or other material that makes up the side of a doorway.

4. **County Mayo:** a county in the northwestern part of Ireland.

269

THE PRAIRIE IS MY GARDEN   1950   Harvey Dunn   South Dakota
Art Museum Collection, Brookings.

brawling riverboatman. In New Orleans, he met a beautiful Cajun[5] girl and married her. Together, they started west for Santa Fe, and Angie was born en route. Both parents died of cholera[6] when Angie was fourteen. She lived with an Irish family for the following three years, then married Ed Lowe when she was seventeen.

Santa Fe was not good for Ed, and Angie kept after him until they started south. It was Apache country, but they kept on until they reached the old Spanish ruin in West Dog. Here there were grass, water, and shelter from the wind.

There was fuel, and there were pinyons and game.[7] And Angie, with an Irish eye for the land, saw that it would grow crops.

The house itself was built on the ruins of the old Spanish building, using the thick walls and the floor. The location had been admirably chosen for defense. The house was built in a corner of the cliff, under the sheltering overhang, so that approach was possible from only two directions, both covered by an easy field of fire from the door and windows.

For seven months, Ed worked hard and steadily. He put in the first crop, built the house, and proved himself a handy man

---

5. **Cajun:** a native of Louisiana originally descended from Acadian French immigrants.

6. **cholera** (käl′ ər ə): an intestinal disease.

7. **pinyons** (pēn yänz) **and game:** *pinyons* are small pine trees with large, edible seeds, and *game* refers to wild birds or animals that are hunted for sport or used as food.

with tools. He repaired the old plow they had bought, cleaned out the spring, and paved and walled it with slabs of stone. If he was lonely for the carefree companions of Santa Fe, he gave no indication of it. Provisions were low, and when he finally started off to the south, Angie watched him go with an ache in her heart.

She did not know whether she loved Ed. The first flush of enthusiasm had passed, and Ed Lowe had proved something less than she had believed. But he had tried, she admitted. And it had not been easy for him. He was an <u>amiable</u> soul, given to whittling and idle talk, all of which he missed in the loneliness of the Apache country. And when he rode away, she had no idea whether she would ever see him again. She never did.

Santa Fe was far and away to the north, but the growing village of El Paso was less than a hundred miles to the west, and it was there Ed Lowe rode for supplies and seed.

He had several drinks—his first in months—in one of the saloons. As the liquor warmed his stomach, Ed Lowe looked around agreeably. For a moment, his eyes clouded with worry as he thought of his wife and children back in Apache country, but it was not in Ed Lowe to worry for long. He had another drink and leaned on the bar, talking to the bartender. All Ed had ever asked of life was enough to eat, a horse to ride, an occasional drink, and companions to talk with. Not that he had anything important to say. He just liked to talk.

Suddenly a chair grated on the floor, and Ed turned. A lean, powerful man with a shock of uncut black hair and a torn, weather-faded shirt stood at bay.[8] Facing him across the table were three hard-faced young men, obviously brothers.

Ches Lane did not notice Ed Lowe watching from the bar. He had eyes only for the men facing him. "You done that deliberate!" The statement was a challenge.

The broad-chested man on the left grinned through broken teeth. "That's right, Ches. I done it deliberate. You killed Dan Tolliver on the Brazos."[9]

"He made the quarrel." Comprehension came to Ches. He was boxed, and by three of the fighting, blood-hungry Tollivers.

"Don't make no difference," the broad-chested Tolliver said. " 'Who sheds a Tolliver's blood, by a Tolliver's hand must die!' "

Ed Lowe moved suddenly from the bar. "Three to one is long odds," he said, his voice low and friendly. "If the gent in the corner is willin', I'll side him."

Two Tollivers turned toward him. Ed Lowe was smiling easily, his hand hovering near his gun. "You stay out of this!" one of the brothers said harshly.

"I'm in," Ed replied. "Why don't you boys light a shuck?"

"No, by—!" The man's hand dropped for his gun, and the room thundered with sound.

Ed was smiling easily, unworried as always. His gun flashed up. He felt it leap in his hand, saw the nearest Tolliver smashed back, and he shot him again as he dropped. He had only time to see Ches Lane with two guns out and another Tolliver down, when something struck him through the stomach

---

8. **at bay:** cornered; with ways of escape cut off.
9. **Brazos** (braz′ əs): a river in central and southeastern Texas that flows into the Gulf of Mexico.

and he stepped back against the bar, suddenly sick.

The sound stopped, and the room was quiet, and there was the <u>acrid</u> smell of powder smoke. Three Tollivers were down and dead, and Ed Lowe was dying. Ches Lane crossed to him.

"We got 'em," Ed said, "we sure did. But they got me."

Suddenly his face changed. "Oh Lord in heaven, what'll Angie do?" And then he crumpled over on the floor and lay still, the blood staining his shirt and mingling with the sawdust.

Stiff-faced, Ches looked up. "Who was Angie?" he asked.

"His wife," the bartender told him. "She's up northeast somewhere, in Apache country. He was tellin' me about her. Two kids, too."

Ches Lane stared down at the crumpled, used-up body of Ed Lowe. The man had saved his life.

One he could have beaten; two he might have beaten; three would have killed him. Ed Lowe, stepping in when he did, had saved the life of Ches Lane.

"He didn't say where?"

"No."

Ches Lane shoved his hat back on his head. "What's northeast of here?"

The bartender rested his hands on the bar. "Cochise," he said. . . .

For more than three months, whenever he could rustle the grub, Ches Lane quartered the country over and back. The trouble was, he had no lead to the location of Ed Lowe's homestead. An examination of Ed's horse revealed nothing. Lowe had bought seed and ammunition. The seed indicated a good water supply, and the ammunition implied trouble. But in the country there was always trouble.

A man had died to save his life, and Ches Lane had a deep sense of obligation. Somewhere that wife waited, if she was still alive, and it was up to him to find her and look out for her. He rode northeast, cutting for sign, but found none. Sandstorms had wiped out any hope of back-trailing Lowe. Actually, West Dog Canyon was more east than north, but this he had no way of knowing.

North he went, skirting the rugged San Andreas Mountains. Heat baked him hot; dry winds parched his skin. His hair grew dry and stiff and alkali-whitened. He rode north, and soon the Apaches knew of him. He fought them at a lonely water hole, and he fought them on the run. They killed his horse, and he switched his saddle to the spare and rode on. They cornered him in the rocks, and he killed two of them and escaped by night.

They trailed him through the White Sands, and he left two more for dead. He fought fiercely and bitterly and would not be turned from his quest. He turned east through the lava beds and still more east to the Pecos. He saw only two white men, and neither knew of a white woman.

The bearded man laughed harshly. "A woman alone? She wouldn't last a month! By now the Apaches got her, or she's dead. Don't be a fool! Leave this country before you die here."

Lean, wind-whipped, and savage, Ches Lane pushed on. The Mescaleros[10] cornered him in Rawhide Draw, and he fought them

---

10. **Mescaleros** (mesk′ə le′ rōs): an Apache people of Texas and New Mexico.

Words to Know and Use | **acrid** (ak′ rid) *adj.* sharp, stinging or irritating to taste or smell

to a standstill. Grimly, the Apaches clung to his trail.

The sheer determination of the man fascinated them. Bred and born in a rugged and lonely land, the Apaches knew the difficulties of survival; they knew how a man could live, how he must live. Even as they tried to kill this man, they loved him, for he was one of their own.

Lane's jeans grew ragged. Two bullet holes were added to the old black hat. The slicker was torn; the saddle, so carefully kept until now, was scratched by gravel and brush. At night he cleaned his guns, and by day he scouted the trails. Three times he found lonely ranch houses burned to the ground, the buzzard- and coyote-stripped bones of their owners lying nearby.

Once he found a covered wagon, its canvas flopping in the wind, a man lying sprawled on the seat with a pistol near his hand. He was dead and his wife was dead, and their canteens rattled like empty skulls.

Leaner every day, Ches Lane pushed on. He camped one night in a canyon near some white oaks. He heard a hoof click on stone, and he backed away from his tiny fire, gun in hand.

The riders were white men, and there were two of them. Joe Tompkins and Wiley Lynn were headed west, and Ches Lane could have guessed why. They were men he had known before, and he told them what he was doing.

Lynn chuckled. He was a thin-faced man with lank yellow hair and dirty fingers. "Seems a mighty strange way to get a woman. There's some as comes easier."

"This ain't for fun," Ches replied shortly. "I got to find her."

Tompkins stared at him. "Ches, you're crazy! That gent declared himself in of his own wish and desire. Far's that goes, the gal's dead. No woman could last this long in Apache country."

At daylight, the two men headed west, and Ches Lane turned south. . . .

The lonely rider who fought so desperately and knew the desert so well soon became a subject of gossip among the Apaches. Over the fires of many a rancheria they discussed this strange rider who seemed to be going nowhere but always riding, like a lean wolf dog on a trail. He rode across the mesas[11] and down the canyons; he studied signs at every water hole; he looked long from every ridge. It was obvious to the Indians that he searched for something—but what?

Cochise had come again to the cabin in West Dog Canyon. "Little warrior too small," he said, "too small for hunt. You join my people. Take Apache for man."

"No." Angie shook her head. "Apache ways are good for the Apache, and the white man's ways are good for white men—and women."

They rode away and said no more, but that night, as she had on many other nights after the children were asleep, Angie cried. She wept silently, her head pillowed on her arms. She was as pretty as ever, but her face was thin, showing the worry and struggle of the months gone by, the weeks and months without hope.

The crops were small but good. Little Jimmy worked beside her. At night, Angie sat alone on the steps and watched the shadows gather down the long canyon, listening to the coyotes yapping from the rim of the Guadalupes,[12] hearing the horses blowing in

---

11. **mesas** (mā′ səs): small, high plateaus with steep sides, found especially in the southwestern United States.

12. **Guadalupes** (gwäd′ə lōō′ pās): a mountain range in Texas and New Mexico.

the corral. She watched, still hopeful, but now she knew that Cochise was right: Ed would not return.

But even if she had been ready to give up this, the first home she had known, there could be no escape. Here she was protected by Cochise. Other Apaches from other tribes would not so willingly grant her peace.

At daylight she was up. The morning air was bright and balmy, but soon it would be hot again. Jimmy went to the spring for water, and when breakfast was over, the children played while Angie sat in the shade

APACHE MEDICINE SONG   1908   Frederic Remington   Sid Richardson Collection of Western Art, Fort Worth, Texas   Wharton photo.

of a huge, old cottonwood and sewed. It was a Sunday, warm and lovely. From time to time, she lifted her eyes to look down the canyon, half smiling at her own foolishness.

The hard-packed earth of the yard was swept clean of dust; the pans hanging on the kitchen wall were neat and shining. The children's hair had been clipped, and there was a small bouquet on the kitchen table.

After a while, Angie put aside her sewing and changed her dress. She did her hair carefully, and then, looking in her mirror, she reflected with sudden pain that she *was* pretty and that she was only a girl.

Resolutely, she turned from the mirror and, taking up her Bible, went back to the seat under the cottonwood. The children left their playing and came to her, for this was a Sunday ritual, their only one. Opening the Bible, she read slowly,

"Though I walk through the valley of the shadow of death, I will fear no evil; for thou art with me; thy rod and thy staff, they comfort me. Thou preparest a table before me in the presence of mine enemies: thou . . ."

"Mommy." Jimmy tugged at her sleeve. "Look!"

Ches Lane had reached a narrow canyon by midafternoon and decided to make camp. There was small possibility he would find another such spot, and he was dead tired, his muscles sodden with fatigue. The canyon was one of those unexpected gashes in the cap rock that gave no indication of its presence until you came right on it. After some searching, Ches found a route to the bottom and made camp under a wind-hollowed overhang. There was water, and there was a small patch of grass.

After his horse had a drink and a roll on the ground, it began cropping eagerly at the rich, green grass, and Ches built a smokeless fire of some ancient driftwood in the canyon bottom. It was his first hot meal in days, and when he had finished he put out his fire, rolled a smoke, and leaned back contentedly.

Before darkness settled, he climbed to the rim and looked over the country. The sun had gone down, and the shadows were growing long. After a half-hour of study, he decided there was no living thing within miles, except for the usual desert life. Returning to the bottom, he moved his horse to fresh grass, then rolled in his blanket. For the first time in a month, he slept without fear.

He woke up suddenly in the broad daylight. The horse was listening to something, his head up. Swiftly, Ches went to the horse and led it back under the overhang. Then he drew on his boots, rolled his blankets, and saddled the horse. Still he heard no sound.

Climbing the rim again, he studied the desert and found nothing. Returning to his horse, he mounted up and rode down the canyon toward the flatland beyond. Coming out of the canyon mouth, he rode right into the middle of a war party of more than twenty Apaches—invisible until suddenly they stood up behind rocks, their rifles leveled. And he didn't have a chance.

Swiftly, they bound his wrists to the saddle horn and tied his feet. Only then did he see the man who led the party. It was Cochise.

Words to Know and Use

resolutely (rez′ ə lo͞ot′ lē) *adv.* determinedly; unwaveringly
fatigue (fə tēg′) *n.* physical or mental exhaustion; weariness

275

He was a lean, wiry Indian of past fifty, his black hair streaked with gray, his features strong and clean-cut. He stared at Lane, and there was nothing in his face to reveal what he might be thinking.

Several of the younger warriors pushed forward, talking excitedly and waving their arms. Ches Lane understood some of it, but he sat straight in the saddle, his head up, waiting. Then Cochise spoke and the party turned, and, leading his horse, they rode away.

The miles grew long and the sun was hot. He was offered no water and he asked for none. The Indians ignored him. Once a young brave rode near and struck him viciously. Lane made no sound, gave no indication of pain. When they finally stopped, it was beside a huge anthill swarming with big red desert ants.

Roughly, they quickly untied him and jerked him from his horse. He dug in his heels and shouted at them in Spanish: "The Apaches are women! They tie me to the ants because they are afraid to fight me!"

An Indian struck him, and Ches glared at the man. If he must die, he would show them how it should be done. Yet he knew the unpredictable nature of the Indian, of his great respect for courage.

"Give me a knife, and I'll kill any of your warriors!"

They stared at him, and one powerfully built Apache angrily ordered them to get on with it. Cochise spoke, and the big warrior replied angrily.

Ches Lane nodded at the anthill. "Is this the death for a fighting man? I have fought your strong men and beaten them. I have left no trail for them to follow, and for months I have lived among you, and now

only by accident have you captured me. Give me a knife," he added grimly, "and I will fight *him!*" He indicated the big, black-faced Apache.

The warrior's cruel mouth hardened, and he struck Ches across the face.

The white man tasted blood and fury. "Woman!" Ches said. "Coyote! You are afraid!" Ches turned on Cochise, as the Indian stood irresolute. "Free my hands and let me fight!" he demanded. "If I win, let me go free."

Cochise said something to the big Indian. Instantly, there was stillness. Then an Apache sprang forward and, with a slash of his knife, freed Lane's hands. Shaking loose the thongs, Ches Lane chafed his wrists to bring back the circulation. An Indian threw a knife at his feet. It was his own bowie knife.

Ches took off his riding boots. In sock feet, his knife gripped low in his hand, its cutting edge up, he looked at the big warrior.

"I promise you nothing," Cochise said in Spanish, "but an honorable death."

The big warrior came at him on cat feet. Warily, Ches circled. He had not only to defeat this Apache but to escape. He permitted himself a side glance toward his horse. It stood alone. No Indian held it.

The Apache closed swiftly, thrusting wickedly with the knife. Ches, who had learned knife fighting in the bayou country of Louisiana, turned his hip sharply, and the blade slid past him. He struck swiftly, but the Apache's forward movement deflected the blade, and it failed to penetrate. However, as it swept up between the Indian's body and arm, it cut a deep gash in the warrior's left armpit.

Words to Know and Use | **irresolute** (ir rez′ ə l $\overline{oo}$ t′) *adj.* wavering in decision, purpose, or opinion; indecisive
deflect (dē flekt′) *v.* to turn to one side

MISSING 1899 Frederic Remington The Thomas Gilcrease Institute of American History and Art, Tulsa, Oklahoma.

The Indian sprang again, like a clawing cat, streaming blood. Ches moved aside, but a backhand sweep nicked him, and he felt the sharp bite of the blade. Turning, he paused on the balls of his feet.

He had had no water in hours. His lips were cracked. Yet he sweated now, and the salt of it stung his eyes. He stared into the malevolent[13] black eyes of the Apache, then moved to meet him. The Indian lunged, and Ches sidestepped like a boxer and spun on the ball of his foot.

The sudden side step threw the Indian past him, but Ches failed to drive the knife into the Apache's kidney when his foot rolled on a stone. The point left a thin red line across the Indian's back. The Indian was quick. Before Ches could recover his balance, he grasped the white man's knife wrist. Desperately, Ches grabbed for the Indian's knife hand and got the wrist, and they stood there straining, chest to chest.

Seeing his chance, Ches suddenly let his knees buckle, then brought up his knee and fell back, throwing the Apache over his head to the sand. Instantly, he whirled and was on his feet, standing over the Apache. The warrior had lost his knife, and he lay there, staring up, his eyes black with hatred.

---

13. **malevolent** (mə lev′ə lənt): malicious; wishing evil or harm to others.

Coolly, Ches stepped back, picked up the Indian's knife, and tossed it to him contemptuously. There was a grunt from the watching Indians, and then his antagonist rushed. But loss of blood had weakened the warrior, and Ches stepped in swiftly, struck the blade aside, then thrust the point of his blade hard against the Indian's belly.

Black eyes glared into his without yielding. A thrust, and the man would be disemboweled,[14] but Ches stepped back. "He is a strong man," Ches said in Spanish. "It is enough that I have won."

Deliberately, he walked to his horse and swung into the saddle. He looked around, and every rifle covered him.

So he had gained nothing. He had hoped that mercy might lead to mercy, that the Apache's respect for a fighting man would win his freedom. He had failed. Again they bound him to his horse, but they did not take his knife from him.

When they camped at last, he was given food and drink. He was bound again, and a blanket was thrown over him. At daylight they were again in the saddle. In Spanish he asked where they were taking him, but they gave no indication of hearing. When they stopped again, it was beside a pole corral, near a stone cabin.

When Jimmy spoke, Angie got quickly to her feet. She recognized Cochise with a start of relief, but she saw instantly that this was a war party. And then she saw the prisoner.

Their eyes met and she felt a distinct shock. He was a white man, a big, unshaven man who badly needed both a bath and a haircut, his clothes ragged and bloody. Cochise gestured at the prisoner.

"No take Apache man, you take white man. This man good for hunt, good for fight. He strong warrior. You take 'em."

Flushed and startled, Angie stared at the prisoner and caught a faint glint of humor in his dark eyes.

"Is this here the fate worse than death I hear tell of?" he inquired gently.

"Who are you?" she asked, and was immediately conscious that it was an extremely silly question.

The Apaches had drawn back and were watching curiously. She could do nothing for the present but accept the situation. Obviously they intended to do her a kindness, and it would not do to offend them. If they had not brought this man to her, he might have been killed.

"Name's Ches Lane, ma'am," he said. "Will you untie me? I'd feel a lot safer."

"Of course." Still flustered, she went to him and untied his hands. One Indian said something, and the others chuckled; then, with a whoop, they swung their horses and galloped off down the canyon.

Their departure left her suddenly helpless, the shadowy globe of her loneliness shattered by this utterly strange man standing before her, this big, bearded man brought to her out of the desert.

She smoothed her apron, suddenly pale as she realized what his delivery to her implied. What must he think of her? She turned away quickly.

"There's hot water," she said hastily, to prevent his speaking. "Dinner is almost ready."

She walked quickly into the house and stopped before the stove, her mind a blank.

---

14. **disemboweled** (dis′ im bou′ əld): having had the bowels, or entrails, removed.

She looked around her as if she had suddenly waked up in a strange place. She heard water being poured into the basin by the door and heard him take Ed's razor. She had never moved the box. To have moved it would—

"Sight of work done here, ma'am."

She hesitated, then turned with determination and stepped into the doorway. "Yes, Ed—"

"You're Angie Lowe."

Surprised, she turned toward him and recognized his own startled awareness of her. As he shaved, he told her about Ed and what had happened that day in the saloon.

"He—Ed was like that. He never considered consequences until it was too late."

"Lucky for me he didn't."

He was younger looking with his beard gone. There was a certain quiet dignity in his face. She went back inside and began putting plates on the table. She was conscious that he had moved to the door and was watching her.

"You don't have to stay," she said. "You owe me nothing. Whatever Ed did, he did because he was that kind of person. You aren't responsible."

He did not answer, and when she turned again to the stove, she glanced swiftly at him. He was looking across the valley.

There was a studied <u>deference</u> about him

when he moved to a place at the table. The children stared, wide-eyed and silent; it had been so long since a man had sat at this table.

Angie could not remember when she had felt like this. She was awkwardly conscious of her hands, which never seemed to be in the right place or doing the right things. She scarcely tasted her food, nor did the children.

Ches Lane had no such <u>inhibitions</u>. For the first time, he realized how hungry he was. After the half-cooked meat of lonely, trailside fires, this was tender and flavored. Hot biscuits, desert honey . . . Suddenly he looked up, embarrassed at his appetite.

"You were really hungry," she said.

"Man can't fix much, out on the trail."

Later, after he'd got his bedroll from his saddle and unrolled it on the hay in the barn, he walked back to the house and sat on the lowest step. The sun was gone, and they watched the cliffs stretch their red shadows across the valley. A quail called <u>plaintively</u>, a mellow sound of twilight.

"You needn't worry about Cochise," she said. "He'll soon be crossing into Mexico."

"I wasn't thinking about Cochise."

That left her with nothing to say, and she listened again to the quail and watched a lone bright star in the sky.

"A man could get to like it here," he said quietly. ❧

Words to Know and Use	**deference** (def' ər əns) *n.* a courteous regard or respect; honor **inhibition** (in' hi bish' ən) *n.* a holding back, especially of an emotion, thought, or action; a restraint **plaintively** (plān' tiv lē) *adv.* sorrowfully or sadly

The Other Pioneers

ROBERTO FÉLIX SALAZAR

Now I must write
Of those of mine who rode these plains
Long years before the Saxon and the Irish came.
Of those who plowed the land and built the towns
And gave the towns soft-woven Spanish names.
Of those who moved across the Rio Grande
Toward the hiss of Texas snake and Indian yell.
Of men who from the earth made thick-walled homes
And from the earth raised churches to their God.
And of the wives who bore them sons
And smiled with knowing joy.

They saw the Texas sun rise golden-red with promised wealth
And saw the Texas sun sink golden yet, with wealth unspent.
"Here," they said. "Here to live and here to love."
"Here is the land for our sons and the sons of our sons."
And they sang the songs of ancient Spain
And they made new songs to fit new needs.
They cleared the brush and planted the corn
And saw green stalks turn black from lack of rain.
They roamed the plains behind the herds
And stood the Indian's cruel attacks.
There was dust and there was sweat.
And there were tears and the women prayed.

And the years moved on.
Those who were first placed in graves
Beside the broad mesquite and the tall nopal.
Gentle mothers left their graces and their arts
And stalwart fathers pride and manly strength.
Salinas, de la Garza, Sánchez, García,
Uribe, González, Martinez, de León:
Such were the names of the fathers.
Salinas, de la Garza, Sánchez, García,
Uribe, González, Martinez, de León:
Such are the names of the sons.

BARILLEROS, SAN FELIPE 1870 Theodore Gentilz
Collection of Larry Sheerin, San Antonio, Texas.

Responding to Reading

First Impressions

1. Jot down what you liked (or disliked) about this story.

Second Thoughts

2. Who or what is the gift of Cochise? Is there more than one gift?

3. How would you describe Angie? Give reasons to support your views.

   Think about
   - her relationship with Cochise and the other Apaches
   - her relationship with Ed
   - her way of overcoming obstacles

4. Contrast Ed Lowe and Ches Lane. Describe each man's strengths and weaknesses. Support your opinions with specific details from the story.

5. The Apaches were famous as warriors. How does Cochise live up to this image? What other words would you use to describe him?

   Think about
   - his opinion of Angie and his treatment of her
   - his treatment of Ches
   - his reasons for bringing Ches to Angie

6. Which character do you find the most interesting? Who do you think faces the greatest test of endurance? Give reasons for your opinions.

Broader Connections

7. How might Apaches today react to the way their people are portrayed in this story? Does the story present a stereotype of Native Americans?

Literary Concepts: Historical Fiction and Flashback

A realistic story that takes place in an actual setting in the past is called **historical fiction**. References are made to actual people and events of that period, while the problems that the characters face are the same problems that real people faced at that time. Consider the setting, characters, and conflicts in "The Gift of Cochise." Why is this story classified as historical fiction?

A **flashback** interrupts the sequence of events to relate an earlier event. Identify one flashback in this story and tell what you learn from it.

Writing Options

1. Predict Angie's future. Remember to consider her past and her present situation when making your predictions.

2. A **stereotype** is a fixed idea of how a certain type of people act. Stereotypical characters act in a predictable way and show traits associated with that stereotype. Choose a character from this story and tell why you do or do not think he or she fits the stereotype of cowboys, women, or Indians presented in most Westerns.

3. Ches's physical appearance changes gradually throughout the story. Skim the selection to find at least three descriptions. Then explain how his physical changes reflect the events in the story.

4. Decide to whom the poem "The Other Pioneers" on page 280 refers. Compare and contrast the experiences of the pioneers in the poem and those of Angie. Present your comparison as a paragraph, a poem, or a series of phrases.

Vocabulary Practice

Exercise A   On your paper, write the letter of the word that is not related in meaning to the other words in the set.

1. (a) lonely (b) solitary (c) united (d) isolated
2. (a) disintegrate (b) crumble (c) separate (d) construct
3. (a) angry (b) sharp (c) stinging (d) acrid
4. (a) bend (b) turn (c) deflect (d) twist
5. (a) politely (b) pleasantly (c) plaintively (d) respectfully
6. (a) antagonist (b) partner (c) enemy (d) opponent
7. (a) fragment (b) fatigue (c) remnant (d) scrap
8. (a) deception (b) honor (c) deference (d) respect
9. (a) worried (b) uneasy (c) anxious (d) amiable
10. (a) shiftless (b) steady (c) immovable (d) solid

Exercise B   On your paper, write the vocabulary word that most closely matches the meaning of the boldfaced word or phrase in each sentence below.

1. **With determination,** Angie went outside to read her Bible.
2. The hungry Ches felt no **restraints** when eating Angie's dinner.
3. Ches smiled **disdainfully** at his opponent.
4. Cochise was **indecisive** about letting Ches fight the warrior.
5. Angie had to fight off **occasional** attacks by bands of Indians.

---

*Words
to Know
and Use*

**acrid
amiable
antagonist
contemptuously
deference
deflect
disintegrate
fatigue
inhibition
irresolute
plaintively
resolutely
shiftless
solitary
sporadic**

extend

Options for Learning

1 • Picture the Plot Create a time line, a flow chart, or some other graphic aid to illustrate the plot of the story. Diagram the action, and show visually at what point the plots intersect and finally join to finish the story. You can use words or drawings to indicate the events.

2 • Ecological Survey The story mentions plants and animals found in a Southwestern desert. Research the ecology of this region and report your findings to your class. You might include discussions of land structures, climate, and plant and animal life. Try to discover how Ches could have found driftwood in the desert canyon.

3 • Model Home Build a model of the Lowe homestead and the surrounding terrain. Include the cliff under which the cabin was built, the cabin, the corral, the field, and the spring. Explain the model to your classmates and point out why the homestead's location was good for defense.

 FACT FINDER

How many years after Angie and Ed left Santa Fe did New Mexico become a state?

Louis L'Amour
1908-1988

When fifteen-year-old Louis L'Amour left his hometown of Jamestown, North Dakota, few would have predicted that he would become an internationally famous writer. L'Amour wandered the world, working as a hay shocker, longshoreman, lumberjack, fruit picker, miner, and elephant handler. During his travels, especially in the American West, he often spent time listening to people tell true stories of the past, people such as former outlaws, gunfighters, old Indian scouts, or wagon masters.

Over the years, L'Amour wrote eighty-six novels, more than four hundred short stories, sixty-five television scripts, poetry, nonfiction, and film scripts. Many of his books, including *How the West Was Won* and *The Broken Gun*, have been made into movies. Although many of his works are classified as Westerns, he preferred to call them "stories of the frontier." A self-educated man, L'Amour carefully researched his novels and short stories, paying special attention to historical and geographical details. He also drew on his own experiences and adventures to make his writing more true to life. Because of this, it has been said that to read a book by Louis L'Amour is to be both entertained and educated.

WRITER'S WORKSHOP

SYNTHESIS

Most writing is a **synthesis,** or combination, of different types of writing. For example, while a narrative tells a story, it includes description to allow the reader to picture the characters, events, and setting. A description often includes narration to prevent it from becoming a list of details. Persuasion usually includes description, narration, or both. In this workshop, you will synthesize all three kinds of writing: description, narration, and persuasion.

You have probably seen several mini-series on television. Shorter than a regular series but longer than a movie, a mini-series typically includes three or more episodes shown over several nights. Your task for this assignment is to choose one of the longer selections in this subunit and propose a mini-series based on that selection. As an independent producer, you need to convince the network executives to accept your proposal. Your proposal will be a detailed plan consisting of four parts:

1. an introduction that tells the purpose of the proposal and "sells" it to network executives
2. a description of characters, including cast recommendations
3. a description of the setting, including locations for filming
4. a scene-by-scene plot summary of each episode

Here is your PASSkey to this assignment.

GUIDED ASSIGNMENT: PROPOSAL FOR A MINI-SERIES

Write a detailed proposal for a TV mini-series based on a selection from this subunit. Include a complete plan that will "sell" your idea to the network.

PURPOSE: To narrate, describe, and persuade

AUDIENCE: Television network executives

SUBJECT: Television mini-series

STRUCTURE: Formal proposal

Prewriting

STEP **1** **Choose the story**   Begin by reviewing "A Trip to the Edge of Survival," "Giving Blood," and "The Gift of Cochise." Choose the one that you think would make the most exciting mini-series.

STEP 2 **List characters and cast** List the characters in the selection. Jot down descriptive details for each character, including significant character traits. Think of an actor or actress who would be ideal for the role. You may wish to make a chart like this one, in which a student planned a mini-series based on *The Odyssey.*

Character	Description	Traits	Casting
Polyphemos, a Cyclops	huge giant with one red eye in center of forehead; very strong	fierce, greedy, not too smart	Arnold Schwarzenegger

◀ STUDENT MODEL

STEP 3 **Describe settings and filming locations** List the settings needed for each scene of the story. Briefly describe each. Think of locations to match that setting. Again, if you wish, use a chart:

Setting	Description	Film Location
Polyphemos' cave	large dark cave surrounded by rocks and boulders, containing huge fireplace	Hollywood set

◀ STUDENT MODEL

STEP 4 **Plot the action** Review the story you have chosen to determine the number and sequence of the scenes you will need. List them in order and briefly summarize each, as in the example below. Keep in mind that television writers have to find visual ways of communicating information that a short story or essay would simply explain. For this reason you may need to add scenes that are not in the original story. In "A Trip to the Edge . . .," for example, you might need to plan a scene involving the wives talking to the police.

Scene	Brief Summary
1	Odysseus and twelve men land on a small, mountainous island.
2	The men smell roasting meat and enter a cave trying to find it.

◀ STUDENT MODEL

STEP 5 **Divide the action** Using your list of scenes, decide how many episodes your mini-series will need and which scenes should be included in each episode. Because a successful mini-series must maintain its audience from beginning to end, conclude each episode with an exciting cliffhanger that will make your viewers want to tune in the following night to see what happens next.

STEP 6 **Sell the idea** Now that you have an overall plan for the mini-series, consider the introduction to your proposal. The introduction should briefly explain your idea and persuade network executives that your mini-series will be a hit. Convince them that the mini-series will be so successful that it is worth the cost of producing it. To do this, make a list of reasons that explain why your mini-series would appeal to a large television audience.

Drafting

Using the charts and lists you have devised, write a draft of your mini-series proposal. Use the outline headings "Introduction," "Descriptions of Characters and Settings," and "Plot Summaries" to separate the different parts of your plan.

STEP 1 **Persuade** Begin with the introduction. Capture the executives' interest in a short paragraph like this one:

Proposal for Odyssey Mini-Series

STUDENT MODEL ▶

Introduction
    Television viewers of all ages enjoy heroic adventures, and there is no greater hero than Odysseus. A mini-series based on his travels will excite and delight family viewers. Monsters like the Cyclops and Charybdis will fascinate children, while the romance between the alluring Circe and handsome Odysseus will provide interest for older viewers. Power struggles, treachery, and intrigue will make the classic story exciting viewing for the 90's. Add exotic locations, costumes, and special effects, and this mini-series will become a major television event.

STEP 2 **Describe** In the second section of your proposal, briefly describe the characters and settings. Devote a paragraph to each main character. You may combine descriptions of minor characters into one paragraph. Next, describe the settings and the film locations.

STEP 3 Narrate Summarize each episode of the mini-series in a separate paragraph. Use narration and description to make clear exactly what happens throughout the episode.

Revising and Editing

When you have completed your draft, ask a classmate to evaluate it according to the checklist below. Then revise your writing.

Revision Checklist

1. Does the introduction clearly state why the mini-series would appeal to television viewers?
2. Will the introduction excite prospective buyers? Is it persuasive?
3. Are the characters described thoroughly, including physical, emotional, and psychological traits?
4. Are the descriptions of locations accurate? Will the readers be able to visualize the settings from the descriptions?
5. Is the action divided into an appropriate number of episodes?
6. Does the proposal clearly narrate what will happen in each episode?
7. Does the ending of each episode entice viewers to watch the next episode?

Editing When you have finished revising your draft, proofread for spelling, clarity, and mechanics.

Presenting

Have some students act as a group of network executives. Present your plan to the group and try to convince them to produce your mini-series. If the group has reasonable concerns or objections to your plan, consider revising it to better meet their needs.

Reflecting on Your Writing

Briefly answer the following questions about your writing. Attach your answers to your paper before handing it in.

1. Which type of writing did you find easiest: persuasive, narrative, or descriptive?
2. In which type of writing do you think you have made the most improvement?
3. Were you able to organize the assignment to your satisfaction?

LANGUAGE
WORKSHOP

JOINING SENTENCES AND SENTENCE PARTS

I have an idea. My idea is for a TV mini-series. The series will be a Western. Most of it will be filmed in Montana. Some scenes will be done in a studio.

You would probably never write something that sounds as childish as the passage above. Still, if you look over your writing, you may find that it sometimes sounds choppy and even boring, because you have strung together too many short sentences. The solution is to combine some of these short related sentences into longer, smoother ones.

Joining Complete Sentences

One way to combine sentences is to join complete sentences with a **conjunction,** or connecting word, like those in the box below.

and	but	or	so	for	yet

REMINDER

When you combine sentences, the capital letter that begins the second sentence becomes a lowercase letter.

If the ideas in two sentences are similar, join them with a comma and the conjunction *and.*

> Joel watched the clouds gather. He feared the worst.
> Joel watched the clouds gather, **and** he feared the worst.

If two sentences express contrasting ideas of equal importance, you can join them with a comma and the conjunction *but.*

> Joel was exhausted. He was afraid to sleep.
> Joel was exhausted, **but** he was afraid to sleep.

Sometimes two sentences offer a choice between ideas of equal importance. Such sentences can generally be joined with a comma and the conjunction *or.*

> The storm could damage the cabin. It could even sink the boat.
> The storm could damage the cabin, **or** it could even sink the boat.

Sometimes writers want to join closely related ideas without interrupting the flow of their writing with a conjunction. In such cases, they might use a semicolon to connect the sentences. A **semicolon** is a powerful punctuation mark—strong enough to glue sentences together without a conjunction.

PUNCTUATION RULE

◄ Use a semicolon (;) to join two sentences when no conjunction is used.

The days seemed long; the nights seemed endless.

Exercise 1 Use the word in parentheses to combine each pair of sentences. Remember to use a comma before a conjunction.

1. The *Cairo III* set out for a simple, week-long fishing trip. Its five-month journey became a test of human endurance. (but)
2. When the crew set out, the Pacific Ocean was calm. It suddenly became wild and dangerous. (but)
3. The ocean swells swamped the deck. Winds destroyed the doors and windows of the cabin. (and)
4. The crew could try to survive day by day. They could give in to the cruelty of nature. (or)
5. Joel Gonzalez was desperate to survive. Each day, his will was tested anew. (but)

Joining Sentence Parts

Two sentences may express such closely related ideas that the sentences use many of the same words. Often you can combine these sentences by eliminating repeated or unnecessary words and then joining the remaining, important sentence parts with a conjunction. In such cases no comma is necessary.

To join similar sentence parts, use *and.*

Fishermen study wind patterns. *They also study* cloud formations.
Fisherman study wind patterns **and** cloud formations.

To join contrasting sentence parts, use *but.*

Fishing requires skill. *Fishing* also involves luck.
Fishing requires skill **but** also involves luck.

When the sentence parts present a choice, use *or.*

The crew could make a sail. *They could* continue to drift aimlessly hoping to be found.
The crew could make a sail **or** continue to drift aimlessly hoping to be found.

Look at the following examples. Notice the difference between joining complete sentences and joining sentence parts.

Joining Sentences   They could eat raw fish, or they could starve.

Joining Parts   They could eat raw fish or starve.

Exercise 2   Work separately or in groups to rewrite the following passage, using the combining techniques in this workshop. Compare your rewritten passage with those of your classmates.

> When my great-grandmother was a child, she traveled across the country. She traveled in a covered wagon. Her father bought land near the Mississippi River. Her father also built a log cabin for his family. He fished. He also trapped.
>
> Even though she was only five years old at the time, my great-grandmother remembers one winter vividly. Her father had stocked the barn with food and wood. He had forgotten to stock the cabin with wood. He kissed his family goodbye. He left for two months of trapping. Her mother, only twenty-three at the time, was alone with two children. The wind howled. The snow began to blow. For ten days they never saw daylight. Snow covered the windows. Snow buried their cabin. Her mother burned all the stove wood. She needed more. She could burn the dining room table. She could burn the beds. Fourteen days later, when they could finally open the cabin door and reach the barn, the baby's cradle was the only piece of furniture left in the cabin.

Exercise 3   Analyzing and Revising Your Writing

LANGUAGE HANDBOOK

For review and practice:
sentence combining,
    pages 898–900
commas,
    pages 966–67
semicolons,
    pages 969, 971
compound sentences,
    pages 950–52, 955

1. Take a paper from your writing portfolio and choose a passage to analyze.

2. Rewrite the passage, using the sentence-combining skills you have learned. Remember that not all sentences should be joined. Your goal should be a variety of sentence types.

3. Compare your revision to the original passage. Which one do you prefer?

4. The next time you revise your work, remember to check for related sentences that might be combined effectively.

STUDY SKILLS
WORKSHOP

SUMMARIZING

A **summary** is a short restatement or retelling of written or spoken material. Writing summaries is an excellent aid to remembering and understanding what you have learned. Summaries can be especially helpful for writing a research paper or studying for a test.

When you write a summary, you use your own words to restate the main points and important details of what you've read. Your completed summary should be no more than one-third as long as the original selection. The following guidelines will help you write summaries.

1. Skim the selection first. Try to understand its general meaning.
2. Reread the selection carefully. Note key words and phrases.
3. Jot down brief notes on the main ideas and the important details.
4. Keep the following points in mind as you write:
    a. Use your own words. Never copy the exact words of the original article.
    b. State the main idea of the entire selection in the first sentence.
    c. Include only important information such as names, places, dates, and other facts.
    d. Keep the information in the same order in which it appears in the original material.

Exercise   Summarize the following paragraphs.

Spanish explorers arrived in what is now Costa Rica in the early 1500's. The Indians who lived there told them stories about deposits of gold and other precious metals supposedly mined in the region. The Spaniards named the land *Costa Rica,* which means rich coast. But the explorers found the area had little mineral wealth.

Today, almost all Costa Ricans are of mixed Spanish and Indian ancestry. About three-fourths of the people live on a fertile plateau in the mountains of central Costa Rica. San Jose, the capital and largest city, lies in this region. Hillsides covered with coffee trees surround San Jose. Coffee ranks as the country's chief export. Bananas, another major export, grow on large plantations near the coasts.

—*The World Book Encyclopedia*

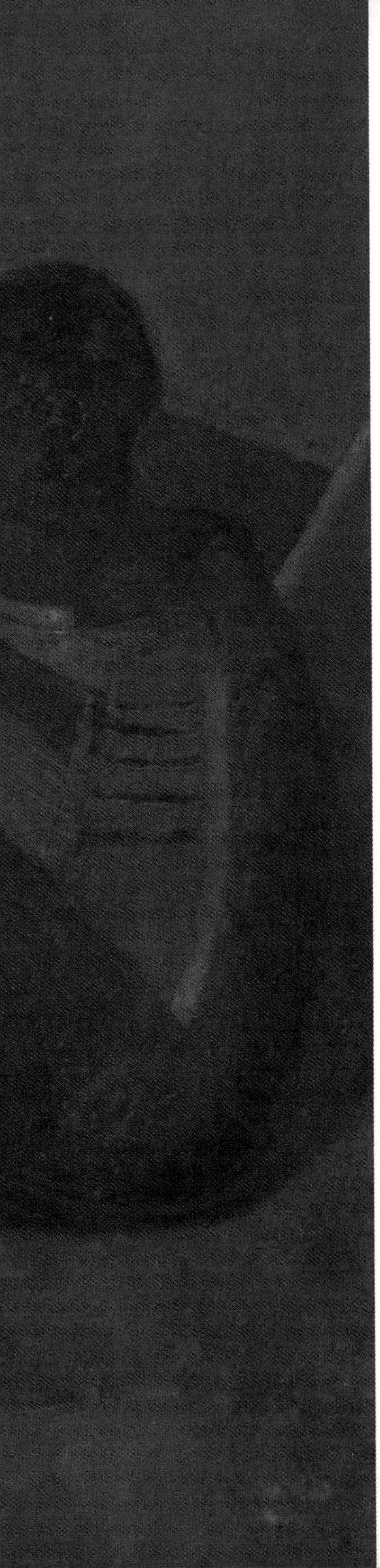

RELATIONSHIPS: PORTRAITS FROM LIFE

" *In a package of minutes*

there is this We.

How beautiful."

Gwendolyn Brooks

■ DIALOGUE 1974 Rufino Tamayo
B. Lewin Galleries,
Palm Springs, California.

Bittersweet Memories

Happy memories that are tinged with sadness or regret are called bittersweet memories. As with bittersweet candy, something about the memory prevents it from being totally satisfying. Since hu-

mans are imperfect, most relationships have flaws. As you read these portraits of relationships, determine what about each memory is sweet and what is bitter.

Fiction

Aunt Zurletha

RUBY DEE

Examine What You Know

Think about a special person from your past. What objects, sounds, or scents do you associate with that person? Read the story to find out what the narrator associates with Aunt Zurletha.

Expand Your Knowledge

This story is set in Harlem, an area in the northern part of New York City on the island of Manhattan. Like many city families in the earlier part of this century, the family in this story runs what is called a **boardinghouse.** In a boardinghouse, extra rooms in the family home are rented to outsiders who also share meals with the family. Because this arrangement is often less expensive than renting an apartment or a hotel room, boarders often stay with a family for many years.

Enrich Your Reading

Making Inferences   An **inference** is a logical guess or conclusion based on known facts or evidence. To make an inference when you read, combine facts the writer provides with what you know to be true from your experience. In this story, for example, Aunt Zurletha is described as "the only roomer that pays her rent in advance." From this statement, you might infer that she always has money and is responsible. As you read, look for statements that will help you make inferences about Aunt Zurletha's character. A chart like the one below might help you organize your thoughts.

Statement from Story	What I Know to Be True	Inference
only roomer to pay rent in advance	You need a good supply of cash to pay bills in advance	—has a steady income —is responsible

■ *A biography of the author can be found on page 303.*

Aunt Zurletha

RUBY DEE

Dedicated to the memories of Ida, Mrs. Adkins, Pearl, Kitty, Miss Kitts, Mrs. Hovington, Hazel, Yolene, and to all the women who work "sleep-in service" and whose day-to-day family is the people they work for.

Aunt Zurletha had pretty red hair, gray eyes, and blue-black skin. A circle of rouge was on each cheek. The shiny red lipstick on her full mouth matched the fingernail polish, which matched the toenail polish. Usually, she wore earrings that looked like diamonds that matched the three rings she always wore.

My brother William said she looked like a witch, which made me wonder when and where he had ever seen a witch. My other brother Curtis said she looked pathetic. "Pathetic" was his new word that year. Everything was "pathetic." My father Hosea said she looked like a hustler. Zurletha the Zero, he used to say. I thought she was pretty, especially when she smiled. Her teeth were even and so white.

Mama used to say, "You can just quit so much talk about Zurletha. She's the only roomer that pays her rent in advance."

I heard her say to Hosea one night, "Who could we turn to when we had that fire in the shop and folks suing you for their clothes and the insurance company practically blaming you for starting your own fire and all the fires in Harlem for the last ten years? Who in this world could we turn to? Tell me. We would have starved to death but for Zurletha. No, I will not let you put her out."

"Now hold on, Mat. Gratitude is a thing you have got to understand. I am grateful—grateful to God who made it possible for me not to go under. That woman was just God's instrument. God's way of showing me—"

"You just mad because you can't get her to that church of yours."

"Mat, the woman needs a church home. She needs something more in her life besides those white folks she works for. She needs to find God."

"Not in that raggedy little broken-down storefront, Hosea. You know how she likes pretty things."

"That is precisely what worries me, Mat. That is precisely why I want her out of here. Take Baby—she practically worships her. And if I catch her one more time messing around in that woman's room—"

"Zurletha doesn't mind. She told me Baby's just having a little fun," Mama said.

"A little fun can leave you dragging a lifetime load. I've seen too much, Mat. I know what I'm talking about."

"All right, Hoséa—that's how you feel, we can keep Baby out of there."

"Playing with them beads and that glass

junk she calls jewelry. Rubbing up against those rabbits she's got hanging up on the door—"

"They are not rabbits, and you know it. Mink, that's what it is. A mink coat, and she's also got a fox stole."

"Don't care if it's dog. I want Baby's mind steady on her books and her grades and on what she is going to do with her life."

"All right, all right, Hosea. Stop preaching at me. Put that light out now. Go on to sleep."

"Keep that door locked when Zurletha's not in there, y'hear."

I didn't understand my father sometimes. Aunt Zurletha—and he made us call her "aunt"—had been living with us on her days off for as long as I can remember. She didn't want us to call her Miss Battles. And Hosea wouldn't let us say just "Zurletha." The people she worked for just called her "Zurlie." I think that's the only thing she didn't like—"Zurlie" this and "Zurlie" that for forty years.

She was always giving us something. Gave Curtis his own radio. Gave William a microscope. My last birthday, last August, she gave me a guitar. You should've heard her play the guitar. We'd come home from Sunday school and hear her singing and stomping her foot. Made us want to dance. Soon after though, she'd stop—especially if Hosea came home to eat before going back to church. Then she'd open her door, and we'd all go in, me first.

She had so many beautiful things. Real crystal glasses that she could tap with her fingernail and make sounds like music. There wasn't too much room to walk, so mostly I sat on her big brass bed. And she'd let me play with the silver candlesticks or try on the jewelry and hats. She had such pretty suitcases, too. Since the guitar, though, whenever she came home, she'd show me how to play different chords. We'd practice very quietly.

One time she took us to the beach on the subway. Hosea was in Washington, and Mama had promised us we could go. It was still dark when I heard her in the kitchen. I got up, and she let me help her pack this big straw basket with all kinds of food she had brought with her the night before. William and Curtis carried the blankets. She carried the basket. I had Curtis's radio. It was a beautiful day, and we had such a good time, too, even Curtis with his smart-alecky self.

Aunt Zurletha had on a silky blue and green bathing suit and some kind of rubber sandals that had lots of straps and curved heels with big holes through them and her pretty red hair was tied in a ponytail, and as always, she had on her jewelry. William and Curtis were whispering behind her back and making fun, saying she looked like a cow-pig. I think she must have heard them talking about her bunion sticking out of her strappy shoes, even though she was laughing and shaking her shoulders to the music on Curtis's radio as she set up the umbrella and opened the blankets. Later, when me and Curtis and William came out of the water, she had the lunch all set out and was stretched out reading *True Love* magazine. The sun was bouncing off her bracelet as I reached over and started twisting it around her arm. She took it off and said, "Here, you can wear it for a while." I put it on my arm and ran out from under the umbrella and started pretending I was a rich lady. William said, "You think you something, huh? She probably stole it." This time I know she heard because just before we started to eat, she took the bracelet off my arm.

"You always have such pretty things, Aunt Zurletha," I said.

JOLIE MADAME 1973 Audrey Flack Australian National Gallery, Canberra.

And she said, "Ought to. I've been working mighty hard for a lotta years. Then, too, my people buy me—or give me—a lot of stuff. Especially when the children were small. We traveled all over then."

"They must be some rich people, man," Curtis said.

"Rich? They got money's mama," Aunt Zurletha said.

"What does money's mama look like, and who's the daddy?" William asked.

Zurletha laughed and took a dainty little bite of one of the sandwiches.

"They probably stole all that money," William said. "Hosea says that rich folks are thieves."

"Not my people," said Zurletha. "My people are just plain smart. And white, too, you know?"

I thought William sounded jealous and mean, too.

"And how come they didn't give you some of that money instead of all that other junk?"

Aunt Zurletha didn't even seem mad.

"It's not junk, William. They give me expensive things. Years ago, too, when I wanted to bake pies to sell, they were going to set me up a place."

"What happened, Aunt Zurletha?" I asked.

Then she told us how her lady got pregnant again and didn't want her to leave, and how they kept promising to set up the pie place but never did what with the traveling and more babies coming; then, being in charge of opening all the different houses; and with her people getting sick and dying one right after the other; and how the children not wanting her to leave, she just finally got out of the notion of a pie place.

"Why you never got married, Aunt Zurletha?" Curtis asked.

"One time I was gonna get married—this was before you children were even thought of. But again, something came up with my people, and we stayed in Europe. I should say we stayed all over Europe for a year. And when I came back, lo and behold he had married somebody else. Never will forget. Said it came to him that I was already married—married to a job was the way he put it."

Sometimes I could just ball up my fist and hit William in the mouth.

"O-o-o, you should have quit that job, Aunt Zurletha, and married what's-his-name."

"Frank. His name was Frank." Aunt Zurletha looked sad for a second. Then she leaned over and started cutting the cake. "Then I wouldn't have you for my kids," she said.

Curtis nudged William and pointed at the kinky gray hair sticking out from under the red wig. Aunt Zurletha must have eyes all around her head, just like Mama. She fixed the wig, so the gray didn't show. And I thought it was strange—just at that moment that song, "Darling, I Am Growing Old" came on the radio. Then Aunt Zurletha started singing and doing a little dance on her tiptoes as she passed out the cake.

I wish I could remember more about Aunt Zurletha, but she was never really home that much. I think often about that last summer, though. Our for-real Aunt Marie was a nurse, and she had arranged for us to go to a summer camp for two weeks. Hosea and Mama just had to get our clothes ready—

that's all. We didn't have to pay. We didn't even think about Aunt Zurletha we were having such a good time. And Mama and Hosea didn't tell us in their letter that she had been in the hospital. We didn't find out until they picked us up at the bus terminal on the way home. I was so ashamed that we hadn't thought about her. I could have drawn her a funny get-well card.

After camp, first thing, I knocked on her door and went in before she said come in. Even though she had the biggest of the three rented rooms, it looked so small and crowded. All her beautiful stuff was packed in boxes and piled on top of the radiator, and beside the window, under the bed—everywhere. It looked like she was planning to move. Everything looked gray, except for the afternoon sun against the window shade. A sweet-smelling spray mingled with the odor of—something like when Hosea found a dead mouse that had gotten caught in the little space between the stove and the sink. I had never seen Aunt Zurletha without the wig and without the red lipstick and the beautiful earrings. Her black, black face was lying on the white, white pillow. It looked smooth like wax. Her hair was corn-rowed, ending in two thin braids, and almost gone in the front and on the sides where the wig used to be. It seemed like she stayed that way for the rest of the summer.

She didn't want us children to come into her room, so I would sit on the little rug outside her door and play some of the things she had showed me on the guitar. Mama would bring food. Hosea used to say, "It's a shame. Why didn't she tell somebody she was so sick?"

Mama said, "Guess she didn't want to worry us. She complained one or two times, but she told me she just didn't have the time to go sit in some doctor's office."

That fall they took her away to the hospital again. And one day while I was in school, Aunt Zurletha died. When I came home, the room was empty. All the boxes, the brass bed, the furs, the lamps, and the glasses, the china ornaments—everything, gone.

"It just so happened, Baby," Mama said, "the people she sold all her things to came today to pick them up."

A bottle of fingernail polish was on the windowsill. It was hard to open. I don't know why, but I started painting my thumbnail. Then I found myself kneeling on the floor, with my head on the windowsill, crying. Crying like I couldn't stop. And the polish spilled all over my middyblouse. Luckily I didn't spill it all. There was a little left, and I promised myself not to ever use it, because it was all I had to remember Aunt Zurletha by.

"Nail polish? That's not what she left you, Baby," Mama said. "She left us all her cash money. She left a will. Enough for each of you to go one year in college."

"I'm hoping they will get scholarships," Hosea said.

"Well, we can see to that when the time comes." Mama started crying.

"Aw, come on now, Mat, sweetheart," Hosea said. "You know Zurletha wanted to go. See how she planned everything. Too bad, though, she never planned time to get with God."

What Hosea said made me scream at him, "Yeah, but she will. And when she does, I hope she'll have on her red wig and her rouge and her fingernail polish with toes to match and all her jewelry, and kiss God with her greasy lipstick on. I bet he'll just hug and kiss her back, and tell her how beautiful she is."

Daddy just looked at me a long time after that. Then he walked across the room and put his arms around me. I couldn't remember the last time he did that. He said, "Come on now. Crying won't bring her back, Baby. If crying would bring her back, maybe I'd cry along with you. Won't find another roomer who—" He went over to Mama, took her by the shoulders, and shook her a little bit before he hugged her and said, "She got to be part of this family, Mat. She really did. We're going to miss her all right. All of us."

That day I felt something that I'd been afraid of all my life tumble down inside my father, and he became a gentler man. From that day, whenever I think about Aunt Zurletha, I hear the music of crystal glasses as they touch tingling around me, and I feel happy. ❧

e x p l a i n

Responding to Reading

First Impressions

1. Would you want Aunt Zurletha to live in your house? Why or why not?

Second Thoughts

2. Each member of the narrator's family has a different opinion of Aunt Zurletha. Whose opinion most closely matches your opinion of her? Whose opinion is least like yours? Explain.

3. In her youth, Zurletha hoped to marry Frank and own a pie shop, but she chose instead to stay with her employers. Do you think her decision was wise? Explain your answers.

    Think about
    • the benefits she gained from her employers
    • the sacrifices she made for her employers
    • her feelings toward her employers

4. Which characters in this story have bittersweet memories of the past? Describe these memories and tell why they are bittersweet.

5. Using your inference chart, list what you consider to be Zurletha's strengths and weaknesses. How would you evaluate her as a person?

6. Why do you think the author includes a dedication at the beginning of this story?

Broader Connections

7. Frank told Zurletha that she was married to her job. What role do you think a job should have in a person's life? Support your opinion with examples from the story and from your own experience.

Literary Concepts: Characterization and Symbolism

Characterization refers to the techniques a writer uses to make a character come alive. Find examples to show how Ruby Dee uses each of the techniques listed below to round out the character of Aunt Zurletha and to make her seem real.

• direct physical description
• the character's own words and actions
• the words and actions of other characters
• the comments of the narrator

A **symbol** is a person, place, or thing that stands for something beyond itself. In literature, objects and images are often used to symbolize abstract ideas. For example, a crown might symbolize royalty or power, and a sunrise might symbolize hope or a new beginning. List objects associated with Aunt Zurletha and tell what you think each one symbolizes.

Writing Options

1. Reread the second to the last sentence in this story. Write a paragraph that explains what this statement means. Use details from the story to support your opinion.

2. Write Zurletha's letter to Frank in which she explains that because the family is staying longer in Europe than planned, their wedding must be delayed.

3. Write a eulogy, or a speech of praise, that someone might read at Zurletha's funeral.

4. Like that of most people, Zurletha's life is filled with ups and downs. Examine Zurletha's life by making two lists: one showing the accomplishments she is proud of and another showing the actions or decisions she regrets.

Options for Learning

1 • Zurletha Talks Back In this story, we learn a lot about what others think of Zurletha but little about her opinions of them. Create a monologue in which Zurletha gives her opinion of each member of the narrator's family. Use details from the story and any inferences you have made to develop your speech. Present the monologue to your class.

2 • Frank Encounter With a classmate, imagine and act out the scene in which Frank tells Zurletha that he has married someone else. Make the scene as emotional as you think it might have been. Present the scene to your classmates.

3 • Just Like Her Make a chart comparing and contrasting Zurletha with someone you know. The person may be old or young.

4 • Impressions Create a mandala or a collage that reveals your impressions of Zurletha. Make sure your finished work represents the whole person, not just her appearance or personality. For more information about creating these forms of art, see pages 29 and 132.

 FACT FINDER

Find out what it would cost to attend a college or a vocational school of your choice for one year.

Ruby Dee

Ruby Ann Wallace, a famous actress whose professional name is Ruby Dee, was born in Cleveland, Ohio, in the 1920's. She has been married to actor Ossie Davis for more than forty-two years and has raised three children. Her own words best sum up her approach to life: "You just try to do everything that comes up. Get up an hour earlier, stay up an hour later, make the time. Then you look back and say 'Well, that was a neat piece of juggling there—school, marriage, babies, career.'"

Dee's enthusiasm and commitment to doing her best to make the world a better place have contributed to her successes in life. Although she is best known for her talents as a stage, film, and television actress, she has also attained fame as a writer and as a political activist. Her acting credits include *Do the Right Thing, A Raisin in the Sun,* and *I Know Why the Caged Bird Sings.* Her writing includes nonfiction, fiction, and poetry.

Personal
Narrative

Li Chang's Million

HENRY GREGOR FELSEN

*E*xamine What You Know

In this narrative, the writer tells about a time when he unintentionally hurt someone's feelings. Without meaning to, have you ever hurt someone by something you said or did? What did you do about it? How did you feel about it? Compare your experience with the experiences of your classmates.

*E*xpand Your Knowledge

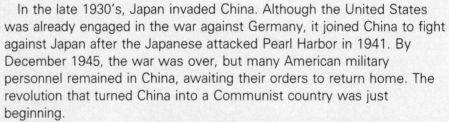

In the late 1930's, Japan invaded China. Although the United States was already engaged in the war against Germany, it joined China to fight against Japan after the Japanese attacked Pearl Harbor in 1941. By December 1945, the war was over, but many American military personnel remained in China, awaiting their orders to return home. The revolution that turned China into a Communist country was just beginning.

During the war, Henry Gregor Felsen was a U.S. Marine sergeant and a combat correspondent. As this selection begins, he makes an unplanned stop in China's capital city, which at that time was called Peiping (pā′ piŋ) or Peking (pē′ kiŋ) and is now called Beijing (bā′ jiŋ). While there, he visits the bazaars, or open-air markets, where customers traditionally haggle, or bargain, with the merchants for the lowest prices they can get.

*W*rite Before You Read

Before reading Felsen's account, take your turn at being an author. The words and phrases below are from "Li Chang's Million." Use them to write what you predict will happen. Then compare and contrast your story line with "Li Chang's Million."

American friend	haggle	poverty and misery
two million dollars	young boy	gift
expensive furs	hurt, sad eyes	next trip

■ *A biography of the author can be found on page 313.*

Li Chang's Million

HENRY GREGOR FELSEN

I don't know what comes to your mind when you think about China. Maybe you picture the way it looks on the map, or the wide, dusty plains, or the great, barren mountain ranges that have not yet been fully explored. Perhaps you think of the great swarms of people in the cities, or pigtails, or the rickshaws,[1] or the temples, or the rivers that teem with houseboats . . . I always think of little Li Chang.

I am Li Chang's American friend, but he doesn't know that. We never spoke, or even smiled, but I am his friend. I am sure he doesn't remember me, just as I am certain I will never forget him. Actually, I don't even know his name. I call him Li Chang because he must have a name, and I want to think of him as more than a small, anonymous boy in the great bazaar in Peiping—a boy whose life I planned to change.

I had flown in to Peiping on a Marine transport plane, and I was staying at the Grand Hotel de Pekin while the mechanics worked over a balky port motor. We wanted perfection out of that motor before we started back across the Pacific.

On the night I met Li Chang, I was bored with sightseeing, although Peiping is the most Chinese of all China's large cities and is as Oriental as a Midwest county seat is American. I was tired of the grandeur of the Forbidden City[2] and fed up with the crush and noise of the Chinese City outside the Tartar Wall.[3] I decided to shop—always a stimulating and <u>strenuous</u> activity in China.

I left the hotel and chose a rickshaw from the clamoring mob of boys that swept over me as soon as I went down the front steps. I told my boy to take me to the bazaar and settled back for the smooth ride.

As I was pulled to the bazaar, I felt that if I was not actually sitting on top of the world, I was only one step down. I had drawn my

1. **rickshaws** (rik′ shôz′): small, two-wheeled carts or carriages pulled by one or two persons.
2. **Forbidden City:** an enclosed part of the city of Beijing where the palaces of former Chinese emperors are located. Access to this area was once forbidden to all but members of the emperor's household.
3. **Tartar Wall:** one of many systems of walls built in the city of Beijing during the Middle Ages to keep out the Tartars, people from Mongolia and Turkey who raided the city during the thirteenth century.

Words to Know and Use | **strenuous** (stren′ yoo əs) *adj.* energetic; requiring great effort

pay before flying to China and had four hundred dollars in my pocket. Four hundred dollars American but no less than two million dollars in the North China currency.

... my two million represented a small fortune.

If there is a more wonderful feeling in this world than being in a strange, Oriental city, halfway around the world from home, with two million dollars in your pocket, I cannot imagine what it would be. True, it was two million in an inflated currency. Dinner cost two thousand dollars, gloves twenty-five thousand, a hotel room eighteen thousand a night, and a good camera went at three hundred thousand. But there is magic in the name and thought of a million dollars; no matter what the currency and despite inflation, my two million represented a small fortune. There were thousands of Chinese in Peiping who would have worked for me night and day for five years for that two million in gaudy[4] bills.

It was a short ride to the bazaar, and when we arrived, I gave my boy the standard hundred dollars for the distance, ignored his cries for more and went toward the archway that was the entrance to the bazaar.

As I went in, I was surrounded by the inevitable crowd of beggars holding out their hands and asking for money in voices that ranged from the most piteous cries to cheerful shouts. The healthy-looking little beggar boys, bold as flies, crowded closest, impudently shouting, "*i mao ch'ien!*"[5] (One

dime money.) Others shouted in English, the usual cry being, "No momma, no poppa, no chow for t'ree day!" And one lad was crying, "No momma, no poppa, no flight pay!"

I waved them away, shouting the only Chinese expression of disapproval I knew—*pu hao*.[6] I had been in China long enough to pass to the second stage of feeling about it. The first stage was one of shock and pity at the appalling poverty. The second, which I with my two million dollars enjoyed at the moment, was one of calloused indifference. I accepted starvation and misery as part of the scene and thought no more about it. To me, all Chinese looked alike and were either trying to beg or sell. As I walked into the bazaar, I don't think I even regarded them as human but as a noisy, annoying, faceless mass. Two million dollars in one's pocket and a good meal in one's stomach can do that.

I wandered around the stalls for about two hours. I examined fur gloves and leather boots, Chinese musical instruments, kimonos, cameras, intricately carved canes, silverware and silks. Whether or not I intended to make a purchase, I haggled loudly and vehemently, in the fashion Chinese approve in a buyer, feeling all the while the wonderful sense of opulence and power the money in my pocket gave to me.

I enjoyed every moment of my slow progress, drinking in the strange Oriental atmosphere, listening to the shrill, singsong talk, examining curious carvings and handicraft, and getting a particular satisfaction

---

4. **gaudy** (gôd′ ē): cheaply colorful and ornate; showy.
5. *i mao ch'ien!* (ē′ mɔu chē ən′): an idiomatic expression meaning ten cents.
6. *pu hao* (bo͞o hɔu): not good.

Hedda Morrison/Oxford University Press, Hong Kong.

out of my blustering arguments over prices, which delighted the ever-present crowd of onlookers.

In the course of this aimless wandering, I suddenly turned down a small alley that was darker and quieter than the others. The lights overhead were less numerous, and noises fewer and softer. I was about to turn back to the clamor of the main line of stalls when my attention was caught by a shop at the very end of this little alley. There were furs exhibited in the window, and having heard that expensive furs could be had cheaply in Peiping, I went to investigate.

As I walked into the shop, a stout Chinese in a long black gown, and wearing a round black skullcap, rose to greet me. With several other men in the shop, he had been drinking tea at a small table. I indicated that I wished to examine the furs, and he showed me a rack of finished coats.

I looked at the coats with a negligent—I will even say sneering—air. I knew that a look of interest in any garment would cause its price to leap, and for that reason I handled the furs as though they were the shoddiest coats I had ever seen.

I looked at one a trifle longer than the others, and the bland Chinese who stood at my elbow spoke for the first time. "*Ting hao*[7]," he said. "Very good."

"*Pu hao*," I grunted in reply. "*Ting pu hao.*"

I was positive the old rascal could speak excellent English. Most of the Chinese merchants can, but they do better business with Americans if they pretend they know no English. "It's very badly made," I said, touching the coat.

"Very well made," the Chinese insisted, slipping his hands into the sleeves of his gown. "Most excellent workmanship."

---

7. *Ting hao* (tēŋ hoʊ): extremely good.

307

I examined the garment carelessly. "Very bad," I said, just for the sake of argument. "See how badly it is sewn. It would be laughed at in America."

I looked up with a smirk still on my lips, hoping to discomfit the man. But he had moved, and when I looked up, I gazed into a pair of hurt, sad eyes.

Sitting across the room, behind a counter, unnoticed by me until this moment, sat a boy who looked to be no more than six or seven years of age. While the old men had been sitting around drinking tea, he had been working—and had not stopped until I had by word and action indicated my low opinion of the way the coat had been sewn.

For a moment I was completely off balance. I let the coat fall from my hand and felt a sudden rush of shame. For the boy sat on a high stool, and before him on the counter were two squares of fur that he was sewing by hand. I walked over to him. With a small needle, he was making a line of stitches as tiny and even as could be done on any machine. It was his work I had criticized.

"Sorry, Junior," I said lightly. "I didn't mean to run down your work."

The boy looked at me in silence. He had the most hurt expression on his face I had ever caused anyone. I looked into his inky-black eyes and noticed there were shadows under them. I noticed how his smooth little face already showed signs of the tired, resigned expression it was growing into. I noticed how his head and shoulders were already bent, and how, even when he rested, his back did not straighten. We stared at one another for a long minute—this child whose

work I had sneered at and I—and then one of the men spoke to him, and he bowed his head and his small fingers took up their slow, painstaking stitching again.

I turned and walked out of the shop. It was late, and the bazaar was closing. The long lines of stalls were boarded up, and their owners were shuffling home. The lights were going out, and the beggars, sleeping on the sidewalk, hardly roused themselves to ask sleepily for alms as I went past. I hailed a dozing rickshaw boy and rode back to the hotel. All I could see was the poverty and misery. The mystery, the romance, the spell of the Orient had been smashed by the hurt look of a child.

I felt ashamed of the way I had acted, and I wanted him to know.

I went up to my room and went to bed, but I couldn't sleep. I kept thinking of the boy and feeling him on my conscience. At an age when he should have been thinking of toys, and at an hour when he should have been in bed, he was sitting behind a counter on a high stool, stitching carefully and slowly, while the long hours and hard work stole the brightness from his eyes and the youth from his body.

I felt ashamed of the way I had acted, and I wanted him to know. I wanted to go back and tell him that it was all right, that his workmanship was the best I had ever seen, and not to feel bad. I wanted to tell him that he ought not to be working but playing—I

Words to Know and Use | **resigned** (ri zīnd′) *adj.* submissive; passively accepting **resign** *v.*

Henri Cartier-Bresson/Magnum Photos, Inc., New York.

thought of him in terms of the children of his age I knew in the States, and how he should be playing as they were and not bending over the monotonous stitching night after night. I wanted to do anything I could to help him, and suddenly it came to me.

I was so excited I rolled out of bed and paced the floor. It was too late tonight, but the next day, as soon as the bazaar opened, I would do it. I took my wallet, opened it, and counted out half the money. Tomorrow, although he did not know it, the little boy, little . . . Li Chang, I called him suddenly, little Li Chang would be a millionaire.

I almost shouted in my joy at that moment. I laughed, felt tears in my eyes, and thought about the look on Li Chang's face when I walked in and gave him a present of a million dollars. I didn't know what that million dollars could do for him. It wasn't a fortune. But it might be enough to rescue him from his dreary fate with that needle. It might buy him a few precious years of care-free childhood before it was gone and he had to work again. Perhaps he could afford to become a boy again. I would ask the men. I would try to buy whatever happiness I could for the little boy I had hurt that night.

I went to sleep with a light heart, impatient for the morning.

I was awakened before dawn by a hand shaking me. It was the pilot of our plane, and he was completely dressed in flying clothes. "Come on, sleepy," he grinned, "get your clothes on. The mechs have fixed the motor, and we have to be in the air at 0500.[8]

We're flying down to Tsingtao[9] to pick up a colonel and then back to Hawaii."

"But I can't leave now," I protested. "I have something important to do. I can't . . ."

The pilot looked at his watch. "A truck is calling for us in half an hour. You can buy that souvenir next trip. We'll be making this run again next month."

As we circled over Peiping, gaining altitude, I looked down on that great walled city and wondered if Li Chang were awake. In a few hours he would be returning to those tiny, never-ending stitches. Perhaps, because of my actions the night before, he would be beaten or treated harshly. If he remembered me at all, it would be as the cause of further sorrow. And I was a thousand feet above him, with his million dollars in my pocket. Next month, the pilot had said. Next trip, Li Chang would have his money.

We flew away from Peiping and from China. When we reached Hawaii, I was ordered back to the States. I have not returned to China since, and I doubt if I shall ever go again. And Li Chang's million went very quickly in this country.

I don't know what you think about when the talk gets around to what's wrong with China. Maybe you think about the lack of communications, or ancestor worship, or politics and civil war. I think of little Li Chang. ❧

---

8. **0500:** five o'clock in the morning.

9. **Tsingtao** (chēŋ' dou): old name for the coastal city of Quingdao, located southeast of Beijing on the Yellow Sea.

Words to Know and Use | **monotonous** (mə nät' 'n əs) *adj.* boring and tedious

Responding to Reading

First Impressions

1. Does your impression of Felsen change during the course of the story? Explain.

Second Thoughts

2. Summarize Felsen's attitude toward the Chinese people as presented in this account. Find examples to support your opinion.

3. How does Felsen's attitude cause conflicts?

4. Felsen decides to give Li Chang half of his money. What does he expect to happen? Is his plan a good one?

> **Think about**
> • what he is trying to accomplish
> • how Li Chang's life might change if he had the money

5. In your opinion, should Felsen feel guilty? Why or why not?

> **Think about**
> • his behavior toward the boy while he is in the shop
> • whether Felsen is or is not Li Chang's friend
> • why Li Chang never gets the money

6. Felsen seems to have bittersweet memories of this visit to Peiping. Discuss why his memories are both bitter and sweet.

Broader Connections

7. Felsen gradually becomes indifferent to the poverty of the beggars around him. Is this reaction natural? Does it happen in this country? How can apathy toward poverty be overcome?

Literary Concept: Mood

The feeling that the writer wants the reader to get from a work of literature is called the **mood.** For example, a story might give you feelings of excitement, anger, sadness, happiness, or pity. Details, dialogue, images, and the use of words with strong connotations can help set the mood. Look at the description of the bazaar on page 306. How would you describe the mood? Give examples to show how the writer creates this mood for you.

Concept Review: Theme The mood may also help transmit the theme of a work. What lesson or theme do you think Felson is trying to convey? Explain how the overall mood of the story reinforces this theme.

Writing Options

1. Li Chang has a hurt expression on his face as he listens to Felsen's criticism of his work. Imagine and write Li Chang's thoughts.

2. Taking into account the fact that this story was written about fifty years ago, create a list of possible ways Felsen might have gotten the money to Li Chang.

3. Write a paragraph that explains how fate is important to the plot of this story.

4. Suppose that somehow Felsen had gotten the money to Li Chang. Write what you think Li Chang might have done with it or whether and how his life might have changed.

Vocabulary Practice

Exercise Replace the boldfaced word or phrase in each title with a word from the list that has nearly the same meaning. Write the new title on your paper.

1. Getting the **Careless** Driver Off the Road
2. **Money** Trading in a World Market
3. **Hard** Climbs: The Hiker's Guide to the Rockies
4. A Feeling of **Richness**: Decorating Tips and Techniques
5. Music Today: **Tedious** or Terrific?
6. Persuasive Speaking: Make Your Point **Strongly**
7. Do the **Poorest Quality** Manufacturers Have the Flashiest Ads?
8. World War II: The **Unavoidable** Conflict
9. Diplomacy in the Office: Dealing with **Hardhearted** Bosses
10. Portraits of Despair: The **Passively Accepting** Faces of the Homeless

Words to Know and Use

calloused
currency
inevitable
monotonous
negligent
opulence
resigned
shoddiest
strenuous
vehemently

extend

Options for Learning

1 • **Money Matters** The author states that his four hundred American dollars is the equivalent of two million Chinese dollars. How many Chinese "dollars," or units of currency, equal the value of one American dollar? After you solve this problem, work with classmates to create other math problems using details from the story. Have others solve the problems.

2 • **Facts About the Fur Industry** Li Chang performs one of a series of steps required to make a fur coat. Find out about the process of making a fur coat, from the breeding of the animals to the selling of the coats. Design a flowchart or other graphic device to show each step in the process. In addition, learn how "fake-fur" coats are made, and make a chart to show your findings.

3 • **Fur-Shop Drama** Rewrite the scene in the fur shop in play form, adding dialogue and stage directions. Plan the setting and gather the props that are needed to act out the scene. Call upon three or four classmates to help you perform the scene for your class.

4 • **Beautiful Peiping** From sources such as travel guides, encyclopedias, books about China, and magazines, find out what Peiping, or Beijing, has to offer tourists. Use your findings to create a travel brochure promoting a trip to Beijing. For more information about writing a travel brochure, see page 198.

5 • **Scale Models** Rickshaws and open-air bazaars were once a common sight in China. Find out what each one looks like. Use details from the story and your imagination to create a model of a rickshaw or a bazaar.

FACT FINDER

How much is an American dollar worth in Chinese currency today?

Henry Gregor Felsen
1916–

Although "Li Chang's Million" was rejected thirty-three times before it was finally bought by *Woman's Day* magazine, Felsen continued writing books, articles and short stories. Many of his books, such as *Hot Rod* and *Street Rod*, are about teenagers and cars. Several of these books have remained so popular that thirty years after their first publication they have been reprinted. Felsen has also published articles in many popular magazines and has written for television.

Born in Brooklyn, New York, Felsen has spent much of his life in the Midwest. When his son Daniel was in ninth grade, Felsen wrote *Letters to a Teenage Son* in which he explained, "I am thinking about you and how to reach you. . . . I can write what I cannot say." Four years later, Felsen published *To My Son in Uniform*, another series of letters to Daniel, who also served in the U.S. Marines. Felsen now lives in Michigan.

Fiction

The Cub

LOIS DYKEMAN KLEIHAUER

Examine What You Know

The following story and *Insight* article are about fathers and their children. Before you read, think about your own father, or about a "typical" father. Jot down phrases that describe your thoughts about such things as his role in the family, his favorite activities, his habits, the way he looks and dresses, and the way his children see him.

Expand Your Knowledge

Coming of age has always been a popular theme for writers. Such stories tell of youngsters taking steps toward growing up. These steps, often called **rites of passage,** signify movement from one phase of life into another. In early Native American groups, for example, an important rite of passage was the first hunt. Today we have many rites of passage by which teenagers progress toward the adult world; high school graduation is an obvious one. Yet there are also informal rites—unofficial but significant changes in a teenager's life. Such changes often involve tests of strength, intelligence, or emotional maturity. In "The Cub," notice the rite of passage the boy goes through and the changes it brings to his life.

Write Before You Read

In your journal or on a piece of paper, write a few paragraphs comparing and contrasting yourself with one or both of your parents. In what ways do you measure up favorably? In what ways do you have a long way to go? In what ways do you want to be like your parent(s) when you grow up? How would you like to be different?

The *Cub*

LOIS DYKEMAN KLEIHAUER

One of his first memories was of his father bending down from his great height to sweep him into the air. Up he went, gasping and laughing with delight. He could look down on his mother's upturned face as she watched, laughing with them, and at the thick shock of his father's brown hair, and at his white teeth.

Then he would come down, shrieking happily, but he was never afraid, not with his father's hands holding him. No one in the world was as strong, or as wise, as his father.

He remembered a time when his father moved the piano across the room for his mother. He watched while she guided it into its new position, and he saw the difference in their hands as they rested, side by side, upon the gleaming walnut. His mother's hands were white and slim and delicate, his father's large and square and strong.

As he grew, he learned to play bear. When it was time for his father to come home at night, he would lurk behind the kitchen door. When he heard the closing of the garage door, he would hold his breath and squeeze himself into the crack behind the door. Then he would be quiet.

It was always the same. His father would open the door and stand there, the backs of his long legs beguilingly close. "Where's the boy?"

He would glance at the conspiratorial smile on his mother's face, and then he would leap and grab his father about the knees, and his father would look down and shout, "Hey, what's this? A bear—a young cub!"

Then, no matter how tightly he tried to cling, he was lifted up and perched upon his father's shoulder, and they would march past his mother, and together they would duck their heads beneath the doors.

And then he went to school. And on the playground, he learned how to wrestle and shout, how to hold back tears, how to get a half nelson[1] on the boy who tried to take his football away from him. He came home at night and practiced his new wisdom on his father. Straining and puffing, he tried to pull his father off the lounge chair while his father kept on reading the paper, only glancing up now and then to ask in mild wonderment, "What are you trying to do, boy?"

He would stand and look at his father. "Gee whiz, Dad!" And then he would realize that his father was teasing him, and he would crawl up on his father's lap and pummel him in affectionate frustration.

And still he grew—taller, slimmer, stronger. He was like a young buck with tiny new horns. He wanted to lock them with any

---

1. **half nelson:** a wrestling hold.

Words to Know and Use

conspiratorial (kən spir′ ə tôr′ ē əl) *adj.* planning together secretly
pummel (pum′ əl) *v.* to beat or hit repeatedly with the fist; thrash

315

SONGS FOR MY FATHER 1980 Juan Gonzalez Nancy Hoffman Gallery, New York.

other young buck's, to test them in combat. He measured his <u>biceps</u> with his mother's tape measure. Exultantly, he thrust his arm in front of his father. "Feel that! How's that for muscle?"

His father put his great thumb into the flexed muscle and pressed, and the boy pulled back, protesting, laughing. "Ouch!"

Sometimes they wrestled on the floor together, and his mother moved the chairs back. "Be careful, Charles—don't hurt him."

After a while his father would push him aside and sit in his chair, his long legs thrust out before him, and the boy would scramble to his feet, half-resentful, half-mirthful over the ease with which his father mastered him.

"Doggone it, Dad, someday—" he would say.

He went out for football and track in high school. He surprised even himself now, there was so much more of him. And he could look down on his mother. "Little one," he called her, or "small fry."

Sometimes he took her wrists and backed her into a chair, while he laughed and she scolded. "I'll—I'll take you across my knee."

"Who will?" he demanded.

"Well—your father still can," she said.

His father—well, that was different.

" *F eel that! How's that for muscle?* "

They still wrestled occasionally, but it distressed his mother. She hovered about them, worrying, unable to comprehend the need for their struggling. It always ended the same way, with the boy upon his back <u>prostrate</u>, and his father grinning down at him. "Give?"

"Give." And he got up, shaking his head.

"I wish you wouldn't," his mother would say, fretting. "There's no point in it. You'll hurt yourselves; don't do it anymore."

Words to Know and Use

biceps (bī′ seps′) *n.* the large muscle in the front of the upper arm
prostrate (präs′ trāt′) *adj.* lying flat on the ground

So for nearly a year they had not wrestled, but he thought about it one night at dinner. He looked at his father closely. It was queer, but his father didn't look nearly as tall or broad-shouldered as he used to. He could even look his father straight in the eyes now.

"How much do you weigh, Dad?" he asked.

His father threw him a mild glance. "About the same; about a hundred and ninety. Why?"

The boy grinned. "Just wondering."

But after a while he went over to his father where he sat reading the paper and took it out of his hands. His father glanced up, his eyes at first questioning and then narrowing to meet the challenge in his son's. "So," he said, softly.

"Come on, Dad."

His father took off his coat and began to unbutton his shirt. "You asked for it," he said.

His mother came in from the kitchen, alarmed. "Oh, Charles! Bill! Don't—you'll hurt yourselves!" But they paid no attention to her. They were standing now, their shirts off. They watched each other, intent and purposeful. The boy's teeth gleamed again. They circled for a moment, and then their hands closed upon each other's arms.

They strained against each other, and then the boy went down, taking his father with him. They moved and <u>writhed</u> and turned, in silence seeking an advantage, in silence pressing it to its conclusion. There was the sound of the thumps of their bodies upon the rug and of the quick, hard intake of breath. The boy showed his teeth occasionally in a grimace of pain. His mother stood at one side, both hands pressed against her ears. Occasionally her lips moved, but she did not make a sound.

After a while the boy pinned his father on his back. "Give!" he demanded.

His father said "Heck, no!" And with a great effort he pushed the boy off, and the struggle began again.

But at the end his father lay prostrate, and a look of bewilderment came into his eyes. He struggled desperately against his son's merciless, restraining hands. Finally he lay quiet, only his chest heaving, his breath coming loudly.

The boy said, "Give!"

The man frowned, shaking his head.

Still the boy knelt on him, pinning him down.

"Give!" he said, and tightened his grip. "Give!"

All at once his father began to laugh, silently, his shoulders shaking. The boy felt his mother's fingers tugging fiercely at his shoulder. "Let him up," she said. "Let him up!"

The boy looked down at his father. "Give up?"

His father stopped laughing, but his eyes were still wet. "Okay," he said. "I give."

The boy stood up and reached a hand to his father to help him up, but his mother was before him, putting an arm about his father's shoulders, helping him to rise. They stood together and looked at him, his father grinning gamely, his mother with baffled pain in her eyes.

The boy started to laugh. "I guess I—" He stopped. "Gosh, Dad, I didn't hurt you, did I?"

"Heck, no, I'm all right. Next time . . ."

"Yeah, maybe next time . . ."

And his mother did not contradict what

they said, for she knew as well as they that there would never be a next time.

For a moment the three of them stood looking at one another, and then, suddenly, blindly, the boy turned. He ran through the door under which he had ducked so many times when he had ridden on his father's shoulders. He went out the kitchen door, behind which he had hidden, waiting to leap out and pounce upon his father's legs.

It was dark outside. He stood on the steps, feeling the air cool against his sweaty body. He stood with lifted head, looking at the stars, and then he could not see them because of the tears that burned his eyes and ran down his cheeks. ❧

I N S I G H T

My Father
ERMA BOMBECK

When I was a little kid, a father was like the light in the refrigerator. Every home had one, but no one really knew what either of them did once the door was shut.

My dad left the house every morning and always seemed glad to see everyone at night.

He opened the jar of pickles when no one else could.

He was the only one in the house who wasn't afraid to go in the basement by himself.

He cut himself shaving, but no one kissed it or got excited about it. It was understood that whenever it rained, he got the car and brought it around to the door. When anyone was sick, he went out to get the prescription filled. . . .

I was afraid of everyone else's father but not my own. Once I made him tea.

It was only sugar water, but he sat on a small chair and said it was delicious. He looked very uncomfortable. . . .

Whenever I played house, the mother doll had a lot to do. I never knew what to do with the daddy doll, so I had him say, "I'm going off to work now," and threw him under the bed.

When I was nine years old, my father didn't get up one morning and go to work. He went to the hospital and died the next day. . . .

I went to my room and felt under the bed for the father doll. When I found him, I dusted him off and put him on my bed.

He never did anything. I didn't know his leaving would hurt so much.

I still don't know why.

e x p l a i n

Responding to Reading

First Impressions

1. Do you identify with Bill, the boy, in any way? Explain your answer.

Second Thoughts

2. Do you find this story believable? Why or why not?

3. What does their wrestling reveal about the relationship between Bill and his father?

   Think about
   - why they wrestle
   - why Bill wants to beat his father
   - why Bill cries when he finally wins

4. Do you think the mother's relationships with her son and her husband change as Bill grows up? Give proof from the story for your answer.

5. How do you feel about the images of a father that Kleihauer and Bombeck describe? How do these images compare with what you wrote earlier about your father or the ''typical'' father?

Writing Options

1. Write a diary entry from the perspective of Bill, his father, or his mother about the night Bill pins down his father.

2. Compare and contrast the endings of ''The Cub'' and the Bombeck article. Explain how each might depict a bittersweet memory.

Vocabulary Practice

Exercise   On your paper, write the letter of the word or phrase that best completes each sentence below.

1. Bill might build up his **biceps** by (a) sleeping (b) lifting weights (c) reading.
2. A **conspiratorial** look between father and son shows that they are (a) angry (b) in agreement (c) scared.
3. A **prostrate** person is (a) standing (b) sitting (c) lying down.
4. To **pummel,** Bill must use his (a) knees (b) brain (c) fists.
5. A wrestler who gets hurt badly might **writhe** (a) in pain (b) in anger (c) in boredom.

> *Words*
> *to Know*
> *and Use*
>
> ---
>
> **biceps**
> **conspiratorial**
> **prostrate**
> **pummel**
> **writhe**

Poetry

Taught Me Purple

EVELYN TOOLEY HUNT

The Secret Heart

ROBERT P. TRISTRAM COFFIN

Examine What You Know

Consider the titles of the two poems you are about to read, ''Taught Me Purple'' and ''The Secret Heart.'' For fun, make predictions about the subjects of the poems based on the titles alone. See in how many different directions your own and your classmates' predictions take you. Use your imagination!

Expand Your Knowledge

You have learned that writers use objects to symbolize ideas or feelings. For example, a heart is often used to symbolize love, while a flame may represent a more intense love, or passion. Writers also use colors to symbolize abstract ideas and feelings. Consider the color purple. Traditionally, this color has symbolized two very different ideas. It may be a symbol of mourning or repentance, but it also stands for royalty or nobility. Likewise, something golden can be a symbol of wealth and power, or it can be a symbol of something precious or gifted in a way that promises future joy or success.

Enrich Your Reading

Interpreting Stanzas The lines in poetry are arranged in groups called **stanzas.** In ''Taught Me Purple'' and ''The Secret Heart,'' each stanza resembles a sentence in that it expresses one main idea. To better understand each poem, read the poem as a series of sentences. That is, read one stanza at a time, stopping briefly after each stanza to describe the central image or to state the main idea in your own words.

■ *Biographies of the authors can be found in the Reader's Handbook.*

Taught Me Purple

EVELYN TOOLEY HUNT

My mother taught me purple
    Although she never wore it.
Wash-gray was her circle,
    The tenement her orbit.

5 My mother taught me golden
    And held me up to see it,
Above the broken molding,
    Beyond the filthy street.

My mother reached for beauty
10 And for its lack she died,
Who knew so much of duty
    She could not teach me pride.

ROYAL GOLD 1988 Kay Buckner Private collection.

*R*esponding *to Reading*

First Impressions of "Taught Me Purple"

1. What is your impression of the mother in this poem? Explain.

Second Thoughts on "Taught Me Purple"

2. What does the speaker mean when she says "My mother taught me purple" and "My mother taught me golden"? Consider what these colors might symbolize to the speaker.

3. How does the reality of the mother's life compare with the ideals she has passed on to her child? Give reasons for your answer.

4. How do you think the speaker feels about her mother? Why?

The *Secret Heart*

ROBERT P. TRISTRAM COFFIN

Across the years he could recall
His father one way best of all.

In the stillest hour of night
The boy awakened to a light.

5 Half in dreams, he saw his sire
With his great hands full of fire.

The man had struck a match to see
If his son slept peacefully.

He held his palms each side the spark
10 His love had kindled in the dark.

His two hands were curved apart
In the semblance of a heart.

He wore, it seemed to his small son,
A bare heart on his hidden one,

15 A heart that gave out such a glow
No son awake could bear to know.

It showed a look upon a face
Too tender for the day to trace.

One instant, it lit all about,
20 And then the secret heart went out.

But it shone long enough for one
To know that hands held up the sun.

©Robert George Young/Masterfile, Toronto.

*R*esponding to Reading

First Impressions of "The Secret Heart"

1. After reading this poem, what image stands out most clearly in your mind? Sketch this image or write a description of it.

Second Thoughts on "The Secret Heart"

2. What do the images in this poem suggest about the feelings of the father and of the son?

   Think about
   • what the fire symbolizes in lines 5-6
   • what the heart symbolizes in lines 11-12
   • what the sun symbolizes in lines 21-22

3. Why do you think the father keeps his true feelings a secret?

Comparing the Poems

4. Which poem is a better example of a bittersweet memory? Why? Support your answer with quotes from the poems.

5. How do the children's feelings toward their parents differ? In what ways are they alike?

*L*iterary Concept: Meter

A regular pattern of stressed and unstressed syllables in a line of poetry is called **meter**. Meter may help emphasize particular words or ideas, or it may create a particular mood. To discover the meter, mark the stressed syllables with a **/** and the unstressed syllables with a ◡. For example,

$$\smile \, / \; \smile \, / \; \smile \, / \; \smile \, /$$
Across the years he could recall

On your paper, copy three more lines from either poem and mark them to show meter. Decide if any lines vary from the pattern.

*W*riting Options

1. Choose one of the parents in the poems and compare him or her with another character in this subunit.

2. Rewrite one of the poems in another form, either as prose or as poetry in free verse, such as "Incident in a Rose Garden" on page 65.

EXPOSITION

Most people have bittersweet memories about their first tries at something. Remember the first time you rode a bike or made pizza or tied a tie or used a typewriter? Your first effort may have been funny or frustrating. Would it have helped if you had had someone to explain the process step by step? This is what you will do in the following assignment.

You are about to explain a process—how to do something—to someone else. You might choose to explain a process that someone else used to create or accomplish something. For example, you might tell how the Great Wall of China was built or explain how a solar-powered car works. On the other hand, you might choose to teach your classmates a skill, such as how to change a bicycle tire or tie-dye a T-shirt. In any case, you will first explain the process in writing; then you will use your writing as the basis for an informal speech.

> **Here is your PASSkey to this assignment.**

GUIDED ASSIGNMENT: PROCESS COMPOSITION AND SPEECH

Write a composition and give a speech in which you explain a process.

PURPOSE: To explain a process

AUDIENCE: Your classmates

SUBJECT: A process of your choice

STRUCTURE: A composition and informal speech

Prewriting

STEP 1 **Think of topics** In a small group, brainstorm for processes that you have tried or that interest you. Think about your hobbies, your job, interesting machines you wonder about, tricks, crafts, special buildings, scientific breakthroughs, and so forth. Remember that the purpose of brainstorming is to get as many ideas on paper as quickly as possible, whether they turn out to be good or bad. Here is a partial list of ideas that one group created.

```
how to develop film                how to apply false
how a radar gun works                 fingernails
how to make doughnuts              how videos are edited
how the Vietnam Veterans           how to set a VCR
   Memorial was made               how paper is recycled
```

◀ STUDENT MODEL

STEP 2 **Choose a topic** From your list choose a topic that interests you and that you think would interest your classmates. Since the purpose of this paper is to describe a process, make sure that the topic you choose can be broken down into several clear steps. If you decide to teach a skill, make sure you have used it enough to be able to clearly explain it to others. If you are sharing new information, make sure that you can find the information necessary for your explanation.

STEP 3 **Gather information and list steps of the process** If your topic is one you need to research, use the library. If you can, observe the process in action. For example, if you are explaining how newspapers are made, go to a printing plant to watch, ask questions, and take notes.

If you are teaching a skill, first list all the necessary supplies and equipment. Then actually go through the process yourself. As you work, take notes about what you do. Try to write every step in the process in the order you do it.

When you are finished, make sure the steps are in chronological order. Then check for any missing or incomplete directions and fill in details.

In explaining a process, a diagram or picture is often more effective than paragraphs of description. Make use of such graphic aids for both your composition and your speech.

Finally, consider possible problems. Think of times when you did not carry out the process successfully. What problems did you have? How did you solve them? Include these ideas in your notes.

Here are one student's notes.

```
Goal: to light an outdoor grill
Supplies: charcoal (5- or 10-pound bag), charcoal
             starter fluid, long kitchen matches
Equipment: outdoor grill, either round bottomed or
              open-ended flat; metal trowel or grill shovel
Steps
  1. Remove metal grill where the meat goes.
  2. Scrape old ashes out of bottom of grill. Make sure
     air can reach bottom.
  3. Pour in enough charcoal to cover two-thirds of
     bottom area.
```

◀ STUDENT MODEL

4. Arrange charcoal in a tight mound.
5. Squeeze or spray charcoal starter at the center of the mound, aiming at the inside coals.
6. Put bottle of charcoal starter away from the grill.
7. Wait 30 seconds. Then light a match, and light the center of the mound. Drop match and stand back.
8. Wait. Do not move mound of charcoal until the center glows red.
9. When center coals are well-lit, use trowel to spread charcoal out, arranging unlit ones near lit ones. Put metal grill back on, and cook when ready.

Problems:
carelessness—you can get burned
Don't squirt more fluid!
being impatient—let coals get going on their own

Drafting

STEP 1 **Write an introduction**   Begin with an introduction that clearly states what you are about to explain. Interest your readers right away with an anecdote, interesting fact, or reason why this process is useful or important. Establish your tone in your introduction.

STEP 2 **Include details**   As you write about the steps in the process, keep your audience in mind. Define any unfamiliar terms and be sure to include all the steps. Don't skip steps that you might do automatically.

Special Tip

In presenting a series of steps, use **transitions** to signal the reader that one step has ended and another has begun. Common transitions include words like *first, next, then, at the same time,* and *finally.*

STEP 3 **Write a conclusion**   Remind your readers what the final results of your process are. You might include an explanation of your feelings about mastering the process, or what you got out of researching the process.

Revising and Editing

Having a peer read your draft is especially important when you are giving directions, since what is perfectly clear to you may not be understandable to someone else. Ask your classmate to question any directions that are unclear.

Revision Checklist
1. Is the purpose of the process clearly stated in the introduction?
2. Does the introduction catch the audience's interest?
3. Are the steps of the process clear?
4. Are terms defined? Are possible problems addressed?

Editing   When you have finished revising your draft, proofread for spelling, clarity, and mechanics.

Presenting

Now you must turn your written composition into a speech.

1. Gather materials. Assemble everything you need to do your demonstration. If your process cannot be demonstrated in the classroom, such as how to light a grill, create visual aids that show the steps.

2. Make notes. Do not read from your paper. Take notes about the main points on note cards. Leave space for reminders.

3. Practice! Practice not only what you will say but also what you will do. Decide at what points during your speech you should do or show something, and put reminders on your note cards.

4. Give your speech. Don't be afraid—your classmates want to hear what you have to say. Be in tune with your audience and look at them. Watch for confused faces as you talk. You may need to go over something again if it is not understood.

Reflecting on Your Writing

Answer the following questions and put them in your portfolio.

1. Was it easier for you to write the paper or to give the speech? Why?

2. Do you think having written this paper will help you give better directions in the future? Explain.

3. Will you be able to transfer what you have learned about writing directions to other types of writing?

LANGUAGE
WORKSHOP

COMBINING WITH WORD ADDITIONS

A successful writer, like a successful chef, knows when and how to combine ingredients to create the most satisfying results. Sometimes you can take a single word from one sentence and add it very effectively to another, related sentence. When you add words to another sentence in this way, place them close to the person, thing, or action they describe.

> Aunt Zurletha rented a room. *It was a* small *room.*
> Aunt Zurletha rented a **small** room.

Sometimes you can combine more than two sentences when one sentence contains the main idea and the others add only one important detail each. In such cases you may have to use a comma or the word *and.*

> The kind woman was never in her room. *The woman was* hard-working. *Her room was* tiny.
> The kind, **hard-working** woman was never in her **tiny** room.

> At the beach Aunt Zurletha wore a bathing suit. *The bathing suit was* silky. *She also wore* rubber sandals.
> At the beach Aunt Zurletha wore a **silky** bathing suit **and rubber sandals.**

Sometimes you may need to change the form of a word when you combine sentences. This usually means adding an ending such as *-y, -ed, -ing,* or *-ly.*

> Aunt Zurletha's hair was tied in a ponytail. *She had* red curls.
> Aunt Zurletha's **red, curly** hair was tied in a ponytail.

> Aunt Zurletha loved to wear jewelry. *Her jewelry* matched.
> Aunt Zurletha loved to wear **matching** jewelry.

PUNCTUATION RULE

Sometimes you will need to use commas between two or more adjectives. If *and* sounds natural between the adjectives and if you can reverse the order of the adjectives without changing meaning, use a comma.

Exercise 1 Combine each group of sentences by adding words from one sentence to another. Eliminate the words in italics. Remember that you may need to change the form of a word.

1. "Li Chang's Million" took place in the city of Peking. *Peking was a* beautiful *city.*
2. The narrator of the story was a pilot. *He was an* American.

3. He felt wealthy with four hundred dollars in his pocket. *His wealth felt* incredible.

4. For two hours he wandered through the bazaar. *He was* aimless.

5. He found a fur shop at the end of a dark alley. *The shop was* small.

6. The pilot examined a fur garment. *He was* careless.

7. Then he saw a pair of eyes. *The eyes were* sad. *The eyes were* hurt.

8. The pilot had criticized the child's work. *The pilot was* insensitive.

9. He decided to give the boy one million yuan. *His decision was* sudden.

10. The pilot was forced to leave before he could complete his plan. *This was* unfortunate.

Exercise 2 Work in groups to rewrite the following passage, eliminating the words in italics and combining the sentences in parentheses.

(One of my bittersweet memories is about my grandfather. *He was a* sweet, funny *man*.) (He lived by himself in the apartment he had shared with my grandmother. *The apartment was* old. *It was* dusty.) (The apartment was in the middle of the city. *The city* bustled.) (My grandfather loved playing card games with me and telling me about the old country he had left as a boy. *The card games were* silly.) As I got older, I talked more, and he talked less. (He listened to me drone on and on about my baseball cards, my new bicycles, my new friends. *He was a* patient *listener*.) Then, somehow, I grew up, and it seemed I was always too busy to see him. (I didn't really forget my grandfather. *He was* lovable. *He was* funny.) I was always making—and then breaking—plans to visit him. He died during my second year of college. (In my headlong rush into life, I had lost him. *I was* careless.) As I had grown up, he had grown old. (Those are my memories of my grandfather. *My memories are* bittersweet.)

Exercise 3   Analyzing and Revising Your Writing

1. Take a paper from your portfolio. Choose a passage to analyze.

2. Rewrite the passage, using the sentence building skills you have learned in this workshop.

3. Check to see that you have punctuated correctly.

4. Compare your revision to the original passage. Which do you prefer?

5. The next time you proofread your work, remember to check for related sentences that might be combined effectively.

SPEAKING AND LISTENING
WORKSHOP

PUBLIC SPEAKING

Do you get butterflies at the idea of speaking in front of an audience—even if it's just a short oral report to your class? If so, you're not alone; everyone gets nervous before speaking in public. If you prepare carefully, however, you'll be able to keep the butterflies under control.

1. PREPARE CAREFULLY.

- **Choose an interesting topic.** If the topic bores you, it will probably bore your audience as well.

- **Collect more information than you need.** The more you know about your topic, the more comfortable you'll feel.

- **Organize your speech.** Write your speech notes on sturdy index cards. Make sure your writing is easy to read, and make sure the cards are numbered in the proper order.

2. REHEARSE THOROUGHLY.

- **Practice, practice, and then practice some more.** Rehearse the speech over and over again, *out loud.* Say it in the shower, in your room before you go to sleep, and especially in front of a mirror. As you get the speech almost memorized, work at making the tone natural and energetic.

- **Impose on your friends and relatives.** Beg if you have to, but get someone you trust to listen to your speech and make suggestions.

3. GO FOR IT!

- **Start strong.** Smile. Take a deep breath. Then use a joke, a story, or an interesting question or statement to grab the audience's attention.

- **Speak directly to your audience.** Make eye contact with the people in your audience. As you look around, talk to each person as if he or she were the only person in the room. If people seem to be losing interest, pump a little energy into your voice, move around a little, speak a little louder or softer, or maybe even skip to your next point.

- **Finish strong.** Summarize your main ideas. Use one last joke, anecdote, or quote to wrap things up.

Exercise Prepare, rehearse, and deliver a two-minute speech on a topic of your choice.

HELP!

Prepare a few interesting charts or other visual aids. They'll give your audience something to look at . . . besides you!

REMINDER

If possible, tape-record your speech. Even if your voice sounds tinny on tape, using a tape recorder will help you get rid of all those *um's* and *ah's,* and it will tell you where to slow down and where to use more emphasis.

$\mathcal{P}$OINTS OF CONFLICT

The conflict, or struggle between opponents, is what makes literature exciting. You read to find out who wins. The most extreme conflicts result in physical battles. Most conflicts, though, are the kind you have daily—conflicts with people who are close to you, and conflicts within your own mind or heart.

In the following selections, individuals struggle with teachers, parents, brothers, sisters, even out-of-this-world opponents.

Fiction

from Annie John
JAMAICA KINCAID

*E*xamine What You Know

This story is about a girl who finds herself in trouble with her teacher. Think about times you or your friends have had run-ins with teachers, parents, or other adults. What usually caused the problem? Whom did you blame for the problem? Discuss these situations with your classmates.

*E*xpand Your Knowledge

Annie John's ancestors were African slaves on the island of Antigua (an tē' gwə) in the Caribbean Sea. In 1493 Christopher Columbus became the first European to reach Antigua, which was inhabited by Carib Indians. In 1632 England claimed the island, and British settlers soon began importing African slaves to work on sugar cane plantations. By 1774 about twenty-six hundred whites lived on Antigua with about thirty-eight thousand slaves. In the 1830's the English issued a proclamation freeing Antigua's slaves. Most of the British settlers left the island in the years that followed, but the English government still controlled the island. Almost 150 years later, in 1981, Antigua won its independence.

*E*nrich Your Reading

Understanding Flashbacks As the narrator tells this story about a day in her life, she jumps back in time to describe important past incidents. Such excursions into the past are called **flashbacks.** In Annie's story the flashbacks come in the form of daydreams. Keep track of which events occur in the present and which are flashbacks.

■ *A biography of the author can be found on page 341.*

from Annie John

JAMAICA KINCAID

Our teacher, Miss Edward, paced up and down in front of the class in her usual way. In front of her desk stood a small table, and on it stood the dunce cap. The dunce cap was in the shape of a coronet,[1] with an adjustable opening in the back so that it could fit any head. It was made of cardboard with a shiny gold paper covering and the word *DUNCE* in shiny red paper on the front. When the sun shone on it, the dunce cap was all aglitter, almost as if you were being tricked into thinking it a desirable thing to wear. As Miss Edward paced up and down, she would pass between us and the dunce cap like an eclipse. Each Friday morning we were given a small test to see how well we had learned the things taught to us all week. The girl who scored lowest was made to wear the dunce cap all day the following Monday. On many Mondays Ruth wore it—only, with her short yellow hair, when the dunce cap was sitting on her head she looked like a girl attending a birthday party in *The Schoolgirl's Own Annual.*[2]

It was Miss Edward's way to ask one of us a question the answer to which she was sure the girl would not know and then put the same question to another girl who she was sure would know the answer. The girl who did not answer correctly would then have to repeat the correct answer in the exact words of the other girl. Many times I had heard my exact words repeated over and over again, and I liked it especially when the girl doing the repeating was one I didn't care about very much. Pointing a finger at Ruth, Miss Edward asked a question the answer to which was "On the third of November 1493, a Sunday morning, Christopher Columbus discovered Dominica." Ruth, of course, did not know the answer, as she did not know the answer to many questions about the West Indies. I could hardly blame her. Ruth had come all the way from England. Perhaps she did not want to be in the West Indies at all. Perhaps she wanted to be in England, where no one would remind her constantly of the terrible things her ancestors had done; perhaps she had felt even worse when her father was a missionary in Africa. I could see how Ruth felt from looking at her face. Her ancestors had been the masters, while ours had been the slaves. She had such a lot to be ashamed of, and by being with us every day she was always being reminded. We could look everybody in the eye, for our ancestors had done nothing wrong except just sit somewhere, defenseless. Of course, sometimes, what with our teachers and our books, it was hard for us to tell on which side we really now belonged—with the masters or the slaves—for it was all history, it was all in the past, and everybody

---

1. **coronet** (kôr′ ə net′): a small crown.
2. ***The Schoolgirl's Own Annual:*** a magazine for girls.

behaved differently now; all of us celebrated Queen Victoria's birthday,[3] even though she had been dead a long time. But we, the descendants of the slaves, knew quite well what had really happened, and I was sure that if the tables had been turned, we would have acted differently; I was sure that if our ancestors had gone from Africa to Europe and come upon the people living there, they would have taken a proper interest in the Europeans on first seeing them, and said, "How nice," and then gone home to tell their friends about it.

I lost track of what was going on around me.

I was sitting at my desk, having these thoughts to myself. I don't know how long it had been since I lost track of what was going on around me. I had not noticed that the girl who was asked the question after Ruth failed—a girl named Hyacinth—had only got a part of the answer correct. I had not noticed that after these two attempts Miss Edward had launched into a harangue[4] about what a worthless bunch we were compared to girls of the past. In fact, I was no longer on the same chapter we were studying. I was way ahead, at the end of the chapter about Columbus's third voyage. In this chapter, there was a picture of Columbus that took up a whole page, and it was in color—one of only five color pictures in the book. In this picture Columbus was seated in the bottom of a ship. He was wearing the usual three-quarter trousers and a shirt with enormous sleeves, both the trousers and shirt made of maroon-colored velvet. His

hat, which was cocked up on one side of his head, had a gold feather in it, and his black shoes had huge gold buckles. His hands and feet were bound up in chains, and he was sitting there staring off into space, looking quite dejected and miserable. The picture had as a title "Columbus in Chains," printed at the bottom of the page. What had happened was that the usually quarrelsome Columbus had got into a disagreement with people who were even more quarrelsome, and a man named Bobadilla, representing King Ferdinand and Queen Isabella, had sent him back to Spain fettered in chains attached to the bottom of a ship. What just deserts,[5] I thought, for I did not like Columbus. How I loved this picture—to see the usually triumphant Columbus, brought so low, seated at the bottom of a boat just watching things go by. Shortly after I first discovered it in my history book, I heard my mother read out loud to my father a letter she had received from her sister, who still lived with her mother and father in the very same Dominica, which is where my mother came from. Ma Chess was fine, wrote my aunt, but Pa Chess was not well. Pa Chess was having a bit of trouble with his limbs; he was not able to go about as he pleased; often he had to depend on someone else to do one thing or another for him. My mother read the letter in quite a state, her voice rising to a higher pitch with each sentence. After she read the part about Pa Chess's stiff limbs, she turned to my father and laughed as she said, "So the great man can no longer just get up and go. How I would love to see his face now!" When I next saw the picture of Columbus sitting there all locked up in his

---

3. **Queen Victoria's birthday:** birthday of Victoria, queen of Great Britain from 1837 to 1901. It was celebrated in Antigua, then a British colony.
4. **harangue** (hər aŋ'): a long, blustering speech.
5. **just deserts** (di zɜrts'): exactly the reward or punishment one deserves.

ORANGE SWEATER 1955 Elmer Bischoff Oil on canvas 48½" x 57". San Francisco
Museum of Modern Art. Gift of Mr. and Mrs. Mark Schorer.

chains, I wrote under it the words "The Great Man Can No Longer Just Get Up and Go." I had written this out with my fountain pen and in Old English lettering—a script I had recently mastered. As I sat there looking at the picture, I traced the words with my pen over and over, so that the letters grew big and you could read what I had written from not very far away. I don't know how long it was before I heard that my name, Annie John, was being said by this bellowing dragon in the form of Miss Edward, bearing down on me.

I had never been a favorite of hers. Her favorite was Hilarene. It must have pained Miss Edward that I so often beat out Hilarene. Not that I liked Miss Edward and wanted her to like me back, but all my other teachers regarded me with much affection, would always tell my mother that I was the most charming student they had ever had, beamed at me when they saw me coming, and were very sorry when they had to write some version of this on my report card: "Annie is an unusually bright girl. She is well behaved in class, at least in the presence of her masters and mistresses, but behind their backs and outside the classroom quite the opposite is true." When my mother read this or something like it, she would burst into tears. She had hoped to display, with a great <u>flourish</u>, my report card to her friends, along with whatever prize I had won. Instead, the report card would have to take a place at the bottom of the old trunk in which she kept any important thing that had to do with me. I became not a favorite of Miss Edward's in the following way: Each Friday afternoon the girls in the lower forms were given, instead of a last lesson period, an extra-long recess. We were to use this in ladylike recreation—walks, chats about the novels and poems we were reading, showing each other the new embroidery stitches we had learned to master in home class, or something just as seemly.[6] Instead, some of the girls would play a game of cricket or rounders or stones, but most of us would go to the far end of the school grounds and play band. In this game, of which teachers and parents disapproved and which was sometimes absolutely forbidden, we would place our arms around each other's waist or shoulders, forming lines of ten or so girls, and then we would dance from one end of the school grounds to the other. As we danced, we would sometimes chant these words: "Tee la la la, come go. Tee la la la, come go." At other times we would sing a popular calypso[7] song which usually had lots of unladylike words to it.

Up and down the schoolyard, away from our teachers, we would dance and sing. At the end of recess—forty-five minutes—we were missing ribbons and other ornaments from our hair, the pleats of our linen tunics became unset, the collars of our blouses were pulled out, and we were soaking wet all the way down to our bloomers.[8] When the school bell rang, we would make a whooping sound, as if in a great panic, and then we would throw ourselves on top of each other as we laughed and shrieked. We would then run back to our classes, where we prepared to file into the auditorium for evening prayers. After that, it was home for the weekend. But how could we go straight home after all that excitement? No sooner were we on the street than we would form little groups, depending on the direction we were headed in. I was never keen on joining them on the way home, because I was sure I would run into my mother. Instead, my friends and I would go to our usual place near the back of the churchyard and sit on the tombstones of people who had been buried there way before slavery was abolished, in 1833. We would sit and sing bad songs and use forbidden words. While some of us watched, the others would walk up and down on the large tombstones, showing off their legs. It was immediately a popular idea; everybody soon wanted to do it. It wasn't long before many girls—the ones whose mothers didn't pay strict attention to what they were doing—started to come to school on Fridays wearing not bloomers under their uniforms but underpants trimmed

---

6. **seemly:** proper; fitting.

7. **calypso** (kə lip′ sō): a type of improvised West Indian singing with a strong rhythmic beat.

8. **bloomers:** a baggy undergarment like shorts, gathered at the knees.

Words to Know and Use | **flourish** (flur′ ish) *n.* a sweeping, showy movement of the arms, legs, or body

JAMAICAN GOTHIC 1968 Karl Parboosingh National Gallery of Jamaica, Kingston Photograph by Jeffrey Ploskonka.

thing that my mother couldn't bring herself to repeat my misdeed to my father in my presence. I got the usual punishment of dinner alone, outside under the breadfruit[9] tree, but added on to that, I was not allowed to go to the library on Saturday, and on Sunday, after Sunday school and dinner, I was not allowed to take a stroll in the botanical gardens, where Gwen was waiting for me in the bamboo grove.

Oh, how I wished the ground would open up and take her in. . . .

That happened when I was in the first form.[10] Now here Miss Edward stood. Her whole face was on fire. Her eyes were bulging out of her head. I was sure that at any minute they would land at my feet and roll away. The small pimples on her face, already looking as if they were constantly irritated, now ballooned into huge, on-the-verge-of-exploding boils. Her head shook from side to side. Her strange bottom, which she carried high in the air, seemed to rise up so high that it almost touched the ceiling. Why did I not pay attention, she said. My impertinence was beyond endurance. She then found a hundred words for the different forms my impertinence took. On she went. I was just getting used to this amazing bellowing when suddenly she was speechless. In

with lace and satin frills. It also wasn't long before an end came to all that. One Friday afternoon Miss Edward, on her way home from school, took a shortcut through the churchyard. She must have heard the commotion we were making, because there she suddenly was, saying, "What is the meaning of this?"—just the very thing someone like her would say if she came unexpectedly on something like us. It was obvious that I was the ringleader. Oh, how I wished the ground would open up and take her in, but it did not. We all shamefacedly slunk home, I with Miss Edward at my side. Tears came to my mother's eyes when she heard what I had done. It was apparently such a bad

---

9. **breadfruit:** a large, round, starchy tropical fruit.
10. **the first form:** a grade in British-style secondary schools; students are about twelve or thirteen years old.

fact everything stopped. Her eyes stopped, her bottom stopped, her pimples stopped. Yes, she had got close enough so that her eyes caught a glimpse of what I had done to my textbook. The glimpse soon led to closer inspection. It was bad enough that I had defaced my schoolbook by writing in it. That I should write under the picture of Columbus "The Great Man . . ." etc. was just too much. I had gone too far this time, defaming one of the great men in history, Christopher Columbus, discoverer of the island that was my home. And now look at me. I was not even hanging my head in remorse. Had my peers ever seen anyone so arrogant, so blasphemous?[11]

I was sent to the headmistress, Miss Moore. As punishment, I was removed from my position as prefect,[12] and my place was taken by the odious[13] Hilarene. As an added punishment, I was ordered to copy Books I and II of *Paradise Lost,* by John Milton, and to have it done a week from that day. I then couldn't wait to get home to lunch and the comfort of my mother's kisses and arms. I had nothing to worry about there yet; it would be a while before my mother and father heard of my bad deeds. What a terrible morning! Seeing my mother would be such a tonic—something to pick me up.

When I got home, my mother kissed me absent-mindedly. My father had got home ahead of me, and they were already deep in conversation, my father regaling her with some unusually outlandish thing the oaf Mr. Oatie had done. I washed my hands and took my place at table. My mother brought me my lunch. I took one smell of it, and I could tell that it was the much-hated breadfruit. My mother said not at all, it was a new kind of rice imported from Belgium, and not breadfruit, mashed and forced through a ricer, as I thought. She went back to talking to my father. My father could hardly get a few words out of his mouth before she was a jellyfish of laughter. I sat there, putting my food in my mouth. I could not believe that she couldn't see how miserable I was and so reach out a hand to comfort me and caress my cheek, the way she usually did when she sensed that something was amiss with me. I could not believe how she laughed at everything he said and how bitter it made me feel to see how much she liked him. I ate my meal. The more I ate of it, the more I was sure that it was breadfruit. When I finished, my mother got up to remove my plate. As she started out the door, I said, "Tell me, really, the name of the thing I just ate."

My mother said, "You just ate some breadfruit. I made it look like rice so that you would eat it. It's very good for you, filled with lots of vitamins." As she said this, she laughed. She was standing half inside the door, half outside. Her body was in the shade of our house, but her head was in the sun. When she laughed, her mouth opened to show off big, shiny, sharp white teeth. It was as if my mother had suddenly turned into a crocodile. 🙐

---

11. **blasphemous** (blas′ fə məs): disrespectful.

12. **prefect** (prē′ fekt): in British-style schools, the student who is in charge when the teacher is not in the room.

13. **odious** (ō′ dē əs): hateful; disgusting.

Words to Know and Use | **defame** (dē fām′) *v.* to attack or injure someone's reputation; disgrace
remorse (ri môrs′) *n.* a deep sense of guilt for having done wrong
arrogant (ar′ ə gənt) *adj.* full of undeserved pride and self-importance; overbearing

explain

Responding to Reading

First Impressions

1. Does Annie seem like a typical young person to you? Why or why not?

Second Thoughts

2. What is your opinion of Annie John?
   Think about
   • her behavior in school
   • her attitudes
   • the conflicts she feels

3. Do you agree with Annie's view of Miss Edward? Explain.

4. Using details from the story, describe the relationship between Annie and her mother.

5. Why do you think Annie sees her mother as a crocodile at the end of the story?

Broader Connections

6. If you were Annie John's teacher, how would you handle her and students like her? Express your ideas in the form of positive and practical advice for teachers.

Literary Concept: Techniques of Humor

Jamaica Kincaid sprinkles humor throughout this story in the form of amusing descriptions, exaggeration, and sarcasm. Notice how **exaggeration,** or overstatement, adds humor to the description of Miss Edward as "the bellowing dragon" with her "strange bottom, which . . . seemed to rise up so high that it almost touched the ceiling." Identify other examples of exaggeration in this story. **Sarcasm** is humorous, ironic criticism. Do you feel that Annie is being sarcastic in her description on page 334 of what her African ancestors would have done? Why or why not?

Concept Review: Conflict Characters in literature struggle with internal conflict (conflicts in their minds) and external conflict (conflict with other characters or forces, such as society). What are Annie John's points of conflict? Identify each as internal or external.

Writing Options

1. Think about some of the other young people you have read about in this book. Choose one, male or female, who could be a good friend for Annie. Explain your choice.

2. Skim the story for information about Annie John's school. Make a chart that compares her school with yours.

3. Write the dialogue Miss Edward might have with Annie's parents if she called them on the day described in this story.

4. Write a letter Ruth might send to a best friend in her native England. Imagine and describe her feelings about Miss Edward and the school.

Vocabulary Practice

Exercise On your paper, write the word from the list that best describes each of Annie's actions below.

1. signing her name with an elaborate swirl
2. feeling sorry about causing her mother to cry
3. bragging about her accomplishments
4. speaking rudely to her teacher
5. writing insulting things about a famous explorer

> *Words to Know and Use*
>
> ___
>
> **arrogant**
> **defaming**
> **flourish**
> **impertinence**
> **remorse**

extend

Options for Learning

1 • Columbus in Chains Draw or paint your version of "Columbus in Chains." Before you start, reread Annie's description of the scene and find drawings and paintings of Columbus that will help you capture his appearance.

2 • Visit Antigua Design and write a tourist brochure advertising Antigua. Do some research so you can include information about recreational activities, places of interest to visit, and hotels and restaurants. You might also include a brief history of the island. Find or draw pictures of Antigua for your brochure.

3 • Annie's Miss Edward Draw a caricature of Miss Edward. Remember that a caricature exaggerates certain physical characteristics or mannerisms to make a point. Use the vivid descriptions in the story as a source of ideas.

FACT FINDER

What happened to Columbus when he returned to Spain in chains?

Jamaica Kincaid

1949-

Although Jamaica Kincaid left her native Antigua after graduating from high school, her stories are set on Antigua or other Caribbean islands. In fact, Kincaid used her own childhood memories to write *Annie John*. The mother-daughter relationship so important in *Annie John* is a strong theme in many of Kincaid's other stories. The Columbus-in-chains incident reflects Kincaid's own childhood anger about the emphasis on white historical figures. "Black Antiguans had historical figures," she says. "I never heard of them in school." Remembering her anger, she advises young people, "Don't be afraid to be angry. It's legitimate and necessary."

Besides *Annie John*, Kincaid has published three other books—*At the Bottom of the River*, *A Small Place*, and *Lucy*. She also writes for *The New Yorker* magazine.

Kincaid lives with her husband, composer Allen Shawn, and their two children in Vermont. Of her adopted homeland, Kincaid says, "What I really feel about America is that it's given me a place to be myself—but myself as I was formed somewhere else."

Autobiography

Fish Eyes
DAVID BRENNER

Examine What You Know

Sibling rivalry is the psychological term for the competitive behavior among brothers and sisters that is normal in most families. Think of your own family and those you have observed. How do children show sibling rivalry? Think of extreme examples as well as normal examples. Discuss them with your class.

Expand Your Knowledge

Popular comedian David Brenner has appeared often on television and in night clubs. Brenner draws much of his humor from everyday experiences. Many of his funniest stories come from his childhood in a big-city neighborhood that provided him with "stockpiles of laughter." In this autobiographical piece, you will read about the rivalry between Brenner and his brother and sister.

Write Before You Read

"Fish Eyes" tells of the practical jokes Brenner and his siblings played on each other when they were young. Describe either a practical joke you have played on a brother, sister, or friend or a memorable one you have heard about. How did your victim feel about the trick? How satisfied did you feel with the trick?

■ *A biography of the author can be found in the Reader's Handbook.*

Fish Eyes

DAVID BRENNER

Ladies and Gentlemen and Children of all ages (drum roll, please), I am proud to bring to you, from its very beginning to its very ending, the very true and hopefully very funny story of little David Brenner and his fish eyes.

Let's have a brief background of the Louis and Estelle Brenner offspring. The oldest, Mel, "Moby Dick"; the middle, Blanche, "Bib"; and the itsy-bitsy little baby, David, "Kingy." Very close and very much in love with one another in spite of great differences in age and lifestyle. Whatever sibling rivalry existed was expressed lovingly in the wildest, weirdest, most bizarre practical jokes and most disturbingly creative attacks. The oldest was the most <u>devious</u>. For example:

My brother offered me a delicious new drink—and I discovered—pure carrot juice. He pretended to join me in drinking some. I didn't pretend, taking the biggest gulp of all time of the most <u>rancid</u>-tasting liquid of all time, almost causing me to throw up on the spot. The oldest rolled on the floor bursting with laughter as I charged upstairs to brush my teeth and gargle. The youngest strikes back. Every night I poured just a few drops of the awful carrot juice into my brother's milk. Every night he complained that his milk tasted rather peculiar

but continued to drink it until all the juice was consumed. As the last glass was finished, I announced what I had been doing. His turn to brush and gargle.

I was never safe in my own house.

The oldest also had the sickest sense of humor. His idea of fun was to sneak up on me while I was reading or sleeping and place a dirty sock of his on my shoulder or over my face. Now remember that this is a man tormenting a boy, a full-grown man with a Ph.D. degree, a college professor, a brilliant intellect.[1] I'd be watching TV and all of a sudden I'm smothered with a dirty gym sock, or I'd be doing my homework and suddenly would smell something rotten, only to see the sock my brother was dangling in front of my forehead. I was never safe in my own house, not even when I went to sleep in the bedroom I shared with my big, <u>demented</u> brother. When he would return home after a date, he would sneak up to the bed and lay a dirty sock over my

---

1. **intellect** (in′ tə lekt′): a person of high intelligence.

Words to Know and Use | **devious** (dē′ vē əs) *adj.* not honest; deceiving; underhanded
rancid (ran′ sid) *adj.* spoiled; smelly; offensive
demented (dē ment′ id) *adj.* mentally deranged; mad; insane

343

David Brenner at age nine poses with his mother, his father, and his brother, who is home from the Korean War. From *Soft Pretzels with Mustard* by David Brenner, Arbor House, New York.

sleeping face. Sometimes he would pile as many as a half-dozen socks on my face. Of course, I struck back as best I could. For these sock wars, we wouldn't put our dirty socks in the clothing hamper to be washed. My mother was always complaining about the missing socks. So as not to aggravate Mother and in order to better aggravate each other, we both began wearing the same socks for a week or so while throwing clean socks into the hamper. My mother was happy, and we developed more deadly sock bombs.

My best attack ended the war forever. While my brother was out on a date, I rigged a series of clothesline pulleys across the ceiling of my bedroom, through which I put a string, on the end of which was a rancid sock. When lowered, this foul article of clothing would come to rest directly above my brother's pillow. A second dreadful sock was rigged so that it could be pulled across his pillow. I then tied the string to my hand and forced myself to stay awake until my brother returned from his date.

In the middle of the night he came home. I faked deep breathing as I heard him climb into our bed. I waited until I heard the familiar sound of his sleeping breathing, then I ever so slowly pulled the string that released the sock so that it hung a few inches above his nose. As he sniffed, twisted and turned onto his side, I pulled the string that brought the other sock slowly sliding up onto and across his pillow, coming to rest directly at his nose. He sniffed, coughed, and opened his watering eyes, and stared at the moldy cloth object perched at the tip of his nose. I then released the pulley string so that the first sock came pummeling from the ceiling. A direct hit—right over his face. My brother gagged and shot up. I rolled around the bed in hysterics. Moby Dick, on the merits of originality and ingenuity, conceded victory and called a truce. So ended the War of the Socks.

Warfare with sister Bib was of an entirely different nature. She had a proof-perfect aim. She could hit just about any target, from any distance, with just about any weapon, her favorite being a rubber band

Words to Know and Use

ingenuity (in′ jə n$\overline{oo}$′ ə tē) *n.* originality, cleverness, skill
concede (kən sēd′) *v.* to admit as certain; acknowledge; grant

with a semistraightened paper clip or a V-shaped wad made from tightly rolled paper. Then, too, she could throw anything, from a sofa pillow to a stale end of a rye bread, with the same deadly skill. I would tease her, she'd pick up something, I'd run as quickly as I could, she'd haul off and throw, I'd get smacked with it. I never learned my lesson. What I should have done was tease her from behind a protective shield or from another city.

Now for the fish-eye incident. One day I challenged a friend of mine to a game of stickball. . . .

The fellow I challenged to a game was the best, or second best, according to me, stickball player in the neighborhood. We were to play longways on my street. Kids from all over the neighborhood came to see the playoff.

We flipped a coin and he won. I would bat first. I got myself positioned at home plate, a small pothole in the street. The first pitch was a big mistake on his part. It was low and on the outside, just where I liked it. I knew it was going to be a home run as soon as the bat left my shoulder, and it would've been, if I hadn't gotten hit in the back of the head with a small red brick.

I collapsed to the street. I didn't know what or who had hit me. I saw who as soon as I rolled over onto my back. There she was, my sister, running across the roofs.

The game was called off. I got to my feet dizzily and staggered toward my house. A huge lump was already coming out on the back of my head. It looked like a person was following me. When I got into the house, I didn't say anything to my mother, because there was an unwritten rule in the streets that one never squeals. It was a sacred law.

I weaved into the kitchen, where my mother was preparing fish for dinner. The lump on my head reflected a large shadow on the wall.

Now, preparing fish for dinner was different in those days. Nowadays you go to a supermarket and there's a fish counter and inside are all the fish already prepared for you. You reach in, you take a white thing wrapped in cellophane paper marked "Fish." It could be anything—a gym sock, anything. When I was a kid, it was a lot different, especially if you were poor. Your mother either went to the local fish market or bought the fish off a pushcart. No matter where you bought it, you had to prepare the fish yourself. It wasn't cleaned. You bought the whole fish, with the head and the tail, a little hat, eyeglasses, sneakers, the works. Then the fisherman would wrap it up in a newspaper. I still feel a little squeamish when I open a newspaper, because as a kid, sometimes you'd open a paper and under the headlines there'd be this open-mouthed carp staring at you.

Next, your mother had to prepare the fish herself. She had to cut off the head and the tail and put in her own mercury.[2] It was entirely different then and it was difficult.

While my mother was preparing the fish for dinner, I was standing there wobbling, thinking of how I could get revenge on my sister. I glanced down on the drainboard of the sink and saw a pair of fish eyes staring at me. I scooped them up and put them in my pocket. I got some Krazy Glue and glued them to my forehead and then climbed into the dirty clothing hamper in the hallway with a flashlight in my mouth, the light flashing inward. I waited until my sister opened the hamper to throw in some of her

---

2. **put in her own mercury:** a joking reference to the fact that today some fish contain poisonous levels of the chemical mercury as a result of water pollution.

delicacies,[3] then I turned on the flashlight. When my sister saw my red cheeks and the four eyes, she fainted, but, as she fell, she slammed the lid of the hamper against the end of my flashlight, lodging it in my throat. Immediately, I climbed out of the hamper and started running down the hall. My mother saw me, thought I had jammed a pipe in my throat and my eyes were coming out of my head. She collapsed on the spot. I charged downstairs. My father glanced up. Nothing ever bothered my father. He just looked at me and said, "How ya doin', four-eyes?"

My father followed me into the kitchen, where I was removing the fish eyes from my forehead, after having successfully extracted the flashlight from my throat. Lou took a long puff on his cigar and slowly blew the smoke up to the kitchen ceiling. He removed the cigar from his mouth and looked at me. Then in his soft, Godfather-type[4] whisper, he spoke: "Kingy, I want you to take those fish eyes into the backyard and throw them into the garbage can or else I'm going to see that you eat them for dinner."

I didn't need more convincing. I ran out into the backyard, opened the garbage can lid and . . . well, I looked into the eyes of the eyes. It was as if we had become friends. I just couldn't throw my new-found friends into the garbage just like that. They were pleading with me to save them, silently promising that they could offer me more fun. I opened the lid and rattled the can noisily, as though I were throwing away the eyes, which was really dumb because there was no way two eyes could make that much noise. You could throw away an entire cow more quietly.

I then carefully put the fish eyes into my pocket and went into the house. I apologized to my sister and mother for the inci-dent. Then I casually walked into the dining room and as silently as possible slid open the top drawer of the dresser where the glue was kept. I took the glue and ducked out into the back alley. I then reglued the fish eyes to my forehead and walked up to 60th Street, the bustling shopping area for the neighborhood.

The neighborhood was terrorized. I was very happy.

I would walk up to a store whose front window was painted halfway up in order to use the space for advertising, and then I would tap on the window lightly but loudly enough to be heard while simultaneously raising my head so that the fish eyes would appear first and then my own wide-open eyes. Women shoppers would scream. I did it to about six stores. The rumor was flying that a monster was loose on 60th Street. The neighborhood was terrorized. I was very happy.

I returned to my house and placed the two fish eyes in the center drawer of my bedroom dresser, a hand-me-down from my brother, who had as a child put a big ball of roofing tar in the center drawer. I think he was trying to corner the black-tar market.

Well, you know the attention span and memory span of young children. It isn't very long. The world is all new and all exciting, and there is so much to enjoy and remember that one forgets so much, such as

---

3. **delicacies:** here, underwear; a humorous reference.
4. **Godfather-type:** gruff, like the voice of Marlon Brando, star of the movie *The Godfather,* as he played the role of a mobster.

a pair of fish eyes casually placed in a drawer.

The summer rolled along. July came and with it a horrific heat spell. The second floor of our house began to stink. Then the first floor. The whole house reeked of a strange and horrible odor. Although we really could not afford to call an exterminator, we were forced to, because we would gag upon entering the house, and my father's search for the dead animal had failed. We had no choice—Morris the Exterminator Man.

He arrived in his exterminator truck, which had a huge water bug on the roof almost as big as the truck itself. The water bug was on its back with its legs up in the air, and Morris's slogan was painted across the side paneling: "Nobody Gets Away Alive from Morris the Bug Killer."

Morris came into the house and sniffed around. He went up the stairs to the second floor. I could hear him open the door to my bedroom and enter. I think I even remember hearing him sniffing around in there. I know I do remember hearing him scream and seeing him charge down the stairs.

"What is it, Morris? Have you found it?"

"Yes, it's a dead animal."

"What kind of animal?"

"I don't really know, Mrs. Brenner. I've never seen anything like it in my life. It's in the center drawer of David's dresser. It's this real small, soft, black animal and from the look of its eyes, I'd say it's been dead at least two years."

My father, mother, sister, and brother snapped their heads in my direction. I leaped to my feet and ran out of the house. There was no way I was going to have fish eyes and tar for dinner.

That's the truth, the whole truth, nothing but the truth about the pair of fish eyes as it all happened during one of those glorious summers so long ago in the days of my wild, woolly, disturbed—and fun-filled—youth. Would I do it all over again if I could? You're darn right I would. ❧

INSIGHT

Fireworks

AMY LOWELL

You hate me and I hate you,
And we are so polite, we two!

But whenever I see you, I burst apart
And scatter the sky with my blazing
   heart.
It spits and sparkles in stars and balls,
Buds into roses—and flares, and falls.

Scarlet buttons, and pale green disks,
Silver spirals and asterisks,
Shoot and tremble in a mist
Peppered with mauve and amethyst.

I shine in the windows and light up the
   trees,
And all because I hate you, if you
   please.

And when you meet me, you rend
   asunder
And go up in a flaming wonder
Of saffron cubes, and crimson moons,
And wheels all amaranths and maroons.

Golden lozenges and spades,
Arrows of malachites and jades,
Patens of copper, azure sheaves.
As you mount, you flash in the glossy
   leaves.

Such fireworks as we make, we two!
Because you hate me and I hate you.

explain

Responding to Reading

First Impressions

1. Which part of "Fish Eyes" did you find the most humorous? See whether your classmates agree.

Second Thoughts

2. Do you find Brenner's family life believable? Before you answer, consider your own family experiences and your observations of other families.

3. Are the feelings expressed in the poem "Fireworks" the same as those Brenner expresses about his family? Explain.

4. Do you think Brenner's father handles the "fish-eyes incident" correctly? Explain.

5. Comedians often exaggerate to make a story funny. Find examples of exaggeration in "Fish Eyes." How does exaggeration add humor to the story?

6. If David Brenner were your age, would you want him as a friend? Why or why not?

Writing Options

1. When the exterminator said he had found a dead animal, Brenner ran out of his house in self-defense. Write what you think happened next.

2. Compare the family relationships in "Fish Eyes" with those in another story you have read in this book.

Vocabulary Practice

Exercise On your paper, write the word from the list that is most closely related to each situation below.

1. David's brother was even sneakier and more dishonest than he.
2. The older brother finally admitted defeat in the sock war.
3. The whole house smelled of rotting fish.
4. Their clever tricks showed the Brenners' originality.
5. David believed that his brilliant brother was quite insane.

Words to Know and Use

concede
demented
devious
ingenuity
rancid

Drama *The* ***Hitchhiker***

LUCILLE FLETCHER

*E*xamine *What You Know*

As a class, create a list of criteria for a good horror story. Include standards regarding types of characters you expect, what kinds of settings are needed, what plot lines are typical, and any other elements that make for high-quality horror. Use a diagram similar to the one below to group your ideas. As you read this play, see whether it meets your criteria.

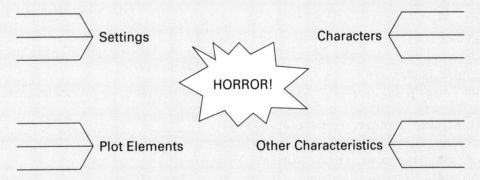

Settings   Characters

HORROR!

Plot Elements   Other Characteristics

*E*xpand *Your Knowledge*

It may be hard for you to imagine a time when television was not part of daily life. Yet in the 1930's and 1940's, families gathered around the radio and listened to such shows as *Amos 'n' Andy, Fibber McGee and Molly, The Green Hornet,* and *Suspense.* The vivid sounds of radio— voices, laughter, screams, trains, creaking doors—helped create pictures in listeners' imaginations.

The sound effects in *The Hitchhiker,* written for radio, helped the radio audience follow Ronald Adams on an eerie car trip along the famous Route 66, a 2,400-mile highway connecting Chicago and California. *The Hitchhiker* was originally produced and narrated by Orson Welles, who later became a famous actor and movie director.

*W*rite *Before You Read*

■ *A biography of the author can be found on page 362.*

What role do you think a hitchhiker might play in a horror story? Write your prediction.

The *Hitchhiker*

A Play for Radio

Welles. Good evening, this is Orson Welles.

Music (in)

Personally I've never met anybody who didn't like a good ghost story, but I know a lot of people who think there are a lot of people who don't like a good ghost story. For the benefit of these, at least, I go on record at the outset of this evening's entertainment with the <u>sober</u> <u>assurance</u> that although blood may be curdled on this program, none will be spilt. There's no shooting, knifing, throttling, axing, or poisoning here. No clanking chains, no cobwebs, no bony and/or hairy hands appearing from secret panels or, better yet, bedroom curtains. If it's any part of that dear old <u>phosphorescent</u> foolishness that people who don't like ghost stories don't like, then again I promise you we haven't got it. What we do have is a thriller. If it's half as good as we think it is, you can call it a shocker; and we present it proudly and without apologies. After all, a story doesn't have to appeal to the heart—it can also appeal to the spine. Sometimes you want your heart to be warmed— sometimes you want your spine to tingle.

The tingling, it's to be hoped, will be quite audible as you listen tonight to *The Hitch-hiker*—That's the name of our story, *The Hitchhiker*—

Sound (automobile wheels humming over concrete road)

Music (something weird and shuddery)

Adams. I am in an auto camp on Route Sixty-six just west of Gallup, New Mexico. If I tell it, perhaps it will help me. It will keep me from going mad. But I must tell this quickly. I am not mad now. I feel perfectly well, except that I am running a slight temperature. My name is Ronald Adams. I am thirty-six years of age, unmarried, tall, dark, with a black mustache. I drive a 1940 Ford V-8, license number 6V-7989. I was born in Brooklyn. All this I know. I know that I am at this moment perfectly sane. That it is not I who have gone mad—but something else—something utterly beyond my control. But I must speak quickly. At any moment the link with life may break. This may be the last thing I ever tell on earth . . . the last night I ever see the stars. . . .

Music (in)

Words to Know and Use

sober (sō′ bər) *adj.* serious, solemn
assurance (ə shoōr′ əns) *n.* the state of being sure of something; confidence; certainty
phosphorescent (fäs′ fə res′ ənt) *adj.* continually giving off light

Adams. Six days ago I left Brooklyn to drive to California. . . .

Mother. Goodbye, Son. Good luck to you, my boy. . . .

Adams. Goodbye, Mother. Here—give me a kiss, and then I'll go. . . .

Mother. I'll come out with you to the car.

Adams. No. It's raining. Stay here at the door. Hey—what is this? Tears? I thought you promised me you wouldn't cry.

Mother. I know, dear. I'm sorry. But I—do hate to see you go.

Adams. I'll be back. I'll be on the coast only three months.

Mother. Oh—it isn't that. It's just—the trip. Ronald—I wish you weren't driving.

Adams. Oh—Mother. There you go again. People do it every day.

Mother. I know. But you'll be careful, won't you? Promise me you'll be extra careful. Don't fall asleep—or drive fast—or pick up any strangers on the road. . . .

Adams. Lord, no. You'd think I was still seventeen to hear you talk—

Mother. And wire me as soon as you get to Hollywood, won't you, son?

Adams. Of course I will. Now don't you worry. There isn't anything going to happen. It's just eight days of perfectly simple driving on smooth, decent, civilized roads, with a hotdog or a hamburger stand every ten miles. . . . (*fade*)

Sound (auto hum)

Music (in)

Adams. I was in excellent spirits. The drive ahead of me, even the loneliness, seemed like a lark. But I reckoned without *him*.

Music (changes to something weird and empty)

Adams. Crossing Brooklyn Bridge that morning in the rain, I saw a man leaning against the cables. He seemed to be waiting for a lift. There were spots of fresh rain on his shoulders. He was carrying a cheap overnight bag in one hand. He was thin, <u>nondescript</u>, with a cap pulled down over his eyes. He stepped off the walk, and if I hadn't swerved, I'd have hit him.

Sound (terrific skidding)

Music (in)

Adams. I would have forgotten him completely, except that just an hour later, while crossing the Pulaski Skyway over the Jersey flats, I saw him again. At least, he looked like the same person. He was standing now, with one thumb pointing west. I couldn't figure out how he'd got there, but I thought probably one of those fast trucks had picked him up, beaten me to the Skyway, and let him off. I didn't stop for him. Then—late that night, I saw him again.

Music (changing)

Adams. It was on the new Pennsylvania Turnpike between Harrisburg and Pittsburgh. It's 265 miles long, with a very high speed limit. I was just slowing down for one of the tunnels—when I saw him—standing under an arc light by the side of the road. I could see him quite distinctly. The bag, the cap, even the spots of fresh rain spattered over his shoulders. He hailed me this time. . . .

Words to Know and Use | **nondescript** (nän′ di skript′) *adj.* colorless; drab; unnoticeable

GAS 1940 Edward Hopper Oil on canvas, 26¼″ × 40¼″
Collection, The Museum of Modern Art, New York Mrs. Simon Guggenheim Fund.

Voice (*very spooky and faint*). Hall-ooo. . . . (*echo as through tunnel*) Hall-ooo . . .!

Adams. I stepped on the gas like a shot. That's lonely country through the Alleghenies,[1] and I had no intention of stopping. Besides, the coincidence, or whatever it was, gave me the willies.[2] I stopped at the next gas station.

Sound (auto tires screeching to stop . . . horn honk)

Mechanic. Yes, sir.

Adams. Fill her up.

Mechanic. Certainly, sir. Check your oil, sir?

Adams. No, thanks.

Sound (gas being put into car . . . bell tinkle, et cetera)

Mechanic. Nice night, isn't it?

Adams. Yes. It—hasn't been raining here recently, has it?

Mechanic. Not a drop of rain all week.

Adams. I suppose that hasn't done your business any harm.

Mechanic. Oh—people drive through here in all kinds of weather. Mostly business, you know. There aren't many pleasure cars out on the turnpike this season of the year.

Adams. I suppose not. (*casually*) What about hitchhikers?

Mechanic (*half laughing*). Hitchhikers *here*?

Adams. What's the matter? Don't you ever see any?

Mechanic. Not much. If we did, it'd be a sight for sore eyes.

Adams. Why?

Mechanic. A guy'd be a fool who started out

---

1. **Alleghenies** (al ə gā′ nēz): the Allegheny Mountain range, which runs across Pennsylvania, Maryland, West Virginia, and Virginia.

2. **gave me the willies:** made me nervous.

to hitch rides on this road. Look at it. It's 265 miles long, there's practically no speed limit, and it's a straightaway. Now what car is going to stop to pick up a guy under these conditions? Would you stop?

Adams. No. (*slowly, with puzzled emphasis*) Then you've never seen anybody?

Mechanic. Nope. Mebbe they get the lift before the turnpike starts—I mean, you know, just before the toll house—but then it'd be a mighty long ride. Most cars wouldn't want to pick up a guy for that long a ride. And you know—this is pretty lonesome country here—mountains, and woods. . . . You ain't seen anybody like that, have you?

Adams. No. (*quickly*) Oh no, not at all. It was—just a—technical question.

Mechanic. I see. Well—that'll be just a dollar forty-nine—with the tax. . . . (*fade*)

Sound (auto hum up)

Music (changing)

Adams. The thing gradually passed from my mind, as sheer coincidence. I had a good night's sleep in Pittsburgh. I did not think about the man all next day—until just outside of Zanesville, Ohio, I saw him again.

Music (dark, ominous note)

Adams. It was a bright, sunshiny afternoon. The peaceful Ohio fields, brown with the autumn stubble, lay dreaming in the golden light. I was driving slowly, drinking it in, when the road suddenly ended in a detour. In front of the barrier, *he* was standing.

Music (in)

Adams. Let me explain about his appearance before I go on. I repeat. There was nothing <u>sinister</u> about him. He was as drab as a mud fence. Nor was his attitude <u>menacing</u>. He merely stood there, waiting, almost drooping a little, the cheap overnight bag in his hand. He looked as though he had been waiting there for hours. Then he looked up. He hailed me. He started to walk forward.

Voice (*far off*). Hall-ooo. . . . Hall-ooo. . . .

Adams. I had stopped the car, of course, for the detour. And for a few moments, I couldn't seem to find the new road. I knew he must be thinking that I had stopped for him.

Voice (*closer*). Hall-ooo. . . . Hallll . . . ooo. . . .

Sound (gears jamming . . . sound of motor turning over hard . . . nervous accelerator)

Voice (*closer*). Halll . . . oooo. . . .

Adams (*panicky*). No. Not just now. Sorry. . . .

Voice (*closer*). Going to California?

Sound (starter starting . . . gears jamming)

Adams (*as though sweating blood*). No. Not today. The other way. Going to New York. Sorry . . . sorry . . . .

Sound (Car starts with squeal of wheels on dirt . . . into auto hum.)

Music (in)

Adams. After I got the car back onto the road again, I felt like a fool. Yet the thought of picking him up, of having him sit beside me, was somehow unbearable. Yet, at the same time, I felt, more than ever, unspeakably alone.

Sound (auto hum up)

Words to Know and Use | **sinister** (sin' is tər) *adj.* mysteriously wicked, evil, or dishonest
menacing (men' əs iŋ) *adj.* threatening harm or evil **menace** *v.*

Adams. Hour after hour went by. The fields, the towns ticked off, one by one. The lights changed. I knew now that I was going to see him again. And though I dreaded the sight, I caught myself searching the side of the road, waiting for him to appear.

Sound (Auto hum up . . . car screeches to a halt . . . impatient honk two or three times . . . door being unbolted.)

Sleepy man's voice. Yep? What is it? What do you want?

Adams (*breathless*). You sell sandwiches and pop here, don't you?

Voice (*cranky*). Yep. We do. In the daytime. But we're closed up now for the night.

Adams. I know. But—I was wondering if you could possibly let me have a cup of coffee—black coffee.

Voice. Not at this time of night, mister. My wife's the cook, and she's in bed. Mebbe farther down the road—at the Honeysuckle Rest. . . .

Sound (door squeaking on hinges as though being closed)

Adams. No—no. Don't shut the door. (*shakily*) Listen—just a minute ago, there was a man standing here—right beside this stand—a suspicious looking man. . . .

Woman's voice (*from distance*). Hen-ry? Who is it, Henry?

Henry. It's nobuddy, Mother. Just a feller thinks he wants a cup of coffee. Go back into bed.

Adams. I don't mean to disturb you. But you see, I was driving along—when I just happened to look—and there he was. . . .

Henry. What was he doing?

Adams. Nothing. He ran off—when I stopped the car.

Henry. Then what of it? That's nothing to wake a man in the middle of his sleep about. (*sternly*) Young man, I've got a good mind to turn you over to the sheriff.

Adams. But—I—

Henry. You've been taking a nip; that's what you've been doing. And you haven't got anything better to do than to wake decent folk out of their hard-earned sleep. Get going. Go on.

Adams. But—he looked as though he were going to rob you.

Henry. I ain't got nothin' in this stand to lose. Now—on your way before I call out Sheriff Oakes. (*fade*)

Sound (auto hum up)

Adams. I got into the car again, and drove on slowly. I was beginning to hate the car. If I could have found a place to stop . . . to rest a little. But I was in the Ozark Mountains of Missouri now. The few resort places there were closed. Only an occasional log cabin, seemingly deserted, broke the monotony of the wild, wooded landscape. I *had* seen him at that roadside stand; I knew I would see him again—perhaps at the next turn of the road. I knew that when I saw him next, I would run him down. . . .

Sound (auto hum up)

Adams. But I did not see him again until late next afternoon. . . .

Sound (of railroad warning signal at crossroads)

Adams. I had stopped the car at a sleepy little junction just across the border into Oklahoma—to let a train pass by—when he appeared, across the tracks, leaning against a telephone pole.

Sound (distant sound of train chugging . . . bell ringing steadily)

Adams (*very tense*). It was a perfectly airless, dry day. The red clay of Oklahoma was baking under the southwestern sun. Yet there were spots of fresh rain on his shoulders. I couldn't stand that. Without thinking, blindly, I started the car across the tracks.

Sound (train chugging closer)

Adams. He didn't even look up at me. He was staring at the ground. I stepped on the gas hard, veering the wheel sharply toward him. I could hear the train in the distance now, but I didn't care. Then something went wrong with the car. It stalled right on the tracks.

Sound (Train chugging closer. Above this, sound of car stalling.)

Adams. The train was coming closer. I could hear its bell ringing and the cry of its whistle. Still he stood there. And now—I knew that he was beckoning—beckoning me to my death.

Sound (Train chugging close. Whistle blows wildly. Then train rushes up and by with pistons going, et cetera.)

Adams. Well—I frustrated him that time. The starter had worked at last. I managed to back up. But when the train passed, he was gone. I was all alone in the hot, dry afternoon.

FIGURE date unknown Bruce McGaw Collection of The Oakland Museum, California.

Words to Know and Use	**veering** (vir′ iŋ) *adj.* turning or swinging **veer** *v.* **beckon** (bek′ 'n) *v.* to call or summon with a silent gesture

Sound (Train retreating. Crickets begin to sing.)

Music (in)

Adams. After that, I knew I had to do something. I didn't know who this man was or what he wanted of me. I only knew that from now on, I must not let myself be alone on the road for one moment.

Sound (Auto hum up. Slow down. Stop. Door opening.)

Adams. Hello, there. Like a ride?

Girl. What do you think? How far you going?

Adams. Amarillo . . . I'll take you to Amarillo.

Girl. Amarillo, Texas?

Adams. I'll drive you there.

Girl. Gee!

Sound (Door closes. Car starts.)

Music (in)

Girl. Mind if I take off my shoes? My dogs[3] are killing me.

Adams. Go right ahead.

Girl. Gee, what a break this is. A swell car, a decent guy, and driving all the way to Amarillo. All I been getting so far is trucks.

Adams. Hitchhike much?

Girl. Sure. Only it's tough sometimes, in these great open spaces, to get the breaks.

Adams. I should think it would be. Though I'll bet if you get a good pickup in a fast car, you can get to places faster than— say, another person, in another car?

Girl. I don't get you.

Adams. Well, take me, for instance. Suppose I'm driving across the country, say, at a nice steady clip of about forty-five miles an hour. Couldn't a girl like you, just standing beside the road, waiting for lifts, beat me to town after town—provided she got picked up every time in a car doing from sixty-five to seventy miles an hour?

Girl. I dunno. Maybe she could and maybe she couldn't. What difference does it make?

Adams. Oh—no difference. It's just a— crazy idea I had sitting here in the car.

Girl (*laughing*). Imagine spending your time in a swell car thinking of things like that!

Adams. What would you do instead?

Girl (*admiringly*). What would I do? If I was a good-looking fellow like yourself? Why—I'd just *enjoy* myself—every minute of the time. I'd sit back and relax, and if I saw a good-looking girl along the side of the road. . . . (*sharply*) Hey! Look out!

Adams (*breathlessly*). Did you see him too?

Girl. See who?

Adams. That man. Standing beside the barbed wire fence.

Girl. I didn't see—anybody. There wasn't nothing but a bunch of steers—and the barbed wire fence. What did you think you was doing? Trying to run into the barbed wire fence?

Adams. There was a man there, I tell you . . . a thin, gray man with an overnight bag in his hand. And I was trying to—run him down.

Girl. Run him down? You mean—kill him?

Adams. He's a sort of—phantom. I'm trying to get rid of him—or else prove that he's real. But (*desperately*) you say you didn't see him back there? You're sure?

---

3. **dogs:** feet.

Girl (*queerly*). I didn't see a soul. And as far as that's concerned, mister. . . .

Adams. Watch for him the next time, then. Keep watching. Keep your eyes peeled on the road. He'll turn up again—maybe any minute now. (*excitedly*) There. Look there—

Sound (Auto sharply veering and skidding. GIRL screams.)

Sound (Crash of car going into barbed wire fence. Frightened lowing[4] of steer.)

Girl. How does this door work? I—I'm gettin' outta here.

Adams. Did you see him that time?

Girl (*sharply*). No. I didn't see him that time. And personally, mister, I don't expect never to see him. All I want to do is to go on living—and I don't see how I will very long, driving with you—

Adams. I'm sorry. I—I don't know what came over me. (*frightened*) Please—don't go. . . .

Girl. So if you'll excuse me, mister—

Adams. You can't go. Listen, how would you like to go to California? I'll drive you to California.

Girl. Seeing pink elephants all the way? No thanks.

Adams (*desperately*). I could get you a job there. You wouldn't have to be a waitress. I have friends there—my name is Ronald Adams—you can check up.

Sound (Door opens.)

Girl. Uhn-huuh. Thanks just the same.

Adams. Listen. Please. For just one minute. Maybe you think I am half-cracked. But this man. You see, I've been seeing this man all the way across the country. He's been following me. And if you could only help me—stay with me—until I reach the coast—

Girl. You know what I think you need, big boy? Not a girl friend. Just a good dose of sleep. . . . There, I got it now.

Sound (Door opens . . . slams.)

Adams. No. You can't go.

Girl (*screams*). Leave your hands offa me, do you hear! Leave your—

Adams. Come back here, please, come back.

Sound (struggle . . . slap . . . footsteps running away on gravel . . . lowing of steer)

Adams. She ran from me as though I were a monster. A few minutes later, I saw a passing truck pick her up. I knew then that I was utterly alone.

Sound (lowing of steer up)

Adams. I was in the heart of the great Texas prairies. There wasn't a car on the road after the truck went by. I tried to figure out what to do, how to get hold of myself. If I could find a place to rest. Or even if I could sleep right here in the car for a few hours, along the side of the road . . . . I was getting my winter overcoat out of the back seat to use as a blanket (Hall-ooo) when I saw him coming toward me (Hall-ooo), emerging from the herd of moving steer. . . .

Voice. Hall-ooo. . . . Hall-oooo. . . .

Sound (auto starting violently . . . up to steady hum)

Music (in)

Adams. I didn't wait for him to come any closer. Perhaps I should have spoken to him then, fought it out then and there. For now he began to be everywhere. Whenever I stopped, even for a moment—for gas, for oil, for a drink of pop,

---

4. **lowing:** mooing.

a cup of coffee, a sandwich—he was there.

Music (faster)

Adams. I saw him standing outside the auto camp in Amarillo that night when I dared to slow down. He was sitting near the drinking fountain in a little camping spot just inside the border of New Mexico.

Music (faster)

Adams. He was waiting for me outside the Navajo Reservation, where I stopped to check my tires. I saw him in Albuquerque,[5] where I bought twelve gallons of gas. . . . I was afraid now, afraid to stop. I began to drive faster and faster. I was in lunar landscape now—the great arid mesa country of New Mexico. I drove through it with the indifference of a fly crawling over the face of the moon.

Music (faster)

Adams. But now he didn't even wait for me to stop. Unless I drove at eighty-five miles an hour over those endless roads—he waited for me at every other mile. I would see his figure, shadowless, flitting before me, still in its same attitude, over the cold and lifeless ground; flitting over dried-up rivers, over broken stones cast up by old glacial upheavals, flitting in the pure and cloudless air. . . .

Music (strikes sinister note of finality)

Adams. I was beside myself when I finally reached Gallup, New Mexico, this morning. There is an auto camp here—cold, almost deserted at this time of year. I went inside and asked if there was a telephone. I had the feeling that if only I could speak to someone familiar, some-

one that I loved, I could pull myself together.

Sound (nickel put in slot)

Operator. Number, please?

Adams. Long distance.

Sound (return of nickel. Buzz.)

Long-distance Opr. This is long distance.

Adams. I'd like to put in a call to my home in Brooklyn, New York. I'm Ronald Adams. The number is Beechwood 2-0828.

Long-distance Opr. Thank you. What is your number?

Adams. 312.

Albuquerque Opr. Albuquerque.

Long-distance Opr. New York for Gallup. *(pause)*

New York Opr. New York.

Long-distance Opr. Gallup, New Mexico, calling Beechwood 2-0828. *(fade)*

Adams. I had read somewhere that love could banish demons. It was the middle of the morning. I knew Mother would be home. I pictured her, tall, white-haired, in her crisp house dress, going about her tasks. It would be enough, I thought, merely to hear the even calmness of her voice. . . .

Long-distance Opr. Will you please deposit three dollars and eighty-five cents for the first three minutes? When you have deposited a dollar and a half, will you wait until I have collected the money?

Sound (clunk of six coins)

Long-distance Opr. All right, deposit another dollar and a half.

---

5. **Albuquerque** (al′ bə kʉr′ kē): a city in New Mexico.

Words to Know and Use

lunar (lo͞o′ nər) *adj.* like or relating to the moon
banish (ban′ ish) *v.* to send or put away; exile; expel

Sound (clunk of six coins)

Long-distance Opr. Will you please deposit the remaining eighty-five cents?

Sound (clunk of four coins)

Long-distance Opr. Ready with Brooklyn—go ahead, please.

Adams. Hello.

Mrs. Whitney. Mrs. Adams's residence.

Adams. Hello. Hello—Mother?

Mrs. Whitney. (*very flat and rather proper . . . dumb, too, in a frizzy sort of way*). This is Mrs. Adams's residence. Who is it you wished to speak to, please?

Adams. Why—who's this?

Mrs. Whitney. This is Mrs. Whitney.

Adams. Mrs. Whitney? I don't know any Mrs. Whitney. Is this Beechwood 2-0828?

Mrs. Whitney. Yes.

Adams. Where's my mother? Where's Mrs. Adams?

Mrs. Whitney. Mrs. Adams is not at home. She is still in the hospital.

Adams. The hospital!

Mrs. Whitney. Yes. Who is this calling, please? Is it a member of the family?

Adams. What's she in the hospital for?

Mrs. Whitney. She's been prostrated for five days. Nervous breakdown. But who is this calling?

Adams. Nervous breakdown? But—my mother was never nervous. . . .

Mrs. Whitney. It's all taken place since the death of her oldest son, Ronald.

Adams. Death of her oldest son, Ronald . . .? Hey—what is this? What number is this?

Mrs. Whitney. This is Beechwood 2-0828. It's all been very sudden. He was killed just six days ago in an automobile accident on the Brooklyn Bridge.

Operator (*breaking in*). Your three minutes are up, sir. (*silence*) Your three minutes are up, sir. (*pause*) Your three minutes are up, sir. (*fade*) Sir, your three minutes are up. Your three minutes are up, sir.

Adams (*in a strange voice*). And so, I am sitting here in this deserted auto camp in Gallup, New Mexico. I am trying to think. I am trying to get hold of myself. Otherwise, I shall go mad. . . . Outside it is night—the vast, soulless night of New Mexico. A million stars are in the sky. Ahead of me stretch a thousand miles of empty mesa, mountains, prairies— desert. Somewhere among them, he is waiting for me. Somewhere I shall know who he is, and who . . . I . . . am. . . .

Music (up)❧

THE BROOKLYN BRIDGE: VARIATION ON AN OLD THEME
1939   Joseph Stella
Collection of Whitney Museum of American Art, New York. Purchase. Photograph by Geoffrey Clements.

Responding to Reading

First Impressions

1. If you were all alone when you heard this story on the radio, how would you feel? Explain your thoughts.

Second Thoughts

2. What do you think really happens to Adams at the end of this play? Give reasons for your answer.

   Think about
   - whether he is dead
   - whether he is mad or insane
   - what else might be going on

3. In your opinion, who is the mysterious hitchhiker? Use information from the play to support your answer.

4. What do you think is the main conflict in this play? Explain.

5. Is *The Hitchhiker* a good horror story? Compare your thoughts with the ideas you had about horror stories before you read the play.

   Think about
   - your reaction to Orson Welles's introduction and his promises
   - whether the play is convincing
   - whether the elements of suspense and surprise are present

Broader Connections

6. Horror stories fascinate movie and television audiences and readers of all ages. Why do you think these stories and films are so popular?

Literary Concept: Foreshadowing

Foreshadowing is a writer's hinting at a future event in the story. In *The Hitchhiker,* the writer drops stronger and stronger hints that the innocent-looking fellow on the road will bring an unusual end to Ronald Adams's story. What are some of these clues?

Concept Review: Mood You remember that **mood** is the feeling, such as happiness or fright or anger, that a reader gets from the story. Foreshadowing, figurative language, images, word choice, setting, and dialogue all contribute to the mood. What is the mood of *The Hitchhiker?* Find words and phrases that help create this mood.

Writing Options

1. Make a chart comparing and contrasting your favorite horror story and *The Hitchhiker.*

2. Consider whether *The Hitchhiker* would be more effective on the radio, as it was originally presented, or as a television play. Write a paragraph stating your opinion in the first sentence and the reasons supporting it in the following sentences. Include an explanation of how this play might be presented on television.

3. What do you think would have happened if Adams had picked up the hitchhiker on the Brooklyn Bridge instead of swerving and going on? Write down your thoughts.

4. The ending of this play leaves the reader hanging, uncertain. Write a scene to follow it that you think will end *The Hitchhiker* in a satisfying way.

Vocabulary Practice

Exercise A Decide whether the following pairs of words are synonyms or antonyms. On your paper, identify each pair as *synonyms* or *antonyms.*

1. phosphorescent—glowing
2. assurance—uncertainty
3. nondescript—boring
4. menacing—friendly
5. banish—welcome

Exercise B On your paper, write the word from the list that is closest in meaning to each term below.

1. evil
2. serious
3. moonlike
4. turning
5. call

> **Words to Know and Use**
>
> ---
>
> **assurance**
> **banish**
> **beckon**
> **lunar**
> **menacing**
> **nondescript**
> **phosphorescent**
> **sinister**
> **sober**
> **veering**

Options for Learning

1 • **Incidents Along the Way** Using tracing paper, outline a map of the United States and trace Adams's route. At the appropriate places along the route, describe each important incident in a phrase. For example, by Brooklyn, you might write "Adams leaves home." You may need to do some research to locate certain places on the map.

2 • **"Get Your Kicks on Route 66"** So goes "Route 66," a song by Bobby Troup. Route 66, one of America's most famous roads, was once an important link between East and West. Find a picture of this great roadway and research whose idea it was, why it was built, and why it became famous. Make a poster showing your information and explain it to your class.

3 • **Signs of the Past** *The Hitchhiker* was first published in 1947. Reread or skim the play and make a list of objects or facts that tell you this play is not set in the present day.

4 • **Produce for Radio** With your class, produce *The Hitchhiker* as a radio play. Some students can play roles, while others can set up the necessary music and sound effects. Tape-record your show and play it for another class.

 **FACT FINDER**

How far is it from Brooklyn, New York, to Gallup, New Mexico?

Lucille Fletcher
1912–

Lucille Fletcher was born in Brooklyn, the same city where Ronald Adams's frightening trip begins. She married another writer, novelist John Douglass Wallop, and the two lived on Maryland's Atlantic coast until Wallop's death in 1985.

During the 1940's, Fletcher kept radio audiences on the edge of their seats with her chilling mystery dramas. One of her most famous radio plays is *Sorry, Wrong Number*, which has been rewritten as a novel and adapted for stage, film, and television. Fletcher wrote twenty plays for the radio series *Suspense*, and she wrote scripts for the television shows *Chrysler Theater* and *Lights Out*. She has also written mystery novels, including *Blindfold* and *And Presumed Dead*, which were made into movies. Her play *Night Watch* was produced on Broadway in 1972.

EXPOSITION

The selections from this subunit all focus on unusual events or effects. Because human beings naturally believe that everything has a cause, we frequently ask ourselves why something has happened. For instance, what causes the Brenner brothers to wage a Dirty Sock War? What causes Annie John to get in so much trouble at school? Why does the hitchhiker keep reappearing?

Writing that speculates about causes gives possible explanations for a specific effect. The effect can be an event (a trial) or an attitude (a desire to win). Cause-effect writing is usually formal in tone. The writer tries to be reasonable, logical, and persuasive because the ultimate goal of this kind of writing is to convince the reader that the explanations given are accurate and true.

> **Here is your PASSkey to this assignment.**

GUIDED ASSIGNMENT:
EXPLANATION OF CAUSE

Explain the cause of an event or a character's attitude in one of the selections from this subunit.

P URPOSE: To explain cause

A UDIENCE: Other people who have read the selection

S UBJECT: An effect from one of the selections

S TRUCTURE: An expository essay

Prewriting

STEP 1 **Choose an effect** Review the selections in the "Points of Conflict" subunit. Pick the selection you find most interesting to write about. Then write a question about a significant effect (an event or attitude) that occurs within the selection. For example, you might ask "Why does Annie John's teacher seem to dislike her so much?" Choose one of the effects referred to in the introduction to this assignment or choose a different one, but make sure that the effect is central to the story. In a small group or with a partner who has picked the same selection as you, review your questions to make sure they refer to an important effect in the selection.

STEP 2 **Speculate on causes**   Now that you have decided on the effect, review the selection and speculate on possible causes. When a writer **speculates,** he or she guesses at or figures out causes that are not specifically mentioned in the selection itself. Remember that most events or attitudes have several causes. Consider what characters say to one another, their behavior, and the insights of the narrator, if there is one. Try to come up with at least three possible causes. List the causes or make a cause-effect chart like the one below, in which a student speculated on the cause of Ches's decision to find Angie in "The Gift of Cochise."

STUDENT MODEL ▶

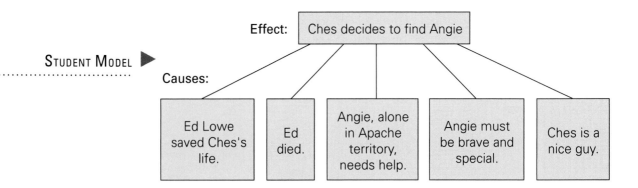

Effect: Ches decides to find Angie

Causes:

| Ed Lowe saved Ches's life. | Ed died. | Angie, alone in Apache territory, needs help. | Angie must be brave and special. | Ches is a nice guy. |

STEP 3 **Support your position**   Consider your causes and select the ones that you think are most important. On a separate piece of paper, list each cause. Under each statement, explain how it helped bring about the effect. Then elaborate on that cause by adding details and quotations from the story, as well as your own reasoning about the cause.

Drafting

STEP 1 **Write an introduction**   The first paragraph, or the introduction, of an expository essay tells the reader exactly **what** you are going to discuss and **how** you are going to prove or explain it. In this case, the **what** is the effect, and the **how** is a general statement of one or more causes in order of importance. You will give more detailed explanations of each cause in the following paragraphs of your paper. The introduction should begin with an interesting comment, question, or incident to grab the reader's attention.

Here is the introduction one student wrote for a cause-effect essay on "The Gift of Cochise," a story from the "Tests of Endurance" subunit.

Why do people sometimes go out of their way to help others who are in need? What makes them want to help even if it might cost them everything they have? In "The Gift of Cochise" by Louis L'Amour, Ches Lane decides to find Angie Lowe, even though his search will take him into dangerous territory. Ches makes this decision because Ed Lowe, Angie's husband, saved his life, and he feels he owes him something. He also decides to go because a lone woman and two children in Apache country need help. Ches figures that Angie and her children must be very brave, and he admires people who take a stand.

◀ STUDENT MODEL

STEP 2 **Write and support your reasons** After your introduction, use the body of your paper to explain and elaborate on the causes of your chosen effect. In each paragraph, restate one of the causes you named in your introduction. Then go on to explain why that cause is a cause, showing your reasoning and using details and quotations from the selections to support your statement. Use the notes you made in prewriting. Then take the next cause and explain it in the following paragraph, and so on.

The student who wrote about "The Gift of Cochise" wrote this body paragraph explaining the first cause mentioned.

Ches felt an obligation to Angie's husband, Ed Lowe. When Ches was cornered by the three angry brothers of a man he'd killed in self-defense, Ed Lowe stood up for him. During the gunfight that followed, the three brothers were killed, but in the process Ed was shot to death too. Ches realized at the time that he could not have killed all three brothers by himself: "One he could have beaten; two he might have beaten; three would have killed him. Ed Lowe, stepping in when he did, had saved the life of Ches Lane." He owed something to Ed, whose dying words were, "Oh Lord in heaven, what'll Angie do?"

◀ STUDENT MODEL

Revising and Editing

Before asking a classmate to review your draft, look for ways you can add variety to your sentence patterns. See if you can combine any sentences to prevent choppiness. Add transitional words and phrases when necessary. Correct any run-ons or sentence fragments.

Once you have completed your draft, ask a classmate to review your work, using the following checklist as a guide.

Editing When you have finished revising your draft, proofread for spelling, clarity, and mechanics.

Presenting

Read your essay to others who picked the same selection as you. As a group pick the best essay and give reasons for your choice.

Reflecting on Your Writing

Answer the following questions about this assignment. Put the answers and your paper in your writing portfolio.

1. Which part of the assignment did you find easiest? Why?
2. If you could spend more time on one part of this assignment, which would it be? Why?

LANGUAGE WORKSHOP

MAKING SUBJECTS AND VERBS AGREE

> A verb and its subject must agree in number.

Using a singular verb with a plural subject, or vice versa, is like playing a record at the wrong speed: the results just don't sound right.

The **number** of a word indicates whether the word is singular or plural. If the subject of a sentence is **singular,** its verb must also be singular. If a subject is **plural,** its verb must also be plural.

The *student* (singular) **sits** (singular) near the back of the class.
The *students* (plural) **sit** (plural) near the back of the class.

Remember that the *s* at the end of a verb, as in *votes* or *practices,* shows that the verb is singular. Most verbs drop the *s* in the plural form.

Generally you can "hear" when the subject and verb of a sentence are in agreement. A sentence like "The student answer the question" is incorrect, and it sounds incorrect. In some cases, however, you may not be sure whether to use a singular or a plural verb with a particular subject.

Beware of Phrases

Watch out when a prepositional phrase appears between the subject and the verb. The subject is never part of such a phrase. Look for the subject outside the phrase.

The subject of the verb is never found in a prepositional phrase.

The *student* with the notebooks *plays* the violin. (*Student,* not *notebooks,* is the subject.)
The *books* at the library *are* all new. (*Books,* not *library,* is the subject.)

Phrases beginning with the words *with, together with, including, as well as,* or *in addition to* are not part of the subject.

Annie John, as well as her parents, *is* at home.
Her *classmates,* in addition to her teacher, *have* left school.

REMINDER

◄ 1. The pronoun *you* can be singular or plural, but it always takes a plural verb.
2. Except in *I am* and *I was,* the pronoun *I* always takes a plural verb.

HELP!

For help in deciding which word is the subject, say the sentence without the phrase. If you have chosen the correct word as the subject, the sentence will ◄ make sense without the phrase.

Exercise 1 Write the verb that agrees with the subject.

1. I, as well as my friends, (love, loves) frightening tales.
2. Sometimes, however, a horror movie, with all its blood and violence, (make, makes) me want to get up and leave the theater.
3. Old-time radio plays, on the other hand, (is, are) just right.
4. Somehow the scenes (seem, seems) more frightening when you use your imagination.
5. Instead of seeing every detail on the screen, I, along with other listeners, (have, has) to "see" things in my mind.
6. Do we all (picture, pictures) the action in a different way?
7. One of my favorite radio dramas (is, are) *Sorry, Wrong Number.*
8. The plot (involve, involves) a sick woman who is home alone.
9. While using the telephone, she accidentally (hear, hears) a murder being planned.
10. The poor woman (has, have) no idea that she will be the victim.

Verbs with Compound Subjects

A **compound subject** is two or more subjects used with the same verb.

Compound subjects that contain the word *and* are plural and take a plural verb.

History and *writing* **are** Annie's favorite subjects.

When the parts of a compound subject are connected by the conjunction *or* or *nor,* the verb agrees with the subject nearer to the verb.

Neither *Annie* nor her *friends* **want** to get in trouble.
Either her *family* or her *teacher* **disapproves** of her behavior.

Exercise 2 Some of the following sentences contain errors in subject-verb agreement. On your paper, write correctly those sentences that have errors. If a sentence has no error, write *Correct.*

1. Annie John and her parents lives in the West Indies.
2. This story about Annie begin in a classroom.
3. Either Annie or the other girls answers Miss Edward's questions.
4. Neither Annie nor her classmates wants to wear the dunce cap.

5. Often Annie and Hilarene competes for class prizes.
6. Annie and her friends plays forbidden games at recess.
7. Either reading or quiet talk is Miss Edward's idea of ladylike recreation.
8. Neither Miss Edward nor Annie's parents understands her behavior.
9. Thoughts and daydreams constantly swims in Annie's head.
10. In Annie's mind a dragon and a crocodile symbolizes her teacher and her mother.

Exercise 3   Rewrite the following passage correcting errors in subject-verb agreement.

All brothers and sisters has war stories. The kids in "Fish Eyes" sounds exactly like my family. Let me tell you my own fish story as I remembers it.

I is nine years old at the time of this tale. My older brother and my parents leaves me home alone. Suddenly sirens or some other screeching noise attract my attention. Three fire trucks and a police car is in our neighbor's yard. I, along with the family dog, rushes into my brother's room to get a good look at the action. Suddenly, a loud boom fills the room. I have tripped on the electrical cord attached to my brother's fish tank. Thirty gallons of water pours into the room. Fish of all sizes fly through the air. Water on the soaked rugs rise to my ankles. Dying fish flop pathetically on the floor. At this moment my brother magically appear. His screams and his anger confront me. Neither six months of my allowance nor my heartfelt apology seem to make a difference to my heartless brother.

Exercise 4   Analyzing and Revising Your Writing

1. Take a paper from your writing portfolio. Choose a passage to analyze.
2. Reread the passage, looking for errors in subject-verb agreement. Look carefully wherever you have used a prepositional phrase or a compound subject.
3. Correct any errors in subject-verb agreement.
4. Remember to check for errors in subject-verb agreement the next time you proofread your work.

LANGUAGE HANDBOOK
....
For review and practice:
subject-verb agreement,
    pages 943–45, 947–49

STUDY SKILLS
WORKSHOP

SQ3R

SQ3R is a step-by-step method to help you study written material more effectively. **SQ3R** consists of five steps: **S**urvey, **Q**uestion, **R**ead, **R**ecord, and **R**eview. Here's how it works.

Survey	Skim the material to get a general idea of what you will be reading. Read the introduction and, if there is one, the summary. Look quickly at titles, headings, topic sentences, and highlighted words or phrases. Also look at illustrations, charts, and other graphics.
Question	Decide what questions you think you should be able to answer at the end of your studying and write them down. Start with the questions that seemed important to you as you skimmed the material. Also include any study questions found in the book or provided by your teacher. Create additional questions suggested by the material's titles, headings, pictures, maps, and charts.
Read	Look for the answers to your questions as you read. Also identify the main ideas in each section.
Record	After you have finished your careful reading, record the answers to your questions in your own words. In addition, make sure you understand any other important points of the selection. Note them, too.
Review	Quickly read over your notes and look over the main ideas in the book so you will remember them. Look up the answers to any questions that remain.

Exercise Apply the SQ3R study method to your next reading assignment for another class. First, survey the material. Then, write a list of questions you should be able to answer after you finish reading. After reading, answer the questions in your own words.

COMMANDING RESPECT

How does a person earn respect? Sometimes just one action is enough. Usually, however, respect is earned more slowly, through a series of conversations, a manner of bearing, a way of living.

Look for reasons the people you read about in this subunit are admired by others. Think about which of these characters would command *your* respect.

Fiction

Thank You, M'am

LANGSTON HUGHES

Examine What You Know

The following story is about a young thief and his victim. How would you react if someone tried to rob you in the street? Would you give in? call for help? defend yourself? Compare your probable reactions with those of the woman in the story.

Expand Your Knowledge

Black author and poet Langston Hughes wrote about the common people of the New York City community of Harlem. In his writing he used **dialect**— the speech patterns of a certain group or region—to make his Harlem characters come alive. In this story Hughes tells of a woman kicking a boy "right square in his blue-jeaned sitter." Later she yells at the boy, "You a lie!" (You're a liar!) Note how the use of dialect makes the story and characters more realistic.

Write Before You Read

The young boy in this story gets caught red-handed committing a crime. Have you ever been caught doing something wrong, such as stealing, lying, or cheating on a test? If so, how did you feel? If not, how might you feel if you were? In your journal, write an explanation of your feelings.

■ *A biography of the author can be found on page 378.*

Thank You, M'am

LANGSTON HUGHES

She was a large woman with a large purse that had everything in it but hammer and nails. It had a long strap, and she carried it slung across her shoulder. It was about eleven o'clock at night, and she was walking alone, when a boy ran up behind her and tried to snatch her purse. The strap broke with the single tug the boy gave it from behind. But the boy's weight and the weight of the purse combined caused him to lose his balance so, instead of taking off full blast as he had hoped, the boy fell on his back on the sidewalk, and his legs flew up. The large woman simply turned around and kicked him right square in his blue-jeaned sitter. Then she reached down, picked the boy up by his shirt front, and shook him until his teeth rattled.

After that the woman said, "Pick up my pocketbook, boy, and give it here."

She still held him. But she bent down enough to permit him to stoop and pick up her purse. Then she said, "Now ain't you ashamed of yourself?"

Firmly gripped by his shirt front, the boy said, "Yes'm."

The woman said, "What did you want to do it for?"

The boy said, "I didn't aim to."

She said, "You a lie!"

By that time two or three people passed, stopped, turned to look, and some stood watching.

"If I turn you loose, will you run?" asked the woman.

"Yes'm," said the boy.

"Then I won't turn you loose," said the woman. She did not release him.

"I'm very sorry, lady, I'm sorry," whispered the boy.

"Um-hum! And your face is dirty. I got a great mind to wash your face for you. Ain't you got nobody home to tell you to wash your face?"

"No'm," said the boy.

"Then it will get washed this evening," said the large woman starting up the street, dragging the frightened boy behind her.

He looked as if he were fourteen or fifteen, frail and willow-wild, in tennis shoes and blue jeans.

The woman said, "You ought to be my son. I would teach you right from wrong. Least I can do right now is to wash your face. Are you hungry?"

"No'm," said the being-dragged boy. "I just want you to turn me loose."

"Was I bothering *you* when I turned that corner?" asked the woman.

"No'm."

"But you put yourself in contact with *me,*"

MADISON II 1982 Philip Reisman
Edwin A. Ulrich Museum of Art, the Wichita State University,
Kansas Endowment Association Art Collection.

said the woman. "If you think that that contact is not going to last awhile, you got another thought coming. When I get through with you, sir, you are going to remember Mrs. Luella Bates Washington Jones."

Sweat popped out on the boy's face and he began to struggle. Mrs. Jones stopped, jerked him around in front of her, put a half nelson about his neck, and continued to drag him up the street. When she got to her door, she dragged the boy inside, down a hall, and into a large kitchenette-furnished room at the rear of the house. She switched on the light and left the door open. The boy could hear other roomers laughing and talking in the large house. Some of their doors were open, too, so he knew he and the woman were not alone. The woman still had him by the neck in the middle of her room.

She said, "What is your name?"

"Roger," answered the boy.

"Then, Roger, you go to that sink and wash your face," said the woman, whereupon she turned him loose—at last. Roger looked at the door—looked at the woman—looked at the door—*and went to the sink.*

"Let the water run until it gets warm," she said. "Here's a clean towel."

"You gonna take me to jail?" asked the boy, bending over the sink.

"Not with that face, I would not take you nowhere," said the woman. "Here I am trying to get home to cook me a bite to eat and you snatch my pocketbook! Maybe you ain't been to your supper either, late as it be. Have you?"

"There's nobody home at my house," said the boy.

"Then we'll eat," said the woman. "I believe you're hungry—or been hungry—to try to snatch my pocketbook!"

"I wanted a pair of blue suede shoes," said the boy.

"Well, you didn't have to snatch *my* pocketbook to get some suede shoes," said Mrs. Luella Bates Washington Jones. "You could of asked me."

"M'am?"

The water dripping from his face, the boy looked at her. There was a long pause. A very long pause. After he had dried his face and, not knowing what else to do, dried it again, the boy turned around, wondering what next. The door was open. He could make a dash for it down the hall. He could run, run, run, run, *run!*

The woman was sitting on the daybed. After a while she said, "I were young once and I wanted things I could not get."

There was another long pause. The boy's mouth opened. Then he frowned, but not knowing he frowned.

The woman said, "Um-hum! You thought I was going to say *but,* didn't you? You thought I was going to say, *but I didn't snatch people's pocketbooks.* Well, I wasn't going to say that." Pause. Silence. "I have done things, too, which I would not tell you, son—neither tell God, if He didn't already know. So you set down while I fix us something to eat. You might run that comb through your hair so you will look presentable."

In another corner of the room behind a screen was a gas plate and an icebox. Mrs. Jones got up and went behind the screen. The woman did not watch the boy to see if he was going to run now, nor did she watch her purse, which she left behind her on the daybed. But the boy took care to sit on the far side of the room where he thought she could easily see him out of the corner of her eye, if she wanted to. He did not trust the woman *not* to trust him. And he did not want to be mistrusted now.

"Do you need somebody to go to the store," asked the boy, "maybe to get some milk or something?"

"Don't believe I do," said the woman, "unless you just want sweet milk yourself. I was going to make cocoa out of this canned milk I got here."

"That will be fine," said the boy.

She heated some lima beans and ham she had in the icebox, made the cocoa, and set the table. The woman did not ask the boy anything about where he lived, or his folks, or anything else that would embarrass him. Instead, as they ate, she told him about her job in a hotel beauty shop that stayed open late, what the work was like, and how all kinds of women came in and out, blondes, redheads, and Spanish. Then she cut him a half of her ten-cent cake.

"Eat some more, son," she said.

When they were finished eating, she got up and said, "Now, here, take this ten dollars and buy yourself some blue suede shoes. And next time, do not make the mistake of latching onto *my* pocketbook *nor nobody else's*—because shoes come by devilish like that will burn your feet. I got to get my rest now. But I wish you would behave yourself, son, from here on in."

She led him down the hall to the front door and opened it. "Good night! Behave yourself, boy!" she said, looking out into the street.

The boy wanted to say something else other than, "Thank you, m'am," to Mrs. Luella Bates Washington Jones, but he couldn't do so as he turned at the barren stoop and looked back at the large woman in the door. He barely managed to say "Thank you" before she shut the door. And he never saw her again. ❧

explain

Responding to Reading

First Impressions

1. Do you approve of the way Mrs. Jones treats Roger? Jot down your explanation on a sheet of paper or in your journal. Then discuss your ideas with classmates.

Second Thoughts

2. Mrs. Jones's actions toward the young thief might differ from what you expected. Why do you think she treats Roger the way she does?

> **Think about**
> • at least three actions she takes
> • her comments about her past
> • her inferences about Roger's life

3. Did you expect Roger to react to Mrs. Jones's treatment of him as he does? Give reasons for your answer.

4. Roger never states his opinion of Mrs. Jones. What do you believe he thinks of her?

> **Think about**
> • why he does not run away
> • why he wants her to trust him
> • why he can barely say, "Thank you, M'am" at the end

5. Is Roger likely to steal again? Explain your opinion.

Broader Connections

6. In some states juvenile offenders receive punishments that are less harsh than those imposed on adults who commit similar crimes. Do you think this is fair? Explain.

7. One of Langston Hughes's purposes for writing was to give a true picture of African-American life. Why would such a purpose have been important?

Literary Concept: Character Motivation

A writer must show, or at least hint at, reasons for characters' actions, or their **motivation.** Review the story and give some reasons that explain why the two main characters behave in the ways they do.

Concept Review: Internal and External Conflict What internal conflicts—conflicts in his own mind—does Roger face? What external conflicts does he have with other people? Do you think he resolves any of these successfully?

Writing Options

1. Write a description of the purse snatching that a bystander might have given. Use your imagination. Feel free to exaggerate and add colorful details.

2. Write a description of what you think Roger's home life might be like. Use details from the story to support your view.

3. Mrs. Jones acts in an unexpected way toward Roger after the attempted robbery. Describe in writing how you might have acted in a similar situation.

4. Mrs. Jones says to Roger, "But you put yourself in contact with *me.* If you think that that contact is not going to last awhile, you got another thought coming." Consider the different meanings of the word *contact.* Make a list of the kinds of contact that occur between Roger and Mrs. Jones.

5. In her conversation with Roger, Mrs. Jones speaks mysteriously of her own past. Using clues from the story, make up a past for Mrs. Jones.

6. Imagine that Mrs. Jones turns Roger in to the police instead of trying to help him. Write up a police report for the attempted theft.

7. Choose three selections from this book that you think Roger should read. Explain your reasons for choosing each.

8. What does Mrs. Jones mean by her statement "Shoes come by devilish like that will burn your feet"? Do you agree with her? Why or why not?

extend

Options for Learning

1 • **Thank You, Mrs. Jones!** Role-play Roger as a grown man telling the effect this incident with Mrs. Jones has had on his life.

2 • **To Catch a Thief** With another classmate, act out Roger's unsuccessful purse-snatching attempt and the moments that follow.

3 • **Neighborhood Watch** Police and community groups provide tips on how to protect yourself from crime. Research some of these tips and present them to the class.

4 • **Talking About Crime** Stage a talk show on the topic of crimes against the elderly. Have your host interview Mrs. Jones, Roger, and other guests. Do some research on the topic to help prepare for your talk show.

 **FACT FINDER**

How many street robberies occur in your community or city in a typical month?

Langston Hughes
1902-1967

Langston Hughes led a lonely childhood, never feeling much support from his separated parents. For much of his youth, he lived like a nomad, moving from place to place. After graduating from high school in Cleveland, he spent a short and unhappy time in Mexico with his father before enrolling at Columbia University in New York. Later he dropped out and held many jobs, including cook, waiter, doorman, farmer, and sailor. Hughes went to Europe, where he was robbed of everything he owned. When he returned to the United States, he began writing and working, and eventually graduated from Lincoln University in Pennsylvania. He spent many years in New York's Harlem, the scene of many of his stories and poems.

Hughes was "discovered" when, while working as a busboy, he left three of his poems at the table where poet Vachel Lindsay was dining. Lindsay was impressed with the young poet's works and presented them at one of his own readings. Soon, Hughes had become well-known.

In his writing Hughes portrayed the lives of African-Americans—their joy and their despair. He wrote without bitterness yet told of the prejudice, discrimination, and poverty his people faced.

Essay

^A *Celebration* of *Grandfathers*

RUDOLFO A. ANAYA
(ro͞o dôl′ fō ä nä′ yä)

Examine What You Know

In this essay the author praises and honors his grandfather. Think of the elderly person that you most admire. Jot down accomplishments or other things about the person's life that command your respect.

Expand Your Knowledge

Although Rudolfo Anaya is a respected and well-known writer of both fiction and nonfiction, he may be most famous for recording and retelling the folk tales, legends, and oral histories of Hispanics and Native Americans. His works have been praised for the way they capture the hearts and souls of Hispanics and their cultural heritage and at the same time express universal truths. Anaya has also written extensively about the people and culture of his native state, New Mexico. Because he believes strongly that young people can learn important lessons from older generations, he has helped start a program in which older people come into schools to share their history and traditions with students.

Enrich Your Reading

Separating Facts from Opinions   A **fact** is a statement that can be proved true, such as "My grandfather was ninety-four when he died." An **opinion** is a statement that cannot be proved. It expresses a person's feelings or beliefs, such as in "My grandfather lived a rewarding life." By mixing facts and opinions, a writer may make readers think that opinions are facts. As you read this essay, separate the facts Anaya presents from his personal opinions. Notice which of his opinions are based on facts. Weigh the facts and the opinions before deciding whether you agree with his message.

■ *A biography of the author can be found in the Reader's Handbook.*

A Celebration of Grandfathers

RUDOLFO A. ANAYA

Buenos días le de Dios, abuelo.*"[1]* God give you a good day, grandfather. This is how I was taught as a child to greet my grandfather, or any grown person. It was a greeting of respect, a cultural value to be passed on from generation to generation, this respect for the old ones.

The old people I remember from my childhood were strong in their beliefs, and as we lived daily with them, we learned a wise path of life to follow. They had something important to share with the young, and when they spoke, the young listened. These old *abuelos* and *abuelitas*[2] had worked the earth all their lives, and so they knew the value of nurturing, they knew the sensitivity of the earth. . . . They knew the rhythms and cycles of time, from the preparation of the earth in the spring to the digging of the *acequias*[3] that brought the water to the dance of harvest in the fall. They shared good times and hard times. They helped each other through the epidemics and the personal tragedies, and they shared what little they had when the hot winds burned the land and no rain came. They learned that to survive one had to share in the process of life. . . .

My grandfather was a plain man, a farmer from the valley called Puerto de Luna on the Pecos River.[4] He was probably a descendant of those people who spilled over the mountain from Taos, following the Pecos River in search of farmland. There in that river valley he settled and raised a large family.

Bearded and walrus-mustached, he stood five feet tall, but to me as a child he was a giant. I remember him most for his silence. In the summers my parents sent me to live with him on his farm, for I was to learn the ways of a farmer. My uncles also lived in that valley, there where only the flow of the river and the whispering of the wind marked time. For me it was a magical place.

I remember once, while out hoeing the fields, I came upon an anthill, and before I knew it I was badly bitten. After he had covered my welts with the cool mud from the irrigation ditch, my grandfather calmly said: "Know where you stand." That is the way he spoke, in short phrases, to the point.

---

1. *Buenos días le de Dios, abuelo* (bwe′ nôs dē′ äs lā dā dyôs ä bwe′ lô) *Spanish.*
2. *abuelos* (ä bwe′ lôs) and *abuelitas* (ä bwe lē′ täs) *Spanish:* grandfathers and grandmothers.
3. *acequias* (ä se′ kyäs) *Spanish:* irrigation ditches.
4. **Puerto de Luna** (pwer′ tô dä lo͞o nä) . . . **Pecos** (pe′ kôs) **River**

One very dry summer, the river dried to a trickle; there was no water for the fields. The young plants withered and died. In my sadness and with the impulse of youth I said, "I wish it would rain!" My grandfather touched me, looked up into the sky and whispered, "Pray for rain." In his language there was a difference. He felt connected to the cycles that brought the rain or kept it from us. His prayer was a meaningful action, because he was a participant with the forces that filled our world; he was not a bystander.

A young man died at the village one summer. A very tragic death. He was dragged by his horse. When he was found, I cried, for the boy was my friend. I did not understand why death had come to one so young. My grandfather took me aside and said: "Think of the death of the trees and the fields in the fall. The leaves fall, and everything rests, as if dead. But they bloom again in the spring. Death is only this small transformation in life."

These are the things I remember, these fleeting images, few words.

I remember him driving his horse-drawn wagon into Santa Rosa in the fall when he brought his harvest produce to sell in the town. What a tower of strength seemed to come in that small man huddled on the seat of the giant wagon. One click of his tongue and the horses obeyed, stopped or turned as he wished. He never raised his whip. How unlike today, when so much teaching is done with loud words and threatening hands.

I would run to greet the wagon, and the wagon would stop. *"Buenos días le de Dios, abuelo,"* I would say. . . . *"Buenos días te de Dios, mi hijo,"*[5] he would answer and smile, and then I could jump up on the wagon and sit at his side. Then I, too, became a king as I rode next to the old man who smelled of earth and sweat and the other deep aromas from the orchards and fields of Puerto de Luna.

We were all sons and daughters to him. But today the sons and daughters are breaking with the past, putting aside *los abuelitos*.[6] The old values are threatened, and threatened most where it comes to these relationships with the old people. If we don't take the time to watch and feel the years of their final transformation, a part of our humanity will be lessened.

I grew up speaking Spanish, and oh! how difficult it was to learn English. Sometimes I would give up and cry out that I couldn't learn. Then he would say, *"Ten paciencia."*[7] Have patience. *Paciencia,* a word with the strength of centuries, a word that said that someday we would overcome. . . . "You have to learn the language of the Americanos," he said. "Me, I will live my last days in my valley. You will live in a new time."

A new time did come; a new time is here. How will we form it so it is fruitful? We need to know where we stand. We need to speak softly and respect others, and to share what we have. We need to pray not for material gain, but for rain for the fields, for the sun to nurture growth, for nights in which we can sleep in peace, and for a harvest in which everyone can share. Simple lessons from a simple man. These lessons he learned from his past, which was as deep and strong as the currents of the river of life.

He was a man; he died. Not in his valley but nevertheless cared for by his sons and daughters and flocks of grandchildren. At

---

5. *mi hijo* (mē ē′ hô) *Spanish:* my son.
6. *los abuelitos* (lôs ä bwe lē′ tôs) *Spanish:* the grandparents.
7. *Ten paciencia* (ten pä syen′ syä) *Spanish.*

MANUEL LA JEUNESSE
1922 Walter Ufer
Courtesy of the Anshutz Collection,
Denver, Colorado
Photograph by
James O. Milmoe.

the end, I would enter his room, which carried the smell of medications and Vicks. Gone were the aroma of the fields, the strength of his young manhood. Gone also was his patience in the face of crippling old age. Small things bothered him; he shouted or turned sour when his expectations were not met. It was because he could not care for himself, because he was returning to that state of childhood, and all those wishes and desires were now wrapped in a crumbling, old body.

"*Ten paciencia,*" I once said to him, and he smiled. "I didn't know I would grow this old," he said. . . .

I would sit and look at him and remember what was said of him when he was a young man. He could mount a wild horse and break it, and he could ride as far as any man. He could dance all night at a dance, then work the *acequia* the following day. He helped the neighbors; they helped him. He married, raised children. Small legends, the kind that make up every man's life.

He was ninety-four when he died. Family, neighbors, and friends gathered; they all agreed he had led a rich life. I remembered the last years, the years he spent in bed. And as I remember now, I am reminded that it is too easy to romanticize old age. Sometimes we forget the pain of the transformation into old age, we forget the natural breaking down of the body. . . . My grandfather pointed to the leaves falling from the tree. So time brings with its transformation the often painful wearing-down process. Vision blurs, health wanes; even the act of walking carries with it the painful reminder of the autumn of life. But this process is something to be faced, not something to be hidden away by false images. Yes, the old can be young at heart, but in their own way, with their own dignity. They do not have to copy the always-young image of the Hollywood star. . . .

I returned to Puerto de Luna last summer to join the community in a celebration of the founding of the church. I drove by my grandfather's home, my uncles' ranches, the neglected adobe washing down into the earth from whence it came. And I wondered, how might the values of my grandfather's generation live in our own? What can we retain to see us through these hard times? I was to become a farmer, and I became a writer. As I plow and plant my words, do I nurture as my grandfather did in his fields and orchards? The answers are not simple.

"They don't make men like that anymore," is a phrase we hear when one does honor to a man. I am glad I knew my grandfather. I am glad there are still times when I can see him in my dreams, hear him in my reverie.[8] Sometimes I think I catch a whiff of that earthy aroma that was his smell. Then I smile. How strong these people were to leave such a lasting impression.

So, as I would greet my *abuelo* long ago, it would help us all to greet the old ones we know with this kind and respectful greeting: *"Buenos días le de Dios."*

8. **reverie** (rev′ ər ē): a daydream or a visionary imagining.

INSIGHT

Legacy II

LEROY V. QUINTANA

Grandfather never went to school
spoke only a few words of English,
a quiet man; when he talked
talked about simple things

planting corn or about the weather
sometimes about herding sheep as a
   child.
One day pointed to the four directions
taught me their names

> El Norte
Poniente   Oriente
> El Sur

He spoke their names as if they were
one of only a handful of things
a man needed to know

Now I look back
only two generations removed
realize I am nothing but a poor fool
who went to college

trying to find my way back
to the center of the world
where Grandfather stood
that day

*R*esponding to Reading

First Impressions

1. How did this essay affect you? Jot down your thoughts in your journal or on a sheet of paper.

Second Thoughts

2. Why does Anaya's grandfather command his respect? Does Anaya persuade you that his grandfather deserves respect? Explain.

3. Summarize the philosophy of Anaya's grandfather toward life and death. Would this philosophy work today?

4. What do you learn about old age from this essay?

5. Anaya states that older people have something important to share with the young. What facts does he use to support this opinion?

6. How does Anaya's attitude toward the elderly compare with the attitude toward the elderly in your community?

   Think about
   • who cares for the elderly in your community
   • whether the elderly still merit respect and honor as in times past

*L*iterary Concept: Essay

An **essay** is a form of nonfiction in which a writer offers his or her opinion on a particular topic. Essays can be formal or informal. **Formal essays** are serious in tone and examine a topic in an orderly, logical manner. **Informal essays** tend to reveal a writer's feelings and personality as well as his or her beliefs. Such essays are usually less structured than formal essays and may use anecdotes, humor, and even exaggeration to make a point. Considering these differences, would you call Anaya's essay formal or informal? Give examples from the essay to support your answer.

*W*riting Options

1. Might Anaya have written a poem like "Legacy"? Write your opinion and support it with details from the essay and the poem.

2. Young people are often criticized for their lack of respect for the elderly. Do you feel that this is a fair criticism? Defend your opinion with facts.

Fiction

Too Soon a Woman

DOROTHY M. JOHNSON

Examine What You Know

This story is about an American pioneer family and their move west. What do you know about the difficulties the pioneers encountered? On a chart like the one below, classify those problems under headings that you create, such as "weather," "food," "travel," and so on. After you read this story, add any new problems you learn about through reading.

Problems the Pioneers Faced

Categories	Weather	Food		

Expand Your Knowledge

In 1775, Daniel Boone and a group of axmen cut a trail through the Appalachian Mountains. This trail, the Wilderness Road, connected Virginia and Kentucky. It was the main route used by early pioneers who wanted to travel west. During the next 140 years, trails pushed farther and farther west as pioneers settled the Great Plains, the Rocky Mountains, and eventually the land beyond the Rockies. Between 1840 and 1870, more than 350,000 pioneers migrated west.

Families who cultivated a piece of land and lived on it were called **homesteaders.** Some homesteaders stayed on the land they first settled. Others, like the family in this story, moved farther west after a time. While this story is not set in a particular time or place, the hardships the characters encounter are typical of the difficulties many pioneers faced in their struggle for a new life.

Enrich Your Reading

Making Inferences Although this story seems easy to read, you will have to make inferences to really understand the characters' feelings and motives. As you read, stop often to question what is going on and why. Use your own experience and details from the story to decide what makes each character act as he or she does.

■ *A biography of the author can be found in the Reader's Handbook.*

Too Soon a Woman

DOROTHY M. JOHNSON

We left the home place behind, mile by slow mile, heading for the mountains, across the prairie where the wind blew forever.

At first there were four of us with the one-horse wagon and its skimpy load. Pa and I walked, because I was a big boy of eleven. My two little sisters romped and trotted until they got tired and had to be boosted up into the wagon bed.

> ## "If you won't take me, I'll travel with any wagon that will."

That was no covered Conestoga,[1] like Pa's folks came west in, but just an old farm wagon, drawn by one weary horse, creaking and rumbling westward to the mountains, toward the little woods town where Pa thought he had an old uncle who owned a little two-bit sawmill.

Two weeks we had been moving when we picked up Mary, who had run away from somewhere that she wouldn't tell. Pa didn't want her along, but she stood up to him with no fear in her voice.

"I'd rather go with a family and look after kids," she said, "but I ain't going back. If you won't take me, I'll travel with any wagon that will."

Pa scowled at her, and her wide blue eyes stared back.

"How old are you?" he demanded.

"Eighteen," she said. "There's teamsters[2] come this way sometimes. I'd rather go with you folks. But I won't go back."

"We're prid'near out of grub," my father told her. "We're clean out of money. I got all I can handle without taking anybody else." He turned away as if he hated the sight of her. "You'll have to walk," he said.

So she went along with us and looked after the little girls, but Pa wouldn't talk to her.

On the prairie, the wind blew. But in the mountains, there was rain. When we stopped at little timber claims along the way, the homesteaders said it had rained all summer. Crops among the blackened stumps were rotted and spoiled. There was no cheer anywhere and little hospitality. The people we talked to were past worrying. They were scared and desperate.

So was Pa. He traveled twice as far each

---

1. **Conestoga:** a broad-wheeled covered wagon used by early pioneers to transport their belongings; originally made in Conestoga Valley, Pennsylvania.

2. **teamsters:** drivers of teams of horses, oxen, or other animals.

LANDSCAPE WITH CHILDREN 1880 Henry Farny Cincinnati Art Museum, Ohio.

day as the wagon. He ranged through the woods with his rifle, but he never saw game. He had been depending on venison,[3] but we never got any except as a grudging[4] gift from the homesteaders.

He brought in a porcupine once; that was fat meat and good. Mary roasted it in chunks over the fire, half crying with the smoke. Pa and I rigged up the tarp[5] sheet for a shelter to keep the rain from putting the fire clean out.

The porcupine was long gone, except for some of the tried-out[6] fat that Mary had saved, when we came to an old, empty cabin. Pa said we'd have to stop. The horse was wore out, couldn't pull any more up those grades[7] on the deep-rutted roads in the mountains.

At the cabin, at least there was shelter. We had a few potatoes left and some cornmeal. There was a creek that probably had fish in it, if a person could catch them. Pa tried it for half a day before he gave up. To this day I don't care for fishing. I remember my father's sunken eyes in his sad face.

He took Mary and me outside the cabin to talk. Rain dripped on us from branches overhead.

"I think I know where we are," he said. "I calculate to get to old John's and back in about four days. There'll be grub in the

---

3. **venison:** deer meat.
4. **grudging:** reluctantly or resentfully given.
5. **tarp:** a type of waterproof canvas cloth.
6. **tried-out:** melted down to make pure.
7. **grades:** rising surfaces; slopes.

town, and they'll let me have some whether old John's still there or not."

He looked at me. "You do like she tells you," he warned. It was the first time he had admitted Mary was on earth since we picked her up two weeks before.

"You're my pardner," he said to me, "but it might be she's got more brains. You mind what she says."

He burst out with bitterness. "There ain't anything good left in the world, or people to care if you live or die. But I'll get grub in the town and come back with it."

He took a deep breath and added, "If you get too all-fired hungry, butcher the horse. It'll be better than starvin'."

He kissed the little girls goodbye and plodded off through the woods with one blanket and the rifle.

The cabin was moldy and had no floor. We kept a fire going under a hole in the roof, so it was full of blinding smoke, but we had to keep the fire so as to dry out the wood.

The third night, we lost the horse. A bear scared him. We heard the racket, and Mary and I ran out, but we couldn't see anything in the pitch dark.

In gray daylight I went looking for him, and I must have walked fifteen miles. It seemed like I had to have that horse at the cabin when Pa came or he'd whip me. I got plumb lost two or three times and thought maybe I was going to die there alone and nobody would ever know it, but I found the way back to the clearing.

That was the fourth day, and Pa didn't come. That was the day we ate up the last of the grub.

The fifth day, Mary went looking for the horse. My sisters whimpered, huddled in a blanket by the fire because they were scared and hungry.

I never did get dried out, always having to bring in more damp wood and going out to yell to see if Mary would hear me and not get lost. But I couldn't cry like the little girls did, because I was a big boy, eleven years old.

It was near dark when there was an answer to my yelling, and Mary came into the clearing.

Mary didn't have the horse—we never saw hide nor hair of that old horse again—but she was carrying something big and white that looked like a pumpkin with no color to it.

She didn't say anything, just looked around and saw Pa wasn't there yet, at the end of the fifth day.

"What's that thing?" my sister Elizabeth demanded.

"Mushroom," Mary answered. "I bet it hefts ten pounds."

"What are you going to do with it now?" I sneered. "Play football here?"

"Eat it—maybe," she said, putting it in a corner. Her wet hair hung over her shoulders. She huddled by the fire.

My sister Sarah began to whimper again. "I'm hungry!" she kept saying.

"Mushrooms ain't good eating," I said. "They can kill you."

"Maybe," Mary answered. "Maybe they can. I don't set up to know all about everything, like some people."

"What's that mark on your shoulder?" I asked her. "You tore your dress on the brush."

"What do you think it is?" she said, her head bowed in the smoke.

"Looks like scars," I guessed.

" 'Tis scars. They whipped me. Now mind' your own business. I want to think."

Elizabeth whimpered, "Why don't Pa come back?"

"He's coming," Mary promised. "Can't come in the dark. Your pa'll take care of you soon's he can."

She got up and rummaged around in the grub box.

"Nothing there but empty dishes," I growled. "If there was anything, we'd know it."

Mary stood up. She was holding the can with the porcupine grease.

"I'm going to have something to eat," she said coolly. "You kids can't have any yet. And I don't want any squalling, mind."

It was a cruel thing, what she did then. She sliced that big, solid mushroom and heated grease in a pan.

The smell of it brought the little girls out of their quilt, but she told them to go back in so fierce a voice that they obeyed. They cried to break your heart.

I didn't cry. I watched, hating her.

I endured the smell of the mushroom frying as long as I could. Then I said, "Give me some."

"Tomorrow," Mary answered. "Tomorrow, maybe. But not tonight." She turned to me with a sharp command: "Don't bother me! Just leave me be."

She knelt there by the fire and finished frying the slice of mushroom.

If I'd had Pa's rifle, I'd have been willing to kill her right then and there.

She didn't eat right away. She looked at the brown, fried slice for a while and said, "By tomorrow morning, I guess you can tell whether you want any."

The girls stared at her as she ate. Sarah was chewing an old leather glove.

When Mary crawled into the quilts with them, they moved away as far as they could get.

I was so scared that my stomach heaved, empty as it was.

Mary didn't stay in the quilts long. She took a drink out of the water bucket and sat down by the fire and looked through the smoke at me.

She said in a low voice, "I don't know how it will be if it's poison. Just do the best you can with the girls. Because your pa will come back, you know. . . . You better go to bed. I'm going to sit up."

And so would you sit up. If it might be your last night on earth and the pain of death might seize you at any moment, you would sit up by the smoky fire, wide-awake, remembering whatever you had to remember, savoring life.

We sat in silence after the girls had gone to sleep. Once I asked, "How long does it take?"

"I never heard," she answered. "Don't think about it."

I slept after a while, with my chin on my chest. Maybe Peter dozed that way at Gethsemane as the Lord knelt praying.[8]

Mary's moving around brought me wide-awake. The black of night was fading.

"I guess it's all right," Mary said. "I'd be able to tell by now, wouldn't I?"

I answered gruffly, "I don't know."

Mary stood in the doorway for a while, looking out at the dripping world as if she found it beautiful. Then she fried slices of the mushroom while the little girls danced with anxiety.[9]

We feasted, we three, my sisters and I, until Mary ruled, "That'll hold you," and would not cook any more. She didn't touch any of the mushroom herself.

That was a strange day in the moldy cabin. Mary laughed and was gay; she told stories,

---

8. **Maybe Peter . . . praying.**: reference to the biblical story in which Jesus visits the Garden of Gethsemane to pray on the night he is arrested and sentenced to be crucified. Jesus asks Peter and two other disciples to keep watch, but they fall asleep. Likewise, the narrator wants to keep watch with Mary, but he falls asleep.

9. **anxiety**: apprehension; uneasiness about what is to come.

and we played "Who's Got the Thimble?" with a pine cone.

In the afternoon we heard a shout, and my sisters screamed and I ran ahead of them across the clearing.

The rain had stopped. My father came plunging out of the woods leading a pack horse—and well I remember the treasures of food in that pack.

He glanced at us anxiously as he tore the ropes that bound the pack.

"Where's the other one?" he demanded.

Mary came out of the cabin then, walking sedately. As she came toward us, the sun began to shine.

My stepmother was a wonderful woman.

❧

I N S I G H T

A Journey

NIKKI GIOVANNI

It's a journey . . . that I propose . . . I am not the guide . . . nor technical assistant . . . I will be your fellow passenger. . .

Though the rail has been ridden . . . winter clouds cover . . . autumn's exuberant quilt . . . we must provide our own guide-posts . . .

I have heard . . . from previous visitors . . . the road washes out sometimes . . . and passengers are compelled . . . to continue groping . . . or turn back . . . I am not afraid. . .

I am not afraid . . . of rough spots . . . or lonely times . . . I don't fear . . . the success of this endeavor . . . I am Ra . . . in a space . . . not to be discovered . . . but invented . . .

I promise you nothing . . . I accept your promise . . . of the same we are simply riding . . . a wave . . . that may carry . . . or crash . . .

It's a journey . . . and I want . . . to go . . .

explain

Responding to Reading

First Impressions

1. Were you surprised by the conclusion of this story? Why or why not?

Second Thoughts

2. What can you infer about Mary's character? Provide details from the story to support your conclusions.

   Think about
   - what you know and can infer about Mary's past
   - ways in which her past affects her present actions and attitudes
   - whether she acts heroically

3. Would you have eaten the mushroom if you had been in Mary's place? Explain.

4. What can you infer about Pa from his actions and words?

   Think about
   - his gruffness at the beginning of the story
   - his reasons for leaving Mary in charge of the children
   - his decision to marry Mary

5. Why do you suppose the writer chose to have an eleven-year-old boy narrate the story? What does his point of view add?

6. Explain how the title "Too Soon a Woman" relates to this story.

7. Compare Mary's outlook on life with that of the speaker in "A Journey."

Literary Concept: Setting

Although the writer does not state the exact time and location in which this story takes place, you can picture the setting from the dialogue, the geographic references, the details about everyday life, and the events in the story. Describe the setting as you imagine it. List the clues that helped you visualize the setting.

Writing Options

1. Look again at the problems you charted. Choose another selection in this book in which the characters face similar conflicts. Explain in writing how the conflicts are alike.

2. Write two or three journal entries that either Mary or Pa might have written about the events in this story.

Poetry

The Courage That My Mother Had

EDNA ST. VINCENT MILLAY

Lineage

MARGARET WALKER

Examine What You Know

In what ways are you like your parents or grandparents? Do you have similar features, mannerisms, talents, and personality traits, or are you very different? How do the speakers in the following poems think they are similar to or different from their relatives?

Expand Your Knowledge

Many people can trace their *lineage,* or ancestry, back for several generations. By examining their roots they learn more about themselves. In these poems the poets compare themselves with their relatives. The poets are from different parts of the United States and from different backgrounds.

Edna St. Vincent Millay grew up in Maine. She writes about her mother, a nurse who raised her three children alone after divorcing her husband. Millay compares her mother to granite, an extremely hard rock quarried in New England and used to build bridges, large buildings, and tombstones. Early New Englanders have traditionally been compared to granite because of their strength and persistence in the face of trouble. Only with toughness and hard work were they able to farm the rocky land.

Margaret Walker, on the other hand, grew up in Alabama. The subject of her poem is her grandmothers, women who were born into slavery and were later freed as a result of the Emancipation Proclamation. Walker, too, remembers her relatives' strength and sturdiness.

Enrich Your Reading

Comparing Poems To get the most out of these poems, take time to compare them. Notice what you learn about Millay and Walker. What are their attitudes toward themselves and toward their subjects? How are their attitudes alike in spite of their different backgrounds?

■ *Biographies of the authors can be found on page 396.*

The Courage That My Mother Had

EDNA ST. VINCENT MILLAY

The courage that my mother had
Went with her, and is with her still:
Rock from New England quarried;
Now granite in a granite hill.

5   The golden brooch my mother wore
She left behind for me to wear;
I have no thing I treasure more:
Yet, it is something I could spare.

Oh, if instead she'd left to me
10 The thing she took into the grave!—
That courage like a rock, which she
Has no more need of, and I have.

THE WINDY DOORSTEP   1910   Abastenia St. Leger
Eberle   Worcester Art Museum, Massachusetts.

*R*esponding to Reading

First Impressions of "The Courage That My Mother Had"

1. What image do you get of the speaker's mother? List the words and phrases that come to mind.

Second Thoughts on "The Courage That My Mother Had"

2. What feelings does the speaker have toward her mother? What feeling do you think is strongest?

3. Based on the poem, what do you think are the speaker's strengths and weaknesses? Explain.

Lineage

MARGARET WALKER

My grandmothers were strong.
They followed plows and bent to toil.
They moved through fields sowing seed.
They touched earth and grain grew.
5   They were full of sturdiness and singing.
My grandmothers were strong.

My grandmothers are full of memories
Smelling of soap and onions and wet clay
With veins rolling roughly over quick hands

10   They have many clean words to say.
My grandmothers were strong.
Why am I not as they?

HARRIET TUBMAN SERIES, NO. 7
1939–40 Jacob Lawrence
Hampton University Museum,
Hampton, Virginia.

Responding to Reading

First Impressions of "Lineage"

1. Does this poem give you the same feeling as the first poem? Why or why not?

Second Thoughts on "Lineage"

2. The speaker compares herself with her grandmothers. In doing so, do you think she judges herself fairly?

Comparing the Poems

3. How are the speakers in these poems alike in their feelings and attitudes toward themselves and their ancestors?

4. Do you sympathize with either of the speakers? Explain.

5. Which speaker's ancestor or ancestors command more of your respect and admiration? Why?

Literary Concept: Imagery

Words and phrases that re-create sensory experiences for the reader are called **imagery**. Often these descriptions connote ideas and feelings beyond the literal meaning of the words. For example, Millay uses this metaphor to describe her mother: "Rock from New England quarried." The word *rock* implies a toughness and inner strength that Millay admires. Find examples of imagery in both poems.

Writing Options

1. Write a poem about someone you admire. Try using imagery to help your reader see why the person commands your respect.

2. Compare one of the poems with "A Celebration of Grandfathers" or another piece in this section.

3. Write a "recipe" showing the ingredients for any one of the subjects of these poems or for your own mother, father, or grandparents. For example, you might write that to make one of Walker's grandmothers you would combine two parts strength, one part love, and a pinch of clay.

Edna St. Vincent Millay
1892-1950

Edna St. Vincent Millay was considered by many to be the voice of the rebellious youth of her time. She wrote in simple, down-to-earth language, mainly about love and life.

Millay began writing poetry as a child. At nineteen, she received national recognition for her first published poem, "Renascence." She used her earnings from this poem to attend Vassar College.

After graduating, Millay became a part of New York City's controversial Greenwich Village scene. From the 1920's through the 1940's, this area's reputation as a center for artists and writers grew. Millay enjoyed life there and created her most successful writing during this period. Although her works often shocked the older generation while voicing the views of her liberated contemporaries, Millay won a Pulitzer Prize in 1923 for her poem *The Ballad of the Harp-Weaver* and for other works. In all, Millay wrote more than twenty volumes of poetry, plays, an opera, and essays. Millay also directed and acted in plays, including those of Floyd Dell (see page 50).

Margaret Walker
1915-

Margaret Walker, the daughter of a well-educated and scholarly Methodist minister, grew up with books. She graduated from high school at age fourteen and went to college at Northwestern University at fifteen. Later she received a Ph.D. from Iowa University.

Early in life, Walker decided to write poetry. She won the Yale Younger Poets Award in 1942 for her first collection of poems, *For My People*. One of her most famous works is a novel, *Jubilee*, the story of her great-grandmother, a slave in Georgia during the time of the Civil War.

Walker taught school for much of her career, most of the time as a professor of English at Jackson State College in Mississippi. There she founded a research institute bearing her name that records the achievements and lives of twentieth-century African Americans.

A friend of Langston Hughes, Walker considers him, W.E.B. Dubois, and Richard Wright as her mentors. Walker says, "I don't think you can write if you don't read. You can't read if you can't think. Thinking, reading, and writing all go together. When I was about eight, I decided that the most wonderful thing, next to a human being, was a book."

EXPOSITION: SUPPORTING GENERALIZATIONS

A **generalization** is a conclusion based on observations, experience, or other kinds of evidence. People generalize all the time. For instance, we generalize that summers in the American Midwest are hot and humid based on evidence such as past daily temperatures, average rainfall, or humidity readings. We make generalizations about people, too. When we say, "Mrs. Franklin is a thoughtful and compassionate person," our conclusion is based on observations of her behavior and our experiences with her.

A common kind of writing about literature that requires making and supporting generalizations is **character analysis.** Analyzing involves looking at the various parts of something and making generalizations about it. In the case of character analysis, you study a character from literature. First, you carefully examine what the character does and says, how he or she behaves, and how other characters relate to him or her. From these details, you draw conclusions about this character's values or traits, such as, "Character X is honest, brave, and intelligent." Finally, you support your conclusion with quotes and details from the story.

> Here is your PASSkey to this assignment.

**GUIDED ASSIGNMENT:
CHARACTER ANALYSIS**

Write a character analysis of one of the main characters from the selections in this subunit. Make and support generalizations about the character using evidence from the story.

PURPOSE: To analyze a character

AUDIENCE: Your teacher and classmates

SUBJECT: A main character

STRUCTURE: A formal composition

Prewriting

STEP **1** **Choose a character** Begin by looking over the selections in this subunit and thinking about the characters in them. Pick the character you find most interesting to analyze. You will probably find that the most complex character is the one that will offer you the best writing possibilities.

STEP 2 **Brainstorm character traits** With a partner, in a small group, or on your own, brainstorm a long list of human values and traits, both good and bad, that any character might possess. For example, you might include honesty, intelligence, courage, independence, greed, power, friendship, selfishness, and fairness. If you get stuck, do a mental inventory of people you know—those you like and dislike. Add their character traits to your list. You might also recall characters from other stories, movies, or television.

STEP 3 **Think about your character** Now, compare your list of character traits and values to the character you have chosen. Decide which values your character finds most important and which qualities he or she shows.

STEP 4 **Find supporting evidence** On your paper, state each character trait as a generalization. For example, you might write, "Mrs. Jones is brave." Then, using elaboration, gather specific evidence that supports each statement. Below each statement, copy quotations and summarize events from the story that show that your character exhibits that trait.

Drafting

STEP 1 **Write an introduction** In your first paragraph, introduce your character and tell from what literary work he or she comes, including the author of the selection. Then state your generalizations. Here is the introduction one student wrote:

STUDENT MODEL ▶

> Sometimes people are almost too good to be true. Lydia, the main character in Paula Jackson's story "Trying Again" is such a person. Lydia is loyal to others, is loving to her family, and always tries to do the right thing—even when her actions are not understood by others.

STEP 2 **State each generalization as a topic sentence** Explain each generalization in a separate paragraph. Include a topic sentence that states the generalization you will support. Then add specific quotations and summaries from the story as supporting details. Finally, explain why the evidence you give proves the stated generalization. Study the student model to see how this is done.

Here is one of the body paragraphs a student wrote. Notice how she introduces, punctuates, and explains her evidence.

Most of all, Lydia tries to do the right thing. When Valerie, her best friend, invites her to go to the mall as a way of making up, Lydia has no idea what is coming. In the jeans store, Valerie says, "If you were really my friend, you'd loan me the money for these jeans. I'll pay you back next week when I get my paycheck." Lydia wants to be friends again with Valerie, but she knows that the only money she has must be spent on her brother's birthday present the next day. As Valerie stands there waiting for the money, Lydia thinks to herself, "My brother would never know I had planned to get him something more expensive. I could lend Valerie the money and still have enough for something smaller." Just when Lydia is about to hand over the money to Valerie, she says, "I'm sorry, I can't!" Lydia had made a promise to herself that this birthday would be the best ever for her brother. She knew that meant buying him the best gift she could afford. It meant doing the right thing even if she lost Valerie as a friend.

Generalization

Evidence from story: quotes and summaries of events

◀ STUDENT MODEL
. . . .

Explanation of why evidence proves generalization

Revising and Editing

When you have completed your draft, ask a classmate to evaluate your work according to the following checklist.

Revision Checklist
. . . .
1. Does the introduction name the selection's title and author, your subject, and the traits and values of that character?
2. Does each paragraph include elaboration: quotations and summaries from the selection?
3. Does the writer explain how and why the evidence given supports the generalization? Are these explanations clear and reasonable?

Editing When you have finished revising your draft, proofread for spelling, clarity, and mechanics.

Presenting

In a small group with other students who analyzed the same character, read your essay. Compare your impression of the character with that of the other students.

LANGUAGE WORKSHOP

PRONOUN AGREEMENT

Most pronoun agreement problems occur when indefinite pronouns are used. **Indefinite pronouns** do not refer to a specific person or thing. Some are singular, some are plural, and some can be either.

Since an indefinite pronoun does not refer to a specific person or thing, you cannot always "hear" whether you are using it correctly. The only way to know for sure is to learn which indefinite pronouns are singular, which are plural, and which are singular or plural, depending on the circumstances.

INDEFINITE PRONOUNS				
Singular	another	anybody	anyone	anything	each
	either	everybody	everyone	everything
	neither	nobody	no one	one
	somebody	someone		
Plural	both	few	many	several
Singular or Plural	all	any	most	none	some

Indefinite Pronouns as Antecedents

The noun or pronoun that a pronoun stands for is called the **antecedent.**

The *boy* read *his* poem to the class.

In the example above, the pronoun *his* stands for the noun *boy. Boy* is the antecedent of *his.* Note that since *boy* is a singular noun, you must use a singular pronoun, *his.*

Sometimes the antecedent of a pronoun is an indefinite pronoun. To be sure that the pronoun and the indefinite pronoun agree in number, you must determine whether the indefinite pronoun is singular or plural.

In these examples the indefinite pronouns are singular, so the possessive pronouns that stand for them must also be singular.

HIS OR HER?
HER OR HIS?
Notice that the phrase "his or her" may be used when the person referred to could be either male or female.

▶   Everyone ate *her* dinner.   No one had *his* or *her* dessert.
Someone borrowed *his* coat.   Something left *its* paw prints here.

When the indefinite pronoun is plural, use a plural form of the possessive pronoun.

Few did *their* homework.   Several offered *their* excuses.

Notice that *all, any, some,* and *none* may be either singular or plural, depending on their meaning in the sentence. They are singular when they refer to one thing and plural when they refer to several things.

Singular   All of the popcorn has butter on *it.*
Plural   All of the potatoes have butter on *them.*

HELP!

Don't be confused by a phrase that appears be-tween an indefinite pro-noun and a possessive pronoun.
Incorrect: One of the boys left their coat. (The possessive pronoun should agree with *one,* not with *boys.*)
Correct: One of the boys left *his* coat.

Exercise 1   Find the indefinite pronoun in each sentence and decide whether it is singular or plural. Then write the correct pronoun.

1. Few of the pioneers made (their, his or her) way to the West safely.
2. Many of these people lost (their, his or her) lives during the trip.
3. Some of the women lost (their, her) lives during childbirth.
4. Few of the elderly kept (their, his or her) health.
5. In "Too Soon a Woman," someone told (his, their) story quietly.
6. Everyone in the family missed (their, her or his) former home.
7. No one mentioned (their, his or her) feelings of homesickness.
8. Each of the young girls listened to (her, their) brother willingly.
9. Despite desperate feelings of hunger, nobody ate (their, his or her) pieces of mushroom until Mary agreed.
10. Everyone in the family recognized the courage of (their, his or her) future stepmother.

Subject-Verb Agreement with Indefinite Pronouns

Sometimes an indefinite pronoun is used as the subject of a sentence. To make sure that the indefinite pronoun agrees with the verb, you must again decide whether it is singular or plural. For the indefinite pronouns that are always singular or always plural, the correct verb will often sound right to you.

Incorrect   *Everyone* **have** a poem to write.
Correct   *Everyone* **has** a poem to write. (*Everyone* is singular; it takes a singular verb, *has.*)

Incorrect   *Both* of the poems **is** in Spanish.
Correct   *Both* of the poems **are** in Spanish. (*Both* is plural; it takes a plural verb, *are.*)

The indefinite pronouns that can be either singular or plural cause the most difficult problems. Treat the pronoun as singular if it refers to one thing. If the pronoun refers to several things, treat it as plural and choose a plural verb to agree with it.

Singular   *All* of the class **was** there.   (*All* refers to one group.)
Plural   *All* of the books **were** read.   (*All* refers to several books.)

Exercise 2   The sentences below contain errors in indefinite pronoun-verb agreement. On your paper, rewrite the sentences correctly.

1. Most of the class have enjoyed reading ''A Celebration of Grandfathers.''
2. All of the Spanish words was translated by our teacher.
3. One of my favorite sections are the description of the old people whom the writer remembers from his childhood.
4. Several in class praises the simplicity of the writing in this narrative.
5. Some of my friends mentions the beautiful descriptions of nature.
6. Everyone in class recognize how important the writer's grandfather is to him.

Exercise 3   Rewrite the following passage, correcting any errors in the agreement of indefinite pronouns and verbs or possessive pronouns.

Everyone have a chance to read their favorite poems during the Thursday morning poetry sessions in English class. Today, since the topic is ''Our Heritage,'' several of my classmates is reading poems about his or her grandparents. One of the students wrote a poem in their native language, Russian. Some of my friends raises their hands to ask for a translation. Both of the teachers comments on the beauty of the Russian language. Then everybody take their turn reading a poem. One of the boys read their favorite poem, ''Legacy II'' by Leroy Quintana. It makes all of the students think about their own feelings toward his or her grandparents.

LANGUAGE HANDBOOK

For review and practice:
indefinite pronouns,
pages 905, 914–15
agreement with indefinite
pronouns, pages 945–47

Exercise 4   Analyzing and Revising Your Writing

1. Reread a passage from one of your papers, looking for errors in the use of indefinite pronouns.
2. Revise any errors in indefinite-pronoun usage.

Speaking and Listening
WORKSHOP

INTERVIEW TIPS

When you write articles or reports, you need to collect information from as many sources as possible. One way to gather information you need is to conduct a personal **interview.**

Before the Interview

1. **Define your purpose.** What information do you hope to gain from the interview?

2. **Prepare your questions.** Think carefully about what you want to find out. Write down clear, direct questions. Don't avoid tough questions, but try to save them for later in the interview.
   - Avoid questions you can answer without the interview.
   - Avoid overly vague questions, like "Is education a good idea?"
   - Avoid leading questions, like "You do think education is a good idea, don't you?"

During the Interview

1. **Be prepared and be on time.** Arrive promptly at your interview, with your questions written out.

2. **Ask your questions.** Use your prepared questions, but don't feel limited by them, if the person you are interviewing leads you in an unexpected direction.

After the Interview

1. **Review and expand your notes.** *Directly* after the interview, fill in the gaps in your notes and make your notes readable.

2. **Find the main ideas and the supporting details.** Shape your report by finding the most important points and the best quotes.

Exercise   Interview a family member, a teacher, or a classmate about a controversial topic, like "Should school be in session twelve months of the year?" Follow the steps in this workshop.

To Tape or Not To Tape?

Advantages
1. You don't have to take notes. You can concentrate on the interview.
2. Your record of the interview will be accurate. You won't forget the details.

Disadvantages
1. Many people are uncomfortable talking in front of a tape recorder.
2. It takes a great deal of time afterwards to play over the tape to find the pertinent information.

P.S. *Never* tape-record an interview without the consent of the person being interviewed.

HIGH EXPECTATIONS: UNEXPECTED RESULTS

" *We never know how high we are*

Till we are called to rise "

Emily Dickinson

SUNSHINE TOURISTS (detail)
1990   Zoltan Szabo
By permission of the artist.

$\mathcal{S}$HEER DETERMINATION

While some people give up easily, others seem to have the courage and determination to see a challenge through to the end. The following selections are all about people who attempt nearly impossible tasks. What traits allow them to persist in their struggles and achieve their goals?

Biography

Frederick Douglass

J. A. ROGERS

Examine What You Know

This biography tells about the life of Frederick Douglass, an African-American freedom fighter who helped end slavery. Discuss what you know about the lives of slaves in the United States during the 1800's. In your discussion, include where and how slaves lived, their family life, lineage, legal rights, and the problems they faced.

Expand Your Knowledge

By 1860, there were about 4 million slaves living in the South, where slavery was still legal. In fact, slaves outnumbered whites in some states.

During the 1800's, a small but growing number of people known as **abolitionists** worked to end slavery. They believed that slavery was immoral. They distributed pamphlets and newspapers, held public meetings, and created a network known as the **underground railroad** to help runaway slaves reach the North. Some abolitionists who were extreme in their beliefs, like John Brown, even resorted to violence. Due in part to the persistent efforts of Frederick Douglass and other abolitionists, on January 1, 1863, President Abraham Lincoln issued the Emancipation Proclamation, which legally freed the slaves forever.

$200 REWARD!

Ran away from his owner [a Lady residing near Upper Marlboro, Prince George's County, Md.] on or about the 12th inst. of this month, a bright Mulatto man named Frank, a carpenter by trade, he is about five feet 9 or 10 inches high, light grey eyes, slow in speech, and very good personal appearance, about twenty-five years of age, his clothing good.

One Hundred dollars will be paid if apprehended within thirty miles of home, if more than thirty, the above reward, provided he be secured in Jail so that his owner gets him again.

W. D. BOWIE,
for the owner,
Buena Vista Post Office, Prince George's Co. Md.
February 14th, 1853.

Enrich Your Reading

Evaluating Opinions   In this biography, the author reveals his opinion of Frederick Douglass both directly and through his choice of words. As you read, watch for **subjective** statements, or statements that show an opinion. Look for supporting facts. Then decide whether you agree with the author's evaluation.

■ *A biography of the author can be found on page 419.*

Frederick Douglass

J. A. ROGERS

Ex-Slave Who Rose to Be a Mighty Champion of Freedom (1817–1895)

Frederick Douglass was not only one of the greatest Americans, colored[1] or white, but he was one of the most inspiring figures in the entire history of the human race. Plutarch[2] contains no figure of more heroic proportions.

None of America's most famous white men had as hard a time as he. None of them came up from such depths of <u>degradation</u> and seeming hopelessness. Lincoln with all his immense difficulties was at least born free, and there was never any law against his learning to read or acquiring an education as there was against Douglass, whose social status until he was past twenty-three was that of an ox or a mule. He had to win his freedom, a very <u>formidable</u> task, before he could reach even near to where Lincoln started. Had he been born white with such great natural gifts as he possessed, what further heights might he not have reached?

No child living in any civilized or semicivilized country today can encounter the handicaps Douglass faced. Born in one of the darkest periods of slavery on an estate owned by Colonel Lloyd in Talbot County, Maryland, his life was one of extreme hardship from the beginning. Hunger, as he said, was his constant companion. His share of corn mush, which a dozen children ate like pigs out of a trough on the kitchen floor, was so scant that he was pinched with hunger.[3] He used to run races against the cat and the dog to reach the bones that were tossed out of the window or to snap up the crumbs that fell under the table. He never tasted white bread, and the great desire of his childhood was to have one of those hot biscuits that were taken to his master's table every day. He suffered intensely from the cold, his only garment, summer and winter, being a long shirt. He had neither shoes nor hat.

While a baby, he was taken away from his mother and put under his grandmother's care. Later he was passed on to his Aunt Katy, who treated him badly. So did the poor whites, among whom he lived. They were ignorant and cruel and would take out

---

1. **colored:** in J. A. Rogers's day, this term and the term *Negro* were commonly used to refer to black men and women.
2. **Plutarch:** famous Greek biographer and moralist who lived in the first century A.D.
3. **pinched with hunger:** made excessively thin by lack of food.

Words to Know and Use

degradation (deg′ rə dā′ shən) *n.* humiliation; disgrace
formidable (fôr′ mə də bəl) *adj.* hard to accomplish; overwhelming

on the slaves their spite against the upper-class whites.

As for his mother, Harriet, she loved him, but she was a slave on a plantation twelve long miles away. To get a glimpse of her little boy, she sometimes stole away after the day's labor and hurried so as to get back in time for work at sunrise. She died when he was eight years old. . . .

At the age of ten, when life seemed gloomiest, relief came. He was sent to live with the Auld family, relatives of the manager of the plantation. Mrs. Auld, who was rather tenderhearted, took a fancy to him. She gave him his first pair of trousers and made him the playmate of her little son, Thomas. Instead of the damp dirt floor of a cabin, he now had carpets to walk on.

"Teach him to read and you'll unfit him to be a slave."

The boy's great ambition was to learn to read, and he begged Mrs. Auld to teach him. Not knowing that she was breaking a state law, she gladly complied. But one day she told her husband, who scolded her sharply and forbade any more lessons.

"Teach him to read," shouted Auld wrathfully, "and you'll unfit him to be a slave. Learning will spoil the best slave in the world. He should know nothing but the will of his master and learn to obey that. The next thing you know he'll be wanting to write, and then he'll be running away with himself."

Auld's order almost broke the heart of the young slave. But it was a turning point in his life. It made him realize, as nothing else could have, the value of education. He made this solemn vow: "Knowledge I mean to have."

Thereafter, anything with print on it became precious to him. He treasured bits of old newspapers as others do bank notes.[4] How he envied all those who had access to books!

From these bits of paper he spelled out the words as best he could, while hiding. Sometimes he used cunning to get his white playmates to help him. Whenever Mrs. Auld caught him, she would snatch away the book or paper, stamping and storming "in the utmost fury." But he did not give up, and after three years of this catch-as-catch-can method he could read.

He learned to write in a manner no less ingenious. While firing a boiler in a Baltimore shipyard, he saw that the carpenters marked letters on the timber according to the part of the ship for which it was intended. Starboard pieces would be marked "S," larboard, "L," and so on.

Between shovelfuls of coal he would copy the letters on any available material, and later, to learn their names, would challenge white boys to see who could make a similar letter the most accurately.

"With my playmates for my teachers," he said, "fences and pavements for my copy-books, and chalk for my pen and ink, I soon learned to write." Appropriating used copy-books, he copied the lessons in margins and

_____

4. **bank notes:** paper money.

Frederick Douglass   UPI/Bettmann Newsphotos, New York.

empty spaces. At night, in the kitchen loft, with a flour barrel as a desk, he copied from the Bible and the hymn book, running the risk of being soundly thrashed if caught. Lincoln's solitary struggles to educate himself, <u>arduous</u> as they were, were easy compared to those of Douglass.

An important event in the life of young Douglass was the secret purchase of a *Columbian Orator* with money earned by shining shoes. Over and over again he read the mighty orations of Pitt, Fox, and Burke until his ambition flamed at white heat.

About this time an event occurred which brought what seemed to him the crowning humiliation of his wretched life. His master,

Words to Know and Use | **arduous** (är′ jo͞o əs) *adj.* difficult to do; hard

Colonel Lloyd, died, and he was sent for to be evaluated with the rest of the estate. He, in whom such noble thoughts burned, to be treated like one of the cattle on the estate!

His new master, Captain Thomas Auld,[5] to make matters worse, was selfish, brutal, and very religious. His piety did not prevent him from going among the slaves during their prayer meetings and showering blows on them.

Auld's wife was also not only unkind but stingy. She gave the slaves barely enough food to keep them alive. To make sure that they would steal none, she kept the key to the meat house in her pocket. Douglass says, "Bread and meat were moldering[6] in there while I was famishing."

Driven by hunger, the young slave would sneak away to friends on a nearby estate for something to eat. For this he would be severely beaten. He did not conceal his resentment after his floggings, which led Auld to decide that he needed breaking in. Accordingly, he sent him to Covey, a poor renter, to whom masters sent their stubborn slaves to have the spirit beaten out of them.

Douglass went not unwillingly, expecting at least that he would get a square meal now and then. Covey was a round-shouldered, bull-necked man, above middle height, ferocious and strong, and with a thin, wolfish face. At once he put Douglass to doing field work. Three days later, on some pretext, he beat Douglass so severely that his back was a mass of wounds.

A few days later he again beat him savagely because a team of unbroken oxen Douglass was driving crashed into a gate. Thereafter, overwork and the lash were Douglass's daily lot. As for study, that was out of the question. The dark night of slavery had closed in on him—he was at the level of the brute creation.

Longingly he would watch the ships sailing by, bound for free lands, and wish he were on them. Only his burning resolution to escape at the first opportunity kept him alive.

In spite of the cruelty he suffered, his spirit remained unbroken. One day Covey, in a greater fit of anger than ever, seized him by the leg to tie him up in order to beat him, and he pushed Covey away. The latter's cousin, Hughes, came rushing up to help Covey, but Douglass, with his six feet of brawn, charged Hughes and sent him flying, then, regardless of the consequences, turned on Covey and gave him the thrashing of his life.

To strike a master meant death, but after what he was experiencing, even death seemed welcome. However, to his great surprise, nothing came of the affair. Covey, knowing that it would hurt both his reputation and his income if the story were known, said nothing. He never tried to beat Douglass again.

Six months later Douglass was hired out to a less brutal master, but, still untamed, he incited his fellow slaves to revolt, for which he was tied to a horse and dragged fifteen miles to jail where, after several weeks, he was released at Auld's request.

He was then sent to a shipyard to learn

---

5. **Captain Thomas Auld:** Douglass's new master, Auld, had the same last name as the master he had had as a child.

6. **moldering:** spoiling and rotting.

Words to Know and Use

pretext (prē′ tekst) *n.* an excuse; a false reason put forth to hide the real one
incite (in sīt′) *v.* to rouse; urge on

411

caulking.[7] His orders were to obey all the carpenters, who would send him on dozens of errands, kicking and beating him when they considered he did not move fast enough. On one occasion he was knocked down and kicked in the eye, as a result of which he could not see for days.

Someone shouted, "Kill him. Knock his brains out."

Another time, four of his tormentors jumped on him at once. "Dear reader," says Douglass in his autobiography, "you can hardly believe this statement, but it is true, and therefore I write it down; no fewer than fifty men stood by and saw the brutal and shameful outrage, and that one's face was beaten and battered most horribly, and no one said, 'That's enough,' but someone shouted, 'Kill him. Knock his brains out.'" After this, Auld took him away from the shipyard, not from sympathy but because his property was being damaged.

Douglass was now allowed to hire himself out with orders to turn over his wages each Saturday. Able to move about now with much more freedom, he began to plan his escape. If only he could reach Philadelphia, ninety miles away! But how was he to get there? The regulations on the railroads and steamships were so strict regarding Negroes that it was difficult for even a free one to buy a ticket. To get one he would have to show his "free" papers to the ticket agent.

Douglass at last got hold of a sailor's uniform and a passport. To avoid buying a ticket, he waited until the train had started and then caught it. He had taken the further precaution of learning sea lingo[8] and imitating a sailor's walk. However, the description on the passport was that of one much darker than he. Fortunately for him, the conductor merely glanced at it. Then another thought worried him: suppose some white man who knew him should be on the train. This was just what happened. There were two such: one a German ship carpenter with whom he had once worked and another with whom he had talked only two days before. Both, however, to his great relief, made no move to betray him.

The next day he arrived in New York. But he was not yet free. There was the Fugitive Slave Law. Slave masters had Negro spies in the North to report runaways, and the judges, who received ten dollars a head for each slave returned to the South, readily issued orders returning them there.

He found work shoveling coal. He was now twenty-one, and hoping to find work at his trade, he went to the shipyards at New Bedford, Massachusetts; but color prejudice was very strong in the North, and he was forced to take a job blowing the bellows in a foundry.

The bellows was to be pumped continuously in order to keep the furnace at a heat that would make the metal run. Since this was purely mechanical, he was determined to use the time to better his education, and nailing a newspaper or other printed matter to a post, he would read as he worked the bellows.

Up to now he had no surname. He had

---

7. **caulking** (kôk′ iŋ) the process of waterproofing a boat by filling the seams with tar.

8. **sea lingo:** specialized vocabulary, or jargon, used by sailors and others who worked around the docks.

Words to Know and Use | **surname** (sur′ nām) *n.* a person's family name or last name

been known only as Frederick. He now decided to call himself Douglass after the hero of Walter Scott's *Marmion*. He also married a freedwoman, Anna Murray.

With freedom he had an increasing desire to help those still in slavery. This determination grew as he read *The Liberator,* published by William Lloyd Garrison, famous abolitionist, whose motto was, "Color prejudice is rebellion against God."

His opportunity came three years later. He was attending an antislavery meeting in Nantucket when someone said that an escaped slave was present. His name was called and shouts came back for him to speak.

Douglass got up in great confusion. He had never spoken in public before. His first words were stammering, but soon his nervousness was lost in his tale and he was pouring out a story such as an antislavery audience had never heard before. Its force and fervor held everyone present spellbound.

When he was finished, there was a rush to him. Parker Pillsbury, who was present, says, "The crowded congregation had been wrought up almost to enchantment as he turned over the terrible apocalypse of his experience in slavery."

Emotion fairly boiled over when Garrison arose and thundered, "What I want to know is: Have we been listening to a thing, a piece of property, or a man?"

"A man! A man!" shouted the audience.

"Shall such a man be sent back to slavery from the soil of Old Massachusetts?" demanded Garrison, swept away by the storm of enthusiasm. "No, a thousand times, no! Sooner let the lightnings of Heaven blast Bunker Hill monument until not one stone shall be left on another."

The abolitionists, quick to realize the worth of this escaped slave, engaged him on the spot. What better than to have a slave of such intelligence and commanding personality and conviction to plead the cause of his own people!

Douglass took the field, and at once it became clear that a newer, greater, and more relentless foe than ever before had arisen against slavery. Across the Northern states he thundered. Raging mobs attacked him in Faneuil Hall, Boston, and at Harrisburg, Pennsylvania. At Richmond, Indiana, he was rotten-egged. But everywhere he showed the spirit he had shown against Covey, the slave killer. At Pendleton, Indiana, when a mob tore down the platform on which he was speaking, he fought back until his arm was broken and he was battered into unconsciousness; but the same night, with his arm in a sling, he was again on the platform. During the Draft Riots[9] in New York, when the greatest massacre of Negroes probably known in American history occurred, he faced frenzied white mobs with the same courage.

As for Jim Crow[10] in the North, he never yielded to it. When the conductor of a train in Massachusetts wanted to send him to the Jim Crow section, he refused. The conductor sent for the train hands to oust him, but he held onto the seat so firmly that it came loose and he was thrown off the train still holding it.

9. **Draft Riots:** riots that occurred in 1863 over conscription, or the draft. In New York in particular, foreign-born laborers rioted for several days to protest being drafted to serve in the Civil War. One point of contention was that wealthy men were able to pay others to serve in their place.

10. **Jim Crow:** laws that legitimized the separation of the races in Southern public facilities. These laws got their nickname from the character in a minstrel show who sang a song that ended with the words "Jump, Jim Crow." The Jim Crow section of a train, for example, would have been the section in which blacks had to sit.

One winter night while on a steamboat plying between Boston and New York, he was shut out on deck, although entitled to a berth. A compassionate white steward, wanting to admit him, hintingly said, "You're an Indian, aren't you?" "No," replied Douglass resolutely, "only a damned nigger."[11]

His courage was as firm as the pigment in his skin.

Everywhere his courage was as firm as the pigment in his skin, though he was constantly running the risk of being caught and returned to his master in the South. At first he used a false name and gave a wrong place of birth, but when the proslavery faction denounced him as a fraud, he boldly published his autobiography with full details.

His book had a wide sale and put the slavers on his track. He fled to England, where he had long been wanting to go to carry on the fight. On the way over, however, his zeal almost cost him his life. An antislavery speech he made aboard the ship so incensed a party of Southerners that they tried to throw him overboard and might have succeeded had not members of the crew and other passengers interfered. This dastardly attack on the high seas brought him immense publicity in England, and world-famed figures [such] as Cobden, Brougham, Peel, and Disraeli[12] invited him to their homes. . . .

He was offered a home in England, but true to his resolve, he declined. "America,"
he said, "is my home and there I mean to spend my life and be spent in the cause of my outraged brethren." His English friends thereupon gave him $20,000, of which $750 was to purchase his freedom and the remainder to found a newspaper.

His liberty now purchased, Douglass went to Rochester, New York, and started his paper, *The North Star,* later *Frederick Douglass' Paper,* through which he fought for not only the emancipation of the slaves but full equality for Negroes. In this he was opposed by many of the abolitionists, who felt that in their attack on slavery they already had a big enough fight. He says, "They did not want a Negro newspaper and even the Negroes ridiculed me." Undismayed, however, he persisted. Later, Rochester was to be very proud of him.

On the lecture platform he worked closely with the white abolitionists, especially Wendell Phillips, Theodore Tilton, and John Brown. When the last begged him to join in his raid on Harper's Ferry,[13] however, he refused. He saw the futility of the attempt

---

11. **nigger:** an extremely offensive term used for a person with black skin.

12. **Cobden . . . Disraeli:** Richard Cobden, English statesman and economist; Henry Peter Brougham, political leader and member of Parliament who was later elected to the House of Lords; Sir Robert Peel, English statesman; Benjamin Disraeli, British politician and author who served as Prime Minister of Britain in 1868 and again from 1874 to 1880.

13. **Harper's Ferry:** On October 6, 1859, John Brown, assisted by seventeen men, including both whites and free blacks, attacked the federal arsenal at Harper's Ferry, Virginia, and took several slaveholders and slaves as hostage. Brown had hoped that his actions would incite a slave rebellion. Instead, Virginia militiamen and troops surrounded the arsenal and fired on the abolitionists and their hostages. Brown surrendered after more than half of his men were killed; he was later hanged for treason.

Words to Know and Use

faction (fak′shən) *n.* a group of people working in a common cause against other groups or the majority
denounce (dē nouns′) *v.* to criticize or condemn
zeal (zēl) *n.* intense enthusiasm; eagerness
incense (in sens′) *v.* to make extremely angry; enrage
emancipation (ē man′ sə pā′ shən) *n.* freedom
futility (fyōō til′ ə tē) *n.* uselessness; fruitlessness

FORWARD #10   1967   Jacob Lawrence
Illustration for *Harriet and the Promised Land*.

and wisely decided that his life could be used to better advantage than in such a quixotic [14] attempt.

In spite of this, he found himself involved. His name was found among John Brown's papers, and to avoid arrest, he fled to Canada and then again to England. What he feared most was not implication in the raid but disclosure of his activities as a station master on the Underground Railway, a system of freeing slaves by aiding their escape from the South and smuggling them into Canada.

In England he was received with even greater acclaim, but his heart was in America and he longed to return. Then sentiment in the North swung in favor of John Brown. The latter was no longer "a traitor and a fanatic" but a martyr, a hero. Douglass, feeling that he would be safe, returned and, when the Civil War broke out, threw all his energies into it. His slogan was "Union and Emancipation; Abolition or Destruction."

Consistent with his policy of equality, he demanded that colored men should be used as soldiers and not merely as servants and laborers. Northern color prejudice opposed him, and Lincoln, whose declared goal was

---

14. **quixotic** (kwiks ät′ik): idealistic and impractical.

Words to Know and Use | **implication** (im′ pli kā′ shən) *n.* an association; connection

415

to save the Union even if it were necessary to retain slavery and color discrimination to do so, obeyed the popular will. But Douglass went on fighting for the use of Negro soldiers until the need for men became so urgent that the Union Army had to use them. Lincoln later admitted, no less than four times, that the Negroes furnished the balance of power which decided the conflict in favor of the North. . . .

With colored soldiers now in the Army, Douglass's next task was to see that they were fairly treated. The South was hanging all colored prisoners. As Horace Greeley said, "Every black soldier now goes to battle with a halter about his neck." Douglass insisted that the North should retaliate on such occasions. He demanded equal pay for the colored soldier with the white, and the same opportunity for promotion.

He fought stubbornly and went often to the White House. At first Lincoln regarded him as a pest. Later, when the Negro soldiers proved their worth, Lincoln learned to appreciate him, and in the darkest moments of the conflict, sent for him to ask his advice.

In spite of this, an attempt was made to bar him from Lincoln's second inaugural ceremony on account of color. Fairbank, a white man who was present, relates the episode thus: "Douglass was stopped at the door. 'Hold on, you can't go in,' someone said. Another interposed and said: 'This is Frederick Douglass.' Douglass replied for himself: 'I don't want to go in as Frederick Douglass, but as a citizen of the United States.' "

At this point Lincoln, noticing the trouble, came over, and with his long arms outstretched over the heads of the crowd, said, "How do you do, Frederick? Come right in!"

Lincoln wanted to know what Douglass thought of his inaugural speech. "Mr. Lincoln," replied Douglass, "I must not detain you with my poor opinion. There are a thousand waiting to shake your hand."

"No, no!" insisted Lincoln, "you must stop a little. There's no man in the country whose opinion I value more than yours. I want to know what you think of it."

"Mr. Lincoln," responded Douglass, "that was a sacred effort."

With the Civil War won, Douglass's next fight was to have the freedmen made citizens. ❧

Responding to Reading

First Impressions

1. What do you think of Frederick Douglass? Jot down the thoughts you had when you finished reading.

Second Thoughts

2. Do you agree with the opinions Rogers expresses in the first sentence in this selection? Why or why not?

    Think about
    - what Douglass accomplished in his life
    - the obstacles that stood in his way
    - what you know about other inspiring figures in history

3. Why was Douglass able to survive hardships and reach his goals?

4. Were the actions Douglass took to achieve his goals justified? Explain.

5. Mr. Auld warned that learning would make Douglass unfit to be a slave. Did Douglass's actions justify Auld's fears? Explain.

6. If you were a slave owner, would you want Douglass as one of your slaves? Give reasons to support your answer.

Broader Connections

7. Douglass broke the law and risked his life in his struggle to learn to read and write. How important is an education in today's world? To what lengths would you go to become educated?

Literary Concept: Biography

A **biography** is a true account of a person's life written by another person. Biographers use first-hand information from the subject (in this case, from Douglass's autobiography) and what others have written or said about the subject. Most biographers write objectively about their subject, but the purpose for writing and feelings about the subject may influence how the biographer presents facts. In your opinion, how objective is this account? In the selection, find three statements that are objective and three that are subjective.

Concept Review: Tone   The **tone** of a piece of writing expresses the writer's attitude toward the subject. Find words or phrases that express Rogers's admiration of Douglass. Does the tone affect your willingness to accept factual statements about Douglass and his achievements?

Writing Options

1. Write an editorial either urging that Douglass receive an award for his efforts on behalf of African Americans or criticizing him for the methods he uses in his antislavery work.

2. Write a poem about Frederick Douglass. Begin by jotting down your thoughts about Douglass, his life, or his contribution to history.

3. Imagine that you were present when Covey or the men at the shipyard beat Douglass or when Douglass spoke at the antislavery meeting in Nantucket. Describe in writing what you saw and heard. Your writing might take the form of an essay, a newspaper article, a letter, or a diary.

Vocabulary Practice

Exercise On your paper, write the word from the list that best completes each sentence. Each word is only used once.

1. Difficult and _____ work, such as picking cotton, is exhausting.
2. If a slave did not _____ immediately with his master's orders, he was often beaten.
3. Slave owners often used a _____ to justify their mistreatment of slaves.
4. It was common for a slave to have a first name but no _____.
5. Although slave masters tried to impress upon their slaves the _____ of trying to escape, many slaves ran away.
6. _____ was a common theme in the songs of the slaves.
7. Slaves who had formerly endured _____ felt pride when they became free men and women.
8. The punishment for escaped slaves who were caught made running away a frightening and a _____ challenge.
9. The idea of slavery can _____, or infuriate, people who believe that slavery is immoral.
10. During the 1800's, one group of Americans demanded an end to slavery while another _____ fought to continue it.
11. The abolitionists used Douglass to _____ others to action.
12. The _____ with which Douglass spoke made people sympathetic to his cause.
13. He would strongly _____, or condemn, slave owners.
14. To protect himself, Douglass tried to avoid _____ in John Brown's raid.
15. Douglass obtained writing materials by _____ discarded copybooks to use as his own.

> *Words to Know and Use*
>
> ___
>
> **appropriating**
> **arduous**
> **comply**
> **degradation**
> **denounce**
> **emancipation**
> **faction**
> **formidable**
> **futility**
> **implication**
> **incense**
> **incite**
> **pretext**
> **surname**
> **zeal**

Options for Learning

1 • **Spirituals**   The songs that slaves sang were called spirituals. While they seemed religious in nature, the words held hidden meanings for the slaves. For example, the song "Go Down, Moses" seemed to be about Moses of the Bible, but Moses was also a code name for Harriet Tubman, a conductor on the underground railroad. Research this spiritual or another song to find out the hidden meanings the words held for the slaves.

2 • **From the Source**   Douglass wrote three autobiographies: *Narrative of the Life of Frederick Douglass, an American Slave; My Bondage and My Freedom;* and *Life and Times of Frederick Douglass.* Choose an excerpt from one of these books to read orally to your class.

3 • **Underground Research**   Find out about famous conductors and routes used on the underground railroad. Draw a map showing some of the routes, and present the information to your class.

4 • **A Dating Game**   Rogers includes dates for only a few of the events in the life of Frederick Douglass. Find out when at least five of the events in this biography occurred and plot them on a time line to show the key events in Douglass's early life.

 **FACT FINDER**

Douglass worked toward the ratification of the Fourteenth and Fifteenth Amendments. What was the purpose of these amendments?

J. A. Rogers
1880–1966

A self-trained writer with no formal education, J.A. Rogers wrote fourteen books and many newspaper articles condemning racism and documenting lives of great achievers of African descent. "Biography will ever be the highest and most civilizing form of literature," he said, "and it will destroy the old slaving-holding dogma of 'Negro' inferiority."

Born in Jamaica, Rogers was one of eleven children. After serving in the Royal Army for four years, he immigrated to the United States in 1906. Later he traveled to Europe and Africa, combing libraries and art galleries to gather material for his books.

In Rogers's challenges to generally accepted ideas about race, he wrote harshly and accusingly. He published most of his books himself.

Fiction

The Way Up
WILLIAM HOFFMAN

Examine What You Know

This story is about a boy who wants to make a name for himself. Think about the various activities you associate with certain classmates. Is there a class clown? a math genius? a fantastic singer or dancer? Discuss the kinds of things you and your friends do to gain recognition. Are some ways of getting recognized more acceptable or more impressive than others?

Expand Your Knowledge

You will discover that an important element in "The Way Up" is a water tower. A water tower is a structure that stores water for a building or for an entire community. Sometimes, a tower stores water for periods of peak use or as a reserve if the main water supply, a reservoir for example, shuts down. A typical water tower consists of a tank with rounded sides sitting on tubular steel legs. The height of the tower may depend on the pressure needed—the higher the tower, the greater the pressure. Some towers are 30 feet high; others may be as high as 130 feet. A walkway called a catwalk circles the tank. This walkway, used by painters and other maintenance workers, is about 2½ feet wide and has a safety railing about 3 feet high. Water companies usually lock the ladders leading up to the catwalk and sometimes weld shut the locks to keep curious climbers off the tower.

Write Before You Read

Look around at your classmates. What will they remember you for ten years from now? What would you like to be remembered for by these classmates? Write down your thoughts in your journal.

■ *A biography of the author can be found on page 432.*

The Way Up

WILLIAM HOFFMAN

Sitting in the back row of English literature class, Jamie looked through an open window toward a rounded silver water tower which poked up through the woods like a great metal tulip. The tower had recently been painted and appeared immaculate in the spring sunlight. Tubular[1] steel legs were hidden at the bottom by newly greening oaks, sycamores, and poplars that bordered the rear grounds of the suburban Richmond High School.

Jamie had made no brag. He had not even spoken the evening he was at Jawbone's house, loafing in the basement playroom with the others.

"Look at Jamie's," Jawbone said. Jawbone was a dark, wiry boy of eighteen who had a jutting chin. He wanted to go to West Point.[2] He stuck a finger on Jamie's picture in the new yearbook. Under the names of the others were accomplishments—teams, organizations, trophies.

"Not even the Glee Club," Nick said, lying on a sofa, his legs hanging over the arm rest at one end. He was a blond boy whose father owned a fancy restaurant downtown.

"They'll never know you been here," Alf said. Alf, the top student, was a heavyset, shaggy boy who'd won his letter in baseball.

More sensitive than the rest, he was immediately sorry. He reached across a chair to punch Jamie's arm. Jamie dodged and smiled, though smiling was like cracking rock.

They meant the remarks good-naturedly. Still, the words made him see what his relationship to them was. He had gone through four years of high school without leaving a mark. He had ridden with them daily, shared their secrets, and eaten in their homes. They considered him a friend. But they expected nothing from him.

At first he was resentful and hurt, as if betrayed. Next he had fantasies of heroic derring-do[3] on the basketball court or baseball diamond—because of his smallness he didn't dream of football glory any longer. After the fantasies, he tried to think of projects. Finally he came up with a plan.

He had spent a lot of time working out details. He was now merely waiting for the right day—or rather night. Recently there had been rain and blustering weather. Even when the sun shone, the wind gusted. This afternoon, however, as he sat in English literature class, Jamie saw that the treetops barely quivered.

His eyes kept returning to the silver water

---

1. **tubular:** in the shape of a tube.
2. **West Point:** the United States Military Academy in southeastern New York State.
3. **derring-do:** reckless, courageous actions.

tower. Other students had attempted the climb. A few inventive ones had gone up as far as the catwalk around the fat belly of the tank, where they had painted skulls and crossbones. A sophomore had lost his nerve halfway and got stuck. The Richmond rescue squad had coaxed him down like a kitten from a light pole. The boy had been so ashamed he had tried to join the Army. Nobody had ever made it to the stubby spike on the crown.

Mr. Tharpe, the principal, understood the tower's temptation and had ordered the ladder above the catwalk taken off. He had also directed that the ladder up the leg be cut high above the ground. Lastly, he had made climbing the tower punishable by expulsion.

The toughest problem was getting from the catwalk to the crown. As the tank served only the school, it wasn't large, but without a ladder the rounded sides appeared unscalable.[4] Jamie concluded that he needed a light hook which could be thrown fifteen to twenty feet.

He found what he wanted in a Richmond boating store—a small, three-pronged, aluminum anchor. Along with the anchor he bought fifty feet of braided nylon line that had a thousand-pound test strength. He also purchased a hacksaw. The clerk packed the things in a strong cardboard box, and as soon as Jamie reached home, he hid them in the back of his closet.

He assembled other equipment as well—tennis shoes, a pair of light cotton gloves, a sweat suit, which would keep him warm in the night air yet allow him to move freely, a billed cap, a small flashlight with a holding ring, and a sheath knife to fasten to his leather belt.

Twice he scheduled attempts on the tower. The first night a thunderstorm washed him out. The second, the moon was too bright, increasing the risk that he would be seen.

Delay made him uneasy. He felt that if he didn't go soon, he might lose his nerve.

*N*obody had ever made it to the stubby spike on the crown.

The bell rang. He went to his locker and then left the building quickly. He wanted to get away without the others seeing him, but Alf called his name. Alf ran down the sidewalk. He adjusted his glasses.

"Want to shoot baskets?" he asked, making an imaginary hook shot. He held up two fingers to indicate a score.

"No, thanks," Jamie answered, moving on.

"You're getting pretty exclusive lately," Alf said.

"I've always been exclusive," Jamie told him, hoping it sounded like a joke.

He spent the afternoon working around the house. He cut the grass and spread some of the lawn fertilizer his father had stored in the garage. When he had a chance, he went up to his room and again checked his equipment. The check was just nervousness. He knew his equipment was right.

After dinner, as he was sure they would, his parents went next door to play cards. He

---

4. **unscalable:** impossible to climb.

Words to Know and Use | **hacksaw** (hak′ sô′) *n.* a saw used to cut metal

and his brother David were left in the house. David was a year younger, although already heavier than Jamie. He had been asked to come out for football and liked to flex his muscles before a mirror.

Jamie sat at his desk and pretended to study so he wouldn't be questioned. He listened to sounds of the night coming through the open window. There was some wind, but not enough to worry him. The sky was cloudy.

When David went down to the kitchen for a sandwich, Jamie undressed, put on the sweat suit, and pulled pajamas over it. He kept his socks on. He slipped his belt through slots in the leather sheath of the knife and buckled it around his waist. Hearing David approach, Jamie got into bed.

"You sick?" David asked, surprised.

"Just sleepy."

"You look kind of <u>queasy</u>."

"I'm okay."

David watched TV and did his exercises before coming to bed. Jamie listened, as he had for weeks, to the pattern of his brother's breathing. In practice, Jamie had gotten up several times and moved around the dark room. Once David had waked. Jamie had explained he was after another blanket.

David breathed softly. When he was completely asleep, his mouth opened and he wheezed slightly. Jamie heard the wheezing now. Still he did not move, although he wanted badly to start. He lay on his back, eyes open, waiting for his parents.

They returned at eleven. He heard them in the kitchen. Finally his mother came to his and David's room. Jamie smelled her perfume. She bent over them, lightly adjusting the covers. He kept his eyes shut until she went out.

SEVENTEEN 1959 Lew Davis Courtesy of Yares Gallery, Scottsdale, Arizona.

As soon as she was gone, he swung his legs out of bed. He stood, listening, but David's breathing did not change. Jamie walked to the closet, slipped off his pajamas, and sat on the floor to pull on his tennis shoes. He tied the laces in double knots.

He put on his baseball cap and fastened the large, red bandanna around his neck. The bandanna, too, was part of his plan. He had bought it in a Richmond ten-cent store. For some time he had been carrying it to school and whipping it out to be seen by Jawbone, Nick, and Alf. Though no name was on it, people would identify it as his—the right people, anyway.

Lastly he worked his fingers into the cotton gloves, gathered the hacksaw and aluminum anchor, and tiptoed to the window. It was already half-raised. Earlier in the week he'd rubbed soap along the metal tracks to prevent squeaking.

The window slid up noiselessly. He unsnapped the screen and lifted it out. David turned in his bed but did not wake. Jamie climbed onto the window ledge, lowered his equipment to the ground, and stepped down to the grass of the back yard. He stood still and listened. David did not stir. Jamie replaced the screen without hooking it and picked up his equipment.

Crouching, he ran—not fast enough to wear himself out, but with the easy lope of a distance runner. He carried the anchor in his right hand, the saw in his left. The damp grass of neighboring yards brushed his feet softly. He stayed in the shadows.

On reaching the high school, he cut behind the main building and headed toward the athletic field. When he was almost to the other side, a dog snarled close behind him. He was afraid that if he continued running, the dog might jump him. He turned and ducked behind a pile of canvas tackling dummies.[5]

The dog leaped out of the dark, its hair bristling, its teeth bared. Jamie talked softly, holding his hands at his sides so as not to excite the boxer. The animal circled, sniffed, and growled.

"King!" a voice from the field house called. It was Carver, the watchman—an erect, dark figure outlined against a door. "Here, boy!"

The dog sprang off toward the field house. Jamie pressed against the ground. Carver leaned over to pat the boxer.

"What's out there?" he asked, turning on his long flashlight. The light brushed across the dummies. Jamie held his breath. Carver talked to the dog. Finally the flashlight went out, and Carver entered the field house. The door slammed.

*T*he steel legs were like those of a giant insect poised over him.

Jamie pushed up and sprinted. He wanted to be well away in case the boxer was still loose. His arms pumped. By the time he reached the woods, he was winded. There was no use even starting up the tower unless he was fresh. He rested against a tree.

When his breath steadied, he walked on through the woods. He didn't need his flashlight. Clouds had slid away from a sickle moon, which laid a pale sheen on his

---

5. **tackling dummies:** upright, matlike objects connected to flexible poles and used for tackling practice in football.

Words to Know and Use | **sheen** (shēn) *n.* brightness; shininess

path. He stopped once to be certain nobody was following.

He walked out of the woods to the tower and under it. Though the tank wasn't large, it was high and seemed to float like a balloon. The silver skin shone eerily. The steel legs were like those of a giant insect poised over him. He touched the steel and kicked a cement footing to rid himself of the sensation. The tank was simply a water tower which could be climbed.

H e didn't hurry. Hurrying might tire him. Methodically he unwound the line from the anchor. He looped the saw onto his belt. He adjusted his cap. Standing away from a leg of the tower, he swung the anchor around his head like a lasso and let fly at the ladder.

The hooks missed by inches. The light anchor clanged against tubular steel, which reverberated like a gong. The sound was loud—loud enough, perhaps, to alert the watchman or the family who lived in a board-and-batten[6] house nearby. Quickly Jamie picked up the anchor, swung it, and threw. A prong clattered over a rung.

He had practiced rope climbing. Two or three afternoons a week he had pulled himself to the I-beam at the top of the gym where ropes were attached to swivels. He had learned to go up without using his legs. Basketball players had stood around to watch, impressed that anybody so slight could climb so well.

"You're turning into a regular Atlas," Nick had said.

Jamie had already tied knots every five feet along the nylon line in order to have a better grip on it. He fingered the line and pulled. As he looked up, he felt doubt. The line was thin, the tower great. He jumped before he had time to think further.

Climbing made him feel better. He reached the bottom of the ladder and easily drew himself onto it. He stopped to loosen the anchor. He wrapped the line around the anchor's shank and hooked it over his left shoulder.

He stepped up slowly. He was attempting to pace himself for the distance. He looked neither up nor down. Doing so might cause dizziness. He narrowed his eyes and tried to see no more than his own gloved hands closing over rungs.

After what seemed a long while, he glanced up to get his bearings[7] on the catwalk. He was disappointed at how far it was above him. He estimated that he had come only a quarter of the way. His excitement was giving him a false sense of time.

He kept on. When he again looked up, he had climbed not quite halfway. His breathing was noisy, and he rested. As he clung to the ladder, he thought how easy it would be to go back now. Nobody knew he was here. He could go down and slip into his bed without ever being missed.

He was angry at himself for considering it. His trouble was thinking too much. To block the thoughts, he stepped up, determined to reach the catwalk without stopping again.

He climbed until his arms and legs ached. He sucked at air. He did not raise his eyes lest the distance to the catwalk discourage him. Occasionally a light wind gusted

---

6. **board-and-batten:** having walls constructed with wide vertical wood strips alternating with thin wood strips that are recessed or protruding.

7. **get his bearings:** figure out his situation.

Words to Know and Use	**methodically** (mə thäd′ ik lē) *adv.* done in a regular, orderly way; systematically **reverberate** (ri vʉr′ bə rāt′) *v.* to re-echo, resound

against his face and chest—not hard enough to worry him, but sufficient to slow his step.

His head banged steel. The blow frightened and pained him, and he clutched at the ladder. The catwalk door was right over him, its heavy padlock swinging from his having hit it.

He put his right leg through the ladder and hooked the foot over a rung to keep from falling in case he lost his balance. He unbuckled his belt to get the hacksaw. Because of the awkwardness of his position, he had to work slowly. His left hand held the lock, his right the saw.

Cutting was more difficult than he'd anticipated. He had to rest and wipe sweat from his face. When the metal finally snapped, he flung the saw from him. It was a long time hitting the ground.

He threw the padlock down, too, glad he had on gloves in case an investigation checked fingerprints. He raised a hand to the trap door and pushed. The thick iron squeaked but gave only a little. He stepped up another rung in order to hunch his shoulders and the back of his head against it. The door rose, teetered, and fell to the catwalk with a loud clang.

He climbed the rest of the way up the ladder, swung off it to the catwalk, and, holding the railing, closed the trap door. As he straightened to look out over the dark land, he had his first real sense of how high he was. Instinctively, he pressed against the tank. He edged around the catwalk until he faced the school. Lights from houses were faint and twinkling, and he saw the skyline milkiness of Richmond itself.

He grinned, thinking of Alf, Nick, and Jawbone. They wouldn't believe it! They were lying down there, warm in their bunks. He waved a hand over them.

He turned to the tank. He was still a good fifteen feet from the top. As he calculated the distance, a cloud passing over gave him a feeling that the tower was falling. Space shifted under him. He grabbed at the tank.

Leaning against it, he considered tying his bandanna to the railing on the school side. In the morning everybody would see it. Going up this far was certainly a victory, and people would be impressed.

He took off the bandanna and hesitated, fingering it. For tying the bandanna to the railing he might be temporarily honored, but if he was the first to reach the top, he would be remembered for years.

He retied the bandanna around his neck and unwound the nylon line from the anchor. In order to throw to the top of the tank from the proper angle, he had to lean out and flap his arm upward. He forced his thigh hard against the railing. Holding the anchor from him, he threw.

The anchor thumped on top of the rounded tower but slid back when he pulled the line. He jumped to keep from being hit. He stumbled and almost fell. Fear surged in him.

He rested against the tank. When he was calmer, he again threw the anchor. He made half a dozen tries, but each time it came sliding back. He didn't have quite the angle he needed to get the anchor to the crown where the spike was. There was simply no way to do it. He had to tie the bandanna to the railing and climb down.

Another idea nagged him. He shook his head as if he'd been asked. He didn't want to step up onto the railing. He'd be crazy to do it. He could, of course, use part of his line to tie himself. Thus if he slipped, he wouldn't fall far.

He wrapped the nylon line twice around

WATCHTOWER 1984
Sigmar Polke Private collection.

his waist. He knotted the middle section to one of the upright supports of the railing.

Cautiously, like a performer mounting the high wire, he stepped up onto the pipe railing. He rested a hand against the tank so that any fall would be toward the catwalk. His left foot dangled. Though his body wished to bend, he straightened it. He was sweating, and the anchor was wet in his grip. He blinked to clear his eyes, being careful not to turn his head toward where he might look down.

He hefted the anchor and with a gentle, looping motion arched it over himself. The anchor slid back and struck him in the side of the face. Standing on the railing, he was unable to dodge. His head throbbed and ached. He touched his cheek, and his hand came away bloody.

He pulled the anchor up from the catwalk. This time he didn't throw it directly over him. When he tugged on the line, the anchor came down. He felt weak and sick.

He balanced the anchor, tossed it, and jerked the line. The anchor did not come back. He jumped to the catwalk and pulled. The anchor held.

He couldn't be certain it was caught on the spike. Perhaps a hook tip was in a seam or had snagged a bolt. He hung all his weight on the line, drawing up his feet to do so. Next he untied the line from the railing support. He dried his hands on his sweat suit and wiped his mouth.

With a great effort, he pulled himself up. When he reached the rounded curve of the roof, he worked his hands under the line that his weight stretched tight. <u>Nausea</u> pumped through him as he bruised his knuckles on the steel. Grunting, he made a final thrust of his body and lay flat against the slope.

His heart beat hard. He sweated yet felt cold in the gusting wind. He raised his head to look at the top of the tower. Two prongs of the anchor had caught the spike.

He crawled up. Because of the slope and his tennis shoes, he could have done it without a line. He lay on his side as he took off the bandanna. He tied the bandanna high on the spike. He tested to make certain the bandanna would not blow loose.

Fear ballooned in him, and he shook harder.

To go down, he merely let his body slide against the steel. He braked himself by gripping the line. His feet jarred against the catwalk. He hated leaving his anchor, but he knew of no way to pull it free. With his knife, he cut the line as high as he could reach. He wound what was left of it around his body and opened the trap door.

As he put a foot on the ladder, a gust of wind caught his cap and blew it off. He snatched for the cap but missed. It fluttered dizzily down and down and down. He couldn't stop looking. The cap seemed to fall forever. He felt the pull of space. He'd tumble the same way if he slipped. He began to shake. He was too weak to climb down that great distance. He backed off.

Fear ballooned in him, and he shook harder. He couldn't stop thinking of the boy who'd gotten stalled halfway up and needed the Richmond rescue squad. The terrible disgrace of it—the sirens, the people gathered around, and the spotlight swinging up. The police would call his parents.

Yet he was unable to force himself to the ladder. The grip was gone from his fingers, and his body was limp. He might climb down a few steps and not be able to hold. He had the sensation of falling, like the cap, of cartwheeling end over end to the ground. He lay flat on the catwalk, his face against steel strips. He was shaking so badly that his temple knocked against the metal.

He gave himself up to fear. As if his mouth had a life of its own, yells came out. He couldn't stop the sounds. He shouted for help. He screamed and begged in a rush of terror.

The wind carried his voice away. Even if he was missed at home and searched for, nobody would think of looking on the tower. He'd have to lie on the catwalk all night. . . . No, he couldn't! With his flashlight he signaled toward the school. There was no response from the watchman. Jamie kept yelling until his voice became faint and hoarse. He wept.

The fright in him was gradually replaced by exhaustion. He lay panting. He felt the heat of shame. He thought of Alf, Nick, and Jawbone seeing him like this. He thought of his parents. Like a person gone blind, he groped for the trap door.

This time he didn't allow himself to look down. Instead he rolled his eyes upward. His fingers measured the position of the hole, and he lowered a trembling foot to a

Words to Know and Use | **nausea** (nō′ shə) *n.* a feeling of sickness in the stomach accompanied by the urge to vomit

rung. As if decrepit, he shifted his weight onto the ladder.

He went down a step. He was holding the rungs too tightly, and his sweating hands made the steel slippery. He felt the pull of space behind him. His breathing was rapid and shallow. He moved the way a small child would, using the same foot first on each rung.

He closed his eyes. His body functioned with no direction from him. He was a passenger cowering inside.

He rested, hanging his armpits over the ladder and leaning his forehead against the steel. For an instant he was drunkenly comfortable. He wobbled on the ladder, almost letting go. He caught himself and cried out.

Again he started down. In the endlessness of his descent, he didn't believe he would ever get to the bottom. His hands would fail, and he would drop off. He imagined his body curving to the ground.

He stopped on the ladder, not understanding. The fact that his foot swung under him and found no support meant nothing. He believed his tiredness had tricked him. A second time he put out the foot. Like one coming from a cave into sunlight, he opened his eyes and squinted. He saw the dark shapes of trees. He was at the base of the ladder. Lying under the tower was his cap.

Wearily, even calmly now, he untied the line from his waist and knotted it to the bottom rung. He wrapped the line around his wrists. He slid down, but he was too weak to brake himself effectively. The line burned his skin. When he hit the ground, he fell backward. He lay looking at the silver tower shining above him.

Using one of the tubular steel legs for support, he pulled himself up, staggered, and stooped for his cap. He turned to get his bearings before stumbling into a jogging run. At the trees he wove to a stop and again looked at the tower. He shuddered.

He breathed deeply. Straightening, he entered the dark woods with the step of a man who wouldn't be hurried and walked back toward the house. ❧

INSIGHT

Thumbprint

EVE MERRIAM

In the heel of my thumb
are whorls, whirls, wheels
in a unique design:
mine alone.
What a treasure to own!
My own flesh, my own feelings.
No other, however grand or base,
can ever contain the same.
My signature,
thumbing the pages of my time.
My universe key,
my singularity.
Impress, implant,
I am myself,
of all my atom parts I am the sum.
And out of my blood and my brain
I make my own interior weather,
my own sun and rain.
Imprint my mark upon the world,
whatever I shall become.

429

Responding to Reading

First Impressions

1. How did you feel as Jamie climbed the water tower? Explain why you felt this way.

Second Thoughts

2. What does Jamie hope to accomplish by climbing the tower? Do you think he is successful in reaching this goal?

3. What makes it possible for Jamie to reach the top of the tower?

   Think about
   - his personality traits
   - the preparations he makes
   - his luck

4. Do you think Jamie will change as a result of his climb? Explain.

5. In your opinion, was Jamie's climb worth the risk? Why or why not?

Broader Connections

6. Is it important for a student to have a list of school accomplishments and activities like those of Jamie's friends? Should a yearbook include such lists? Explain your opinion.

Literary Concept: Suspense

Suspense is a growing feeling of anxiety and excitement that makes a reader extremely curious about the outcome of a story. A writer creates suspense by raising questions in the reader's mind about possible endings to the conflict. As you read this story, you were probably anxious to know if Jamie would reach the top of the tower and return safely to the ground. One way Hoffman builds suspense is by carefully detailing Jamie's preparations for the climb. In what other ways does he create suspense?

Concept Review: Character Motivation Once Jamie starts climbing the tower, what motivates him to keep going? Why does he refuse to give in to fear? Are his reasons believable?

Writing Options

1. Write the conversation Jamie's friends might have when they learn Jamie climbed the tower.

2. List the phrases or lines in the poem ''Thumbprint'' that best express Jamie's thoughts and actions. Explain why you chose these phrases.

3. Write your prediction of the next few days in Jamie's life as a result of his climbing of the water tower.

4. Write what might have appeared under Jamie's yearbook picture if it had been published after the events in this story. Hint at, but do not state, what he did.

Vocabulary Practice

Exercise Write the letter of the word or phrase that best completes each sentence below.

1. You could make a long **descent** from a   (a) mountain   (b) riverbed   (c) valley   (d) meadow.

2. We could tell Jamie felt **queasy** because he was holding his   (a) feet   (b) stomach   (c) ankle   (d) neck.

3. A **hacksaw** is made especially to cut   (a) meat   (b) trees   (c) wood planks   (d) metal.

4. When you do something **methodically** as Jamie did, you do it in a way that is   (a) confused   (b) without a method   (c) orderly   (d) disorderly.

5. If Jamie was **cowering,** he was probably   (a) annoyed   (b) afraid   (c) disgusted   (d) curious.

6. When the falling anchor hit the steel tank, making it **reverberate,** the sound   (a) died down   (b) echoed   (c) stopped suddenly   (d) could barely be heard.

7. Jamie had **nausea,** which means he felt   (a) healthy   (b) immaculate   (c) sick   (d) confident.

8. A **sheen** on the path means that it was   (a) muddy   (b) shiny   (c) dimly lighted   (d) rocky.

9. As Jamie climbed down he felt **decrepit,** which means   (a) weak and tired   (b) happy and confident   (c) depressed   (d) triumphant.

10. A tower would appear **immaculate** if it were   (a) filthy and old   (b) clean and shiny   (c) smeared with mud   (d) hidden by a cloud.

> *Words to Know and Use*
>
> ---
>
> **cowering**
> **decrepit**
> **descent**
> **hacksaw**
> **immaculate**
> **methodically**
> **nausea**
> **queasy**
> **reverberate**
> **sheen**

Options for Learning

1 • Cost of the Climb Make a list of the equipment Jamie collected for his climb. Consult local stores to find out how much each item costs at current prices. Then add up the total cost to discover how much Jamie would have to spend today for the climb.

2 • Mood Music Choose background music for an imaginary film version of "The Way Up." Select appropriate music for the different parts of the story. Perform some of the music for your classmates or play recorded versions of it for them.

3 • The Principal Speaks Imagine that the next morning the principal, Mr. Tharpe, sees the bandanna tied to the top of the tower. Write and deliver the speech Mr. Tharpe might make.

4 • Private Eye Suppose the principal wants to learn who climbed the tower. He hires a detective to work on the case. Reread the story carefully to discover clues Jamie left that would help the detective solve the case. List the clues and explain how each one might help.

 **FACT FINDER**

If the water tower were seventy-five feet high, how many times your height would it be?

William Hoffman
1925–

William Hoffman, originally from West Virginia, writes novels, short stories, and plays set in and around Virginia, where he now lives with his wife. Critics agree, though, that Hoffman's works are not limited by their settings, and that they appeal to a wide range of readers. Hoffman frequently writes of people's connection to their own community, as well as of parent-child relationships, husband-wife relationships, struggles between old and new values, ties to the land, and the lure of the sea. Hoffman's stories have appeared in *Cosmopolitan*, *McCall's*, and several literary magazines. His books include the novel *Godfires* and *By Land, By Sea*, a collection of short stories.

Hoffman served with the U.S. Army from 1943 to 1946. Later, he taught at Hampden-Sydney College in Virginia. Besides being a writer and teacher, Hoffman has also raised horses and managed a grocery company.

Biography

The United States vs. Susan B. Anthony

MARGARET TRUMAN

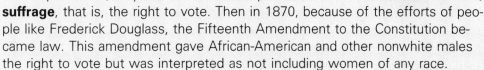

Examine What You Know

Discuss what you know about the struggle for women's rights. What has been achieved so far? What rights still need to be gained?

Expand Your Knowledge

For almost one hundred years after America won its independence, only white males were permitted **suffrage**, that is, the right to vote. Then in 1870, because of the efforts of people like Frederick Douglass, the Fifteenth Amendment to the Constitution became law. This amendment gave African-American and other nonwhite males the right to vote but was interpreted as not including women of any race.

Susan B. Anthony was the daughter of Quakers who strongly supported abolition and equal rights for women. In 1852, Anthony's anger over women's inequality grew after she was refused permission to speak at a rally because she was female. After a second confrontation involving her fellow teachers, she joined the women's suffrage movement.

In 1920, fourteen years after her death, the Nineteenth Amendment was passed. It gave all female citizens the right to vote.

Enrich Your Reading

Understanding Specialized Vocabulary This selection contains many legal terms. Use the definitions below plus the footnotes that accompany the selection for a clearer understanding of the legal process.

- **bill of indictment** a description of crimes that a person is accused of committing
- **grand jury** a jury that determines if there is enough evidence to try an accused person
- **post a bond** deliver money to a court to obtain temporary release of an accused person with the understanding that the person will return for the trial
- **test case** a legal case to decide whether a law conforms to the U.S. Constitution

■ *A biography of the author can be found on page 445.*

The United States vs. Susan B. Anthony

MARGARET TRUMAN

Susan B. Anthony has never been one of my favorite characters. Stern-eyed and grim-lipped, she seemed utterly devoid of warmth and humor and much too quick to <u>dominate</u> the women she worked with. I always thought her personality could be summed up in one word: battle-ax.[1] On top of that drawback, she was a <u>fanatic</u>. She joined the woman's suffrage movement in 1852, when she was thirty-two years old. From then until her death in 1906, she could think of little else.

The fanatics of one generation have a habit of turning into the heroes and heroines of the next, as Susan B. Anthony proved. And since I've been making a study of heroines, I decided to give Miss Anthony a second look. I have to report that my original assessment of her character was much too harsh. . . .

Susan B. Anthony was a stern and single-minded woman. Like most crusaders for causes—especially unpopular causes—she had little time for fun and games. But I have a sneaky feeling that behind her severe manner and unremitting[2] devotion to duty, she may actually have had a sense of humor. Let me tell you about my favorite episode in Susan B. Anthony's career, and perhaps you'll agree.

It began on Friday morning, November 1, 1872. Susan was reading the morning paper at her home in Rochester. There, at the top of the editorial page of the *Democrat and Chronicle*, was an exhortation[3] to the city's residents:

> Now register! Today and tomorrow are the only remaining opportunities. If you were not permitted to vote, you would fight for the right, undergo all privations[4] for it, face death for it. You have it now at the cost of five minutes' time to be spent in seeking your place of registration and having your name entered. And yet, on election day, less than a week hence, hundreds of you are likely to lose your votes because you have not thought it worthwhile to give the five minutes. Today and tomorrow are your only opportunities. Register now!

---

1. **battle-ax:** derogatory slang term for a woman who is harsh and domineering.
2. **unremitting:** not stopping; persistent.
3. **exhortation:** warning.
4. **privations:** lack of the ordinary necessities of life.

Susan B. Anthony read the editorial again. Just as she thought, it said nothing about being addressed to men only. With a gleam in her eye, she put down the paper and summoned her sister Guelma, with whom she lived. The two women donned their hats and cloaks and went off to call on two other Anthony sisters who lived nearby. Together, the four women headed for the barber shop on West Street, where voters from the Eighth Ward were being registered.

For some time, Susan B. Anthony had been looking for an opportunity to test the Fourteenth Amendment to the Constitution as a weapon to win the vote for women. Adopted in 1868, the amendment had been designed to protect the civil rights—especially the voting rights—of recently freed slaves. It stated that:

> All persons born or naturalized in the United States, and subject to the jurisdiction thereof, are citizens of the United States and of the State wherein they reside. No State shall make or enforce any law which shall abridge the privileges or immunities of citizens of the United States, nor shall any State deprive any person of life, liberty, or property without due process of law, nor deny to any person within its jurisdiction the equal protection of the laws.

The amendment did not say that "persons" meant only males, nor did it spell out "the privileges and immunities of citizens." Susan B. Anthony felt perfectly justified in concluding that the right to vote was among the privileges of citizenship and that it extended to women as well as men. I'm sure she must have also seen the humor of outwitting the supposedly superior males who wrote the amendment.

To insist on being admitted to . . . the voting booth was absolutely outrageous.

It was bad enough for a bunch of women to barge into one sacred male precinct[5]—the barber shop—but to insist on being admitted to another holy of holies—the voting booth—was absolutely outrageous. Mustaches twitched, throats were cleared, a whispered conference was held in the corner.

Susan had brought along a copy of the Fourteenth Amendment. She read it aloud, carefully pointing out to the men in charge of registration that the document failed to state that the privilege of voting extended only to males.

Only one man in the barber shop had the nerve to refuse the Anthony sisters the right to register. The rest buckled under Susan's determined <u>oratory</u> and allowed them to sign the huge, leather-bound voter registration book. If the men in the barber shop thought they were getting rid of a little band of crackpots the easy way, they were wrong. Susan urged all her followers in Rochester to register. The next day, a dozen women invaded the Eighth Ward barber shop, and

---

5. **precinct:** the grounds immediately surrounding a holy place, such as a church. Truman is equating the barbershop with a sacred place.

Susan B. Anthony at her desk
Frances Benjamin Johnston
The Bettmann Archive, New York.

another thirty-five appeared at registration sites elsewhere in the city. The *Democrat and Chronicle,* which had inadvertently prompted the registrations, expressed no editorial opinion on the phenomenon, but its rival, the *Union and Advertiser,* denounced the women. If they were allowed to vote, the paper declared, the poll inspectors[6] "should be prosecuted to the full extent of the law."

The following Tuesday, November 5, was Election Day. Most of the poll inspectors in Rochester had read the editorial in the *Union and Advertiser* and were too intimidated to allow any of the women who had registered to vote. Only in the Eighth Ward did the males weaken. Maybe the inspectors were *Democrat and Chronicle* readers, or perhaps they were more afraid of Susan B. Anthony than they were of the law. What-

ever the reason, when Susan and her sisters showed up at the polls shortly after 7A.M., there was only a minimum of fuss. A couple of inspectors were hesitant about letting the women vote, but when Susan assured them that she would pay all their legal expenses if they were prosecuted, the men relented, and one by one, the women took their ballots and stepped into the voting booth. There were no insults or sneers, no rude remarks. They marked their ballots, dropped them into the ballot box, and returned to their homes.

Susan B. Anthony's feat quickly became the talk of the country. She was applauded in some circles, vilified in others. But the day of reckoning was not long in arriving.

---

6. **poll inspectors:** people whose job it is to make sure that votes are cast according to the law.

Words to Know and Use

inadvertently (in′ ad vʉrt′ ′nt lē) *adv.* unintentionally
phenomenon (fə näm′ ə nən′) *n.* an extremely unusual occurrence
intimidate (in tim′ ə dāt′) *v.* to make afraid

436

On November 28, Deputy U.S. Marshal E. J. Keeney appeared at her door with a warrant[7] for her arrest. She had violated Section 19 of the Enforcement Act of the Fourteenth Amendment, which held that anyone who voted illegally was to be arrested and tried on criminal charges.

Susan B. Anthony was a great believer in planning ahead. The day after she registered, she decided to get a legal opinion on whether or not she should attempt to vote. A number of lawyers turned her away, but she finally found one who agreed to consider the case. He was Henry R. Selden, a former judge of the Court of Appeals, now a partner in one of Rochester's most prestigious law firms.

On the Monday before Election Day, Henry Selden informed his new client that he agreed with her interpretation of the Fourteenth Amendment and that in his opinion, she had every right to cast her ballot. The U.S. Commissioner of Elections in Rochester, William C. Storrs, did not <u>concur</u>.

E. J. Keeney, the marshal dispatched to arrest Susan B. Anthony, was not at all happy with his assignment. He nervously twirled his tall felt hat while waiting for her to come to the front door. When she finally appeared, he blushed and stammered, shifted uncomfortably from one foot to the other, and finally blurted out, "The Commissioner wishes to arrest you."

Susan couldn't help being amused at Keeney's embarrassment. "Is this your usual method of serving a warrant?" she asked calmly. With that, the marshal recovered his official dignity, presented her with the warrant, and told her that he had come to escort her to the office of the Commissioner of Elections.

When Susan asked if she could change into a more suitable dress, the marshal saw his opportunity to escape. "Of course," he said, turning to leave. "Just come down to the Commissioner's office whenever you're ready."

"I'll do no such thing," Susan informed him curtly. "You were sent here to arrest me and take me to court. It's your duty to do so."

"Don't you want to handcuff me, too?"

Keeney had no choice but to wait while his prisoner went upstairs and put on a more appropriate outfit. When she returned, she thrust out her wrists and said, "Don't you want to handcuff me, too?"

"I assure you, madam," Marshal Keeney stuttered, "it isn't at all necessary."

With the U.S. Marshal at her side, Susan was brought before the Federal Commissioner of Elections, William C. Storrs. Her arrest was recorded, and she was ordered to appear the next day for a hearing. It was conducted by U.S. District Attorney Richard Crowley and his assistant, John E. Pound.

Susan answered District Attorney Crowley's questions politely. She said that she thought the Fourteenth Amendment gave her the right to vote. She admitted that she

---

7. **warrant:** a legal document authorizing an officer to make an arrest, a search, or a seizure.

had consulted an attorney on the question but said that she would have voted even if he had not advised her to do so. When Crowley asked if she had voted deliberately to test the law,[8] she said, "Yes, sir. I have been determined for three years to vote the first time I happened to be at home for the required thirty days before an election."

The District Attorney's next step was to convene a grand jury to draw up a bill of indictment. He and his assistant fell to wrangling over a suitable trial date. Susan interrupted them. "I have lecture dates that will take me to central Ohio," she said. "I won't be available until December 10."

"But you're supposed to be in custody[9] until the hearing," Crowley informed her.

"Is that so?" said Susan coolly. "I didn't know that."

The District Attorney backed down without an argument and scheduled the grand jury session for December 23.

Sixteen women had voted in Rochester. All sixteen were arrested and taken before the grand jury, but Susan alone was brought to trial. The District Attorney had decided to single her out as a test case. The three poll inspectors who had allowed the women to vote were also arrested. The grand jury indicted them too, set bail at five hundred dollars each, and ordered their trial set for the summer term of the U.S. District Court.

Susan Anthony's case now involved nineteen other men and women. All of them—including Susan—were liable to go to prison if they were found guilty and the judge was in a sentencing mood. Prison in the 1870's was a very unpleasant place. There were no minimum security setups where a <u>benevolent</u> government allowed corrupt politicians, crooked labor leaders, and political agitators to rest and rehabilitate, as we do today. Prison meant a cold cell, wretched food, the company of thieves and murderers.

For a while it looked as if Susan might be behind bars even before her trial. She refused to post a bond for her five-hundred-dollar bail. Henry Selden paid the money for her. "I could not see a lady I respected put in jail," he said.

It must be agonizing to sweat out the weeks before a trial. There is time to look ahead and brood about the possibility of an unfavorable verdict and time to look back, perhaps with regret, at the decision that placed you in the hands of the law. But Susan B. Anthony had no regrets. Nor did she appear to have any anxieties about her trial. She had already proven her <u>fortitude</u> by devoting twenty years of her life to fighting for the right to vote. If she won her case, the struggle would be over. But even if she lost, Susan was not ready to give up the fight. . . .

The trial of *The United States* vs. *Susan B. Anthony* opened on the afternoon of June 17, 1873, with the tolling of the Canandaigua Courthouse bell. The presiding justice was Ward Hunt, a prim, pale man, who owed his judgeship to the good offices of Senator Roscoe Conkling, the Republican boss of New York State. Conkling was a fierce foe of woman suffrage, and Hunt, who had no wish to offend his powerful patron, had written his decision before the trial started.

---

8. **test the law:** breaking a law thought to be unconstitutional hoping that the law will be changed.

9. **in custody:** under arrest.

| *Words to Know and Use* | **benevolent** (bə nev′ ə lənt) *adj.* charitable; kind; compassionate |
| | **fortitude** (fôrt′ ə tōōd′) *n.* the inner strength needed to bear misfortune calmly; resoluteness |

District Attorney Crowley opened the arguments for the prosecution.[10] They didn't make much sense at the time, and in retrospect, they sound nothing short of ridiculous. The District Attorney mentioned that Susan B. Anthony was a woman and therefore she had no right to vote. His principal witness was an inspector of elections for the Eighth Ward, who swore that on November 5 he had seen Miss Anthony put her ballot in the ballot box. To back up his testimony, the inspector produced the voter registration book with Susan B. Anthony's signature in it.

"*I direct that you find the defendant guilty.*"

Henry Selden's reply for the defense was equally simple. He contended that Susan Anthony had registered and voted in good faith, believing that it was her constitutional right to do so. When he attempted to call his client to the stand, however, District Attorney Crowley announced that she was not competent to testify in her own behalf. Judge Hunt agreed, and the only thing Henry Selden could do was read excerpts from the testimony Susan had given at her previous hearings when presumably she was no less incompetent than she was right now.

Henry Selden tried to make up for this gross injustice by making his closing argument a dramatic, three-hour speech on behalf of woman suffrage. District Attorney Crowley replied with a two-hour rehash of the original charge.

By the afternoon of June 18, the case of *The United States* vs. *Susan B. Anthony* was ready to go to the jury. It was impossible to predict what their verdict might be, so Judge Hunt, determined to make it the verdict he and Roscoe Conkling wanted, took matters into his own hands. "Gentlemen of the jury," he said, "I direct that you find the defendant guilty."

Henry Selden leaped to his feet. "I object, your honor," he thundered. "The court has no power to direct the jury in a criminal case."

Judge Hunt ignored him. "Take the verdict, Mr. Clerk," he said.

The clerk of the court must have been another Conkling man. "Gentlemen of the jury," he intoned as if the whole proceeding was perfectly normal, "hearken to the verdict as the court hath recorded it. You say you find the defendant guilty of the offense charged. So say you all."

The twelve jurymen looked stunned. They had not even met to discuss the case, much less agree on a verdict. When Henry Selden asked if the clerk could at least poll the jury, Judge Hunt rapped his gavel sharply and declared, "That cannot be allowed. Gentlemen of the jury, you are discharged."

An enraged Henry Selden lost no time in introducing a motion for a new trial on the grounds that his client had been denied the right to a jury verdict. Judge Hunt denied the motion. He turned to Susan B. Anthony and said, "The prisoner will stand up. Has the prisoner anything to say why sentence shall not be pronounced?"

Thus far in the trial, Susan B. Anthony

---

10. **prosecution:** the State as the party that begins and carries on a criminal proceeding in court.

Words
to Know
and Use

retrospect (re′ trə spect′) *n.* a looking back to or rethinking of past events
competent (käm′ pə tənt) *adj.* capable; legally fit

439

had remained silent. Now, she rose to her feet and said slowly, "Yes, your honor, I have many things to say."

Without further preliminaries, she launched into a scathing <u>denunciation</u> of Judge Hunt's conduct of her trial. ". . . In your ordered verdict of guilty," she said, "you have trampled underfoot every vital principle of our government. My natural rights, my civil rights, my political rights, are all alike ignored. Robbed of the fundamental privilege of citizenship, I am degraded from the status of a citizen to that of a subject; and not only myself individually, but all of my sex, are, by your honor's verdict, doomed to political subjection under this so-called Republican government."

Judge Hunt reached for his gavel, but Susan B. Anthony refused to be silenced.

"May it please your honor," she continued. "Your denial of my citizen's right to vote is the denial of my right to a trial by a jury of my peers as an offender against law, therefore, the denial of my sacred rights to life, liberty, property, and—"

"The court cannot allow the prisoner to go on," Judge Hunt cried out.

Susan ignored him and continued her impassioned <u>tirade</u> against the court. Hunt frantically rapped his gavel and ordered her to sit down and be quiet. But Susan, who must have been taking delight in his consternation, kept on talking. She deplored the fact that she had been denied the right to a fair trial. Even if she had been given such a trial, she insisted, it would not have been by her peers. Jury, judges, and lawyers were not her equals, but her superiors, because they could vote and she could not.

Susan was <u>adamant</u> about the fact that she had been denied the justice guaranteed in the Constitution to every citizen of the United States.

Judge Hunt was sufficiently cowed[11] by now to try to defend himself. "The prisoner has been tried according to the established forms of law," he sputtered.

"Yes, your honor," retorted Susan, overlooking his <u>blatant</u> lie, "but by forms of law all made by men, interpreted by men, administered by men, in favor of men, and against women; and hence your honor's ordered verdict of guilty, against a United States citizen for the exercise of that citizen's right to vote, simply because that citizen was a woman and not a man. But yesterday, the same man-made forms of law declared it a crime punishable with a one-thousand-dollar fine and six months imprisonment for you, or me, or any of us, to give a cup of cold water, a crust of bread, or a night's shelter to a panting fugitive while he was tracking his way to Canada. And every man or woman in whose veins coursed a drop of human sympathy violated that wicked law, reckless of consequences, and was justified in so doing. As, then, the slaves who got their freedom must take it over, or under, or through the unjust forms of law, precisely so now must women, to get their right to a voice in this government, take it, and I have taken mine, and mean to take it at every opportunity."

Judge Hunt flailed his gavel and gave the by now futile order for the prisoner to sit down and be quiet. Susan kept right on talking.

"When I was brought before your honor for trial," she said, "I hoped for a broad and

---

11. **cowed:** intimidated.

Words to Know and Use | **denunciation** (dē nun′ sē ā′ sʰhən) *n.* a public accusation; a strong condemnation
tirade (tī′ rād′) *n.* a long impassioned speech, especially one that denounces
adamant (ad′ ə mənt) *adj.* not giving in; unyielding; unrelenting
blatant (blāt′ ′nt) *adj.* glaringly conspicuous; obvious

AN
ACCOUNT OF THE PROCEEDINGS
ON THE
TRIAL OF
SUSAN B. ANTHONY,
ON THE
Charge of Illegal Voting,
AT THE
PRESIDENTIAL ELECTION IN NOV., 1872,
AND ON THE
TRIAL OF
BEVERLY W. JONES, EDWIN T. MARSH
AND WILLIAM B. HALL,
THE INSPECTORS OF ELECTION BY WHOM HER VOTE WAS RECEIVED.

ROCHESTER, N. Y.:
DAILY DEMOCRAT AND CHRONICLE BOOK PRINT, 8 WEST MAIN ST.
1874.

Susan B. Anthony (left)
confers with Elizabeth Cady
Stanton. The invitation to
Anthony's trial (above)
UPI/Bettmann Newsphotos,
New York.

liberal interpretation of the Constitution and its recent amendments. One that would declare all United States citizens under its protection. But failing to get this justice—failing, even, to get a trial by a jury *not* of my peers—I ask not leniency at your hands—but to take the full rigors of the law."

With that Susan finally obeyed Judge Hunt's orders and sat down. Now he had to reverse himself and order her to stand up so he could impose sentence. As soon as he pronounced the sentence—a fine of one hundred dollars plus the costs of prosecuting the trial—Susan spoke up again. "May it please your honor," she said, "I shall never pay a dollar of your unjust penalty. All the stock in trade I possess is a ten-thousand-dollar debt, incurred by publishing my paper—*The Revolution*—four years ago, the sole object of which was to educate all women to do precisely as I have done, rebel against your man-made, unjust, unconstitutional forms of law that tax, fine, imprison, and hang women while they deny them the right of representation in the government; and I shall work on with might and main to pay every dollar of that honest debt, but not a penny shall go to this unjust claim. And I shall earnestly and persistently continue to urge all women to the practical recognition of the old Revolutionary maxim, that 'Resistance to tyranny is obedience to God.' "

Judge Hunt must have had strict orders not only to see that the defendant was convicted, but to do everything he could to prevent the case from going on to a higher court. He allowed Susan to walk out of the courtroom without imposing a prison sentence in lieu of[12] her unpaid fine. If he had sent her to prison, she could have been released on a writ of habeas corpus[13] and would have had the right to appeal.[14] As it was, the case was closed.

Although she was disappointed that her case would not go to the Supreme Court as she had originally hoped, Susan knew that she had struck an important blow for woman's suffrage. Henry Selden's arguments and her own speech at the end of the trial were widely publicized, and Judge Hunt's conduct of the trial stood as proof that women were treated unjustly before the law.

Susan did not forget the election inspectors who had allowed her to cast her ballot. The men were fined twenty-five dollars each and sent to jail when they refused to pay. In all, they spent about a week behind bars before Susan, through the influence of friends in Washington, obtained presidential pardons for each of them. In the meantime, her followers, who included some of the best cooks in Rochester, saw to it that the men were supplied with delicious hot meals and home-baked pies.

True to her promise, Susan paid the legal expenses for the three inspectors. With the help of contributions from sympathetic admirers, she paid the costs of her own trial. But she never paid that one-hundred-dollar fine. Susan B. Anthony was a woman of her word as well as a woman of courage. 🔊

---

12. **in lieu of:** in place of.

13. **writ of habeus corpus:** a legal document requesting that a person appear in court.

14. **right to appeal:** the right to have legal issues, not facts, that arose during a trial reviewed by another court.

explain

Responding to Reading

First Impressions

1. In your journal or on a sheet of paper, list words and phrases that describe your impressions of Susan B. Anthony.

Second Thoughts

2. Based on the information in this account, how effective was Anthony in her efforts to gain suffrage for women?

>   **Think about**
>   • her short-term goals
>   • her long-term or ultimate goal

3. In your opinion, what is wrong or unfair about Anthony's trial?

4. Why does the judge avoid putting Anthony in jail? Do you think she thought in advance that she would not be sent to jail? Give reasons for your answer.

5. Reread the first two paragraphs of this selection. What do you think caused Truman's opinion of Anthony to change? Do you think that the details Truman presents support her new point of view?

Broader Connection

6. How far should equality for women go? Is there anything that a woman should not be allowed to do? Explain your opinion.

Literary Concept: Character

One way to learn about a subject is to examine the words and actions of others. Consider the reactions of the poll inspectors, the lawyer Henry Selden, Marshal E. J. Keeney, District Attorney Crowley, and Judge Ward Hunt to Susan B. Anthony. What can you infer about her character from the behavior of each of these men toward her? Give reasons to support your conclusions.

Concept Review: Biography   You have learned that in a biography, the writer's opinion of the subject can affect what and how facts are presented. For example, by mixing facts with opinions or by using loaded language, the writer can influence the reader's perception of the subject. In your opinion, how objective is this account? Support your opinion with evidence from the selection.

Writing Options

1. Imagine that it is 1873 and you have just heard about Susan B. Anthony's trial. Write a letter to Judge Hunt expressing your opinion of his actions.

2. Write a newspaper article about Anthony's attempt to register to vote or about her subsequent trial. Remember that an account in a newspaper should include only the facts of the incident, not the writer's opinions. Have a friend review your paper to eliminate statements that express your personal bias.

3. In the 1988 Presidential election, only 50.2 percent of those eligible to vote cast a ballot. With several classmates, create a questionnaire that asks people's views on the importance of voting. Ask as many people as you can to complete your questionnaire. Present to your class any conclusions you draw about why so many people do not vote.

4. Compare Susan B. Anthony with Frederick Douglass in terms of personality, methods, and sheer determination.

Vocabulary Practice

Exercise Read each pair of words below. On your paper, write *Synonyms* if the pair are synonyms. Write *Antonyms* if they are antonyms.

1. fanatic—extremist
2. denunciation—praise
3. retrospect—review
4. oratory—speech
5. phenomenon—event
6. fortitude—cowardice
7. tirade—recommendation
8. dominate—control
9. intimidate—soothe
10. concur—disagree
11. inadvertently—accidentally
12. competent—capable
13. adamant—unyielding
14. blatant—hidden
15. benevolent—kind

Words to Know and Use

adamant
benevolent
blatant
competent
concur
denunciation
dominate
fanatic
fortitude
inadvertently
intimidate
oratory
phenomenon
retrospect
tirade

Options for Learning

1 • Stage a Debate Imagine that you and several classmates are citizens of Rochester, New York, during 1873. Debate the question "Is Susan B. Anthony an admirable person or a troublemaker?"

2 • Voting Milestones Research the history of suffrage in America from colonial to modern times. Find out when each group of citizens, such as eighteen-year-olds, received the right to vote. Create a time line illustrating milestones in voting history.

3 • Cartoon Capers The newspapers of 1872 and 1873 published political cartoons about Anthony's efforts to gain the vote for women. Draw a cartoon about the events in this account. Remember that political cartoons often attack, ridicule, or criticize a public person or event. Your cartoon may favor either side.

4 • Test Case Challenge Susan B. Anthony's trial was meant to test, or challenge, existing laws. Sometimes a test case that loses in a lower court is sent by appeal to the Supreme Court. Research the history of one of the following cases tried by the Supreme Court: *Dred Scott* v. *Sanford,* 1857; *Brown* v. *Board of Education,* 1954; *Hazelwood School District* v. *Kuhlmeier,* 1988.

 FACT FINDER

What percentage of the people who voted in the last presidential election were women?

Margaret Truman
1924–

When Franklin Delano Roosevelt died suddenly on April 12, 1945, Harry S Truman became President of the United States. He moved into the White House with his wife, Bess, and his daughter, Margaret. They stayed for seven years.

After graduating from George Washington University, Truman sang professionally in operas, acted, lectured, and worked in radio and television. As the President's daughter, Margaret had a tough time. She was the object of ridicule and scorn—particularly over her singing. She received scathing reviews, and few people took her seriously.

Truman is known today for her eight murder mysteries, all of which center around famous sites in Washington, D. C. Although the stories are based on her knowledge of political life in the nation's capital, she says her mysteries are "pure fiction."

Truman has also written an autobiography, *Souvenir,* which was her first book; biographies of her parents; and the collection of biographies, *Women of Courage,* from which this selection comes.

WRITER'S WORKSHOP

EXPOSITION

A **biography** is the true-life story of someone important. A book-length biography typically includes accounts of the person's childhood and descriptions of his or her family, as well as a discussion of the significant achievements that help define his or her life. Biographies also analyze the qualities that make (or made) the person special in some way.

In this subunit you have read two biographies of people whose determination and strength of character eventually made them famous. Not all biographies are about famous people, however. Equally important are biographies of unknown people whose greatness was recognized only by the few people who knew them. Your task in this assignment is to research and write a biography about someone you respect.

GUIDED ASSIGNMENT: RESEARCH BIOGRAPHY

Research and write a biography about someone you admire. You may write about someone who is famous, such as a sports star or entertainer, or about a friend, a relative, a neighbor, or someone else in your community.

> Here is your PASSkey to this assignment.

PURPOSE: To research and write about a person's life

AUDIENCE: Your classmates

SUBJECT: A person whom you respect

STRUCTURE: A multi-paragraph biography

Prewriting

STEP 1 **Select a subject**   First, you must decide who will be the subject of your biography. With some classmates, list a number of categories such as authors, family members, sports figures, community leaders, historical figures, and so on. Then think of specific people in each group. Once you have brainstormed several possibilities, select as your subject the one you find most interesting to write about. Keep in mind that this person should be someone you really admire.

STEP 2 **List questions**   With a partner, in a small group, or on your own, consider what you need to know about the person you have selected in order to write a good biography. Write down several questions that your research will attempt to answer. One important question is "Why do I admire this person?" Another question might be "What is this person generally famous for?" Keep going until you have a long list of questions. Then choose the ones you want to focus on.

STEP 3 **Research your subject** Once you have a focus for your writing, you are ready to begin to research your subject. At this point, you may wish to review the Guidelines for Research and Report Writing section in the *Writer's Handbook.* This handbook provides detailed information on all the stages of report writing.

How you research your subject depends on whether you have selected a famous subject or not. If your subject is a well-known person, you will use **secondary research.** This means you will use sources written by other people. If your subject is not famous, you will need to do **primary research.** That is, you will do the interviewing and legwork yourself.

Secondary research When investigating the life of a famous person, start in your library. Consult the card catalog under your subject's name to see whether the library has any books about him or her. Look up your subject's name in a reference book called *The Biography Index,* which lists books and articles about famous people. People of recent fame may not have books written about them yet. If this is the case with your subject, you may find *The Readers' Guide to Periodical Literature* helpful. Another resource you might find useful is *The New York Times Index,* which lists by subject all the articles appearing in that newspaper in any given year.

Once you have located several sources on your subject, you are ready to read them and take notes. Review your list of questions from Step 2. When you come across an answer to one of the questions, write it down. Also, record any other information which seems useful or interesting. Include direct quotations when a source makes a point you too want to make. Be sure to record information about each source you use. Take notes on index cards—one idea or fact per card. When you organize your notes, you can easily rearrange the cards until their order satisfies you. Use a separate notecard to record information about each source.

Primary research A library will not be much help in researching a subject who is not famous. The questions you designed in Step 2 will have to be answered through your own observations and interviews. You probably have firsthand information about your subject if you know him or her personally, so begin by answering your own questions as completely and specifically as you can. Add to this information by interviewing your subject and other people who know him or her. Refer to the **Speaking and Listening Workshop** on page 403 for help with interviewing techniques.

STEP **4** **Organize your information**   Once you have completed your research, you need to organize your information. Read over your notecards, looking for three or four main ideas or categories. Then sort your cards into piles, creating a separate pile for each main idea. You will probably find that your categories roughly match the main questions you chose to focus on in Step 2.

Drafting

STEP **1** **Introduce your subject**   Begin with your subject's name and a brief description of what he or she, whether famous or not, is best known for. Also mention the outstanding qualities this person possesses. With your classmates discuss ways to make this paragraph more than just a list of facts. What can you say that will capture and hold a reader's attention?

STEP **2** **Describe the subject**   Next, write paragraphs describing the qualities or accomplishments of your subject. Begin a new paragraph for each main idea. Use your grouped notecards to help you develop these paragraphs. Use quotations from your sources when appropriate. Here are two of the paragraphs one student wrote who researched his neighbor, an elderly woman named Mrs. Bella Thompkins. The first paragraph tells how she treated young children; the second describes her relationships with teenagers.

STUDENT MODEL ▶

Mrs. Thompkins was more than just a loving grandmother. In a way, she became a grandmother to everyone. She often invited the younger neighborhood children over for cookies and milk. Janey Reed, a nine-year-old, said of Mrs. Thompkins, "She was always friendly. She always asked me over, and we would play games or have snacks."

She also befriended children who were older and needed understanding and a sympathetic ear more than cookies and milk. One sophomore girl said that Mrs. Thompkins often listened to her troubles. She asked her questions and helped her figure out what she thought. Mrs. Thompkins didn't force her own opinions on anyone else. "She never told me what to do," the sophomore said. "She helped me figure out the situation for myself."

STEP 3 **Write a conclusion**   You might finish your biography with a brief summary of the person's accomplishments. Emphasize the qualities that made you choose this person as your subject rather than someone else. You might include an especially meaningful quotation from the person or from someone else about that person.

STEP 4 **List your sources**   At the end of your paper, include a bibliography that credits all your sources.

Revising and Editing

After you have completed your rough draft, use the following checklist to help you evaluate and revise your work, or ask a classmate to review your work according to the checklist.

Revision Checklist

1. Does the opening paragraph introduce the subject and include a brief description of the person and his or her achievements?
2. Does the body of the biography clearly and specifically explain the person's most obvious qualities?
3. Does the essay contain quotations and/or summaries from several sources that support the biography's main points?
4. Does the biography include a list of sources at the end?

Editing   When you have finished revising your draft, proofread for spelling, clarity, and mechanics.

Publishing

Make copies of everyone's work and publish them as a volume of collected biographies. Form an editorial committee to decide on a title for your collection.

Reflecting on Your Writing

Place your answers to the following questions in your writing portfolio.

1. What did you learn about research techniques?
2. What research steps would you do differently next time?
3. After you had written your biography, did you admire your subject more or less? Why?

USING EFFECTIVE TRANSITIONS

A transition is a "passage" from one place, subject, or experience to another. Good writing is full of **transitions**—words, phrases, or even entire sentences that help the reader move from one idea to another. These transitions may connect details to a main idea, or the main idea in one paragraph to the main idea of the next. Sometimes they signal a change in direction.

The chart below shows different kinds of transitions, such as time and place, and words and phrases commonly used to make such transitions.

TRANSITIONS	WORDS AND PHRASES
Time	after, before, during, finally, first, meanwhile, sometimes, when, whenever, immediately
Place	above, around, beneath, down, here, there
Order of Importance	first, second, mainly, most important
Cause and Effect	as a result, because, therefore, so, for that reason, consequently
Contrast	on the other hand, yet, but, however, in contrast
Comparison	as, than, in the same way, similarly, likewise

Exercise 1   Read the following passage. Choose and write the correct transition from the two shown in parentheses.

To Jamie, the evening seemed endless. He couldn't wait for his adventure to begin. **1.** (To sum up, In the meantime) he checked and rechecked his equipment. **2.** (On the contrary, Then) he waited patiently for his parents to go next door to play cards. **3.** (After a while, Likewise) he pretended to go to bed so that his brother wouldn't get suspicious. **4.** (As soon as, Also) he heard his parents come in downstairs, he knew the time was near. **5.** (Below, Above) his bedroom, in the kitchen, Jamie's parents rustled around, cleaning up for the night. **6.** (Finally, First) his mother appeared in Jamie's room for a good-night check on her sleeping sons.

7. (As soon as, Moreover) she left the room, Jamie started to act. He slipped off his pajamas, which he had put on over his clothes, tied up the laces on his shoes, put on his gloves, gathered up his equipment, and tiptoed to the window.

8. (Earlier, Later) in the week, Jamie had rubbed soap along the window track. **9.** (Nevertheless, As a result), the window slid up noiselessly. **10.** (At long last, Afterward) his adventure was about to begin.

Exercise 2 Work in groups to add transitional words, phrases, or sentences to the paragraphs below. Try to make stronger links between the ideas within the paragraphs and between the paragraphs themselves.

It was 10 A.M., the first day of Sports Camp. "Sports Camp!" Ginny mumbled under her breath. "They should call it Survival Camp!" The flimsy-looking rope bridge swayed back and forth, a long and scary forty feet above the ground. She heard the instructor's cheery voice saying, "You can do it, Ginny. Just go for it!"

She took a deep breath. She took one tiny step onto the rope. She began to inch her way slowly toward the far end. Her legs began to shake as if they were made of spaghetti. The bridge began to sway. The sky seemed to be spinning. She was determined not to turn back. She reached the end!

She thought back on what she had done. She was proud of herself for overcoming her fear. She was glad she wouldn't have to cross that particular bridge again!

Exercise 3 Style   Skim one of the selections you have read. Write down at least five transitional words, phrases, or sentences. Then tell what ideas each transition connects.

Exercise 4 Analyzing and Revising Your Writing

1. Reread a passage of your writing, looking for places where transitions might improve the flow of your work.
2. Rewrite that section of the paper, adding appropriate transitions.
3. Compare your revision with the original piece. In what ways is the revision an improvement?

VOCABULARY
WORKSHOP

LEVELS OF LANGUAGE

FORMAL OR INFORMAL?

How do you know when to use formal English and when to use informal English? First, don't think of them as two separate categories. Instead, imagine them as two ends of a spectrum.

Informal

↑ Conversation
Letters between friends

Writing for magazines and newspapers

Formal speeches
Reports for school or work
Professional documents
↓

Formal

▶ Standard English, which follows accepted grammatical rules and guidelines, can be divided into formal and informal English. **Formal English** is found primarily in writing but is appropriate in any situation that is serious, dignified, or ceremonial. **Informal English,** also known as conversational English, is appropriate in everyday situations. It is used in magazines, newspapers, casual letters, and conversation.

Decide what kind of language to use by asking yourself, *Who is my audience?* and *What is my purpose?* This chart lists the characteristics of formal and informal English.

	Formal	**Informal**
Tone	Serious, academic	Personal, friendly
Vocabulary and Mechanics	May use difficult words Avoids contractions Uses correct grammar	Uses simpler words Often uses contractions Uses correct grammar
Organization	Longer, more carefully constructed sentences	Similar to conversational English

CORRECT FORM

To put your letter in correct business form, see Correct Business Letter Form in the Language Handbook.

▶ **Exercise** The following letter was written in response to a help-wanted advertisement. Rewrite the letter in formal English.

Hi Mr. Koren,
  I'd love the job you advertised. Would you believe I was just flipping through the pages of this paper looking for the comics when I saw your ad? What amazing luck! I'm a *real* animal lover! You'll never find someone who loves animals more than I do. When I was seven I was bringing home every stray animal I'd find on the streets. Ask my mother if you don't believe me. In school I'm the pres. of the Animal Care Club. For the past three summers I've volunteered at Save-a-Stray Farm, our local animal shelter. Do you think I'd have a chance of getting your job? PLEASE!!!! I know I'd be great at it.

Making Adjustments

Have you ever made plans for or looked forward to something only to have it turn out much differently than you expected? Sometimes even when people meet their goals, the results surprise or disappoint them. The ability to be flexible when faced with unexpected events is an important life skill.

In the following selections look first for the expectations. Then evaluate the adjustments the characters make in order to deal with the unexpected results.

Autobiography

^A *Measure of Freedom*

JADE SNOW WONG

Examine What You Know

"A Measure of Freedom" describes a conflict between a sixteen-year-old girl and her parents. Do you have conflicts with your parents about where you can go, when to come home, and when to do homework? On a chart like the one below, list conflicts you have experienced, the positions you and your parents have taken, and the results.

Conflict	Your Position	Parents' Position	Result

Expand Your Knowledge

In this autobiographical account, Jade Snow Wong describes her life as a member of a Chinese immigrant family living in San Francisco in 1938. At that time Chinese parents expected unquestioned obedience from their children. The head of the family was the oldest man in the household, and women were traditionally considered family property. After marriage a woman followed her husband's wishes. To the Chinese, such family obligations were foremost—even more important than loyalty to their country.

Many of these basic ideas about family life came from Confucius (kən fyōo' shəs), a Chinese philosopher and teacher who lived from about 551 to 479 B.C. Confucius's teachings influenced Chinese culture for almost two thousand years. Today, however, many of these ancient customs have become less rigid, especially among Chinese families in the United States.

Write Before You Read

Does one person have authority in your family, or is it shared? Are family rules strict, flexible, or nonexistent? Do you have any input in family decisions? Write your responses and thoughts in your journal.

■ *A biography of the author can be found on page 466.*

A Measure of Freedom

JADE SNOW WONG

Without much enthusiasm, Jade Snow decided upon junior college. Now it was necessary to inform Mama and Daddy. She chose an evening when the family was at dinner. All of them were in their customary places, and Daddy, typically, was in conversation with Older Brother about the factory:

"Blessing, when do you think Lot Number fifty-one twenty-six will be finished? I want to ask for a check from our jobber so that I can have enough cash for next week's payroll."

To which Older Brother replied, "As soon as Mama is through with the seams in Mrs. Lee's and Mrs. Choy's bundles, the women can finish the hems. Another day, probably."

Mama had not been consulted; therefore she made no comment. Silence descended as the Wongs continued their meal, observing the well-learned <u>precept</u> that talk was not permissible while eating.

Jade Snow considered whether to break the silence. Three times she thought over what she had to say, and still she found it worth saying. This also was according to family precept.

"Daddy," she said, "I have made up my mind to enter junior college here in San Francisco. I will find a steady job to pay my expenses, and by working in the summers I'll try to save enough money to take me through my last two years at the university."

Then she waited. Everyone went on eating. No one said a word. Apparently no one was interested enough to be curious. But at least no one objected. It was settled.

Junior college was at first disappointing in more ways than one. There was none of the glamour usually associated with college because the institution was so young that it had not yet acquired buildings of its own. Classes were held all over the city wherever accommodations were available. The first days were very confusing to Jade Snow, especially when she discovered that she must immediately decide upon a college major.[1]

---

1. **major:** the subject in which a student specializes.

455

DEPARTING Gu Daxiang From *Contemporary Chinese Photographs* by members of the China Modern Photo Salon, 1985.

While waiting to register, she thumbed through the catalog in search of a clue. English . . . mathematics . . . chemistry . . . in the last semester of high school she had found chemistry particularly fascinating: so with a feeling of assurance she wrote that as her major on the necessary forms and went to a sign-up table.

"I wish to take the lecture and laboratory classes for Chemistry 1A," she informed the gray-haired man who presided there.

He looked at her, a trifle impatiently she thought.

"Why?"

"Because I like it." To herself she sounded reasonable.

"But you are no longer in high school. Chemistry here is a difficult subject on a university level, planned for those who are majoring in medicine, engineering, or the serious sciences."

Jade Snow set her chin stubbornly. "I still want to take Chemistry 1A."

Sharply he questioned: "What courses in mathematics have you had? What were your grades?"

Finally Jade Snow's annoyance rose to the surface. "Straight A's. But why must you ask? Do you think I would want to take a course I couldn't pass? Why don't you sign me up and let the instructor be the judge of my ability?"

"Very well," he replied stiffly. "I'll accept you in the class. And for your information, young lady, I am the instructor!"

With this inauspicious[2] start, Jade Snow began her college career.

To take care of finances, she now needed to look for work. Through a friend she learned that a Mrs. Simpson needed someone to help with household work. "Can you cook?" was Mrs. Simpson's first question.

Jade Snow considered a moment before answering. Certainly she could cook Chi-

---

2. **inauspicious** (in′ ô spish′ əs): unfavorable; unlucky.

nese food, and she remembered a common Chinese saying, "A Chinese can cook foreign food as well as, if not better than, the foreigners, but a foreigner cannot cook Chinese food fit for the Chinese." On this reasoning it seemed safe to say "Yes."

After some further discussion Jade Snow was hired. Cooking, she discovered, included everything from pastries, puddings, meats, steaks, and vegetables, to sandwiches. In addition, she served the meals, washed dishes, kept the house clean, did the light laundry and ironing for Mr. and Mrs. Simpson and their career daughter—and always appeared in uniform, which she thoroughly disliked. In return she received twenty dollars a month. At night, she did her studying at home, and sometimes after a hard day she was so tired that the walk from the Simpson flat to the streetcar on Chestnut Street was a blessed respite, a time to relax and admire the moon if she could find it, and to gather fresh energy for whatever lay ahead. . . .

Of her college courses, Latin was the easiest. This was a surprise, for everyone had told her of its horrors. It was much more logical than French, almost mathematical in its orderliness and precision, and actually a snap after nine years of Chinese.

Chemistry, true to the instructor's promise, was difficult, although the classes were anything but dull. It turned out that he was a very nice person with a keen sense of humor and a gift for enlivening his lectures with stories of his own college days. There were only two girls in a class of more than fifty men—a tense blond girl from Germany, who always ranked first, and Jade Snow, who usually took second place.

But if Latin was the easiest course and chemistry the most difficult, sociology[3] was the most stimulating. Jade Snow had chosen it without thought, simply to meet a requirement; but that casual decision completely revolutionized her thinking, shattering her Wong-constructed conception of the order of things. This was the way it happened:

Today we recognize that children are individuals . . .

After several uneventful weeks during which the class explored the historical origins of the family and examined such terms as "norms," "mores," "folkways,"[4] there came a day when the instructor stood before them to discuss the relationship of parents and children. It was a day like many others, with the students listening in varying attitudes of interest or indifference. The instructor was speaking casually of ideas to be accepted as standard. Then suddenly upon Jade Snow's astounded ears there fell this statement:

"There was a period in our American history when parents had children for economic reasons, to put them to work as soon as possible, especially to have them help on the farm. But now we no longer regard children in this way. Today we recognize that children are individuals and that parents can no longer demand their unquestioning obedience. Parents should do their best to understand their children, because young people also have their rights."

---

3. **sociology:** the study of human society.
4. **"norms," "mores," "folkways":** terms from the field of sociology referring to rules and customs of social groups.

Words to Know and Use	**respite** (res′ pit) *n.* a temporary relief; break **conception** (kən sep′ shən) *n.* a mental impression or idea

457

The instructor went on talking, but Jade Snow heard no more, for her mind was echoing and re-echoing this startling thought. "Parents can no longer demand unquestioning obedience from their children. They should do their best to understand. Children also have their rights." For the rest of that day, while she was doing her chores at the Simpsons', while she was standing in the streetcar going home, she was busy translating the idea into terms of her own experience.

"My parents demand unquestioning obedience. Older Brother demands unquestioning obedience. By what right? I am an individual besides being a Chinese daughter. I have rights too."

Could it be that Daddy and Mama, although they were living in San Francisco in the year 1938, actually had not left the Chinese world of thirty years ago? Could it be that they were forgetting that Jade Snow would soon become a woman in a new America, not a woman in old China? In short, was it possible that Daddy and Mama could be wrong?

For days Jade Snow gave thought to little but her devastating discovery that her parents might be subject to error. As it was her habit always to act after reaching a conclusion, she wondered what to do about it. Should she tell Daddy and Mama that they needed to change their ways? One moment she thought she should, the next she thought not. At last she decided to overcome her fear in the interests of education and better understanding. She would at least try to open their minds to modern truths. If she

succeeded, good! If not, she was prepared to suffer the consequences.

In this spirit of patient martyrdom, she waited for an opportunity to speak.

It came, surprisingly, one Saturday. Ordinarily that was a busy day at the Simpsons', a time for entertaining, so that Jade Snow was not free until too late to go anywhere even had she had a place to go. But on this particular Saturday the Simpsons were away for the weekend, and by three in the afternoon Jade Snow was ready to leave the apartment with unplanned hours ahead of her. She didn't want to spend these rare hours of freedom in any usual way. And she didn't want to spend them alone.

She had never telephoned a boy before . . .

"Shall I call Joe?" she wondered. She had never telephoned a boy before, and she debated whether it would be too forward. But she felt too happy and carefree to worry much, and she was confident that Joe would not misunderstand.

Even before reporting to Mama that she was home, she ran downstairs to the telephone booth and gave the operator Joe's number. His mother answered and then went to call him while Jade Snow waited in embarrassment.

"Joe." She was suddenly tongue-tied. "Joe, I'm already home."

That wasn't at all what she wanted to say. What did she want to say?

"Hello! Hello!" Joe boomed back. "What's the matter with you? Are you all right?"

"Oh, yes, I'm fine. Only, only . . . well, I'm

Words
to Know
and Use

devastating (dev′ əs tāt′ iŋ) *adj.* overwhelming devastate *v.*
martyrdom (märt′ ər dəm) *n.* long, severe suffering

through working for the day." That was really all she had to say, but now it sounded rather pointless.

"Isn't that wonderful? It must have been unexpected." That was what was nice and different about Joe. He always seemed to know without a lot of words. But because his teasing was never far behind his understanding he added quickly, "I suppose you're going to study and go to bed early."

Jade Snow was still not used to teasing and didn't know how to take it. With an effort she swallowed her shyness and disappointment. "I thought we might go for a walk . . . that is, if you have nothing else to do . . . if you would care to . . . if . . ."

Joe laughed. "I'll go you one better. Suppose I take you to a movie. I'll even get all dressed up for you, and you get dressed up too."

Jade Snow was delighted. Her first movie with Joe! What a wonderful day. In happy anticipation she put on her long silk stockings, lipstick, and the nearest thing to a suit she owned—a hand-me-down jacket and a brown skirt she had made herself. Then with a bright ribbon tying back her long black hair she was ready.

Daddy didn't miss a detail of the preparations as she dashed from room to room. He waited until she was finished before he demanded, "Jade Snow, where are you going?"

"I am going out into the street," she answered.

"Did you ask my permission to go out into the street?"

"No, Daddy."

"Do you have your mother's permission to go out into the street?"

"No, Daddy."

A sudden silence from the kitchen indicated that Mama was listening.

Daddy went on: "Where and when did you learn to be so daring as to leave this house without permission of your parents? You did not learn it under my roof."

It was all very familiar. Jade Snow waited, knowing that Daddy had not finished. In a moment he came to the point.

"And with whom are you going out into the street?"

It took all the courage Jade Snow could muster, remembering her new thinking, to say nothing. It was certain that if she told Daddy that she was going out with a boy whom he did not know, without a chaperone, he would be convinced that she would lose her maidenly purity before the evening was over.

"Very well," Daddy said sharply. "If you will not tell me, I forbid you to go! You are not too old to whip."

That was the moment.

Suppressing all anger, and in a manner that would have done credit to her sociology instructor addressing his freshman class, Jade Snow carefully turned on her mentally rehearsed speech.

"That is something you should think more about. Yes, I am too old to whip. I am too old to be treated as a child. I can now think for myself, and you and Mama should not demand unquestioning obedience from me. You should understand me. There was a time in America when parents raised children to make them work, but now the foreigners regard them as individuals with rights of their own. I have worked too, but

Words to Know and Use | **anticipation** (an tis' ə pā' shən) *n.* pleasurable expectation

459

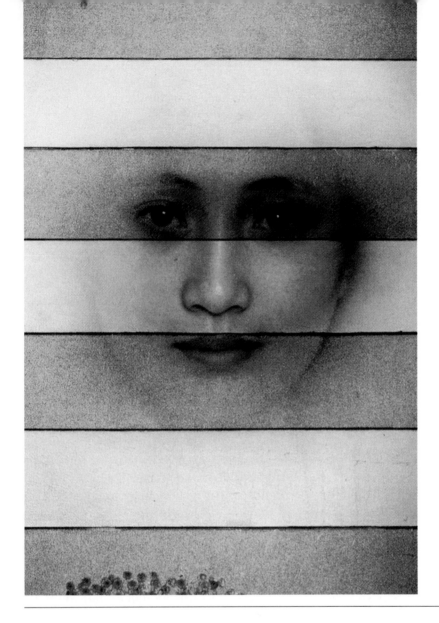

HURDLES Zhang Qi
From *Contemporary Chinese Photographs*
by members of the China
Modern Photo Salon, 1985.

now I am an individual besides being your fifth daughter."

It was almost certain that Daddy blinked, but after the briefest pause he gathered himself together.

"Where," he demanded, "did you learn such an unfilial[5] theory?"

Mama had come quietly into the room and slipped into a chair to listen.

"From my teacher," Jade Snow answered triumphantly, "who you taught me is supreme after you, and whose judgment I am not to question."

Daddy was feeling pushed. Thoroughly aroused, he shouted:

"A little learning has gone to your head! How can you permit a foreigner's theory to put aside the practical experience of the Chinese, who for thousands of years have preserved a most superior family pattern? Confucius had already presented an organized philosophy of manners and conduct when the foreigners were unappreciatively persecuting Christ. Who brought you up?

---

5. **unfilial** (un fil′ ē əl): unfit for a son or daughter.

Who clothed you, fed you, sheltered you, nursed you? Do you think you were born aged sixteen? You owe honor to us before you satisfy your personal <u>whims</u>."

Daddy thundered on, while Jade Snow kept silent.

"What would happen to the order of this household if each of you four children started to behave like individuals? Would we have one peaceful moment if your personal desires came before your duty? How could we maintain our self-respect if we, your parents, did not know where you were at night and with whom you were keeping company?"

With difficulty Jade Snow kept herself from being swayed by fear and the old familiar arguments. "You can be bad in the daytime as well as at night," she said defensively. "What could happen after eleven that couldn't happen before?"

Daddy was growing more excited. "Do I have to justify my judgment to you? I do not want a daughter of mine to be known as one who walks the streets at night. Have you no thought for our reputations if not for your own? If you start going out with boys, no good man will want to ask you to be his wife. You just do not know as well as we do what is good for you."

Mama fanned Daddy's <u>wrath</u>, "Never having been a mother, you cannot know how much grief it is to bring up a daughter. Of course we will not permit you to run the risk of corrupting your purity before marriage."

"Oh, Mama!" Jade Snow retorted. "This is America, not China. Don't you think I have any judgment? How can you think I would go out with just any man?"

"Men!" Daddy roared. "You don't know a thing about them. I tell you, you can't trust any of them."

Now it was Jade Snow who felt pushed. She delivered the balance of her declaration of independence:

"Both of you should understand that I am growing up to be a woman in a society greatly different from the one you knew in China. You expect me to work my way through college—which would not have been possible in China. You expect me to exercise judgment in choosing my employers and my jobs and in spending my own money in the American world. Then why can't I choose my friends? Of course independence is not safe. But safety isn't the only consideration. You must give me the freedom to find some answers for myself."

Mama found her tongue first. "You think you are too good for us because you have a little foreign book knowledge."

"You will learn the error of your ways after it is too late," Daddy added darkly.

By this Jade Snow knew that her parents had conceded defeat. Hoping to soften the blow, she tried to explain: "If I am to earn my living, I must learn how to get along with many kinds of people, with foreigners as well as Chinese. I intend to start finding out about them now. You must have confidence that I shall remain true to the spirit of your teachings. I shall bring back to you the new knowledge of whatever I learn."

Daddy and Mama did not accept this offer graciously. "It is as useless for you to tell me such ideas as 'The wind blows across a deaf ear.' You have lost your sense of balance," Daddy told her bluntly. "You are shameless. Your skin is yellow. Your features are for-

---

Words to Know and Use | **whim** (hwim) *n.* a sudden wish or desire; passing notion
wrath (rath) *n.* great anger; rage

461

ever Chinese. We are content with our proven ways. Do not try to force foreign ideas into my home. Go. You will one day tell us sorrowfully that you have been mistaken."

After that there was no further discussion of the matter. Jade Snow came and went without any questions being asked. In spite of her parents' dark predictions, her new freedom in the choice of companions did not result in a rush of undesirables. As a matter of fact, the boys she met at school were more concerned with copying her lecture notes than with anything else.

As for Joe, he remained someone to walk with and talk with.

As for Joe, he remained someone to walk with and talk with. On the evening of Jade Snow's seventeenth birthday he took her up Telegraph Hill and gave her as a remembrance a sparkling grown-up bracelet with a card which read: "Here's to your making Phi Beta Kappa."[6] And there under the stars he gently tilted her face and gave her her first kiss.

Standing straight and awkward in her full-skirted red cotton dress, Jade Snow was caught by surprise and without words. She felt that something should stir and crash within her, in the way books and movies described, but nothing did. Could it be that she wasn't in love with Joe, in spite of liking and admiring him? After all, he was twenty-three and probably too old for her anyway.

Still she had been kissed at seventeen,

which was cause for rejoicing. Laughing happily, they continued their walk.

But while the open rebellion gave Jade Snow a measure of freedom she had not had before and an outer show of assurance, she was deeply troubled within. It had been simple to have Daddy and Mama tell her what was right and wrong; it was not simple to decide for herself. No matter how critical she was of them, she could not discard all they stood for and accept as a substitute the philosophy of the foreigners. It took very little thought to discover that the foreign philosophy also was subject to criticism and that for her there had to be a middle way.

In particular, she could not reject the fatalism that was at the core of all Chinese thinking and behavior, the belief that the broad pattern of an individual's life was ordained by fate, although within that pattern he was capable of perfecting himself and accumulating a desirable store of good will. Should the individual not benefit by his good works, still the rewards would pass on to his children or his children's children. Epitomized by the proverbs: "I save your life, for your grandson might save mine," and "Heaven does not forget to follow the path a good man walks," this was a fundamental philosophy of Chinese life, which Jade Snow found fully as acceptable as some of the so-called scientific reasoning expounded in the sociology class, where heredity and environment were assigned all the responsibility for personal success or failure.

There was good to be gained from both concepts if she could extract and retain her

---

6. **Phi Beta Kappa:** an honorary society of college students with high academic standing.

---

own personally applicable combination.[7] She studied her neighbor in class, Stella Green, for clues. Stella had grown up reading Robert Louis Stevenson,[8] learning to swim and play tennis, developing a taste for roast beef, mashed potatoes, sweets, aspirin tablets, and soda pop, and she looked upon her mother and father as friends. But it was very unlikely that she knew where her great-grandfather was born, or whether or not she was related to another strange Green she might chance to meet. Jade Snow had grown up reading Confucius, learning to embroider and cook rice, developing a taste for steamed fish and bean sprouts, tea, and herbs, and she thought of her parents as people to be obeyed. She knew not only where her ancestors were born but where they were buried and how many chickens and roast pigs should be brought annually to their graves to feast their spirits. She knew all of the branches of the Wong family, the relation of each to the other, and understood why Daddy must help support the distant cousins in China who <u>bore</u> the sole responsibility of carrying on the family heritage by periodic visits to the burial grounds in Fragrant Mountains. She knew that one could purchase in a Chinese stationery store the printed record of her family tree relating their Wong line and other Wong lines back to the original Wong ancestors. In such a scheme the individual counted for little weighed against the family, and after sixteen years it was not easy to sever roots.

There were, alas,[9] no books or advisers to guide Jade Snow in her search for balance between the pull from two cultures. If she chose neither to reject nor accept *in toto*,[10] she must sift both and make her decisions alone. It would not be an easy search. But pride and determination, which Daddy had given her, prevented any thought of turning back. &

---

7. **extract . . . combination:** find and develop what was most useful for her from each way of thinking.
8. **Robert Louis Stevenson:** 1850–1894; the Scottish writer of *Treasure Island, Dr. Jekyll and Mr. Hyde,* and *Kidnapped.*
9. **alas** (ə las′): an exclamation used to express regret.
10. **in toto** *Latin:* as a whole.

Words to Know and Use | **bear** (ber) *v.* to support or hold up; sustain; past tense—**bore** (bôr)

Responding to Reading

First Impressions

1. Are any of Jade Snow's experiences similar to yours? Jot down your thoughts.

Second Thoughts

2. In what ways is Jade Snow's family like a typical American family? In what ways is it different?

   Think about
   - the way her family makes decisions
   - her parents' concerns about their daughter
   - the roles of different family members
   - how her family conflicts compare with those you listed

3. In your opinion is Jade Snow right to stand up to her parents? How do you feel about the way she does it? Support your opinions with reasons.

4. What do you think of the parents' side of the argument?

5. Why do Jade Snow's parents eventually give in?

6. By the end of this selection, how independent is Jade Snow? What adjustments has she made? Explain.

Broader Connections

7. How will you raise your own teenagers? How independent will you allow them to be?

Literary Concept: Point of View

Jade Snow Wong wrote her autobiography in the third person rather than from the usual first-person point of view because, according to Chinese tradition, it is unbecoming to talk about yourself using the first person. In using *she* instead of *I*, what attitude does Wong convey about herself? Find other examples in the story that support your answer.

Concept Review: Author's Purpose   The usual purpose of an autobiography is to share the author's life with the reader. What other purposes does this autobiography seem to fulfill?

Writing Options

1. Review the father's comments in his argument with Jade Snow. Rewrite these comments as one of your parents might say them to you.

2. Are there times when your personal needs are more important to you than the needs and rules of your family? How do you handle such conflicts? Write about some specific instances.

3. Jade Snow wondered whether she was being too aggressive in phoning Joe. What is your opinion about girls' calling boys? Support your opinion with reasons.

4. List the facts you have learned about Chinese culture and family life from this selection.

Vocabulary Practice

Exercise Choose the word from the list that best completes each sentence below.

1. To Jade Snow's father, obedience to family was more important than satisfying a personal _____.
2. After a long day of cooking, Jade Snow needed a _____ before doing homework.
3. How would you handle a _____ that required you not to talk during meals?
4. Some young Chinese displayed patience and even _____ as they held back their ideas, waiting for a proper time to confront their parents.
5. Jade Snow would _____ total responsibility for her decisions; she asked no one to make them for her.
6. Jade Snow's angry father expressed his _____ when she went against Chinese family traditions.
7. Jade Snow's refusal to follow her parents' rules was _____ to them.
8. Jade Snow's parents had one _____ of the role of daughters, and she had another.
9. Jade Snow could not quite let go of her belief in _____, the idea that events are determined by forces apart from ourselves.
10. Jade Snow glowed with _____ of her upcoming date with Joe.

> *Words to Know and Use*
>
> **anticipation**
> **bear**
> **conception**
> **devastating**
> **fatalism**
> **martyrdom**
> **precept**
> **respite**
> **whim**
> **wrath**

Options for Learning

1 • How Strict Are Parents? Conduct a poll of your classmates on the strictness of their parents. Use a scale of 1 to 5 with 1 indicating "not strict" and 5 "exceedingly strict." Summarize the results for your class.

2 • Choose a College Major Jade Snow has to choose a major in junior college just as you will have to if you attend school after high school. Do some research to find out in what fields you might major in a college or junior college. Choose a major you might like and list college courses you would take for that major.

3 • Debate the Issues Jade Snow and her parents argue about several issues. Choose one of these issues and stage a debate about it. The class can then vote on who wins.

4 • Confucius Says. . . Find books with the sayings of Confucius and choose one saying that you like. Then use a calligraphy pen to write the saying artistically, so that it can be framed and displayed.

 **FACT FINDER**

What other name did the Chinese have for Confucius?

Jade Snow Wong
1922–

In 1903 Jade Snow Wong's father came from China to America, where he founded a factory that made overalls. Jade Snow admired her father's individualism, and she too longed to be independent. After graduating from college, she set up a successful pottery business in San Francisco's Chinatown. Then she decided to try becoming a writer. Her first book, *Fifth Chinese Daughter,* from which this piece comes, was published in 1950. "I think it is my responsibility to try to create understanding between Chinese and Americans," she says. Wong's second book, *No Chinese Stranger,* tells of her marriage to her Chinese-American husband and of her four children, her career, and her lecture tours to the Far East.

Poetry

Prospective Immigrants Please Note

ADRIENNE RICH

Lost

BRUCE IGNACIO

Examine What You Know

As you know, the United States is a nation of immigrants and descendants of immigrants. Only one group can claim to be original inhabitants—the Native Americans. What might this group have in common with America's newest arrivals?

Expand Your Knowledge

Before the sixteenth century, Native Americans were the only people living in what is now the United States. Since then, wave after wave of immigrants from all over the world have settled in America. Early Spanish settlers were followed by northern Europeans and British and by Africans, who came as slaves. Groups from eastern and southern Europe and Russia came later. In recent decades most immigrants have come from Mexico, the Caribbean islands, and Asia. For most of these immigrants, leaving their native lands was both an opportunity and a great risk.

Native Americans were drastically affected by the multitude of immigrants who moved westward, pushing the Indians from their land. Tribes were moved by force onto reservations. One well-known move was the Long Walk of the Navahos referred to in Ignacio's poem "Lost." In 1864 the U.S. Army forced eight thousand Navaho on this three-hundred mile trek from their tribal lands to Fort Sumner, New Mexico. Many died on the walk. After four years of captivity, the Navaho reluctantly moved to reservation lands. Even today, many Navaho remember the Long Walk with great bitterness.

Enrich Your Reading

■ *Biographies of the authors can be found in the Reader's Handbook.*

Summarizing Stanzas Stanzas in a poem are groups of lines separated by spaces. Each stanza expresses a thought. To understand these two poems more easily, summarize the main idea in each stanza after you have read it.

Prospective Immigrants Please Note

ADRIENNE RICH

Either you will
go through this door
or you will not go through.

If you go through
5 there is always the risk
of remembering your name.

Things look at you doubly
and you must look back
and let them happen.

10 If you do not go through
it is possible
to live worthily

to maintain your attitudes
to hold your position
15 to die bravely

but much will blind you,
much will evade you,
at what cost who knows?

The door itself
20 makes no promises.
It is only a door.

Responding to Reading

First Impressions of "Prospective Immigrants Please Note"

1. What are your first thoughts about the message of this poem?

Second Thoughts on "Prospective Immigrants Please Note"

2. What do you think the door symbolizes? Explain your answer.

3. What choices does the speaker offer prospective immigrants? Does he or she suggest which choice is best? Give reasons for your answer.

Lost

BRUCE IGNACIO

CONTEMPORARY SIOUX INDIAN (detail)
'8 James Bama Buffalo Bill Historical Center,
dy, Wyoming.

I know not of my forefathers
nor of their beliefs
For I was brought up in the city.
Our home seemed smothered and surrounded
5 as were other homes on city sites.
When the rain came
I would slush my way to school
as though the street were a wading pool.
Those streets were always crowded.
10 I brushed by people with every step,
Covered my nose once in awhile,
Gasping against the smell of perspiration on humid days.
Lights flashed everywhere
until my head became a signal, flashing on and off.
15 Noise so unbearable
I wished the whole place would come to a standstill,
leaving only peace and quiet

And still, would I like this kind of life? . . .
The life of my forefathers
20 who wandered, not knowing where they were going,
but just moving, further and further
from where they had been,
To be in quiet,
to kind of be lost in their dreams and wishing,
25 as I have been to this day,
I awake.

Then I recalled this trail
    Swept away by the north wind,
It wasn't for me to follow,
30   The trail of the Long Walk.

Deciding between two cultures,
    I gave a second thought,
Reluctantly I took the new one,
    The paved rainbow highway.
35 I had found a new direction.

*R*esponding to Reading

First Impressions of "Lost"

1. Describe the speaker of this poem.

Second Thoughts on "Lost"

2. In the first stanza, how does the speaker feel about the life he leads now? Why?

3. What would the speaker's life be like if he chose the second option? What would he have to do to achieve that lifestyle?

4. Do you agree with the speaker's final choice? Explain.

Comparing the Poems

5. What would the door in Rich's poem mean to the speaker in "Lost"? Would the speaker go through it? Support your answer with information from the poems.

6. Compare and contrast the themes of these two poems.

*L*iterary Concept: Alliteration

Alliteration is the repetition of consonant sounds at the beginning of words. Poets use alliteration to emphasize words, to tie lines together, to reinforce meaning, and to add sound effects. Note this example of alliteration in "Lost": "Our home <u>s</u>eemed <u>s</u>mothered and <u>s</u>urrounded." What effect does this alliteration create? Find other examples of alliteration in both poems.

Concept Review: Sensory Images   Find sensory images in "Lost." Identify whether each one appeals to sight, hearing, touch, taste, smell, or a combination of senses.

*W*riting Options

1. Write a brief explanation of the title of each poem.

2. Choose either poem and list the advantages and disadvantages of the two choices it proposes.

Fiction

Brothers Are the Same

BERYL MARKHAM

Examine What You Know

"Brothers Are the Same" tells of a boy in Africa who faces a test of manhood. What tests or accomplishments signal adulthood in our society? Think of the special customs of different ethnic groups as well as the more common signs, such as learning to drive a car and voting for the first time. Create a class list.

Expand Your Knowledge

This story is set in the eastern part of Africa, on Tanzania's vast Serengeti Plain. In the background rises snow-covered Mount Kilimanjaro, Africa's tallest peak. The Serengeti's rich grasslands attract animals like wildebeests, gazelles, and also lions which feed on these grazing animals.

The Serengeti and surrounding areas are also home to the nomadic, cattle-raising Masai people. For more than a hundred years, the Masai hindered the European development of East Africa through furious and continual raids on cattle ranches, trade caravans, and safaris. The Masai's fierceness also enabled them to resist capture as slaves.

The Masai live in groups of four to eight families and wander in search of grazing land for their cattle. They make temporary settlements of mud huts surrounded by a thornbush fence. Their main source of food is their cattle: the Masai drink both the milk and the blood of cattle.

Write Before You Read

This story tells of a young man's fear. Describe a time in your life when you were afraid but faced your fear and overcame it.

■ *A biography of the author can be found on page 484.*

Brothers Are the Same

BERYL MARKHAM

They are tall men, cleanly built and straight as the shafts of the spears they carry, and no one knows their tribal history, but there is some of Egypt in their eyes and the look of ancient Greece about their bodies. They are the Masai.

They are the color of worn copper and, with their graceful women, they live on the Serengeti Plain, which makes a carpet at the feet of high Kilimanjaro. In all of Africa there are today no better husbandmen of cattle.

But once they were warriors and they have not forgotten that, nor have they let tradition die. They go armed, and to keep well-tempered the mettle[1] of their men, each youth among them must, when his hour comes, prove his right to manhood. He must meet in combat the only worthy enemy his people recognize—the destroyer of their cattle, the marauding master of the plains—the lion.

Thus, just before the dawning of a day in what these Masai call the Month of the Little Rains, such a youth with such a test before him lay in a cleft of rock and watched the shadowed outlines of a deep ravine. For at least eight of his sixteen years, this youth, this young Temas,[2] had waited for his moment. He had dreamed of it and lived it in a dozen ways—all of them glorious.

In all of the dreams, he had confronted the lion with casual courage, he had presented his spear on the charging enemy with steadiness born of brave contempt—and always he had won the swift duel with half a smile on his lips. Always—in the dreams.

Now it was different. Now as he watched the place where the real lion lay, he had no smile.

He was Masai and legend said that no Masai had ever feared.

He did not fear the beast. He was sure that in his bones and in his blood and in his heart he was not afraid. He was Masai, and legend said that no Masai had ever feared.

Yet in his mind Temas now trembled.

---

1. **mettle:** character; spirit.
2. **Temas** (tä′ mäs)

Words to Know and Use	**marauding** (mə rôd′ iŋ) *adj.* raiding; plundering **maraud** *v.* **cleft** (kleft) *n.* a crack or crevice **contempt** (kən tempt′) *n.* scorn

Fear of battle was a nonexistent thing—but fear of failure could be real, and was. It was real and living—and kept alive by the nearness of an enemy more formidable than any lion—an enemy with the hated name Medoto.[3]

He thought of Medoto—of that Medoto who lay not far away in the deep grass watching the same ravine. Of that Medoto who, out of hate and jealousy over a mere girl, now hoped in his heart that Temas would flinch at the moment of his trial. That was it. That was the thing that kept the specter[4] of failure dancing in his mind, until already it looked like truth.

There were ten youths hidden about the ravine, and they would stage and witness the coming fight. They had tracked the lion to this, his lair, and when the moment came, they would drive him, angered, upon Temas and then would judge his courage and his skill. Good or bad, that judgment would, like a brand mark, cling to him all his life.

But it was Medoto who would watch the closest for a sign, a gesture, a breath of fear in Temas. It was Medoto who would spread the word—Medoto who surely would cry "Coward!" if he could.

Temas squirmed under the heavy, unwholesome thought, then lifted his head and pierced the dim light with his eyes. To the east, the escarpment[5] stood like a wall against the rising sun. But to the north and to the west and to the south there were no horizons; the gray sky and the gray plain were part and counterpart, and he was himself a shadow in his cleft of rock.

He was a long shadow, a lean shadow. The *shuka*[6] that he wore was now bound about his waist, giving freedom to his legs and arms. His necklace and bracelets were of shining copper, drawn fine and finely spiraled, and around each of his slender ankles there was a copper chain.

His long hair, bound by beaded threads, was a <u>chaste</u> black column that lay between his shoulders, and his ears were pierced and hung with gleaming pendants. His nose was straight, with nostrils delicately flanged. The bones of his cheeks were high, the ridges of his jaw were hard, and his eyes were long and dark and a little brooding. He used them now to glance at his weapons, which lay beside him—a spear, a rawhide shield. These, and a short sword at his belt, were his armament.

He lowered his glance to the place he watched. The ravine was overgrown with a thicket of thorns, and the light had not burst through it yet. When it did, the lion within it would wake, and the moment would come.

A feeling almost of hopelessness surged through him. It did not seem that he, Temas, could in this great test prove equal to his comrades. All had passed it; all had earned the warrior's title—and none had faltered. Even Medoto—especially Medoto—had proven brave and more than ready for his cloak of manhood. Songs were sung about Medoto. In the evenings in the *manyatta*[7] when the cattle drowsed and the old men drank their honey wine, the girls

---

3. **Medoto** (mə dō′ tō)
4. **specter** (spek′ tər): a ghost or spirit.
5. **escarpment** (e skärp′ mənt): a steep slope or cliff.
6. *shuka* (shoo′ kə): a loose, flowing Masai garment.
7. *manyatta* (män yä′ tə): a Masai camp.

Words to Know and Use | **chaste** (chāst) *adj.* plain or pure

473

Whistling thorn trees in the Serengeti   1970   Eliot Porter
Courtesy of the photographer.

would gather, and the young men, too, and they would chant to the heroes of their hearts.

But none chanted to Temas. Not yet. Perhaps they never would—not one of them. Not even . . .

He shook his head in anger. He had not meant to think of her—of Kileghen[8] of the soft, deep-smiling eyes and the reedbuck's grace. Even she, so rightly named after the star Venus, had only last night sung to Medoto, and he to her, laughing the while, as

Temas, the yet unproven, had clung to the saving shadows, letting his fury burn. Could she not make up her mind between them? Must it always be first one and then the other?

He saw it all with the eye of his memory—all too clearly. He saw even the sneer of Medoto on the day the elder warrior, the chief of them all, had tendered Temas his spear with the wise words: "Now at last this

_____

8. **Kileghen** (kēl′ ə gən)

weapon is your own, but it is only wood and steel and means nothing until it changes to honor, or to shame, within your grasp. Soon we shall know!"

And soon they should! But Medoto had laughed then. Medoto had said, "It seems a heavy spear, my comrade, for one so slight—a big weight for any but a man!" And Temas had made no answer. How could he with Kileghen leaning there against the *boma*[9] as though she heard nothing, yet denying her innocence with that quiet, ever-questing smile? At whom had she smiled? At Medoto for his needless malice—or at Temas for his acceptance of it?

summarize Why does Temas think of Medoto as his enemy?

He did not know. He knew only that he had walked away carrying the unstained spear a little awkwardly. And that the joy of having it was quickly dead.

Now he spat on the earth where he rested. He raised a curse against Medoto—a harsh, a bitter curse. But in the midst of it he stiffened and grew tense. Suddenly he lay as still as sleep and watched only the ravine and listened, as to the tone of some familiar silence.

It was the silence of a waking lion, for morning light had <u>breached</u> the thicket, and within his lair the lion was roused.

Within his lair the lion sought wakefulness as suspicion came to him on the cool, unmoving air. Under the bars of sunlight that latticed his flanks and belly, his coat was short and shining. His mane was black and evenly grown. The muscles of his forelegs were not corded, but flat, and the muscles of

his shoulders were <u>laminated</u> like sheaths of metal.

Now he smelled men. Now as the sunlight fell in streams upon his sorrel coat and warmed his flanks, his suspicion and then his anger came alive. He had no fear. Whatever lived he judged by strength—or lack of it—and men were puny. And yet the scent of them kindled fire in his brooding eyes and made him contemplate his massive paws.

He arose slowly, without sound—almost without motion—and peered outward through the wall of thorns. The earth was mute, expectant, and he did not break the spell. He only breathed.

The lion breathed and swung his tail in easy, rhythmic arcs and watched the slender figure of a human near him in a cleft of rock.

Temas had risen, too. On one knee now, he waited for the signal of the lifted spears.

Of his ten comrades he could see but two or three—a tuft of warrior's feathers, here and there a gleaming arm. Presently all would leap from the places where they hid, and the Masai battle cry would slash through the silence. And then the lion would act.

But the silence held. The <u>interminable</u> instant hung like a drop that would not fall, and Temas remembered many of the rules, the laws that governed combat with a lion—but not enough, for stubbornly, wastefully, foolishly, his mind nagged at fear of disgrace—fear of failure. Fear of Medoto's ringing laughter in the *manyatta*—of Kileghen's ever-questing smile.

---

9. ***boma*** (bō′ mə): the wall around a Masai camp.

Words to Know and Use	**breach** (brēch) *v.* to break through; pierce **laminate** (lam′ i nāt′) *v.* to form into thin sheets or layers **interminable** (in tur′ mi nə bəl) *adj.* seeming to last forever; endless

"I shall fail," he thought. "I shall fail before Medoto, and through his eyes she will see my failure. I must fail," he said, "because now I see that I am trembling."

And he was. His hand was loose upon the long steel spear—too loose; the arm that held the rawhide shield was hot and too unsteady. If he had ever learned to weep, he would have wept—had there been time.

But the instant vanished—and with it, silence. From the deep grass, from the shade of anthills, from clustered rocks, warriors sprang like flames, and as they sprang they hurled upon the waiting lion their shrill, arrogant challenge, their scream of battle.

Suddenly the world was small and inescapable.

Suddenly the world was small and inescapable. It was an arena whose walls were tall young men that shone like worn gold in the sun, and in this shrunken world there were Temas and the lion.

He did not know when or how he had left the rock. It was as if the battle cry had lifted him from it and placed him where he stood—a dozen paces from the thicket. He did not know when the lion had come forward to the challenge, but the lion was there.

The lion waited. The ring of warriors waited. Temas did not move.

His long Egyptian eyes swept around the circle. All was perfect—too perfect. At every point a warrior stood blocking the lion from improbable retreat—and of these Medoto was one. Medoto stood near—a little behind Temas and to the right. His shield bore proud colors of the proven warrior. He was lean and proud, and upon his level stare

he weighed each movement Temas made, though these were hesitant and few.

For the lion did not seek escape, nor want it. His shifting yellow eyes burned with even fire. They held neither fear nor fury—only the hard and regal wrath of the challenged tyrant. The strength of either of his fore-arms was alone greater than the entire strength of any of these men; his speed in the attack was blinding speed, shattering speed. And with such knowledge, with such sureness of himself, the lion stood in the tawny grass and stared his scorn while the sun rose higher and warmed the scarcely breathing men.

The lion would charge. He would choose one of the many and charge that one. Yet the choice must not be his to make, for through the generations—centuries, perhaps—the code of the Masai decreed that the challenger must draw the lion upon him. By gesture and by voice it can be done. By movement, by courage.

Temas knew the time for this had come. He straightened where he stood and gripped his heavy spear. He held his shield before him, tight on his arm, and he advanced, step by slow step.

The gaze of the lion did not at once swing to him. But every eye was on him, and the strength of one pair—Medoto's—burned in his back like an unhealed scar.

A kind of anger began to run in Temas's blood.

A kind of anger began to run in Temas's blood. It seemed unjust to him that in this crucial moment, at this first great trial of his courage, his enemy and harshest judge must be a witness. Surely Medoto could see the points of sweat that now rose on his forehead and about his lips as he moved upon the embattled lion. Surely Medoto could see—or sense—the hesitance of his advance—almost hear, perhaps, the pounding of his heart!

clarify **What is Temas most worried about?**

He gripped the shaft of his spear until pain stung the muscles of his hand. The lion had crouched, and Temas stood suddenly within the <u>radius</u> of his leap. The circle of warriors had drawn closer, tighter, and there was no sound save the sound of their uneven breathing.

The lion crouched against the reddish earth, head forward. The muscles of his massive quarters were <u>taut</u>, his body was a drawn bow. And, as a swordsman unsheaths his blade, so he unsheathed his fangs and chose his man.

It was not Temas.

As if in contempt for this confused and untried youth who paused within his reach, the lion's eyes passed him by and fastened hard upon the stronger figure of another, upon the figure of Casaro,[10] a warrior of many combats and countless victories.

All saw it. Temas saw it, and for an instant—for a shameless breath of time—he felt an overwhelming ease of heart, relief, deliverance, not from danger, but from trial. He swept his glance around the ring. None watched him now. All action, all thought was frozen by the duel of wills between Casaro and the beast.

Slowly the veteran Casaro sank upon one knee and raised his shield. Slowly the lion gathered the power of his body for the leap. And then it happened.

From behind Temas, flung by Medoto's hand, a stone no larger than a grain of maize shot through the air and struck the lion.

No more was needed. The bolt was loosed.

But not upon Casaro, for if from choice the regal prowler of the wilderness had first preferred an opponent worthy of *his* worth, he now, under the sting of a hurled pebble, preferred to kill that human whose hand was guilty.

He charged at once, and as he charged, the young Temas was, in a breath, transformed from doubting boy to man. All fear was gone—all fear of fear—and as he took the charge, a light almost of ecstasy burned in his eyes, and the spirit of his people came to him.

Over the rim of his shield he saw fury take form. Light was blotted from his eyes as the dark shape descended upon him—for the lion's last leap carried him above the shield, the spear, the youth, so that, looking upward from his crouch, Temas, for a sliver of time, was <u>intimate</u> with death.

He did <u>not yield</u>. He did not think or feel or consciously react. All was simple. All now happened as in the dreams, and his mind was an observer of his acts.

He saw his own spear rise in a swift arc, his own shield leap on his bended arm, his own eyes seek the vital spot—and miss it.

But he struck. He struck hard, not wildly or too soon, but exactly at the precise, the ripened moment and saw his point drive full

---

10. **Casaro** (cha̅ sär′ o̅)

477

into the shoulder of the beast. It was not enough. In that moment his spear was torn from his grasp, his shield vanished, claws furrowed the flesh of his chest ripping deep. The weight and the power of the charge overwhelmed him.

He was down. Dust and blood and grass and the pungent lion smell were mingled, blended, and in his ears an enraged, triumphant roar overlaid the shrill, high human cry of his comrades.

His friends were about to make the kill that must be his. Yet his hands were empty, he was caught, he was being dragged. He had scarcely felt the long crescentic[11] teeth close on his thigh, it had been so swift. Time itself could not have moved so fast.

A lion can drag a fallen man, even a fighting man, into thicket or deep grass with incredible ease and with such speed as to outdistance even a hurled spear. But sometimes this urge to plunder first and destroy later is a saving thing. It saved Temas. That and his Masai sword, which now was suddenly in his hand.

Perhaps pain dulled his reason, but reason is a sluggard ally[12] to any on the edge of death. Temas made a cylinder of his slender body, and, holding the sword flat against his leg, he whirled, and whirling, felt the fangs tear loose the flesh of his thigh, freeing it, freeing him. And, as he felt it, he lunged.

It was quick. It was impossible, it was mad, but it was Masai madness, and it was done. Dust clothed the tangled bodies of the lion and the youth so that those who clamored close to strike the saving blows saw nothing but this cloud and could not aim into its formless shape. Nor had they need

to. Suddenly, as if *En-Gai* himself—God and protector of these men of wilderness—had stilled the scene with a lifted hand, all movement stopped, all sound was dead.

The dust was gone like a vanquished shadow, and the great rust body of the lion lay quiet on the rust-red earth. Over it, upon it, his sword still tight in his hand, the youth lay breathing, bleeding. And, beyond that, he also smiled.

What happened in the battle with the lion?

He could smile because the chant of victory burst now like drumbeats from his comrades' throats—the paeans[13] of praise fell on him where he lay; the sun struck bright through shattered clouds; the dream was true. In a dozen places he was hurt, but these would heal.

And so he smiled. He raised himself, and swaying slightly like any warrior weak in sinew but strong in spirit from his wounds, he stood with pride and took his accolade.

And then his smile left him. It was outdone by the broader, harder smile of another—for Medoto was tall and straight before him, and with his eyes and with his lips Medoto seemed to say: "It is well—this cheering and this honor. But it will pass—and we two have a secret, have we not? We know who threw the stone that brought the lion upon you when you stood hoping in

---

11. **crescentic** (kri sen′ tik): having the thin, curved shape of a new moon.
12. **reason . . . ally:** logical thought is not much help.
13. **paeans** (pē′ ənz): words, cheers, or songs of praise.

your heart that it would charge another. You stood in fear then, you stood in coward-ice. We two know this, and no one else. But there is one who might, if she were told, look not to you but to the earth in shame when you pass by. Is this not so?"

Yes, it was so, and Temas, so lately happy, shrank within himself and swayed again. He saw the young Kileghen's eyes and did not wish to see them. But for Medoto's stone, the spear of Temas would yet be virgin, clean, unproved—a thing of futile vanity.

He straightened. His comrades—the true warriors, of which even now he was not one—had in honor to a fierce and van-quished enemy laid the dead lion on a shield and lifted him. In triumph and with songs of praise (mistaken praise!) for Temas, they were already beginning their march toward the waiting *manyatta*.

Words to Know and Use | **vanity** (van′ ə tē) *n.* excessive pride; conceit

Temas turned from his field of momentary triumph, but Medoto lingered at his side.

And now it will come, Temas thought. Now what he has said with his eyes he will say with his mouth, and I am forced to listen. He looked into Medoto's face—a calm, unmoving face—and thought: It is true that this, my enemy, saw the shame of my first fear. He will tell it to everyone—and to her. So, since I am lost, it is just as well to strike a blow against him. I am not so hurt that I cannot fight at least once more.

clarify What does Temas think Medoto will say?

His sword still hung at his side. He grasped it now and said, "We are alone and we are enemies. What you are about to charge me with is true—but, if I was a coward before the lion, I am not a coward before you, and I will not listen to sneering words!"

For a long moment, Medoto's eyes peered into the eyes of Temas. The two youths stood together on the now-deserted plain and neither moved. Overhead the sun hung low and red and poured its burning light upon the drying grass, upon the thorn trees that stood in lonely clusters, upon the steepled shrines of drudging ants. There was no sound of birds, no rasping of cicada wings, no whispering of wind.

And into this dearth, into this poverty of sound, Medoto cast his laugh. His lips parted, and the low music of this throat was laughter without mirth; there was sadness in it, a note of incredulity, but not more, not mockery, not challenge.

He stared into the proud, unhappy face of Temas. He plunged the shaft of his spear into the earth and slipped the shield from his arm. At last he spoke.

He said, "My comrade, we who are Masai know the saying: 'A man asks not the motives of a friend but demands reason from his enemy.' It is a just demand. If, until now, I have seemed your enemy, it was because I feared you would be braver than I, for when I fought my lion, my knees trembled and my heart was white—until that charge was made. No one knew that, and I am called Medoto, the unflinching, but I flinched. I trembled."

He stepped closer to Temas. He smiled. "It is no good to lie," he said. "I wanted you to fail, but when I saw you hesitate, I could not bear it because I remembered my own hour of fear. It was then I threw the stone—not to shame you, but to save you from shame—for I saw that your fear was not fear of death, but fear of failure—and this I understood. You are a greater warrior than I—than any—for who but the bravest would do what you have done?" Medoto paused and watched a light of wonderment kindle in Temas's eye. The hand of Temas slipped from his sword; his muscles relaxed. Yet for a moment he did not speak, and as he looked at Medoto, it was clear to both that the identical thought, the identical vision, had come to each of them. It was the vision that must and always will come to young men everywhere, the vision of a girl.

Now this vision stood between them, and nothing else. But it stood like a barrier, the last barrier.

And Medoto destroyed it. Deliberately, casually, he reached under the folds of his flowing *shuka* and brought from it a slender belt of leather crusted with beads. It was the work and the possession of a girl, and both knew which girl. Kileghen's handiwork was rare enough but recognized in many places.

"This," said Medoto, "this, I was told to bring, and I was told in these words: 'If in his battle the young Temas proves himself a warrior and a man, make this belt my gift to him so that I may see him wear it when he returns. But if he proves a coward, Medoto, the belt is for you to keep.'"

Medoto looked at the bright gift in his hands. "It is yours, Temas!" He held it out. "I meant to keep it. I planned ways to cheat you of it, but I do not think a man can cheat the truth. I have seen you fight better than I have ever fought, and now this gift belongs to you. It is her wish and between us you are at last her choice." He laid the belt on the palm of Temas's open hand and reached once more for his shield and spear. "We will return now," Medoto said, "for the people are waiting. She is waiting. I will help you walk."

But Temas did not move. Through the sharp sting of his wounds, above his joy in the promise that now lay in his hands, he felt another thing, a curious, swelling pride in this new friendship. He looked into the face of Medoto and smiled, timidly, then broadly. And then he laughed and drew his sword and cut the beaded belt in half.

"No," he said. "If she has chosen, then she must choose again, for we are brothers now and brothers are the same!"

He entwined one half of the severed belt in the arm band of Medoto, and the other half he hung, as plainly, on himself.

"We begin again," he said, "for we are equal to each other, and this is a truth that she must know. She must make her choice on other things but skill in battle, since only men may judge a warrior for his worth!"

It was not far to the *manyatta* and they walked it arm in arm. They were tall together, and strong and young, and somehow full of song. Temas walked brokenly for he was hurt, and yet he sang:

> *Oi-Konyek of the splendid shield*
> *Has heard the lowing of the kine . . .*

And when they entered the gates of the *manyatta*, there were many of every age to welcome Temas, for his lion had been brought and his story told. They cheered and cried his name and led him past the open doors to the peaceful earthen houses to the *singara*,[14] which is the place reserved for warriors.

Medoto did not leave him, nor he Medoto, and it was strange to some to see the enemies transformed and strong in friendship, when yesterday their only bond was hate.

It was strange to one who stood against the *boma* wall, a slender girl of fragile beauty and level, seeking eyes. She was as young as morning, as anticipant. But this anticipation quickly dimmed as she saw the token she had made, one half borne hopefully by Medoto, the other as hopefully carried by Temas!

Both sought her in the gathered crowd, both caught her glance and gave the question with their eyes. Both, in the <u>smug</u>, self-satisfied way of men, swaggered a little.

So the girl paused for an instant and frowned a woman's frown. But then, with musing, lidded eyes, she smiled a woman's smile—and stranger yet, the smile had more of triumph in it, and less of wonder, than it might have had. ❧

---

14. **singara** (siŋ ä′ rə).

Words to Know and Use | **smug** (smug) *adj.* annoyingly self-satisfied

Responding to Reading

First Impressions

1. Do you think this story would make a good movie? Explain.

Second Thoughts

2. What is the most important lesson Temas learns from his test of manhood? Explain your answer.

3. Notice how Temas changes his opinion of Medoto during the story. Are his opinions justified? Give reasons for your answer.

   Think about
   - Medoto's behavior toward Temas
   - how well Temas understands Medoto's attitude toward him
   - Medoto's words and actions after the lion is killed

4. What is Temas's greatest obstacle in this test? Support your answer with information from the story.

5. Medoto says Temas is a braver warrior than he is. Explain why you agree or disagree.

6. What do you think of Kileghen? Explain your opinion.

   Think about
   - her behavior toward Medoto before Temas's test
   - her instructions to Medoto about the belt
   - what the final paragraph reveals about her

Broader Connections

7. Temas seems more afraid of failure in front of his friends than he is of the lion. Is fear of failing in front of peers common among your friends? What effects can such fear have? Explain and give some examples.

Literary Concept: Climax

A story's **climax** is the turning point of the action, the peak of interest and intensity when the outcome of the plot becomes clear. The events or complications building up to the climax are called the **rising action.** The events following the climax bring the story to a close and are called the **falling action.** What moment in this story do you think is the climax? Create a plot diagram indicating events in the rising action, the climax, and the falling action. See Elements of Fiction, page 17, for a plot diagram model.

Concept Review: Characterization What methods does Markham use to describe Temas's character? Provide examples from the story.

*W*riting Options

1. Use a web diagram to describe the Masai. In a circle write "Masai." Draw a number of spokes radiating from the circle. At the end of each spoke, write something you have learned about the Masai from the story.

2. Describe what might have happened if Medoto had not thrown the stone at the lion.

3. Imagine that you are Kileghen. Whom will you choose—Temas or Medoto? Write your thoughts explaining your choice.

4. Medoto tells Temas, "A man asks not the motives of a friend but demands reason from his enemy." Explain the meaning of this Masai saying.

*V*ocabulary Practice

Exercise On your paper, answer the following questions.

1. Would a strong odor be **pungent** or **chaste**?
2. Would a boring movie seem **taut** or **interminable**?
3. Would you prefer a close friend to be **intimate** or **smug**?
4. Would a **marauding** group more likely be surrounded by **vanquished** or happy neighbors?
5. If people say you are conceited, are they accusing you of **vanity** or **contempt**?
6. If you were given an **accolade**, would you be proud or ashamed?
7. If you **breach** a wall, do you go over, around, or through it?
8. Would you feel comfortable standing within the **radius** of a lion's leap? Why or why not?
9. Does a **cleft** in a wall jut out or sink in?
10. Are layers of plastic used to **laminate** or **breach** paper?

Words to Know and Use

accolade
breach
chaste
cleft
contempt
interminable
intimate
laminate
marauding
pungent
radius
smug
taut
vanity
vanquished

Options for Learning

1 • **More About the Masai** Research the Masai, who live in the African nations of Kenya and Tanzania. Use encyclopedias and books about the peoples of East Africa. Also check the *National Geographic Index* and the *Readers' Guide to Periodical Literature.* Focus your research on one aspect of Masai culture, for example, their clothing, their settlements, or how their lives have changed in modern times. Present your information as an oral report. Use photos, pictures, or diagrams to illustrate your talk.

2 • **Be a Storyteller** Create the story that Temas might one day tell his children about the day he proved he was a man by killing a lion. Tell your story from the first-person point of view to a fifth- or sixth-grade class.

3 • **Masai Artist** Do some research to find pictures of Masai jewelry and weapons. Use what you find as a guide for designing and making a model of Masai jewelry or weaponry.

4 • **Lion Behavior** Read about lions and compare the behavior of the lion in this story to typical lion behavior. Is Markham's portrayal accurate? Present a report explaining your findings.

 **FACT FINDER**

How high is Mount Kilimanjaro?

Beryl Markham
1902–1986

Until the early 1980's Beryl Markham was most famous as the first person to fly solo from east to west across the Atlantic Ocean. She made the trip, which took twenty-one hours and twenty-five minutes, in 1936. In 1983 *West With the Night*, her book about the flight, was reissued. It had been largely ignored when first published shortly after World War II. However, changing ideas about women's roles helped make this story popular in the 1980's.

Born in England, Beryl Markham moved with her father to East Africa when she was four. She grew up with native children and watched her father turn a wilderness area into a working farm. As a child in Africa, Markham, like Temas, was attacked by a lion. She remembered "an immense roar that encompassed the world and dissolved [her] in it."

From 1931 to 1936, Markham worked as a pilot, flying mail, passengers, and supplies to remote African areas. After her trans-Atlantic flight, she returned to Africa and trained race horses. In later years, she wrote short stories.

Fiction

Say It with Flowers

TOSHIO MORI (tō shē ō mō rē)

Examine What You Know

If you don't already have a job, you probably will join the work force in the next few years. With your classmates talk about the problems you or people you know encounter with their work, their bosses, or their co-workers. As you read this story, decide whether the problems Teruo (te rōō ō) faces in his job are typical of those faced by employees.

Expand Your Knowledge

Toshio Mori drew his stories from everyday life in the late 1930's and early 1940's in the Japanese-American community where he lived. This story is one of several set in the fictional community of Yokohama, California, which he named after a large seaport in Japan. Like the narrator of this story, Mori worked for much of his life in a plant nursery, that is, a place where young trees, flowers, and other plants are grown.

Enrich Your Reading

Relating Cause and Effect   Often, events in a story cause a change in a character's attitude toward himself or herself, toward another character, or toward life. This change in attitude affects the character's actions. In this story you will find that as Teruo learns more about his job, his feelings about himself and his job change. Create a cause-and-effect chart like the one below to track the way each event affects Teruo's attitude. The first event and its effect have been supplied. Use your chart to predict how Teruo will resolve his conflict.

Cause	Effect
Teruo takes a job in a flower shop.	→ feels happy and motivated

A biography of the author can be found on page 495.

Say It with Flowers

TOSHIO MORI

He was a queer one to come to the shop and ask Mr. Sasaki for a job, but at the time I kept my mouth shut. There was something about this young man's appearance which I could not altogether harmonize with a job as a clerk in a flower shop. I was a delivery boy for Mr. Sasaki then. I had seen clerks come and go, and although they were of various sorts of temperaments and conducts, all of them had the technique of waiting on the customers or acquired one eventually. You could never tell about a new one, however, and to be on the safe side I said nothing and watched our boss readily take on this young man. Anyhow, we were glad to have an extra hand.

Mr. Sasaki undoubtedly remembered last year's rush when Tommy, Mr. Sasaki and I had to do everything and had our hands tied behind our backs for having so many things to do at one time. He wanted to be ready this time. "Another clerk and we'll be all set for any kind of business," he used to tell us. When Teruo came around looking for a job, he got it, and Morning Glory Flower Shop was all set for the year as far as our boss was concerned.

When Teruo reported for work the fol-lowing morning, Mr. Sasaki left him in Tommy's hands. Tommy was our number one clerk for a long time.

"Tommy, teach him all you can," Mr. Sasaki said. "Teruo's going to be with us from now on."

"Sure," Tommy said.

"Tommy's a good florist. You watch and listen to him," the boss told the young man.

"All right, Mr. Sasaki," the young man said. He turned to us and said, "My name is Teruo." We shook hands.

We got to know one another pretty well after that. He was a quiet fellow with very little words for anybody, but his smile disarmed a person. We soon learned that he knew nothing about the florist business. He could identify a rose when he saw one, and gardenias and carnations too; but other flowers and materials were new to him.

"You fellows teach me something about this business, and I'll be grateful. I want to start from the bottom," Teruo said.

Tommy and I nodded. We were pretty sure by then he was all right. Tommy ea-gerly went about showing Teruo the florist game. Every morning for several days Tommy repeated the prices of the flowers for him. He told Teruo what to do on telephone orders, how to keep the greens fresh, how to make bouquets, corsages, and sprays.[1] "You need a little more time to learn how to make big funeral pieces," Tommy said. "That'll come later."

In a couple of weeks, Teruo was just as good a clerk as we had had in a long time. He was curious almost to a fault and was a glutton for work. It was about this time our boss decided to move ahead his yearly business trip to Seattle. Undoubtedly he was satisfied with Teruo, and he knew we could get along without him for a while. He went off and left Tommy in full charge.

During Mr. Sasaki's absence I was often in the shop helping Tommy and Teruo with the customers and the orders. One day when Teruo learned that I once had worked in the nursery and had experience in flower growing, he became inquisitive.

"How do you tell when a flower is fresh or old?" he asked me. "I can't tell one from the other. All I do is follow your instructions and sell the ones you tell me to sell first, but I can't tell one from the other."

I laughed, "You don't need to know that, Teruo," I told him. "When the customers ask you whether the flowers are fresh, say yes firmly. 'Our flowers are always fresh, madam.' "

Teruo picked up a vase of carnations. "These flowers came in four or five days ago, didn't they?"

"You're right. Five days ago," I said.

"How long will they keep if a customer bought them today?" Teruo asked.

"I guess in this weather they'll hold a day or two," I said.

"Then they're old," Teruo almost gasped. "Why, we have fresh ones that last a week or so in the shop."

"Sure, Teruo. And why should you worry about that?" Tommy said. "You talk right to the customers, and they'll believe you. 'Our flowers are always fresh? You bet they are! Just came in a little while ago from the market.' "

Teruo looked at us calmly. "That's a hard thing to say when you know it isn't true."

"You've got to get it over with sooner or later," I told him. "Everybody has to do it. You too, unless you want to lose your job."

"You got to play the game when you're in it."

"I don't think I can say it convincingly again," Teruo said. "I must've said yes forty times already when I didn't know any better. It'll be harder next time."

"You've said it forty times already, so why can't you say yes forty million times more? What's the difference? Remember, Teruo, it's your business to live," Tommy said.

"I don't like it," Teruo said.

"Do we like it? Do you think we're any different from you?" Tommy asked Teruo. "You're just a green kid. You don't know any better, so I don't get sore, but you got to play the game when you're in it. You understand, don't you?"

Teruo nodded. For a moment he stood

1. **sprays:** small branches or plant sprigs covered with leaves, berries, or flowers.

Words to Know and Use | **inquisitive** (in kwiz′ ə tiv) *adj.* tending to ask many questions; eager to learn; curious

487

and looked curiously at us for the first time and then went away to water the potted plants.

In the ensuing weeks we watched Teruo develop into a slick sales clerk, but for one thing. If a customer forgot to ask about the condition of the flowers, Teruo did splendidly. But if someone should mention about the freshness of the flowers, he wilted right in front of the customer's eyes. Sometimes he would sputter. On other occasions he would stand gaping speechless, without a comeback. Sometimes, looking embarrassedly at us, he would take the customer to the fresh flowers in the rear and complete the sale.

"Don't do that any more, Teruo," Tommy warned him one afternoon after watching him repeatedly sell the fresh ones. "You know we got plenty of the old stuff in the front. We can't throw all that stuff away. First thing you know the boss'll start losing money, and we'll all be thrown out."

"I wish I could sell like you," Teruo said. "Whenever they ask me, 'Is this fresh? How long will it keep?' I lose all sense about sell-

GREENHOUSE BULBS ©1986 Peggy Flora Zalucha Collection of the artist.

488

ing the stuff and begin to think of the difference between the fresh and the old stuff. Then the trouble begins."

"Remember, the boss has to run the shop so he can keep it going," Tommy told him. "When he returns next week, you better not let him see you touch the fresh flowers in the rear."

On the day Mr. Sasaki came back to the shop, we saw something unusual. For the first time I watched Teruo sell old stuff to a customer. I heard the man plainly ask him if the flowers would keep good, and very clearly I heard Teruo reply, "Yes, sir. These flowers'll keep good." I looked at Tommy, and he winked back. When Teruo came back to make it into a bouquet, he looked as if he had just discovered a snail in his mouth. Mr. Sasaki came back to the rear and watched him make the bouquet. When Teruo went up front to complete the sale, Mr. Sasaki looked at Tommy and nodded approvingly.

When I went out to the truck to make my last delivery for the day, Teruo followed me. "Gee, I feel rotten," he said to me. "Those flowers I sold won't last longer than tomorrow. I feel lousy. I'm lousy. The people'll get to know my word pretty soon."

"Forget it," I said. "Quit worrying. What's the matter with you?"

"I'm lousy," he said, and went back to the store.

Then one early morning the inevitable happened. While Teruo was selling the fresh flowers in the back to a customer, Mr. Sasaki came in quietly and watched the <u>transaction</u>. The boss didn't say anything at the time. All day Teruo looked sick. He didn't know whether to explain to the boss or shut up.

While Teruo was out to lunch, Mr. Sasaki called us aside. "How long has this been going on?" he asked us. He was pretty sore.

"He's been doing it off and on. We told him to quit it," Tommy said. "He says he feels rotten selling the old flowers."

"Old flowers!" snorted Mr. Sasaki. "I'll tell him plenty when he comes back. Old flowers! Maybe you can call them old at the wholesale market, but they're not old in a flower shop."

"He feels guilty fooling the customers," Tommy explained.

The boss laughed impatiently. "That's no reason for a businessman."

When Teruo came back, he knew what was up. He looked at us for a moment and then went about cleaning the stems of the old flowers.

"Teruo," Mr. Sasaki called.

Teruo approached us as if steeled for an attack.

"You've been selling fresh flowers and leaving the old ones go to waste. I can't afford that, Teruo," Mr. Sasaki said. "Why don't you do as you're told? We all sell the flowers in the front. I tell you they're not old in a flower shop. Why can't you sell them?"

"I don't like it, Mr. Sasaki," Teruo said. "When the people ask me if they're fresh, I hate to answer. I feel rotten after selling the old ones."

"Look here, Teruo," Mr. Sasaki said. "I don't want to fire you. You're a good boy, and I know you need a job, but you've got to be a good clerk here or you're going out. Do you get me?"

"I get you," Teruo said.

In the morning we were all at the shop early. I had an eight o'clock delivery, and the others had to rush with a big funeral order. Teruo was there early. "Hello," he greeted us cheerfully as we came in. He was unusually high-spirited, and I couldn't account for it. He was there before us and had already filled out the eight o'clock package for me.

He was almost through with the funeral frame, padding it with wet moss and covering it all over with brake fern, when Tommy came in. When Mr. Sasaki arrived, Teruo waved his hand and cheerfully went about gathering the flowers for the funeral piece. As he flitted here and there, he seemed as if he had forgotten our presence, even the boss. He looked at each vase, sized up the flowers, and then cocked his head at the next one. He did this with great deliberation, as if he were the boss and the last word in the shop. That was all right, but when a customer soon after came in, he swiftly attended him as if he owned all the flowers in the world. When the man asked Teruo if he was getting fresh flowers, without batting an eye he escorted the customer into the rear and eventually showed and sold the fresh ones. He did it with so much grace, dignity and swiftness that we stood around like his stooges.[2] However, Mr. Sasaki went on with his work as if nothing had happened.

Along toward noon Teruo attended his second customer. He fairly ran to greet an old lady who wanted a cheap bouquet around fifty cents for a dinner table. This time he not only went back to the rear for the fresh ones but added three or four extras. To make it more irritating for the boss, who was watching every move, Teruo used an extra lot of maidenhair[3] because the old lady was appreciative of his art of making bouquets. Tommy and I watched the boss fuming inside of his office.

When the old lady went out of the shop, Mr. Sasaki was furious. "You're a blockhead. You have no business sense. What are you doing here?" he said to Teruo. "Are you crazy?"

Teruo looked cheerful enough. "I'm not crazy, Mr. Sasaki," he said. "And I'm not dumb. I just like to do it that way, that's all."

The boss turned to Tommy and me. "That boy's a sap,"[4] he said. "He's got no head."

Teruo laughed and walked off to the front with a broom. Mr. Sasaki shook his head. "What's the matter with him? I can't understand him," he said.

While the boss was out to lunch, Teruo went on a mad spree. He waited on three customers at one time, ignoring our presence. It was amazing how he did it. He hurriedly took one customer's order and had him write a birthday greeting for it, jumped to the second customer's side and persuaded her to buy roses because they were the freshest of the lot. She wanted them delivered, so he jotted the address down on the sales book and leaped to the third customer.

"I want to buy that orchid in the window," she stated without deliberation.

---

2. **stooges:** assistants to comedians who act as straight men or victims to pranks.

3. **maidenhair:** a fern with delicate fronds, used to provide fullness in bouquets.

4. **sap:** slang for a fool or stupid person.

Words to Know and Use | **deliberation** (di lib′ ər ā′ shən) *n.* the quality of being careful, unhurried, and methodical
spree (sprē) *n.* a period of unrestrained activity

"Do you have to have orchid, madam?"

"No," she said. "But I want something nice for tonight's ball, and I think the orchid will match my dress. Why do you ask?"

"If I were you, I wouldn't buy that orchid," he told her. "It won't keep. I could sell it to you and make a profit, but I don't want to do that and spoil your evening. Come to the back, madam, and I'll show you some of the nicest gardenias in the market today. We call them Belmont, and they're fresh today."

> ## "If he was the boss, he couldn't do those things."

He came to the rear with the lady. We watched him pick out three of the biggest gardenias and make them into a corsage. When the lady went out with her package, a little boy about eleven years old came in and wanted a twenty-five-cent bouquet for his mother's birthday. Teruo waited on the boy. He was out in the front, and we saw him pick out a dozen of the two-dollar-a-dozen roses and give them to the kid.

Tommy nudged me. "If he was the boss, he couldn't do those things," he said.

"In the first place," I said, "I don't think he could be a boss."

"What do you think?" Tommy said. "Is he crazy? Is he trying to get himself fired?"

"I don't know," I said.

When Mr. Sasaki returned, Teruo was waiting on another customer, a young lady.

"Did Teruo eat yet?" Mr. Sasaki asked Tommy.

"No, he won't go. He says he's not hungry today," Tommy said.

PEOPLE'S FLOWERS   1971   Richard Estes
Thyssen-Bornemisza Collection, Lugano, Switzerland.

We watched Teruo talking to the young lady. The boss shook his head. Then it came. Teruo came back to the rear and picked out a dozen of the very fresh white roses and took them out to the lady.

"Aren't they lovely!" we heard her exclaim.

We watched him come back, take down a box, place several maidenhairs and asparagus,[5] place the roses neatly inside, sprinkle a few drops, and then give it to her. We watched him thank her, and we noticed her smile and thanks. The girl walked out.

Mr. Sasaki ran excitedly to the front. "Teruo! She forgot to pay!"

Teruo stopped the boss on the way out. "Wait, Mr. Sasaki," he said. "I gave it to her."

"What!" the boss cried indignantly.

"She came in just to look around and see the flowers. She likes pretty roses. Don't you think she's wonderful?"

"What's the matter with you?" the boss said. "Are you crazy? What did she buy?"

"Nothing, I tell you," Teruo said. "I gave it to her because she admired it, and she's pretty enough to deserve beautiful things, and I liked her."

"You're fired! Get out!" Mr. Sasaki spluttered. "Don't come back to the store again."

"And I gave her fresh ones too," Teruo said.

Mr. Sasaki rolled out several bills from his pocketbook. "Here's your wages for this week. Now get out," he said.

"I don't want it," Teruo said. "You keep it and buy some more flowers."

"Here, take it. Get out," Mr. Sasaki said.

Teruo took the bills and rang up the cash register. "All right, I'll go now. I feel fine. I'm happy. Thanks to you." He waved his hand to Mr. Sasaki. "No hard feelings."

On the way out Teruo remembered our presence. He looked back. "Goodbye. Good luck," he said cheerfully to Tommy and me.

He walked out of the shop with his shoulders straight, head high, and whistling. He did not come back to see us again. ❧

---

5. **asparagus:** a plant with fine, fernlike leaves, used to provide fullness in bouquets.

INSIGHT

Identity

JULIO NOBOA POLANCO

Let them be as flowers,
always watered, fed, guarded, admired,
but harnessed to a pot of dirt.

I'd rather be a tall, ugly weed,
clinging on cliffs, like an eagle
wind-wavering above high, jagged rocks.

To have broken through the surface of
stone, to live, to feel exposed to the
madness of the vast, eternal sky.
To be swayed by the breezes of an
ancient sea, carrying my soul, my seed,
beyond the mountains of time or into
the abyss of the bizarre.

I'd rather be unseen, and if then
shunned by everyone, than to be a
pleasant-smelling flower, growing in
clusters in the fertile valley, where
they're praised, handled, and plucked
by greedy, human hands.

I'd rather smell of musty, green stench
than of sweet, fragrant lilac.
If I could stand alone, strong and free,
I'd rather be a tall, ugly weed.

Responding to Reading

First Impressions

1. Would you hire Teruo to work for you? In your journal or on a sheet of paper, explain your answer.

Second Thoughts

2. Why was it so difficult for Teruo to follow Mr. Sasaki's directions for selling flowers?

3. Do you agree with the way Teruo resolves the conflict he experiences in his job?

    Think about
    - the steps he takes to deal with his problems
    - his timing
    - another way he might have solved the problem

4. Did you expect that Teruo would be fired, and that he would be happy about it? Why or why not?

5. The narrator says that he does not think Teruo could be a boss. Do you agree or disagree? Why?

6. In your opinion will Teruo's actions cause Mr. Sasaki or any of his employees to adjust their approach to business? Explain.

Broader Connections

7. Mr. Sasaki lies to his customers but justifies his actions by saying that if he did not sell the old flowers, he would go out of business. Do you think that business people today must be slightly dishonest in order to succeed? Give reasons to support your opinion.

Literary Concept: Point of View

You probably noticed right away that this story is written from a first-person point of view. The narrator expresses his opinions and feelings about the characters and events. What do you learn about the narrator's values from this story? In what ways does his interpretation of events influence your reaction to the story?

Concept Review: Climax The climax of a story is the point at which the conflict is resolved. Examine the cause and effect chart you made. At what point does Teruo act as if he's made his decision? Is that the climax? Support your opinion with evidence from the story.

Writing Options

1. Explain why Teruo would or would not agree with the speaker in "Identity." Which other characters you have read about might agree with the speaker? Give reasons for your answers.

2. This subunit is entitled "Making Adjustments." Write about a time when you had to adjust to accommodate another person's way of thinking or acting. Explain how successful you were at changing your ways.

3. Teruo has definite ideas about the business world. Considering his approach to business and ethics, in what occupations might Teruo find success? List them.

4. Imagine that one of Teruo's customers returns to the flower shop either to complain about flowers that did not last or to praise Teruo for his salesmanship. Write the conversation that might occur between the customer and Mr. Sasaki.

Vocabulary Practice

Exercise On your paper, write the word from the list that best completes each sentence.

1. Teruo could not _____ his ideas with those of his boss.
2. His quiet yet friendly behavior hinted at his mild _____.
3. With his cheerful smile, Teruo could _____ even the most unhappy customer.
4. Teruo's _____ nature caused him to ask many questions about the flower business.
5. The boys told Teruo to respond with a _____ when a customer asked about the freshness of the flowers.
6. Teruo acted with _____ when he carefully chose and arranged flowers on his last day of work.
7. When Teruo began his selling _____, he moved like a whirlwind through the shop.
8. The other clerks began to _____ at Teruo as he waited on three customers at once.
9. In one _____, Teruo discouraged a woman from buying orchids and sold her fresh gardenias instead.
10. In the _____ weeks after his firing, how do you think Teruo will feel?

*Words
to Know
and Use*

**comeback
deliberation
disarm
ensuing
gape
harmonize
inquisitive
spree
temperament
transaction**

e x t e n d

Options for Learning

1 • **Business Ethics** Ask a local businessperson to discuss this story with you. Either summarize the story or have the person read it. Report to your classmates the merchant's reactions to both Teruo's and Mr. Sasaki's behavior.

2 • **Get the Inside Story** Interview a local florist about the business of selling flowers. Ask questions such as: What skills or background do you need to enter this business? How do you choose which flowers to sell?

3 • **Welcome!** Predict what business Teruo might run ten years from now. What might Teruo say to new employees on their first day? How might he explain his approach to business? What helpful hints might he give to motivate and train his employees? Present Teruo's speech for new employees.

4 • **Better Business** The Better Business Bureau exists nationwide to promote ethical business practices and to aid consumers in their complaints against businesses. Contact the Better Business Bureau office in your community to find out what procedures you should follow to file a complaint.

 **FACT FINDER**

How much do one dozen long-stemmed white roses cost in your community?

Toshio Mori
1910-1980

Toshio Mori was born and raised in California. In his youth he considered becoming a professional baseball player or entering the ministry, but at the age of twenty-two, he decided instead to write. To achieve this goal, he worked diligently in his family's nursery all day and concentrated on writing at night.

During World War II he was sent to live at the Topaz, Utah, Relocation Center, one of the ten camps in which Japanese Americans were detained after Japan's attack on Pearl Harbor in 1941. There Mori worked as a historian for the documentation division of the camp and helped create a camp magazine called *Trek*.

Eventually, Mori became the first Japanese American to have a collection of short stories published in the United States. "Say It with Flowers" comes from that collection. Mori's works have also appeared in magazines and anthologies. He wrote one novel, *Woman from Hiroshima*, for which he won the Jane Addams Peace Association and Women's International League for Peace and Freedom Honor Award in 1981.

Besides being a nurseryman and writer, Mori lectured both at high schools and at universities. He especially enjoyed teaching senior citizens.

W RITER'S
WORKSHOP

PERSUASION

Persuasive writing is used to influence the opinions of others. A writer who uses persuasion starts out with a strong opinion about an important issue that is controversial. The writer presents his or her opinion and then uses reasons and facts to convince others to agree with that opinion. Sometimes the writer urges readers to take action.

All of the selections in this subunit deal with making an adjustment of some kind. Several of the characters struggle with the problems of adjusting to new cultures and customs. For this assignment you will be asked to persuade others to agree with your opinion on the issue of how foreigners should adapt to American culture. You will respond to the following editorial.

Adapting to America

If America is to be "one nation under God," then its citizens must unite under one cultural banner. Although we must never lose sight of America's rich variety of ethnic groups, it's time to cast aside differences in color, language, and heritage in order to create a single American culture. We must not cater to the values, tastes, and languages of the many foreigners who move to our country. Instead, we must insist on a national language and a national culture. If immigrants choose to settle in our country, then they must also choose to adopt our cultural values and our language, which is an expression of those values. It is not our duty, nor is it in our national interest, to adjust our standards to satisfy all ethnic groups; for if we bend our standards to meet the needs of each nationality, then we weaken the national fabric that holds us together.

> Here is your **PASSkey to** this assignment.

GUIDED ASSIGNMENT: LETTER TO THE EDITOR

Write a letter to the editor of a newspaper in response to the editorial, "Adapting to America." In the letter, persuade readers to adopt your opinion on the issue of how foreigners should adapt to American culture.

P URPOSE: To persuade opinion

A UDIENCE: The newspaper and its readers

S UBJECT: Adapting to American culture

S TRUCTURE: Formal letter

Prewriting

STEP 1 **Take a side**   Read the editorial carefully and be sure you understand the opinion it expresses. Think about the issue. Then decide whether you agree or disagree.

STEP 2 **State your opinion**   Write your opinion in a sentence that clearly reflects your position. Here's how one student stated his opinion on a similar issue. In this case, he was responding to an editorial that claimed that foreign language study should not be required in high school.

> Opinion: High school students should be required to study a foreign language.

◀ STUDENT MODEL

STEP 3 **Consider your audience**   When writing to persuade, think about your readers. Before you prepare your arguments, ask yourself the following questions.

1. How much do most of your readers know about the issue? Will you need to provide background information for them?
2. Are your readers likely to have a strong opinion for or against your position already, or are they neutral?
3. What kind of evidence will appeal to your readers?

STEP 4 **Brainstorm supporting evidence**   To persuade your readers, you will have to provide strong reasons and/or facts that support or elaborate on your opinion. Since it is unlikely that you will be able to find statistics on this particular topic, you will probably draw your evidence from your own experience and observations. Brainstorm the reasons that you might use to support your opinion. Be careful not to include any statements you cannot support. List everything you think of now; later you can edit your list.

The student who formed his opinion on foreign language study in high school came up with this list when he brainstormed supporting evidence:

1. It's good to know a foreign language.
2. Studying another language helps with English.
3. Knowing a foreign language is helpful for travel.
4. We can understand other cultures better.
5. Speaking a foreign language makes us sound smarter.
6. All other major industrial countries require foreign language study.

◀ STUDENT MODEL

7. By not speaking another language, Americans isolate themselves from the world.
8. In the field of international business, speaking a foreign language is a big asset.
9. To compete economically with other countries, we should speak their language.
10. Many foreigners know our language, but we don't know theirs.
11. Students may not be able to fit a foreign language class into their schedules.

STEP 5 **Select the best reasons** Next, you need to evaluate and edit your initial list of supporting evidence. Eliminate any statement that doesn't support your opinion, that is too vague to be persuasive, that repeats a previous statement, or that will not appeal to your audience. The student who compiled the list above discovered that he could eliminate statements 1 and 5 because they were too vague, 11 because it didn't support his opinion, and 8 because 9 repeated it but said it better. Statement 2 was a good reason but would not have appealed to his audience.

STEP 6 **Organize your evidence** In order to present your ideas logically and effectively, group together related ideas. For example, statements 6, 7, and 10 in the list above can be grouped because all of them relate to Americans' knowledge versus the knowledge of people of other countries. Then decide which are your most effective arguments and how you will order them. The student above decided that statement 9 was his strongest argument, and he chose to begin with it.

Drafting

STEP 1 **Introduce the issue and your position** Begin your letter by referring to the editorial to which you are responding. You might briefly mention the opinion expressed in the editorial and then proceed to express your own position on the issue, as in this example:

STUDENT MODEL ▶

To the Editor:

In a recent editorial you claimed that foreign language study in high school took valuable time away from other subjects. Although language study may replace other subjects, I think that all high school students should be required to study a foreign language.

STEP 2 **Persuade with reasons**   In the body of your letter, support your opinion by presenting the evidence you have selected. You may choose to start with your strongest reasons. Elaborate on each reason, explaining its implications or providing examples.

STEP 3 **Conclude with strength**   To complete your draft of the letter, add a closing statement that summarizes your position and reinforces its importance.

Revising and Editing

Review the draft you composed. Use the following checklist to help you evaluate and revise your work. Then write your letter in the modified block form as shown in Correct Business Letter Form in the **Writer's Handbook.**

Revision Checklist
....

1. Do you respond to the issue addressed in the editorial?
2. Is your position stated clearly?
3. Have you provided sufficient and persuasive support for your position?
4. Have you organized supporting evidence logically and effectively?
5. Have you elaborated sufficiently on the evidence you provide?

Editing   When you have finished revising your draft, proofread it for spelling, clarity, and mechanics.

Presenting

Pair up with a classmate who took the opposite point of view. Read your letters to each other and see if either can persuade the other to change his or her opinion.

Reflecting on Your Writing

Attach the answers to the following questions to your letter and put it in your writing portfolio.

1. What have you learned about persuasion from this assignment?
2. Were you able to keep your audience in mind as you wrote?

LANGUAGE WORKSHOP

ADDING PHRASES

One way to combine sentences is to take a descriptive phrase from one sentence and, without changing its form, simply add it to another sentence. When you use this method, place the phrase as near as possible to the person, thing, or action it describes. Notice that in the second set of examples, three sentences were combined.

> The clerks were hard-working. *The clerks were* in the shop.
> The clerks **in the shop** were hard-working.

> The fresh flowers were hidden. *They were* in refrigerated cases. *The cases were* near the back of the shop.
> The fresh flowers were hidden **in refrigerated cases near the back of the shop.**

Often you can add a phrase from one sentence that simply renames something in another sentence. A group of words that renames a noun is called an **appositive phrase.** Set off an appositive phrase with commas.

> Mr. Sasaki hired a new clerk. *Mr. Sasaki was* the shop owner.
> Mr. Sasaki, **the shop owner,** hired a new clerk.

> Teruo quickly learned what to do. *Teruo was* the new clerk.
> Teruo, **the new clerk,** quickly learned what to do.

Sometimes you have to change the form of one of the words you insert by adding *-ly, -ing,* or *-ed.* Look at these examples.

> The corsage had daisies. *They* surround some roses.
> The corsage had daisies **surrounding** some roses.
> The customers loved the roses. *The roses had a* peach color.
> The customers loved the **peach-colored** roses.

Exercise 1 Combine the following sentences by eliminating the words in italics. Hints for combining are provided in parentheses.

1. Temas was sixteen. *Temas was* the boy in the story. (Use a pair of commas.)
2. When a boy is sixteen, he must prove his manhood. *This is true* in the Masai tribe. (Move the phrase near the person it describes.)

3. To succeed, the boy must kill a lion. *The boy must kill the lion* with a spear. *This action must be* brave. (Use *-ly.*)

4. For the test Temas wore pendants. *The pendants were* in his ears. *The pendants* gleamed. (Use *-ing.*)

5. Medoto seemed to laugh at him. *Medoto was* Temas's enemy. (Use a pair of commas.)

Exercise 2   Work in groups to rewrite the following passage, using combining techniques to join some of the shorter sentences. Be sure that the revised sentences are correctly punctuated.

Balancing two cultures is never easy. It is not easy in one household. It's like walking a tightrope. The tightrope goes across a deep chasm. I know. My mother's family came here when she was six years old. They came from a tiny village in Greece. For years she's told me about her early life. She struggled to become a "real" American. But last summer I finally understood what she went through. I understood in Greece.

I spent the summer with my great-aunt. I spent it in Thira. Thira is my mother's home village. I loved the narrow streets. They have cobblestones. I loved the tiny, white houses. They cling precariously to the mountainside. The mountainside is steep.

In that village I would always be a stranger. I would always be a stranger from a totally different world. For example, a teenage girl in the village never talked to unrelated young men. She never talked to them except in the company of a chaperone. And she never wore blue jeans!

Yes, I loved the world my mother left behind. But I could never be a part of that world. My mother made that long journey for me.

Exercise 3   Analyzing and Revising Your Writing

1. Review one of your earlier writing assignments, looking for related sentences that might be combined.

2. Rewrite one or two paragraphs, using phrases to combine some related sentences.

3. Compare your revised sentences to the original ones. Which sentences do you prefer? The next time you revise your writing, remember to check for related sentences that you might combine.

LANGUAGE HANDBOOK
....
For review and practice:
appositives,
   pages 965–66

LIFE SKILLS
WORKSHOP

FORMS AND APPLICATIONS

What do these have in common: applying for a job, applying to college, applying for a driver's license? The answer is simple—forms! Sometimes it seems as if we're all drowning in a sea of forms and applications. Use the following guidelines to help you complete this task more efficiently.

1. **Read all directions.** Skim the entire form before you write anything and gather all the information you need—your social security number, your parents' birthdates, the names and addresses of all your previous employers, and so forth.

2. **Be neat.** Use a good pen with blue or black ink and your best handwriting or printing. When you are filling out a form at home, use a typewriter if possible. Do not use a pencil unless you are specifically told to do so.

3. **Fill out the form line by line.** Read the directions for each line before you fill it in. Sometimes there is very little space for the information, so plan ahead. If you make a mistake, carefully draw a line through the error and write the correction above the line.

4. **Be prepared to answer some basic questions.** For example, on an employment form you will often be asked for names of two or three references—people who know you well and would be willing to confirm your abilities. Teachers, coaches, or employers with whom you have a good relationship make good references. Be sure to get their permission, their complete addresses and daytime telephone numbers.

5. **Complete every line if you can.** If you find an item that does not apply to you, write, "Does not apply" in that space. When you are finished, check the entire form carefully for accuracy, spelling, and completeness.

Exercise   As a homework assignment, find a blank form and bring it to class. Look for a form that requires extensive information such as an application for credit, an employment application, or a bank form. Exchange forms with a partner and fill out your partner's form. Then, discuss any problems you encountered. Report your findings to the class.

LESSONS LEARNED

Many of life's most important lessons are not learned in a classroom. Experience—trying, failing, trying again, and finally succeeding—can be the greatest teacher of all. As you read each of the following selections, decide what valuable lessons the characters learned and think about how they were learned.

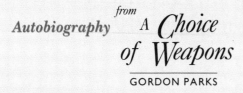

e x p l o r e

Autobiography *from* A *Choice* of *Weapons*

GORDON PARKS

*E*xamine What You Know

You have probably heard the old saying "A picture is worth a thousand words." What does this mean to you? Describe a photograph that sticks in your mind. Why is it so memorable? Why is it worth a thousand words?

*E*xpand Your Knowledge

Gordon Parks, an African American with a number of talents, first won fame as a photographer. He got his start in 1942 in the photography department of the Farm Security Administration (FSA) in Washington, D.C. In this excerpt from his autobiography, *A Choice of Weapons,* Parks has just arrived in Washington. He feels quite excited about seeing the city, beginning his job with the FSA, and meeting his boss, Roy Stryker.

To understand the time period portrayed in this article, you need to look back thirteen years from 1942. On October 29, 1929, the stock market crashed and millions of Americans lost their money and jobs as a severe economic depression spread. When Franklin D. Roosevelt became President in 1933, he proposed a series of programs to help end the Depression. He called these programs the New Deal. Under the New Deal, Roosevelt created the FSA, which offered poor farmers low-interest, long-term loans and set up migrant worker camps and medical associations in poor communities. In addition, the FSA sent out photographers to document the lives of poor farmers and other Depression-era Americans.

*W*rite Before You Read

In this selection, someone teaches Parks a crucial lesson about photography. This teacher uses an interesting method, however. He sends Parks out into the world to learn by experience. In your journal or on a sheet of paper, write about a lesson you have learned through experience.

■ *A biography of the author can be found on page 514.*

from
A Choice of Weapons

GORDON PARKS

A tall blond girl who said her name was Charlotte came forward and greeted me. "Mr. Stryker will be with you in a minute," she said. She had just gotten the words out when he bounced out and extended his hand. "Welcome to Washington. I'm Roy," were his first words. "Come into the office and let's get acquainted." I will like this man, I thought.

He motioned me to a chair opposite his desk, but before he could say anything his telephone rang. "It's Arthur Rothstein phoning from Montana," Charlotte called from the outer office. The name flashed my thoughts back to the night on the dining car when I first saw it beneath the picture of the farmer and his two sons running toward their shack through the dust storm.

"Arthur? This is Roy."

I'm here, I thought; at last I'm here.

As he talked, I observed the chubby face topped with a mane of white hair, the blinking piercingly curious eyes, enlarged under thick bifocal lenses. There was something boyish, something fatherly, something tyrannical, something kind and good about him. He did not seem like anyone I had ever known before.

They talked for about ten minutes. "That was Rothstein," Stryker said, hanging up. "He had bad luck with one of his cameras." The way he said this pulled me in as if I were already accepted, as if I had been there for years. The indoctrination had begun. "Now tell me about yourself and your plans," he said with a trace of playfulness in his voice. I spent a lot of time telling him perhaps more than he bargained for. After I had finished, he asked me bluntly, "What do you know about Washington?"

"Nothing much," I admitted.

"Did you bring your cameras with you?"

"Yes, they're right here in this bag." I took out my battered Speed Graphic and a Rolleiflex and proudly placed them on his desk.

He looked at them approvingly and then asked me for the bag I had taken them from. He then took all my equipment and locked it in a closet behind him. "You won't be needing those for a few days," he said flatly. He lit a cigarette and leaned back in his chair and continued, "I have some very specific things I would like you to do this week. And I would like you to follow my instructions faithfully. Walk around the city. Get to know it. Buy yourself a few

---

*Words
to Know
and Use* | **indoctrination** (in dak′ trə nā′ sнən) *n.* instruction in a set of beliefs

505

things—you have money, I suppose."

"Yes, sir."

"Go to a picture show, the department stores, eat in the restaurants and drugstores. Get to know this place." I thought his orders were a bit <u>trivial</u>, but they were easy enough to follow. "Let me know how you've made out in a couple of days," he said after he had walked me to the door.

"I will," I promised casually. And he smiled oddly as I left.

I walked toward the business section and stopped at a drugstore for breakfast. When I sat down at the counter, the white waiter looked at me as though I were crazy. "Get off of that stool," he said angrily. "Don't you know colored[1] people can't eat in here? Go round to the back door if you want something." Everyone in the place was staring at me now. I retreated, too stunned to answer him as I walked out the door.

I found an open hot dog stand. Maybe this place would serve me. I approached the counter <u>warily</u>. "Two hot dogs, please."

"To take out?" the boy in the white uniform snapped.

"Yes, to take out," I snapped back. And I walked down the street, gulping down the sandwiches.

I went to a theater.

"What do you want?"

"A ticket."

"Colored people can't go in here. You should know that."

I remained silent, observing the ticket seller with more surprise than anything else. She looked at me as though I were insane. What is this, I wondered. Was Stryker playing some sort of joke on me? Was this all planned to <u>exasperate</u> me? Such discrimination here in Washington, D.C., the nation's capital? It was hard to believe.

Everyone in the place was staring at me now.

Strangely, I hadn't lost my temper. The experience was turning into a weird game, and I would play it out—follow Roy's instructions to the hilt.[2] I would try a department store now; and I chose the most imposing one in sight, Julius Garfinckel.[3] Its name had confronted me many times in full-page advertisements in fashion magazines. Its owners must have been filled with national pride—their ads were always identified with some sacred Washington monument. Julius Garfinckel. Julius Rosenwald. I lumped them with the names of Harvey Goldstein and Peter Pollack[4]—Jews who had helped shift the course of my life. I pulled myself together and entered the big store, with nothing particular in mind. The men's hats were on my right, so I <u>arbitrarily</u> chose that department. The salesman appeared a little on edge, but he sold me a hat. Then leaving I saw an advertisement for camel's-hair coats on an upper floor. I had

---

1. **colored:** at the time of the story, a term commonly used to refer to African Americans.

2. **to the hilt:** thoroughly; entirely.

3. **Julius Garfinckel:** an expensive department store in Washington, D.C., owned by a rich businessman who donated money to worthy causes.

4. **Julius Rosenwald, Harvey Goldstein, Peter Pollack:** wealthy men who provided grants and/or other help to Parks and others in the arts.

Words to Know and Use

trivial (triv′ ē əl) *adj.* unimportant; insignificant
warily (wer′ ə lē) *adv.* cautiously; guardedly
exasperate (eg zas′ pər āt) *v.* to irritate or annoy greatly
arbitrarily (är′ bə trer′ ə lē) *adv.* based on one's own judgment, choice, or whim

wanted one since the early days at the Minnesota Club[5]. It was possible now. The elevator operator's face brought back memories of the doorman at the Park Central Hotel on that first desperate morning in New York.

"Can I help you?" His question was shadowed with arrogance.

"Yes. Men's coats, please." He hesitated for a moment, then closed the door, and we went up.

The game had temporarily ended on the first floor as far as I was concerned. The purchase of the hat had relieved my doubts about discrimination here; the coat was the goal now. The floor was bare of customers. Only four salesmen stood eying me as I stepped from the elevator. None of them offered assistance, so I looked at them and asked to be shown a camel's-hair coat.

No one moved. "They're to your left," someone volunteered.

I walked to my left. There were the coats I wanted, several racks of them. But no one attempted to show them to me.

"Could I get some help here?" I asked.

One man sauntered over. "What can I do for you?"

"I asked you for a camel's-hair coat."

"Those aren't your size."

"Then where are my size?"

"Probably around to your right."

"Probably around to my right?" The game was on again. "Then show them to me."

"That's not my department."

"Then whose department is it?"

"Come to think of it, I'm sure we don't have your size in stock."

"But you don't even know my size."

"I'm sorry. We just don't have your size."

"Well, I'll just wait here until you get one my size." Anger was at last beginning to take over. There was a white couch in the middle of the floor. I walked over and sprawled out leisurely on it, took a newspaper from my pocket and pretended to read. My blackness stretched across the white couch commanded attention. The manager arrived, posthaste[6], a generous smile upon his face. My ruse had succeeded, I thought.

"I'm the manager of this department. What can I do for you?"

"Oh, am I to have the honor of being waited on by the manager? How nice," I said, smiling with equal graciousness.

"Well, you see, there's a war on. And we're very short of help. General Marshall was in here yesterday and *he* had to wait for a salesman. Now please understand that—"

"But I'm not General Marshall, and there's no one here but four salesmen, you and me. But I'll wait here until they're not so busy. I'll wait right here." He sat down in a chair beside me and we talked for a half hour—about weather, war, food, Washington, and even camel's-hair coats. But I was never shown one. Finally, after he ran out of conversation, he left. I continued to sit there under the gaze of the four puzzled salesmen and the few customers who came to the floor. At last the comfort of the couch made me sleepy; and by now the whole thing had become ridiculous. I wouldn't have accepted a coat if they had given me the entire rack. Suddenly I thought of my camera, of Stryker. I got up and hurried out of the store and to his office. He was out to lunch

---

5. **Minnesota Club:** a private men's club in St. Paul, Minnesota, where Parks once worked as a bellboy.

6. **posthaste:** with great speed or rapidity.

when I got back. But I waited outside his door until he returned.

"I didn't expect you back so soon," he said. "I thought you'd be out seeing the town for a couple of days."

"I've seen enough of it in one morning," I replied sullenly. "I want my cameras."

"What do you intend to do with them?"

"I want to show the rest of the world what your great city of Washington, D.C., is really like, I want—"

"Okay. Okay." The hint of that smile was on his face again. And now I was beginning to understand it. "Come into my office and tell me all about it," he said. He listened patiently. He was sympathetic; but he didn't return my equipment.

"You'll have to prove yourself to them."

"Young man," he finally began, "you're going to face some very hard facts down here. Whatever else it may be, this is a Southern city. Whether you ignore it or tolerate it is up to you. I purposely sent you out this morning so that you can see just what you're up against." He paused for a minute to let this sink in. Then he continued. "You're going to find all kinds of people in Washington, and a good cross-section of the types are right here in this building. You'll have to prove yourself to them, especially the lab people. They are damned good technicians—but they are all Southerners. I can't predict what their attitudes will be toward you, and I warn you I'm not going to try to influence them one way or the other.

It's completely up to you. I do think they will respect good craftsmanship. Once you get over that hurdle, I honestly believe you will be accepted as another photographer—not just as a Negro[7] photographer. There is a certain amount of resentment against even the white photographers until they prove themselves. Remember, these people slave in hot darkrooms while they think about the photographers enjoying all the glamor and getting all the glory. Most of them would like to be on the other end."

We were walking about the building now, and as he introduced me to different people, his words took on meaning. Some smiled and extended their hands in welcome. Others, especially those in the laboratory, kept working and acknowledged me with cold nods, making their <u>disdain</u> obvious. Any triumph over them would have to be well earned, I told myself. Stryker closed the door when we were back in his office. "Go home," he advised, "and put it on paper."

"Put what on paper?" I asked puzzled.

"Your plan for fighting these things you say you just went through. Think it out constructively. It won't be easy. You can't take a picture of a white salesman, waiter or ticket seller and just say they are prejudiced. That isn't enough. You've got to <u>verbalize</u> the experience first, then find logical ways to express it in pictures. The right words too are important; they should <u>underscore</u> your photographs. Think in terms of images and words. They can be mighty powerful when they are fitted together properly."

I went home that evening and wrote. I

---

7. **Negro:** another term commonly used to refer to African Americans at the time of this story.

*Words
to Know
and Use*

disdain (dis dān') *n.* contempt or scorn
verbalize (vur' bəl īz') *v.* to put into words; express
underscore (un' dər skôr') *v.* to emphasize or stress

The Arthur Rothstein photograph of the farmer and his two sons described on page 505
The Bettmann Archive, New York.

wrote of just about every injustice that I had ever experienced. Kansas, Minnesota, Chicago, New York and Washington were all forged together in the heat of the blast.

Images and words images and words images and words—I fell asleep trying to arrange an acceptable marriage of them.

Stryker read what I had written with a troubled face. I watched his eyes move over the lines, his brows furrow from time to time. When he had finished, we both sat quietly for a few minutes. "You've had quite a time," he finally said, "but you have to simplify all this material. It would take many years and all the photographers on the staff to fulfill what you have put down here. Come outside; I want to show you something." He took me over to the file and opened a drawer marked "Dorothea Lange." "Spend the rest of the day going through this set of pictures. Each day take on another drawer. And go back and write more specifically about your visual approach to things."

For several weeks I went through hundreds of photographs by Lange, Russell Lee, Jack Delano, Carl Mydans, John Vachon, Arthur Rothstein, Ben Shahn, Walker Evans, John Collier and others. The disaster of the thirties was at my fingertips: the gutted cotton fields, the eroded farmland, the crumbling South, the unending lines of dispossessed migrants, the pitiful shacks, the shameful city ghettos, the breadlines and bonus marchers[8], the gaunt faces of men, women and children caught up in the tragedy; the horrifying spectacles of sky blackened with locusts, and swirling dust, and towns flooded with muddy rivers[9]. There were some, no doubt, who laid these tragedies to God. But research accompanying these stark photographs accused man himself—especially the lords of the land. In their greed and passion for wealth, they had gutted the earth for cotton; overworked the farms; exploited the tenant farmers and sharecroppers[10] who, broken, took to the highways with their families in search of work. They owned the ghettos as well as the impoverished souls who inhabited them. No, the indictment was against man, not God; the proof was there in those ordinary

---

8. **breadlines and bonus marchers:** Starving men and women waited in long lines for bread and soup from charities. Twenty thousand bonus marchers, veterans of World War I, camped in Washington, D.C., in 1932 demanding advance payment of a war bonus due them in 1945.

9. **horrifying spectacles . . . rivers:** In the mid-1930's, farmers of Oklahoma, Texas, New Mexico, Colorado, and Texas saw natural disasters such as locusts, dust storms, and floods devastate their land.

10. **sharecropper:** a farmer who grows crops on rented land for a share of the crops.

Words to Know and Use

gutted (gut' 'd) *adj.* ruined; destroyed
stark (stark) *adj.* bleak; desolate

509

AMERICAN GOTHIC 1930 Grant Wood The Art Institute of Chicago Friends of American Art Collection.

"AMERICAN GOTHIC," WASHINGTON, D.C., 1942 Gordon Parks By permission of Gordon Parks, New York.

steel files. It was a raw slice of contemporary America—clear, hideous and beautifully detailed in images and words. I began to get the point. . . .

Using my camera effectively against <u>intolerance</u> was not so easy as I had assumed it would be. One evening, when Stryker and I were in the office alone, I confessed this to him. "Then at least you have learned the most important lesson," he said. He thought for a moment, got up and looked down the corridor, then called me to his side. There was a Negro charwoman[11] mopping the floor. "Go have a talk with her before you go home this evening. See what she has to say about life and things. You might find her interesting."

This was a strange suggestion, but after he had gone I went through the empty building searching for her. I found her in a notary public's[12] office and introduced myself. She was a tall, <u>spindly</u> woman with sharp features. Her <u>hair</u> was swept back from graying temples; a sharp intelligence shone in the eyes behind the steel-rimmed glasses. We started off awkwardly, neither of us knowing my reason for starting the conversation. At first it was a meaningless exchange of words. Then, as if a dam had broken within her, she began to spill out her life story. It was a pitiful one. She had struggled alone after her mother had died and her father had been killed by a lynch mob. She had gone through high school, married

---

11. **charwoman:** a cleaning woman for an office building.

12. **notary public:** an official authorized to certify documents.

Words to Know and Use

intolerance (in täl′ ər əns) *n.* a lack of respect for the opinions or beliefs of others
spindly (spind′ lē) *adj.* tall and very thin, often looking frail or weak

and become pregnant. Her husband was accidentally shot to death two days before the daughter was born. By the time the daughter was eighteen, she had given birth to two illegitimate children, dying two weeks after the second child's birth. What's more, the first child had been stricken with paralysis a year before its mother died. Now this woman was bringing up these grandchildren on a salary hardly suitable for one person.

"Who takes care of them while you are at work?" I asked after a long silence.

"Different neighbors," she said, her heavily veined hands tightening about the mop handle.

"Can I photograph you?" The question had come out of an elaboration of thoughts. I was escaping the humiliation of not being able to help.

"I don't mind," she said.

My first photograph of her was unsubtle. I overdid it and posed her, Grant Wood style, before the American flag, a broom in one hand, a mop in the other, staring straight into the camera. Stryker took one look at it the next day and fell speechless.

"Well, how do you like it?" I asked eagerly.

He just smiled and shook his head. "Well?" I insisted.

"Keep working with her. Let's see what happens," he finally replied. I followed her for nearly a month—into her home, her church and wherever she went. "You're learning," Stryker admitted when I laid the photographs out before him late one evening. "You're showing you can involve yourself in other people. This woman has done you a great service. I hope you understand this." I did understand. ❧

INSIGHT

The Artist

ISABELLE C. CHANG

There was once a king who loved the graceful curves of the rooster. He asked the court artist to paint a picture of a rooster for him. For one year he waited, and still this order was not fulfilled. In a rage, he stomped into the artist's studio and demanded to see the artist.

Quickly the artist brought out paper, paint, and brush. In five minutes a perfect picture of a rooster emerged from his skillful brush. The king turned purple with anger, saying, "If you can paint a perfect picture of a rooster in five minutes, why did you keep me waiting for over a year?"

"Come with me," begged the artist. He led the king to his storage room. Paper was piled from the floor to the ceiling. On every sheet was a painting of a rooster.

"Your Majesty," explained the artist, "it took me more than one year to learn how to paint a perfect rooster in five minutes."

Life is short; art is long.

511

*R*esponding to Reading

First Impressions

1. Does this piece make you want to see more of Parks's photography? Why or why not?

Second Thoughts

2. What lesson does Gordon Parks learn from Stryker? How important is that lesson? Explain your answer.

> **Think about**
> - Parks's experiences in the store and restaurant
> - his reaction to other photographers' pictures
> - his encounter with the charwoman
> - his goal

3. How would you rate Stryker as a teacher and Parks as a student? Use information from the selection to support your answer.

4. Study Parks's first photograph of the charwoman on page 510. Why do you think Parks came to consider it "unsubtle"?

5. Why do you think Parks chose the title *A Choice of Weapons* for his autobiography?

6. Read Stryker's comments in the last paragraph about Parks's second attempt to photograph the charwoman. What do you think Stryker means?

Broader Connections

7. Do you think photography can be an effective tool in fighting problems such as injustice, prejudice, homelessness, and poverty? What other methods can be effective?

*L*iterary Concept: Style

Style refers to the way a selection is written—not what is said but how it is said. Every writer has a unique, personal style. A number of elements make up a writer's style. These include description, tone, point of view, use of dialogue, and methods of characterization. What are some important elements of Parks's style? Give examples. What makes his style different from other autobiographies you have read in this book, such as "Fool's Paradise" or "A Measure of Freedom"?

Writing Options

1. Write a story or poem to accompany Parks's photograph of the charwoman. Use facts about her life given in this selection.

2. Use what you learn about Parks in this selection and in his biography on page 514 to compare his personality and life with the personality and life of the charwoman. List the similarities and differences.

3. Explain whether you think Parks would agree or disagree that the fable "The Artist" applies to his early experiences with photography.

4. In the preface of an autobiography, writers often thank people who influenced their lives and helped them with the book. Write an acknowledgment Parks might include in his book thanking Stryker for his help.

Vocabulary Practice

Exercise Choose one item from each of the three columns below. Then write a brief story based on these three items.

Characters	Incidents	Conditions
a judge who makes decisions **arbitrarily**	treating someone with **intolerance**	with great **disdain**
an **exasperated** photographer	behaving **warily** to avoid **humiliation**	in a **gutted** ghost town
a **spindly** police officer	pulling off a clever **ruse**	as part of one's **indoctrination**
a scientist who cannot **verbalize** ideas	writing an **unsubtle** letter to a friend	on a **stark** landscape
	trying to **underscore** someone's foolishness	filled with **trivial** information

> **Words to Know and Use**
>
> **arbitrarily**
> **disdain**
> **exasperate**
> **gutted**
> **humiliation**
> **indoctrination**
> **intolerance**
> **ruse**
> **spindly**
> **stark**
> **trivial**
> **underscore**
> **unsubtle**
> **verbalize**
> **warily**

e x t e n d

Options for Learning

1 • **Create a Photo Exhibit** Make a display of photographs by at least four of the photographers mentioned in this selection. One of the photographers might be Parks. Place a notebook at the end of the display. Invite other students to look at the exhibit and write down their reactions and feelings.

2 • **Be the Photographer** Plan a photo shoot in your own community. Make sure you have a specific purpose in mind. What do you want to accomplish with your photos? Create a display of your finished work and discuss with your classmates the problems, successes, and failures you experienced.

3 • **More About Parks** Gordon Parks has written three autobiographical books: *The Learning Tree, A Choice of Weapons,* and *To Smile in Autumn.* Read one of these autobiographies to learn more about his experiences and accomplishments. Report what you learn to your class.

 **FACT FINDER**

Find out what steps are involved in developing black-and-white film.

Gordon Parks
1912-

Gordon Parks was born in Fort Scott, Kansas, the fifteenth and last child of a poor farm family. As a young man, Parks cleaned floors, played the piano, worked as a busboy, played semipro basketball, and served as a railroad dining car waiter. He became fascinated with magazine photographs by FSA photographers and eventually bought his own camera in a pawnshop. He was soon able to leave the railroad and earn a living by doing fashion photography. As time allowed, Parks pursued more serious photographic goals, eventually winning an award for a series of photos on Chicago slums. This led him to a job at the FSA. From there, he went to the Office of War Information, the Standard Oil Company, and *Life* magazine, where he stayed for twenty years.

Parks finally left *Life* to write, compose the music, and direct a film based on his autobiographical book *The Learning Tree*. He has written novels, four volumes of poetry, essays, and photography books and has directed television documentaries and other movies. He has even composed a symphony and the musical score and lyrics for *Martin,* a ballet tribute to Martin Luther King, Jr.

Fiction

Just Try to Forget

NATHANIEL BENCHLEY

Examine What You Know

"Just Try to Forget" tells of a father's experience while watching his son's swim meet. How do you feel about your parents and others watching you participate in activities such as sports events, concerts, ceremonies, or other events?

Expand Your Knowledge

This story about a boys' swim meet focuses on a two-hundred-yard relay race. Each of four team members swims fifty yards (four lengths of the pool) in this race. A key element in the relay is teamwork. Each swimmer must anticipate how the previous swimmer will finish so that seconds will not be lost between laps. The first swimmer enters the water with the starting gun. The second swimmer's feet may not leave the wall or block until the first swimmer touches the wall, although his or her body can be extended out over the water. The same rule applies to the third and fourth swimmers.

Another important element in the relay is the order in which the swimmers race. Usually, the fastest swimmer races last as the anchor of the team, either to catch up or to hold the team's lead.

Write Before You Read

■ *A biography of the author can be found on page 525.*

Describe the pressures you feel when you compete in sporting events or in other activities, such as trying out for a play, applying for a job, or auditioning for a position in the band.

Just Try to Forget

NATHANIEL BENCHLEY

Arthur Dobson held open the door of the school gymnasium for his wife, then followed her in. The smell of steam heat and liniment and disinfectant was the same as it had been twenty years before, and he could hear the scurrying, pounding feet of basketball players, punctuated by the sharp tweets of the referee's whistle. It never changes, Dobson thought. Every smell and every sound is still the same. He led his wife past the basketball court, then through another door and up a short flight of steps to the gallery above the swimming pool.

The room was of white tile and glass brick, and it was steaming hot and echoed hollowly with a noise of its own. Dobson and his wife sat down behind a railing overlooking the pool, and Dobson took off his topcoat and put it on the seat beside him.

"I'm getting nervous already," his wife said. "Do you think they have a chance?"

"All I know is what Larry said," Dobson replied. "He didn't seem to think so."

"I don't really care, so long as Larry wins his race," she said. "I think he'd die if he didn't win it, with you here, and all."

"He can't win it or not win it," said Dobson. "He's in the two-hundred-yard relay, so there are three others with him."

"I know, but still . . ." His wife took off her coat and peered down at the green, transparent water of the pool. "It looks awfully long, doesn't it?" she said.

Dobson looked at the pool and estimated that he could swim about one length— maybe two, if he took it easy. "Long enough," he said.

Two lanky, muscular figures wearing the bright blue trunks of the rival school walked out of a door at one end of the pool and dived flatly into the water, hitting it with a double crack like pistol shots. Then more boys in blue trunks came out and followed them, until the whole squad was swimming up and down the length of the pool. At the diving board, two boys took turns doing unbelievably complicated dives, and Dobson and his wife watched them with a kind of uneasy respect.

"It looks as though Larry were right," Dobson said after a while. "They look pretty good."

"I know," said his wife. "Much too good."

Then Larry's team, wearing red trunks, appeared and dived into the water and

---

Words to Know and Use | **transparent** (trans per′ ənt) *adj.* able to be seen through; clear

swam up and down the pool. At first, Dobson had trouble recognizing his son among the twisting, thrashing bodies. The boys all swam alike, with long, powerful strokes, and they made insane-looking, bottoms-up turns at either end of the pool, and Dobson thought back on the summer, many years ago, when he had had some difficulty teaching Larry to swim. As long as Dobson held him, he would splash and paddle gleefully, but the minute Dobson took his hands away he would become panic-stricken and sink. It wasn't until children younger than he had begun to swim that Larry, without any help from his father, took his first strokes. He's certainly improved since then, Dobson thought. I had no idea he could swim this well. Even last summer, he wasn't swimming like this. Then Dobson looked at the others, in the blue trunks, and they seemed to be swimming just a little better. I guess it always looks that way, he thought. The other guys always look frighteningly good, even if they aren't. But this time they *are* better—there's no getting around it.

When the warm-up was over, the two teams retired, and the officials began arranging their lists and checking their watches. It was the final meet of the season, the letter meet, and the gallery was full of spectators, both students and adults. From below came the sounds of more spectators, who were standing or sitting along the edge of the pool beneath the gallery, and the whole place hummed and echoed and rang with noise. Dobson removed his jacket, put it next to his topcoat, and loosened his tie. He fought down an urge to light a cigarette and locked his hands together in his lap. His wife reached across and clutched them briefly, and her hand was cold and wet. He smiled at her. "It's no good worrying now," he said. "Larry's race isn't until the very last."

There was a patter of applause as the rival team, wearing blue sweat suits, filed out and took places on benches set in three rows at the shallow end of the pool. A moment later, the air was shattered with cheers and whistles as Larry's team, in red sweat suits, came out and sat beside them. Presently, two boys from each team peeled off their sweat suits and dived into the pool, then pulled themselves out, shook hands all around, and waited, nervously flapping their arms and wrists. Dobson looked at his son, who was sitting on the back row of benches, staring straight ahead of him and chewing a thumbnail. I wish I hadn't come, Dobson thought. I wish I'd made up some excuse to stay at home. He remembered a time when he was young and his father had come to watch him play football, and he had spent the entire, miserable game on the bench. Parents should stay away from athletic contests, he told himself. They ought to be barred by law. Larry continued to chew his thumbnail, and Dobson felt sick.

A manager with a megaphone announced the first event, which was the fifty-yard freestyle race, and gave the names of the contestants. The starter pointed a blank pistol upward and told the boys to take their marks. There was complete silence as they stood in a row at the edge of the pool, gripping the rim with their toes. The starter said, "Get set," and the boys crouched, their hands on a level with their feet. There was a pause. The pistol banged, and after what seemed to Dobson like an unnaturally long wait, the boys shot forward, cracked into the water, and churned off down the pool.

The crowd shouted and called and cheered and chanted, and the noise swelled to a roar as the swimmers reached the far end of the pool, made their frantic, ducking turns, and headed back for the finish line. They were almost indistinguishable in the boiling spray, but the two in the farthest lane, the ones in the blue trunks, pulled steadily ahead in the final yards, and finished first and second. Dobson settled back in his seat.

"That makes the score eight to one already," he said to his wife. "This is going to be murder."

It seemed to him that Larry was getting smaller and paler.

But Larry's team placed first and third in the next event, and first and second in the one after that, and somehow, unbelievably, they managed to gain a slight lead. It was never a big enough lead to be safe, and at one point the score was tied, and Dobson saw and pitied the agony of the one boy in each event who failed to score. Some drooped forlornly in the gutter, some cried, and some had to be helped from the pool by consoling teammates, who said futile things to them and patted them on the bottom while they dragged themselves to the benches. As the final event came closer, Dobson looked more often at his son, and it seemed to him that Larry was getting smaller and paler with each race. I wish to God he'd swum first, Dobson thought. I wish it was all over, so he wouldn't have to wait like this. Even if he'd lost, I wish it was all over.

The diving took a long time, with each of the four contestants doing six dives, and the next-to-last event was the medley relay[1]

race, which Larry's team won, putting them ahead 37–30. When the score was announced, Dobson's wife gave a little shout and grabbed him. "We've won!" she cried. "They can't possibly catch us now!"

"It looks that way," Dobson replied with a certain amount of relief. "It certainly looks that way."

A student behind him touched his arm. "No, sir," he said. "They can still tie us. The last race counts seven points, and there's no score for second."

"Oh!" said Dobson. "Damn!" he added, half to himself.

He saw Larry and his three teammates strip off their sweat suits, jump into the water, then climb out, shake hands, and stand around fluttering their hands and breathing deeply. The boys from the other school did the same, and they looked big and unnaturally husky. They didn't seem as nervous as the boys on Larry's team. The noise from the crowd was such that the manager had to shout three times for quiet before he could announce the event, and when Larry was announced as swimming third in the relay, Dobson had an odd feeling at the sound of the name. His wife slid her hand into his. "I don't think I'm going to be able to watch," she said. "You tell me what happens."

The first two swimmers took their marks, and a tense silence hung until the crack of the gun. Then, as the swimmers leaped out at the water, the spectators came to their feet and shouted and cheered and stamped, and the noise grew and swelled until Dobson couldn't hear his own voice.

The swimmers thrashed down the pool

1. **medley relay:** a relay in which each leg of the race is swum in a different stroke.

Words to Know and Use

indistinguishable (in′ di stiŋ′ gwish ə bəl) *adj.* unable to be separated visually or recognized
forlornly (fôr lôrn′ lē) *adv.* hopelessly, miserably
consoling (kən sōl′ iŋ) *adj.* comforting **console** *v.*

518

and then back, and the one in red trunks was slightly ahead as they touched the starting line and two more swimmers sprang out. Dobson didn't watch the second boys; all he saw was Larry, who had moved up to the starting line, breathing in deep gulps, his eyes fixed glassily ahead of him. An official squatted beside Larry's feet, and Larry crouched lower and lower as his teammate in the pool approached him. The red-trunked boy was leading by about two yards when he reached the edge, and it seemed to Dobson that Larry was in the air and in the water at almost the same instant. Then Dobson's throat closed and he couldn't make a sound, but beside him his wife was screaming and pounding the rail, her voice all but lost in the growing pandemonium.[2]

Larry finished his lap three or four yards ahead, but as the two last swimmers raced down and turned, the one in blue trunks began to gain. He closed the gap slowly, and the members of both teams crowded

---

2. **pandemonium** (pan′ də mō′ nē əm)**:** wild and noisy disorder; confusion.

OLYMPIC BACKSTROKE SWIMMING TRIAL   1977   Joe Wilder, M.D.   Private Collection.

around the finish line, jumping and beckoning and bellowing, and then the red-trunked boy put on a final, <u>frenzied</u> spurt and held his lead to the finish line. Larry and his teammates spilled into the water, hugging one another and falling down and shouting, and the blue-trunked boy clung to the gutter, exhausted and miserable.

Dobson sat back and looked at his wife. "Wow!" he said. And she laughed.

Down below, members of both teams clustered around the officials, and then, suddenly, the ones in blue leaped into the air and shouted, and Dobson saw a boy in red trunks hit the water with his fist. There was some commotion and a lot of noise from the crowd, and Dobson was unable to hear distinctly what the manager said through the megaphone, but he caught the words "Thirty-seven to thirty-seven."

Unbelieving, he turned to a student in the crowd. "What happened?" Dobson asked. "I couldn't hear."

"We were disqualified," the student answered sourly. "Dobson jumped the gun."

For almost a full minute, neither Dobson nor his wife said anything. Then he put on his coat and helped her on with hers, and as they walked slowly down the stairs she took his arm. "What are we going to say to him?" she asked in a small voice. "What *can* we say?"

"I wish I knew," he replied. "I wish to God I knew."

They went out to the car and stood beside it smoking while they waited for Larry. Dobson's mind was a jumble of things he wanted to say, but even as he thought of them, they seemed inadequate, and he knew that none of them would do any good. He thought of going in and seeing Larry in the locker room, and then quickly decided against it. I guess it's best to wait out here, he thought. He'll come out when he wants to.

After what seemed like an hour, Larry came out of the gym and walked slowly toward them. His hair was wet and slicked back, and his eyes were red—possibly from the chlorine in the pool, Dobson thought, knowing that wasn't the reason. Without a word, Larry opened a door of the car and dropped into the back seat. Dobson got in front, and, after a moment's hesitation, his wife got in back with Larry.

"Do you want to drive around for a while?" Dobson asked as he started the engine.

"Whatever you say," Larry replied. "I don't care."

They drove through the streets of the town and then out into the bleak, snow-spotted country. For several minutes nobody spoke, and then Dobson cleared his throat. "Would you like me to tell you something?" he asked.

"Sure," said Larry, without enthusiasm.

"When I was in school, I wanted to play baseball," Dobson said. "More than anything else, I wanted to make the baseball team. The only trouble was I wasn't good enough. I got in a couple of games as a pinch-hitter, and once they let me play right field, but I dropped the only fly that came my way, and they yanked me out." He looked into the rear-view mirror and saw the incredulous expression on his wife's face. He continued, "The last game in my senior year—the letter game—we were behind four to three in the ninth inning. We had a man on third, and the coach sent me in to

Words to Know and Use | **frenzied** (fren′ zēd) *adj.* with a wild outburst of feeling or action; frantic

bunt down toward first. On the first ball pitched, I tried to bunt, and the ball hit my right thumb and broke it. Technically, I was eligible for a letter, but I never collected it. I couldn't look at any of the team again."

"*I* couldn't look at any of the team again."

Larry laughed shortly. "I never heard about that," he said.

"I didn't tell many people," Dobson replied, with another look into the rear-view mirror. "But what I'm getting at is that these things are horrible when they happen—you think you'll never live them down—but sooner or later it gets so you can bear to think of them again. It may take a long while, but eventually it happens."

Larry was quiet for a minute. "I guess I was just trying too hard," he said, at last.

"I know," Dobson replied. "And I promise you, next year we won't come up here to watch."

Larry looked at his father in the mirror. "OK," he said, and smiled. 🍃

I N S I G H T

Every Good Boy Does Fine

DAVID WAGONER

I practiced my cornet in a cold garage
Where I could blast it till the oil in drums
Boomed back; tossed free throws till I couldn't move my thumbs;
Sprinted through tires, tackling a headless dummy.

In my first contest, playing a wobbly solo,
I blew up in the coda, alone on stage,
And twisting like my hand-tied necktie, saw the judge
Letting my silence dwindle down his scale.

At my first basketball game, gangling away from home
A hundred miles by bus to a dressing room,
Under the showering voice of the coach, I stood in a towel,
Having forgotten shoes, socks, uniform.

In my first football game, the first play under the lights
I intercepted a pass. For seventy yards, I ran
Through music and squeals, surging, lifting my cleats,
Only to be brought down by the safety man.

I took my second chances with less care, but in dreams
I saw the bald judge slumped in the front row,
The coach and team at the doorway, the safety man
Galloping loud at my heels. They watch me now.

You who have always horned your way through passages,
Sat safe on the bench while some came naked to court,
Slipped out of arms to win in the long run,
Consider this poem a failure, sprawling flat on a page.

Responding to Reading

First Impressions

1. Do you sympathize with any character in this story? Explain.

Second Thoughts

2. Are Mr. and Mrs. Dobson typical parents? Give reasons for your answer.

3. Do you think Mr. Dobson acts appropriately after the meet? Is there anything else he should have said or done? Explain your answer.

4. Does the relationship between Larry and his father change during this story?

> **Think about**
> • Mrs. Dobson's comment that Larry would die if he didn't win with his father at the meet
> • why Mr. Dobson comes to the meet
> • what happens after the meet

5. Does any character learn a lesson from this meet? If so, what is the lesson and who learns it?

6. Mr. Dobson says that "parents should stay away from athletic contests." Do you agree or disagree? Explain.

Broader Connections

7. How important is winning to you? What do you do when you lose? In your opinion, how should someone handle losing?

Literary Concept: Falling Action and Resolution

You know that the action of the plot builds to a climax, or turning point. The **falling action** is what takes place after the climax. Although the greatest suspense is over, the reader wants to know how it all ends. The falling action blends with the **resolution,** or the part that ties up all the loose ends of the plot and closes the story. Identify the climax of "Just Try to Forget." Then summarize the events of the falling action and the resolution. Is the resolution effective in bringing the story to a close? Explain your answer.

Concept Review: Descriptive Details   Descriptive details make the swim meet lively and interesting. List precise adjectives, adverbs, nouns, action verbs, and colorful phrases that accomplish this.

Writing Options

1. What do you think the speaker in the poem "Every Good Boy Does Fine" might say to Larry after the swim meet? Use ideas from the poem and the story to support your opinions.

2. Write a motto that either Larry or the speaker in "Every Good Boy Does Fine" might find useful.

3. List the emotions you think Larry or his father experiences at different times during the meet or make a line graph showing these emotional changes as highs or lows of feeling.

4. Write a "how to" memo to parents explaining how they should behave at their children's sports events, plays, and concerts.

Vocabulary Practice

Exercise On your paper, write the word from the list that is most clearly related to the situation described in each item below.

1. The spectator stands filled rapidly for the meet. John could not find his parents in the mob, but he knew they were there.
2. The members of the defeated team left the pool area with heads down and tears in their eyes.
3. The visiting team arrived just ten minutes before starting time. Frantically they changed into their swimsuits.
4. The water was as clear as glass.
5. Instead of criticizing the swimmers for the loss, the coach tried to lift their spirits.

Words to Know and Use

consoling
forlornly
frenzied
indistinguishable
transparent

Options for Learning

1 • **Ask the Athletes** Design and pass out a questionnaire asking athletes in your school how they cope with losing a game or meet. Collect the questionnaires, summarize the results, and share them with your class. Your findings might make an interesting article for your school newspaper.

2 • **The Next Day** With other students, improvise a skit to dramatize a meeting between the coach and Larry's team the day after the meet. Perform the skit for your class.

3 • **Pantomiming Parents** Do a pantomime of parents watching the meet in this story. You might perform a series of scenes, each one portraying the behavior of a different parent. Stage the show for your class.

4 • **Tell Your Story** Tell a sports story of your own to the class. Recall and tell a story from gym class, a school team, Little League, or a neighborhood or family pickup game. The focus of your story may be the players, spectators, or referees.

 **FACT FINDER**

How many meters long is a two-hundred-yard race?

Nathaniel Benchley
1915-1981

When he graduated from Harvard University, Nathaniel Benchley said it seemed the only thing he could do was write. Since his father, Robert Benchley, was a famous humorist, Nathaniel Benchley tried to make his own mark with a different kind of writing than his father's: low-key humor combined with melodrama, satire, and a happy ending. After working briefly at *The New York Herald Tribune* and *Newsweek* and serving in the navy during World War II, he began a thirty-five-year career writing novels, biographies, short stories, books for children and young adults, essays, plays and screenplays. His most famous novel, *The Off-Islanders,* was filmed in 1966 as the comedy *The Russians Are Coming! The Russians Are Coming!*

Benchley said he began writing children's books with fantastical plots and young adult historical fiction in the 1960's because of his personal battle with television. "I want to get young people in the habit of reading instead of staring at the tube."

Fiction

Beauty Is Truth

ANNA GUEST

Examine What You Know

As you might have guessed from the title, the concept of beauty is an important element in this story. What images, thoughts, feelings, and words does the word *beauty* bring to your mind? Use a diagram like the one below to organize your ideas.

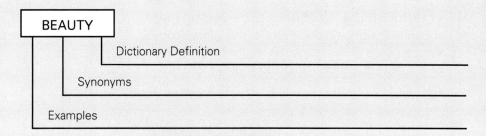

Expand Your Knowledge

The main character in "Beauty Is Truth" wonders how her teacher can be "so stirred up" by a poem written about a Greek urn, or vase. The poem, "Ode on a Grecian Urn," was written in 1819 by John Keats, one of England's most famous Romantic poets. It describes the picture that appears on a Grecian urn—a forest scene in which young men and women chase each other and enjoy themselves while a piper plays nearby. In the poem the speaker compares the never-changing beauty and joyfulness of the scene to the short-lived but real beauty that occurs in everyday life. The speaker ends by expressing Keats own philosophy:

> "Beauty is truth, truth beauty,—that is all
> Ye know on earth, and all ye need to know."

Write Before You Read

What is beautiful in your life? Would *beautiful* describe a relationship, a place, or something else in your life? Describe this beauty in your journal or on a sheet of paper. Use vivid and precise details to make your ideas clear.

Beauty Is Truth

ANNA GUEST

At 125th Street, they all got off, Jeanie and her friend Barbara and a crowd of other boys and girls who went to the same downtown high school. Through the train window, Jeanie thought she saw the remaining passengers look at them with relief and disdain. Around her, the boys and girls pressed forward with noisy gaiety. They were all friends now. They were home again in Harlem.

A tall boy detached himself from a group, bowed low and swept his cap before him in a courtly salute.

"Greetings, Lady Jeanie. Greetings, Barbara."

Jeanie bit her lip. Frowning, she pulled her coat closer and shrugged. Barbara smiled and dimpled, pleased for her friend.

"I told you he likes you," she whispered. "Look, he's waiting. Want me to go on ahead?"

Jeanie really was wasting an opportunity. Norman was keen. She saw Jeanie's head, slightly bowed and thrust forward. It was no use. She was an odd girl, but Barbara liked her anyway. The boy swung gracefully back to his group.

"Coming to the show tonight?" Barbara asked.

"No, I can't. I'm so far behind in my homework, I'd better try to do some before they decide to throw me out." Jeanie still frowned.

"Want a Coke or something?" asked Barbara as they passed the big ice-cream parlor window, cluttered with candy boxes and ornate with curly lettering. They could see the jukebox near the door and some boys and girls sitting down at a table. It looked warm and friendly.

Jeanie shook her head, one brief shake.

"I think I'll stop in. I'm awful thirsty," said Barbara.

Jeanie shrugged.

"So long, then."

"So long."

She walked along the busy street, aimlessly looking in the store windows, turned the corner, and walked the few blocks to her house. Though it was chilly, each brownstone or gray stoop had its cluster of people clinging to the iron railings. Some children on skates played a desperate game of hockey with sticks that were not hockey sticks. When a car approached, they did not interrupt their game until it was almost too late. Amid shouts from the driver and wild jeers from the children, the car passed, and the game was resumed in all its concentrated intensity.

Her little brother Billy was playing in front of the stoop[1] with three or four other kids. They were bending over something on the sidewalk, in a closed circle. Pitching pennies again, she thought with repugnance. She was going to pass them and started up the three stone steps to the doorway. A window on the ground floor opened, and Fat Mary leaned out, dressed only in a slip and a worn, brown sweater.

"Now you're going to catch it, Billy Boy. Your sister's going to tell your mama you been pitching pennies again."

Jeanie did not pause.

Billy sprang up. "Hi, Jeanie. Jeanie, gimme a nickel. I need a nickel. A nickel, a nickel. I gotta have a nickel."

The other little boys took up the chant. "A nickel, a nickel. Billy needs a nickel."

She threw them a furious glance and went in. Two little girls sat on the second landing, playing house. They had a set of toy dishes spread out on the top stair and held dolls in their laps. She stepped over them, careful not to disturb their arrangements.

The kitchen smelled dank and unused, and the opening of the door dislodged a flake of green-painted plaster. It fell into the sink, with a dry powdering. A black dress someone had given her mother lay over the chair before the sewing machine. It reminded her that her sleeve had torn half out, dressing after gym. She really should sew it, but the sight of the black dress waiting to be made over made her dislike the thought of sewing. She would just have to wear her coat in school tomorrow. Lots of kids did. She did not like her shape anyway, so big and chesty.

She hung her coat on a hook in the room she shared with her mother and stood irresolute. Her mother would be coming in soon and would expect to find the potatoes peeled and the table laid. She caught sight of a comic book and, unwillingly attracted by the garish colors, read one side. "Ah!" she thought in disgust. "Billy!" She thought of her homework. She was so far behind in social studies that she could probably never make it up. It was hardly worth trying. Mercantilism. The rise of the merchant class. She would probably fail. And gym, all those cuts in gym. Miss Fisher, her grade advisor, had called her down yesterday and warned her. "Ah!" she said again. Miss Fisher was all right. She had even been encouraging. "I know you can do it," she had said.

She sat down on the bed and opened her loose-leaf notebook at random. A page fell out. She was about to jam it back in, when the freshly inked writing caught her eye. Today's English. Some poem about a vase and youths and maidens. Miss Lowy had brought in some pictures of vases with people on them, dressed in togas or whatever they were, spinning and reading from scrolls. Why did everybody get so excited about the Greeks? It was so long ago. "Wonderful! Wonderful!" Miss Lowy had exclaimed. How could anybody get so stirred up over a poem? She meant it too. You could tell from her expression.

"Listen, boys and girls. Listen." A lifted arm enjoined them.

"Beauty is truth, truth beauty,—that is all
Ye know on earth, and all ye need to know."

---

1. **stoop:** a small platform with steps at the door of a house or apartment building.

Words to Know and Use

jeer (jir) *n.* a rude, ridiculing remark or comment; taunt
intensity (in ten′ sə tē) *n.* a high degree of emotion or action
repugnance (ri pug′ nəns) *n.* extreme dislike or distaste
garish (gar′ ish) *adj.* overly bright; flashy; gaudy

MARBLE PLAYERS 1938 Allan Rohan Crite The Boston Athenaeum, Massachusetts.

There it was, copied into her notebook. Caught by something in the lines, she tried to find the poem in her tattered anthology, not bothering about the index but riffling the pages to and fro. John Keats, at last—*On First Looking into Chapman's Homer*. More Greeks. Here it was—*Ode on a Grecian Urn*. The poem, all squeezed together in the middle of the page, looked dry and dusty, withered and far away, at the bottom of a dry well. She saw, not so much words, as an uninteresting, meandering pattern. The big *THOU* at the opening repelled her. She turned the page to find that the poem went on. Recognizing the last lines, she heard them again, falling so roundly, so perfectly, from the lips of Miss Lowy. She turned back to the beginning. Why "Grecian," why not "Greek"? With an effort, she began to dig the poem out of its constricted print.

"Thou foster child of silence and slow times," its soft susurrus[2] carried her on. She read the poem through to the end, trying to remember her teacher's cadences.[3]

2. **susurrus** (sə sʉr′ əs): a whispering, murmuring sound.

3. **cadences** (kād′ 'ns əs): inflections or variations in stress or pitch when speaking.

Words to Know and Use | **anthology** (an thäl′ ə jē) *n.* a collection of literary works compiled in one book

"Write about beauty and truth. Write about life," Miss Lowy had said.

She tore a page out of her notebook and opened her pen. Pulling over a chair, she rested her book on the sooty windowsill. She stared out at the dusk falling sadly, sadly, thickening into darkness over the coal yards.

A crash of the kitchen door caused a reverberation in the windowsill. The notebook slipped out of her hands.

"Where'd you get that bottle of pop?" she heard her mother's voice, hard and sounding more Southern than usual.

A high-pitched, wordless sniveling came in reply.

"I asked you. Where'd you get that pop? You better tell me."

"A lady gave me a nickel. A lady came down the street and ask me—"

"You lying. I know where you got that money. Gambling, that's what you was doing."

"I was only pitching pennies, Ma. It's only a game, Ma."

"Gambling and stealing and associating with bad friends. I told you to stay away from them boys. Didn't I? Didn't I?" Her mother's voice rose. "I'm going to give you a beating you ain't going to forget."

Billy wailed on a long descending note.

Jeanie could hear each impact of the strap and her mother's heavy breathing.

"I want you to grow up good, not lying and gambling and stealing," her mother gasped, "and I'm going to make you good. You ain't never going to forget this." When it had been going on forever, it stopped. A final slap of the strap. "And you ain't going to get any supper either. You can go now.

You can go to bed and reflect on what I told you."

He stumbled past her, whimpering, fists grinding into eyes, and into the dark little <u>alcove</u> which was his room. Jeanie heard the groan of the bed as he threw himself on it. She felt a pain in her fingers and saw them still pressed tightly around the pen.

Her mother appeared in the doorway. She wore her hat and coat.

"Come help me get supper, Jeanie. You should have got things started." Her voice was tired and <u>tremulous</u> and held no <u>reproach</u>.

"I don't want any supper, Ma."

Her mother came in and sat down heavily on the bed, taking off her hat and letting her coat fall open.

"I had a hard day. I worked hard every minute," she said. "I brought you something extra nice for dessert. I stood on line to get some of them tarts from Sutter's."

Jeanie rose and silently put her mother's hat on the shelf. She held out her hand for her mother's coat and hung it up.

Together they opened the paper bags on the kitchen table. She set the water to boil.

As they ate in silence, the three tarts shone like subtle jewels on a plate at one end of the chipped porcelain table. Her mother looked tired and stern.

"You better fix your brother up a plate," she said, still stern. "Put it on a tray. Here, take this." And she put on the tray the most luscious, the most perfect of the tarts. "Wait." She went heavily over to her swollen black handbag, took out a small clasp purse, opened it, and carefully, seriously, deliberately, picked out a coin, rejected it, and took out another. "Give him this." It was a quarter.

Words to Know and Use

alcove (al′ kōv′) *n.* a small section of a room that is set back from the main part; nook
tremulous (trem′ yoo ləs) *adj.* quivering; shaking
reproach (ri prōch′) *n.* blame; rebuke

After the dishes were washed, Jeanie brought her books into the kitchen and spread them out under the glaring overhead light. Billy had been asleep, huddled in his clothes. Tears had left dusty streaks on his face.

Her mother sat in the armchair, ripping out the sides of the black dress. Her spectacles made her look strange. *"Beauty is truth,"* Jeanie read in her notebook. Hastily, carelessly, defiantly disregarding margins and doubtful spellings, letting her pen dig into the paper, she began to write: "Last night my brother Billy got a terrible beating. . . ."

Scramble to borrow the social studies homework from a girl in her homeroom, say hello to Barbara, undress for gym, dress again, the torn sleeve, bookkeeping—a blot, get another piece of ledger paper. "This is the third I've given you. You might say thank you." Get to English early. Slip her composition in under the others, sit in the last seat. Don't bother me. I am in a bad mood. Rows and rows of seats. Rows and rows of windows opposite. She could even read the writing on some of the blackboards, but who cared? A boy leaned far out of the window before closing it. Other heads turning. Would he fall? No, he was safe. Heads turned back. A poem about a skylark.[4] From where she sat, she could see about a square foot of sky, drained of all color by the looming school walls. Miss Lowy read clearly, standing all alone at the front of the room in her clean white blouse and with her smooth blond hair.

Miss Lowy, maybe you see skylarks. Me, I'd be glad to see some sky, she thought and nearly uttered it. Around her, students were writing in their notebooks. Miss Lowy was about to speak to her. Better start writing something. Sullen, Mr. MacIver had called her last week. She felt about for her notebook and pen. It had been a mistake to write as she had done about her brother's beating. They would laugh if they knew. Shirley, who was the class secretary, and Saul, with the prominent forehead. No, he would not laugh. He was always writing about spaceships and the end of the world. No danger, though, that her story would be read. Only the best manuscripts were read. She remembered keenly the blotched appearance of the paper, the lines crossed out, and the words whose spelling she could never be sure of. Oh, well, she didn't care. Only one more period and then the weekend. "Lady Jeanie's too proud to come to our party. Jeanie, what are you waiting for? Jeanie's waiting for a Prince Charming with a red Cadillac to come and take her away." If Barbara asked her again, she would go with her, maybe. There was going to be a party at Norma's Saturday night, with Cokes and sandwiches and records and dancing, everybody chipping in. "Jeanie, I need a nickel. Mama, I need a dollar. I need, I need."

The bell rang, and the pens dropped, the books were closed with a clatter. She slipped out ahead of the pushing, jostling boys and girls.

Monday, Miss Lowy had on still another perfect white blouse. She stood facing the class, holding a sheaf of papers in her hand. Most of the students looked at her expectantly. Marion, who nearly always got 90, whispered to her neighbor. Michael, who had but recently come from Greece—ah, but that was a different Greece—grumbled and shifted in his seat. He would have to do his composition over. He always did.

"I spent a very enjoyable time this weekend reading your work," said Miss Lowy, waiting for the class to smile.

---

4. **A poem . . . skylark:** Percy Bysshe Shelley, a British poet, wrote a famous poem called "To a Skylark."

"Seriously, though, many of your pieces were most interesting, even though they were a trifle <u>unconventional</u> about spelling and punctuation." A smile was obviously indicated here too, and the class obeyed. She paused. "Sometimes, however, a piece of writing is so honest and human that you forgive the technical weaknesses. Not that they aren't important," she said hastily, "but what the writer has to say is more significant."

The three best students in the class looked confused. It was their pride not to have technical errors.

"When you hear this," Miss Lowy continued, "I think you'll agree with me. I know it brought tears to my eyes."

The class looked incredulous.

"It's called 'Evening Comes to 128th Street.'" Her face took on that rapt look.

Jeanie's heart beat painfully. She picked up a pencil but dropped it, so unsteady were her fingers. Even the back of Shirley's head was listening. Even the classes in the other wing of the building, across the courtyard, seemed fixed, row on row, in an attitude of listening. Miss Lowy read on. It was all there, the coal yards and Fat Mary, the stoop and the tarts from Sutter's, Billy asleep with the tears dried on his face, the clasp purse and the quarter.

" 'The funny part of it was, when I woke him, Billy wasn't mad. He was glad about the quarter and ate his supper, dessert and all, but Mama never did eat her tart, so I put it away.' "

A <u>poignancy</u> of remembrance swept over Jeanie, then shame and regret. It was no business of theirs, these strange white people.

No one spoke. The silence was unbearable. Finally Marion, the incomparable Marion, raised her hand.

"It was so real," she said, "you felt you were right there in that kitchen."

"You didn't know who to feel sorry for," said another student. "You wanted to cry with the mother and you wanted to cry with Billy."

"With the girl too," said another.

Several heads nodded.

"You see," said Miss Lowy. "It's literature. It's life. It's pain and truth and beauty."

Jeanie's heart beat so, it made a mist come before her eyes. Through the blur she heard Miss Lowy say it was good enough to be sent in to *Scholastic*. It showed talent; it showed promise. She heard her name called and shrank from the eyes turned upon her.

After school, she hurried out and caught the first train that you could catch only if you left immediately and did not stroll or stop the least bit to talk to someone. She did not want to meet anyone, not even Barbara.

Was that Billy among the kids on the stoop?

"Billy," she called, "Billy."

What would she say to him? Beauty is truth, truth beauty?

"Billy," she called again urgently.

Billy lifted his head and, seeing who it was, tore himself reluctantly away from his friends and took a step toward her. ❧

Words to Know and Use | **unconventional** (un′ kən ven′ shən əl) *adj.* not conforming to customary or accepted rules
poignancy (poin′ yən sē) *n.* a sharp, emotionally painful feeling

532

explain.

Responding to Reading

First Impressions

1. What is your reaction to this story? Write your impressions in your journal or on a sheet of paper.

Second Thoughts

2. Summarize the main problems Jeanie experiences.

   Think about
   • the problems she faces with her friends
   • the problems she faces at school
   • the problems within her family
   • the problems within herself

3. In your opinion, does Jeanie's self-image change as a result of this episode? Give reasons to support your point of view.

4. What do the mother's actions and words reveal about her character? Is there anything beautiful about her? Explain.

5. Who learns lessons in this story? What are the lessons? Support your answer with details from the story.

6. The teacher finds beauty in a truthful account of Jeanie's life. Do you agree with her? Explain.

7. Are you left with a hopeful or hopeless feeling after reading this story? Tell why you think as you do.

Broader Connections

8. Jeanie's problems are not very different from those of some of your classmates. If you were her teacher, what services and advice would you suggest to help her and others with the same problems?

Literary Concept: Characterization

You know that **characterization** refers to the ways a writer creates and develops a character. In this story you learn that Jeanie is sensitive and easily embarrassed by her life. How does Guest show these aspects of Jeanie's personality? Give examples from the story to support your answer. What other character traits does Jeanie have?

*W*riting Options

1. Describe in writing how you would feel if a teacher read your composition aloud to the class.

2. Write an account of an hour in your day in the style Guest uses on page 531, paragraph 3, to describe Jeanie's busy day at school. Use the same point of view that Guest uses.

3. Create a chart in which you contrast Jeanie and her classmates. Use criteria such as intelligence, neatness, appearance, and personality.

4. Write a few sentences or paragraphs to show how you would complete Miss Lowy's assignment: "Write about beauty and truth. Write about life."

*V*ocabulary Practice

Exercise Write on your paper the word from the list that best completes each sentence.

1. The family used a(n) _____ off the kitchen as an extra bedroom.
2. Although Jeanie sometimes dressed in bright colors, the colors were never _____.
3. Miss Lowy read "Ode on a Grecian Urn" with a(n) _____ that revealed her passion for the work.
4. The class could expect a(n) _____ from Miss Lowy if they behaved rudely.
5. Although Miss Lowy politely called the spellings _____, she meant that the words were spelled incorrectly.
6. Jeanie would have felt even more _____ and nervous if Miss Lowy had asked her to read her composition aloud.
7. Jeanie was afraid her classmates would _____ and laugh at her work.
8. Jeanie felt a distaste or _____ for the dingy buildings that blocked her view of the sky.
9. Miss Lowy read from the students' literary _____, which contained many works by famous writers.
10. Jeanie wrote with a(n) _____ and drive that enabled her to ignore the noise and activity around her.

*Words
to Know
and Use*
___

**alcove
anthology
garish
intensity
jeer
poignancy
reproach
repugnance
tremulous
unconventional**

Options for Learning

1 • Chance Meetings Think of another character you have read about in this book who might share Jeanie's ideas or experiences. With another student, act out a meeting between Jeanie and the other character. Begin by deciding where they will meet and under what circumstances the meeting will occur. Briefly outline the topics or ideas that the characters will discuss. Practice your skit before presenting it to your class.

2 • Jeanie's World Think about the places, people, sights, sounds, and colors that make up Jeanie's world. Then choose an art form that lends itself to representing the various aspects of Jeanie's life. You might choose to create a collage, a montage, a triptych (a set of three illustrated panels, often hinged so that the two side panels may be folded over the middle panel), a mobile, or a painting. Display your finished artwork, and ask others to comment on it.

3 • Your Name in Print Miss Lowy says that Jeanie's composition is good enough to be published. Find out what you have to do to get an article published in one of the *Scholastic* magazines or in *Seventeen* magazine, which first published "Beauty Is Truth." Check the copyright page of the magazine for information on submitting manuscripts or write to the editor in chief for guidelines. Present your findings to your class.

4 • Design a Diorama This story includes at least four very different settings. Design a diorama, that is, a miniature three-dimensional scene, that depicts one of these settings. You might create your diorama in a shoe box. Use details from the story and what you know to create the scene you choose.

5 • Lead a Discussion Lead a discussion about the meaning of the poem "Ode on a Grecian Urn." Find the poem and make copies of it for your classmates. Spend time reading and thinking about the poem until you feel that you understand it. You may wish to confer with your teacher about ways to approach the poem.

6 • Delve into the Details Anna Guest brings this story to life by including details that describe the characters and the setting. List details that helped you visualize Jeanie's family, Miss Lowy, and Jeanie's classmates or that helped you visualize the setting. Compare your list with the lists of two or three of your classmates. Circle the details that are most important to your understanding of the characters or the setting.

FACT FINDER

Describe a skylark and tell where you might find one.

WORKSHOP

NARRATION

All of the main characters in this subunit learned important lessons as a result of their experiences. Sometimes the events were simple and brief. Sometimes they occurred over a long period of time. In each case, however, the experience gave the writer (and reader) a chance to reflect on the larger significance of an important universal truth.

To *reflect* means to think about something carefully and deeply—to wonder about it. Reflection does not mean settling for easy answers or solutions, but instead involves looking for meaningful and significant understanding. For example, if your parents allowed your brother or sister to do something forbidden to you, you might reflect on the nature of justice. You might consider that deciding what is fair depends on one's point of view and in some cases involves more than simply equal treatment. In a similar way, writers of reflective essays usually use an event, experience, or observation as a springboard to discuss a complex issue or universal truth. Reflective writing, therefore, often combines many of the kinds of writing you have practiced so far. For instance, a reflective essay may begin with narration and description. Then, as the writer explores the deeper significance of a specific experience, he or she may make generalizations, analyze causes, evaluate alternatives, or attempt to persuade the reader.

> **Here is your PASSkey to this assignment.**

GUIDED ASSIGNMENT: REFLECTIVE ESSAY

Write an essay about an experience during your freshman year that in some way relates to an idea, issue, problem, or concept of universal significance.

P URPOSE: To reflect

A UDIENCE: Your teacher and classmates

S UBJECT: A freshman experience

S TRUCTURE: A multi-paragraph essay

Prewriting

STEP 1 **Think of incidents**   In a small group, brainstorm typical freshmen activities and experiences. List as many incidents as you can. You might include such things as going to school on the first day, getting lost, attending your first high school dance, being intimidated by older students, and so on. Do not limit your experience to school; consider anything that has happened during the year. In order to jog your memory, run through a mental diary month-by-month or check your journal or assignment notebook.

STEP **2** **Choose an incident that leads to a lesson** Look at your list of memories. From which incidents did you learn something? Which experiences have to do with the problems or concerns of life in general? From which incidents could you draw a larger significance? Circle the incident you think has the best possibilities for reflection and writing.

STEP **3** **Reflect** What lesson or larger truth can you learn from the incident? Do some careful thinking about what caused the incident or what resulted from it. How might it relate to other people's experiences? Try to state several generalizations or universal truths that relate to the incident.

One student chose to write about getting lost on the first day of classes. She reflected on the experience and came up with some ideas that seemed larger than the incident itself.

Getting Lost

Everybody gets lost sometimes.
Getting lost equals confusion.
People who don't ask for help are afraid to show their
    ignorance.
Being lost is being out of control.

◀ STUDENT MODEL

STEP **4** **Explore your ideas through freewriting** Freewriting is a technique writers use to help them explore their topics. It means to write steadily for a full page without stopping to plan or correct errors. You simply write down ideas as they occur to you. For this assignment, use freewriting to explore your ideas about the truth or issue you selected. Freewriting is a form of brainstorming, so don't be too critical of your ideas as you write.

Here is a portion of one student's freewriting:

Getting Lost as a Freshman = Confusion

◀ STUDENT MODEL

Getting lost the first day of school is confusing. It's
not knowing where you are and this is how lots of people
go through their lives. Lots of people don't have any
idea about what's happening. They're clueless, and some
of them are too afraid to ask somebody else for help. I

wonder why. Maybe they don't like to seem stupid. Maybe they have to pretend to be in control of every situation. If you're in trouble, doesn't it make sense to ask? If somebody could make you less confused, wouldn't you want to be?

STEP 5 **Select your best ideas** Review your freewriting. Underline ideas that you think are worth developing further in your rough draft. If you like, ask a classmate to look over your freewriting and mark ideas worth exploring further.

Drafting

STEP 1 **Organize your essay** Decide how to organize your essay. There are several different ways you might do this. One way is to begin by narrating the personal experience fully and then to reflect on its universal significance. Another way is to begin by exploring the meaning of a general concept and then to use the personal experience to illustrate the concept. A third way combines the first two by narrating part of the experience and then pausing to reflect on that specific part before moving on to the next aspect of the experience.

STEP 2 **Reflect and narrate** As you write your rough draft, keep in mind that your main purpose is to reflect, not to narrate. The narrative part of your essay should be shorter than the reflective part.

Special Tip

Since this composition includes narration of a personal experience, write in the first-person point of view. Continue in the first-person even during the reflective part of the composition. Good reflective essays express the real concerns of the writer, so feel free to be honest and personal.

Revising and Editing

Before asking a classmate to review your draft, try these elaboration techniques to improve your narrative reflection.

1. Replace two verbs with strong **action** verbs.
2. Add two descriptive **adjectives** to further clarify nouns.

3. Add two **adverbs** to make verbs more specific.

4. Add a **comparison** in the form of a **simile** or **metaphor** to explain a feeling or thought you describe.

5. Use an **example** to better explain an idea.

6. Decide if **dialogue** would improve the narrative part of your essay. If so, add it.

After you have used elaboration to improve your draft, ask a classmate to evaluate your work according to the following checklist.

Revision Checklist

1. Is this experience narrated clearly with specific details?

2. Does the writer use the experience in order to reflect on a significant issue or universal truth of some kind?

3. Are the experience and the reflection well suited to each other?

4. Is it clear that the writer has examined the issue, concept, or universal truth carefully and completely?

5. Are there aspects of the reflection that are not clear?

6. Is the composition organized in a way that makes sense?

Editing   When you have finished revising your draft, proofread for spelling, clarity, and mechanics.

Publishing

Collect the compositions together in a volume entitled "Reflections on Freshman Year." Appoint an editorial committee to decide how to organize the compositions.

Reflecting on Your Writing

Place the answers to the following questions in your writing portfolio.

1. Was the freewriting portion of your planning helpful to you?

2. What did you learn about writing about concepts?

3. What part, if any, of the assignment did you enjoy? Why?

LANGUAGE WORKSHOP

AVOIDING UNNECESSARY SHIFTS IN TENSE

Time. You can measure it in seconds, minutes, hours, and days. You can measure it by seasons, holidays, school years, things you've done, and things you hope to do.

Every action you can imagine—or write about—takes place at some point in time. So naturally, since verbs describe action, they also tell time. In fact, all verbs change form, or **tense,** to show when an action occurs. To make sure your reader understands exactly when a particular action takes place, you must use the correct tense.

Every verb has six tenses formed by using the principal parts of the verb and certain helping verbs such as *be* and *have.*

As you can see from the chart, the tenses of a verb cover a range of situations in time.

Tense	Example	Use
• **Present**	*she walks*	For action that is happening now
• **Past**	*she walked*	For action that was completed in the past
• **Future**	*she will walk*	For action that will occur in the future
• **Present perfect**	*she has walked*	For action that was completed at an indefinite time in the past or that began in the past and continues into the present
• **Past perfect**	*she had walked*	To show an action in the past that came before another action in the past
• **Future perfect**	*she will have walked*	To show an action in the future that will happen before another future action or time

> Use the same tense to show two or more actions that occur at the same time.

In most of your writing, the action in any one sentence or paragraph takes place in one time period. To show this kind of consistent action, keep the same tense for all the verbs in the sentence or paragraph. Do not change tenses within or between sentences unless such a change clarifies your meaning.

Incorrect   Jeanie sits at her desk and looked out the window.
Correct   Jeanie sits at her desk and looks out the window.
Correct   Jeanie sat at her desk and looked out the window.

One type of sentence that *does* require a shift in verb tense is a sentence involving a sequence of events. For example, the sentence below describes a sequence in which first Jeanie finishes her poem and then the class ends. Notice how the change in verb tense shows this flow from one period of time to another.

> Jeanie *will have finished* (future perfect) her poem by the time the class *ends.* (present)

Whenever you proofread your writing, check for unnecessary changes in verb tense that may confuse your reader.

Exercise 1   Rewrite each sentence to correct any unnecessary shift in tenses. If the tenses need no correction, write *Correct.*

1. ''Beauty Is Truth'' takes place in Harlem, where Jeanie and her friends will live.
2. While Jeanie rode the train home, she looks out the window.
3. Her friend Barbara stopped at the soda parlor, but Jeanie heads home.
4. Billy pitched pennies on the front stoop as Jeanie starts up the front steps.
5. Jeanie will have thought about school and then opened her notebook.
6. As she starts her homework, Jeanie heard her mother's voice.
7. Because Billy pitched pennies, his mother punished him.
8. Jeanie's mother had worked hard all day, and now she needs some help with dinner.
9. The next day, Jeanie's heart beat fast when Miss Lowy reads her paper.
10. Jeanie had written the truth, and her words will have been beautiful.

Exercise 2   Work in groups to revise the following paragraphs. Look carefully at each sentence with italicized verbs and decide how to correct improper shifts in tense. Write the corrected sentence.

Annie *had worked* long and hard in preparation for the piano competition. Forty-two talented young musicians from across the state *compete* in the first round. Six months later, there *will be* four finalists, including Annie. When the final competition was over, only one contestant *will be* left—Annie!

Three days later, with the applause of the crowd still in her ears, Annie arrived at Miss Salkind's studio for her weekly lesson. Without a word about Annie's triumph, the wrinkled old woman *points* to the piano and *will say,* "Begin." For the next hour, Annie *had played* the same piece over and over. Miss Salkind *stopped* her constantly and *criticizes* every passage. Annie *feels* the tears of frustration behind her eyes and finally *has blurted* out, "If I'm so terrible, how did I win the competition?"

"Dear girl," *replies* Miss Salkind, with a surprisingly gentle smile. "You must not care what others think, whether good or bad. Instead you must focus on the music."

LANGUAGE HANDBOOK

For review and practice:
principal parts of verbs,
    page 933
verb tenses,
    pages 938–40
tense shifts,
    pages 939–40

Exercise 3   Style   Choose a passage of two or three paragraphs from one of the selections you have read. List each verb in the passage and write its tense. If a shift in tense occurs, explain why the writer used a different tense at that point.

Exercise 4   Analyzing and Revising Your Writing   Review a piece of your writing, looking for improper shifts in verb tenses. Correct any errors in tense that you find.

STUDY SKILLS
WORKSHOP

TAKING OBJECTIVE TESTS

You are undoubtedly familiar with **objective tests**—tests whose questions require a choice of right or wrong answers. Here are the four most common types of questions used in objective tests and some hints to help you succeed in answering them.

True-False You are given a statement and asked to tell whether the statement is true or false.

1. If any part of a statement is false, all of it is false.
2. Words such as *all, always, only,* and *never* often appear in false statements.
3. Words such as *some, a few, usually, often,* and *most* often appear in true statements.

Matching You are asked to match items in one column with items in another column.

1. Check the directions. See whether each item is used only once.
2. Read all items before starting.
3. Match those you know first. Cross out items as you use them.

Multiple Choice You are asked to choose the best answer from a group of answers given on the test.

1. Read all choices first and eliminate incorrect answers.
2. Choose the most complete or most accurate answer.
3. Pay particular attention to choices that read ''none of the above'' or ''all of the above.''

Completion You fill in a blank in a statement on the exam.

1. Make sure your answer makes sense in terms of space provided. If several words are needed, be sure you write all of them down.
2. Write clearly, using proper spelling, grammar, punctuation, and capitalization.

Exercise   Write an objective test based on the story ''Beauty Is Truth'' on page 527. Include three true-false questions, three multiple-choice questions, one completion question, and a matching question with five items to match against five other items. Exchange tests with a classmate and answer your partner's test questions.

TEST-TAKING TIPS
1. Survey the test quickly.
2. Plan your time.
3. Read all directions and questions carefully.
4. Save time for reviewing answers.

TURNING POINTS: MOMENTS TO REMEMBER

" *The difficulty in life is the choice.* "

George Moore

GATE TO THE ISLES   1980
Winifred Nicholson   © Estate of
Winifred Nicholson.

545

$\mathcal{O}$PPORTUNITY KNOCKS

When a lucky break comes our way, we say that opportunity knocks. Then we must decide whether to take advantage of the opportunity or ignore it. An opportunity presents a possibility, not a sure thing. Accepting the challenge it represents is risky—you could get hurt along the way. Read to see how the characters in this subunit react to the opportunities presented to them.

explore

Fiction

Three Wise Guys:
Un Cuento de Navidad/A Christmas Story
(ōōn kwen' tō dä nä vē däd')

SANDRA CISNEROS *(sis' ner' ōs)*

Examine What You Know

What is the best gift you ever received? What is the worst? Talk with your classmates about gifts and what makes them good or bad. Then work together to make a list of criteria for a "good" gift. As you read, think about whether you would consider the Travis brothers' gift good or bad.

Expand Your Knowledge

In Mexico, as in many other Latin American countries, the celebration of Jesus Christ's birthday stretches from the evening of December twenty-fourth, which is called Nochebuena (nô che bwe' nä), or Good Night, to January sixth, which is known as El Día de los Reyes (el dē' ä dä lôs re' yes), or Day of the Three Kings. According to the Bible, three wise men came from foreign lands to honor Christ by offering precious gifts: gold; frankincense, a sweet-smelling incense; and myrrh, a perfumed oil. To commemorate this event, children in Latin America traditionally receive gifts on Day of the Three Kings rather than on Christmas Eve or Christmas Day.

The Bible reveals few details about the wise men, but in the first century A.D. they were thought to be priests and astrologers, men of wisdom, or philosophers. In the second century, the scholar Tertullian made popular his theory that the wise men fulfilled a prophecy from the Old Testament that kings bearing gifts would come to Israel. From that time on, the wise men were often pictured as kings.

Write Before You Read

Imagine that a large, brightly wrapped holiday package is delivered to your family. What would you want it to contain? What would other members of your family want? Write your thoughts in your journal or on a sheet of paper.

■ *A biography of the author can be found on page 555.*

Three Wise Guys:
Un Cuento de Navidad/A Christmas Story

SANDRA CISNEROS

The big box came marked DO NOT OPEN TILL XMAS, but the mama said not until the Day of the Three Kings. Not until El Día de los Reyes, the sixth of January, do you hear? That is what the mama said exactly, only she said it all in Spanish. Because in Mexico where she was raised, it is the custom for boys and girls to receive their presents on January sixth and not Christmas, even though they were living on the Texas side of the river now. Not until the sixth of January.

Today the big box had arrived.

Yesterday the mama had risen in the dark same as always to reheat the coffee in a tin saucepan and warm the breakfast tortillas. The papa had gotten up coughing and spitting up the night, complaining how the evening before the buzzing of the *chicharras*[1] had kept him from sleeping. By the time the mama had the house smelling of oatmeal and cinnamon, the papa would be gone to the fields, the sun already tangled in the trees and the *urracas*[2] screeching their rubber-screech cry. The boy Rubén and the girl Rosalinda would have to be shaken awake

for school. The mama would give the baby Gilberto his bottle, and then she would go back to sleep before getting up again to the chores that were always waiting. That is how the world had been.

But today the big box had arrived. When the boy Rubén and the girl Rosalinda came home from school, it was already sitting in the living room in front of the television set that no longer worked. Who had put it there? Where had it come from? A box covered with red paper with green Christmas trees and a card on top that said: *Merry Christmas to the González Family. Frank, Earl, and Dwight Travis. P.S. DO NOT OPEN TILL XMAS.* That's all.

Two times the mama was made to come into the living room, first to explain to the children and later to their father how the brothers Travis had arrived in the blue pickup and how it had taken all three of those big men to lift the box off the back of the truck and bring it inside and how she had had to nod and say thank-you thank-you thank-you over and over because those were the only words she knew in English. Then the brothers Travis had nodded as well the way they always did when they came and brought the boxes of clothes or the tur-

---

1. **chicharras** (che chä′ räs) *Spanish*: cicadas or locusts.
2. **urracas** ($\overline{oo}$ rä′ käs) *Spanish*: magpies; noisy black-and-white feathered birds related to crows and jays.

key each November or the canned ham on Easter ever since the children had begun to earn high grades at the school where Dwight Travis was the principal.

But this year the Christmas box was bigger than usual. What could be in a box so big? The boy Rubén and the girl Rosalinda begged all afternoon to be allowed to open it, and that is when the mama had said the sixth of January, the Day of the Three Kings. Not a day sooner.

It seemed the weeks stretched themselves wider and wider since the arrival of the big box. The mama got used to sweeping around it because it was too heavy for her to push in a corner, but since the television no longer worked ever since the afternoon the children had poured iced tea through the little grates in the back, it really didn't matter if it obstructed the view. Visitors that came inside the house were told and told again the story of how the box had arrived, and then each was made to guess what was inside.

It was the *comadre*[3] Elodia who suggested over coffee one afternoon that the big box held a portable washing machine that could be rolled away when not in use, the kind she had seen in her Sears, Roebuck catalog. The mama said she hoped so, because the wringer washer she had used for the last ten years had finally gotten tired and quit. These past few weeks she had to boil all the clothes in the big pot she used for cooking the Christmas tamales. Yes. She hoped the big box was a portable washing machine. A washing machine, even a portable one, would be good.

But the neighbor man Cayetano said, What foolishness, *comadre*. Can't you see the box is too small to hold a washing machine, even a portable one? Most likely God has

heard your prayers and sent a new color TV. With a good antenna you could catch all the Mexican soap operas, the neighbor man said. You could distract yourself with the complicated troubles of the rich and then give thanks to God for the blessed simplicity of your poverty. A new TV would surely be the end to all your miseries.

Each night when the papa came home from the fields, he would spread newspapers on the cot in the living room where the boy Rubén and the girl Rosalinda slept, and sit facing the big box in the center of the room. Each night he imagined the box held something different. The day before yesterday he guessed a new record player. Yesterday an ice chest filled with beer. Today the papa sat with his bottle of beer, fanning himself with a magazine, and said in a voice as much a plea as a prophecy: air conditioner.

But the boy Rubén and the girl Rosalinda were sure the big box was filled with toys. They had even punctured a hole in one corner with a pencil when their mother was busy cooking, although they could see nothing inside but blackness.

Only the baby Gilberto remained uninterested in the contents of the big box and seemed each day more fascinated with the exterior of the box rather than the interior. One afternoon he tore off a fistful of paper, which he was chewing when his mother swooped him up with one arm, rushed him to the kitchen sink, and forced him to swallow handfuls of lukewarm water in case the red dye of the wrapping paper might be poisonous.

When Christmas Eve finally came, the family González put on their good clothes and went to midnight mass. They came

---

3. **comadre** (kô mä′ drā) *Spanish*: woman friend; godmother.

home to a house that smelled of tamales and atole[4], and everyone was allowed to open one present before going to sleep, but the big box was to remain untouched until the sixth of January.

On New Year's Eve the little house was filled with people, some related, some not, coming in and out. The friends of the papa came with bottles, and the mama set out a bowl of grapes to count off the New Year. That night the children did not sleep in the living-room cot as they usually did, because the living room was crowded with big-fannied ladies and fat-stomached men sashaying[5] to the accordion music of the Midget Twins from McAllen. Instead the children fell asleep on a lump of handbags and crumpled suit jackets on top of the mama and the papa's bed, dreaming of the contents of the big box.

All night they whispered last-minute wishes.

Finally the fifth of January. And the boy Rubén and the girl Rosalinda could hardly sleep. All night they whispered last-minute wishes. The boy thought perhaps if the big box held a bicycle, he would be the first to ride it, since he was the oldest. This made his sister cry, until the mama had to yell from her bedroom on the other side of the plastic curtains, Be quiet or I'm going to give you each the stick, which sounds worse in Spanish than it does in English. Then no one said anything. After a very long time, long after they heard the mama's wheezed breathing and their papa's piped snoring, the children closed their eyes and remembered nothing.

The papa was already in the bathroom

coughing up the night before from his throat when the *urracas* began their clownish chirping. The boy Rubén awoke and shook his sister. The mama frying the potatoes and beans for breakfast nodded permission for the box to be opened.

With a kitchen knife the boy Rubén cut a careful edge along the top. The girl Rosalinda tore the Christmas wrapping with her fingernails. The papa and the mama lifted the cardboard flaps, and everyone peered inside to see what it was the brothers Travis had brought them on the Day of the Three Kings.

There were layers of balled newspaper packed on top. When these had been cleared away, the boy Rubén looked inside. The girl Rosalinda looked inside. The papa and the mama looked.

This is what they saw: the complete *Encyclopaedia Britannica Junior*, twenty-four volumes in red imitation leather with gold embossed letters beginning with volume 1, Aar-Bel, and ending with volume 24, Yel-Zyn. The girl Rosalinda let out a sad cry as if her hair was going to be cut again. The boy Rubén pulled out volume 4, Ded-Fem. There were many pictures and many words, but there were more words than pictures. The papa flipped through volume 22, but because he could not read English words, simply put the book back and grunted, What can we do with this? No one said anything and shortly after, the screen door slammed.

Only the mama knew what to do with the contents of the big box. She withdrew volumes 6, 7, and 8, marched off to the dinette set in the kitchen, placed two on Rosalinda's chair so she could better reach the table, and

---

4. **atole** (ä tô′ lā): a Mexican drink from corn meal.
5. **sashaying** (sa shā′ iŋ): walking slowly in such a way as to show off.

CHRISTMAS '58   Jan Hoy   Chalk pastel 17″ × 19″   Courtesy of the artist.

put one underneath the plant stand that danced.

When the boy and the girl returned from school that day, they found the books stacked into squat pillars against one living-room wall and a board placed on top. On this were arranged several plastic doilies and framed family photographs. The rest of the volumes the baby Gilberto was playing with, and he was already rubbing his sore gums along the corners of volume 14.

The girl Rosalinda also grew interested in the books. She took out her colored pencils and painted blue on the lids of all the illustrations of women, and with a red pencil dipped in spit she painted their lips and fingernails red-red. After a couple of days, when all the pictures of women had been colored in this manner, she began to cut out some of the prettier pictures and paste them on looseleaf paper.

One volume suffered from being exposed to the rain when the papa improvised a hat during a sudden shower. He forgot it on the hood of the car when he drove off. When the children came home from school, they set it on the porch to dry. But the pages puffed up and became so fat, the book was impossible to close.

Only the boy Rubén refused to touch the books. For several days he avoided the principal because he didn't know what to say in case Mr. Travis were to ask how they were enjoying the Christmas present.

On the Saturday after New Year's, the mama and the papa went into town for groceries and left the boy in charge of watching his sister and baby brother. The girl Rosalinda was stacking books into spiral staircases and making her paper dolls descend them in a fancy manner.

Perhaps the boy Rubén would not have bothered to open the volume left on the kitchen table if he had not seen his mother wedge her name-day[6] corsage in its pages. On the page where the mama's carnation lay pressed between two pieces of kleenex was a picture of a dog in a spaceship. FIRST DOG IN SPACE the caption said. The boy turned to another page and read where cashews came from. And then about the man who invented the guillotine. And then about Bengal tigers. And about clouds. All afternoon the boy read, even after the mama and the papa came home. Even after the sun set, until the mama said time to sleep and put the light out.

In their bed on the other side of the plastic curtain the mama and the papa slept. Across from them in the crib slept the baby Gilberto. The girl Rosalinda slept on her end of the cot. But the boy Rubén watched the night sky turn from violet. To blue. To gray. And then from gray. To blue. To violet once again. ❧

---

6. **name-day:** the church feast day of the saint after whom one is named.

e x p l a i n

Responding to Reading

First Impressions

1. How would you react if you received a set of encyclopedias? Write a few sentences to explain your feelings.

Second Thoughts

2. In the past, the Travis brothers gave the González family gifts of clothing and food. Why do you think they choose to give the family a set of encyclopedias this time?

3. Do you think the gift was a "good" one? Consider your criteria for a good gift when forming your answer.

4. What effect does the gift have on Rubén? Give evidence from the story to support your answer.

   Think about
   - his first reaction to the gift
   - his avoidance of Principal Travis
   - the last two paragraphs

5. What effect do you predict the encyclopedias will have on the rest of the family in the near and distant future? Explain.

6. What do you learn about each family member from the uses he or she finds for the gift?

7. How do you suppose the Travis brothers might react if they saw how their gift was used?

8. To whom does the title refer? In what ways might you interpret the phrase "wise guys"?

Broader Connections

9. Of what value would a set of encyclopedias be to a poor or immigrant family in the United States today? How might knowledge from reading improve their lives? Give reasons for your answer.

Literary Concepts: Suspense and Idiom

Suspense refers to the growing feeling of tension and excitement created in the reader's mind. It keeps the reader wondering about how a story will end. What causes suspense in this story? Find sentences that help create this feeling.

An **idiom** is a common phrase or expression that has a different meaning from the actual, or literal, meaning of the individual words. Two idioms Cisneros uses in this story are "spitting up the night" and "give you a stick." What is the literal meaning of these idioms? What idioms do you know have similar meanings?

Concept Review: Point of View This story is written from a third-person point of view; the narrator is not one of the characters. Is the narrator's knowledge of the characters and their thoughts limited or all-knowing? In what ways does the point of view influence your opinion of each character's behavior?

Writing Options

1. Describe a gift you would give the González family. Tell why you think the gift is appropriate.

2. Cisneros includes many facts about the customs and traditions surrounding the celebration of a Mexican-American Christmas. Make a list of the customs and traditions detailed in this story.

3. Imagine that you are a film director. Write a detailed character sketch for one member of the González family or a detailed description of the main setting for your film.

4. In a paragraph, name the first topic you would look up if you were given a set of encyclopedias and give reasons for your choice.

e x t e n d

Options for Learning

1 • **Think Fast** How many uses can you find for a set of encyclopedias in addition to those presented in this story? Have a contest in which you and your classmates write as many uses as you can think of in three minutes' time. Decide which player has (1) the most ideas, (2) the cleverest idea, (3) the most practical idea, and (4) the funniest idea.

2 • **Insightful Thoughts** Many selections in this book are accompanied by *Insights,* short literary works that reinforce the theme of the story or present another side of an issue. Decide on the theme of this story. Then find a poem or another short work that focuses on the theme. Read your insight and lead a discussion on its relationship to "Three Wise Guys."

3 • **Slick Sales** Imagine that you are an encyclopedia salesperson. Create a sales pitch to sell your product. Include solid reasons why your product is worth the expense. Practice your speech, varying your tone and emphasis, before presenting it to the class.

4 • **Before and After** The González family's feelings about their mystery package change during this story. Draw one cartoon that shows the family's expressions before they open the box and another cartoon that shows their expressions after opening the box. Use thought bubbles to show what the characters are thinking.

 **FACT FINDER**

When did the first dog travel in space? What was its name?

Sandra Cisneros
1954-

Sandra Cisneros believes that she writes by obsession, not by inspiration. "If I were asked what it is I write about, I would have to say I write about those ghosts inside that haunt me . . . of that which even memory does not like to mention." To her, writing is a way of dealing with the poverty, loneliness, and feelings of instability she faced as a child in inner-city Chicago.

A graduate of Loyola University in Chicago, she later attended the University of Iowa's prestigious Writer's Workshop. It was there that she discovered her unique style—a blend of her mother's working-class English and her father's gentle Spanish. To date, she has written one novel and more than thirty-nine other works. She has received many fellowships, grants, awards, and honors for her work, both in this country and abroad.

Cisneros shares her writing talent by lecturing and teaching.

Fiction

Red Dress—1946

ALICE MUNRO

Examine What You Know

For many students, high school offers the opportunity to begin a "new life." What expectations did you have for yourself as you began high school? Did you expect to do well academically, to become popular, or to "blossom" in some other way? So far, to what degree has reality matched your expectations? Share your ideas with your classmates. As you read this story, compare your experiences with those of the narrator.

Expand Your Knowledge

A popular trend in modern writing is to write about the real problems of everyday life. Characters in **contemporary realistic fiction** are often ordinary people who face psychological problems or who have problems dealing with basic human relationships, such as the relationship between a mother and her daughter. Alice Munro, a modern Canadian writer, usually writes about women who are not heroic, but ordinary. Her plots, too, involve ordinary, not dangerous or fantastic, situations. The presented conflicts are not earth-shattering, yet they are very important to the characters. Although this story is set in 1946, when bobby socks, penny loafers, and crinolines were the fashion, the problems the main character faces are very similar to those faced by teenagers today.

Write Before You Read

The narrator in this story is embarrassed by her mother. Why are teenagers sometimes embarrassed by their parents? Do you think parents are ever embarrassed by their teenagers? Write your thoughts in your journal or on a sheet of paper.

■ *A biography of the author can be found on page 569.*

Red Dress—1946

ALICE MUNRO

My mother was making me a dress. All through the month of November I would come from school and find her in the kitchen, surrounded by cut-up red velvet and scraps of tissue-paper pattern. She worked at an old treadle machine[1] pushed up against the window to get the light and also to let her look out, past the stubble fields and bare vegetable garden, to see who went by on the road. There was seldom anybody to see.

The red velvet material was hard to work with—it pulled—and the style my mother had chosen was not easy either. She was not really a good sewer. She liked to make things; that is different. Whenever she could, she tried to skip basting and pressing, and she took no pride in the fine points of tailoring, the finishing of buttonholes and the overcasting of seams as, for instance, my aunt and my grandmother did. Unlike them, she started off with an inspiration, a brave and dazzling idea; from that moment on, her pleasure ran downhill. In the first place she could never find a pattern to suit her. It was no wonder; there were no patterns made to match the ideas that blossomed in her head. She had made me, at various times when I was younger, a flowered organdy dress with a high Victorian neckline edged in scratchy lace, with a poke bonnet to match; a Scottish plaid outfit with a velvet jacket and tam; an embroidered peasant blouse worn with a full red skirt and black laced bodice.[2] I had worn these clothes with docility, even pleasure, in the days when I was unaware of the world's opinion. Now, grown wiser, I wished for dresses like those my friend Lonnie had, bought at Beale's store.

I had to try it on. Sometimes Lonnie came home from school with me, and she would sit on the couch watching. I was embarrassed by the way my mother crept around me, her knees creaking, her breath coming heavily. She muttered to herself. Around the house she wore no corset[3] or stockings; she wore wedge-heeled shoes and ankle socks; her legs were marked with lumps of blue-green veins. I thought her squatting position shameless, even obscene; I tried to keep talking to Lonnie so that her attention would be taken away from my mother as much as possible. Lonnie wore the composed, polite, appreciative expression that

---

1. **treadle** (tred′ 'l) **machine:** a nonelectric sewing machine powered by the operator's stepping on a pedal.
2. **bodice** (bäd′ is): a kind of vest.
3. **corset:** a tight-fitting undergarment intended to give a desired figure to the wearer.

Words to Know and Use | **composed** (kəm pōzd′) *adj.* calm; tranquil

557

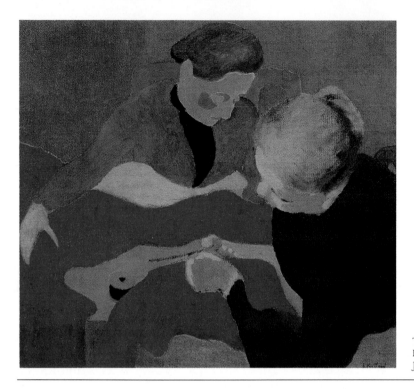

THE DRESSMAKERS 1891
Edouard Vuillard
Josephowitz Collection.

was her disguise in the presence of grown-ups. She laughed at them and was a ferocious <u>mimic</u>, and they never knew.

My mother pulled me about and pricked me with pins. She made me turn around; she made me walk away; she made me stand still. "What do you think of it, Lonnie?" she said around the pins in her mouth.

"It's beautiful," said Lonnie, in her mild, sincere way. Lonnie's own mother was dead. She lived with her father, who never noticed her, and this, in my eyes, made her seem both <u>vulnerable</u> and privileged.

"It *will* be, if I can ever manage the fit," my mother said. "Ah, well," she said theatrically, getting to her feet with a woeful creaking and sighing, "I doubt if she appreciates it." She enraged me, talking like this to Lonnie, as if Lonnie were grown up and I were still a child. "Stand still," she said, hauling the pinned and basted dress over my head. My head was muffled in velvet, my body exposed in an old cotton school slip. I felt like a great, raw lump, clumsy and goose-pimpled. I wished I was like Lonnie, light boned, pale, and thin; she had been a blue baby.[4]

"Well, nobody ever made me a dress when I was going to high school," my mother said, "I made my own, or I did without." I was afraid she was going to start again on the story of her walking seven miles to town and finding a job waiting on tables in a boardinghouse so that she could go to high school. All the stories of my mother's life which had once interested me had begun to seem <u>melodramatic</u>, <u>irrelevant</u>, and tiresome.

"One time I had a dress given to me," she said. "It was a cream-colored cashmere wool with royal blue piping down the front and lovely mother-of-pearl buttons. I wonder what ever became of it?"

---

4. **blue baby:** a baby born with a certain blood and respiratory defect that requires blood transfusions. Being a blue baby may have made Lonnie so pale and thin.

Words to Know and Use

mimic (mim′ ik) *n.* someone who imitates
vulnerable (vul′ nər ə bəl) *adj.* easily hurt; sensitive
melodramatic (mel′ ō drə mat′ ik) *adj.* sensational and extavagantly emotional
irrelevant (ir rel′ ə vənt) *adj.* not to the point; not relating to the subject

When we got free, Lonnie and I went upstairs to my room. It was cold, but we stayed there. We talked about the boys in our class, going up and down the rows saying, "Do you like him? Well, do you half like him? Do you *hate* him? Would you go out with him if he asked you?" Nobody had asked us. We were thirteen, and we had been going to high school for two months. We did questionnaires in magazines, to find out whether we had personality and whether we would be popular. We read articles on how to make up our faces to <u>accentuate</u> our good points and how to carry on a conversation on the first date and what to do when a boy tried to go too far. When we were not doing schoolwork, we were occupied most of the time with the garnering, passing on, and discussing of sexual information. We had made a pact to tell each other everything. But one thing I did not tell was about this dance, the high school Christmas Dance for which my mother was making me a dress. It was that I did not want to go.

At high school I was never comfortable for a minute.

At high school I was never comfortable for a minute. I did not know about Lonnie. Before an exam she got icy hands and palpitations,[5] but I was close to despair at all times. When I was asked a question in class, any simple little question at all, my voice was apt to come out squeaky, or else hoarse and trembling. My hands became slippery with sweat when they were required to work the

blackboard compass. I could not hit the ball in volleyball; being called upon to perform an action in front of others made all my reflexes come undone. I hated Business Practice because you had to rule pages for an account book, using a straight pen, and when the teacher looked over my shoulder, all the delicate lines wobbled and ran together. I hated Science; we perched on stools under harsh lights, behind tables of unfamiliar, fragile equipment, and were taught by the principal of the school, a man with a cold, self-relishing voice—he read the Scriptures every morning—and a great talent for inflicting humiliation. I hated English because the boys played bingo at the back of the room while the teacher, a stout, gentle girl, slightly cross-eyed, read Wordsworth at the front. She threatened them; she begged them, her face red and her voice as unreliable as mine. They offered burlesqued[6] apologies, and when she started to read again they took up rapt postures, made swooning faces, crossed their eyes, flung their hands over their hearts. Sometimes she would burst into tears, there was no help for it; she had to run out into the hall. Then the boys made loud mooing noises; our hungry laughter—oh, mine too—pursued her. There was a carnival atmosphere of brutality in the room at such times, scaring weak and suspect people like me.

But what was really going on in the school was not Business Practice and Science and English; there was something else that gave life its urgency and brightness. That old building, with its rock-walled, clammy basements and black cloakrooms and pictures of

---

5. **palpitations** (pal′ pə tā′ sʰənz): rapid or fluttering heartbeats.

6. **burlesqued** (bər leskd′): insultingly comical.

dead royalties and lost explorers, was full of the tension and excitement of sexual competition, and in this, in spite of daydreams of vast successes, I had premonitions of total defeat. Something had to happen to keep me from that dance.

With December came snow, and I had an idea. Formerly I had considered falling off my bicycle and spraining my ankle, and I had tried to manage this as I rode home along the hard-frozen, deeply rutted country roads. But it was too difficult. However, my throat and bronchial tubes were supposed to be weak; why not expose them? I started getting out of bed at night and opening my window a little. I knelt down and let the wind, sometimes stinging with snow, rush in around my bared throat. I took off my pajama top. I said to myself the words "blue with cold," and as I knelt there, my eyes shut, I pictured my chest and throat turning blue, the cold, grayed blue of veins under the skin. I stayed until I could not stand it any more, and then I took a handful of snow from the windowsill and smeared it all over my chest before I buttoned my pajamas. It would melt against the flannelette, and I would be sleeping in wet clothes, which was supposed to be the worst thing of all. In the morning, the moment I woke up, I cleared my throat, testing for soreness, coughed experimentally, hopefully, touched my forehead to see if I had fever. It was no good. Every morning, including the day of the dance, I rose defeated and in perfect health.

The day of the dance I did my hair up in steel curlers. I had never done this before, because my hair was naturally curly, but today I wanted the protection of all possible female rituals. I lay on the couch in the kitchen, reading *The Last Days of Pompeii*,[7] and wishing I was there. My mother, never satisfied, was sewing a white lace collar on the dress; she had decided it was too grown-up looking. I watched the hours. It was one of the shortest days of the year. Above the couch, on the wallpaper, were old games of X's and O's, old drawings and scribblings my brother and I had done when we were sick with bronchitis. I looked at them and longed to be back safe behind the boundaries of childhood.

When I took out the curlers, my hair, both naturally and artificially stimulated, sprang out in an exuberant, glossy bush. I wet it, combed it, beat it with the brush, and tugged it down along my cheeks. I applied face powder, which stood out chalkily on my hot face. My mother got out her Ashes of Roses cologne, which she never used, and let me splash it over my arms. Then she zipped up the dress and turned me around to the mirror. The dress was princess style, very tight in the midriff.

"Well, I wish I could take a picture," my mother said. "I am really, genuinely proud of that fit. And you might say thank you for it."

"Thank you," I said.

The first thing Lonnie said when I opened the door to her was, "What did you do to your hair?"

"I did it up."

"Get me a comb and I'll do the front in a roll. It'll look all right. It'll even make you look older."

I sat in front of the mirror, and Lonnie stood behind me, fixing my hair. My mother seemed unable to leave us. I wished she

---

7. **Pompeii** (päm′ pā′ ē): a Roman city destroyed by a volcano.

would. She watched the roll take shape and said, "You're a wonder, Lonnie. You should take up hairdressing."

"That's a thought," Lonnie said. She had on a pale blue crepe dress with a peplum[8] and bow; it was much more grownup than mine even without the collar. Her hair had come out as sleek as the girl's on the bobby-pin card. I had always thought secretly that Lonnie could not be pretty because she had crooked teeth, but now I saw that, crooked teeth or not, her stylish dress and smooth hair made me look a little like a golliwog,[9] stuffed into red velvet, wide-eyed, wild haired, with a suggestion of delirium.

My mother followed us to the door and called out into the dark, "Au reservoir!" This was a traditional farewell of Lonnie's and mine; it sounded foolish and desolate coming from her, and I was so angry with her for using it that I did not reply. It was only Lonnie who called back cheerfully, encouragingly, "Good night!"

The gymnasium smelled of pine and cedar. Red and green bells of fluted paper hung from the basketball hoops; the high, barred windows were hidden by green boughs. Everybody in the upper grades seemed to have come in couples. Some of the grade 12 and 13 girls had brought boyfriends who had already graduated, who were young businessmen around the town. These young men smoked in the gymnasium. Nobody could stop them; they were free. The girls stood beside them, resting their hands casually on male sleeves, their faces bored, aloof, and beautiful. I longed to be like that. They behaved as if only they—the older ones—were really at the dance, as if the rest of us,

whom they moved among and peered around, were, if not invisible, inanimate; when the first dance was announced—a Paul Jones—they moved out languidly, smiling at each other as if they had been asked to take part in some half-forgotten childish game. Holding hands and shivering, crowding up together, Lonnie and I and the other grade 9 girls followed.

I didn't dare look at the outer circle as it passed me, for fear I should see some unmannerly hurrying up. When the music stopped, I stayed where I was, and half raising my eyes I saw a boy named Mason Williams coming reluctantly toward me. Barely touching my waist and my fingers, he began to dance with me. My legs were hollow; my arm trembled from the shoulder; I could not have spoken. This Mason Williams was one of the heroes of the school; he played basketball and hockey and walked the halls with an air of royal sullenness and barbaric contempt. To have to dance with a nonentity like me was as offensive to him as having to memorize Shakespeare. I felt this as keenly as he did and imagined that he was exchanging looks of dismay with his friends. He steered me, stumbling, to the edge of the floor. He took his hand from my waist and dropped my arm.

"See you," he said. He walked away.

It took me a minute or two to realize what had happened and that he was not coming back. I went and stood by the wall alone. The physical education teacher, dancing past energetically in the arms of a grade 10

---

8. **peplum:** a short, skirtlike section of fabric attached to the waist of a dress and extending around the hips.

9. **golliwog** (gäl′ ē wäg′): a kind of grotesque doll made famous by Florence K. Upton in her children's books of the early 1900's.

Words to Know and Use
aloof (ə lo͞of′) *adj.* reserved and cool
inanimate (in an′ ə mit) *adj.* not possessing life; like an object
nonentity (nän′ en′ tə tē) *n.* a person of little or no importance

561

boy, gave me an inquisitive look. She was the only teacher in the school who made use of the words *social adjustment*, and I was afraid that if she had seen, or if she found out, she might make some horribly public attempt to make Mason finish out the dance with me. I myself was not angry or surprised at Mason. I accepted his position, and mine, in the world of school, and I saw that what he had done was the realistic thing to do. He was a Natural Hero, not a Student Council type of hero bound for success beyond the school; one of those would have danced with me courteously and patronizingly and left me feeling no better off. Still, I hoped not many people had seen. I hated people seeing. I began to bite the skin on my thumb.

When the music stopped, I joined the surge of girls to the end of the gymnasium. Pretend it didn't happen, I said to myself. Pretend this is the beginning, now.

The band began to play again. There was movement in the dense crowd at our end of the floor; it thinned rapidly. Boys came over; girls went out to dance. Lonnie went. The girl on the other side of me went. Nobody asked me. I remembered a magazine article Lonnie and I had read, which said *Be gay! Let the boys see your eyes sparkle, let them hear laughter in your voice! Simple, obvious, but how many girls forget!* It was true, I had forgotten. My eyebrows were drawn together with tension; I must look scared and ugly. I took a deep breath and tried to loosen my face. I smiled. But I felt absurd, smiling at no one. And I observed that girls on the dance floor, popular girls, were not smiling; many of them had sleepy, sulky faces and never smiled at all.

Girls were still going out to the floor. Some, despairing, went with each other. But most went with boys. Fat girls, girls with pimples, a poor girl who didn't own a good dress and had to wear a skirt and sweater to the dance; they were claimed; they danced away. Why take them and not me? Why everybody else and not me? I have a red velvet dress; I did my hair in curlers; I used a deodorant and put on cologne. *Pray,* I thought. I couldn't close my eyes but I said over and over again in my mind, *Please, me, please,* and I locked my fingers behind my back in a sign more <u>potent</u> than crossing, the same secret sign Lonnie and I used not to be sent to the blackboard in Math.

It did not work. What I had been afraid of was true. I was going to be left. There was something mysterious the matter with me, something that could not be put right like bad breath or overlooked like pimples, and everybody knew it, and I knew it; I had known it all along. But I had not known it for sure; I had hoped to be mistaken. Certainty rose inside me like sickness. I hurried past one or two girls who were also left and went into the girls' washroom. I hid myself in a cubicle.

That was where I stayed. Between dances girls came in and went out quickly. There were plenty of cubicles; nobody noticed that I was not a temporary occupant. During the dances, I listened to the music, which I liked but had no part of anymore. For I was not going to try anymore. I only wanted to hide in here, get out without seeing anybody, get home.

One time after the music started somebody stayed behind. She was taking a long time running the water, washing her hands, combing her hair. She was going to think it

Words to Know and Use | **potent** (pōt′ 'nt) *adj.* effective or powerful

UNTITLED   Susan Kahn   Collection of The Montclair Art Museum, New Jersey.

funny that I stayed in so long. I had better go out and wash my hands, and maybe while I was washing them she would leave.

It was Mary Fortune. I knew her by name because she was an officer of the Girls' Athletic Society and she was on the honor roll and she was always organizing things. She had something to do with organizing this dance; she had been around to all the classrooms asking for volunteers to do the decorations. She was in grade 11 or 12.

"Nice and cool in here," she said. "I came in to get cooled off. I get so hot."

She was still combing her hair when I finished my hands. "Do you like the band?" she said.

"It's all right." I didn't really know what to say. I was surprised at her, an older girl, taking this time to talk to me.

"I don't. I can't stand it. I hate dancing when I don't like the band. Listen. They're so choppy. I'd just as soon not dance as dance to that."

I combed my hair. She leaned against a basin, watching me.

"I don't want to dance and don't particularly want to stay in here. Let's go and have a cigarette."

"Where?"

"Come on, I'll show you."

At the end of the washroom, there was a door. It was unlocked and led into a dark closet full of mops and pails. She had me hold the door open, to get the washroom light, until she found the knob of another door. This door opened into darkness.

"I can't turn on the light or somebody might see," she said. "It's the janitor's room." I reflected that athletes always seemed to know more than the rest of us about the school as a building; they knew where things were kept, and they were always coming out of unauthorized doors with a bold, preoccupied air. "Watch out where you're going," she said. "Over at the far end there's some stairs. They go up to a closet on the second floor. The door's locked at the top, but there's like a partition between the stairs and the room. So if we sit on the steps, even if by chance someone did come in here, they wouldn't see us."

"Wouldn't they smell smoke?" I said.

"Oh, well. Live dangerously."

There was a high window over the stairs, which gave us a little light. Mary Fortune had cigarettes and matches in her purse. I had not smoked before except the cigarettes Lonnie and I made ourselves, using papers and tobacco stolen from her father; they came apart in the middle. These were much better.

"The only reason I even came tonight," Mary Fortune said, "is because I'm responsible for the decorations and I wanted to see, you know, how it looked once people got in there and everything. Otherwise why bother? I'm not boy crazy."

In the light from the high window I could see her narrow, scornful face, her dark skin pitted with acne, her teeth pushed together at the front, making her look adult and commanding.

"Most girls are. Haven't you noticed that? The greatest collection of boy-crazy girls you could imagine is right here in this school."

I was grateful for her attention, her company, and her cigarette. I said I thought so too.

"Like this afternoon. This afternoon I was trying to get them to hang the bells and junk. They just get up on the ladders and fool around with boys. They don't care if it ever gets decorated. It's just an excuse. That's the only aim they have in life, fooling around with boys. As far as I'm concerned, they're idiots."

We talked about teachers and things at school. She said she wanted to be a physical education teacher, and she would have to go to college for that, but her parents did not have enough money. She said she planned to work her own way through; she wanted to be independent anyway. She would work in the cafeteria, and in the summer she would do farm work, like picking tobacco. Listening to her, I felt the acute phase of my unhappiness passing. Here was someone who had suffered the same defeat as I had—I saw that—but she was full of energy and self-respect. She had thought of other things to do. She would pick tobacco.

We stayed there talking and smoking during the long pause in the music when, outside, they were having doughnuts and coffee. When the music started again, Mary said, "Look, do we have to hang around here any longer? Let's get our coats and go.

Words to Know and Use | **preoccupied** (prē äk′ yōō pīd′) *adj.* lost in thought
acute (ə kyōōt′) *adj.* serious; critical

We can go down to Lee's and have a hot chocolate and talk in comfort; why not?"

We felt our way across the janitor's room, carrying ashes and cigarette butts in our hands. In the closet, we stopped and listened to make sure there was nobody in the washroom. We came back into the light and threw the ashes into the toilet. We had to go out and cut across the dance floor to the cloakroom, which was beside the outside door.

A dance was just beginning. "Go round the edge of the floor," Mary said. "Nobody'll notice us."

I followed her. I didn't look at anybody. I didn't look for Lonnie. Lonnie was probably not going to be my friend any more, not as much as before, anyway. She was what Mary would call boy crazy.

I found that I was not so frightened, now that I had made up my mind to leave the dance behind. I was not waiting for anybody to choose me. I had my own plans. I did not have to smile or make signs for luck. It did not matter to me. I was on my way to have a hot chocolate with my friend.

A boy said something to me. He was in my way. I thought he must be telling me that I had dropped something or that I couldn't go that way or that the cloakroom was locked. I didn't understand that he was asking me to dance until he said it over again. It was Raymond Bolting from our class, whom I had never talked to in my life. He thought I meant yes. He put his hand on my waist and almost without meaning to, I began to dance.

W̲e moved to the middle of the floor. I was dancing. My legs had forgotten to tremble and my hands to sweat. I was dancing with a boy who had asked me. Nobody told him to; he didn't have to; he just asked me. Was

it possible? Could I believe it? Was there nothing the matter with me after all?

I thought I ought to tell him there was a mistake, that I was just leaving, that I was going to have a hot chocolate with my girlfriend. But I did not say anything. My face was making certain delicate adjustments, achieving with no effort at all the grave, absent-minded look of those who were chosen, those who danced. This was the face that Mary Fortune saw, when she looked out of the cloakroom door, her scarf already around her head. I made a weak waving motion with the hand that lay on the boy's shoulder, indicating that I apologized, that I didn't know what had happened, and also that it was no use waiting for me. Then I turned my head away and when I looked again she was gone.

R̲aymond Bolting took me home, and Harold Simons took Lonnie home. We all walked together as far as Lonnie's corner. The boys were having an argument about a hockey game, which Lonnie and I could not follow. Then we separated into couples, and Raymond continued with me the conversation he had been having with Harold. He did not seem to notice that he was now talking to me instead. Once or twice I said, "Well, I don't know; I didn't see that game," but after a while I decided just to say, "H'm hmm," and that seemed to be all that was necessary.

One other thing he said was, "I didn't realize you lived such a long ways out." And he sniffled. The cold was making my nose run a little too, and I worked my fingers through the candy wrappers in my coat pocket until I found a shabby Kleenex. I didn't know whether to offer it to him or not, but he sniffled so loudly that I finally said, "I just have this one Kleenex; it probably isn't even clean; it probably has ink on it. But if I was to tear it in half, we'd each have something."

"Thanks," he said. "I sure could use it."

It was a good thing, I thought, that I had done that, for at my gate, when I said, "Well, good night" and after he said, "Oh, yeah. Good night," he leaned toward me and kissed me, briefly, with the air of one who knew his job when he saw it, on the corner of my mouth. Then he turned back to town, never knowing he had been my rescuer, that he had brought me from Mary Fortune's territory into the ordinary world.

I went around the house to the back door, thinking, I have been to a dance and a boy has walked me home and kissed me. It was all true. My life was possible. I went past the kitchen window and I saw my mother. She was sitting with her feet on the open oven door, drinking tea out of a cup without a saucer. She was just sitting and waiting for me to come home and tell her everything that had happened. And I would not do it; I never would. But when I saw the waiting kitchen and my mother in her faded, fuzzy paisley kimono, with her sleepy but doggedly expectant face, I understood what a mysterious and oppressive obligation I had, to be happy, and how I had almost failed it, and would be likely to fail it every time, and she would not know. ❧

I N S I G H T

Long Distance

CAROLE GREGORY

That phone call, the one that you wait for
but never expect to come
was phoned today. And
that voice, the voice you ache for
but seldom expect to hear
spoke today. And that
loneliness, the loneliness you hurt from
but always held inside,
flies out like thin stones across water.

Words to Know and Use | **oppressive** (ə pres′ iv) *adj.* weighing heavily on one's mind or spirits; distressing
obligation (äb′ lə ga′ shən) *n.* a sense of duty; responsibility

Responding to Reading

First Impressions

1. Is the narrator someone you would like to know? Why or why not?

Second Thoughts

2. In what ways do the narrator's expectations about herself and others affect the events in this story? Explain.

3. On what does the narrator base her assumptions about other people? In your opinion, is she a good judge of people? Why or why not?

4. Does the narrator's level of self-confidence change during the story? Why or why not? Give examples to illustrate your answer.

5. Compare and contrast the narrator and Mary. What is the narrator's opinion of Mary by the end of the story? Do you share that opinion?

6. Does the narrator's attitude toward her mother change during the story? Explain.

> **Think about**
> • her feelings as her mother makes the red dress
> • her feelings as she and Lonnie leave for the dance
> • her thoughts as she returns home from the dance

7. Explain the last sentence of the story. In your opinion, is this "oppressive obligation . . . to be happy" a common expectation of parents for their children? Explain.

Broader Connections

8. The narrator says that attraction to the opposite sex, not learning, was "what was really going on" in her school. Is this true at your school? Describe what you see happening.

Literary Concept: First-Person Point of View

In a story told from the **first-person point of view**, the reader sees the action and other characters through the narrator's eyes and learns the narrator's thoughts and feelings. "Red Dress—1946" is told from the main character's point of view. How does this point of view affect your perception of her and of the other characters? How might the story have differed if it had been told by the mother's or Mary's point of view?

Concept Review: Conflict Are the conflicts in this story primarily internal or external? Give reasons to support your opinion.

Writing Options

1. Suppose you are the narrator, just home from the dance. Write a diary entry that expresses your private thoughts about the dance.

2. Write a paragraph explaining how the thoughts of the speaker in "Long Distance" parallel those of the narrator in "Red Dress—1946."

3. A "female ritual" the narrator performs to prepare for the dance is setting her hair. List rituals that girls and boys go through today to get ready for special occasions.

4. Write what you think might be Mason Williams's thoughts as he dances with the narrator.

Vocabulary Practice

Exercise A Refer to the word list to answer each question below. Some questions have more than one correct answer.

1. What words describe a mood?
2. What words describe a manner of behaving?
3. What word can only be used to describe an object?
4. What is a word for a bad feeling about the future?
5. What word describes a strong pain?
6. What is a word for a type of comedian?
7. What is a word for a task that has to be done?

Exercise B Antonyms Write the word that is most nearly opposite in meaning to the capitalized word.

1. IRRELEVANT: (a) ruined (b) significant (c) unnecessary (d) undecided
2. POTENT: (a) powerful (b) weak (c) crucial (d) silly
3. OPPRESSIVE: (a) lighthearted (b) painful (c) visible (d) heavy
4. ACCENTUATE: (a) downplay (b) highlight (c) speed (d) immigrate
5. NONENTITY: (a) nobody (b) celebrity (c) zero (d) outsider
6. VULNERABLE: (a) worried (b) weak (c) tough (d) useless
7. ALOOF: (a) reserved (b) friendly (c) shy (d) honest
8. COMPOSED: (a) calm (b) sleepy (c) nervous (d) clever

Words to Know and Use

accentuate
acute
aloof
composed
inanimate
irrelevant
melodramatic
mimic
nonentity
obligation
oppressive
potent
premonition
preoccupied
vulnerable

e x t e n d

Options for Learning

1 • **Then and Now** From this story you have learned something about what it was like to be a teenager in 1946. What were some other characteristics of that time? Search your library for books, magazines, and newspaper articles about the 1940's. Look for information about music, movies, dances, clothes, heroes, cars, and popular food. Talk to relatives who lived then. Make a chart that compares life then and now.

2 • **A "Then" Dance** Research the popular dances of the 1940's. Choose one dance to learn with a partner. Find an appropriate recording in your local library or your school's music department. Perform the dance for classmates or teach it to them.

3 • **What Will I Say?** Review the conversation that the narrator and Mary Fortune have during the dance. With a partner, act out your version of the next conversation that might occur between them.

4 • **How to be Popular** Ever since *Seventeen* magazine first came out in 1944, teen magazines have advised teenagers on how to be popular. Check the *Readers' Guide to Periodical Literature* for articles on how to be popular. Read three of the articles and write a review in which you summarize each article and give your opinion of its accuracy and value to teens.

 **FACT FINDER**

Find out the names of some of the most popular songs of 1946.

Alice Munro
1931-

Peaceful Canadian towns that change little over the years, rolling fields of golden wheat—such scenes have served as the setting for the life of Alice Munro. Born into a farm family, Munro has spent much of her life in rural Ontario, Canada. She attended the University of Western Ontario and then remained in Ontario, where she was married and raised three daughters.

Munro's rural background provides the setting for many of her stories. Yet readers with different backgrounds and lifestyles enjoy following the lives of Munro's down-to-earth characters. "I want to write the story that will zero in and give you intense . . . moments of experience," she says.

Munro published her first collection of stories, *Dance of the Happy Shades and Other Stories*, in 1968. In 1990 she published her seventh collection, *Friend of My Youth*. Munro has received three Governor General's Literary Awards, Canada's highest prize for literature.

Autobiography

from I Know Why the Caged Bird Sings

MAYA ANGELOU
(mī yə an′ jə lo͞o)

Examine What You Know

Angelou took the title of her autobiography from a line of the poem "Sympathy" by Paul Laurence Dunbar. Three lines of "Sympathy" suggest Angelou's reasons.

> I know why the caged bird sings, ah me,
>   When his wing is bruised and his bosom sore,—
> When he beats his bars and he would be free

Talk about the ways people are "caged" by society or by themselves. As you read, watch for similarities between Angelou and a caged bird.

Expand Your Knowledge

Maya Angelou was born Marguerite Johnson. "Maya" came from her brother Bailey's habit of addressing her as "Mya Sister." She has written five autobiographical books. *I Know Why the Caged Bird Sings*, her first and most famous book, tells about her life until the age of sixteen.

In the early 1930's, when Angelou's parents separated, she and Bailey were sent to live with their grandmother, whom they called Momma, in the rural community of Stamps, Arkansas. At that time, Stamps was a small, segregated town in the southwest corner of the state. Angelou's grandmother owned a general store in the part of town Angelou refers to as Black Stamps.

After a traumatic experience that took place in St. Louis when she was eight, Angelou withdrew into herself and barely spoke for five years. The recollection you will read begins after her return to Stamps.

Write Before You Read

One woman in this excerpt, Mrs. Flowers, helps create a turning point in young Angelou's life. Consider some turning points in your life. Write about a person who influenced you in a significant way.

■ *A biography of the author can be found on page 579.*

from I Know Why the Caged Bird Sings

MAYA ANGELOU

For nearly a year, I sopped around the house, the Store, the school and the church, like an old biscuit, dirty and inedible. Then I met, or rather got to know, the lady who threw me my first lifeline.

Mrs. Bertha Flowers was the aristocrat of Black Stamps. She had the grace of control to appear warm in the coldest weather, and on the Arkansas summer days it seemed she had a private breeze which swirled around, cooling her. She was thin without the taut look of wiry people, and her printed voile dresses and flowered hats were as right for her as denim overalls for a farmer. She was our side's answer to the richest white woman in town.

Her skin was a rich black that would have peeled like a plum if snagged, but then no one would have thought of getting close enough to Mrs. Flowers to ruffle her dress, let alone snag her skin. She didn't encourage familiarity. She wore gloves, too.

I don't think I ever saw Mrs. Flowers laugh, but she smiled often. A slow widening of her thin black lips to show even, small white teeth, then the slow effortless closing. When she chose to smile on me, I always wanted to thank her. The action was so graceful and inclusively benign.[1]

She was one of the few gentlewomen I have ever known and has remained throughout my life the measure of what a human being can be.

Momma had a strange relationship with her. Most often when she passed on the road in front of the Store, she spoke to Momma in that soft yet carrying voice, "Good day, Mrs. Henderson." Momma responded with "How you, Sister Flowers?"

Mrs. Flowers didn't belong to our church, nor was she Momma's familiar.[2] Why on earth did she insist on calling her Sister Flowers? Shame made me want to hide my face. Mrs. Flowers deserved better than to be called Sister. Then, Momma left out the verb. Why not ask, "How *are* you, *Mrs.* Flowers?" With the unbalanced passion of the young, I hated her for showing her ignorance to Mrs. Flowers. It didn't occur to me for many years that they were as alike as sisters, separated only by formal education.

---

1. **inclusively benign:** good-natured and kindly in a way that takes others in.
2. **familiar:** a close friend or confidant.

571

ANNA WASHINGTON DERRY 1927 Laura Wheeler Waring National Museum of American Art, Smithsonian Institution, Washington, D.C./Art Resource, New York.

Although I was upset, neither of the women was in the least shaken by what I thought an unceremonious greeting. Mrs. Flowers would continue her easy gait[3] up the hill to her little bungalow,[4] and Momma kept on shelling peas or doing whatever had brought her to the front porch.

Occasionally, though, Mrs. Flowers would drift off the road and down to the Store and Momma would say to me, "Sister, you go on and play." As I left I would hear the beginning of an intimate conversation. Momma persistently using the wrong verb, or none at all.

"Brother and Sister Wilcox is sho'ly the meanest—" "Is," Momma? "Is?" Oh, please, not "is," Momma, for two or more. But they talked, and from the side of the building where I waited for the ground to open up and swallow me, I heard the soft-voiced Mrs. Flowers and the textured voice of my grandmother merging and melting. They were interrupted from time to time by giggles that must have come from Mrs. Flowers

---

3. **gait** (gāt): manner or style of walking.
4. **bungalow:** a small, one-story house or cottage.

(Momma never giggled in her life). Then she was gone.

She appealed to me because she was like people I had never met personally. Like women in English novels who walked the moors[5] (whatever they were) with their loyal dogs racing at a respectful distance. Like the women who sat in front of roaring fireplaces, drinking tea incessantly from silver trays full of scones and crumpets.[6] Women who walked over the "heath"[7] and read morocco-bound[8] books and had two last names divided by a hyphen. It would be safe to say that she made me proud to be Negro, just by being herself.

She acted just as refined as whitefolks in the movies and books, and she was more beautiful, for none of them could have come near that warm color without looking gray by comparison.

It was fortunate that I never saw her in the company of powhitefolks. For since they tend to think of their whiteness as an evenizer, I'm certain that I would have had to hear her spoken to commonly as Bertha, and my image of her would have been shattered like the unmendable Humpty-Dumpty.

One summer afternoon, sweet-milk fresh in my memory, she stopped at the Store to buy provisions. Another Negro woman of her health and age would have been expected to carry the paper sacks home in one hand, but Momma said, "Sister Flowers, I'll send Bailey up to your house with these things."

She smiled that slow dragging smile, "Thank you, Mrs. Henderson. I'd prefer Marguerite, though." My name was beautiful when she said it. "I've been meaning to talk to her, anyway." They gave each other age-group looks.

Momma said, "Well, that's all right then. Sister, go and change your dress. You going to Sister Flowers's."

The chifforobe[9] was a maze. What on earth did one put on to go to Mrs. Flowers's house? I knew I shouldn't put on a Sunday dress. It might be sacrilegious. Certainly not a housedress, since I was already wearing a fresh one. I chose a school dress, naturally. It was formal without suggesting that going to Mrs. Flowers's house was equivalent to attending church.

I trusted myself back into the Store.

"Now, don't you look nice." I had chosen the right thing, for once.

"Mrs. Henderson, you make most of the children's clothes, don't you?"

"Yes, ma'am. Sure do. Store-bought clothes ain't hardly worth the thread it take to stitch them."

"I'll say you do a lovely job, though, so neat. That dress looks professional."

Momma was enjoying the seldom-received compliments. Since everyone we knew (except Mrs. Flowers, of course) could sew competently, praise was rarely handed out for commonly practiced craft.

"I try, with the help of the Lord, Sister Flowers, to finish the inside just like I does the outside. Come here, Sister."

---

5. **moors:** an area of open, rolling, marshy wasteland most often covered with heather; often associated with Scotland.

6. **scones and crumpets:** Scones are small, sweet biscuits; crumpets are rolls similar to English muffins.

7. **heath** (hēth): a moor.

8. **morocco-bound:** bound, or covered, in soft leather.

9. **chifforobe** (shif′ ə rōb′): a chest of drawers combined with a small closet for storing clothes.

Words to Know and Use

incessantly (in ses′ ənt lē) *adv.* continuously; nonstop
sacrilegious (sak rə lij′ əs) *adj.* disrespectful toward a sacred person, place, or thing

573

I had buttoned up the collar and tied the belt, apronlike, in back. Momma told me to turn around. With one hand she pulled the strings, and the belt fell free at both sides of my waist. Then her large hands were at my neck, opening the button loops. I was terrified. What was happening?

"Take it off, Sister." She had her hands on the hem of the dress.

"I don't need to see the inside, Mrs. Henderson, I can tell . . ." But the dress was over my head and my arms were stuck in the sleeves. Momma said, "That'll do. See here, Sister Flowers, I French-seams around the armholes." Through the cloth film, I saw the shadow approach. "That makes it last longer. Children these days would bust out of sheet-metal clothes. They so rough."

Words mean more than what is set down on paper.

"That is a very good job, Mrs. Henderson. You should be proud. You can put your dress back on, Marguerite."

"No ma'am. Pride is a sin. And 'cording to the Good Book, it goeth before a fall."

"That's right. So the Bible says. It's a good thing to keep in mind."

I wouldn't look at either of them. Momma hadn't thought that taking off my dress in front of Mrs. Flowers would kill me stone dead. If I had refused, she would have thought I was trying to be "womanish" and might have remembered St. Louis. Mrs. Flowers had known that I would be embarrassed, and that was even worse. I picked up the groceries and went out to wait in the hot sunshine. It would be fitting if I got a sunstroke and died before they came outside. Just dropped dead on the slanting porch.

There was a little path beside the rocky road, and Mrs. Flowers walked in front, swinging her arms and picking her way over the stones.

She said, without turning her head, to me, "I hear you're doing very good schoolwork, Marguerite, but that it's all written. The teachers report that they have trouble getting you to talk in class." We passed the triangular farm on our left and the path widened to allow us to walk together. I hung back in the separate unasked and unanswerable questions.

"Come and walk along with me, Marguerite." I couldn't have refused even if I wanted to. She pronounced my name so nicely. Or more correctly, she spoke each word with such clarity that I was certain a foreigner who didn't understand English could have understood her.

"Now no one is going to make you talk—possibly no one can. But bear in mind, language is man's way of communicating with his fellow man and it is language alone which separates him from the lower animals." That was a totally new idea to me, and I would need time to think about it.

"Your grandmother says you read a lot. Every chance you get. That's good, but not good enough. Words mean more than what is set down on paper. It takes the human voice to infuse them with the shades of deeper meaning."

I memorized the part about the human voice infusing words. It seemed so valid and poetic.

She said she was going to give me some

Words to Know and Use | **infuse** (in fyo͞oz′) v. to inject; add to

books and that I not only must read them, I must read them aloud. She suggested that I try to make a sentence sound in as many different ways as possible.

"I'll accept no excuse if you return a book to me that has been badly handled." My imagination boggled at the punishment I would deserve if in fact I did abuse a book of Mrs. Flowers's. Death would be too kind and brief.

The odors in the house surprised me. Somehow I had never connected Mrs. Flowers with food or eating or any other common experience of common people. There must have been an outhouse, too, but my mind never recorded it.

The sweet scent of vanilla had met us as she opened the door.

"I made tea cookies this morning. You see, I had planned to invite you for cookies and lemonade so we could have this little chat. The lemonade is in the icebox."

It followed that Mrs. Flowers would have ice on an ordinary day, when most families in our town bought ice late on Saturdays only a few times during the summer to be used in the wooden ice-cream freezers.

She took the bags from me and disappeared through the kitchen door. I looked around the room that I had never in my wildest fantasies imagined I would see. Browned photographs leered or threatened from the walls, and the white, freshly done curtains pushed against themselves and against the wind. I wanted to gobble up the room entire and take it to Bailey, who would help me analyze and enjoy it.

"Have a seat, Marguerite. Over there by the table." She carried a platter covered with a tea towel. Although she warned that she hadn't tried her hand at baking sweets for some time, I was certain that, like everything else about her, the cookies would be perfect.

They were flat, round wafers, slightly browned on the edges and butter-yellow in the center. With the cold lemonade they were sufficient for childhood's lifelong diet. Remembering my manners, I took nice little ladylike bites off the edges. She said she had made them expressly for me and that she had a few in the kitchen that I could take home to my brother. So I jammed one whole cake in my mouth and the rough crumbs scratched the insides of my jaws, and if I hadn't had to swallow, it would have been a dream come true.

As I ate, she began the first of what we later called "my lessons in living." She said that I must always be intolerant of ignorance but understanding of illiteracy. That some people, unable to go to school, were more educated and even more intelligent than college professors. She encouraged me to listen carefully to what country people called mother wit. That in those homely sayings was couched the collective wisdom of generations.

When I finished the cookies, she brushed off the table and brought a thick, small book from the bookcase. I had read *A Tale of Two Cities*[10] and found it up to my standards as a romantic novel. She opened the first page, and I heard poetry for the first time in my life.

"It was the best of times and the worst of times . . ." Her voice slid in and curved down through and over the words. She was nearly singing. I wanted to look at the pages. Were

---

10. *A Tale of Two Cities:* a novel written by Charles Dickens.

Words to Know and Use | illiteracy (il lit' ər ə sē) *n.* a lack of knowledge of how to read and write

575

they the same that I had read? Or were there notes, music, lined on the pages, as in a hymn book? Her sounds began cascading gently. I knew from listening to a thousand preachers that she was nearing the end of her reading, and I hadn't really heard, heard to understand, a single word.

"How do you like that?"

It occurred to me that she expected a response. The sweet vanilla flavor was still on my tongue and her reading was a wonder in my ears. I had to speak.

I said, "Yes, ma'am." It was the least I could do, but it was the most also.

"There's one more thing. Take this book of poems and memorize one for me. Next time you pay me a visit, I want you to recite."

I have tried often to search behind the sophistication of years for the enchantment I so easily found in those gifts. The essence escapes but its aura remains. To be allowed, no, invited, into the private lives of strangers and to share their joys and fears was a chance to exchange the Southern bitter wormwood for a cup of mead with Beowulf or a hot cup of tea and milk with Oliver Twist.[11] When I said aloud, "It is a far, far better thing that I do, than I have ever done . . ." tears of love filled my eyes at my selflessness.

On that first day, I ran down the hill and into the road (few cars ever came along it) and had the good sense to stop running before I reached the Store.

I was liked, and what a difference it made. I was respected not as Mrs. Henderson's grandchild or Bailey's sister but for just being Marguerite Johnson.

Childhood's logic never asks to be proved (all conclusions are absolute). I didn't question why Mrs. Flowers had singled me out for attention, nor did it occur to me that Momma might have asked her to give me a little talking to. All I cared about was that she had made tea cookies for *me* and read to *me* from her favorite book. It was enough to prove that she liked me. ❧

---

11. **a chance to exchange . . . with Oliver Twist:** Angelou would like to exchange the bitterness of her life in the South, where they drink a liquor made from the bitter oil of the wormwood plant, for a storybook life in England, where famous literary characters such as Beowulf drank mead, a sweet beer-like drink, and Oliver Twist drank tea with milk.

INSIGHT

Metaphor

EVE MERRIAM

Morning is
a new sheet of paper
for you to write on.

Whatever you want to say,
all day,
until night
folds it up
and files it away.

The bright words and the dark words
are gone
until dawn
and a new day
to write on.

Words to Know and Use

cascading (kas kād ′iŋ) *n.* falling or flowing, like a waterful **cascade** *v.*
sophistication (sə fis′ tə kā′ shən) *n.* the state of being worldly-wise or experienced
essence (es′ əns) *n.* the basic or most important quality
aura (ô′ rə) *n.* the atmosphere or feeling that surrounds a person, object, or event

Responding to Reading

First Impressions

1. Describe your image of Mrs. Flowers. In your journal or on a sheet of paper, jot down any words or phrases that come to mind.

Second Thoughts

2. What does Angelou mean when she says that Mrs. Flowers is "the measure of what a human being can be"? Why does Angelou admire Mrs. Flowers so much? Give reasons for your answers.

3. In what ways is young Angelou like a caged bird? Support your answer with details from the story.

4. In what ways does Mrs. Flowers fulfill Angelou's needs?

5. Although Angelou's grandmother and Mrs. Flowers are very different, they get along very well. Why?

Broader Connections

6. Angelou is embarrassed by her grandmother's common way of speaking. Are people judged by the level of language they use? When is it important to speak well? Do you think that a person's manner of speaking reflects his or her intelligence and worth?

Literary Concept: Figurative Language

Figurative language is language that conveys meaning beyond the literal meaning of the words. Angelou uses two kinds of figurative language, similes and metaphors, to express exactly what she saw, heard, thought, and felt.

You have learned that a **simile** compares two things using *like* or *as*, while a **metaphor** compares two things directly without the use of *like* or *as*. Find at least two similes and two metaphors in this selection. Explain each comparison that is made and tell how it affects your concept of the person, action, or setting.

Concept Review: Theme One way to identify the theme of a work of literature is to focus on what the main character learns about life or human nature. Think about what Angelou learns from her visit with Mrs. Flowers. How would you summarize the theme of this selection?

Writing Options

1. Mrs. Flowers tells Angelou to be "intolerant of ignorance but understanding of illiteracy." What is your opinion of this advice? Give reasons to support your opinion.

2. Explain how this selection fits the theme "Opportunity Knocks."

3. Angelou credits Mrs. Flowers with throwing her a lifeline. Predict how her contact with this woman could change her life.

4. Imagine that young Angelou and Mrs. Flowers have just read the poem "Metaphor." Write a scene in which they discuss the meaning of the poem.

5. Describe someone you know who reminds you of Mrs. Flowers.

Vocabulary Practice

Exercise A An **analogy** shows a relationship between words. To complete an analogy, determine the relationship between the first pair of words. Then decide which word from the list best completes the second analogy. Write the word on your paper.

1. *Glow* is to *radiance* as _____ is to *atmosphere.*
2. *Beauty* is to *ugliness* as _____ is to *inexperience.*
3. *Drifting* is to *snow* as _____ is to *water.*
4. *Disease* is to *medicine* as _____ is to *education.*
5. *Democrat* is to *democracy* as _____ is to *aristocracy.*

Exercise B Read each question. On a separate sheet of paper, write your answer and explain why you think as you do.

1. How might a religious person like Momma respond to a **sacrilegious** comment?
2. If Marguerite were to read **incessantly**, would she most likely finish a novel quickly or slowly?
3. What might an educated woman like Mrs. Flowers do to **infuse** book knowledge into an uneducated woman like Momma?
4. How might Mrs. Flowers have spoken or acted if she had wanted to encourage **familiarity?**
5. Is the **essence** of a person visible or invisible?

Words to Know and Use

aristocrat
aura
cascading
essence
familiarity
illiteracy
incessantly
infuse
sacrilegious
sophistication

extend

Options for Learning

1 • Cascading Voices Angelou compares Mrs. Flowers's reading voice to music. Choose an excerpt from one of the literary works mentioned in this selection or a work you like to read to your class. Practice reading the piece aloud, pausing after each unit of thought. Change the pitch, volume, and tone of your voice until you feel comfortable with your interpretation.

2 • Portrait Painter From the details given in this selection, paint or draw a portrait of Mrs. Flowers. Include an object that you think symbolizes her character.

3 • On-Stage Action Create a monologue in which Mrs. Flowers presents her version of the events in this excerpt, or develop a scene involving Mrs. Flowers and another character. Find clues in the story about how Mrs. Flowers moves, speaks, and dresses. Perform your monologue or dialogue for your class.

4 • Mother Wit Mrs. Flowers advises Marguerite to pay attention to "mother wit," that is, proverbs or sayings used to pass on knowledge. "A watched pot never boils" is one example of mother wit. With several classmates, compile a list of these sayings that you collect from adults. Present your favorites to the class by illustrating them, acting them out, or by creating a story with a saying as the moral.

FACT FINDER

What are the titles of Angelou's other autobiographical works?

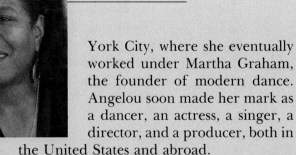

Maya Angelou
1928 -

Although Maya Angelou's formal education ended after high school, she has continued to search for knowledge of herself and the world around her. "I believe all things are possible for a human being, and I don't think there's anything in the world I can't do."

Angelou's life bears evidence that she lives by this philosophy. After high school, she worked days to support herself and her son while she studied dance at night. Her talent led to a scholarship to study dance in New York City, where she eventually worked under Martha Graham, the founder of modern dance. Angelou soon made her mark as a dancer, an actress, a singer, a director, and a producer, both in the United States and abroad.

Angelou, who is fluent in six languages, began writing in the mid-1960's. She has written poems, songs, stage and screenplays, television specials, short stories, magazine articles, and five autobiographical works. Angelou has also toured the country as a lecturer and visiting professor to various colleges and universities.

WRITER'S WORKSHOP

CREATIVE EXPRESSION

People write poetry for various reasons. Poems may be written to express emotions, to explore ideas, to convey experiences, or to paint pictures with words in an original way. Poems can surprise, amuse, challenge, and entertain us.

Poetry is different from other kinds of writing. Although a poem might narrate an incident or describe a setting, it uses language and images in a special way. Most poems are relatively brief, and therefore each word carries much more weight than it might in an essay or a story. Poets choose each word carefully and frequently use figurative language, such as similes, metaphors, and personification, to create strong images.

Poets pay special attention not only to *what* they want to say but also to *how* they say it. Some poems rhyme at the ends of lines and follow specific rhythmic patterns, similar to music. Others seem to have no regular structure. Skimming through the poems in this book will give you an idea of the many forms a poem can take.

For example, notice the different forms in these lines quoted from Nikki Giovanni's "A Journey" and Amy Lowell's "Fireworks."

> It's a journey . . . that I propose . . . I am not the guide . . . nor technical assistant . . . I will be your fellow passenger. . .

> You hate me and I hate you,
> And we are so polite, we two!

The selections in this subunit revolve around memories of childhood events that were very important to the writer or main character. These events may have been turning points, or they may have been the first glimmer of opportunity for future success. In this workshop, you will write a poem that expresses a similar memory of your own.

Here is your PASSkey to this assignment.

GUIDED ASSIGNMENT: POETRY

Remember an incident in your life that was a turning point or a significant opportunity for you. Write a poem about it.

PURPOSE: To write creatively

AUDIENCE: Your classmates

SUBJECT: A memory of a turning point

STRUCTURE: A poem

Prewriting

Step 1 **Brainstorm for ideas** Try to recall times in your life that were significant turning points. Also consider any events that offered you opportunities for future success. Jot down anything that comes to mind. You should end up with a list similar to the following one created by a student:

- I tried out for the junior high school band.
- My best friend moved away.
- My mother got a full-time job.
- My older brother joined the army.
- I wrote my first short story.

◀ STUDENT MODEL

Step 2 **Choose an event** Look over your list. Consider the importance of each event and how much you remember about it. Which one had consequences for you that stretched far beyond the immediate circumstances of the event? Choose the one that you think will be the easiest to write about.

The student who compiled the list in step 1 reviewed her options and selected the last item. She chose to compose a poem about writing her first short story because that event was a turning point in her life—it led to her avid interest in writing. She also had vivid memories about it, and the idea seemed to lend itself to a poem.

Step 3 **Think of details** Brainstorm details about the event you selected. Start by imagining yourself back in the situation. What did you see, hear, taste, and feel? What was the atmosphere? Recall what happened. Visualize the scene in your mind's eye.

On a piece of paper, make a chart with three headings: Images, Feelings, and What Happened. Under each heading, write in sentences or phrases any specific images that illustrate the event. Refer to the Figurative Language Workshop on page 584 for suggestions on using similes, metaphors, and personification. Don't forget to include sensory details—the sounds or smells or sights connected with the event. Try to add words that will convey some of that part of your memory, to make the event more real for your readers.

If you have trouble thinking of a variety of words, try looking in a thesaurus or reviewing some of the poetry in this book. Sometimes one or two words will start a whole list of associations.

Here is a portion of the chart made by the student who was remembering writing her first short story.

Images	Feelings	What Happened
blank paper	threatened	at first,
white, clean	challenged	nothing
too white, empty	Do I dare disturb	story filled my
clean as a yard	it?	head
of snow	Will I dirty it	I got excited.
clicking and	up?	Ideas poured
clacking of	paper making fun	out.
typewriter	of me	
pouring black	excitement	
letters onto		
white paper		
like water		

Step 4 **Be selective** Review your chart carefully. Select the most important details to include in your poem. Look over the various images and choose the ones that are most specific, vivid, and original. Ask a classmate to review your details and images. Revise any items that he or she identifies as confusing, vague, or unoriginal.

Drafting

Step 1 **Organize your poem** One way to organize your poem is to tell about the events in the order in which they happened. However, poems that delight readers often contain mysteries and surprises. You might want to begin with an unusual image first and then gradually tell the story. Don't give everything away. Let your readers use their imagination. Here is the beginning of the student's first draft.

Evil blank paper—a threat and a challenge
My mind as closed and empty as this white
Will floodgates open and ideas pour across it?

Notice how the student begins her poem. Instead of beginning with a topic sentence, as she would in writing an essay, she starts her poem with a striking image that will amuse and interest the reader.

Step 2 **Write in lines** Decide how to break your poem into separate lines. As you know, lines of poetry do not have to extend to the right-hand margin of the page. A line might be as short as a single word. Poets sometimes give a full line to each important image or detail. Look at some poems in this book for ways in which lines can be broken. Write several different drafts with varying line lengths. Choose the draft that you like best.

Revising and Editing

Once you have completed the rough draft of your poem, ask a classmate to review your work according to the following checklist. Then revise your paper using those ideas that you think will improve it.

> ### Revision Checklist
> ....
> 1. Does the poem center on a turning point or opportunity?
> 2. Does the poem begin in such a way that you want to read further?
> 3. Does the poem avoid telling the reader everything? Does it require the reader to use his or her imagination?
> 4. Are the images specific, vivid, and original?

Editing   When you have finished revising your poem, proofread it for spelling, clarity, and mechanics.

Presenting

Organize a poetry reading in your class. After each student reads his or her poem aloud, discuss what made the event in the poem a true turning point.

Reflecting on Your Writing

Answer the following questions about this assignment. Put the answers and your poem in your writing portfolio.

1. Compare writing poetry to writing essays. Which do you find easier? Why?
2. What was the most difficult part about writing this poem? Why?
3. Would you like to write more poetry? Why or why not?
4. Having completed this assignment, will you read poetry differently in the future? Explain.

USING FIGURATIVE LANGUAGE

Whether you are writing or reading poetry or other forms of literature, you should understand the use of figurative language.

Figurative language is language in which words communicate ideas beyond the exact meanings of those words. It is different from **literal language,** which uses only the ordinary meanings of words. For example, the familiar expression "It was raining cats and dogs" is a figurative statement. Its meaning has nothing to do with animals. A literal statement that expresses the same idea is "It was raining extremely hard."

Figurative language can link ideas in fresh, often surprising ways. Specific types of figurative language are known as **figures of speech.** Simile, metaphor, and personification are the figures of speech used most frequently by writers.

A **simile** is a comparison between two unlike things that have something in common. A simile always uses the word *like* or *as* to make a comparison. Here is an example from the poem "Long Distance."

> the loneliness . . . flies out like thin stones across water.

Like a simile, a **metaphor** also compares unlike things that have something in common. But a metaphor does not use the word *like* or *as.* Look at the first stanza in the poem "Metaphor." How are morning and a blank sheet of paper different? Why do you think the poet chose to use them together in this metaphor?

> Morning is a new sheet of paper for you to write on.

Personification is a figure of speech in which human qualities are given to an object, animal, or idea. Look at the following sentence from *I Know Why the Caged Bird Sings.* What items are personified? What human qualities does the writer give them?

> Browned photographs leered or threatened from the walls, and the white, freshly done curtains pushed against themselves and against the wind.

Exercise 1   Find the figure of speech in each of the following quotations and identify it as a *simile,* a *metaphor,* or *personification.* Then explain the comparison each makes.

Word Play
....
Think about the meta-
  phors we use
  every day:
This is a wild-goose
  chase!
That's for the birds!
Only fifty cents? That's
  chicken feed!
It's a dog-eat-dog world!
I hate all this red tape!
Don't spill the beans!
I'm getting out of this rat
  race!
Can you think of others?

1. . . . summer was dead, but autumn had not yet been born.

—"The Scarlet Ibis," James Hurst

2. I sopped around the house . . . like an old biscuit, dirty and inedible.

—*I Know Why the Caged Bird Sings,* Maya Angelou

3. The Truth
is quite messy
like
a wind blown room

—"The Truth Is Quite Messy," William J. Harris

4. The pine tree pointed his finger to the sky,
And the oak spread out his arms

—"The Creation," James Weldon Johnson

Exercise 2   Style   In small groups skim through the selections you have read. Find and write down two examples each of simile, metaphor, and personification. Discuss how the writing would be different if literal language had been used.

Exercise 3   Write similes to describe three of the following items.

sand in your shoes	when school lets out
a stadium crowd	an angry face

Exercise 4   Write metaphors to describe two of the following things.

snake   fire   closet   computer   music

Exercise 5   Use personification to describe two of the following objects.

a pencil sharpener	a skyscraper	a slide
a video game	an empty house	a car

Exercise 6   Analyzing and Revising Your Writing

1. Review a piece of your writing. Choose a passage that could be improved with a figure of speech.
2. Rewrite the necessary sentences, adding the figurative language.
3. Compare your revised sentences with the original ones. Which version do you prefer?

VOCABULARY
WORKSHOP

DENOTATION AND CONNOTATION

The definition of a word found in a dictionary is that word's **denotation,** or direct, specific meaning. Many words have more than one denotation, and some words have several. As a writer looking for just the right word, however, you have to consider more than just denotation, because many words have other associations, either positive or negative, attached to them. These added ideas and feelings are called **connotations.**

WORD PLAY

Which would you rather have—

a cheap or an inexpensive radio?

a whim or a daydream?

an exasperated or a maniacal teacher?

a worthy or a brilliant idea?

Some words, such as *house,* have only a denotative meaning. These words can be thought of as neutral. A word like *home,* however, has a positive connotation, suggesting a welcoming, comfortable place. In contrast, the word *shack* has a negative connotation, suggesting a shabby, run-down place.

When you read, notice the shades of meaning that the writer's words carry. When you write, think carefully about each word you choose.

Exercise 1   Tell whether each of the following words has a *positive* or *negative* connotation.

1. thrifty	**6.** slim
2. stingy	**7.** silly
3. careful	**8.** good-natured
4. picky	**9.** gaudy
5. skinny	**10.** colorful

Exercise 2   Write three paragraphs about a school dance or another event.

1. In the first paragraph describe the event with words that have *positive* connotations.
2. Next, write the paragraph using words with *negative* connotations.
3. Finally, rewrite the paragraph using words without either a positive or negative slant. That is, describe the event objectively.

DECISIONS AND CONSEQUENCES

The hardest decisions to make are the ones with the most important consequences. When the consequences are life or death—as in the selections in this subunit—the choices become crucial. As you read put yourself in the place of the characters faced with the decisions. Make your own choice. Then read about the unusual and unexpected consequences—both good and bad—of the characters' decisions.

Fiction

Button, Button

RICHARD MATHESON

Examine What You Know

"Button, Button" examines how people react when faced with temptation. How strong of a temptation is money to you? Would you do something unusual or even immoral to get it? Look at the following ways people make easy money. Decide which if any would be a temptation to you.

play the lottery
do a daring stunt
make yourself look foolish
do something illegal
do something immoral

Expand Your Knowledge

Richard Matheson uses elements of both science fiction and fantasy in his writing. **Science fiction** is based on real or imagined scientific developments and often gives an imaginary or fantastical view of the future. **Fantasy,** which is highly imaginative, features characters and settings that could never be found in the real world. Typical fantasy characters might be ghosts, dragons, and sorcerers.

Enrich Your Reading

Making Predictions   The main character in "Button, Button" faces a crucial choice. As you read, try to make reasonable predictions about what choice she will make, what will happen as a result, and how the story will end. Use your own knowledge of the way people behave and notice clues in the story that foreshadow later events.

■ *A biography of the author can be found on page 597.*

Button, Button

RICHARD MATHESON

The package was lying by the front door—a cube-shaped carton sealed with tape, their name and address printed by hand: "Mr. and Mrs. Arthur Lewis, 217 E. Thirty-seventh Street, New York, New York 10016." Norma picked it up, unlocked the door, and went into the apartment. It was just getting dark.

After she put the lamb chops in the broiler, she sat down to open the package.

Inside the carton was a push-button unit fastened to a small wooden box. A glass dome covered the button. Norma tried to lift it off, but it was locked in place. She turned the unit over and saw a folded piece of paper Scotch-taped to the bottom of the box. She pulled it off: "Mr. Steward will call on you at 8:00 P.M."

Norma put the button unit beside her on the couch. She reread the typed note, smiling.

A few moments later, she went back into the kitchen to make the salad.

The doorbell rang at eight o'clock. "I'll get it," Norma called from the kitchen. Arthur was in the living room, reading.

There was a small man in the hallway. He removed his hat as Norma opened the door. "Mrs. Lewis?" he inquired politely.

"Yes?"

"I'm Mr. Steward."

"Oh, yes." Norma repressed a smile. She was sure now it was a sales pitch.

"May I come in?" asked Mr. Steward.

"I'm rather busy," Norma said, "I'll get you your whatchamacallit, though." She started to turn.

"Don't you want to know what it is?"

Norma turned back. Mr. Steward's tone had been <u>offensive.</u> "No, I don't think so," she replied.

"It could prove very valuable," he told her.

"*Monetarily?*" she challenged.

Mr. Steward nodded. "Monetarily," he said.

Norma frowned. She didn't like his attitude. "What are you trying to sell?" she asked.

"I'm not selling anything," he answered.

Arthur came out of the living room. "Something wrong?"

Mr. Steward introduced himself.

"*Oh,* the—" Arthur pointed toward the living room and smiled. "What is that gadget, anyway?"

"It won't take long to explain," replied Mr. Steward. "May I come in?"

"If you're selling something—," Arthur said.

Mr. Steward shook his head. "I'm not."

TRANSECTION #24 1977 Clarence Holbrook Carter
Courtesy of the artist.

Arthur looked at Norma. "Up to you," she said.

He hesitated. "Well, why not?" he said.

They went into the living room and Mr. Steward sat in Norma's chair. He reached into an inside coat pocket and withdrew a small sealed envelope. "Inside here is a key to the bell-unit dome," he said. He set the envelope on the chair-side table. "The bell is connected to our office."

"What's it for?" asked Arthur.

"If you push the button," Mr. Steward told him, "somewhere in the world someone you don't know will die. In return for which you will receive a payment of $50,000."

Norma stared at the small man. He was smiling.

"What are you talking about?" Arthur asked him.

Mr. Steward looked surprised. "But I've just explained," he said.

"Is this a practical joke?" asked Arthur.

"Not at all. The offer is completely genuine."

"You aren't making sense," Arthur said. "You expect us to believe—"

"Whom do you represent?" demanded Norma.

Mr. Steward looked embarrassed. "I'm afraid I'm not at liberty to tell you that," he said. "However, I assure you, the organization is of international scope."

"I think you'd better leave," Arthur said, standing.

Mr. Steward rose. "Of course."

"And take your button unit with you."

"Are you sure you wouldn't care to think about it for a day or so?"

Arthur picked up the button unit and the envelope and thrust them into Mr. Steward's hands. He walked into the hall and pulled open the door.

"I'll leave my card," said Mr. Steward. He placed it on the table by the door.

When he was gone, Arthur tore it in half and tossed the pieces onto the table.

Norma was still sitting on the sofa. "What do you think it was?" she asked.

"I don't care to know," he answered.

She tried to smile but couldn't. "Aren't you curious at all?"

"No." He shook his head.

After Arthur returned to his book, Norma went back to the kitchen and finished washing the dishes.

"Why won't you talk about it?" Norma asked.

Arthur's eyes shifted as he brushed his teeth. He looked at his reflection in the bathroom mirror.

"Doesn't it <u>intrigue</u> you?"

"It offends me," Arthur said.

"I know, but"—Norma rolled another curler in her hair—"doesn't it intrigue you, too?"

"You think it's a practical joke?" she asked as they went into the bedroom.

"If it is, it's a sick one."

Norma sat on her bed and took off her slippers. "Maybe it's some kind of psychological research."

Arthur shrugged. "Could be."

"Maybe some <u>eccentric</u> millionaire is doing it."

"Maybe."

"Wouldn't you like to know?"

Arthur shook his head.

"*Why?*"

"Because it's immoral," he told her.

Norma slid beneath the covers. "Well, I think it's intriguing," she said.

Arthur turned off the lamp and leaned over to kiss her. "Good night," he said.

"Good night." She patted his back.

Norma closed her eyes. Fifty thousand dollars, she thought.

In the morning, as she left the apartment, Norma saw the card halves on the table. Impulsively, she dropped them into her purse. She locked the front door and joined Arthur in the elevator.

While she was on her coffee break, she took the card halves from her purse and held the torn edges together. Only Mr. Steward's name and telephone number were printed on the card.

After lunch, she took the card halves from her purse again and Scotch-taped the edges together. "Why am I doing this?" she thought.

Just before five, she dialed the number.

"Good afternoon," said Mr. Steward's voice.

Norma almost hung up but restrained herself. She cleared her throat. "This is Mrs. Lewis," she said.

"*Yes,* Mrs. Lewis," Mr. Steward sounded pleased.

"I'm curious."

"That's natural," Mr. Steward said.

"Not that I believe a word of what you told us."

"Oh, it's quite authentic," Mr. Steward answered.

"Well, whatever—" Norma swallowed. "When you said someone in the world would die, what did you mean?"

"Exactly that," he answered. "It could be anyone. All we guarantee is that you don't know them. And, of course, that you wouldn't have to watch them die."

"For $50,000," Norma said.

"That is correct."

She made a scoffing sound. "That's crazy."

"Nonetheless, that is the <u>proposition</u>," Mr. Steward said. "Would you like me to return the button unit?"

Norma stiffened. "*Certainly not.*" She hung up angrily.

The package was lying by the front door; Norma saw it as she left the elevator. Well, of all the nerve, she thought. She glared at the carton as she unlocked the door. I just

Words to Know and Use | intrigue (in trēg′) *v.* to arouse the interest or curiosity of; fascinate
eccentric (ek sen′ trik) *adj.* out of the ordinary; odd
proposition (präp′ ə zish′ ən) *n.* a plan, proposal, deal, or scheme

won't take it in, she thought. She went inside and started dinner.

Later, she went into the front hall. Opening the door, she picked up the package and carried it into the kitchen, leaving it on the table.

She sat in the living room, looking out the window. After a while, she went back into the kitchen to turn the cutlets in the broiler. She put the package in a bottom cabinet. She'd throw it out in the morning.

"Maybe some eccentric millionaire is playing games with people," she said.

Arthur looked up from his dinner. "I don't understand you."

"What does *that* mean?"

"*Let it go*," he told her.

Norma ate in silence. Suddenly, she put her fork down. "Suppose it's a genuine offer?" she said.

Arthur stared at her.

"*Suppose it's a genuine offer?*"

"All right, suppose it is?" He looked incredulous. "What would you like to do? Get the button back and push it? *Murder* someone?"

Norma looked disgusted. "*Murder.*"

"How would you define it?"

"If you don't even *know* the person?" Norma said.

Arthur looked astounded. "Are you saying what I think you are?"

"If it's some old Chinese peasant ten thousand miles away? Some diseased native in the Congo?"[1]

"How about a baby boy in Pennsylvania?" Arthur countered. "Some beautiful little girl on the next block?"

"Now you're loading things."

"The point is, Norma," he continued, "what's the difference whom you kill? It's still murder."

"The point *is*," Norma broke in, "if it's

someone you've never seen in your life and never *will* see, someone whose death you don't even have to *know* about, you *still* wouldn't push the button?"

Arthur stared at her, appalled. "You mean *you would?*"

"Fifty thousand dollars, Arthur."

"What has the amount—"

"*Fifty thousand dollars,* Arthur," Norma interrupted. "A chance to take that trip to Europe we've always talked about."

"Norma, no."

"A chance to buy that cottage on the island."

"Norma, *no*." His face was white.

She shuddered. "All right, take it easy," she said. "Why are you getting so upset? It's only talk."

After dinner, Arthur went into the living room. Before he left the table, he said, "I'd rather not discuss it anymore, if you don't mind."

Norma shrugged. "Fine with me."

She got up earlier than usual to make pancakes, eggs, and bacon for Arthur's breakfast.

"What's the occasion?" he asked with a smile.

"No occasion." Norma looked offended. "I wanted to do it, that's all."

"Good," he said. "I'm glad you did."

She refilled his cup. "Wanted to show you I'm not—" She shrugged.

"Not what?"

"Selfish."

"Did I say you were?"

"Well"—she gestured vaguely—"last night. . . ."

Arthur didn't speak.

"All that talk about the button," Norma

---

1. **the Congo:** an African nation now known as Zaire.

SEVEN A.M. NEWS 1976–78
Alfred Leslie
Collection of Joseph D. and Janet M. Shein,
Merion, Pennsylvania.

said. "I think you—well, misunderstood me."

"In what way?" His voice was guarded.

"I think you felt"—she gestured again—"that I was only thinking of myself."

"Oh."

"I wasn't."

"Norma—"

"Well, I *wasn't*. When I talked about Europe, a cottage on the island—"

"Norma, why are we getting so involved in this?"

"I'm not involved at all." She drew in a shaking breath. "I'm simply trying to indicate that—"

"*What?*"

"That I'd like for *us* to go to Europe. Like for *us* to have a cottage on the island. Like for *us* to have a nicer apartment, nicer furniture, nicer clothes, a car. Like for us to finally have a *baby*, for that matter."

"Norma, we will," he said.

"*When?*"

He stared at her in dismay. "Norma—"

"*When?!*"

"Are you"—he seemed to draw back slightly—"are you really saying—"

"I'm saying that they're probably doing it for some research project!" she cut him off. "That they want to know what average people would do under such a circumstance! That they're just *saying* someone would die, in order to study reactions, see if there'd be guilt, anxiety, whatever! You don't think they'd *kill* somebody, do you?!"

Arthur didn't answer. She saw his hands trembling. After a while, he got up and left.

When he'd gone to work, Norma remained at the table, staring into her coffee. I'm going to be late, she thought. She shrugged. What difference did it make? She should be home, anyway, not working in an office.

While she was stacking dishes, she turned abruptly, dried her hands, and took the package from the bottom cabinet. Opening it, she set the button unit on the table. She stared at it for a long time before taking the key from its envelope and removing the glass dome. She stared at the button. How ridiculous, she thought. All this furor over a meaningless button.

Reaching out, she pressed it down. For *us*, she thought angrily.

She shuddered. Was it *happening*? A chill of horror swept across her.

In a moment, it had passed. She made a contemptuous noise. *Ridiculous*, she thought. To get so worked up over nothing.

She threw the button unit, dome, and key into the wastebasket and hurried to dress for work.

She had just turned over the supper steaks when the telephone rang. She picked up the receiver. "Hello?"

"Mrs. Lewis?"

"Yes?"

"This is the Lenox Hill Hospital."

She felt unreal as the voice informed her of the subway accident—the shoving crowd, Arthur pushed from the platform in front of the train. She was conscious of shaking her head but couldn't stop.

As she hung up, she remembered Arthur's life-insurance policy for $25,000, with double indemnity[2] for—

"*No*." She couldn't seem to breathe. She struggled to her feet and walked into the kitchen numbly. Something cold pressed at her skull as she removed the button unit from the wastebasket. There were no nails or screws visible. She couldn't see how it was put together.

Abruptly, she began to smash it on the sink edge, pounding it harder and harder, until the wood split. She pulled the sides apart, cutting her fingers without noticing. There were no transistors in the box, no wires or tubes.

The box was empty.

She whirled with a gasp as the telephone rang. Stumbling into the living room, she picked up the receiver.

"Mrs. Lewis?" Mr. Steward asked.

It wasn't her voice shrieking so; it couldn't be. *"You said I wouldn't know the one that died!"*

"My dear lady," Mr. Steward said. "Do you really think you knew your husband?" ❧

---

2. **double indemnity:** a clause in some life insurance policies in which the insurance company offers to pay double the value of the policy in case of accidental death.

Responding to Reading

First Impressions

1. Did you like the story? Why or why not?

Second Thoughts

2. Why does Norma push the button? Which of her reasons are justified and which are not?

3. Whom or what does Mr. Steward represent? Support your opinion.

4. Mr. Steward asks Norma if she thinks she really knew her husband. Do you think she did? Explain.

5. Judging from what you know about people, would most people push the button? Explain.

6. Name a character from another selection who would *not* push the button. Support your answer with facts about that character.

Broader Connections

7. What would you do for a million dollars? For example, would you give up your best friend? Do you think that everyone has a price? Explain your answer.

Literary Concept: Character Traits

A **character trait** is a quality that a character shows, such as courage, greed, or honesty. You can infer character traits from a character's actions, appearance, speech, and thoughts and from what the narrator or other characters say about him or her. List character traits of Norma and Arthur. Use the list to compare and contrast these two characters.

Concept Review: Conflict   What conflicts, both internal and external, does Norma face in this story?

Writing Options

1. Write the next episode in Norma's life after Arthur's death. For example, will the police or the insurance company investigate his death? Will Norma tell anyone about Mr. Steward and the button unit?

2. Change one element in the story—a character, an idea, or a conversation, for example. Describe how the change would affect the rest of the story.

3. Do you think Norma got what she deserved? Write a statement explaining your opinion.

4. Imagine that Mr. Steward selects another family to receive the box. Write a scene portraying his sales pitch and the next family's reaction. You may use your own family, another family you know, or a completely fictional family.

5. Now that you know the ending of "Button, Button," review the story to find and list clues that foreshadow this conclusion.

Vocabulary Practice

Exercise On your paper, write the letter of the word in each group that does not have a meaning similar to the other three words.

1. (a) aggressive (b) obnoxious (c) offensive (d) timid
2. (a) normal (b) ordinary (c) eccentric (d) usual
3. (a) sentimentally (b) monetarily (c) financially (d) cost-related
4. (a) refusal (b) proposition (c) deal (d) proposal
5. (a) bore (b) intrigue (c) fascinate (d) interest

Words to Know and Use

eccentric
intrigue
monetarily
offensive
proposition

Options for Learning

1 • **Modern Temptation** For a week, look for ways in which our society tempts people with easy money. Create a list that includes what you hear on the radio, see on television, or read in newspapers. Arrange these temptations from the least harmful in your view to the most harmful, and present them to your class.

2 • **Amateur Psychologist** Make up a situation, similar to the one in the story, that will test a person's moral values. With a friend, act out this temptation for the class. For instance, can you tempt a friend to keep money that he or she has found? Create your scene with yourself in the role of someone like Mr. Steward.

3 • **Act It Out** Plan a play version of this story. Enlist other students to perform the play and help you videotape it. Play the tape for another class and ask the class to evaluate the story.

4 • **Box Builder** Design and build your version of the button unit. Demonstrate how it works for your class.

 **FACT FINDER**

Do most life insurance policies have double indemnity clauses?

*R*ichard *Matheson*
1926-

Richard Matheson weaves fantasy, science fiction, and even horror into his tales of ordinary people who have been thrust into critical situations. "I don't like stories about distant planets or distant futures or underground kingdoms of hunchbacked elves," he says. Rather, he has always been fascinated by fantasy. "The first book I ever borrowed from the library, when I was about seven years old, was called *Pinocchio in Af-rica*, which no one's ever heard of but me." Matheson has written fantastical novels, short stories, and screenplays for both movies and television. The short story "Button, Button" was later adapted by Matheson for the television series *The Twilight Zone*.

Matheson, an amateur actor, says he has no trouble switching from novels and short stories to screenplays. "When I write short stories or novels, I see them on a screen in my mind and I describe what I see."

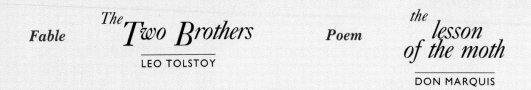

Fable **The Two Brothers**
LEO TOLSTOY

Poem **the lesson of the moth**
DON MARQUIS

Examine What You Know

What are your basic attitudes toward life? On paper, copy each pair of opposing attitudes below, connecting each pair with a line, or continuum. Then place an **X** on each continuum to show where your attitude lies. For example, are you usually cautious or adventurous? Place your **X** near your answer. Compare your ratings with those of a few classmates.

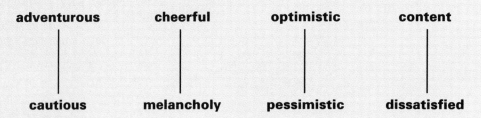

adventurous	**cheerful**	**optimistic**	**content**
cautious	**melancholy**	**pessimistic**	**dissatisfied**

Expand Your Knowledge

Both Tolstoy and Marquis wrote in several **genres** (zhän′ rəz), or forms of literature. Two forms Tolstoy used were fables and folk tales. A **fable** is a brief tale with a moral. **Folk tales** are stories that have been passed down by word of mouth from generation to generation. The characters in these tales often stand for important human qualities, such as courage or honesty.

Marquis usually wrote poetry. His poems, he humorously insisted, were written by a gigantic cockroach. This cockroach, named archy, wrote "the lesson of the moth." Archy typed by hurling himself at the keys. Unable to hit the shift key, archy could type no capital letters, apostrophes, quotation marks, or question marks. Thus, the poem has none of these.

Write Before You Read

■ *Biographies of the authors can be found on page 603.*

Marquis's poem describes one attitude toward life as "come easy, go easy." Write a brief phrase or sentence describing your attitude toward life.

The Two Brothers

LEO TOLSTOY

Two brothers set out on a journey together. At noon they lay down in a forest to rest. When they woke up they saw a stone lying next to them. There was something written on the stone, and they tried to make out what it was.

"Whoever finds this stone," they read, "let him go straight into the forest at sunrise. In the forest a river will appear; let him swim across the river to the other side. There he will find a she-bear and her cubs. Let him take the cubs from her and run up the mountain with them, without once looking back. On the top of the mountain he will see a house, and in that house he will find happiness."

When they had read what was written on the stone, the younger brother said:

"Let us go together. We can swim across the river, carry off the bear cubs, take them to the house on the mountain, and together find happiness."

"I am not going into the forest after bear cubs," said the elder brother, "and I advise you not to go. In the first place, no one can know whether what is written on this stone is the truth—perhaps it was written in jest. It is even possible that we have not read it correctly. In the second place, even if what is written here is the truth—suppose we go into the forest and night comes, and we cannot find the river. We shall be lost. And if we do find the river, how are we going to swim across it? It may be broad and swift. In the

TWO MEN CONTEMPLATING THE MOON 1918 Caspar-David Friedrich
Schloss Pillnitz, Dresden/
The Bridgeman Art Library, London.

third place, even if we swim across the river, do you think it is an easy thing to take her cubs away from a she-bear? She will seize us, and, instead of finding happiness, we shall perish, and all for nothing. In the fourth place, even if we succeeded in carrying off the bear cubs, we could not run up a mountain without stopping to rest. And, most important of all, the stone does not tell us what kind of happiness we should find in that house. It may be that the happiness awaiting us there is not at all the sort of happiness we would want."

"In my opinion," said the younger

brother, "you are wrong. What is written on the stone could not have been put there without reason. And it is all perfectly clear. In the first place, no harm will come to us if we try. In the second place, if we do not go, someone else will read the inscription on the stone and find happiness, and we shall have lost it all. In the third place, if you do not make an effort and try hard, nothing in the world will succeed. In the fourth place, I should not want it thought that I was afraid of anything."

The elder brother answered him by saying: "The proverb says: 'In seeking great happiness small pleasures may be lost.' And also: 'A bird in the hand is worth two in the bush.'"

The younger brother replied: "I have heard: 'He who is afraid of the leaves must not go into the forest.' And also: 'Beneath a stone no water flows.'"

Then the younger brother set off, and the elder remained behind.

No sooner had the younger brother gone into the forest than he found the river, swam across it, and there on the other side was the she-bear, fast asleep. He took her cubs, and ran up the mountain without looking back. When he reached the top of the mountain the people came out to meet him with a carriage to take him into the city, where they made him their king.

He ruled for five years. In the sixth year, another king, who was stronger than he, waged war against him. The city was conquered, and he was driven out.

Again the younger brother became a wanderer, and he arrived one day at the house of the elder brother. The elder brother was living in a village and had grown neither rich nor poor. The two brothers rejoiced at seeing each other, and at once began telling of all that had happened to them.

"You see," said the elder brother, "I was right. Here I have lived quietly and well, while you, though you may have been a king, have seen a great deal of trouble."

"I do not regret having gone into the forest and up the mountain," replied the younger brother. "I may have nothing now, but I shall always have something to remember, while you have no memories at all." ❧

Responding to Reading

First Impressions of "The Two Brothers"

1. Do you identify more closely with the younger brother or the older brother? Why?

Second Thoughts on "The Two Brothers"

2. What are the pros and cons of each brother's philosophy, or approach to life?

3. Which brother's approach to life do you think Tolstoy favors? Give reasons for your answer.

4. Which brother is happier at the end? Explain.

the lesson of the moth

DON MARQUIS

STREET LIGHT
1909 Giacomo Balla
Oil on canvas, 68¾″ ×
45¼″ Collection,
The Museum
of Modern Art,
New York Hillman
Periodicals Fund.

i was talking to a moth
the other evening
he was trying to break into
an electric light bulb
5 and fry himself on the wires

why do you fellows
pull this stunt i asked him
because it is the conventional
thing for moths or why
10 if that had been an uncovered
candle instead of an electric
light bulb you would
now be a small unsightly cinder
have you no sense

15 plenty of it he answered
but at times we get tired
of using it
we get bored with the routine
and crave beauty
20 and excitement
fire is beautiful
and we know that if we get
too close it will kill us
but what does that matter
25 it is better to be happy
for a moment
and be burned up with beauty

than to live a long time
and be bored all the while

30 so we wad all our life up
into one little roll
and then we shoot the roll
that is what life is for
it is better to be a part of beauty
35 for one instant and then cease to
exist than to exist forever
and never be a part of beauty
our attitude toward life
is come easy go easy
40 we are like human beings
used to be before they became
too civilized to enjoy themselves

and before i could argue him
out of his philosophy
45 he went and immolated[1] himself
on a patent cigar lighter
i do not agree with him
myself i would rather have
half the happiness and twice
50 the longevity[2]

but at the same time i wish
there was something i wanted
as badly as he wanted to fry himself
                                    archy

1. **immolate** (im′ə lāt′): to kill or destroy.
2. **longevity** (län jev′ ə tē): length of life.

Responding to Reading

First Impressions of "the lesson of the moth"

1. Write several words that describe your feelings toward the speaker in this poem. Compare your description with your classmates'.

Second Thoughts on "the lesson of the moth"

2. What is the lesson of the moth? Do you agree with this lesson? Explain.

3. Explain the moth's attitude toward humans, as stated in lines 40-42. Do you agree or disagree with this view? Why?

Comparing the Selections

4. Which brother's attitude toward life is similar to the moth's? Would this brother be likely to make a decision with the extreme consequences the moth chose? Give reasons for your answer.

5. Do both selections have the same message? If you think they do, what is the message? If they do not, how do the messages differ?

Literary Concept: Genre

Each of these writers chose a different **genre,** or form of literature. The four main genres are fiction, nonfiction, poetry, and drama. Even though these two selections are in different genres, what do they have in common? What main differences do you see? Which piece brings out its message more powerfully? Is genre a factor in the effectiveness of that piece?

Writing Options

1. Choose a character from one of the two selections. Write a scene in which he defends his attitude toward life in a conversation with a character of your choice from another selection in this book.

2. Compose your own version of "the lesson of the moth," writing about people instead of a moth.

Leo Tolstoy
1828-1910

Leo Tolstoy's early life in a wealthy, aristocratic Russian family was a mixture of happiness and tragedy. His mother died before he was two, but life went on at the family's forty-two-room estate. Tolstoy was tutored at home and spent much time fishing, fencing, riding horses, and swimming. Shortly after his family moved to Moscow, his father and grandmother died.

Tolstoy was not sure what to do with his life until he joined the army and wrote his autobiography, *Childhood*, an immediate success. He later started a school and wrote a number of innovative textbooks. He married Sonya Behrs, farmed his family's estate, and wrote *War and Peace*, considered one of the greatest and longest novels ever written. He followed this success with another classic, *Anna Karenina*.

Though wealthy and successful, Tolstoy was dissatisfied. He developed beliefs based on simplicity, love, goodness, and peace. He wrote about his ideas and organized relief for starving Russians. Finally, he even gave up the rights to the great wealth earned from his books. His wife was outraged over this because she wanted to provide a comfortable life for her thirteen children. To escape her anger, Tolstoy left home to lead a solitary life. On the trip, however, the eighty-two-year-old Tolstoy caught a fever and died.

Don Marquis
1878-1937

One day, the "biggest cockroach you ever saw" scampered across Don Marquis's desk at the *New York Sun*, the newspaper he worked for. This gave Marquis the idea for a comic character, archy, the philosophical cockroach poet. Later, Marquis created mehitabel (mə hit′ə bel), the joyful, adventurous alley cat. Through such characters, Marquis expressed his views on life from 1912 to 1925 in his newspaper column. Marquis also wrote novels, plays, short stories, poems, and humorous essays.

Before he became a successful writer, Marquis held a variety of jobs: drugstore clerk, sewing machine salesman, truck driver, poultry plucker, printer, cook, railroad-track straightener, and schoolteacher. After he successfully launched his daily column, the "Sun Dial," in the *Sun*, a well-known writer said, "Most of us didn't consult the leading editorials to know what to think. The almost universal reflex was 'let's see what Don says about it.'"

Article

Not to Go with the Others

JOHN HERSEY

Examine What You Know

To many people, the phrase *concentration camp* is synonymous with *death camp*. What do you know about the concentration camps in Europe during World War II? Where were they? What kinds of people were imprisoned and for what reasons? Share your knowledge in a classroom discussion.

Expand Your Knowledge

THE LAST WALK Hans Jelinek
Library of Congress, Washington, D.C.

In 1938 and early 1939, Austria and Czechoslovakia were occupied by the German army under the leadership of Adolf Hitler. While other countries protested, no one did anything to halt the takeover. Then in September of 1939, Germany invaded Poland. This incident drove France and England to finally declare war on Germany. It also marked the beginning of World War II. Soon Hitler and his forces occupied much of Europe and turned east to invade Russia.

One of the most tragic aspects of the war was the imprisonment and killing of millions of Jewish people and non-Jewish political resisters by the German army. Prisoners were held in more than thirty concentration camps located in Poland and western Germany.

By early 1945, the Allied Forces were closing in on the German forces. Around this time, John Hersey was working in Moscow as a correspondent for *Time* magazine. A few days after the Russians drove the German troops out of the Polish city of Lodz (lôdz), Hersey toured the area and heard the story you are about to read.

Enrich Your Reading

■ *A biography of the author can be found in the Reader's Handbook.*

Visualizing and Clarifying Frantizek Zaremski (frän tē′ zhek zä rem′ skē), the person whom this article is about, finds himself in a life-or-death situation. To fully appreciate the dangers he faces, use the details the writer provides to **visualize**, or picture in your mind, the setting and action. Questions that appear within the text will help you **clarify**, or make clear in your own mind, what Zaremski is going through.

Not to Go with the Others

JOHN HERSEY

In the third year of the war, Franti-zek Zaremski was arrested by the invaders on a charge of spreading underground literature—specifi-cally, for carrying about his person a poem a friend from Gdynia had given him, which began:

Sleep, beloved Hitler, planes will come by night . . .

After he had spent six weeks of a three-year sentence for this crime in the Gestapo[1] prison at Inowroczon, Zaremski was sent to Kalice to do carpentry. By bad luck, at the time when his term expired, the Russians had broken through at the Vistula,[2] and his captors, instead of releasing him, took him, in their general panic, to the transfer camp for Polish political prisoners at Rodogoszcz,[3] where he was placed in Hall Number Four with nine hundred men. Altogether there were between two and three thousand men and women—no Jews, only "Aryan"[4] Poles suspected or convicted of political activity—in the prison.

Late in the evening of Wednesday, January 17, 1945, three days before Lodz was to fall to the Russians, all the prisoners were gathered on the third and fourth floors of the main building, even those who were sick, and there they all lay down on wooden bunks and floors to try to sleep. At about two in the morning guards came and ordered the inmates to get up for roll call.

They divided the prisoners into groups of about twenty each and lined up the groups in pairs. Zaremski was in the second group. SS[5] men led it down concrete stairs in a brick-walled stairwell at one end of the building and halted it on a landing of the stairway, near a door opening into a large loft on the second floor. The first group had apparently been led down to the ground floor.

Someone gave an order that the prisoners should run in pairs into the loft as fast as they could. When the first pairs of Zaremski's group ran in, SS men with their backs to the wall inside the room began to shoot at them from behind. Zaremski's turn came. He ran in terror. A bullet burned through his trouser leg. Another grazed his thigh. He fell down and feigned[6] death.

Others, from Zaremski's and later groups,

---

1. **Gestapo** (gǝ stä′ pō): the secret police force of Nazi Germany.
2. **Vistula** (vis′ choo lǝ): Vistula River.
3. **Rodogoszcz** (rô dô′ gôshch)
4. **Aryan** (ar′ ē ǝn): a term used by the Nazis to mean a "Nordic" or "Caucasoid" person of non-Jewish descent.
5. **SS:** a quasi-military unit of the Nazi party, used as a special police force.
6. **feigned** (fānd): pretended.

ran into the hall and were shot and fell dead or wounded on top of Zaremski and those who had gone first. At one time Zaremski heard the Polish national anthem being sung somewhere.

Finally the running and shooting ended, and there ensued some shooting on the upper floors, perhaps of people who had refused to run downstairs.

SS men with flashlights waded among the bodies, shining lights in the faces of the prostrate victims. Any wounded who moaned or moved, or any whose eyes reacted when the shafts of light hit their faces, were dispatched with pistol shots. Somehow Zaremski passed the test of pretense.

clarify At this moment, what is Zaremski's predicament?

As dawn began to break, Zaremski heard the iron doors of the main building being locked, and he heard some sort of grenades or bombs being thrown into the lowest hall and exploding there; they seemed to him to make only smoke, but they may have been incendiaries.[7] Later, in any case, the ground floor began to burn. Perhaps benzine or petrol had been poured around. Zaremski was still lying among the bodies of others.

There were several who were still alive, and they began jumping out of the burning building, some from windows on the upper stories. A few broke through a skylight to the roof, tied blankets from the prisoners' bunks into long ropes and let themselves down outside. Zaremski, now scurrying about the building, held back to see what would happen. Those who jumped or climbed down were shot at leisure in the camp enclosure by SS men in the turrets on the walls, and Zaremski decided to try to stay inside.

On the fourth floor, at the top of the reinforced concrete staircase, in the bricked stairwell at the end of the building, Zaremski found the plant's water tank, and for a time he and others poured water over the wounded lying on the wooden floors in the main rooms. Later Zaremski took all his clothes off, soaked them in the tank, and put them back on. He lay down and kept pouring water over himself. He put a soaked blanket around his head.

clarify What immediate danger does Zaremski face?

The tank was a tall one, separated from the main room by the stairwell's brick wall, and when the fire began to eat through the wooden floor of the fourth story and the heat in the stairwell grew unbearable, Zaremski climbed up and got right into the water in the tank. He stayed immersed there all day long. Every few minutes he could hear shots from the wall turrets. He heard floors of the main halls fall and heard the side walls collapse. The staircase shell and the concrete stairs remained standing.

It was evening before the shooting and the fire died down. When he felt sure both had ended, Zaremski pulled himself out of the tank and lay awhile on the cement floor beside it. Then, his strength somewhat restored, he made his way down the stairs, and on the way he found six others who were wounded but could walk.

The seven went outside. Dusk. All quiet. They thought the Germans had left, and they wanted to climb the wall and escape. The first three climbed up and dropped away in apparent safety, but then the lights flashed on in the turrets and bursts of firing broke out. Three of the remaining four decided to take their chances at climbing out after total darkness;

---

7. **incendiaries** (in sen′ dē er′ ēz): bombs designed to cause fires or explosions.

THE NEW ORDER
William Sharp
Library of Congress,
Washington, D.C.

they did not know whether the first three had been killed or had escaped. Only Zaremski decided to stay.

The three climbed, but this time the lights came sooner, and the guards killed all three while they were still scaling the wall.

clarify What are Zaremski's choices?

Zaremski crept into the camp's storehouse in a separate building. Finding some damp blankets, he wrapped them around himself and climbed into a big box, where he stayed all night. Once during the night he heard steps outside the building, and in the early morning he heard walking again. This time the footsteps approached the storeroom door. The door opened. The steps entered. Through the cracks of the box Zaremski sensed that the beam of a flashlight was probing the room. Zaremski could hear box tops opening and slamming and a foot kicking barrels. He held the lid of his box from the inside. Steps came near, a hand tried the lid, but Zaremski held tight, and the searcher must have decided the box was locked or nailed down. The footsteps went away.

Later two others came at different times and inspected the room, but neither tried Zaremski's box; the third hunter locked the door from the outside.

Much later Zaremski heard a car start and drive away.

Much later still—some time on the nineteenth of January in the year of victory—Zaremski heard the Polish language being spoken, even by the voices of women and children. He jumped out of the box and broke the window of the storehouse and climbed out to his countrymen. 🍂

*R*esponding to Reading

First Impressions

1. What words and phrases best describe Zaremski? Write your thoughts in your journal or on a sheet of paper.

Second Thoughts

2. In your opinion, is Zaremski's survival due more to luck or to his sensible thinking? Give reasons to support your response.

3. What motivates the SS men to kill the prisoners?

    Think about
    - the closeness of the Russian troops to the concentration camp
    - the fate of war criminals

4. What, if anything, did you learn about concentration camps from Hersey's account of Zaremski's ordeal?

5. Compare Zaremski with other survivors you know or have read about. What do they have in common? In what ways are their methods of survival different?

*L*iterary Concept: *Journalistic Style*

Writing in the **journalistic style** common to newspaper and magazine correspondents, Hersey relates Zaremski's experience without stating his opinion about his subject. Journalistic writing is characterized by short sentences, a reliance on factual information that is presented in an unbiased manner, and sometimes the use of quotations. Does Hersey's style help you identify with Zaremski? Would you have preferred a more personal style of writing? How does Hersey's style contrast with other styles in this book, such as that of J. A. Rogers or Margaret Truman?

*W*riting Options

1. List the actions Zaremski takes to ensure his survival.

2. Rewrite one paragraph from this selection in a more personal style.

3. Write a paragraph that discusses the theme of this selection.

Fiction

The Scarlet Ibis (ī' bis)

JAMES HURST

*E*xamine What You Know

Expectations play an important role in this story. How are you affected by other people's expectations of you? Are you affected differently by high and low expectations? Jot down your feelings about the expectations the following people have of you:

parents   friends   neighbors   teachers   coaches   society

*E*xpand Your Knowledge

The narrator of this story is an adult who relives a painful turning point in his life. Although the story covers several years, the climax occurs in 1918, near the end of World War I. The story is set in the southeastern part of the United States in a rural area much like the one in which the writer, James Hurst, grew up.

You will find that Hurst mentions several trees and flowers from his hometown, calling them by local names he learned as a boy. For example, the "bleeding tree" is named for the white sap that runs like blood from this tree when the bark is cut. "Graveyard flowers" are sweet-smelling gardenias, which, because they bloom year after year, are often planted in cemeteries. The match-size limbs of the "toothbrush tree" were once dipped in salt and used as toothbrushes.

*E*nrich Your Reading

Understanding the Exposition The beginning of a story presents information the reader needs to understand the plot. In this part of the story, called the **exposition**, the setting and characters are introduced, the mood is established, and the conflict is revealed. In "The Scarlet Ibis," the exposition is unusual in that it begins as a flashback, jumps to the present, and then returns to a past time.

As you read the first few paragraphs, pay attention to the mood the writer creates through his highly detailed description. Watch for objects and colors that may act as symbols later in the story. Look for images that may foreshadow events to come.

■ *A biography of the author can be found on page 622.*

The *Scarlet Ibis*

JAMES HURST

It was in the clove[1] of seasons, summer was dead but autumn had not yet been born, that the ibis lit in the bleeding tree. The flower garden was stained with rotting brown magnolia petals, and ironweeds grew <u>rank</u> amid the purple phlox. The five o'clocks by the chimney still marked time, but the oriole nest in the elm was untenanted and rocked back and forth like an empty cradle. The last graveyard flowers were blooming, and their smell drifted across the cotton field and through every room of our house, speaking softly the names of our dead.

It's strange that all this is still so clear to me, now that summer has long since fled and time has had its way. A grindstone stands where the bleeding tree stood, just outside the kitchen door, and now if an oriole sings in the elm, its song seems to die up in the leaves, a silvery dust. The flower garden is prim, the house a gleaming white, and the pale fence across the yard stands straight and spruce.[2] But sometimes (like right now), as I sit in the cool, green-draped parlor, the grindstone begins to turn, and time with all its changes is ground away— and I remember Doodle.

Doodle was just about the craziest brother a boy ever had. Of course, he wasn't crazy crazy like old Miss Leedie, who was in love with President Wilson and wrote him a letter every day, but was a nice crazy, like someone you meet in your dreams. He was born when I was six and was, from the outset, a disappointment. He seemed all head, with a tiny body which was red and shriveled like an old man's. Everybody thought he was going to die—everybody except Aunt Nicey, who had delivered him. She said he would live because he was born in a caul,[3] and cauls were made from Jesus' nightgown. Daddy had Mr. Heath, the carpenter, build a little mahogany coffin for him. But he didn't die, and when he was three months old, Mama and Daddy decided they might as well name him. They named him William Armstrong, which is like tying a big tail on a small kite. Such a name sounds good only on a tombstone.

I thought myself pretty smart at many things, like holding my breath, running, jumping, or climbing the vines in Old Woman Swamp, and I wanted more than anything else someone to race to Horsehead Landing, someone to box with, and someone to perch with in the top fork of the great pine behind the barn, where across the

---

1. **clove:** cleft, gap, ravine.
2. **spruce:** neat and trim.
3. **caul** (kôl): a thin membrane that sometimes envelops a baby's head at birth.

Words to Know and Use

rank (raŋk) *adj.* growing wildly and vigorously; overgrown

fields and swamps you could see the sea. I wanted a brother. But Mama, crying, told me that even if William Armstrong lived, he would never do these things with me. He might not, she sobbed, even be "all there." He might, as long as he lived, lie on the rubber sheet in the center of the bed in the front bedroom where the white marquisette curtains billowed out in the afternoon sea breeze, rustling like palmetto fronds.[4]

It was bad enough having an invalid[5] brother, but having one who possibly was not all there was unbearable, so I began to make plans to kill him by smothering him with a pillow. However, one afternoon as I watched him, my head poked between the iron posts of the foot of the bed, he looked straight at me and grinned. I skipped through the rooms, down the echoing halls, shouting, "Mama, he smiled. He's all there! He's all there!" and he was.

When he was two, if you laid him on his stomach, he began to move himself, straining terribly. The doctor said that with his weak heart this strain would probably kill him, but it didn't. Trembling, he'd push himself up, turning first red, then a soft purple, and finally collapse back onto the bed like an old worn-out doll. I can still see Mama watching him, her hand pressed tight across her mouth, her eyes wide and unblinking. But he learned to crawl (it was his third winter), and we brought him out of the front bedroom, putting him on the rug before the fireplace. For the first time he became one of us.

As long as he lay all the time in bed, we called him William Armstrong, even though it was formal and sounded as if we were referring to one of our ancestors, but with his creeping around on the deerskin rug and beginning to talk, something had to be done about his name. It was I who renamed him. When he crawled, he crawled backwards, as if he were in reverse and couldn't change gears. If you called him, he'd turn around as if he were going in the other direction, then he'd back right up to you to be picked up. Crawling backward made him look like a doodlebug, so I began to call him Doodle, and in time even Mama and Daddy thought it was a better name than William Armstrong. Only Aunt Nicey disagreed. She said caul babies should be treated with special respect since they might turn out to be saints. Renaming my brother was perhaps the kindest thing I ever did for him, because nobody expects much from someone called Doodle.

Although Doodle learned to crawl, he showed no signs of walking, but he wasn't idle. He talked so much that we all quit listening to what he said. It was about this time that Daddy built him a go-cart and I had to pull him around. At first I just paraded him up and down the piazza,[6] but then he started crying to be taken out into the yard, and it ended up by my having to lug him wherever I went. If I so much as picked up my cap, he'd start crying to go with me and Mama would call from wherever she was, "Take Doodle with you."

He was a burden in many ways. The doctor had said that he mustn't get too excited, too hot, too cold, or too tired and that he must always be treated gently. A long list of don'ts went with him, all of which I ignored once we got out of the house. To discourage his coming with me, I'd run with him across the ends of the cotton rows and careen him around the corners on two wheels. Some-

---

4. **palmetto fronds:** the fanlike leaves of a kind of palm tree.

5. **invalid** (in′ və lid): weak and sickly; not well.

6. **piazza** (pē az′ ə): a large, covered porch.

times I accidentally turned him over, but he never told Mama. His skin was very sensitive, and he had to wear a big straw hat whenever he went out. When the going got rough and he had to cling to the sides of the go-cart, the hat slipped all the way down over his ears. He was a sight. Finally, I could see I was licked. Doodle was my brother and he was going to cling to me forever, no matter what I did, so I dragged him across the burning cotton field to share with him the only beauty I knew, Old Woman Swamp. I pulled the go-cart through the saw-tooth fern, down into the green dimness where the palmetto fronds whispered by the stream. I lifted him out and set him down in the soft rubber grass beside a tall pine. His eyes were round with wonder as he gazed about him, and his little hands began to stroke the rubber grass. Then he began to cry.

"For heaven's sake, what's the matter?" I asked, annoyed.

"It's so pretty," he said. "So pretty, pretty, pretty."

After that day Doodle and I often went down into Old Woman Swamp. I would gather wildflowers—wild violets, honeysuckle, yellow jasmine, snakeflowers, and water lilies—and with wire grass we'd weave them into necklaces and crowns. We'd bedeck ourselves with our handiwork and loll about thus beautified, beyond the touch of the everyday world. Then when the slanted rays of the sun burned orange in the tops of the pines, we'd drop our jewels into the stream and watch them float away toward the sea.

There is within me (and with sadness I have watched it in others) a knot of cruelty borne by the stream of love, much as our blood sometimes bears the seed of our destruction, and at times I was mean to Doodle. One day I took him up to the barn loft and showed him his casket, telling him how we all had believed he would die. It was covered with a film of Paris green[7] sprinkled to kill the rats, and screech owls had built a nest inside it.

Doodle studied the mahogany box for a long time, then said, "It's not mine."

"It is," I said. "And before I'll help you down from the loft, you're going to have to touch it."

"I won't touch it," he said sullenly.

"Then I'll leave you here by yourself," I threatened, and made as if I were going down.

Doodle was frightened of being left. "Don't go leave me, Brother," he cried, and he leaned toward the coffin. His hand, trembling, reached out, and when he touched the casket he screamed. A screech owl flapped out of the box into our faces, scaring us and covering us with Paris green. Doodle was paralyzed, so I put him on my shoulder and carried him down the ladder, and even when we were outside in the bright sunshine, he clung to me, crying, "Don't leave me. Don't leave me."

When Doodle was five years old, I was embarrassed at having a brother of that age who couldn't walk, so I set out to teach him. We were down in Old Woman Swamp and it was spring and the sick-sweet smell of bay flowers hung everywhere like a mournful song. "I'm going to teach you to walk, Doodle," I said.

He was sitting comfortably on the soft grass, leaning back against the pine. "Why?" he asked.

I hadn't expected such an answer. "So I won't have to haul you around all the time."

---

7. **Paris green:** a poisonous green powder used as an insecticide.

"I can't walk, Brother," he said.

"Who says so?" I demanded.

"Mama, the doctor—everybody."

"Oh, you can walk," I said, and I took him by the arms and stood him up. He collapsed onto the grass like a half-empty flour sack. It was as if he had no bones in his little legs.

"Don't hurt me, Brother," he warned.

"Shut up. I'm not going to hurt you. I'm going to teach you to walk." I heaved him up again, and again he collapsed.

This time he did not lift his face up out of the rubber grass. "I just can't do it. Let's make honeysuckle wreaths."

"Oh yes you can, Doodle," I said. "All you got to do is try. Now come on," and I hauled him up once more.

It seemed so hopeless from the beginning that it's a miracle I didn't give up. But all of us must have something or someone to be proud of, and Doodle had become mine. I did not know then that pride is a wonderful, terrible thing, a seed that bears two vines, life and death. Every day that summer we went to the pine beside the stream of Old Woman Swamp, and I put him on his feet at least a hundred times each afternoon. Occasionally I too became discouraged because it didn't seem as if he was trying, and I would say, "Doodle, don't you *want* to learn to walk?"

He'd nod his head, and I'd say, "Well, if you don't keep trying, you'll never learn." Then I'd paint for him a picture of us as old men, white-haired, him with a long white beard and me still pulling him around in the go-cart. This never failed to make him try again.

Finally one day, after many weeks of practicing, he stood alone for a few seconds. When he fell, I grabbed him in my arms and hugged him, our laughter pealing through the swamp like a ringing bell. Now we knew

RICHARD AT AGE FIVE 1944 Alice Neel
Robert Miller Gallery, New York.

it could be done. Hope no longer hid in the dark palmetto thicket but perched like a cardinal in the lacy toothbrush tree, brilliantly visible.

"Yes, yes," I cried, and he cried it too, and the grass beneath us was soft and the smell of the swamp was sweet.

With success so <u>imminent</u>, we decided not to tell anyone until he could actually walk. Each day, barring rain, we sneaked into Old Woman Swamp, and by cotton-picking time Doodle was ready to show what he could do. He still wasn't able to walk far, but we could wait no longer. Keeping a nice secret is very hard to do, like holding your breath. We chose to reveal all on October eighth, Doodle's sixth birthday, and for weeks ahead we mooned around the house, promising everybody a most spectacular surprise. Aunt Nicey said that, after so much talk, if we produced anything less tremendous than the Resurrection,[8] she was going to be disappointed.

At breakfast on our chosen day, when Mama, Daddy, and Aunt Nicey were in the dining room, I brought Doodle to the door in the go-cart just as usual and had them turn their backs, making them cross their hearts and hope to die if they peeked. I helped Doodle up, and when he was standing alone, I let them look. There wasn't a sound as Doodle walked slowly across the room and sat down at his place at the table. Then Mama began to cry and ran over to him, hugging him and kissing him. Daddy hugged him too, so I went to Aunt Nicey, who was thanks praying in the doorway, and began to waltz her around. We danced together quite well until she came down on my big toe with her brogans,[9] hurting me so badly I thought I was crippled for life.

Doodle told them it was I who had taught him to walk, so everyone wanted to hug me, and I began to cry.

"What are you crying for?" asked Daddy, but I couldn't answer. They did not know that I did it for myself; that pride, whose slave I was, spoke to me louder than all their voices, and that Doodle walked only because I was ashamed of having a crippled brother.

Within a few months Doodle had learned to walk well, and his go-cart was put up in the barn loft (it's still there) beside his little mahogany coffin. Now, when we roamed off together, resting often, we never turned back until our destination had been reached, and to help pass the time, we took up lying.[10] From the beginning Doodle was a terrible liar and he got me in the habit. Had anyone stopped to listen to us, we would have been sent off to Dix Hill.

My lies were scary, involved, and usually pointless, but Doodle's were twice as crazy. People in his stories all had wings and flew wherever they wanted to go. His favorite lie was about a boy named Peter who had a pet peacock with a ten-foot tail. Peter wore a golden robe that glittered so brightly that when he walked through the sunflowers they turned away from the sun to face him. When Peter was ready to go to sleep, the peacock spread his magnificent tail, enfolding the boy gently like a closing go-to-sleep flower, burying him in the glorious iridescent, rustling vortex.[11] Yes, I must admit it. Doodle could beat me lying.

Doodle and I spent lots of time thinking about our future. We decided that when we were grown we'd live in Old Woman Swamp and pick dog-tongue for a living. Beside the stream, he planned, we'd build us a house of whispering leaves and the swamp birds would be our chickens. All day long (when

---

8. **the Resurrection:** the rising of Jesus Christ from the dead after his death and burial.

9. **brogans:** heavy ankle-high work shoes.

10. **lying:** an expression meaning "telling tall tales."

11. **vortex:** a whirlwind of feathers.

*Words
to Know
and Use* | **imminent** (im′ ə nənt) *adj.* approaching; near; close at hand

we weren't gathering dog-tongue) we'd swing through the cypresses on the rope vines, and if it rained we'd huddle beneath an umbrella tree and play stickfrog. Mama and Daddy could come and live with us if they wanted to. He even came up with the idea that he could marry Mama and I could marry Daddy. Of course, I was old enough to know this wouldn't work out, but the picture he painted was so beautiful and serene that all I could do was whisper Yes, yes.

Once I had succeeded in teaching Doodle to walk, I began to believe in my own infallibility, and I prepared a terrific development program for him, unknown to Mama and Daddy, of course. I would teach him to run, to swim, to climb trees, and to fight. He, too, now believed in my infallibility, so we set the deadline for these accomplishments less than a year away, when, it had been decided, Doodle could start school.

That winter we didn't make much progress, for I was in school and Doodle suffered from one bad cold after another. But when spring came, rich and warm, we raised our sights again. Success lay at the end of summer like a pot of gold, and our campaign got off to a good start. On hot days, Doodle and I went down to Horsehead Landing, and I gave him swimming lessons or showed him how to row a boat. Sometimes we descended into the cool greenness of Old Woman Swamp and climbed the rope vines or boxed scientifically beneath the pine where he had learned to walk. Promise hung about us like the leaves, and wherever we looked, ferns unfurled and birds broke into song.

That summer, the summer of 1918, was blighted.[12] In May and June there was no rain and the crops withered, curled up, then died under the thirsty sun. One morning in July a hurricane came out of the east, tipping over the oaks in the yard and splitting the limbs of the elm trees. That afternoon it roared back out of the west, blew the fallen oaks around, snapping their roots and tearing them out of the earth like a hawk at the entrails[13] of a chicken. Cotton bolls were wrenched from the stalks and lay like green walnuts in the valleys between the rows, while the cornfield leaned over uniformly so that the tassels touched the ground. Doodle and I followed Daddy out into the cotton field, where he stood, shoulders sagging, surveying the ruin. When his chin sank down onto his chest, we were frightened, and Doodle slipped his hand into mine. Suddenly Daddy straightened his shoulders, raised a giant knuckly fist, and with a voice that seemed to rumble out of the earth itself began cursing the weather and the Republican Party.[14] Doodle and I, prodding each other and giggling, went back to the house, knowing that everything would be all right.

And during that summer, strange names were heard through the house: Château-Thierry, Amiens, Soissons, and in her blessing at the supper table, Mama once said, "And bless the Pearsons, whose boy Joe was lost at Belleau Wood."[15]

So we came to that clove of seasons.

---

12. **blighted:** withered; damaged; destroyed.

13. **entrails:** inner organs of people or animals.

14. **Republican Party:** in 1918, most Southerners were Democrats.

15. **Chateau-Thierry** (shȧ tō′ tē er′ ē), **Amiens** (ȧm′ ē ǝnz), **Soissons** (swȧ′ sōn′) . . . **Belleau** (be lō′) **Wood:** famous battles of World War I fought in France near the end of the war.

---

infallibility (in fal′ ǝ bil′ ǝ tē) *n.* the state of being unable to make an error

School was only a few weeks away, and Doodle was far behind schedule. He could barely clear the ground when climbing up the rope vines, and his swimming was certainly not passable. We decided to double our efforts, to make that last drive and reach our pot of gold. I made him swim until he turned blue and row until he couldn't lift an oar. Wherever we went, I purposely walked fast, and although he kept up, his face turned red and his eyes became glazed. Once, he could go no further, so he collapsed on the ground and began to cry.

"Aw, come on, Doodle," I urged. "You can do it. Do you want to be different from everybody else when you start school?"

"Does it make any difference?"

"It certainly does," I said. "Now, come on," and I helped him up.

As we slipped through dog days,[16] Doodle began to look feverish, and Mama felt his forehead, asking him if he felt ill. At night he didn't sleep well, and sometimes he had nightmares, crying out until I touched him and said, "Wake up, Doodle. Wake up."

It was Saturday noon, just a few days before school was to start. I should have already admitted defeat, but my pride wouldn't let me. The excitement of our program had now been gone for weeks, but still we kept on with a tired doggedness. It was too late to turn back, for we had both wandered too far into a net of expectations and left no crumbs behind.

Daddy, Mama, Doodle, and I were seated at the dining-room table having lunch. It was a hot day, with all the windows and doors open in case a breeze should come. In the kitchen Aunt Nicey was humming softly. After a long silence, Daddy spoke.

"It's so calm, I wouldn't be surprised if we had a storm this afternoon."

"I haven't heard a rain frog," said Mama, who believed in signs, as she served the bread around the table.

"I did," declared Doodle. "Down in the swamp."

"He didn't," I said contrarily.

"You did, eh?" said Daddy, ignoring my denial.

"I certainly did," Doodle reiterated, scowling at me over the top of his iced-tea glass, and we were quiet again.

Suddenly, from out in the yard, came a strange croaking noise. Doodle stopped eating, with a piece of bread poised ready for his mouth, his eyes popped round like two blue buttons. "What's that?" he whispered.

I jumped up, knocking over my chair, and had reached the door when Mama called, "Pick up the chair, sit down again, and say excuse me."

By the time I had done this, Doodle had excused himself and had slipped out into the yard. He was looking up into the bleeding tree. "It's a great big red bird!" he called.

The bird croaked loudly again, and Mama and Daddy came out into the yard. We shaded our eyes with our hands against the hazy glare of the sun and peered up through the still leaves. On the topmost branch a bird the size of a chicken, with scarlet feathers and long legs, was perched precariously. Its wings hung down loosely, and as we watched, a feather dropped away and floated slowly down through the green leaves.

---

16. **dog days:** the hot, uncomfortable days of August, named for the Dog Star which rises and sets with the sun at that time.

HOT, HOT MORNING
Zoltan Szabo
By permission of the artist.

"It's not even frightened of us," Mama said.

"It looks tired," Daddy added. "Or maybe sick."

Doodle's hands were clasped at his throat, and I had never seen him stand still so long. "What is it?" he asked.

Daddy shook his head. "I don't know, maybe it's—"

At that moment the bird began to flutter, but the wings were uncoordinated, and amid much flapping and a spray of flying feathers, it tumbled down, bumping through the limbs of the bleeding tree and landing at our feet with a thud. Its long, graceful neck jerked twice into an S, then straightened out, and the bird was still. A white veil came over the eyes, and the long white beak unhinged. Its legs were crossed and its clawlike feet were delicately curved at rest. Even death did not mar its grace, for it lay on the earth like a broken vase of red flowers, and we stood around it, awed by its exotic beauty.

"It's dead," Mama said.

"What is it?" Doodle repeated.

"Go bring me the bird book," said Daddy.

I ran into the house and brought back the bird book. As we watched, Daddy thumbed through its pages. "It's a scarlet ibis," he said, pointing to a picture. "It lives in the tropics—South America to Florida. A storm must have brought it here."

Sadly, we all looked back at the bird. A scarlet ibis! How many miles it had traveled to die like this, in *our* yard, beneath the bleeding tree.

"Let's finish lunch," Mama said, nudging us back toward the dining room.

"I'm not hungry," said Doodle, and he knelt down beside the ibis.

"We've got peach cobbler for dessert," Mama tempted from the doorway.

Words to Know and Use | **exotic** (eg zät′ ik) *adj.* striking; extremely unusual

Doodle remained kneeling. "I'm going to bury him."

"Don't you dare touch him," Mama warned. "There's no telling what disease he might have had."

"All right," said Doodle. "I won't."

Daddy, Mama, and I went back to the dining-room table, but we watched Doodle through the open door. He took out a piece of string from his pocket and, without touching the ibis, looped one end around its neck. Slowly, while singing softly "Shall We Gather at the River," he carried the bird around to the front yard and dug a hole in the flower garden, next to the petunia bed. Now we were watching him through the front window, but he didn't know it. His awkwardness at digging the hole with a shovel whose handle was twice as long as he was made us laugh, and we covered our mouths with our hands so he wouldn't hear.

When Doodle came into the dining room, he found us seriously eating our cobbler. He was pale, and lingered just inside the screen door. "Did you get the scarlet ibis buried?" asked Daddy.

Doodle didn't speak but nodded his head.

"Go wash your hands, and then you can have some peach cobbler," said Mama.

"I'm not hungry," he said.

"Dead birds is bad luck," said Aunt Nicey, poking her head from the kitchen door. "Specially *red* dead birds!"

As soon as I had finished eating, Doodle and I hurried off to Horsehead Landing. Time was short, and Doodle still had a long way to go if he was going to keep up with the other boys when he started school. The sun, gilded with the yellow cast of autumn, still burned fiercely, but the dark green woods through which we passed were shady and cool. When we reached the landing, Doodle said he was too tired to swim, so we got into a skiff and floated down the creek with the tide. Far off in the marsh a rail was scolding, and over on the beach locusts were singing in the myrtle trees. Doodle did not speak and kept his head turned away, letting one hand trail limply in the water.

After we had drifted a long way, I put the oars in place and made Doodle row back against the tide. Black clouds began to gather in the southwest, and he kept watching them, trying to pull the oars a little faster. When we reached Horsehead Landing, lightning was playing across half the sky and thunder roared out, hiding even the sound of the sea. The sun disappeared and darkness descended, almost like night. Flocks of marsh crows flew by, heading inland to their roosting trees; and two egrets, squawking, arose from the oyster-rock shallows and careened away.

Doodle was both tired and frightened, and when he stepped from the skiff he collapsed onto the mud, sending an armada of fiddler crabs rustling off into the marsh grass. I helped him up, and as he wiped the mud off his trousers, he smiled at me ashamedly. He had failed and we both knew it, so we started back home, racing the storm. We never spoke (What are the words that can <u>solder</u> cracked pride?), but I knew he was watching me, watching for a sign of mercy. The lightning was near now, and from fear he walked so close behind me he kept stepping on my heels. The faster I walked, the faster he walked, so I began to

Words to Know and Use | **solder** (säd′ ər) *v.* to join or bond together

run. The rain was coming, roaring through the pines, and then, like a bursting Roman candle, a gum tree ahead of us was shattered by a bolt of lightning. When the deafening peal of thunder had died, and in the moment before the rain arrived, I heard Doodle, who had fallen behind, cry out, "Brother, Brother, don't leave me! Don't leave me!"

The knowledge that Doodle's and my plans had come to naught[17] was bitter, and that streak of cruelty within me awakened. I ran as fast as I could, leaving him far behind with a wall of rain dividing us. The drops stung my face like nettles,[18] and the wind flared the wet glistening leaves of the bordering trees. Soon I could hear his voice no more.

I hadn't run too far before I became tired, and the flood of childish spite evanesced[19] as well. I stopped and waited for Doodle. The sound of rain was everywhere, but the wind had died and it fell straight down in parallel paths like ropes hanging from the sky. As I waited, I peered through the downpour, but no one came. Finally I went back and found him huddled beneath a red nightshade bush beside the road. He was sitting on the ground, his face buried in his arms, which were resting on his drawn-up knees. "Let's go, Doodle," I said.

He didn't answer, so I placed my hand on his forehead and lifted his head. Limply, he fell backwards onto the earth. He had been bleeding from the mouth, and his neck and the front of his shirt were stained a brilliant red.

"Doodle! Doodle!" I cried, shaking him, but there was no answer but the ropy rain. He lay very awkwardly, with his head thrown far back, making his vermilion neck appear unusually long and slim. His little legs, bent sharply at the knees, had never before seemed so fragile, so thin.

I began to weep, and the tear-blurred vision in red before me looked very familiar. "Doodle!" I screamed above the pounding storm and threw my body to the earth above his. For a long long time, it seemed forever, I lay there crying, sheltering my fallen scarlet ibis from the heresy of rain. ❧

---

17. **come to naught:** come to nothing or worthlessness.
18. **nettles:** a kind of weed covered with stinging hairs.
19. **evanesced** (ev′ ə nes′d): disappeared, vanished.

INSIGHT

Woman with Flower

NAOMI LONG MADGETT

I wouldn't coax the plant if I were you.
Such watchful nurturing may do it
    harm.
Let the soil rest from so much digging
And wait until it's dry before you water
    it.
The leaf's inclined to find its own
    direction;
Give it a chance to seek the sunlight for
    itself.

Much growth is stunted by too careful
    prodding,
Too eager tenderness.
The things we love we have to learn to
    leave alone.

Words to Know and Use

vermilion (vər mil′ yən) *adj.* a bright red or scarlet
heresy (her′ i sē) *n.* an opinion that opposes commonly held views and beliefs

619

e x p l a i n

Responding to Reading

First Impressions

1. How did you feel at the end of the story? Why?

Second Thoughts

2. For what reasons does the narrator help his brother Doodle?

3. What different feelings does the narrator have toward Doodle? Do any of his feelings change over time? Explain.

4. Should the narrator feel guilty about Doodle's death? Give reasons for your answer.

    Think about
    • the ways in which he helps Doodle
    • whether or not he causes Doodle any harm
    • what Doodle's life would have been like without the narrator

5. In some ways, the scarlet ibis symbolizes Doodle and his life. How are the scarlet ibis and Doodle alike and how are they different?

    Think about
    • each one's physical characteristics
    • how and for what each one struggles
    • the way each dies

6. How does Doodle feel about himself and his brother? Why?

Broader Connections

7. The narrator says "There is within me . . . a knot of cruelty borne by the stream of love." Explain this statement. Think about your relationships with people you love or relationships you have observed between others. Are we cruelest to those we love?

Literary Concept: Figurative Language

Hurst uses **figurative language** to help the reader visualize the narrator's memories. For example, a **simile** in the first paragraph compares the swaying of an empty oriole's nest with an empty cradle. The story begins with a **metaphor** that compares the time of year to a clove, a gap or V-shaped crevice like that between two mountains. What details support this metaphor? Find four other similes or metaphors and explain the comparison in each one.

Concept Review: Foreshadowing The writer's use of hints to indicate what will happen later in a story is called **foreshadowing**. Identify five examples of foreshadowing and explain their significance.

Concept Review: Idiom Explain the meaning of the idiom ''all there'' on page 611.

Writing Options

1. Create a time line that indicates the main events in Doodle's life.

2. Write a comparison of this story with another selection you have read, such as ''A Mother in Mannville,'' ''On Being Seventeen, Bright, and Unable to Read,'' or ''the lesson of the moth.''

3. Explain what Doodle's ''lies'' reveal about his inner thoughts and dreams.

4. Explain your feelings about the narrator's thoughts on pride on page 613.

5. What advice does the poem ''Woman with Flower'' seem to offer the narrator of ''The Scarlet Ibis''? Do you agree with the message in this poem?

6. Chart the changes in weather in this story and explain why each is important.

Vocabulary Practice

Exercise A Read the pairs of words below. On your paper, write *Synonym* if the words are synonyms. Write *Antonym* if they are antonyms.

1. doggedness—determination
2. imminent—distant
3. infallibility—perfection
4. precariously—shakily
5. rank—sparse
6. reiterate—repeat
7. solder—separate
8. heresy—belief

Exercise B Using the spectrum scale below as a model, create two scales, one for **vermilion**, another for **exotic**. To begin, place the word on one end of the scale. Then add three or four more related words.

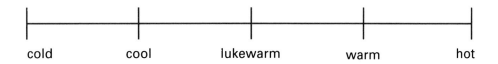

cold   cool   lukewarm   warm   hot

Options for Learning

1 • **Botanical Illustrations** Botany is the study of plants. Choose five trees, shrubs, or flowers mentioned in the story to research. Illustrate each one and write a caption listing some facts about it.

2 • **Where Did You Get That Nickname?** Just as Doodle was nicknamed by the narrator, many people are given nicknames by family or friends to fit their personality or appearance. Survey your classmates on their feelings about nicknames. Do they like them? Do they have one? What is its origin? Create a chart that shows your findings to share with your class.

3 • **Medicine Then and Now** Ask a doctor to read "The Scarlet Ibis" and discuss with you Doodle's possible medical problems. Consider such questions as: What probably caused Doodle's death? How would Doodle be treated today? Report your findings to your class.

4 • **In the Mind's Eye** Draw or paint the strongest image that this story leaves in your mind. Your work of art may be realistic or abstract in style.

5 • **Critics on Camera** Imagine that you and one or two classmates host a show that reviews popular literary works. Your topic this week is "The Scarlet Ibis." Briefly summarize the plot and then critique the story. Videotape your show and play it for your class.

 **FACT FINDER**

Find three uses of different plants in the nightshade family.

James Hurst
1922–

James Hurst grew up in North Carolina on a farm near the sea. Today, he lives not far from the place where he was born. In his garden grow many of the flowers mentioned in "The Scarlet Ibis."

After attending North Carolina State College and serving in the United States Army during World War II, Hurst studied singing at the world-renowned Juilliard School of Music in New York and later in Rome, Italy. In 1951, Hurst began a thirty-four year career in the international department of a large New York bank. During his early years at the bank, he wrote and published short stories and a play.

His most famous short story, "The Scarlet Ibis," was first published in *The Atlantic Monthly* in July 1960. It won the "Atlantic First" award for that year. Hurst says that there are three "characters" in the story— Doodle, the narrator, and the setting, which comments on the inner action. When asked about the meaning of the story, Hurst replied, "I hesitate to respond since authors seldom understand what they write. That is why we have critics. I venture to say, however, that it comments on the tenacity and the splendor of the human spirit."

WORKSHOP

EXPOSITION

Exposition involves conveying information in a clear, precise manner. A newspaper article is one of the best examples of expository writing. A reporter writing a story has one primary purpose: to relate the facts of a situation to readers accurately and in an interesting way. Though a journalist often relies on narration and description and at times on evaluation or persuasion, these are not characteristics of a typical newspaper article. Unlike a travel brochure, which might contain a good deal of figurative language to entice the reader, the newspaper article limits description to the essential details of the situation. These details frequently come in the form of answers to the "five W's and an H": *who, what, when, where, why,* and *how.*

A successful reporter knows that his or her readers have only a limited amount of time to spend on the daily news, so newspaper articles get to the point quickly with clear and direct sentences.

The selections in this subunit all explore important decisions and consequences. Each piece also includes unusual or explosive events, any one of which would make an excellent subject for a news story.

Here is your PASSkey to this assignment.

GUIDED ASSIGNMENT: NEWSPAPER ARTICLE

Write a newspaper article on a major event from one of the selections. Write the article as if the event had just happened and include quotations from the characters. Add a personal commentary at the end.

PURPOSE: To inform

AUDIENCE: Readers of a newspaper

SUBJECT: A major event from a selection

STRUCTURE: A newspaper article

Prewriting

Step **1** **Select an event to write about** Review the selections in this subunit. Pick the piece you found most interesting. Depending on the length of the selection, you may be able to write about the selection as a whole, or you may have to limit yourself to a single major event within the selection.

Step 2 **Plan your lead**   The first paragraph of a newspaper article is called the **lead,** and its purposes are to briefly summarize the main points of the story and to interest the reader. On a separate piece of paper, write down the five W's and an H—*who, what, when, where, why,* and *how.* Skip several lines between questions, and in the spaces answer the questions with information from the selection you picked.

Step 3 **Fill in details**   Determine what additional details your readers will want or need to know in order to understand the event. Skim the selection and take notes only on those important details. Then have a classmate review your lead information. Ask him or her what questions come to mind concerning the subject of your article. Make sure that your notes include answers to your classmate's questions.

Step 4 **Consider your own feelings**   For this assignment, you will also add a commentary, which means that you will give your personal opinion about the story's subject in the last paragraph of your article. Your commentary might give your personal answers to any or all of the following questions:

- Did the characters make the right decision?
- Were the consequences appropriate?
- How might you have handled the situation differently?

Drafting

Step 1 **Write the lead**   Use the notes you made that summarize the who, what, when, where, why, and how of the event. Combine the information into two or three clear, straightforward sentences. Keep the paragraph short and to the point.

Step 2 **Write short paragraphs**   In the body of the article, you will give the details. Include quotations from the characters to help make your article lively and specific. You may use quotations directly from the selection itself, or you may use made-up responses to an "interview." Quotations give a story authenticity and often reveal the emotional reactions or opinions of those involved in the event. Here is one paragraph from a student's article about Odysseus' adventure in the Cyclops's cave.

STUDENT MODEL ▶   Though obviously a very brave and clever man, Odysseus downplayed his own heroism. One of his men, Mr. Arrestes, explained, "Old Oddy is just like that. He tried to warn us not to rush into the cave, but we were too hungry to listen. If he hadn't come up with the idea of getting Polyphemos drunk and blinding him, we'd all be digested by now."

Step 3 **Write your conclusion**   Your conclusion will present your commentary on the event. Write your remarks in the third person, avoiding statements that begin with "I think." Use your concluding paragraph to briefly answer some or all of the questions in Step 4 of prewriting.

The conclusion is your chance to tie together the points you have made in your article. You should try to summarize your main idea in a clear final statement.

The student who wrote about Odysseus gave his opinion in this way:

> It is obvious from his actions that Odysseus is a very clever fellow who will probably go far in the world. However, his tendency to laugh at his opponents, as when he mocked Polyphemos after leaving the island, shows a lack of consistent good judgment. If Odysseus' common sense doesn't improve, he may be headed for trouble. At any rate, he's a fascinating figure, and his future conquests are well worth watching.

◀ STUDENT MODEL

Step 4 **Decide on a headline**   Your headline must have a strong impact if it is to attract the attention of a reader who may only have time to read a few stories. At the same time it needs to let readers know what the article is about. Limit your headline to a few words. Here is the headline used by the student who wrote about Odysseus' adventure with the Cyclops:

> Clever Hero Outwits One-Eyed Giant!

◀ STUDENT MODEL

Revising and Editing

Once you have completed your draft, ask a classmate to review your article according to the following checklist. Make sure your reviewer gives you specific answers to all of the questions in the checklist. Then revise your article using the ideas that you feel will improve it.

Revision Checklist

1. Does the headline of the article attract the reader's attention?
2. Does the article's lead paragraph briefly answer the five W's and an H?
3. Are the sentences and paragraphs specific, clear, and generally short?
4. Is the article organized in a way that is easy to follow?
5. Are all the essential details of the event reported? Are they reported accurately?
6. Does the article include quotations?
7. Is the last paragraph of the article a personal commentary?

Editing When you have finished revising your article, proofread for spelling, clarity, and mechanics.

Presenting

Collect the articles from the class and appoint editors, layout-and-design editors, proofreaders, and photography editors. Work in teams to organize the articles into an actual newspaper. Select the most sensational ones to be the lead articles, that is, the ones that will go on the front page. Proofread, design the layout, enlarge headlines, and find and copy photographs to illustrate the stories. Make the first page eye-catching. Decide on a good method of reproducing and distributing the newspaper throughout the school.

Reflecting on Your Writing

Answer the following questions about this assignment. File the answers in your writing portfolio.

1. What was the most difficult part of writing the news article? Why?
2. Did you keep the audience in mind as you wrote?
3. Would you like to learn more about journalism as a possible career? Why or why not?

ADVANCED SENTENCE COMBINING

You have already learned that combining sentences can often make your writing smoother, more coherent, and less repetitive. You have learned how to combine sentences by using conjunctions to join sentences and sentence parts and by inserting a key word or phrase from one sentence into another. Here are some other useful sentence-combining techniques.

Inserting Word Groups

Use the word *who* to add information about a person or a group of persons.

> The couple received a package. *They* lived at 217 E. Thirty-seventh Street.
> The couple **who** lived at 217 E. Thirty-seventh Street received a package.

> Norma Lewis answered the door. *She* was in the kitchen making a salad.
> Norma Lewis, **who** was in the kitchen making a salad, answered the door.

In both examples, combining the sentences makes the writing more coherent. In the first example, the added words tell which couple received a package. Because the added words are **essential** to the meaning of the sentence, no comma is needed. In the second example, the added words supply additional information that is unnecessary, or **nonessential,** to the meaning. Therefore, the added words are set off with commas.

Use *that* or *which* to add information about things or ideas.

> The gadget was odd. *The gadget* arrived in the carton.
> The gadget **that** arrived in the carton was odd.

> Mr. Steward's offer bothered the couple. *The offer* was unusual.
> Mr. Steward's offer, **which** was unusual, bothered the couple.

In the first example, the added words are necessary to the main idea of the sentence; therefore, *that* is used. In the second example, the information is not necessary to the sentence; therefore, *which* is used and commas set off the added words.

Exercise 1 Combine each pair of sentences by eliminating the words in italics. Remember to use correct punctuation.

1. Arthur Lewis was not interested in Mr. Steward's offer. *Arthur Lewis* was a decent man. (Use *who* and commas.)
2. The offer intrigued Norma Lewis. *The offer* gave the couple money in return for a human life. (Use *that*.)
3. Fifty-thousand dollars would make a big difference in the Lewises' lives. *Fifty-thousand dollars* is a large sum of money. (Use *which* and commas.)
4. After Norma called Mr. Steward, the package was returned to them. *The package* contained the deadly push-button unit. (Use *that*.)
5. Finally Norma pushed the button. *Norma* couldn't stop thinking about the money. (Use *who* and commas.)

Showing Relationships

You may discover that the ideas in two sentences are related in a particular way, such as by time or through cause-and-effect. You can often combine these sentences by subordinating the less important information found in one sentence to the information in the other sentence. The combining word you choose will show the relationship that exists between the ideas.

You can use the words *when* or *after* to show time, the word *because* to show why something happened, and the word *although* to explain under what conditions something occurred. In the following examples, notice how the combining word shows the connection between the two ideas.

The two brothers disagreed. They tried to interpret the writing on the stone.
The two brothers disagreed **when** they tried to interpret the writing on the stone.

One brother became a king. He was not afraid to take a chance.
One brother became a king **because** he was not afraid to take a chance.

He remained satisfied with his life. He had lost his kingdom to a stronger man.
He remained satisfied with his life, **although** he had lost his kingdom to a stronger man.

The combining words *although* and *though* are always preceded by a comma.

There are times when the subordinate idea may be placed at the beginning of the sentence, followed by a comma.

Although he had lost his kingdom to a stronger man, he remained satisfied with his life.

Here are some other words that can be used in sentence combining to show relationships of time, cause, and condition.

When	Why	Condition
before	as	considering (that)
until	for	whether (or not)
while	since	unless

Exercise 2   Rewrite the following passage. Combine the sentences in parentheses using *that, which, although, because,* or *when*. Be sure to punctuate the revised sentences correctly.

(The ibis is a wading bird. It lives in marshes or near water.) (This bird looks similar to a stork. It has long legs and a long neck.) (The white ibis is the most common. There are other colors as well.) (The red ibis is rarely seen in the United States. It prefers tropical climates.) (Interestingly, the red ibis's color fades to pink. It is in captivity.) (Black and white ibises once had a special significance. They were considered sacred by ancient Egyptians.) (Egyptian artists often painted pictures of these long-billed birds. They decorated the tombs of important people.)

Exercise 3   Analyzing and Revising Your Writing

1. Take a piece of writing from your writing portfolio.
2. Reread it, looking for related sentences that might be combined.
3. Rewrite one or two paragraphs in which some related sentences can be combined.
4. Check to see that you have punctuated your new sentences correctly.
5. Compare your revised sentences with the original ones. Which sentences do you prefer? Remember to check for related sentences that you might combine the next time you proofread your writing.

LANGUAGE HANDBOOK
For review and practice:
clauses and complex
sentences, pages 952–55
subordinating conjunctions,
   page 953

THINKING SKILLS
WORKSHOP

FACT AND OPINION

A **fact** is a statement that can be proved. An **opinion** cannot be proved.

Fact "The Scarlet Ibis" was written by James Hurst.
Opinion "The Scarlet Ibis" is a great short story.

The first statement is a fact because it can be proved. You can check the truth of the statement by looking at reference books or even communicating directly with the author. The second statement is an opinion. It merely expresses what some people think about the story.

Some types of nonfiction writing, such as newspaper articles, present facts with as few personal opinions as possible. Other nonfiction writing focuses on the writer's opinions about the facts.

When you read and write, make sure you can separate fact from opinion. You should also be able to evaluate whether an opinion is reasonable or not.

Evaluating Opinions   One guideline for evaluating opinions is the relationship between the opinions and the facts. Does the writer support each opinion with facts? Are there other facts that do not support the opinion that the writer has avoided mentioning? Another guideline is the qualifications of the writer. Is the writer likely to have thorough knowledge of the subject? A third guideline is the writer's purpose. Is the writer trying to inform or to persuade? Why would the purpose make a difference?

Exercise   Tell whether each statement below is a fact or an opinion. If it is a fact, tell how it could be proved.

1. In Mexico, January 6 is the Day of the Three Kings.
2. Clothing made at home is better than store-bought clothing.
3. The scarlet ibis is a beautiful bird.
4. The black and white ibis of Egypt was once considered sacred.
5. Leo Tolstoy was Russian.
6. A metaphor makes a comparison between unlike things.
7. The best poetry contains metaphors.
8. The inventor of the telephone was born in Scotland.
9. The telephone is the most important invention of this century.
10. Moths are four-winged flying insects related to butterflies.

JUDGMENT WORDS

Opinions often contain judgment words. These are words that express personal feelings.

awful   fine
magnificent   clever
terrible   terrific
ridiculous

What judgment words can you find in the exercise sentences?

AWAKENINGS

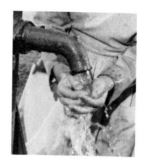

The body can sleep, the mind can sleep, and the spirit can sleep. It does not require a miracle to awaken the body—but to awaken the mind or spirit is a much more difficult challenge.

You are about to read a play

about people whose spirits need awakening. As you read about blind and deaf Helen Keller, her family, and her teacher, decide what causes their awakenings—miracles or human endeavor.

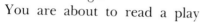

Drama

The *Miracle Worker*

WILLIAM GIBSON

Examine What You Know

The play you are about to read is based on the life of Helen Keller. Brainstorm to find out what you and your classmates already know about this remarkable woman. Appoint someone to keep a record of these facts. At the end of each act, go over the list, adding new facts and correcting any errors in the information you recorded earlier.

Expand Your Knowledge

The Miracle Worker takes place in Alabama approximately twenty years after the Civil War. Three attitudes that were common at that time influence the relationships between the characters in the play. First, many Southerners still felt bitter about losing the war and therefore distrusted people from Northern states. Second, women were expected to yield to men in all matters. Finally, people with handicaps or disabilities were to be avoided and were often locked away in hospitals or asylums to separate them from the rest of society.

As you read, try to determine which characters demonstrate these attitudes and which characters try to fight them.

Enrich Your Reading

Understanding Staging The staging of *The Miracle Worker* is different than in most plays. In this play, curtains do not open and close between scenes, and sets are designed only to suggest a particular place, not to show it realistically. There are no solid walls; objects such as a bed or a porch rail are used to set the scene. Look at the diagram on the next page. Notice that the stage is divided into two parts: one area represents the Keller home, and the other area is used for any other setting that is needed.

■ *A biography of the author can be found on page 705.*

Playwright William Gibson states that "the convention of the staging is one of cutting through time and place, and its essential qualities are fluidity and spatial counterpoint." In other words, the lighting and the open, unwalled sets are designed to let the action move smoothly forward and backward through time and from place to place, without interruption. The stage lights focus on one area of the stage and then shift the focus to another area to show a change in scene or setting. Occasionally, actions occur in two settings at the same time, as when Annie says, "Coming!" in Boston and the Kellers in Alabama seem to hear her.

The stage directions on page 635 explain how the stage is arranged. As you read, use the diagram below to help you understand the staging. Watch for directions about lighting that indicate a change in setting.

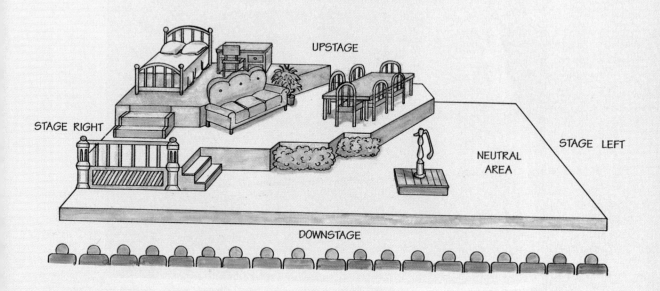

The *Miracle Worker*

WILLIAM GIBSON

Helen Keller and Anne Sullivan, 1890   American Foundation for the Blind, New York.

CHARACTERS

A Doctor	James
Kate	Anagnos
Keller	Annie Sullivan
Helen	Viney
Martha	Blind Girls
Percy	A Servant
Aunt Ev	Offstage Voices

Time: The 1880's.

Place: In and around the Keller homestead in Tuscumbia, Alabama; also, briefly, the Perkins Institution for the Blind, in Boston.

The playing space is divided into two areas by a more or less diagonal line, which runs from downstage right to upstage left.

The area behind this diagonal is on platforms and represents the Keller house. Inside we see, down right, a family room; and up center, elevated, a bedroom. On stage level near center, outside a porch, there is a water pump.

The other area, in front of the diagonal, is neutral ground. It accommodates various places as designated at various times—the yard before the Keller home, the Perkins Institution for the Blind, the garden house, and so forth.

The convention of the staging is one of cutting through time and place, and its essential qualities are fluidity and spatial counterpoint. To this end, the less set there is, the better; in a literal set, the fluidity will seem merely episodic. The stage therefore should be free, airy, unencumbered by walls. Apart from certain practical items—such as the pump, a window to climb out of, doors to be locked—locales should be only skeletal suggestions, and the movement from one to another should be accomplishable by little more than lights.

ACT ONE

It is night over the Keller homestead.

Inside, three adults in the bedroom are grouped around a crib, in lamplight. They have been through a long vigil, and it shows in their tired bearing and disarranged clothing. One is a young gentlewoman with a sweet girlish face, Kate Keller; the second is an elderly Doctor, *stethoscope at neck, thermometer in fingers;* the third is a hearty gentleman in his forties with chin whiskers, Captain Arthur Keller.

Doctor. She'll live.

Kate. Thank God.

(The Doctor leaves them together over the crib, packs his bag.)

Doctor. You're a pair of lucky parents. I can tell you now, I thought she wouldn't.

Keller. Nonsense, the child's a Keller; she has the <u>constitution</u> of a goat. She'll outlive us all.

Doctor *(amiably).* Yes, especially if some of you Kellers don't get a night's sleep. I mean you, Mrs. Keller.

Keller. You hear, Katie?

Kate. I hear.

Keller *(indulgent).* I've brought up two of them, but this is my wife's first; she isn't battle-scarred yet.

Kate. Doctor, don't be merely considerate. Will my girl be all right?

Doctor. Oh, by morning she'll be knocking down Captain Keller's fences again.

Words to Know and Use

vigil (vij′ əl) *n.* a time of staying awake during the usual hours of sleep in order to keep watch over or guard something or someone.
constitution (kän′ stə too′ shən) *n.* the physical makeup of someone or something

635

Kate. And isn't there anything we should do?

Keller (*jovial*). Put up stronger fencing, ha?

Doctor. Just let her get well; she knows how to do it better than we do.

(*He is packed, ready to leave.*)

Main thing is the fever's gone. These things come and go in infants; never know why. Call it acute congestion[1] of the stomach and brain.

Keller. I'll see you to your buggy, Doctor.

Doctor. I've never seen a baby with more <u>vitality</u>, that's the truth.

(*He beams a goodnight at the baby and* Kate, *and* Keller *leads him downstairs with a lamp. They go down the porch steps and across the yard, where the* Doctor *goes off left;* Keller *stands with the lamp aloft.* Kate, *meanwhile, is bent lovingly over the crib, which emits a bleat; her finger is playful with the baby's face.*)

Kate. Hush. Don't you cry now; you've been trouble enough. Call it acute congestion, indeed. I don't see what's so cute about a congestion, just because it's yours. We'll have your father run an editorial in his paper, the wonders of modern medicine. They don't know what they're curing even when they cure it. Men, men and their battle scars; we women will have to—

(*But she breaks off, puzzled, moves her finger before the baby's eyes.*)

Will have to—Helen?

(*Now she moves her hand, quickly.*)

Helen.

(*She snaps her fingers at the baby's eyes twice, and her hand falters; after a moment she calls out, loudly.*)

Captain, will you come—

(*But she stares at the baby, and her next call is directly at her ears.*)

Captain!

(*And now, still staring,* Kate *screams.* Keller *in the yard hears it, and runs with the lamp back to the house.* Kate *screams again, her look intent on the baby and terrible.* Keller *hurries in and up.*)

Keller. Katie? What's wrong?

Kate. Look.

(*She makes a pass with her hand in the crib, at the baby's eyes.*)

Keller. What, Katie? She's well; she needs only time to—

Kate. She can't see. Look at her eyes.

(*She takes the lamp from him, moves it before the child's face.*)

She can't *see!*

Keller (*hoarsely*). Helen.

Kate. Or hear. When I screamed, she didn't blink. Not an eyelash—

Keller. Helen. Helen!

Kate. She can't *hear* you!

Keller. *Helen!*

(*His face has something like fury in it, crying the child's name.* Kate, *almost fainting, presses her knuckles to her mouth, to stop her own cry. The room dims out quickly.*

Time, in the form of a slow tune of distant belfry chimes that approaches in a crescendo

------

1. **acute congestion:** severe blockage.

Words to Know and Use | **vitality** (vī tal′ ə tē) *n.* energy; strength

and then fades, passes; the light comes up again on a day five years later, on three kneeling children and an old dog outside around the pump.

The dog is a setter named Belle, *and she is sleeping. Two of the children are black,* Martha *and* Percy. *The third child is* Helen, *six and a half years old, quite* unkempt, *in body a* vivacious *little person with a fine head; attractive, but noticeably blind, one eye larger and protruding. Her gestures are abrupt, insistent, lacking in human* restraint, *and her face never smiles. She is flanked by the other two, in a litter of paper doll cutouts; and while they speak,* Helen's *hands thrust at their faces in turn, feeling baffledly at the movements of their lips.)*

Martha *(snipping).* First I'm gonna cut off this Doctor's legs, one, two, now then—

Percy. Why you cuttin' off that Doctor's legs?

Martha. I'm gonna give him a operation. Now I'm gonna cut off his arms, one, two. Now I'm gonna fix up—

(She pushes Helen's *hand away from her mouth.)*

You stop that.

Percy. Cut off his stomach; that's a good operation.

Martha. No, I'm gonna cut off his head first; he got a bad cold.

Percy. Ain't gonna be much of that Doctor left to fix up, time you finish all them opera—

(But Helen *is poking her fingers inside his mouth, to feel his tongue; he bites at them, annoyed, and she jerks them away.* Helen *now fingers her own lips, moving them in imitation, but soundlessly.)*

Martha. What you do, bite her hand?

Percy. That's how I do. She keep pokin' her fingers in my mouth; I just bite 'em off.

Martha. What she tryin' do now?

Percy. She tryin' *talk.* She gonna get mad. Looka her tryin' talk.

*(*Helen *is scowling, the lips under her fingers moving in ghostly silence, growing more and more frantic; until in a bizarre rage, she bites at her own fingers. This sends* Percy *off into laughter, but alarms* Martha.*)*

Martha. Hey, you stop now.

(She pulls Helen's *hand down.)*

You just sit quiet and—

(But at once Helen *topples* Martha *on her back, knees pinning her shoulders down, and grabs the scissors.* Martha *screams.* Percy *darts to the bell string on the porch, yanks it, and the bell rings.*

Inside, the lights have been gradually coming up on the main room, where we see the family informally gathered, talking, but in pantomime; Kate *sits darning socks near a cradle, occasionally rocking it.* Captain Keller *in spectacles is working over newspaper pages at a table. A* benign *visitor in a hat,* Aunt Ev, *is sharing the sewing basket, putting the finishing touches on a big, shapeless doll made out of towels. An* indolent *young man,* James Keller, *is at the window watching the children.*

With the ring of the bell, Kate *is instantly on her feet and out the door onto the porch, to take in the scene. Now we see what these five years have done to her. The girlish playfulness is gone; she is a woman steeled in grief.)*

Kate *(for the thousandth time).* Helen.

Words to Know and Use

unkempt (un kempt') *adj.* messy; untidy
vivacious (vī vā' shəs) *adj.* animated; full of life
restraint (ri strānt') *n.* self-control
benign (bi nīn') *adj.* good-natured; kindly
indolent (in' də lənt) *adj.* lazy; idle

(She is down the steps at once to them, seizing Helen's *wrists and lifting her off* Martha. Martha *runs off in tears and screams for momma, with* Percy *after her.)*

Let me have those scissors.

(Meanwhile the family inside is alerted, Aunt Ev *joining* James *at the window.* Captain Keller *resumes work.)*

James *(blandly)*. She only dug Martha's eyes out. Almost dug. It's always almost. No point worrying till it happens, is there?

(They gaze out, while Kate *reaches for the scissors in* Helen's *hand. But* Helen *pulls the scissors back. They struggle for them for a moment; then* Kate *gives up, lets* Helen *keep them. She tries to draw* Helen *into the house.* Helen *jerks away.* Kate *next goes down on her knees, takes* Helen's *hands gently, and using the scissors like a doll, makes* Helen *caress and cradle them; she points* Helen's *finger housewards.* Helen's *whole body now becomes eager; she surrenders the scissors.* Kate *turns her toward the door and gives her a little push.* Helen *scrambles up and toward the house, and* Kate, *rising, follows her.)*

Aunt Ev. How does she stand it? Why haven't you seen this Baltimore man? It's not a thing you can let go on and on, like the weather.

James. The weather here doesn't ask permission of me, Aunt Ev. Speak to my father.

Aunt Ev. Arthur. Something ought to be done for that child.

Keller. A refreshing suggestion. What?

*(Kate *entering turns* Helen *to* Aunt Ev, *who gives her the towel doll.)*

Aunt Ev. Why, this very famous oculist[2] in Baltimore I wrote you about. What was his name?

Kate. Dr. Chisholm.

Aunt Ev. Yes, I heard lots of cases of blindness that people thought couldn't be cured, he's cured. He just does wonders. Why don't you write to him?

Keller. I've stopped believing in wonders.

Kate *(rocks the cradle)*. I think the Captain will write to him soon. Won't you Captain?

Keller. No.

James *(lightly)*. Good money after bad, or bad after good. Or bad after bad—

Aunt Ev. Well, if it's just a question of money, Arthur, now you're marshal you have this Yankee money. Might as well—

Keller. Not money. The child's been to specialists all over Alabama and Tennessee. If I thought it would do good, I'd have her to every fool Doctor in the country.

Kate. I think the Captain will write to him soon.

Keller. Katie, how many times can you let them break your heart?

Kate. Any number of times.

*(Helen, *meanwhile, sits on the floor to explore the doll with her fingers, and her hand pauses over the face. This is no face, a blank area of towel, and it troubles her. Her hand searches for features, and taps questioningly for eyes, but no one notices. She then yanks at her aunt's dress, and taps again vigorously for eyes.)*

Aunt Ev. What, child?

(Obviously not hearing, Helen *commences to go around, from person to person, tapping for eyes, but no one attends or understands.)*

Kate *(no break)*. As long as there's the least chance. For her to see. Or hear, or—

Keller. There isn't. Now I must finish here.

---

2. **oculist** (äk′ yo͞o list): an eye doctor.

Kate. I think, with your permission, Captain, I'd like to write.

Keller. I said no, Katie.

Aunt Ev. Why, writing does no harm, Arthur, only a little bitty letter. To see if he can help her.

Keller. He can't.

Kate. We won't know that to be a fact, Captain, until after you write.

Keller (rising, emphatic). Katie, he can't.

(He collects his papers.)

James (facetiously). Father stands up; that makes it a fact.

Keller. You be quiet! I'm badgered enough here by females without your impudence.

(James shuts up, makes himself scarce. Helen now is groping among things on Keller's desk, and paws his papers to the floor. Keller is exasperated.)

Katie.

(Kate quickly turns Helen away, and retrieves the papers.)

I might as well try to work in a henyard as in this house—

James (placating). You really ought to put her away, Father.

Kate (staring up). What?

James. Some asylum. It's the kindest thing.

Aunt Ev. Why, she's your sister, James, not a nobody—

James. Half sister, and half-mentally defective; she can't even keep herself clean. It's not pleasant to see her about all the time.

Kate. Do you dare? Complain of what you can see?

Keller (very annoyed). This discussion is at an end! I'll thank you not to broach it again, Ev.

(Silence descends at once. Helen gropes her way with the doll, and Keller turns back for a final word, explosive.)

I've done as much as I can bear; I can't give my whole life to it! The house is at sixes and sevens[3] from morning till night over the child. It's time some attention was paid to Mildred here instead!

Kate (gently dry). You'll wake her up, Captain.

Keller. I want some peace in the house. I don't care how, but one way we won't have it is by rushing up and down the country every time someone hears of a new quack. I'm as sensible to this affliction as anyone else; it hurts me to look at the girl.

Kate. It was not our affliction I meant you to write about, Captain.

(Helen is back at Aunt Ev, fingering her dress, and yanks two buttons from it.)

Aunt Ev. Helen! My buttons.

(Helen pushes the buttons into the doll's face. Kate now sees, comes swiftly to kneel, lifts Helen's hands to her own eyes in question.)

Kate. Eyes?

(Helen nods energetically.)
She wants the doll to have eyes.

(Another kind of silence now, while Kate takes pins and buttons from the sewing basket and attaches them to the doll as eyes. Keller stands, caught, and watches morosely. Aunt

---

3. **at sixes and sevens:** in a state of disorder.

| Words to Know and Use | impudence (im′ pyōō dəns) n. shameless or disrespectful boldness impudent adj. morosely (mə rōs′ lē) adv. gloomily; sullenly |

639

Photographs from the 1962 film version of *The Miracle Worker*, United Artists, starring Anne Bancroft and Patty Duke.

Ev *blinks, and conceals her emotions by inspecting her dress.)*

Aunt Ev. My goodness me, I'm not decent.

Kate. She doesn't know better, Aunt Ev. I'll sew them on again.

James. Never learn with everyone letting her do anything she takes it into her mind to—

Keller. You be quiet!

James. What did I say now?

Keller. You talk too much.

James. I was agreeing with you!

Keller. Whatever it was. Deprived child, the least she can have are the little things she wants.

(James, *very wounded, stalks out of the room onto the porch; he remains here, sulking.)*

Aunt Ev (*indulgently*). It's worth a couple of buttons. Kate, look.

(Helen *now has the doll with eyes, and cannot contain herself for joy; she rocks the doll, pats it vigorously, kisses it.*)

This child has more sense than all these men Kellers, if there's ever any way to reach that mind of hers.

(But Helen *suddenly has come upon the cradle, and unhesitatingly overturns it; the swaddled baby tumbles out, and* Captain Keller *barely manages to dive and catch it in time.*)

Keller. Helen!

(All are in commotion. The baby screams, but Helen, *unperturbed, is laying her doll in its place.* Kate, *on her knees, pulls her hands off the cradle, wringing them.* Helen *is bewildered.*)

Kate. Helen, Helen, you're not to do such things; how can I make you understand—

Keller (*hoarsely*). Katie.

Kate. How can I get it into your head, my darling, my poor—

Keller. Katie, some way of teaching her an iota of discipline has to be—

Kate (*flaring*). How can you discipline an afflicted child? Is it her fault?

(Helen's *fingers have fluttered to her mother's lips, vainly trying to comprehend their movements.*)

Keller. I didn't say it was her fault.

Kate. Then whose? I don't know what to do! How can I teach her, beat her—until she's black and blue?

Keller. It's not safe to let her run around loose. Now there must be a way of confining her, somehow, so she can't—

Kate. Where, in a cage? She's a growing child; she has to use her limbs!

Keller. Answer me one thing. Is it fair to Mildred here?

Kate (*inexorably*). Are you willing to put her away?

(Now Helen's *face darkens in the same rage as at herself earlier, and her hand strikes at* Kate's *lips.* Kate *catches her hand again, and* Helen *begins to kick, struggle, twist.*)

Keller. Now what?

Kate. She wants to talk, like—be like you and me.

(She holds Helen, *struggling, until we hear from the child her first sound so far, an <u>inarticulate</u>, weird noise in her throat such as an animal in a trap might make; and* Kate *releases her. The second she is free,* Helen *blunders away, collides violently with a chair, falls, and sits weeping.* Kate *comes to her, embraces, caresses, soothes her, and buries her own face in her hair, until she can control her voice.*)

Every day she slips further away. And I don't know how to call her back.

Aunt Ev. Oh, I've a mind to take her up to Baltimore myself. If that Doctor can't help her, maybe he'll know who can.

Keller (*presently, heavily*). I'll write the man, Katie.

(He stands with the baby in his clasp, staring at Helen's *head, hanging down on* Kate's *arm.*

The lights dim out, except the one on Kate *and* Helen. *In the twilight,* James, Aunt Ev, *and* Keller *move off slowly, formally, in separate*

Words to Know and Use | **inarticulate** (in' är tik' yo͞o lit) *adj.* **1** not spoken so others can understand; not expressed clearly **2** not able to speak understandably

641

directions; Kate, *with* Helen *in her arms, remains, motionless, in a image that overlaps into the next scene and fades only when it is well underway.*

Without pause, from the dark down left we hear a man's voice with a Greek accent speaking.)

Anagnos. —who could do nothing for the girl, of course. It was Dr. Bell who thought she might somehow be taught. I have written the family only that a suitable governess, Miss Annie Sullivan, has been found here in Boston—

(The lights begin to come up, down left, on a long table and chair. The table contains equipment for teaching the blind by touch—a small replica of the human skeleton, stuffed animals, models of flowers and plants, piles of books. The chair contains a girl of twenty, Annie Sullivan, *with a face that in repose is grave and rather obstinate and when active is impudent,* combative, *twinkling with all the life that is lacking in* Helen's, *and handsome. There is a crude vitality to her. Her suitcase is at her knee.* Anagnos, *a stocky, bearded man, comes into the light only toward the end of his speech.)*

Anagnos. —and will come. It will no doubt be difficult for you there, Annie. But it has been difficult for you at our school too, hm? Gratifying, yes, when you came to us and could not spell your name, to accomplish so much here in a few years, but always an Irish battle. For independence.

(He studies Annie, *humorously; she does not open her eyes.)*

This is my last time to counsel you, Annie, and you do lack some—by some I mean *all*—what, tact or talent to bend. To others. And what has saved you on more than one occasion here at Perkins is that there was nowhere to expel you to. Your eyes hurt?

Annie. My ears, Mr. Anagnos.

(And now she has opened her eyes. They are inflamed, vague, slightly crossed, clouded by the granular growth of trachoma;[4] and she often keeps them closed to shut out the pain of light.)

Anagnos *(severely).* Nowhere but back to Tewksbury, where children learn to be saucy. Annie, I know how dreadful it was there, but that battle is dead and done with. Why not let it stay buried?

Annie *(cheerily).* I think God must owe me a resurrection.

Anagnos *(a bit shocked).* What?

Annie *(taps her brow).* Well, he keeps digging up that battle!

Anagnos. That is not a proper thing to say, Annie. It is what I mean.

Annie *(meekly).* Yes. I know what I'm like. What's this child like?

Anagnos. Like?

Annie. Well—bright or dull, to start off.

Anagnos. No one knows. And if she is dull, you have no patience with this?

Annie. Oh, in grown-ups you have to, Mr. Anagnos. I mean in children it just seems a little—precocious. Can I use that word?

Anagnos. Only if you can spell it.

Annie. Premature. So I hope at least she's a bright one.

---

4. **They are . . . trachoma** (trə kō′ mə): Annie's eyes are red, swollen, and not clear, with a grainy surface caused by trachoma, a contagious eye infection.

Words to Know and Use | **combative** (kəm bat′ iv) *adj.* ready or eager to fight
resurrection (rez′ ə rek′ shən) *n.* a bringing back to life; a rebirth

Anagnos. Deaf, blind, mute—who knows? She is like a little safe, locked, that no one can open. Perhaps there is a treasure inside.

Annie. Maybe it's empty, too?

Anagnos. Possible. I should warn you; she is much given to tantrums.

Annie. Means something is inside. Well, so am I, if I believe all I hear. Maybe you should warn *them*.

Anagnos *(frowns)*. Annie, I wrote them no word of your history. You will find yourself among strangers now, who know nothing of it.

Annie. Well, we'll keep them in a state of blessed ignorance.

Anagnos. Perhaps *you* should tell it?

Annie *(bristling)*. Why? I have enough trouble with people who don't know.

Anagnos. So they will understand. When you have trouble.

Annie. The only time I have trouble is when I'm right.

(But she is amused at herself, as is Anagnos.)

Is it my fault it's so often? I won't give them trouble, Mr. Anagnos. I'll be so ladylike they won't notice I've come.

Anagnos. Annie, be—humble. It is not as if you have so many offers to pick and choose. You will need their affection, working with this child.

Annie *(humorously)*. I hope I won't need their pity.

Anagnos. Oh, we can all use some pity.

(Crisply)

So. You are no longer our pupil; we throw you into the world, a teacher. If the child can be taught. No one expects you to work miracles, even for twenty-five

dollars a month. Now, in this envelope a loan, for the railroad, which you will repay me when you have a bank account. But in this box, a gift. With our love.

(Annie opens the small box he extends, and sees a garnet ring. She looks up, blinking, and down.)

I think other friends are ready to say goodbye.

(He moves as though to open doors.)

Annie. Mr. Anagnos.

(Her voice is trembling.)

Dear Mr. Anagnos, I—

(But she swallows while getting the ring on her finger, and cannot continue until she finds a woebegone joke.)

Well, what should I say? I'm an ignorant, opinionated girl, and everything I am I owe to you?

Anagnos *(smiles)*. That is only half true, Annie.

Annie. Which half? I crawled in here like a drowned rat. I thought I died when Jimmie died, that I'd never again—come alive. Well, you say with love so easy, and I haven't *loved* a soul since, and I never will, I suppose; but this place gave me more than my eyes back. Or taught me how to spell, which I'll never learn anyway; but with all the fights and the trouble I've been here, it taught me what help is and how to live again; and I don't want to say goodbye. Don't open the door; I'm crying.

Anagnos *(gently)*. They will not see.

(He moves again as though opening doors, and in comes a group of girls, eight-year-olds to seventeen-year-olds; as they walk, we see they are blind. Anagnos shepherds them in with a hand.)

A Child. Annie?

Annie *(her voice cheerful)*. Here, Beatrice.

(As soon as they locate her voice, they throng joyfully to her, speaking all at once. Annie is down on her knees to the smallest, and the following are the more intelligible fragments in the general hubbub.)

Children. There's a present. We bought you a going-away present, Annie!

Annie. Oh, now, you shouldn't have—

Children. We did, we did. Where's the present?

Smallest Child *(mournfully)*. Don't go, Annie, away.

Children. Alice has it. Alice! Where's Alice? Here I am! Where? Here!

(An arm is aloft of the group, waving a present; Annie *reaches for it.)*

Annie. I have it. I have it, everybody. Should I open it?

Children. Open it! Everyone be quiet! Do, Annie! She's opening it. Ssh!

(A setting of silence while Annie *unwraps it. The present is a pair of smoked glasses, and she stands still.)*

Is it open, Annie?

Annie. It's open.

Children. It's for your eyes, Annie. Put them on, Annie! 'Cause Mrs. Hopkins said your eyes hurt since the operation. And she said you're going where the sun is *fierce*.

Annie. I'm putting them on now.

Smallest Child *(mournfully)*. Don't go, Annie, where the sun is fierce.

Children. Do they fit all right?

Annie. Oh, they fit just fine.

Children. Did you put them on? Are they pretty, Annie?

Annie. Oh, my eyes feel hundreds of percent better already, and pretty. Why, do you know how I look in them? Splendiloquent. Like a race horse!

Children *(delighted)*. There's another present! Beatrice! We have a present for Helen, too! Give it to her, Beatrice. Here Annie!

(This present is an elegant doll, with movable eyelids and a momma sound.)

It's for Helen. And we took up a collection to buy it. And Laura dressed it.

Annie. It's beautiful!

Children. So don't forget; you be sure to give it to Helen from us, Annie!

Annie. I promise it will be the first thing I give her. If I don't keep it for myself, that is; you know I can't be trusted with dolls!

Smallest Child *(mournfully)*. Don't go, Annie, to her.

Annie *(her arm around her)*. Sarah, dear. I don't *want* to go.

Smallest Child. Then why are you going?

Annie *(gently)*. Because I'm a big girl now, and big girls have to earn a living. It's the only way I can. But if you don't smile for me first, what I'll just have to do is—

(She pauses, inviting it.)

Smallest Child. What?

Annie. Put *you* in my suitcase, instead of this doll. And take *you* to Helen in Alabama!

(This strikes the children as very funny, and they begin to laugh and tease the smallest child, who after a moment does smile for Annie.)

Anagnos *(then)*. Come, children. We must get the trunk into the carriage and Annie into her train, or no one will go to Alabama. Come, come.

(He shepherds them out, and Annie *is left alone on her knees with the doll in her lap. She reaches for her suitcase, and by a subtle change in the color of the light, we go with her thoughts into another time. We hear a boy's voice whispering; perhaps we see shadowy intimations of these speakers in the background.)*

Boy's Voice. Where we goin', Annie?

Annie *(in dread)*. Jimmie.

Boy's Voice. Where we goin'?

Annie. I said—I'm takin' care of you—

Boy's Voice. Forever and ever?

Man's Voice *(impersonal)*. Annie Sullivan, aged nine, virtually blind. James Sullivan, aged seven—What's the matter with your leg, Sonny?

Annie. Forever and ever.

Man's Voice. Can't he walk without that crutch?

(Annie shakes her head, and does not stop shaking it.)

Girl goes to the women's ward. Boy to the men's.

Boy's Voice *(in terror)*. Annie! Annie, don't let them take me—Annie!

Anagnos *(offstage)*. Annie! Annie?

(But this voice is real, in the present, and Annie *comes up out of her horror, clearing her head with a final shake. The lights begin to pick out* Kate *in the* Keller *house, as* Annie *in a bright tone calls back.)*

Annie. Coming!

(This word catches Kate, *who stands half turned and attentive to it, almost as though hearing it. Meanwhile,* Annie *turns and hurries out, lugging the suitcase.*

*The room dims out; the sound of railroad wheels begins from off left, and maintains itself in a constant rhythm underneath the fol-*lowing scenes; the remaining lights have come up on the* Keller *homestead.* James *is lounging on the porch, waiting. In the upper bedroom which is to be* Annie's, Helen *is alone, puzzledly exploring, fingering and smelling things, the curtains, empty drawers in the bureau, water in the pitcher by the washbasin, fresh towels on the bedstead. Downstairs in the family room,* Kate, *turning to a mirror, hastily adjusts her bonnet, watched by a black servant in an apron,* Viney.)*

Viney. Let Mr. Jimmy go by hisself. You been pokin' that garden all day; you ought to rest your feet.

Kate. I can't wait to see her, Viney.

Viney. Maybe she ain't gone be on this train neither.

Kate. Maybe she is.

Viney. And maybe she ain't.

Kate. And maybe she is. Where's Helen?

Viney. She upstairs, smellin' around. She know somethin' funny's goin' on.

Kate. Let her have her supper as soon as Mildred's in bed, and tell Captain Keller when he comes that we'll be delayed tonight.

Viney. Again?

Kate. I don't think we need say *again*. Simply delayed will do.

(She runs upstairs to Annie's *room,* Viney *speaking after her.)*

Viney. I mean that's what he gone say. "What, again?"

*(*Viney *works at setting the table. Upstairs* Kate *stands in the doorway, watching* Helen's *groping explorations.)*

Kate. Yes, we're expecting someone. Someone for my Helen.

*(*Helen *happens upon her skirt, clutches her leg.* Kate *in a tired dismay, kneels to tidy her hair and soiled pinafore.)*

Oh, dear, this was clean not an hour ago.

(Helen *feels her bonnet, shakes her head darkly, and tugs to get it off.* Kate *retains it with one hand, diverts* Helen *by opening her other hand under her nose.*)

Here. For while I'm gone.

(Helen *sniffs, reaches, and pops something into her mouth, while* Kate *speaks a bit guiltily.*)

I don't think one peppermint drop will spoil your supper.

(*She gives* Helen *a quick kiss, and hurries downstairs again. Meanwhile* Captain Keller *has entered the yard from around the rear of the house, newspaper under arm, cleaning off and munching on some radishes. He sees* James *lounging at the porch post.*)

Keller. Jimmie?

James *(unmoving).* Sir?

Keller *(eyes him).* You don't look dressed for anything useful, boy.

James. I'm not. It's for Miss Sullivan.

Keller. Needn't keep holding up that porch; we have wooden posts for that. I asked you to see that those strawberry plants were moved this evening.

James. I'm moving your—Mrs. Keller, instead. To the station.

Keller *(heavily).* Mrs. Keller. Must you always speak of her as though you haven't met the lady?

(Kate *comes out on the porch, and* James *inclines his head.*)

James *(ironic).* Mother.

(*He starts off the porch, but sidesteps* Keller's *glare like a blow.*)

I said mother!

Kate. Captain.

Keller. Evening, my dear.

Kate. We're off to meet the train, Captain. Supper will be a trifle delayed tonight.

Keller. What, again?

Kate *(backing out).* With your permission, Captain?

(*And they are gone,* Keller *watches them off-stage, morosely.*

Upstairs, Helen *meanwhile has groped for her mother, touched her cheek in a meaningful gesture, waited, touched her cheek, waited, then found the open door, and made her way down. Now she comes into the family room, touches her cheek again;* Viney *regards her.*)

Viney. What you want, honey, your momma?

(Helen *touches her cheek again.* Viney *goes to the sideboard, gets a tea-cake, gives it into* Helen's *hand;* Helen *pops it into her mouth.*)

Guess one little tea-cake ain't gone ruin your appetite.

(*She turns* Helen *toward the door.* Helen *wanders out onto the porch, as* Keller *comes up the steps. Her hands encounter him, and she touches her cheek again, waits.*)

Keller. She's gone.

(*He is awkward with her. When he puts his hand on her head, she pulls away.* Keller *stands regarding her, heavily.*)

She's gone; my son and I don't get along; you don't know I'm your father; no one likes me; and supper's delayed.

(Helen *touches her cheek, waits.* Keller *fishes in his pocket.*)

Here, I brought you some stick candy; one nibble of sweets can't do any harm.

(*He gives her a large stick candy;* Helen *falls to it.* Viney *peers out the window.*)

Viney (reproachfully). Cap'n Keller, now how'm I gone get her to eat her supper you fill her up with that trash?

Keller (roars). Tend to your work!

(Viney beats a rapid retreat. Keller thinks better of it, and tries to get the candy away from Helen, but Helen hangs on to it; and when Keller pulls, she gives his leg a kick. Keller hops about. Helen takes refuge with the candy down behind the pump, and Keller then irately flings his newspaper on the porch floor, stamps into the house past Viney, and disappears.

The lights half dim on the homestead, where Viney and Helen, going about their business, soon find their way off. Meanwhile, the railroad sounds off left have mounted in a crescendo to a climax typical of a depot at arrival time. The lights come up on stage left, and we see a suggestion of a station. Here Annie in her smoked glasses and disarrayed by travel is waiting with her suitcase, while James walks to meet her. She has a battered paper-bound book, which is a Perkins report, under her arm.)

James (coolly). Miss Sullivan?

Annie (cheerily). Here! At last. I've been on trains so many days I thought they must be backing up every time I dozed off—

James. I'm James Keller.

Annie. James?

(The name stops her.)

I had a brother Jimmie. Are you Helen's?

James. I'm only half a brother. You're to be her governess?

Annie (lightly). Well. Try!

James (eyeing her). You look like half a governess.

(Kate enters. Annie stands moveless, while James takes her suitcase. Kate's gaze on her is doubtful, troubled.)

Mrs. Keller, Miss Sullivan.

(Kate takes her hand.)

Kate (simply). We've met every train for two days.

(Annie looks at Kate's face, and her good humor comes back.)

Annie. I changed trains every time they stopped. The man who sold me that ticket ought to be tied to the tracks—

James. You have a trunk, Miss Sullivan?

Annie. Yes.

(She passes James a claim check and he bears the suitcase out behind them. Annie holds the battered book. Kate is studying her face, and Annie returns the gaze. This is a mutual appraisal, southern gentlewoman and working-class Irish girl, and Annie is not quite comfortable under it.)

You didn't bring Helen. I was hoping you would.

Kate. No, she's home.

(A pause. Annie tries to make ladylike small talk, though her energy now and then erupts. She catches herself up, whenever she hears it.)

Annie. You—live far from town, Mrs. Keller?

Kate. Only a mile.

Annie. Well, I suppose I can wait one more mile. But don't be surprised if I get out to push the horse!

Kate. Helen's waiting for you, too. There's been such a bustle in the house; she expects something, heaven knows what.

(Now she voices part of her doubt, not as such, but Annie *understands it.)*

I expected—a desiccated spinster.[5] You're very young.

Annie *(resolutely).* Oh, you should have seen me when I left Boston. I got much older on this trip.

Kate. I mean, to teach anyone as difficult as Helen.

Annie. *I* mean to try. They can't put you in jail for trying!

Kate. Is it possible, even? To teach a deaf-blind child *half* of what an ordinary child learns—has that ever been done?

Annie. Half?

Kate. A tenth.

Annie *(reluctantly).* No.

(Kate's face loses its remaining hope, still appraising her youth.)

Dr. Howe did wonders, but—an ordinary child? No, never, But then I thought when I was going over his reports—

(She indicates the one in her hand.)

—he never treated them like ordinary children. More like—eggs everyone was afraid would break.

Kate *(a pause).* May I ask how old you are?

Annie. Well, I'm not in my teens, you know! I'm twenty.

Kate. All of twenty.

(Annie takes the bull by the horns, valiantly.)

Annie. Mrs. Keller, don't lose heart just because I'm not on my last legs. I have three big advantages over Dr. Howe that money couldn't buy for you. One is his work behind me. I've read every word he wrote about it and he wasn't exactly what you'd call a man of few words. Another is

being young; why, I've got energy to do anything. The third is, I've been blind.

(But it costs her something to say this.)

Kate *(quietly).* Advantages.

Annie *(wry).* Well, some have the luck of the Irish; some do not.

(Kate smiles; she likes her.)

Kate. What will you try to teach her first?

Annie. First, last, and—in between, language.

Kate. Language.

Annie. Language is to the mind more than light is to the eye. Dr. Howe said that.

Kate. Language.

(She shakes her head.)

We can't get through to teach her to sit still. You *are* young, despite your years, to have such—confidence. Do you, inside?

(Annie studies her face; she likes her, too.)

Annie. No, to tell you the truth, I'm as shaky inside as a baby's rattle!

(They smile at each other, and Kate *pats her hand.)*

Kate. Don't be.

(James returns to usher them off.)

We'll do all we can to help, and to make you feel at home. Don't think of us as strangers, Miss Annie.

Annie *(cheerily).* Oh, strangers aren't so strange to me. I've known them all my life!

(Kate smiles again, Annie *smiles back, and they precede* James *offstage.*

The lights dim on them, having simultaneously risen full on the house. Viney *has*

---

5. **desiccated** (des′ i kāt′ id) **spinster:** a dried-up, old, unmarried woman—a belittling expression.

already entered the family room, taken a water pitcher, and come out and down to the pump. She pumps real water. As she looks offstage, we hear the clop of hoofs, a carriage stopping, and voices.)

Viney. Cap'n Keller! Cap'n Keller, they comin'!

(She goes back into the house, as Keller *comes out on the porch to gaze.)*

She sure 'nuff came, Cap'n.

*(*Keller *descends, and crosses toward the carriage; this conversation begins offstage and moves on.)*

Keller *(very courtly).* Welcome to Ivy Green, Miss Sullivan. I take it you are Miss Sullivan—

Kate. My husband, Miss Annie, Captain Keller.

Annie *(her best behavior).* Captain, how do you do.

Keller. A pleasure to see you, at last. I trust you had an agreeable journey?

Annie. Oh, I had several! When did this country get so big?

James. Where would you like the trunk, father?

Keller. Where Miss Sullivan can get at it, I imagine.

Annie. Yes, please. Where's Helen?

Keller. In the hall, Jimmie—

Kate. We've put you in the upstairs corner room, Miss Annie. If there's any breeze at all this summer, you'll feel it—

(In the house, the setter Belle *flees into the family room, pursued by* Helen *with groping hands. The dog doubles back out the same door, and* Helen, *still groping for her, makes her way out to the porch. She is messy; her hair tumbled, her pinafore now ripped, her shoelaces untied.* Keller *acquires the suitcase,*

and Annie *gets her hands on it too, though still endeavoring to live up to the general air of propertied manners.)*

Keller. And the suitcase—

Annie *(pleasantly).* I'll take the suitcase, thanks.

Keller. Not at all, I have it, Miss Sullivan.

Annie. I'd like it.

Keller *(gallantly).* I couldn't think of it, Miss Sullivan. You'll find in the South we—

Annie. Let me.

Keller. —view women as the flowers of civiliza—

Annie *(impatiently).* I've got something in it for Helen!

(She tugs it free; Keller *stares.)*

Thank you. When do I see her?

Kate. There. There is Helen.

*(*Annie *turns, and sees* Helen *on the porch. A moment of silence. Then* Annie *begins across the yard to her, lugging her suitcase.)*

Keller *(sotto voce[6]).* Katie—

*(*Kate *silences him with a hand on his arm. When* Annie *finally reaches the porch steps, she stops, contemplating* Helen *for a last moment before entering her world. Then she drops the suitcase on the porch with intentional heaviness.* Helen *starts with the jar, and comes to grope over it.* Annie *puts forth her hand, and touches* Helen's*.* Helen *at once grasps it, and commences to explore it, like reading a face. She moves her hand on to* Annie's *forearm, and dress; and* Annie *brings her face within reach of* Helen's *fingers, which travel over it, quite without timidity, until they encounter and push aside the smoked glasses.* Annie's *gaze is grave, unpitying, very attentive. She puts her hands on* Helen's *arms, but*

---

6. **sotto voce** (sät′ ō vō′ chē) *Italian:* in a low tone of voice, so as not to be overheard.

Helen *at once pulls away, and they confront each other with a distance between. Then* Helen *returns to the suitcase, tries to open it, cannot.* Annie *points* Helen's *hand overhead.* Helen *pulls away, tries to open the suitcase again;* Annie *points her hand overhead again.* Helen *points overhead, a question; and* Annie, *drawing* Helen's *hand to her own face, nods.* Helen *now begins tugging the suitcase towards the door. When* Annie *tries to take it from her, she fights her off and backs through the doorway with it.* Annie *stands a moment, then follows her in, and together they get the suitcase up the steps into* Annie's *room.)*

Kate. Well?

Keller. She's very rough, Katie.

Kate. I like her, Captain.

Keller. Certainly rear a peculiar kind of young woman in the North. How old is she?

Kate *(vaguely).* Ohh—Well, she's not in her teens, you know.

Keller. She's only a child. What's her family like, shipping her off alone this far?

Kate. I couldn't learn. She's very close-mouthed about some things.

Keller. Why does she wear those glasses? I like to see a person's eyes when I talk to—

Kate. For the sun. She was blind.

Keller. Blind.

Kate. She's had nine operations on her eyes. One just before she left.

Keller. Blind, good heavens, do they expect one blind child to teach another? Has she experience at least? How long did she teach there?

Kate. She was a pupil.

Keller *(heavily).* Katie, Katie. This is her first position?

Kate *(bright voice).* She was valedictorian—

Keller. Here's a houseful of grownups can't cope with the child. How can an inexperienced, half-blind Yankee schoolgirl manage her?

(James moves in with the trunk on his shoulder.)

James *(easily).* Great improvement. Now we have two of them to look after.

Keller. You look after those strawberry plants!

(James stops with the trunk. Keller *turns from him without another word, and marches off.)*

James. Nothing I say is right.

Kate. Why say anything?

(She calls.)

Don't be long, Captain. We'll have supper right away—

(She goes into the house, and through the rear door of the family room. James *trudges in with the trunk, takes it up the steps to* Annie's *room, and sets it down outside the door. The lights elsewhere dim somewhat.*

Meanwhile, inside, Annie *has given* Helen *a key. While* Annie *removes her bonnet,* Helen *unlocks and opens the suitcase. The first thing she pulls out is a voluminous shawl. She fingers it until she perceives what it is; then she wraps it around her, and acquiring* Annie's *bonnet and smoked glasses as well, dons the lot. The shawl swamps her, and the bonnet settles down upon the glasses, but she stands before a mirror cocking her head to one side, then to the other, in a mockery of adult action.* Annie *is amused, and talks to her as one might to a kitten, with no trace of company manners.)*

Annie. All the trouble I went to, and that's how I look?

(Helen then comes back to the suitcase, gropes for more, lifts out a pair of female drawers.)

Oh, no. Not the drawers!

(But Helen, *discarding them, comes to the elegant doll. Her fingers explore its features, and when she raises it and finds its eyes open and close, she is at first startled, then delighted. She picks it up, taps its head vigorously, taps her own chest, and nods questioningly. Annie takes her finger, points it to the doll, points it to* Helen, *and touching it to her own face, also nods.* Helen *sits back on her heels, clasps the doll to herself and rocks it. Annie studies her, still in bonnet and smoked glasses like a caricature of herself, and addresses her humorously.)*

All right, Miss O'Sullivan. Let's begin with doll.

(She takes Helen's *hand. In her palm, Annie's forefinger points, thumb holding her other fingers clenched.)*

D.

(Her thumb next holds all her fingers clenched, touching Helen's *palm.)*

O.

(Her thumb and forefinger extend.)

L.

(Same contact repeated.)

L.

(She puts Helen's *hand to the doll.)*

Doll.

James. You spell pretty well.

(Annie, *in one hurried move, gets the drawers swiftly back into the suitcase, the lid banged shut, and her head turned, to see* James *leaning in the doorway.)*

Finding out if she's ticklish? She is.

(Annie *regards him stonily, but after a scowling moment,* Helen *tugs at her hand again, imperious.* Annie *repeats the letters, and* Helen *interrupts her fingers in the middle, feeling each of them, puzzled.* Annie *touches* Helen's *hand to the doll, and begins spelling into it again.)*

James. What is it, a game?

Annie *(curtly)*. An alphabet.

James. Alphabet?

Annie. For the deaf.

(Helen *now repeats the finger movements in air, exactly, her head cocked to her own hand, and* Annie's *eyes suddenly gleam.)*

Ho. How *bright* she is!

James. You think she knows what she's doing?

(He takes Helen's *hand, to throw a meaningless gesture into it; she repeats this one too.)*

She imitates everything; she's a monkey.

Annie *(very pleased)*. Yes, she's a bright little monkey, all right.

(*She takes the doll from* Helen *and reaches for her hand;* Helen *instantly grabs the doll back.* Annie *takes it again, and* Helen's *hand next, but* Helen *is incensed now. When* Annie *draws her hand to her face to shake her head no, then tries to spell to her,* Helen *slaps at* Annie's *face.* Annie *grasps* Helen *by both arms, and swings her into a chair, holding her pinned there, kicking, while glasses, doll, bonnet fly in various directions.* James *laughs.)*

James. She wants her doll back.

Annie. When she spells it.

James. Spell, she doesn't know the thing has a name, even.

Annie. Of course not. Who expects her to, now? All I want is her fingers to learn the letters.

James. Won't mean anything to her.

(Annie *gives him a look. She then tries to form* Helen's *fingers into the letters, but* Helen *swings a haymaker[7] instead, which* Annie *barely ducks, at once pinning her down again.)*

Doesn't like that alphabet, Miss Sullivan. You invent it yourself?

(Helen *is now in a rage, fighting tooth and nail to get out of the chair, and* Annie *answers while struggling and dodging her kicks.)*

Annie. Spanish monks under a—vow of silence. Which I wish *you'd* take!

(*And suddenly releasing* Helen's *hands, she comes and shuts the door in* James's *face.* Helen *drops to the floor, groping around for the doll.* Annie *looks around desperately, sees her purse on the bed, rummages in it, and comes up with a battered piece of cake wrapped in newspaper. With her foot she moves the doll deftly out of the way of* Helen's *groping; and going on her knee, she lets* Helen *smell the cake. When* Helen *grabs for it,* Annie *removes the cake and spells quickly into the reaching hand.)*

Cake. From Washington, up north; it's the best I can do.

(Helen's *hand waits, baffled.* Annie *repeats it.)*

C, a, k, e. Do what my fingers do; never mind what it means.

(*She touches the cake briefly to* Helen's *nose, pats her hand, presents her own hand.* Helen

---

7. **haymaker:** a powerful punch meant to cause a knockout.

spells the letters rapidly back. Annie *pats her hand enthusiastically, and gives her the cake.* Helen *crams it into her mouth with both hands.* Annie *watches her, with humor.)*

Get it down fast; maybe I'll steal that back, too. Now.

(She takes the doll, touches it to Helen's *nose, and spells again into her hand.)*

D, o, l, l. Think it over.

*(*Helen *thinks it over, while* Annie *presents her own hand. Then* Helen *spells three letters.* Annie *waits a second, then completes the word for* Helen *in her palm.)*

L.

(She hands over the doll, and Helen *gets a good grip on its leg.)*

Imitate now, understand later. End of the first les—

(She never finishes, because Helen *swings the doll with a furious energy. It hits* Annie *squarely in the face, and she falls back with a cry of pain, her knuckles up to her mouth.* Helen *waits, tensed for further combat. When* Annie *lowers her knuckles, she looks at blood on them. She works her lips, gets to her feet, finds the mirror, and bares her teeth at herself. Now she is furious herself.)*

You little wretch, no one's taught you any manners? I'll—

(But rounding from the mirror, she sees the door slam. Helen *and the doll are on the outside, and* Helen *is turning the key in the lock.* Annie *darts over, to pull the knob; the door is locked fast. She yanks it again.)*

Helen! Helen, let me out of—

(She bats her brow at the folly of speaking but James, *now downstairs, hears her and turns to see* Helen *with the key and doll groping her way down the steps.* James *takes in the whole situation, makes a move to intercept but then changes his mind, lets her pass, and amusedly follows her out onto the porch. Upstairs,* Annie *meanwhile rattles the knob, kneels, peers through the keyhole, gets up. She goes to the window, looks down, frowns.* James *from the yard sings gaily up to her,)*

James. Buffalo girl, are you coming out tonight,
Coming out tonight—
Coming out—

(He drifts back into the house. Annie *takes a handkerchief, nurses her mouth, stands in the middle of the room, staring at door and window in turn; and so catches sight of herself in the mirror, her cheek scratched, her hair dishevelled, her handkerchief bloody, her face disgusted with herself. She addresses the mirror, with some irony.)*

Annie. Don't worry. They'll find you; you're not lost. Only out of place.

(But she coughs, spits something into her palm, and stares at it, outraged.)

And toothless.

(She winces.)

Oo! It hurts.

(She pours some water into the basin, dips the handkerchief, and presses it to her mouth. Standing there, bent over the basin in pain—with the rest of the set dim and unreal, and the lights upon her taking on the subtle color of the past—she hears again, as do we, the faraway voices; and slowly she lifts her head to them. The boy's voice is the same; the others are cracked old crones[8] in a nightmare; and perhaps we see their shadows.)

Boy's Voice. It hurts, Annie, it hurts.

First Crone's Voice. Keep that brat shut up, can't you, girlie. How's a body to get any sleep in this darn ward?

---

8. **crones:** ugly, withered old women; hags.

THE MIRACLE WORKER   653

Boy's Voice. It hurts. It hurts.

Second Crone's Voice. Shut up, you!

Boy's Voice. Annie, when are we goin' home? You promised!

Annie. Jimmie—

Boy's Voice. Forever and ever, you said forever—

(Annie *drops the handkerchief, averts to the window, and is arrested there by the next cry.)*

Annie, Annie, you there? Annie! It *hurts!*

Third Crone's Voice. Grab him; he's fallin'!

Boy's Voice. *Annie!*

Doctor's Voice *(a pause, slowly)*. Little girl. Little girl, I must tell you your brother will be going on a—

(But Annie *claps her hands to her ears, to shut this out; there is instant silence.*

As the lights bring the other areas in again, James *goes to the steps to listen for any sound from upstairs.* Keller, *re-entering from left, crosses toward the house; he passes* Helen *en route to her retreat under the pump.* Kate *reenters the rear door of the family room, with flowers for the table.)*

Kate. Supper is ready, Jimmie. Will you call your father?

James. Certainly.

(But he calls up the stairs, for Annie's *benefit.)*

Father! Supper!

Keller *(at the door)*. No need to shout; I've been cooling my heels for an hour. Sit down.

James. Certainly.

Keller. Viney!

(Viney backs in with a roast, while they get settled around the table.)

Viney. Yes, Cap'n, right here.

Kate. Mildred went directly to sleep, Viney?

Viney. Oh, yes, that babe's an angel.

Kate. And Helen had a good supper?

Viney *(vaguely)*. I dunno, Miss Kate, somehow she didn't have much of a appetite tonight—

Kate *(a bit guiltily)*. Oh, dear.

Keller *(hastily)*. Well, now. Couldn't say the same for my part. I'm famished. Katie, your plate.

Kate *(looking)*. But where is Miss Annie?

(A silence.)

James *(pleasantly)*. In her room.

Keller. In her room? Doesn't she know hot food must be eaten hot? Go bring her down at once, Jimmie.

James *(rises)*. Certainly. I'll get a ladder.

Keller *(stares)*. What?

James. I'll need a ladder. Shouldn't take me long.

Kate *(stares)*. What shouldn't take you—

Keller. Jimmie, do as I say! Go upstairs at once and tell Miss Sullivan supper is getting cold—

James. She's locked in her room.

Keller. Locked in her—

Kate. What on earth are you—

James. Helen locked her in and made off with the key.

Kate *(rising)*. And you sit here and say nothing?

James. Well, everybody's been telling me not to say anything.

(He goes serenely out and across the yard whistling. Keller *thrusting up from his chair, makes for the stairs.)*

Kate. Viney, look out in back for Helen. See if she has that key.

Viney. Yes, Miss Kate.

(Viney *goes out the rear door.*)

Keller (*calling down*). She's out by the pump!

(Kate *goes out on the porch after* Helen, *while* Keller *knocks on* Annie's *door, then rattles the knob, imperiously.*)

Miss Sullivan! Are you in there?

Annie. Oh, I'm here, all right.

Keller. Is there no key on your side?

Annie (*with some asperity*[9]). Well, if there was a key in here, *I* wouldn't be in here. Helen took it; the only thing on my side is me.

Keller. Miss Sullivan. I—

(*He tries, but cannot hold it back.*)

Not in the house ten minutes, I don't see *how* you managed it!

(*He stomps downstairs again, while* Annie *mutters to herself.*)

Annie. And even I'm not on my side.

Keller (*roaring*). Viney!

Viney (*reappearing*). Yes, Cap'n?

Keller. Put that meat back in the oven!

(Viney *bears the roast off again, while* Keller *strides out onto the porch.* Kate *is with* Helen *at the pump, opening her hands.*)

Kate. She has no key.

Keller. Nonsense, she must have the key. Have you searched in her pockets?

Kate. Yes. She doesn't have it.

Keller. Katie, she must have the key.

Kate. Would you prefer to search her yourself, Captain?

Keller. No, I would not prefer to search her! She almost took my kneecap off this evening, when I tried merely to—

(James *reappears carrying a long ladder, with* Percy *running after him to be in on things.*)

Take that ladder back!

James. Certainly.

(*He turns around with it.* Martha *comes skipping around the upstage corner of the house to be in on things, accompanied by the setter* Belle.)

Kate. She could have hidden the key.

Keller. Where?

Kate. Anywhere. Under a stone. In the flower beds. In the grass—

Keller. Well, I can't plow up the entire grounds to find a missing key! Jimmie!

James. Sir!

Keller. Bring me a ladder!

James. Certainly.

(Viney *comes around the downstage side of the house to be in on things; she has over her shoulder,* Mildred, *bleating.* Keller *places the ladder against* Annie's *window and mounts.* Annie, *meanwhile, is running about making herself presentable, washing the blood off her mouth, straightening her clothes, tidying her hair. Another black servant enters to gaze in wonder, increasing the gathering ring of spectators.*)

Kate (*sharply*). What is Mildred doing up?

Viney. Cap'n woke her, ma'am, all that hollerin'.

Keller. Miss Sullivan!

(Annie *comes to the window, with as much air of gracious normality as she can manage;* Keller *is at the window.*)

Annie (*brightly*). Yes, Captain Keller?

Keller. Come out!

Annie. I don't see how I can. There isn't room.

Keller. I intend to carry you. Climb onto my shoulder and hold tight.

---

9. **asperity** (ə sper′ ə tē): harshness, rudeness.

Annie. Oh, no. It's—very chivalrous of you, but I'd really prefer to—

Keller. Miss Sullivan, follow instructions! I will not have you also tumbling out of our windows.

(Annie obeys, with some misgivings.)

I hope this is not a sample of what we may expect from you. In the way of simplifying the work of looking after Helen.

Annie. Captain Keller, I'm perfectly able to go down a ladder under my own—

Keller. I doubt it, Miss Sullivan. Simply hold onto my neck.

(He begins down with her, while the spectators stand in a wide and somewhat awe-stricken circle, watching. Keller *half-misses a rung, and* Annie *grabs at his whiskers.)*

My *neck,* Miss Sullivan!

Annie. I'm sorry to inconvenience you this way—

Keller. No inconvenience, other than having that door taken down and the lock replaced, if we fail to find that key.

Annie. Oh, I'll look everywhere for it.

Keller. Thank you. Do not look in any rooms that can be locked. There.

(He stands her on the ground. James *applauds.)*

Annie. Thank you very much.

(She smooths her skirt, looking as composed and ladylike as possible. Keller *stares around at the spectators.)*

Keller. Go, go, back to your work. What are you looking at here? There's nothing here to look at.

(They break up, move off.)

Now would it be possible for us to have supper, like other people?

(He marches into the house.)

Kate. Viney, serve supper. I'll put Mildred to sleep.

(They all go in. James *is the last to leave, murmuring to* Annie *with a gesture.)*

James. Might as well leave the l, a, d, d, e, r, hm?

*(Annie *ignores him, looking at* Helen; James *goes in too. Imperceptibly the lights commence to narrow down.* Annie *and* Helen *are now alone in the yard, seated at the pump, where she has been oblivious to it all, a battered little savage,* playing with *her doll in a picture of innocent contentment.* Annie *comes near, leans against the house, and taking off her smoked glasses, studies her, not without awe. Presently* Helen *rises, gropes around to see if anyone is present;* Annie *evades her hand, and when* Helen *is satisfied she is alone, the key suddenly protrudes out of her mouth. She takes it in her fingers, stands thinking, gropes to the pump, lifts a loose board, drops the key into the well, and hugs herself gleefully.* Annie *stares. But after a moment she shakes her head to herself; she cannot keep the smile from her lips.)*

Annie. You *devil.*

(Her tone is one of great respect, humor, and acceptance of challenge.)

You think I'm so easily gotten rid of? You have a thing or two to learn first. I have nothing else to do.

(She goes up the steps to the porch, but turns for a final word, almost of warning.)

And nowhere to go.

(And presently she moves into the house to the others, as the lights dim down and out, except for the small circle upon Helen *solitary at the pump, which ends the act.)*

e x p l a i n

Responding to Reading

First Impressions

1. Write a list of words that describe your feelings as you finished reading this act. Save your list; you will refer to it later.

Second Thoughts

2. Describe Helen. Discuss both her negative and positive qualities. Find evidence in the play to support your ideas.

3. How does each family member react to Helen?

4. The scenes from Annie's past reveal a painful childhood. What strengths did Annie gain from her experiences? What problems does she still face because of her past?

5. Annie explains her goals for Helen by quoting Dr. Howe, who said, "Language is to the mind more than light is to the eye." What does this sentence mean? Do you agree with it?

6. Consider the problems Annie Sullivan faces at the end of Act One. Which do you think will be the hardest to overcome?

   Think about
   - Helen's reactions to her
   - Captain Keller's attitude toward her
   - the family's feelings about Helen
   - James's actions and words at the end of this act
   - Annie's memories of her past

7. Although the play focuses primarily on the relationship between Annie and Helen, there is a second plot, or **subplot**, that concerns James's relationship with his family. What conflicts exist between James and each of his family members?

Literary Concept: Flashback

As you know, the events in most stories move forward in chronological order, the order in which they happen in time. Sometimes, however, a writer may interrupt the plot to present a conversation, a scene, or an event that happened before the beginning of a story. This interruption in the chronological order of events is called a **flashback**. What purpose do the flashbacks to Annie's life in the asylum serve in this story? How are they connected to Annie's present life?

Writing Options

1. The key Helen hides is a symbol for other ideas. Write a paragraph that explains what the key represents.

2. Make a chart that shows the ways in which Annie and Helen are alike and the ways in which they are different.

3. Write the telegram Annie might send to Dr. Anagnos after her first day with Helen. Because you must pay for each word in a telegram, convey your message in twenty-five words or fewer.

Vocabulary Practice

Exercise On your paper, write the word from the list that best completes each sentence below.

1. During Helen's illness, her parents stayed by her bedside day and night, keeping a ____ until her fever broke.
2. Helen had a strong ____, or physical makeup.
3. Aunt Ev's ____ manner made her seem pleasant and kind.
4. Although Helen tried to communicate, her speech was ____ and sounded more like an animal's cry for help.
5. Tangled hair and messy clothes made Helen look ____.
6. Unlike hard-working and ambitious Annie, James was ____.
7. Annie thought she deserved a ____, or rebirth.
8. Based on her ____ of the new governess at the station, Kate judged that Annie was too young to be Helen's teacher.
9. When Captain Keller spoke ____, everyone else felt gloomy, too.
10. Both Annie and Helen had ____ personalities that made them outgoing and spirited.
11. Annie's ____ nature helped her fight for her beliefs.
12. Captain Keller criticized James for his ____ when James responded in a rude and sarcastic manner.
13. Helen's uncontrollable rages showed her lack of ____.
14. Helen was ____ to the sounds and commotion around her.
15. Helen had a ____ and zest for living.

Words to Know and Use

---

appraisal
benign
combative
constitution
impudence
inarticulate
indolent
morosely
oblivious
restraint
resurrection
unkempt
vigil
vitality
vivacious

Reading On

Before you read on, review the conflicts that exist between Annie and Helen, between James and his father, and within Annie herself. As you read Act Two, notice how these conflicts grow and intensify. Watch for events that lead to a physical confrontation between Helen and Annie. Try to predict whether and how the conflicts will be resolved.

ACT TWO

It is evening.

The only room visible in the Keller *house is* Annie's, *where by lamplight,* Annie *is at a desk writing a letter. At her bureau,* Helen *in her customary unkempt state is tucking her doll in the bottom drawer as a cradle, the contents of which she has dumped out, creating as usual a fine disorder.*

Annie *mutters each word as she writes her letter, slowly, her eyes close to and almost touching the page, to follow with difficulty her penwork.*

Annie. ". . . and, nobody, here, has, attempted, to, control, her. The, greatest, problem, I, have, is, how, to, disipline, her, without, breaking, her, spirit."

(Resolute voice)

"But, I, shall, insist, on, reasonable, obedience, from, the, start—"

(At which point Helen, *groping about on the desk, knocks over the inkwell.* Annie *jumps up, rescues her letter, rights the inkwell, grabs a towel to stem the spillage, and then wipes at* Helen's *hands; as always* Helen *pulls free, but not until* Annie *first gets three letters into her palm.)*

Ink.

*(*Helen *is enough interested in and puzzled by this spelling that she proffers her hand again; so* Annie *spells, and impassively dunks it back in the spillage.)*

Ink. It has a name.

(She wipes the hand clean, and leads Helen *to her bureau, where she looks for something to engage her. She finds a sewing card, with needle and thread, and going to her knees, shows* Helen's *hand how to connect one row of holes.)*

Down. Under. Up. And be careful of the needle—

*(*Helen *gets it, and* Annie *rises.)*

Fine. You keep out of the ink, and perhaps I can keep out of—the soup.

(She returns to the desk, tidies it, and resumes writing her letter, bent close to the page.)

"These, blots, are, her, handiwork. I—"

(She is interrupted by a gasp; Helen *has stuck her finger, and sits sucking at it, darkly. Then with vengeful resolve she seizes her doll, and is about to dash its brains out on the floor when* Annie, *diving, catches it in one hand, which she at once shakes with hopping pain but otherwise ignores, patiently.)*

All right, let's try <u>temperance.</u>

(Taking the doll, she kneels, goes through the motion of knocking its head on the floor, spells into Helen's *hand.)*

Bad, girl.

(She lets Helen *feel the grieved expression on her face.* Helen *imitates it. Next, she makes* Helen *caress the doll and kiss the hurt spot and hold it gently in her arms, then spells into her hands,)*

Good, girl.

(She lets Helen *feel the smile on her face.* Helen *sits with a scowl, which suddenly clears. She pats the doll, kisses it, wreathes her face in a large, artificial smile, and bears the doll to the washstand, where she carefully sits it.* Annie *watches, pleased.)*

Very good girl—

(Whereupon Helen *elevates the pitcher and*

Words to Know and Use | **temperance** (tem′ pər əns) *n.* self-restraint; moderation

dashes it on the floor instead. Annie leaps to her feet, and stands inarticulate; Helen calmly gropes back to sit by the sewing card and needle.

Annie *manages to achieve self-control. She picks up a fragment or two of the pitcher, sees Helen is puzzling over the card, and resolutely kneels to demonstrate it again. She spells into Helen's hand.*

Kate, *meanwhile, coming around the corner with folded sheets on her arm, halts at the doorway and watches them for a moment in silence; she is moved, but level.)*

Kate *(presently)*. What are you saying to her?

(Annie, glancing up, is a bit embarrassed, and rises from the spelling, to find her company manners.)

Annie. Oh, I was just making conversation. Saying it was a sewing card.

Kate. But does that—

(She imitates with her fingers)

—mean that to her?

Annie. No. No, she won't know what spelling is till she knows what a word is.

Kate. Yet you keep spelling to her? Why?

Annie *(cheerily)*. I like to hear myself talk!

Kate. The Captain says it's like spelling to the fence post.

Annie *(a pause)*. Does he, now.

Kate. Is it?

Annie. No, it's how I watch you talk to Mildred.

Kate. Mildred.

Annie. Any baby. Gibberish, grown-up gibberish, baby-talk gibberish, do they understand one word of it to start? Some-

how they begin to. If they hear it. I'm letting Helen hear it.

Kate. Other children are not—impaired.

Annie. Ho, there's nothing impaired in that head; it works like a mousetrap!

Kate *(smiles)*. But after a child hears how many words, Miss Annie, a million?

Annie. I guess no mother's ever minded enough to count.

(She drops her eyes to spell into Helen's hand, again indicating the card; Helen spells back, and Annie is amused.)

Kate *(too quickly)*. What did she spell?

Annie. I spelt card. She spelt cake!

(She takes in Kate's quickness and shakes her head, gently.)

No, its only a finger-game to her, Mrs. Keller. What she has to learn first is that things have names.

Kate. And when will she learn?

Annie. Maybe after a million and one words.

(They hold each other's gaze; Kate then speaks quietly.)

Kate. I should like to learn those letters, Miss Annie.

Annie *(pleased)*. I'll teach you tomorrow morning. That makes only half a million each!

Kate *(then)*. It's her bedtime.

(Annie reaches for the sewing card. Helen objects; Annie insists, and Helen gets rid of Annie's hand by jabbing it with the needle. Annie gasps and moves to grip Helen's wrist; but Kate intervenes with a proffered sweet, and Helen drops the card, crams the sweet into her mouth, and scrambles up to search

her mother's hands for more. Annie *nurses her wound, staring after the sweet.*)

I'm sorry, Miss Annie.

Annie *(indignantly)*. Why does she get a reward? For stabbing me?

Kate. Well—*(then tiredly)*. We catch our flies with honey, I'm afraid. We haven't the heart for much else, and so many times she simply cannot be <u>compelled</u>.

Annie *(<u>ominous</u>)*. Yes. I'm the same way myself.

(Kate *smiles and leads* Helen *off around the corner.* Annie, *alone in her room, picks up things; and in the act of removing* Helen's *doll, gives way to unmannerly temptation. She throttles it. She drops it on her bed and stands pondering. Then she turns back, sits decisively, and writes again, as the lights dim on her.*)

(grimly)

"The, more, I, think, the, more, certain, I, am, that, obedience, is, the, gateway, through, which, knowledge, enters, the, mind, of, the, child—"

(On the word obedience *a shaft of sunlight hits the water pump outside, while* Annie's *voice ends in the dark, followed by a distant cockcrow. Daylight comes up over another corner of the sky, with* Viney's *voice heard at once.*)

Viney. Breakfast ready!

(Viney *comes down into the sunlight beam, and pumps a pitcherful of water. While the pitcher is brimming, we hear conversation from the dark. The light grows to the family room of the house, where all are either entering or already seated at breakfast, with* Keller *and* James *arguing the war.* Helen *is wandering around the table to explore the contents of the other plates. When* Annie *is in her chair, she watches* Helen. Viney *re-enters, sets the pitcher on the table;* Kate *lifts the almost empty biscuit plate with an inquiring look;* Viney *nods and bears it off back, neither of them interrupting the men.* Annie, *meanwhile, sits with fork quiet, watching* Helen, *who at her mother's plate, pokes her hand among some scrambled eggs.* Kate *catches* Annie's *eyes on her, smiles with wry gesture.* Helen *moves on to* James's *plate, the male talk continuing,* James *deferential and* Keller *overriding.*)

James. —no, but shouldn't we give the devil his due, Father? The fact is we lost the South two years earlier when he outthought us behind Vicksburg.[10]

Keller. *Outthought* is a peculiar word for a butcher.

James. Harness maker, wasn't he?

Keller. I said butcher; his only virtue as a soldier was numbers, and he led them to slaughter with no more regard than for so many sheep.

James. But even if in that sense he was a butcher, the fact is he—

Keller. And a drunken one, half the war.

James. Agreed, Father. If his own people said he was, I can't argue he—

Keller. Well, what is it you find to admire in such a man, Jimmie, the butchery or the drunkenness?

James. Neither, Father, only the fact that he beat us.

---

10. **The fact is . . . Vicksburg.:** James and Keller are discussing General Ulysses S. Grant, the commander of the Union army at Vicksburg, Mississippi, during the Civil War. Vicksburg, on the Mississippi River, had been captured by Grant in 1863.

Words to Know and Use	**compel** (kəm pel′) *v.* to force
	ominous (äm′ ə nəs) *adj.* threatening; foreshadowing evil
	deferential (def′ ər en′ shəl) *adj.* showing courteous regard or respect

Keller. He didn't.

James. Is it your contention we won the war, sir?

Keller. He didn't beat us at Vicksburg. We lost Vicksburg because Pemberton gave Bragg five thousand of his cavalry; and Loring, whom I knew personally for a nincompoop before you were born, marched away from Champion's Hill with enough men to have held them. We lost Vicksburg by stupidity verging on treason.

James. I would have said we lost Vicksburg because Grant was one thing no Yankee general was before him—

Keller. Drunk? I doubt it.

James. Obstinate.

Keller. Obstinate. Could any of them compare even in that with old Stonewall? If he'd been there, we would still have Vicksburg.

James. Well, the butcher simply wouldn't give up; he tried four ways of getting around Vicksburg, and on the fifth try he got around. Anyone else would have pulled north and—

Keller. He wouldn't have got around if we'd had a Southerner in command, instead of a half-breed Yankee traitor like Pemberton—

(While this background talk is in progress, Helen *is working around the table, ultimately toward* Annie's *plate. She messes with her hands in* James's *plate, then in* Keller's, *both men taking it so for granted they hardly notice. Then* Helen *comes groping with soiled hands past her own plate, to* Annie's; *her hand goes to it, and* Annie, *who has been waiting, deliberately lifts and removes her hand.* Helen *gropes again.* Annie *firmly pins her by the wrist, and removes her hand from the table.* Helen *thrusts her hands again;* Annie *catches them; and* Helen *begins to flail*

and make noises. The interruption brings Keller's *gaze upon them.)*

What's the matter there?

Kate. Miss Annie. You see, she's accustomed to helping herself from our plates to anything she—

Annie *(evenly).* Yes, but *I'm* not accustomed to it.

Keller. No, of course not. Viney!

Kate. Give her something, Jimmie, to quiet her.

James *(blandly).* But her table manners are the best she has. Well.

(He pokes across with a chunk of bacon at Helen's *hand, which* Annie *releases; but* Helen *knocks the bacon away and stubbornly thrusts at* Annie's *plate.* Annie *grips her wrists again; the struggle mounts.)*

Keller. Let her this time, Miss Sullivan; it's the only way we get any adult conversation. If my son's half merits that description.

(He rises).

I'll get you another plate.

Annie *(gripping Helen).* I have a plate, thank you.

Kate *(calling).* Viney! I'm afraid what Captain Keller says is only too true; she'll persist in this until she gets her own way.

Keller *(at the door).* Viney, bring Miss Sullivan another plate—

Annie *(stonily).* I have a plate; nothing's wrong with the *plate.* I intend to keep it.

(Silence for a moment, except for Helen's *noises as she struggles to get loose. The* Keller's *are a bit nonplussed, and* Annie *is too darkly intent on* Helen's *manners to have any thoughts now of her own.)*

James. Ha. You see why they took Vicksburg?

Keller *(uncertainly).* Miss Sullivan. One plate or another is hardly a matter to struggle with a <u>deprived</u> child about.

Annie. Oh, I'd sooner have a more—

(Helen begins to kick; Annie moves her ankles to the opposite side of the chair.)

—heroic issue myself, I—

Keller. No, I really must insist you—

(Helen bangs her toe on the chair and sinks to the floor, crying with rage and <u>feigned</u> injury. Annie keeps hold of her wrists, gazing down, while Kate rises.)

Now she's hurt herself.

Annie *(grimly).* No, she hasn't.

Keller. Will you please let her hands go?

Kate. Miss Annie, you don't know the child well enough yet, she'll keep—

Annie. I know an ordinary tantrum well enough, when I see one, and a badly spoiled child—

James. Hear, hear.

Keller *(very annoyed).* Miss Sullivan! You would have more understanding of your pupil if you had some pity in you. Now kindly do as I—

Annie. Pity?

(She releases Helen to turn equally annoyed on Keller across the table. Instantly Helen scrambles up and dives at Annie's plate. This time Annie intercepts her by pouncing on her wrists like a hawk, and her temper boils.)

For this <u>tyrant</u>? The whole house turns on her whims. Is there anything she wants she doesn't get? I'll tell you what I pity, that the sun won't rise and set for her all her life, and every day you're telling her it will. What good will your pity do her

when you're under the strawberries, Captain Keller?

Keller *(outraged).* Kate, for the love of heaven will you—

Kate. Miss Annie, please, I don't think it serves to lose our—

Annie. It does you good, that's all. It's less trouble to feel sorry for her than to teach her anything better, isn't it?

Keller. I fail to see where you have taught her anything yet, Miss Sullivan!

Annie. I'll begin this minute, if you'll leave the room, Captain Keller!

Keller *(astonished).* Leave the—

Annie. Everyone, please.

(She struggles with Helen, while Keller endeavors to control his voice.)

Keller. Miss Sullivan, you are here only as a paid teacher. Nothing more, and not to lecture—

Annie. I can't *un*teach her six years of pity if you can't stand up to one tantrum! Old Stonewall, indeed. Mrs. Keller, you promised me help.

Kate. Indeed I did, we truly want to—

Annie. Then leave me alone with her. Now!

Keller *(in a wrath).* Katie, will you come outside with me? At once, please.

(He marches to the front door. Kate and James follow him. Simultaneously Annie releases Helen's wrists, and the child again sinks to the floor, kicking and crying her weird noises. Annie steps over her to meet Viney coming in the rear doorway with biscuits and a clean plate, surprised at the general commotion.)

Viney. Heaven sakes—

Annie. Out, please.

(She backs Viney *out with one hand, closes the door on her astonished mouth, locks it, and removes the key.* Keller, *meanwhile, snatches his hat from a rack, and* Kate *follows him down the porch steps.* James *lingers in the doorway to address* Annie *across the room with a bow.*)

James. If it takes all summer, general.

(Annie *comes over to his door in turn, removing her glasses grimly. As* Keller *outside begins speaking,* Annie *closes the door on* James, *locks it, removes the key, and turns with her back against the door to stare ominously at* Helen, *kicking on the floor.*

James *takes his hat from the rack, and going down the porch steps, joins* Kate *and* Keller *talking in the yard,* Keller *in a sputter of ire.*)

Keller. This girl, this—cub of a girl—*presumes!* I tell you, I'm of half a mind to ship her back to Boston before the week is out. You can inform her so from me!

Kate (*eyebrows up*). I, Captain?

Keller. She's a *hireling!* Now I want it clear, unless there's an apology and complete change of manner, she goes back on the next train! Will you make that quite clear?

Kate. Where will you be, Captain, while I am making it quite—

Keller. At the office!

(*He begins off left, finds his napkin still in his irate hand, is uncertain with it, dabs his lips with dignity, gets rid of it in a toss to* James, *and marches off.* James *turns to eye* Kate.)

James. Will you?

(Kate's *mouth is set, and* James *studies it lightly.*)

I thought what she said was exceptionally intelligent. I've been saying it for years.

Kate (*not without scorn*). To his face?

(*She comes to relieve him of the white napkin, but reverts again with it.*)

Or will you take it, Jimmie? As a flag?

(James *stalks out, much offended; and* Kate, *turning, stares across the yard at the house. The lights narrowing down to the following pantomime in the family room, leave her motionless in the dark.*

Annie, *meanwhile, has begun by slapping both keys down on a shelf out of* Helen's *reach. She returns to the table, upstage.* Helen's *kicking has subsided, and when from the floor her hand finds* Annie's *chair empty, she pauses.* Annie *clears the table of* Kate's, James's, *and* Keller's *plates. She gets back to her own across the table just in time to slide it deftly away from* Helen's *pouncing hand. She lifts the hand and moves it to* Helen's *plate, and after an instant's exploration,* Helen *sits again on the floor and drums her heels.* Annie *comes around the table and resumes her chair. When* Helen *feels her skirt again, she ceases kicking, waits for whatever is to come, renews some kicking, waits again.* Annie, *retrieving her plate, takes up a forkful of food, stops it halfway to her mouth, gazes at it devoid of appetite, and half-lowers it; but after a look at* Helen *she sighs, dips the forkful toward* Helen *in a for-your-sake toast, and puts it in her own mouth to chew, not without an effort.*

Helen *now gets hold of the chair leg and half-succeeds in pulling the chair out from under her.* Annie *bangs it down with her rear, heavily, and sits with all her weight.* Helen's *next attempt to topple it is unavailing, so her fingers dive in a pinch at* Annie's *flank.* Annie, *in the middle of her mouthful, almost loses it with startle, and she slaps down her fork to round on* Helen. *The child comes up with curiosity to feel what* Annie *is doing, so* Annie *resumes eating, letting* Helen's *hand follow the movement of her fork to her mouth; where-*

upon Helen *at once reaches into* Annie's plate. Annie *firmly removes her hand to her own plate.* Helen *in reply pinches* Annie's thigh, *a good, mean pinchful that makes* Annie *jump.* Annie *sets the fork down and sits with her mouth tight.* Helen *digs another pinch into her thigh, and this time* Annie *slaps her hand smartly away.* Helen *retaliates with a roundhouse fist*[11] *that catches* Annie *on the ear, and* Annie's *hand leaps at once in a forceful slap across* Helen's *cheek.* Helen *is the startled one now.* Annie's *hand in compunction falters to her own face, but when* Helen *hits at her again,* Annie *deliberately slaps her again.* Helen *lifts her fist irresolute for another roundhouse;* Annie *lifts her hand resolute for another slap; and they freeze in this posture, while* Helen *mulls it over. She thinks better of it, drops her fist, and giving* Annie *a wide berth, gropes around to her mother's chair, to find it empty. She blunders her way along the table upstage, and encountering the empty chairs and missing plates, she looks bewildered. She gropes back to her mother's chair, again touches her cheek and indicates the chair, and waits for the world to answer.*

Annie *now reaches over to spell into her hand, but* Helen *yanks it away. She gropes to the front door, tries the knob, and finds the door locked, with no key. She gropes to the rear door, and finds it locked, with no key. She commences to bang on it.* Annie *rises, crosses, takes her wrists, draws her, resisting, back to the table, seats her, and releases her hands upon her plate. As* Annie *herself begins to sit,* Helen *writhes out of her chair, runs to the front door, and tugs and kicks at it.* Annie *rises again, crosses, draws her by one wrist back to the table, seats her, and sits.* Helen *escapes back to the door, knocking over her mother's chair en route.* Annie *rises again in*

pursuit, and this time lifts Helen *bodily from behind and bears her kicking to her chair. She deposits her and once more turns to sit.* Helen *scrambles out, but as she passes,* Annie *catches her up again from behind and deposits her in the chair.* Helen *scrambles out on the other side, for the rear door, but* Annie *at her heels catches her up and deposits her again in the chair. She stands behind it.* Helen *scrambles out to her right, and the instant her feet hit the floor,* Annie *lifts and deposits her back. She scrambles out to her left, and is at once lifted and deposited back. She tries right again and is deposited back, and tries left again and is deposited back; and now feints* Annie *to the right but is off to her left, and is promptly deposited back. She sits a moment and then starts straight over the tabletop, dishware notwithstanding.* Annie *hauls her in and deposits her back, with her plate spilling in her lap, and she melts to the floor and crawls under the table, laborious among its legs and chairs; but* Annie *is swift around the table and waiting on the other side when she surfaces, immediately bearing her aloft.* Helen *clutches at* James's *chair for anchorage, but it comes with her, and halfway back she abandons it to the floor.* Annie *deposits her in her chair and waits.* Helen *sits tensed motionless. Then she tentatively puts out her left foot and hand,* Annie *interposes her own hand, and at the contact* Helen *jerks hers in. She tries her right foot;* Annie *blocks it with her own, and* Helen *jerks hers in. Finally, leaning back, she slumps down in her chair, in a sullen biding.*

Annie *backs off a step and watches;* Helen *offers no move.* Annie *takes a deep breath. Both of them and the room are in considerable*

---

11. **roundhouse fist:** a clenched fist used to throw—as Helen does—a wide, curving punch.

Words to Know and Use | **retaliate** (ri tal′ ē āt′) *v.* to return an injury or wrong

disorder, *two chairs down and the table a mess, but* Annie *makes no effort to tidy it; she only sits on her own chair and lets her energy refill. Then she takes up knife and fork and resolutely addresses her food.* Helen's *hand comes out to explore, and seeing it,* Annie *sits without moving. The child's hand goes over her hand and fork, pauses—*Annie *still does not move—and withdraws. Presently it moves for her own plate, slaps about for it, and stops, thwarted. At this,* Annie *again rises, recovers* Helen's *plate from the floor and a handful of scattered food from the deranged tablecloth, drops it on the plate, and pushes the plate into contact with* Helen's *fist. Neither of them now moves for a pregnant moment—until* Helen *suddenly takes a grab of food and wolfs it down.* Annie *permits herself the humor of a minor bow and warming her hands together; she wanders off a step or two, watching.* Helen *cleans up the plate.*

After a glower of indecision, she holds the empty plate out for more. Annie *accepts it, and crossing to the removed plates, spoons food from them onto it. She stands debating the spoon, tapping it a few times on* Helen's *plate; and when she returns with the plate, she brings the spoon, too. She puts the spoon first into* Helen's *hand, then sets the plate down.* Helen, *discarding the spoon, reaches with her hand, and* Annie *stops it by the wrist; she replaces the spoon in it.* Helen *impatiently discards it again, and again* Annie *stops her hand, to replace the spoon in it. This time* Helen *throws the spoon on the floor.* Annie, *after considering it, lifts* Helen *bodily out of the chair and, in a wrestling match on the floor, closes her fingers upon the spoon and returns her with it to the chair.* Helen *again throws the spoon on the floor.* Annie *lifts her out of the chair again; but in the struggle over the spoon* Helen, *with* Annie *on her back, sends her sliding over her head.* Helen *flees back to her chair and scrambles into it. When*

Annie *comes after her, she clutches it for dear life.* Annie *pries one hand loose, then the other, then the first again, then the other again, and then lifts* Helen *by the waist, chair and all, and shakes the chair loose.* Helen *wrestles to get free, but* Annie *pins her to the floor, closes her fingers upon the spoon, and lifts her kicking under one arm. With her other hand, she gets the chair in place again and plunks* Helen *back on it. When she releases her hand,* Helen *throws the spoon at her.*

Annie *now removes the plate of food.* Helen, *grabbing, finds it missing, and commences to bang with her fists on the table.* Annie *collects a fistful of spoons and descends with them and the plate on* Helen; *she lets her smell the plate, at which* Helen *ceases banging, and* Annie *puts the plate down and a spoon in* Helen's *hand.* Helen *throws it on the floor.* Annie *puts another spoon in her hand.* Helen *throws it on the floor.* Annie *puts another spoon in her hand.* Helen *throws it on the floor. When* Annie *comes to her last spoon, she sits next to* Helen *and, gripping the spoon in* Helen's *hand, compels her to take food in it up to her mouth.* Helen *sits with lips shut.* Annie *waits a stolid moment, then lowers* Helen's *hand. She tries again;* Helen's *lips remain shut.* Annie *waits, lowers* Helen's *hand. She tries again; this time* Helen *suddenly opens her mouth and accepts the food.* Annie *lowers the spoon with a sigh of relief, and* Helen *spews the mouthful out at her face.* Annie *sits a moment with eyes closed, then takes the pitcher and dashes its water into* Helen's *face, who gasps astonished.* Annie, *with* Helen's *hand, takes up another spoonful and shoves it into her open mouth.* Helen *swallows involuntarily, and while she is catching her breath,* Annie *forces her palm open, throws four swift letters into it, then another four, and bows toward her with devastating pleasantness.)*

Annie. Good girl.

(Annie lifts Helen's hand to feel her face, nodding; Helen grabs a fistful of her hair and yanks. The pain brings Annie to her knees, and Helen pummels her. They roll under the table, and the lights commence to dim out on them.

Simultaneously the light at left has been rising, slowly, so slowly that it seems at first we only imagine what is intimated in the yard: a few ghostlike figures, in silence, motionless, waiting. Now the distant belfry chimes commence to toll the hour, also very slowly, almost—it is twelve—interminably; the sense is that of a long time passing. We can identify the figures before the twelfth stroke, all facing the house in a kind of watch; Kate is standing exactly as before, but now with the baby Mildred sleeping in her arms; and placed here and there, unmoving, are Aunt Ev in her hat with a hanky to her nose, and the two black children, Percy and Martha, with necks outstretched eagerly, and Viney with a knotted kerchief on her head and a feather duster in her hand.

The chimes cease, and there is silence. For a long moment, none of the group moves.)

Viney *(presently).* What am I gone do, Miss Kate? It's noontime; dinner's comin'; I didn't get them breakfast dishes out of there yet.

(Kate says nothing, stares at the house; Martha shifts Helen's doll in her clutch, and it plaintively says momma.)

Kate *(presently).* You run along, Martha.

(Aunt Ev blows her nose.)

Aunt Ev *(wretchedly).* I can't wait out here a minute longer, Kate. Why, this could go on all afternoon, too.

Kate. I'll tell the captain you called.

Viney *(to the children).* You hear what Miss Kate say? Never you mind what's going on here.

(Still no one moves.)

You run along, tend your own bizness.

(Finally Viney turns on the children with the feather duster.)

Shoo!

(The two children divide before her. She chases them off. Aunt Ev comes to Kate, in her dignity.)

Aunt Ev. Say what you like, Kate, but that child is a *Keller.*

(She opens her parasol, preparatory to leaving.)

I needn't remind you that all the Kellers are cousins to General Robert E. Lee.[12] I don't know *who* that girl is.

(She waits, but Kate, staring at the house, is without response.)

The only Sullivan I've heard of—from Boston too, and I'd think twice before locking her up with that kind—is that man John L.[13]

(And Aunt Ev departs, with head high. Presently Viney to Kate, her arms out for the baby.)

Viney. You give me her, Miss Kate; I'll sneak her in back, to her crib.

(But Kate is moveless until Viney starts to take the baby; Kate looks down at her before relinquishing her.)

Kate *(slowly).* This child never gives me a minute's worry.

Viney. Oh, yes, this one's the angel of the family, no question bout *that.*

(She begins off rear with the baby, heading around the house; and Kate now turns her back on it, her hand to her eyes. At this moment there is the slamming of a door, and when Kate wheels, Helen is blundering down the porch steps into the light, like a ruined bat. Viney halts, and Kate runs in. Helen collides with her mother's knees, and reels off and back to clutch them as her savior. Annie, with smoked glasses in hand, stands on the porch, also much undone, looking as though she had indeed just taken Vicksburg. Kate, taking in Helen's ravaged state, becomes steely in her gaze up at Annie.)

Kate. What happened?

(Annie meets Kate's gaze, and gives a factual

---

12. **General Robert E. Lee:** the commander of the Confederate army during the Civil War.

13. **John L. [Sullivan]:** a world heavyweight boxing champion during the 1800's.

Words to Know and Use | **ravaged** (rav′ ijd) *adj.* violently destroyed; ruined

report, too exhausted for anything but a flat voice.)

Annie. She ate from her own plate.

(She thinks a moment.)

She ate with a spoon. Herself.

(Kate *frowns, uncertain with thought, and glances down at* Helen.)

And she folded her napkin.

(Kate's *gaze now wavers, from* Helen *to* Annie, *and back.*)

Kate (softly). Folded—her napkin?

Annie. The room's a wreck, but her napkin is folded.

(She pauses, then,)

I'll be in my room, Mrs. Keller.

(She moves to reenter the house; but she stops at Viney's voice.)

Viney (cheery). Don't be long, Miss Annie. Dinner will be ready right away!

(Viney *carries* Mildred *around the back of the house.* Annie *stands unmoving, takes a deep breath, stares over her shoulder at* Kate *and* Helen; *then inclines her head graciously and goes with a slight stagger into the house. The lights in her room above steal up in readiness for her.*

Kate *remains alone with* Helen *in the yard, standing protectively over her, in a kind of wonder.*)

Kate. (slowly). Folded her napkin.

(She contemplates the wild head in her thighs; and moves her fingertips over it, with such a tenderness and something like a fear of its strangeness, that her own eyes close. She whispers, bending to it,)

My Helen—folded her napkin—

(And still erect, with only her head in surrender, Kate for the first time that we see, loses her protracted war with grief; but she will not let a sound escape her, only the grimace of tears comes, and sobs that shake her in a grip of silence. But Helen feels them, and her hand comes up in its own wondering, to interrogate her mother's face, until Kate buries her lips in the child's palm.

Upstairs, Annie enters her room, closes the door, and stands back against it. The lights, growing on her with their special color, commence to fade on Kate and Helen. Then Annie goes wearily to her suitcase and lifts it to take it toward the bed. But it knocks an object to the floor, and she turns back to regard it. A new voice comes in a cultured murmur, hesitant as with the effort of remembering a text.)

Man's Voice. This—soul—

(Annie puts the suitcase down, and kneels to the object. It is the battered Perkins report, and she stands with it in her hand, letting memory try to speak.)

This—blind, deaf, mute—woman—

(Annie sits on her bed, opens the book, and finding the passage, brings it up an inch from her eyes to read, her face and lips following the overheard words, the voice quite factual now.)

Can nothing be done to <u>disinter</u> this human soul? The whole neighborhood would rush to save this woman, if she were buried alive by the caving in of a pit, and labor with zeal until she were dug out. Now, if there were one who had as much patience as zeal, he might awaken her to a consciousness of her immortal—

(When the boy's voice comes, Annie *closes her eyes, in pain.)*

Boy's Voice. Annie? Annie, you there?

Annie. Hush.

Boy's Voice. Annie, what's that noise?

(Annie tries not to answer; her own voice is drawn out of her, unwilling.)

Annie. Just a cot, Jimmie.

Boy's Voice. Where they pushin' it?

Annie. To the deadhouse.

Boy's Voice. Annie. Does it hurt, to be dead?

(Annie escapes by opening her eyes; her hand works restlessly over her cheek. She retreats into the book again, but the cracked old crones interrupt, whispering. Annie *slowly lowers the book.)*

First Crone's Voice. There is schools.

Second Crone's Voice. There is schools outside—

Third Crone's Voice. —schools where they teach blind ones, worse'n you—

First Crone's Voice. To read—

Second Crone's Voice. To read and write—

Third Crone's Voice. There is schools outside where they—

First Crone's Voice. There is schools—

(Silence. Annie *sits with her eyes shining, her hand almost in a caress over the book. Then,)*

Boy's Voice. You ain't going to school, are you, Annie?

Annie *(whispering).* When I grow up.

Boy's Voice. You ain't either, Annie. You're goin' to stay here take care of me.

Annie. I'm goin' to school when I grow up.

Boy's Voice. You said we'll be together, forever and ever and ever—

Annie *(fierce).* I'm goin' to school when I grow up!

Doctor's Voice *(slowly).* Little girl. Little girl, I must tell you. Your brother will be going on a journey, soon.

(Annie sits rigid, in silence. Then the boy's voice pierces it, a shriek of terror.)

Boy's Voice. *Annie!*

(It goes into Annie *like a sword; she doubles onto it. The book falls to the floor. It takes her a racked moment to find herself and what she was engaged in here. When she sees the suitcase she remembers and lifts it once again toward the bed. But the voices are with her and she halts with suitcase in hand.)*

First Crone's Voice. Goodbye, Annie.

Doctor's Voice. Write me when you learn how.

Second Crone's Voice. Don't tell anyone you came from here. Don't tell anyone—

Third Crone's Voice. Yeah, don't tell anyone you come from—

First Crone's Voice. Yeah, don't tell anyone—

Second Crone's Voice. Don't tell any—

(The echoing voices fade. After a moment, Annie *lays the suitcase on the bed; and the last voice comes faintly, from far away.)*

Boy's Voice. Annie. It hurts, to be dead. Forever.

(Annie falls to her knees by the bed, stifling her mouth in it. When at last she rolls blindly away from it, her palm comes down on the open report. She opens her eyes, regards it dully, and then, still on her knees, takes in the print.)

Man's Voice *(factual).* —might awaken her to a consciousness of her immortal nature. The chance is small indeed; but with a smaller chance they would have dug desperately for her in the pit; and is the life of the soul of less importance than that of the body?

(Annie *gets to her feet. She drops the book on the bed and pauses over her suitcase; after a moment, she unclasps and opens it. Standing before it, she comes to her decision. She at once turns to the bureau, and taking her things out of its drawers, commences to throw them into the open suitcase.*

In the darkness down left, a hand strikes a match, and lights a hanging oil lamp. It is Keller's *hand, and his voice accompanies it, very angry. The lights, rising here before they fade on* Annie, *show* Keller *and* Kate *inside a suggestion of a garden house, with a bay-window seat toward center and a door at back.)*

Keller. Katie, I will not *have* it! Now you did not see when that girl after supper tonight went to look for Helen in her room—

Kate. No.

Keller. The child practically climbed out of her window to escape from her! What kind of teacher *is* she? I thought I had seen her at her worst this morning, shouting at me, but I come home to find the entire house disorganized by her—Helen won't stay one second in the same room, won't come to the table with her, won't let herself be bathed or undressed or put to bed by her, or even by Viney now; and the end result is that *you* have to do more for the child than before we hired this girl's services! From the moment she stepped off the train, she' been nothing but a burden, incompetent, impertinent, ineffectual, immodest—

Kate. She folded her napkin, Captain.

Keller. What?

Kate. Not ineffectual. Helen did fold her napkin.

Keller. What in heaven's name is so extraordinary about folding a napkin?

Kate *(with some humor).* Well. It's more than you did, Captain.

Keller. Katie, I did not bring you all the way out here to the garden house to be frivolous. Now, how does Miss Sullivan propose to teach a deaf-blind pupil who won't let her even touch her?

Kate *(a pause).* I don't know.

Keller. The fact is, today she scuttled any chance she ever had of getting along with the child. If you can see any point or purpose to her staying on here longer, it's more than—

Kate. What do you wish me to do?

Keller. I want you to give her notice.

Kate. I can't.

Keller. Then if you won't, I must. I simply will not—

(He is interrupted by a knock at the back door. Keller, *after a glance at* Kate, *moves to open the door.* Annie, *in her smoked glasses, is standing outside.* Keller contemplates her heavily.)*

Miss Sullivan.

Annie. Captain Keller.

(She is nervous, keyed up to seizing the bull by the horns again, and she assumes a cheeriness which is not unshaky.)

Viney said I'd find you both over here in the garden house. I thought we should— have a talk?

Keller *(reluctantly).* Yes, I—Well, come in.

(Annie enters and is interested in this room;

Words to Know and Use | **ineffectual** (in' e fek' cho͞o əl) *adj.* having no effect; useless
contemplate (kän' təm plāt) *v.* to consider; think about intently

she rounds on her heel, anxiously, studying it. Keller *turns the matter over to* Kate, *sotto voce.)*

Katie.

Kate *(turning it back, courteously).* Captain.

(Keller clears his throat, makes ready.)

Keller. I, ah—wanted first to make my position clear to Mrs. Keller, in private. I have decided I—am not satisfied—in fact, am deeply dissatisfied—with the manner in which—

Annie *(intent).* Excuse me, is this little house ever in use?

Keller *(with patience).* In the hunting season. If you will give me your attention, Miss Sullivan.

(Annie turns her smoked glasses upon him; they hold his unwilling stare.)

I have tried to make allowances for you because you come from a part of the country where people are—women, I should say—come from who—well, for whom—

(It begins to elude him.)

allowances must—be made. I have decided, nevertheless, to—that is, decided I—

(vexedly.)

Miss Sullivan, I find it difficult to talk through those glasses.

Annie *(eagerly, removing them).* Oh, of course.

Keller *(dourly).* Why do you wear them? The sun has been down for an hour.

Annie *(pleasantly, at the lamp).* Any kind of light hurts my eyes.

(A silence; Keller ponders her, heavily.)

Keller. Put them on. Miss Sullivan, I have decided to—give you another chance.

Annie *(cheerfully).* To do what?

Keller. To—remain in our employ.

(Annie's eyes widen.)

But on two conditions. I am not accustomed to rudeness in servants or women, and that is the first. If you are to stay, there must be a radical change of manner.

Annie *(a pause).* Whose?

Keller *(exploding).* Yours, young lady, isn't it obvious? And the second is that you persuade me there's the slightest hope of your teaching a child who flees from you now like the plague, to anyone else she can find in this house.

Annie *(a pause).* There isn't.

(Kate stops sewing, and fixes her eyes upon Annie.)

Kate. What, Miss Annie?

Annie. It's hopeless here. I can't teach a child who runs away.

Keller *(nonplussed).* Then—do I understand you—propose—

Annie. Well, if we all agree it's hopeless, the next question is what—

Kate. Miss Annie.

(She is leaning toward Annie, *in deadly earnest; it commands both* Annie *and* Keller.*)*

I am not agreed. I think perhaps you—underestimate Helen.

Annie. I think everyone else here does.

Kate. She did fold her napkin. She learns, she learns. Do you know she began talking when she was six months old? She could say "water." Not really—"wahwah." "Wahwah," but she meant water. She knew what it meant, and only six months old; I never saw a child so—bright, or outgoing—

(Her voice is unsteady, but she gets it level.)

It's still in her, somewhere, isn't it? You should have seen her before her illness, such a good-tempered child—

Annie *(agreeably).* She's changed.

(A pause, Kate not letting her eyes go; her appeal at last is unconditional and very quiet.)

Kate. Miss Annie, put up with it. And with us.

Keller. Us!

Kate. Please? Like the lost lamb in the parable, I love her all the more.

Annie. Mrs. Keller, I don't think Helen's worst handicap is deafness or blindness. I think it's your love. And pity.

Keller. Now what does that mean?

Annie. All of you here are so sorry for her you've kept her—like a pet, why, even a dog you housebreak. No wonder she won't let me come near her. It's useless for me to try to teach her language or anything else here. I might as well—

Kate *(cuts in).* Miss Annie, before you came we spoke of putting her in an asylum.

(Annie turns back to regard her. A pause.)

Annie. What kind of asylum?

Keller. For mental defectives.

Kate. I visited there. I can't tell you what I saw, people like—animals, with—*rats* in the halls, and—

(She shakes her head on her vision.)

What else are we to do, if you give up?

Annie. Give up?

Kate. You said it was hopeless.

Annie. Here. Give up, why, I only today saw what has to be done, to begin!

(She glances from Kate to Keller, who stare, waiting; and she makes it as plain and simple as her nervousness permits.)

I—want complete charge of her.

Keller. You already have that. It has resulted in—

Annie. No, I mean day and night. She has to be dependent on me.

Kate. For what?

Annie. Everything. The food she eats, the clothes she wears, fresh—

(She is amused at herself, though very serious.)

—air, yes, the air she breathes, whatever her body needs is a—primer,[14] to teach her out of. It's the only way; the one who lets her have it should be her teacher.

(She considers them in turn; they digest it, Keller frowning, Kate perplexed.)

Not anyone who *loves* her. You have so many feelings they fall over each other like feet. You won't use your chances and you won't let me.

Kate. But if she runs from you—*to us*—

Annie. Yes, that's the point. I'll have to live with her somewhere else.

Keller. What!

Annie. Till she learns to depend on and listen to me.

Kate *(not without alarm).* For how long?

Annie. As long as it takes.

(A pause. She takes a breath.)

I packed half my things already.

Keller. Miss—Sullivan!

(But when Annie attends upon him, he is speechless, and she is merely earnest.)

Annie. Captain Keller, it meets both your conditions. It's the one way I can get back in touch with Helen, and I don't see how I

---

14. **primer** (prim′ ər): a simple book that gives the first principles or basic information on a subject.

can be rude to you again if you're not around to interfere with me.

Keller *(red-faced).* And what is your intention if I say no? Pack the other half, for home, and abandon your charge to—to—

Annie. The asylum?

(She waits, appraises Keller's *glare and* Kate's *uncertainty, and decides to use her weapons.)*

I grew up in such an asylum. The state almshouse.

(Kate's head comes up on this, and Keller *stares hard;* Annie's *tone is cheerful enough, albeit level as gunfire.)*

Rats—why, my brother Jimmie and I used to play with the rats because we didn't have toys. Maybe you'd like to know what Helen will find there, not on visiting days? One ward was full of the—old women, crippled, blind, most of them dying; but even if what they had was catching, there was nowhere else to move them; and that's where they put us. There were younger ones across the hall, with TB, and epileptic fits, and some insane. The youngest were in another ward to have babies they didn't want; they started at thirteen, fourteen. They'd leave afterwards, but the babies stayed, and we played with them, too, but not many of them lived. The first year we had eighty; seventy died. The room Jimmie and I played in was the deadhouse, where they kept the bodies till they could dig—

Kate *(closes her eyes).* Oh, my dear—

Annie. —the graves.

(She is immune to Kate's *compassion.)*

No, it made me strong. But I don't think you need send Helen there. She's strong enough.

(She waits again; but when neither offers her a word, she simply concludes.)

No, I have no conditions, Captain Keller.

Kate *(not looking up).* Miss Annie.

Annie. Yes.

Kate *(a pause).* Where would you—take Helen?

Annie. Ohh—*(brightly)* Italy?

Keller *(wheeling).* What?

Annie. Can't have everything. How would this garden house do? Furnish it, bring Helen here after a long ride so she won't recognize it, and you can see her every day. If she doesn't know. Well?

Kate *(a sigh of relief).* Is that all?

Annie. That's all.

Kate. Captain.

*(Keller *turns his head; and* Kate's *request is quiet but firm.)*

With your permission?

Keller *(teeth in cigar).* Why must she depend on you for the food she eats?

Annie *(a pause).* I want control of it.

Keller. Why?

Annie. It's a way to reach her.

Keller *(stares).* You intend to *starve* her into letting you touch her?

Annie. She won't starve; she'll learn. All's fair in love and war. Captain Keller, you never cut supplies?

Keller. This is hardly a war!

Annie. Well, it's not love. A <u>siege</u> is a siege.

Keller *(heavily)*. Miss Sullivan. Do you *like* the child?

Annie *(straight in his eyes)*. Do you?

(A long pause.)

Kate. You could have a servant here—

Annie *(amused)*. I'll have enough work without looking after a servant! But the boy Percy could sleep here, run errands—

Kate *(also amused)*. We can let Percy sleep here, I think, Captain?

Annie *(eagerly)*. And some old furniture, all our own—

Kate *(also eager)*. Captain? Do you think that walnut bedstead in the barn would be too—

Keller. I have not yet consented to Percy! Or to the house, or to the proposal! Or to Miss Sullivan's—staying on when I—

(But he erupts in an irate surrender.)

Very well, I consent to everything!

(He shakes his cigar at Annie.*)*

For two weeks. I'll give you two weeks in this place, and it will be a miracle if you get the child to tolerate you.

Kate. Two weeks? Miss Annie, can you accomplish anything in two weeks?

Keller. Anything or not, two weeks; then the child comes back to us. Make up your mind, Miss Sullivan, yes or no?

Annie. Two weeks. For only one miracle?

(She nods at him, nervously.)

I'll get her to tolerate me.

(Keller marches out and slams the door. Kate on her feet regards Annie *who is facing the door.)*

Kate *(then)*. You can't think as little of love as you said.

(Annie glances questioning.)

Or you wouldn't stay.

Annie *(a pause)*. I didn't come here for love. I came for money!

(Kate shakes her head to this with a smile; after a moment, she extends her open hand. Annie looks at it, but when she puts hers out it is not to shake hands, it is to set her fist in Kate's *palm.)*

Kate *(puzzled)*. Hm?

Annie. A. It's the first of many. Twenty-six!

(Kate squeezes her fist, squeezes it hard, and hastens out after Keller. Annie *stands as the door closes behind her, her manner so apprehensive that finally she slaps her brow, holds it, sighs, and, with her eyes closed, crosses herself for luck.*

The lights dim into a cool silhouette scene around her, the lamp paling out, and now, in formal entrances, persons appear around Annie with furniture for the room. Percy crosses the stage with a rocking chair and waits. Martha, from another direction, bears in a stool. Viney bears in a small table, and the other black servant rolls in a bed partway from left; and Annie, *opening her eyes to put her glasses back on, sees them. She turns around in the room once and goes into action, pointing out locations for each article. The servants place them and leave, and then* Annie *darts around, interchanging them. In the midst of this— while* Percy *and* Martha *reappear with a tray of food and a chair, respectively—*James *comes down from the house with* Annie's *suitcase and stands viewing the room and her quizzically;* Annie *halts abruptly under his eyes, embarrassed, then seizes the suitcase from his hand, explaining herself brightly.)*

Annie. I always wanted to live in a doll's house!

(She sets the suitcase out of the way and continues. Viney *at left appears to position a rod with drapes for a doorway, and the other servant at center pushes in a wheelbarrow loaded with a couple of boxes of* Helen's *toys and clothes.* Annie *helps lift them into the room, and the servant pushes the wheelbarrow off. In none of this is any heed taken of the imaginary walls of the garden house. The furniture is moved in from every side and itself defines the walls.*

Annie *now drags the box of toys into center, props up the doll conspicuously on top. With the people melted away, except for* James, *all is again still. The lights turn again without pause, rising warmer.)*

James. You don't let go of things easily, do you? How will you—win her hand now, in this place?

Annie *(curtly).* Do I know? I lost my temper, and here we are!

James *(lightly).* No touching, no teaching. Of course, you *are* bigger—

Annie. I'm not counting on force; I'm counting on her. That little imp is dying to know.

James. Know what?

Annie. Anything. Any and every crumb in God's creation. I'll have to use that appetite too.

(*She gives the room a final survey, straightens the bed, arranges the curtains.*)

James *(a pause).* Maybe she'll teach you.

Annie. Of course.

James. That she isn't. That there's such a thing as—dullness of heart. Acceptance. And letting go. Sooner or later we all give up, don't we?

Annie. Maybe you all do. It's my idea of the original sin.

James. What is?

Annie *(witheringly)*. Giving up.

James *(nettled)*. You won't open her. Why can't you let her be? Have some—pity on her, for being what she is—

Annie. If I'd ever once thought like that, I'd be dead!

James *(pleasantly)*. You will be. Why trouble?

(Annie turns to glare at him; he is mocking.)

Or will you teach me?

(And with a bow, he drifts off.

Now in the distance there comes the clopping of hoofs, drawing near and nearer, up to the door; and they halt. Annie wheels to face the door. When it opens this time, the Kellers— Kate in traveling bonnet, Keller also hatted— are standing there with Helen between them; she is in a cloak. Kate gently cues her into the room. Helen comes in groping, baffled but interested in the new surroundings; Annie evades her exploring hand, her gaze not leaving the child.)

Annie. Does she know where she is?

Kate *(shakes her head)*. We rode her out in the country for two hours.

Keller. For all she knows, she could be in another town—

(Helen stumbles over the box on the floor and in it discovers her doll and other battered toys, is pleased, sits by them, then becomes puzzled and suddenly very wary. She scrambles up and back to her mother's thighs; but Annie steps in, and it is hers that Helen embraces. Helen recoils, gropes, and touches her cheek instantly.)

Kate. That's her sign for me.

Annie. I know.

(Helen waits, then recommences her groping,

more urgently. Kate stands indecisive and takes an abrupt step toward her, but Annie's hand is a barrier.)

In two weeks.

Kate. Miss Annie, I—Please be good to her. These two weeks, try to be very good to her—

Annie. I will.

(Kate, turning then, hurries out. The Kellers cross back to the main house.

Annie *closes the door.* Helen *starts at the door jar and rushes it.* Annie *holds her off.* Helen *kicks her, breaks free, and careens around the room like an imprisoned bird, colliding with furniture, groping wildly, repeatedly touching her cheek in a growing panic. When she has covered the room, she commences her weird screaming.* Annie *moves to comfort her, but her touch sends* Helen *into a paroxysm[15] of rage. She tears away, falls over her box of toys, flings its contents in handfuls in* Annie's *direction, flings the box too, reels to her feet, rips curtains from the window, bangs and kicks at the door, sweeps objects off the mantelpiece and shelf, a little tornado incarnate, all destruction, until she comes upon her doll and, in the act of hurling it, freezes. Then she clutches it to herself, and in exhaustion sinks sobbing to the floor.* Annie *stands contemplating her, in some awe.)*

Two weeks.

(She shakes her head, not without a touch of disgusted bewilderment.)

What did I get into now?

(The lights have been dimming throughout, and the garden house is lit only by moonlight now, with Annie *lost in the patches of dark.*

Kate, *now hatless and coatless, enters the family room by the rear door, carrying a lamp.*

---

15. **paroxysm** (par′ əks iz′əm): a sudden outburst.

Keller, *also hatless, wanders simultaneously around the back of the main house to where* James *has been waiting, in the rising moonlight, on the porch.)*

Keller. I can't understand it. I had every intention of dismissing that girl, not setting her up like an empress.

James. Yes, what's her secret, sir?

Keller. Secret?

James *(pleasantly)*. That enables her to get anything she wants out of you? When I can't.

(James *turns to go into the house, but* Keller *grasps his wrist, twisting him half to his knees.* Kate *comes from the porch.)*

Keller *(angrily)*. She does *not* get anything she—

James *(in pain)*. Don't—don't—

Kate. Captain.

Keller. He's afraid.

(He throws James *away from him, with contempt.)*

What *does* he want out of me?

James *(an outcry)*. My God, don't you know?

(He gazes from Keller *to* Kate.*)*

Everything you forgot, when you forgot my mother.

Keller. What!

(James *wheels into the house.* Keller *takes a stride to the porch, to roar after him.)*

One thing that girl's secret is not; she doesn't fire one shot and disappear!

(Kate *stands rigid, and* Keller *comes back to her.)*

Katie. Don't mind what he—

Kate. Captain, *I* am proud of you.

Keller. For what?

Kate. For letting this girl have what she needs.

Keller. Why can't my son be? He can't bear me; you'd think I treat him as hard as this girl does Helen—

(He breaks off, as it dawns in him.)

Kate *(gently)*. Perhaps you do.

Keller. But he has to learn some respect!

Kate *(a pause, wryly)*. *Do* you like the child?

(She turns again to the porch, but pauses, reluctant.)

How empty the house is, tonight.

(After a moment she continues on in. Keller *stands moveless, as the moonlight dies on him.*

The distant belfry chimes toll two o'clock, and with them, a moment later, comes the boy's voice on the wind, in a whisper.)

Boy's Voice. Annie. Annie.

(In her patch of dark Annie, *now in her nightgown, hurls a cup into a corner as though it were her grief, getting rid of its taste through her teeth.)*

Annie. No! No pity, I won't have it.

(She comes to Helen, *prone on the floor.)*

On either of us.

(She goes to her knees, but when she touches Helen's *hand, the child starts up awake, recoils, and scrambles away from her under the bed.* Annie *stares after her. She strikes her palm on the floor, with passion.)*

I *will* touch you!

(She gets to her feet and paces in a kind of anger around the bed, her hand in her hair, and confronting Helen *at each turn.)*

How, how? How do I—

*(Annie *stops. Then she calls out urgently, loudly.)*

Percy! Percy!

(*She moves swiftly to the drapes, at left.*)

Percy, wake up!

(Percy's *voice comes in a thick sleepy mumble, unintelligible.*)

Get out of bed and come in here. I need you.

(Annie *darts away, finds and strikes a match, and touches it to the hanging lamp. The lights come up dimly in the room, and* Percy *stands bare to the waist in torn overalls, between the drapes, with eyes closed, swaying.* Annie *goes to him, pats his cheeks vigorously.*)

Percy. You awake?

Percy. No'm.

Annie. How would you like to play a nice game?

Percy. Whah?

Annie. With Helen. She's under the bed. Touch her hand.

(*She kneels* Percy *down at the bed, thrusting her hand under it to contact* Helen's. Helen *emits an animal sound and crawls to the opposite side, but commences sniffing.* Annie *rounds the bed with* Percy *and thrusts his hand again at* Helen. *This time* Helen *clutches it, sniffs in recognition, and comes scrambling out after* Percy, *to hug him with delight.* Percy, *alarmed, struggles, and* Helen's *fingers go to his mouth.*)

Percy. Lemme go. Lemme go—

(Helen *fingers her own lips, as before, moving them in dumb imitation.*)

She tryin' talk. She gonna hit me—

Annie (*grimly*). She *can* talk. If she only knew. I'll show you how. She makes letters.

(*She opens* Percy's *other hand, and spells into it.*)

This one is C. C.

(*She hits his palm with it a couple of times, her eyes upon* Helen *across him.* Helen *gropes to feel what* Percy's *hand is doing, and when she encounters* Annie's, *she falls back from them.*)

She's mad at me now, though; she won't play. But she knows lots of letters. Here's another, A. C, a. C, a.

(*But she is watching* Helen, *who comes groping, consumed with curiosity.* Annie *makes the letters in* Percy's *hand, and* Helen *pokes to question what they are up to. Then* Helen *snatches* Percy's *other hand and quickly spells four letters into it.* Annie *follows them aloud.*)

C, a, k, e! She spells cake; she gets cake.

(*She is swiftly over to the tray of food, to fetch cake and a jug of milk.*)

She doesn't know yet it means this. Isn't it funny? She knows how to spell it and doesn't *know* she knows?

(*She breaks the cake into two pieces, and extends one to each;* Helen *rolls away from her offer.*)

Well, if she won't play it with me, I'll play with you. Would you like to learn one she doesn't know?

Percy. No'm.

(*But* Annie *seizes his wrist and spells to him.*)

Annie. M, i, l, k. M is this. I, that's an easy one, just the little finger. L is this—

(*And* Helen *comes back with her hand, to feel the new word.* Annie *brushes her away and continues spelling aloud to* Percy. Helen's *hand comes back again and tries to get in.* Annie *brushes it away again.* Helen's *hand insists, and* Annie *puts it away rudely.*)

No, why should I talk to you? I'm teaching Percy a new word. L. K is this—

(Helen *now yanks their hands apart. She butts*
Percy *away and thrusts her palm insistently.*
Annie's *eyes are bright with glee.*)

Ho, you're *jealous,* are you!

(Helen's *hand waits, intractably*[16] *waits.*)

All *right.*

(Annie *spells into it* milk; *and* Helen *after a*
moment spells it back to Annie. Annie *takes*
her hand, with her whole face shining. She
gives a great sigh.)

Good! So I'm finally back to where I can
touch you, hm? Touch and go! No love
lost, but here we go.

(She *puts the jug of milk into* Helen's *hand*
and squeezes Percy's *shoulder.*)

You can go to bed now; you're earned
your sleep. Thank you.

(Percy, *stumbling up, weaves his way out*
through the drapes. Helen *finishes drinking,*
and holds the jug out for Annie. *When* Annie
takes it, Helen *crawls onto the bed and makes*
for sleep. Annie *stands, looks down at her.*)

Now all I have to teach you is—one word.
Everything.

(She *sets the jug down. On the floor, now*
Annie *spies the doll, stoops to pick it up, and*
with it dangling in her hand, turns off the
lamp. A shaft of moonlight is left on Helen *in*
the bed, and a second shaft on the rocking
chair; and Annie, *after putting off her smoked*
glasses, sits in the rocker with the doll. She is
rather happy, and dangles the doll on her
knee, and it makes its momma sound. Annie
whispers to it in mock solicitude.)

Hush, little baby. Don't—say a word—

(She *lays it against her shoulder, and begins*

rocking with it, patting its diminutive behind;
she talks the lullaby to it, humorously at
first.)

Momma's gonna buy you—a mockingbird:
If that—mockingbird don't sing—

(The *rhythm of the rocking takes her into the*
tune, softly, and more tenderly.)

Momma's gonna buy you a diamond
ring:
If that diamond ring turns to brass—

(A *third shaft of moonlight outside now rises*
to pick out James *at the main house, with one*
foot on the porch step; he turns his body, as if
hearing the song.)

Momma's gonna buy you a looking
glass:
If that looking glass gets broke—

(In *the family room, a fourth shaft picks out*
Keller *seated at the table, in thought; and he,*
too, lifts his head, as if hearing.)

Momma's gonna buy you a billy goat:
If that billy goat won't pull—

(The *fifth shaft is upstairs in* Annie's *room,*
and picks out Kate, *pacing there; and she*
halts, turning her head, too, as if hearing.)

Momma's gonna buy you a cart and
bull:
If that cart and bull turns over,
Momma's gonna buy you a dog named
Rover:
If that dog named Rover won't bark—

(With *the shafts of moonlight on* Helen, *and*
James, *and* Keller, *and* Kate, *all moveless, and*
Annie *rocking the doll, the curtain ends the*
act.)

---

16. **intractably** (in trak′tə blē): stubbornly.

$e\ x\ p\ l\ a\ i\ n$

Responding to Reading

First Impressions

1. Look at the list of words you wrote for First Impressions after Act One. Do the same words still apply or have your feelings changed?

Second Thoughts

2. Reread Annie's opinions about discipline and obedience on pages 660 and 662. How do her beliefs lead to her physical conflict with Helen?

3. Captain Keller and Annie feel sorry for Helen for different reasons. How does their pity for Helen affect their approaches to dealing with her?

4. Why does Annie insist on taking Helen to the garden house?

5. What "miracle" does Annie hope to achieve?

6. What do you learn about both James and Captain Keller during their debate about General Ulysses S. Grant?

7. How are Annie's actions and tactics like those of General Grant?

   Think about
   • Annie's tactics for gaining control of Helen throughout the act
   • her battle with Helen at the breakfast table
   • her decision to talk about her experiences in the asylum
   • the reasons Keller allows Annie to stay
   • the manner in which she uses Percy to reach Helen

8. Reread the conversation on page 680 that takes place outside. What does Keller want from James? What does James need from his father?

L*iterary Concept: Conflict*

As the plot develops in Act Two, many of the conflicts introduced in Act One build to a climax, while new conflicts surface. The reasons for these conflicts are also revealed. Identify the causes of each conflict listed below. Can you identify any other conflicts?

1. the physical conflict between Annie and Helen

2. the conflict between Annie and Captain Keller

3. the conflict between Captain Keller and James

4. the conflict within Annie

Writing Options

1. Choose a character and a scene from Act Two. Write a poem that describes the character's feelings, thoughts, or viewpoints during the scene you chose.

2. Helen is not the only one who has trouble communicating with others. Imagine that you are any other character in this play. Write a letter to another character with whom you have trouble communicating. In your letter, tell what you really feel.

3. At the end of Act Two, Annie sings a lullaby, which James, Captain Keller, and Kate all seem to hear. Why do you think the act ends in this way? Write a paragraph that explains your thoughts.

4. Although Helen cannot see, speak, or hear, she can think. Write the interior monologue she might have with herself either during the scene at the breakfast table or during the scene with Percy in the garden house.

Vocabulary Practice

Exercise On your paper write the word whose meaning is not related to the other words in the row.

1. contemplate   watch   study   tremble
2. insolent   respectful   deferential   polite
3. uncover   disinter   disregard   expose
4. interminably   quickly   continuously   endlessly
5. force   make   invite   compel
6. ruined   destroyed   ravaged   untouched
7. intervene   interview   interrupt   interfere
8. retaliate   repay   compromise   punish
9. voyage   trip   siege   journey
10. moderation   self-control   addiction   temperance
11. oppressor   tyrant   peacemaker   dictator
12. feigned   put-on   artificial   sincere
13. threatening   menacing   ominous   harmless
14. underprivileged   deprived   disadvantaged   crazed
15. ineffectual   influential   unproductive   useless

Words to Know and Use

compel
contemplate
deferential
deprived
disinter
feigned
ineffectual
interminably
intervene
ominous
ravaged
retaliate
siege
temperance
tyrant

Reading On

In the last act the action comes to a climax as emotions reach their peak. As you read, look for the turning point of the story. Watch for changes in the characters' attitudes that might result in a resolution of their conflicts. Finally, look for the "miracle" referred to in the title.

ACT THREE

The stage is totally dark, until we see Annie *and* Helen *silhouetted on the bed in the garden house.* Annie's *voice is audible, very patient, and worn; it has been saying this for a long time.*

Annie. Water, Helen. This is water. W, a, t, e, r. It has a *name.*

(A silence. Then,)

Egg, e, g, g. It has a *name,* the name stands for the thing. Oh, it's so simple, simple as birth, to explain.

(The lights have commenced to rise, not on the garden house but on the homestead. Then,)

Helen, Helen, the chick *has* to come out of its shell, sometime. You come out, too.

(In the bedroom upstairs, we see Viney *unhurriedly washing the window, dusting, turning the mattress, readying the room for use again; then in the family room a diminished group at one end of the table—*Kate, Keller, James*—finishing up a quiet breakfast; then outside, down right, the other black servant on his knees, assisted by* Martha, *working with a trowel around a new trellis and wheelbarrow. The scene is one of everyday calm, and all are oblivious to* Annie's *voice.)*

There's only one way out, for you, and it's language. To learn that your fingers can talk. And say anything, anything you can name. This is a mug. Mug, m, u, g. Helen, it has a *name.* It—has—a—*name*—

(Kate rises from the table.)

Keller *(gently).* You haven't eaten, Katie.

Kate *(smiles, shakes her head).* I haven't the appetite. I'm too—restless, I can't sit to it.

Keller. You should eat, my dear. It will be a long day, waiting.

James *(lightly).* But it's been a short two weeks. I never thought life could be so—noiseless, went much too quickly for me.

(Kate and Keller gaze at him, in silence. James becomes uncomfortable.)

Annie. C, a, r, d. Card. C, a—

James. Well, the house has been practically normal, hasn't it?

Keller *(harshly).* Jimmie.

James. Is it wrong to enjoy a quiet breakfast, after five years? And you two even seem to enjoy each other—

Keller. It could be even more noiseless, Jimmie, without your tongue running every minute. Haven't you enough feeling to imagine what Katie has been undergoing, ever since—

(Kate stops him, with her hand on his arm.)

Kate. Captain.

(to James.*)*

It's true. The two weeks have been normal, quiet, all you say. But not short. Interminable.

(She rises and wanders out; she pauses on the porch steps, gazing toward the garden house.)

Annie *(fading).* W, a, t, e, r. But it means *this.* W, a, t, e, r. *This.* W, a, t—

James. I only meant that Miss Sullivan is a boon.[17] Of contention, though, it seems.

Keller *(heavily).* If and when you're a parent, Jimmie, you will understand what separation means. A mother loses a—protector.

James *(baffled).* Hm?

---

17. **boon:** a gift or blessing. James implies that although Annie has brought the gift of peace, her presence has also created disputes, or quarrels.

Keller. You'll learn; we don't just keep our children safe. They keep us safe.

(He rises, with his empty coffee cup and saucer.)

There are, of course, all kinds of separation. Katie has lived with one kind for five years. And another is disappointment. In a child.

(He goes with the cup out the rear door. James sits for a long moment of stillness. In the garden house, the lights commence to come up. Annie, haggard at the table, is writing a letter, her face again almost in contact with the stationery. Helen, apart on the stool, and for the first time as clean and neat as a button, is quietly crocheting an endless chain of wool, which snakes all around the room.)

Annie. "I, feel, every, day, more, and, more, in—"

(She pauses, and turns the pages of a dictionary open before her; her finger descends the words to a full stop. She elevates her eyebrows, then copies the word.)

"—adequate."

(In the main house James pushes up, and goes to the front doorway, after Kate.)

James. Kate?

(Kate turns her glance. James is rather weary.)

I'm sorry. Open my mouth, like that fairy tale, frogs jump out.

Kate. No. It has been better. For everyone.

(She starts away, up center.)

Annie *(writing)*. "If, only, there, were, someone, to, help, me, I, need, a, teacher, as, much, as, Helen—"

James. Kate.

(Kate halts, waits.)

What does he want from me?

Kate. That's not the question. Stand up to the world, Jimmie; that comes first.

James *(a pause, wryly)*. But the world is him.

Kate. Yes. And no one can do it for you.

James. Kate.

(His voice is humble.)

At least we—Could you—be my friend?

Kate. I am.

(Kate turns to wander, up back of the garden house. Annie's murmur comes at once; the lights begin to die on the main house.)

Annie. "—my, mind, is, undisciplined, full, of, skips, and, jumps, and—"

(She halts, rereads, frowns.)

Hm.

(Annie puts her nose again in the dictionary, flips back to an earlier page, and fingers down the words; Kate presently comes down toward the bay window with a trayful of food.)

Disinter—disinterested—disjoin—dis—

(She backtracks, indignant.)

Disinterested, disjoin—Where's discipline?

(She goes a page or two back, searching with her finger, muttering.)

What a dictionary; have to know how to spell it before you can look up how to spell it; disciple, *discipline!* Diskipline.

(She corrects the word in her letter.)

(But her eyes are bothering her; she closes them in exhaustion and gently fingers the eyelids. Kate watches her through the window.)

Kate. What are you doing to your eyes?

(Annie glances around; she puts her smoked glasses on and gets up to come over, assuming a cheerful energy.)

Annie. It's worse on my vanity! I'm learning to spell. It's like a surprise party; the most unexpected characters turn up.

Kate. You're not to overwork your eyes, Miss Annie.

Annie. Well.

(She takes the tray, sets it on her chair, and carries chair and tray to Helen.*)*

Whatever I spell to Helen I'd better spell right.

Kate *(almost wistful)*. How—<u>serene</u> she is.

Annie. She learned this stitch yesterday. Now I can't get her to stop!

(She disentangles one foot from the wool chain and sets the chair before Helen. Helen, *at its contact with her knee, feels the plate, promptly sets her crocheting down, and tucks the napkin in at her neck; but* Annie *withholds the spoon. When* Helen *finds it missing, she folds her hands in her lap and quietly waits.* Annie *twinkles at* Kate *with mock devoutness.)*

Such a little lady; she'd sooner starve than eat with her fingers.

(She gives Helen *the spoon, and* Helen *begins to eat, neatly.)*

Kate. You've taught her so much, these two weeks. I would never have—

Annie. Not enough.

(She is suddenly gloomy; shakes her head.)

Obedience isn't enough. Well, she learned two nouns this morning, key and water; brings her up to eighteen nouns and three verbs.

Kate *(hesitant)*. But—not—

Annie. No. Not that they mean things. It's still a finger game, no meaning.

(She turns to Kate, *abruptly.)*

Mrs. Keller—

(But she defers it; she comes back, to sit in the bay and lift her hand.)

Shall we play our finger game?

Kate. How will she learn it?

Annie. It will come.

(She spells a word; Kate *does not respond.)*

Kate. How?

Annie *(a pause)*. How does a bird learn to fly?

(She spells again.)

We're born to use words, like wings; it has to come.

Kate. How?

Annie *(another pause, wearily)*. All right. I don't know how.

(She pushes up her glasses, to rub her eyes.)

I've done everything I could think of. Whatever she's learned here—keeping herself clean, knitting, stringing beads, meals, setting-up exercises each morning; we climb trees; hunt eggs; yesterday a chick was born in her hands—all of it I spell; everything we do, we never stop spelling. I go to bed with—writer's cramp from talking so much!

Kate. I worry about you, Miss Annie. You must rest.

Annie. Now? She spells back in her *sleep;* her fingers make letters when she doesn't know! In her bones, those five fingers know; that hand aches to—speak out, and something in her mind is asleep. How do I—nudge that awake? That's the one question.

Kate. With no answer.

Words to Know and Use | **serene** (sə rēn′) *adj.* untroubled; having a peaceful spirit

Annie *(long pause).* Except keep at it. Like this.

(She again begins spelling—I, need—and Kate's *brows gather, following the words.)*

Kate. More—time?

(She glances at Annie, *who looks her in the eyes, silent.)*

Here?

Annie. Spell it.

(Kate spells a word—no—shaking her head; Annie *spells two words—why, not—back, with an impatient question in her eyes; and* Kate *moves her head in pain to answer it.)*

Kate. Because I can't—

Annie. Spell it! If she ever learns, you'll have a lot to tell each other. Start now.

(Kate painstakingly spells in air. In the midst of this the rear door opens, and Keller *enters with the setter* Belle *in tow.)*

Keller. Miss Sullivan? On my way to the office, I brought Helen a playmate—

Annie. Outside please, Captain Keller.

Keller. My dear child, the two weeks are up today; surely you don't object to—

Annie *(rising).* They're not up till six o'clock.

Keller *(indulgent).* Oh, now. What difference can a fraction of one day—

Annie. An agreement is an agreement. Now you've been very good, I'm sure you can keep it up for a few more hours.

(She escorts Keller *by the arm over the threshold; he obeys, leaving* Belle.*)*

Keller. Miss Sullivan, you are a tyrant.

Annie. Likewise, I'm sure. You can stand there, and close the door if she comes.

Kate. I don't think you know how eager we are to have her back in our arms—

Annie. I do know; it's my main worry.

Keller. It's like expecting a new child in the house. Well, she *is,* so—composed, so— *(Gently.)* Attractive. You've done wonders for her, Miss Sullivan.

Annie *(not a question).* Have I.

Keller. If there's anything you want from us in repayment, tell us; it will be a privilege to—

Annie. I just told Mrs. Keller. I want more time.

Kate. Miss Annie—

Annie. Another week.

(Helen lifts her head, and begins to sniff.)

Keller. We miss the child. *I* miss her, I'm glad to say, that's a different debt I owe you—

Annie. Pay it to Helen. Give *her* another week.

Kate *(gently).* Doesn't she miss us?

Keller. Of course she does. What a wrench[18] this unexplainable—<u>exile</u> must be to her. Can you say it's not?

Annie. No. But I—

(Helen is off the stool, to grope about the room; when she encounters Belle, *she throws her arms around the dog's neck in delight.)*

Kate. Doesn't she need affection too, Miss Annie?

Annie *(wavering).* She—never shows me she needs it, she won't have any—caressing or—

Kate. But you're not her mother.

---

18. **wrench:** a sudden feeling of anguish or grief.

Keller. And what would another week accomplish? We are more than satisfied. You've done more than we ever thought possible, taught her constructive—

Annie. I can't promise anything. All I can—

Keller *(no break).*—things to do, to behave like—even look like—a human child, so manageable, contented, cleaner, more—

Annie *(withering).* Cleaner.

Keller. Well. We say cleanliness is next to godliness, Miss—

Annie. Cleanliness is next to nothing. She has to learn that everything has its name! That words can be her *eyes,* to everything in the world outside her, and inside too. What is she without words? With them, she can think, have ideas, be reached; there's not a thought or fact in the world that can't be hers. You publish a newspaper, Captain Keller. Do I have to tell you what words are? And she has them already—

Keller. Miss Sullivan.

Annie. —eighteen nouns and three verbs. They're in her fingers now. I need only time to push *one* of them into her mind! One, and everything under the sun will follow. Don't you see what she's learned here is only clearing the way for that? I can't risk her unlearning it. Give me more time alone with her, another week to—

Keller. Look.

(He points, and Annie *turns.* Helen *is playing with* Belle's *claws; she makes letters with her fingers, shows them to* Belle, *waits with her palm, then* manipulates *the dog's claws.)*

What is she spelling?

(A silence.)

Kate. Water?

*(*Annie *nods.)*

Keller. Teaching a dog to spell. *(A pause.)* The dog doesn't know what she means any more than she knows what you mean, Miss Sullivan. I think you ask too much, of her and yourself. God may not have meant Helen to have the—eyes you speak of.

Annie *(toneless).* I mean her to.

Keller *(curiously).* What is it to you?

*(*Annie's *head comes slowly up.)*

You make us see how we indulge her for our sake. Is the opposite true, for you?

Annie *(then).* Half a week?

Keller. An agreement *is* an agreement.

Annie. Mrs. Keller?

Kate *(simply).* I want her back.

(A wait; Annie *then lets her hands drop in surrender, and nods.)*

Keller. I'll send Viney over to help you pack.

Annie. Not until six o'clock. I have her till six o'clock.

Keller *(consenting).* Six o'clock. Come, Katie.

(Kate, leaving the window, joins him around back, while Keller *closes the door; they are shut out.*

Only the garden house is daylit now, and the light on it is narrowing down. Annie *stands watching* Helen *work* Belle's *claws. Then she settles beside them on her knees, and stops* Helen's *hand.)*

Annie *(gently).* No.

(She shakes her head, with Helen's *hand to her face, then spells.)*

Dog. D, o, g. Dog.

689

(She touches Helen's *hand to* Belle. Helen *dutifully pats the dog's head, and resumes spelling to its paw.)*

Not water.

(Annie rolls to her feet, brings a tumbler of water back from the tray, and kneels with it, to seize Helen's *hand and spell.)*

Here, water. *Water.*

(She thrusts Helen's *hand into the tumbler.* Helen *lifts her hand out dripping, wipes it daintily on* Belle's *hide; and taking the tumbler from* Annie, *endeavors to thrust* Belle's *paw into it.* Annie *sits watching, wearily.)*

I don't know how to tell you. Not a soul in the world knows how to tell you. Helen, Helen.

(She bends in compassion to touch her lips to Helen's *temple, and instantly* Helen *pauses, her hands off the dog, her head slightly averted. The lights are still narrowing, and* Belle *slinks off. After a moment,* Annie *sits back.)*

Yes, what's it to me? They're satisfied. Give them back their child and dog, both house broken; everyone's satisfied. But me, and you.

*(*Helen's *hand comes out into the light, groping.)*

Reach. *Reach!*

*(*Annie, *extending her own hand, grips* Helen's; *the two hands are clasped, tense in the light, the rest of the room changing in shadow.)*

I wanted to teach you—oh, everything the earth is full of, Helen, everything on it that's ours for a wink, and it's gone; and what we are on it, the—light we bring to it and leave behind in—words. Why, you can see five thousand years back in a light of words, everything we feel, think, know—and share, in words, so not a soul

is in darkness, or done with, even in the grave. And I know, I *know,* one word and I can—put the world in your hand—and whatever it is to me, I won't take less! How, how, how do I tell you that *this—*

(She spells.)

—means a *word,* and the word means this *thing,* wool?

(She thrusts the wool at Helen's *hand;* Helen *sits, puzzled.* Annie *puts the crocheting aside.)*

Or this—s, t, o, o, l—means this *thing,* stool?

(She claps Helen's *palm to the stool.* Helen *waits, uncomprehending.* Annie *snatches up her napkin, spells.)*

Napkin!

(She forces it in Helen's *hand, waits, discards it, lifts a fold of the child's dress, spells.)*

Dress!

(She lets it drop, spells.)

F, a, c, e, face!

(She draws Helen's *hand to her cheek and pressing it there, staring into the child's responseless eyes, hears the distant belfry begin to toll, slowly: one, two, three, four, five, six.)*

On the third stroke, the lights stealing in around the garden house show us figures waiting: Viney, *the other servant,* Martha, Percy *at the drapes, and* James *on the dim porch.* Annie *and* Helen *remain, frozen. The chimes die away. Silently* Percy *moves the drape rod back out of sight;* Viney *steps into the room—not using the door—and unmakes the bed; the other servant brings the wheelbarrow over, leaves it handy, rolls the bed off;* Viney *puts the bed linens on the top of a waiting boxful of* Helen's *toys and loads the box on the wheel-*

barrow; Martha *and* Percy *take out the chairs, with the trayful, then the table; and* James, *coming down and into the room, lifts* Annie's *suitcase from its corner.* Viney *and the other servant load the remaining odds and ends on the wheelbarrow, and the servant wheels it off.* Viney *and the children departing leave only* James *in the room with* Annie *and* Helen. James *studies the two of them, without mockery, and then, quietly going to the door and opening it, bears the suitcase out, and housewards. He leaves the door open.*

Kate *steps into the doorway and stands.* Annie, *lifting her gaze from* Helen, *sees her; she takes* Helen's *hand from her cheek and returns it to the child's own, stroking it there twice, in her mother sign, before spelling slowly into it,)*

M, o, t, h, e, r. Mother.

(Helen, with her hand free, strokes her cheek, suddenly forlorn. Annie *takes her hand again.)*

M, o, t, h—

(But Kate *is trembling with such impatience that her voice breaks from her, harsh.)*

Kate. Let her *come!*

(Annie lifts Helen *to her feet, with a turn, and gives her a little push. Now* Helen *begins groping, sensing something, trembling herself; and* Kate, *falling one step in onto her knees, clasps her, kissing her.* Helen *clutches her, tight as she can.* Kate *is inarticulate, choked, repeating* Helen's *name again and again. She wheels with her in her arms, to stumble away out the doorway.* Annie *stands unmoving, while* Kate *in a blind walk carries* Helen *like a baby behind the main house, out of view.*

Annie *is now alone on the stage. She turns, gazing around at the stripped room, bidding it silently farewell, impassively, like a defeated general on the deserted battlefield. All that*

remains is a stand with a basin of water; and here Annie *takes up an eyecup, bathes each of her eyes, empties the eyecup, drops it in her purse, and tiredly locates her smoked glasses on the floor. The lights alter subtly; in the act of putting on the glasses,* Annie *hears something that stops her, with head lifted. We hear it too, the voices out of the past, including her own now, in a whisper,)*

Boy's Voice. You said we'd be together, forever—You promised, forever and—*Annie!*

Anagnos's Voice. But that battle is dead and done with. Why not let it stay buried?

Annie's Voice *(whispering).* I think God must owe me a resurrection.

Anagnos's Voice. What?

(A pause, and Annie *answers it herself, heavily.)*

Annie. And I owe God one.

Boy's Voice. Forever and ever—

(Annie shakes her head.)

—forever, and ever, and—

(Annie covers her ears.)

—forever, and ever, and ever—

(It pursues Annie; *she flees to snatch up her purse, wheels to the doorway, and* Keller *is standing in it. The lights have lost their special color.)*

Keller. Miss—Annie.

(He has an envelope in his fingers.)

I've been waiting to give you this.

Annie *(after a breath).* What?

Keller Your first month's salary.

(He puts it in her hand.)

With many more to come, I trust. It doesn't express what we feel; it doesn't pay our debt. For what you've done.

Annie. What have I done?

Keller. Taken a wild thing and given us back a child.

Annie *(presently)*. I taught her one thing, no. Don't do this, don't do that—

Keller. It's more than all of us could, in all the years we—

Annie. I wanted to teach her what language is. I wanted to teach her yes.

Keller. You will have time.

Annie. I don't know how. I know without it to do nothing but obey is—no gift. Obedience without understanding is a—blindness, too. Is that all I've wished on her?

Keller *(gently)*. No, no—

Annie. Maybe. I don't know what else to do. Simply go on, keep doing what I've done, and have—faith that inside she's—That inside it's waiting. Like water, underground. All I can do is keep on.

Keller. It's enough. For us.

Annie. You can help, Captain Keller.

Keller. How?

Annie. Even learning no has been at a cost. Of much trouble and pain. Don't undo it.

Keller. Why should we wish to—

Annie *(abruptly)*. The world isn't an easy place for anyone. I don't want her just to obey, but to let her have her way in everything is a lie, to *her*. I can't—

(Her eyes fill; it takes her by surprise, and she laughs through it.)

And I don't even love her. She's not my child! Well. You've got to stand between that lie and her.

Keller. We'll try.

Annie. Because *I* will. As long as you let me stay, that's one promise I'll keep.

Keller. Agreed. We've learned something too, I hope. *(A pause.)* Won't you come now, to supper?

Annie. Yes.

(She wags the envelope, ruefully.)

Why doesn't God pay His debts each month?

Keller. I beg your pardon?

Annie. Nothing. I used to wonder how I could—

(The lights are fading on them, simultaneously rising on the family room of the main house, where Viney is polishing glassware at the table set for dinner.)

—earn a living.

Keller. Oh, you do.

Annie. I really do. Now the question is, can I survive it!

(Keller smiles, offers his arm.)

Keller. May I?

(Annie takes it, and the lights lose them as he escorts her out.

Now in the family room the rear door opens, and Helen steps in. She stands a moment, then sniffs in one deep, grateful breath; and her hands go out vigorously to familiar things, over the door panels, and to the chairs around the table, and over the silverware on the table, until she meets Viney; she pats her flank approvingly.)

Viney. Oh, we glad to have you back too, prob'ly.

(Helen hurries groping to the front door, opens and closes it, removes its key, opens and closes it again to be sure it is unlocked, gropes back to the rear door and repeats the procedure, removing its key and hugging herself gleefully.

Aunt Ev is next in by the rear door, with a relish tray; she bends to kiss Helen's cheek.

Helen *finds* Kate *behind her, and thrusts the keys at her.)*

Kate. What? Oh.

(to Ev.)

Keys.

(She pockets them; lets Helen *feel them.)*

Yes, *I'll* keep the keys. I think we've had enough of locked doors, too.

*(*James, *having earlier put* Annie's *suitcase inside her door upstairs and taken himself out of view around the corner, now reappears and comes down the stairs as* Annie *and* Keller *mount the porch steps. Following them into the family room, he pats* Annie's *hair in passing, rather to her surprise.)*

James. Evening, General.

(He takes his own chair opposite.)

Viney *bears the empty water pitcher out to the porch. The remaining suggestion of garden house is gone now, and the water pump is unobstructed.* Viney *pumps water into the pitcher.*

Kate, *surveying the table, breaks the silence.)*

Kate. Will you say grace, Jimmie?

(They bow their heads, except for Helen, *who palms her empty plate and then reaches to be sure her mother is there.* James *considers a moment, glances across at* Annie, *lowers his head again, and obliges.)*

James (*lightly*). And Jacob was left alone, and wrestled with an angel until the breaking of the day; and the hollow of Jacob's thigh was out of joint, as he wrestled with him; and the angel said, Let me go, for the day breaketh. And Jacob said, I will not let thee go, except thou bless me. Amen.

(Annie *has lifted her eyes suspiciously at* James, *who winks expressionlessly and inclines his head to* Helen.)

Oh, you angel.

(*The others lift their faces;* Viney *returns with the pitcher, setting it down near* Kate; *then goes out the rear door; and* Annie *puts a napkin around* Helen.)

Aunt Ev. That's a very strange grace, James.

Keller. Will you start the muffins, Ev?

James. It's from the Good Book, isn't it?

Aunt Ev (*passing a plate*). Well, of course it is. Didn't you know?

James. Yes, I knew.

Keller (*serving*). Ham, Miss Annie?

Annie. Please.

Aunt Ev. Then why ask?

James. I meant it *is* from the Good Book and therefore a fitting grace.

Aunt Ev. Well. I don't know about *that*.

Kate (*with the pitcher*). Miss Annie?

Annie. Thank you.

Aunt Ev. There's an awful *lot* of things in the Good Book that I wouldn't care to hear just before eating.

(*When* Annie *reaches for the pitcher,* Helen *removes her napkin and drops it to the floor.* Annie *is filling* Helen's *glass when she notices it. She considers* Helen's *bland expression a moment, then bends, retrieves it, and tucks it around* Helen's *neck again.*)

James. Well, fitting in the sense that Jacob's thigh was out of joint, and so is this piggie's.

Aunt Ev. I declare, James—

Kate. Pickles, Aunt Ev?

Aunt Ev. Oh, I should say so; you know my opinion of your pickles—

Kate. This is the end of them, I'm afraid. I didn't put up nearly enough last summer; this year I intend to—

(*She interrupts herself, seeing* Helen *deliberately lift off her napkin and drop it again to the floor. She bends to retrieve it, but* Annie *stops her arm.*)

Keller (*not noticing*). Reverend looked in at the office today to complain his hens have stopped laying. Poor fellow, *he* was out of joint; all he could—

(*He stops too, to frown down the table at* Kate, Helen, *and* Annie *in turn, all suspended in midmotion.*)

James (*not noticing*). I've always suspected those hens.

Aunt Ev. Of what?

James. I think they're Papist.[19] Has he tried—

(*He stops, too, following* Keller's *eyes.* Annie *now stoops to pick the napkin up.*)

Aunt Ev. James, now you're pulling my—lower extremity,[20] the first thing you know we'll be—

(*She stops, too, hearing herself in the silence.* Annie, *with everyone now watching, for the third time puts the napkin on* Helen. Helen *yanks it off, and throws it down.* Annie *rises, lifts* Helen's *plate, and bears it away.* Helen, *feeling it gone, slides down and commences to*

---

19. **Papist** (pā′ pist): Roman Catholic.
20. **lower extremity:** a leg.

kick up under the table; the dishes jump. Annie *contemplates this for a moment; then, coming back, takes* Helen's *wrists firmly and swings her off the chair.* Helen, *struggling, gets one hand free, and catches at her mother's skirt. When* Kate *takes her by the shoulders,* Helen *hangs quiet.)*

Kate. Miss Annie.

Annie. No.

Kate *(a pause).* It's a very special day.

Annie *(grimly).* It will be, when I give in to that.

(She tries to disengage Helen's *hand;* Kate *lays hers on* Annie's.*)*

Kate. Please. I've hardly had a chance to welcome her home—

Annie. Captain Keller.

Keller *(embarrassed).* Oh. Katie, we—had a little talk, Miss Annie feels that if we indulge Helen in these—

Aunt Ev. But what's the child done?

Annie. She's learned not to throw things on the floor and kick. It took us the best part of two weeks and—

Aunt Ev. But only a napkin; it's not as if it were breakable!

Annie. And everything she's learned *is*? Mrs. Keller, I don't think we should—play tug-of-war for her. Either give her to me or you keep her from kicking.

Kate. What do you wish to do?

Annie. Let me take her from the table.

Aunt Ev. Oh, let her stay. My goodness, she's only a child; she doesn't have to wear a napkin if she doesn't want to her first evening—

Annie *(level).* And ask outsiders not to interfere.

Aunt Ev *(astonished).* Out—outsi—I'm the child's *aunt*!

Kate *(distressed).* Will once hurt so much,

Miss Annie? I've—made all Helen's favorite foods, tonight.

(A pause.)

Keller *(gently).* It's a homecoming party, Miss Annie.

(Annie after a moment releases Helen. *But she cannot accept it. At her own chair, she shakes her head and turns back, intent on* Kate.*)*

Annie. She's testing you. You realize?

James *(to* Annie*).* She's testing *you*.

Keller. Jimmie, be quiet.

(James sits, tense.)

Now she's home, naturally she—

Annie. And wants to see what will happen. At your hands. I said it was my main worry. Is this what you promised me not half an hour ago?

Keller *(reasonably).* But she's *not* kicking, now—

Annie. And not learning not to. Mrs. Keller, teaching her is bound to be painful, to everyone. I know it hurts to watch, but she'll live up to just what you demand of her, and no more.

James *(palely).* She's testing *you*.

Keller *(testily).* Jimmie.

James. I have an opinion. I think I should—

Keller. No one's interested in hearing your opinion.

Annie. *I'm* interested. Of course she's testing me. Let me keep her to what she's learned, and she'll go on learning from me. Take her out of my hands, and it all comes apart.

(Kate closes her eyes, digesting it; Annie *sits again, with a brief comment for her.)*

Be bountiful; it's at her expense.

(She turns to James, *flatly.)*

Please pass me more of—her favorite foods.

(Then Kate *lifts* Helen's *hand, and turning her toward* Annie, *surrenders her;* Helen *makes for her own chair.)*

Kate *(low).* Take her, Miss Annie.

Annie *(then).* Thank you.

(But the moment Annie, *rising, reaches for her hand,* Helen *begins to fight and kick, clutching to the tablecloth, and uttering laments.* Annie *again tries to loosen her hand, and* Keller *rises.)*

Keller *(tolerant).* I'm afraid you're the difficulty, Miss Annie. Now I'll keep her to what she's learned; you're quite right there—

(He takes Helen's *hands from* Annie, *pats them;* Helen *quiets down.)*

—but I don't see that we need send her from the table; after all, she's the guest of honor. Bring her plate back.

Annie. If she was a seeing child, none of you would tolerate one—

Keller. Well, she's not, I think some compromise is called for. Bring her plate, please.

(Annie's *jaw sets, but she restores the plate, while* Keller *fastens the napkin around* Helen's *neck; she permits it.*)

There. It's not unnatural. Most of us take some <u>aversion</u> to our teachers, and occasionally another hand can smooth things out.

(*He puts a fork in* Helen's *hand;* Helen *takes it. Genially,*)

Now. Shall we start all over?

(*He goes back around the table and sits.* Annie *stands watching.* Helen *is motionless, thinking things through, until with a wicked glee she deliberately flings the fork on the floor. After another moment, she plunges her hand into her food, and crams a fistful into her mouth.*)

James (*wearily*). I think we've started all over—

(Keller *shoots a glare at him, as* Helen *plunges her other hand into* Annie's *plate.* Annie *at once moves in to grasp her wrist; and* Helen, *flinging out a hand, encounters the pitcher. She swings with it at* Annie. Annie, *falling back, blocks it with an elbow, but the water flies over her dress.* Annie *gets her breath, then snatches the pitcher away in one hand, hoists* Helen *up bodily under the other arm and starts to carry her out, kicking.* Keller *stands.*)

Annie (*savagely polite*). Don't get up!

Keller. Where are you going?

Annie. Don't smooth anything else out for me; don't interfere in any way! I treat her like a seeing child because I *ask* her to see. I *expect* her to see. Don't undo what I do!

Keller. Where are you taking her?

Annie. To make her fill this pitcher again!

(*She thrusts out with* Helen *under her arm, but* Helen *escapes up the stairs and* Annie *runs after her.* Keller *stands rigid.* Aunt Ev *is astounded.*)

Aunt Ev. You let her speak to you like that, Arthur? A creature who *works* for you?

Keller (*angrily*). No. I don't.

(*He is starting after* Annie *when* James, *on his feet with shaky resolve, interposes his chair between them in* Keller's *path.*)

James. Let her go.

Keller. What!

James (*a swallow*). I said—let her go. She's right.

(Keller *glares at the chair and him.* James *takes a deep breath, then headlong,*)

She's right, Kate's right, I'm right, and you're wrong. If you drive her away from here, it will be over my dead—chair. Has it never occurred to you that on one occasion you might be <u>consummately</u> wrong?

(Keller's *stare is unbelieving, even a little fascinated.* Kate *rises in trepidation,*[21] *to <u>mediate</u>.*)

Kate. Captain.

(Keller *stops her with his raised hand; his eyes stay on* James's *pale face, for a long hold. When he finally finds his Voice, it is gruff.*)

Keller. Sit down, everyone.

(*He sits.* Kate *sits.* James *holds onto his chair.* Keller *speaks mildly.*)

Please sit down, Jimmie.

---

21. **trepidation:** fearful uncertainty or apprehension.

Words to Know and Use | **aversion** (ə vur′ zhən) *n.* an intense dislike
consummately (kən sum′ it lē) *adv.* completely
mediate (mē′ dē āt′) *v.* to settle a dispute or an argument by bringing the two sides together

697

(James *sits, and a moveless silence prevails;* Keller's *eyes do not leave him.*

Annie *has pulled* Helen *downstairs again by one hand, the pitcher in her other hand, down the porch steps, and across the yard to the pump. She puts* Helen's *hand on the pump handle, grimly.)*

Annie. All right. Pump.

(Helen *touches her cheek, waits uncertainly.)*

No, she's not here. Pump!

(She forces Helen's *hand to work the handle, then lets go. And* Helen *obeys. She pumps till the water comes. Then* Annie *puts the pitcher in her other hand and guides it under the spout, and the water tumbling half into and half around the pitcher douses* Helen's *hand.* Annie *takes over the handle to keep water coming, and does automatically what she has done so many times before, spells into* Helen's *free palm,)*

Water. W, a, t, e, r. *Water.* It has a— name—

(And now the miracle happens. Helen *drops the pitcher on the slab under the spout. It shatters. She stands transfixed.* Annie *freezes on the pump handle. There is a change in the sundown light, and with it a change in* Helen's *face, some light coming into it we have never seen there, some struggle in the depths behind it; and her lips tremble, trying to remember something the muscles around them once knew, till at last it finds its way out, painfully, a baby sound buried under the debris of years of dumbness.)*

Helen. Wah. Wah.

(And again, with great effort.) Wah. Wah.

(Helen *plunges her hand into the dwindling water, spells into her own palm. Then she gropes frantically.* Annie *reaches for her hand, and* Helen *spells into* Annie's *hand.)*

Annie *(whispering).* Yes.

(Helen *spells into it again.)*

Yes!

(Helen *grabs at the handle, pumps for more water, plunges her hand into its spurt, and grabs* Annie's *to spell it again.)*

Yes! Oh, my dear—

(She falls to her knees to clasp Helen's *hand, but* Helen *pulls it free, stands almost bewildered, then drops to the ground, pats it swiftly, holds up her palm, imperious.* Annie *spells into it,)*

Ground.

(Helen *spells it back.)*

Yes!

(Helen *whirls to the pump, pats it, holds up her palm, and* Annie *spells into it.)*

Pump.

(Helen *spells it back.)*

Yes! Yes!

(Now Helen *is in such an excitement she is possessed, wild, trembling, cannot be still, turns, runs, falls on the porch steps, claps it, reaches out her palm, and* Annie *is at it instantly to spell,)*

Step.

(Helen *has no time to spell back now. She whirls, groping, to touch anything, encounters the trellis, shakes it, thrusts out her palm, and* Annie, *while spelling to her, cries wildly at the house.)*

Words to Know and Use | **transfixed** (trans fikst') *adj.* motionless **transfix** *v.*

Trellis. Mrs. Keller! *Mrs. Keller!*

(Inside, Kate *starts to her feet.* Helen *scrambles back onto the porch, groping, and finds the bell string, tugs it. The bell rings; the distant chimes begin tolling the hour; all the bells in town seem to break into speech, while* Helen *reaches out and* Annie *spells feverishly into her hand.* Kate *hurries out, with* Keller *after her.* Aunt Ev *is on her feet, to peer out the window. Only* James *remains at the table, and with a napkin wipes his damp brow. From up right and left the servants—*Viney, *the two black children, the other servant—run in, and stand watching from a distance as* Helen, *ringing the bell, with her other hand encounters her mother's skirt. When she throws a hand out,* Annie *spells into it,)*

Mother.

*(*Keller *now seizes* Helen's *hand. She touches him, gestures a hand, and* Annie *again spells,)*

Papa—She *knows!*

*(*Kate *and* Keller *go to their knees, stammer-*

ing, clutching Helen *to them; and* Annie *steps unsteadily back to watch the threesome,* Helen *spelling wildly into* Kate's *hand, then into* Keller's, Kate *spelling back into* Helen's. *They cannot keep their hands off her and rock her in their clasp.*

Then Helen *gropes, feels nothing, turns all around, pulls free, and comes with both hands groping to find* Annie. *She encounters* Annie's *thighs.* Annie *kneels to her,* Helen's *hand pats* Annie's *cheek impatiently, points a finger, and waits; and* Annie *spells into it,)*

Teacher.

*(*Helen *spells back, slowly;* Annie *nods.)*

Teacher.

(She holds Helen's *hand to her cheek. Presently* Helen *withdraws it, not jerkily, only with reserve, and retreats a step. She stands thinking it over, then turns again and stumbles back to her parents. They try to embrace her, but she has something else in mind. It is to get the keys, and she hits* Kate's *pocket until* Kate *digs them out for her.*

Annie, *with her own load of emotion, has retreated, her back turned, toward the pump, to sit.* Kate *moves to* Helen, *touches her hand questioningly, and* Helen *spells a word to her.* Kate *comprehends it, their first act of verbal communication, and she can hardly utter the word aloud, in wonder, gratitude, and deprivation. It is a moment in which she simultaneously finds and loses a child.)*

Kate. Teacher?

*(*Annie *turns; and* Kate, *facing* Helen *in her direction by the shoulders, holds her back, holds her back, and then* relinquishes *her.* Helen *feels her way across the yard rather shyly, and when her moving hands touch An-*

nie's skirt, she stops. Then she holds out the keys and places them in Annie's *hand. For a moment neither of them moves. Then* Helen *slides into* Annie's *arms, and lifting away her smoked glasses, kisses her on the cheek.* Annie *gathers her in.*

Kate, *torn both ways, turns from this, gestures the servants off, and makes her way into the house, on* Keller's *arm. The servants go, in separate directions.*

The lights are half down now, except over the pump. Annie *and* Helen *are here, alone in the yard.* Annie *has found* Helen's *hand, almost without knowing it, and she spells slowly into it, her voice unsteady, whispering,)*

Annie. I, love, Helen.

(She clutches the child to her, tight this time, not spelling, whispering into her hair.)

Forever, and—

(She stops. The lights over the pump are taking on the color of the past, and it brings Annie's *head up, her eyes opening, in fear; and as slowly as though drawn she rises, to listen, with her hand on* Helen's *shoulders. She waits, waits, listening with ears and eyes both, slowly here, slowly there; and hears only silence. There are no Voices. The color passes on, and when her eyes come back to* Helen, *she can breathe the end of her phrase without fear,)*

—ever.

(In the family room, Kate *has stood over the table, staring at* Helen's *plate, with* Keller *at her shoulder. Now* James *takes a step to move her chair in, and* Kate *sits, with head erect, and* Keller *inclines his head to* James; *so it is Aunt Ev, hesitant, and rather humble, who moves to the door.*

---

relinquish (ri liŋ′ kwish) *v.* to let go or give up; to surrender

Outside, Helen *tugs at* Annie's *hand, and An-*
nie comes with it. Helen *pulls her toward the*
house; and hand in hand, they cross the yard,
and ascend the porch steps, in the rising lights,
to where Aunt Ev *is holding the door open for*
them.

The curtain ends the play.)

Fable for When There's No Way Out

MAY SWENSON

Grown too big for his skin,
and it grown hard,

without a sea and atmosphere—
he's drunk it all up—

his strength's inside him now,
but there's no room to stretch.

He pecks at the top
but his beak's too soft;

though instinct or ambition shoves,
he can't get through.

Barely old enough to bleed
and already bruised!

In a case this tough
what's the use

if you break your head
instead of the lid?

Despair tempts him
to just go limp;

Maybe the cell's
already a tomb,

and beginning end
in this round room.

Still, stupidly he pecks
and pecks, as if from under

his own skull—
yet makes no crack . . .

No crack until
he finally cracks,

and kicks and stomps.
What a thrill

and shock to feel
his little gaff poke

through the floor!
A way he hadn't known or meant.

Rage works if reason won't.
When locked up, bear down.

explain

Responding to Reading

First Impressions

1. Which part of Act Three affected you most? Jot down your feelings.

Second Impressions

2. Annie's two weeks alone with Helen come to an end. At this point, how have Annie's problems changed, if at all?

3. Do you think the Kellers' decision to bring Helen home is wise? Give reasons for your answer.

   Think about
   - the importance of affection to Helen
   - what Helen has accomplished in the two weeks
   - what Annie believes Helen still needs to learn
   - other reasons Annie might have for keeping Helen longer

4. What happens to resolve the conflict between James and his father?

   Think about
   - Kate's response to James's question about his father on page 686
   - Captain Keller's reaction when James stops him from following Annie

5. Helen takes the house keys from her mother and gives them to Annie. What is the significance of this gesture for Helen, Annie, and Kate?

6. Several references are made to a resurrection, or rebirth. What characters experience a resurrection? Explain your opinion.

7. How does the subunit title, "Awakenings," relate to the play?

Broader Connections

8. Annie says that "obedience without understanding is a—blindness, too." In what ways does this statement apply to your life? When might following orders without understanding cause more harm than good?

Literary Concept: Theme

The Miracle Worker has more than one theme. Think about language and communication and the lessons each character learns. Then figure out three themes of this play. Which is most important? Explain.

Concept Review: Conflict Review the conflicts listed on page 683. How is each of these conflicts resolved by the end of Act Three?

Writing Options

1. A motto can describe the goals or philosophy of an individual or a group. A motto can be a single word, a phrase, or a sentence, such as "Honesty is the best policy." Write a motto that expresses Annie's philosophy of life.

2. Choose a quote from the play that you find particularly meaningful. Explain its importance to the play and its importance to you.

3. Choose two characters in this play who are alike in some way. Compare them, listing their similarities.

4. In *The Miracle Worker,* Helen is compared to a chick waiting to hatch. Read the poem "Fable for When There's No Way Out" on page 701. Explain how Helen is like the bird in this poem. Write your comparison as a chart or in paragraph form.

Vocabulary Practice

Exercise Write the letter of the word pair that best expresses a relationship similar to that of the first pair.

1. AVERSION : EMOTION ::
   (a) broccoli : distaste
   (b) anger : war
   (c) measles : illness
   (d) exercise : muscles
2. CONSUMMATELY : PARTIALLY ::
   (a) totally : scarcely
   (b) courageously : bravely
   (c) skillfully : carefully
   (d) peacefully : calmly
3. EXILE : HOMECOMING ::
   (a) catastrophe : calamity
   (b) debt : obligation
   (c) law : legality
   (d) illness : recovery
4. MANIPULATE : HANDS ::
   (a) write : book
   (b) hear : sound
   (c) talk : voice
   (d) sing : melody
5. MEDIATE : DISPUTE ::
   (a) think : brain
   (b) teach : lesson
   (c) perspire : relaxation
   (d) argue : cooperation
6. RELINQUISH : RETAIN ::
   (a) squeeze : compress
   (b) uncover : bury
   (c) cry : sniffle
   (d) sever : split
7. SERENE : SERENITY ::
   (a) mean : amenity
   (b) obsessed : obesity
   (c) noble : nobility
   (d) sensible : sensation
8. TRANSFIXED : MOTIONLESS ::
   (a) polite : courteous
   (b) excited : bored
   (c) horrified : calm
   (d) qualified : useless

> *Words to Know and Use*
>
> aversion
> consummately
> exile
> manipulate
> mediate
> relinquish
> serene
> transfixed

e x t e n d

*O*ptions for Learning

1 • Construct a Stage Set Using the stage directions on page 635, construct a model of the set for *The Miracle Worker*. Experiment by sketching several designs before you begin construction. Decide the size of your model and gather the materials you will use. Then skim the play for details about furniture and other props that are important to the action, such as the breakfast table, and the dresser in Annie's room. Construct your model using the information that is provided and your own imagination.

2 • Get the Facts Research the life of either Annie Sullivan or Helen Keller. Gather information from at least three sources. Some sources to consider are Helen's autobiography, *The Story of My Life;* biographies such as *Teacher: Anne Sullivan Macy* by Helen Keller and *Helen and Teacher: The Story of Helen Keller and Anne Sullivan Macy* by Joseph P. Lash; and encyclopedias. Compare your findings with the information presented in this play. Present your findings orally, or visually on a chart.

3 • A Different Way of Living Interview a person who works with blind, deaf, or blind and deaf people to find out how he or she instructs students. To locate a subject for your interview, check the public-service pages in your telephone book under the heading "Human Services," or contact one of the following organizations:

- a regional office of the Helen Keller National Center for Deaf-Blind Youths and Adults
- your state office of blindness and visual services or office of vocational rehabilitation
- state or private schools for the deaf and blind
- state colleges and universities

Prepare an oral report for your class to share what you learned.

4 • High-Tech for the Handicapped Today, people who are blind and/or deaf often use high-tech, computerized devices to get around and to communicate with others. Find out about the Mowat Sensor, Lazar Canes, the TDD (Telecommunication Device for the Deaf), and other inventions to aid the handicapped by contacting one of the organizations listed in the previous activity. Present your findings in a visual display.

5 • Actions Louder Than Words With your classmates, act out a scene that you especially like from the play. Presenting a scene that includes Helen is a challenge, even to professional actors. Therefore, take time to block the scene, that is, to plan each actor's movements. The student who plays Helen might rehearse wearing a blindfold to better understand Helen's problems. When you are comfortable with your interpretation, present the scene for the rest of your class.

6 • Language Options Annie used a manual sign language to communicate with Helen. Research other language systems that are used to communicate with blind and deaf people, such as braille, print on palm, and American Sign Language. Create a display to show the origins of each language and how letters and words of the language are formed.

7 • Picture Helen

William Gibson uses many adjectives to describe Helen's physical appearance and her personality. Skim the play and list at least ten words or phrases that help you know Helen. For example, early in the play, Helen is described as *vivacious*. Then use the words and phrases you listed to write a description of Helen. Draw a picture of Helen as you imagine her, to accompany your paragraph.

 **FACT FINDER**

Who became Helen's companion after Annie Sullivan Macy died?

William Gibson
1914-

William Gibson is a novelist, poet, and dramatist who was born in New York City and educated at the City College of New York. *Two For the Seesaw*, one of his most successful plays, brought fame both to Gibson and to its leading lady, Anne Bancroft. Bancroft later played the part of Annie Sullivan in *The Miracle Worker*.

When asked how he became interested in Helen Keller, William Gibson is said to have replied, "I was never interested in her, the play is about her teacher [Annie Sullivan], and for that reason is not named *The Miracle Workee*." When he read Keller's autobiography, *The Story of My Life*, he discovered letters that Annie had written printed in the back of the book. They included a "blow-by-blow" account of the tactics she used during the first two months she was with Helen. "I thought these among the most extraordinary letters I had ever read, and I drew . . . the play almost exclusively from them," Gibson said.

Even though Gibson had no television set and had never written a play for television, *The Miracle Worker* was highly acclaimed when it first aired in 1957. His contract stipulated that 10 percent of his pay would go to a charity chosen by Helen herself. In 1959, Gibson rewrote the television script for the stage, changing the emphasis slightly to show that "everyone in the family was to be significantly affected by the work of the child [Helen], and we were to see it liberate the teacher from her past, as much as the pupil from her present."

Gibson went on to write *Monday After the Miracle* (1983), a second play about Annie Sullivan and Helen Keller. This play deals with their continuing relationship after *The Miracle Worker* ends. Today, William Gibson lives in Stockbridge, Massachusetts.

WORKSHOP

LITERARY ANALYSIS

A literary analysis is an in-depth discussion of a literary work. The writer of the analysis studies the work and writes his or her interpretation for an audience who is familiar with the selection. The writer focuses on an important point and shows how the literature supports his or her idea.

High school and college literature courses frequently require you to write literary analyses. Usually the test or assignment provides a focus for your writing, but sometimes you will have to determine this on your own.

In this assignment you will write a literary analysis of *The Miracle Worker* that focuses on two characters. You will choose the characters and support a generalization about them by comparing and contrasting them, using evidence from the play as support for your interpretation.

> **Here is your PASSkey to this assignment.**

GUIDED ASSIGNMENT:
CHARACTERS IN CONTRAST

Write a composition that compares and contrasts two characters in *The Miracle Worker.*

PURPOSE: To inform

AUDIENCE: Other readers of *The Miracle Worker*

SUBJECT: Two characters from *The Miracle Worker*

STRUCTURE: A comparison/contrast composition

Prewriting

Step 1 **Choose characters**   Start with the character you find most interesting. As a second character, select one who is in conflict with your character. You might compare and contrast Helen and Annie, Captain Keller and Kate Keller, Captain Keller and James Keller, Annie and James, or another combination you find exciting.

Step 2 **Establish your point**   What point do you want to make in your comparison? Work in pairs or in small groups to think of generalizations you can make about the characters. Consider what themes the play expresses about human nature. Think about the subunit title, "Awakenings," and about the lessons the characters learn. After choosing your generalization, write it in one sentence. This will be your **thesis statement,** the focus of your paper. For example, your thesis statement might be one of the following:

> Both James and Helen are isolated because neither can communicate with others.
>
> Kate is a stronger person than her husband.
>
> Both Annie and Helen are survivors, but Annie is the stronger of the two.

Note: You may switch Steps 1 and 2 if you wish. You might choose to start with your point and then find characters who will help you prove it.

Step 3 **Take notes on each character** Study your two characters individually by looking back through the play. Design a chart like the one below to help you see the characters' likenesses and differences. Make up categories appropriate to your characters and generalization. As you fill in your chart, look for lines in the play that support what you write. When you note a trait or attitude exhibited by the character, also jot down the line, or briefly describe the passage that shows that quality.

One student compared and contrasted Doodle and the narrator from "The Scarlet Ibis." Part of the chart she made is shown below.

◀ STUDENT MODEL

	Doodle	Narrator
Motivation	wants to please narrator never cares for own self	wants Doodle to be normal proud of his own achievements
Good Qualities	tries in spite of pain kind, calm accepts own frailties unselfish and uncomplaining	works hard for goal treats Doodle as an equal mostly patient but pushes motivates Doodle energetic
Faults	unmotivated for himself	expectations too high

Step 4 **Compare your characters**   Examine your chart. Circle the traits and attitudes that the characters share. These will be compared in your essay. Star the qualities they do not share. These will be contrasted. Cross out details that have nothing to do with your thesis.

Step 5 **Organize your evidence**   There are two ways to organize a comparing and contrasting essay. One way is to use the **block pattern,** spending the first half of the essay discussing one character and the second half discussing the other character. In the second half, show how the second character is like and different from the first character. To organize your notes for a block-pattern essay, list your points of comparison and contrast by character and plan to write a paragraph on each character.

Another method of organization is called the **alternating pattern.** In this organizational plan, you group the differences and similarities under general points of comparison. Then you show how the characters compare on each point. For example, you pick a quality, such as courage, and discuss the similarities and differences in the manner or extent to which both characters exhibit that quality. Then you do the same for your other points or qualities. To organize your notes for the alternating pattern, establish general points and make subpoints comparing and contrasting the characters on that point. Plan to write a paragraph about each general point.

Drafting

Step 1 **Write your introduction**   Begin by identifying the literary work you are analyzing. State what characters you are comparing and contrasting and make your thesis statement. Here is the introduction to the comparison/contrast essay the student wrote about "The Scarlet Ibis."

STUDENT MODEL ▶

> Even though his brother died, the narrator in "The Scarlet Ibis" should not feel guilty. Without his brother, Doodle's life would have been nothing. A comparison of the two brothers will show that even though Doodle was more emotionally mature than his older brother, his brother gave him a reason for living.

Step 2 **Turn your notes into paragraphs**   Begin each paragraph with a topic sentence that clearly indicates which character or what quality or point you will describe in that paragraph. After making a generalization about the character, quality, or point, include a brief summary or quotation that illustrates your statement. Elaborate on how your evidence supports your generalizations. Then start a new paragraph about the next character, quality, or point.

Revising and Editing

Once you have completed your draft, ask a classmate to review your essay using the following checklist. Then revise your paper using those ideas that you feel will improve it.

Revision Checklist

1. Does the introduction mention the literary work being discussed?
2. Does the introduction include a clear statement of who is being compared and what generalization is being made?
3. Is the essay organized in a way that is clear and easy to follow?
4. Does evidence in the form of quotations or summaries support the generalizations?
5. Does the comparison and contrast support the writer's thesis statement?

Editing When you have finished revising your analysis, proofread for spelling, clarity, and mechanics.

Presenting

In a small group with others who wrote about different characters than you did, read your essay aloud. Notice how your classmates chose different approaches and have different insights about the characters.

Reflecting on Your Writing

Answer the following questions about this assignment. Place the answers and your paper in your writing portfolio.

1. What was the most difficult thing about writing this essay? Why?
2. Which part of your essay is the strongest? Why?
3. As you wrote this essay, did you develop new insights into the characters of the play? Explain.

LANGUAGE
WORKSHOP

ACHIEVING SENTENCE VARIETY

One way to add interest to your writing is to vary the structure of the sentences you use. In this workshop you will review three different kinds of sentence structure.

Simple Sentences

REMINDER

The **subject** of a sentence names the person or thing about which something is said. The **predicate** tells what the subject did or what happened. The **simple predicate** is the *verb*.

A **simple sentence** is a sentence that contains only one subject and one predicate. The subject or predicate of a simple sentence may be compound, but the parts are considered one unit. Each of the following sentences is a simple sentence with one compound part.

Compound Subject   *Helen* and *Annie* had a violent fight at the dinner table.

Compound Predicate   They *slapped each other* and *wrestled around on the floor.*

Compound Sentences

A **compound sentence** consists of two or more simple sentences joined together. The parts of a compound sentence may be joined by a coordinating conjunction *(and, or, but)* or by a semicolon *(;).* In the following examples, the subject is underlined once; the verb is underlined twice.

<u>Helen</u> slapped Annie, **and** <u>Annie</u> slapped her back.
<u>Helen</u> <u>wanted</u> to eat with her hands, **but** <u>Annie</u> <u>made</u> her use a spoon.
<u>Helen</u> <u>threw</u> the napkin on the floor; <u>Annie</u> picked it up.

Complex Sentences

HELP!

Can you tell the difference between a **phrase** and a **clause**?
A clause has a subject and a verb. A phrase does not.
Phrase: at the movie
Clause: after the movie ended

A **complex sentence** contains one independent, or main, clause and one or more subordinate clauses.

Remember that a **clause** is a group of words that contains a verb and a subject. A simple sentence is a clause. A compound sentence has two clauses.

A clause that can stand as a sentence by itself is an **independent**

clause. All the clauses in a compound sentence are independent clauses, because they can stand by themselves.

A **subordinate** clause cannot stand alone as a sentence, usually because it begins with a word that makes the meaning incomplete. Look at these examples:

> Helen was born. (This is an independent clause. It has a subject and a verb and the meaning is complete.)
>
> when Helen was born (This is a subordinate clause. It has a subject and verb, but adding the word *when* makes the meaning incomplete. The reader wonders *What happened when Helen was born?*)

Now look at examples of complex sentences.

┌─ **Subordinate Clause** ─┐ ┌─ **Independent Clause** ─┐
When Helen was born, she was a perfect baby.

┌── **Independent Clause** ──┐ ┌── **Subordinate Clause** ──┐
She became blind and deaf after she had brain fever.

The next time you write or revise, look for opportunities to vary the types of sentences you use.

Exercise 1 For each sentence, write *Simple, Compound,* or *Complex* to show what kind of structure it has.

1. "The Scarlet Ibis" is a hauntingly beautiful story.
2. The writer included vivid descriptions of nature and crafted a sensitive, powerful plot.
3. The main characters in the story are two brothers.
4. The brothers in this story love each other, but they spend a great deal of time fighting.
5. The younger brother was handicapped, but he went everywhere with his older brother.
6. Doodle had many successes in his life because he was so determined.
7. A scarlet ibis was rarely seen in the South; a storm must have carried the exotic bird there.
8. The red bird's death foreshadowed Doodle's tragic death.
9. Both the bird and Doodle lived in worlds where they could not survive.
10. The narrator was haunted by his brother's death because he felt responsible for it.

Exercise 2   Work in groups to revise the following passage by varying sentence structure. Include all three types of sentences. You may add or delete words if necessary. Compare your revisions with those of other groups to see the various ways writers work.

Helen Keller's story is told in *The Miracle Worker.* Her story does not end there. At age ten Helen could read and write in Braille. Then she took lessons from a teacher of the deaf. The teacher taught her to speak. She learned to speak well. She was able to attend Radcliffe College. She graduated with honors in 1904. Helen wanted to do more. She was concerned about conditions for the handicapped. She worked on the staffs of many organizations. She gave lectures. She wrote books. She raised money. She traveled to more than twenty-five countries. There she helped civilians and soldiers. They had been blinded during World War II.

Exercise 3   Analyzing and Revising Your Writing

1. Take a piece of writing from your writing portfolio.
2. Reread it, looking for opportunities to vary your sentence structure.
3. Rewrite one or two paragraphs in which you can add a variety of kinds of sentences. Remember that not all sentences should be revised. Your goal should be strong, varied sentences.

LANGUAGE HANDBOOK

For review and practice: sentence structure, pages 950–55

Speaking and Listening

DRAMATIC READING

Professional dramatic readings are usually done with the actors sitting or standing on stage. They use a script, although they often have most of their lines memorized. Generally, no scenery, props, or costumes are used. The actors must rely on their voices and bodies to hold the attention of the audience. When you read plays or other selections aloud in class, use the same techniques that actors do.

1. Prepare.   Make sure you have read the material before class. If possible, practice reading out loud. As you read, look for the high points—the moments of tension, excitement, and humor.

2. Project.   Nothing is more annoying than a speaker who cannot be heard, so **project** your voice to all corners of the room. Don't shout, but speak forcefully and aim your voice outwards. You can also use your voice to bring out the high points of the selection. It will help if you hold the book and your head up when you read. For example, try raising the **volume,** or loudness, then dropping it suddenly to create tension.

3. Create a character.   If you are reading dialogue in a play or story, try creating a special voice for your character.

4. Pause.   Nothing builds suspense like silence. Practice using pauses at key moments to create tension. Don't be afraid to hold a pause: the audience won't go to sleep. Note: Do not pause between speeches in drama. When you have a part in a play, say your line the moment the previous character finishes.

5. Think and react.   Don't let yourself go on automatic pilot when you read. Think about what you're saying. If you are reading a play, listen to what the other character says. Don't let your attention waver!

6. Use your whole body.   Don't be afraid to move! Use hand gestures and facial expressions to emphasize words and phrases, even if you are sitting at your desk. Try some exaggerated gestures for humor or dramatic effect: a quick turn of your head, perhaps, or a shake of your fist. Getting your body into the act will improve your vocal presentation.

Exercise   Singly or in groups, choose a poem, monologue, or play scene. Use the steps above to prepare a dramatic reading for the class.

THE CLASSIC TRADITION

" *or never was a story*

of more woe

Than this of Juliet

and her Romeo. "

William Shakespeare

*Funeral procession from
Franco Zeffirelli's* Romeo and Juliet
Memory Shop, New York.

715

Drama

The *Tragedy of Romeo and Juliet*
WILLIAM SHAKESPEARE

Examine What You Know

Imagine that a movie or television producer is looking for a story that will be a sure-fire success. Which of the following topics would you suggest that the producer consider? Talk about your choices with your classmates.

- a passionate romance between two young lovers
- a friendship that is so intense that it leads to death
- a long-lasting and deadly feud between two powerful families
- a hatred so deep that it can be satisfied only by revenge
- the role of fate in determining the future

William Shakespeare managed to deal with all of these themes in *The Tragedy of Romeo and Juliet*. In doing so, he created a drama that has fascinated audiences for nearly four centuries because its topics concern all people in all ages. You may be surprised at how many connections you can make between this drama and your own life.

Expand Your Knowledge

William Shakespeare is considered by many to be the greatest playwright—and one of the greatest English poets—of all time. His plays have been produced more often and in more countries than those of any other playwright. Shakespeare began his career in the theater during the **Elizabethan Age,** that is, during the reign of Queen Elizabeth I of England, from 1558 to 1603. Like her father, Henry VIII, Elizabeth was a strong supporter of the arts—literature, painting, sculpture, theater, and music. As a result, artists of all types were held in high esteem—and even supported—by members of the upper class.

Besides being respected by the rich and powerful people of his day, Shakespeare also became very popular with the common people, for whom plays were one of the few forms of entertainment available. The theater became one of the few places where the working class and the educated upper classes mixed.

Elizabethan Drama

An Elizabethan play was likely to be either a comedy or a tragedy. Traditionally, a **comedy** was defined as "a play that begins with trouble and ends in peace." By the last act, solutions were provided to all the problems that the characters faced. A **tragedy,** on the other hand, was "a play that begins in calm and ends in tempest," or violence. A tragedy usually ended with the death of one or more of the main characters.

In both kinds of plays, the audience demanded to see many characters, colorful costumes, lots of action, and special effects. For example, comic scenes often included broad, slapstick humor and characters who looked or acted funny. Tragedies often included realistic sword fights and bloody death scenes. Actors wore pig bladders filled with red liquid that flowed like blood when the actors were "stabbed."

Elizabethan audiences did not expect the plots of their plays to be original. In fact, people often preferred plays about familiar stories, especially those taken from myths, legends, and history. *The Tragedy of Romeo and Juliet*, for example, is thought to be based on the poem "The Tragicall History of Romeus and Juliet," written in 1562 by English author Arthur Brooke. The plot of both stories is similar to that of the Roman myth of Pyramus and Thisbe. The audience's enjoyment was in seeing how Shakespeare would retell the tale in his own way.

DEATH OF MERCUTIO   Edwin Austin Abbey   Yale University Art Gallery, New Haven, Connecticut.

Shakespeare and the Globe Theatre

Until past the mid-1500's, plays were performed wherever the actors could find an audience—in bear baiting arenas, in open-air saloons, on makeshift platforms, or in an open field. Then, in 1576, James Burbage built a structure called The Theatre in a field outside London. It was the first building in England designed specifically for the presenting of plays. Soon there were several theaters competing for audiences. One of the most famous was the Globe Theatre, built in 1598. Most of Shakespeare's plays were performed there, for Shakespeare was one of its owners and an actor in its company, the King's Men. The picture on this page shows what the Globe probably looked like before its destruction by fire in 1613.

The Globe had no roof and very few seats, but it could accommodate almost two thousand people, since most of them stood in the yard that surrounded the stage. This area was called the pit, and the people who stood to watch the play were called groundlings. They paid a penny apiece. For a higher admission price, a person could sit above the crowds in the partially enclosed galleries.

Elizabethan theater relied heavily on the audience's imagination. Theaters had no curtains, no lights, and very little scenery. Instead, simple props were used to let the audience know where a particular scene took place, whether in a market, a tomb, or a bedroom. Actors used the words of the play and their own skills to set the scene.

Scale model of Shakespeare's Globe Theatre.
Folger Shakespeare Library, Washington, D.C.

Keep in mind that there were no female actors in Shakespeare's time, for it was considered improper for women to appear on stage. Consequently, the female roles, such as those of Juliet and the Nurse, were played by young male actors.

Enrich Your Reading

Although you will probably find reading this play difficult at first, it will become easier as you get used to Shakespeare's language and style of writing. The play includes many Elizabethan expressions, some of which are mild swear words, like *zounds,* a shortened form of "by God's wounds," and *marry,* a shortened form of "by the Virgin Mary." Some words are no longer used as they were, such as *soft,* meaning "wait a minute," and *an,* meaning "if." In addition, Shakespeare includes many puns and jokes that you may not understand. His audience, however, delighted in the wordplay and understood the double meanings he intended. The Guide for Reading in the right margin of the play's text will help you with many of the strange words and explain some of the jokes.

Shakespeare makes great use of figurative language and imagery, particularly light images, throughout *The Tragedy of Romeo and Juliet.* Watch for references to the sun, the moon, the stars, shadows, and other representations of light and dark. Also watch for **allusions,** or references to other literary works. Shakespeare makes several allusions to classical mythology.

Most of this play is written in **blank verse,** a form of poetry in unrhyming lines that sounds similar to everyday speech. Sometimes a line of poetry is split between two characters. When this happens, you will notice a large indent in the second character's line. Because this tale of "star-crossed lovers" was intended to be spoken aloud, reading it aloud may be the best way to get the meaning from the written words.

■ *A biography of the author can be found on page 845.*

The *Tragedy of* *Romeo and Juliet*

WILLIAM SHAKESPEARE

CHARACTERS

THE MONTAGUES

Lord Montague (män′ tə gyo͞o′)

Lady Montague

Romeo, son of Montague

Benvolio (ben vō′ lē ō), nephew of
   Montague and friend of Romeo

Balthasar (bäl′ thə sär′), servant to Romeo

Abram, servant to Montague

THE CAPULETS

Lord Capulet (kap′ yo͞o let′)

Lady Capulet

Juliet, daughter of Capulet

Tybalt (ti′ bält), nephew of Lady Capulet

Nurse to Juliet

Peter, servant to Juliet's Nurse

Sampson ⎫
            ⎬ servants to Capulet
Gregory ⎭

An old man of the Capulet family

OTHERS

Prince Escalus (es′ kə lus), ruler of Verona

Mercutio (mər kyo͞o′ shē ō′), kinsman of the
   Prince and friend of Romeo

Friar Laurence, a Franciscan priest

Friar John, another Franciscan priest

Count Paris, a young nobleman, kinsman of
   the Prince

Apothecary (ə päth′ ə ker′ ē)

Page to Paris

Chief Watchman

Three Musicians

An Officer

**Citizens of Verona, Gentlemen and
   Gentlewomen of both houses, Maskers,
   Torchbearers, Pages, Guards, Watchmen,
   Servants, and Attendants.**

Time: The fourteenth century

Place: Verona (və rō′ nə); Mantua (man′
cho͞o wə) in northern Italy

THE PROLOGUE

The CHORUS *is one actor who serves as a narrator. He enters from the back of the stage to introduce and explain the theme of the play. His job is to ''hook'' the audience's interest by telling them just enough to quiet them down and make them eager for more. In this prologue, or preview, the narrator explains that the play will be about a feud between two families (the Capulets and the Montagues). In addition, the narrator says that the feud will end in tragedy. As you read the prologue, determine what the tragedy will be.*

GUIDE FOR READING

[Enter Chorus.]

Chorus. Two households, both alike in dignity,
In fair Verona, where we lay our scene,
From ancient grudge break to new mutiny,
Where civil blood makes civil hands unclean.
5 From forth the fatal loins of these two foes,
A pair of star-crossed lovers take their life,
Whose misadventured piteous overthrows
Doth with their death bury their parents' strife.
The fearful passage of their death-marked love,
10 And the continuance of their parents' rage,
Which, but their children's end, naught could remove,
Is now the two hours' traffic of our stage,
The which if you with patient ears attend,
What here shall miss, our toil shall strive to mend.

[Exit.]

3-4 ancient . . . unclean: A new outbreak of fighting **(mutiny)** between families has caused the citizens of Verona to have one another's blood on their hands.

6 star-crossed: doomed. The position of the stars when the lovers were born was not favorable. In Shakespeare's day, people took astrology and horoscopes very seriously.

11 but: except for; **naught:** nothing.

12 two hours' . . . stage: the action that will take place on the stage during the next two hours.

15 What . . . mend: We will fill in the details that have been left out of the prologue.

ACT ONE

Scene 1 *A public square in Verona.*

As the scene opens, two young Capulet servants swagger across the stage joking and bragging. When they happen to meet servants from the rival house of Montague, a quarrel begins that grows into an ugly street fight. Finally the ruler of Verona, Prince Escalus, appears. He is angry about the violence in his city and warns that the next offenders will receive the death penalty. The crowd fades away and the stage is set for the entrance of Romeo, heir of the Montague family. Romeo, lovesick and miserable, can talk of nothing but his love for Rosaline and her cruelty in refusing to love him back.

[Enter Sampson *and Gregory, servants of the house of Capulet, armed with swords and bucklers (shields).]*

Sampson. Gregory, on my word, we'll not carry coals.

Gregory. No, for then we should be colliers.

Sampson. I mean, an we be in choler, we'll draw.

Gregory. Ay, while you live, draw your neck out of
5   collar.

Sampson. I strike quickly, being moved.

Gregory. But thou art not quickly moved to strike.

Sampson. A dog of the house of Montague moves me.

Gregory. To move is to stir, and to be valiant is to
10   stand. Therefore, if thou art moved, thou runnest
     away.

Sampson. A dog of that house shall move me to stand.
     I will take the wall of any man or maid of
     Montague's.

15 **Gregory.** That shows thee a weak slave, for the weakest
     goes to the wall.

Sampson. 'Tis true; and therefore women, being the
     weaker vessels, are ever thrust to the wall. Therefore
     I will push Montague's men from the wall and thrust
20   his maids to the wall.

Gregory. The quarrel is between our masters and us
     their men.

Sampson. 'Tis all one. I will show myself a tyrant.
     When I have fought with the men, I will be cruel
25   with the maids: I will cut off their heads.

Gregory. The heads of the maids?

Sampson. Ay, the heads of the maids, or their
     maidenheads. Take it in what sense thou wilt.

Gregory. They must take it in sense that feel it.

30 **Sampson.** Me they shall feel while I am able to stand;
     and 'tis known I am a pretty piece of flesh.

Gregory. 'Tis well thou art not fish; if thou hadst, thou
     hadst been poor-John. Draw thy tool! Here comes
     two of the house of Montagues.

[Enter Abram *and* Balthasar, *servants to the* Montagues.]*

1-5 we'll not carry coals: We won't stand to be insulted. (Those involved in the dirty work of hauling coal were often the targets of jokes and insults.) Here the comic characters Gregory and Sampson are bragging about how brave they are. Their boasts include several bad jokes based on words that sound alike: **collier** means "coal dealer"; **in choler** means "angry"; **collar** refers to a hangman's noose.

13 take the wall: walk nearest to the wall. People of higher rank had the privilege of walking closer to the wall, to avoid any water or garbage that might be in the street. *What claim is Sampson making about himself and anyone from the rival house of Montague?*

17-28 Sampson's tough talk includes boasts about his ability to overpower women.

33 poor-John: a salted fish, considered fit only for poor people to eat.

35 **Sampson.** My naked weapon is out. Quarrel! I will back thee.

Gregory. How? turn thy back and run?

Sampson. Fear me not.

Gregory. No, marry. I fear thee!

40 **Sampson.** Let us take the law of our sides; let them begin.

Gregory. I will frown as I pass by, and let them take it as they list.

Sampson. Nay, as they dare. I will bite my thumb at
45 them; which is disgrace to them, if they bear it.

Abram. Do you bite your thumb at us, sir?

Sampson. I do bite my thumb, sir.

Abram. Do you bite your thumb at us, sir?

Sampson. *[Aside to* Gregory] Is the law of our side if I
50 say ay?

Gregory. *[Aside to* Sampson] No.

Sampson. No, sir, I do not bite my thumb at you, sir; but I bite my thumb, sir.

Gregory. Do you quarrel, sir?

55 **Abram.** Quarrel, sir? No, sir.

Sampson. But if you do, sir, I am for you. I serve as good a man as you.

Abram. No better.

Sampson. Well, sir.

[Enter Benvolio, nephew of Montague *and first cousin of* Romeo.]

60 **Gregory.** *[Aside to* Sampson] Say "better." Here comes one of my master's kinsmen.

Sampson. Yes, better, sir.

Abram. You lie.

Sampson. Draw, if you be men. Gregory, remember
65 thy swashing blow.

[They fight.]

Benvolio. Part, fools! *[Beats down their swords.]* Put up your swords. You know not what you do.

35 During the next few speeches in this comic scene, watch what happens when the foolish, boastful servants actually meet their rivals face to face.

39 *marry:* a short form of "by the Virgin Mary" and so a mild swear word.
40–51 Gregory and Sampson decide to pick a fight by insulting the Montague servants with a rude gesture **(bite my thumb)**. To appreciate the humor in this scene, think about what the servants say openly, what they say in asides, and what they actually do.

49 *Aside:* privately, in a way that keeps the other characters from hearing what is said. Think of it as a whisper that the audience happens to overhear.

60–65 From the corner of his eye, Gregory can see Tybalt, a Capulet, arriving on the scene. With help on the way, his interest in fighting suddenly returns. He reminds Sampson to use **swashing,** or smashing, blows.

66 As you read the next few lines, think about the different attitudes shown by Benvolio and Tybalt. *How would you describe the contrast between them?*

[Enter Tybalt, hot-headed nephew of Lady Capulet and first cousin of Juliet.]

Tybalt. What, art thou drawn among these heartless hinds?
    Turn thee, Benvolio! look upon thy death.

70 **Benvolio.** I do but keep the peace. Put up thy sword,
    Or manage it to part these men with me.

Tybalt. What, drawn, and talk of peace? I hate the word
    As I hate hell, all Montagues, and thee.
    Have at thee, coward!

[They fight.]

[Enter several of both houses, who join the fray; then enter Citizens and Peace Officers, with clubs.]

75 **Officer.** Clubs, bills, and partisans! Strike! beat them
    down!

Citizens. Down with the Capulets! Down with the
    Montagues!

[Enter old Capulet and Lady Capulet.]

Capulet. What noise is this? Give me my long sword,
80   ho!

Lady Capulet. A crutch, a crutch! Why call you for a
    sword?

Capulet. My sword, I say! Old Montague is come
    And flourishes his blade in spite of me.

[Enter old Montague and Lady Montague.]

85 **Montague.** Thou villain Capulet!—Hold me not, let
    me go.

Lady Montague. Thou shalt not stir one foot to seek
    a foe.

[Enter Prince Escalus, with attendants. At first no one hears him.]

Prince. Rebellious subjects, enemies to peace,
90   Profaners of this neighbor-stained steel—
    Will they not hear? What, ho! you men, you beasts,
    That quench the fire of your pernicious rage
    With purple fountains issuing from your veins!
    On pain of torture, from those bloody hands
95   Throw your mistempered weapons to the ground
    And hear the sentence of your moved prince.

68-74 Tybalt misunderstands that Benvolio is trying to stop the fight. He challenges Benvolio.
68 *heartless hinds:* cowardly servants.

72 *drawn . . . peace:* You have your sword out, and yet you have the nerve to talk of peace?
74 *Have at thee:* Defend yourself.

75 *bills and partisans:* spears.

81-88 *A crutch . . . sword:* You need a crutch more than a sword. *How do both wives respond to their husbands' "fighting words"?*

89-96 The Prince is furious about the street fighting caused by the feud. He commands all the men to put down their weapons and pay attention.
pernicious: destructive.

Three civil brawls, bred of an airy word
By thee, old Capulet, and Montague,
Have thrice disturbed the quiet of our streets
100 And made Verona's ancient citizens
Cast by their grave beseeming ornaments
To wield old partisans, in hands as old,
Cankered with peace, to part your cankered hate.
If ever you disturb our streets again,
105 Your lives shall pay the forfeit of the peace.
For this time all the rest depart away.
You, Capulet, shall go along with me;
And, Montague, come you this afternoon,
To know our farther pleasure in this case,
110 To old Freetown, our common judgment place.
Once more, on pain of death, all men depart.

[Exeunt all but Montague, Lady Montague, *and* Benvolio.*]*

Montague. Who set this ancient quarrel new abroach?
Speak, nephew, were you by when it began?
Benvolio. Here were the servants of your adversary
115 And yours, close fighting ere I did approach.
I drew to part them. In the instant came
The fiery Tybalt, with his sword prepared;
Which, as he breathed defiance to my ears,
He swung about his head and cut the winds,
120 Who, nothing hurt withal, hissed him in scorn.
While we were interchanging thrusts and blows,
Came more and more, and fought on part and part,
Till the Prince came, who parted either part.

Lady Montague. O, where is Romeo? Saw you him
125 today? Right glad I am he was not at this fray.

Benvolio. Madam, an hour before the worshiped sun
Peered forth the golden window of the East,
A troubled mind drave me to walk abroad,
Where, underneath the grove of sycamore
130 That westward rooteth from the city's side,
So early walking did I see your son.
Towards him I made, but he was ware of me
And stole into the covert of the wood.
I—measuring his affections by my own,
135 Which then most sought where most might not be found,
Being one too many by my weary self—
Pursued my humor, not pursuing his,

97-103 Three . . . hate: The Prince holds Capulet and Montague responsible for three recent street fights, probably started by an offhand remark or insult **(airy word)**. He warns the old men that they will be put to death if any more fights occur.

Exeunt *(Latin):* they leave. When one person leaves the stage, the direction is *Exit.*
112 Who . . . abroach: Who reopened this old argument?
114 adversary: enemy.
115 ere: before.

120 withal: by this.

122 on part and part: some on one side, some on the other.
114-123 *According to Benvolio, what kind of person is Tybalt? How might Tybalt be likely to act if he meets Benvolio again?*
125 fray: fight.

128 drave: drove.

130 rooteth: grows.

132-138 made: moved; **covert:** covering. Romeo saw Benvolio coming toward him and hid in the woods. Benvolio decided to respect Romeo's privacy and went away. *What does this action tell you about Benvolio?*

And gladly shunned who gladly fled from me.
Montague. Many a morning hath he there been seen,
140   With tears augmenting the fresh morning's dew,
Adding to clouds more clouds with his deep sighs;
But all so soon as the all-cheering sun
Should in the farthest East begin to draw
The shady curtains from Aurora's bed,
145   Away from light steals home my heavy son
And private in his chamber pens himself,
Shuts up his windows, locks fair daylight out,
And makes himself an artificial night.
Black and portentous must this humor prove
150   Unless good counsel may the cause remove.

Benvolio. My noble uncle, do you know the cause?

Montague. I neither know it nor can learn of him.

Benvolio. Have you importuned him by any means?

Montague. Both by myself and many other friends;
155   But he, his own affections' counselor,
Is to himself—I will not say how true—
But to himself so secret and so close,
So far from sounding and discovery,
As is the bud bit with an envious worm
160   Ere he can spread his sweet leaves to the air
Or dedicate his beauty to the sun.
Could we but learn from whence his sorrows grow,
We would as willingly give cure as know.

[Enter Romeo lost in thought.]

Benvolio. See, where he comes. So please you step
165   aside, I'll know his grievance, or be much denied.

Montague. I would thou wert so happy by thy stay
To hear true shrift. Come, madam, let's away.

[Exeunt Montague and Lady.]

Benvolio. Good morrow, cousin.

Romeo.   Is the day so young?

170 **Benvolio.** But new struck nine.

Romeo.   Ay me! sad hours seem long.
Was that my father that went hence so fast?

Benvolio. It was. What sadness lengthens Romeo's
hours?

139-150 Romeo has been wandering through the woods at night, often in tears. At daybreak he returns home and locks himself in his darkened room. Montague is deeply concerned about his son's behavior and feels he needs guidance.

153 importuned: demanded.

155 his own affections' counselor: Romeo keeps to himself.

158-163 So far from . . . know: Finding out what Romeo is thinking is nearly impossible. Montague compares his son to a young bud destroyed by the bite of an envious worm. He wants to find out what is bothering Romeo so he can help him.

167 shrift: confession.

168 cousin: any relative or close friend. The informal version is **coz.**

Romeo. Not having that which having makes them
175 short.

Benvolio. In love?

Romeo. Out—

Benvolio. Of love?

180 **Romeo.** Out of her favor where I am in love.

Benvolio. Alas that love, so gentle in his view,
Should be so tyrannous and rough in proof!

Romeo. Alas that love, whose view is muffled still,
Should without eyes see pathways to his will!
185 Where shall we dine?—O me! What fray was
here?—
Yet tell me not, for I have heard it all.
Here's much to do with hate, but more with love.
Why then, O brawling love! O loving hate!
190 O anything, of nothing first create!
O heavy lightness! serious vanity!
Misshapen chaos of well-seeming forms!
Feather of lead, bright smoke, cold fire, sick health!
Still-waking sleep, that is not what it is!
195 This love feel I, that feel no love in this.
Dost thou not laugh?

Benvolio.   No, coz, I rather weep.

Romeo. Good heart, at what?

Benvolio.   At thy good heart's oppression.

200 **Romeo.** Why, such is love's transgression.
Griefs of mine own lie heavy in my breast,
Which thou wilt propagate, to have it prest
With more of thine. This love that thou hast shown
Doth add more grief to too much of mine own.
205 Love is a smoke raised with the fume of sighs;
Being purged, a fire sparkling in lovers' eyes;
Being vexed, a sea nourished with lovers' tears.
What is it else? A madness most discreet,
A choking gall, and a preserving sweet.
210 Farewell, my coz.

Benvolio.   Soft! I will go along.
An if you leave me so, you do me wrong.

Romeo. Tut! I have lost myself; I am not here:
This is not Romeo, he's some other where.

175-180 *Why has Romeo been so
depressed?*

181-184 *love:* refers to Cupid, the god
of love. Cupid is pictured as a blind boy
with wings and a bow and arrow.
Anyone hit by one of his arrows falls in
love instantly. Since he is blind, love is
blind. He looks gentle, but in reality he
can be a harsh master.

188-196 Romeo, confused and upset,
tries to describe his feelings about love
in phrases like "loving hate." Look for
other expressions in this speech made
up of pairs of words that contradict
each other. *Has love ever made you
feel this way?*

197-204 Benvolio expresses his
sympathy for Romeo. Romeo replies
that this is one more problem caused
by love. He now feels worse than
before because he must carry the
weight of Benvolio's sympathy along
with his own grief.

206 *purged:* cleansed (of the smoke).
207 *vexed:* troubled.

211 *Soft:* Wait a minute.

Benvolio. Tell me in sadness, who is that you love? 215

Romeo. What, shall I groan and tell thee?

Benvolio.   Groan? Why, no;
But sadly tell me who.

Romeo. Bid a sick man in sadness make his will.
Ah, word ill urged to one that is so ill! 220
In sadness, cousin, I do love a woman.

Benvolio. I aimed so near when I supposed you loved.

Romeo. A right good markman! And she's fair I love.

Benvolio. A right fair mark, fair coz, is soonest hit.

Romeo. Well, in that hit you miss. She'll not be hit 225
With Cupid's arrow. She hath Dian's wit,
And, in strong proof of chastity well armed,
From Love's weak childish bow she lives unharmed.
She will not stay the siege of loving terms,
Nor bide the encounter of assailing eyes, 230
Nor ope her lap to saint-seducing gold.
O, she is rich in beauty; only poor
That, when she dies, with beauty dies her store.

Benvolio. Then she hath sworn that she will still live
chaste? 235

Romeo. She hath, and in that sparing makes huge waste;
For beauty, starved with her severity,
Cuts beauty off from all posterity.
She is too fair, too wise, wisely too fair,
To merit bliss by making me despair. 240
She hath forsworn to love, and in that vow
Do I live dead that live to tell it now.

Benvolio. Be ruled by me: forget to think of her.

Romeo. O, teach me how I should forget to think!

Benvolio. By giving liberty unto thine eyes: 245
Examine other beauties.

Romeo.   'Tis the way
To call hers (exquisite) in question more.
These happy masks that kiss fair ladies' brows,
Being black, puts us in mind they hide the fair. 250
He that is strucken blind cannot forget
The precious treasure of his eyesight lost.
Show me a mistress that is passing fair,

---

215 *sadness:* seriousness

221-222 Romeo seems unaware of how foolish his dramatic confession sounds. Benvolio responds with appropriate but gentle sarcasm.
222-225 Romeo and Benvolio talk of love in terms of archery, another reference to Cupid and his love arrows.
225-228 *She'll . . . unharmed:* The girl isn't interested in falling in love. She is like Diana, the goddess of chastity, the moon, and the hunt, who avoided Cupid's arrows.

229-231 She is unmoved by Romeo's declaration of love, his adoring looks, and his wealth.

234-238 Since she has vowed to remain chaste, she will die without children, and her beauty will not be passed on to future generations *(posterity).*

240-241 *To merit . . . despair:* The girl will reach heaven *(bliss)* by being chaste, which causes Romeo *despair,* or hopelessness. *forsworn to:* sworn not to.

245-246 *What is Benvolio's advice?*

247-248 *'Tis . . . more:* That would only make me appreciate my own love's beauty more.
249 Masks were worn by Elizabethan women to protect their complexions from the sun.

What doth her beauty serve but as a note
255 Where I may read who passed that passing fair?
Farewell. Thou canst not teach me to forget.

Benvolio. I'll pay that doctrine, or else die in debt.

[Exeunt.]

257 *I'll pay . . . debt:* I'll convince you you're wrong, or die trying.

*R*esponding to Reading

1. What is your first impression of Romeo? In your journal or on a sheet of paper, jot down words that describe him.

2. What is Romeo's attitude toward love?

   Think about
   • why he says he loves the girl
   • his actions and attitude when she rejects him

3. Consider Benvolio's and Tybalt's actions in the scene. Which character would you want for a friend? Explain.

4. Why doesn't Shakespeare give reasons for the feud between the Capulets and Montagues? What reasons might cause such bitter rivalry?

5. Do you think Prince Escalus's angry warnings will stop the feuding? Why or why not?

Scene 2   *A street near the Capulet house.*

This scene opens with Count Paris, a young nobleman, asking Capulet for permission to marry his daughter, Juliet. Capulet says that Juliet is too young but gives Paris permission to court her and try to win her favor. He also invites Paris to a party he is giving that night.

   Romeo finds out about the party and discovers that Rosaline, the girl who rejected him, will be present. Benvolio urges Romeo to go to the party to see how Rosaline compares with the other women.

[Enter Capulet with Paris, a kinsman of the Prince, and Servant.]

Capulet. But Montague is bound as well as I,
   In penalty alike; and 'tis not hard, I think,
   For men so old as we to keep the peace.

1 *bound:* obligated.

"But now, my lord, what say you to my suit?"

Paris. Of honorable reckoning are you both,
5   And pity 'tis you lived at odds so long.
    But now, my lord, what say you to my suit?

Capulet. But saying o'er what I have said before:
    My child is yet a stranger in the world,
    She hath not seen the change of fourteen years;
10   Let two more summers wither in their pride
    Ere we may think her ripe to be a bride.

Paris. Younger than she are happy mothers made.

Capulet. And too soon marred are those so early made.
    The earth hath swallowed all my hopes but she;
15   She is the hopeful lady of my earth.
    But woo her, gentle Paris, get her heart;
    My will to her consent is but a part.
    An she agree, within her scope of choice
    Lies my consent and fair according voice.
20   This night I hold an old accustomed feast,
    Whereto I have invited many a guest,
    Such as I love, and you among the store,

4 *reckoning:* reputation.

6 *what say . . . suit:* Paris is asking for Capulet's response to his proposal to marry Juliet.

8-13 *My child . . . made:* Capulet repeats his claim that Juliet, still thirteen, is too young for marriage. He further argues that girls are hurt by becoming mothers too soon.

14 *The earth . . . she:* All my children are dead except Juliet.

16 *woo her:* try to win her affection.

18-19 *An . . . voice:* I will give my approval to the one she chooses.

20 *old accustomed feast:* a traditional or annual party.

One more, most welcome, makes my number more.
At my poor house look to behold this night
25 Earth-treading stars that make dark heaven light.
Such comfort as do lusty young men feel
When well-appareled April on the heel
Of limping Winter treads, even such delight
Among fresh female buds shall you this night
30 Inherit at my house. Hear all, all see,
And like her most whose merit most shall be;
Which, on more view of many, mine, being one,
May stand in number, though in reck'ning none.
Come, go with me. *[To* Servant, *giving him a paper.]*
35   Go, sirrah, trudge about
Through fair Verona; find those persons out
Whose names are written there, and to them say,
My house and welcome on their pleasure stay.

[Exeunt Capulet *and* Paris.]

Servant. Find them out whose names are written here!
40 It is written that the shoemaker should meddle with
his yard and the tailor with his last, the fisher with
his pencil and the painter with his nets; but I am
sent to find those persons whose names are here
writ, and can never find what names the writing
45 person hath here writ. I must to the learned. In
good time!

[Enter Benvolio *and* Romeo.]

Benvolio. Tut, man, one fire burns out another's
burning;
One pain is lessened by another's anguish; Turn
50 giddy, and be holp by backward turning;
One desperate grief cures with another's languish.
Take thou some new infection to thy eye,
And the rank poison of the old will die.

Romeo. Your plantain leaf is excellent for that.

55 **Benvolio.** For what, I pray thee?

Romeo.   For your broken shin.

Benvolio. Why, Romeo, art thou mad?

Romeo. Not mad, but bound more than a madman is;
Shut up in prison, kept without my food,
60 Whipped and tormented and—God-den, good
fellow.

29-33 Among . . . none: Tonight at the party you will witness **(inherit)** the loveliest young girls in Verona, including Juliet. When you see all of them together, your opinion of Juliet may change.

35 sirrah: a term used to address a servant.

38 My house . . . stay: My house and my welcome wait for their pleasure. *What does Capulet send the servant to do?*

39-42 The servant is bewildered and frustrated because he has been asked to read—a skill he does not have. He confuses the craftsmen and their tools, tapping a typical source of humor for Elizabethan clowns, then goes off to seek help.

45-46 In good time: What luck; he is referring to the arrival of Romeo and Benvolio, who look like men who can read.

47-53 Tut, man . . . die: Benvolio is still trying to convince Romeo that the best way he can be helped **(holp)** in his love for Rosaline is to find someone else. Notice that he compares love to a disease that can only be cured by another disease.

58-61 Romeo is giving Benvolio a dismal picture of how he feels when he is interrupted by Capulet's servant. **God-den:** good evening.

Servant. God gi' go-den. I pray, sir, can you read?

Romeo. Ay, mine own fortune in my misery.

Servant. Perhaps you have learned it without book. But
65   I pray, can you read anything you see?

Romeo. Ay, if I know the letters and the language.

Servant. Ye say honestly. Rest you merry!

*[Romeo's joking goes over the clown's head. He concludes
that Romeo cannot read and prepares to seek someone who
can.]*

Romeo. Stay, fellow; I can read.   *[He reads.]*
  "Signior Martino and his wife and daughters;
70   County Anselmo and his beauteous sisters;
  The lady widow of Vitruvio;

62 *God gi' go-den:* God give you a
good evening.

67 *Rest you merry:* Stay happy; a
polite form of *goodbye.*

*"Stay, fellow; I can read.
'Signior Martino and his wife . . .' "*

Signior Placentio and his lovely nieces;
Mercutio and his brother Valentine;
Mine uncle Capulet, his wife, and daughters;
My fair niece Rosaline and Livia;
Signior Valentio and his cousin Tybalt;
Lucio and the lively Helena."

[Gives back the paper.]
A fair assembly. Whither should they come?

Servant. Up.

Romeo. Whither?

Servant. To supper, to our house.

Romeo. Whose house?

Servant. My master's.

Romeo. Indeed I should have asked you that before.

Servant. Now I'll tell you without asking. My master is
the great rich Capulet; and if you be not of the
house of Montagues, I pray come and crush a cup of
wine. Rest you merry!

[Exit.]

Benvolio. At this same ancient feast of Capulet's
Sups the fair Rosaline whom thou so lovest,
With all the admired beauties of Verona.
Go thither, and with unattainted eye
Compare her face with some that I shall show,
And I will make thee think thy swan a crow.

Romeo. When the devout religion of mine eye
Maintains such falsehood, then turn tears to fires;
And these, who, often drowned, could never die,
Transparent heretics, be burnt for liars!
One fairer than my love? The all-seeing sun
Ne'er saw her match since first the world begun.

Benvolio. Tut! you saw her fair, none else being by,
Herself poised with herself in either eye;
But in that crystal scales let there be weighed
Your lady's love against some other maid
That I will show you shining at this feast,
And she shall scant show well that now shows best.

Romeo. I'll go along, no such sight to be shown,
But to rejoice in splendor of mine own.

[Exeunt.]

75 Notice that Romeo's beloved Rosaline, a Capulet, is invited to the party. (This is the first time in the play that her name is mentioned.) Mercutio, a friend of both Romeo and the Capulets, is also invited.
78 *Whither:* where.

87-88 *crush a cup of wine:* slang for "drink some wine."

92-94 *Go . . . crow:* Go to the party and, with unbiased eyes, compare Rosaline with the other beautiful girls.

95-98 *When . . . liars:* If the love I have for Rosaline, which is like a religion, changes because of such lies (that others could be more beautiful), let my tears be turned to fire and my eyes be burned. *To what does Romeo compare Rosaline's beauty?*

101-106 *Tut . . . best:* You've seen Rosaline alone; now compare her with some other woman. *How does Benvolio think Rosaline will stack up against the other girls?*

107-108 Romeo agrees to go to the party, but only to see Rosaline.

*R*esponding to Reading ─────────────────────────────

1. At this point, what is your view of Capulet as a father?

2. How do you think Capulet feels about Paris as a possible son-in-law?

   Think about
   • Capulet's discussion of Juliet's age
   • the advice he gives Paris regarding Juliet
   • why he invites Paris to the party

3. In your opinion, does Benvolio give Romeo good advice? Explain.

Scene 3   *Capulet's house.*

In this scene, you will meet Juliet, her mother, and her nurse. The Nurse, a merry and slightly crude servant, has been in charge of Juliet since her birth. Once she starts talking, she can't stop. Just before the party, Juliet's mother asks if Juliet has thought about getting married. Lady Capulet is matchmaking, trying to convince her daughter that Paris would make a good husband. Juliet responds just as you might if your parents set up a blind date for you—without much enthusiasm.

[Enter Lady Capulet *and* Nurse.*]*

Lady Capulet. Nurse, where's my daughter? Call her
   forth to me.

Nurse. Now, by my maidenhead at twelve year old,
   I bade her come. What, lamb! what, ladybird!
5   God forbid! Where's this girl? What, Juliet!

[Enter Juliet.*]*

Juliet. How now? Who calls?

Nurse. Your mother.

Juliet. Madam, I am here. What is your will?

Lady Capulet. This is the matter—Nurse, give leave
10   awhile,
   We must talk in secret. Nurse, come back again;
   I have remembered me, thou's hear our counsel.
   Thou knowest my daughter's of a pretty age.

Nurse. Faith, I can tell her age unto an hour.

15 **Lady Capulet.** She's not fourteen.

4–5 *What:* a call like "Hey, where are you?"

9–12 *give leave . . . counsel:* Lady Capulet seems flustered or nervous. First she tells the Nurse to leave, then she remembers that the Nurse knows Juliet as well as anyone and asks her to stay and listen. *of a pretty age:* of an attractive age, ready for marriage.

Nurse.   I'll lay fourteen of my teeth—
And yet, to my teen be it spoken, I have but four—
She's not fourteen. How long is it now
To Lammastide?

20 **Lady Capulet.** A fortnight and odd days.

Nurse. Even or odd, of all days in the year,
Come Lammas Eve at night shall she be fourteen.
Susan and she (God rest all Christian souls!)
Were of an age. Well, Susan is with God;
25 She was too good for me. But, as I said,
On Lammas Eve at night shall she be fourteen;
That shall she, marry; I remember it well.
'Tis since the earthquake now eleven years;
And she was weaned (I never shall forget it),
30 Of all the days of the year, upon that day.
For I had then laid wormwood to my dug,
Sitting in the sun under the dovehouse wall.
My lord and you were then at Mantua—
Nay, I do bear a brain—But, as I said,
35 When it did taste the wormwood on the nipple
Of my dug and felt it bitter, pretty fool,
To see it tetchy and fall out with the dug!
Shake, quoth the dovehouse! 'Twas no need, I trow,
To bid me trudge.
40 And since that time it is eleven years,
For then she could stand alone; nay, by the rood,
She could have run and waddled all about;
For even the day before, she broke her brow;
And then my husband (God be with his soul!
45 'A was a merry man) took up the child.
"Yea," quoth he, "dost thou fall upon thy face?
Thou wilt fall backward when thou has more wit,
Wilt thou not, Jule?" And, by my holidam,
The pretty wretch left crying, and said "Ay."
50 To see now how a jest shall come about!
I warrant, an I should live a thousand years,
I never should forget it. "Wilt thou not, Jule?"
quoth he,
And, pretty fool, it stinted, and said "Ay."

55 **Lady Capulet.** Enough of this. I pray thee hold thy
peace.

Nurse. Yes, madam. Yet I cannot choose but laugh

17 _teen:_ sorrow.

19 _Lammastide:_ August 1, a religious feast day and the day after Juliet's birthday. The feast day is now a little more than two weeks **(_a fortnight_)** away
21–54 The Nurse now begins to babble on about various memories of Juliet's childhood. She talks of her dead daughter, Susan, who was the same age as Juliet. Susan probably died in infancy, allowing for the Nurse to become a wet nurse to (breast-feed) Juliet. She remembers an earthquake that happened on the day she stopped breast-feeding Juliet **(_she was weaned_)**.

31 _laid wormwood to my dug:_ applied wormwood, a plant with a bitter taste, to her breast in order to discourage the child from breast-feeding.

37 _tetchy:_ touchy; cranky.
38–39 _shake . . . trudge:_ When the dovehouse shook, I knew enough to leave.

41 _by the rood:_ The rood is the cross on which Christ was crucified. The expression means something like "by God."
43 _broke her brow:_ cut her forehead.

46–54 _"Yea" . . . "Ay":_ To quiet Juliet after her fall, the Nurse's husband makes a crude joke, asking the baby whether she'll fall the other way (on her back) when she's older. Although at three Juliet doesn't understand the question, she stops crying **(_stinted_)** and innocently answers, "Yes." The Nurse finds this story so funny, she can't stop retelling it.

To think it should leave crying and say "Ay."
And yet, I warrant, it had upon its brow
60 A bump as big as a young cock'rel's stone;
A perilous knock; and it cried bitterly.
"Yea," quoth my husband, "fallst upon thy face?
Thou wilt fall backward when thou comest to age,
Wilt thou not, Jule?" It stinted, and said "Ay."

65 **Juliet.** And stint thou too, I pray thee, nurse, say I.

Nurse. Peace, I have done. God mark thee to his grace!
Thou wast the prettiest babe that e'er I nursed.
An I might live to see thee married once,
I have my wish.

70 **Lady Capulet.** Marry, that "marry" is the very theme
I came to talk of. Tell me, daughter Juliet,
How stands your disposition to be married?

Juliet. It is an honor that I dream not of.

Nurse. An honor? Were not I thine only nurse,
75 I would say thou hadst sucked wisdom from thy teat.

Lady Capulet. Well, think of marriage now. Younger
than you,
Here in Verona, ladies of esteem,
Are made already mothers. By my count,
80 I was your mother much upon these years
That you are now a maid. Thus then in brief:
The valiant Paris seeks you for his love.

Nurse. A man, young lady! lady, such a man
As all the world—why he's a man of wax.

85 **Lady Capulet.** Verona's summer hath not such a
flower.

Nurse. Nay, he's a flower, in faith—a very flower.

Lady Capulet. What say you? Can you love the
gentleman?
90 This night you shall behold him at our feast.
Read o'er the volume of young Paris' face,
And find delight writ there with beauty's pen;
Examine every several lineament,
And see how one another lends content;
95 And what obscured in this fair volume lies
Find written in the margent of his eyes.
This precious book of love, this unbound lover,

67 e'er: ever.

70 Lady Capulet uses the word **marry** in two different senses. The first **marry** means "by the Virgin Mary"; the second means "to wed."

80–81 I was . . . maid: I was your mother at about your age, yet you are still unmarried.

84 a man of wax: a man so perfect he could be a wax statue. Sculptors used to use wax figures as models for their works.

91–98 Read . . . cover: Lady Capulet uses an extended metaphor that compares Paris to a book that Juliet should read. Look for the similarities she points out.
93 several lineament: separate feature. Lady Capulet points out how each of Paris' features makes the others look even better.
96 margent . . . eyes: She compares Paris' eyes to the margin of the page of a book where notes are written that explain the content.

To beautify him only lacks a cover.
The fish lives in the sea, and 'tis much pride
100 For fair without the fair within to hide.
That book in many's eyes doth share the glory,
That in gold clasps locks in the golden story;
So shall you share all that he doth possess,
By having him making yourself no less.

105 **Nurse.** No less? Nay, bigger! Women grow by men.

Lady Capulet. Speak briefly, can you like of Paris' love?

Juliet. I'll look to like, if looking liking move;
But no more deep will I endart mine eye
Than your consent gives strength to make it fly.

[Enter a Servingman.*]*

110 **Servingman.** Madam, the guests are come, supper
served up, you called, my young lady asked for, the
nurse cursed in the pantry, and everything in
extremity. I must hence to wait. I beseech you follow
straight.

115 **Lady Capulet.** We follow thee. *[Exit* Servingman.*]* Juliet,
the County stays.

Nurse. Go, girl, seek happy nights to happy days.

[Exeunt.]

97–100 *This . . . hide:* This beautiful book (Paris) only needs a cover (wife) to become even better. He may be hiding even more wonderful qualities inside.

105 The Nurse can't resist one of her earthy comments. She notes that women get bigger (pregnant) when they marry.
107 *I'll look . . . move:* Juliet's playful answer means "I'll look at him with the intention of liking him, if simply looking can make me like him."

113 *extremity:* confusion. The servant is upset because everything is happening at once, and he can't handle it. ***straight:*** immediately.
116 *the County stays:* Count Paris is waiting for you.

*R*esponding to Reading

1. Contrast the personalities and characteristics of Lady Capulet and the Nurse.

2. What is the Nurse's attitude toward Juliet?
   Think about
   • her role in raising Juliet
   • her memories
   • her response to Lady Capulet's suggestion that Juliet consider Paris

3. Would Juliet be more likely to share secrets and ask favors of her mother or her Nurse?

4. At this point, what can you tell about Juliet's personality?

5. How would you feel in Juliet's place if your parents set up a blind date in hope that it might lead to marriage?

Scene 4 *A street near the Capulet house.*

It is the evening of the Capulet masque, or costume ball. Imagine the guests proceeding through the darkened streets with torches to light the way.
  Romeo and his two friends, Mercutio and Benvolio, join the procession. Their masks will prevent them from being recognized as Montagues. Mercutio and Benvolio are in a playful, partying mood, but Romeo is still depressed by his unanswered love for Rosaline. Romeo has also had a dream that warned him of the harmful consequences of this party. He senses trouble.

[*Enter* Romeo, Mercutio, Benvolio, *with five or six other* Maskers; Torchbearers.]

Romeo. What, shall this speech be spoke for our
  excuse? Or shall we on without apology?

Benvolio. The date is out of such prolixity.
  We'll have no Cupid hoodwinked with a scarf,
5   Bearing a Tartar's painted bow of lath,
  Scaring the ladies like a crowkeeper;
  Nor no without-book prologue, faintly spoke
  After the prompter, for our entrance;
  But let them measure us by what they will,
10   We'll measure them a measure, and be gone.

Romeo. Give me a torch. I am not for this ambling;
  Being but heavy, I will bear the light.

Mercutio. Nay, gentle Romeo, we must have you
  dance.

15 **Romeo.** Not I, believe me. You have dancing shoes
  With nimble soles; I have a soul of lead
  So stakes me to the ground I cannot move.

Mercutio. You are a lover. Borrow Cupid's wings
  And soar with them above a common bound.

20 **Romeo.** I am too sore enpierced with his shaft
  To soar with his light feathers, and so bound
  I cannot bound a pitch above dull woe.
  Under love's heavy burden do I sink.

Mercutio. And, to sink in it, should you burden love—
25   Too great oppression for a tender thing.

Romeo. Is love a tender thing? It is too rough,
  Too rude, too boist'rous, and it pricks like thorn.

1–10 shall this . . . be gone: Romeo asks whether they should send a messenger announcing their arrival at the party. Benvolio replies that this custom is out of date. He then lists all the things they won't use to make such an announcement. For example, **We'll have . . . crowkeeper:** We won't send someone dressed as a blindfolded Cupid, carrying a bow and looking like a scarecrow. Let them think what they want. We'll **measure them a measure** (dance one dance with them) and go.

12 heavy: sad. In spite of his mood, Romeo makes a joke based on the meanings of *heavy* and *light*.
13–33 As you read these lines, try to visualize each man. Romeo is overcome with sadness because of his lovestruck condition. Mercutio is determined to cheer him up. He is making fun of Romeo, but he is doing it in a friendly way.

Mercutio. If love be rough with you, be rough with love.
Prick love for pricking, and you beat love down.
30   Give me a case to put my visage in.
A visor for a visor! What care I
What curious eye doth quote deformities?
Here are the beetle brows shall blush for me.

Benvolio. Come, knock and enter, and no sooner in
35   But every man betake him to his legs.

Romeo. A torch for me! Let wantons light of heart
Tickle the senseless rushes with their heels;
For I am proverbed with a grandsire phrase,
I'll be a candle-holder and look on;
40   The game was ne'er so fair, and I am done.

Mercutio. Tut, dun's the mouse, the constable's own
    word!
If thou art Dun, we'll draw thee from the mire
Of, save your reverence, love, wherein thou stickst
45   Up to the ears. Come, we burn daylight, ho!

Romeo. Nay, that's not so.

Mercutio.   I mean, sir, in delay
We waste our lights in vain, like lamps by day.
Take our good meaning, for our judgment sits
50   Five times in that ere once in our five wits.

Romeo. And we mean well in going to this masque;
But 'tis no wit to go.

Mercutio. Why, may one ask?

Romeo. I dreamt a dream tonight.

55 **Mercutio.** And so did I.

Romeo. Well, what was yours?

Mercutio. That dreamers often lie.

Romeo. In bed asleep, while they do dream things
    true.

60 **Mercutio.** O, then I see Queen Mab hath been with you.
She is the fairies' midwife, and she comes
In shape no bigger than an agate stone
On the forefinger of an alderman,
Drawn with a team of little atomies
65   Athwart men's noses as they lie asleep;
Her wagon spokes made of long spinners' legs,

30–33 Give . . . for me: Give me a mask for an ugly face. I don't care if people notice my ugliness. Here, look at my heavy eyebrows.

35 betake . . . legs: dance.

36–39 Let . . . look on: Let playful people tickle the grass **(rushes)** on the floor with their dancing. I'll stick with the old saying **(grandsire phrase)** and hold a candle and watch the dancers.

41–45 Tut . . . daylight: Mercutio jokes using various meanings of the word *dun*, which sounds like Romeo's last word, *done*. He concludes by saying they should not waste time **(burn daylight)**.

60–102 In this famous speech Mercutio tries to cheer up Romeo by spinning a tale about how Queen Mab brings dreams to people. Queen Mab, queen of the fairies, was a folktale character well known to Shakespeare's audience. Mercutio is a born storyteller. He dominates the stage with his vivid descriptions, puns, and satires of people and professions. Don't worry about understanding everything in the speech. Read it instead for the language Mercutio uses and the dreamlike scene he creates.
62 agate stone: jewel for a ring.
64 atomies: tiny creatures. Note the description of Mab's tiny and delicate carriage.
66 spinners' legs: spiders' legs.

"And we mean well in going to this masque; But 'tis no wit to go."

The cover, of the wings of grasshoppers;
Her traces, of the smallest spider's web;
Her collars, of the moonshine's wat'ry beams;
70 Her whip, of cricket's bone; the lash, of film;
Her wagoner, a small grey-coated gnat,
Not half so big as a round little worm
Pricked from the lazy finger of a maid;
Her chariot is an empty hazelnut,
75 Made by the joiner squirrel or old grub,
Time out o' mind the fairies' coachmakers.
And in this state she gallops night by night
Through lovers' brains, and then they dream of love;
O'er courtiers' knees, that dream on curtsies straight;
80 O'er lawyers' fingers, who straight dream on fees;
O'er ladies' lips, who straight on kisses dream,
Which oft the angry Mab with blisters plagues,
Because their breaths with sweetmeats tainted are.
Sometime she gallops o'er a courtier's nose,
85 And then dreams he of smelling out a suit,
And sometime comes she with a tithe-pig's tail
Tickling a parson's nose as 'a lies asleep,
Then dreams he of another benefice.
Sometime she driveth o'er a soldier's neck,
90 And then dreams he of cutting foreign throats,
Of breaches, ambuscadoes, Spanish blades,
Of healths five fathom deep; and then anon
Drums in his ear, at which he starts and wakes,
And being thus frighted, swears a prayer or two
95 And sleeps again. This is that very Mab
That plaits the manes of horses in the night
And bakes the elflocks in foul sluttish hairs,
Which once untangled much misfortune bodes.
This is the hag, when maids lie on their backs,
100 That presses them and learns them first to bear,
Making them women of good carriage.
This is she—

Romeo.   Peace, peace, Mercutio, peace!
Thou talkst of nothing.

105 **Mercutio.**   True, I talk of dreams;
Which are the children of an idle brain,
Begot of nothing but vain fantasy;
Which is as thin of substance as the air,
And more inconstant than the wind, who woos
110 Even now the frozen bosom of the North

68 traces: harness.

75 joiner: carpenter.

79–81 *What does Mab make lawyers and ladies dream of?*

84–85 Sometime she . . . suit: Sometimes Mab makes a member of the king's court dream of receiving the king's special favors.

88 benefice: well-paying position for a church parson.

91 ambuscadoes: ambushes; **Spanish blades:** high-quality Spanish swords.

96 plaits: braids.

105–112 True . . . South: Mercutio is trying to keep Romeo from taking his dreams too seriously.

And, being angered, puffs away from thence,
Turning his face to the dew-dropping South.

Benvolio. This wind you talk of blows us from
ourselves.
115   Supper is done, and we shall come too late.

Romeo. I fear, too early; for my mind misgives
Some consequence, yet hanging in the stars,
Shall bitterly begin his fearful date
With this night's revels and expire the term
120   Of a despised life, closed in my breast,
By some vile forfeit of untimely death.
But he that hath the steerage of my course
Direct my sail! On, lusty gentlemen!

Benvolio. Strike, drum.

[Exeunt.]

116–121 *my mind . . . death:* Romeo will not be cheered. He fears that some terrible event, caused by the stars, will begin at the party. Remember the phrase "star-crossed lovers" from the prologue of this act.

*R*esponding to Reading

1. What kind of person is Mercutio?

2. What is Mercutio's purpose in his dream speech? Do you think he accomplishes his purpose? Explain.

3. Do you sympathize with Romeo and his continual depression? Why or why not?

4. Reread Romeo's last speech in this scene. What is he afraid of? Do you think his fears are justified? Why or why not?

Scene 5   *A hall in Capulet's house; the scene of the party.*

This is the scene of the party at which Romeo and Juliet finally meet. Romeo and his friends, disguised in their masks, arrive as uninvited guests. As he watches the dancers, Romeo suddenly sees Juliet and falls in love at first sight. At the same time, Tybalt recognizes Romeo's voice and knows he is a Montague. He alerts Capulet and threatens to kill Romeo. Capulet, however, insists that Tybalt behave himself and act like a gentleman. Promising revenge, Tybalt leaves. Romeo and Juliet meet and kiss in the middle of the dance floor. Only after they part do they learn each other's identity.

[Servingmen come forth with napkins.]

First Servingman. Where's Potpan, that he helps not to take away? He shift a trencher! he scrape a trencher!

Second Servingman. When good manners shall lie all in one or two men's hands, and they unwashed too,
5 'tis a foul thing.

First Servingman. Away with the joint-stools, remove the court-cupboard, look to the plate. Good thou, save me a piece of marchpane and, as thou lovest me, let the porter let in Susan Grindstone and Nell.
10 Anthony, and Potpan!

Second Servingman. Ay, boy, ready.

First Servingman. You are looked for and called for, asked for and sought for, in the great chamber.

Third Servingman. We cannot be here and there too.
15 Cheerly, boys! Be brisk awhile, and the longer liver take all.

[Exeunt.]

[Maskers appear with Capulet, Lady Capulet, Juliet, all the Guests, and Servants.]

Capulet. Welcome, gentlemen! Ladies that have their toes
Unplagued with corns will have a bout with you.
20 Ah ha, my mistresses! which of you all
Will now deny to dance? She that makes dainty,
She I'll swear hath corns. Am I come near ye now?
Welcome, gentlemen! I have seen the day
That I have worn a visor and could tell
25 A whispering tale in a fair lady's ear,
Such as would please. 'Tis gone, 'tis gone, 'tis gone!
You are welcome, gentlemen! Come, musicians, play.
A hall, a hall! give room! and foot it, girls.

[Music plays and they dance.]

More light, you knaves! and turn the tables up,
30 And quench the fire, the room is grown too hot.
Ah, sirrah, this unlooked-for sport comes well.
Nay, sit, nay, sit, good cousin Capulet,
For you and I are past our dancing days.
How long is't now since last yourself and I
35 Were in a mask?

Second Capulet. By'r Lady, thirty years.

1–16 The opening lines of the scene are a comic conversation among three servants as they do their work.
2 *trencher:* wooden plate.

7–8 *plate:* silverware and plates.
marchpane: marzipan, a sweet made from almond paste.

17–31 Capulet is welcoming his guests and inviting them all to dance. At the same time, like a good host, he is trying to get the party going. He alternates talking with his guests and telling the servants what to do.
21–22 *She that . . . corns:* Any woman too shy to dance will be assumed to have **corns,** ugly and painful growths on the toes.
24 *visor:* mask.

31–45 The dancing has begun, and Capulet and his relative are watching as they talk about days gone. *Although the two old men are speaking, whom do you think the audience is watching?*

Capulet. What, man? 'Tis not so much, 'tis not so
much!
'Tis since the nuptial of Lucentio,
40 Come Pentecost as quickly as it will,
Some five-and-twenty years, and then we masked.

Second Capulet. 'Tis more, 'tis more! His son is elder, sir;
His son is thirty.

Capulet. Will you tell me that?
45 His son was but a ward two years ago.

Romeo. *[To a* Servingman] What lady's that, which doth
enrich the hand of yonder knight?

Servant. I know not, sir.

Romeo. O, she doth teach the torches to burn bright!
50 It seems she hangs upon the cheek of night
Like a rich jewel in an Ethiop's ear—
Beauty too rich for use, for earth too dear!
So shows a snowy dove trooping with crows
As yonder lady o'er her fellows shows.
55 The measure done, I'll watch her place of stand
And, touching hers, make blessed my rude hand.
Did my heart love till now? Forswear it, sight!
For I ne'er saw true beauty till this night.

Tybalt. This, by his voice, should be a Montague.
60 Fetch me my rapier, boy. What, dares the slave
Come hither, covered with an antic face,
To fleer and scorn at our solemnity?
Now, by the stock and honor of my kin,
To strike him dead I hold it not a sin.

65 **Capulet.** Why, how now, kinsman? Wherefore storm
you so?

Tybalt. Uncle, this is a Montague, our foe;
A villain, that is hither come in spite
To scorn at our solemnity this night.

70 **Capulet.** Young Romeo is it?

Tybalt. 'Tis he, that villain Romeo.

Capulet. Content thee, gentle coz, let him alone.
'A bears him like a portly gentleman,
And, to say truth, Verona brags of him
75 To be a virtuous and well-governed youth.
I would not for the wealth of all this town
Here in my house do him disparagement.

46–47 Romeo has spotted Juliet across the dance hall, and he is immediately hypnotized by her beauty.

51–52 *Ethiop's ear:* the ear of an Ethiopian (African). **for earth too dear:** too precious for this world.

55–58 *The measure . . . night:* When the dance is over, Romeo will "bless" his hand by touching that of this beautiful woman. He swears that he has never loved before this moment because he's never seen true beauty before. *What seems to be Romeo's standard for falling in love?*

59–64 Tybalt recognizes Romeo's voice and tells his servant to get his sword *(rapier).* He thinks Romeo has come to mock *(fleer)* their party. *What does Tybalt want to do to Romeo?*

72–101 Capulet is not concerned about Romeo's presence and notes that the boy has a reputation for being well-mannered. He insists that Tybalt calm down and enjoy the party.

Therefore be patient, take no note of him.
It is my will; the which if thou respect,
80   Show a fair presence and put off these frowns,
An ill-beseeming semblance for a feast.

Tybalt. It fits when such a villain is a guest.
I'll not endure him.

Capulet.   He shall be endured.
85   What, goodman boy? I say he shall. Go to!
Am I the master here, or you? Go to!
You'll not endure him? God shall mend my soul!
You'll make a mutiny among my guests!
You will set cock-a-hoop! You'll be the man.

90   **Tybalt.** Why, uncle, 'tis a shame.

Capulet.   Go to, go to!
You are a saucy boy. Is't so, indeed?
This trick may chance to scathe you. I know what.
You must contrary me! Marry, 'tis time.—
95   Well said, my hearts!—You are a princox—go!
Be quiet, or—More light, more light!—For shame!
I'll make you quiet; what!—Cheerly, my hearts!

Tybalt. Patience perforce with willful choler meeting
Makes my flesh tremble in their different greeting.
100   I will withdraw; but this intrusion shall,
Now seeming sweet, convert to bitter gall.

[Exit.]

Romeo. If I profane with my unworthiest hand
This holy shrine, the gentle fine is this:
My lips, two blushing pilgrims, ready stand
105   To smooth that rough touch with a tender kiss.

Juliet. Good pilgrim, you do wrong your hand too much,
Which mannerly devotion shows in this;
For saints have hands that pilgrims' hands do touch,
110   And palm to palm is holy palmers' kiss.

Romeo. Have not saints lips, and holy palmers too?

Juliet. Ay, pilgrim, lips that they must use in prayer.

Romeo. O, then, dear saint, let lips do what hands do!
They pray; grant thou, lest faith turn to despair.

115   **Juliet.** Saints do not move, though grant for prayers'
sake.

85 *goodman boy:* a term used to address an inferior. In an angrier tone Capulet tells Tybalt that he's acting childishly and in an ungentlemanly manner. **Go to:** Stop, that's enough!
89 *set cock-a-hoop:* cause everything to be upset.

93–94 *scathe:* harm; ***what:*** what I'm doing. You dare to challenge my authority?
95–97 Capulet interrupts his angry speech with concerned comments to his guests and servants.

98–101 *Patience . . . gall:* Tybalt says he will restrain himself, being forced to; but his suppressed anger ***(choler)*** makes his body shake. *What do you think he might do about his anger?*

102–121 Think of this part of the scene as a close-up involving only Romeo and Juliet. With the party going on around them, Romeo and Juliet are at center stage, ignoring everyone else. They touch the palms of their hands together. Their conversation revolves around Romeo's comparison of his lips to pilgrims ***(palmers)*** who have traveled to visit a holy shrine, Juliet. Juliet goes along with his comparison because she feels the same way he does.

"For saints have hands that pilgrims' hands do touch, And palm to palm is holy palmers' kiss."

Romeo. Then move not while my prayer's effect I take.
Thus from my lips, by thine my sin is purged.

[Kisses her.]

Juliet. Then have my lips the sin that they have took.

120 **Romeo.** Sin from my lips? O trespass sweetly urged!
Give me my sin again.

[Kisses her.]

118 In the midst of the dancers, Romeo kisses Juliet.

Juliet. You kiss by the book.

Nurse. Madam, your mother craves a word with you.

Romeo. What is her mother?

125 **Nurse.**   Marry, bachelor,
    Her mother is the lady of the house.
    And a good lady, and a wise and virtuous.
    I nursed her daughter that you talked withal.
    I tell you, he that can lay hold of her
130   Shall have the chinks.

    Romeo.   Is she a Capulet?
    O dear account! my life is my foe's debt.

Benvolio. Away, be gone, the sport is at the best.

Romeo. Ay, so I fear; the more is my unrest.

135 **Capulet.** Nay, gentlemen, prepare not to be gone;
    We have a trifling foolish banquet towards.

[They whisper in his ear.]

    Is it e'en so? Why then, I thank you all.
    I thank you, honest gentlemen. Good night.
    More torches here! *[Exeunt* Maskers.*]* Come on then,
140   let's to bed.
    Ah, sirrah, by my fay, it waxes late;
    I'll to my rest.

[Exeunt all but Juliet *and* Nurse.*]*

Juliet. Come hither, nurse. What is yond gentleman?

Nurse. The son and heir of old Tiberio.

145 **Juliet.** What's he that now is going out of door?

Nurse. Marry, that, I think, be young Petruchio.

Juliet. What's he that follows there, that would not
    dance?

Nurse. I know not.

150 **Juliet.** Go ask his name.—If he be married,
    My grave is like to be my wedding bed.

Nurse. His name is Romeo, and a Montague,
    The only son of your great enemy.

Juliet. My only love, sprung from my only hate!
155   Too early seen unknown, and known too late!
    Prodigious birth of love it is to me

122 *kiss by the book:* Juliet could mean "You kiss like an expert, someone who has studied the correct method." Or she could be teasing Romeo, meaning "You kiss coldly, as though you had learned it by reading a book."

123–130 Because of the Nurse's message from Lady Capulet, Juliet leaves, and Romeo is left to talk with the Nurse. She informs him that Juliet is Capulet's daughter and a good catch—whoever wins her shall become rich **(have the chinks).**

132 *my life . . . debt:* my life belongs to my enemy. *How does Romeo react when he learns that Juliet is Capulet's daughter?*

136 *towards:* coming up.

143–148 Juliet asks the Nurse to identify various guests as they leave the house. *What does she really want to know?*

151 In this line Juliet tells her own fortune, although she doesn't know it.

155–156 *Too early . . . too late:* I fell in love with him before I learned who he is. ***Prodigious:*** abnormal, unlucky.

That I must love a loathed enemy.

Nurse. What's this? what's this?

Juliet. A rhyme I learnt even now
160 Of one I danced withal.

[One calls within, "Juliet."]

Nurse. Anon, anon!
Come, let's away; the strangers all are gone.

[Exeunt.]

157 *How does Juliet feel about the fact that she's fallen in love with the son of her father's enemy?*

Responding to Reading

1. Why do you think Romeo and Juliet fall in love with each other? How serious is their love? Explain.

2. What causes Capulet and his nephew Tybalt to react so differently to Romeo's presence at the party? Which reaction would you likely have had?

3. What conflicts are shown in this scene? Which do you consider most serious?

e x p l a i n

Responding to Reading

First Impressions

1. Write one or two sentences describing Romeo and one or two describing Juliet.

Second Thoughts

2. How similar are Romeo and Juliet to each other? Consider their attitudes toward love, their actions and discussion during the party, and their reactions later.

3. In your opinion, does Romeo understand his own feelings? Explain.

   Think about
   - his love for Rosaline
   - his reaction to Benvolio's and Mercutio's attempts to help him
   - the effect the sight of Juliet has on him

4. What if the characters were in modern clothing and spoke modern-day English? Which characters, situations, and conflicts would seem realistic? Which would not?

5. In your opinion, which character is the most troubled at this point in the play? Explain your choice.

Literary Concept: Foil

A **foil** is a character whose personality or actions are in striking contrast to those of another character. By using a foil, a writer highlights the other character's traits or mood. Shakespeare frequently uses a foil to emphasize the qualities of a character. For example, in Scene 4 Mercutio's merry mood, jokes, and teasing make him a foil for Romeo, who is depressed and full of self-pity.

In Scene I, how does Benvolio act as a foil for Tybalt? In Scene 3, how does the Nurse act as a foil for Lady Capulet?

Writing Options

1. Imagine that you are a gossip columnist assigned to cover the party at the Capulet mansion. Write a newspaper column in which you name guests and describe their clothing. Include any "hot" gossip from the party that would interest your readers.

2. Rewrite Romeo and Juliet's conversation in Scene 5 as modern teenagers might say it.

3. Capulet and Tybalt have a serious disagreement about how to deal with the party crashers, Romeo and his friends. Make two lists detailing the arguments presented by each side. Then write your own idea about what should be done in this situation.

4. Write a brief diary entry that Juliet might have written after talking to her mother about Paris and the upcoming party.

e   x   t   e   n   d

Options for Learning

1 **• Book Jacket** Choose one scene from Act One that you think would make an enticing cover illustration for a new edition of *Romeo and Juliet*. Design the book cover to include the title, the author, and your painted or drawn illustration.

2 **• Comedy Tonight!** Act out one of the comic speeches. You and a friend could be the servants in Scene I or Scene 5, or the Nurse and Lady Capulet in Scene 3. Exaggerate movements, gestures, and voice inflections. Present your scene to the class.

3 **• Casting Director** You have met most of the characters in this play. Cast the play with current film, television, and stage actors. Explain your choices.

4 **• Party Outfits** Research costume designs of the Elizabethan theater. Find pictures of stage productions of *Romeo and Juliet* and study the costumes. Then design an original outfit that either Juliet or Romeo might have worn to the party. Draw your costume and show it to the class.

PROLOGUE

In a sonnet the Chorus *summarizes what has happened so far in the play. He reviews how Romeo and Juliet have fallen in love and suggests both the problems and delights they now face. He also includes hints about what will result from the events of Act One.*

[Enter Chorus.]

Chorus. Now old desire doth in his deathbed lie,
    And young affection gapes to be his heir.
    That fair for which love groaned for and would die,
    With tender Juliet matched, is now not fair.
5   Now Romeo is beloved, and loves again,
    Alike bewitched by the charm of looks;
    But to his foe supposed he must complain,
    And she steal love's sweet bait from fearful hooks.
    Being held a foe, he may not have access
10   To breathe such vows as lovers use to swear,
    And she as much in love, her means much less
    To meet her new beloved anywhere;
    But passion lends them power, time means, to meet,
    Temp'ring extremities with extreme sweet.

[Exit.]

GUIDE FOR READING

1–4 old . . . heir: Romeo's love for Rosaline **(old desire)** is now dead. His new love **(young affection)** replaces the old. Compared to Juliet, Rosaline no longer seems so lovely.

6 *What attracted Romeo and Juliet to each other?*
7 But . . . complain: Juliet, a Capulet, is Romeo's enemy; yet she is the one to whom he must plead **(complain)** his love.
9–12 *What problem now faces Romeo and Juliet?*

14 Temp'ring . . . sweet: moderating great difficulties with extreme delights.

ACT TWO

Scene 1   *A lane by the wall of Capulet's orchard.*

Later in the evening of the party, Romeo returns alone to the Capulet home, hoping for another glimpse of Juliet. He climbs the wall and hides outside, in the orchard. Meanwhile, Benvolio and Mercutio come looking for him, but he remains hidden behind the wall. Mercutio makes fun of Romeo and his lovesick condition. Keep in mind that Mercutio and Benvolio think Romeo is still in love with Rosaline, since they know nothing about his meeting with Juliet.

[Enter Romeo alone.]

Romeo. Can I go forward when my heart is here?
    Turn back, dull earth, and find thy center out.

[Climbs the wall and leaps down within it.]

[Enter Benvolio with Mercutio.]

1–2 Can . . . out: How can I leave when Juliet is still here? My body **(dull earth)** has to find its heart **(center).**

Benvolio. Romeo! my cousin Romeo! Romeo!

Mercutio. He is wise,
5 And, on my life, hath stol'n him home to bed.

Benvolio. He ran this way, and leapt this orchard wall.
Call, good Mercutio.

Mercutio.   Nay, I'll conjure too.
Romeo! humors! madman! passion! lover!
10 Appear thou in the likeness of a sigh;
Speak but one rhyme, and I am satisfied!
Cry but "Ay me!" pronounce but "love" and "dove";
Speak to my gossip Venus one fair word,
One nickname for her purblind son and heir,
15 Young Adam Cupid, he that shot so trim
When King Cophetua loved the beggar maid!
He heareth not, he stirreth not, he moveth not;
The ape is dead, and I must conjure him.
I conjure thee by Rosaline's bright eyes,
20 By her high forehead and her scarlet lip,
By her fine foot, straight leg, and quivering thigh,
And the demesnes that there adjacent lie,
That in thy likeness thou appear to us!

Benvolio. An if he hear thee, thou wilt anger him.

25 **Mercutio.** This cannot anger him. 'Twould anger him
To raise a spirit in his mistress' circle
Of some strange nature, letting it there stand
Till she had laid it and conjured it down.
That were some spite; my invocation
30 Is fair and honest and in his mistress' name
I conjure only but to raise up him.

Benvolio. Come, he hath hid himself among these trees
To be consorted with the humorous night.
Blind is his love, and best befits the dark.

35 **Mercutio.** If love be blind, love cannot hit the mark.
Now will he sit under a medlar tree
And wish his mistress were that kind of fruit
As maids call medlars when they laugh alone.
Oh, Romeo, that she were, O, that she were
40 An open et cetera, thou a pop'rin pear!
Romeo, good night. I'll to my truckle bed;
This field-bed is too cold for me to sleep.
Come, shall we go?

---

8 conjure: use magic to call him.

10–23 Appear . . . us: Mercutio makes a series of loud jokes about Romeo's lovesickness. He tries to make Romeo appear by teasing him and suggestively naming parts of Rosaline's body. **demesnes:** areas.

25–31 'Twould . . . raise up him: It would anger him if I called a stranger to join his lover **(mistress),** but I'm only calling Romeo to join her.

33 To be . . . night: to join with the night, which is as gloomy as Romeo is.

36 medlar: a fruit that looks like a small, brown apple.

41–45 Romeo . . . found: Mercutio jokes that he will go to his child's bed **(truckle bed)** since he is so "innocent."

Benvolio.   Go then, for 'tis in vain
45   To seek him here that means not to be found.

[*Exeunt.*]

*R*esponding to Reading ——————————————————————

    1. How do you think Romeo feels about the jokes Mercutio makes at his expense?

    2. While Mercutio makes fun of Romeo, Benvolio says, "An if he hear thee, thou wilt anger him." What contrast does this show between Mercutio and Benvolio? Whose approach do you think is more likely to be helpful to Romeo?

    3. His friends still believe that Romeo is in love with Rosaline. Would they feel differently toward him if they knew the truth? Why or why not?

Scene 2   *Capulet's orchard.*

The following is one of the most famous scenes in all literature. The speeches contain some of the most beautiful poetry Shakespeare ever wrote.

* Juliet appears on the balcony outside her room. She cannot see Romeo, who stands in the garden just below. At the beginning of the scene, both characters are speaking private thoughts to themselves. Romeo, however, can hear Juliet as she expresses her love for him despite his family name. Eventually, he speaks directly to her, and they declare their love for each other. Just before dawn Romeo leaves to make plans for their wedding.*

[*Enter* Romeo.]

Romeo. He jests at scars that never felt a wound.

[*Enter* Juliet *above at a window.*]

But soft! What light through yonder window breaks?
   It is the East, and Juliet is the sun!
   Arise, fair sun, and kill the envious moon,
5   Who is already sick and pale with grief
   That thou her maid art far more fair than she.
   Be not her maid, since she is envious;
   Her vestal livery is but sick and green,
   And none but fools do wear it; cast it off.

1 *He jests:* Mercutio makes jokes.
What is Romeo saying about Mercutio?

2–9 *But soft...cast it off:* Romeo sees Juliet at her window. For a moment he is speechless (***But soft:*** be still), but then he describes her beauty in glowing images of light and the heavenly bodies. He compares Juliet's beauty to the sun and says the moon looks sick and green because it is jealous of her.

10 It is my lady; O, it is my love!
O that she knew she were!
She speaks, yet she says nothing. What of that?
Her eye discourses; I will answer it.
I am too bold; 'tis not to me she speaks.
15 Two of the fairest stars in all the heaven,
Having some business, do entreat her eyes
To twinkle in their spheres till they return.
What if her eyes were there, they in her head?
The brightness of her cheek would shame those stars
20 As daylight doth a lamp; her eyes in heaven
Would through the airy region stream so bright
That birds would sing and think it were not night.
See how she leans her cheek upon her hand!
O that I were a glove upon that hand,
25 That I might touch that cheek!

Juliet.   Ay me!

Romeo. She speaks.
O, speak again, bright angel! for thou art
As glorious to this night, being o'er my head,
30 As is a winged messenger of heaven
Unto the white-upturned wond'ring eyes
Of mortals that fall back to gaze on him
When he bestrides the lazy-pacing clouds
And sails upon the bosom of the air.

35 **Juliet.** O Romeo, Romeo! wherefore art thou Romeo?
Deny thy father and refuse thy name!
Or, if thou wilt not, be but sworn my love,
And I'll no longer be a Capulet.

Romeo. *[Aside]* Shall I hear more, or shall I speak at
40 this?

Juliet. 'Tis but thy name that is my enemy.
Thou art thyself, though not a Montague.
What's Montague? It is nor hand, nor foot,
Nor arm, nor face, nor any other part
45 Belonging to a man. O, be some other name!
What's in a name? That which we call a rose
By any other name would smell as sweet.
So Romeo would, were he not Romeo called,
Retain that dear perfection which he owes
50 Without that title. Romeo, doff thy name;
And for that name, which is no part of thee,
Take all myself.

11–14 O that . . . speaks: Romeo shifts back and forth between wanting to speak to Juliet and being afraid. *Why is he reluctant to let her know he is in the garden?*

15–22 Two of . . . not night: Romeo compares Juliet's eyes to stars in the sky.

26 Remember that Juliet does not know that Romeo is listening.

28–34 thou art . . . of the air: He compares Juliet to an angel **(winged messenger of heaven)** who stands over **(bestrides)** the clouds.

35–38 wherefore: why. Juliet asks why the man she loves is named Montague, a name that she is supposed to hate. *What does she ask him to do? What does she promise to do?*

46–52 Juliet tries to convince herself that a name is just a meaningless word that has nothing to do with the person. She asks Romeo to get rid of **(doff)** his name.

Romeo.   I take thee at thy word.
Call me but love, and I'll be new baptized;
55 Henceforth I never will be Romeo.

Juliet. What man art thou that, thus bescreened in night,
So stumblest on my counsel?

Romeo.   By a name
60 I know not how to tell thee who I am.
My name, dear saint, is hateful to myself,
Because it is an enemy to thee.
Had I it written, I would tear the word.

Juliet. My ears have yet not drunk a hundred words
65 Of that tongue's utterance, yet I know the sound.
Art thou not Romeo, and a Montague?

Romeo. Neither, fair saint, if either thee dislike.

Juliet. How camest thou hither, tell me, and wherefore?
70 The orchard walls are high and hard to climb,
And the place death, considering who thou art,
If any of my kinsmen find thee here.

Romeo. With love's light wings did I o'erperch these walls;
75 For stony limits cannot hold love out,
And what love can do, that dares love attempt.
Therefore thy kinsmen are no let to me.

Juliet. If they do see thee, they will murder thee.

Romeo. Alack, there lies more peril in thine eye
80 Than twenty of their swords! Look thou but sweet,
And I am proof against their enmity.

Juliet. I would not for the world they saw thee here.

Romeo. I have night's cloak to hide me from their sight;
85 And but thou love me, let them find me here.
My life were better ended by their hate
Than death prorogued, wanting of thy love.

Juliet. By whose direction foundst thou out this place?

Romeo. By love, that first did prompt me to enquire.
90 He lent me counsel, and I lent him eyes.
I am no pilot, yet, wert thou as far
As that vast shore washed with the farthest sea,

53–55 Romeo startles Juliet by speaking aloud.

56–58 How dare you, hiding **(bescreened),** listen to my private thoughts **(counsel)**?

68–69 How . . . wherefore: How did you get here, and why did you come?

73–78 With . . . thee: Love helped me climb **(o'erperch)** the walls. Neither walls nor your relatives are a hindrance **(let)** to my love. (Romeo is carried away with emotion, but Juliet is more realistic.) *What warning does she give?*

80–81 Look . . . enmity: Smile on me, and I will be defended against your family's hatred **(enmity).**

86–87 My life . . . love: I'd rather die from their hatred than have my death postponed **(prorogued)** if you don't love me.

*"If they do see thee,
they will murder thee."*

I would adventure for such merchandise.

Juliet. Thou knowest the mask of night is on my face;
95   Else would a maiden blush bepaint my cheek
For that which thou hast heard me speak tonight.
Fain would I dwell on form—fain, fain deny
What I have spoke; but farewell compliment!
Dost thou love me? I know thou wilt say "Ay";
100   And I will take thy word. Yet, if thou swearst,
Thou mayst prove false. At lovers' perjuries,
They say Jove laughs. O gentle Romeo,
If thou dost love, pronounce it faithfully.
Or if thou thinkst I am too quickly won,
105   I'll frown, and be perverse, and say thee nay,
So thou wilt woo; but else, not for the world.
In truth, fair Montague, I am too fond,
And therefore thou mayst think my 'havior light;
But trust me, gentleman, I'll prove more true
110   Than those that have more cunning to be strange.
I should have been more strange, I must confess,
But that thou overheardst, ere I was ware,
My true love's passion. Therefore pardon me,
And not impute this yielding to light love,
115   Which the dark night hath so discovered.

94–98 Thou . . . compliment: Had I known you were listening, I would have gladly **(fain)** behaved more properly, but now it's too late for good manners **(farewell compliment).** *Why is Juliet embarrassed that Romeo overheard her?*

101–102 At . . . laughs: Jove (the king of the gods) laughs at lovers who lie to each other. *Why is Juliet worried?*

104–110 if . . . strange: You might think I've fallen in love too easily and that I am too forward. But I'll be truer to you than those who hide their feelings **(be strange)** and play romantic games.

Romeo. Lady, by yonder blessed moon I swear,
That tips with silver all these fruit-tree tops—

Juliet. O, swear not by the moon, the inconstant moon,
That monthly changes in her circled orb,
120   Lest that thy love prove likewise variable.

Romeo. What shall I swear by?

Juliet.   Do not swear at all;
Or if thou wilt, swear by thy gracious self,
Which is the god of my idolatry,
125   And I'll believe thee.

Romeo.   If my heart's dear love—

Juliet. Well, do not swear. Although I joy in thee,
I have no joy of this contract tonight.
It is too rash, too unadvised, too sudden;
130   Too like the lightning, which doth cease to be
Ere one can say "It lightens." Sweet, good night!
This bud of love, by summer's ripening breath,
May prove a beauteous flow'r when next we meet.
Good night, good night! As sweet repose and rest
135   Come to thy heart as that within my breast!

Romeo. O, wilt thou leave me so unsatisfied?

Juliet. What satisfaction canst thou have tonight?

Romeo. The exchange of thy love's faithful vow for mine.

140 **Juliet.** I gave thee mine before thou didst request it;
And yet I would it were to give again.

Romeo. Wouldst thou withdraw it? For what purpose, love?

Juliet. But to be frank and give it thee again.
145   And yet I wish but for the thing I have.
My bounty is as boundless as the sea,
My love as deep; the more I give to thee,
The more I have, for both are infinite.
I hear some noise within. Dear love, adieu!

[Nurse calls within.]

150 Anon, good nurse! Sweet Montague, be true.
Stay but a little, I will come again.

[Exit.]

118–120 *swear . . .* **variable:** *Why doesn't Juliet want Romeo to swear by the moon?*

128–131 *I have . . .* **lightens:** Juliet is worried about their love **(contract)**, which has happened as quickly as lightning and could be gone as fast. *What is Juliet's attitude at this point? Do you agree with her feelings about the relationship?*

150–151 *Anon:* Right away! Juliet calls to her nurse but meanwhile asks Romeo to wait till she returns. The Nurse's repeated calls begin to create urgency and tension.

Romeo. O blessed, blessed night! I am afeard,
    Being in night, all this is but a dream,
    Too flattering-sweet to be substantial.

[Re-enter Juliet, *above.]*

155 **Juliet.** Three words, dear Romeo, and good night
    indeed.
    If that thy bent of love be honorable,
    Thy purpose marriage, send me word tomorrow,
    By one that I'll procure to come to thee,
160   Where and what time thou wilt perform the rite;
    And all my fortunes at thy foot I'll lay
    And follow thee my lord throughout the world.

Nurse. *[Within]* Madam!

Juliet. I come, anon.—But if thou meanst not well,
165   I do beseech thee—

Nurse. *[Within]*   Madam!

Juliet. By-and-by I come.—
    To cease thy suit and leave me to my grief.
    Tomorrow will I send.

170 **Romeo.**   So thrive my soul—

Juliet. A thousand times good night! *[Exit.]*

Romeo. A thousand times the worse, to want thy light!
    Love goes toward love as schoolboys from their books;
    But love from love, towards school with heavy looks.

[Enter Juliet *again, above.]*

175 **Juliet.** Hist! Romeo, hist! O for a falc'ner's voice
    To lure this tassel-gentle back again!
    Bondage is hoarse and may not speak aloud;
    Else would I tear the cave where Echo lies,
    And make her airy tongue more hoarse than mine
180   With repetition of my Romeo's name.
    Romeo!

Romeo. It is my soul that calls upon my name.
    How silver-sweet sound lovers' tongues by night,
    Like softest music to attending ears!

185 **Juliet.** Romeo!

Romeo.   My sweet?

Juliet. What o'clock tomorrow
    Shall I send to thee?

157–160 *If that . . . rite:* I'll send a messenger to you tomorrow. If your intention is to marry me, tell the messenger where and when the ceremony will be. Although in love, Juliet continues to be practical and wants proof that Romeo's intentions are serious.

173–174 *Love . . . looks:* The simile means that lovers meet as eagerly as schoolboys leave their books; lovers separate with the sadness of boys going to school.

175–181 *Hist . . . name:* Listen, Romeo, I wish I could speak your name as loudly as a falconer calls his falcon *(tassel-gentle),* but because of my parents, I must whisper. Echo was a nymph in Greek mythology whose unreturned love for Narcissus caused her to waste away until only her voice was left.

187–188 The ever-practical Juliet asks for details.

Romeo. By the hour of nine.

190 **Juliet.** I will not fail. 'Tis twenty years till then.
I have forgot why I did call thee back.

Romeo. Let me stand here till thou remember it.

Juliet. I shall forget, to have thee still stand there,
Rememb'ring how I love thy company.

195 **Romeo.** And I'll still stay, to have thee still forget,
Forgetting any other home but this.

Juliet. 'Tis almost morning. I would have thee gone—
And yet no farther than a wanton's bird,
That lets it hop a little from her hand,
200 Like a poor prisoner in his twisted gyves,
And with a silk thread plucks it back again,
So loving-jealous of his liberty.

197–202 *I would . . . liberty:* I know you must go, but I want you close to me like a pet bird that a thoughtless child *(wanton)* keeps on a string.

Romeo. I would I were thy bird.

Juliet. Sweet, so would I.
205 Yet I should kill thee with much cherishing.
Good night, good night! Parting is such sweet sorrow,
That I shall say good night till it be morrow.

[Exit.]

Romeo. Sleep dwell upon thine eyes, peace in thy
210 breast!
Would I were sleep and peace, so sweet to rest!
Hence will I to my ghostly father's cell,
His help to crave and my dear hap to tell.

[Exit.]

212–213 *ghostly father:* spiritual advisor or priest. *dear hap:* good fortune

Responding to Reading

1. At this point in the play, you have learned a great deal about the personalities of the two main characters. Describe your impressions of Romeo and Juliet.

2. In this scene both Romeo and Juliet experience the overwhelming emotions of love. In what ways are their responses to each other and their situation similar? How are they different?

3. If Juliet were in the same situation today, would her responses be similar or different? Explain.

Scene 3 *Friar Laurence's cell in the monastery.*

Romeo goes from Capulet's garden to the monastery where Friar Laurence lives. The friar knows Romeo well and often gives him advice. As the scene begins, Friar Laurence is gathering herbs in the early morning. He talks of good and bad uses for herbs. Keep this in mind, since Friar Laurence's skill at mixing herbs becomes important later in the play. Romeo tells the friar that he loves Juliet and wants to marry her. The friar is amazed that Romeo has forgotten about Rosaline so easily and suggests that Romeo might be acting in haste. Eventually, however, he agrees to marry Romeo and Juliet, hoping that the marriage might end the feud between their families.

[*Enter* Friar Laurence *alone, with a basket.*]

Friar Laurence. The grey-eyed morn smiles on the
　　frowning night,
　　Chequ'ring the Eastern clouds with streaks of light;
　　And flecked darkness like a drunkard reels
5　　From forth day's path and Titan's fiery wheels.
　　Now, ere the sun advance his burning eye
　　The day to cheer and night's dank dew to dry,
　　I must upfill this osier cage of ours
　　With baleful weeds and precious-juiced flowers.
10　The earth that's nature's mother is her tomb,
　　What is her burying grave, that is her womb;
　　And from her womb children of divers kind
　　We sucking on her natural bosom find;
　　Many for many virtues excellent,
15　None but for some, and yet all different.
　　O, mickle is the powerful grace that lies
　　In plants, herbs, stones, and their true qualities;
　　For naught so vile that on the earth doth live
　　But to the earth some special good doth give;
20　Nor aught so good but, strained from that fair use,
　　Revolts from true birth, stumbling on abuse.
　　Virtue itself turns vice, being misapplied,
　　And vice sometime's by action dignified.
　　Within the infant rind of this small flower
25　Poison hath residence, and medicine power;
　　For this, being smelt, with that part cheers each part;
　　Being tasted, slays all senses with the heart.
　　Two such opposed kings encamp them still
　　In man as well as herbs—grace and rude will;

1–31 Friar Laurence begins his speech by describing how night changes into day. He then speaks of the herbs he is collecting. The friar is particularly fascinated with the idea that in herbs as well as man both good and evil can exist.
5 Titan is the god whose chariot pulls the sun into the sky each morning.
8 osier cage: willow basket.

10–11 The earth . . . womb: The same earth that acts as a tomb, or burial ground, is also the womb, or birthplace, of useful plants.

16–19 mickle: great. The Friar says that nothing from the earth is so evil that it doesn't do some good.

24–27 Within . . . heart: He holds a flower that can be used either as a poison or a medicine. If the flower is smelled, its fragrance can improve health in each part of the body; if eaten, it causes death.
29 grace and rude will: good and evil. Both exist in people as well as in plants.

30   And where the worser is predominant,
       Full soon the canker death eats up that plant.

[Enter Romeo.*]*

Romeo. Good morrow, father.

Friar Laurence.   Benedicite!
       what early tongue so sweet saluteth me?
35   Young son, it argues a distempered head
       So soon to bid good morrow to thy bed.
       Care keeps his watch in every old man's eye,
       And where care lodges sleep will never lie;
       But where unbruised youth with unstuffed brain
40   Doth couch his limbs, there golden sleep doth reign.
       Therefore thy earliness doth me assure
       Thou art uproused with some distemp'rature;
       Or if not so, then here I hit it right—
       Our Romeo hath not been in bed tonight.

45 **Romeo.** That last is true, the sweeter rest was mine.

Friar Laurence. God pardon sin! Wast thou with
       Rosaline?

Romeo. With Rosaline, my ghostly father? No.
       I have forgot that name, and that name's woe.

50 **Friar Laurence.** That's my good son! But where hast
       thou been then?

Romeo. I'll tell thee ere thou ask it me again.
       I have been feasting with mine enemy,
       Where on a sudden one hath wounded me
55   That's by me wounded. Both our remedies
       Within thy help and holy physic lies.
       I bear no hatred, blessed man, for, lo,
       My intercession likewise steads my foe.

Friar Laurence. Be plain, good son, and homely in thy
60   drift.
       Riddling confession finds but riddling shrift.

Romeo. Then plainly know my heart's dear love is set
       On the fair daughter of rich Capulet;
       As mine on hers, so hers is set on mine,
65   And all combined, save what thou must combine
       By holy marriage. When, and where, and how
       We met, we wooed, and made exchange of vow,
       I'll tell thee as we pass; but this I pray,
       That thou consent to marry us today.

33 Benedicite (bā′ nä dē′ chē ta′): God bless you.

35–44 it argues . . . tonight: Only a disturbed **(distempered)** mind could make you get up so early. Old people may have trouble sleeping, but it is not normal for someone as young as you. Or were you up all night?

46–47 God . . . Rosaline: The Friar is shocked that Romeo has not been to bed yet. *Where does he think Romeo has been?*

52–61 Romeo tries to explain the situation and asks for help for both himself and his enemy (Juliet). In his excitement, Romeo talks in riddles, which confuse the Friar. The Friar tells Romeo to talk clearly.

70 **Friar Laurence.** Holy Saint Francis! What a change
is here!
Is Rosaline, that thou didst love so dear,
So soon forsaken? Young men's love then lies
Not truly in their hearts, but in their eyes.
75 Jesu Maria! What a deal of brine
Hath washed thy sallow cheeks for Rosaline!
How much salt water thrown away in waste,
To season love, that of it doth not taste!
The sun not yet thy sighs from heaven clears,
80 Thy old groans ring yet in mine ancient ears.
Lo, here upon thy cheek the stain doth sit
Of an old tear that is not washed off yet.
If e'er thou wast thyself, and these woes thine,
Thou and these woes were all for Rosaline.
85 And art thou changed? Pronounce this sentence then:
Women may fall when there's no strength in men.

Romeo. Thou chidst me oft for loving Rosaline.

Friar Laurence. For doting, not for loving, pupil mine.

Romeo. And badest me bury love.

90 **Friar Laurence.**   Not in a grave
To lay one in, another ought to have.

Romeo. I pray thee chide not. She whom I love now
Doth grace for grace and love for love allow.
The other did not so.

95 **Friar Laurence.**   O, she knew well
Thy love did read by rote, that could not spell.
But come, young waverer, come go with me.
In one respect I'll thy assistant be;
For this alliance may so happy prove
100 To turn your households' rancor to pure love.

Romeo. O, let us hence! I stand on sudden haste.

Friar Laurence. Wisely, and slow. They stumble that
run fast.

[Exeunt.]

73–74 Young . . . eyes: *How would you paraphrase this sentence?*

75–85 brine: salt water. The Friar is referring to the tears Romeo has been shedding for Rosaline. *What is his opinion of Romeo's rapid change of affections from one girl to another?*

86 Women . . . men: If men are so weak, women may be forgiven for sinning.
87–88 chidst: scolded. The Friar replies that he scolded Romeo for being lovesick, not for loving.

92–96 She whom . . . spell: Romeo says that the woman he loves feels the same way about him. That wasn't true of Rosaline. The Friar replies that Rosaline knew that he didn't know what real love is.

99–100 This marriage may work out well and turn the feud between your families into love.

102–103 *How is the Friar's warning similar to Juliet's fears in the previous scene?*

Responding to Reading

1. If you were Friar Laurence, would you agree to perform the wedding? Why or why not?

2. Do you think Friar Laurence has a good understanding of Romeo? What does he think of Romeo?

3. How wise do you think Friar Laurence is?

   Think about
   - his discussion of plants and people
   - his reaction and advice to Romeo
   - his reason for agreeing to marry Romeo and Juliet

Scene 4 *A street.*

Several hours after his meeting with Friar Laurence, Romeo meets Benvolio and Mercutio in the street. He is excited and happy; his mood is key to the comic nature of this scene, which includes much talk of swordplay and many suggestive jokes. Mercutio makes fun of Tybalt and teases Romeo. The Nurse comes to carry a message from Romeo to Juliet. Romeo tells her that Juliet should meet him at Friar Laurence's cell for their secret marriage ceremony.

[Enter Benvolio *and* Mercutio.*]*

Mercutio. Where the devil should this Romeo be?
  Came he not home tonight?

Benvolio. Not to his father's. I spoke with his man.

3 man: servant.

Mercutio. Why, that same pale hard-hearted wench,
5   that Rosaline,
  Torments him so that he will sure run mad.

Benvolio. Tybalt, the kinsman to old Capulet,
  Hath sent a letter to his father's house.

7–13 Tybalt . . . dared: The hot-headed Tybalt has sent a letter to Romeo, challenging him to a duel. He is obviously still angry about Romeo crashing the Capulet party. Benvolio says that Romeo will do more than answer the letter; he will accept Tybalt's challenge and fight him.

Mercutio. A challenge, on my life.

10 **Benvolio.** Romeo will answer it.

Mercutio. Any man that can write may answer a letter.

Benvolio. Nay, he will answer the letter's master, how
  he dares, being dared.

Mercutio. Alas, poor Romeo, he is already dead!
15   stabbed with a white wench's black eye; shot through

the ear with a love song; the very pin of his heart cleft with the blind bow-boy's butt-shaft; and is he a man to encounter Tybalt?

Benvolio. Why, what is Tybalt?

20 **Mercutio.** More than Prince of Cats, I can tell you. O, he's the courageous captain of compliments. He fights as you sing pricksong—keeps time, distance, and proportion; rests me his minim rest, one, two, and the third in your bosom! the very butcher of a
25 silk button, a duelist, a duelist! a gentleman of the very first house, of the first and second cause. Ah, the immortal *passado!* the *punto reverso!* the *hay!*

Benvolio. The what?

Mercutio. The pox of such antic, lisping, affecting
30 fantasticoes—these new tuners of accent! "By Jesu, a very good blade! a very tall man! a very good whore!" Why, is not this a lamentable thing, grandsire, that we should be thus afflicted with these strange flies, these fashion-mongers, these
35 perdona-mi's, who stand so much on the new form that they cannot sit at ease on the old bench? O, their bones, their bones!

[Enter Romeo, no longer moody.]

Benvolio. Here comes Romeo! here comes Romeo!

Mercutio. Without his roe, like a dried herring. O,
40 flesh, flesh, how art thou fishified! Now is he for the numbers that Petrarch flowed in. Laura, to his lady, was but a kitchen wench (marry, she had a better love to berhyme her) Dido a dowdy, Cleopatra a gypsy, Helen and Hero hildings and harlots, Thisbe
45 a grey eye or so, but not to the purpose. Signior Romeo, *bon jour!* There's a French salutation to your French slop. You gave us the counterfeit fairly last night.

Romeo. Good morrow to you both. What counterfeit
50 did I give you?

Mercutio. The slip, sir, the slip. Can you not conceive?

Romeo. Pardon, good Mercutio. My business was great, and in such a case as mine a man may strain courtesy.

---

17 blind bow-boy's butt-shaft: Cupid's dull practice arrows; Mercutio suggests that Romeo fell in love with very little work on Cupid's part.

20–27 More than . . . hay: Mercutio mocks Tybalt's name. **Prince of Cats** refers to a cat in a fable named "Tybalt" that was known for its slyness. Then Mercutio makes fun of Tybalt's fancy new method of dueling, comparing it to precision singing **(pricksong)**. *Passado, punto, reverso,* and *hay* were terms used in the new dueling style.

29–37 The pox . . . their bones: As in his previous speech, Mercutio makes fun of people, who like Tybalt, try to impress everyone with their knowledge of the latest fashions in dueling.

39–45 without his roe: he is only part of himself. Mercutio makes fun of Romeo's name and his lovesickness. **numbers:** verses. Mercutio mentions Petrarch, who wrote sonnets to his love, Laura. He then makes insulting comments about famous lovers of the past.

46–51 bon jour: *(French)* good day. Here's a greeting to match your fancy French trousers *(slop).* You did a good job of getting away from us last night. (A piece of counterfeit money was called a **slip**.)

51–97 In these lines, Romeo and Mercutio have a battle of wits. They keep trying to top each other with funnier comments and cleverer puns.

55 **Mercutio.** That's as much as to say, such a case as yours constrains a man to bow in the hams.

Romeo. Meaning, to curtsy.

Mercutio. Thou hast most kindly hit it.

Romeo. A most courteous exposition.

60 **Mercutio.** Nay, I am the very pink of courtesy.

Romeo. Pink for flower.

Mercutio. Right.

Romeo. Why, then is my pump well-flowered.

Mercutio. Well said! Follow me this jest now till thou
65   hast worn out thy pump, that, when the single sole of it is worn, the jest may remain, after the wearing, solely singular.

Romeo. Oh, single-soled jest, solely singular for the singleness!

70 **Mercutio.** Come between us, good Benvolio! My wits faint.

Romeo. Switch and spurs, switch and spurs! or I'll cry a match.

Mercutio. Nay, if our wits run the wild-goose chase, I
75   am done; for thou hast more of the wild goose in one of thy wits than, I am sure, I have in my whole five. Was I with you there for the goose?

Romeo. Thou wast never with me for anything when thou wast not there for the goose.

80 **Mercutio.** I will bite thee by the ear for that jest.

Romeo. Nay, good goose, bite not!

Mercutio. Thy wit is a very bitter sweeting; it is a most sharp sauce.

Romeo. And is it not, then, well served in to a sweet
85   goose?

Mercutio. O, here's a wit of cheveril, that stretches from an inch narrow to an ell broad!

Romeo. I stretch it out for that word "broad," which, added to the goose, proves thee far and wide a
90   broad goose.

Mercutio. Why, is not this better now than groaning

---

63 _pump:_ shoe; **_well-flowered:_** shoes were "pinked," or punched out in flowerlike designs.

72–73 _Switch . . . match:_ Keep going, or I'll claim victory.

77 _Was . . . goose?:_ Have I proved that you are a foolish person **_(goose)?_**

86 _cheveril:_ kid skin, which is flexible. Mercutio means that a little wit stretches a long way.

for love? Now art thou sociable, now art thou Romeo;
now art thou what thou art, by art as well as by
nature. For this driveling love is like a great natural
that runs lolling up and down to hide his bauble in a
hole.

Benvolio. Stop there, stop there!

Mercutio. Thou desirest me to stop in my tale against
the hair.

Benvolio. Thou wouldst else have made thy tale large.

Mercutio. O, thou art deceived! I would have made it
short; for I was come to the whole depth of my tale,
and meant indeed to occupy the argument no
longer.

[Enter Nurse *and* Peter, *her servant. He is carrying a large
fan.]*

Romeo. Here's goodly gear!

Mercutio. A sail, a sail!

Benvolio. Two, two! a shirt and a smock.

Nurse. Peter!

Peter. Anon.

Nurse. My fan, Peter.

Mercutio. Good Peter, to hide her face; for her fan's
the fairer of the two.

Nurse. God ye good morrow, gentlemen.

Mercutio. God ye good-den, fair gentlewoman.

Nurse. Is it good-den?

Mercutio. 'Tis no less, I tell ye, for the bawdy hand of
the dial is now upon the prick of noon.

Nurse. Out upon you! What a man are you!

Romeo. One, gentlewoman, that God hath made
himself to mar.

Nurse. By my troth, it is well said. "For himself to
mar," quoth'a? Gentlemen, can any of you tell me
where I may find the young Romeo?

Romeo. I can tell you; but young Romeo will be older

95 **95–97** *great natural:* an idiot like a jester or clown who carries a fool's stick *(bauble).* Mercutio is happy that Romeo is his old playful self again.

100

105

106–107 *Goodly gear:* something fine to joke about. A sail indicates that the Nurse in all her petticoats looks like a huge ship coming toward them.

110

110 *Anon:* Right away.

111 Fans were usually carried only by fine ladies. The Nurse is trying to pretend that she is more than a servant.

115

120

125

when you have found him than he was when you sought him. I am the youngest of that name, for fault of a worse.

Nurse. You say well.

130 **Mercutio.** Yea, is the worst well? Very well took, i' faith! wisely, wisely.

Nurse. If you be he, sir, I desire some confidence with you.

Benvolio. She will endite him to some supper.

135 **Mercutio.** A bawd, a bawd, a bawd! So ho!

Romeo. What hast thou found?

Mercutio. No hare, sir; unless a hare, sir, in a lenten pie, that is something stale and hoar ere it be spent.

[Sings.]

        "An old hare hoar,
140   And an old hare hoar,
        Is very good meat in Lent.
        But a hare that is hoar,
        Is too much for a score
        When it hoars ere it be spent."

145 Romeo, will you come to your father's? We'll to dinner thither.

Romeo. I will follow you.

Mercutio. Farewell, ancient lady. Farewell, *[sings]* lady, lady, lady.

[Exeunt Mercutio *and* Benvolio.*]*

150 **Nurse.** Marry, farewell! I pray you, sir, what saucy merchant was this that was so full of his ropery?

Romeo. A gentleman, nurse, that loves to hear himself talk and will speak more in a minute than he will stand to in a month.

155 **Nurse.** An 'a speak anything against me, I'll take him down, an 'a were lustier than he is, and twenty such Jacks; and if I cannot, I'll find those that shall. Scurvy knave! I am none of his flirt-gills; I am none of his skainsmates. *[Turning to* Peter.*]* And thou must
160 stand by too, and suffer every knave to use me at his pleasure?

Peter. I saw no man use you at his pleasure. If I had,

132–134 *confidence:* The Nurse means *conference;* she uses big words without understanding their meaning. Benvolio makes fun of this by using *endite* instead of *invite.*
135–145 Mercutio calls the Nurse a *bawd,* or woman who runs a house of prostitution. His song uses the insulting puns *hare,* a rabbit or a prostitute, and *hoar,* old.

151 *ropery:* roguery, or jokes.

158–161 The Nurse is angry that Mercutio treated her like one of his loose women *(flirt-gills)* or his gangsterlike friends *(skainsmates).* She then complains that Peter did not come to her defense.

my weapon should quickly have been out, I warrant
you. I dare draw as soon as another man, if I see
165   occasion in a good quarrel, and the law on my side.

Nurse. Now, afore God, I am so vexed that every part
about me quivers. Scurvy knave! Pray you, sir, a
word; and as I told you, my young lady bade me
enquire you out. What she bid me say, I will keep to
170   myself; but first let me tell ye, if ye should lead her
into a fool's paradise, as they say, it were a very gross
kind of behavior, as they say; for the gentlewoman is
young; and therefore, if you should deal double with
her, truly it were an ill thing to be offered to any
175   gentlewoman, and very weak dealing.

Romeo. Nurse, commend me to thy lady and mistress.
I protest unto thee—

169–175 The Nurse warns Romeo that he'd better mean what he said about marrying Juliet. She holds back her own news to make sure that Romeo's love is genuine.

176 *commend me:* give my respectful greetings.

"Now, afore God, I am so vexed that every part about me quivers. Scurvy Knave!"

Nurse. Good heart, and i' faith I will tell her as much.
Lord, Lord! she will be a joyful woman.

180 **Romeo.** What wilt thou tell her, nurse? Thou dost not
mark me.

Nurse. I will tell her, sir, that you do protest, which, as
I take it, is a gentlemanlike offer.

Romeo. Bid her devise
185 Some means to come to shrift this afternoon;
And there she shall at Friar Laurence' cell
Be shrived and married. Here is for thy pains.

Nurse. No, truly, sir; not a penny.

Romeo. Go to! I say you shall.

190 **Nurse.** This afternoon, sir? Well, she shall be there.

Romeo. And stay, good nurse, behind the abbey wall.
Within this hour my man shall be with thee
And bring thee cords made like a tackled stair,
Which to the high topgallant of my joy
195 Must be my convoy in the secret night.
Farewell. Be trusty, and I'll quit thy pains.
Farewell. Commend me to thy mistress.

Nurse. Now God in heaven bless thee! Hark you, sir.

Romeo. What sayst thou, my dear nurse?

200 **Nurse.** Is your man secret? Did you ne'er hear say,
Two may keep counsel, putting one away?

Romeo. I warrant thee my man's as true as steel.

Nurse. Well, sir, my mistress is the sweetest lady. Lord,
Lord! when 'twas a little prating thing—O, there is a
205 nobleman in town, one Paris, that would fain lay
knife aboard; but she, good soul, had as lief see a
toad, a very toad, as see him. I anger her sometimes,
and tell her that Paris is the properer man; but
I'll warrant you, when I say so, she looks as pale as
210 any clout in the versal world. Doth not rosemary and
Romeo begin both with a letter?

Romeo. Ay, nurse, what of that? Both with an R.

Nurse. Ah, mocker! that's the dog's name. R is for
the—No; I know it begins with some other letter;
215 and she hath the prettiest sententious of it, of you
and rosemary, that it would do you good to hear it.

184–187 Romeo tells the Nurse to have Juliet come to Friar Laurence's cell this afternoon using the excuse that she is going to confession **(shrift)**. There she will receive forgiveness for her sins **(be shrived)** and be married.

193 tackled stair: a rope ladder. **topgallant:** highest point.

196–201 quit thy pains: reward you. The Nurse asks Romeo if his servant can be trusted and quotes the saying that two can keep a secret, but not three.

203–207 The Nurse, as is her way, begins to babble on and on. She mentions Paris's proposal but says Juliet would rather look at a toad than at Paris.

210–216 clout . . . world: old cloth in the entire world. **Doth not . . . hear it:** The Nurse tries to recall a clever saying that Juliet made up about Romeo and rosemary, the herb for remembrance, but she cannot remember it. She is sure that the two words couldn't begin with *R* because this letter sounds like a snarling dog. The Nurse mistakenly says **sententious** when she means *sentences*.

Romeo. Commend me to thy lady.

Nurse. Ay, a thousand times. *[Exit* Romeo.*]* Peter!

Peter. Anon.

220 **Nurse.** Peter, take my fan, and go before, and apace.

[Exeunt.]

220 *apace:* quickly.

*R*esponding to Reading

1. Why does Mercutio think Romeo is in such a good mood? Why do you think Romeo doesn't share his plans with his friends?

2. Which character do you like better—Mercutio or Benvolio? How do their personalities differ?

Think about

• how each thinks Romeo will respond to Tybalt's challenge
• their behavior and attitudes

3. What is the Nurse's opinion of Romeo? Why does she feel this way?

Scene 5   *Capulet's orchard.*

Juliet is a nervous wreck, having waited for more than three hours for the Nurse to return. When the Nurse does arrive, she simply can't come to the point. Juliet gets more and more upset, until the Nurse finally reveals the wedding arrangements.

[Enter Juliet.*]*

Juliet. The clock struck nine when I did send the nurse;
In half an hour she promised to return.
Perchance she cannot meet him. That's not so.
O, she is lame! Love's heralds should be thoughts,
5   Which ten times faster glide than the sun's beams
Driving back shadows over lowering hills.
Therefore do nimble-pinioned doves draw Love,
And therefore hath the wind-swift Cupid wings.
Now is the sun upon the highmost hill
10   Of this day's journey, and from nine till twelve
Is three long hours; yet she is not come.
Had she affections and warm youthful blood,
She would be as swift in motion as a ball;
My words would bandy her to my sweet love,
15   And his to me.

4–6 *Love's . . . hills:* Love's messengers should be thoughts, which travel ten times faster than sunbeams.

14 *bandy:* toss.

But old folks, many feign as they were dead—
Unwieldy, slow, heavy, and pale as lead.

[Enter Nurse *and* Peter.]

O God, she comes! O honey nurse, what news?
Hast thou met with him? Send thy man away.

20 **Nurse.** Peter, stay at the gate.

[Exit Peter.]

Juliet. Now, good sweet nurse—O Lord, why lookst
    thou sad?
Though news be sad, yet tell them merrily;
If good, thou shamest the music of sweet news
25 By playing it to me with so sour a face.

Nurse. I am aweary, give me leave awhile.
Fie, how my bones ache! What a jaunce have I had!

Juliet. I would thou hadst my bones, and I thy news.
Nay, come, I pray thee speak. Good, good nurse,
30 speak.

Nurse. Jesu, what haste! Can you not stay awhile?
Do you not see that I am out of breath?

Juliet. How art thou out of breath when thou hast
    breath
35 To say to me that thou art out of breath?
The excuse that thou dost make in this delay
Is longer than the tale thou dost excuse.
Is thy news good or bad? Answer to that.
Say either, and I'll stay the circumstance.
40 Let me be satisfied, is't good or bad?

Nurse. Well, you have made a simple choice; you know
not how to choose a man. Romeo? No, not he.
Though his face be better than any man's, yet his leg
excels all men's; and for a hand and a foot, and a
45 body, though they be not to be talked on, yet they
are past compare. He is not the flower of courtesy,
but, I'll warrant him, as gentle as a lamb. Go thy
ways, wench; serve God. What, have you dined at
home?

50 **Juliet.** No, no. But all this did I know before.
What say he of our marriage? What of that?

Nurse. Lord, how my head aches! What a head have I!
It beats as it would fall in twenty pieces.

16 feign as: act as if.

21–22 The Nurse teases Juliet by putting on a sad face as if the news were bad.

26–27 give me . . . I had: Leave me alone for a while. I ache all over because of the running back and forth I've been doing.

39–40 Say . . . bad: Tell me if the news is good or bad, and I'll wait for the details.
41 simple: foolish.

My back o' t' other side—ah, my back, my back!
55 Beshrew your heart for sending me about
To catch my death with jauncing up and down!

Juliet. I' faith, I am sorry that thou art not well.
Sweet, sweet, sweet nurse, tell me, what says my love?

Nurse. Your love says, like an honest gentleman, and a
60 courteous, and a kind, and a handsome, and, I
warrant, a virtuous—Where is your mother?

Juliet. Where is my mother? Why, she is within.
Where should she be? How oddly thou repliest!
"Your love says, like an honest gentleman,
65 'Where is your mother?' "

Nurse. O God's Lady dear!
Are you so hot? Marry come up, I trow.
Is this the poultice for my aching bones?
Henceforward do your messages yourself.

70 **Juliet.** Here's such a coil! Come, what says Romeo?

Nurse. Have you got leave to go to shrift today?

Juliet. I have.

Nurse. Then hie you hence to Friar Laurence' cell;
There stays a husband to make you a wife.
75 Now comes the wanton blood up in your cheeks:
They'll be in scarlet straight at any news.
Hie you to church; I must another way,
To fetch a ladder, by the which your love
Must climb a bird's nest soon when it is dark.
80 I am the drudge, and toil in your delight;
But you shall bear the burden soon at night.
Go; I'll to dinner; hie you to the cell.

Juliet. Hie to high fortune! Honest nurse, farewell.

[Exeunt.]

Scene 6 *Friar Laurence's cell.*

Friar Laurence cautions Romeo to be more sensible in his love for Juliet. When she arrives, the two confess their love to each other and prepare to be married by Friar Laurence.

[Enter Friar Laurence *and* Romeo.*]*

Friar Laurence. So smile the heavens upon this holy act
That after-hours with sorrow chide us not!

55–56 *Beshrew . . . down:* Curse you for making me endanger my health by running around. *Considering the Nurse's feelings for Juliet, is this really an angry curse?*

66–69 *O God's . . . yourself:* Are you so eager? Control yourself *(come up)*. Is this the treatment I get for my pain? From now on, run your own errands.

70 *coil:* fuss.

71–73 *Have you . . . cell:* Do you have permission to go to confession today? Then go quickly to Friar Laurence's cell, where Romeo wants to marry you.

77–79 The Nurse will get the ladder that Romeo will use to climb to Juliet's room after they are married.

1–2 *So smile . . . us not:* May heaven bless this act and not blame us for it in the future *(after-hours).*

Romeo. Amen, amen! But come what sorrow can,
It cannot countervail the exchange of joy

5 That one short minute gives me in her sight.
Do thou but close our hands with holy words,
Then love-devouring death do what he dare—
It is enough I may but call her mine.

Friar Laurence. These violent delights have violent
10 ends
And in their triumph die, like fire and powder,
Which, as they kiss, consume. The sweetest honey
Is loathsome in his own deliciousness
And in the taste confounds the appetite.
15 Therefore love moderately: long love doth so;
Too swift arrives as tardy as too slow.

[Enter Juliet.*]*

Here comes the lady. O, so light a foot
Will ne'er wear out the everlasting flint.
A lover may bestride the gossamer
20 That idles in the wanton summer air,
And yet not fall; so light is vanity.

Juliet. Good even to my ghostly confessor.

Friar Laurence. Romeo shall thank thee, daughter, for
us both.

25 **Juliet.** As much to him, else is his thanks too much.

Romeo. Ah, Juliet, if the measure of thy joy
Be heaped like mine, and that thy skill be more
To blazon it, then sweeten with thy breath
This neighbor air, and let rich music's tongue
30 Unfold the imagined happiness that both
Receive in either by this dear encounter.

Juliet. Conceit, more rich in matter than in words,
Brags of his substance, not of ornament.
They are but beggars that can count their worth;
35 But my true love is grown to such excess
I cannot sum up sum of half my wealth.

Friar Laurence. Come, come with me, and we will
make short work;
For, by your leaves, you shall not stay alone
40 Till Holy Church incorporate two in one.

[Exeunt.]

3–8 come what . . . mine: No future sorrow can outweigh **(countervail)** the joy Juliet brings me. Once we're married, I don't even care if I die.

9–16 These . . . slow: The Friar compares Romeo's passion to gunpowder and the fire that ignites it: both are destroyed; then to honey, whose sweetness can destroy the appetite. He reminds Romeo to practice moderation in love. *How likely is it that Romeo will follow this advice?*

19–21 A lover . . . vanity: A lover can walk across a spider's web **(gossamer),** almost like walking on air.

22 ghostly confessor: spiritual advisor.

25 As much to him: The same greeting to Romeo that he offers to me.
26–31 If you are as happy as I am and have more skill to proclaim it, then sweeten the air by singing of our happiness to the world.

32–33 Conceit . . . ornament: True understanding **(conceit)** needs no words.

39–40 you shall . . . one: Until I have performed the wedding ceremony, I will not allow you to be alone together.

"But my true love is grown to such excess I cannot sum up sum of half my wealth."

Responding to Reading

1. Why does the Nurse put Juliet through so much torture before giving her Romeo's message?

2. What does Friar Laurence mean when he warns Romeo that "violent delights have violent ends"? Is this warning justified? Why or why not?

3. If you were either Romeo or Juliet, how would you plan to announce your marriage to your parents?

Responding to Reading

First Impressions

1. How do you feel about the speed of this romance?

Second Thoughts

2. Do you think Romeo and Juliet do the right thing by marrying before anyone can object? Why or why not?

   Think about
   • how long they've known each other
   • why Juliet proposes marriage
   • what their families might do if they find out about the romance

3. In your opinion, do Friar Laurence and the Nurse act responsibly in helping Romeo and Juliet to marry? Explain.

4. What are the possible consequences of this marriage ceremony?

   Think about
   • how both sets of parents will react
   • how Tybalt will react
   • how Paris will react

5. What is the best thing that could happen in the remaining acts of the play? What is the worst thing that could happen?

Literary Concept: Soliloquy

A **soliloquy** is a speech that a character gives when he or she is alone. Its purpose is to let the audience know what the character is thinking.
Reread Friar Laurence's soliloquy in Scene 3, lines 1–31. What important ideas does he discuss? Reread Juliet's soliloquy in Scene 5, lines 1–17. How would you describe her emotional state?

Writing Options

1. Imagine that you are a close friend of either Romeo or Juliet. Write the advice you would give your friend before the wedding took place.

2. How closely does this romance resemble modern love and courtship? Compare Romeo and Juliet's actions and feelings with those of couples today.

3. Remember that **foreshadowing** is the technique of giving clues that usually warn of bad things to come. Find and list examples of foreshadowing in this act.

4. Think about the Nurse. Why do you think she participates in this plan? Is she out for her own gain, or does she truly think that the young couple will be happy? Write your opinion.

e x t e n d

Options for Learning

1 • **On Stage** Find out about the theaters in London during Shakespeare's time. Use encyclopedias and other reference works to find answers to the following questions. Present your findings to the class.

Besides the Globe Theatre, what other theaters existed in London?

What features did all theaters have in common? What features differed?

What kind of social standing did actors have at the time?

2 • **Balcony Setting** Shakespeare gives very little description of the setting for Romeo and Juliet's secret talk. Imagine that you are the set designer planning the scenery for Act 2, Scene 2. Draw a picture or build a model of what the audience would see on stage. Ignore any stage settings you've seen for the play; rely as much as possible on your own imagination.

3 • **Cupid's Arrows** Shakespeare's plays are filled with allusions to Greek and Roman mythology. In this play, Cupid, the Roman god of love, is mentioned frequently. Find at least two Roman myths in which Cupid plays an important part. Using details from this play, the myths, and other sources you find through research, illustrate Cupid as you imagine him.

4 • **Mercutio's Mockery** Throughout this act, Mercutio makes fun of Romeo's lovesick condition. Decide whether Mercutio is genuinely worried about his friend or is simply laughing at him. Then act out his teasing as it would sound today. Make sure his attitude toward Romeo is reflected in your performance.

ACT THREE

Scene 1 *A public place.*

Act Two ended with the joyful Romeo and Juliet secretly married. Their happiness, however, is about to end abruptly. In this scene, Mercutio, Benvolio, and Romeo meet Tybalt on the street. Tybalt insults Romeo, but Romeo, who has just returned from his wedding, remains calm. Mercutio, on the other hand, is furious with Tybalt, and they begin to fight. As Romeo tries to separate them, Tybalt stabs Mercutio, who later dies. Romeo then challenges Tybalt, kills him, and flees. The Prince arrives and demands an explanation. He announces that Romeo will be killed if he does not leave Verona immediately.

[Enter Mercutio, Benvolio, Page and Servants.]

Benvolio. I pray thee, good Mercutio, let's retire.
The day is hot, the Capulets abroad,
And if we meet, we shall not scape a brawl,
For now, these hot days, is the mad blood stirring.

GUIDE FOR READING

3–4 we shall . . . stirring: We shall not avoid a fight since the heat makes people angry.

5 **Mercutio.** Thou art like one of those fellows that, when he enters the confines of a tavern, claps me his sword upon the table and says "God send me no need of thee!" and by the operation of the second cup draws him on the drawer, when indeed there is
10 no need.

8–9 by the . . . drawer: feeling the effects of a second drink, is ready to fight **(draw on)** the waiter who's pouring drinks **(drawer)**.

Benvolio. Am I like such a fellow?

Mercutio. Come, come, thou art as hot a Jack in thy mood as any in Italy; and as soon moved to be moody, and as soon moody to be moved.

13–14 as soon moved . . . to be moved: as likely to get angry and start a fight.

15 **Benvolio.** And what to?

Mercutio. Nay an there were two such, we should have none shortly, for one would kill the other. Thou! why, thou wilt quarrel with a man that hath a hair more or a hair less in his beard than thou hast. Thou
20 wilt quarrel with a man for cracking nuts, having no other reason but because thou hast hazel eyes. What eye but such an eye would spy out such a quarrel? Thy head is as full of quarrels as an egg is full of meat; and yet thy head hath been beaten as addle as an egg for quarreling. Thou hast quarreled with a
25 man for coughing in the street, because he hath wakened thy dog that hath lain asleep in the sun.

16–31 Picture Mercutio and Benvolio playfully roughing each other up as this conversation proceeds. Mercutio teases his friend by insisting that Benvolio is quick to pick a fight. However, everyone knows that Benvolio is gentle and peace loving. Mercutio could have been describing himself.

Didst thou not fall out with a tailor for wearing his new doublet before Easter? with another for tying
30   his new shoes with old riband? And yet thou wilt tutor me from quarreling!

Benvolio. An I were so apt to quarrel as thou art, any man should buy the fee simple of my life for an hour and a quarter.

35 **Mercutio.** The fee simple? O simple!

[Enter Tybalt and others.]

Benvolio. By my head, here come the Capulets.

Mercutio. By my heel, I care not.

Tybalt. Follow me close, for I will speak to them. Gentlemen, good den. A word with one of you.

40 **Mercutio.** And but one word with one of us? Couple it with something; make it a word and a blow.

Tybalt. You shall find me apt enough to that, sir, an you will give me occasion.

45 **Mercutio.** Could you not take some occasion without giving?

Tybalt. Mercutio, thou consortest with Romeo.

Mercutio. Consort? What, dost thou make us minstrels? An thou make minstrels of us, look to hear nothing
50   but discords. Here's my fiddlestick; here's that shall make you dance. Zounds, consort!

Benvolio. We talk here in the public haunt of men. Either withdraw unto some private place And reason coldly of your grievances,
55   Or else depart. Here all eyes gaze on us.

Mercutio. Men's eyes were made to look, and let them gaze. I will not budge for no man's pleasure, I.

[Enter Romeo.]

Tybalt. Well, peace be with you, sir. Here comes my man.

60 **Mercutio.** But I'll be hanged, sir, if he wear your livery. Marry, go before to field, he'll be your follower! Your worship in that sense may call him man.

Tybalt. Romeo, the love I bear thee can afford

29–30 *doublet:* jacket. ***riband:*** ribbon or laces.

32–34 *An I . . . quarter:* If I picked fights as quickly as you do, anybody could own me for the smallest amount of money.

36 *What do you predict will happen now that Tybalt has appeared?*

38–57 As you read this exchange, ask yourself, *Who is responsible for starting this fight?*

41–44 Mercutio dares Tybalt to add a punch *(blow)* to whatever he has to say. Tybalt says he'll do so if Mercutio gives him an excuse.

47–51 *consortest:* keep company with. Tybalt means "You are friendly with Romeo." Mercutio pretends to misunderstand him, assuming that Tybalt is insulting him by calling Romeo and himself a **consort,** a group of traveling musicians. He then refers to his sword as his **fiddlestick,** the bow for a fiddle.
52–55 Benvolio steps between Tybalt and Mercutio, trying to keep peace between them. *What does he suggest they do?*

58–61 When Romeo enters, Mercutio again pretends to misunderstand Tybalt. By ***my man,*** Tybalt means "the man I'm looking for." Mercutio takes it to mean "my servant." (**Livery** is a servant's uniform.) He assures Tybalt that the only place Romeo would follow him as a servant is to the dueling field.

No better term than this: thou art a villain.

65 **Romeo.** Tybalt, the reason that I have to love thee
Doth much excuse the appertaining rage
To such a greeting. Villain am I none.
Therefore farewell. I see thou knowst me not.

Tybalt. Boy, this shall not excuse the injuries
70 That thou hast done me; therefore turn and draw.

Romeo. I do protest I never injured thee,
But love thee better than thou canst devise
Till thou shalt know the reason of my love;
And so, good Capulet, which name I tender
75 As dearly as mine own, be satisfied.

Mercutio. O calm, dishonorable, vile submission!
Alla stoccata carries it away.

[Draws.]

Tybalt, you ratcatcher, will you walk?

Tybalt. What wouldst thou have with me?

80 **Mercutio.** Good King of Cats, nothing but one of your
nine lives. That I mean to make bold withal, and, as
you shall use me hereafter, dry-beat the rest of the
eight. Will you pluck your sword out of his pilcher
by the ears? Make haste, lest mine be about your ears
85 ere it be out.

Tybalt. I am for you.

[Draws.]

Romeo. Gentle Mercutio, put thy rapier up.

Mercutio. Come, sir, your *passado!*

[They fight.]

Romeo. Draw, Benvolio; beat down their weapons.
90 Gentlemen, for shame! forbear this outrage!
Tybalt, Mercutio, the Prince expressly hath
Forbid this bandying in Verona streets.
Hold, Tybalt! Good Mercutio!

*[Tybalt, under Romeo's arm, thrusts Mercutio
in, and flies with his Men.]*

Mercutio. I am hurt.
95 A plague o' both your houses! I am sped.
Is he gone and hath nothing?

65–68 I forgive your anger because I have reason to love you. *What reason is Romeo referring to? Who else knows about this reason?*

69 *Boy:* an insulting term of address to Romeo.

74 *tender:* cherish.

76–78 Mercutio is disgusted by Romeo's calm response to Tybalt and assumes that Romeo is afraid to fight. ***Alla stoccata*** is a move used in sword fighting. Mercutio calls Tybalt a ***ratcatcher,*** an insult based on Tybalt's name. Then he dares him to step aside and fight ***(walk)***.

81–83 *I mean . . . eight:* I intend to take one of your nine lives (as a cat has) and give a beating to the other eight.

88 Be on your guard; I'm about to attack. (A ***passado*** is a move used in sword fighting.)

89–93 Imagine a sword fight between Tybalt and Mercutio. Romeo, off to the side with Benvolio, is frantic at what is happening. He wants desperately to stop this fighting ***(bandying)*** between his friend and his new in-law. He steps between the duellers and manages to hold Mercutio, but Tybalt stabs Mercutio under Romeo's arm.

95 *A plague . . . sped:* I curse both the Montagues and the Capulets. I am destroyed.

Tybalt, under Romeo's arm, thrusts Mercutio in,

Benvolio. What, art thou hurt?

Mercutio. Ay, ay, a scratch, a scratch. Marry, 'tis enough.

100 Where is my page? Go, villain, fetch a surgeon.

[Exit Page.]

Romeo. Courage, man. The hurt cannot be much.

Mercutio. No, 'tis not so deep as a well, nor so wide as a church door; but 'tis enough, 'twill serve. Ask for me tomorrow, and you shall find me a grave man. I

105 am peppered, I warrant, for this world. A plague o' both your houses! Zounds, a dog, a rat, a mouse, a cat, to scratch a man to death! A braggart, a rogue, a villain, that fights by the book of arithmetic! Why the devil came you between us? I was hurt under your

110 arm.

Romeo. I thought all for the best.

Mercutio. Help me into some house, Benvolio,
Or I shall faint. A plague o' both your houses!
They have made worms' meat of me. I have it,

115 And soundly too. Your houses!

[Exit, supported by Benvolio.]

Romeo. This gentleman, the Prince's near ally,
My very friend, hath got this mortal hurt
In my behalf—my reputation stained

102–110 Picture Mercutio lying on the ground, bleeding, surrounded by horrified friends. Even as he is dying, he continues to joke and to make nasty remarks about Tybalt. He makes a pun on the word **grave.**

116–122 My true friend is dying because of me. My reputation has been damaged by a man who has been my relative for only an hour. My love for Juliet has made me less manly and brave.

With Tybalt's slander—Tybalt, that an hour
120   Hath been my kinsman, O sweet Juliet,
    Thy beauty hath made me effeminate
    And in my temper softened valor's steel!

[Re-enter Benvolio.]

Benvolio. O Romeo, Romeo, brave Mercutio's dead!
    That gallant spirit hath aspired the clouds,
125   Which too untimely here did scorn the earth.

124 aspired: soared to.

Romeo. This day's black fate on mo days doth depend;
    This but begins the woe others must end.

126–127 This awful day will be followed by more of the same.

[Re-enter Tybalt.]

Benvolio. Here comes the furious Tybalt back again.

Romeo. Alive in triumph, and Mercutio slain?
130   Away to heaven respective lenity,
    And fire-eyed fury be my conduct now!
    Now, Tybalt, take the "villain" back again
    That late thou gavest me, for Mercutio's soul
    Is but a little way above our heads,
135   Staying for thine to keep him company.
    Either thou or I, or both, must go with him.

129–136 Romeo sees Tybalt still living, while Mercutio lies dead. *What challenge does Romeo make to Tybalt?*

Tybalt. Thou, wretched boy, that didst consort him here,
    Shalt with him hence.

140 **Romeo.**   This shall determine that.

[They fight. Tybalt falls.]

140 Imagine the sword fight between the two men, which probably goes on for several minutes. The fight ends with Romeo running his sword through Tybalt.

Benvolio. Romeo, away, be gone!
    The citizens are up, and Tybalt slain.
    Stand not amazed. The Prince will doom thee death
    If thou art taken. Hence, be gone, away!

141–144 Don't just stand there! The Prince will sentence you to death if he catches you.

145 **Romeo.** O, I am fortune's fool!

Benvolio.   Why dost thou stay?

145 I am fortune's fool: Fate has made a fool of me.

[Exit Romeo.]

[Enter Citizens.]

Citizen. Which way ran he that killed Mercutio?
    Tybalt, that murderer, which way ran he?

Benvolio. There lies that Tybalt.

150 **Citizen.**   Up, sir, go with me.
    I charge thee in the Prince's name obey.

[*Enter* Prince *with his* Attendants, Montague,
Capulet, *their* Wives, *and* others.*]*

Prince. Where are the vile beginners of this fray?

Benvolio. O noble Prince, I can discover all
    The unlucky manage of this fatal brawl.
155   There lies the man, slain by young Romeo,
    That slew thy kinsman, brave Mercutio.

Lady Capulet. Tybalt, my cousin! O my brother's child!
    O Prince! O cousin! O husband! O, the blood is
    spilled
160   Of my dear kinsman! Prince, as thou art true,

153–154 Benvolio says he can tell
(*discover*) what happened.

160–161 *as thou . . .* **Montague:** If
your word is good, you will sentence
Romeo to death for killing a Capulet.

"And fire-eyed fury be my conduct now!"

For blood of ours shed blood of Montague.
O cousin, cousin!

Prince. Benvolio, who began this bloody fray?

Benvolio. Tybalt, here slain, whom Romeo's hand did
165   slay.
Romeo, that spoke him fair, bid him bethink
How nice the quarrel was, and urged withal
Your high displeasure. All this—uttered
With gentle breath, calm look, knees humbly
170   bowed—
Could not take truce with the unruly spleen
Of Tybalt deaf to peace, but that he tilts
With piercing steel at bold Mercutio's breast;
Who, all as hot, turns deadly point to point,
175   And, with a martial scorn, with one hand beats
Cold death aside and with the other sends
It back to Tybalt, whose dexterity
Retorts it. Romeo he cries aloud,
"Hold, friends! friends, part!" and swifter than his
180   tongue,
His agile arm beats down their fatal points,
And 'twixt them rushes; underneath whose arm
An envious thrust from Tybalt hit the life
Of stout Mercutio, and then Tybalt fled,
185   But by-and-by comes back to Romeo,
Who had but newly entertained revenge,
And to't they go like lightning; for, ere I
Could draw to part them, was stout Tybalt slain;
And, as he fell, did Romeo turn and fly.
190   This is the truth, or let Benvolio die.

Lady Capulet. He is a kinsman to the Montague;
Affection makes him false, he speaks not true.
Some twenty of them fought in this black strife,
And all those twenty could but kill one life.
195   I beg for justice, which thou, Prince, must give.
Romeo slew Tybalt; Romeo must not live.

Prince. Romeo slew him; he slew Mercutio.
Who now the price of his dear blood doth owe?
Montague. Not Romeo, Prince; he was Mercutio's
200   friend;
His fault concludes but what the law should end,
The life of Tybalt.

164–190 Benvolio explains what has just happened. *How accurate is his retelling?*

166–167 *Romeo that . . . was:* Romeo talked calmly *(fair)* and told Tybalt to think how trivial *(nice)* the argument was.

171–172 *Could . . . peace:* All this could not quiet Tybalt's anger; he would not listen to pleas for peace.

181–182 *His agile . . . rushes:* He rushed between them and pushed down their swords.

186 *entertained:* thought of.

191–192 *Why does Lady Capulet think Benvolio is lying? What wild accusation does she go on to make?*

201–202 Romeo is guilty only of avenging Mercutio's death, which the law would have done anyway.

"I beg for justice, which thou, Prince, must give. Romeo slew Tybalt; Romeo must not live."

Prince.   And for that offense
             Immediately we do exile him hence.
205   I have an interest in your hate's proceeding,
             My blood for your rude brawls doth lie a-bleeding;
             But I'll amerce you with so strong a fine
             That you shall all repent the loss of mine.
             I will be deaf to pleading and excuses;
210   Nor tears nor prayers shall purchase out abuses.
             Therefore use none. Let Romeo hence in haste,
             Else, when he is found, that hour is his last.
             Bear hence this body, and attend our will.
             Mercy but murders, pardoning those that kill.

[Exeunt.]

204–215 The Prince banishes Romeo from Verona. He angrily points out that one of his own relatives, Mercutio, is now dead because of the feud. The Prince promises that if Romeo does not leave Verona immediately, he will be put to death.

*R*esponding to Reading

1. Whose fault is the fight between Mercutio and Tybalt? Support your opinion with lines from the play.

2. Is Romeo right to challenge Tybalt? Would you have done the same in his place? Explain.

3. Capulet and Montague both present arguments to the Prince. Whose side would you take? Why?

4. Do you think the Prince's decision is wise? Explain.

Scene 2 *Capulet's orchard.*

The scene begins with Juliet impatiently waiting for night to come so that Romeo can climb to her bedroom on the rope ladder. Suddenly the Nurse enters with the terrible news of Tybalt's death and Romeo's banishment. Juliet mourns for the loss of her cousin and her husband and threatens to kill herself. To calm her, the Nurse promises to find Romeo and bring him to Juliet before he leaves Verona.

[Enter Juliet alone.]

Juliet. Gallop apace, you fiery-footed steeds,
    Toward Phoebus' lodging! Such a wagoner
    As Phaëton would whip you to the West,
    And bring in cloudy night immediately.
5   Spread thy close curtain, love-performing night,
    That runaways' eyes may wink, and Romeo
    Leap to these arms, untalked of and unseen.
    Lovers can see to do their amorous rites
    By their own beauties; or, if love be blind,
10   It best agrees with night. Come, civil night,
    Thou sober-suited matron, all in black,
    And learn me how to lose a winning match,
    Played for a pair of stainless maidenhoods.
    Hood my unmanned blood bating in my cheeks.
15   With thy black mantle; till strange love, grown bold,
    Think true love acted simple modesty.
    Come, night; come, Romeo, come; thou day in night;
    For thou wilt lie upon the wings of night
    Whiter than new snow on a raven's back.
20   Come, gentle night; come, loving, black-browed night;
    Give me my Romeo; and, when he shall die,
    Take him and cut him out in little stars,
    And he will make the face of heaven so fine
25   That all the world will be in love with night
    And pay no worship to the garish sun.
    O, I have bought the mansion of a love,
    But not possessed it; and though I am sold,
    Not yet enjoyed. So tedious is this day
30   As is the night before some festival
    To an impatient child that hath new robes
    And may not wear them. Oh, here comes my nurse,

[Enter Nurse, wringing her hands, with the ladder of cords in her lap.]

1–4 Juliet is wishing for nightfall, when Romeo is to come to her room. ***Phoebus*** is the god whose chariot pulls the sun across the sky; ***Phaëton*** was his son, who lost control of the chariot when he drove it too fast.

14–16 *Hood . . . modesty:* Juliet asks that the darkness hide her blushing cheeks on her wedding night.

22–26 *What does Juliet think should happen to Romeo after he dies?*

27–32 *I have . . . wear them:* Juliet protests that she has gone through the wedding ceremony **(*bought the mansion*)** but is still waiting to enjoy the rewards of marriage. She then compares herself to an excited, impatient child on the night before a holiday or festival.

And she brings news; and every tongue that speaks
But Romeo's name speaks heavenly eloquence.
35   Now, nurse, what news? What hast thou there? the cords
That Romeo bid thee fetch?

Nurse.   Ay, ay, the cords.

Juliet. Ay me! what news? Why dost thou wring thy
40   hands?

Nurse. Ah, well-a-day! he's dead, he's dead, he's dead!
We are undone, lady, we are undone!
Alack the day! he's gone, he's killed, he's dead!

Juliet. Can heaven be so envious?

45   **Nurse.**   Romeo can,
Though heaven cannot. O Romeo, Romeo!
Who ever would have thought it? Romeo!

Juliet. What devil art thou that dost torment me thus?
This torture should be roared in dismal hell.
50   Hath Romeo slain himself? Say thou but "I,"
And that bare vowel "I" shall poison more
Than the death-darting eye of a cockatrice.
I am not I, if there be such an "I,"
Or those eyes shut, that make thee answer "I."
55   If he be slain, say "I," or if not, "no."
Brief sounds determine of my weal or woe.

Nurse. I saw the wound, I saw it with mine eyes,
(God save the mark!) here on his manly breast.
A piteous corse, a bloody piteous corse;
60   Pale, pale as ashes, all bedaubed in blood,
All in gore blood. I swounded at the sight.

Juliet. O, break, my heart! poor bankrout, break
at once!
To prison, eyes; ne'er look on liberty!
65   Vile earth, to earth resign; end motion here,
And thou and Romeo press one heavy bier!

Nurse. O Tybalt, Tybalt, the best friend I had!
O courteous Tybalt! honest gentleman!
That ever I should live to see thee dead!

70   **Juliet.** What storm is this that blows so contrary?
Is Romeo slaughtered, and is Tybalt dead?
My dear-loved cousin, and my dearer lord?

36–37 cords . . . fetch: the rope ladder Romeo told you to get.

41–47 well-a-day: an expression used when someone has bad news. The Nurse wails and moans without clearly explaining what has happened. Juliet misunderstands and assumes that Romeo is dead.

50–55 Juliet's *I* means "aye," or yes. She is in agony, thinking Romeo dead, and begs the Nurse to answer clearly. A **cockatrice** is a mythological beast whose glance killed its victims.

58–61 God . . . mark: an expression meant to scare off evil powers, similar to "Knock on wood." The Nurse says she saw the corpse **(corse)**, covered **(bedaubed)** in blood and gore. She fainted **(swounded)** at the sight of it.
62–66 Juliet says her heart is broken and bankrupt **(bankrout)**. She wants to be buried with Romeo, or share his casket **(bier)**.

70–74 Juliet is trying to make sense of what the Nurse has said.

Then, dreadful trumpet, sound the general doom!
For who is living, if those two are gone?

75 **Nurse.** Tybalt is gone, and Romeo banished;
Romeo that killed him, he is banished.

Juliet. O God! Did Romeo's hand shed Tybalt's blood?

Nurse. It did! it did! alas the day, it did!

Juliet. O serpent heart, hid with a flow'ring face!
80 Did ever dragon keep so fair a cave?
Beautiful tyrant! fiend angelical!
Dove-feathered raven! wolvish-ravening lamb!
Despised substance of divinest show!
Just opposite to what thou justly seemst,
85 A damned saint, an honorable villain!
O nature, what hadst thou to do in hell
When thou didst bower the spirit of a fiend
In mortal paradise of such sweet flesh?
Was ever book containing such vile matter
90 So fairly bound? O, that deceit should dwell
In such a gorgeous palace!

Nurse.   There's no trust,
No faith, no honesty in men; all perjured,
All forsworn, all naught, all dissemblers.
95 Ah, where's my man? Give me some aqua vitae.
These griefs, these woes, these sorrows make me old.
Shame come to Romeo!

Juliet.   Blistered be thy tongue
For such a wish! He was not born to shame.
100 Upon his brow shame is ashamed to sit;
For 'tis a throne where honor may be crowned
Sole monarch of the universal earth.
O, what a beast was I to chide at him!

Nurse. Will you speak well of him that killed your
105 cousin?

Juliet. Shall I speak ill of him that is my husband?
Ah, poor my lord, what tongue shall smooth thy
name
When I, thy three-hours' wife, have mangled it?
110 But wherefore, villain, didst thou kill my cousin?
That villain cousin would have killed my husband.
Back, foolish tears, back to your native spring!
Your tributary drops belong to woe,
Which you, mistaking, offer up to joy.

79–91 In her grief Juliet cries out a series of contradictory phrases, which show her conflicting feelings. A **fiend** is a demon. *How are* **fiend angelical** *and* **dove-feathered raven** *contradictory? What is Juliet's first reaction to the news that Romeo killed Tybalt?*

92–94 There's . . . dissemblers: All men are liars and pretenders.

95 where's . . . vitae: Where's my servant? Give me some brandy.

98–103 Blistered . . . him: Juliet has now recovered a bit from the shock of the news. *How does she respond to the Nurse's wish that shame come to Romeo?*

106–117 Shall . . . husband: Juliet is in turmoil. She is ashamed that she criticized her husband. She realizes that if he hadn't killed Tybalt, Tybalt would have killed him.

115   My husband lives, that Tybalt would have slain;
    And Tybalt's dead, that would have slain my
    husband.
    All this is comfort; wherefore weep I then?
    Some word there was, worser than Tybalt's death,
120   That murdered me. I would forget it fain;
    But O, it presses to my memory
    Like damned guilty deeds to sinners' minds!
    "Tybalt is dead, and Romeo—banished."
    That "banished," that one word "banished,"
125   Hath slain ten thousand Tybalts. Tybalt's death
    Was woe enough, if it had ended there;
    Or, if sour woe delights in fellowship
    And needly will be ranked with other griefs,
    Why followed not, when she said "Tybalt's dead,"
130   Thy father, or thy mother, nay, or both,
    Which modern lamentation might have moved?
    But with a rearward following Tybalt's death,
    "Romeo is banished"—to speak that word
    Is father, mother, Tybalt, Romeo, Juliet,
135   All slain, all dead. "Romeo is banished"—
    There is no end, no limit, measure, bound,
    In that word's death; no words can that woe sound.
    Where is my father and my mother, nurse?

Nurse. Weeping and wailing over Tybalt's corse.
140   Will you go to them? I will bring you thither.

Juliet. Wash they his wounds with tears? Mine shall be
    spent,
    When theirs are dry, for Romeo's banishment.
    Take up those cords. Poor ropes, you are beguiled,
145   Both you and I, for Romeo is exiled.
    He made you for a highway to my bed;
    But I, a maid, die maiden-widowed.
    Come, cords; come, nurse. I'll to my wedding bed;
    And death, not Romeo, take my maidenhead!

150 **Nurse.** Hie to your chamber. I'll find Romeo
    To comfort you. I wot well where he is.
    Hark ye, your Romeo will be here at night.
    I'll to him; he is hid at Laurence' cell.

Juliet. O, find him! give this ring to my true knight
155   And bid him come to take his last farewell.

[Exeunt.]

119–125 *What is Juliet wishing she hadn't heard?*

125–137 Juliet says that if the news of Tybalt's death had been followed by the news of her parents' deaths, she would have felt normal *(modern)*, or expected, grief. To follow the story of Tybalt's death with the terrible news of Romeo's banishment creates a sorrow so deep it cannot be expressed in words.

144 *beguiled:* cheated.

147–149 *But I . . . maidenhead:* I will die a widow without ever really having been a wife. Death, not Romeo, will be my husband.

151 *wot:* know.

Responding to Reading

1. Explain Juliet's emotional stress. What upsets her the most? Would you feel the same way?

2. How might Juliet's reaction have been different if the Nurse had told her right away of Romeo's banishment?

3. At this point, what do you think of the Nurse?

   Think about
   - why she takes so long to tell the news
   - whom she blames for the bad events
   - why she volunteers to take the message

Scene 3   *Friar Laurence's cell.*

Friar Laurence tells Romeo of his banishment, and Romeo collapses in grief. When he learns from the Nurse that Juliet, too, is in despair, he threatens to stab himself. The friar reacts by suggesting a plan. Romeo is to spend a few hours with Juliet and then escape to Mantua. While he is away, the friar will announce the wedding and try to get a pardon from the Prince.

[Enter Friar Laurence.]

Friar Laurence. Romeo, come forth; come forth, thou
   fearful man.
   Affliction is enamored of thy parts,
   And thou art wedded to calamity.

    3–4 *Affliction . . . calamity:* Trouble follows you everywhere.

[Enter Romeo.]

5 **Romeo.** Father, what news? What is the Prince's doom?
   What sorrow craves acquaintance at my hand
   That I yet know not?

    5 *doom:* sentence.

Friar Laurence.   Too familiar
   Is my dear son with such sour company.
10   I bring thee tidings of the Prince's doom.

Romeo. What less than doomsday is the Prince's doom?

    11 *doomsday:* death.

Friar Laurence. A gentler judgment vanished from his
   lips—
   Not body's death, but body's banishment.

    12 *vanished:* came.

15 **Romeo.** Ha, banishment? Be merciful, say "death";
   For exile hath more terror in his look,
   Much more than death. Do not say "banishment."

    15 *Why does Romeo think death would be a more merciful punishment than banishment?*

Friar Laurence. Hence from Verona art thou banished.
Be patient, for the world is broad and wide.

20 **Romeo.** There is no world without Verona walls,
But purgatory, torture, hell itself.
Hence banished is banisht from the world,
And world's exile is death. Then "banishment,"
Is death mistermed. Calling death "banishment,"
25 Thou cuttst my head off with a golden axe
And smilest upon the stroke that murders me.

Friar Laurence. O deadly sin! O rude unthankfulness!
Thy fault our law calls death; but the kind Prince,
Taking thy part, hath rushed aside the law,
30 And turned that black word death to banishment.
This is dear mercy, and thou seest it not.

Romeo. 'Tis torture, and not mercy. Heaven is here,
Where Juliet lives; and every cat and dog
And little mouse, every unworthy thing,
35 Live here in heaven and may look on her;
But Romeo may not. More validity,
More honorable state, more courtship lives
In carrion flies than Romeo. They may seize
On the white wonder of dear Juliet's hand

20–26 *without:* outside. Being exiled to the rest of the world (that is, the world away from Juliet) is as bad as being dead. And yet you smile at my misfortune!

27–31 The Friar is very angry at Romeo's reaction to the news. He reminds Romeo that the crime he committed deserves the death penalty, according to law. The Prince has shown Romeo mercy, and Romeo doesn't appreciate it.
32–46 Romeo refuses to listen to reason. He is obsessed with the word *banished,* just as Juliet was. He compares himself to the animals—and even the flies that live off the dead *(carrion)*—that will be able to see Juliet while he will not.

"Hence from Verona art thou banished. Be patient, for the world is broad and wide."

40 And steal immortal blessing from her lips,
    Who, even in pure and vestal modesty,
    Still blush, as thinking their own kisses sin;
    But Romeo may not—he is banished.
    This may flies do, when I from this must fly;
45 They are free men, but I am banished.
    And sayst thou yet that exile is not death?
    Hadst thou no poison mixed, no sharp-ground knife,
    No sudden mean of death, though ne'er so mean,
    But "banished" to kill me—"banished"?
50 O friar, the damned use that word in hell;
    Howling attends it! How hast thou the heart,
    Being a divine, a ghostly confessor,
    A sin-absolver, and my friend professed,
    To mangle me with that word "banished"?

55 **Friar Laurence.** Thou fond mad man, hear me a little
    speak.

    Romeo. O, thou wilt speak again of banishment.

    Friar Laurence. I'll give thee armor to keep off that
    word;
60 Adversity's sweet milk, philosophy,
    To comfort thee, though thou art banished.

    Romeo. Yet "banished"? Hang up philosophy!
    Unless philosophy can make a Juliet,
    Displant a town, reverse a prince's doom,
65 It helps not, it prevails not. Talk no more.

    Friar Laurence. O, then I see that madmen have no
    ears.

    Romeo. How should they, when that wise men have
    no eyes?

70 **Friar Laurence.** Let me dispute with thee of thy estate.

    Romeo. Thou canst not speak of that thou dost not
    feel.
    Wert thou as young as I, Juliet thy love,
    An hour but married, Tybalt murdered,
75 Doting like me, and like me banished,
    Then mightst thou speak, then mightst thou tear
    thy hair,
    And fall upon the ground, as I do now,
    Taking the measure of an unmade grave.

    [Nurse *knocks within.*]

47–49 *Hadst . . . to kill me:* Couldn't you have killed me with poison or a knife instead of with that awful word?

55 *fond:* foolish.

60–62 The Friar offers philosophical comfort and counseling *(adversity's sweet milk)* as a way to overcome hardship.

70 *dispute:* discuss; ***estate:*** situation.

71–79 You can't understand how I feel because you haven't been through what I have.

Friar Laurence. Arise; one knocks. Good Romeo, hide
    thyself.

Romeo. Not I; unless the breath of heartsick groans
    Mist-like infold me from the search of eyes.

[Knock.]

80

Friar Laurence. Hark, how they knock! Who's there?
    Romeo, arise;
    Thou wilt be taken.—Stay awhile!—Stand up;

85

[Knock.]

Run to my study.—By-and-by!—God's will,
    What simpleness is this.—I come, I come!

[Knock.]

Who knocks so hard? Whence come you? What's your
    will?

90

Nurse. *[Within.]* Let me come in, and you shall know
    my errand.
    I come from Lady Juliet.

Friar Laurence.   Welcome then.

[Enter Nurse.]

Nurse. O holy friar, O, tell me, holy friar,

95

    Where is my lady's lord, where's Romeo?

Friar Laurence. There on the ground, with his own
    tears made drunk.

Nurse. O, he is even in my mistress' case,
    Just in her case! O woeful sympathy!
    Piteous predicament! Even so lies she,
    Blubb'ring and weeping, weeping and blubbering.
    Stand up, stand up! Stand, an you be a man.
    For Juliet's sake, for her sake, rise and stand!
    Why should you fall into so deep an O?

100

105

Romeo. *[Rises]* Nurse—

Nurse. Ah sir! ah sir! Well, death's the end of all.

Romeo. Spakest thou of Juliet? How is it with her?
    Doth not she think me an old murderer,
    Now I have stained the childhood of our joy
    With blood removed but little from her own?
    Where is she? and how doth she? and what says
    My concealed lady to our canceled love?

110

80–91 When a knock sounds, the Friar frantically tries to get Romeo to hide.

99–105 *O he . . . an O:* The Nurse says that Romeo is in exactly the same condition as Juliet. She tells Romeo to stand up and be a man and asks why he's in such deep grief *(so deep an O)*.

113 *concealed lady:* secret bride.

Nurse. O, she says nothing, sir, but weeps and weeps;
115   And now falls on her bed, and then starts up,
    And Tybalt calls; and then on Romeo cries,
    And then down falls again.

Romeo.   As if that name,
    Shot from the deadly level of a gun,
120   Did murder her; as that name's cursed hand
    Murdered her kinsman. O tell me, friar, tell me,
    In what vile part of this anatomy
    Doth my name lodge? Tell me, that I may sack
    The hateful mansion.

[Draws his dagger.]

125 **Friar Laurence.**   Hold thy desperate hand.

    Art thou a man? Thy form cries out thou art;
    Thy tears are womanish, thy wild acts denote
    The unreasonable fury of a beast.
    Unseemly woman in a seeming man!
130   Or ill-beseeming beast in seeming both!
    Thou hast amazed me. By my holy order,
    I thought thy disposition better tempered.
    Hast thou slain Tybalt? Wilt thou slay thyself?
    And slay thy lady too that lives in thee,
135   By doing damned hate upon thyself?
    Why railst thou on thy birth, the heaven, and earth?
    Since birth and heaven and earth, all three do meet
    In thee at once; which thou at once wouldst lose.
    Fie, fie, thou shamest thy shape, thy love, thy wit,
140   Which, like a usurer, aboundst in all,
    And usest none in that true use indeed
    Which should bedeck thy shape, thy love, thy wit.
    Thy noble shape is but a form of wax,
    Digressing from the valor of a man;
145   Thy dear love sworn but hollow perjury,
    Killing that love which thou hast vowed to cherish;
    Thy wit, that ornament to shape and love,
    Misshapen in the conduct of them both,
    Like powder in a skilless soldier's flask,
150   Is set afire by thine own ignorance,
    And thou dismembered with thine own defense.
    What, rouse thee, man! Thy Juliet is alive,
    For whose dear sake thou wast but lately dead.
    There art thou happy. Tybalt would kill thee,
155   But thou slewest Tybalt. There art thou happy.

118–124 *that name:* the name *Romeo.* Romeo says his name is a bullet that kills Juliet just as his hand killed her kinsman Tybalt. Romeo asks where in his body *(hateful mansion)* his name can be found so that he can cut the name out. *What is Romeo about to do?*

125–142 *Hold:* stop. You're not acting like a man. Would you send your soul to hell by committing suicide *(doing damned hate)*? Why do you curse your birth, heaven, and earth? You are refusing to make good use of your advantages just as a miser refuses to spend his money.

152–158 The Friar tells Romeo to count his blessings instead of feeling sorry for himself. He lists the things Romeo has to be thankful for. *What three blessings does the Friar mention?*

The law, that threatened death, becomes thy friend
And turns it to exile. There art thou happy.
A pack of blessings light upon thy back;
Happiness courts thee in her best array;
160　But, like a misbehaved and sullen wench,
Thou poutst upon thy fortune and thy love.
Take heed, take heed, for such die miserable.
Go get thee to thy love, as was decreed,
Ascend her chamber, hence and comfort her.
165　But look thou stay not till the watch be set,
For then thou canst not pass to Mantua,
Where thou shalt live till we can find a time
To blaze your marriage, reconcile your friends,
Beg pardon of the Prince, and call thee back
170　With twenty hundred thousand times more joy
Than thou wentst forth in lamentation.
Go before, nurse. Commend me to thy lady,
And bid her hasten all the house to bed,
Which heavy sorrow makes them apt unto.
175　Romeo is coming.

Nurse. O Lord, I could have stayed here all the night
To hear good counsel. O, what learning is!
My lord, I'll tell my lady you will come.

Romeo. Do so, and bid my sweet prepare to chide.
[Nurse *offers to go and turns again.*]

180　**Nurse.** Here is a ring she bid me give you, sir.

Hie you, make haste, for it grows very late.
[*Exit.*]

Romeo. How well my comfort is revived by this!

Friar Laurence. Go hence; good night; and here stands
all your state:
185　Either be gone before the watch be set,
Or by the break of day disguised from hence.
Sojourn in Mantua. I'll find out your man,
And he shall signify from time to time
Every good hap to you that chances here.
190　Give me thy hand. 'Tis late. Farewell; good night.

Romeo. But that a joy past joy calls out on me,
It were a grief so brief to part with thee.
Farewell.
[*Exeunt.*]

163–166 Go and spend the night with Juliet. But leave before the guards take their places at the city gates, so you can escape to Mantua.

167–171 *till we . . . lamentation:* The Friar intends to announce *(blaze)* the marriage at the right time, get the families *(friends)* to stop their feud, ask the Prince to pardon Romeo, and have Romeo return to a happier situation.

176–177 *How does the Nurse react to the advice the Friar has just given Romeo?*

179 *bid . . . chide:* Tell Juliet to get ready to scold me for the way I've behaved.

182 *How has Romeo's mood changed since he threatened to kill himself?*
183–189 *and here . . . here:* This is what your fate depends on: either leave before the night watchmen go on duty, or get out at dawn in a disguise. Stay awhile in Mantua. I'll find your servant and send messages to you about what good things are happening here.

Scene 4   *Capulet's house.*

In this scene, Paris visits the Capulets, who are mourning the death of Tybalt. He says he realizes that this is no time to talk of marriage. Capulet, however, disagrees; he decides that Juliet should marry Paris on Thursday, three days away. He tells Lady Capulet to inform Juliet immediately.

[Enter Capulet, Lady Capulet, and Paris.]

Capulet. Things have fall'n out, sir, so unluckily
    That we have had no time to move our daughter.
    Look you, she loved her kinsman Tybalt dearly,
    And so did I. Well, we were born to die.
5   'Tis very late; she'll not come down tonight.
    I promise you, but for your company,
    I would have been abed an hour ago.

Paris. These times of woe afford no time to woo.
    Madam, good night. Commend me to your
10   daughter.

Lady Capulet. I will, and know her mind early
    tomorrow;
    Tonight she's mewed up to her heaviness.

[Paris offers to go and Capulet calls him again.]

Capulet. Sir Paris, I will make a desperate tender
15   Of my child's love. I think she will be ruled
    In all respects by me; nay more, I doubt it not.
    Wife, go you to her ere you go to bed;
    Acquaint her here of my son Paris' love
    And bid her (mark you me?) on Wednesday next—
20   But, soft! what day is this?

Paris.   Monday, my lord.

Capulet. Monday! ha, ha! Well, Wednesday is too soon.
    A Thursday let it be—a Thursday, tell her,
    She shall be married to this noble earl.
25   Will you be ready? Do you like this haste?
    We'll keep no great ado—a friend or two;
    For hark you, Tybalt being slain so late,
    It may be thought we held him carelessly,
    Being our kinsman, if we revel much.
30   Therefore we'll have some half a dozen friends,
    And there an end. But what say you to Thursday?

1–2 Such terrible things have happened that we haven't had time to persuade *(move)* Juliet to think about your marriage proposal.

8 Sad times are not good times for talking of marriage.

11–13 *and know . . . heaviness:* I'll know early tomorrow what she intends to do; tonight she's locked up with her sorrow. *What reason do Lord and Lady Capulet think causes Juliet to be sad?*

14–31 Capulet thinks Juliet will obey him and pledges her in marriage to Paris (makes a **desperate tender,** or bold offer). He decides the wedding will be on Thursday and only a small ceremony, since the family is mourning Tybalt's death. He is so sure that Juliet will accept Paris that he calls Paris "son" already.

Paris. My lord, I would that Thursday were tomorrow.

Capulet. Well, get you gone. A Thursday be it then.
　Go you to Juliet ere you go to bed;
35　Prepare her, wife, against this wedding day.
　Farewell, my lord.—Light to my chamber, ho!
　Afore me, it is so very very late
　That we may call it early by-and-by.
　Good night.

[Exeunt.]

34–36 Capulet tells his wife to go to Juliet right away and inform her of his decision.

37–38 *it is . . . by-and-by:* It's so late at night that soon we'll be calling it early in the morning.

*R*esponding to Reading

1. Why do both Romeo and Juliet react so strongly to Romeo's banishment?

2. The Friar and Romeo disagree about the seriousness of Romeo's punishment. Who is right? Why?

3. What do you think of the Friar's long-range plan to solve Romeo's problem? Is it likely to work? What might go wrong?

4. In what other ways than the Friar's might Romeo and Juliet have dealt with the problem of banishment?

5. In Scene 4, Capulet decides that Juliet will marry Paris immediately. Why do you think he is suddenly in such a hurry to see her wed?

6. What do you think of Capulet's attitude toward Juliet? Is he correct in his thinking? Explain.

Scene 5　*Capulet's orchard.*

Romeo and Juliet have spent the night together, but before daylight, Romeo leaves for Mantua. As soon as he leaves, Lady Capulet comes in to tell Juliet of her father's decision—that she will marry Count Paris on Thursday. Juliet is very upset and refuses to go along with the plan. Juliet's father goes into a rage at her disobedience and tells her that she will marry Paris or he will disown her.

*　The Nurse advises Juliet to wed Paris, since her marriage to Romeo is over and Paris is a better man anyway. Juliet, now angry with the Nurse, decides to go to Friar Laurence for help.*

[Enter Romeo *and* Juliet *above, at the window.]*

Juliet. Wilt thou be gone? It is not yet near day.
It was the nightingale, and not the lark,
That pierced the fearful hollow of thine ear.
Nightly she sings on yond pomegranate tree.
5   Believe me, love, it was the nightingale.

Romeo. It was the lark, the herald of the morn;
No nightingale. Look, love, what envious streaks
Do lace the severing clouds in yonder East.
Night's candles are burnt out, and jocund day
10   Stands tiptoe on the misty mountain tops.
I must be gone and live, or stay and die.

Juliet. Yond light is not daylight; I know it, I.
It is some meteor that the sun exhales
To be to thee this night a torchbearer
15   And light thee on thy way to Mantua.
Therefore stay yet; thou needst not to be gone.

Romeo. Let me be ta'en, let me be put to death.
I am content, so thou wilt have it so.
I'll say yon grey is not the morning's eye,
20   'Tis but the pale reflex of Cynthia's brow;
Nor that is not the lark whose notes do beat
The vaulty heaven so high above our heads.
I have more care to stay than will to go.
Come, death, and welcome! Juliet wills it so.
25   How is't, my soul? Let's talk; it is not day.

Juliet. It is, it is! Hie hence, be gone, away!
It is the lark that sings so out of tune,
Straining harsh discords and unpleasing sharps.
Some say the lark makes sweet division;
30   This doth not so, for she divideth us.
Some say the lark and loathed toad changed eyes;
O, now I would they had changed voices too,
Since arm from arm that voice doth us affray,
Hunting thee hence with hunt's-up to the day!
35   O, now be gone! More light and light it grows.

Romeo. More light and light—more dark and dark our
woes!

[Enter Nurse, *hastily.]*

Nurse. Madam!

Juliet. Nurse?

2–5 *It was . . . nightingale:* The nightingale sings at night; the lark sings in the morning. *What is Juliet trying to get Romeo to believe?*

6 *herald:* messenger.

9–10 *night's candles:* stars. *How is day personified here?*

12–25 Juliet continues to pretend it is night to keep Romeo from leaving, even though she knows that it is morning. Romeo gives in and says he'll stay if Juliet wishes it, even if staying means death.

26–28 Romeo's mention of death frightens Juliet. She becomes serious and urges Romeo to go quickly.

29 *division:* melody.

31–34 The toad's large, brilliant eyes would be more suitable for the lark. *affray:* frighten. *hunt's-up:* a morning song for hunters.

"Therefore stay yet;
thou needst not to be gone."

40 **Nurse.** Your lady mother is coming to your chamber.
    The day is broke; be wary, look about.

[Exit.]

Juliet. Then, window, let day in, and let life out.

Romeo. Farewell, farewell! One kiss, and I'll descend.

[He starts down the ladder.]

Juliet. Art thou gone so, my lord, my love, my friend?
45   I must hear from thee every day in the hour,
    For in a minute there are many days.
    O, by this count I shall be much in years
    Ere I again behold my Romeo!

47 much in years: very old.

Romeo. Farewell!
50   I will omit no opportunity
    That may convey my greetings, love, to thee.

Juliet. O, thinkst thou we shall ever meet again?

Romeo. I doubt it not; and all these woes shall serve
    For sweet discourses in our time to come.

55 **Juliet.** O God, I have an ill-divining soul!
    Methinks I see thee, now thou art below,
    As one dead in the bottom of a tomb.
    Either my eyesight fails, or thou lookst pale.

55–57 I have . . . tomb: Juliet sees an evil vision of the future. *What is her vision?*

Romeo. And trust me, love, in my eye so do you.
60   Dry sorrow drinks our blood. Adieu! adieu!

[Exit.]

60 Dry . . . blood: People believed that sorrow drained the blood from the heart, causing a sad person to look pale. Romeo leaves Juliet by climbing down from her balcony.

Juliet. O Fortune, Fortune! all men call thee fickle.
    If thou art fickle, what dost thou with him
    That is renowned for faith? Be fickle, Fortune,
    For then I hope thou wilt not keep him long
65   But send him back.

61–63 fickle: changeable in loyalty or affection. Juliet asks fickle Fortune why it has anything to do with Romeo, who is the opposite of fickle.

Lady Capulet. *[Within.]* Ho, daughter! are you up?

Juliet. Who is't that calls? It is my lady mother.
    Is she not down so late, or up so early?
    What unaccustomed cause procures her hither?

69 What . . . hither: What unusual reason brings her here?

[Enter Lady Capulet.]

70 **Lady Capulet.** Why, how now, Juliet?

Juliet.   Madam, I am not well.

Lady Capulet. Evermore weeping for your cousin's
    death?
    What, wilt thou wash him from his grave with tears?
75   An if thou couldst, thou couldst not make him live.
    Therefore have done. Some grief shows much of
    love;
    But much of grief shows still some want of wit.

Juliet. Yet let me weep for such a feeling loss.

80 **Lady Capulet.** So shall you feel the loss, but not the
    friend
    Which you weep for.

Juliet.   Feeling so the loss,
    I cannot choose but ever weep the friend.

85 **Lady Capulet.** Well, girl, thou weepst not so much for
    his death
    As that the villain lives which slaughtered him.

Juliet. What villain, madam?

Lady Capulet.   That same villain Romeo.

90 **Juliet.** *[Aside.]* Villain and he be many miles
    asunder.—
    God pardon him! I do, with all my heart;
    And yet no man like he doth grieve my heart.

Lady Capulet. That is because the traitor murderer
95   lives.

Juliet. Ay, madam, from the reach of these my hands.
    Would none but I might venge my cousin's death!

Lady Capulet. We will have vengeance for it, fear
    thou not.
100   Then weep no more. I'll send to one in Mantua,
    Where that same banished runagate doth live,
    Shall give him such an unaccustomed dram
    That he shall soon keep Tybalt company;
    And then I hope thou wilt be satisfied.

105 **Juliet.** Indeed I never shall be satisfied
    With Romeo till I behold him—dead—
    Is my poor heart so for a kinsman vexed.
    Madam, if you could find out but a man
    To bear a poison, I would temper it;
110   That Romeo should, upon receipt thereof,
    Soon sleep in quiet. O, how my heart abhors

72–74 *What does Lady Capulet think Juliet is crying about?*

76–78 have . . . wit: Stop crying **(have done)**. A little grief is evidence of love, while too much grief shows a lack of good sense **(want of wit)**.

90–114 In these lines Juliet's words have double meanings. In order to avoid lying to her mother, she chooses her words carefully. They can mean what her mother wants to hear, but they can also mean what we know Juliet really has in mind.

101 runagate: runaway.

102 unaccustomed dram: poison.
What does Lady Capulet plan to do about Romeo?

105–114 Dead could refer either to Romeo or to Juliet's heart. Juliet says that if her mother could find someone to carry a poison to Romeo, she would mix **(temper)** it herself. *What hidden meaning lies in lines 108–112?*

To hear him named and cannot come to him,
To wreak the love I bore my cousin Tybalt
Upon his body that hath slaughtered him!

115 **Lady Capulet.** Find thou the means, and I'll find such
a man.
But now I'll tell thee joyful tidings, girl.

Juliet. And joy comes well in such a needy time.
What are they, I beseech your ladyship?

120 **Lady Capulet.** Well, well, thou hast a careful father,
child;
One who, to put thee from thy heaviness,
Hath sorted out a sudden day of joy
That thou expects not nor I looked not for.

125 **Juliet.** Madam, in happy time! What day is that?

Lady Capulet. Marry, my child, early next Thursday
morn
The gallant, young, and noble gentleman,
The County Paris, at Saint Peter's Church,
130 Shall happily make thee there a joyful bride.

Juliet. Now by Saint Peter's Church, and Peter too,
He shall not make me there a joyful bride!
I wonder at this haste, that I must wed
Ere he that should be husband comes to woo.
135 I pray you tell my lord and father, madam,
I will not marry yet; and when I do, I swear
It shall be Romeo, whom you know I hate,
Rather than Paris. These are news indeed!

Lady Capulet. Here comes your father. Tell him so
140 yourself,
And see how he will take it at your hands.

[Enter Capulet and Nurse.]

Capulet. When the sun sets the air doth drizzle dew,
But for the sunset of my brother's son
It rains downright.
145 How now? a conduit, girl? What, still in tears?
Evermore show'ring? In one little body
Thou counterfeitst a bark, a sea, a wind:
For still thy eyes, which I may call the sea,
Do ebb and flow with tears; the bark thy body is,
150 Sailing in this salt flood; the winds, thy sighs,
Who, raging with thy tears and they with them,

136–138 and when . . . Paris: Once
again, Juliet uses a double meaning.
She mentions Romeo to show her
mother how strongly opposed she is to
marrying Paris, yet what she really
means is that she loves Romeo.

143 my brother's son: Tybalt.

145–153 conduit: fountain. Capulet
compares Juliet to a boat, an ocean,
and the wind because of her excessive
crying.

Without a sudden calm will overset
Thy tempest-tossed body. How now, wife?
Have you delivered to her our decree?

155 **Lady Capulet.** Ay, sir; but she will none, she gives you
   thanks.
   I would the fool were married to her grave!

Capulet. Soft! take me with you, take me with you,
   wife.
160 How? Will she none? Doth she not give us thanks?
   Is she not proud? Doth she not count her blest,
   Unworthy as she is, that we have wrought
   So worthy a gentleman to be her bridegroom?

Juliet. Not proud you have, but thankful that you have.
165 Proud can I never be of what I hate,
   But thankful even for hate that is meant love.

Capulet. How, how, how, how, choplogic? What is this?
   "Proud"—and "I thank you"—and "I thank you
   not"—
170 And yet "not proud"? Mistress minion you,
   Thank me no thankings, nor proud me no prouds,
   But fettle your fine joints 'gainst Thursday next
   To go with Paris to Saint Peter's Church,
   Or I will drag thee on a hurdle thither.
175 Out, you green-sickness carrion! out, you baggage!
   You tallow-face!

Lady Capulet.   Fie, fie; what, are you mad?

Juliet. Good father, I beseech you on my knees,

[She kneels down.]

Hear me with patience but to speak a word.

180 **Capulet.** Hang thee, young baggage! disobedient
   wretch!
   I tell thee what—get thee to church a Thursday
   Or never after look me in the face.
   Speak not, reply not, do not answer me!
185 My fingers itch. Wife, we scarce thought us blest
   That God had lent us but this only child;
   But now I see this one is one too much,
   And that we have a curse in having her.
   Out on her, hilding!

190 **Nurse.**   God in heaven bless her!
   You are to blame, my lord, to rate her so.

158 take me with you: Let me understand you. Capulet, like his wife, simply can't believe that Juliet won't go along with his plan for marriage.

164–160 I'm not pleased, but I am grateful for your intentions.

167–176 How . . . tallow-face: Capulet is furious with Juliet. He rages, calls her names, and threatens her. He calls her a person who argues over fine points **(choplogic)**, and says she is a spoiled child **(minion)**. He tells her to prepare herself **(fettle your fine joints)** for the wedding or he'll haul her there in a cart for criminals **(hurdle)**. He calls her an anemic piece of dead flesh **(green-sickness carrion)** and a coward **(tallow-face)**.

177 Fie . . . mad: Lady Capulet is worried by her husband's violent anger and tries to calm him.

185 My fingers itch: I feel like hitting you.

189 hilding: good-for-nothing person.
190–197 The Nurse dares to stand up for Juliet but is rudely dismissed by Capulet, who considers her nothing more than a lowly servant.

Capulet. And why, my Lady Wisdom? Hold your tongue,
    Good Prudence. Smatter with your gossips, go!

195 **Nurse.** I speak no treason.

Capulet.   O, God-i-god-en!

Nurse. May not one speak?

Capulet: Peace, you mumbling fool!
    Utter your gravity o'er a gossip's bowl,
200   For here we need it not.

Lady Capulet.   You are too hot.

Capulet. God's bread! it makes me mad. Day, night, late, early,
    At home, abroad, alone, in company,
205   Waking or sleeping, still my care hath been
    To have her matched; and having now provided
    A gentleman of princely parentage,
    Of fair demesnes, youthful, and nobly trained,
    Stuffed, as they say, with honorable parts,
210   Proportioned as one's thought would wish a man—
    And then to have a wretched puling fool,
    A whining mammet, in her fortunes tender,
    To answer "I'll not wed, I cannot love;
    I am too young, I pray you pardon me"!
215   But, an you will not wed, I'll pardon you.
    Graze where you will, you shall not house with me.
    Look to't, think on't; I do not use to jest.
    Thursday is near; lay hand on heart, advise:
    An you be mine, I'll give you to my friend;
220   An you be not, hang, beg, starve, die in the streets,
    For, by my soul, I'll ne'er acknowledge thee,
    Nor what is mine shall never do thee good.
    Trust to't. Bethink you. I'll not be forsworn.
    [Exit.]

Juliet. Is there no pity sitting in the clouds
225   That sees into the bottom of my grief?
    O sweet my mother, cast me not away!
    Delay this marriage for a month, a week;
    Or if you do not, make the bridal bed
    In that dim monument where Tybalt lies.

230 **Lady Capulet.** Talk not to me, for I'll not speak a word.
    Do as thou wilt, for I have done with thee.
    [Exit.]

---

194 *Smatter:* chatter.

199 *Utter . . . bowl:* Save your words of wisdom for a gathering of gossips.

202–223 Capulet complains that day and night he's tried to get Juliet a good husband, and now that he has, she acts like a crying *(puling)* fool, a whining doll *(mammet)*. He will not put up with this. She will marry or he'll put her out of his house. He will not break his promise to Paris *(be forsworn)*.

Juliet. O God!—O nurse, how shall this be prevented?
My husband is on earth, my faith in heaven.
235 How shall that faith return again to earth
Unless that husband send it me from heaven
By leaving earth? Comfort me, counsel me.
Alack, alack, that heaven should practice stratagems
Upon so soft a subject as myself!
240 What sayst thou? Hast thou not a word of joy?
Some comfort, nurse.

Nurse.   Faith, here it is.
Romeo is banisht; and all the world to nothing
That he dares ne'er come back to challenge you;
245 Or if he do, it needs must be by stealth.
Then, since the case so stands as now it doth,
I think it best you married with the County.
O, he's a lovely gentleman!
Romeo's a dishclout to him. An eagle, madam,
250 Hath not so green, so quick, so fair an eye
As Paris hath. Beshrew my very heart,

233–237 How shall . . . earth: Juliet is worried about the sin of being married to two men. She goes on to ask how heaven can play such tricks **(practice stratagems)** on her.

242–251 The Nurse gives Juliet advice. She says that since Romeo is banished, he's no good to her; Juliet should marry Paris. Romeo is a dishcloth **(dishclout)** compared to Paris.

251 beshrew: curse.

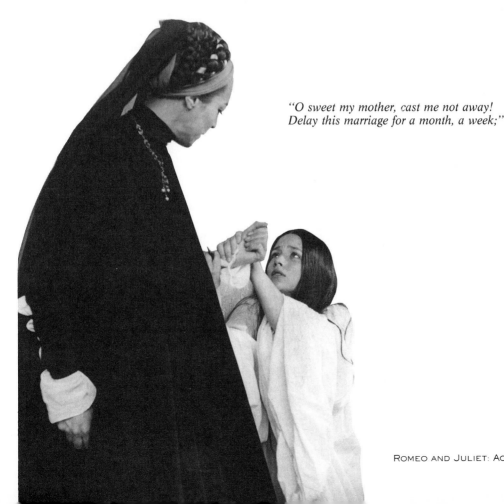

"O sweet my mother, cast me not away!
Delay this marriage for a month, a week;"

I think you are happy in this second match,
For it excels your first; or if it did not,
Your first is dead—or 'twere as good he were
255   As living here and you no use of him.

Juliet. Speakst thou this from thy heart?

Nurse. And from my soul too; else beshrew them both.

Juliet. Amen!

Nurse. What?

260 **Juliet.** Well, thou hast comforted me marvelous much.
    Go in; and tell my lady I am gone,
    Having displeased my father, to Laurence' cell,
    To make confession and to be absolved.

Nurse. Marry, I will; and this is wisely done.

[Exit.]

265 **Juliet.** Ancient damnation! O most wicked fiend!
    Is it more sin to wish me thus forsworn,
    Or to dispraise my lord with that same tongue
    Which she hath praised him with above compare
    So many thousand times? Go, counselor!
270   Thou and my bosom henceforth shall be twain.
    I'll to the friar to know his remedy.
    If all else fail, myself have power to die.

[Exit.]

252–254 This new marriage will be better than the first, which is as good as over.

258 *Amen:* I agree. Curse your heart and soul!

260–269 *What message does Juliet give to the Nurse for her parents?*

265–270 Now that Juliet is alone, she says what she really thinks. She calls the Nurse an old devil *(ancient damnation)*. She doesn't know whether to be angrier at the Nurse for telling her to break her wedding vows or for criticizing Romeo after having praised him. ***Go . . . twain:*** Leave me. You and my secrets will be separated *(twain)* from now on. *How has Juliet's relationship with the Nurse changed?*

*R*esponding to Reading

1. Discuss the reaction of Juliet's parents to her refusal to marry Paris. Is their reaction typical of parents? Is it justified?

2. Think about what you learned of Capulet earlier in the play. Do you think he means the harsh things he says to Juliet in this scene? Why or why not?

3. What do you think of the advice the Nurse gives to Juliet? Does her advice surprise you? Why or why not?

4. Do you agree with Juliet's reaction to the Nurse at the end of the scene?

e x p l a i n

Responding to Reading

First Impressions

1. If you were either Romeo or Juliet, what would be your strongest feeling at the end of this act?

Second Thoughts

2. Which event in this act causes the most problems for Romeo and Juliet? Why?

3. What do you think of Juliet's refusal to marry Paris?

   Think about
   - the future of her marriage with Romeo
   - her parents' reaction
   - the Nurse's advice
   - how strong you think Juliet is

4. Consider Romeo's behavior throughout this act. Do you sympathize with him? Do you respect him? Give reasons for your opinions.

   Think about
   - his attitudes toward Tybalt before and after Mercutio's death
   - his conduct in Friar Laurence's cell
   - his attitude when he leaves Juliet

5. Consider the actions of the Nurse and Friar Laurence in this act. Which character would you trust more if you were Romeo or Juliet? Which would you trust if you were one of their parents? Explain.

6. At the end of Act Three, what are Juliet's choices of action?

Literary Concept: Plot Structure

For a five-act play the standard plot diagram looks like this:

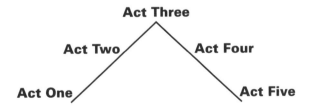

Act Three

Act Two   **Act Four**

Act One   **Act Five**

The first act gives the **exposition,** the second act contains the **rising action,** the third contains the **climax,** and the fourth and fifth acts contain the **falling action** and **resolution.** What is the turning point, or climax, in this third act? How do Acts One and Two conform to the diagram?

Writing Options

1. What if Mercutio had killed Tybalt instead of the reverse? Write what you think might have happened.

2. Although Capulet said earlier that he would abide by Juliet's choice of a husband, he is angry when she refuses the choice he makes for her. Write him a letter telling him what you think of his actions in Scene 5.

3. Using modern language, rewrite Mercutio's death speech in Scene 1, lines 102–115, or Friar Laurence's lecture to Romeo in Scene 3, lines 125–151.

4. Briefly summarize the events in Act Three. Then predict two possible endings for the story.

e x t e n d

Options for Learning

1 • Acting Choose one part of a scene from this act to perform for your classmates. You might try one of the duels, Romeo's discussion with Friar Laurence, or Capulet's angry speech to Juliet. Choose acting partners and practice before presenting the scene to your class. Pretend that you really are the character you portray and be sure to respond to the other actor's words and actions.

2 • Background Music Select music for a performance of two incidents from Act Three: the fight between Romeo and Tybalt in Scene 1 and Juliet and Romeo's parting at the beginning of Scene 5. For each scene select an appropriate piece of music. Then, with other class members, read the two passages aloud with your selections as background.

3 • Remember Me! Suppose that as they parted, Romeo and Juliet had exchanged mementoes that would remind each of the other. Create a memento for each character to give the other. Your memento might be anything from a collage or an ornament to a book or a box filled with keepsakes.

4 • Asking for Advice Since Juliet can no longer confide in the Nurse, suppose that she visits a therapist to discuss her problems. With a classmate improvise the conversation between Juliet and the therapist.

ACT FOUR

Scene 1   *Friar Laurence's cell.*

When Juliet arrives at Friar Laurence's cell, she is upset to find Paris there making arrangements for their wedding. When Paris leaves, the panicked Juliet tells the Friar that if he has no solution to her problem, she will kill herself. The Friar explains his plan. Juliet will drink a potion he has made from his herbs that will put her in a deathlike coma. When she wakes up two days later in the family tomb, Romeo will be waiting for her, and they will escape to Mantua together.

[*Enter* Friar Laurence *and* Paris.]

Friar Laurence. On Thursday, sir? The time is very
    short.

Paris. My father Capulet will have it so,
    And I am nothing slow to slack his haste.

5 **Friar Laurence.** You say you do not know the lady's
    mind.
    Uneven is the course; I like it not.

Paris. Immoderately she weeps for Tybalt's death,
    And therefore have I little talked of love;
10   For Venus smiles not in a house of tears.
    Now, sir, her father counts it dangerous
    That she do give her sorrow so much sway,
    And in his wisdom hastes our marriage
    To stop the inundation of her tears,
15   Which, too much minded by herself alone,
    May be put from her by society.
    Now do you know the reason of this haste.

Friar Laurence. [*Aside.*] I would I knew not why it should
    be slowed.—
20 Look, sir, here comes the lady toward my cell.

[*Enter* Juliet.]

Paris. Happily met, my lady and my wife!

Juliet. That may be, sir, when I may be a wife.

Paris. That may be must be, love, on Thursday next.

Juliet. What must be shall be.

25 **Friar Laurence.**   That's a certain text.

3–4 ***My . . . haste:*** Capulet is eager to have the wedding on Thursday and so am I.

5–7 ***You say . . . not:*** You don't know how Juliet feels about this. It's a difficult (**uneven**) plan, and I don't like it. *What is the Friar's real reason for wanting to slow down the wedding preparations?*

8–17 *According to Paris, what is Capulet's reason for wanting Juliet to marry so quickly?*

22–32 As in the last scene of Act Three, Juliet chooses her words carefully to avoid lying and to avoid telling her secret. *Whom does* him *refer to in line 29?*

Paris. Come you to make confession to this father?

Juliet. To answer that, I should confess to you.

Paris. Do not deny to him that you love me.

Juliet. I will confess to you that I love him.

30 **Paris.** So will ye, I am sure, that you love me.

Juliet. If I do so, it will be of more price,
   Being spoke behind your back, than to your face.

Paris. Poor soul, thy face is much abused with tears.

Juliet. The tears have got small victory by that,
35   For it was bad enough before their spite.

Paris. Thou wrongst it more than tears with that
   report.

Juliet. That is no slander, sir, which is a truth;
   And what I spake, I spake it to my face.

40 **Paris.** Thy face is mine, and thou hast slandered it.

Juliet. It may be so, for it is not mine own.
   Are you at leisure, holy father, now,
   Or shall I come to you at evening mass?

Friar Laurence. My leisure serves me, pensive
45   daughter, now.
   My lord, we must entreat the time alone.

Paris. God shield I should disturb devotion!
   Juliet, on Thursday early will I rouse ye.
   Till then, adieu, and keep this holy kiss.

   [Exit.]

50 **Juliet.** O, shut the door! and when thou hast done so,
   Come weep with me—past hope, past cure, past
   help!

Friar Laurence. Ah, Juliet, I already know thy grief;
   It strains me past the compass of my wits.
55   I hear thou must, and nothing may prorogue it,
   On Thursday next be married to this County.

Juliet. Tell me not, friar, that thou hearst of this,
   Unless thou tell me how I may prevent it.
   If in thy wisdom thou canst give no help,
60   Do thou but call my resolution wise
   And with this knife I'll help it presently.
   God joined my heart and Romeo's, thou our hands;

34–35 The tears . . . spite: The tears haven't ruined my face: it wasn't all that beautiful before they did their damage.

40 Paris says he owns Juliet's face (since she will soon marry him). Insulting her face, he says, insults him, its owner.

46 We must ask you to leave.

54–55 compass: limit. **prorogue:** postpone.

59–62 If . . . hands: If you can't help me, at least tell me that my plan (**resolution**) is right.

And ere this hand, by thee to Romeo's sealed,
Shall be the label to another deed,

65 Or my true heart with treacherous revolt
Turn to another, this shall slay them both.
Therefore, out of thy long-experienced time,
Give me some present counsel; or, behold,
'Twixt my extremes and me this bloody knife

70 Shall play the umpire, arbitrating that
Which the commission of thy years and art
Could to no issue of true honor bring.
Be not so long to speak. I long to die
If what thou speakst not of remedy.

75 **Friar Laurence.** Hold, daughter, I do spy a kind
of hope,
Which craves as desperate an execution
As that is desperate which we would prevent.
If, rather than to marry County Paris,

80 Thou hast the strength of will to slay thyself,
Then is it likely thou wilt undertake
A thing like death to chide away this shame,
That copest with death himself to scape from it;
And, if thou darest, I'll give thee remedy.

85 **Juliet.** O, bid me leap, rather than marry Paris,
From off the battlements of yonder tower,
Or walk in thievish ways, or bid me lurk
Where serpents are; chain me with roaring bears,
Or shut me nightly in a charnel house,

90 O'ercovered quite with dead men's rattling bones,
With reeky shanks and yellow chapless skulls;
Or bid me go into a new-made grave
And hide me with a dead man in his shroud—
Things that, to hear them told, have made me

95 tremble—
And I will do it without fear or doubt,
To live an unstained wife to my sweet love.

Friar Laurence. Hold, then. Go home, be merry, give
consent

100 To marry Paris. Wednesday is tomorrow.
Tomorrow night look that thou lie alone:
Let not the nurse lie with thee in thy chamber.
Take thou this vial, being then in bed,
And this distilled liquor drink thou off;

105 When presently through all thy veins shall run
A cold and drowsy humor; for no pulse

64–74 Before I sign another wedding agreement *(deed)*, I will use this knife to kill myself. If you, with your years of experience *(long-experienced time)*, can't help me, I'll end my sufferings *(extremes)* and solve the problem myself.

79–84 If you are desperate enough to kill yourself, then you'll try the desperate solution I have in mind.

85–97 Juliet replies that she will do anything. *What does Juliet say she would rather face than marry Paris?* **charnel house:** a storehouse for bones from old graves; **reeky shanks:** stinking bones; **chapless:** without jaws. The description in lines 89–93 comes closer to Juliet's future than she knows.

98–130 The Friar explains his desperate plan to Juliet.

103 vial: small bottle.

106 humor: liquid.

Shall keep his native progress, but surcease;
No warmth, no breath, shall testify thou livest;
The roses in thy lips and cheeks shall fade
110 To paly ashes, thy eyes' windows fall
Like death when he shuts up the day of life;
Each part, deprived of supple government,
Shall, stiff and stark and cold, appear like death;
And in this borrowed likeness of shrunk death
115 Thou shalt continue two-and-forty hours,
And then awake as from a pleasant sleep.
Now, when the bridegroom in the morning comes
To rouse thee from thy bed, there art thou dead.
Then, as the manner of our country is,
120 In thy best robes uncovered on the bier
Thou shalt be borne to that same ancient vault
Where all the kindred of the Capulets lie.
In the meantime, against thou shalt awake,
Shall Romeo by my letters know our drift;
125 And hither shall he come; and he and I
Will watch thy waking, and that very night
Shall Romeo bear thee hence to Mantua.
And this shall free thee from this present shame,
If no inconstant toy nor womanish fear
130 Abate thy valor in the acting it.

Juliet. Give me, give me! O, tell me not of fear!

Friar Laurence. Hold! Get you gone, be strong and prosperous
In this resolve. I'll send a friar with speed
135 To Mantua, with my letters to thy lord.

Juliet. Love give me strength! and strength shall help afford.
Farewell, dear father.

[Exeunt.]

107–116 Your pulse will stop **(surcease),** and you will turn cold, pale, and stiff, as if you were dead. This condition will last for forty-two hours.

117–122 *What will happen when Paris comes to wake Juliet on Thursday?*

124 *drift:* plan.

129–130 *inconstant toy:* foolish whim. *Abate thy valor:* weaken your courage.

Responding to Reading

1. What is your opinion of Paris? Do you think he would be a better husband for Juliet than Romeo? Explain your opinion.

2. What motivates Friar Laurence to come up with his plan?

3. What do you think of the Friar's plan? Explain your answer.

4. If you were Juliet, would you try the Friar's solution? Why or why not?

Scene 2 *Capulet's house.*

Capulet is making plans for the wedding on Thursday. Juliet arrives and apologizes to him, saying that she will marry Paris. Capulet is so relieved that he reschedules the wedding for the next day, Wednesday.

[Enter Capulet, Lady Capulet, Nurse, and Servingmen.]

Capulet. So many guests invite as here are writ.

[Exit a Servingman.]

    Sirrah, go hire me twenty cunning cooks.

Servingman. You shall have none ill, sir; for I'll try if
    they can lick their fingers.

5 **Capulet.** How canst thou try them so?

Servingman. Marry, sir, 'tis an ill cook that cannot lick
    his own fingers. Therefore he that cannot lick his
    fingers goes not with me.

Capulet. Go, begone.

[Exit Servingman.]

10 We shall be much unfurnished for this time.
    What, is my daughter gone to Friar Laurence?

Nurse. Ay, forsooth.

Capulet. Well, he may chance to do some good on her.
    A peevish self-willed harlotry it is.

[Enter Juliet.]

15 **Nurse.** See where she comes from shrift with merry
    look.

Capulet. How now, my headstrong? Where have you
    been gadding?

Juliet. Where I have learnt me to repent the sin
20 Of disobedient opposition
    To you and your behests, and am enjoined
    By holy Laurence to fall prostrate here
    To beg your pardon. Pardon, I beseech you!
    Henceforward I am ever ruled by you.

25 **Capulet.** Send for the County. Go tell him of this.
    I'll have this knot knit up tomorrow morning.

Juliet. I met the youthful lord at Laurence' cell
    And gave him what becomed love I might,

1–8 Capulet is having a cheerful conversation with his servants about the wedding preparations. One servant assures him that he will test *(try)* each cook he hires by making the cook taste his own food *(lick his own fingers)*.

10 *unfurnished:* unprepared.

14 A silly, stubborn girl she is. *What does calling Juliet "it" suggest about Capulet's attitude toward her?*

15 *shrift:* confession.

17–18 How are you, my stubborn *(headstrong)* daughter? Where have you been wandering around *(gadding)*?
19–23 *Where I . . . pardon:* where I have learned to regret disobeying your orders *(behests)*. Friar Laurence has ordered *(enjoined)* me to bow before you and ask you to forgive me.

25–26 *knot knit up:* wedding, from the expression "tying the knot." Capulet declares that the wedding will be the next day, Wednesday, instead of Thursday. *What does moving the wedding up by one day do to Friar Laurence's plan?*

Not stepping o'er the bounds of modesty.

30 **Capulet.** Why, I am glad on't. This is well. Stand up.
This is as't should be. Let me see the County.
Ay, marry, go, I say, and fetch him hither.
Now, afore God, this reverend holy friar,
All our whole city is much bound to him.

33–34 *What is ironic about Capulet's praise of Friar Laurence?*

35 **Juliet.** Nurse, will you go with me into my closet
To help me sort such needful ornaments
As you think fit to furnish me tomorrow?

35 *closet:* bedroom.

Lady Capulet. No, not till Thursday. There is time
enough.

38–44 Lady Capulet urges her husband to wait until Thursday as originally planned. She needs time to get food **(provisions)** ready for the wedding party.

40 **Capulet.** Go, nurse, go with her. We'll to church
tomorrow.

[*Exeunt* Juliet *and* Nurse.]

Lady Capulet. We shall be short in our provision.
'Tis now near night.

Capulet. Tush, I will stir about,
45 And all things shall be well, I warrant thee, wife.
Go thou to Juliet, help to deck up her.
I'll not to bed tonight; let me alone.
I'll play the housewife for this once. What, ho!
They are all forth; well, I will walk myself
50 To County Paris, to prepare him up
Against tomorrow. My heart is wondrous light,
Since this same wayward girl is so reclaimed.

45–51 Capulet is so set on Wednesday that he promises to make the arrangements himself.

[*Exeunt.*]

Scene 3 *Juliet's bedroom.*

Juliet sends her mother away and prepares to take the drug the Friar has given her. She is confused and frightened but finally puts the vial to her lips and drinks.

[*Enter* Juliet *and* Nurse.]

Juliet. Ay, those attires are best; but, gentle nurse,
I pray thee leave me to myself tonight;
For I have need of many orisons
To move the heavens to smile upon my state,
5 Which, well thou knowest, is cross and full of sin.

3–5 *orisons:* prayers. *Why is Juliet's upcoming marriage "cross and full of sin"?*

[*Enter* Lady Capulet.]

Lady Capulet. What, are you busy, ho? Need you my
help?

Juliet. No madam; we have culled such necessaries
As are behooveful for our state tomorrow.

10   So please you, let me now be left alone,
And let the nurse this night sit up with you;
For I am sure you have your hands full all
In this so sudden business.

Lady Capulet.   Good night.
15   Get thee to bed and rest, for thou hast need.

[Exeunt Lady Capulet and Nurse.]

Juliet. Farewell! God knows when we shall meet again.
I have a faint cold fear thrills through my veins
That almost freezes up the heat of life.
I'll call them back again to comfort me.
20   Nurse!—What should she do here?
My dismal scene I needs must act alone.
Come, vial.
What if this mixture do not work at all?
Shall I be married then tomorrow morning?
25   No, no! This shall forbid it. Lie thou there.

[Lays down a dagger.]

What if it be a poison which the friar
Subtly hath ministered to have me dead,
Lest in this marriage he should be dishonored
Because he married me before to Romeo?
30   I fear it is; and yet methinks it should not,
For he hath still been tried a holy man.
How if, when I am laid into the tomb,
I wake before the time that Romeo
Come to redeem me? There's a fearful point!
35   Shall I not then be stifled in the vault,
To whose foul mouth no healthsome air breathes in,
And there die strangled ere my Romeo comes?
Or, if I live, is it not very like
The horrible conceit of death and night,
40   Together with the terror of the place—
As in a vault, an ancient receptacle
Where for this many hundred years the bones
Of all my buried ancestors are packed;
Where bloody Tybalt, yet but green in earth,
45   Lies fest'ring in his shroud; where, as they say,

8–9 *we have . . . tomorrow:* We have
picked out *(culled)* everything
appropriate for tomorrow.

16–25 *farewell . . . there:* Juliet
wonders when she'll see her mother
and nurse again. She starts to call back
the Nurse but realizes she must be
alone to drink the potion. She keeps
her knife near her in case the potion
doesn't work.

*26–31 Why does Juliet think the Friar
might have given her poison?*

*32–37 In these lines what fear does
Juliet express?*

38–45 Next Juliet fears the vision
(conceit) she might have on waking in
the family tomb and seeing the rotting
body of Tybalt.

"Romeo, I come!
this do I drink to thee."

At some hours in the night spirits resort—
Alack, alack, is it not like that I,
So early waking—what with loathsome smells,
And shrieks like mandrakes torn out of the earth,
50   That living mortals, hearing them, run mad—
O, if I wake, shall I not be distraught,
Environed with all these hideous fears,
And madly play with my forefather's joints,
And pluck the mangled Tybalt from his shroud,
55   And, in this rage, with some great kinsman's bone
As with a club dash out my desp'rate brains?
O, look! methinks I see my cousin's ghost
Seeking out Romeo, that did spit his body
Upon a rapier's point. Stay, Tybalt, stay!
60   Romeo, I come! this do I drink to thee.

[She drinks and falls upon her bed within the curtains.]

46–56 She fears that the smells together with sounds of ghosts screaming might make her lose her mind. ***Mandrake*** root was thought to look like the human form and, when pulled from the ground, to scream and drive people mad.

57–60 Juliet thinks she sees Tybalt's ghost searching for Romeo. She cries to the ghost to stop *(stay)* and, with Romeo's name on her lips, quickly drinks the potion.

Responding to Reading

1. Do you think that concern for Juliet's well-being is Capulet's reason for insisting on her hasty marriage to Paris? Explain your opinion.

2. Consider all the fears that Juliet discusses in her soliloquy in Scene 3. Which makes the most sense to you? Why?

3. Do you think Juliet is courageous or foolish to take the drug? Why?

Scene 4   *Capulet's house.*

It is now the next morning, nearly time for the wedding. The household is happy and excited as everyone makes final preparations.

[Enter Lady Capulet and Nurse.]

Lady Capulet. Hold, take these keys and fetch more spices, nurse.

Nurse. They call for dates and quinces in the pastry.

[Enter Capulet.]

Capulet. Come, stir, stir, stir! The second cock hath
5   crowed,
   The curfew bell hath rung, 'tis three o'clock.

3 *pastry:* the room where baking is done.

4–6 Capulet tells everyone to wake up *(stir)*.

Look to the baked meat, good Angelica;
Spare not for cost.

Nurse.   Go, you cot-quean, go,
10 Get you to bed! Faith, you'll be sick tomorrow
For this night's watching.

Capulet. No, not a whit. What, I have watched ere now
All night for lesser cause, and ne'er been sick.

Lady Capulet. Ay, you have been a mouse-hunt in your
15 time;
But I will watch you from such watching now.

[Exeunt Lady Capulet and Nurse.]

Capulet. A jealous hood, a jealous hood!

[Enter three or four Servants, with spits and logs and baskets.]

                                          Now, fellow,
What is there?

20 **First Servant.** Things for the cook, sir; but I know not
what.

Capulet. Make haste, make haste. *[Exit Servant.]* Sirrah,
fetch drier logs.
Call Peter; he will show thee where they are.

25 **Second Servant.** I have a head, sir, that will find out
logs
And never trouble Peter for the matter.

Capulet. Mass, and well said, merry whoreson, ha!
Thou shalt be loggerhead. *[Exit Servant.]* Good faith,
30 'tis day.
The County will he here with music straight,
For so he said he would. *[Music within.]* I hear him
near.
Nurse! Wife! What, ho! What, nurse, I say!

[Reenter Nurse.]

35 Go waken Juliet; go and trim her up.
I'll go and chat with Paris. Hie, make haste,
Make haste! The bridegroom he is come already:
Make haste, I say.

[Exeunt.]

7–8 In his happy mood he even calls the Nurse by her name, Angelica. He tells her to attend to the meat and to spend any amount of money necessary.
9 cot-quean: The Nurse playfully calls Capulet a "cottage queen," or a housewife. This is a joke about his doing women's work (arranging the party).
12–13 I've stayed up all night for less important things and never gotten sick.
14–17 Lady and Lord Capulet joke about his being a woman chaser (**mouse-hunt**) as a young man. He jokes about her jealousy (**jealous hood**).

28–31 The joking between Capulet and his servants includes the mild oath **Mass,** short for "by the Mass," and **loggerhead,** a word for a stupid person and a pun, since the servant is searching for drier logs. **straight:** right away.

Scene 5 *Juliet's bedroom.*

The joyous preparations suddenly change into plans for a funeral when the Nurse discovers Juliet on her bed, apparently dead. Lord and Lady Capulet, Paris, and the Nurse are overcome with grief. Friar Laurence tries to comfort them and instructs them to bring Juliet's body to the Capulet family tomb. The scene abruptly switches to humor, in a foolish conversation between the servant Peter and the musicians hired to play at the wedding.

[Enter Nurse.]

Nurse. Mistress! what, mistress! Juliet! Fast, I warrant
   her, she.
   Why, lamb! why, lady! Fie, you slugabed!
   Why, love, I say! madam! sweetheart! Why, bride!
5   What, not a word? You take your pennyworths now,
   Sleep for a week; for the next night, I warrant,
   The County Paris hath set up his rest
   That you shall rest but little. God forgive me,
   Marry and amen, how sound is she asleep!
10   I needs must wake her. Madam, madam, madam!
   Aye, let the County take you in your bed,
   He'll fright you up, i' faith. Will it not be?

[Opens the curtains.]

   What, dressed and in your clothes and down again?
   I must needs wake you. Lady! lady! lady!
15   Alas, alas! Help, help! my lady's dead!
   O well-a-day that ever I was born!
   Some aqua vitae, ho! My lord! my lady!

[Enter Lady Capulet.]

Lady Capulet. What noise is here?

Nurse.   O lamentable day!

20 **Lady Capulet.** What is the matter?

Nurse.   Look, look! O heavy day!

Lady Capulet. O me, O me! My child, my only life!
   Revive, look up, or I will die with thee!
   Help! help! Call help.

[Enter Capulet.]

25 **Capulet.** For shame, bring Juliet forth; her lord is
   come.

1–12 The Nurse chatters as she bustles around the room arranging things. She calls Juliet a **slugabed,** or sleepyhead, who is trying to get her rest now, since after the wedding, Paris won't let her get much sleep. When Juliet doesn't answer, the Nurse opens the curtains that enclose the bed.

17 *aqua vitae:* an alcoholic drink.

19 *lamentable:* filled with grief; mournful.

Nurse. She's dead, deceased; she's dead! Alack the day!

Lady Capulet. Alack the day, she's dead, she's dead,
    she's dead!

30 **Capulet.** Ha! let me see her. Out alas! she's cold,
    Her blood is settled, and her joints are stiff;
    Life and these lips have long been separated.
    Death lies on her like an untimely frost
    Upon the sweetest flower of all the field.

35 **Nurse.** O lamentable day!

Lady Capulet.   O woeful time!

Capulet. Death, that hath ta'en her hence to make me
    wail,
    Ties up my tongue and will not let me speak.

[Enter Friar Laurence and Paris, with Musicians.]

40 **Friar Laurence.** Come, is the bride ready to go to
    church?

Capulet. Ready to go, but never to return.
    O son, the night before thy wedding day
    Hath death lain with thy wife. See, there she lies,
45   Flower as she was, deflowered by him.
    Death is my son-in-law, Death is my heir;
    My daughter he hath wedded. I will die
    And leave him all. Life, living, all is Death's.

Paris. Have I thought long to see this morning's face,
50   And doth it give me such a sight as this?

Lady Capulet. Accursed, unhappy, wretched, hateful
    day!
    Most miserable hour that e'er time saw
    In lasting labor of his pilgrimage!
55   But one, poor one, one poor and loving child,
    But one thing to rejoice and solace in,
    And cruel Death hath catched it from my sight!

Nurse. O woe! O woeful, woeful, woeful day!
    Most lamentable day, most woeful day
60   That ever ever I did yet behold!
    O day! O day! O day! O hateful day!
    Never was seen so black a day as this.
    O woeful day! O woeful day!

Paris. Beguiled, divorced, wronged, spited, slain!

33–34 Death . . . field: *What simile does Capulet use to describe what has happened to Juliet?*

48 Life . . . Death's: Life, the living, and everything else belongs to Death.

53–57 This is the most miserable hour that time ever saw in its long journey. I had only one child to make me happy, and Death has taken *(catched)* her from me.

64 Beguiled: tricked.

65 Most detestable Death, by thee beguiled,
By cruel cruel thee quite overthrown!
O love! O life! not life, but love in death!

Capulet. Despised, distressed, hated, martyred, killed!
Uncomfortable time, why camest thou now
70 To murder, murder our solemnity?
O child! O child! my soul, and not my child!
Dead art thou, dead! alack, my child is dead,
And with my child my joys are buried!

69–70 why . . . solemnity: Why did Death have to come to murder our celebration?

Friar Laurence. Peace, ho, for shame! Confusion's cure
75 lives not
In these confusions. Heaven and yourself
Had part in this fair maid! now heaven hath all,
And all the better is it for the maid.
Your part in her you could not keep from death,
80 But heaven keeps his part in eternal life.
The most you sought was her promotion,
For 'twas your heaven she should be advanced;
And weep ye now, seeing she is advanced
Above the clouds, as high as heaven itself?
85 O, in this love, you love your child so ill
That you run mad, seeing that she is well.
She's not well married that lives married long,
But she's best married that dies married young.
Dry up your tears and stick your rosemary
90 On this fair corse, and, as the custom is,
In all her best array bear her to church;
For though fond nature bids us all lament,
Yet nature's tears are reason's merriment.

74–88 The Friar comforts the family. He says that the cure for disaster **(confusion)** cannot be found in cries of grief. Juliet's family and heaven once shared her; now heaven has all of her. All the family ever wanted was the best for her; now she's in heaven—what could be better than that? It is best to die young, when the soul is still pure, without sin.

89–93 Do what is customary. Put rosemary, an herb, on her corpse **(corse)**, and take her, in her finest clothes **(best array)**, to church. Though it's natural to cry, common sense tells us we should rejoice for the dead.

Capulet. All things that we ordained festival
95 Turn from their office to black funeral—
Our instruments to melancholy bells,
Our wedding cheer to a sad burial feast;
Our solemn hymns to sullen dirges change;
Our bridal flowers serve for a buried corse;
100 And all things change them to the contrary.

94 ordained festival: intended for the wedding.

98 sullen dirges: sad, mournful tunes.

Friar Laurence. Sir, go you in; and, madam, go with
him;
And go, Sir Paris. Every one prepare
To follow this fair corse unto her grave.
105 The heavens do lower upon you for some ill;
Move them no more by crossing their high will.

105–106 The heavens . . . will: The fates **(heavens)** frown on you for some wrong you have done. Don't tempt them by refusing to accept their will (Juliet's death).

[Exeunt Capulet, Lady Capulet, Paris, *and* Friar.*]*

First Musician. Faith, we may put up our pipes, and be gone.

Nurse. Honest good fellows, ah, put up, put up,
110 For well you know this is a pitiful case.

[Exit.]

Second Musician. Aye, by my troth, the case may be amended.

[Enter Peter.*]*

Peter. Musicians, oh, musicians, "Heart's ease, heart's ease." Oh, an you will have me live, play "Heart's ease."

115 **First Musician.** Why "Heart's ease"?

Peter. Oh, musicians, because my heart itself plays "My heart is full of woe." Oh, play me some merry dump, to comfort me.

First Musician. Not a dump we, 'tis no time to play
120 now.

Peter. You will not, then?

First Musician. No.

Peter. I will then give it you soundly.

First Musician. What will you give us?

125 **Peter.** No money, on my faith, but the gleek. I will give you the minstrel.

First Musician. Then will I give you the serving creature.

Peter. Then will I lay the serving creature's dagger on
130 your pate. I will carry no crotchets. I'll re you, I'll fa you, do you note me?

First Musician. An you re us and fa us, you note us.

Second Musician. Pray you put up your dagger, and put out your wit.

135 **Peter.** Then have at you with my wit! I will drybeat you with an iron wit, and put up my iron dagger. Answer me like men:
    "When griping grief the heart doth wound
    And doleful dumps the mind oppress,
140 Then music with her silver sound—"

114–157 After the tragedy of Juliet's "death," Shakespeare injects a light and witty conversation between Peter and the musicians. Peter asks them to play "Heart's Ease," a popular song of the time and a *dump,* a sad song. They refuse, and insults and puns are traded. Peter says that instead of money he'll give them a jeering speech *(gleek),* and he insults them by calling them minstrels. In return they call him a servant. Then both make puns using notes of the singing scale, *re* and *fa.*

Why "silver sound"? Why "music with her silver
sound"?—What say you, Simon Catling?

First Musician. Marry, sir, because silver hath a sweet
sound.

145 **Peter.** Pretty! What say you, Hugh Rebeck?

Second Musician. I say "silver sound" because
musicians sound for silver.

Peter. Pretty too! What say you, James Soundpost?

Third Musician. Faith, I know not what to say.

150 **Peter.** Oh, I cry you mercy, you are the singer. I will
say for you. It is "music with her silver sound"
because musicians have no gold for sounding.
  "Then music with her silver sound
    With speedy help doth lend redress."

[Exit.]

155 **First Musician.** What a pestilent knave is this same!

Second Musician. Hang him, Jack! Come, we'll in here.
Tarry for the mourners, and stay dinner.

[Exeunt.]

Responding to Reading

1. Contrast Capulet's happy mood in Scene 4 with his anguish in Scene 5.
Does he genuinely love Juliet? Explain your opinion.

2. What is similar about the expressions of grief in Scene 5, lines 51–73?
How deeply do you think the characters feel? Explain your opinion.

3. Friar Laurence knows that Juliet is not dead. Is he admirable for
consoling the family or shameful for lying to them? Explain your
opinion.

Responding to Reading

First Impressions

1. What do you think of Juliet and the actions she has taken in this act?

Second Thoughts

2. Why is Friar Laurence's plan dangerous? What might go wrong?

   Think about
   • the uncertainties involved in dealing with drugs
   • Juliet's fears about waking up too early
   • the importance of timing to both Romeo and Juliet

3. Why doesn't Friar Laurence tell Juliet's parents about her secret marriage? Consider the consequences to both himself and Juliet.

4. The Nurse used to be Juliet's advisor and close friend. How is Juliet's anger with her important in Act Four? Do you think that Juliet would have acted differently if the Nurse had been involved in the conversation with Friar Laurence?

5. At this point which characters, if any, have earned your sympathy? Why?

6. Should any characters feel guilty? Which ones, and why?

Literary Concept: Comic Relief

In his tragedies Shakespeare often includes **comic relief,** or humorous scenes that relieve the overall emotional intensity. At the end of Scene 5, the conversation between Peter and the musicians is comic relief. It is meant to relieve the audience's tension after the grief-filled scene in which Juliet's body is discovered.

How do you feel about this conversation? Do you think it adds to the play, or would you cut it out? Explain your opinion. Find two other examples of comic relief in this act.

Writing Options

1. Give any character in this act a piece of your mind. Tell the character why his or her behavior is wrong or foolish. For example, you might criticize Capulet for his treatment of Juliet, or Juliet for taking the potion, or the Friar for planning the trick.

2. Describe another plan that Friar Laurence could have used to rescue Juliet from a second marriage and reunite her with Romeo.

3. Suppose that at this point Friar Laurence has to defend his actions to his superior in the church. Write a list of arguments that support the decisions he has made and the actions he has taken.

4. If Juliet were a teenager today confronted with a similar problem, what options would she have? List some choices for her and put a star by the one you would advise her to make.

e x t e n d

Options for Learning

1 • **Visions of Horror** In Scene 3 Juliet imagines the horrible things she might see when she awakes inside the family tomb. Reread lines 41–59 and try to visualize the inside of the tomb. Imagine what she describes. Paint or draw the picture in Juliet's mind.

2 • **Debate Interpretation** You might judge Capulet as either self-centered and egotistical, or genuinely concerned about his daughter's welfare. You might see Friar Laurence as an immoral priest trying to cover up his wrongdoing, or as a gentle person who's trying to do the best he can for two young people. Decide how you feel about one of these characters and find a classmate with the opposite point of view. Using lines from the text as your evidence, debate the character's values and worth for your class.

3 • **Comic Relief** Shakespeare chose to relieve the tension caused by Juliet's "death" by creating a comic scene between Peter and the musicians. Improvise a different scene with different characters that performs the same function. You may introduce new characters as Shakespeare did.

4 • **Good Grief!** With several classmates act out the part of Scene 5 in which Juliet's body is discovered and everyone responds to her "death."

ACT FIVE

Scene 1 *A street in Mantua.*

Balthasar, Romeo's servant, comes from Verona to tell him that Juliet is dead and lies in the Capulet's tomb. Since Romeo has not yet received any word from the Friar, he believes Balthasar. He immediately decides to return to Verona in order to die next to Juliet. He sends Balthasar away and sets out to find a pharmacist who will sell him poison.

[*Enter* Romeo.]

Romeo. If I may trust the flattering truth of sleep,
My dreams presage some joyful news at hand.
My bosom's lord sits lightly in his throne,
And all this day an unaccustomed spirit
5 Lifts me above the ground with cheerful thoughts.
I dreamt my lady came and found me dead
(Strange dream that gives a dead man leave to think!)
And breathed such life with kisses in my lips
10 That I revived and was an emperor.
Ah me! how sweet is love itself possessed,
When but love's shadows are so rich in joy!

[*Enter* Romeo's *servant*, Balthasar, *booted.*]

News from Verona! How now, Balthasar?
Dost thou not bring me letters from the friar?
15 How doth my lady? Is my father well?
How fares my Juliet? That I ask again,
For nothing can be ill if she be well.

Balthasar. Then she is well, and nothing can be ill.
Her body sleeps in Capels' monument,
20 And her immortal part with angels lives.
I saw her laid low in her kindred's vault
And presently took post to tell it you.
O, pardon me for bringing these ill news,
Since you did leave it for my office, sir.

25 **Romeo.** Is it e'en so? Then I defy you, stars!
Thou knowst my lodging. Get me ink and paper
And hire posthorses. I will hence tonight.

Balthasar. I do beseech you, sir, have patience
Your looks are pale and wild and do import
30 Some misadventure.

GUIDE FOR READING

1–5 If I can trust my dreams, something joyful is about to happen. My heart **(bosom's lord)** is happy and I am content.

6–10 *What was Romeo's dream?*

17 If Juliet is well, no news can be bad.

18–24 Balthasar replies that Juliet is well, since although her body is dead, her soul **(her immortal part)** is with the angels. As soon as he saw her in the tomb, he immediately rode to Mantua **(presently took post)** to tell Romeo. He asks forgiveness for bringing bad news but reminds Romeo that he had given Balthasar the duty **(office)** of bringing important news.
25 I defy you stars: Romeo angrily challenges fate, which has caused him so much grief.

29–30 import some misadventure: suggest that something bad will happen.

Romeo.　　　　　　　Tush, thou art deceived.
Leave me and do the thing I bid thee do.
Hast thou no letters to me from the friar?

Balthasar. No, my good lord.

35 **Romeo.**　　　　　　　No matter. Get thee gone
And hire those horses. I'll be with thee straight.

[Exit Balthasar.]

Well, Juliet, I will lie with thee tonight.
Let's see for means. O mischief, thou art swift
To enter in the thoughts of desperate men!
40 I do remember an apothecary,
And hereabouts he dwells, which late I noted
In tattered weeds, with overwhelming brows,
Culling of simples. Meager were his looks,
Sharp misery had worn him to the bones;
45 And in his needy shop a tortoise hung,
An alligator stuffed, and other skins
Of ill-shaped fishes; and about his shelves
A beggarly account of empty boxes,
Green earthen pots, bladders, and musty seeds,
50 Remnants of packthread, and old cakes of roses
Were thinly scattered, to make up a show.
Noting this penury, to myself I said,
"An if a man did need a poison now
Whose sale is present death in Mantua,
55 Here lives a caitiff wretch would sell it him."
O, this same thought did but forerun my need,
And this same needy man must sell it me.
As I remember, this should be the house.
Being holiday, the beggar's shop is shut.
60 What, ho! apothecary!

[Enter Apothecary.]

Apothecary. Who calls so loud?

Romeo. Come hither, man. I see that thou art poor.
Hold, there is forty ducats. Let me have
A dram of poison, such soon-speeding gear
65 As will disperse itself through all the veins
That the life-weary taker may fall dead,
And that the trunk may be discharged of breath
As violently as hasty powder fired
Doth hurry from the fatal cannon's womb.

37 *What does Romeo mean?*

38–43 ***Let's see for means:*** Let me find a way *(means)* to join Juliet in death. ***apothecary:*** pharmacist ***tattered weeds:*** ragged clothes. ***Culling of simples:*** sorting herbs.

45–51 Romeo describes the items in the apothecary's shop.

52 ***penury:*** poverty.

53–55 Although it is a crime to sell poison, the apothecary is such a miserable person *(caitiff wretch)* that he would probably do it for the money.

63–69 ***ducats:*** gold coins. Forty ducats was a large sum of money. Romeo asks for fast-acting *(soon-speeding)* poison.

70 **Apothecary.** Such mortal drugs I have; but Mantua's law
Is death to any he that utters them.

Romeo. Art thou so bare and full of wretchedness
And fearest to die? Famine is in thy cheeks,
75 Need and oppression starveth in thine eyes,
Contempt and beggary hangs upon thy back:
The world is not thy friend, nor the world's law;
The world affords no law to make thee rich;
Then be not poor, but break it and take this.

80 **Apothecary.** My poverty but not my will consents.

Romeo. I pay thy poverty and not thy will.

Apothecary. Put this in any liquid thing you will
And drink it off, and if you had the strength
Of twenty men, it would dispatch you straight.

85 **Romeo.** There is thy gold—worse poison to men's souls,
Doing more murder in this loathsome world,
Than these poor compounds that thou mayst not sell.
90 I sell thee poison; thou hast sold me none.
Farewell. Buy food and get thyself in flesh.
Come, cordial and not poison, go with me
To Juliet's grave; for there must I use thee.

[Exeunt.]

70–72 Such . . . them: I have such deadly drugs, but selling them is a crime punishable by death.

73–79 Romeo argues that the man lives in such misery he has no reason to fear death or the law. He urges the apothecary to improve his situation by selling the poison.

80 I'm doing this for the money, not because I think it's right.
81 I'm not paying your conscience.

84 *dispatch you straight:* kill you instantly.

92 Romeo refers to the poison as a ***cordial,*** a drink believed to be good for the heart.

Scene 2 *Friar Laurence's cell in Verona.*

Friar Laurence's messenger arrives saying that he was unable to deliver the letter to Romeo. Friar Laurence, his plans ruined, rushes to the Capulet vault before Juliet awakes. He intends to hide her in his room until Romeo can come to take her away.

[Verona. Friar Laurence's cell.]

[Enter Friar John.]

Friar John. Holy Franciscan friar, brother, ho!

[Enter Friar Laurence.]

Friar Laurence. This same should be the voice of Friar John.
Welcome from Mantua. What says Romeo?
5 Or, if his mind be writ, give me his letter.

Friar John. Going to find a barefoot brother out,
  One of our order to associate me,
  Here in this city visiting the sick,
  And finding him, the searchers of the town,
10 Suspecting that we both were in a house
  Where the infectious pestilence did reign,
  Sealed up the doors, and would not let us forth,
  So that my speed to Mantua there was stayed.

Friar Laurence. Who bare my letter, then, to Romeo?

15 **Friar John.** I could not send it—here it is again—
  Nor get a messenger to bring it thee,
  So fearful were they of infection.

Friar Laurence. Unhappy fortune! By my brotherhood,
  The letter was not nice, but full of charge,
20 Of dear import, and the neglecting it
  May do much danger. Friar John, go hence,
  Get me an iron crow and bring it straight
  Unto my cell.

Friar John.   Brother, I'll go and bring it thee.

  [Exit.]

25 **Friar Laurence.** Now must I to the monument alone.
  Within this three hours will fair Juliet wake.
  She will beshrew me much that Romeo
  Hath had no notice of these accidents;
  But I will write again to Mantua,
30 And keep her at my cell till Romeo come—
  Poor living corse, closed in a dead man's tomb!

  [Exeunt.]

6–13 Friar John explains why he didn't go to Mantua. He had asked another friar *(One of our order)*, who had been caring for the sick, to go with him. The health officials of the town, believing that the friars had come into contact with the deadly disease, the plague *(infectious pestilence)*, locked them up to keep them from infecting others.

14 bare: carried (bore).

19–21 The letter wasn't trivial *(nice)* but rather contained instructions *(charge)* of great importance *(dear import)*. The fact that it wasn't sent *(neglecting it)* may cause great harm. *What would the letter have told Romeo that he does not know?*
22 iron crow: crowbar. *Why might Friar Laurence need a crowbar?*

25–28 Now I must hurry to Juliet's side, since she'll awaken in three hours. Juliet will be furious with me *(beshrew me)* when she discovers that Romeo doesn't know what has happened.

Responding to Reading

1. Why does Romeo feel optimistic at the beginning of Scene 1? How could his dream be interpreted as a bad sign instead of a good one?

2. Would you have expected Romeo to react any differently to the news of Juliet's death? Why or why not?

3. What is Romeo's plan? Is his plan consistent with his personality and behavior so far? Explain your answer.

4. Why is Friar Laurence so upset that his message did not reach Romeo? What are the possible consequences of the lack of communication?

Scene 3   *The cemetery that contains the Capulets' tomb.*

In the dark of night Paris comes to the cemetery to put flowers on Juliet's grave. At the same time Romeo arrives, and Paris hides. Romeo opens the tomb and Paris assumes that he is going to harm the bodies. He challenges Romeo, who warns him to leave. They fight and Romeo kills Paris. When Romeo recognizes the dead Paris, he lays his body inside the tomb as Paris requested. Romeo declares his love for Juliet, drinks the poison, and dies. Shortly after, Friar Laurence arrives and discovers both bodies. When Juliet wakes up, the Friar urges her to leave with him before the guard comes. Juliet refuses and when the Friar leaves, she kills herself with Romeo's dagger. The guards and the Prince arrive, followed by the Capulets and Lord Montague, whose wife has just died because of Romeo's exile. Friar Laurence and both servants explain has what happened. Capulet and Montague finally end their feud and promise to erect statues honoring Romeo and Juliet.

[Enter Paris *and his* Page *with flowers and a torch.]*

Paris. Give me thy torch, boy. Hence, and stand aloof.
    Yet put it out, for I would not be seen.
    Under yond yew tree lay thee all along,
    Holding thine ear close to the hollow ground.
5   So shall no foot upon the churchyard tread
    (Being loose, unfirm, with digging up of graves)
    But thou shalt hear it. Whistle then to me,
    As signal that thou hearst something approach.
    Give me those flowers. Do as I bid thee, go.

10 **Page.** *[Aside]* I am almost afraid to stand alone
    Here in the churchyard; yet I will adventure.

[Withdraws.]

Paris. Sweet flower, with flowers thy bridal bed I strew

[He strews the tomb with flowers.]

    (O woe! thy canopy is dust and stones)
    Which with sweet water nightly I will dew;
15   Or, wanting that, with tears distilled by moans.
    The obsequies that I for thee will keep
    Nightly shall be to strew thy grave and weep.

[The Page *whistles.]*

    The boy gives warning something doth approach.
    What cursed foot wanders this way tonight

1–9 Paris wants nobody to know that he is visiting Juliet's tomb. He tells his servant to keep his ear to the ground and whistle if anyone comes near.

12–17 Paris promises to decorate Juliet's grave with flowers, as he does now, and with either perfume **(sweet water)** or his tears. He will perform these honoring rites **(obsequies)** every night.

20　To cross my obsequies and true love's rite?
　　What, with a torch? Muffle me, night, awhile.

[Withdraws.]

[Enter Romeo *and* Balthasar *with a torch, a mattock, and a crow of iron.]*

Romeo. Give me that mattock and the wrenching iron.
　　Hold, take this letter. Early in the morning
　　See thou deliver it to my lord and father.
25　Give me the light. Upon thy life I charge thee,
　　Whate'er thou hearest or seest, stand all aloof
　　And do not interrupt me in my course.
　　Why I descend into this bed of death
　　Is partly to behold my lady's face,
30　But chiefly to take thence from her dead finger
　　A precious ring—a ring that I must use
　　In dear employment. Therefore hence, be gone.
　　But if thou, jealous, dost return to pry
　　In what I farther shall intend to do,
35　By heaven, I will tear thee joint by joint
　　And strew this hungry churchyard with thy limbs.
　　The time and my intents are savage-wild,
　　More fierce and more inexorable far
　　Than empty tigers or the roaring sea.

40　**Balthasar.** I will be gone, sir, and not trouble you.

　　Romeo. So shalt thou show me friendship. Take thou
　　that. Live, and be prosperous; and farewell, good
　　fellow.

　　Balthasar. *[Aside]* For all this same, I'll hide me
45　hereabout.
　　His looks I fear, and his intents I doubt.

[Withdraws.]

　　Romeo. Thou detestable maw, thou womb of death,
　　Gorged with the dearest morsel of the earth,
　　Thus I enforce thy rotten jaws to open,
50　And in despite I'll cram thee with more food.

[Romeo opens the tomb.]

　　Paris. This is that banisht haughty Montague
　　That murdered my love's cousin—with which grief
　　It is supposed the fair creature died—
　　And here is come to do some villainous shame

19–22 What cursed . . . awhile: who dares to interrupt my ritual? Is he even carrying a torch? Let the darkness hide me. **mattock . . . iron:** ax and crowbar.

23–24 *What might Romeo have written to his father?*

28–32 *What two reasons does Romeo give for going into Juliet's tomb?*

32 In dear employment: for an important purpose.
33–39 Romeo threatens that if Balthasar returns because he is curious **(jealous),** Romeo will rip him apart and throw his bones around the churchyard. His intention is more unstoppable **(inexorable)** than a hungry **(empty)** tiger or the waves of an ocean.

44–45 Balthasar decides to hide in the cemetery in spite of what he has just promised Romeo. *Who else is hiding in the cemetery at this point?*

47–50 Romeo addresses the tomb as though it were devouring people. He calls it a hateful stomach **(destestable maw)** that is filled **(gorged)** with the dearest morsel of earth, Juliet. He uses his crowbar to open its **rotten jaws** and feeds himself to it.

55   To the dead bodies. I will apprehend him.
     Stop thy unhallowed toil, vile Montague!
     Can vengeance be pursued further than death?
     Condemned villain, I do apprehend thee.
     Obey, and go with me; for thou must die.

60   **Romeo.** I must indeed; and therefore came I hither.
     Good gentle youth, tempt not a desp'rate man.
     Fly hence and leave me. Think upon these gone;
     Let them affright thee. I beseech thee, youth,
     Put not another sin upon my head
65   By urging me to fury. O, be gone!
     By heaven, I love thee better than myself.
     For I come hither armed against myself.
     Stay not, be gone. Live, and hereafter say
     A madman's mercy bid thee run away.

70   **Paris.** I do defy thy conjuration
     And apprehend thee for a felon here.

     Romeo. Wilt thou provoke me? Then have at
     thee, boy!

     [They fight.]

     Page. O Lord, they fight! I will go call the watch.

     [Exit.]

75   **Paris.** O, I am slain! *[Falls.]* If thou be merciful,
     Open the tomb, lay me with Juliet.

     [Dies.]

     Romeo. In faith, I will. Let me peruse this face.
     Mercutio's kinsman, noble County Paris!
     What said my man when my betossed soul
80   Did not attend him as we rode? I think
     He told me Paris should have married Juliet.
     Said he not so? or did I dream it so?
     Or am I mad, hearing him talk of Juliet,
     To think it was so? O, give me thy hand,
85   One writ with me in sour misfortune's book!
     I'll bury thee in a triumphant grave.
     A grave? O, no, a lantern, slaughtered youth,
     For here lies Juliet, and her beauty makes
     This vault a feasting presence full of light.
90   Death, lie thou there, by a dead man interred.

     [Lays Paris *in the tomb.]*

55–59 apprehend: arrest. Recognizing Romeo, Paris speaks these lines to himself. He is angry with Romeo, believing that Romeo's having killed Tybalt caused Juliet to die of grief for her cousin. *What does he think Romeo intends to do at the tomb?*

60–69 Romeo rejects Paris' challenge. He tells Paris to think of those already killed and leave before Romeo is forced to kill him too. Romeo swears that he has come to harm himself, not Paris.

70–71 I reject your appeal **(defy thy conjuration)** and arrest you as a criminal.

77–90 Romeo discovers that the man he has just killed is Paris, whom he vaguely remembers was supposed to marry Juliet. He says that like himself, Paris has been a victim of bad luck. He will bury him with Juliet, whose beauty fills the tomb with light. Paris' corpse **(Death)** is being buried **(interred)** by a dead man in that Romeo expects to be dead soon.

How oft when men are at the point of death
Have they been merry! which their keepers call
A lightning before death. O, how may I
Call this a lightning? O my love! my wife!
95 Death, that hath sucked the honey of thy breath,
Hath had no power yet upon thy beauty.
Thou art not conquered. Beauty's ensign yet
Is crimson in thy lips and in thy cheeks,
And death's pale flag is not advanced there.
100 Tybalt, liest thou there in thy bloody sheet?
O, what more favor can I do to thee
Than with that hand that cut thy youth in twain
To sunder his that was thine enemy?
Forgive me, cousin! Ah, dear Juliet,
105 Why art thou yet so fair? Shall I believe
That unsubstantial Death is amorous,
And that the lean abhorred monster keeps
Thee here in dark to be his paramour?
For fear of that I still will stay with thee
110 And never from this palace of dim night
Depart again. Here, here will I remain
With worms that are thy chambermaids. O, here
Will I set up my everlasting rest
And shake the yoke of inauspicious stars
115 From this world-wearied flesh. Eyes, look your last!
Arms, take your last embrace! and, lips, O you
The doors of breath, seal with a righteous kiss
A dateless bargain to engrossing death!
Come, bitter conduct; come, unsavory guide!
120 Thou desperate pilot, now at once run on
The dashing rocks thy seasick weary bark!
Here's to my love! *[Drinks.]* O true apothecary!
Thy drugs are quick. Thus with a kiss I die.

[Falls.]

[Enter Friar Laurence, *with lantern, crow, and spade.]*

Friar Laurence. Saint Francis be my speed! how
125 oft tonight
Have my old feet stumbled at graves! Who's there?

Balthasar. Here's one, a friend, and one that knows
you well.

Friar Laurence. Bliss be upon you! Tell me, good
130 my friend,

95–99 Romeo notices that death has had no effect on Juliet's beauty. The sign *(ensign)* of beauty is still in Juliet's red lips and rosy cheeks.

101–103 *O what . . . enemy:* I can best repay you (Tybalt) by killing your enemy (myself) with the same hand that cut your youth in two *(twain)*.

105–108 Romeo can't get over how beautiful Juliet still looks. He asks whether Death is loving *(amorous)* and whether it has taken Juliet as its lover *(paramour)*.

112–115 *O, here . . . flesh:* Here I will cause my death *(everlasting rest)* and rid myself of the burden *(shake the yoke)* of an unhappy fate *(inauspicious stars)*.

118 *dateless:* eternal; neverending. Romeo means that what he is about to do can never be undone.
120–121 *thy seasick weary bark:* Romeo compares himself to the pilot of a ship *(bark)* who is going to crash on the rocks because he is so weary and sick.

"Death, that hath sucked the honey of thy breath, Hath had no power yet upon thy beauty."

What torch is yond that vainly lends his light
To grubs and eyeless skulls? As I discern,
It burneth in the Capels' monument.

Balthasar. It doth so, holy sir; and there's my master,
135   One that you love.

Friar Laurence. Who is it?

Balthasar.   Romeo.

Friar Laurence. How long hath he been there?

Balthasar. Full half an hour.

140 **Friar Laurence.** Go with me to the vault.

Balthasar.   I dare not, sir.
My master knows not but I am gone hence,
And fearfully did menace me with death
If I did stay to look on his intents.

145 **Friar Laurence.** Stay then; I'll go alone. Fear comes
upon me.
O, much I fear some ill unthrifty thing.

Balthasar. As I did sleep under this yew tree here,
I dreamt my master and another fought,
150   And that my master slew him.

Friar Laurence.   Romeo!

[Stoops and looks on the blood and weapons.]

Alack, alack, what blood is this which stains
The stony entrance of this sepulcher?
What mean these masterless and gory swords
155   To lie discolored by this place of peace?

[Enters the tomb.]

Romeo! O, pale! Who else? What, Paris too?
And steeped in blood? Ah, what an unkind hour
Is guilty of this lamentable chance!
The lady stirs.

[Juliet rises.]

160 **Juliet.** O comfortable friar! where is my lord?
I do remember well where I should be,
And there I am. Where is my Romeo?

Friar Laurence. I hear some noise. Lady, come from
that nest

141–144 I can't go with you to the tomb. My master threatened me with death if I stayed here.

145–147 The Friar fears that something unlucky **(unthrifty)** has happened.

151–155 Why are these bloody swords lying here at the tomb **(sepulcher)**, a place that should be peaceful? (The swords are also **masterless**, or without their owners.)

160 comfortable: comforting.

165 Of death, contagion, and unnatural sleep.
     A greater power than we can contradict
     Hath thwarted our intents. Come, come away.
     Thy husband in thy bosom there lies dead;
     And Paris too. Come, I'll dispose of thee
170 Among a sisterhood of holy nuns.
     Stay not to question, for the watch is coming.
     Come, go, good Juliet. I dare no longer stay.

Juliet. Go, get thee hence, for I will not away.

[Exit Friar Laurence.]

     What's here? A cup, closed in my true love's hand?
175 Poison, I see, hath been his timeless end.
     O churl! drunk all, and left no friendly drop
     To help me after? I will kiss thy lips.
     Haply some poison yet doth hang on them
     To make me die with a restorative.

[Kisses him.]

180 Thy lips are warm!

Chief Watchman. *[Within]* Lead, boy. Which way?

Juliet. Yea, noise? Then I'll be brief. O happy dagger!

[Snatches Romeo's dagger.]

     This is thy sheath; there rust, and let me die.

[She stabs herself and falls.]

[Enter Watchmen with the Page of Paris.]

Page. This is the place. There, where the torch doth
185 burn.

Chief Watchman. The ground is bloody. Search about
     the churchyard.
     Go, some of you; whoe'er you find attach.

[Exeunt some of the Watch.]

     Pitiful sight! here lies the County slain;
190 And Juliet bleeding, warm, and newly dead,
     Who here hath lain this two days buried.
     Go, tell the Prince; run to the Capulets;
     Raise up the Montagues; some others search.

[Exeunt others of the Watch.]

     We see the ground whereon these woes do lie,
195 But the true ground of all these piteous woes

163–173 The Friar hears noise and wants Juliet to get out of the awful tomb. He says that a greater force than they can fight **(contradict)**, meaning God or fate, has ruined their plans **(thwarted our intents).** He informs her of Romeo's and Paris' deaths and says he'll find a place for her in a convent of nuns. *Why is the Friar so anxious to leave?*

175 *timeless:* happening before its proper time.

176–180 Juliet calls Romeo a miser **(churl)** for not leaving some poison for her. She kisses him, hoping that perhaps **(haply)** some of the poison is still on his lips.

183 From this point on, the churchyard will be filled with people and lights.

188 *attach:* arrest.

193 *Raise up:* awaken.

194–196 We see the earth **(ground)** these bodies lie on. But the real cause **(true ground)** of these deaths is yet for us to discover **(descry).**

"O happy dagger! This is thy sheath; there rust, and let me die."

We cannot without circumstance descry.

[*Reenter some of the* Watch, *with* Balthasar.]

Second Watchman. Here's Romeo's man. We found
  him in the churchyard.

Chief Watchman. Hold him in safety till the Prince
200   come hither.

199–205 The guards arrest Balthasar
and Friar Laurence as suspicious
characters.

[Reenter Friar Laurence and another Watchman.]

Third Watchman. Here is a friar that trembles, sighs, and weeps.
We took this mattock and this spade from him
As he was coming from this churchyard side.

205 **Chief Watchman.** A great suspicion! Stay the friar too.

[Enter the Prince and Attendants.]

Prince. What misadventure is so early up,
That calls our person from our morning rest?

[Enter Capulet, Lady Capulet, and others.]

Capulet. What should it be, that they so shriek abroad?

Lady Capulet. The people in the street cry "Romeo,"
210   Some "Juliet," and some "Paris"; and all run,
With open outcry, toward our monument.

Prince. What fear is this which startles in our ears?

212 *startles:* causes alarm.

Chief Watchman. Sovereign, here lies the County Paris slain;
215   And Romeo dead, and Juliet, dead before,
Warm and new killed.

Prince. Search, seek, and know how this foul murder comes.

Chief Watchman. Here is a friar, and slaughtered
220   Romeo's man,
With instruments upon them fit to open
These dead men's tombs.

Capulet. O heavens! O wife, look how our daughter bleeds!
225   This dagger hath mista'en, for, lo, his house
Is empty on the back of Montague,
And it missheathed in my daughter's bosom!

225–227 This dagger has missed its target. It should rest in the sheath *(house)* that Romeo wears. Instead it is in Juliet's bosom.

Lady Capulet. O me! this sight of death is as a bell
That warns my old age to a sepulcher.

[Enter Montague and others.]

230 **Prince.** Come, Montague; for thou art early up
To see thy son and heir now early down.

Montague. Alas, my liege, my wife is dead tonight!
Grief of my son's exile hath stopped her breath.
What further woe conspires against mine age?

232–234 My son's exile has caused my wife to die. What other sadness plots against me in my old age?

235 **Prince.** Look, and thou shalt see.

Montague. O thou untaught! what manners is in this,
  To press before thy father to a grave?

Prince. Seal up the mouth of outrage for a while,
  Till we can clear these ambiguities
240 And know their spring, their head, their true
  descent;
  And then will I be general of your woes
  And lead you even to death. Meantime forbear,
  And let mischance be slave to patience.
245 Bring forth the parties of suspicion.

Friar Laurence. I am the greatest, able to do least,
  Yet most suspected, as the time and place
  Doth make against me, of this direful murder;
  And here I stand, both to impeach and purge
250 Myself condemned and myself excused.

Prince. Then say at once what thou dost know in this.

Friar Laurence. I will be brief, for my short date
  of breath
  Is not so long as is a tedious tale.
255 Romeo, there dead, was husband to that Juliet;
  And she, there dead, that Romeo's faithful wife.
  I married them; and their stol'n marriage day
  Was Tybalt's doomsday, whose untimely death
  Banisht the new-made bridegroom from this city;
260 For whom, and not for Tybalt, Juliet pined.
  You, to remove that siege of grief from her,
  Betrothed and would have married her perforce
  To County Paris. Then comes she to me
  And with wild looks bid me devise some mean
265 To rid her from this second marriage,
  Or in my cell there would she kill herself.
  Then gave I her (so tutored by my art)
  A sleeping potion; which so took effect
  As I intended, for it wrought on her
270 The form of death. Meantime I writ to Romeo
  That he should hither come as this dire night
  To help to take her from her borrowed grave,
  Being the time the potion's force should cease.
  But he which bore my letter, Friar John,
275 Was stayed by accident, and yesternight
  Returned my letter back. Then all alone

236–237 what manners . . . grave:
What kind of behavior is this, for a son
to die before his father?
238–245 Seal . . . descent: Stop your
emotional outbursts until we can find
out the source *(spring)* of these
confusing events *(ambiguities)*. Wait
(forbear) and let's find out what
happened.

246–250 Friar Laurence confesses that
he is most responsible for these
events. He will both accuse *(impeach)*
himself and clear *(purge)* himself of
guilt.

259 It was Romeo's banishment, not
Tybalt's death, that made Juliet sad.

272 borrowed: temporary.

At the prefixed hour of her waking
Came I to take her from her kindred's vault;
Meaning to keep her closely at my cell
280 Till I conveniently could send to Romeo.
But when I came, some minute ere the time
Of her awaking, here untimely lay
The noble Paris and true Romeo dead.
She wakes; and I entreated her come forth
285 And bear this work of heaven with patience;
But then a noise did scare me from the tomb,
And she, too desperate, would not go with me,
But, as it seems, did violence on herself.
All this I know, and to the marriage
290 Her nurse is privy; and if aught in this
Miscarried by my fault, let my old life
Be sacrificed, some hour before his time,
Unto the rigor of severest law.

Prince. We still have known thee for a holy man.
295 Where's Romeo's man? What can he say in this?

Balthasar. I brought my master news of Juliet's death;
And then in post he came from Mantua
To this same place, to this same monument.
This letter he early bid me give his father,
300 And threatened me with death, going in the vault,
If I departed not and left him there.

Prince. Give me the letter. I will look on it.
Where is the County's page that raised the watch?
Sirrah, what made your master in this place?

305 **Page.** He came with flowers to strew his lady's grave;
And bid me stand aloof, and so I did.
Anon comes one with light to ope the tomb;
And by-and-by my master drew on him;
And then I ran away to call the watch.

310 **Prince.** This letter doth make good the friar's words,
Their course of love, the tidings of her death;
And here he writes that he did buy a poison
Of a poor 'pothecary, and therewithal
Came to this vault to die and lie with Juliet.
315 Where be these enemies? Capulet, Montague,
See what a scourge is laid upon your hate,
That heaven finds means to kill your joys with love!
And I, for winking at your discords too,

289–293 and to . . . law: Her nurse can bear witness to the secret marriage. If I am responsible for any of this, let the law punish me with death.

297 in post: at full speed.

303–304 Where . . . this place: The Prince asks for Paris's servant, who notified the guards **(raised the watch)**. Then he asks the servant why Paris was at the cemetery.

307–309 Soon **(Anon),** someone with a light came and opened the tomb. Paris drew his sword, and I ran to call the guards.

310 Romeo's letter shows that Friar Laurence has told the truth.
315–319 Where are the enemies whose feud started all this trouble? Capulet and Montague, look at the punishment your hatred has brought on you. Heaven has killed your children **(joys)** with love. For shutting my eyes to your arguments **(discords)**, I have lost two relatives (Mercutio and Paris). We all have been punished.

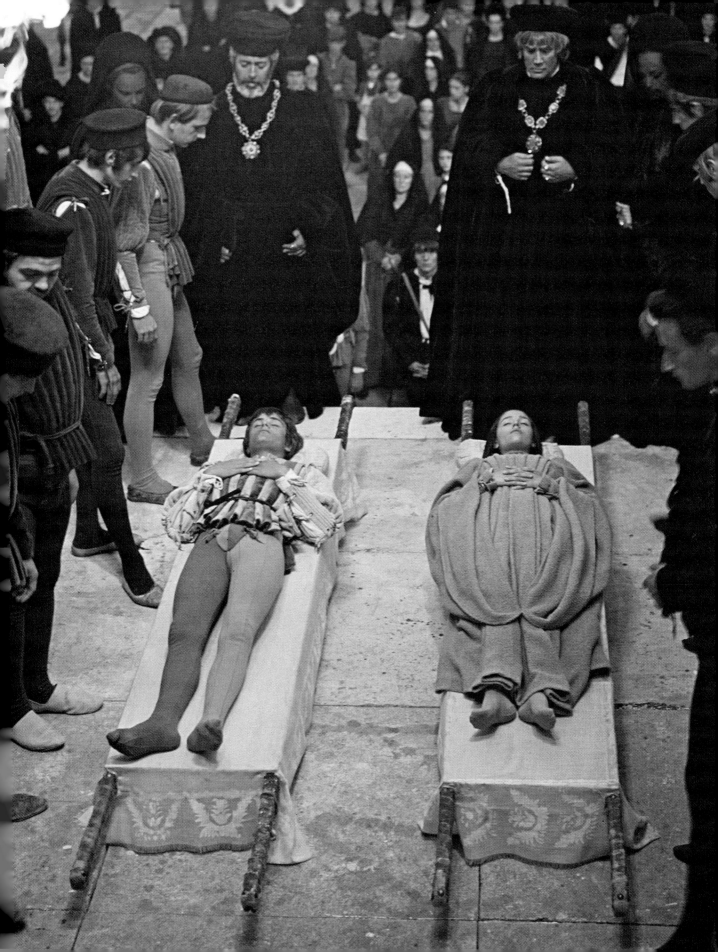

Have lost a brace of kinsmen. All are punished.

320 **Capulet.** O brother Montague, give me thy hand.
This is my daughter's jointure, for no more
Can I demand.

Montague.   But I can give thee more;
For I will raise her statue in pure gold,
325 That whiles Verona by that name is known,
There shall no figure at such rate be set
As that of true and faithful Juliet.

Capulet. As rich shall Romeo's by his lady's lie—
Poor sacrifices of our enmity!

330 **Prince.** A glooming peace this morning with it brings.
The sun for sorrow will not show his head.
Go hence, to have more talk of these sad things;
Some shall be pardoned, and some punished;
For never was a story of more woe
335 Than this of Juliet and her Romeo.

[Exeunt.]

321 *jointure:* dowry, the payment a bride's father makes to the groom. Capulet means that no one could demand more of a bride's father than he has already paid.
324–327 *at such rate be set:* be valued so highly. *What does Montague promise to do for the memory of Juliet?*

328–329 Capulet promises to do the same for Romeo as Montague will do for Juliet. Their children have become sacrifices to their hatred **(enmity)**.

*R*esponding to Reading

1. Are Romeo's actions in this scene consistent with his previous behavior? Explain.

   Think about
   - his threat to his servant
   - his discussion and fight with Paris
   - his words to Tybalt's corpse
   - his final words to Juliet

2. Does your opinion of Paris change in this scene? Why or why not?

3. How would you judge the Friar for his actions in this scene?

   Think about
   - why he leaves the tomb after Juliet awakens
   - what might have happened if he had stayed in the tomb
   - his statement that the law could punish him
   - the Prince's apparent forgiveness of him

4. Is the final reconciliation between Montague and Capulet believable? Why or why not?

Responding to Reading

First Impressions

1. What is your first reaction to the suicides of Romeo and Juliet? Jot down your feelings.

Second Thoughts

2. In your judgment, do Romeo and Juliet act nobly or cowardly in choosing suicide? Consider other actions they might have chosen.

3. What events in this act could be due to fate? How much responsibility do you think fate bears in the tragedy? Explain.

4. The Prince blames Montague, Capulet, and himself for this tragedy. Who do you think should take the most blame? Explain.

   Think about
   • the actions of Romeo and Juliet
   • the actions of Friar Laurence and the Nurse
   • Tybalt and Paris

5. Do you think either Romeo or Juliet grows in character from the beginning of the play to the end? Support your answer with evidence from the play.

Literary Concept: Tragedy

A **tragedy** is a drama in which events turn out disastrously for the main characters, often resulting in death. While fate is a major cause of the tragic ending, weaknesses or flaws within characters also contribute significantly. What are the flaws in the characters of Romeo and Juliet? What flaws in other characters contribute to the tragedy?

Concept Review: Plot   Review the plot diagram you made on page 807. In a tragedy the resolution of the plot is called a **catastrophe.** What events from Act Four can you now list as part of the falling action? What events from Act Five can you list as belonging to the resolution, or catastrophe?

Writing Options

1. Do you think Shakespeare glorifies suicide in this play or condemns it? Write your opinion and support it with details from the play.

2. Choose one character whose actions you think are stupid or evil. Write a letter to the character and bluntly state your opinion of his or her actions.

3. Many songs make references to Romeo and Juliet. Write lyrics to a song of your own that summarize the story.

4. Write a new ending to the play that avoids suicide but is believable. You may write in play form or simply describe your suggested change.

e x t e n d

*O*ptions for Learning

1 • Advertising Several movies have been made from this play. Make a poster that a movie theater might display to advertise the movie. Emphasize parts of the story that have box-office appeal, such as fight scenes and romance. Illustrate the poster with an enticing scene. Display your finished poster.

2 • Lights, Action, Camera! Videotape one segment of the play. Plan which scene you will shoot and where you will shoot it. Arrange for classmates to act out the roles. Figure out lighting and camera angles before you start. You might want to film parts of the scene twice and then edit together the best takes before showing your film to the class.

3 • Whodunit? In the style of *Sixty Minutes* or another television investigative magazine, act out a documentary that attempts to answer the question of who should be held responsible for the deaths of Romeo and Juliet. Decide on the guilty characters and report on their actions throughout the play. Interview them, asking tough questions. Have eyewitnesses back up your accusations. Build a convincing case that these characters are responsible.

4 • West Side Story Watch the movie *West Side Story*. As you watch, take notes comparing the movie's plot to that of *Romeo and Juliet*. Present your findings in an oral report to the class.

William Shakespeare
1564–1616

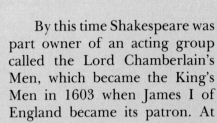

Even though William Shakespeare is probably the most famous writer who ever lived, we know surprisingly few facts about him. He was born in Stratford-on-Avon, a small town less than a hundred miles northwest of London, probably on April 23. Shakespeare's family was middle-class. His father was a glove maker who later became mayor of the town. His mother was a distant relative of a wealthy family who lived not far from Stratford.

Scholars assume that Shakespeare went to a local grammar school, as was the custom for middle-class youth. There he probably studied Latin and read works by ancient Roman writers. This was the extent of his formal education. At age eighteen he married Anne Hathaway, a local woman seven or eight years older than he. They had a daughter in 1583 and twins—a boy and a girl—in 1585.

Sometime after the birth of the twins, Shakespeare moved to London, apparently without his family. There are no records of what he did during the next seven years. However, by 1592, he was one of the most successful playwrights in London. By 1596, the year that *The Tragedy of Romeo and Juliet* was first performed, ten of his plays had been produced in London.

By this time Shakespeare was part owner of an acting group called the Lord Chamberlain's Men, which became the King's Men in 1603 when James I of England became its patron. At that time, acting troupes were a business; their members shared the profits they made in producing plays. Shakespeare was a good businessman as well as a master dramatist. He owned shares in the Globe Theatre, where most of his plays were first performed. From his business interests and plays, he made a good deal of money.

From 1592 to 1594, London suffered outbreaks of the plague. As a result, theaters were closed during most of this period. Since there was no market for plays, Shakespeare used this time to write poetry. His first long poem, *Venus and Adonis,* was published in 1593, and others were published soon after.

Shakespeare resumed writing plays in 1594 and continued until 1613. His success enabled him to buy a beautiful home in Stratford, and, about five years before his death, he retired there to live with his family. By then he possessed a royal coat of arms and lived as a gentleman. While there are no records of his death, the monument that marks his grave at Holy Trinity Church suggests he died in April 1616.

WRITER'S WORKSHOP

WRITER'S CHOICE

Compared to the Writer's Workshops you have completed so far, this final workshop allows you greater freedom of choice. However, it also requires greater responsibility on your part. Each of the previous workshops explained in detail the steps necessary for successfully planning, drafting, and revising the assigned essay. This workshop, however, provides you with several possible topics and brief instructions. You must rely on what you have learned about specific forms and strategies to complete the assignment. Refer to earlier workshops for suggestions whenever doing so will help you. Remember to keep your purpose, audience, subject, and structure in mind as you write. You may find it helpful to make a PASSkey for the assignment you choose.

A. Narration and Description: Has This Ever Happened to You?

Have you ever felt like Romeo or Juliet? Have you ever been in a situation in which parents or peers strongly disapproved of your feelings for someone else? Write an essay in which you narrate and describe your personal Romeo-and-Juliet experience.

Prewriting Freewrite for fifteen minutes about your experience. Recall what happened, how you felt, and how things eventually turned out. Review your freewriting and add further details that help capture the experience.

Drafting Using your freewriting and notes, write a first draft. As you write, be aware of the need for specific, vivid description and clear organization. You will probably want to use chronological order.

Revising Review the Revision Checklists for narrative and descriptive writing on pages 53 and 143. Check your draft against both lists, looking for ways you can improve your essay.

B. News Report: Double Suicide Shocks Verona!

What do you think the front page of the *Verona Daily Gazette* looked like the morning after Romeo and Juliet were discovered in the tomb? Write a headline story and include a brief commentary at the end.

Prewriting Review the play for details that answer the questions *who,* *what, when, where, why,* and *how*. Decide how much background information the typical Verona reader would need and think of ways to explain the families' relationship. Make up quotes from surviving characters that will help explain the events. Decide what point you will make in your commentary.

Drafting Using your notes, write a draft of your newspaper story. Begin with a strong lead. Present your information concisely but thoroughly. Use quotes to present information and to add human interest.

Revising Ask a classmate to review your draft based on the Revision Checklist on page 626. Use your classmate's comments and suggestions to write a final draft.

C. Recommendation and Persuasion: A Matchmaker's Proposal

Imagine that you have been hired by Romeo's or Juliet's parents as a matchmaker. You are to find a suitable mate for either Romeo or Juliet in order to break up the relationship between the two. Suppose you had all of the characters in this book to choose from. Whom would you pick and why? Write a proposal in which you recommend a match for either Romeo or Juliet.

Prewriting Decide whether to write about Romeo or Juliet. Think about the personality and tastes of your chosen character and decide what kind of person would be a good match. Review the characters you've read about in the text this year. Pick the match and make notes explaining why you think you've made the right choice.

Drafting Using your notes, write a draft. Early in your proposal, describe Romeo's or Juliet's character and what kind of person would be a good match. Then introduce the character you've picked for him or her and explain why. Be sure to include specific references.

Revising Check the Revision Checklist for the proposal for a television mini-series on page 287 to help you with revision. Ask a classmate for suggestions and revise your draft.

D. Causal Analysis: Who Is to Blame?

What factors caused the tragedy of Romeo and Juliet? Their parents? The feud? The well-meaning but misguided assistance of others? Fate? Themselves? A combination of these? Something else? Write an essay in which you analyze the factors responsible for the tragedy. After exploring the various causes, discuss which one you believe to be most responsible.

Prewriting Make a list of all the possible causal factors. For each factor, write down details that show how it contributed to the tragedy.

Drafting Using your list and notes, write a draft. As you write, keep in mind the need for specific details from the text and the importance of clear explanations. Remember to state which factor you believe to be most responsible for the tragedy and to support your argument with solid reasons, which you elaborate with detailed explanations.

Revising Check your draft against the Revision Checklist on page 366 and ask a classmate for suggestions. Revise your draft and write a final essay.

E. Persuasion: Advice from Shakespeare

Based on *Romeo and Juliet,* what advice do you think Shakespeare would have for young people? Do you think he believed that Romeo and Juliet truly loved each other, or was he implying that they were merely infatuated with each other and acting irrationally? Write a letter from Shakespeare to young lovers in which he reflects on Romeo and Juliet's actions and offers advice.

Prewriting Decide whether you believe Shakespeare's portrayal of Romeo and Juliet serves as a warning or a model. Review the comments characters make about the nature of love. Formulate three statements that Shakespeare might make about his characters and decide what advice each statement would lead him to make.

Drafting Using your notes, write a draft of a letter from Shakespeare. Write a paragraph about each of the three statements and the advice it leads to. Use specific examples to support your points.

Revising Make up a Revision Checklist suitable for a letter of advice. Ask a classmate to review your draft. Use your classmate's comments and suggestions to write a final letter.

SELF-ASSESSMENT

Year-End Portfolio Review

Assignment Write a one-page essay in which you report on your achievement this year as a writer.

Prewriting Review your Writing Portfolio. Take extensive notes on what you find there. Be as objective as possible. Think about the aspects of your writing that were weakest at the beginning of the year. Decide which essays were the best and take notes on the areas in which you improved. Identify some features of your writing that still need improving. Consider the parts of the writing process (Prewriting, Drafting, Revising, Editing) that are your strengths. Make a list of goals for next year's writing.

Drafting Using your notes and lists, write a draft of your essay. As you write, be sure to apply the various standards of good writing you've worked on this year. Keep in mind the need for

- an interesting opening that tells your audience where you are going
- specific details (facts, observations, quotations, summaries) that support and illustrate each main point
- thoughtful explanations and careful reasoning
- effective, logical organization

Conclude your essay with your goals for next year's writing.

Revising and Editing Design your own Revision Checklist for this assignment and use it to review your essay as honestly as you can. Write a final draft. When you have finished revising, proofread for spelling, clarity, and mechanics.

LANGUAGE
WORKSHOP

CONFUSING VERB PAIRS

It's easy to tell a pine tree from a palm tree or a hawk from a sparrow. It's not so simple, though, to tell a pine tree from a spruce tree or a red-tailed hawk from a red-shouldered hawk.

The same is true for words. Whenever two words look similar or have similar meanings, there may be difficulty. This workshop focuses on several pairs of verbs that are often confused.

Using *Bring/Take*, *Learn/Teach*, and *Let/Leave*

	Present	Past	Past Participle
·*Bring* and *Take*	bring	brought	(have) brought
	take	took	(have) taken
·*Learn* and *Teach*	learn	learned	(have) learned
	teach	taught	(have) taught
·*Let* and *Leave*	let	let	(have) let
	leave	left	(have) left

Bring involves action directed toward the speaker. *Take* indicates action directed away from the speaker.

> *Bring* that book to me, please.
> *Take* this awful costume away, please!

Learn means "to gain knowledge or skill." *Teach* means "to help someone learn."

> I *am learning* my lines for our skit in the talent show.
> Last year Mr. McGovern *taught* us about Elizabethan England.

Let means "to allow or to permit." *Leave* means "to go away from."

> The theater owner *will let* us perform there next month.
> The last group *left* without taking the props.

Using *Lie/Lay, Rise/Raise,* and *Sit/Set*

	Present	**Past**	**Past Participle**
·*Lie* and *Lay*	lie	lay	(have) lain
	lay	laid	(have) laid
·*Rise* and *Raise*	rise	rose	(have) risen
	raise	raised	(have) raised
·*Sit* and *Set*	sit	sat	(have) sat
	set	set	(have) set

Lie means "to rest in a flat position" or "to be in a certain place." *Lie* never has a direct object. *Lay* means "to place." *Lay* always has a direct object.

> The script *was lying* on the stage floor.
> The actors *will lay* their props on the floor. (*Props* is the direct object.)

Rise means "to go upward." *Rise* does not take a direct object. *Raise* means "to lift" or "to make something go up." *Raise* always has a direct object.

> Thick, smoky mist *rises* to the ceiling of the stage.
> The stagehands *raise* the curtains at the beginning of the play. (*Curtains* is the direct object.)

Sit means "to occupy a seat." *Sit* never takes a direct object. *Set* means "to place." *Set* always has a direct object.

> My father *sits* next to my mother at the production.
> He *sets* a large box of roses on an empty seat. (*Box* is the direct object.)

Exercise 1   In many of the following sentences, there is an error in the use of a verb. Rewrite these sentences, correcting the error. If a sentence has no error, write *Correct.*

1. Ms. Schultz has learned us about Shakespeare's plays.
2. We learned about life in Shakespearean England just in time for our class production of *Romeo and Juliet.*
3. On a large table in the front of the classroom, Ms. Schultz has set a miniature model of the Globe Theatre.

4. We set together in a circle and read the play.
5. Will you bring your costume home with you tonight?
6. Don't leave those students go home without their scripts.
7. If you set next to me, we can help each other memorize lines.
8. Could you rise the shades so that we can see our scripts better?
9. After practicing the sword fight, Nick and Tony were so exhausted they laid down on the stage gasping for breath.
10. We are giving the play to rise money for the day-care center.
11. Our class president will bring the profits to the center's director.
12. Later, if Ms. Schultz leaves us go, we will visit the center to see how our donation was used.

Exercise 2   Work in groups to correct errors in verbs in the following passage.

After my class had taught about Shakespeare, we went to see the film of *Romeo and Juliet.* All twenty-five of us set down in the first three rows at the theater. Ms. Schultz sat her purse and her briefcase on the seat beside her. Before the curtain raised, Ms. Schultz reviewed the story with us so we wouldn't be confused by all the characters. When the lights were lowered, the class clown, Jimmy Smith, laid down across three empty seats and started to snore. Ms. Schultz was not amused. Suddenly the curtains were risen. In front of us, in glorious colors, lay the bustling town of Verona. I sat my box of tissues on my lap because I knew that once the film began, I'd need them. Sit me down in front of a tragic story like this, and I'll end up in tears.

LANGUAGE HANDBOOK

For review and practice: commonly confused verbs, pages 941–42

LIFE SKILLS

WORKSHOP

FINDING A SUMMER JOB

How would you go about finding a summer job? The first step is to find out what's available. A good place to start is the guidance department in your school. Employers looking for reliable help often contact schools. Help-wanted ads in your local newspaper are also a good place to look. Finally, don't forget personal contacts: ask your friends and family members for help.

After you have identified a promising job possibility, you need to contact the employer. You may call an employer directly or send a letter and a resumé of your work and school experience. Whether you write or phone, it's important to create a good impression. Offer specific information about yourself, including why you would like the job and why you would do well at it. Be honest, and be polite.

If a particular employer is interested in meeting you, you will be scheduled for an interview. Many employers think that an interview is the most important part of applying for a job, so be prepared!

1. Take copies of your resumé to the interview. If you don't have a resumé, neatly write or type a paragraph detailing your work and school experience. Ask a teacher or counselor to go over it with you.

2. Find out as much as you can about the job and the company so that you can talk knowledgeably about them.

3. Practice introducing yourself to the employer until you feel comfortable doing it. Practicing in front of a mirror often helps.

4. Choose clothing that is neat and appropriate. For example, don't wear jeans to a job interview at a bank.

5. Think about your strengths and weaknesses. Make a list of the valuable things you can bring to the job. Be honest. If you have little or no experience with a particular job, say so.

6. Anticipate questions that the employer might ask. Practice answering these kinds of questions before the interview.

7. Make sure you know exactly where the interview will be held. Get there a few minutes early. Don't be late! Don't be late!

HELP!

Here are some things employers look for in interviews:

friendliness and courtesy

self-confidence

experience

good speaking and listening skills

punctuality

honesty

Exercise   Make a list of at least five summer jobs you would like to have. Then imagine that an employer has called you for an interview for one of those jobs. Make a list of the questions that the employer might ask you at the interview. Then answer your own questions. With a partner, take turns playing the parts of the employer and the job seeker.

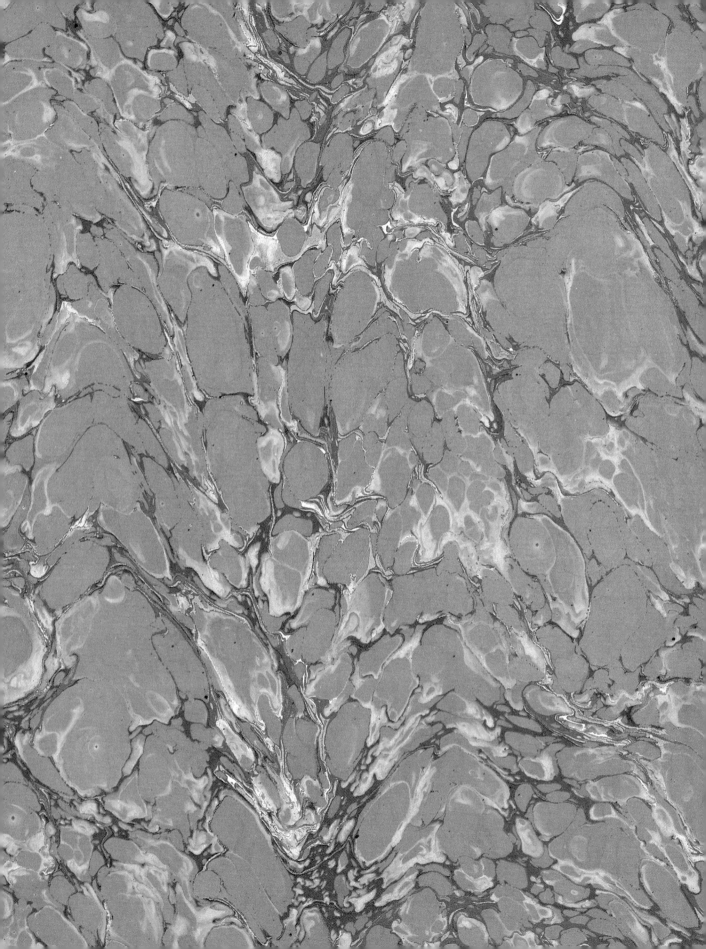

Handbook Contents

GLOSSARY

The **glossary** is an alphabetical listing of words from the selections, with meanings. The glossary gives the following information:

1. **The entry word broken into syllables.**

2. **The pronunciation of each word.** The **respelling** is shown in parentheses. The Pronunciation Key on the next page shows the symbols for the sounds of letters and key words that contain those sounds.

   A **primary accent** ′ is placed after the syllable that is stressed the most when the word is spoken. A **secondary accent** ′ is placed after a syllable that has a lighter stress.

3. **The part of speech of the word.** These abbreviations are used:

   n. noun   *v.* verb   *adj.* adjective   *adv.* adverb

4. **The meaning of the word.** The definitions listed in the glossary apply to selected ways a word is used in these selections.

1. entry word
3. part of speech

def er en tial (def′ ər en′ shəl)
adj. showing courteous regard or respect

2. respelling
4. meaning

A

a bate (ə bāt') *v.* to lessen or decrease; subside

a bom i na bly (ə bäm' ə nə blē) *adv.* disgustingly

ac cen tu ate (ak sen' cho͞o āt') *v.* emphasize

ac co lade (ak' ə lād') *n.* praise or other sign of respect

ac rid (ak' rid) *adj.* sharp, stinging or irritating to taste or smell

a cute (ə kyo͞ot') *adj.* serious; critical

ad a mant (ad' ə mənt) *adj.* not giving in; unyielding; unrelenting

a dren al in (a dren' ə lin) *n.* a hormone that triggers increased muscular strength

ad ver sar y (ad' vər ser' ē) *n.* an opponent; enemy

af fa ble (af' ə bəl) *adj.* friendly; pleasant and easygoing

a ghast (ə gast') *adj.* horrified, in disbelief

al cove (al' kōv') *n.* a small section of a room that is set back from the main part; nook

a loof (ə lo͞of') *adj.* reserved and cool

a mi a ble (ā' mē ə bəl) *adj.* having a pleasant, friendly disposition; affable

an tag o nist (an tag' ə nist) *n.* a person who opposes or competes against another person; opponent

an thol o gy (an thäl' ə jē) *n.* a collection of literary works compiled in one book

an ti ci pa tion (an tis' ə pā' shən) *n.* pleasurable expectation

ap palled (ə pôld') *adj.* filled with horror; shocked

ap prais al (ə prāz' el) *n.* a sizing up or an evaluation

ap pre hen sion (ap' rē hen' shən) *n.* a feeling of anxiety, worry, or dread

ap pro pri at ing (ə prō' prē āt' iŋ) *adj.* taking for one's own use, especially without permission **appropriate** *v.*

ar bi trar i ly (är' bə trer' ə lē) *adv.* based on one's own judgment, choice, or whim

ar du ous (är' jo͞o əs) *adj.* difficult to do; hard

a ris to crat (ə ris' tə krat') *n.* a person from the upper class

ar ro gant (ar' ə gənt) *adj.* full of undeserved pride and self-importance; overbearing

a skew (ə skyo͞o') *adj.* crooked; on one side

as sur ance (ə sho͞or' əns) *n.* the state of being sure of something; confidence; certainty

au ra (ô' rə) *n.* the atmosphere or feeling that surrounds a person, object, or event

a vail (ə vāl') *v.* to be of help or advantage to, as in achieving an end

a ver sion (ə vur' zhən) *n.* an intense dislike

B

balk (bôk) *v.* to stubbornly refuse to move or act

ban ish (ban' ish) *v.* to send or put away; exile; expel

bar rio (bär' ē ō) *n.* in Spanish-speaking countries or areas, a section or suburb of a city

bear (ber) *v.* to support or hold up; sustain; past tense—**bore** (bôr)

beck on (bek' 'n) *v.* to call or summon with a silent gesture

be nev o lent (bə nev' ə lənt) *adj.* charitable; kind; compassionate

be nign (bi nīn') *adj.* good-natured; kindly

be wil der ment (bē wil' dər mənt) *n.* hopeless confusion

bi ceps (bī' seps') *n.* the large muscle in the front of the upper arm

bla tant (blāt' 'nt) *adj.* glaringly conspicuous; obvious

blunt (blunt) *adj.* abrupt; rudely straightforward or honest

breach (brēch) *v.* to break through; pierce

C

cal loused (kal' əst) *adj.* unfeeling or insensitive

cas cad ing (kas kād' iŋ) *n.* falling or flowing, like a waterfall **cascade** *v.*

cat a stroph ic (kat' ə sträf' ik) *adj.* disastrous; tragic

cha os (kā' äs) *n.* disorder; confusion

chaste (chāst) *adj.* plain or pure

chide (chīd) *v.* to scold

clad (klad) *adj.* clothed or dressed

clar i ty (klar' ə tē) *n.* the quality of being easily seen; clearness

cleft (kleft) *n.* a crack or crevice

co in ci dence (kō in' sə dəns) *n.* an accidental occurrence of related events at about the same time

com bat ive (kəm bat' iv) *adj.* ready or eager to fight

come back (kum' bak') *n.* a witty answer or response

com mun ion (kə myōōn' yən) *n.* a close relationship with deep understanding; intimacy

com pel (kəm pel') *v.* to force

com pe tent (käm' pə tənt) *adj.* capable; legally fit

com ply (kəm plī') *v.* to obey; submit

com posed (kəm pōzd') *adj.* calm; tranquil

com pul so ry (kəm pul' sə rē) *adj.* that must be done, required, or undergone; mandatory, obligatory

con cede (kən sēd') *v.* to admit as certain; acknowledge; grant

con cep tion (kən sep' shən) *n.* a mental impression or idea

con cur (kən kʉr') *v.* to agree with

con sol ing (kən sōl' iŋ) *adj.* making someone feel less sad or disappointed, comforting **console** *v.*

con spir a to ri al (kən spir' ə tôr' ē əl) *adj.* planning together secretly

con sti tu tion (kän' stə tōō' shən) *n.* the physical makeup of a person

con sum mate ly (kən sum' it lē) *adv.* completely

con ta gious (kən tā' jəs) *adj.* infectious; spreading easily from person to person

con tem plate (kän' təm plāt) *v.* to consider; to think about intently

con tempt (kən tempt') *n.* scorn

con temp tu ous ly (kən temp' chōō əs lē') *adv.* with contempt or scorn; disdainfully

con tend er (kən tend' ər) *n.* an opposer; one who fights against someone or something else

cow er ing (kou' ər iŋ) *adj.* crouching and trembling out of fear; cringing **cower** *v.*

cur ren cy (kʉr' ən sē) *n.* money, especially paper money

cy lin dri cal (sə lin' dri kəl) *adj.* having the tubelike shape of a cylinder

D

de cep tive (dē sep' tiv) *adj.* not truthful; dishonest

de crep it (dē krep' it) *adj.* worn out by old age, illness, or long use; weak, frail, feeble

de fame (dē fām') *v.* to attack or injure someone's reputation; disgrace

def er ence (def' ər əns) *n.* a courteous regard or respect; honor

def er en tial (def' ər en' shəl) *adj.* showing courteous regard or respect

de flect (dē flekt') *v.* to turn to one side

deg ra da tion (deg' rə dā' shən) *n.* humiliation; disgrace

de lib er a tion (di lib' ər ā' shən) *n.* the quality of being careful, unhurried, and methodical

de ment ed (dē ment' id) *adj.* mentally deranged; mad; insane

de nounce (dē nouns') *v.* to criticize or condemn

de nun ci a tion (dē nun' sē ā' shən) *n.* a public accusation; a strong condemnation

dep ri va tion (dep' rə vā' shən) *n.* a forcible taking away or loss of something

de prived (dē prīvd') *adj.* underprivileged

de scent (dē sent') *n.* a way down, a going down; a fall

de spond ent (di spän′ dənt) *adj.* having lost hope; depressed

dev as tat ing (dev′ əs tāt′ iŋ) *adj.* overwhelming **devastate** *v.*

de vi ous (dē′ vē əs) *adj.* not honest; deceiving; underhanded

dig ni ty (dig′ nə tē) *n.* self-respect

dis arm (dis ärm′) *v.* to overcome the hostility of, especially by using charm

dis con so late (dis cän′ sə lit) *adj.* dejected; extremely unhappy, beyond cheering up

dis dain (dis dān′) *n.* contempt or scorn

dis in te grate (dis in′ tə grāt′) *v.* to separate into small parts; break apart

dis in ter (dis′ in tʉr′) *v.* to dig up or bring to light

dis po si tion (dis′ pə zish′ ən) *n.* a person's usual nature or frame of mind

doc ile (dös′ əl) *adj.* easy to manage; obedient

dog ged ness (dôg′ id nəs) *n.* persistence; stubbornness

dom i nate (däm′ ə nāt′) *v.* to control by superior power or influence; overpower

dot ing (dōt′ iŋ) *adj.* foolishly or overly fond

E

eaves drop (ēvz′ dräp′) *v.* to listen secretly to a private conversation

ec cen tric (ək sen′ trik) *adj.* out of the ordinary; odd

ec sta sy (ek′ stə sē) *n.* a feeling of overwhelming joy or delight; bliss

e lu sive (i loo′ siv) *adj.* hard to catch

e man ci pa tion (ē man′ sə pā′ shən) *n.* freedom

em i nent (em′ ə nənt) *adj.* standing in a high position when compared to others; famous; distinguished

en su ing (en soo′ iŋ) *adj.* coming afterward; following

es sence (es′ əns) *n.* the basic or most important quality

e va sion (ē vā′ zhən) *n.* an avoiding, using deceit or cleverness

ev o lu tion (ev′ ə loo′ shən) *n.* the process of development, as from a simple to a complex form

ex as per ate (eg zas′ pər āt′) *v.* to irritate or annoy greatly

ex hil a rat ed (eg zil′ ə rat′ id) *adj.* invigorated; stimulated

ex ile (eks′ īl) *n.* a long period of time living away from home usually by force; banishment

ex ot ic (eg zät′ ik) *adj.* **1** unique; striking **2** foreign; alien

F

fac tion (fak′ shən) *n.* a group of people working in a common cause against other groups or the majority

fac ul ty (fak′ əl tē) *n.* a mental ability or power, such as will or reason

fal si fy (fôl′ sə fī′) *v.* to make untrue

fa mil i ar i ty (fə mil′ ē er′ ə tē) *n.* behavior that implies a close, personal relationship

fa na tic (fə nat′ ik) *n.* a person whose extreme enthusiasm is unreasonable; a zealot

fa tal ism (fāt′ ′l iz′əm) *n.* the belief that all events are determined by fate and are therefore inevitable

fa tigue (fə tēg′) *n.* physical or mental exhaustion; weariness

feigned (fānd) *adj.* pretended; faked

flour ish (flʉr′ ish) *n.* a sweeping, showy movement of the arms, legs, or body

fore bod ing (fôr bōd′ iŋ) *n.* a feeling that something bad is about to happen

for lorn ly (fôr lôrn′ lē) *adv.* hopelessly, miserably

for mi da ble (fôr′ mə də bəl) *adj.* hard to accomplish; overwhelming

for ti tude (fôrt′ ə tood′) *n.* the inner strength needed to bear misfortune calmly; resoluteness

fren zied (fren′ zēd) *adj.* with a wild outburst of feeling or action; frantic

fu til i ty (fyoo til′ ə tē) *n.* uselessness; fruitlessness

G

gam ut (gam′ ət) *n.* the entire range or series of something

gape (gāp) *v.* to stare with the mouth open

gar ish (gar′ ish) *adj.* overly bright; flashy; gaudy

gaunt (gônt) *adj.* very thin; lean

glade (glād) *n.* an open space in a wood or forest

glut ton (glut′ ′n) *n.* a person or animal who eats too much because of greed

gro tesque (grō tesk′) *adj.* distorted; highly unattractive; ugly

gut ted (gut′ ′d) *adj.* ruined; destroyed

H

hack saw (hak′ sô′) *n.* a saw used to cut metal

har mo nize (här′ mə nīz′) *v.* to bring into agreement

her e sy (her′ i sē) *n.* an opinion that opposes established or commonly held views and beliefs; dissension

hu mil i a tion (hyo͞o mil′ ē ā′ shən) *n.* hurt pride caused by being made to feel foolish; extreme embarrassment

I

il lit er a cy (il lit′ ər ə sē) *n.* a lack of knowledge of how to read and write

im mac u late (im mak′ yo͞o lit) *adj.* perfectly clean, spotless

im mi nent (im′ ə nənt) *adj.* approaching; near; close at hand

im pel (im pel′) *v.* to force, drive, or urge

im per ti nence (im pʉrt′ 'n əns) *n.* not showing proper courtesy; disrespect

im pli ca tion (im′ pli kā′ shən) *n.* an association; connection

im pov er ished (im päv′ ər ishd) *adj.* very poor   **impoverish** *v.*

im pu dence (im′ pyo͞o dəns) *n.* shameless or disrespectful boldness   **impudent** *adj.*

in ad e quate (in ad′ i kwət) *adj.* not good enough for what is needed or not equal to what is required

in ad vert ent ly (in′ ad vʉrt′ 'nt lē) *adv.* unintentionally

in an i mate (in an′ ə mit) *adj.* not possessing life; like an object

in ar ti cu late (in′ är tik′ yo͞o lit) *adj.* not spoken so others can understand; not expressed clearly

in cense (in sens′) *v.* to make extremely angry; enrage

in ces sant ly (in ses′ ənt lē) *adv.* continuous; non-stop

in cite (in sīt′) *v.* to rouse; urge on

in cred u lous ly (in krej′ o͞o ləs lē′) *adv.* in an unbelieving way; skeptically

in dig nant ly (in dig′ nənt lē) *adv.* angrily; resentfully

in dis tin guish a ble (in′ di stiŋ′ gwish ə bəl) *adj.* unable to be separated visually or recognized

in doc tri na tion (in dak′ trə nā′ shən) *n.* instruction in a set of beliefs

in do lent (in′ də lənt) *adj.* lazy; idle

in ef fec tu al (in′ e fek′ cho͞o əl) *adj.* having no effect; useless

in ev i ta ble (in ev′ i tə bəl) *adj.* certain to occur

in fal li bil i ty (in fal′ ə bil′ ə tē) *n.* the state of being unable to make an error

in fat u a tion (in fach′ o͞o ā′ shən) *n.* a short-lived, absorbing affection or passion; love

in fuse (in fyo͞oz′) *v.* to inject; add to

in ge nu i ty (in′ jə no͞o′ ə tē) *n.* originality, cleverness, skill

in hi bi tion (in′ hi bish′ ən) *n.* a holding back, especially of an emotion, thought, or action; a restraint

in quis i tive (in kwiz′ ə tiv) *adj.* tending to ask many questions; eager to learn; curious

in stinc tive (in stiŋk′ tiv) *adj.* having a natural tendency; spontaneous

in ten si ty (in ten′ sə tē) *n.* a high degree of emotion or action

in ter mi na ble (in tʉr′ mi nə bəl) *adj.* seeming to last forever; endless

in ter vene (in′ tər vēn′) *v.* to come between

in ti mate (in′ tə mət) *adj.* closely acquainted; familiar

in tim i date (in tim′ ə dāt′) *v.* to make afraid

in tol er ance (in täl′ ər əns) *n.* a lack of respect for the opinions or beliefs of others

in trigue (in trēg′) *v.* to arouse interest or curiosity; fascinate

ir rel e vant (ir rel′ ə vənt) *adj.* not to the point; not relating to the subject

ir res o lute (ir rez′ ə lo͞ot′) *adj.* wavering in decision, purpose, or opinion; indecisive

J

jeer (jir) *n.* a rude, ridiculing remark or comment; taunt

K

kin dling (kind′ liŋ) *n.* pieces of dry wood or other material that can be easily lighted to start a fire; tinder

L

lam i nate (lam′ i nāt′) *v.* to form into thin sheets or layers

leer (lir) *n.* a sly look revealing triumph or evilness

le git i mate (lə jit′ ə mət) *adj.* legal; acceptable

lu nar (lo͞o′ nər) *adj.* like or relating to the moon

M

mal ice (mal′ is) *n.* the desire to harm or hurt another

ma neu ver ing (mə no͞o′ vər iŋ) *adj.* directing or guiding in a skillful manner   **maneuver** *v.*

ma nip u late (mə nip′ yo͞o lāt′) *v.* to work or operate, as with the hands

ma raud ing (mə rôd′ iŋ) *adj.* raiding; plundering   **maraud** *v.*

mar tyr dom (märt′ ər dəm) *n.* long, severe suffering

me di ate (mē′ dē āt′) *v.* to settle a dispute or an argument by bringing two sides together

mel o dra mat ic (mel′ ō drə mat′ ik) *adj.* sensational and extravagantly emotional

men a cing (men′ əs iŋ) *adj.* threatening harm or evil **menace** *v.*

me thod i cal ly (mə thäd′ ik lē) *adv.* done in a regular, orderly way; systematically

mim ic (mim′ ik) *n.* someone who imitates

mon e tar i ly (man′ ə ter′ ə lē) *adv.* having to do with money; financially

mo no to nous (mə nät′ 'n əs) *adj.* boring and tedious

mo rose ly (mə rōs′ lē) *adv.* gloomily; sullenly

N

nau se a (nô′ shə) *n.* a feeling of sickness in the stomach accompanied by the urge to vomit

neg li gent (neg′ lə jənt) *adj.* careless or indifferent

niche (nich) *n.* a recess or hollow; a nook

non de script (nän′ di skript′) *adj.* colorless; drab; unnoticeable

non en ti ty (nän′ en′ tə tē) *n.* a person of little or no importance

O

ob li ga tion (äb′ lə gā′ shən) *n.* a sense of duty; responsibility

ob liv i ous (ə bliv′ ē əs) *adj.* not noticing

ob ses sion (əb sesh′ ən) *n.* the state of being preoccupied with an idea or desire

of fen sive (ə fen′ siv) *adj.* causing anger or resentment; obnoxious

om i nous (äm′ ə nəs) *adj.* threatening; foreshadowing evil

op pres sive (ə pres′ iv) *adj.* weighing heavily on one's mind or spirits; distressing

op u lence (äp′ yoo ləns) *n.* wealth or richness

or a to ry (ôr′ ə tôr′ ē) *n.* skill in public speaking; elocution

P

pang (paŋ) *n.* a sudden, sharp twinge of distress

parched (pärchd) *adj.* very hot and thirsty

pau per (pô′ pər) *n.* a poor person

per sist ent (pər sist′ ənt) *adj.* refusing to give up; stubborn or persevering

phe nom e non (fə näm′ ə nən′) *n.* an extremely unusual occurrence

phos phor es cent (fäs′ fə res′ ənt) *adj.* continually giving off light

plac id (plas′ id) *adj.* undisturbed; peaceful; quiet; calm

plain tive ly (plān′ tiv lē) *adv.* sorrowfully or sadly

poign an cy (poin′ yən sē) *n.* a sharp, emotionally painful feeling

pon der ous (pän′ dər əs) *adj.* heavy and massive

po tent (pōt′ 'nt) *adj.* effective or powerful

pre car ious ly (prē ker′ ē əs lē) *adv.* insecurely; in a manner that is not safe

pre cept (prē′ sept′) *n.* a commandment or rule of conduct

pre dic a ment (prē dik′ ə mənt) *n.* a difficult or embarrassing situation

prel ude (prel′ yood′) *n.* an introduction to an event, action, or performance

prem o ni tion (prem′ ə nish′ ən) *n.* a feeling that something bad is about to happen

pre oc cu pied (prē äk′ yoo pīd′) *adj.* lost in thought

pre text (prē′ tekst) *n.* an excuse; a false reason put forth to hide the real one

pro fu sion (prō fyoo′ zhən) *n.* an abundance; a large amount

prop o si tion (präp′ ə zish′ ən) *n.* a plan, proposal, deal, or scheme

pros pects (prä′ spekts′) *n.* chances for success

pros trate (präs′ trāt′) *adj.* lying flat on the ground

psy cho log i cal (sī′ kə läj′ i kəl) *adj.* of the mind; mental

pum mel (pum′ əl) *v.* to beat or hit repeatedly with the fist; thrash

pun gent (pun′ jənt) *adj.* sharp, bitter

pu ny (pyoo′ nē) *adj.* of very little size or strength; slight; weak

Q

quea sy (kwē′ zē) *adj.* nauseated; feeling uncomfortable and uneasy

R

ra di us (rā′ dē əs) *n.* range, scope, or extent

ran cid (ran′ sid) *adj.* spoiled; smelly; offensive

rank (raŋk) *adj.* growing wildly and vigorously; overgrown

rav aged (rav′ ijd) *adj.* violently destroyed; ruined **ravage** *v.*

rav e nous (rav′ ə nəs) *adj.* wildly hungry; famished

re dun dant (ri dun′ dənt) *adj.* more than enough; superfluous

re fined (ri fīnd′) *adj.* elegant and cultivated **refine** *v.*

re fuge (ref′ yo͞oj) *n.* a place of safety and protection

re ha bil i tate (re′ hə bil′ ə tāt′) *v.* to restore or return to order the privileges or reputation that one has lost

re it er ate (rē it′ ə rāt′) *v.* to repeat

re li a ble (ri lī′ ə bəl) *adj.* trustworthy; dependable

re lin quish (ri liŋ′ kwish) *v.* to let go or give up; to surrender

re morse (ri môrs′) *n.* a deep sense of guilt for having done wrong

re nun ci a tion (ri nun′ sē ā′ shən) *n.* the act of giving up or denying an idea or claim to something

re proach (ri prōch′) *n.* a blame; rebuke

re pug nance (ri pug′ nəns) *n.* extreme dislike or distaste

re signed (ri zīnd′) *adj.* submissive; passively accepting **resign** *v.*

res o lute ly (rez′ ə lo͞ot′ lē) *adv.* determinedly; unwaveringly

re spect a bil i ty (ri spek′ tə bil′ ə tē) *n.* the quality or state of being respectable or honorable

res pite (res′ pit) *n.* a temporary relief; break

re straint (ri strānt′) *n.* self-control

res ur rec tion (rez′ ə rek′ shən) *n.* a bringing back to life; a rebirth

re tal i ate (ri tal′ ē āt′) *v.* to return an injury or wrong

ret ri bu tion (re′ trə byo͞o′ shən) *n.* punishment for bad behavior or for a wrong one has committed; penalty

ret ro spect (re′ trə spekt′) *n.* a looking back to or rethinking of past events

re ver ber ate (ri vʉr′ bə rāt′) *v.* to re-echo, resound

re vert (ri vʉrt′) *v.* to go back to a previous state

rogue (rōg) *n.* **1** an archaic term for a wandering beggar or tramp **2** a rascal

ru in ous (ro͞o′ ə nəs) *adj.* disastrous, bringing ruin

ruse (ro͞oz) *n.* trick; deception

S

sac ri le gious (sak′ rə lij′ əs) *adj.* disrespectful toward a sacred person, place, or thing

scourge (skʉrj) *n.* a means of harsh punishment or great suffering

se cure (si kyo͞or′) *v.* to take possession or hold of; acquire

se nile (sē′ nīl) *adj.* showing signs of breakdown caused by old age, especially confusion or loss of memory

se rene sə rēn′) *adj.* untroubled; having a peaceful spirit

sev ered (sev′ ərd) *adj.* cut apart or cut off **sever** *v.*

sheen (shēn) *n.* brightness; shininess

shift less (shift′ lis) *adj.* lazy

shod di est (shäd′ ē əst) *adj.* most poorly made

shriv el (shriv′ əl) *v.* to wither; waste

siege (sēj) *n.* a stubborn, continued effort to win or control something

sig nif i cance (sig nif′ ə kəns) *n.* importance

sin is ter (sin′ is tər) *adj.* mysteriously wicked, evil, or dishonest

smug (smug) *adj.* annoyingly self-satisfied

snare (snar) *n.* a trap; anything dangerous that tempts people

so ber (sō′ bər) *adj.* serious, solemn

sol der (säd′ ər) *v.* to join or bond together

sol i tar y (säl′ ə ter′ ē) *adj.* **1** unfrequented; remote **2** single; alone

sol i tude (säl′ ə tood′) *n.* the state of being alone; remoteness

so phis ti ca tion (sə fis′ tə kā′ shən) *n.* the state of being worldly-wise or experienced

spher i cal (sfer′ i kəl) *adj.* shaped like a ball or globe

spin dly (spind′ lē) *adj.* tall and very thin, often looking frail or weak

spo ra dic (spə rad′ ik) *adj.* occurring from time to time; occasional

spree (sprē) *n.* a period of unrestrained activity

stark (stark) *adj.* bleak; desolate

stealth (stelth) *n.* secret behavior

sto ic (stō′ ik) *adj.* calm and unemotional, especially while in pain; uncomplaining

stren u ous (stren′ yo͞o əs) *adj.* energetic; requiring great effort

stu por (sto͞o′ pər) *n.* a condition in which the mind and senses are dulled

suc cumb (sə kum′) *v.* to give in

sul len (sul′ ən) *adj.* resentful; ill-humored

sur name (sʉr′ nām) *n.* a person's family name or last name

T

taut (tôt) *adj.* tense, tightly stretched

tem per a ment (tem′ pər ə mənt) *n.* a person's usual nature or disposition

tem per ance (tem′ pər əns) *n.* self-restraint; moderation

ter rain (ter rān′) *n.* ground, especially with regard to topographical features

ti rade (tī′ rād′) *n.* a long impassioned speech, especially one that denounces

trans ac tion (tran zak′ shən) *n.* an exchange of money for a product or service

trans fixed (trans fikst′) *adj.* motionless   **transfix** *v.*

trans form (trans fôrm′) *v.* to change the appearance, form, or character of someone or something

trans lu cent (trans loo′ sənt) *adj.* letting light through but scattering it in such a way that objects on the other side cannot be clearly seen; partially transparent

trans par ent (trans per′ ənt) *adj.* able to be seen through, clear

trem u lous (trem′ yoo ləs) *adj.* quivering; shaking

trivial (triv′ ē əl) *adj.* unimportant; insignificant

ty rant (tī′ rənt) *n.* a person who uses his or her authority or ability to control others in a cruel or unjust manner; one who rules with absolute power

U

un con ven tion al (un′ kən ven′ shən əl) *adj.* not conforming to customary or accepted rules

un der score (un′ dər skôr′) *v.* to emphasize or stress

u nique (yoo nēk′) *adj.* having no equal; unlike anything else

un kempt (un kempt′) *adj.* messy; untidy

un per ceived (un pər sēvd′) *adj.* not seen

un sub tle (un sut′ 'l) *adj.* overly obvious

V

van i ty (van′ ə tē) *n.* excessive pride; conceit

van quished (van′ kwisht) *adj.* defeated; conquered   **vanquish** *v.*

veer ing (vir′ iŋ) *adj.* turning or swinging   **veer** *v.*

ve he ment ly (vē′ ə mənt lē) *adv.* fiercely

ver bal ize (vur′ bəl īz′) *v.* to put into words; express

ver mil ion (vər mil′ yən) *n.* a bright red or scarlet

vex a tion (veks ā′ shən) *n.* anger or annoyance

vi gil (vij′ əl) *n.* the act or a time of staying awake during the usual hours of sleep as in order to keep watch over or guard something or someone

vile (vīl) *adj.* evil; offensive

vir tu ous (vur′ choo əs) *adj.* having moral excellence, right action and thinking, goodness

vis u al ize (vizh′ oo əl īz′) *v.* to form a mental image of something

vi tal i ty (vī tal′ ə tē) *n.* energy; strength

vi va cious (vī vā′ shəs) *adj.* animated; full of life

vul ner a ble (vul′ nər ə bəl) *adj.* easily hurt; sensitive

W

war i ly (wer′ ə lē) *adv.* cautiously; guardedly

whim (hwim) *n.* a sudden wish or desire; passing notion

with drawn (with drôn′) *adj.* shy reserved

wrath (rath) *n.* great anger; rage

writhe (rīth) *v.* to make twisting and turning movements; contort the body, often in pain

XYZ

zeal (zēl) *n.* intense enthusiasm; eagerness

LITERARY TERMS

Act   An act is a major unit of action in a play. Acts in a play are comparable to chapters in a book. Each act may contain several scenes. *A Sunny Morning* is a one-act play, while *The Tragedy of Romeo and Juliet* is a five-act play.

Alliteration   The repetition of consonant sounds at the beginning of two or more words is called alliteration. Poets use alliteration to emphasize words, to tie lines together, to reinforce meaning, and to add sound effects. Note this example of alliteration from Bruce Ignacio's poem "Lost":

> Our home seemed smothered and
>   surrounded
> as were other homes on city sites.

Allusion   An allusion is a reference to a well-known work of literature, a famous person, or a historical event with which the reader is assumed to be familiar. "The Scarlet Ibis" contains an allusion to the children's story "Hansel and Gretel," in which the main characters leave a trail of bread crumbs to mark their path through the forest.

> It was too late to turn back, for
> we had both wandered too far into
> a net of expectations and had left
> no crumbs behind.

Anecdote   An anecdote is a brief story told to entertain or to make a point. In "A Celebration of Grandfathers," for example, Rudolfo Anaya includes anecdotes about his grandfather to support his thesis that the elderly should be honored.

Aside   An aside is a remark that is spoken in an undertone by a character in a play and that is heard by the audience but not by the other characters on stage. Asides tell the audience what a character is thinking or feeling.

Assonance   Assonance is the repetition of vowel sounds within two or more words, as in this line from "Annabel Lee" by Edgar Allan Poe:

> And so all the night-tide, I lie down
>   by the side

Author's Purpose   Authors write for any of four main purposes: to entertain, to inform, to express opinions, and to persuade. An author may have several of these purposes for writing, but one is usually most important.

Autobiography   An autobiography is the story of a person's life written by that person. An autobiography is usually told from the first-person point of view. Because the writer chooses what incidents to include, the account also reveals the writer's self-image. "Fool's Paradise" is an example of autobiography.

Biography   A biography is a form of nonfiction in which a writer gives a factual account of someone else's life. A biography may tell either about a person's whole life or about only a part of the person's life. It is written in the third person. An example of a biography is "Frederick Douglass."

Blank Verse   Blank verse is unrhymed poetry written with an alternating pattern of stressed and unstressed syllables. The rhythm created by this pattern resembles the natural rhythm of spoken English. The plays of William Shakespeare were written mainly in blank verse.
See *Meter.*

Cast of Characters   In a play the cast of characters is given at the beginning of the script, before the first act. It is a list of all the characters in the play, usually in the order in which they will appear.

Catastrophe   The resolution of the plot in a tragedy is called the catastrophe. Traditionally, the catastrophe falls within the last two acts of a play and involves the death of a hero.
See *Tragedy*.

Character   A character is a person or animal who takes part in the action of a work of literature. Generally, the plot of a story focuses on one or more main characters.

Main characters are those who are most important in the story. The other characters in the story are called *minor characters*. The most important role of minor characters is to keep the plot of the story moving along.

Characterization   Characterization refers to the techniques a writer uses to create and develop a character. A writer reveals a character through physical description; through the character's actions, feelings, and words; through a narrator's direct comments about the character; and through the words, actions, and feelings of other characters.

Chronological Order   The progression of events in the order in which they occur in time is called chronological order or time order. Chronological order is a common form for organizing the details in a piece of writing. Most biographies use this order.

Climax   The climax is the turning point in the plot of a literary work. It is at this peak of interest and intensity, usually near the end of a story, when the outcome of the conflict in the plot becomes clear. The climax may occur because of a decision the main character reaches or because of a discovery or an event. The climax usually results in a change in the characters or a solution to the problem.

Colloquialism   A colloquialism is an expression used in informal conversation but not accepted as good usage in formal speech or writing. For example, in "Beauty Is Truth" by Anna Guest, the narrator's mother states that she "stood on line for tarts," meaning she waited in a line to buy tarts. Colloquialisms and other kinds of informal language are used by writers to make characters seem more true to life.
See *Idiom, Slang*.

Comic Relief   Comic relief is a humorous scene, incident, or speech in the course of a serious literary work. In drama it is sometimes used to relieve the emotional intensity of a previous scene. For example, in Act Four of *The Tragedy of Romeo and Juliet*, a comic scene relieves the tension and dark mood that result from Juliet's "death."

Conflict   Conflict is the struggle between opposing forces that is the basis of the plot of a story. *External conflict* occurs between a character and a force of nature, between two characters, or between a character and society. *Internal conflict* occurs when a character struggles within himself or herself, such as to make a decision.

Description   Description is writing that creates a picture of a scene, event, or character. To create description, writers often use sensory images—words and phrases that appeal to the reader's senses—and figurative language. Sometimes a description provides details about the actions or attitudes of a character. Notice the descriptive details in *I Know Why the Caged Bird Sings* by Maya Angelou.

> Her skin was a rich black that would have peeled like a plum if snagged, but then no one would have thought of getting close enough to Mrs. Flowers to ruffle her dress, let alone snag her skin.

See *Imagery, Figurative Language*.

Dialect   The form of a language as it is spoken in a certain place or among a certain group of people is called dialect. In this example of dialect from James Herriot's *All Things Bright and Beautiful,* notice how letters are dropped from words.

> "There's a nice little green 'un here. But he's a bit older than t'others. Matter of fact I've got 'im talkin'."

Dialogue   Dialogue is a conversation between two or more characters. Dialogue is used in all kinds of writing, but it makes up almost the entire body of a play. In a play the words each character says are written in lines next to the character's name, as in this excerpt from *A Sunny Morning* by Serafín and Joaquín Álvarez Quintero:

> **Don Gonzalo.** Are you speaking to me, señora?
> **Doña Laura.** Yes, to you.

In other kinds of writing, the words each character speaks are commonly set off by quotation marks.

Drama   Drama is literature that is meant to be performed for an audience. In a drama, or play, actors and actresses play the roles of the characters, telling the story through their words and actions. Like fiction, drama has the elements of character, setting, plot, and theme.

Generally, the script for a play includes both a list of the characters and stage directions that tell the actors and actresses how to move or speak their lines. These directions also provide suggestions for special effects, music, lighting, and scenery.

A play is made up of one or more acts. Each act may contain several scenes.

See also *Act, Cast of Characters, Dialogue, Scene, Stage Directions.*

Epic Hero   An epic hero is a well-known character of high social position whose main qualities are those that are valuable to his or her society. The hero of an epic is usually strong and courageous, often to the point of seeming superhuman. The hero is often cunning and crafty in dealings with others. Nevertheless, since the hero represents all humans, he or she must struggle to overcome human weaknesses such as pride or greed.

See *Epic Poem, Hero.*

Epic Poem   An epic poem is a long narrative poem that tells the adventures of a hero whose actions help decide the fate of a nation or of a group of people. The style of an epic poem is formal and grand. *The Odyssey* is one of the most famous epic poems of all time.

See *Epic Hero.*

Epic Simile   An epic simile is a long comparison that may go on for several lines. It does not always use the words *like* or *as.* Homer uses epic similes throughout *The Odyssey.*

Essay   An essay is a short nonfiction work that deals with one subject. In an essay the author might give an opinion, try to persuade, or simply narrate an interesting event. Essays can be formal or informal. Formal essays examine a topic in a thorough, serious, and highly organized manner. Informal essays reflect the writer's feelings and personality. An example of an informal essay is "A Celebration of Grandfathers."

Eulogy   A eulogy is a formal speech of praise, usually for someone who has died.

Euphemism   A euphemism is a word or phrase that is used instead of a more direct but distasteful or offensive word or phrase. For example, a euphemism like "passed away" might be substituted for the word *died.*

Exaggeration An exaggeration, or over-statement, is a statement in which an idea is magnified or overemphasized to an extreme degree. Writers often exaggerate to emphasize.
See *Hyperbole.*

Exposition The exposition is the part of a plot that provides background information and introduces the story's setting, its conflict, and often its main character or characters. The ex-position usually occurs at the beginning of a literary work.
See *Plot.*

External Conflict See *Conflict.*

Fable A fable is a brief story that is written to teach a lesson about human nature. Many fables, such as those by Aesop, have animals as the main characters. ''The Two Brothers'' is one of many fables written by Leo Tolstoy.

Falling Action The falling action occurs af-ter the climax in a work of fiction or drama and shows the effects of the climax. The suspense is over, but the results of the decision or action that caused the climax are not yet fully worked out.
See *Plot, Resolution.*

Fantasy Fantasy is a type of fiction that is highly imaginative and could not really happen. In a fantasy the setting might be a nonexistent and unrealistic world, the plot might involve magic, or characters might employ extrahuman powers. An example is ''Button, Button'' by Richard Matheson.

Fiction Fiction is writing that comes from a writer's imagination. Fiction is not factual but may be based on facts, real experiences, or people the writer has known. Fiction may take the form of a short story or a novel. Its main purpose is to entertain, but it often also serves to instruct or enlighten.

Figurative Language Language that con-veys meaning beyond the literal meaning of the words is called figurative language. Writers commonly use figurative language to create effects, to emphasize ideas, and to call upon emotions. Special types of figurative language, called *figures of speech,* are simile, metaphor, hyperbole, and personification.
See *Hyperbole, Metaphor, Personification, Simile.*

Flashback A flashback is an interruption in the chronological order of events in a story in order to present a conversation or event that happened before the beginning of the story. This background information helps explain the present actions or attitude of a character.

Folk Tale A folk tale is a simple story about humans or animals that has been handed down by word of mouth from one generation to the next generation. Folk tales are often set in the distant past.

Foreshadowing Foreshadowing is the technique of hinting about an event that will occur later in a story. For example, in *The Hitch-hiker,* the writer drops stronger and stronger hints that the innocent-looking fellow on the road will cause an unusual end to the story.

Form Form refers to the shape of a poem, that is, to the way the words are arranged on the page. A poem is written in lines, which may or may not be sentences. In some poems the lines are grouped into stanzas.
See *Stanza.*

Formal Essay See *Essay.*

Free Verse Free verse is poetry without regular patterns of rhyme and meter. It often sounds like everyday conversation when it is read aloud. ''Saying Yes'' is a poem written in free verse.

Genre   Genre is the term used to specify the distinct types or categories into which literary works are grouped. The four main literary genres are fiction, poetry, nonfiction, and drama.

Hero   In an older literary work, the hero is traditionally a character who exhibits extraordinary powers such as strength, courage, or intelligence. In modern literature the hero can be simply the most important character in a story.

Historical Fiction   Historical fiction is realistic fiction that takes place in an actual setting in the past. It contains references to actual people and events of that period, while the problems that the characters face are the same problems that real people faced then.

Humor   Humor in literature takes many forms. It can be an amusing description, an exaggeration, or a sarcastic remark. Humor is often created by the use of hyperbole or irony or through the writer's tone. "Fish Eyes," from David Brenner's autobiography, is an example of a work that contains several forms of humor.
See *Hyperbole, Irony, Tone.*

Hyperbole   Hyperbole is a figure of speech in which an exaggeration is made for emphasis or humorous effect. In *An American Childhood,* Annie Dillard uses hyperbole when she states that "we could have run through every backyard in North America until we got to Panama."
See *Figurative Language.*

Idiom   A common phrase or expression that has a different meaning from the actual meaning of the individual words is called an idiom. For example, when the narrator in "Say It with Flowers" says that he and his boss "had our hands tied behind our backs for having so many things to do at one time," he means that they had so much to do that they felt helpless.

Imagery   Imagery refers to words and phrases that appeal to the reader's senses. Most imagery appeals to the sense of sight, but imagery can appeal to other senses as well. These lines from Bruce Ignacio's poem "Lost" appeal to the senses of touch and smell:

> I brushed by people with every step,
> Covered my nose once in a while,
> Gasping against the smell of
>   perspiration on humid days.

Informal Essay   See *Essay.*

Informative Article   Informative articles are a type of nonfiction that present facts about a specific subject. This type of writing is found in textbooks, newspapers, magazines, pamphlets, books, directions, encyclopedias, and so on. The information is generally organized into several main ideas supported by details.

Internal Conflict   See *Conflict.*

Irony   Irony is the contrast between what is expected and what actually exists or happens. The irony in "The Necklace" is owing to the fact that the Loisels spend ten years working to replace a paste necklace.

Jargon   The specialized vocabulary and idioms of people in a particular field or profession are called jargon. Writers sometimes use jargon to make a work more true-to-life and accurate.
See *Idiom.*

Metaphor   A metaphor is a figure of speech that compares two things that have something in common. Unlike similes, metaphors do not use the word *like* or *as.* In these lines from

"Lost," the speaker's head is compared to a signal.

> Lights flashed everywhere until
> my head became a signal, flashing
> on and off.

See *Figurative Language, Simile.*

Meter   Meter is the regular pattern of stressed and unstressed syllables in a line of poetry. The meter of a poem emphasizes the musical quality of the language. In addition, it may serve to call attention to particular words or ideas or to create a particular mood.
See *Rhythm.*

Mood   Mood is the feeling that the writer wants the reader to get from a work of literature, such as excitement, anger, sadness, happiness, or pity. The use of connotation, details, dialogue, imagery, figurative language, foreshadowing, setting, and rhythm can help set the mood.

Motive   A character's reason for action is a motive. In "Brothers Are the Same" by Beryl Markham, Teruo's motive for killing the lion is to prove his bravery and manhood.
See *Character.*

Myth   A myth is a traditional story, usually involving magic or supernatural beings, that explains how something connected with humans or nature came to be. Most myths were at one time believed to be true, and they were often tied to the society's religion. The story "Snake Boy" by Jamake Highwater is based on a myth from the Cheyenne tribe.

Narrative   A narrative is any writing that tells a story. A narrative recounts a series of related events to tell a reader about something that happened. The events of a narrative can be real or imaginary. Some common types of narrative include anecdotes, autobiographies, biographies, myths, narrative poems, novels, and short stories.

Narrator   The narrator is the teller of a story. Sometimes the narrator is a character in the story. At other times the narrator is an outside voice created by the writer.
See *Point of View.*

Nonfiction   Nonfiction is prose writing about real people, places, things, and ideas. Biographies and autobiographies, histories, diaries, editorial articles, essays, journals, research reports, and news articles are all examples of nonfiction.

Novel   A novel is an extended work of fiction that focuses on several ideas. It is much longer and more complex than a short story.

Personification   A personification is a figure of speech in which human qualities are attributed to an object, animal, or idea. For example, in "Incident in a Rose Garden," the speaker personifies death as "a smiling man with glowing eyes."
See *Figurative Language.*

Persuasion   Persuasion is a type of writing intended to convince the reader to adopt a particular opinion or to perform a certain action. Effective persuasion appeals to both the intellect and the emotions.

Play   See *Drama.*

Plot   The sequence of actions and events in a literary work is called the plot. Most plots center on a conflict which the characters struggle to resolve. Plots usually follow a specific pattern having five stages: exposition, rising action, climax, falling action, and resolution.
See *Climax, Conflict, Exposition, Falling Action, Resolution, Rising Action.*

Poetry   Poetry is a special type of literature in which words are chosen and arranged to create a certain effect. Poets carefully select words for their sounds and connotations and combine them in different and unusual ways in order to communicate ideas, feelings, experiences, and different points of view. Like fiction, poems can also tell stories. Poets use form, rhyme, rhythm, alliteration, assonance, imagery, figurative language, speaker, and theme—known collectively as the elements of poetry—to convey the sounds, emotions, pictures, and ideas they want to express.

Some poems follow strict rules for form, rhythm, and rhyme, while those that follow no rules are said to be written in free verse.

See *Alliteration, Assonance, Blank Verse.*

Point of View   Point of view is the perspective from which a story is told. In a story told from the first-person point of view, the narrator tells the story using the pronouns *I* and *me* and is usually a character in the story. "Say It with Flowers" is told from the first-person point of view.

In a story told from a third-person point of view, such as "A Retrieved Reformation," the narrator is outside the story. The story is told using the pronouns *he, she,* and *they.* If a story is told from the third-person limited point of view, as "The Stolen Party" is, the narrator tells what only one character sees, thinks, and feels. If a story is told from a third-person omniscient point of view, as in "Three Wise Guys: Un Cuento de Navidad/A Christmas Story," the narrator sees into the minds of all the characters.

See *Narrator.*

Realistic Fiction   Realistic fiction is a type of fiction that is set in the modern, real world. The characters act like real people and use ordinary human abilities to deal with problems typical of the modern world.

Repetition   The literary technique in which a word or group of words is repeated throughout a selection is called repetition. Poets often repeat a word or phrase to give special emphasis to a thought or action.

Resolution   The final part of the plot of a story is called the resolution. The resolution, which often blends with the falling action, explains how the conflict is resolved and may also answer the reader's remaining questions pertaining to the plot.

See *Plot.*

Rhyme   Rhyme is the repetition of the vowel and consonant sounds at the ends of two or more words—as in *one* and *sun,* for example. Many traditional poems contain rhyme at the ends of lines. Rhyme that occurs within a line is called internal rhyme.

Rhyme Scheme   The pattern of rhyme within a poem is called the rhyme scheme. Rhyme scheme is indicated by using a different letter of the alphabet for every rhyming sound. In these lines from "The Secret Heart" by Robert P. Tristram Coffin, notice that words at the end of each pair of lines rhyme.

Across the years he could <u>recall</u>	a
His father one way best of <u>all</u>.	a
In the stillest hour of <u>night</u>	b
The boy awakened to a <u>light</u>.	b

Rhythm   The pattern of accented and unaccented syllables in poetry is called rhythm. Rhythm brings out the musical quality of language; it can also create mood and emphasize ideas. The accented or stressed syllables are marked with ╱, while the unaccented syllables are marked with ⌣. The pattern these syllables make in a line of poetry may be divided into units. Each unit is called a foot. Notice the rhythm in these lines from Amy Lowell's poem "Fireworks."

You hate me and I hate you,
And we are so polite, we two!

See *Meter.*

Rising Action   In fiction and drama, the rising action forms the second stage in the development of the plot. During the rising action the conflict in a story becomes obvious. Complications arise and suspense begins to build as the main characters struggle to resolve their problem.

See *Plot.*

Sarcasm   Sarcasm is a type of humor that contains ironic criticism yet is funny. A sarcastic remark may seem complimentary, but it is actually meant as a criticism.

Scene   Scenes are the episodes into which the action of a play is divided. The setting of each scene differs either in time or in place. In long plays, scenes are grouped into acts. The play *A Sunny Morning* has just one scene, while *The Tragedy of Romeo and Juliet* has at least three scenes in each of its five acts.

Science Fiction   Science fiction is fiction that is based on real or possible scientific developments. It frequently presents both an imaginary view into the future and the writer's concerns about problems in today's society.

Sensory Images   Sensory images are words and phrases that appeal to any of the five senses: sight, hearing, touch, taste, and smell.

See *Figurative Language, Imagery.*

Setting   The setting of a story is the time and place in which the action occurs. A story may be set in the past, the present, or the future; during the day or at night; during a particular time of year or in a certain historical period. The place may be real or imaginary.

Sometimes the setting is clear and well-defined; at other times it is left to the reader's imagination.

Setting, along with plot, character, and theme, is one of the main elements of fiction.

Short Story   A short story is a work of fiction that can be read in one sitting. It usually tells about one or two major characters and one major conflict. The four elements of a short story are character, plot, setting, and theme. An example of a short story is "The Necklace" by Guy de Maupassant.

Simile   A simile is a comparison of two things using the word *like* or *as.* In these lines from Homer's epic poem *The Odyssey,* Homer uses similes to compare the Cyclops' manner of eating to that of a mountain lion.

> Then he dismembered them and
>   made his meal,
> gaping and crunching like a
>   mountain lion—
> everything: innards, flesh, and
>   marrow bones.

Writers use similes to intensify emotional responses, create vivid images, and to help the reader look at a familiar object in a new way.

See *Figurative Language.*

Slang   Slang is very informal, everyday speech outside the standard version of a language. Slang terms can be new words or established words and phrases that have taken on new meanings. Slang terms usually go out of date quickly. An example of outdated slang is *stir,* which is used in O. Henry's story "A Retrieved Reformation" to mean "prison."

Soliloquy   A soliloquy is a speech that a character in a play makes when he or she is alone. Its purpose is to let the audience know what the character is thinking. An example of a soliloquy occurs in Act Two, Scene 5, lines 1-16, of *The Tragedy of Romeo and Juliet,* when Juliet, alone on her balcony, voices her feelings about Romeo.

Sound Devices See *Alliteration, Assonance, Rhyme, Rhythm.*

Speaker In poetry the speaker is the voice that talks to the reader. The speaker of a poem might be compared to the narrator of a work of fiction. Although the speaker often expresses feelings that the poet wants to convey, the speaker may not be the voice of the poet, not even in a poem that uses the pronouns *I* or *me.* Instead, the speaker might be a young child, a tree, or even a spirit.

Stage To stage a play is to produce it for an audience. Staging involves determining the physical appearance of the set, the lighting, and even the position of the actors on the stage.

Stage Directions Stage directions are instructions to the actors and director in a play. They tell the actors how to speak or act. They also give directions about setting, props, and lighting. Stage directions often appear in italics and are commonly set off from the dialogue by parentheses or brackets.

Stanza A group of lines that form a unit in poetry is called a stanza. A stanza is comparable to a paragraph in prose. The number of lines may vary from stanza to stanza, or it may be uniform.

Stereotype Stereotype refers to something or someone that conforms to a fixed or general pattern, without individual distinguishing qualities. Often a stereotype is a mental picture that members of a group believe typifies all members of some other group.

Style Style refers to the special way in which a writer expresses ideas. It describes not the ideas themselves but rather how they are presented. Every writer has a unique style. Some elements that make up a writer's style are sentence length, use of descriptive language, tone, point of view, use of dialogue, use of irony, and methods of characterization.

Surprise Ending A surprise ending is an unexpected plot twist at the conclusion of a story.

Suspense Suspense is the growing feeling of anxiety and excitement that makes a reader curious about the outcome of a story. A writer creates suspense through techniques that raise questions in the reader's mind about possible endings to the conflict.

Symbol A symbol is a person, place, or thing that stands for something beyond itself. In literature, objects and images are often used to symbolize abstract ideas. For example, a crown might symbolize royalty or power.

Theme The theme of a literary work is the message or insight about life or human nature that the writer presents to the reader. Although some works are written purely for entertainment and do not have a clear-cut theme, in most serious works the writer makes at least one point about life or the human condition.

Because the theme is not usually stated directly, the reader has to figure it out. One way to discover the theme of a work is to consider what happens to the main character. The importance of that event, stated in terms that apply to all human beings, is the theme.

Time Order See *Chronological Order.*

Tone The tone of a work of literature reflects the writer's attitude toward his or her subject.

It might be humorous, admiring, sad, angry, or bitter, depending on how the writer feels about the subject. Tone is not measurable, but you can sense the writer's attitude by examining his or her word choice and the kinds of statements that he or she makes.

Topic Sentence   The topic sentence is the sentence that tells the main idea of the paragraph in which it occurs. It is often the first or last sentence in the paragraph. The other sentences in the paragraph support, or explain more about, that main idea.

Tragedy   A tragedy is a drama that begins in calm and ends in violence, often with the death of one or more of the main characters. In some tragedies, however, the characters do not die but end up devastated. While fate is a major cause of the tragic ending, weaknesses or flaws within the characters also contribute significantly to their troubles. In a tragedy the resolution of the plot is called the catastrophe.

True-Life Adventure   True-life adventures are a type of nonfiction commonly found in popular magazines and books. They are true tales of heroic deeds or exciting adventures and are usually told in chronological order. "A Trip to the Edge of Survival" by Ron Arias is an example of a true-life adventure.

Turning Point   See *Climax.*

BIOGRAPHIES OF THE AUTHORS

RUDOLFO A. ANAYA

Rudolfo A. Anaya *(1937–   )* is an American author of Mexican heritage whose family has lived in the Southwest for several generations. His writing is grounded in the landscape of New Mexico and inspired by the stories and myths of his people—a tradition that he values and is determined will not be lost. Anaya has received numerous awards for his novels, plays, screenplays, short stories, children's stories, essays and articles. He has collected and published works of many other Chicano writers.

Erma Bombeck *(1927–   )* has been named by the World Almanac as one of the twenty-five most influential women in America, a distinction in addition to her many awards. Her humorous newspaper column, based on the daily life of a housewife, reaches more than 30 million readers in seven hundred newspapers across the country. Bombeck has appeared on several television talk shows and was a regular on ABC's *Good Morning, America.* Her books include *At Wit's End, Aunt Erma's Cope Book,* and *The Grass Is Always Greener over the Septic Tank.*

DAVID BRENNER

David Brenner *(1945–   )* grew up in west Philadelphia. As a teenager, he was elected class comedian and class president. Brenner first found professional success as a producer, director, and writer of serious documentary films on subjects such as the welfare system. He won many awards for these. He is best known as a very successful professional comedian, often acting as guest host for *The Tonight Show,* and hosting his own show, *Nightlife.* The story of his life and what he calls his "extremely good luck" is told in his books *Nobody Ever Sees You Eat Tuna Fish* and *Soft Pretzels with Mustard.*

Diana Chang a contemporary Chinese-American novelist and poet, is also a painter whose work has been exhibited in solo and group shows. She taught creative writing at Barnard College for ten years and is the author of several novels. About the poem "Saying Yes," Chang remarks, "To my surprise, 'Saying Yes' has been reprinted very often. I can only suppose it's because it is sincere and simple. If you want to be a writer, do try to bear these two qualities in mind."

DIANA CHANG

Isabelle C. Chang *(1925–   ),* author of *Chinese Fairy Tales, Tales from Old China,* and *The Magic Pole,* has also published books on cooking: *What's Cooking at Chang's* and *Gourmet on the Go.* A gifted storyteller, a librarian and media specialist, and the former director of the public library of Shrewsbury, Massachusetts, Chang is now working with a colleague on a novel about education. The story, she says, will recognize that there exists today a "civil war between technology and the humanities."

Alice Childress *(1920–   ),* an author and playwright, worked for eleven years as an actress and director with the American Negro Theater in New York City. She has been awarded many honors. Critics praise her writing for the realism of the characters, her honest treatment of racial issues, and her compassion for all human beings. Some of her works are controversial and have been banned in some areas. Childress has been called "a crusader and writer who resists compromise." One of her most acclaimed novels, *A Hero Ain't Nothin' but a Sandwich,* is a powerful study of teenage drug addiction.

Robert Tristram Coffin *(1892–1955)* was born in Brunswick, Maine, was educated at Bowdoin and Princeton, and was a Rhodes scholar at Oxford. In 1936 he was awarded the Pulitzer Prize for poetry, but he was also a novelist, a biographer, a lecturer, and an essayist. His intense interest in his home state reached its peak in the 1950 collection of essays called *Maine Doings.*

Nikki Giovanni *(1943–   )* is considered one of the major writers of the 1960's African American literary renaissance and has received many awards for her poetry, nonfiction, and recordings. Born in Knoxville, Tennessee, Giovanni graduated with honors from Fisk University and also attended the University of Pennsylvania and Columbia University. A teacher and lecturer as well as a writer, Giovanni founded her own publishing company at the age of twenty-seven. Commenting about her strong opinions, Giovanni says, "It seems to always fall on me to tell the truth, and, hey, I don't mind. It's not nearly as bad a job as some people think."

Carole Gregory *(1945–   ),* also known as Carole Gregory Clemmons, was born in Youngstown, Ohio, and graduated from Youngstown State University. Her poetry has appeared in *New Black Poetry, Nine Black Poets,* and *To Gwen with Love,* an anthology dedicated to poet Gwendolyn Brooks, as well as in numerous reviews. Gregory has worked in the fields of communications— including for *Look* magazine—and education and development.

W. C. Heinz *(1915–   )* was born in Mount Vernon, New York. In his youth he dreamed of becoming a sports star but soon realized he lacked the necessary skill. Instead, Heinz decided to write about heroes like Babe Ruth, Jack Dempsey, and Red Grange. As his writing career evolved, however, he covered a variety of newsworthy subjects. He concludes, "There is only one story. . . . That is man against adversity." Heinz is a respected newspaper feature writer and war correspondent and an award-winning sportswriter.

James Herriot *(1916–   )* is a practicing veterinarian as well as the author of books including the bestsellers *All Things Bright and Beautiful, All Creatures Great and Small* and *All Things Wise and Wonderful.* Herriot's books are humorous and heartwarming collections of anecdotes from his veterinary practice. Because of the British veterinary system's ban on advertising, the names and the community in the books are fictitious; even James Herriot is a pen name for the real James Wight. Herriot's accounts reflect his love for his profession and English rural life.

John Hersey *(1914–   )* is famous both as a reporter and as a novelist. His first novel, *A Bell for Adano,* won a Pulitzer Prize, and he became even more famous for *Hiroshima,* a nonfiction account of the results of the dropping of the atomic bomb. Born in Tientsin, China, the son of missionaries, Hersey lived there until age eleven. He graduated from Yale University in 1936 and, after study in Cambridge, England, worked for a time for the novelist Sinclair Lewis. For many years a traveling correspondent for *Time* and *Life* magazines, Hersey based several of his books on his experiences abroad. He has successfully combined his fiction and journalism skills to write of important world events and make them real to his readers.

Evelyn Tooley Hunt *(1904–   )* was born in Hamburg, New York. She graduated from William Smith College in Geneva, New York, where she edited the literary magazine. She received the Sidney Lanier Memorial Award for her first collection of poems, *Look Again, Adam,* published in 1961. Hunt's interest in different cultures is apparent in her writing. She is perhaps best known for her variations of haiku, a kind of Japanese poetry. She signs these poems Tao-Li.

Bruce Ignacio, a Native American of northern Ute ancestry, was born in Fort Duchesne, Utah. From 1967 through 1970, he attended the Institute of American Indian Arts in Santa Fe, New Mexico, where he studied creative writing and jewelry making. He worked making jewelry until 1985 when he became a carpenter. Ignacio now lives with his wife and three daughters on the Wampanoag Indian Reservation, Martha's Vineyard, Massachusetts. He continues to make jewelry and small carvings known as fetishes.

Dorothy M. Johnson *(1905–1984)* was an award-winning writer of Western stories and an honorary member of Montana's Blackfoot tribe, by whom she was given the name *Kills-Both-Places.* In such books as *Warrior for a Lost Nation*—her biography of Sitting Bull—and *Buffalo Woman,* Johnson demonstrates her understanding of the Indian people. A magazine editor, news editor, and professor of journalism, she wrote many stories and articles and more than fifteen books. Johnson's works *The Hanging Tree, The Man Who Shot Liberty Valance,* and *A Man Called Horse* were made into films.

Amy Lowell *(1874–1925)* was born into a wealthy and distinguished New England family. She began writing verse at age twenty-eight, but it was not until twelve years later that her work achieved recognition. Known for her outspokenness and eccentric behavior, Lowell became a leader of a new poetry movement called imagism. She lectured widely and wrote critical works and articles proposing a new freedom in verse forms and subject matter. After her death she was awarded the 1926 Pulitzer Prize for her collection *What's O'Clock.*

Naomi Long Madgett *(1923–   )* began writing poetry in her youth. Her first collection was published days after her graduation from high school. Her poems have appeared in magazines, journals, and more than ninety anthologies both in this country and abroad. Madgett is professor emeritus at Eastern Michigan University.

Eve Merriam *(1916–1992)* was primarily a poet and a playwright. She won many awards for plays, television scripts, poetry, and fiction. A very prolific author, Merriam published more than thirty books, twelve of them for young people, and several, such as *Growing Up Female in America: Ten Lives,* concerned with women's rights. Merriam said, "I am fortunate in that my work is my main pleasure." She found poetry the most satisfying genre to write.

EVE MERRIAM
© 1990 Layle Silbert

Julio Noboa Polanco *(1949–   )* is an American poet of Puerto Rican parentage. Born in the Bronx, a section of New York City, he later attended school on Chicago's West Side, and it was there, as an eighth grader, that he wrote "Identity." Although Noboa Polanco values his Hispanic heritage, he is also deeply interested in other cultures. He holds a bachelor's degree in anthropology and a master's degree in education. He now lives in San Antonio, where he writes reports and articles for a national policy institute on Latino issues, the Tomas Rivera Center at Trinity University.

Leroy V. Quintana *(1944–   )* is a native of Albuquerque, New Mexico. He was raised by his grandparents in a home rich with the tradition of storytelling, a calling he inherited. Quintana interrupted his college education by serving in the U.S. Army and fighting in Vietnam from 1967 to 1968 as an infantryman and with a reconnaissance team of the 101st Airborne Division. He returned to graduate from the University of New Mexico. He has been a social services caseworker, a writer for the *Albuquerque Tribune,* and, having received a master's degree in psychology, a marriage and family counselor. Today he is an English professor at Mesa College in San Diego.

LEROY V. QUINTANA

David Raymond *(1958–   )* was born in Norwalk, Connecticut. He attended college in a program for special students, from which he graduated with honors. Raymond now lives in Westport, Connecticut, where he works in real estate development, renovation, and design. He recently completed an intensive architectural program at Harvard University and plans to do more work in the field of design.

Adrienne Rich *(1929–   )* has received a number of prestigious awards for her poetry, including a Guggenheim Fellowship. Born in Baltimore and an honors graduate from Radcliffe College, she taught creative writing and English at several universities before coming to Cornell University as professor-at-large. Rich's poems are noted for their bold and intense statements about personal experiences and political and social issues. She is a leader in a newly defined female literature.

DAVID RAYMOND

May Swenson *(1919–1989)* was born in Utah and graduated from Utah State University. She taught at several universities and worked as an editor at New Directions, a New York publishing house. An award-winning poet, she experimented with typing words on a page so that the poem appeared in the shape of an object; she also used sound creatively. In *Poems to Solve,* written for children, she presented thirty-five poems containing riddles, extended metaphors, hidden meanings, and ideas to puzzle and challenge the reader.

THE WRITING PROCESS

Everyone who reads and writes belongs to a special community, a community of readers and writers. You, too, are part of this community. When you read, you discover meaning that reflects who you are as well as what the writer is trying to communicate. When you write, you discover ideas about yourself, about the world, and about what you read.

On the following pages you will find practical information that you can apply in many different writing situations.

The Reader's Journal

Like all readers, you observe, question, predict, and make connections as you read. You experience feelings such as excitement and amusement. One place to record these responses to literature is in a Reader's Journal. Your journal then can provide you with a rich source of writing ideas. Your journal can also serve as the place to record notes as you prepare for a writing assignment.

Here are some tips for keeping a journal:

- Carry your journal with you or keep it in a convenient place.
- Date and label your journal entries.
- Record words, passages, and lines that trigger ideas, along with your response to these ideas.
- Set aside part of your journal for the journal writing that is suggested throughout this book.
- Set aside another part of your journal for observations, quotations, and imaginative writing that is not tied to a literary selection.

The Writing Process

Writing is a process unique to each writer and to each writing experience. However, the following activities need to take place during most writing experiences.

- **Exploring ideas:** reflecting on what you know, what you need to know, and where you might find what you need
- **Gathering material:** remembering, imagining, reading, observing, interviewing, discussing
- **Making connections:** finding the way ideas fit together, letting new ideas surface, elaborating and pushing ideas to their limits
- **Clarifying communication:** rethinking content, reorganizing structure, correcting mechanics and usage

In most books about writing, each of these activities is tied to a specific stage of the writing process. The traditional stages are listed below in the same order that they appear in the Writer's Workshops in this text. It is important to understand, however, that the stages are only guides. Any activity can take place at any point in the process. The more you write, the more you should develop your own personal process, moving in and out of the writing stages in the manner that works best for you.

Stage 1. Prewriting   This is the planning stage where you think of ideas, do research, and organize your material.

Stage 2. Drafting   When you draft, you begin to put your ideas on paper, following any notes, graphics, or outlines you have made. Drafting is a time to let ideas flow without concern for spelling and punctuation. These errors can be corrected later.

Stage 3. Revising and Editing   When you revise, you refine your draft by improving word choice, and sentence structure, clarifying organization, eliminating unnecessary details, and adding new ideas when necessary. When you are satisfied with your revision, you edit, or proofread your work looking for errors in capitalization, punctuation, grammar, and spelling.

Stage 4. Publishing or Presenting   This is the time to share your writing with others.

The Writer as Decision-Maker

During the writing process, writers make a series of decisions that give direction or redirection to their writing. These decisions concern the key issues of purpose, audience, subject, and structure. These elements are highlighted in the **PASSkey** to writing that accompanies each Writer's Workshop in this text. In order to keep your writing focused, you may find it helpful to create a **PASSkey** when you are writing for other classes, as well. Following is a list of questions to guide you in thinking about these issues as you write.

Purpose

Is a purpose stated in the assignment?
What do I really want to accomplish in this piece:
   to express ideas or feelings? to inform? to entertain? to analyze? to persuade?
How do I want my audience to respond?

Audience

Who will read my writing?
What do my readers know or need to know?
What might they find interesting?

Subject

What information must I pull together or research?
Will I need to fill in details from my imagination?
How detailed will I need to be for my audience?

Structure

Is a structure or form named in the assignment?
What is the most effective organization to accomplish my purpose?
What should the final product look like?

The Writer as Problem-Solver

Everyone's writing process is personal. Many writers, however, experience the same kinds of difficulties. The questions they ask tend to sound like these:

1. Where do I start? Where do I get ideas? What do I do with them?
2. Who can help me? When should I ask for help?
3. How do I know what's wrong with my writing? How do I fix it?

On the following pages are some strategies to help you deal with these common problems.

Strategies: Word Webs and Brainstorming The notes in your journal can be a good starting point for many writing assignments. When you need to explore ideas further, generate new ideas, or discover connections among ideas, you might want to try using a **word web.** A word web is a diagram showing a central idea and related ideas. Here is an example.

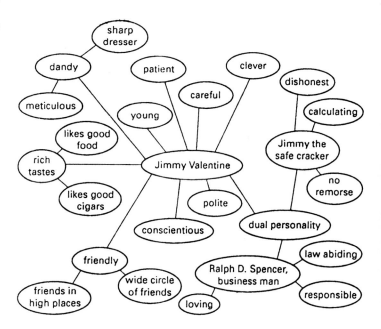

This word web shows the central idea "Jimmy Valentine" surrounded by words and phrases that describe his qualities. It would be useful for writing a character sketch on Jimmy.

To create a word web like the one above, write a central idea in the middle of a page and draw a circle around it. Outside the circle, write related ideas. Circle each one and draw a line connecting it to the central idea. Do the same for each related idea.

Brainstorming is similar to making a word web. In brainstorming, though, you write down every idea that comes to mind, whether it is related or not. Brainstorming can be done alone, but it is even more productive when done in a group.

Strategies: Charts and Diagrams Charts and diagrams can help you discover connections as well as pinpoint where you need to gather more material. You will discover a wide variety of useful charts and diagrams in this book—both on the Explore pages and with the Writer's Workshop assignments.

Strategies: Peers as Partners Because you are part of a community of readers and writers, you can work with a partner at any point in the writing process. You can codevelop a writing plan, bounce ideas off a friend, ask a classmate to read a rough draft or a cleaned-up copy, or in some cases teamwrite a piece. Involving peers in your problem-solving process can help you in exploring and clarifying ideas, in seeing a subject from a different point of view, and in identifying and eliminating problems in communication.

When you want some feedback on a piece of writing, you can read it aloud to a classmate and then ask that person two simple questions: What do you like? What don't you like?

A way to get more detailed feedback, especially for longer pieces, is to give a classmate the piece of writing along with the following questions. You can use the answers to these questions as a guide for talking about your writing with your partner.

- What did you like the best? the least?
- What message do you think I am trying to get across? Summarize it for me.
- What do you want to know more about? What parts went on too long?
- Did the beginning work for you? Did the ending?
- Did you have any trouble following my ideas?

Strategies: Self-Evaluation Sometimes a first draft of a piece of writing needs little revision. Other times you may have to write several drafts, perhaps going back to do more research or to rethink the

ideas. When trying to figure out what's wrong with a piece of writing that just isn't working, you can start with a quick check like the following:

- The main point I am trying to make is _____.
- I want my reader to respond to my writing by thinking or feeling that _____.
- In looking back over the piece, I like _____.
- I don't like _____.

At this point you'll want to review the personal goals you set when identifying the purpose of your writing and to decide how close you've come to meeting your goals. One good evaluation strategy is to read your writing aloud. As you read, listen for the following problems:

- ideas that are unclear or unnecessary
- ideas that don't make logical connections
- abrupt transitions from one idea to the next
- a dull or choppy style
- words that don't sound quite right or aren't right for your audience

Strategies: The Final Edit It would be wonderful to know all the rules of grammar, spelling, capitalization, punctuation, and usage, all the synonyms for every word, all the meanings for every word you read or hear. The next best thing is to know where to get the information you need to refine your writing. Here are some ideas.

- **To check spelling:** dictionary, spelling dictionary, computer spellchecker
- **To check punctuation, capitalization, grammar, and usage:** the Language Handbook in this text
- **To check word meanings and synonyms:** dictionary, thesaurus

One point to check carefully when writing about literature is the accuracy of your quotations and the correct spellings of any names and titles. The literature itself is your source for this information.

When you edit your writing or that of a partner, use the proofreading symbols in the box on the next page.

Proofreading Symbols

Symbol	Meaning	Example
∧	insert	leson
≡	capitalize	douglass
/	lowercase	History
∼	transpose	veiw
ℒ	take out	lots of
¶	paragraph	¶ The
⊙	add a period	slavery
∧	add a comma	Finally

The Writer as Learner

After you have completed a piece of writing, take time to think about your writing process. Questions like these can help you to focus on various aspects of the writing and learning experience:

- Am I pleased with my final product?
- Did I become involved in my topic?
- Did I learn something from writing about this topic?
- Which aspects of the writing were easiest for me? Which were the most difficult?
- What aspect of writing is becoming easier?
- What was the biggest problem I encountered? How did I solve the problem? How might I avoid the problem next time?
- When I compare this piece of writing with others in my working folder or portfolio, can I see changes in my writing style? in my writing skill?
- Have I seen anything in the writing done by my peers or by professional writers that I would like to try myself?

Another way to learn from a writing experience is through an objective evaluation of your final product. The evaluation may be conducted by a teacher or a peer reader. The goal is the same: to contribute to your growth as a writer and to heighten your sense of writing as communication.

Strategies: The Evaluation Task Each kind of writing has certain characteristics unique to that writing. An evaluator, however, can assess the strengths and weaknesses of most writing using general guidelines in three key areas:

(1) content
(2) form
(3) grammar, usage, and mechanics.

The following is a description of a well-developed piece of writing, which you might use when you are acting as a peer evaluator and when judging whether your own work is ready for a final evaluation or in need of further revision.

Content

The content of a well-developed piece of writing

- Is clearly focused throughout the piece
- Keeps a consistent tone and point of view
- Uses precise verbs, nouns, and modifiers
- Elaborates on ideas with supporting details, examples, and summaries, as appropriate
- Demonstrates a clear sense of purpose
- Demonstrates a clear sense of audience through choice of language and details

Form

The form of a well-developed piece of writing

- Shows clear relationships among ideas through effective transitions
- Includes sentences with a variety of structures

Grammar, Usage, Mechanics

The final draft of a well-developed piece of writing

- Contains few if any minor errors in grammar and usage
- Contains few if any minor errors in spelling, capitalization, and punctuation

The Writer as Communicator

When the time comes to share your writing, you have many choices. A few of these choices are listed below:

- Trade papers with the classmate who helped you refine your ideas.
- Trade papers with a classmate unfamiliar with your work.
- Read your writing aloud to a small group of classmates or to the class.
- Ask a classmate to read your writing aloud.
- Read your writing to younger children or to adults in your family or community.
- Discuss the ideas explored in your writing and the conclusions you arrived at.
- Choose appropriate ideas to share in a discussion and save others for future use.

- Present a dramatic reading with sound effects.
- Tape record a reading of the piece.
- Stage your work as simple Readers Theater or as a more elaborate performance.
- Publish a booklet of your own writing or of writing by many contributors.
- Display your writing in the class or school.
- Submit your writing to the school newspaper or literary magazine.
- Mail your writing to a magazine or newspaper with a wider circulation.
- Add your writing to your notebook or portfolio for later sharing.

Whatever option you choose, share your work in the spirit of learning and growing in your role as communicator.

WRITING WITH COMPUTERS

In this age of "electronic miracles," we've become accustomed to having computers help us out. Computers can help us drive our automobiles and cook our food. Thanks to computer technology, we can phone the next-door neighbor or a friend on another continent. Now the same technology can make the task of writing easier, faster, and more effective.

What Is a Word Processor?

A computer becomes a word processor when a word-processing software program is loaded into it. Programs for word processing are contained on a storage device, such as a floppy disk. The computer works in combination with a printer, which on command will print on paper any text that has been composed. Although computers vary and individual word-processing programs may differ in the features they offer, all word processing offers certain benefits to assist writers.

Type Without Knowing How

Perhaps the simplest and most elementary benefit of word processing is that it allows nontypers to produce printed words on a page. It's true that the computer's keyboard is like a typewriter and that to word process you must key in the words. However, because the word processor makes it so easy to correct errors and automatically takes care of many of the spacing and formatting decisions, it is not necessary to possess extensive typing skills.

Face the Blank Page Bravely

Even during the beginning stages of writing, when you're still thinking about a writing topic, word processing can help make your job easier. The screen light on many computers is adjustable and can be dimmed. Try free-writing with the screen dimmed, typing any ideas that come to mind. Not being able to see what you're typing frees you from concerns about form and correctness. It also keeps you from trying to rewrite prematurely. After you've exhausted your supply of ideas, turn up the monitor screen and review what you've written. Then, you can tell the computer to store your ideas, print them out, or both.

Extend Your Memory

A computer can store, or "remember," a great deal of material. You can use this fact to your advantage both while you're organizing your ideas and while you're composing. In a computer, a body of information is called a file. Word processors store written material as files. For example, if you have a list of questions that help you explore writing ideas, you can create a file to store it. If you'd like to keep an ongoing list of ideas, you can give it a file of its own, calling it up and adding to it as needed.

Some word processors let you work on more than one file at a time. This allows you to move back and forth between drafting and prewriting while the computer stores the other file for you. For example, suppose a great idea hits you during the drafting stage. Simply call up your idea file, store the inspiration, and return to your drafting. Later, you can refer to your idea file, pull out the idea, and insert it in the appropriate place in your text.

Handle Words with Confidence

Word processing simplifies adding or deleting material and moving words or passages around on the page. "Cut-and-paste" commands allow you to arrange and rearrange items in a writing plan or outline. You can also develop the points in your outline in order, or skip around as you fill in material. You can update and correct information quickly and without mess.

Throughout the planning and drafting stages, you have the option of working on-screen or making a paper copy (called a *hard copy*) of your text.

Find Your Own Drafting Style

The cut-and-paste feature is extremely useful during the drafting stage as well because it allows the word processor to accommodate alternative writing styles.

If you work best by first organizing and then writing, you could review your idea file on-screen or print out your ideas on paper to form prewriting notes. Then, use the cut-and-paste command to form a plan. Finally, expand your plan into sentences.

An alternative drafting method is to write and organize as you go. Produce text quickly and experiment on the spot with several ways of expressing an idea, or with several plans for developing it. Later, you can delete unneeded text or reorganize your draft.

The word processor also gives you the flexibility to use different approaches in your writing. For example, you may want to follow the outline as you write, or you may want to write parts of the composition out of order—say, the conclusion first or the middle sections interspersed with the introduction and the conclusion.

Be Two People at Once

Competent writers are constantly aware of—and concerned with—the impact of their words on the reader. Word processing enables you to become author and audience at the same time. In fact, some word-processing programs have a "split-screen" feature that permits you to view onscreen more than one file at a time. The split screen is divided into separate sections called *windows,* and each window displays a portion of a file. You can move back and forth between windows and make changes, creating two versions of text simultaneously. You can experiment by moving words and even entire passages around. You can try a variety of locations for the same paragraph. The split screen allows you to test the merits of several versions and choose the one you consider to be the most effective.

Choose the Best Word

Word-processing programs have a "search and replace" function that indicates the number of times a given word is used in the text. If in revising your writing you suspect that you've overused a word, use this function to learn how many times it's mentioned in your text. (Some programs even display the location in the text of each occurrence.) Then, you can decide in each case whether to keep the word or to replace it with another.

Some word-processing programs have a built-in thesaurus to help you find a synonym. If yours does not, use your own thesaurus or a dictionary.

Produce a Perfect Paper

One of the best features of the word processor is its ability, at the stroke of a key, to produce a hard copy that is free of deletions, inserts, carets, smudges, and other marks. You can edit your writing onscreen or the "old-fashioned" way—with pencil on paper.

If you prefer, the word processor can print a copy with wide spacing and/or wide margins so that you can easily pencil in corrections. In this case, after careful proofreading you would add each of your corrections onto the screen and then print out a clean final version.

Spell Perfectly

Another feature of many processors, the *spelling checker,* automatically scans the text for misspelled or unfamiliar words. Spelling checkers call up each questionably spelled word so that you can check it against a built-in dictionary or one of your own.

Become a More Effective Writer

Without a doubt, word processors make composing and revising easier. They enable you to concentrate your efforts on the most important aspect of writing: saying what you have to say in the best possible way.

GUIDELINES FOR RESEARCH AND REPORT WRITING

A private eye summarizes an investigation. A sportswriter explains the academic probation of a star player. A newspaper reporter covers the trial of a local politician. A student uses the library to write a term paper about film versions of *Romeo and Juliet*. All these people have conducted research to find and evaluate information. Despite differences in style and purpose, each person has written a report or research paper that presents information to others.

The following section provides an overview of the steps needed to complete a formal research paper. Though the focus is on writing a paper for school, this process may be adapted to any kind of research task.

Discovering a Topic

Finding the right topic is crucial for success. Use the suggestions in The Writing Process on pages 878–880 to explore possibilities. Strategies such as brainstorming, word webs, lists, charts, diagrams, and peer conferences can help you find a topic.

Evaluating a Topic

Once you have possible topics, you need to eliminate the unsuitable ones, using questions such as the following to trim your list.

1. Are you interested enough in the topic to spend a long time with it?
2. Is there enough information available on it? A subject that is too recent or too technical may not have enough materials.
3. Is the topic too simple? If you can learn everything you need to know in one article, the topic does not need research.
4. Is the topic too broad? Some topics, such as the causes of World War I or the effects of pollution, are just too big to handle in a short paper.

Limiting a Topic

Once you have chosen what you think is a good topic, you need to narrow its scope; otherwise, you'll be overwhelmed with information. You can begin by reading about your subject in an encyclopedia or other reference book, looking for ways to whittle down your topic. For example, you might begin by exploring cultural traditions of Mexico, then narrow your topic to Mexican dance masks.

As you limit your topic, try to focus on the purpose of your paper. If you are interested in air bags, deciding whether to evaluate their effectiveness or to report the history of their development will help focus your hunt for information.

Finding Sources

After narrowing your topic, you need to search for and collect information, using the tools listed below.

The Card Catalog   The card catalog provides a guide to all material in the library, using three categories, **title cards, author cards,** and **subject cards.** Begin by looking up your subject, but don't give up if it doesn't seem to be there. You may have to look up a variety of headings before you strike gold.

Many public libraries offer a **computerized catalog system** that is more compact and often easier to use than the card catalog. If you know the author, title, or subject of a book, the computer will tell you if the library has that book. If you need a listing of the books the library has on a certain subject, type in the subject and the computer will list titles and call numbers of books available.

Readers' Guide to Periodical Literature This source will list current magazine articles on your subject.

Encyclopedias   Generally, encyclopedias are a good starting point. They provide basic information and often suggest other books and articles. There are general encyclopedias as well as sets of special-purpose references that focus on one subject. Here is a partial listing.

- *The World Book Encyclopedia*
- *Encyclopaedia Britannica*
- *Collier's Encyclopedia*
- *The Baseball Encyclopedia*
- *Harper Encyclopedia of Science*

Specialized Reference Books   The reference section of your library contains all kinds of books that may prove helpful. The librarian can point you in the right direction.

- **Almanacs and Yearbooks** provide up-to-date facts and statistics. *The Guinness Book of World Records* is an example.
- **Specialized Dictionaries** focus on a particular field of knowledge or part of the language. You can find dictionaries on such subjects as architecture, ballet, botany, biographies, slang, and many others.
- **Atlases** contain maps as well as other information on topics such as population, temperatures, weather, and so on.

People in the Know   Interviews with people who are knowledgeable about your topic can add fresh insight. You'll be surprised at how cooperative such people are if approached in the right way.

Evaluating Possible Sources

Researching a report can be time-consuming. To make the best use of your time, you should learn to quickly review the parts of a book to determine whether it will be a useful source of information.

Title Page   This page gives the complete title of the book, the names of authors or editors, the name of the publisher, and the place of publication.

Copyright Page   On this page you will find the date of publication. You can then decide if the material in the book is current enough for your purpose. For example, a 1965 copyright date on a book about nuclear energy would indicate that the information in that particular book is probably out of date.

Foreword, Preface, or Introduction Pages   These pages contain important background information, such as the author's purpose in writing the book or the method used in collecting the information.

Table of Contents   This is a summary or outline of the contents of the book, arranged in order of appearance. These pages are especially important because they quickly tell you whether the book discusses your topic and whether the coverage is detailed enough for your purposes.

Text   This is the body of the book. Look briefly at the text of any book you are interested in using. Can you understand the language and the level of discussion? Don't bother using a book that is too technical or too scholarly.

Appendices   Some books may have appendices at the back which contain additional information such as maps, charts, tables, illustrations, or graphs.

Notes and Bibliography   Here the author credits the sources used in the preparation of the book and lists other books that may be of interest to readers who need further information.

Glossary   This is a dictionary at the back of the book that lists unusual or technical terms used in the text.

Index   This is an alphabetical list of subjects covered in the book. Each entry is followed by page numbers that enable you to locate specific information. If your research subject is part of a chapter listed in the table of contents, a look at the index will tell you where it is located and how many pages are devoted to it.

Creating Bibliography Cards

Use bibliography cards to keep track of your sources. Once you have looked through an article or book and decided it may be useful, record essential information on a 3" × 5" index card, using a separate card for each source. You need to include the full title, complete names of authors, and complete publishing information. Carefully record your information in the exact format used in the bibliography, described on pages 889–890. If you get all the details in the right order now, you'll save time and effort later on.

Also list the library call number on each card; if you use more than one library, give the name as well. Finally, since your cards will also serve as a way of coding your notes, assign a number to each card and put it in the upper right hand corner.

Sample Bibliography Card

```
                                        ④
Cordry, Donald.  Mexican Masks.
   Austin: U of Texas P, 1980.


Evanston Public Library         391.434
```

Taking Notes

Format   Most researchers write notes on 4″ × 6″ index cards to avoid confusing them with the smaller bibliography cards. The notes should be in the following format: 1) a heading, which gives the general idea, 2) the body of the note, 3) a page reference, and 4) a source number which matches the note card to the bibliography card. Use a separate card for each note.

Sample Note Card

Heading   **Source Number**

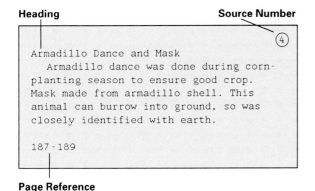

```
                                        ④
Armadillo Dance and Mask
   Armadillo dance was done during corn-
planting season to ensure good crop.
Mask made from armadillo shell. This
animal can burrow into ground, so was
closely identified with earth.

187-189
```

Page Reference

Knowing When   Deciding when to take a note is difficult. The basic question you need to ask is: How important is this information for my topic? Here are some things to look for:

1. The main concepts of the topic
2. Results of research or studies
3. Important dates and facts
4. Key people involved
5. Interesting examples or stories
6. Contrasting opinions of experts
7. Special terms

Quoting or Summarizing   Whenever possible, you should summarize the information you find in your own words. Keep your emphasis on what is important, being careful not to get bogged down in details. Also, label opinions; if you are reporting what Dr. Jones thinks, be sure to say so in your note.

Statements that are memorable, clever, famous, or written in an interesting way should be quoted directly. Copy them word for word and mark the beginning and end with quotation marks. If the quotation is too long to copy completely, you can combine summary with direct quotation.

Plagiarism   The uncredited use of someone else's ideas or words is called plagiarism. This occurs when a direct quote is presented as if it were your own words or when someone else's ideas are summarized without credit being given.

Organizing Your Material

State Your Controlling Purpose   Once you've assembled your information, you need a game plan for your paper. The first step is to state a controlling purpose, a sentence that sums up the aim of your paper. Your controlling purpose will help you move in the right direction as you organize and write your paper.

Examples
To explain how masked dances played an important role in Mexican culture.

To show how the problems described in "Giving Blood" by Roberta Silman reflect the larger problems faced by today's blood suppliers.

To compare the science of robotics with the science-fiction image of robots.

Constructing an Outline   Outlining can help you think through a paper before the writing starts. Though some writers work better without outlines, many find them necessary.

One way to begin an outline is to turn your controlling purpose into a question. This can help you break down your topic into its major parts, which then become the main headings of an outline.

Then review your notes, paying special attention to the headings on the note cards. Group the notes into separate piles, putting similar ones together. Your groups can help you organize your outline into headings and subheadings.

Example
    Masked Dances of Mexico
        I. History of mask dances
            A. Before 1500
            B. After 1500
        II. Types of dances and masks
            A. Historical
                1. Spaniards vs. Indians
                2. May 5th (Cinco de Mayo) victory
            B. Nature-related
                1. Armadillo
                2. Tiger
            C. Religious
                1. Moors and Christians
                2. Nativity

Writing from Your Outline

Your main purpose now is to get your ideas down in writing. In the draft, don't aim for perfect, error-free writing; simply get your ideas down in a form that you will be able to follow when it's time for revision.

Incorporating Your Notes

You'll need to decide how best to present the information from your notes. Usually, you should use only key phrases, weaving them into your own sentences. Summarize as much as possible in your own words.

Sometimes you may wish to quote an entire passage. Longer quotations—those more than four typed lines—should be set off from the text. Indent the entire quote ten characters in from the left margin. In this case no quotation marks are needed.

Phrases
Roosevelt spoke of "the need to find a program that uplifts rather than degrades."

Whole Sentences
The next step was to produce an airplane that could go faster than sound, but according to Isaac Asimov. "There was talk of the <u>sound barrier</u> as though it were something physical that could not be approached without destruction."

Long Passages
In <u>Psychology: A Biographical Approach</u>, Malinda Jo Levin presents an interesting way of looking at dreams:

> Recently it has become popular to talk of dreams in relation to creativity. Elias Howe supposedly perfected the sewing machine while in a dream state.

Be careful not to let quotations overrun your paper. You need to put the information together in a clear, easy-to-follow way.

Documenting Your Sources

Any information that you use from your sources must be documented, or credited to its original source. To accomplish this, you can use **parenthetical documentation.** In most cases, you will list only the author's last name and a page reference in parentheses after the paraphrased, summarized, or quoted material. Refer to the following example and guidelines.

Example

> "Covering the face with a mask is the equivalent of temporarily removing the identity and the soul (alma) of the mask wearer" (Cordry 3).

Guidelines for Documentation

1. **Works by one author.** Give the author's last name in parentheses at the end of a sentence, followed by the page numbers (Jones 58).
2. **Works by more than one author.** List all the last names in parentheses, or give one last name followed by *et al.* (Smith, Jones, and Wilcox 87) or (Smith *et al.* 87).
3. **Works with no author listed.** When citing an article that does not identify the author, use the title of the work or a shortened version of it ("Cochise" 398).
4. **Two works by the same author.** If you use more than one work by the same author, give the title, or a shortened version, after the author's last name (Jones, *Indian Wars* 398).
5. **Two works cited at the same place.** If you use more than one source to support a point, use a semicolon to separate the entries (Jones 398; Smith 87).

Compiling the Bibliography

Once you have completed your draft, gather the bibliography cards for every source you have cited. Use these cards to create your Bibliography or Works Cited, following these guidelines.

Guidelines for Final Bibliography

1. Arrange all bibliography entries by the last name of the author or editor.
2. If no author or editor is provided, alphabetize each entry by the first word of the title. If the first word is *A, An,* or *The,* begin with the second word of the title.
3. Begin the first line of each entry at the left margin. If the entry runs to a second or third line, indent those lines five spaces.
4. Single-space each bibliography entry, but double-space between entries.
5. Put a period at the end of each entry.
6. Bibliography entries contain page numbers only when they refer to parts within whole works.

Sample Bibliography Entries

Whole Books

A. One author

Webster, Charles. *From Paracelsus to Newton: Magic and the Making of Modern Science.* Cambridge: Cambridge UP, 1983.

B. Two authors

Gilbert, Sandra M., and Susan Gubar. *The Madwoman in the Attic: The Woman Writer and the Nineteenth Century Literary Imagination.* New Haven: Yale UP, 1979.

C. Two or more authors

Gatto, Joseph, *et al. Exploring Visual Design.* 2nd ed. Worcester: Davis, 1987.

Use *et al.,* Latin for *and others,* instead of listing all authors.

D. No author given

Literary Market Place: The Directory of American Book Publishing. 1984 ed. New York: Bowker, 1984.

E. An editor, but no single author

Saddlemyer, Ann, ed. *Letters to Molly: John Millington Synge to Maire O'Neill.* Cambridge: Harvard UP, 1984.

When you have cited several works from a collection, you may write one entry for the entire collection or list each work separately.

F. Two or three editors

Emanuel, James A., and Theodore L. Gross, eds. *Dark Symphony: Negro Literature in America.* New York: Macmillan, 1968.

Parts Within Books

A. A poem, short story, essay, or chapter from a collection of works by one author

Angelou, Maya. "Remembering." <u>Poems.</u> New York: Bantam, 1986. 11.

B. A poem, short story, essay, or chapter from a collection of works by several authors

Welty, Eudora. "The Corner Store." <u>Prose Models</u>. Ed. Gerald Levin. New York: Harcourt, 1984. 20–22.

C. A novel or play from a collection

Serling, Rod. <u>Requiem for a Heavyweight.</u> <u>Twelve American Plays</u>. Ed. Richard Corbin and Miriam Balf. New York: Scribner's, 1973. 57–89.

Steinbeck, John. <u>The Red Pony</u>. <u>The Short Novels of John Steinbeck</u>. New York: Viking, 1963. 355–649.

Magazines, Encyclopedias, Newspapers, Interviews

A. An article from a quarterly or monthly magazine

Batten, Mary. "Life Spans." <u>Science Digest</u> Feb. 1984: 46–51.

B. An article from a weekly magazine

Powell, Bill. "Coping with the Markets." <u>Newsweek</u> 27 Apr. 1987: 54.

C. A magazine article with no author given

"How the New Tax Law Affects America." <u>Nation's Accountants</u> 24 Sept. 1986: 66–69.

D. An article from a daily newspaper

James, Noah. "The Comedian Everyone Loves to Hate." <u>New York Times</u> 22 Jan. 1984, sec. 2: 23.

E. An encyclopedia article

"Western Frontier Life." <u>The World Book Encyclopedia</u>. 1993 ed.

F. A signed review

Ludlow, Arthur. "Glass Houses." Rev. of <u>Rolling Breaks and Other Movie Business</u> by Aljean Harmetz. <u>Movies</u> Aug. 1983: 76.

G. An unsigned, untitled review

Rev. of <u>Harry and Son</u>. <u>American Film</u> Mar. 1984: 78.

H. An interview

Farquharson, Reginald W. Personal interview. 26 May 1990.

Revising

Research papers almost always need revising before they fully meet the needs of the writer and reader. Find someone to read your paper carefully, using the following questions as a guide.

1. Is the purpose for writing clear?
2. Are ideas presented clearly, one at a time?
3. Is more information needed anywhere?
4. Should some of the information be cut out?

MLA Manuscript Guidelines

Typing or Printing   Type your final draft on a typewriter, or if you are using a word processor, print out a letter-quality copy. Do not justify the lines. If you have to write your final copy by hand, use dark blue or black ink and make sure your handwriting is neat and legible. Use only one side of the paper.

Paper   Use 8½-by-11-inch, white, nonerasable paper.

Margins   Except for page numbers, leave one-inch margins on all sides of the paper. Indent the first line of each paragraph five spaces from the left margin. Indent set-off quotations (those of more than four lines) ten spaces from the left margin. Do not indent long quotations from the right.

Spacing   The entire paper—including the heading and title on the first page, the body of the paper, quotations, and the Works Cited list—should be double-spaced.

Heading and Title   One inch from the top of the first page and flush with the left margin, type your name, your teacher's name, the course name, and the date on separate lines. Below this heading, center the title on the page. Do not underline the title or surround it with quotation marks. Do not use all capital letters for the title.

CORRECT BUSINESS LETTER FORM

Business letters have six parts: the **heading,** the **inside address,** the **salutation,** the **body,** the **closing,** and the **signature.** These six parts can be arranged in either **block form** or **modified block form.**

Block Form and Modified Block Form

For all business letters, use plain white 8½ × 11″ paper, whether you handwrite or type them. In **block form,** all parts begin at the left margin. Use this form only when you type the letter. In **modified block form** the heading, closing, and signature are aligned near the right margin, and the other parts are at the left margin.

BLOCK FORM

1246 Prairie Avenue
Minneapolis, Minnesota 55435   ◀ **Heading**
April 4, 19–

U.S. Cycling Federation   ◀ **Inside Address**
1750 East Boulder Street
Colorado Springs, Colorado 80409

Dear Sir or Madam: ◀ **Salutation**   **Body** ▼

I am interested in joining a cycling club and in participating in bike races that your organization sponsors. Please send me information about clubs in my area and instructions for entering federation races.

Thank you for your assistance.

Yours truly,   ◀ **Closing**
Jose Martinez   ◀ **Signature**
Jose Martinez

MODIFIED BLOCK FORM

Heading ▶
631 Inca Lane
St. Louis, Missouri 63101
April 3, 19–

Edgar Drexler, Manager   ◀ **Inside Address**
Sutton's Department Store
432 Oak Street
St. Louis, Missouri 63142

Dear Mr. Drexler: ◀ **Salutation**   **Body** ▼

In March I purchased a pair of All World basketball shoes in your sporting goods department for $39.95. Enclosed is a copy of the sales receipt.

I wore these shoes for less than one week before the sole came loose on the left shoe. When I took them back to the store, the sales clerk said they could not be returned. I feel this is unfair because the shoes I bought were obviously defective. I am requesting a full refund or an exchange for another brand. Your prompt attention to this problem would be appreciated.

Closing ▶   Very truly yours,
Signature ▶   *Benjamin Erickson*
Benjamin Erickson

Heading The heading is written at the top of the page. The first line contains your street address; the second line contains your town or city, state, and ZIP code. Separate the city and state with a comma and write out the name of the state. The third line gives the date of the letter. Place the heading at the left or the right margin, depending on whether you use the block form or the modified block form.

Inside Address The inside address tells to whom the letter is being sent. Place the inside address at the left margin at least four lines below the heading. On the first line you should place the name of the receiver. If there is room, place the person's title on the same line, separated from the name by a comma. Otherwise, place the title on the next line. If you do not know the name of the person who will receive your letter, use the person's title or the name of the department. On the succeeding lines, place the company name and address, including the city, state, and ZIP code.

Salutation   Position the salutation two lines below the inside address. Begin with the word *Dear,* follow it by the name of the person to whom you are writing, and end with a colon. Use only the person's last name, preceded by a title such as *Mr., Mrs., Ms., Dr.,* or *Professor.* If you do not know the person's name, use a general salutation such as *Ladies and Gentlemen.* Another alternative is to write to a department or to a position within a company. The following forms are acceptable:

Dear Mr. Allen:	Dear Sir or Madam:
Dear Ms. Kreutzer:	Dear Customer Service
Dear Mrs. Jackson:	Department:
	Dear Editor:

Body   The body, the main part of the letter in which you write your message, begins two spaces below the salutation. The body may contain a single paragraph or several paragraphs. Leave a space between each paragraph.

Closing   The closing is placed two lines below the body, in line with the heading. Closings commonly used for business letters include *Sincerely, Sincerely yours,* and *Very truly yours.* Note that only the first word is capitalized and that the closing ends with a comma.

Signature   Type or print your name four spaces below the closing, and sign your name in the space between.

LANGUAGE
HANDBOOK

USING THE LANGUAGE HANDBOOK

This language handbook outlines some of the common errors people make in both written and spoken English. The handbook does not focus on learning rules and terms. Its goal is to help you communicate more effectively by providing concentrated review and practice in the areas where usage problems often occur.

THE PARTS OF SPEECH

While terminology is not emphasized in this book, it is important to have a basic knowledge of the parts of speech so that you can communicate about language.

You have studied the eight parts of speech many times over the years. Here is a quick review.

Noun   A noun is a word that names a person, place, thing, or idea.
   writer   New York   baseball   sympathy

Pronoun   A pronoun is a word used in place of a noun or another pronoun.
   she   his   themselves   anyone   who   which

Verb   A verb is a word that tells about an action, or a state of being.
   run   work   think   is

Adjective   An adjective is a word that modifies a noun or a pronoun.
   these   huge   green   several   ten   delicious

Adverb   An adverb is a word that modifies a verb, an adjective, or another adverb.
   slowly   outside   later   very   quickly

Preposition   A preposition is a word used with a noun or a pronoun to show how the noun or pronoun is related to some other word in the sentence.
   before   on   in   across   over   to

Conjunction   A conjunction is a word that connects words or groups of words.
   and   but   both   because   however

Interjection   An interjection is a word or group of words that shows feeling or emotion.
   wow   good grief   look out   ouch   hooray

SECTION 1: WRITING COMPLETE SENTENCES

A *sentence* is a group of words that expresses a complete thought. A sentence begins with a capital letter and ends with either a period, a question mark, or an exclamation point.

The Parts of a Sentence

A sentence that expresses a complete thought always has a subject and a verb. In addition, the sentence may contain other elements such as objects that complete the meaning of the sentence.

You have studied the parts of a sentence many times during your school years. The following diagrams will serve as a quick review.

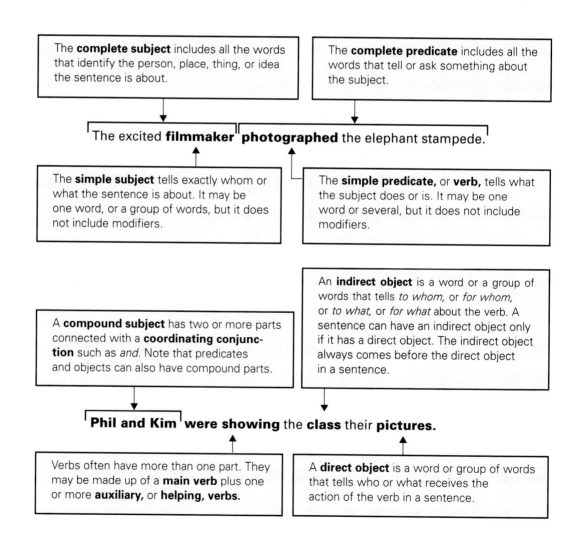

The **complete subject** includes all the words that identify the person, place, thing, or idea the sentence is about.

The **complete predicate** includes all the words that tell or ask something about the subject.

The excited **filmmaker** **photographed** the elephant stampede.

The **simple subject** tells exactly whom or what the sentence is about. It may be one word, or a group of words, but it does not include modifiers.

The **simple predicate,** or **verb,** tells what the subject does or is. It may be one word or several, but it does not include modifiers.

An **indirect object** is a word or a group of words that tells *to whom,* or *for whom,* or *to what,* or *for what* about the verb. A sentence can have an indirect object only if it has a direct object. The indirect object always comes before the direct object in a sentence.

A **compound subject** has two or more parts connected with a **coordinating conjunction** such as *and.* Note that predicates and objects can also have compound parts.

Phil and Kim **were showing** the **class** their **pictures.**

Verbs often have more than one part. They may be made up of a **main verb** plus one or more **auxiliary,** or **helping, verbs.**

A **direct object** is a word or group of words that tells who or what receives the action of the verb in a sentence.

Sentence Usage

Have you ever tried to finish a jigsaw puzzle when some of the pieces were missing? It's a very frustrating situation. As a writer, you must be sure to give your reader all the pieces of a sentence. If your sentences do not express complete thoughts, your reader will be confused and frustrated. You won't have communicated the whole picture.

Avoiding Sentence Fragments

A group of words that does not express a complete thought is a *sentence fragment*.

Many sentence fragments lack a subject or a verb, or both. To correct a fragment, add the missing part or parts.

Fragment	Announced their intentions to the crowd. (*Who* or *what* announced their intentions? The subject is missing.)
Sentence	The *candidates* announced their intentions to the crowd.
Fragment	A group of volunteers, who had waited all day for the results. (What did the volunteers do? The predicate is missing.)
Sentence	A group of volunteers, who had waited all day for the results, *studied* the TV screen.
Fragment	Onto the stage. (Both the subject and the predicate are missing.)
Sentence	The *winner bounded* onto the stage.

QUICK TIP   If you want to locate sentence fragments in your own writing, try reading your work aloud. If a sentence doesn't "sound right," you might discover that the subject or predicate is missing. Asking *who* or *what* will help you decide what to add in order to complete the sentence.

Exercise 1 Sentence Fragments   On a piece of paper, write *Sentence* after the number of each complete sentence. Change each fragment into a sentence by adding words.

Example	About traditional Native American culture.
Answer	*We have a lot to learn* about traditional Native American culture.

BETWEEN FRIENDS

Sentence fragments are always acceptable in casual conversation.

FRAGMENTS IN OTHER PLACES

Sentence fragments are useful and acceptable in certain situations. For example, when you are taking notes, you can invent your own kind of shorthand. Fragments are also acceptable when writing dialogue that imitates real-life conversations. Outlines, study notes, and directions are situations where using fragments works well.

1. Too many people have misconceptions about the Native Americans of the past.
2. Teepees, tomahawks, or feathered headdresses.
3. In actuality, tribes differed dramatically from one another.
4. Life among the Sioux, Navajo, or Shawnee.
5. Because of differences in geographical location.
6. Native Americans lived in various types of dwellings, ranging from wigwams, to long houses, to pueblos.
7. Canoes, peace pipes, and moccasins were not a part of every tribe's culture.
8. Numerous scattered tribes, each with a unique, rich heritage.
9. An appreciation of the balance of nature.
10. Native Americans have made many contributions to our culture.

Avoiding Run-on Sentences

A *run-on sentence* is two or more sentences written as one sentence.

Run-on sentences can be confusing because they combine ideas that need to be separated.

To correct run-on sentences, put a period or other end mark at the end of each complete sentence and begin each complete sentence with a capital letter.

Run-on   The flood victims were rescued they were taken to a temporary shelter.

Correct   The flood victims were rescued. They were taken to a temporary shelter.

Sometimes a run-on is created when a writer uses a comma instead of an end mark to separate two complete thoughts. This error is called a **comma splice**. Comma splices are corrected in the same way as run-ons.

Comma Splice   The barn needed repairs, it finally collapsed.
Correct   The barn needed repairs. It finally collapsed.

QUICK TIP As you read your writing aloud, listen for the place where you pause naturally at the end of a complete thought. Have you used the correct punctuation at that point?

Exercise 2   Run-on Sentences   Correct the following run-on sentences by adding capitalization and punctuation to show where each complete thought begins and ends.

Example   *The Miracle Worker* is a drama about the life of Helen Keller, the play was also made into a movie.

Answer   *The Miracle Worker* is a drama about the life of Helen Keller. The play was also made into a movie.

1. Helen Keller's life began in Tuscumbia, Alabama her father owned the local newspaper.
2. The child was very bright she was talking and running before her first birthday.
3. At 19 months old a high fever left her very ill it affected her sight and hearing.
4. In a few weeks she lost all speech, she was never to see or hear again.
5. Her inability to communicate made Helen angry her family had great difficulty disciplining her.
6. In desperation the Keller family took Helen to Washington D.C. there she met Alexander Graham Bell.
7. The inventor of the telephone was interested in education of the deaf his advice was to find a teacher for Helen.
8. The teacher was Annie Sullivan her own blindness had been cured by surgery.
9. Helen's temper tantrums were violent she once knocked out her teacher's two front teeth.
10. After two weeks Sullivan got through to Helen, Annie Sullivan helped Helen discover language.
11. Sullivan had spent hours finger spelling words onto Helen's hands, the word *water* finally broke through Helen's silence.
12. Five years of a child's loneliness were over Helen had found a new way to communicate.
13. The teacher and pupil encouraged each other soon Helen was reading and writing.
14. Word of Sullivan's success spread even President Cleveland wanted to meet Helen and her teacher.
15. In Boston Helen lived at Perkins School for the Blind she made many friends.
16. Helen Keller wanted to speak she was unable to learn.
17. Her vocal cords were too weak and untrained, her words were difficult to understand.
18. Her friendships with Alexander Graham Bell and Mark Twain were important to her they helped her financially.

19. Helen pursued her studies in Boston, at the age of nineteen she applied to Radcliffe College.

20. She graduated with honors in 1904 her multiple handicaps never held her back.

Exercise 3 Complete Sentences Write *Sentence, Fragment,* or *Run-on* for each of the following groups of words. Correct any fragments by adding words to make complete sentences. Correct any run-ons or comma splices by adding capitalization and punctuation.

1. In the early 1900's the most popular writer of short stories was O. Henry.

2. His real name was William Sydney Porter.

3. His stories first appeared in newspapers and magazines they were translated into many languages.

4. Porter was born in North Carolina, his mother died when he was three.

5. Jobs as a clerk at a drugstore, a bank teller, and a newspaper columnist.

6. In 1896, he was accused of stealing from a bank where he worked.

7. He was sentenced to five years in prison, he was released two years early for good conduct.

8. Porter wrote some of his first stories in prison.

9. Used the name O. Henry.

10. He moved to New York in 1901, where he experienced poverty and hardship.

11. 251 stories in ten years.

12. O. Henry lived in Texas, Central America, and New York his stories reflected his travels.

13. His stories often end with a surprise twist, this style greatly influenced American fiction.

14. Ordinary people such as taxi drivers, shop clerks, and office workers appeared in most of his stories.

15. A prize for the best American short story bears his name, it is awarded every year.

Combining Sentences

When you correct run-on sentences, try not to end up with too many short sentences. Although short sentences can be effective, too many will make your writing choppy and boring. To add interest and variety to your writing, combine related sentences and sentence parts. Combined sentences will sound smoother and show your reader the relationship between ideas.

One way to combine sentences is to create compound sentence parts.

A **compound subject** consists of two or more subjects that share the same verb. A **compound predicate** has two or more verbs that share the same subject.

Study the examples below to see how compound parts are formed. Notice that the parts are connected with a **coordinating conjunction** such as *and*.

COORDINATING CONJUNCTIONS

Coordinating conjunctions are words that connect words or groups of words. Here is a list of coordinating conjunctions: *and, but, or, for, so, yet, nor.*

Short Sentences	Fishing vessels filled the harbor. Sailboats were there also.
Combined	*Fishing vessels* and *sailboats* filled the harbor. (compound subject)
Short Sentences	The lobsterman hauled up his traps. He pulled them onto the deck.
Combined	The lobsterman *hauled up his traps* and *pulled them onto the deck.* (compound predicate)

Note Creating compounds is just one of the many ways sentences can be combined. Refer to the Language Workshops on pages 288, 328, 500 and 627 for other sentence combining techniques.

QUICK TIP As you revise and improve your writing, vary the length of your sentences. Use compound subjects and predicates to write long sentences, but also include some short sentences for emphasis.

Exercise 4 Combining Sentences Combine each pair of sentences by joining either their subjects or their predicates. If you wish, you may add or delete words to make the new sentences read smoothly.

1. Anoles, often called American chameleons, are related to chameleons. Anoles are not true chameleons.
2. Chameleons have the ability to change color. Many other kinds of lizards also have the ability to change color.
3. Contrary to popular belief, chameleons do not change colors to match their backgrounds. Also, they do not alter patterns to match their backgrounds.
4. Light intensity can cause chameleons to alter their color. Mood can also.
5. Courting rituals encourage the most dramatic color and pattern transformations. Defensive actions encourage these changes also.

6. Male chameleons puff themselves up to scare rivals away from their territory. They also change to vibrant colors to scare rivals away.
7. A chameleon's eyes are as fascinating as its ability to change color. Its tongue is fascinating also.
8. Each eye takes in a radius of 180 degrees. Each eye moves independently of the other.
9. Thus, a chameleon can hunt its prey without moving its head or body. It can spy on its predators in this same way.
10. A chameleon's sticky tongue thrusts at a victim. Then the tongue reels the victim in.

REMINDER
Don't overdo the use of conjunctions. If you use *and* too often in a sentence, you'll end up with a weak sentence that bores your reader. When you write, think of other ways to combine your ideas.
Weak: Andrew earns money by walking dogs, and he mows lawns, and he repairs bicycles.
Improved: Andrew earns money by walking dogs, mowing lawns, and repairing bicycles.

Exercise 5   Sentence Review   Write *Sentence, Fragment,* or *Run-on* for each of the following groups of words. Correct fragments by adding missing sentence parts. Correct run-ons by making separate sentences or combining sentence parts. Be sure to use correct capitalization and punctuation.

1. Arielle loves the library, she welcomes the quiet.
2. After being in the noisy halls and cafeteria.
3. Leisurely browsing through numerous magazines.
4. Sometimes studies with friends.
5. Read twenty books last year.
6. Often recommended by friends.
7. She enjoys science fiction, she especially likes Ray Bradbury's work.
8. Because futuristic plots appeal to her.
9. Isaac Asimov is another favorite author, she is always looking for his titles.
10. Fantasy also appeals to her.
11. *The Hobbit*, a fantasy novel by J.R.R. Tolkien.
12. The librarian who is impressed with Arielle's motivation.
13. Many students and adults enjoy science-fiction movies.
14. They prefer science-fiction movies to science-fiction novels.
15. Arielle is different she prefers reading.
16. Books let you use your imagination.
17. Imagines strange-looking creatures and settings.
18. She did love one science-fiction film, it was *2001 - A Space Odyssey*.
19. Perhaps one day she will write her own books.
20. Another student in another library reading Arielle's books.

SECTION 2: USING NOUNS

A *noun* is a word that names a person, place, thing, or idea.

Persons	Charles Dickens, child, coach, Zeus
Places	Dallas, lake, restaurant, skating rink
Things	radio, umbrella, pizza, ticket
Ideas	love, freedom, safety, anger

Classes of Nouns

Nouns may be classified in many ways. The following chart reviews the various types of nouns.

Common Noun   A general name such as *singer, state, house, river*.

Proper Noun   A specific name such as *Paul McCartney, California, The White House, Amazon River*. Note that proper nouns are always capitalized.

Concrete Noun   Anything that can be seen, heard, smelled, touched, or tasted, such as *forest, thunder, odor, cloth, banana*.

Abstract Noun   Something that cannot be recognized through the senses, such as *pity, truth, ability, love*.

Compound Noun   A noun made of two or more words. Compound nouns may be written as one word, as two words, or with a hyphen such as *football, high school, great-grandmother*.

Collective Noun   A noun that names a group of people or things, such as *audience, herd, team, family*.

Noun Usage

Nouns change form to show singular or plural number and to show possession.

Although nouns pose relatively few problems in your speech and writing, sometimes their changes in form can cause confusion.

The following rules will help you form the plural and the possessive of most nouns.

LOOKING INTO WORDS

Can a proper noun become a common noun? An **eponym** is a person whose name becomes a common word. During the Civil War, Ambrose Burnside was a general whose picture was constantly in the newspapers. Men across America copied the bushy whiskers on the side of his face. Soon the whiskers were called *burnsides*, and we know them today as *sideburns*.

WORD PLAY

There are many unusual collective nouns, especially those that refer to groups of animals: a *plague* of locusts, a *wedge* of swans, a *skulk* of foxes, a *pride* of lions. People who love to play with words have made up some original collective nouns that you won't find in a dictionary, like a *click* of photographers and a *string* of yo-yo players.

Forming Plurals

PLURAL FACTS

Sometimes the plurals of words are more familiar than the singular. Do you know that if you have only one of a pair of *dice*, it is a *die*? Or that if you are collecting *data* and have only one fact it is *datum*? There are even plural nouns that have no singulars such as *pliers, suds, overalls, athletics,* and *pajamas.*

Form the plural of most nouns by adding -s, -es, or -ies.

1. **Most nouns form the plural by simply adding -s to the singular:**

car	cat	hammer	stove	bulb
cars	*cats*	*hammers*	*stoves*	*bulbs*

2. **Nouns that end in -s, -sh, -ch, -x, or -z form the plural by adding -es.** Even if you forget this exact rule, you can see from the following examples that adding -es to such words just looks and sounds right.

glass	dish	match	tax	buzz
glasses	*dishes*	*matches*	*taxes*	*buzzes*

3. **For most singular nouns ending in -o, add -s to form the plural. For a few nouns that end in an -o preceded by a consonant add -es.**

studio	radio	photo	tomato	hero	echo
studios	*radios*	*photos*	*tomatoes*	*heroes*	*echoes*

4. **If a noun ends in -y with a vowel before it, add -s to form the plural. If the -y follows a consonant, change the -y to -i and add -es.**

toy	ray	key	lady	country
toys	*rays*	*keys*	*ladies*	*countries*

5. **For most nouns ending in f or fe, change the f to v and add -es or -s. Since there is no rule, you must memorize such words.**

life	calf	knife	thief	shelf	loaf
lives	*calves*	*knives*	*thieves*	*shelves*	*loaves*

   For some nouns ending in *f,* add -s to make the plural:

   roofs   chiefs   reefs   beliefs

6. **Some nouns have the same form for both singular and plural.**

   deer   sheep   moose   salmon   trout

7. **For some nouns, the plural is formed in a special way.**

man	goose	ox	woman	mouse	child
men	*geese*	*oxen*	*women*	*mice*	*children*

8. **For a compound noun written as one word, form the plural by changing the last word in the compound to its plural form:**

stepchild	firefly
stepchildren	*fireflies*

If the compound noun is written as separate or as hyphenated words, change the most important word to the plural form:

brother-in-law   life jacket
brothers-in-law   *life jackets*

Exercise 1   Plural Nouns   Write the plural form of each noun.

1. chief   **6.** sky   **11.** echo   **16.** spy
2. year   **7.** knife   **12.** tomato   **17.** goose
3. deer   **8.** tooth   **13.** bunch   **18.** calf
4. passer-by   **9.** rodeo   **14.** raindrop **19.** wish
5. coach   **10.** fox   **15.** moose   **20.** copy

Exercise 2   Plural Nouns   Change the italicized singular nouns to their correct forms.

1. The Aegean Sea is dotted with *island*.
2. The islands are full of mountains and *volcano*.
3. On either side are two mountainous *country*, Greece and Turkey.
4. The Greek *city* of the Aegean were built along the coast.
5. It was easier to travel by sea than to cross mountains and *valley*.
6. The many *city-state* of Greece had powerful navies.
7. Ships were often wrecked in stormy *sea*.
8. The natural world was explained in myths about gods and *hero*.
9. The *child* of ancient Greece learned history and religion from myths.
10. They also played with toys like tops and *yo-yo*.

Forming Possessives

Nouns not only name things, they also show possession, ownership, or that something is part of a person. There are only three rules for forming the possessives of nouns.

1. If a noun is singular, add 's to form the possessive.

George   horse   child   man   Mr. Harris
George's   *horse's*   *child's*   *man's*   *Mr. Harris's*

2. If the noun is plural and already ends in -s, add just the apostrophe.

doctors   committees
doctors' advice   *committees'* officers

3. If the noun is plural and does not end in -s, add 's.

people   jury
people's opinion   *jury's* decision

Exercise 3   Possessive Nouns   Write the possessive forms of these nouns.

1. secretaries
2. banker
3. James
4. Peggy
5. artist
6. photographer
7. Mr. Briggs
8. Ms. Holmes
9. Charles Smith
10. customers
11. day
12. hours
13. Lee
14. Ms. Voss
15. designers

Exercise 4   Possessive Nouns   Write the following sentences, adding the possessive forms of the noun in parentheses.

1. The first (Americans) homes varied from tribe to tribe.
2. (Tribes) homes in wet climates were raised off the ground.
3. The (Iroquois) long houses were covered in bark.
4. After ten years the (house) bark would decay.
5. The (men) task was to rebuild the houses.
6. (Parents) bunks were on the bottom.
7. The (family) possessions were kept on the bunks.
8. Each (group) cooking was done over a fire.
9. The (builder) plans included holes in the roof.
10. The (fire) smoke escaped through the holes.

Exercise 5   Noun Usage Review   Each sentence below has one error in either the plural or possessive form. Find the error and write the word correctly.

1. Noah Websters *American Dictionary* is a landmark.
2. He is Americas most famous dictionary maker.
3. Teaching changed the lawyers life.
4. Britain was at war with the colony's.
5. Schoolbook's were rare and very British.
6. While still in his twenty's, Webster published three textbooks.
7. The spelling books success gave Webster a good income.
8. He invented American spelling's for certain words.
9. Webster wanted Americas language to be unique.
10. Webster traveled to printing press's all over New England.
11. He convinced the American persons to adopt his ideas.
12. The sales of the first American English dictionarys were not great.
13. His works lack of recognition is surprising.
14. Noah Webster and George Washington were both revolutionary's.
15. Websters ideas are found in today's dictionaries.

SECTION 3: USING PRONOUNS

A *pronoun* is a word that replaces a noun or another pronoun. The noun or pronoun that a pronoun replaces is called the *antecedent* of the pronoun.

Nick whistled nervously as he walked through the alley. (The pronoun *he* refers to the noun *Nick. Nick* is the antecedent of *he*.)

Classes of Pronouns

There are many types of pronouns. The following chart gives a summary. Note that this section will deal only with the pronouns that cause the most serious problems in writing or speaking.

Classes of Pronouns
Personal
I, you, he, she, it, we, they, me, her, him, us, them, my, mine, your, yours, hers, his, its, our, ours, your, yours, their, theirs
Reflexive and Intensive
myself, yourself, himself, herself, itself, ourselves, yourselves, themselves
Demonstrative
this, that, these, those
Interrogative
who, whose, whom, which, what
Relative
who, whose, whom, which, what, that
Indefinite
all, another, any, anybody, anyone, anything, both, each, either, everybody, everyone, everything, few, many, more, most, much, neither, nobody, none, no one, nothing, one, other, several, some, somebody, someone, something, such

Pronoun Usage

If you listen to a conversation or look back at some of your writing, you will realize just how frequently pronouns are used. In fact, the sentence you just read contains four pronouns.

Most of the time English speakers automatically use pronouns correctly. There are a few situations, however, that cause confusion.

Personal Pronouns

Like nouns, personal pronouns are used to refer to people, places, things, and ideas. Unlike nouns, however, personal pronouns change form, or case, according to their use in a sentence. As you can see in the following chart, personal pronouns are divided into three cases: **nominative, objective,** and **possessive.**

Forms of Personal Pronouns			
	Nominative	**Objective**	**Possessive**
Singular	I	me	my, mine
	you	you	your, yours
	she, he, it	her, him, it	her, hers, his, its
Plural	we	us	our, ours
	you	you	your, yours
	they	them	their, theirs

Nominative Forms as Subjects

Use the nominative form of a pronoun for subjects.

The nominative forms of pronouns are used as subjects of the verb. Generally, people don't make mistakes when only one pronoun is used. Problems are more likely to occur when two or more pronouns are used together as the subject of the sentence.

Incorrect   Her and me arrived at the dance in the same dress. (*Her* and *me* are used incorrectly as subjects. They are not nominative forms.)

Correct   *She* and *I* arrived at the dance in the same dress.

QUICK TIP   To decide which pronoun to use, try saying each pronoun separately with the rest of the sentence. Let your "ear" tell you which is correct. For example, *Her arrived* or *Me arrived* sounds wrong. *She arrived* and *I arrived* sound natural.

Another problem occurs when a pronoun is used together with a noun as the subject of a sentence.

Incorrect Us boys refused to go along with the idea. (*Us* is used incorrectly as part of the subject. It is not a nominative pronoun.)

Correct *We boys* refused to go along with the idea.

QUICK TIP To decide whether *we* or *us* is correct, try the sentence without the noun. *We refused* sounds right; *us refused* does not.

Exercise 1 Pronouns as Subjects Write the correct pronoun for each sentence. If you are unsure of an answer, refer to the boxed QUICK TIPS for help.

1. Will, Molly, and (I, me) are studying different ways to communicate.
2. (We, Us) have learned the American Sign Language alphabet.
3. Molly and (I, me) used headphones.
4. (We, Us) were trying to learn how to read lips.
5. Will and (she, her) learned many words.
6. Molly, Will and (I, me) volunteered to interpret a song for deaf students at the school assembly.
7. I played the piano; Will and (she, her) practiced signing.
8. If we were deaf, we wouldn't hear the music, but (we, us) would feel the vibrations.
9. Will's father has been blind since birth. (He, Him) uses the raised dot system of Braille to read.
10. Will and (he, him) often order a printed copy and a Braille copy of the same book.
11. (Them and us, They and we) have tried to learn Braille together.
12. Will, his sister, and (we, us) have great difficulty understanding the raised dots on the page.
13. Will and (she, her) can't read many words per minute with their fingers.
14. (He, Him) made the Braille poster at school.
15. (We, Us) students have found that there are many interesting ways for people to communicate information.

Nominative Forms as Predicate Pronouns

Use the nominative form of a pronoun for predicate pronouns.

The nominative forms of pronouns are also used as predicate pronouns. A **predicate pronoun** is a pronoun that follows a linking verb and is linked by the verb to the subject. You may be confused by predicate pronouns because you may often hear the wrong forms used.

BETWEEN FRIENDS

Most people consider *It's me* acceptable in informal conversation. However, in formal speaking and writing, use the grammatically correct forms *It is I...This is she*.

Incorrect	It was him at the door. (The linking verb *was* needs the nominative pronoun *he* to follow it.)
Correct	It was *he* at the door.
Incorrect	The winners are Maria and her. (The linking verb *are* needs the nominative pronoun *she* to follow it.)
Correct	The winners are Maria and *she*.

Although the correct use of predicate pronouns is not difficult, you must be sure that you understand what these pronouns are and how they are used. If you have trouble recognizing predicate pronouns, remember these points:

1. Predicate pronouns follow linking verbs, such as *is, was, were, will be, could have been* and other forms of the verb *be*. For more about linking verbs, see page 932.

2. The predicate pronoun usually means the same thing as the subject.

> **QUICK TIP** You can usually tell when a predicate pronoun is needed by reversing the subject and the pronoun. The reversed sentence should still make sense.
>
> He was the visitor. The visitor was he.

Exercise 2 Predicate Pronouns Write the correct pronoun for each sentence.

1. Speaking of Grandma, it is (she, her) who always stresses correct grammar and etiquette.
2. Now it is (I, me) who repeat some of her rules, much to the dismay of my youngest brother.
3. In all honesty, though, the strongest grammarians in the family have always been Grandma and (I, me)!
4. Isn't it (she, her) who noisily clears her throat if anyone uses "My friend and me" as the subjects of a sentence instead of "My friend and I"?
5. As for Dad, it was (he, him) who looked very sheepish when she caught him with his finger in the frosting.
6. And the cousins—was it (they, them) who drank from the milk carton and lived to tell about it?

7. When we call her "Mrs. Manners," Grandma replies with a smile, "Yes, it is (I, me)."
8. If I were (she, her), I would be a bit more lenient with my brothers.
9. But my brothers take it all in stride; Gram's biggest fans are (they, them) and (I, me).
10. One of the most positive influences in our lives has certainly been (she, her).

Exercise 3 Nominative Pronoun Review Write the correct pronoun from those given in parentheses.

1. The boy's father and (he, him) discussed the prospect of buying a computer.
2. "Both Marcia and (I, me) will benefit," Jake explained patiently.
3. "(She, Her) and (I, me) will use it for our homework," he said.
4. "(We, Us) juniors will be responsible for a research paper this year," he continued.
5. "And as for Mom, wasn't it (she, her) who insisted we become computer literate?" Jake added.
6. "Your mother and (I, me) both think you ought to learn word processing," his father stated.
7. (He, Him) and his father looked up to see Jake's mother enter the room.
8. Just then, Jake and (they, them) heard the telephone ring, and his father answered it.
9. "Yes. This is (he, him)," Jake's father said.
10. Then he added before hanging up, "My family and (I, me) will be here all day."
11. Jake's mother inquired, "Mrs. Long from the electronics store—was it (she, her)?"
12. Jake's father had a secretive smile as he answered, "Yes, it was (she, her)."
13. "(We, Us) parents aren't so bad after all," he said to Jake.
14. "Your Mom and (I, me) ordered a computer just in time for your research paper," he added.
15. With much ceremony, Jake's mother proclaimed, "Your Dad and (I, me) are happy to announce that our computer will be delivered this afternoon."

Objective Forms of Personal Pronouns

Use the objective form of a pronoun for direct objects, indirect objects, and objects of prepositions.

Remember that a **direct object** is the person or thing that receives the action of the verb. An **indirect object** always comes before the direct object and tells *to whom* or *to what*, or *for whom* or *for what* the action of the verb is done.

> Daniel invited *us* to swim tomorrow. (*Us* is the direct object of the verb *invited*.)
>
> The record company sent *her* a new tape. (*Her* is the indirect object of the verb *sent*. *Tape* is the direct object.)

A pronoun can also be the object of a preposition. For more about prepositions, see pages 920-922.

> Can you align the handlebars for *me*? (*Me* is the object of the preposition *for*.)

As with nominative forms, most of the confusion with objective pronouns occurs when two pronouns or a pronoun and a noun are used together.

Incorrect   Will Janet be studying with you and I?
Correct   Will Janet be studying with you and *me*?

QUICK TIP   To decide which pronoun to use, try each pronoun separately with the verb. *Studying with I* sounds wrong. *Studying with me* sounds correct.

Exercise 4   Nominative and Objective Pronouns   Write the correct form of the pronoun from those given in parentheses.

1. Martha and (I, me) watched the movie *Glory* before (we, us) wrote our paper on the Civil War.
2. Mrs. Collins told Martha and (I, me) that it might give (we, us) an idea for a topic.
3. She knew that (we, us) students would rather watch a movie than read a book for homework.
4. It was (she, her) who taught us about the role African American soldiers played in the Civil War.
5. It seems (they, them) were eager to fight in the war against slavery, but at first the North rejected (they, them).
6. Frederick Douglass called upon President Lincoln; Douglass urged (he, him) to use African Americans in the war.
7. Congress finally authorized (they, them) to fight, but (they, them) were not to be paid as much as white soldiers.
8. The courage of the 54th Regiment stirred (we, us) students.

9. As for my classmates, Amy and Li, the cruelty suffered by the troops proved the most shocking to (she, her) and (he, him).
10. It was (they, them) who decided to research the treatment African American troops received by both the South and the North.
11. The battles fought by the 54th Massachusetts Regiment seemed the most interesting to Martha and (me, I).
12. Martha said that her father and (she, her) would rent *Glory.*
13. Martha's father is a Civil War buff and he enjoyed watching the movie with (she, her) and (I, me) and discussing it with (we, us).
14. The movie gave (he, him) and (we, us) an insight into the relationship between Colonel Shaw and his regiment.
15. Between Martha and (I, me), we have seen *Glory* four times.

Interrogative Pronouns (*Who* and *Whom*)

Use *who* as the subject of the verb.
Use *whom* as the direct object and object of the preposition.

The interrogative pronouns *who* and *whom* are often confused by speakers and writers. To use *who* and *whom* correctly, first decide how the pronoun is used in the sentence. If the pronoun is used as a subject of the verb, choose *who.*

Incorrect   Whom sings that song?
Correct   *Who* sings that song? (*Who* is the subject of the verb.)

If the pronoun is used as the direct object of a verb or the object of a preposition, choose *whom.*

Incorrect   Who are you visiting?
Correct   *Whom* are you visiting? (*Whom* is the direct object of the verb. The subject is *you.*)

Incorrect   With who do you travel?
Correct   With *whom* do you travel? (*Whom* is the object of the preposition *with.*)

Exercise 5   Who and Whom   Write the correct pronoun from those given in parentheses.

1. (Who, Whom) has heard of Susan B. Anthony?
2. (Who, Whom) fought harder for women's rights?
3. For (who, whom) did Anthony pledge to fight?
4. (Who, Whom) did Anthony battle in the courts?
5. (Who, Whom) called the Woman's Rights Convention the "Tomfoolery Convention"?

6. (Who, Whom) was in the reform movement?
7. (Who, Whom) can imagine a time when women could not vote?
8. With (who, whom) did she register to vote in 1872?
9. With (who, whom) did she work to open the University of Rochester to women?
10. (Who, Whom) would have thought it would take a century after Susan B. Anthony's birth for women to be given the right to vote?

Possessive Pronouns

Never use an apostrophe in a possessive pronoun.

The possessive forms of pronouns never cause problems in speaking. However, because some possessive forms sound identical to certain contractions, people sometimes make mistakes when writing them.

Possessive Pronouns	Contractions
its	it's (it is)
their	they're (they are)
whose	who's (who is)
your	you're (you are)

QUICK TIP   Remember that the apostrophe in a contraction is used to join two words. Read a sentence carefully to decide if the word in question makes sense as two words. If it does, it is a contraction and needs an apostrophe. If it does not make sense, use the correct possessive pronoun.

Exercise 6   Possessive Pronouns   Write the correct word from those given in parentheses.

1. (Its, It's) almost time to take another standardized test.
2. (Whose, Who's) worried about how his or her scores will compare with those of students in other states?
3. Taking a standardized test takes (its, it's) toll on your nerves.
4. (Whose, Who's) hands get sweaty as they fill in the bubbles on the answer sheet?
5. Before taking a timed test, (your, you're) best preparation is to learn test-taking strategies.
6. Before a test always ask teachers if (their, they're) counting a penalty for wrong answers.
7. If there's no penalty, guess at answers even if (your, you're) unsure.

8. Even if you see an answer that seems correct, (its, it's) important to read each choice.
9. Some students get (their, they're) best results if they eliminate all the answers that are obviously wrong.
10. (You're, Your) guaranteed to do better if you stay calm.

Reflexive and Intensive Pronouns

Reflexive and intensive pronouns can only be used when they refer to another word in the sentence.

Reflexive and intensive pronouns are used to add emphasis to a sentence. They are formed by adding *-self* or *-selves* to certain personal pronouns. See page 905 for a complete list of these pronouns.

When some people are unsure about which personal pronoun to use, they incorrectly choose a reflexive pronoun. Reflexive pronouns are not used correctly unless they refer (reflect back) to someone or something already mentioned in the sentence.

We helped ourselves to pizza. (*Ourselves* refers back to *we*.)

Jackson himself won the tug-of-war. (*Himself* refers back to *Jackson*.)

| **Incorrect** | Maria and myself will be ready. (*Myself* does not refer to another word in the sentence.) |
| **Correct** | Maria and *I* will be ready. |

| **Incorrect** | The profit was split between Andy and myself. |
| **Correct** | The profit was split between Andy and *me*. |

Exercise 7 Reflexive and Intensive Pronouns   Write the correct pronoun from those given in parentheses.

1. Kristin and (I, myself) worked as librarian's assistants.
2. "Could you help my friend and (me, myself) with the *Readers' Guide to Periodical Literature*?" one boy asked.
3. Mrs. Cameron, the librarian, gave that assignment to (us, ourselves).
4. As it turned out, that young man was already familiar with the *Readers' Guide* and could have helped (him, himself).
5. He had simply wanted attention from Kristin and (me, myself)!
6. At the end of the period, Mrs. Cameron excused (her, herself) and left us in charge.
7. The job of checking out students' books was given to (me, myself).

8. Kristen assigned (her, herself) another job.
9. Soon Mrs. Cameron returned to the library to see (us, ourselves) confidently in charge.
10. "I'd better watch out for my job, or you two may take it away from (me, myself)!" she laughed.

Indefinite Pronouns

Indefinite pronouns do not refer to a particular person or thing. Because it is hard to remember which of these pronouns are singular and which are plural, problems in agreement often occur.

First, remember that the **antecedent** of a pronoun is the noun or pronoun to which the pronoun refers.

The *runner* talked about *his* Olympic medals. (*Runner* is the antecedent of *his*.)

Next, keep this rule in mind.

A pronoun must agree with its antecedent in number.

If the antecedent of a pronoun is singular, a singular pronoun is required. If the antecedent is plural, the pronoun must be plural.

Incorrect	In the final race, a *rider* can change *their* position in a matter of seconds.
Correct	In the final race, a *rider* can change *his* or *her* position in a matter of seconds.

When an indefinite pronoun is the antecedent, you must decide whether it is singular or plural. Only then can you make it agree with another pronoun in the sentence. The following indefinite pronouns are always singular: *another, anyone, anybody, anything, each, either, everybody, everyone, everything, neither, nobody, no one, one, somebody,* and *someone.*

Incorrect	Does *everyone* have *their* map to the game? (*Everyone* is the antecedent. It is singular. The possessive pronoun *their* is plural and therefore does not agree.)
Correct	Does *everyone* have *his* map to the game?
Incorrect	Is *anyone* willing to read *their* poem?
Correct	Is *anyone* willing to read *his* or *her* poem? (The phrase *his or her* is singular. It shows that the indefinite pronoun may refer to a male or a female.)

These indefinite pronouns are plural: *both, few, many, several.*

Both of the cities have cancelled *their* summer festivals.

All, some, any, and *none* may be either singular or plural, depending on the meaning of the sentence.

Singular   *Some* of the garden has lost *its* beauty.
Plural   *Some* of the flowers have lost *their* scent.

Don't be confused by a phrase that appears between an indefinite pronoun and a possessive pronoun. Such a phrase is not part of the subject and does not affect agreement.

Incorrect   One of the boys left their jacket. (The possessive pronoun should agree with *one*, not with *boys*.)
Correct   One of the boys left *his* jacket.

Exercise 8   Indefinite Pronoun Agreement   Find and correct the errors in agreement in these sentences. Write *Correct* if there is no error.

  1. Everyone in our English class keeps a daily journal of their own writing.
  2. Once a month each of the students reads an entry from their journal.
  3. In the beginning of the semester few of us wanted to share his thoughts.
  4. None of the students were confident that their entries would be appreciated.
  5. Yet nobody in the class has ever said anything critical about their classmates' work.
  6. Many of the writers found his or her writing had improved by the end of the semester.
  7. Several have chosen to publish sections of his or her journals in the school literary magazine.
  8. Either of the Wong twins will read their entry today.
  9. Each of the boys filled their first notebook and began another.
  10. Some in the class think that journal writing has been their most rewarding writing experience.

Exercise 9   Pronoun Usage Review   Select the correct word from those in parentheses.

  1. Sixteen-year-old Jessica and her family agree about (their, they're) taste in music.
  2. Guess (whose, who's) interested in jazz?
  3. (She, Her) and her family have developed a love for this music.

4. Everyone in the family has (his or her, their) own cassette player and earphones.

5. "Just between you and (I, me), early jazz, or ragtime, is my favorite," Jessica claims.

6. But (its, it's) the blues that her father prefers.

7. His friends and (he, him) frequent jazz concerts all year long.

8. One of the great blues singers, Sarah Vaughan, has always been (their, they're) favorite.

9. Her brother listens to Dixieland; this music had (its, it's) beginnings in New Orleans.

10. "As for (me, myself)," he says, "give me Louis Armstrong and his trumpet any time."

11. (Whose, Who's) always buying tapes in this family?

12. Either of the girls will lend us (her, their) Scott Joplin tape.

13. Each of the music lovers received jazz albums for (his or her, their) birthday gifts.

14. (Their, They're) all in agreement that Duke Ellington is one of the most influential composers in jazz history.

15. (Who, Whom) hasn't heard of his big band?

16. Of (who, whom) do you think when "jazz clarinetist" is mentioned?

17. (Its, It's) Benny Goodman, of course.

18. Jessica's mother loves Count Basie; she says, "I'll take Goodman and (he, him) over the Beatles any day!"

19. Speaking of her mother, it is (she, her) who has a beautiful voice, reminiscent of Billie Holiday, the blues singer.

20. (We, Us) jazz fans love all aspects of the music—the sound, the personalities, and the rich history.

SECTION 4: USING MODIFIERS

Modifiers are words that change or limit the meaning of other words. Two kinds of modifiers are adjectives and adverbs.

Adjectives

An *adjective* is a word that modifies a noun or a pronoun.

An adjective tells *which one? what kind? how many? how much?*

that book, *orange* sweater, *two* dogs, *more* rain

Classes of Adjectives

The following chart shows the various types of adjectives.

Articles   *A, an,* and *the* are adjectives referred to as articles.
The article *the* is the **definite article** because it points out a specific person, place, thing, or group.
A and *an* are **indefinite articles** because they do not refer to specific items. Use *an* before a vowel sound. Use *a* before a consonant sound. Remember, it is the sound, not the spelling, that determines the correct choice: *an* elephant, *an* honor, *an* igloo, *a* lamp.

Proper Adjectives   These adjectives are formed from proper nouns and are always capitalized: *Danish* furniture, *French* class.

Predicate Adjectives   These adjectives follow linking verbs and describe the subject of the sentence: The birds were *silent*. The soup smelled *wonderful*.

Nouns as Adjectives   Nouns can also become modifiers when they describe other nouns: *Florida* tan, *essay* exam, *grass* skirt.

Adverbs

An *adverb* modifies a verb, an adjective, or another adverb.

Adverbs tell *where, when, how,* or *to what extent.*

sat *here*   closed *today*   spoke *softly*   *very* quickly
exceptionally fast   *almost* done   *not* finished

WORD PLAY
....
A kind of pun that uses
adverbs is called a "Tom
Swiftie." "I love camp-
ing," said Tom *intently.*
"I have a terrible cold,"
said Tom *infectiously.*

Many adverbs are formed by adding *-ly* to an adjective.

careful + *-ly* = carefully   happy + *-ly* = happily

Here is a list of commonly used adverbs that do not end in *-ly.*

		Commonly Used Adverbs		
afterwards	fast	low	often	there
almost	forth	more	seldom	today
already	hard	near	slow	tomorrow
also	here	never	soon	too
back	instead	next	still	well
even	late	not	straight	yesterday
far	long	now	then	yet

Adjective or Adverb?

If you have trouble deciding whether to use an adjective or an adverb in a sentence ask yourself the following questions:

1. Which word does the modifier describe? Use an adverb if the modified word is an action verb, an adjective, or an adverb. Use an adjective if the modified word is a noun or pronoun.
2. What does the modifier tell about the word it describes? Use an adverb if the modifier tells *how, when, where,* or *to what extent.* Use an adjective if the modifier tells *which one, what kind, how many,* or *how much.*

Which modifier correctly completes the following sentence—the adjective *mournful* or the adverb *mournfully*?

The lost child cried _____ for his mother.

The adverb *mournfully* is the correct choice because the modifier describes the verb *cried.*

Exercise 1   Adjective or Adverb?   Choose the correct modifier from the two in parentheses. Then write the word it modifies.

Example   My evening at orchestra practice turned out to be an
                     (extreme, extremely) bizarre experience.
Answer   extremely   bizarre

1. First of all, I was (awful, awfully) tired during my solo violin practice.

2. The (handsome, handsomely) director of the string section expected us to practice until 9:00 P.M.
3. We consider him to be a (relentless, relentlessly) instructor.
4. I kept glancing (nervous, nervously) at the clock.
5. Then at 8:45 P.M. the lights (sudden, suddenly) flickered and went out.
6. Some musicians (near, nearly) screamed, but I was thrilled to be in the dark with my violin.
7. Thunder clapped and heavy torrents of rain fell (continual, continually).
8. Then the conductor of the orchestra strode (confident, confidently) onto the stage.
9. "Never mind the dark. I'll call out the name of each piece and you will play by memory," he said (loud, loudly).
10. It became (frightening, frighteningly) apparent that I would have to continue to practice.

Adverb or Predicate Adjective?

Use an adverb to modify an action verb. Use an adjective after a linking verb.

Most verbs are action verbs, and can be modified by adverbs. Linking verbs such as *be* or *seem*, however, are never modified by an adverb. Instead, they are often followed by an adjective which actually modifies the subject and not the verb. An adjective used in this way is called a **predicate adjective.**

> The play is *long*. (*Long* is a predicate adjective modifying *play*.)
> The tortillas seemed *fresh*. (*Fresh* is a predicate adjective modifying *tortillas*.)

Some verbs, such as *appear, look, sound, feel, taste, grow*, and *smell*, can be used either as action verbs or linking verbs. Because of this, you may not be sure whether to use an adverb or a predicate adjective. To help you decide, think about which word the adjective or adverb modifies. Use an adjective if it modifies the subject. Use an adverb if it modifies the verb.

> The thief looked *suspicious* to the bank teller. (The predicate adjective *suspicious* modifies the subject, *thief*, not the linking verb, *looked*.)

> The thief looked *suspiciously* at the customers. (Here the adverb *suspiciously* modifies the action verb *looked*.)

> **QUICK TIP**   If you are uncertain about whether to use an adverb or an adjective after a verb like *feel, sound, smell,* or *look,* ask yourself the following questions:
> 1. Does the modifier tell *how, when, where,* or *to what extent* about an action verb? If it does, use an adverb.
> 2. Can you substitute *is* or *was* for the verb? If you can, use an adjective.
>
> The garage *seemed* empty.   The garage *is* empty.

Exercise 2   Adverb or Predicate Adjective?   Choose the correct modifier for each of the following sentences.

1. Looking through my summer journal, I recall that on the first day of camp each youngster seemed (anxious, anxiously).
2. I looked (curious, curiously) at the girls who would be in my care.
3. One angry child sounded (furious, furiously) as he scolded his mother for making him take off his cowboy hat.
4. Anne Bicknell, the camp director, looked (kind, kindly) at the sea of anxious faces.
5. Agitated counselors and campers became (calm, calmly) as Anne introduced herself to the group.
6. The grilled hot dogs on the campfire smelled (delicious, deliciously).
7. With singing and storytelling, the children's enthusiasm grew (quick, quickly).
8. Steaming mugs of cocoa were tasted (careful, carefully).
9. Even the most active youngsters grew (weary, wearily) with each passing hour.
10. By the end of the day, the usually dreaded camp cots looked (wonderful, wonderfully) to the tired campers.

Prepositional Phrases as Modifiers

So far in this section, you have learned about single-word modifiers. As you will see, however, groups of words can also modify.

Prepositions are words that show how one word is related to another word. Read these sentences. Notice how each expresses a different relationship.

The radio is *on the table.*
The radio is *near the table.*
The radio is *beside the table.*

Dorothy pulled a muscle *before the final race.*
Dorothy pulled a muscle *after the final race.*
Dorothy pulled a muscle *during the final race.*

In the first group of sentences at the bottom of page 920, you can see that the words *on, near,* and *beside* show the relationship of *table* to *radio.* In the next group of sentences, *before, after,* and *during* show the relationship of *race* to *pulled a muscle.*

You can see that prepositions do not show relationships by themselves. They begin a **phrase.** A phrase is a group of words that belong together but that do not have a subject and verb. *On the table* and *before the final race* are examples of prepositional phrases.

> A *preposition* **is a word used with a noun or pronoun, called its** *object*, **to show how the noun or pronoun is related to some other word in the sentence.**

> A *prepositional phrase* **consists of a preposition, its object, and any modifiers of the object.**

Here is a list of words often used as prepositions. Most of these prepositions show relationships of place or time. Some show other relationships among people and things. Study the prepositions and notice the relationship that each shows.

Commonly Used Prepositions				
about	at	down	near	to
above	before	during	of	toward
across	behind	except	off	under
after	below	for	on	underneath
against	beneath	from	onto	until
along	beside	in	out	up
among	between	inside	over	upon
around	but (except)	into	since	with
as	by	like	through	without

Prepositional phrases do the same work in a sentence as adjectives and adverbs.

> **A prepositional phrase that modifies a noun or pronoun is called an** *adjective phrase.*

Like adjectives, adjective phrases tell *which one, what kind, how many*, or *how much*.

The procession passed the statue *of Lincoln.*

He was washing the window *over the sink.*

A room *on the third floor* is available.

A prepositional phrase that modifies a verb is called an *adverb phrase.*

Like adverbs, adverb phrases tell *how, when, where*, and *to what extent* about verbs.

The crowd ate *in shifts.*

The geyser erupted *at noon.*

They swam *under the bridge.*

Exercise 3   Prepositional Phrases   Add prepositional phrases to the following nouns and verbs. Do not use the same preposition more than twice. Then use your noun or verb and its phrase in a sentence.

Example   dust
Answer   dust from the trail
The dust from the trail made Diana choke and sneeze.

1. lamp
2. skidded
3. sandwich
4. helmet
5. exploded
6. found
7. hammer
8. landed
9. wallet
10. weeds
11. sock
12. had fallen
13. limped
14. ice cube
15. was dripping

REMINDER
....
Some modifiers cannot be compared. For example, something that is *unique* is one of a kind. It cannot be *more* or *less* unique than something else. Other modifiers that do not take comparisons are *equal, fatal, final,* and *absolute.*

Modifiers in Comparisons

Comparing people, things, and actions is one way of learning about the world. You might say, for example, "These new stereo speakers are *better* than the old ones. The sound is *clearer*, but they are *more expensive*." Or you might say, "This engine runs *smoothly*, but that one runs *more smoothly*."

In comparisons, modifiers have special forms or spellings.

The Comparative

When you compare one person, thing, or action with another, use the **comparative** form of the modifier.

> Rob is *taller* than John.
> Aretta left the party *earlier* than Chris.

The comparative form is made in two ways:

1. **For short modifiers like *calm* and *soon*, add -er.**
   calm + er = calmer   soon + er = sooner
   happy +er = happier   near + er = nearer

2. **For longer modifiers like *delicious* and *bravely*, use *more*.**

   > more delicious   more bravely

   Most modifiers ending in *-ful* or *-ous* form the comparative with *more*.

   > more thoughtful   more gracious   more carefully

The Superlative

When you compare a person, thing, or action with all others of its kind, use the **superlative** form of the modifier. In fact, whenever you compare a person, thing, or action with more than one other person, thing, or action, use the superlative.

> Lynn is the *tallest* person in the class.
> Of all the clerks, Debbie works *most efficiently*.

The superlative form of modifiers is made by adding *-est* or by using *most*. For modifiers that take *-er* in the comparative, add *-est* for the superlative. Those that use *more* to form the comparative use *most* for the superlative.

Modifier	Comparative	Superlative
full	fuller	fullest
dim	dimmer	dimmest
fast	faster	fastest
practical	more practical	most practical
softly	more softly	most softly

FEW, LESS

Few (fewer, fewest) is used for things that can be counted: *I have a few dishes to finish washing. Less (lesser, least)* is used for things that cannot be counted: *There seems to be less flu this year than there was last year.*

FARTHER AND FURTHER

Farther and *farthest* compare distances; *further* and *furthest* compare times, amounts, and degrees: *The hospital is only ten miles farther. This problem requires further attention.*

Irregular Comparisons

Some modifiers make their comparative and superlative forms by complete word changes.

Modifier	Comparative	Superlative
good	better	best
well	better	best
bad	worse	worst
little	less *or* lesser	least
much	more	most
many	more	most
far	farther	farthest

To make a negative comparison, use *less* or *least* before the modifier: *important, less important, least important.*

Exercise 4 Comparisons   Find the errors in comparison in the following sentences and write the sentences correctly. If a sentence has no errors, write *Correct.*

Example   The more interesting thing we studied was pioneer life.
Answer   The most interesting thing we studied was pioneer life.

1. One of the most famous pioneer trails in the American frontier was the Santa Fe Trail.
2. In the 1840's, American traders needed a directer route to Santa Fe than the old route through Mexico.
3. Compared to the old trail, the Santa Fe Trail was shortest.
4. The Santa Fe Trail was soon the busier of all the routes to the West.
5. To pull heavy wagons along the trail, mules were used instead of horses because mules worked hardest.
6. The "mule skinners" who drove the mule trains were some of the most fearsome men in the West.
7. They boasted that their eight-foot-long whips were the deadlier weapons in the West.
8. Later, traders discovered that oxen were best draft animals than mules.
9. Bullwhackers drove the oxen with rawhide whips that could kill a rattlesnake more fast than a gun.
10. More of the travelers on the Santa Fe Trail were traders, not settlers.

11. Of all the products carried west along the trail, shoes were probably the more popular items.
12. Compared to the traders, the settlers were least prepared for the dangers.
13. Life on the Santa Fe Trail was harshest than the life they had known back East.
14. Despite the dangers, more of the travelers reached their destination in good health.
15. By 1880, when the first rail train arrived in Santa Fe, one of the more colorful chapters in American travel was over.

Exercise 5 Review of Comparisons   Choose the correct modifier for each of the following sentences.

1. It is still possible to follow one of the (more scenic, most scenic) historic routes in America, the Santa Fe Trail.
2. Arrow Rock, Missouri, is one of the (older, oldest) starting points for the trail.
3. At some country stores, it's possible to buy the (tougher, toughest) beef jerky you can imagine.
4. Fort Osage, a restored trading post on the Missouri River, is in (better, best) condition than ever before.
5. Museum guides in authentic costumes make Fort Osage one of the (more realistic, most realistic) stops on the trail.
6. Pawnee Rock, located in central Kansas, was the (higher, highest) landmark for travelers to see.
7. In many places throughout the prairie, old wagon wheel ruts are the (more vivid, most vivid) reminders of the trail.
8. In Colorado, the thick adobe walls of Bent's Fort have been reconstructed in the (more, most) authentic way possible.
9. The Santa Fe Trail still leads to one of the (more enchanting, most enchanting) city plazas in New Mexico.
10. To make it (easier, more easy) to explore, the Santa Fe Trail has been made a National Historic Trail by the National Park Service.

Avoiding Double Comparisons

Do not use -er and *more,* or -est and *most,* at the same time.

Incorrect	My house is more nearer to school than yours.
Correct	My house is *nearer* to school than yours.
Incorrect	Her research paper is the most longest in the class.
Correct	Her research paper is the *longest* in the class.

Exercise 6 Double Comparisons Rewrite the following sentences. Correct all the errors in the use of comparative and superlative forms.

Example   Learning the elements of the short story was the most easiest lesson of the term.

Answer   Learning the elements of the short story was the *easiest* lesson of the term.

1. The setting, or time and place of a story, is the most simplest element for me to remember.
2. One of my favorite stories, Jack London's "To Build a Fire," was set in the most coldest of places.
3. Solid characterization in a story will make it more better than a story with shallow characters.
4. O. Henry stands out as an author who created some of the most oddest of characters.
5. The plot of a story is the storyline; it can range from the most simplest story to the most complex.
6. Some plots may be fascinating, while others could not be more duller.
7. The element of conflict, or the stuggle between opposing forces, may range from mild arguments to the most cruelest of battles.
8. Conflict in a story is more easier to discover than the theme.
9. The theme, a comment about life, is the most hardest to explain.
10. The most finest short stories have a meaningful theme.

Avoiding Illogical Comparisons

An **illogical comparison** may seem correct at first, but if you look or listen more closely, you will notice that its meaning is not quite clear. Sometimes an illogical comparison occurs when one thing is compared to the group to which it belongs.

Molly was funnier than any girl in her class.

The sentence actually says that Molly is *not* a girl in her class. To avoid this kind of mistake, use the word *other* in this kind of comparison.

Molly was funnier than any *other* girl in her class.

Illogical comparisons can also occur when the comparison is not clear.

Confusing   Michael was more distrustful of the dog than Paul. (Did Michael distrust both the dog and Paul?)

Clear   Michael was more distrustful of the dog than Paul *was.*

Exercise 7 Illogical Comparisons Rewrite the following sentences, correcting the errors in comparison. If a sentence is already correct, write *Correct*.

Example Maria Elena likes books better than Christina.
Answer Maria Elena likes books better than Christina *does*.

1. My sister, Maria Elena, loves reading and writing poetry more than any person in my family.
2. Then again, she has a more sensitive nature than I have.
3. She enjoys Edna St. Vincent Millay more than my mother.
4. Word images appealed to her more than they did to any child.
5. Imagine having a sister who enjoys poetry more than her teachers!
6. Her English teacher calls on Maria Elena for examples of alliteration more than any student in the class.
7. My most recent poem was better than any poem I've written.
8. However, rhyme and rhythm don't come as easily to me as Maria Elena.
9. She just laughs and says that I can fix the engine of any car far better than she can.
10. Even though she is my sister, she makes me laugh more than any person I know.

Special Problems with Modifiers

Certain adjectives and adverbs are frequently used incorrectly. Study the following pages to avoid these errors.

Them and Those

> **Them is always a pronoun. It is never used as a modifier.
> Those is a pronoun when used alone; it is an adjective when
> followed by a noun.**

With *them* and *those,* the most common mistake is using *them* as an adjective. Remember that *them* is always a pronoun; use *those,* not *them,* as a modifier.

Incorrect Where did you hide them cookies?
Correct Where did you hide *those* cookies?

This and That, These and Those

> **Use this and that to modify singular nouns. Use these and
> those to modify plural nouns.**

The adjectives *this* and *that* modify singular nouns. *These* and *those* modify plural nouns. When these modifiers are used with words such as *kind, sort,* and *type,* be especially careful to use them correctly.

Incorrect   Those kind of movies are frightening. (*Kind* is singular, so it should be modified by either *this* or *that.*)

Correct   *That* kind of movie is frightening.

Bad and Badly

Use *bad* as an adjective. Use *badly* as an adverb.

Bad is an adjective, used to modify nouns and pronouns. Like other adjectives, *bad* sometimes follows a linking verb. *Badly* is always an adverb; in formal language, it should not be used with a linking verb.

Incorrect   She feels badly about missing the party.

Correct   She feels *bad* about missing the party.

Good and Well

Good is always an adjective. *Well* is usually an adverb.

Many people believe that they can substitute the words *good* and *well* for each other. The two words do have similar meanings, but *good* is always an adjective, modifying a noun or a pronoun.

Incorrect   Evan prepared the meal good.

Correct   Evan prepared the meal *well.*

Well usually functions as an adverb that means "expertly" or "properly." But *well* may also mean "in good health"; in that case, it is an adjective, used after a linking verb.

> Thanks to expert medical care, my mother seems *well.* (adjective)
> Toby performed *well* at the local comedy club. (adverb)

QUICK TIP   Since *good* and *well* can both be adjectives, they can both be used as predicate adjectives after linking verbs. To decide which word to use in a sentence, remember that *well* refers to health, while *good* refers to happiness, comfort, or pleasure.

Stephanie telephoned the clinic because she didn't feel *well.*
Dennis felt *good* after he swam thirty laps.

BETWEEN FRIENDS

Many people say *I feel badly* to indicate strong emotion; this expression has become acceptable in informal conversation. (Literally, this sentence means "to feel, or touch, things poorly"!) In formal speaking and writing, however, use the grammatically correct form: *I feel bad.*

Exercise 8 Problem Modifiers Write the correct modifier from those in parentheses.

1. My teacher promised to give me some tips on study habits after I did so (bad, badly) on the exam.
2. In order to do a (good, well) job on any test, you must do more than simply read the chapter.
3. Find yourself one of (them, those) quiet areas, away from any distractions.
4. You should perform (good, well) on a test if you take notes on the chapter.
5. To do this correctly, look for (them, those) main ideas in each section.
6. Jot down (this, these) kinds of ideas in your notebook.
7. Do not feel (bad, badly) if you end up with several pages of notes.
8. It is far easier to study a few pages than it is to learn one of (them, those) entire chapters.
9. My friend Marcus does (good, well) on tests by using "tricks" to remember facts.
10. Would you like to learn (that, those) kinds of gimmicks?
11. If the main exports of a country were corn, oil, and wheat, he could recall (them, those) products by remembering the first letters— C O W !
12. These little tricks may seem silly but they usually work (good, well).
13. My history instructor admits that she used (this, these) sort of method in her college studies.
14. You might consolidate all of (them, those) notes onto one piece of paper or a note card.
15. Have a friend or family member quiz you. You'll feel (good, well) when you are able to answer all the questions!

The Double Negative

Do not use two negatives together.

The most common negative words are *no, not, never, nothing,* and *none.* Sometimes you will hear people use two negative words together, especially with a contraction such as *didn't* or *couldn't.* This kind of error is called a **double negative.**

| **Incorrect** | The graduate didn't show no embarrassment when his mother hugged him. |
| **Correct** | The graduate didn't show *any* embarrassment when his mother hugged him. |

Remember that the *-n't* in a contraction means *not*. If you pair such a contraction with another negative word, you end up with a double negative.

Hardly, barely, and *scarcely* are often used as negative words. Do not use them after contractions like *haven't* or *couldn't.*

Incorrect   Rosa couldn't hardly sleep at night.
Correct   Rosa *could hardly* sleep at night.

Exercise 9   Double Negatives   Rewrite the sentences below correcting the double negatives. If a sentence contains no double negatives, write *Correct.*

Example   Being an active listener isn't no easy task.
Answer   Being an active listener isn't an easy task.

1. Active listening is not never the same as hearing.
2. Passive listeners haven't never been able to tell the difference between truth and lies.
3. Active listeners won't hear nothing without evaluating what they hear.
4. If you don't ever prepare for listening, you won't learn as much.
5. Some listeners haven't barely sat down before the lecture begins.
6. They haven't no idea how rude they are being as they fumble with notebooks and pens.
7. You can't hear nothing under those circumstances.
8. It is important to listen quietly; don't ever distract your fellow listeners.
9. If you can't hear nothing, make that clear to the speaker at the beginning.
10. If you need to have something explained or repeated, don't ever interrupt the speaker; wait until he or she is finished.

Exercise 10   Modifier Usage Review I   The following sentences contain italicized errors in the use of modifiers. On your paper, write each sentence, correcting the error.

1. *Hardly no* students of architecture are ignorant of the accomplishments of Frank Lloyd Wright.
2. Wright was born in Wisconsin on June 8, 1867; his mother, Anna, felt *real strongly* about his becoming an architect.
3. As a boy he worked on his uncle's farm, laboring the *most longest* hours imaginable.
4. Frank attended the University of Wisconsin where he was disappointed to find that they didn't offer *no* architecture courses.

5. *Awful bored,* he went to Chicago and became employed in an architectural office.
6. Later Wright started his own architectural firm, which allowed him to combine two of his *more stronger* interests, nature and design.
7. He designed "prairie houses"—long, low buildings with flowing spaces, few doors, and none of *them* boxlike rooms.
8. The Frederick Robie house and Fallingwater are two of his houses that fit in especially *good* with the environment.
9. Taliesin, his home and retreat, was one of his *more famous* designs.
10. Many Americans *felt confidently* of Frank Lloyd Wright's ability to design beautiful, thought-provoking buildings.

Exercise 11 Modifier Usage Review II Write the correct modifier from those in parentheses.

1. There are more colorful posters in English class than in (any, any other) room in school.
2. Each deals with one of (them, those) poetry terms that are important to remember.
3. The *Onomatopoeia* poster looks (good, well) with all its "BUZZES," "CLANGS," "HISSES," and other words that sound like noises.
4. The poster on *Hyperbole* (which means "exaggeration") is (real, really) funny.
5. "I must have killed a million mosquitoes!" a young boy claims as (aggressive, aggressively) as he can.
6. The *Personification* poster shows a cloud dancing (graceful, gracefully) across the sky.
7. Of all the poetry terms, *personification* is the (easier, easiest) to remember since it means giving the characteristics of a person to an inanimate object.
8. The (worse, worst) poster of all is just too childish.
9. Under the words *Alliteration—the Repetition of Initial Consonant Sounds,* there is the (silliest, most silly) cartoon imaginable.
10. "Seven Students Sing (Soft, Softly) Serenades," it proclaims.

SECTION 5: USING VERBS

A *verb* is a word that expresses an action or a state of being.

Heather *leaped* across the stream.
Carlos *is* always late on Mondays.

Kinds of Verbs

These two sentence charts illustrate and define the different kinds of verbs.

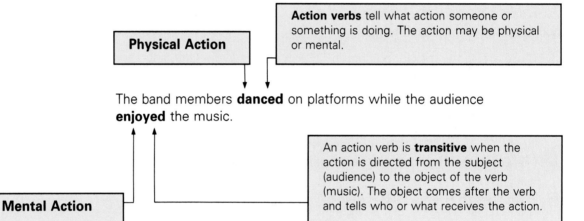

| Physical Action |

Action verbs tell what action someone or something is doing. The action may be physical or mental.

The band members **danced** on platforms while the audience **enjoyed** the music.

An action verb is **transitive** when the action is directed from the subject (audience) to the object of the verb (music). The object comes after the verb and tells who or what receives the action.

| Mental Action |

A **linking verb** shows a state of being. Instead of expressing action, it shows that something exists. Linking verbs are **intransitive** because they never take an object. A linking verb (*feel*) links the subject (*band*) to a word in the predicate (*exhausted*). The most common linking verbs are forms of *be,* and *look, smell, taste, feel, appear, sound, seem, become,* and *grow.*

The band **will feel** exhausted after playing for three hours.

Helping verbs or auxilliary verbs help the action or linking verb. The most common helping verbs are forms of *be:* (am, is, was, were, be, been, being); forms of *have:* (have, has, had); forms of *do:* (do, does, did), and can, could, will, would, shall, should, may, might, must.

Verb Usage

Review this handbook section to determine if you need practice using verbs correctly.

The Principal Parts of Verbs

Every verb has many different forms. These forms are based on the verb's four **principal parts:** the **present,** the **present participle,** the **past,** and the **past participle.**

Present	Present Participle	Past	Past Participle
crash	(is) crashing	crashed	(have) crashed
disappear	(is) disappearing	disappeared	(have) disappeared
spy	(is) spying	spied	(have) spied

With thousands of verbs in the English language, how does anyone ever remember all their principal parts? Fortunately, this is much simpler than it seems. For example, the present participle of a verb always ends in *-ing* and is always used with a form of the helping verb *be.* You use the present participle dozens of times each day, in sentences like these:

I *am going* to gym class.
Sara *is applying* for a job in the library.

Regular Verbs

Almost all English verbs are **regular verbs.** With regular verbs, the past is always formed by adding *-d* or *-ed* to the present. The past form never uses a helping verb. The past participle is the same as the past, but it is always used with a form of the helping verb *have* or *be.*

Present	Present Participle	Past	Past Participle
jump	(is) jumping	jumped	(have) jumped
climb	(is) climbing	climbed	(have) climbed
dance	(is) dancing	danced	(have) danced
try	(is) trying	tried	(have) tried
hurry	(is) hurrying	hurried	(have) hurried

SPELLING TIP: Note that a few regular verbs such as *spy, slip, try,* or *hurry,* change their spelling slightly when *-ing* or *-ed* is added.

Irregular Verbs

Verbs that do not add -*ed* or -*d* to the present to form the past and the past participle are **irregular verbs.**

Present	Present Participle	Past	Past Participle
cost	(is) costing	cost	(have) cost
lose	(is) losing	lost	(have) lost
wear	(is) wearing	wore	(have) worn
sing	(is) singing	sang	(have) sung
take	(is) taking	took	(have) taken

Because the principal parts of irregular verbs are formed in a variety of ways, you must memorize those you don't already know or refer to a dictionary.

QUICK TIP If you are not sure about a verb form, look it up in a dictionary. If the verb is regular, usually only one form will be listed. If the verb is irregular, the dictionary will give the irregular forms. It will give two forms if the past and past participle are the same: *say, said.* It will give all three principal parts if they are all different: *sing, sang, sung.* Look at this entry for the irregular verb *begin.*

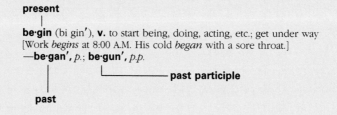

Irregular verbs can be divided into five main groups.

Group 1 The irregular verbs in this group have the same form for the present, the past, and the past participle. *Hit, let,* and *put* are also in this group.

Present	Present Participle	Past	Past Participle
burst	(is) bursting	burst	(have) burst
cost	(is) costing	cost	(have) cost
cut	(is) cutting	cut	(have) cut
set	(is) setting	set	(have) set

Group 2   The irregular verbs in this group have the same form for the past and the past participle.

Present	Present Participle	Past	Past Participle
bring	(is) bringing	brought	(have) brought
lead	(is) leading	led	(have) led
lose	(is) losing	lost	(have) lost
sit	(is) sitting	sat	(have) sat
teach	(is) teaching	taught	(have) taught

Exercise 1 Irregular Verbs   Write the past or past participle of each verb in parentheses.

1. Somebody had already (lead) the lions into the arena.
2. These running shoes (cost) twice as much as my old ones.
3. Ms. Hanover has (teach) for over twenty years.
4. A radiator hose (burst), and the car engine overheated.
5. Juanita (cut) herself with the paring knife.
6. Somehow I had (lose) track of the time.
7. Anne has (sit) on the bench all season.
8. Mike (lead) by just three votes.
9. I had (hit) the target on the first try.
10. The convention (bring) welcome business to the town.
11. Gas once (cost) less than fifty cents a gallon.
12. Suddenly my brother (burst) into my room.
13. Dad (teach) me how to hang wallpaper.
14. Coach Williams has (lead) our team to the playoffs.
15. I (lose) my favorite pen.

Group 3   The irregular verbs in this group form the past participle by adding -n or -en to the past.

Present	Present Participle	Past	Past Participle
break	(is) breaking	broke	(have) broken
choose	(is) choosing	chose	(have) chosen
freeze	(is) freezing	froze	(have) frozen
speak	(is) speaking	spoke	(have) spoken
steal	(is) stealing	stole	(have) stolen

Exercise 2 Irregular Verbs   Most of the following sentences have errors in verb forms. On your paper, rewrite those sentences, correcting the errors. If a sentence has no error, write *Correct*.

1. The bickering lawyers have finally choosed a jury.
2. My hands and feet have froze in the icy wind.

WORD PLAY ....

Verbs are not usually confused with nouns unless they are homographs. **Homographs** are two words that are spelled the same but have different meanings and different pronunciations. I'll be a *graduate* when I *graduate* from high school. *Lead* me to the *lead*. The doctor *wound* the bandage around the *wound*.

3. Carol has broke Mom's antique vase.
4. The sign reads, "Spanish is spoken here."
5. A pickpocket must have stole my wallet during the rally.
6. Have you spoken to your parents about the class trip?
7. Kay accidentally teared up her bus pass.
8. Pablo spoke clearly into the microphone.
9. Matt's new shoes have already wore down at the heels.
10. Michael has broke his new pair of prescription sunglasses.
11. Cynthia may have broke the computer.
12. The team has chose Jim as captain.
13. Jan's tears were almost froze on her cheeks.
14. My baby sister just spoke her first word.
15. These jeans are already wore out.

Group 4 The irregular verbs in this group change a vowel to form the past and the past participle. The vowel changes from **i** in the present form to **a** in the past form and **u** in the past participle.

Present	Present Participle	Past	Past Participle
begin	(is) beginning	began	(have) begun
drink	(is) drinking	drank	(have) drunk
ring	(is) ringing	rang	(have) rung
shrink	(is) shrinking	shrank	(have) shrunk
sing	(is) singing	sang	(have) sung
sink	(is) sinking	sank	(have) sunk
swim	(is) swimming	swam	(have) swum

Exercise 3 Irregular Verbs Write the past or the past participle form of each verb given in parentheses in the following sentences.

1. Emilia (begin) baby-sitting last year and now has many clients.
2. Someone must have (drink) all the skim milk.
3. We (ring) the bell several times, but no one answered.
4. How many times have the Beach Boys (sing) "California Girls"?
5. Those curtains (shrink) in the wash.
6. A Japanese freighter (sink) during the hurricane.
7. Have you (swim) out to the raft yet, or is the water too cold?
8. It seemed as if we (drink) a gallon of cold water that day.
9. Has the warning bell (ring) yet?
10. They (swim) their laps in record time.
11. Have you (swim) in the ocean before?
12. After the victory, the bells (ring) wildly.
13. Most of the candidates have already (begin) their campaigns.
14. My new sweater (shrink) to half its size.
15. The cast (sing) the opera in English, not Italian.

Group 5 The irregular verbs in this group form the past participle from the present form, often adding -n or -en. In the following list, notice the similarity between the present and past participle forms.

Present	Present Participle	Past	Past Participle
come	(is) coming	came	(have) come
do	(is) doing	did	(have) done
drive	(is) driving	drove	(have) driven
eat	(is) eating	ate	(have) eaten
fall	(is) falling	fell	(have) fallen
give	(is) giving	gave	(have) given
go	(is) going	went	(have) gone
grow	(is) growing	grew	(have) grown
know	(is) knowing	knew	(have) known
ride	(is) riding	rode	(have) ridden
rise	(is) rising	rose	(have) risen
run	(is) running	ran	(have) run
see	(is) seeing	saw	(have) seen
take	(is) taking	took	(have) taken
throw	(is) throwing	threw	(have) thrown
write	(is) writing	wrote	(have) written

Exercise 4 Irregular Verbs   Write the past or past participle of each verb in parentheses.

1. The sun has (rise) before six every day this week.
2. Have you (do) your English assignment?
3. We have (give) our old car to my cousin.
4. Mr. Torres has (run) in marathons before.
5. Cary (throw) the ball to the shortstop for an easy out.
6. Have you ever (eat) raw fish?
7. My, how you have (grow)!
8. He (know) the answer to every question in the trivia quiz.
9. We have (take) pictures of everyone except the principal.
10. Have you ever (ride) a bike on a long trip?
11. The dictator had finally (fall) from power.
12. The job (come) along just in time.
13. A gymnast (do) back flips across the mat.
14. I have (take) a poll of the entire school.
15. Dennis (see) a strange object in the night sky.
16. Has everyone (give) up on the project?
17. Anna has (go) to City Hall with her grandparents.
18. The candidate (run) her campaign honestly.
19. S.E. Hinton has also (write) *The Outsiders* and *Rumble Fish.*
20. Dad has never (drive) a car with a stick shift.

Verb Tenses

Use the correct verb tense to show when an action occurs.

All verbs change form to show the time when an action occurs. These changes in form are called **tenses**. Every verb has six tenses, formed by using its principal parts and certain helping verbs such as *be* and *have*.

PROGRESSIVE FORMS

Each of the verb tenses also has a progressive form which shows continuous action. To form the progressive, add a form of the verb *be* to the verb's present participle.
Example:
I *am walking.*
I *have been walking.*

Tense	Form	Use
Present	Add *-s* or *-es* for third-person singular.	To show an action that happens now: *It works!* To tell about something that happens regularly: *We eat lunch every day.* To tell about constant action: *The clock ticks away the seconds.*
Past	Add *-d* or *-ed* to the present. Use the past form of an irregular verb.	To show an action that was completed in the past: *I ate dinner.*
Future	Use *will* or *shall* with the present form.	To show an action that will occur in the future: *The race will begin soon.*
Present Perfect	Use *has* or *have* with the past participle.	To show an action that was completed at an indefinite time in the past or that began in the past and continues into the present: *She has worked on this project for months.*
Past Perfect	Use *had* with the past participle.	To show an action in the past that came before another action in the past: *I had read the book before I saw the movie.*
Future Perfect	Use *will have* or *shall have* with the past participle.	To show an action in the future that will happen before another future action or time: *By the time we arrive, the play will have begun.*

Exercise 5   Verb Tenses   Change the italicized verb to the form given in parentheses. If the italicized verb is already in the correct form, write *Correct*.

Example   According to some writers, a good proofreader *discover* errors that no one else has found. (future)

Answer   According to some writers, a good proofreader *will discover* errors that no one else has found.

1. Many writers *learn* the skill of proofreading. (present perfect)
2. You *read* each sentence carefully to check usage. (present)
3. Jay *trade* his composition with a friend. (past)
4. New eyes *find* different mistakes. (future)
5. Tom *proofread* his work aloud. (present)
6. A sentence *sound* awkward if it's incorrect. (future)
7. Jill *catch* less obvious errors by reading her writing backwards. (past perfect)
8. She *cover* everything on the page except the sentence she is checking. (present)
9. Nan *develop* a proofreading checklist. (present perfect)
10. She *use* her checklist before she types the final copy of her paper. (future perfect)

Improper Shifts in Tense

Use the same tense to show two or more actions that occur at the same time.

In your speech and writing, the action in any one sentence or paragraph will usually take place in the same time period. To express this kind of consistent action, use the same tense for all the verbs in the sentence and paragraph.

Incorrect   She *paints* the picture, and then she *framed* it.
Correct   She *paints* the picture, and then she *frames* it.

There are times, however, when shifting verb tense—even in the same sentence—makes your meaning clearer. For example, two different tenses are needed to show a sequence of events.

You *will have left* (future perfect) the gym by the time the game *starts*. (present)

Check your writing carefully to avoid any illogical shifts in verb tense. Always be sure that your verbs express action in the past, present, or future without confusing your reader.

Exercise 6   Shifts in Tense   Write the verb needed to avoid a shift in tense.

Example   Gordon photographs people and (writes, wrote) about them.
Answer   writes

1. The queen boarded the ship and (knights, knighted) the explorer.
2. The bus (rattles, rattled) into town and stopped at the inn.
3. The batter (hit, hits) a home run and ties the score.
4. Sandra directs the ensemble and (plays, played) piano in it.
5. When the alarm sounds, it (is, was) time to get up.
6. Patrick Henry stood and (delivers, delivered) his speech.
7. Luis (speaks, spoke) Spanish and understands French.
8. When the sun sets, the temperature (drops, dropped).
9. Sondheim composed music, and Lapine (writes, wrote) lyrics.
10. Please mail the letters when you (leave, left).

Exercise 7   Verb Review   Write the correct verb from the two given in parentheses.

1. The Masai people have (live, lived) on the plains of East Africa for centuries.
2. Many Masai still (roam, roamed) across the land, looking for the best food for their cattle.
3. The Masai have always (built, builded) circles of huts and surrounded them with barricades.
4. The barricades enclose the cattle and keep them (hid, hidden) from thieves.
5. The Masai have never (ate, eaten) their cattle unless their people were starving.
6. The Masai have always (did, done) what they wanted.
7. Young Masai men were (teached, taught) to stain their hair and faces and to paint their legs with white patterns.
8. Recently, however, the Kenyan government has (force, forced) them to adapt to modern life.
9. In the past, young warriors (will hunt, hunted) lions with only a spear.
10. They (spent, spended) seven years in the bush for survival training.
11. However, the government has (threw, thrown) out this tradition and now requires the young men to attend school.
12. In the past, the Masai (buyed, bought) what they needed by trading their cattle.
13. Nowadays, however, most Masai have (chosen, chose) to use cash.
14. Because they are considered fierce warriors, some Masai have (finded, found) jobs as security guards in the city.
15. Life for Masai herders seems to (change, changed) every day.

Commonly Confused Verbs

Do not confuse *lie* and *lay, rise* and *raise, sit* and *set.*

There are three pairs of verbs that often cause problems: *lie* and *lay, rise* and *raise,* and *sit* and *set.* Study the chart below to learn the correct use of these words.

	Present	**Past**	**Past Participle**
Lie and *Lay*	lie	lay	(have) lain
	lay	laid	(have) laid
Rise and *Raise*	rise	rose	(have) risen
	raise	raised	(have) raised
Sit and *Set*	sit	sat	(have) sat
	set	set	(have) set

Lie means "to rest in a flat position," "to be in a certain place," or "to exist." *Lie* never has a direct object.

> Some trash *was lying* on the floor of the car.

Lay means "to place." It almost always has a direct object.

> The mason *will lay* the bricks on the driveway. (*Bricks* is the direct object.)

Rise means "to go upward." *Rise* does not take a direct object.

> The temperature *has risen* 20 degrees.

Raise means "to lift" or to make something go up. *Raise* almost always has a direct object.

> The stagehand *raises* the curtain every evening. (Curtain is the direct object.)

Sit means "to occupy a seat." *Sit* never takes a direct object.

> We *have sat* in the same seats each time.

Set means "to place." *Set* almost always has a direct object.

> The waiter *set* a full plate on the table. (*Plate* is the direct object.)

Exercise 8   Confusing Verbs   Write the correct verb form of the two given in parentheses.

1. In class we wondered why people rarely (set, sit) down to write letters anymore.
2. Many find it more convenient to simply (raise, rise) a telephone to their ear and make a call.
3. The reason (lays, lies) in the fact that speed and convenience are of the utmost importance to most people today.
4. Why spend time writing when you can (lay, lie) on a couch comfortably and chat?
5. Still, a lot of people are thrilled when the mail carrier (sets, sits) a letter in the mailbox.
6. One student (raised, rose) another good point.
7. She received a diary as a birthday gift but (lay, laid) it aside and never wrote in it.
8. It was (laying, lying) on her closet floor for months.
9. She promised to (set, sit) it on her desk and try her hand at writing down her thoughts.
10. She mentioned that writing in a journal might (raise, rise) her spirits at times.
11. At that point the teacher agreed and (rose, raised) from his chair.
12. "For homework, (sit, set) a good example for your friends and family and write a letter," he said.
13. He then (lay, laid) the chalk down and passed out the class notebooks.
14. "Now (sit, set) quietly and think before you begin your journal entries," he said.
15. Suddenly the bell rang and everyone (rose, raised) from their seats and left.

SECTION 6: SUBJECT AND VERB AGREEMENT

A verb must agree in number with its subject.

If the subject of a sentence is singular, its verb must also be singular. If a subject is plural, its verb must also be plural. This is called **subject-verb agreement.**

> The parrot (singular) <u>whistles</u> (singular) folk songs.
> The parrots (plural) <u>whistle</u> (plural) folk songs.

The singular and plural forms of verbs rarely cause problems.

REMINDER

The **number** of a word refers to whether the word is singular or plural. When a word refers to one thing, it is **singular**. When it refers to more than one thing, it is **plural**.

Verb Forms			
Singular		**Plural**	
I	dig	we	dig
you	dig	you	dig
he, she, it	digs	they	dig

VERB FORMS

Except for *be*, the only difference between singular and plural verbs in the present tense is in the third person present, which always ends in *-s*.

The verb *be* does not follow the usual pattern. In the following chart notice that *be* has special forms in both the present and past tenses in all three persons.

Forms of *Be*				
	Present Tense		**Past Tense**	
	Singular	Plural	Singular	Plural
First Person	I am	we are	I was	we were
Second Person	you are	you are	you were	you were
Third Person	he, she, it is	they are	he, she, it was	they were

Exercise 1 Agreement in Number On your paper, write the form of the verb that agrees in number with the subject of each of the following sentences. Then tell whether the verb form is singular or plural.

Example Certain skills (improves, improve) with practice.
Answer improve, plural

1. Oral presentations (is, are) difficult.
2. Many students (fears, fear) speaking before their peers.

3. It (makes, make) them feel self-conscious and nervous.
4. Perhaps they (was, were) once forgetful or fidgety during an oral presentation.
5. Maybe their friends (was, were) not attentive to the speech or behaved rudely.
6. (Was, Were) you ever that way?
7. A list of tips (follows, follow).
8. Students (is, are) better off if they prepare beforehand.
9. They (has, have) to have some notes or an outline.
10. Preparation (is, are) essential to avoid panic.
11. A speaker also (needs, need) to consider his or her audience.
12. Reactions (differs, differ) depending upon the type of group listening.
13. Presenters also (needs, need) to speak clearly, project their voices, and avoid mumbling.
14. Some mannerisms (does, do) detract from speeches; these include excessive hand gestures and swaying from side to side.
15. One thing (seem, seems) certain—if the presenter appears enthusiastic, his or her listeners will be more attentive.

Phrases Between a Subject and Verb

Do not be fooled by other nouns in a sentence. Be sure that the verb agrees with its subject.

You will have a problem with subject-verb agreement if you cannot identify the subject in a sentence. To find the subject, first find the verb and then ask *who?* or *what?* before it.

Watch out when a prepositional phrase appears between the subject and verb. Do not be fooled by the noun that appears in the phrase. Make the verb agree in number with the subject.

> The <u>tree</u> with dark purple leaves <u>is</u> a Japanese maple. (*Tree,* not *leaves,* is the subject.)
>
> The paintings on the wall <u>are</u> by a local artist. (*Paintings,* not *wall,* is the subject.)

PREPOSITIONS

Commonly used prepositions include *about, above, across, after, as, at, before, between, by, during, for, from, in inside, into, like, near, of, off, on, over, since, through, to, until, up, upon, with, without.* Compound prepositions include *according to, along with, because of, due to, in addition to, in front of, instead of, next to, on top of, out of.*

QUICK TIP To decide which word is the subject, say the sentence without the phrase. If you have chosen the correct word as the subject, the sentence will still make sense without the phrase.

Exercise 2 Sentences with Phrases Choose the verb that agrees with the subject.

1. The editors, after much discussion, (approves, approve) the story.
2. A copy of the pages (go, goes) to the designer.
3. The designer, along with the editors, (chooses, chose) a typeface.
4. The copyeditors with great care (checks, check) spelling and grammar.
5. The text with the corrections (is, are) typed into a computer.
6. The typesetting machine next to the computers (prints, print) the text.
7. The author with the help of the editors (makes, make) corrections.
8. The mechanics of the book (is, are) made into color film negatives.
9. Printing plates of each color (are, is) made from the film.
10. Copies of the printed book (is, are) sent to stores and libraries.

Indefinite Pronouns as Subjects

Use a singular verb with a singular indefinite pronoun and a plural verb with a plural indefinite pronoun.

Indefinite pronouns do not refer to a definite person or thing. Some indefinite pronouns are singular, some are plural, and some can be either.

Indefinite Pronouns			
Singular	another	anybody	anyone	anything
	either	everybody	everyone	everything
	neither	nobody	no one	one
	someone	something	each	somebody
Plural	both few many several			
Singular or Plural	all any most none some			

MEMORY TRICK

One way to remember which indefinite pronouns are singular is to look at the word endings. Many of the singular words have endings that refer to one thing: *-other, -one, -body,* or *-thing.* Also many of the singular pronouns are compound (*anything, someone*); none of the plural pronouns are compound.

For the indefinite pronouns that are always singular or plural, the correct verb choice will often be the one that sounds right to you.

Incorrect Everyone have a map of the race course.
Correct Everyone has a map of the race course. (*Everyone* is singular; it takes a singular verb, *has.*)

Incorrect Both of the cats catches mice.
Correct Both of the cats catch mice. (*Both* is plural; it takes a plural verb, *catch.*)

The indefinite pronouns that are either singular or plural cause the greatest number of agreement problems. Treat the pronoun as singular if it refers to one thing. If the pronoun refers to several things, treat it as plural.

Singular   All of the paper <u>was</u> recycled. (*All* refers to one quantity of paper.)

Plural   All of the paper cups <u>were</u> crushed. (*All* refers to several paper cups.)

Exercise 3 Indefinite Pronouns   Rewrite the following sentences, correcting all errors in subject-verb agreement. If the sentence is correct, write *Correct.*

Example   Some of the seniors raves about their writing course this year.

Answer   Some of the seniors *rave* about their writing course this year.

1. Most of the first term is devoted to the study of poetry.
2. Nobody in class seem apathetic or disinterested.
3. Everyone is reminded that poems do not have to rhyme.
4. Each of the students attempt to write an ode to a person or object.
5. Everybody are encouraged to create an *elegy,* a mournful poem lamenting the dead.
6. One of the popular assignments call for writing haiku.
7. Nobody in the class mind the limerick-writing exercise.
8. None of the students resists when song lyrics are examined.
9. All of them hope to write their own "Top 40" hit someday.
10. All of the would-be writers gains tremendous respect for poets and their craft.

REMINDER
Remember that nouns ending in -s are usually plural, whereas verbs ending in -s are usually singular.

Exercise 4 Review   Write the subject of each of the following sentences. Then write the form of the verb that agrees in number with the subject.

Example   The architecture in America (is, are) the result of a number of influences.

Answer   Architecture is

1. Some of our buildings (is, are) copies of the classical, or ancient Roman and Greek styles.
2. This type of architecture (has, have) become known as Greek Revival.
3. Many of our banks, homes, and state and federal buildings (was, were) actually modelled after ancient, columned temples.

4. One of the other influences (was, were) the Middle Ages.
5. The Gothic style of architecture (is, are) seen in Trinity Church in New York City.
6. Several of the Gothic characteristics (appears, appear) on the building —long slender spires, arches, stained glass, and steep roofs.
7. Everybody (has, have) probably heard of the Victorian period from 1837–1901.
8. Americans at that time (was, were) taken with the fanciful, elaborate designs of King Louis XV of France.
9. One (calls, call) this the Rococo Revival style.
10. All of these influences (contributes, contribute) to the rich, varied assortment of structures throughout our country.

Compound Subjects

Use a plural verb with most compound subjects joined by *and*. Use a verb that agrees with the subject nearer the verb when the words in a compound subject are joined by *or* or *nor*.

A compound subject is two or more subjects used with the same verb. Most compound subjects that contain the word *and* are plural and take a plural verb.

My sister and brother are twins.
The windows and doors need locks.

When the parts of a compound subject are connected by the conjunctions *or* or *nor,* look at the subject closest to the verb to decide if the verb should be singular or plural.

Neither the bookstore nor the drugstores carry that sports magazine.
Neither the drugstores nor the bookstore carries that sports magazine.

A paper or two oral reports are required this semester.
Two oral reports or a paper is required this semester.

REMINDER
. . . .
If a compound subject is preceded by *each, every,* or *many a,* use a singular verb. Each adult and child re-ceives a life preserver. Many a cat and dog has run away.

Exercise 5 Compound Subjects Choose the verb that agrees with the subject of each sentence.

1. The news and events of the day (reach, reaches) Americans through a variety of means.
2. A radio or television (delivers, deliver) crucial information to millions of people each day.

3. Listening to the news on radio and viewing the news on TV (creates, create) an informed society.
4. Neither the radio nor television (has, have) been around nearly as long as the newspaper.
5. People's appetite and desire for information (makes, make) it probable that some type of newspaper has been around since ancient times.
6. Progress and the invention of the printing press (was, were) instrumental in furthering this means of conveying reports and ideas.
7. Colonial newspapers and newsletters (was, were) delivered in Boston in 1704.
8. Editorials and advertisements (appear, appears) in today's paper, just as in the papers of the 1700's.
9. Publishers and journalists (has, have) made names for themselves over the years.
10. Neither a radio nor a television news broadcast (is, are) able to replace the familiar daily routine of "reading the paper."

Agreement Problems with *Doesn't* and *Don't*

Use *doesn't* with singular subjects and with the personal pronouns *he, she,* and *it.* Use *don't* with plural subjects and with the personal pronouns *I, we, you,* and *they.*

NOTE

When finding the verb in words such as *doesn't* and *don't,* do not include *n't. N't* is a contraction for *not,* which is an adverb.

The words *don't* and *doesn't* often create agreement problems. Keep in mind that these words are contractions for *do not* and *does not.*

Incorrect Doesn't the <u>movies</u> begin at six o'clock?
Correct Don't the <u>movies</u> begin at six o'clock?

Incorrect Don't the <u>movie</u> begin at six o'clock?
Correct Doesn't the <u>movie</u> begin at six o'clock?

Exercise 6 *Doesn't* and *Don't* Choose the form of the verb that agrees in number with the subject.

1. (Doesn't, Don't) the play *Romeo and Juliet* seem like a timeless story?
2. It takes place in Verona, Italy, (don't, doesn't) it?
3. Yes, but (doesn't, don't) the story of the star-crossed lovers seem modern?
4. (Doesn't, Don't) the musical play *West Side Story* remind you of *Romeo and Juliet?*
5. (Doesn't, Don't) the modern lovers Tony and Maria play the parts of Romeo and Juliet?

Exercise 7 Subject-Verb Agreement Review   Choose the
form of the verb that agrees with the subject.

1. Each of us (has, have) a favorite novel.
2. My favorite (happens, happen) to be *To Kill a Mockingbird.*
3. The trials and tribulations of a Southern family (is, are) related in a
   warm, beautiful style.
4. The word *trial* (has, have) a double meaning in the novel.
5. The widowed father of a Maycomb, Alabama, family (is, are) a
   dedicated attorney named Atticus Finch.
6. He (doesn't, don't) hesitate to defend a wrongly accused black man.
7. Prejudice and hatred (is, are) all too prevalent in the town.
8. Scout and Jem Finch (is, are) Atticus's children.
9. The point of view in the novel (is, are) first person as told by Scout.
10. All of the children of the neighborhood (fears, fear) the nearby
    Radley home.
11. Neither logic nor lectures (makes, make) them feel otherwise.
12. Scout and Jem (believes, believe) that Boo Radley may be sinister or
    harmful.
13. Several conflicts with the Radley household only (adds, add) to their
    suspicions.
14. Jem (doesn't, don't) understand the ugly prejudice of the town.
15. A dangerous incident and a touching message (brings, bring) the
    story to a close.

SECTION 7: SENTENCE STRUCTURE

A *sentence* is a group of words that expresses a complete thought. A sentence may be *simple, compound,* or *complex.*

Simple Sentences

Throughout this book you have been studying sentences. You know that a sentence has two basic parts, the **subject** and the **predicate.**

Subject	Predicate
Actors	spoke.
The actors on the stage	spoke their lines with emotion.

You also know that all of the parts of a sentence may be **compound.** That is, they may have more than one part.

Compound Subject The *coach* and the *team* discussed strategy.
Compound Verb The girls *talked* and *laughed.*
Compound Object The store accepts *cash* or *credit.*

You can see that each of these sentences expresses one main idea. These sentences are called **simple** sentences.

A simple sentence is a sentence that contains only one subject and one predicate. Remember, however, that the subject and predicate, or any part of the subject or predicate, may be compound.

Compound Sentences

Sometimes two sentences are so closely related in thought that you join them together. Then you have a different kind of sentence. You have a sentence that has more than one subject and more than one predicate. This is called a **compound sentence.**

A *compound sentence* consists of two or more simple sentences joined together.

The parts of a compound sentence may be joined by a coordinating conjunction or by a semicolon (;). Study the following examples.

My uncle gave me a book, *and* I read it from cover to cover.
We need scientists, *but* we need laboratory workers even more.
You can take the course now, *or* you can wait until next year.
Mother threw the coat away; it was worn out.

Since compound sentences are made up of two or more simple sentences, they may be long. To help the reader keep the thoughts in order, put a comma before the coordinating conjunction.

> Patty did a routine on the parallel bars, *and* Liz and Amy performed on the trampoline.

The only compound construction you have studied that requires a comma is the compound sentence. You do not need a comma to separate two subjects, two predicates, or two parts of any other compound constructions.

Exercise 1 Simple and Compound Sentences   On your paper, write the following sentences. Underline the subjects once and the verbs twice. Label each sentence *Simple* or *Compound*. Remember that a simple sentence may have one or more compound parts.

Example   Alligators <u>seem</u> slow, but they <u>can move</u> quickly.
               Compound.

1. The Native Americans of the Southwest have unique crafts.
2. Theodore Roosevelt and Franklin D. Roosevelt were Presidents with strong personalities.
3. The movie was dull, but the book was exciting.
4. Fog and drizzle closed the runways, and all flights were canceled.
5. The judge heard the evidence and then dismissed the case.
6. Dr. Jekyll was the kind doctor; Mr. Hyde was evil.
7. The filter should be replaced regularly, or the furnace will not work.
8. Vanilla and unsweetened chocolate smell good but taste bitter.
9. The state suffered a dry spell, and farm production dropped.
10. The railroad is on strike, so my parents drove to work this morning.

Combining Related Thoughts

Before you make a compound sentence from two simple sentences, you must be sure that the simple sentences are related in thought.

Some pairs of sentences go together and some do not.

> It looked like rain. We went anyhow. (Will these two simple sentences make a good compound sentence? Yes, because they are closely related in thought. Use *but* to join them.)

> I like horseback riding. Jockeys are very small. (The ideas are not related. These two sentences should not be joined into a compound sentence.)

Exercise 2 Writing Compound Sentences Find the six pairs
of sentences that are related in thought. Write them as compound
sentences using coordinating conjunctions or semicolons. Remember to
use commas correctly where necessary.

  1. Elizabeth has the flu. She is not very sick.
  2. Most trees lose their leaves in the winter. Evergreens live up to their
     name.
  3. Todd and Doug were the winners. It started to snow after the
     match.
  4. Have a good time in New York. See all you can.
  5. You can make pizza with sausage. You can try it with vegetables.
  6. The potatoes were raw. Some of the meat was burned.
  7. Arizona is a beautiful state in the Southwest. Rhode Island was
     founded by Roger Williams.
  8. Lori and Jovita walked to the basketball game. Lori's mother picked
     them up when it was over.
  9. The best feature of the game was the raising of the flag. Our
     quarterback sprained his ankle.
  10. Cross-country skiing is a popular winter sport. Many Midwestern
     states provide hills for snowboarding.

Complex Sentences

In order to understand complex sentences, you must first learn about
clauses.

> **A clause is a group of words that contains a verb and its
> subject.**

From this definition you can see that a simple sentence is a clause
because it has both a verb and a subject.

> <u>We</u> <u>heard</u> a loud explosion.
> The <u>blacksmith</u> <u>forged</u> a horseshoe.

Your study of sentences will be clearer, however, if you think of a
clause as a part of a sentence. A clause is a group of words containing a
subject and a verb within a sentence.

Compound sentences contain two clauses, each with a subject and a
verb.

> Tall <u>tales</u> <u>are</u> not true, but <u>they</u> <u>are</u> amusing.
> <u>Don</u> <u>walked</u> into the store, and <u>he</u> <u>asked</u> for a job.

Independent and Subordinate Clauses

A clause that can stand as a sentence by itself is an **independent clause.** All the clauses in compound sentences are independent clauses. They can all stand as simple sentences by themselves.

Now look at clauses of a different kind.

<u>as</u> the clock struck twelve

<u>after</u> the movie was over

Neither group of words above is a complete thought. Each leaves you wondering: "Then what?" Now, with your finger, cover the first word in each group of words. What happens? Each group of words becomes a complete sentence.

When a word like *as* or *after* introduces a clause, it subordinates the clause. That is, it makes the clause depend on an independent clause to complete its meaning. Words like *as* or *after* are called **subordinating conjunctions** because they introduce **subordinate clauses.**

Subordinate clauses cannot stand alone as sentences.

Not every subordinate clause begins with a subordinating conjunction, but many do. The following words are used frequently as subordinating conjunctions.

Words Often Used as Subordinating Conjunctions			
after	because	so that	whatever
although	before	than	when
as	if	though	whenever
as if	in order that	till	where
as long as	provided	unless	wherever
as though	since	until	while

Caution: These words are subordinating words only when they introduce a clause. Some can be used in other ways.

Not all subordinate clauses begin with subordinating conjunctions. The following words can also introduce subordinate clauses:

that	who, whom, whose	which
what	whoever, whomever	how

PHRASE OR CLAUSE?

Don't confuse a phrase with a clause. A clause has a subject and a verb. A phrase does not.

Phrase in the river
Clause When the doctor arrived

Exercise 3 Subordinate Clauses   Use a variety of subordinating words to make subordinate clauses out of these sentences.

1. My shoes are tight.
2. The bus pulled away.
3. The Ferris wheel stopped.
4. The cookies are done.
5. There is no answer.
6. The battery works.
7. Some insects bite.
8. We ate the cake.
9. The buzzer sounded.
10. It snowed last night.

Now that you know about independent clauses and subordinate clauses, you are ready to learn what a complex sentence is.

A *complex sentence* is a sentence that contains one independent clause and one or more subordinate clauses.

```
     ┌─────── Independent ───────┐┌─────── Subordinate ───────┐
My father gave me the cameo that belonged to his mother.
  ┌─ Independent ─┐┌───── Subordinate ─────┐
I never know what you'll say next.
```

QUICK TIP   When the subordinate clause comes at the beginning of the sentence, it is followed by a comma.

When I looked at my watch**,** I knew I had missed the bus.

Exercise 4 Subordinate Clauses   On your paper, write the following sentences. Draw one line under each subordinate clause and two lines under each independent clause. Two sentences do not have subordinate clauses.

Example   People dream while they sleep.

1. We arrived after the mayor had made her acceptance speech.
2. Do you know where the Isle of Skye is located?
3. Reading that book in ten days will be difficult.
4. The evergreen tree that my grandparents planted is over twenty feet high.
5. If the storm becomes worse, will the game be postponed?
6. We followed a trail that gave us a good view of the mountains and the lake.
7. The Council scheduled the meeting for two weeks from today.
8. When the referee penalized the forward, the fans objected.
9. Penguins are social animals that nest in huge colonies.
10. Alan, who played superbly, won the piano competition.

Exercise 5 Sentence Structure   Tell whether each sentence is *Simple, Compound,* or *Complex.*

1. Colonists settled Roanoke Island, but then they disappeared.
2. After I wrote my report, I proofread it and made a clean copy.
3. The airlines know that some passengers will never appear, and overbook most flights.
4. Astronomers have identified a cloud of comets that is made of dust, rock fragments, and frozen gases.
5. Foreign leaders who visit Washington, D.C., stay at Blair House.
6. Meteorites blaze only a few seconds, but their trails can be seen for miles.
7. We tried the exercises on the videotape, but we couldn't quite master them.
8. After the polls close, the election judges count the ballots.
9. A bola is a weighted rope; it is used to catch cattle.
10. Hiawatha was the hero of a poem by Longfellow.

Exercise 6 Sentence Structure Review   Rewrite and combine the sentence sets below. Follow the directions given in parentheses. Use correct punctuation.

1. Tourists expect the coast of Peru to be a jungle. The coastline is actually arid. (Use *but* to form a compound sentence.)
2. An airplane trip from Chicago to Orlando takes less than three hours. An auto trip takes about twenty-four hours. (Use a semicolon to make a compound sentence.)
3. We were sailing near the cove. The wind died. (Use *when* to make a complex sentence.)
4. Sara sprained her ankle. She completed the marathon. (Use *although* to make the complex sentence.)
5. Connie read the novel. She did not see the movie. (Use *but* to form a compound sentence.)
6. I preferred ball point pens. I tried a fine-line marker. (Use *until* to make a complex sentence.)
7. The hurricane hit Galveston, Texas. Many people were left homeless. (Use *after* to make a complex sentence.)
8. Irma will have forty dollars in her savings account. She doesn't make a withdrawal. (Use *if* to form a complex sentence.)
9. Many investigative reporters faithfully follow one rule. They never reveal a source. (Use a semicolon to form a compound sentence.)
10. You are not sure about the store's hours. Phone first. (Use *if* to form a complex sentence.)

SECTION 8: USING CAPITALIZATION

Rules of Capitalization

Capitalization is one way to call attention to important, meaningful words. The most familiar uses of capitalization are at the beginning of sentences and for proper nouns, like names. The other uses of capitalization most often distinguish general nouns from specific ones. In general, the words that are capitalized fall into the following categories: names of people, personal titles, nationalities, and religions; geographical names and structures; organizations; historical events; and first words and titles. More specific rules and examples of capitalization are listed below. Use this section as a reference when you are in doubt about just what to capitalize.

Proper Nouns and Adjectives

Capitalize proper nouns and adjectives.

A **proper noun** is the name of a specific person, place, thing, or idea. Proper nouns are capitalized. Common nouns are not. A **proper adjective** is an adjective formed by a proper noun; it is also capitalized.

Common Noun	writer
Proper Noun	Shakespeare
Proper Adjective	Shakespearean

Names of People and Personal Titles

Capitalize people's names and initials that stand for names.

Eleanor Roosevelt	I.F. Stone	John F. Kennedy

Capitalize titles and abbreviations for titles used before people's names or in direct address.

Justice William Douglas	Ms. Grace Longey
Senator Margaret Chase Smith	Dr. Lionel Warren, Jr.

Capitalize a title used without a person's name if it refers to a head of state or a person in another important position.

the President of the United States	the Secretary of State
the Chief Justice of the Supreme Court	the Pope

Family Relationships

Capitalize the titles indicating family relationships when the titles are used as names or parts of names.

Uncle **A**rnold and **M**om tease **G**randma about her fear of cats.

If the title is preceded by an article or a possessive adjective, it is not capitalized.

My mom's dream is to travel to Asia.

Races, Languages, Nationalities, and Religions

Capitalize the names of races, languages, nationalities, and religions and any adjectives formed from these names.

Egyptian	**S**wahili	**B**uddhism	**V**ietnamese
French	**C**aucasian	**J**udaism	**A**frican
Navaho jewelry		**J**apanese restaurant	**I**talian pasta

The Supreme Being and Sacred Writings

Capitalize all words referring to God and religious scriptures.

the **L**ord	**A**llah	the **B**ible
the **K**oran	the **T**orah	**J**esus **C**hrist

REMINDER

Do not capitalize *god* when the word means the spirits worshipped by ancient peoples.

The Pronoun *I*

Always capitalize the pronoun *I*.

Ben and **I** ran in the marathon.

Geographical Names

In a geographical name, capitalize the first letter of each word except articles and prepositions.

Continents	**A**ustralia **A**sia **S**outh **A**merica
Bodies of Water	The **G**ulf of **M**aine **N**iagara **F**alls the **P**acific **O**cean
Land Forms	**M**ount **B**lue **C**ape **C**od the **M**ohave **D**esert
World Regions	the **M**iddle **E**ast **S**outheast **A**sia
Public Areas	**Z**ion **N**ational **P**ark the **A**lamo the **O**ld **N**orth **B**ridge
Political Units	**N**evada the **P**rovince of **B**ritish **C**olumbia
Roads, Highways	**R**oute 80 the **A**ppalachian **T**rail **R**odeo **D**rive

REMINDER

In official documents, words like *city, state,* and *county* are capitalized when they are part of a political unit: the City of San Francisco, the County of Hartford.

Directions and Sections

Capitalize names of sections of the country or the world, and any adjectives that come from those sections.

The **S**outh has many battlefields.
John has a **M**idwestern accent.

Do not capitalize compass directions or adjectives that merely indicate direction or a general location.

Drive west on Percy Street.
The storm moved eastward.

Bodies of the Universe

Capitalize the names of the planets in the solar system and other objects in the universe, except words like sun and moon.

Pluto   **H**alley's **C**omet   a phase of the moon

> **QUICK TIP**   Capitalize the word *earth* only when it is used in conjunction with the names of other planets. The word *earth* is not capitalized when the article *the* precedes it.
> From the vantage point of space, astronauts have said the earth is a beautiful planet.

Structures

Capitalize the names of specific monuments, bridges, and buildings.

the **J**efferson **M**emorial   **T**rinity **C**hurch   the **G**olden **G**ate **B**ridge

Organizations and Institutions

▶

Capitalize all words except prepositions and conjunctions in the names of organizations and institutions. Also capitalize abbreviations of these names.

Democratic **P**arty   **K**ennedy **H**igh **S**chool
Securities and **E**xchange **C**ommission

REMINDER
Do not capitalize words such as school, company, church, college, and hospital when they are not used as parts of names.

Events, Documents, and Periods of Time

Capitalize the names of historical events, documents, and periods of time.

World War I   Bill of Rights   the Renaissance
the Battle of Gettysburg

Months, Days, and Holidays

Capitalize the names of months, days, and holidays but not the names of seasons.

April   Friday   Thanksgiving   spring

Time Abbreviations

Capitalize the abbreviations *B.C., A.D., A.M.,* and *P.M.*

The official school day begins at 8:10 **A.M.**

School Subjects and Class Names

Do not capitalize the general names of school subjects. Do capitalize the titles of specific courses and of courses that are followed by a number. School subjects that are languages are always capitalized.

English 101   physics   Introduction to Anthropology

Capitalize class names only when they refer to a specific group or event or when they are used in direct address.

The freshmen are collecting canned goods for the Freshman Class food drive.

Sentences and Poetry

Capitalize the first word of every sentence.

The guitarist had blisters on his fingertips.

Capitalize the first word of every line of poetry.

Whose woods these are I think I know.
His house is in the village though;

from "Stopping by Woods on a Snowy Evening," Robert Frost

REMINDER
....
Sometimes, especially in modern poetry, the first word of every line of a poem is not capitalized.

Quotations

Capitalize the first word of a direct quotation.

Abraham Lincoln said, "**N**o man is good enough to govern another man without that other's consent."

Letter Parts

Capitalize the first word in the greeting of a letter. Also capitalize the title, person's name, and words such as *Sir* and *Madam*.

Dear **S**ir or **M**adam: **D**ear **M**s. **W**all,

Capitalize only the first word in the complimentary close.

Sincerely yours,   **V**ery truly yours,

Outlines and Titles

Capitalize the first word of each item in an outline and letters that introduce major subsections.

I. **I**nstruments
   A. **G**uitars
      1. **A**coustic
      2. **E**lectric
   B. **S**axophones

Capitalize the first, last, and all other important words in titles. Do not capitalize conjunctions, articles, or prepositions with fewer than five letters.

Book Title	*All Things Bright and Beautiful*
Newspaper	*The Boston Globe*
Play	*West Side Story*
Television Series	*The Victory Garden*
Short Story	"A River Runs Through It"
Song	"Twist and Shout"
Work of Art	*The Green Violinist*

The word *the* at the beginning of a title and the word *magazine* are capitalized only when they are part of the formal name.

*T*ime magazine   *Audubon Magazine*   *The New York Times*

Exercise Capitalization   Rewrite the items below, capitalizing where necessary.

1. Lake superior in canada is the largest lake on earth.
2. The dutch grow 3 billion flowers a year.
3. An international language called esperanto was invented by a pole, dr. zemenhof, in the 1880's.
4. The largest painting in the world is *the battle of gettysburg* painted by paul phillipoeaux.
5. You can see the golden gate bridge from coit tower in san francisco.
6. president john f. kennedy, the thirty-fifth president of the united states, was the first catholic elected to that office.
7. In the fall of 1990, columbus day was observed on monday, october 8.
8. The junior class officers held a meeting in the biology lab.
9. Indonesia is made up of over thirteen thousand islands covering an area equal in size to mexico.
10. the world's largest desert, the sahara, covers part of the african countries of chad, nigeria, libya, algeria, egypt, mali, and mauritania.
11. The french exchange students visited the russian and spanish classes.
12. friedrich wilhelm nietzsche wrote, "as an artist, a man has no home in europe save in paris."
13. The english built the longest bridge in the world and called it the humber estuary bridge.
14. Almost two thousand spanish galleons lie in the atlantic ocean off the eastern coast of florida.
15. The phoenicians, who once lived where jordan, lebanon, and syria are today, had an alphabet that was adopted by the greeks and romans.
16. My father moved from europe to the pacific northwest.
17. I told mom to drive north on highway 12 and turn west on route 56.
18. We compared the atmospheres of saturn, mars, and earth for an astronomy 102 project at iowa state university.
19. Maria and i went to reverend barry's 7:00 p.m. lecture on the relationship of god to religion and the bible.
20. The pyramid age in egypt lasted from 2686 to 2181 b.c.
21. The battle of the bulge took place in the ardennes forest in belgium during world war II.
22. Mr. tobas announced that the play *our town* would be performed in may.
23. many cable television channels still run *the brady bunch* series.
24.   I. importance of mammals
      II. bodies of mammals
        a. skin and hair
        b. skeleton

SECTION 9: USING PUNCTUATION

When you talk, you use all kinds of body language to help your listeners understand what you want to communicate. You scowl, wave your hands, shake your head, and lift your eyebrows to show what you mean. When you write those same words you can't help your readers with facial expressions. Instead, you have to rely on punctuation marks to show them where to stop, pause, question or exclaim. Specific rules and examples of correct punctuation are listed in this section.

End Marks

The punctuation marks that show where a sentence ends are called **end marks.** The three end marks are the **period,** the **question mark,** and the **exclamation point.**

The Period

Use a period at the end of a declarative sentence. A declarative sentence is a sentence that makes a statement.

Your library books are on the desk.

Use a period at the end of most imperative sentences. An **imperative sentence** is a sentence that gives a command or makes a request.

Please answer the phone.

Use a period at the end of an indirect question. An **indirect question** indicates that someone has asked a question. However, it does not give the reader the exact words of the question.

Dan asked if you had seen his backpack.

Notice how a **direct question** differs:

''Have you seen my backpack?'' asked Dan.

A direct question shows the exact words of the person asking the question. A direct question ends with a question mark.

Use a period after an abbreviation or after an initial. When an abbreviation is the last word in a sentence, use one period.

ft. (*feet*)	Dr. (doctor)
Oct. (*October*)	B.C. (Before Christ)
Harry S. Truman	P.M. (post meridian)
They spent their vacation in Washington, D.C.	

Use a period after each number or letter that shows a division of an outline or that precedes an item in a list.

I. Fiction
  A. Novels
    1. Mysteries
    2. Historic

Things to Do
1. dry cleaners
2. cash check
3. buy shampoo

Use a period as a decimal and to separate dollars and cents.

$ 722.50 $1.01 .0014

The Question Mark

Use a question mark at the end of an interrogative sentence. An **interrogative sentence** asks a question.

Can we do our homework on a word processor?

The Exclamation Point

Use an exclamation point at the end of an exclamatory sentence. An **exclamatory sentence** shows strong feeling.

That's wonderful news!
You're a great swimmer!

Use an exclamation point after a strong interjection. An **interjection** is one or more words that show strong feeling.

Unbelievable! Super! Never!

When an interjection is followed by a sentence, the sentence may end with any of the three end marks.

Oh no! I forgot my driver's license.
Help! How do I do this?
Wow! That was scary!

Exercise 1 End Marks Rewrite the following sentences, adding the correct punctuation.

1. Reading can make someone want to travel
2. Have you ever read about a foreign place and yearned to visit there
3. The mysteries of Pompeii and ancient Egypt come alive in words
4. Johanna asked how students could ever afford to travel far from home
5. Did you know that there are inexpensive hotels for young people to stay in all over the world

6. These dormitories are called Youth Hostels
7. If you join the organization, you can stay in hostels abroad and in the USA
8. Great Where do I sign up
9. Glen asked if there were any rules
10. You must arrive at a hostel by bicycle or by foot
11. Please return to the hostel by 9:30 PM
12. Is it true you have to share in the daily chores
13. What if you want to visit the great capitals of Europe
14. Hurray There are hostels near wilderness areas and major cities
15. I can't believe hostels often cost only $1050 per night

The Comma

Commas in a Series

NO COMMAS

Do not use commas when the items in a series are joined by *and, or,* or *nor.*

The sick cat didn't eat or drink or open its eyes.

Use a comma after every item in a series except the last. A **series** consists of three or more items of the same kind. Your writing might include a series of words, phrases, or other sentence parts.

Words	John Updike is a novelist, a poet, and an essayist.
Phrases	I cleaned under the table, behind the chairs, and on top of the counter.
Clauses	The dentist explained what the procedure was, why it was necessary, and what it would cost.

Use commas after the adverbs *first, second,* and so on, when they introduce a series of items.

SEMICOLONS IN SERIES

Note the use of semicolons in a series using first, etc. For more about semicolons, see page 969.

We will review three testing formats: first, multiple choice; second, essay; third, fill-ins.

Use commas between two or more adjectives of equal rank that modify the same noun.

QUICK TIP   To determine whether adjectives are of equal rank, try placing *and* between them. If *and* sounds natural, and if you can reverse the order of the adjectives without changing the meaning, then a comma is needed.

David admired the dark, mysterious painting.
The warm, dry, slow breeze rustled the curtains.

Commas with Introductory Elements

Use a comma to separate an introductory word, phrase, or clause from the rest of the sentence. The comma may be omitted if there would be little pause in speaking the words aloud.

> Yes, we are going to the basketball game tonight.
> Because I injured my ankle, I won't be playing.
> At first I thought you were wrong. (No comma is needed)

Commas with Interrupters

Use commas to set off words or groups of words that interrupt the flow of thought in a sentence.

> Fiona, however, has never been to a professional game.
> The reason, I believe, is a lack of interest.

The same words and phrases are not set off by commas when they are used as basic parts of the sentence.

> I believe this book is the finest novel I've read this year.

Use commas to set off nouns of direct address.

When you are speaking to someone, you use that person's name. When you do, you use a **noun of direct address.**

> Upstairs, Luke, is a new jacket for you.
> Luiz, hurry up!

Use commas to set off most appositives.

Appositives are words placed immediately after other words to make those other words clearer or more definite. Most appositives are nouns. Nouns used as appositives are called **nouns in apposition.**

> The slalom race, the most difficult race of the day, was thrilling.
> Alison, the fastest of the girls, won the race.

◄ COMMON INTERRUPTERS
....
however
of course
in fact
by the way
after all
I believe
I suppose
in my opinion
nevertheless
for example
on the other hand
in the first place

Exercise 2 Commas and End Marks Rewrite the following sentences, adding end marks and commas as needed.

1. The landscape of the Southwestern USA has inspired writers artists and photographers
2. Have you seen the red yellow and purple mountains of this area
3. One artist who painted some of the most memorable Western scenes was Georgia O'Keeffe

4. Georgia a talented and independent student attended boarding school in Danville Tenn
5. She painted the essential forms of sun-bleached animal skulls and twisted magnified seashells
6. Reviewers asked whether her paintings had deeper meanings
7. Of course it was difficult to be a successful woman painter at that time
8. Three environments became the source of O'Keeffe's landscapes: first New York City, NY; second Lake George, NY; and third Albuquerque N M
9. Almost unpopulated at the time northern New Mexico became a center for artists and writers
10. In fact many artists inspired by O'Keeffe's paintings have chosen to live in beautiful historic Santa Fe
11. What an inspiring landscape
12. Melanie I've got tickets to the O'Keeffe exhibit at the museum
13. Please meet me in front of the painting of the clouds
14. O'Keeffe's paintings continue to awe to inspire and to shock her viewers
15. Yes the brilliant light rugged beauty and vast sky of the Southwest is captured in her art

Commas in Quotations, Compound Sentences, and Clauses

Use commas to set off a direct quotation from the rest of the sentence. Do not use commas with indirect quotations.

> Janet said, "This lace dress is over one hundred years old."
> "This lace dress is over one hundred years old," Janet said.
> Janet said that my lace dress is over one hundred years old.

Use a comma before the conjunction that joins the two main clauses in a compound sentence.

> The dog came in the house, and now it's hungry.

Be sure to notice whether a sentence is compound or is a simple sentence with a compound predicate. Do not use commas to separate the elements in a compound predicate.

> Jonathan ran into the bedroom and picked up the phone.

A comma is not necessary when the main clauses of a compound sentence are very short and are joined by the conjunction *and*.

> We were hot and we were tired.

Exercise 3   Commas   Rewrite the following sentences, adding commas where they are needed. If no commas are needed, write *Correct*.

1. A play is similar to a novel but it has no narration.
2. Novels have plots and so do plays.
3. The novelist describes the setting and characters.
4. The playwright may show the setting in one act and then change it in another.
5. The audience learns about characters from listening to the dialogue watching the action and observing how the characters react to each other.
6. The actors either address the audience or they address each other.
7. Props small articles the actors use on stage are described in the stage directions.
8. Set designers draw sketches of the set and lighting designers plan how and where lights will be used.
9. Arthur Miller author of *The Crucible* is one of America's most famous playwrights.
10. "I have never read one of Arthur Miller's plays" said Marcy.
11. "You will have a chance" said Hannah "next year in English class."
12. Hannah said that watching a play was her favorite activity.
13. Nancy asked "Have you seen the local production of *Our Town?*"
14. "Plays seem so real" Hannah said "especially if you sit close to the stage."
15. "I would like to see a Shakespearean play" said Nancy.

Other Uses for Commas

Commas in Dates, Place Names, and Letters

In dates, use a comma between the day of the month and the year. When only the month and the year are given, no comma is needed. In a sentence, a comma follows the year.

Friday, October 12, 1999   January 1999
February 20, 1895, was the day the abolitionist Frederick Douglass died.

Use a comma between the name of a city or town and the name of its state or country. In a sentence, a comma follows the state or country. Do not put a comma between the state and the ZIP code. If the address is part of a sentence, use a comma after each part.

65 Riverview Road, Manchester, Connecticut 06040

Use a comma in the salutation of a friendly letter or after the closing of a friendly letter or a business letter. (Use a colon in the salutation of a business letter.)

Dear Aunt Louise,   Sincerely yours,

Commas to Avoid Confusion

Use a comma to separate words that might be misread.

Unclear	Whatever flew by flew by again
Clear	Whatever flew by, flew by again.

Unclear	Outside everyone was wet.
Clear	Outside, everyone was wet.

Exercise 4   Commas   Rewrite the following items, adding commas where needed. If no additional commas are needed, write *Correct.*

1. Dear Uncle Jacob
2. It has been years since our meeting in Phoenix Arizona.
3. At that time on March 17 1982 we were celebrating my parents' anniversary.
4. Even as a six-year-old I was fascinated with your stories about life in Bogota Colombia.
5. Now it is more than ten years later; I will be 17 in August 1992.
6. I still remember what you said to me: "Whatever you do do well."
7. My favorite subject at school is Spanish the language of your country.
8. I would like to visit Colombia South America some day.
9. In the meantime I read the works of South American authors like Gabriel Garcia Marquez Isabel Allende and Carlos Fuentes.
10. Please write to me at 116 Saguaro Street Tempe Arizona 85280.

Sincerely

Robert

Exercise 5   End Mark and Comma Review   On your paper, write the following sentences, adding periods, question marks, exclamation points, and commas where they are needed. If the punctuation is correct, write *Correct.*

1. Who was the first woman named to the U S Supreme Court
2. San Francisco Oakland and Palo Alto are located near San Francisco Bay
3. At the tent sale on Saturday Julio bought a red pickup truck

4. Gen Robert E Lee surrendered at Appomattox
5. Your Honor may I approach the bench
6. Shirley MacLaine the noted actress is also a best-selling author
7. The *Titanic* was supposed to be unsinkable but it sank on its first voyage after striking an iceberg
8. Robin Williams was born in Chicago Illinois on July 21 1952
9. Wow Did you see that incredible catch by the right fielder
10. Henry David Thoreau the nineteenth-century American author and philosopher lived in seclusion at Walden Pond for two years
11. Watch out for that truck
12. The President decided therefore to veto the bill
13. Mark Twain wrote *The Adventures of Tom Sawyer*
14. Mothers Against Drunk Driving or MADD is a growing group
15. If the amount is $991 or more round it off to ten dollars
16. Abe Cohn a specialist in intensive-care nursing was consulted about the patient
17. No Dallas is not the capital of Texas
18. Please meet me at 8:00 AM at the station and we will talk further
19. When there is a new mail carrier, we get our neighbor's letters and magazines
20. After dialing Tony's number Rita had second thoughts and quickly hung up

The Semicolon

A **semicolon** separates sentence elements. It indicates a more definite break than a comma does, but not as abrupt a break as a period.

Use a semicolon to separate the items of a series if one or more of these items contains commas.

> In the contest, first prize is a free trip; second prize, a gift certificate; and third prize, a free meal.

Use a semicolon to join the parts of a compound sentence if no coordinating conjunction is used. Remember that a semicolon may be used only if the clauses are closely related.

> George pumped air into the tire; it was flat.

Use a semicolon before a conjunctive adverb that joins the clauses of a compound sentence. Remember that in this case, the adverb is followed by a comma.

> New Mexico is a dry state; nevertheless, it does rain occasionally.

CONJUNCTIVE ADVERBS

Therefore, however, otherwise, consequently, besides, nevertheless, moreover.

The Colon

Use a colon to introduce a list of items. A word or phrase such as *these* or *the following items* is often followed by a colon.

> The team is missing the following: two pairs of cleats, one soccer ball, one referee whistle, and six jerseys.

Use a colon to introduce a long or formal quotation.

> Susan B. Anthony said in a speech: "Woman must not depend upon the protection of man, but must be taught to protect herself."

Use a colon between two independent clauses when the second clause explains the first. The first word following a colon is never capitalized unless it is a proper noun or the start of a quotation.

> I understand why you're angry: no one listened to you all evening.

Use a colon after the greeting in a formal letter.

> Dear Sir or Madam: Dear Ms. Douglas:

Use a colon between numbers showing hours and minutes.

> 7:30 P.M.   12:55 A.M.

The Hyphen

Use a hyphen between the syllables divided at the end of a line.

> Every member of our family attended my grad-
> uation ceremony.

Use a hyphen in compound numbers from twenty-one to ninety-nine.

> thirty-eight candles

▶ **Use a hyphen in fractions.**

> one-third of the population

Use a hyphen in certain compound nouns.

> mother-in-law   drive-in

Use a hyphen between the words that make up a compound adjective when the modifier is used before a noun.

> eighteen-speed mountain bike

WORD BREAKS

To determine if a word needs a hyphen, look it up in a dictionary.
Use these rules for hyphenating a word at the end of a line:
1. A word may be divided only between syllables. Therefore only words with two or more syllables may be hyphenated.
2. At least two letters of the hyphenated word must fall on each line.

Exercise 6   Semicolons, Colons, and Hyphens   Rewrite the following sentences, adding semicolons, colons, and hyphens where necessary.

1. Dear Sir or Madam
2. I have a number of complaints about your company let me list them.
3. First of all, your advertising is false second, your product is shoddy and third, you have ignored my previous letter.
4. I am an avid catalog user nevertheless, your reading light may be my last purchase.
5. I have made over twenty two purchases from other catalogs.
6. All of these were well made products.
7. None of these purchases have made me lose my self control.
8. There are two things wrong with the Good Night Light it doesn't work and it is dangerous.
9. Instead of lighting up the pages of my book, it actually started flashing and smoking. I found that frightening.
10. I called you at 2 30 P.M. the next day and was told someone would call back later.
11. It's obvious you are avoiding me you never returned my call.
12. I would like you to do the following return my call, answer my letter, and refund my money.
13. The Good Night Light is a fire hazard therefore I demand you stop selling it to the public.
14. I expect a response by 12 00 P.M. on Friday.
15. My mother in law is a lawyer her specialty is consumer protection.

Apostrophes

Use an apostrophe to form the possessive of nouns.

To form the possessive of a singular noun, add an apostrophe and an -s even if the noun ends in -s.

> teacher**'s**   Charles**'s**   woman**'s**

To form the possessive of a plural noun that ends in -s, add an apostrophe only. To form the possessive of a plural noun that does not end in -s, add both an apostrophe and -s.

> friends**'**   women**'s**   geese**'s**

To form the possessive of an indefinite pronoun, add an apostrophe and an -s.

> everyone**'s**   anybody**'s**

PRONOUN LISTS

For a list of indefinite and possessive personal pronouns, see pages 905 and 906.

APOSTROPHE USE
....

Use an apostrophe to
show the omission of
letters in dialect, archaic
speech, or poetry.
"What are we havin' for
supper?"

Do not use an apostrophe with a personal pronoun to show possession.

theirs	hers	ours	its	yours

▶ **Use an apostrophe in contractions to show where letters have been omitted.** Contractions are usually avoided in formal writing.

won't = will not   we'll = we will   Bill's = Bill is or Bill has
doesn't = does not   shouldn't = should not

Use an apostrophe to show the omission of figures in a date.

a reunion of the class of '70
the San Francisco earthquake of '16

Use an apostrophe to show the plurals of letters, numbers, signs, and words referred to as words.

There can be either one *l* or two *l*'s in the name Philip.

Exercise 7   Apostrophes   For each of the following sentences, rewrite each word that has an error in apostrophe usage. If a sentence has no errors, write *Correct.*

1. There are 150 lifeboat stations around Great Britain's coast.
2. The stations purpose is to be available to aid any ship in danger.
3. The institution owes its existence to Sir William Hillarys' persistence in preventing terrible tragedies at sea.
4. He convinced the people of Britain to donate money for lifeboats to be handled by local fishermen and lighthouse keeper's.
5. In 1838, the Longstone Lighthouse keepers daughter Grace Darling called her father's attention to a paddlesteamer in trouble in the pounding storm.
6. In a minutes time, the boat, with 63 people on board, broke up into many pieces on the rocks.
7. The Darling's lifeboat was small, and they couldn't tell if there were any survivors.
8. Its no small feat to risk each others life without knowing if there were lives to be saved.
9. In two harrowing trips, the Darling's rescued nine survivors.
10. That dramatic rescue in 38 marked a new surge in interest in the life-saving organizations' importance to British life at sea.

Quotation Marks

Direct and Indirect Quotations

Use quotation marks to begin and end a direct quotation. Do not use quotation marks to set off an indirect quotation. Indirect quotations are often signaled by the word *that*.

> Steve said, ''There's a bat trapped in the attic.'' (direct quotation)
> Steve said that there's a bat trapped in the attic. (indirect quotation)

To punctuate a direct quotation, enclose the exact words used by a speaker or writer in quotation marks. The first word of the quotation is capitalized. Commas are always placed inside the quotation marks. When the end of the quotation falls at the end of the sentence, the period falls inside the quotation marks.

> The bus driver announced, ''The next stop is Green Street.''

Put question marks and exclamation points inside the quotation marks if they are a part of the quotation. Put question marks and exclamation points outside the quotation marks if they are not part of the quotation. Always put commas and periods inside the quotation marks.

> Ginny asked, ''Are you going to the dance?''
> Did John say, ''I can't come tonight''?
> ''I don't have a jacket to wear,'' said Ted.

Enclose both parts of a divided quotation in quotation marks. Do not capitalize the first word of the second part unless it begins a new sentence.

> ''One reason I stayed,'' said Jackson, ''was to meet the director.''
> ''The director has never spoken here before,'' said Andy. ''That's why so many people hope to see him tonight.''

In punctuating dialogue, begin a new paragraph to indicate a new speaker.

> No one had come to the house for days. Ivan wandered from room to room, just waiting for something to happen.
> ''Please stop that roaming about,'' Greg said.
> ''Why hasn't anyone wondered what's happened to us?'' Ivan whined.
> Greg answered, ''Who cares about two misfits like us?''

In quoting passages of more than one paragraph, use a quotation mark at the beginning of each paragraph and at the end of the last paragraph only.

> Rosa said, "I have seen two professional baseball games. I was too young to appreciate the action.
>
> "The sport I loved best as a young girl was basketball. It made the most sense to me."

Setting Off Titles in Special Ways

Use quotation marks to enclose the titles of short stories, poems, essays, magazine articles, chapters, television episodes, and songs.

Short Story	"The Gift of the Magi"
Poem	"Paul Revere's Ride"
Essay	"How Harmful is TV?"
Magazine Article	"A Day in the Windy City"
Chapter	Chapter 2, "Public Art in City Spaces"
Song	"Yesterday"

The titles of books, newspapers, magazines, movies, television series, plays, works of art, and long musical compositions are underlined in writing and italicized in print.

Book	*The Sun Also Rises*
Newspaper	*Los Angeles Times*
Magazine	*National Geographic*
Movie	*Gone with the Wind*
Television Series	*This Old House*
Play	*The Crucible*
Work of Art	Pablo Picasso's *Three Dancers*
Long Musical Composition	Copland's *Appalachian Spring*

Exercise 8   Quotation Marks and Underlining   Rewrite the following sentences, adding quotation marks where necessary. Indicate italics by underlining. If a sentence has no errors, write *Correct.*

1. Shakespeare's plays have been popular for over four hundred years said Gretchen.
2. His first plays were historic dramas said Gary. They were based on the life of King Henry VI.
3. Didn't he write poetry as well? Janice inquired.
4. Mr. Ponti said that some of Shakespeare's sonnets are beautiful love poems.

5. The play of Romeo and Juliet is a love story and a tragedy.
6. Did Sasha say I haven't read Hamlet?
7. Holly wrote an essay titled Shakespeare the Actor.
8. Chapter 4 in our literature text is called The Bard of Stratford-on-Avon.
9. I once read a magazine article called Who Wrote Shakespeare's Plays?
10. Dianne asked Is there controversy about the authorship of the plays?
11. Yes, The London Times once featured a series of articles about the mystery.
12. I believe he wrote all the plays, said Dan, without any help from other writers.
13. Shakespeare's play Macbeth has been made into a movie a number of times, said Ted. It has been criticized as being too graphic to appear on a big screen.
14. Jane said that Shakespeare wrote 37 plays and 154 sonnets.
15. Shakespeare's plays appear in over one hundred languages, said Jeremy. They are read and performed all over the world. It is said that on any given day, somebody somewhere is reading, watching, or listening to Shakespeare.

Index of Fine Art

Index of Skills

Literary Terms

Reading and Critical Thinking Skills

All Responding to Reading *questions draw upon a variety of critical thinking skills.*

Grammar, Usage, and Mechanics

Writing Skills, Modes, and Formats

Writer
　　as communicator, 882
　　as decision-maker, 879–80
　　as learner, strategies of, 881
　　as problem-solver, strategies of, 879–80
Writing process, 878–82
　　writing with computers, 883–84
　　see also Drafting; Journal writing;
　　　　Prewriting; Proofreading;
　　　　Publishing/presenting; Revising and
　　　　editing; Self-assessment

*V*ocabulary Skills

Analogy, 578, 703
Antonym, 185, 361, 444, 568, 621, 659
Colloquialism, 419, 865. *See also* Dialect;
　　Idiom; Slang
Connotation, 30, 38, 92, 123, 133, 175, 205,
　　304, 311, 320, 395, 586, 604
Context clues, 49, 207
　　antonym, 185, 361, 444, 568, 621, 659
　　contrast, 418, 465
　　definition and restatement, 111, 418, 465,
　　　　494, 534, 659
　　example, 111, 230, 418, 465, 534
　　inference, 147, 252, 385, 443, 659
　　synonym, 185, 312, 361, 444, 465, 596, 621
Denotation, 28, 29, 30, 38, 61, 78, 103, 123,
　　131, 195, 213, 214, 230, 252, 264, 282,
　　312, 319, 340, 377, 418, 431, 465, 483,
　　494, 513, 524, 534, 553, 568, 578, 586,
　　596, 684
Dialect, 213, 372, 866
Glossary, 857–63
Idiom, 554, 621, 868
Jargon. *See* Specialized vocabulary
Levels of language, 452
　　see also Colloquialism; Dialect; Idiom; Slang
Slang, 30, 871
Specialized vocabulary, 254, 342, 433
Synonym, 185, 312, 361, 444, 465, 596, 621

*R*esearch and Study Skills

Opportunities for developing research and
　　study skills also appear in the Options for
　　Learning activities that follow many
　　selections.

Note taking, 41, 291
Reading rates, 239
Report. *See* Writing Skills, Modes, and
　　Formats Index
Research guidelines, 446–49, 885–90
　　bibliography, 886–87, 889–90

documentation. *See* bibliography
　　drafting, 448
　　evaluation and revision, 449, 886
　　organizing information, 448–49, 887–88
　　primary research, 447–48
　　revising and editing, 449, 890
　　secondary research, 447
　　sources, 449, 885–86
　　topic selection, 446, 885
　　writing from outline, 888
Skimming and scanning, 29, 124, 132, 185,
　　196, 222, 264, 282, 291, 340, 362, 704,
　　705
　　see also Reading rates
SQ3R, 370
Story Grammar, 18
Summarizing, 291, 887
Test-taking, 543

*S*peaking, Listening, and Viewing Skills

Dramatic reading, 419, 579, 713
　　an apology, 265
　　an argument, 132
　　a dialogue, 569, 579, 808
　　a monologue, 303, 579
　　a pantomime, 50, 79, 525
　　poetry and songs, 39, 196
　　a press conference, 196
　　a radio play, 362
　　a radio or television documentary, 844
　　role-playing, 29, 265, 378, 579, 704
　　a skit, 525, 535, 569, 597
　　a story, recreating, 104, 303, 313, 378, 525,
　　　　597, 704, 751, 777, 808
　　a talk-show conversation, 89, 378
Interviewing, 223, 265, 403, 495, 622, 704,
　　844, 853
Listening, 58, 905–906, 908
Public speaking, 327, 330, 495, 514, 853, 901,
　　905, 912, 933, 939, 962, 965
　　a class debate, 223, 445, 466
　　leading a discussion, 514, 535, 555, 622
　　a radio or television report, 223
　　a report to the class, 124, 223, 283, 378,
　　　　419, 484, 495, 514, 535, 622, 704, 777,
　　　　844
　　a speech, 432, 555
Reading aloud, 54, 89, 108, 146, 195, 196,
　　235, 287, 366, 367, 399, 400, 419, 499,
　　555, 579, 583, 709, 808, 878, 882
Story telling, 196, 378, 484, 525, 579
Viewing, 514
　　videotaping, 39, 597, 844

Index of Titles and Authors

Page numbers that appear in italics refer to biographical information.

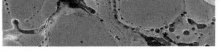

Acknowledgments

(continued from page iv)

Ruby Dee and Marian Searchinger: "Aunt Zurletha," from *My One Good Nerve* by Ruby Dee. Copyright © 1987 by Ruby Dee. All rights reserved. No part of this publication may be reproduced or transmitted in any form or by any means, electronic or mechanical, including photocopy, recording, or any information storage and retrieval system, without permission in writing from the author.

Doubleday, a division of Bantam, Doubleday, Dell Publishing Group: Excerpts ("the lesson of the moth") from *Archy and Mehitabel* by Don Marquis. Copyright 1927 by Doubleday, a division of Bantam, Doubleday, Dell Publishing Group, Inc. Used by permission of the publisher.

Farrar, Straus & Giroux, Inc.: Excerpt from *Annie John* by Jamaica Kincaid. Copyright © 1983, 1984, 1985 by Jamaica Kincaid. Reprinted by permission of Farrar, Straus & Giroux, Inc.

Henry Gregor Felsen: "Li Chang's Million" by Henry Gregor Felsen. By permission of the author.

Carole Gregory: "Long Distance," From *Nine Black Poets*. By permission of the author.

Harcourt Brace Jovanovich, Inc.: "The Necklace" by Guy de Maupassant, translated by Newbury LeB. Morse, from *Adventures in Reading*, Grade 9, Laureate Edition (Adventures in Literature Program), edited by Evan Lodge and Marjorie Braymer. Copyright © 1963 by Harcourt Brace Jovanovich, Inc. Reprinted by permission of the publisher.

HarperCollins Publishers: Excerpt from *An American Childhood* by Annie Dillard. Copyright © 1987 by Annie Dillard. "Snake Boy," from *Anpao* by Jamake Highwater. Text copyright © 1977 by Jamake Highwater. Excerpts from *A Choice of Weapons* by Gordon Parks. Copyright © 1965, 1966 by Gordon Parks. Reprinted by permission of HarperCollins Publishers.

John Hersey: "Not To Go with the Others," from *Here to Stay* by John Hersey, published by Alfred A. Knopf, Inc. 1963. By permission of the author.

Henry Holt and Company, Inc.: Excerpt from Chapter 1, "Fool's Paradise," from *Homecoming* by Floyd Dell. Copyright 1933, © 1961 by Floyd Dell. Reprinted by permission of Henry Holt and Company, Inc.

Houghton Mifflin Company: "Fireworks," from *The Complete Poetical Works of Amy Lowell* by Amy Lowell. Copyright © 1955 by Houghton Mifflin Co. Copyright © 1983 by Houghton Mifflin Co., Brinton P. Roberts, and G. D'Andelot Belin, Esquire. Reprinted by permission of Houghton Mifflin Co.

Evelyn Tooley Hunt: "Taught Me Purple," from *Negro Digest*, 1964 by Evelyn Tooley Hunt. By permission of the author.

James Hurst: "The Scarlet Ibis" by James Hurst from *The Atlantic Monthly,* July 1960. Copyright © 1988 by James Hurst. By permission of the author.

Indiana University Press: "Every Good Boy Does Fine," from *New and Selected Poems* by David Wagoner. By permission of Indiana University Press.

Sterling Lord Literistic, Inc.: "Giving Blood," from *Blood Relations* by Roberta Silman. Copyright © 1977 by Roberta Silman. Reprinted by permission of Sterling Lord Literistic, Inc.

Macmillan Publishing Company: "A Mother in Mannville," from *When the Whippoorwill* by Marjorie Kinnan Rawlings. Copyright 1940 by Marjorie Kinnan Rawlings; copyright renewed © 1968 by Norton Baskin. Reprinted with permission of Charles Scribner's Sons, an imprint of Macmillan Publishing Company. *The Miracle Worker* by William Gibson. Copyright © 1956, 1957 by William Gibson; copyright © 1959, 1960 by Tamarack Productions, Ltd., and George S. Klein and Leo Garel as trustees under three separate deeds of trust. Reprinted with permission of Atheneum Publishers, an imprint of Macmillan Publishing Company. "The Secret Heart," from *Collected Poems* by Robert P. Tristram Coffin. Copyright 1935 by Macmillan Publishing Company, renewed © 1963 by Margaret Coffin Halvosa. "Frederick Douglass," from *The World's Great Men of Color* by J. A. Rogers. Copyright 1947 by J.A. Rogers, renewed © 1974 by Helga M. Rogers; copyright © 1972 by Macmillan Publishing Company. Reprinted with permission of Macmillan Publishing Company.

Naomi Long Madgett: "Woman with Flower," from *Star by Star* by Naomi Long Madgett, Lotus Press, Detroit, © 1965, 1970. Reprinted by permission of the author.

McIntosh and Otis, Inc.: "The Day the Sun Came Out" by Dorothy M. Johnson. Copyright © 1953 by Dorothy M. Johnson; copyright renewed © 1981 by Dorothy M. Johnson. Originally published in *Cosmopolitan* under the title "Too Soon a Woman". Reprinted by permission of McIntosh and Otis, Inc.

Marian Reiner for Eve Merriam: "Metaphor" and "Thumbprint," from *A Sky Full of Poems* by Eve Merriam. Copyright © 1964, 1970, 1973 by Eve Merriam. Reprinted by permission of Marian Reiner for the author.

Estate of Norma Millay Ellis: "The Courage That My Mother Had," from *Collected Poems* by Edna St. Vincent Millay, Harper & Row. Copyright © 1954, 1982 by Norma Millay Ellis. Reprinted by permission of Elizabeth Barnett, Literary Executor.

William Morris Agency, Inc.: *The Hitchhiker* by Lucille Fletcher. Copyright 1947 by Lucille Fletcher. "One Throw" by W.C. Heinz. Copyright © 1960 by W.C. Heinz. Reprinted by permission of William Morris Agency, Inc. on behalf of the authors.

William Morrow & Company, Inc.: "The United States vs. Susan B. Anthony," from *Women of Courage* by Margaret Truman. Copyright © 1976 by Margaret Truman. "A Journey," from *Those Who Ride the Night Winds* by Nikki Giovanni. Copyright © 1983 by Nikki Giovanni. By permission of William Morrow & Co., Inc. "Fish Eyes," from *Nobody Ever Sees You Eat Tunafish* by David Brenner. Copyright © 1986 by David Brenner. By permission of Arbor House, a division of William Morrow & Co.

The New York Times: "On Being Seventeen, Bright and Unable to Read" by David Raymond, April 25, 1976 (op-ed). Copyright © 1976 by The New York Times Company. Reprinted by permission.

The New Yorker: "Just Try to Forget" by Nathaniel Benchley, March 26, 1955 issue. Copyright © 1955, 1983 The New Yorker Magazine, Inc. Reprinted by permission.

Julio Noboa: "Identity" by Julio Noboa. By permission of the author.

W. W. Norton & Company, Inc.: "Prospective Immigrants Please Note," from *The Fact of a Doorframe,* Poems Selected and New, 1950–1984 by Adrienne Rich; copyright © 1984 by Adrienne Rich, copyright © 1975, 1978 by W. W. Norton & Company, Inc. Copyright © 1981 by Adrienne Rich. By permission of W. W. Norton & Company, Inc.

North Point Press: "Brothers Are the Same," excerpted from *The Splendid Outcast* by Beryl Markham. Copyright © 1987 by Beryl Markham. Reprinted by permission of North Point Press.

Harold Ober Associates, Inc.: "Thank You, M'am," from *The Langston Hughes Reader* by Langston Hughes. Copyright © 1958 by Langston Hughes; copyright renewed 1986 by George Houston Bass. Reprinted by permission of Harold Ober Associates, Inc.

NAL Penguin, Inc.: "The Two Brothers," from *Fables and Fairy Tales* by Leo Tolstoy, translated by Ann Dunnigan. Copyright © 1962. By permission of NAL Penguin, Inc.

People Weekly, Time Magazine, Inc.: "A Trip to the Edge of Survival" by Ron Arias, Meg Grant, and Peter Castro, *People Weekly,* 7/11/88 issue. Copyright © 1988 The Time Inc. Magazine Co. All rights reserved.

Leroy V. Quintana: "Legacy II," from *The Face of Poetry* by Leroy V. Quintana. By permission of the author.

Random House, Inc.: Specified excerpts from *The Odyssey of Homer,* translated by Robert Fitzgerald. Copyright © 1961, 1963 by Robert Fitzgerald and renewed 1989 by Benedict R. C. Fitzgerald on behalf of the Fitzgerald children. Reprinted by permission of Vintage Books, a division of Random House, Inc. Chapter 15 from *I Know Why the Caged Bird Sings* by Maya Angelou. Copyright © 1969 by Maya Angelou. "The Artist," from *Tales of Old China* by Isabelle C. Chang. Copyright © 1969 by Isabelle Chang. Reprinted by permission of Random House, Inc.

Flora Roberts, Inc.: "The Pocketbook Game," from *Like One of the Family* by Alice Childress. Copyright © 1956, renewed 1984 by Alice Childress. Used by permission of Flora Roberts, Inc.

St. Martin's Press, Inc. and Harold Ober Associates, Inc.: Excerpt from *All Things Bright and Beautiful* by James Herriot. Copyright © 1973, 1974 by James Herriot. By permission of St. Martin's Press and Harold Ober Associates, Inc.

South Dakota Review: "Lost" by Bruce Ignacio, first published in *South Dakota Review,* summer, 1969. Reprinted with editor's permission.

The Estate of May Swenson: "Fable for When There's No Way Out" by May Swenson. Copyright © 1967 by May Swenson. Used by permission of The Estate of May Swenson.

Texas Christian University: "Everybody Knows Tobie" by Daniel Garza, first published in *Descant, The Literary Magazine of Texas Christian University.*

University of Washington Press: Abridged from *Fifth Chinese Daughter* by Jade Snow Wong. Copyright 1945, 1948, 1950 by Jade Snow Wong, renewed © 1978 by Jade Snow Wong. By permission of University of Washington Press.

University Press of New England: "Incident in a Rose Garden," from *Night Life* by Donald Justice. Copyright © 1967 by Donald Justice. By permission of University Press of New England.

Lucinda Vardey Agency, Ltd.: "The Stolen Party" by Liliana Heker. Copyright © 1982 by Liliana Heker. Translation copyright © 1985 by Alberto Manguel. Permission given by Lucinda Vardey Agency, Ltd. on behalf of Alberto Manguel.

The authors and editors have made every effort to trace the ownership of all copyrighted selections found in this book and to make full acknowledgment for their use.

Illustrations

Robert Borja, 133; Rebecca Brown, 588; Rebecca Brown with Montelle Cade, 86; Diane McKnight, 633; Michele Mitchell, 224, 372; Richard Nichols, 379; Julie Pace, 92. MAPS: Keith Kraus and Linda Gebhardt, 153, 243, 268, 332.

Author Photographs

AP/Wide World Photos: Alice Childress 875, Robert Fitzgerald 197, Annie Dillard 231, William Gibson 705, James Herriot 875, Louis L'Amour 283, Don Marquis 603, Gordon Parks 514, Adrienne Rich 877, Jade Snow Wong 466; The Bettmann Archive: Floyd Dell 50, O. Henry 39, Homer 197, Guy de Maupassant 79, William Shakespeare 845; Canapress Photo Service: Alice Munro 569; Nancy Crampton: Nikki Giovanni 875; Culver Pictures: Edna St. Vincent Millay 396, Marjorie Kinnan Rawlings 29; Henry Curth: Jamake Highwater 124; © 1990 Sigrid Estrada: Jamaica Kincaid 341; Globe Photos: Ruby Dee 303, Margaret Truman 445; Ruben Guzman: Sandra

Cisneros 555; Historical Picture Services, Chicago: Leo Tolstoy 603; Jim Hogopian: Richard Matheson 597; The Houghton Library, Harvard University: Amy Lowell 876; Henri Cartier-Bresson/Magnum Photos Inc.: Langston Hughes 378; Elliott Erwitt/Magnum Photos Inc.: John Hersey 876; Mansfield Library, University of Montana: Dorothy Johnson 876; Steven V. Mori: Toshio Mori 495; New York Times Pictures: Nathaniel Benchley 525; Joyce Ravid: Roberta Silman 265; Jim Ripley: William Hoffman 423; Gordon Robotham: Diana Chang 874; Peter Serling: Ron Arias 253; UPI/Bettmann: Maya Angelou 579, Beryl Markham 484; Vassar College Library: Lucille Fletcher 362; Wesleyan University Press: Donald Justice 68.

Miscellaneous art credits

iii WOODLAND ENCOUNTER 1980 Bev Doolittle © 1980 The Greenwich Workshop, Inc., Trumbull, Connecticut; x ULYSSES DERIDING POLYPHEMUS 1829 Joseph William Mallord Turner National Gallery of Art, London; xii DIALOGUE 1974 Rufino Tamayo B. Lewin Galleries, Palm Springs, California; xiv SUNSHINE TOURISTS 1990 Zoltan Szabo By permission of the artist; xvi GATE TO THE ISLES 1980 Winifred Nicholson © Estate of Winifred Nicholson; xvii Photofest, New York; 4,112 SEATED GIRL WITH DOG (detail) 1944 Milton Avery Collection of Roy R. Neuberger, New York; 6 © Peggi Roberts/Stockworks; 7 © Richard Hutchins/Photo Researchers, New York; 16 ALBERT'S SON (detail) 1959 Andrew Wyeth National Gallery of Oslo, photograph by Jacques Lathion; 59 LOVER'S LANE (detail) 1988 Susan Slyman Jay Johnson America's Folk Heritage Gallery, New York; 113,119 THE FOUR WORLDS (detail) 1954 Joe Herrera Private collection; 150 HEAD OF ODYSSEUS 2nd century B.C. Agesander, Athanadoros, and Polydoros Sperlonga Museum, Italy; 151 ULYSSES ESCAPING FROM POLYPHEMUS 510 B.C. The Sappho Painter Krater The State Museum of Baden, Karlsruhe, Germany; 206 PORTRAIT OF NITO (detail) 1961 Peter Hurd Phoenix Art Museum; 240,266 THE OUTLIER (detail) 1909 Frederic Remington The Brooklyn Museum, bequest of Miss Charlotte R. Stillman; 241 © Peter Serling, New York; 254 © CNRI/SPL/Photo Researchers, Inc., New York; 294 JOLIE MADAME (detail) 1973 Audrey Flack Australia National Gallery, Canberra; 304 RICKSHAW, TAIWAN (detail) Dong Kingman Collection of the artist; 314 SONGS FOR MY FATHER (detail) 1980 Juan Gonzalez Nancy Hoffman Gallery, New York; 331 ORANGE SWEATER (detail) 1955 Elmer Bischoff San Francisco Museum of Art Gift of Mr. and Mrs. Mark Schorer; 342 THE GIFT 1986 Charles Hewitt Courtesy of the artist; 371 MANUEL LA JEUNESSE (detail) 1922 Walter Ufer Courtesy of the Anschutz Collection, Denver, Colorado Photograph by James O. Milmoe; 385 MUSHROOM (detail) 1972 Bob Timberlake Heritage Gallery, Lexington, North Carolina; 406 FORWARD #10 (detail) 1967 Jacob Lawrence illustration from *Harriet Tubman and the Promised Land* By permission of the artist; 420 Henryk Kaiser/Leo deWys, New York; 407 Library of Congress, Washington, D.C.; 433 The Bettmann Archive, New York; 453 *A CONTEMPORARY SIOUX INDIAN* (detail) 1978 James Bama Buffalo Bill Historical Center, Cody, Wyoming; 471 SIMBA (detail) © 1988 The Greenwich Workshop, Inc., Trumbull, Connecticut; 503 (detail) Arthur Rothstein/The Bettmann Archive, New York; 504 Photograph by Cecil Layne By permission of Gordon Parks; 515 © Peter Glass/Monkmeyer Press, New York; 546 UNTITLED (detail) Susan Kahn Collection of the Montclair Art Museum, New Jersey; 570 STILL LIFE WITH HAT (detail) 1983 Warren Brandt Fischbach Gallery, New York; 587 TRANSECTION #24 (detail) 1977 Clarence Holbrook Carter Courtesy of the artist; 609 © Fred Whitehead/Animals Animals, New York 631, 640, 669, 678, 693, 699, 720, 731, 747, 757, 770, 775, 781, 785, 791, 799, 805, 817, 836, 837 Photofest New York; 656,741 Shooting Star, Los Angeles; 651 Wisconsin Center for Film and Theater; 665,696 Museum of Modern Art Film Stills Archive, New York 665, 696. 841 Memory Shop, New York; 733, 769, 783 British Film Institute, London.

McDougal, Littell and Company has made every effort to locate the copyright holders for the images used in this book and to make full acknowledgment for their use.